Contract
Cases and Materials

H. G. Beale BA
Barrister, Professor of Law,
University of Warwick

W. D. Bishop MA, BCL
Partner,
Puttnam, Hayes and Bartlett Ltd,
(Consultant Economists)

M. P. Furmston TD, BCL, MA, LLM
Bencher of Gray's Inn, Professor of Law,
University of Bristol

Butterworths
London, Edinburgh
1990

United Kingdom	Butterworth & Co (Publishers) Ltd, 88 Kingsway, LONDON WC2B 6AB and 4 Hill Street, EDINBURGH EH2 3JZ
Australia	Butterworths Pty Ltd, SYDNEY, MELBOURNE, BRISBANE, ADELAIDE, PERTH, CANBERRA and HOBART
Canada	Butterworths Canada Ltd, TORONTO and VANCOUVER
Ireland	Butterworth (Ireland) Ltd, DUBLIN
Malaysia	Malayan Law Journal Sdn Bhd, KUALA LUMPUR
New Zealand	Butterworths of New Zealand Ltd, WELLINGTON and AUCKLAND
Puerto Rico	Equity de Puerto Rico, Inc, HATO REY
Singapore	Malayan Law Journal Pte Ltd, SINGAPORE
USA	Butterworth Legal Publishers, AUSTIN, Texas; BOSTON, Massachusetts; CLEARWATER, Florida (D & S Publishers); ORFORD, New Hampshire (Equity Publishing); ST PAUL, Minnesota; and SEATTLE, Washington

Reprinted 1991

A CIP Catalogue record for this book is available from the British Library.

ISBN 0 406 51751 7

Typeset by Phoenix Photosetting, Chatham, Kent
Printed and bound in Great Britain by Billing and Sons Ltd, Worcester

Preface

In this second edition we have maintained the same general approach as underlay the first. We think that a modern casebook should present the student with a broad selection of cases and statutes together with enough critical material to stimulate thought about the subject. The casebook of Professor Smith and the late Professor Thomas, first produced in 1957 and now in its eighth edition (1987), goes a long way to achieving these objectives and our work on this book has served to remind us how good a collection Smith & Thomas is. We consider, however, that there is room for a collection with a somewhat different approach which, in addition to setting out the essential core of cases and statutes, seeks to achieve a number of other aims. Since the first edition of the book in 1985 there have been a number of important new cases and statutes, which are included in the book, but the majority of the changes are in pursuit of these further aims.

One is to bring home the relationship of contract to other legal categories, particularly restitution and tort. In the new edition we have tried to provide a slightly fuller introduction to negligence, for readers who have not studied tort, and to give a very brief guide to the important but baffling cases on the recovery of economic loss. At the same time we have expanded the short introductory section on contractual liability, with the aim of exploring and questioning more fully the conceptual bases of the three types of liability.

A second aim is to consider the theoretical question of why contracts are enforced and what policies or values the law may be adopting. We had received a number of comments that the first edition contained too few readings on this point and we have included a number of additional extracts, both in the Introduction and in the section on Legal Theory. (The latter is kept in the middle of the book because we think students will find it easier once they have mastered some of the substance but will tend to ignore it if it is left to the very end.)

A third aim of the first edition was to consider how the rules of contract law operate both inside and outside the courtroom. The new edition tries to show the range of cases actually handled by the courts and to bring out more clearly that contract, although for the most part a general body of rules which can be applied to any agreement, actually falls to be applied in each case in a particular context. The general rule may be applied in a different way, or at least has a rather different operation, according to the nature of the contract in question; and the context may lead to the development of specialised rules applying only to particular types of contract. A much expanded chapter on Implied Terms briefly shows how the courts have given a characteristic shape to three types of contract.

Besides being a body of rules for deciding disputes, contract is a system guiding those who wish to make agreements. We have tried to introduce material, such as extracts from actual contracts, which show the law of contract in this light, and to introduce the reader to empirical investigations of how the rules operate in practice and economic analysis of how the rules may be expected to influence the behaviour of contracting parties. The first edition was criticised for not giving an adequate explanation of the microeconomic concepts employed; we have sought to put this right.

The attempt to achieve these objectives while at the same time illustrating the main features of a body of law which continues to evolve in interesting ways has posed many difficult problems as to choice of materials. Inevitably it has not been possible to include full extracts from every well known case as well as the critical and contextual material. The careful reader will note that there is in fact a shift in the balance between cases and other materials in the course of the book. We have been very much aware of the traditional use of contract law as a training ground for legal technique and have included in the earlier sections most of the old favourites. Later we have increased the proportion of extracts from books and articles while seeking to present all the most important cases at least in summary form where considerations of space prevented full extracts. In black letter terms this inevitably means a loss of coverage but consultation with users of the first edition confirmed our initial view that there are significant gains. In this edition we have shifted the balance slightly further in favour of critical extracts. Meanwhile, we are aware that not all teachers take the material in the same order as the book and in the new edition we have tried to provide the reader with fairly full notes and questions throughout.

One way of saving space is to leave out topics altogether. There are a number of topics which are still discussed in contract textbooks but which are, in our experience, not taught in many undergraduate courses. We think, for instance, of gaming and wagering contracts and minors' contracts. We have said little about these topics. In this edition we have shortened the coverage of Illegal Contracts so as to concentrate on two main heads, contracts involving the commission of a crime or a tort and contracts in restraint of trade. At the same time fuller notes have been provided.

We recognise that even with these omissions most contract teachers will probably not seek to cover all the material in this book. We thought it better however to offer a choice rather than to impose our own selection. It may help teachers to know that throughout the book we have tried to assemble the materials into packages that can be conveniently studied within a pattern of twenty-four weekly or twelve fortnightly tutorials (that is about thirty-five pages for a weekly or seventy for a fortnightly tutorial). Even this may be too much if students are to have time to think about what they are reading, particularly if they are in their first year of study. As an experiment, we suggest a 'core' of readings which can be set to first year students, leaving enough space for additional material to be read on particular topics which the teacher or student wants to pursue in more detail. Our list follows this Preface.

The production of a book of this kind leaves many debts of gratitude. We are particularly grateful to those contract teachers who took the trouble to return the questionnaire about the book; to Kate Love, who read much of the material to ensure that it was readily comprehensible to a student teacher, and whose comments led to a good deal of 'fine tuning'; to Ken Foster, Tom Hervey and John Wightman for advice and suggestions; to Jill Poole for reading the proofs; to our publishers for their help and encouragement; to the University of Warwick which allowed Hugh Beale study leave in order to work on the new edition; and most of all to our families for being at all times patient and encouraging.

Throughout the text, references to 'Cheshire, Fifoot and Furmston' are to *Cheshire, Fifoot and Furmston's Law of Contract* (11th ed, 1986) and those to 'Treitel' are to *The Law of Contract* (by G. H. Treitel, 7th ed, 1987).

H.G.B.
W.B.
M.P.F.

In the first edition of this book we added to the preface the following:

> Our original plan was that the whole of the book should be written jointly. Each of the chapters has been the subject of joint discussion; many have been drafted by one hand and revised by another; a few of the most intractable have been written in turn by all three of us. The three authors are equally responsible for editorial decisions and all errors and infelicities. However, during the three years between conception and delivery, two of us have from time to time been distracted by other demands on our time and a greater burden in the execution of the work has therefore fallen on the uncomplaining shoulders of Hugh Beale. We should like the reader who finds value in this book to know that Hugh Beale was first among equals in producing it.

In this edition Bill Bishop's participation has been largely confined to the economic readings and linked material. Every part of the book has been through the hands of at least two of the co-editors and all three take joint responsibility for it. But, again, Hugh Beale has taken the lead in the enterprise.

W.B.
M.P.F.

Contents

Suggested 'core' readings for first year students

Please note that this selection assumes that the readings from this book will be supplemented by either full lectures or quite wide reading in a textbook.

1. *Introductory readings:* 3–32; 63–67 (Adams & Brownsword); 71–78 (economic analysis); 79–81 (Beale & Dugdale).
2. *Consideration:* 91–93 (introduction to consideration); 98–108, 112–113 (performance of existing duty, requirements contracts, commercial credits); 114–124 (exchange, Fuller); 124–128 (economics of gratuitous promises); 131–133 (formal requirements).
3. *Reliance; Intention:* 133–141 (estoppel), 146–151 (Atiyah), 154–157 (intention).
4. *Offer and acceptance I:* 167–176 (offers in correspondence; advertisements and displays of goods); 180–181 (acceptance by conduct); 184–189 (unilateral contracts); 190–195 (differing proposals).
5. *Postal rules; Uncertainty:* 196–199; 213–214; 217–221; 224–228 (contracts which do not materialise).
6. *Communication mistakes:* 231–237; 237–241; (rectification); 241–242 (mutual mistake); 243–246 (mistaken expectations).
7. *Express terms:* 259–265 (term or representation); 267–275 (ticket cases); 277 (signature).
8. *Misrepresentation:* 285–288; 292–297; 300 (limits to rescission); 297–300 (damages); 301–305; 308–313 (clauses restricting liability).
9. *Interpretation; Implied terms:* 317–325; 327–328; implied terms under SGA.
10. *Frustration:* 247–354; 305–308 (economic analysis); 358–362 (frustration of purpose); LR (FC) Act 1943.
11. *Expectation mistake:* 372–387; 394–404 (duty to disclose).
12. *Express and constructive conditions:* 410–412, 418–421 (substantial performance), 423–433.
13. *Termination:* 436–438, 443–445 (anticipatory repudiation); 453–459. LC Report 457–459 (nature of termination).
14. *Damages:* 463–466, 475–476 (remoteness); 473–474 (economic analysis); 481–483 (mitigation); 495–502 (problem cases); 502–508 (consumer surplus).
15. *Liquidated damages; other remedies:* 508–524; 525–528 (specific performance); 528–531 (economic analysis); 543–547 (action for price).
16. *Contract theory:* Collins; Cohen; Fuller; Atiyah; Leff.
17. *Changing the bargain:* 592–593; 598–600 (consideration); 602–614 (promissory estoppel); 616–618 (economic analysis).
18. *Duress, etc.:* 639–645 (economic duress); 648–656 (undue influence); 658–661 (poor and ignorant persons); 669–673 (a general doctrine?).
19. *Exclusion clauses at common law:* 679–685, 574 (main purpose), 689–699 (substantive doctrine).
20. *UCTA 1977:* 705–708, 713–714, 716–717.
21. *The problem with exclusion clauses; reasonableness:* 700–703; 718–730 (reasonableness).
22. *Contracts involving commission of crime or tort:* pp 753–766.
23. *Contracts in restraint of trade:* pp 776–792.
24. *Privity:* 804–812; 814–822 (agency); 825–827 (indemnities); (burdens).

Acknowledgements

Grateful acknowledgment is made to all authors and publishers of extract material, and in particular to the following for permission to reprint material from the sources indicated:

Professor J. N. Adams and R. Brownsword: 'The Ideologies of Contract Law' (1987) 7 Legal Studies 205, 205–214, 217–222.

Professors V. A. Aivazian, M. J. Trebilcock and M. Penny: 'The Law of Contract Modifications: The Uncertain Quest for a Benchmark of Enforceability' (1984) 22 Osgoode Hall LJ 173, at 187–205.

American Sociological Association: Macaulay, 'Non-Contractual Relations in Business', American Sociological Review; vol 55 (1963), pp 55–60.

Professor P. S. Atiyah: *Essays on Contract*, pp 19–31, 33–41; 184–187, 209–210, 226–230, 232–235, 238–239, 241; *'Sale of Goods'* (7th ed, 1985) 329–330; 'Freedom of Contract and the New Right' (1988) 20 Skriftserien, Juridiska Fakullteten 1 Stockholm, pp 11–13.

Baltic and International Maritime Conference: Uniform Time Charter ('Baltime 1939') and Uniform General Charter ('Gencon').

Basil Blackwell Publisher Ltd: Beale and Dugdale, 'Contracts between Businessmen' (1975) 2 British Journal of Law and Society 45, 45–48, 48–51, 55; Lewis, 'Contracts Between Businessmen: Reform of the Law of Firm Offers' (1982) 9 Journal of Law and Society 153, 153, 158–160, 162–165, 166, 168–169, 170–171; Ferguson 'The Adjudication of Commercial Disputes and the Legal System in Modern England' (1980) 7 Brit J Law & Society 141, 142–148, 151–154.

Bendix Ltd: *Force Majeure* clause from standard conditions of sale.

Butterworths & Co (Canada) Ltd: Trebilcock, in *Studies in Contract Law*: pp 390–396, 399–404, 404–408, 412–421; Butterworths Pty Ltd: Ellinghaus, 'An Australian Contract Law?' (1989) J of Contract Law 13, 19–20.

California Law Review and Fred B. Rothman & Co: Sweet, 'Liquidated Damages in California' (1972) 60 California LR 86–89.

Cambridge Law Journal and Authors: Hamson, 'Illegal Contracts and Limited Interests' (1949) IO CLJ 249, 258–25; Shand, 'Unblinkering the Unruly Horse' (1972A) CLJ 144, 164; Spencer, 'Signature, Consent and the Rule in *L'Estange v Graucob*' [1973] CLJ 103, 108, 114–116.

Hugh Collins: *The law of contract* (1986) pp 1–2, 8–15, 156–158.

The Construction Plant-hire Association: Model Conditions for the Hiring of Plant (1979).

Consumer Credit Trade Association: specimen form hire purchase contract.

Professor B. Coote: 'Another look at Bowmakers' (1972) 35 MLR 38, 42–44.

Duke Law Journal: Muris, (1982) Duke LJ 1053, 1062–1066.

Eclipse Publication Ltd: Industrial Relations Law Reports.

Faber and Faber: Lord Radcliffe, *The Law and its Compass*, pp 46–52 and 54–55.

Peter Gabel and Jay Feinman: 'Contract Law as Ideology' in *The Politics of Law* (ed Kairys), chapter 8.

Grain and Feed Trade Association, Contract No 119.

P. J. Hare Limited: 'Terms of Payment' clause from the standard conditions of sale used by firm.

Harvard Law Review Association: Cohen, 'The Basis of Contract' (1933) 46 Harvard LR 553, 571–589, 591–592; Priest, 'Breach and Remedy for the Tender of Non-conforming Goods' (1978) 91 Harvard LR 960, 963, 965, 967–968.

Harvard University Press: Fried, Contract as Promise: A Theory of Contractual Obligations (1981), pp 14–17, 69–73.

The Controller of Her Majesty's Stationery Office: Law Revision Committee, Sixth Interim Report (Statute of Frauds and the Doctrine of Consideration), Cmd 5449, 1937, pp 6, 7, 8, 33 and 34; Law Commission, First Report on Exemption Clauses (No 24, 1969), paras 68, 69, 73, 79; Second Report on Exemption Clauses, (No 69, 1975), paras 11, 54, 56, 141–143 and 146; Report on Pecuniary Restitution (No 121, 983), para 2.32 and note of dissent; Working Paper No 60 (Firm Offers), paras 55 and 56; Law Commission Working Paper No 93, Transfer of Land: Formalities for Deeds and Escrows (1985), 4.2–3; Report No 160, Sale and Supply of Goods (Cmnd 137, 1987), paras 2.26, 3.5–.12, 4.1–.6, 4.10–.24, 6.10–.20 and page 70; Report No 154, (Cmnd 9700, 1986), paras 2.7, 2.10–.13, 2.15, 2.17, 2.22–.24.

Incorporated Council of Law Reporting: Law Reports and Weekly Law Reports.

Indiana University Trustees and Fred B. Rothman & Co: Schwartz, 'The Private Law Treatment of Defective Products in Sales Situations' (1973) 49 Indiana LJ 8, 21–22.

International Encyclopaedia of Comparative Law: Excerpts from Stewart Macaulay 'The Standardised Contracts of United States Automobile Manufacturers': Int Enc Comp L VII, Ch 3 Contracts in General S3–21/29 Tübingen/The Hague 1974 reprinted with permission.

Archibald Kenrick & Sons Ltd: sets of Conditions.

Law Book Company: Commonwealth Law Reports.

Little, Brown and Company: Kessler and Sharp, *Contracts, Cases and*

Materials (1953), p 5; Kronman and Posner, *Economics of Contract Law* (1979), pp 1–5; Posner, *Economic Analysis of Law* (2nd ed, 1977), pp 66–70, 75–77, 88–92, 94–95.

Lloyds of London Press Ltd: Lloyds Law Reports.

McGill Law Journal: Slayton, 'The unequal bargain doctrine' (1976) 22 McGill LJ 94, 106.

National Consumer Council: Buying problems (1984), para 3.12.

Napier: *The contract of employment in Labour Law in Britain* (ed R. Lewis, (1986), pp 327–331, 337–339, 347–348.

New Zealand Council of Law Reporting: New Zealand Law Reports.

New Zealand Tonnage Committee: New Zealand Southbound Trade Bill of Lading (1978) (some of the terms and conditions have since been updated, and more recent versions are available and in use).

Northwestern University Press: Macneil, 'Contracts: Adjustment of Long-Term Economic Relations Under Classical, Neo-Classical and Relational Contract Law' (1978), 72 Northwestern University LR 854, 859–870, 873–874, 901.

Ohio State University Press: Gilmore, *The Death of Contract*, 87–88 and 90.

Oxford University Press: Atiyah, *The Rise and Fall of Freedom of Contract* (1979), pp 337–338; Lawson & Ruden, *Law of Property* (2nd edn, 1982), pp 26–32; Reiter, 'The Control of Contract Power' (1981) 1 Oxford J of Legal Studies 347, 348–350, 358–361; Anson, *Law of Contract* (26th edn), pp 268–269.

RIBA Publications Limited: Clause 30 of the JCT Form of Building Contract 1963.

Sweet & Maxwell Ltd: Grodecki, 'In Pari Delicto' (1955) 71 LQR 254, 265–269; Reynolds, 'Warranty, Condition and Fundamental Term' (1963) 79 LQR 534, 539; Simpson, 'Innovation in Nineteenth Century Contract Law' (1975) 91 LQR 247, 268; Atiyah, 'Promises, Obligations and The Law of Contract' (1978) LQR 193, 201–205, 208–209, 211–212, 214–220; Harris, Ogus and Phillips, Contract Remedies and the Consumer Surplus (1979) 95 LQR 581, 583, 585, 588, 590–593, 595–597. English Reports. Property and Compensation Reports.

Times Publishing Co: Times Law Reports.

Professor G. H. Treitel: 'Some problems of breach of contract' (1967) 30 MLR 139, 149–150.

United Dominions Trust Ltd: specimen Guarantee and Indemnity Agreement.

The University of Bristol: Alumni Foundation Form of Covenant.

University of Chicago Law Review: Kronman, 'Specific Performacne' (1978) 44 U of Chicago LR 351, 357–363, 365–369.

University of Chicago Press: Journal of Law & Economics: Epstein, 'Unconscionability: a Critical Re-appraisal', (1975) 18 JLE 293–294. The

Journal of Legal Studies: Posner and Rosenfield, 'Impossibility and Related Doctrines in Contract Law: An Economic Analysis' (1977) 6 J Legal Studies 83, 87, 88, 89, 90, 91, 92; Posner, 'Gratuitous promises in economics and law' (1977) 6 J Legal Studies 411, 411–415, 417–418, 421–424; Kronman, 'Mistake Disclosure Information and the Law of Contracts' (1978) 7 J Legal Studies, 1, 2–5, 13–15, 25; Bishop, 'The Contract-Tort Boundary and the Economics of Insurance' (1983) 12 J Legal Studies 241, 254–256, 259; Rea, 'Efficiency Implications of Penalties and Liquidated Damages' (1984) 13 J Legal Studies 147, 159–161; Danzig, 'Hadley v Baxendale: a Study in the Industrialization of the Law' (1975) 4 JLS 249, 279–283.

University of Maryland: Kennedy, 'Distributive and Paternalist Motives in Contract and Tort Law' (1982) 41 Maryland LR 563, 580–583.

University of Toronto Law Journal: Furmston, 'The Analysis of Illegal Contracts' (1966) 16 University of Toronto LJ 267, 267–268; Ramsay, 'Consumer Redress Mechanisms for Poor-Quality and Defective Products' (1981) 21 of Toronto LJ, 117, 134–136.

The University of Wisconsin Press: Friedman, *Contract Law in America* (1965), pp 11–12, 186–187, 189–190, 217.

Virginia Law Review Association and Fred B. Rothman & Co: Macneil, 'Efficient Breach of Contract: Circles in the Sky' (1982) 68 Virginia LR 947, 957; Macneil, 'Restatement (Second) of Contracts and Presentation' (1974) 60 Virginia LR 589, 588–596; Leff, 'Economic Analysis of Law: Some Realism About Nominalism' (1974) 60 Virginia LR 451, 456–458 and 478–479.

Westland plc: part of warranty clause.

West Publishing Co: Feeral Reporter (1946); Atlantic Reporter (1969); North Eastern Reporter (1891, 1917); North Western Reporter (1965); Pacific Reporter (1958, 1960).

Yale Law Journal Company and Fred B. Rothman & Company and the authors: Corbin, 'Conditions in the Law of Contract', vol 28, pp 739, 759; Fuller & Perdue, 'The Reliance Interest in Contract Damages', vol 46, pp 52–65; Schartz, 'The Case for Specific Performance', vol 89, pp. 271, 280–89; Kronman, 'Paternalism and the Law of Contracts', vol 92, pp 763–64, 766, 771–72, 774–75, 778–78, 786–87, 797–98; Whitford, 'Comment on A Theory of the Consumer Product Waranty', vol 91, pp 1371–1372; Dalton, 'An Essay in the Deconstruction of Contract Doctrine' (1985) 94 Yale LJ 997, 1015–1019; Kronman, 'Contract Law and Distributive Justice' (1980) 89 Yale LJ 472, 477–483.

Almost all extracts have been reproduced without footnotes.

Table of statutes

References in **bold** type indicate where the section of an Act is set out in part or in full. References to *Statutes* are to Halsbury's Statutes of England (Fourth Edition) showing the volume and page at which the annotated text of the Act will be found.

Table of cases

Case names and page references printed in bold type indicate that an extract from the judgment of a case is set out in the text. Names of the cases noted at any length are also shown in bold type.

U

Section 1
Introduction

CHAPTER 1
Contracts and contract law

(a) The scope of contract law

What is contract law? What is it for? Both questions are of fundamental importance, but it is surprisingly difficult to give a definitive answer to either. Contract law is most obviously the law relating to agreements or promises. As we shall see, it is primarily concerned with agreements that involve one party, or each party, giving an undertaking or promise to the other. It governs such questions as which agreements the law will enforce, what obligations are imposed by the agreement in question and what remedies are available if the obligations are not performed. Thus one answer to the first question might be that contract law is the law based on liability for breach of promise. When a lawyer says that on a particular set of facts contractual liability will arise, she usually means liability in this sense, predicated upon a promise which has been broken. In the next chapter we will explore the main characteristics of contractual liability and compare it with liability in tort and in restitution. However, 'contract law' is also used to mean the whole collection of rules which apply to contracts, and these include many rules which are not 'contractual' in the sense of being based on a promise to do something. For example, if one party induces the other to enter a contract by fraud or misrepresentation, the innocent party may be able to claim compensation based largely not on contract but on tort or statute. Despite the conceptual differences, the rules on misrepresentation as between contracting parties are 'part of' contract law. There is no precise consensus among lawyers as to just which rules fall into this wider category: for instance, in the next chapter we will look at some cases which involve tortious not contractual liability, but which are concerned with a series of contracts.

We shall see that there is even some controversy over the exact scope of contractual liability in the narrow sense. The traditional view is that it is predicated upon breach of a promise that formed part of an agreed exchange between the parties, and that unless there was to be some exchange there cannot be contractual liability. Some commentators now argue that there may also be contractual liability when there was simply a promise by one party to another with nothing in exchange but the other party has relied on the promise in some way. We will explore the extent to which English contract law recognises such 'reliance' liability in section 2. For the moment it is enough to think of contractual liability as based on promises forming part of agreed exchanges, but to note that sometimes there is only a rather attenuated form of exchange.

While contract law is primarily concerned with supporting the social institution of exchange, the law is not as broad as the institution. An

3

enormous proportion of our life is carried on on the basis of exchanges that are in some sense agreements, but many of them are not governed by what is usually thought of as contract law. Some are not governed by law at all, like domestic arrangements over household chores made by spouses or flatmates. Others are so complex that although they are to some extent still governed by contract law, the latter only plays a fairly small part in a scheme governed also by other common law principles and heavily dependent on special rules developed for the particular transactions. These have come to be viewed as legal subjects in their own right. Company law is an example, and to a lesser extent the law of employment.

Even in these cases it would be a mistake to think of contract law as irrelevant. There is no such thing as a contract in the abstract. Every contract is made, or is found by the court to exist, in a particular context – a contract to sell goods to a consumer, a contract to charter the services of a ship, a contract to look after an elderly relative in exchange for a share in his property when he dies: the possibilities are almost endless. Sometimes few other legal rules are relevant. Then the obligations of the parties fall to be determined almost entirely by purely contractual principles. At other times there are many other rules, yet contract may still be in the background providing the framework for the transaction and the general principles on which the court or contract drafter can rely.

In this book we will be studying mainly the general rules of contract, but we will not ignore the special rules governing particular types of contract. The needs and difficulties which led to their development can tell us a good deal about the value of the general rules. We also have to remember that the courts always have to apply even the general rules in the context of the particular contract. Sometimes there is nothing particularly difficult in the context and the general rule is applied straightforwardly. At other times we shall see that the need to fit the rules to the contexts seems to produce some rather odd results. But usually the courts keep the general rules fairly abstract and then apply these rules rather differently in the various contexts with which they are confronted. We shall see countless examples.

Professor Ian Macneil has suggested a distinction which has excited a good deal of academic interest in the last few years. This is between 'discrete' and 'relational' exchanges. Many simple exchanges are to be completed within a short time scale. What each party is to do can easily be agreed and the exchange will not involve the parties in any longer term relationship to each other, nor involve anyone else. The casual purchase of fruit from a roadside stall is a simple example. Such exchanges can be treated in isolation from any other and there is little relevant background to consider (hence 'discrete'). Other exchanges may be much more complex. Firstly, the parties may expect to be co-operating with each other over a long enough period that it is hard for them to decide at the outset exactly what each of them is to do; they will have to adjust their relationship as it progresses. An employment contract is an example. Secondly, other people may be involved in the project – for instance in a large construction project or a distribution chain. The parties may try to deal with these complexities in various ways: for instance they may enter flexible long-term contracts, perhaps with several parties, or they may make a series of short-term contracts. In either event the law may have to treat this 'relational' contracting differently, for instance by providing mechanisms for allowing flexibility or by recognising that the short term contracts need to be considered in the context of the understandings and expectations engendered by the longer-term relationship from which they sprang. Whether the modern law of contract caters adequately for relational contracting is an open question which will be explored later (see especially below, p 620).

There are so many different contracts and within the area of 'contract law' there are in fact so many special rules, both statutory and common law, governing particular contracts that many commentators prefer to speak of a law of *contracts*. One went so far as to describe the idea of a unitary law as the artificial construct of law teachers in the latter part of the nineteenth century (Gilmore, *The Death of Contract*). Whatever the origin of the unitary theory, it seems to have many judges among its adherents (eg below p 434), and though this might be because they have never escaped the baleful influence of their contract(s) teachers, a more plausible hypothesis is that the unitary approach has its uses. If, for instance, the court faces a set of facts where there is no authority relating to the particular type of contract, it is obviously helpful to be able to fall back on general principles developed in relation to other types of contract. On the other hand, it has to be admitted that sometimes the unitary theory hinders the development of a solution which would be particularly appropriate to one type of contract but would be inappropriate for the majority of contract types. The fact that there seem to be more rules applying to single contract types derived from eighteenth century cases (see, eg, below, p 658) than from modern ones lends some support to Gilmore's thesis. But for the moment it is not necessary to decide on the merits of the singular versus the plural, if indeed there is any one answer; it is sufficient to bear in mind that there are many different contract types and that some do have idiosyncratic rules.

Thus the core of this book is an analysis of the law relating to promises and agreements. The book does not, however, stop there. Firstly, to get a proper picture of what contract law is, it is necessary to see it in the context of other legal rules which are not so closely related as to be thought of as 'part of' the subject. In particular it is important to compare liability in contract with liability in tort and in restitution, to see how the rules interconnect and how the concepts differ. The materials in the second chapter of this Introduction are chosen for this purpose.

(b) The function of contract law

Secondly, the book also attempts to answer the second question, what is contract law for? No study of an area of law will be complete without an attempt to analyse the rules in terms of their function: we need to answer such questions as what is the purpose of this rule, does it achieve the desired effect, and could the effect be reached more easily by other means? This type of analysis is much less well-developed than the traditional legal one, but it is equally important.

So what is contract law for? By the end of the book it will become very clear that there is no one answer, because contract law has many 'purposes', but the central one is to support and to control the millions of agreements that collectively make up the 'market economy'.

We live in a 'mixed' economy, one in which the allocation of resources is determined partly by administrative decisions of public officials and partly through the private sector. For instance, for the majority of the population, the provision of education is largely undertaken and controlled by the State, and the division of the myriad tasks involved is a matter of administrative decision; whereas the provision of food is left to private enterprise, to the many individuals and companies who are primarily motivated by the quest for profit. Of course, neither scheme is purely public or private: the education authorities operate through contracts with their suppliers, their employees and quite possibly between different organs of the authorities, while the food market is heavily influenced by subsidies, taxes and regulations. But the mainspring of each system is different, and so is the legal regime. If a person wishes to complain about a failure in the provision of education, any legal remedy will usually be in administrative or perhaps criminal law, whereas failure to provide food will normally give rise to remedies only if a breach of contract is involved.

In order to have a stable capitalist or mixed economy, the law must guarantee the freedom of individuals and the protection of property, real, personal and intellectual. These laws form the link between persons and resources, including labour. The private enterprise system depends, however, on the exchange of resources. Some exchanges can take place simultaneously without any promises being involved, so that one can say simply that resource x, which was A's, is now the property of B; unless A has given some additional undertaking, such as that x is of a particular quality or will last a certain length of time, contract law has nothing to say about such a trade. But for the most part the process of exchange involves a period of time, and the extension of credit by one party to the other—maybe credit in the normal sense of having to wait to be paid, maybe credit in the sense of having to trust that the other will do as he promised or that some assurance he gave about the goods will turn out to be true. It is here that contract law comes in. For instance, the law will support the exchange by enforcing what the parties agreed if one party defaults; and it provides a set of rules which apply when something goes wrong and the agreement is silent as to what is to happen. This simultaneously provides a mechanism for deciding existing disputes and provides a set of 'standard terms' for each type of contract, so saving parties contracting in the future the need to negotiate a complete set of terms for themselves.

Contract law operates most obviously in the context of dispute resolution in the courtroom. But it will be apparent that contract law also has an importance outside the courtroom: by empowering the parties to make an agreement that the law will then enforce, it enables them to make exchanges that might otherwise carry too great a risk, whether of disruption by some contingency or of default by the other party. They can arrange matters so that the risk is shared, and they can devise remedies to coerce each other into performance. There are limits to what the law permits in this respect, as we shall see, but the planning function of contract law is an essential one. We shall return frequently to the theme of how proper contract planning can avoid a particular problem.

Thus the book will concentrate on what we see as being the core of contract law, the commercial agreements made between business and business, business and employee, and business and consumer. How is contract law's function in relation to these to be described or assessed? A first step is to look at the agreements which are actually made in commerce. This will not only give context to the disputes in the cases in the book; it will also show how contract draftsmen react to the factual problems and legal rules with which they are confronted, and re-emphasizes the 'planning' aspect of contract law. Readers will of course be familiar with the many simple contracts each of us makes each day when buying goods in a shop, taking a bus or getting a haircut. They may not be so familiar with more complex commercial transactions, and for this reason chapter 3 of the Introduction contains a number of specimen contract documents, with some notes to explain the main features of each one. Each contract is of a type which will feature in some case later in the book. In addition, there will be frequent examples of particular types of contract clause throughout.

A second step is to attempt to analyse the court's decisions not just in terms of logic and consistency with authority, but also in terms of underlying policy. Is the court, consciously or unconsciously, adopting a rule which supports the market, and if so, how does the rule do so? We shall see that a given situation may give rise to several possible approaches. For example, the fact that contract law operates as a dispute resolution mechanism in the courtroom, and at the same time as a device for future contract planning, often gives rise to a tension between 'flexibility' and 'certainty'. The court may have to choose between a solution which will produce an apparently fair solution to the dispute before it, but which will lead to considerable uncertainty in future contracting, and a rule which will be easier to apply but less fair. Which should the court adopt? Some of the policies the courts can pursue are explored in readings contained in chapter 4.

One of these policies needs separate mention. So far, we have described contract law as supporting the institution of private exchange by creating power in the parties to commit themselves to legally enforceable agreements. It is important to note, however, that at the same time as it creates this power, contract law goes some way to controlling its exercise. In some cases the control takes the form of frustrating the intentions of the parties for the good of the rest of society: thus contracts which involve the commission of serious crimes or which are for some other reason contrary to public policy may be unenforceable (see Section 9). More frequently the control is for the supposed benefit of the parties themselves. Contract power can be abused or used unwisely; people are occasionally caught in extreme need, are sometimes rash and are frequently ill-informed. The law may step in to protect them against the consequences of the agreements they made in these circumstances, especially if the other party has contributed to the situation or has taken advantage of it. The most obvious forms of the policing of bargains will be found in Section 8, but the theme of control pervades the whole of contract law. The preliminary readings in chapter 4 of this Introduction also deal with this aspect of contract law. In the context of private consumers, there are now so many statutory controls over contracting that 'consumer law' is treated as a subject in its own right; we do not see it as conceptually distinct from contract, but for reasons of space only a selection of the controls will be covered in this book.

We have presented contract law as being primarily concerned with exchanges, and in terms of the number of contracts made and their economic importance this must be correct. However we want to re-emphasise that contract law is sometimes concerned with situations that involve 'exchanges' of a most marginal nature, if they are exchanges at all. We shall see a number of cases where family arrangements that were not obviously profit-seeking exchanges were nonetheless enforced as contracts, and a few cases where liability was imposed on a party and was justified in terms of there being a contract, although it is extremely doubtful whether the parties were thinking in those terms. In other words, contract law is not just the law that is applied to what we normally think of as exchanges; it is also a mode of analysis, a justification for legal intervention, that can be used by a judge in other situations. The book contains several examples of this, eg *Tanner v Tanner* (below, p 17) and *De la Bere v Pearson* (below, p 134). Whether it is always an appropriate analysis for the other situations is another question; sometimes contractual liability may be imposed because for some reason the court finds itself unable to impose liability on any other basis, yet it may not seem right to impose the full consequences of contractual liability (see, for example, p 152 below). These marginal cases may seem to take up the courts' time and space in the book that is out of all proportion to their economic significance, but legally they are very important: they mark the boundaries of the subject, and often illuminate clearly what is understood by contractual liability, as opposed to liability in, say, restitution.

(c) Contract as a dynamic body of rules

Much of the law of consumer protection mentioned earlier is of fairly recent origin, and this serves to emphasize the point that contract law is dynamic, always developing and sometimes changing rapidly as new problems confront the courts and legislature. Sometimes the problem is an internal legal one: for instance, the growth of the doctrine of consideration as a limitation on what promises will be enforced (see Section 2) seems to have been prompted by the adoption in the sixteenth century of a new form of action, the action of assumpsit, to enforce promises. Before that, promises were actionable in the royal courts only if they were part of one of a recognised type of exchange such as a sale, or were made in a sealed covenant or bond. The new action might have led to the enforceability of any promise, however informal and even if nothing was to be received in return, but it came to be limited by the consideration doctrine. More often new developments in contract law have been prompted by changes in society: thus, the rules on offer and acceptance (to be discussed in Section 3) seem to have been a response to the growth of contracting between parties at a distance when a reliable postal system was established in the early nineteenth century; many of the rules governing exemption clauses (see Section 8, chapter 34) are a response to the increased use of pre-printed standard form contracts in the late nineteenth and twentieth centuries.

The American writer Horwitz has argued that during the nineteenth century, when much of the framework of modern contract law was established in a recognisable form, the courts were actively transforming the law in order to create the conditions necessary for economic growth and social development (see (1974) 87 Harvard LR 917). The thesis has been doubted. Firstly, it is not clear that there was a transformation; rather, there was very little contract law before the nineteenth century and the courts were developing rules to govern many situations for the first time (see Simpson (1979) 47 Chicago LR 533). Secondly, the relationship between the law and economic development seems to have been much more complex than the theory suggests (see Rubin, GR and Sugarman, D (eds) *Law, Economy and Society 1750–1914*, pp 3–12). But no one doubts that there is a connection.

There is also a clear connection between the development of contract law and contemporary political thought. In his *Rise and Fall of Freedom of Contract* Atiyah has traced the influence of notions of *laissez faire* on the nineteenth century law and then the gradual increase in controls over contracts as the more collective notions underlying the welfare state emerged. During the last decade this trend seems to have been reversed again; Atiyah argues that this reflects the thinking of the 'New Right' (see his *Introduction to the Law of Contract* (4th ed, 1989), pp 30–39).

Frequently the need for a solution to a new problem has made the judges look to other legal systems. During the nineteenth century the judges were much influenced by Roman law (which many of them would have studied) and by continental writers such as Pothier. We shall see that the introduction of continental ideas has not always met with success, because of the conceptual differences between the common law and the civil law, but it is remarkable to what extent the civil law systems do in fact reach similar results to the common law. Perhaps this should not surprise us: the needs of an effective legal framework for the use of resources in producing goods and services will be essentially the same in every society of a given type. As Holmes wrote over a century ago:

> The substance of the law at any given time pretty nearly corresponds, so far as it goes, with what is then understood to be convenient; but its form and machinery, and the degree to which it is able to work out desired results, depend very much upon its past.

(*The Common Law* (1882), pp 1–2.) We will occasionally refer to the civil law's solution to problems, but more often we will compare the devices employed in other common law jurisdictions, notably the United States, where the law started from the same base as ours but has in many ways developed rather differently.

(d) Economic and empirical analysis

Looking at specimen contracts certainly gives some idea of the function of contract law, but it is only a starting point, and the fact that a draftsman has confronted a problem in this way or that can only tell us a limited amount: it does not tell us, for instance, whether his device was effective to achieve what he had in mind, even if we are sure what that was. The same is true of court decisions: not only may we be unsure what end the court was pursuing, but we may have little idea beyond instinct as to the results the rule enunciated is likely to produce in future situations. For a more rigorous analysis we must turn to other academic disciplines. In the context of contract, the most intensively used discipline to date is micro-economics. This by no means provides all the answers, but a limited amount of simple economic analysis can give extremely interesting and valuable insights into the way that contracting parties are likely to react to various rules of law, and into the costs involved in the different legal approaches. The book contains a number of readings from the 'law and economics' literature, and after many of the cases there will be questions designed to prompt an economic analysis of the problems. For those who, like two of your editors, have no training in economics, a basic introduction to the necessary concepts is contained in chapter 4 of the Introduction.

Even economic analysis gives only theoretical models of the likely impact of a rule of law under certain, often quite limiting, assumptions. Ascertaining the 'real' function of the law requires empirical investigation. Unfortunately only a very limited amount of work has so far been done in this field: on both sides of the Atlantic there are fewer than twenty significant empirical pieces on contract law. Extracts from many of the pieces will be found below. They present a sharp contrast to the blackletter law of the contract texts, and even the economists' models: to give the flavour some extracts are given in chapter 5 of the Introduction. The extracts show that contract law is not always the answer to the businessman or -woman's prayer; indeed, it sometimes seems an irrelevance. This work is important for at least two reasons. From an academic viewpoint, it is part of the analysis of the function and the limits of law. It is also important from a strictly practical viewpoint. The pieces bring out that 'using' contract law— even just making enforceable contracts—is an expensive business. A lawyer who is consulted about a contract dispute or drafting a contract, and who immediately recommends litigation or the negotiation of a long and complex agreement, will scare clients away. Before giving advice the lawyer must weigh the costs of litigation or negotiation against the likely benefits, and the more the lawyer knows about the way contract functions in practice, the better his or her advice is likely to be.

(e) Plan of the book

It may be helpful to end this Introduction with a summary of what is to follow in the later sections, so that the reader has some idea of what is to come. Section 2 deals with the question of what agreements or promises are recognized by the law as being contractual and thus prima facie enforceable. Section 3 covers the questions of whether an effective agreement has been reached. The core of the book is then contained in Sections 4 and 5, which cover respectively the topics of the liabilities under various agreements and the remedies available when some disruption occurs. Section 6 explores 'contract theory': in many respects the readings in Section 6 are chosen to develop themes mentioned in this Introduction. Section 7 deals with changes in the agreement, a difficult and important topic given the long-term nature of many contracts. Section 8 is on policing, though as mentioned above this theme crops up regularly in the other sections. Section 9 covers agreements that are unenforceable for reasons of illegality or public policy, and the book ends with a section dealing with contracts involving or affecting more than two parties.

CHAPTER 2

Contract, tort and restitution

The aim of this chapter is to introduce some of the basic concepts which underlie the three categories of personal liability recognised by the common law, contract, tort and restitution. It looks at the different ideas on which each type of liability is founded and the remedies available, in particular the way in which compensation is measured.

(a) Contract

Contractual liability is based on the defendant's failure to perform an undertaking or 'promise'. We shall see that the promise may be express or the court may infer one from the circumstances, but a promise is one of the essential elements of contractual liability and if the court finds that the defendant did not promise anything there can be no contractual liability. (The plaintiff must also have accepted the defendant's promise and have provided 'consideration' for it, see below).

Taylor v Brewer (1813) 1 M&S 290, 105 ER 108, King's Bench

Walsh had worked for a committee which had been formed to manage the sale of lottery tickets. The committee had, on 4 January 1810, resolved that 'any service to be rendered by Walsh should, after the third lottery, be taken into consideration, and such remuneration be made as should be deemed right.' Walsh had become bankrupt and his debts had been assigned to the plaintiff, who sued the members of the committee for recompense for the work Walsh had done. Lord Ellenborough nonsuited the plaintiff, whose counsel moved to set aside the nonsuit.

Park moved to set aside the nonsuit, on the ground that the bankrupt was entitled to some recompense; inasmuch as an agreement with a person that he should do work, and should have what is right for it, did not import that he should have nothing for his trouble if his employer should be so minded, but that he should have a reasonable reward: it should have been left therefore to the jury to consider what was reasonable, as was done in *Peacock v Peacock*.

Lord Ellenborough CJ. In that case the defendant expressly told the plaintiff that he should have a share in the business, leaving only unsettled what particular share he was to have: but here, I own it struck me, was an engagement accepted by the bankrupt on no definite terms, but only in confidence that if his labour deserved any thing he should be recompensed for it by the defendants. This was throwing himself upon the mercy of those with whom he contracted; and the same thing does not unfrequently happen in contracts with several of the departments of Government.

Grose J. I consider the resolution to import that the committee were to judge whether any or what recompense was right.

Le Blanc J. It seems to me to be merely an engagement of honour.

Bayley J. The fair meaning of the resolution is this, that it was to be in the breast of the committee whether he was to have any thing, and if any thing, then how much.

Rule refused

NOTE

Lord Ellenborough describes Walsh as 'contracting' with the defendants, but he was probably not using 'contract' to refer to any legal obligation: it seems to have been the court's unanimous view that the committee was promising nothing. Compare the words of Le Blanc J.

Often the question whether a promise has been made is put in terms of whether an offer has been made by the defendant, or, when the defendant has made some statement that might have been an undertaking, whether the statement was intended as a binding commitment.

Carlill v Carbolic Smoke Ball Co [1893] 1 QB 256, Court of Appeal

The defendants inserted in the Pall Mall Gazette and other newspapers the advertisement reproduced on p 59. The plaintiff, on the faith of this advertisment, bought a smoke ball and used it as directed three times a day from 20 November 1891 to 17 January 1892, when she caught influenza. Hawkins J held that she was entitled to £100, and the defendants appealed.

Lindley LJ . . . The first observation I will make is that we are not dealing with any inference of fact. We are dealing with an express promise to pay 100*l* in certain events. Read the advertisement how you will, and twist it about as you will, here is a distinct promise expressed in language which is perfectly unmistakable—'100*l* reward will be paid by the Carbolic Smoke Ball Company to any person who contracts the influenza after having used the ball three times daily for two weeks according to the printed directions supplied with each ball.'

We must first consider whether this was intended to be a promise at all, or whether it was a mere puff which meant nothing. Was it a mere puff? My answer to that question is No, and I base my answer upon this passage: '1000*l* is deposited with the Alliance Bank, shewing our sincerity in the matter.' Now, for what was that money deposited or that statement made except to negative the suggestion that this was a mere puff and meant nothing at all? The deposit is called in aid by the advertiser as proof of his sincerity in the matter—that is, the sincerity of his promise to pay this 100*l* in the event which he has specified. I say this for the purpose of giving point to the observation that we are not inferring a promise; there is the promise, as plain as words can make it.

Then it is contended that it is not binding. In the first place, it is said that it is not made with anybody in particular. Now that point is common to the words of this advertisement and to the words of all other advertisements offering rewards. They are offers to anybody who performs the conditions named in the advertisement, and anybody who does perform the condition accepts the offer. In point of law this advertisement is an offer to pay 100*l* to anybody who will perform these conditions, and the performance of the conditions is the acceptance of the offer. That rests upon a string of authorities, the earliest of which is *Williams v Carwardine*, which has been followed by many other decisions upon advertisements offering rewards.

Bowen LJ. . . . We were asked to say that this document was a contract too vague to be enforced.

The first observation which arises is that the document itself is not a contract at all, it is only an offer made to the public. The defendants contend next, that it is an offer the terms of which are too vague to be treated as a definite offer, inasmuch as there is no limit of time fixed for the catching of the influenza, and it cannot be supposed that the advertisers seriously meant to promise to pay money to every person who catches the influenza at any time after the inhaling of the smoke ball. It was urged also, that if you look at this document you will find much vagueness as to the persons with whom the contract was intended to be made—that, in the first place, its terms are wide enough to include persons who may have used the smoke ball before the advertisement was issued; at all events, that it is an offer to the world in general, and, also, that it is unreasonable to suppose it to be a definite offer, because nobody in their senses would contract themselves out of the opportunity of checking the experiment which was going to be made at their own expense. It is also contended that the advertisment is rather in the nature of a puff or a proclamation than a promise or offer intended to mature into a contract when accepted. But the main point seems to be that the vagueness of the document shews that no contract whatever was intended. It seems to me that in order to arrive at a right conclusion we must read this advertisement in its plain meaning, as the public would understand it. It was intended to be issued to the public and to be read by the public. How would an ordinary person reading this document construe it? It was intended unquestionably to have some effect, and I think the effect which it was intended to have, was to make people use the smoke ball, because the suggestions and allegations which it contains are directed immediately to the use of the smoke ball as distinct from the purchase of it. It did not follow that the smoke ball was to be purchased from the defendants directly, or even from agents of theirs directly. The intention was that the circulation of the smoke ball should be promoted, and that the use of it should be increased. The advertisement begins by saying that a reward will be paid by the Carbolic Smoke Ball Company to any person who contracts the increasing epidemic after using the ball. It has been said that the words do not apply only to persons who contract the epidemic after the publication of the advertisement, but include persons who had previously contracted the influenza. I cannot so read the advertisement. It is written in colloquial and popular language, and I think that it is equivalent to this; '100*l* will be paid to any person who shall contract the increasing epidemic after having used the carbolic smoke ball three times daily for two weeks'. And it seems to me that the way in which the public would read it would be this, that if anybody, after the advertisement was published, used three times daily for two weeks the carbolic smoke ball, and then caught cold, he would be entitled to the reward. Then again it was said: 'How long is this protection to endure? Is it to go on for ever, or for what limit of time?' . . .

I . . . have myself no hesitation in saying that I think, on the construction of this advertisement, the protection was to enure during the time that the carbolic smoke ball was being used. My brother, the Lord Justice who preceded me, thinks that the contract would be sufficiently definite if you were to read it in the sense that the protection was to be warranted during a reasonable period after use. I have some difficulty myself on that point; but it is not necessary for me to consider it further, because the disease here was contracted during the use of the carbolic smoke ball.

Was it intended that the 100*l* should, if the conditions be fulfilled, be paid? The advertisement says that 1000*l* is lodged at the bank for the purpose. Therefore, it cannot be said that the statement that 100*l* would be paid was intended to be a mere puff. I think it was intended to be understood by the public as an offer which was to be acted upon.

But it was said there was no check on the part of the persons who issued the advertisement, and that it would be an insensate thing to promise 100*l* to a person who used the smoke ball unless you could check or superintend his manner of using it. The answer to that argument seems to be that if a person chooses to make extravagant promises of this kind he probably does so because it pays him to make them, and, if he has made them, the extravagance of the promises is no reason in law why he should not be bound by them.

[Further extracts from this case will be found below, p 184.]

NOTES

1. At the time many exaggerated claims were made in advertisements for quack medicine and the case excited a good deal of interest. See Simpson (1985) 14 J Legal Studies 345.
2. The doctrines of intention to create legal relations and offer and acceptance are examined in greater detail in chapters 8 and 9 respectively.
3. The Carbolic Smoke Ball Company's advertisement contained a promise and the Court held that it was contractually binding. There are many examples of promises which are held not to be intended as legal

commitments, especially promises made on social occasions or in domestic contexts: see chapter 8.

4. You will notice that although the Lord Justices are discussing whether the advertisement was intended as a contract or as a mere puff, they do not consider what the defendants actually intended. Normally in contract the subjective intentions of the parties are irrelevant; intention is judged 'objectively', that is, as it would reasonably appear to the other party. It is what you say or do that is important, not what you mean. This is explored in more detail below, pp 168–170 and 231ff.

Kleinwort Benson Ltd v Malaysia Mining Corpn Bhd [1989] 1 All ER 785, Court of Appeal

The defendants' wholly owned subsidiary, Metals, had been set up to operate as a ring-dealing member of the London Metal Exchange. This required large sums of money and the plaintiffs granted Metals an acceptance credit/multi-currency cash loan facility to a maximum of £5m. During negotiations the plaintiffs sought a guarantee of the loan from the defendants, but the defendants refused. Instead the defendants furnished to the plaintiffs two 'letters of comfort' each of which stated, in paragraph 3, that 'It is our policy to ensure that the business of [Metals] is at all times in a position to meet its liabilities to you under the loan facility arrangements.' The letters also stated that the defendants would not reduce their current financial interest in Metals until the loans had been repaid.

In 1985 the tin market collapsed (for an account see *Maclaine Watson & Co Ltd v Department of Trade and Industry* [1988] 3 All ER 257) and Metals went into liquidation without repaying the plaintiffs. The plaintiffs brought an action against the defendants to recover the amount owing and Hirst J upheld their claim.

Ralph Gibson LJ. The central question in this case, in my judgment, is that considered in *Esso Petroleum Co Ltd v Mardon* [1976] QB 801, [1976] 2 All ER 5, on which counsel for the plaintiffs relied in this court but which was not cited to Hirst J. That question is whether the words of para 3, considered in their context, are to be treated as a warranty or contractual promise. Paragraph 3 contains no express words of promise. Paragraph 3 is in its terms a statement of present fact and not a promise as to future conduct. I agree with the submission of counsel for the defendants that, in this regard, the words of para 3 are in sharp contrast with the words of para 2 of the letter: 'We confirm that we will not' etc. The force of this point is not limited, as Hirst J stated it, to the absence from para 3 of the words 'We confirm'. The real contrast is between the words of promise, namely 'We will not' in para 2, and the words of statement of fact, 'It is our policy' in para 3. Hirst J held that, by the words of para 3, the defendants gave an undertaking that now and at all times in the future, so long as Metals should be under any liability to the plaintiffs under the facility arrangements, it is *and will be* the defendants' policy to ensure that Metals is in a position to meet their liabilities. To derive that meaning from the words it is necessary to add the words emphasised, namely 'and will be', which do not appear in para 3. In short, the words of promise as to the future conduct of the defendants were held by Hirst J to be part of the necessary meaning of the words used in para 3. The question is whether that view of the words can be upheld.

The absence of express words of warranty as to present facts or the absence of express words of promise as to future conduct does not conclusively exclude a statement from the status of warranty or promise. . . .

The evidence does not show that the words used in para 3 were intended to be a promise as to the future conduct of the defendants but, in my judgment, it shows the contrary.

The concept of a comfort letter was, as counsel for the defendants acknowledged, not shown to have acquired any particular meaning at the time of the negotiations in this case with reference to the limits of any legal liability to be assumed under its terms by a parent company. A letter, which the parties might have referred to at some stage as a letter of comfort, might, after negotiation, have emerged containing in para 3 in express terms the words used by Hirst J to state the meaning which he gave to para 3. The court would not, merely because the parties had referred to the document as a comfort letter, refuse to give effect to the meaning of the words used. But in this case it is clear, in my judgment, that the concept of a comfort letter, to which the parties had resort when the defendants refused to assume joint and several liability or to give a guarantee, was known by both sides at least to extend to or to include a document under which the defendants would give comfort to the plaintiffs by assuming, not a legal liability to ensure repayment of the liabilities of its subsidiary, but a moral responsibility only. Thus, when the defendants by Mr John Green in June 1984 told the plaintiffs that Mr Green would recommend that credit lines for Metals be covered by a letter of comfort rather than by guarantee, the response of Mr Irwin, before any draft of a comfort letter had been prepared, was '. . . that a letter of comfort would not be a problem, but that [he] would probably have to charge a higher rate'. The comfort letter was drafted in terms which in para 3 do not express any contractual promise and which are consistent with being no more than a representation of fact. If they are treated as no more than a representation of fact, they are in that meaning consistent with the comfort letter containing no more than the assumption of moral responsibility by the defendants in respect of the debts of Metals. There is nothing in the evidence to show that, as a matter of commercial probability or common sense, the parties must have intended para 3 to be a contractual promise, which is not expressly stated, rather than a mere representation of fact which is so stated.

Next, the first draft of the comfort letter was produced by the plaintiffs. Paragraph 1 contained confirmation that the defendants knew of and approved of the granting of the facilities in question by the plaintiffs to Metals, and para 2 contained the express confirmation that the defendants would not reduce their current financial interests in Metals until (in effect) facilities had been paid or the plaintiffs consented. Both are relevant to the present and future moral responsibility of the defendants. If the words of para 3 are to be treated as intended to express a contractual promise by the defendants as to their future policy, which Hirst J held the words to contain, then the recitation of the plaintiffs' approval and the promise now to reduce their current financial interest in Metals, would be of no significance. If the defendants have promised that at all times in the future it will be the defendants' policy to ensure that Metals is in a position to meet its liabilities to the plaintiffs under the facility, it would not matter whether they had approved or disapproved, or whether they had disposed of their shares in Metals. Contracts may, of course, contain statements or promises which are caused to be of no separate commercial importance by the width of a later promise in the same document. Where, however, the court is examining a statement which is by its express words no more than a representation of fact, in order to consider whether it is shown to have been intended to be of the nature of a contractual promise or warranty, it seems to me to be a fact suggesting at least the absence of such intention if, as in this case, to read the statement as a contractual promise is to reduce to no significance two paragraphs included in the plaintiffs' draft, both of which have significance if the statement is read as a representation of fact only.

That point can be made more plainly thus: if para 3 in its original or in its final form was intended to contain a binding legal promise by the defendants to ensure the ability of Metals to pay the sums due under the facility, there was no apparent need or purpose for the plaintiffs, as bankers, to waste ink on paras 1 and 2.

As I have said, the absence of express words of promise does not by itself prevent a statement from being treated as a contractual promise. The example given in argument by counsel for the plaintiffs, namely of the shop stating by a notice that it is its policy to accept, within 14 days of purchase, the return in good condition of any goods bought and to refund the price without question, seems to me to be a case in which a court would be likely to hold that the notice imported a promise that the policy would continue over the 14-day period. It would be difficult on those facts to find any sensible commercial explanation for the notice other than a contractual promise not to change the policy over the 14-day period. It would not be satisfactory or convincing to regard the notice as no more than the assumption of a moral responsibility by the shop giving such a notice to its customers. In such a case, and in the absence of any relevant factual context indicating otherwise, it seems to me that the court would probably hold that the statement was shown to have been intended to be a contractual promise.

In this case, however, the opposite seems to me to be clear . . . .

If my view of this case is correct, the plaintiffs have suffered grave financial loss as a result of the collapse of the tin market and the following decision by the defendant company not to honour a moral responsibility which it assumed in order to gain for its subsidiary the finance necessary for the trading operations which the defendants wished that subsidiary to pursue. The defendants have demonstrated, in my judgment, that they made no relevant contractual promise to the plaintiffs which could support the judgment in favour of the plaintiffs. The consequences of the decision of the defendants to repudiate their moral responsibility are not matters for this court.

I would allow this appeal.

[Nicholls and Fox LJJ agreed.]

Appeal allowed.

NOTES

1. Ralph Gibson's example of the statement of policy in a shop suggests that similar words may be construed differently in different contexts. To a consumer a statement of policy may reasonably appear to be a contractual undertaking (though what should the consumer think if the shop had earlier refused to give an explicit promise?). In addition, as *Carlill's* case illustrates, there is a tendency to treat statements by businesses intended to drum up trade as contractual. See also *Esso Petroleum Ltd v Commissioners of Customs and Excise*, below p 161.

2. Ralph Gibson refers to a 'warranty'. This word has a number of legal meanings (eg below, p 260), but here it is used to mean a contractual undertaking that a statement of fact, eg about goods sold, is or will be true. Thus the seller of a machine may 'warrant' that it is capable of a certain speed of operation and will remain so for a given period of time.

3. Just like statements of 'policy', statements of fact will be construed differently in different contexts. We shall see later (below, pp 259–263) that when the parties have definitely entered a contract, it is common for important statements made about the subject matter (eg by the seller about the goods sold) to be treated as warranties, so that if the statement is incorrect the seller is liable for breach of contract. On the other hand, statements made by manufacturers in advertisements for goods which the public can buy through retail outlets are not regarded as contractual promises even though they are clearly designed to induce consumers to buy the goods. The courts have persisted in holding that such statements do not show any 'intention to contract': eg *Lexmead Ltd v Lewis* [1982] AC 225, 262–263. Note that in *Carlill's* case it was the promise to pay £100 if the user caught 'flu which was enforced, not the statement that the ball would cure influenza within 24 hours. Presumably a statement suggesting that a consumer would have a direct right against the advertiser ('Your Bealemobile will not break down for two years—and if it does Beale will give you a new one') might be construed as a contractual promise.

4. The nearest the courts have come to enforcing statements made to induce purchase from a third party are cases in which the plaintiff has individually sought the defendant's advice before buying. In *Wells (Merstham) Ltd v Buckland Sand and Silica Co Ltd* [1965] 2 QB 170 the plaintiffs, who were chrysanthemum growers, asked the defendant sand merchants whether their sand had the low oxide content necessary for propagating cuttings. When the defendants said it did, the plaintiffs bought some of the defendants' sand from a third party. When the sand turned out to have a high oxide content the defendants were held liable in contract.

5. Whether statements are construed as promises or not may also change over time as judges' perceptions change. In *Maddison v Alderson* (1883) 8 App Cas 467 a woman had for years acted as housekeeper to Alderson and because of his straitened circumstances had 'begun to leave wages in

his hand'. In 1860 she was thinking of leaving but he persuaded her to stay by indicating that in his will he would leave her a life interest in his farm. He drew up a will to this effect and read it over to her, asking 'whether she was satisfied'; but the will was not properly witnessed. She continued to look after him without wages for the rest of his life. After Alderson's death she brought an action against his personal representative for possession of the farm. The jury found that there was a contract, but the House of Lords held that she was not entitled to recover. The main reason was that there was not sufficient written evidence to satisfy the Statute of Frauds (which required contracts for the disposition of interests in land to be evidenced in writing, see below, p 131); but every member of the House doubted whether Alderson had made a binding promise. Lord Fitzgerald said:

> . . . although Alderson probably made representations to her of the benefits he intended to confer on her if she remained with him during his life, there never was any agreement binding on him to do so.

In *Schaefer v Schuhmann* [1972] AC 572 the facts were almost identical but the Privy Council decided that a contractual promise had been made. Lord Simon dissented on the ground that the two cases were indistinguishable.

6. The court may infer that the parties were making promises to each other and thus that there was a contract between them even though it is extremely improbable that the parties thought they were making a contract. *Wells v Buckland Sand* (above) may be one example; the next case is even clearer.

Tanner v Tanner [1975] 3 All ER 776, Court of Appeal
In 1968 the plaintiff, a married man, formed an association with the defendant, a single woman, who took his name. The defendant was the tenant of a rent-controlled flat, where the plaintiff frequently visited her. In 1969 she gave birth to twins of whom the plaintiff was the father. In 1970 the parties decided that it would be best to purchase a house to provide accommodation for the defendant and the twins. The plaintiff made it clear to the defendant, however, that he did not intend to marry her. He purchased a house in his own name and himself provided the purchase price by means of a mortgage. The defendant made no contribution to the purchase. She gave up her rent-controlled tenancy, and brought a good deal of furniture from her flat to the house; she also spent £150 on furnishings for the house. She and the twins moved into the house and occupied the ground floor flat. The rest of the house was let and the defendant managed the lettings for the plaintiff. After the defendant had moved into the house the plaintiff stopped paying to her the £5 a week maintenance for the twins that he had previously paid and did not pay her anything for herself or the twins. She obtained a social security allowance. The plaintiff formed an association with another woman whom he later married. He wanted to get the defendant and the twins out of the house so that he could live there himself with his new wife and her family. He offered the defendant £4,000 to leave the house; the house was likely to fetch £6,400 if it were sold furnished; but the defendant refused the offer saying that the house was supposed to be for herself and the children until they left school. By letter dated 16th July 1973 the plaintiff purported to terminate forthwith the licence under which he

alleged the defendant had been occupying the ground floor flat. She refused to vacate the house. The plaintiff brought proceedings claiming possession of the house. The judge found that the defendant had made no contribution in cash or kind from which it could be inferred that she was to have any proprietary interest in the house; accordingly he made an order for possession in the plaintiff's favour and the defendant moved out of the house in pursuance of that order. The defendant appealed against the order for possession. She and the children had been rehoused by the local authority and she did not ask to be put back into the house.

Lord Denning MR . . . [It] seems to me plain on the evidence that the house was acquired in the contemplation and expectation that it would provide a home for Miss MacDermott and the twin daughters. The babies were only eight months old at the time. She gave up her flat in Steele's Road (where she was protected by the Rent Acts) to move into this house. It was obviously provided for her as a house for herself and the twins for the foreseeable future.

It is said that the; were only licensees—bare licensees—under a licence revocable at will; and that he was entitled in law to turn her and the twins out on a moment's notice. I cannot believe that this is the law. This man had a moral duty to provide for the babies of whom he was the father. I would go further. I think he had a legal duty towards them. Not only towards the babies. But also towards their mother. She was looking after them and bringing them up. In order to fulfil his duty towards the babies, he was under a duty to provide for the mother too. She had given up her flat where she was protected by the Rent Acts—at least in regard to rent and it may be in regard also to security of tenure. She had given it up at his instance so as to be able the better to bring up the children. It is impossible to suppose that in that situation she and the babies were bare licensees whom he could turn out at a moment's notice. He recognised this when he offered to pay her £4,000 to get her out. What then was their legal position? She herself said in evidence: 'The house was supposed to be ours until the children left school.' It seems to me that enables an inference to be drawn, namely that in all the circumstances it is to be implied that she had a licence—a contractual licence—to have accommodation in the house for herself and the children so long as they were of school age and the accommodation was reasonably required for her and the children. There was, it is true, no express contract to that effect, but the circumstances are such that the court should imply a contract by him—or, if need be, impose the equivalent of a contract by him—whereby they were entitled to have the use of the house as their home until the girls had finished school. It may be that if circumstances changed—so that the accommodation was not reasonably required—the licence might be determinable. But it was not determinable in the circumstances in which he sought to determine it, namely to turn her out with the children and to bring in his new wife with her family. It was a contractual licence of the kind which is specifically enforceable on her behalf, and which he can be restrained from breaking; and he could not sell the house over her head so as to get her out in that way. That appears from *Binions v Evans*.

If therefore the lady had sought an injunction restraining him from determining the licence, it should have been granted. The order for possession ought not to have been made. . . .

But what is to be done? The judge ordered possession in six weeks. Thereupon the local housing authority (as they usually do when an order for possession is made) provided accommodation for Miss MacDermott and the children. She moved out in pursuance of the order and does not ask to be put back now. Seeing that the order ought not to have been made and we reverse it, what is to be done? It seems to me that this court has ample power, when it reverses an order of the court below, to do what is just and equitable to restore the position as fairly as it can in the circumstances. The plaintiff has obtained an unjust benefit and should make restitution. In the circumstances the courts can and should assess compensation to be payable by him. He has not been paying any maintenance for these children for years—ever since she went into the house. It seems to me a reasonable sum for loss of this licence (which she ought not to have lost) would be £2,000. So I would allow the appeal and say that the order for possession shall be set aside, and as compensation to her for being wrongly turned out, the sum of £2,000 to be payable by Mr Tanner. I would allow the appeal accordingly.

[Browne and Brightman LJJ delivered judgments to the same effect.]

Appeal allowed

NOTE

It may be legitimate to infer a contract when neither party gave any thought to the legal position, but what if both actually believed at the time that no contract was involved? In *Upton-on-Severn RDC v Powell* [1942] 1 All ER 220 the defendant, who was entitled to free service from the Pershore fire brigade, called the police and asked for 'the fire brigade'. The police thought he lived in the Upton district and sent the Upton brigade, who came thinking 'that they were rendering gratuitous services in their own area'. The defendant also thought he was getting a free service. The court held that he was under a contractual obligation to pay for the service he had received, but the case has been severely criticised (eg Treitel, p 30.)

Re Hudson (1885) 54 LJ Ch 811, Pearson J

Hudson had promised to give £20,000 to the Jubilee Fund of the Congregational Union, in five annual instalments of £4,000 each, for the liquidation of chapel debts. On his death the last two instalments remained unpaid and unprovided for. His executors sought a declaration that his estate was not liable for the two instalments.

Pearson J. Mr Cookson [counsel for the Congregational Union] admitted very fairly at the beginning that, unless he could shew that there was a legal debt due from the estate of the testator, he had no case at all; and it was therefore necessary for him to shape the case so as to satisfy the Court that there was a positive legal contract entered into by the testator to pay the whole of this sum of 20,000*l*, which rendered the estate of Mr Hudson liable for so much of the 20,000*l* as was not paid by him during his lifetime. I do not mean to go into all the cases that have been cited. The first question is whether or not there is any contract at all to pay—I mean a contract in the legal sense of the word 'contract'; was there any consideration of any sort or description for Mr Hudson's promise to pay 20,000*l*—anything that could be considered a consideration either in this Court or elsewhere? I am utterly at a loss to ascertain that there was any consideration . . .

Mr Cookson says that there really was a consideration, because the consideration was the risks and liabilities which the parties were to undertake who composed themselves into a committee and became the distributors of the fund. In the first place, there was no duty between themselves and Mr Hudson which they undertook at that time—there was no binding obligation between themselves and Mr Hudson; and I put it to Mr Cookson just now when he was pressing this point: Supposing that at the end of the year, before any more instalments than one had been paid, this committee had chosen to dissolve itself and to relinquish any trouble whatever in the distribution of the fund whether it was gathered in or not, was there any obligation between Mr Hudson and the committee which would have given Mr Hudson any control over the committee, or have made the committee liable to him for not discharging its duty in distributing the fund which is said to be the consideration for the contract? Of course there was none. It was voluntary on the part of both parties—voluntary on the part of Mr Hudson, and voluntary on the part of the committee. The whole thing from beginning to end was nothing more than this: an intention of this gentleman to contribute to the fund, and an intention of the committee, so long as the different members of it remained members of that committee, to dispose of that fund according to the purposes for which it was contributed. There really is in this matter nothing whatever in the shape of a consideration which could form a contract between the parties.

NOTES

1. If Hudson had made his promise in a deed under seal (for the requirements for this see below, p 120), it would have been enforceable even though there was no consideration for it. In *Morley v Boothby* (1825) 3 Bing 107, at 111–112, Best CJ said:

> The common law protected men against improvident contracts. If they bound themselves by deed, it was considered that they must have determined upon what they were about to do, before they made so solemn an engagement; and therefore it was not necessary to the validity of the instrument, that any consideration should appear upon it. In all other cases the contract was invalid, unless the party making the promise was to obtain some advantage, or the party to whom it was made, was to suffer some inconvenience in consequence of the one making or the other accepting the promise [ie there was consideration].

The doctrine of consideration and the function of the deed are considered in more detail in Section 2, chapter 7.

2. Lack of consideration will prevent a person who has promised a gift from being sued for it. If the person has done what is legally sufficient actually to complete the gift (for instance, a gift of a chattel may be completed by actually delivering the chattel to the donee), she can't get the gift back just because the donee provided no consideration.

3. If Hudson's promise had been made by deed, or if there had been consideration for it (for instance if he had asked that in exchange for the money a new chapel be named for him), his estate would have been liable for the full amount promised, not just the amount disbursed by the committee. As his promise was one to pay money, the Congregational Union would have been able to bring an action for the price, at least if they had performed their side of the bargain. (See below, chap 24). If the defendant has failed to perform some other kind of promise—eg to convey property or to perform some service—the plaintiff's normal remedy will be to bring an action for damages. The damages should compensate the plaintiff for not getting what was promised, not merely reimburse the amount by which the plaintiff was left worse off than before.

> The rule of the common law is, that where a party sustains a loss by reason of a breach of contract, he is, so far as money can do it, to be placed in the same situation, with respect to damages, as if the contract had been performed.

(Parke B in *Robinson v Harman* (1848) 1 Exch 850 at 855.)

Sometimes a plaintiff will be able to get an order of specific performance, forcing the defendant to perform on pain of being in contempt of court, but specific performance is treated as an extraordinary remedy in English law. It is only granted routinely in contracts for the sale of land. (See further below, chap 24).

(b) Tort and contract

Donoghue v Stevenson [1932] AC 562, House of Lords (Scotland)

The appellant alleged that she and a friend had visited Minchella's cafe in Paisley, where the friend had ordered some ginger beer for the appellant. The ginger beer, which was in an opaque glass bottle, was opened by Minchella, who poured part of it over some ice cream in a tumbler. The appellant drank part of the mixture and then poured out the remaining ginger beer. The decomposed remains of a snail floated out with the ginger beer. The appellant suffered shock and gastric illness as the result of drinking the ginger beer, and sued the manufacturer of the ginger beer for negligence. The respondent manufacturer pleaded that these allegations disclosed no cause of action; his plea was rejected by the Lord Ordinary. On appeal the Second Division dismissed the appellant's action, holding that a manufacturer does not owe any duty to anyone with whom he does not have a contract, unless the article is inherently dangerous or the manufacturer actually knows that it is in a dangerous condition. The appellant appealed to the House of Lords.

Lord Atkin . . . [I]n English law there must be, and is, some general conception of relations giving rise to a duty of care, of which the particular cases found in the books are but instances. The liability for negligence, whether you style it such or treat it as in other systems as a species of 'culpa,' is no doubt based upon a general public sentiment of moral wrongdoing for which the offender must pay. But acts or omissions which any moral code would censure cannot in a practical world be treated so as to give a right to every person injured by them to demand relief. In this way rules of law arise which limit the range of complainants and the extent of their remedy. The rule that you are to love your neighbour becomes in law, you must not injure your neighbour; and the lawyer's question, Who is my neighbour? receives a restricted reply. You must take reasonable care to avoid acts or omissions which you can reasonably foresee would be likely to injure your neighbour. Who, then, in law is my neighbour? The answer seems to be—persons who are so closely and directly affected by my act that I ought reasonably to have them in contemplation as being so affected when I am directing my mind to the acts or omissions which are called in question. . . .

My Lords, if your Lordships accept the view that this pleading discloses a relevant cause of action you will be affirming the proposition that by Scots and English law alike a manufacturer of products, which he sells in such a form as to show that he intends them to reach the ultimate consumer in the form in which they left him with no reasonable possibility of intermediate examination, and with the knowledge that the absence of reasonable care in the preparation or putting up of the products will result in an injury to the consumer's life or property, owes a duty to the consumer to take that reasonable care.

It is a proposition which I venture to say no one in Scotland or England who was not a lawyer would for one moment doubt. It will be an advantage to make it clear that the law in this matter, as in most others, is in accordance with sound common sense. I think that this appeal should be allowed.

Lord Macmillan. . . . It humbly appears to me that the diversity of view which is exhibited in [the] cases . . . is explained by the fact that in the discussion of the topic which now engages your Lordships' attention two rival principles of the law find a meeting place where each has contended for supremacy. On the one hand, there is the well established principle that no one other than a party to a contract can complain of a breach of that contract. On the other hand, there is the equally well established doctrine that negligence apart from contract gives a right of action to the party injured by that negligence—and here I use the term negligence, of course, in its technical legal sense, implying a duty owed and neglected. The fact that there is a contractual relationship between the parties which may give rise to an action for breach of contract, does not exclude the co-existence of a right of action founded on negligence as between the same parties, independently of the contract, though arising out of the relationship in fact brought about by the contract. Of this the best illustration is the right of the injured railway passenger to sue the railway company either for breach of the contract of safe carriage or for negligence in carrying him. And there is no reason why the same set of facts should not give one person a right of action in contract and another person a right of action in tort.

Where, as in cases like the present, so much depends upon the avenue of approach to the question, it is very easy to take the wrong turning. If you begin with the sale by the manufacturer to the retail dealer, then the consumer who purchases from the retailer is at once seen to be a stranger to the contract between the retailer and the manufacturer and so disentitled to sue upon it. There is no contractual relation between the manufacturer and the consumer; and thus the plaintiff, if he is to succeed, is driven to try to bring himself within one or other of the exceptional cases where the strictness of the rule that none but a party to a contract can found on a breach of that contract has been mitigated in the public interest, as it has been in the case of a person who issues a chattel which is inherently dangerous or which he knows to be in a dangerous condition. If, on the other hand, you disregard the fact that the circumstances of the case at one stage include the existence of a contract of sale between the manufacturer and the retailer, and approach the question by asking whether there is evidence of carelessness on the part of the manufacturer, and whether he owed a duty to be careful in a question with the party who has been injured in consequence of his want of care, the circumstance that the injured party was not a party to the incidental contract of sale becomes irrelevant, and his title to sue the manufacturer is unaffected by that circumstance. . . . I have no hesitation in affirming that a person who for gain engages in the business of manufacturing articles of food and drink intended for consumption by members of the public in the form in which he issues them is under a duty to take care in the manufacture of these articles. That duty, in my opinion, he owes to those whom he intends to consume his products. He manufactures his commodities for human consumption; he intends and contemplates that they shall be consumed. By reason of that very fact he places himself in a relationship with all the potential consumers of his commodities, and that relationship which he assumes and desires for his own ends imposes upon him a duty to take care to avoid injuring them. He owes them a duty not to convert by his own carelessness an article which he issues to them as wholesome and innocent into an article which is dangerous to life and health.

[Lord Thankerton delivered a judgment to the same effect, Lords Buckmaster and Tomlin dissented.]

Appeal allowed.

NOTES

1. Why could Donoghue not sue Minchella?
2. If she had bought the ginger beer herself, would she have been better advised to sue Stevenson in tort or Minchella in contract? Why? [She could, of course, do both, but that might be unnecessarily expensive.)
3. In the consumer context, the difficulties faced by plaintiffs who have been injured by defective products in proving that the manufacturer or producer was negligent were one of the reasons behind the introduction of 'strict' product liability by the Consumer Protection Act 1987. In fact the 'development risk defence' contained in s 4(1)(e)

   . . . . that the state of scientific and technical knowledge at the relevant time was not such that a producer of products of the same description as the product in question might be expected to have discovered the defect. . . .

   means that the producer's liability is far from strict, though it is for the producer to show that the defence applies rather than for the consumer to prove negligence. The Act applies where the defective product has caused death or personal injury, or property damage of more than £275. (See generally, Clark, *Product Liability*, 1989).
4. The rule that only a party to a contract may sue on it has caused difficulties in other contexts too. Building contracts are an example. A common situation is that an employer engages a contractor to do work and the contractor (with the consent of the employer and sometimes as the result of the employer's direction or 'nomination') employs a subcontractor to do part of it. If the work is done badly by the subcontractor, does the employer have a remedy against the subcontractor? (It will usually have one against the contractor—but they may have reached a final settlement of all claims between them before the problem became apparent, or the contractor may have become insolvent.) Frequently there is no contract between the employer and the 'sub', so the employer may try to recover in tort. If the sub was negligent and the building has actually collapsed, damaging the employer's property or causing personal injury, the employer will recover for the damage or injury on the basis of *Donoghue v Stevenson*. What if it hasn't yet collapsed but will do so shortly if it is not repaired? Or if it isn't dangerous but the defect makes it useless? Can there be liability in tort where there has been no physical injury or damage to property? Recent

cases on these issues have raised fundamental issues about the law of tort and its relationship to contract.

Donoghue v Stevenson involved a negligent act leading to physical injury. The original decision was about the liability of manufacturers for defective products, but the courts came gradually to accept Lord Atkin's 'neighbour principle' as a guideline (see the extract from Lord Wilberforce's judgment in *Anns v London Borough of Merton*, quoted by Lord Roskill in *Junior Books v Veitchi*, below, p 25). It is now almost universally the case that a defendant who has acted carelessly and has caused personal injury or property damage to a plaintiff will be liable provided that it was foreseeable that the plaintiff might be injured in the way that occurred. Where the defendant's negligence consisted of a careless statement leading to merely financial loss, however, it was long thought that there was no liability in tort; the plaintiff could only recover if there it could be shown that the defendant had broken a contract under which he was obliged to use care in giving information. However, in 1963 the House of Lords held in *Hedley Byrne & Co Ltd v Heller & Partners* that there might be liability in tort for negligent misstatement if there was a sufficiently close relationship between the parties, though in that case the defendants could not be liable because they had given the information 'without responsibility'.

Hedley Byrne & Co Ltd v Heller & Partners Ltd [1964] AC 465, House of Lords

Hedley Byrne, who were advertising agents, asked their bank to obtain a credit reference on Easipower Ltd. The bank enquired of Easipower's bankers, Hellers, and were told, in confidence and 'without responsibility', that Easipower was 'good for its ordinary business engagements'. Relying on this information, Hedley Byrne booked advertising time and space for Easipower on the basis that they were personally responsible to the television and newspaper companies concerned, and when Easipower went into liquidation, Hedley Byrne lost over £17,000 on these contracts. McNair J held Hellers were negligent, but that they owed no duty of care to Hedley Byrne. The Court of Appeal agreed with the latter point. The House of Lords held that it was unnecessary to decide whether Hellers were negligent, as they could not be liable in the light of their disclaimer. However, the House of Lords said that in some circumstances there might be liability for negligent advice or misrepresentation if responsibility were not disclaimed.

Lord Reid. . . . [A] negligently made article will only cause one accident, and so it is not very difficult to find the necessary degree of proximity or neighbourhood between the negligent manufacturer and the person injured. But words can be broadcast with or without the consent or the foresight of the speaker or writer. It would be one thing to say that the speaker owes a duty to a limited class, but it would be going very far to say that he owes a duty to every ultimate 'consumer' who acts on those words to his detriment. It would be no use to say that a speaker or writer owes a duty but can disclaim responsibility if he wants to. He, like the manufacturer, could make it part of a contract that he is not to be liable for his negligence: but that contract would not protect him in a question with a third party, at least if the third party was unaware of it.

So it seems to me that there is good sense behind our present law that in general an innocent but negligent misrepresentation gives no cause of action. There must be something more than the mere misstatement. I therefore turn to the authorities to see what more is required. The most natural requirement would be that expressly or by implication from the circumstances the speaker or writer has undertaken some responsibility, and that appears to me not to conflict with any authority which is binding on this House. Where there is a contract there is no difficulty as regards the contracting parties: the question is whether there is a warranty. The refusal of English law to recognise any jus quaesitum tertii causes some difficulties, but they are not relevant, here. Then there are cases where a person does not merely make a statement but performs a gratuitous service. I do not intend to examine the cases about that, but at least they show that in some cases that person owes a duty of care apart from any contract, and to that extent they pave the way to holding that there can be a duty of care in making a statement of fact or opinion which is independent of contract . . . [Lord Haldane in *Robinson v National Bank of Scotland Ltd*] did not think that a duty to take care must be limited to cases of fiduciary relationship in the narrow sense of relationships which had been recognised by the Court of Chancery as being of a fiduciary character. He speaks of other special relationships, and I can see no logical stopping place short of all those relationships where it is plain that the party seeking information or advice was trusting the other to exercise such a degree of care as the circumstances required, where it was reasonable for him to do that, and where the other gave the information or advice when he knew or ought to have known that the inquirer was relying on him. I say 'ought to have known' because in questions of negligence we now apply the objective standard of what the reasonable man would have done.

A reasonable man, knowing that he was being trusted or that his skill and judgment were being relied on, would, I think, have three courses open to him. He could keep silent or decline to give the information or advice sought: or he could give an answer with a clear qualification that he accepted no responsibility for it or that it was given without that reflection or inquiry which a careful answer would require: or he could simply answer without any such qualification. If he chooses to adopt the last course he must, I think, be held to have accepted some responsibility for his answer being given carefully, or to have accepted a relationship with the inquirer which requires him to exercise such care as the circumstances require.

[Lord Morris, Lord Hodson, Lord Devlin and Lord Pearce delivered speeches to the same effect.]

Lord Devlin. . . . I think that there is ample authority to justify your Lordships in saying now that the categories of special relationships which may give rise to a duty to take care in word as well as in deed are not limited to contractual relationships or to relationships of fiduciary duty, but include also relationships which in the words of Lord Shaw in *Nocton v Lord Ashburton* are 'equivalent to contract,' that is, where there is an assumption of responsibility in circumstances in which, but for the absence of consideration, there would be a contract.

The differences between *Hedley Byrne* and *Donoghue v Stevenson* are twofold. Firstly, *Hedley Byrne* involved a statement, not an act, and secondly, the plaintiff had not suffered physical injury or damage, only financial loss. In contract it is immaterial whether the plaintiff's loss is physical or financial and in *Hedley Byrne* Lord Devlin (at p 517) said that he could see no logical distinction between the two. But his has been a lone voice. The courts have treated cases of negligent misstatement as an exception to the rule that pure economic loss is not recoverable in tort and have said that where the negligence consisted of an action, purely economic loss is not normally recoverable: negligent statement apart, tort compensates only for physical harm and any financial consequences flowing directly from it, such as loss of earnings after an injury (see *Spartan Steel and Alloys Ltd v Martin & Co (Contractors) Ltd* [1973] QB 27). The only concession made was that the plaintiff can recover the cost of curing a dangerous defect before it has actually caused an injury (*Anns v Merton London Borough Council* [1978] AC 728). Even then the plaintiff can normally recover only any cost involved in removing the danger, not the whole cost of repairing the defect: *D and F Estates Ltd v Church Comrs for England* [1989] AC 177. In that case plastering had been done defectively and the plaster fell off the walls. Lord Bridge said (at p 207):

> It seems to me clear that the cost of replacing the defective plaster itself, either as carried out in 1980 or as intended to be carried out in future, was not an item of damage for which the builder of Chelwood House could possibly be made liable in negligence under the

principle of *Donoghue v Stevenson* or any legitimate development of that principle. To make him so liable would be to impose upon him for the benefit of those with whom he had no contractual relationship the obligation of one who warranted the quality of the plaster as regards materials, workmanship and fitness for purpose. I am glad to reach the conclusion that this is not the law . . .

5. Suppose that Miss Donoghue had seen the snail before she had drunk any of the ginger beer, and thus had avoided injury; or that the bottle had contained water. Could her friend (who had paid for the ginger beer) have recovered the cost of it from the manufacturer in tort? It used to be thought not. In *Dutton v Bognor Regis UDC* [1972] 1 QB 373 Stamp LJ said:

> . . . [A] distinction has been drawn between constructing a dangerous article and constructing one which is defective or of inferior quality. I may be liable to one who purchases in the market a bottle of ginger beer which I have carelessly manufactured and which is dangerous and causes injury to person or property; but it is not the law that I am liable to him for the loss he suffers because what is found inside the bottle and for which he has paid money is not ginger beer but water. I do not warrant, except to an immediate purchaser, and then by the contract and not in tort, that the thing I manufacture is reasonably fit for its purpose.
> . . . the distinction between the case of the manufacturer of a dangerous thing which causes damage and that of a thing which turns out to be defective and valueless lies I think not in the nature of the injury but in the character of the duty. I have a duty not carelessly to put out a dangerous thing which may cause damage to one who may purchase it, but the duty does not extend to putting out carelessly a defective or useless or valueless thing.

Liability under Consumer Protection Act 1987 is similarly limited; even though property damage is recoverable if it exceeds £275, there is no liability for the loss of or damage to the product itself: s 5(2).

Junior Books Ltd v Veitchi Co Ltd [1983] 1 AC 520, [1982] 3 All ER 201, House of Lords

The respondents, the owners, engaged a building company to build a factory for them, under a form of building contract which required the builders to employ for certain tasks subcontractors 'nominated' by the owners. The owners nominated the appellant subcontractors to lay a special concrete floor in the main production area, and the appellants duly entered a subcontract with the builders. There was no contract between the owners and the nominated subcontractors. Two years after the floor had been laid it developed cracks, and rather than have perpetual maintenance to keep the floor usable, the owners wanted to have it replaced, which they alleged would be cheaper. They brought an action against the subcontractors alleging that the subcontractors had laid the floor negligently, and claiming the cost of replacing the floor and the economic loss which would result from closing the factory and moving the machinery out of it while the work was done. The subcontractors replied that, as there was no allegation that the floor was dangerous, the owners' claim disclosed no cause of action. The Lord Ordinary and, on appeal, the Court of Session, rejected this contention, and held that the owners were entitled to proceed with their action. The subcontractors appealed.

Lord Roskill. . . . [In] *Anns v Merton London Borough Council*, Lord Wilberforce . . . said: 'the position has now been reached that in order to establish that a duty of care arises in a particular situation, it is not necessary to bring the facts of that situation within those of previous situations in which a duty of care has been held to exist. Rather the question has to be approached in two stages. First one has to ask whether, as between the alleged wrongdoer and the person who has suffered damage there is a sufficient relationship of proximity or neighbourhood such that, in the reasonable contemplation of the former, carelessness on his part may be likely to cause damage to the latter—in which case a prima facie duty of care arises. Secondly, if the first question is answered affirmatively, it is necessary to consider whether there are any considerations which ought to negative, or to reduce or limit the scope of the duty or the class of person to whom it is owed or the damages to which a breach of it may give rise: . . .'

Applying those statements of general principle as your Lordships have been enjoined to do both by Lord Reid and by Lord Wilberfore rather than to ask whether the particular situation which has arisen does or does not resemble some earlier and different situation where a duty of care has been held or has not been held to exist, I look for the reasons why, it being conceded that the appellants owed a duty of care to others not to construct the flooring so that those others were in peril of suffering loss or damage to their persons or their property, that duty of care should not be equally owed to the respondents. The appellants, though not in direct contractual relationship with the respondents, were as nominated subcontractors in almost as close a commercial relationship with the respondents as it is possible to envisage short of privity of contract. Why then should the appellants not be under a duty to the respondents not to expose the respondents to a possible liability to financial loss for repairing the flooring should it prove that that flooring had been negligently constructed? It is conceded that if the flooring had been so badly constructed that to avoid imminent danger the respondents had expended money upon renewing it the respondents could have recovered the cost of so doing. It seems curious that, if the appellants' work had been so bad that to avoid imminent danger expenditure had been incurred, the respondents could recover that expenditure, but that if the work was less badly done so that remedial work could be postponed they cannot do so. Yet this is seemingly the result of the appellants' contentions . . .

Turning back to the present appeal I therefore ask first whether there was the requisite degree of proximity so as to give rise to the relevant duty of care relied on by the respondents. I regard the following facts as of crucial importance in requiring an affirmative answer to that question. (1) The appellants were nominated sub-contractors. (2) The appellants were specialists in flooring. (3) The appellants knew what products were required by the respondents and their main contractors and specialised in the production of those products. (4) The appellants alone were responsible for the composition and construction of the flooring. (5) The respondents relied upon the appellants' skill and experience. (6) The appellants as nominated sub-contractors must have known that the respondents relied upon their skill and experience. (7) The relationship between the parties was as close as it could be short of actual privity of contract. (8) The appellants must be taken to have known that if they did the work negligently (as it must be assumed that they did) the resulting defects would at some time require remedying by the respondents expending money upon the remedial measures as a consequence of which the respondents would suffer financial or economic loss.

My Lords, reverting to Lord Devlin's speech in *Hedley Byrne & Co Ltd v Heller & Partners Ltd*, it seems to me that all the conditions existed which give rise to the relevant duty of care owed by the appellants to the respondents.

I then turn to Lord Wilberforce's second proposition. On the facts I have just stated, I see nothing whatsoever to restrict the duty of care arising from the proximity of which I have spoken. During the argument it was asked what the position would be in a case where there was a relevant exclusion clause in the main contract. My Lords, that question does not arise for decision in the instant appeal, but in principle I would venture the view that such a clause according to the manner in which it was worded might in some circumstances limit the duty of care just as in the *Hedley Byrne* case the plaintiffs were ultimately defeated by the defendants' disclaimer of responsibility. But in the present case the only suggested reason for limiting the damage (ex hypothesi economic or financial only) recoverable for the breach of the duty of care just enunciated is that hitherto the law has not allowed such recovery and therefore ought not in the future to do so. My Lords, with all respect to those who find this a sufficient answer, I do not. I think this is the next logical step forward in the development of this branch of the law. I see no reason why what was called during the argument 'damage to the pocket' simpliciter should be disallowed when 'damage to the pocket' coupled with physical damage has hitherto always been allowed. I do not think that this development, if development it be, will lead to untoward consequences. The concept of proximity must always involve, at least in most cases, some degree of reliance—I have already mentioned the words 'skill' and 'judgment' in the speech of Lord Morris of Borth-y-Gest in *Hedley Byrne* [1964] AC 465 at 503. These words seem to me to be an echo, be it conscious or unconscious, of the language of section 14 (1) of the Sale of Goods Act 1893. My Lords, though the analogy is not exact, I do not find it unhelpful for I think the concept of proximity of which I have spoken and the reasoning of Lord Devlin in the *Hedley Byrne* case involve factual considerations not unlike those involved in a claim under section 14 (1); and as between an ultimate purchaser and a manufacturer would not easily be found to exist in the ordinary everyday transaction of purchasing chattels when it is obvious that in truth the real reliance was upon the immediate vendor and not upon the manufacturer. . .

[Lords Fraser and Russell agreed, Lord Keith delivered a separate concurring judgment and Lord Brandon dissented.]

Appeal dismissed.

NOTES

1. This seems to suggest that, whereas liability in tort for physical injury rests on foreseeability of the harm, liability for purely economic loss (including having spent good money on a worthless item) depends on the existence of a 'special relationship' between plaintiff and defendant. What do you think are the essential elements of such a relationship, judging from the facts of *Junior Books* and *Hedley Byrne*? For instance would there be a relationship between an employer and a subcontractor selected not by him but by the contractor? Between a nominated sub-subcontractor and the contractor? Between the owners of a newspaper and a reader who wrote in for advice? Between the owners and another reader who had not written in but who relied on the advice published in an article? Why is there no special relationship between a manufacturer of brand name goods and someone who buys the goods relying on the manufacturer's advertisement?

2. *Junior Books* marks a high water mark. Later cases have all involved different facts on which either there was no special relationship between the parties, or there were other factors which suggested that *Junior Books* type liability would be inappropriate. But the overall tone has been hostile to *Junior Books*, Lord Bridge in the *D & F Estates* case remarking that it 'is so far dependent upon the unique, albeit non-contractual, relationship between the pursuer and the defender . . . that the decision cannot be regarded as laying down any principle of general application in the law of tort. . . .'

3. Most of the cases considered so far have been ones in which the plaintiff could not have sued the defendant directly in contract because there was no contract between them. Sometimes the plaintiff who has suffered personal injury or property damage will have both causes of action—for instance, a passenger who has been injured through the negligence of a bus driver may sue the bus company for a breach of the contract of carriage, or as vicariously liable in tort for the driver's negligence. (Needless to say, the plaintiff will only recover one set of damages.) Usually it will not matter how the action is framed, but sometimes there are advantages in suing in one way rather than the other: for instance, the limitation periods may differ.

4. However, the courts have been reluctant to allow plaintiffs to recover purely economic loss in tort when the parties already have a contract with each other. In *Greater Nottingham Co-operative Society Ltd v Cementation Piling and Foundations Ltd* [1988] 2 All ER 971 the facts were indistinguishable from *Junior Books* except that the employer and the nominated subcontractor had actually entered into a direct contract

with one another (in addition to the normal contracts each had with the main contractor). It was held that this was enough to prevent there being liability for economic loss in tort—the contract, rather than the law of tort, should govern their relationship (see also *Tai Hing Cotton Mill Ltd v Liu Chong Hing Bank Ltd* [1986] AC 80, in which the Privy Council said that there was no advantage in creating new liabilities in tort when the parties are in a contractual relationship, and *The Aliakmon* [1986] AC 785).

5. Even if a subcontractor is liable to an employer in tort under *Junior Books*, the employer's recovery may be less full than it would be if there were a contract between them. Suppose the facts had been these: the subcontractors had been selected because the price at which they offered to do the work (say £50,000) was £25,000 less than any of the other tenders. The subcontractors started work only to discover that they had seriously underestimated the work, tried to cut corners to save money and consequently laid the floor with defects that reasonable care and skill would have prevented. If the owners can get the floor relaid for £85,000, and their other losses will amount to £10,000, how much do you think they would recover in a tort action against the subcontractors? One possible answer is £95,000: but is this the amount by which they are out of pocket by reason of their reliance on the subcontractors? If they had employed another subcontractor, they would have had to pay him an extra £25,000: should this be taken into account, so that they recover only £70,000? If they recover the full £95,000, they seem to be compensated for losing the 'profit' they were making on the original subcontract, and while that is wholly proper in an action for breach of contract, is it the correct measure of damages in tort? It would be the equivalent of allowing Miss Donoghue's friend to recover the normal price of a bottle of ginger beer, although she had paid Minchella less than that price because he was offering a 'special' that week. In *Doyle v Olby (Ironmongers) Ltd* [1969] 2 QB 158, a case of fraud, Lord Denning MR said:

Damages for fraud and conspiracy are assessed differently from damages for breach of contract. . . . [In] *McConnel v Wright,* Lord Collins MR pointed out the difference. It was an action for fraudulent statements in a prospectus whereby a man was induced to take up shares. Lord Collins said of the action for fraud:

It is not an action for breach of contract, and, therefore, no damages in respect of prospective gains which the person contracting was entitled by his contract to expect to come in, but it is an action of tort—it is an action for a wrong done whereby the plaintiff was tricked out of certain money in his pocket, and, therefore, prima facie, the highest limit of his damages is the whole extent of his loss, and that loss is measured by the money which was in his pocket. . . .

On principle the distinction seems to be this: in contract, the defendant has made a promise and broken it. The object of damages is to put the plaintiff in as good a position, as far as money can do it, as if the promise had been performed. In fraud, the defendant has been guilty of a deliberate wrong by inducing the plaintiff to act to his detriment. The object of damages is to compensate the plaintiff for all the loss he has suffered, so far, again, as money can do it.

(c) Restitution and contract

Bailey v West 105 Rhode I 61, 249 A 2d 414 (1969), Supreme Court of Rhode Island

In April 1962 the defendant and his trainer went to Belmont Park in New York, where the defendant bought 'Bascom's Folly' from a Dr Strauss, and arranged to have the horse shipped to Suffolk Downs in East Boston, Massachusetts. Upon its arrival the trainer discovered that the horse was lame, and notified the defendant, who ordered him to reship the horse by van to the seller at Belmont Park. On 3 May the seller refused to accept delivery, and the van driver, Kelly called the trainer to ask for further instructions. On the same day Kelly took the horse to the plaintiff's farm, and there it remained until July 1966, when the plaintiff sold it to a third party. It appeared that the plaintiff had been told by Kelly that there was a dispute as to the ownership of the horse. In a separate action the court had determined that the defendant was liable to Dr Strauss for the price of the horse, and the plaintiff brought this action for the reasonable value of feeding, care and maintenance of the horse. The trial judge awarded him the cost of board for five months subsequent to May 1962. The plaintiff appealed and the defendant cross-appealed.

Paolino J. While 'Bascom's Folly' was residing at his horse farm, plaintiff sent bills for his feed and board to defendant at regular intervals. According to testimony elicited from defendant at the trial, the first such bill was received by him some two or three months after 'Bascom's Folly' was placed on plaintiff's farm. He also stated that he immediately returned the bill to plaintiff with the notation that he was not the owner of the horse nor was it sent to plaintiff's farm at his request. The plaintiff testified that he sent bills monthly to defendant and that the first notice he received from him disclaiming ownership was '. . . maybe after a month or two or so' subsequent to the time when the horse was left in plaintiff's care. . . .

I

The defendant alleges in his brief and oral argument that the trial judge erred in finding a contract 'implied in fact' between the parties. We agree.

The source of the obligation in a contract 'implied in fact', as in express contracts, is in the intention of the parties. We hold that there was no mutual agreement and 'intent to promise' between the plaintiff and defendant so as to establish a contract 'implied in fact' for defendant to pay plaintiff for the maintenance of this horse. From the time Kelly delivered the horse to him plaintiff knew there was a dispute as to its ownership, and his subsequent actions indicated he did not know with whom, if anyone, he had a contract. After he had accepted the horse, he made inquiries as to its ownership and, initially, and for some time thereafter, sent his bills to both defendant and Dr Strauss, the original seller.

There is also uncontroverted testimony in the record that prior to the assertion of the claim which is the subject of this suit neither defendant nor his trainer had ever had any business transactions with plaintiff, and had never used his farm to board horses. Additionally, there is uncontradicted evidence that this horse, when found to be lame, was shipped by defendant's trainer not to plaintiff's farm, but back to the seller at Belmont Park. What is most important, the trial justice expressly stated that he believed the testimony of defendant's trainer that he had instructed Kelly that defendant would not be responsible for boarding the horse on any farm.

From our examination of the record we are constrained to conclude that the trial justice overlooked and misconceived material evidence which establishes beyond question that there never existed between the parties an element essential to the formulation of any true contract, namely, an 'intent to contract'.

II

The defendant's second contention is that, even assuming the trial justice was in essence predicating defendant's liability upon a quasi-contractual theory, his decision is still unsupported by competent evidence and is clearly erroneous . . .

[T]he essential elements of a quasi-contract are a benefit conferred upon defendant by plaintiff, appreciation by defendant of such benefit, and acceptance and retention by defendant of such benefit under such circumstances that it would be inequitable to retain the benefit without payment of the value thereof . . .

The key question raised by this appeal with respect to the establishment of a quasi-contract is whether or not plaintiff was acting as a 'volunteer' at the time he accepted the horse for boarding at his farm. There is a long line of authority which has clearly enunciated the general rule that '. . . if a performance is rendered by one person without any request by another, it is very unlikely that this person will be under a legal duty to pay compensation'. 1 A Corbin, Contracts §234.

The Restatement of Restitution, §2 (1937) provides: 'A person who officiously confers a benefit upon another is not entitled to restitution therefor.' Comment *a* in the above-mentioned section states in part as follows:

'. . . Policy ordinarily requires that a person who has conferred a benefit . . . by way of giving another services . . . should not be permitted to require the other to pay therefor, unless the one conferring the benefit had a valid reason for so doing. A person is not required to deal with another unless he so desires and, ordinarily, a person should not be required to become an obligor unless he so desires.'

. . . [I]t is clear that plaintiff cannot recover . . .

Knowing at the time he accepted the horse for boarding that a controversy surrounded its ownership, plaintiff could not reasonably expect remuneration from defendant, nor can it be said that defendant acquiesced in the conferment of a benefit upon him. The undisputed testimony was that defendant, upon receipt of plaintiff's first bill, immediately notified him that he was not the owner of 'Bascom's Folly' and would not be responsible for its keep.

It is our judgment that the plaintiff was a mere volunteer who boarded and maintained 'Bascom's Folly' at his own risk and with full knowledge that he might not be reimbursed for expenses he incurred incident thereto.

NOTES

1. Why was there no contract between the plaintiff and the defendant?
2. The general principle underlying liability in restitution is, as Lord Mansfield put it in *Moses v Macferlan* (1760) 2 Burr 1005, at 1012,

   that the defendant, upon the circumstances of the case, is obliged by the ties of natural justice and equity to refund the money.

   However this general principle is not a rule of law; in order to recover, the plaintiff must show that his case falls within one of a limited number of categories. For instance, he may recover if he has paid money to the defendant under a mistake of fact or in pursuance of an ineffective contract, or that he has paid money to the use of the defendant.
3. Didn't the defendant in *Bailey v West* receive a benefit at the plaintiff's expense? Why then was he not unjustly enriched?
4. There are also dicta in English law to the effect that a person who 'officiously' confers an unrequested benefit on another has no right of restitution. Thus in *Falcke v Scottish Imperial Insurance Co* (1886) 34 Ch D 234, at 248–249, Bowen LJ said:

   The general principle is, beyond all question, that work and labour done or money expended by one man to preserve or benefit the property of another do not according to English law . . . if standing alone, create any obligation to repay the expenditure. Liabilities are not to be forced upon people behind their backs any more than you can confer a benefit upon a man against his will.

   The exact extent of liability in English law for unsolicited actions or expenditures to preserve life or property of the defendant is unclear. See Goff & Jones, *Law of Restitution* (3rd edn), pp 337–350. There are some cases where there seems to be liability: one is the supply of necessaries to a lunatic (cf *Re Rhodes*, below). It is thought that another is if essential medical services are rendered to an unconscious person. In the Canadian case of *Matheson v Smiley* [1932] 1 WWR 758, the Manitoba Court of Appeal allowed a doctor to claim for services rendered in an unsuccessful attempt to save the life of a man who had shot himself with intent to commit suicide. Do you think the suicide would have welcomed the doctor's attentions?

Re Rhodes (1890) 44 Ch D 94, Court of Appeal

From 1855 until her death in 1881, Miss Rhodes lived in a private lunatic asylum, at a cost of £140 per year. This was paid by her brother, partly from the income from her property and the balance out of his own pocket. After the brother's death, his son, who was his executor, continued to do the same, the deficiency being made good sometimes by him and sometimes by his brother and sisters. No claim was ever made against Miss Rhodes' estate during her lifetime, nor were any accounts ever kept, but after her death the brothers and sisters claimed from her estate the amount they had spent out of their own pockets.

Cotton LJ. The case raises several questions, one of which is of considerable importance; and, although in the view which we take, that question is not necessary to the decision of the case, yet, as it has been fully argued, we think we ought to express our opinion upon it. That question is, whether there can be an implied contract on the part of a lunatic not so found by inquisition to repay out of her property sums expended for necessaries supplied to her. Now the term 'implied contract' is a most unfortunate expression, because there cannot be a contract by a lunatic. But whenever necessaries are supplied to a person who by reason of disability cannot himself contract, the law implies an obligation on the part of such person to pay for such necessaries out of his own property. It is asked, can there be an implied contract by a person who cannot himself contract in express terms? The answer is, that what the law implies on the part of such a person is an obligation, which has been improperly termed a contract, to repay money spent in supplying necessaries. I think that the expression 'implied contract' is erroneous and very unfortunate . . .

[W]e all agree with the view that I have thus expressed in order to prevent any doubt from arising in consequence of our having declined to settle the question in the case to which I have alluded. . .

[W]e must look to the facts of the case in order to see whether the payments for the lunatic were made with the intention of constituting thereby a debt against the lunatic's estate. . .

[A]lthough they had no particular intention of making a gift, they contributed the money; and, if they intended to be repaid, it is very strange that they make no claim on their own behalf, but leave their brother to make it for them. In my opinion, the true effect of the evidence is that all these persons—the Appellant, and his brother and sisters, and the father—did provide this money under circumstances from which no implied obligation could arise.

Lindley LJ . . . I do not doubt that the cost of necessaries can be recovered against a lunatic's estate in a proper case.

Then we come to the question of fact. Now, in order to raise an obligation to repay, the money must have been expended with the intention on the part of the person providing it that it should be repaid. I think that that intention is not only not proved, but expressly negatived in the present case. I do not believe that the brother ever intended to constitute himself a creditor of his sister so as to render her estate liable to repay him. He was a kind and affectionate brother; but if he had had any such an intention, being a man of business, he would naturally have kept some kind of account between himself and his sister. There is no real ground for saying that he ever dreamt of repayment. Since his death his children maintained this lady by contribution, and, while there is no direct evidence to shew that the money contributed was a gift, there is still less evidence to shew any intention to be repaid.

Upon the facts, then, I come to the conclusion that the constitution of a debt between themselves and the lunatic was the last thing that the person who made the payments contemplated.

[Lopes LJ concurred.]

NOTES

1. What are the differences between an express contract, an implied contract and quasi-contract (or restitution)? If the plaintiffs in *Re Rhodes* had not acted gratuitously, on which basis would they have recovered?
2. At first instance Kay J had said that Miss Rhodes might have been placed

in an asylum at very much less than £140 per year, and he was not satisfied that the extra expense was a necessary. The Court of Appeal disagreed, pointing out that what is a necessary must be determined 'having regard to the station in life and the means of the person in question'. But this raises an important point about restitutionary liability: it will normally be based on the benefit to the defendant. The amount spent by the plaintiff is not directly relevant (see below, p 368), nor is any amount which the defendant had promised the plaintiff. In the Canadian case of *Deglman v Guaranty Trust Co of Canada and Constantineau* [1954] 3 DLR 785, the respondent was the nephew of the deceased. When he was 20 he lived with his aunt for about six months. She promised him that if he would be good to her and do such services as she might request during her lifetime, she would make adequate provision for him in her will and, in particular, would leave him a house she owned. He drove his aunt on trips to Montreal and elsewhere, did chores about the house and performed other minor services. The Supreme Court of Canada held that the respondent had performed these services in the expectation of receiving the promised reward, but that any contract was unenforceable under the Statute of Frauds (RSO 1950, c 371) s 4, which provided that no action could be brought on a contract concerning land unless the agreement was in writing or there was a written note of it signed by the other party. Nor did the respondent's actions constitute sufficient part performance to take the case out of the statute (the Statute of Frauds is dealt with below, p 131). However, the respondent was awarded $3,000 in restitution as the reasonable value of his services.

3. In this chapter we have presented what may be called the orthodox view of the divisions between contract, tort and restitution. On this view, contractual liability is based on promise and leads to damages for loss of expectaton; tort is based on negligence and foreseeability of harm (or, where the loss is purely economic, a special relationship 'equivalent to contract') and leads to damages for reliance loss; and restitutionary liability is viewed as based upon unjust enrichment and leading to recovery of the benefit received by the defendant at the plaintiff's expense. Even on the orthodox view, the divisions are not as neat as this: for instance, we shall see examples of 'contractual liability' which can only be described as based on 'promise' in a highly fictitious sense (eg below, pp 318 ff). But the real challenge to the analysis presented here comes from Atiyah, who argues that much of contractual liability is in fact based on the receipt of a benefit by the defendant or reliance by the plaintiff, and that the element of 'promise' is grossly exaggerated by the traditional view. We will explore this controversy in section 6.

CHAPTER 3
Specimen contracts

The notes which follow each form are not intended to be exhaustive. They point out some of the distinctive clauses of each type of contract, particularly clauses which will be involved in cases to be considered later in the book.

Standard form buyer's order (see pp 34–35)

NOTES ON STANDARD FORM BUYER'S ORDER

1. The boxes on the face of the form are for the items which will be expressly agreed on each occasion; the back contains a set of standard terms.
2. Some of the 'back of order' conditions differ significantly from the general law (ie the rules that would apply in the absence of express agreement). For instance, a buyer cannot normally cancel an order without the seller's consent merely because a strike means that he no longer requires the goods: compare the second clause.
3. The 'Delivery' clause comes closer to the position under the general law, the only difference being that under the general law the buyer could only cancel the whole of the undelivered part. A clause which merely restates the general rule is still useful, because the other party may be much less unhappy about the buyer exercising a right he claims if the buyer can point to a clear provision for it in the contract documents.
4. The 'Statement' clause clearly contemplates payment being due after delivery. Under the general law the buyer would have to tender payment as a condition of obtaining delivery, see below, p 413.

Established 1791

PURCHASE ORDER

THE KENRICK GROUP

PO Box 9, Union Street,
Kenrick Way, West Bromwich, West Midlands B70 6DB.

Telephone: 021 553 2741
Telex: 336470 Kenric G

NIXDORF COMPUTER Ref.

VAT REG No. 351 4280 77

To:

Purchase Order Number
Page
Supplier Number
Order Date
Requisition Number

Please supply the following goods and / or services, subject to the conditions printed overleaf.

ITEM No.	QTY	UNIT	ARTICLE No.	DESCRIPTION	PRICE	UNIT	% DISCOUNT	DELIVERY IN WEEK

for and on behalf of
THE KENRICK GROUP

.... *Buyer*

.... *Director*

manufacturers of

Builders' Hardware, SHEPHERD castors

D.I.Y. Products

and

Sub-Contract Engineers

THE KENRICK GROUP
Archibald Kenrick & Sons Ltd
Registered No 18712C England
Kenrick Hardware Ltd
Registered No 22942 England
Kenrick Engineering Ltd
Registered No 993932 England

KENRICK

CONDITIONS

No goods are to be supplied or services rendered, without an official order. No alteration is to be made to an order without confirmation in writing.

An order may be cancelled or suspended by The Kenrick Group in the event of Strikes, Lock-outs, Accidents, actions of the Queen's enemies, Acts of God or other events beyond their control.

CARRIAGE	Unless specifically agreed otherwise all deliveries are to be Carriage Paid.
PROPERTY	Property in goods supplied against an official order shall pass to The Kenrick Group upon acceptance by them at their Works (or other place of delivery specified on the order) but without prejudice to the right of subsequent rejection of goods found to be inferior in quality, defective or not in accordance with the order.
DELIVERY	The right is reserved to cancel the whole or any part of an order not delivered within the time stated on the order form. Goods delivered before required delivery date will be treated as delivered on 1st day of following month.
PACKAGES	Packages are not to be charged, but will be returned, if required, as soon as practicable.
DELIVERY NOTE	A Delivery Note, quoting the order number, is to accompany or precede all deliveries.
INVOICES	A separate invoice is to be rendered for each order and for each delivery against an order. The invoice must quote the order number and be sent immediately after delivery has been made.
STATEMENT	A monthly Statement of Account is to be rendered and should be received by the 8th day of the following month. The right is reserved to put forward to the following month Statements not received within this time.
DEFECTIVE EQUIPMENT	Employer's Liability (Defective Equipment) Act 1969. Acceptance of this order is to be regarded as an undertaking by the Supplier of goods and equipment to be responsible for and to indemnify The Kenrick Group against all claims of whatsoever nature and all costs and expenses in any defect in the goods supplied, other than a defect wholly attributable to the negligence or fault of The Kenrick Group or their employees or agents.

Standard form sales quotation

(Kenrick Hardware Ltd, a division of the Kenrick Group: the face of the sales form, which is merely a sheet bearing the company letterhead, is omitted).

CONDITIONS OF SALE

1 Quotations
Unless otherwise expressly stated, quotations remain valid for a period of 30 days from their date. They apply only to the quantities and are not to be taken to apply to orders for other quantities.

2 Price variations
Prices quoted are those current at the time of the quotation, but goods will be invoiced at the price ruling at the time of delivery. Price increase subsequent to the placing of an order will be notified to the customer by the Company and will be deemed to have been accepted, unless specific notification of cancellation has been received within 7 days of the despatch by the company of the notification of the price increase. The component price is based on the LME material price at date of quotation. Any cost variation will be shown in the component price and you will be advised monthly. All prices quoted exclude VAT. Tooling terms—30% deposit required with order, with the remainder due 30 days from submission of samples. Tooling prices quoted are full cost. Tooling will become your property upon final payment.

Any normal day to day maintenance eg replacement of ejector pins, core pins and cleaning will be carried out at the expense of Kenrick. Any major refurbishment, rebuilding or modifications required on tooling, costs to be negotiated and agreed prior to commencing of work.

3 Order quantity
The company reserves the right to supply up to + or − 5% on your order quantity requirements.

Normal minimum quantity will be one day's production, if not stated otherwise in our quotation.

4 Carriage
Carriage charges of goods delivered within the United Kingdom will be paid by the Company on any delivery exceeding £250.00 in value.

5 Delivery
Delivery dates are given in good faith, but the Company can accept no responsibility for damages or losses of any description whatsoever, which may be caused by delays in delivery. Delivery of samples—sample delivery date is assessed on toolroom load at date of quotation, this may vary at order date. Delivery of production quantities to be agreed at time of order.

6 Force majeure
Should the manufacture or delivery of any of the goods or constituent parts thereof at any of the Company's works or delivery of the goods to you elsewhere, whether by the Company or an independent carrier, be prevented or hindered directly or indirectly by fire, the elements or civil commotion, strikes or lock-outs, industrial dispute, shortage of raw materials or fuel, notwithstanding that the Company has taken all reasonable steps to procure the same, shortage of labour breakdown or partial failure of plant or machinery, the late receipt of your specification or other necessary information, acts, orders or regulations of Government, delay on the part of any independent sub-contractor or supplier or any other cause whatsoever beyond the reasonable control of the Company, then the time for delivery of the goods shall be extended for a reasonable period having regard to the effect of the delaying cause on the manufacture or delivery of the goods.

7 Defective goods
If the goods or any part thereof are defective in quality or state or (save for discrepancy in weight) otherwise not in accordance with the Contract then, if the Company and you do not agree that you should accept the goods at an agreed value or that the goods should be made good at the Company's expense, provided that the Company is notified in writing within 14 days of receipt of goods, the Company undertakes to accept a return of the relevant goods and, at your option, either to:

(a) Repay or allow you the invoice price thereon and any transport costs between the place of delivery and such place of return we shall be nominated by the Company borne by you, or,

(b) Replace them as soon as may be reasonably practical.

This undertaking is given and shall be accepted by you in lieu of any other legal remedy. AQL 2½% BS6001 General Inspection Cover 2. Supply is subject to acceptable quality levels being agreed prior to production.

8 Technical information

Draft angles and tolerances to be fully indicated before tool design commences. Position of ejector pins and gate marks to be negotiated. Where possible it is requested that the standard KHL logo appears on all components. Special container requirements may invalidate this quotation.

9 Damage in transit

The Company can accept no responsibility for damage in transit unless such damage is reported in writing to the carriers and to the Company, such report being delivered to the carriers and the Company within 3 days of receipt of the goods. Any liability of the Company will be limited to the replacement of the damaged or lost article or articles only, for no other liability whatsoever, howsoever caused.

10 Design work

Any responsibility for original design work carried out by KHL is transferred to the client on acceptance of said design.

11 Payment

Unless specifically agreed otherwise payment of Accounts become due at the end of the month following despatch of goods.

12 Contract

The Company shall be entitled, without prejudice to its other rights and remedies, either to terminate, wholly or in part, any or every such Contract in any of the following events:

(a) If any debt is due and payable by you to the Company but is unpaid.

(b) If you have failed to provide any letter of credit, Bill of Exchange or any other security required by the Contract, provided that in such event the aforesaid rights of termination or suspension shall apply only in regard to the particular Contract in respect of which you shall have so failed.

(c) If you have failed to take delivery of any goods under any Contract between you and the Company otherwise than in accordance with your contractual rights.

(d) If you become insolvent or, being a body corporate, have passed a resolution for voluntary winding-up, except where solely for the purpose of reconstruction or have suffered an Order of the Court for your winding-up to be made or have had a Receiver appointed or, being an individual or partnership have suspended payment of your debts in whole or in part or have proposed or entered into any composition or arrangement with your creditors or have had a Receiving Order in Bankruptcy made against you.

The Company shall be entitled to exercise its aforesaid rights of termination or suspension at any time during which the event or default rise thereto has not ceased or been remedied and in the event of any suspension the Company shall be entitled, as a condition of resuming delivery under any Contract between it and you, to require pre-payment of or such security as it may require for the payment of the price of any further delivery.

13 Law

Any contract arising from this quotation shall in all respects be construed and operate as an English Contract and in conformity with English law and English Court shall be jurisdiction.

NOTES ON STANDARD FORM SALES QUOTATION

1. The conditions of sale are much longer than the conditions of purchase used by the same company. One reason for this is that the general law of sale seems more favourable to the buyer than the seller: see further below, pp 325–335.
2. This form can be used for sending quotations to buyers, or for acknowledging orders sent by buyers. If a quotation is made on this form, the quotation is valid for 30 days. Suppose a buyer orders the goods quoted: is the seller bound to fill the order, or can it turn the order down if it would have difficulty in filling it? See below, pp 173–176.
3. In the absence of some provision like cl 2, the contract would be 'fixed price'. Note the absence of any equivalent provision in the buying form.
4. Clauses 5 and 6 also present a contrast to the 'Delivery' clause in the purchasing form. Clause 5 deals primarily with liability to pay compensation for late delivery, whereas cl 6 prevents the buyer from cancelling the order on the ground of delay, where the delay was the result of what the clause calls *force majeure*. At common law *force majeure* is no defence.
5. Clause 7 curtails the buyer's remedies if the goods are defective. For the effect of such clauses, which are now subject to statutory control, see below, p 705ff.
6. Clause 12 protects the sellers by giving the power to suspend deliveries or to terminate contracts in much wider circumstances than the general law provides. For instance, the general law does not allow a seller to terminate a contract merely because the buyer is late in paying (below, p 436) or has become insolvent (below, p 448); nor does it allow termination of one contract because of a default on another (below, p 449).
7. We have reproduced the purchasing and sales form of a single group of companies in order to show how the group's interests, and therefore its standard terms, differ according to whether it is buying or selling. What would be the effect of another company, using conditions of sale similar to Kenricks', sending its form as an acknowledgement (acceptance) of an order from Kenricks on the order form above? See below, p 190ff.

Conditions for the hiring of plant (see pp 39–42)

AGREEMENT No........................

From:
(Owner)

HIRE CONTRACT OFFER

TO BE KEPT BY HIRER.

To (Hirer)......................................

Dear Sirs, We thank you for your order/enquiry for hire of plant and set out below a schedule of plant which we offer to hire at the hire rates and terms noted and subject to the Model Conditions attached hereto.
The plant is offered subject to being available to the Owner when the Hirer's acceptance of the Contract is received by the Owner.
Please return the ACCEPTANCE Form duly signed on your behalf.

Your Ref/Order No......................... Date of Offer ....19 ....

PERIOD OF HIRE: From   19   To   19

SCHEDULE OF PLANT (Where interdependent items of plant are hired as a group it should be so stated or indicated by means of a bracket)

CURRENT HIRE RATES AND TERMS

CHARGEABLE ITEMS — All operator items will be charged at rates current at the time the work is carried out to include any increases from National Agreements and/or Statutory Regulations (see Clause 26).

OPERATOR:	BASIS OF CHARGE		BASIS OF CHARGE
Basic Wages		MACHINE:	
Overtime..............		Fuel.............	
Maintenance..........		Oils and Greases........	
Condition Payments ...		Consumable Stores	
Bonus.................		TRANSPORT OF PLANT:	
Holiday Pay		To Site...............	
Travelling Time		From Site	
Fares		VAT (if applicable)	
Lodging Allowance			
Radius/ Travel Allowance		ADDITIONAL INSURANCES –	
Statutory Contributions .		If requested and specified by the Hirer in respect of his liabilities under Clauses 8 and 13, and subject to the agreement of the Owner and confirmation of cover within the terms and limitations of the Owner's insurance policies .	
ADMINISTRATIVE COSTS ON OPERATOR CHARGES			(see Footnote 1) *

SITE ADDRESS (Exact Location and Telephone Number)

DATE OF DELIVERY: /   /19

SIGNATURE
For and on behalf of Owner...

FOOTNOTES* (1) UNLESS OTHERWISE AGREED THE HIRER IS RESPONSIBLE FOR INSURING AGAINST HIS LIABILITIES UNDER CLAUSES 8 AND 13.
(2) ACCEPTANCE OF THE PLANT ON SITE IMPLIES ACCEPTANCE OF ALL TERMS AND CONDITIONS STATED ON THIS OFFER (SEE CLAUSE 3) UNLESS OTHERWISE AGREED.

TERMS OF PAYMENT

CPA/9/79   Copyright CPA

These revised general conditions for the hiring of plant ("Model Conditions") are the result of several years' negotiations between the Contractors' Plant Association representing the plant hire industry, the Federation of Civil Engineering Contractors representing the main client industry of civil engineering and the Office of Fair Trading, and having regard to the provisions of the Restrictive Trade Practices Acts and latterly of the Unfair Contract Terms Act 1977.

The revised conditions have been approved by the Contractors' Plant Association and the Federation of Civil Engineering Contractors for use in their unaltered (i.e. "Model Conditions") form.

The Department of Prices and Consumer Protection and the Office of Fair Trading have agreed for the purposes of Section 21 (2) of the Restrictive Trade Practices Act 1976 that the recommendation of these revised conditions ("Model Conditions") is not to be regarded as warranting investigation by the Restrictive Practices Court.

If any amendments are made to these Model Conditions by the contracting parties, they will cease to be the Model Conditions mentioned above and must not be referred to as such.

See also Footnote at end of Model Conditions.

MODEL CONDITIONS FOR THE HIRING OF PLANT (WITH EFFECT FROM SEPTEMBER 1979)

1. DEFINITIONS

(a) The "Owner" is the Company, firm or person letting the plant on hire and includes their successors, assigns or personal representatives.

(b) The "Hirer" is the Company, firm, person, Corporation or public authority taking the Owner's plant on hire and includes their successors or personal representatives.

(c) "Plant" covers all classes of plant, machinery, equipment and accessories therefor which the Owner agrees to hire to the Hirer.

(d) A "day" shall be 8 hours unless otherwise specified in the Contract.

(e) A "week" shall be seven consecutive days.

(f) A "working week" covers the period from starting time on Monday to finishing time on Friday.

(g) The hire period shall commence from the time when the plant leaves the Owner's depot or place where last employed and shall continue until the plant is received back at the Owner's named depot or equal.

2. EXTENT OF CONTRACT

No conditions other than specifically set forth in the Offer and Acceptance and herein shall be deemed to be incorporated in or to form part of the Contract.

3. ACCEPTANCE OF PLANT

Acceptance of the plant on site implies acceptance of all terms and conditions herein unless otherwise agreed.

4. UNLOADING AND LOADING

The Hirer shall be responsible for unloading and loading the plant at site, and any personnel supplied by the Owner shall be deemed to be under the Hirer's control and shall comply with all directions of the Hirer.

5. DELIVERY IN GOOD ORDER AND MAINTENANCE: INSPECTION REPORTS

(a) Unless notification in writing to the contrary is received by the Owner from the Hirer in the case of plant supplied with an operator within four working days, and in the case of plant supplied without an operator within three working days, of the plant being delivered to the site, the plant shall be deemed to be in good order, save for either an inherent fault or a fault not ascertainable by reasonable examination, in accordance with the terms of the Contract and to the Hirer's satisfaction, provided that where plant requires to be erected on site, the periods above stated shall be calculated from date of completed erection of plant. The Hirer shall be responsible for its safekeeping, use in a workmanlike manner within the Manufacturer's rated capacity and return on the completion of the hire in equal good order (fair wear and tear excepted).

(b) The Hirer shall when hiring plant without Owner's operator or driver take all reasonable steps to keep himself acquainted with the state and condition of the plant. If such plant be continued at work or in use in an unsafe and unsatisfactory state, the Hirer shall be solely responsible for any damage, loss or accidents whether directly or indirectly arising therefrom.

(c) The current Inspection Report required under the relevant legislation, or a copy thereof, shall be supplied by the Owner if requested by the Hirer and returned on completion of hire.

6. SERVICING AND INSPECTION

The Hirer shall at all reasonable times allow the Owner, his Agents or his Insurers to have access to the plant to inspect, test, adjust, repair or replace the same. So far as reasonably possible, such work will be carried out at times to suit the convenience of the Hirer.

7. TIMBER MATS OR EQUIVALENTS

If the ground is soft or unsuitable for the plant to work on or travel over without timbers or equivalents the Hirer shall supply and lay suitable timbers or equivalents in a suitable position for the plant to travel over or work on.

8. HANDLING OF PLANT

When a driver or operator is supplied by the Owner with the plant, the Owner shall supply a person competent in operating the plant and such person shall be under the direction and control of the Hirer. Such drivers or operators shall for all purposes in connection with their employment in the working of the plant be regarded as the servants or agents of the Hirer (but without prejudice to any of the provisions of Clause 13) who alone shall be responsible for all claims arising in connection with the operation of the plant by the said drivers or operators. The Hirer shall not allow any other person to operate such plant without the Owner's previous consent to be confirmed in writing.

9. BREAKDOWN, REPAIRS AND ADJUSTMENT

(a) When the plant is hired without the Owner's driver or operator any breakdown or the unsatisfactory working of any part of the plant must be notified immediately to the Owner. Any claim for breakdown time will only be considered from the time and date of notification.

(b) Full allowance will be made to the Hirer for any stoppage due to breakdown of plant caused by the development of either an inherent fault or a fault not ascertainable by reasonable examination or fair wear and tear and for all stoppages for normal running repairs in accordance with the terms of the Contract.

(c) The Hirer shall not, except for punctures, repair the plant without the written authority of the Owner. Punctures are however the responsibility of the Hirer. Allowance for hire charges and for the reasonable cost of repairs will be made by the Owner to the Hirer where repairs have been authorised.

(d) The Hirer shall be responsible for all expense involved arising from any breakdown and all loss or damage incurred by the Owner due to the Hirer's negligence, misdirection or misuse of the plant, whether by the Hirer or his servants, and for the payment of hire at the appropriate idle time rate during the period the plant is necessarily idle due to such breakdown or damage. The Owner will be responsible for the cost of repairs to the plant involved in breakdowns from all other causes and will bear the cost of providing spare parts.

10. OTHER STOPPAGES

No claims will be admitted (other than those allowed for under "Breakdown" or for "Idle Time", as herein provided), for stoppages through causes outside the Owner's control, including bad weather or ground conditions nor shall the Owner be responsible for the cost or expense of recovering any plant from soft ground.

11. LOSS OF USE OF OTHER PLANT DUE TO BREAKDOWN

Each item of plant specified in the Contract is hired as a separate unit and the breakdown or stoppage of one or more units or vehicles (whether the property of the Owner or otherwise) through any cause whatsoever, shall not entitle the Hirer to compensation or allowance for the loss of working time by any other unit or units of plant working in conjunction therewith, provided that where two or more items of plant are hired together as a unit, such item shall be deemed a unit for the purpose of breakdown.

12. CONSEQUENTIAL LOSSES

Save in respect of the Owner's liability if any under Clauses 5, 8 and 9, the Owner accepts no liability nor responsibility for any consequential loss or damage due to or arising through any cause beyond his control.

Copyright C.P.A.

13. HIRER'S RESPONSIBILITY FOR LOSS AND DAMAGE

(a) For the avoidance of doubt it is hereby declared and agreed that nothing in this Clause affects the operation of Clauses 5, 8 and 9 of this Agreement.

(b) During the continuance of the hire period the Hirer shall subject to the provisions referred to in sub paragraph (a) make good to the Owner all loss of or damage to the plant from whatever cause the same may arise, fair wear and tear excepted, and except as provided in Clause 9 herein, and shall also fully and completely indemnify the Owner in respect of all claims by any person whatsoever for injury to person or property caused by or in connection with or arising out of the use of the plant and in respect of all costs and charges in connection therewith whether arising under statute or common law. In the event of loss of or damage to the plant, hire charges shall be continued at idle time rates until settlement has been effected.

(c) Notwithstanding the above the Owner shall accept liability for damage, loss or injury due to or arising

(i) prior to delivery of any plant to the site of the Hirer where the plant is in transit by transport of the Owner or as otherwise arranged by the Owner,

(ii) during the erection of any plant, where such plant requires to be completely erected on the site, always provided that such erection is under the exclusive control of the Owner or his Agent.

(iii) during the dismantling of any plant, where plant requires to be dismantled after use prior to removal from site, always provided that such dismantling is under the exclusive control of the Owner or his Agent.

(iv) after the plant has been removed from the site and is in transit on to the Owner by transport of the Owner or as otherwise arranged by the Owner.

(v) where plant is travelling to or from a site under its own power with a driver supplied by the Owner.

14. NOTICE OF ACCIDENTS

If the plant is involved in any accident resulting in injury to persons or damage to property, immediate notice must be given to the Owner by telephone and in respect of any claim not within the Hirer's agreement for indemnity, no admission, offer, promise of payment or indemnity shall be made by the Hirer without the Owner's consent in writing.

15. RE-HIRING, ETC.

The plant or any part thereof shall not be re-hired, sub-let, or lent to any third party without the written permission of the Owner.

16. CHANGE OF SITE

The plant shall not be moved from the site to which it was delivered or consigned without the authority of the Owner, such authority to be confirmed in writing.

17. RETURN OF PLANT FOR REPAIRS

If during the hire period the Owner decides that urgent repairs to the plant are necessary he may arrange for such repairs to be carried out on site or at any location of his nomination. In that event the Owner shall be obliged to replace the plant with similar plant if available, the Owner paying all transport charges involved. In the event of the Owner being unable to replace the plant he shall be entitled to determine the Contract forthwith by giving written notice to the Hirer. If such determination occurs:

(a) within three months from the commencement of hire the Owner shall pay all transport charges involved, or,

(b) more than three months but less than six months from the commencement of hire the Owner shall be liable only for the cost of reloading and return transport.

18. BASIS OF CHARGING

(a) The Hirer shall render to the Owner for each working week an accurate statement of the number of hours the plant has worked each day. Where the plant is accompanied by the Owner's driver or operator, the Hirer shall sign the employee's Time Record Sheets daily or weekly. The signature of the Hirer's representative shall bind the Hirer to accept the hours shown on the Time Record Sheets.

(b) Full allowance will be made for breakdown periods resulting from mechanical or electrical faults or absence of driver or operator supplied by the Owner except where breakdown is due to the Hirer's misuse, misdirection or negligence, subject however to the provisions of Clause 8 of this Agreement.

(c) Breakdown time shall be allowed for not exceeding 8 hours each day on Monday to Friday less the actual daily hours worked.

(d) Plant shall be hired out at "per day" or "per week" or "per hour" for a minimum period, for a day of 8 hours or for a week of 40 hours or such other period as may be mutually agreed between the Owner and the Hirer. In the case of plant hired "per week" for a minimum period, odd days at the beginning and at the end of the hire period shall be charged pro rata.

(e) Stoppages due to changing of tyres and repairs to punctures will be chargeable as working time up to a maximum of 2 hours for any one stoppage and any excess will be treated as breakdown time.

(f) In the case of plant which requires to be dismantled for the purpose of transportation, if the Owner agrees to a modification of the hire charge for the period required for assembling on site and dismantling upon completion of hire, such modification of the hire charge and the period for which it shall apply shall be stated on the Hire Contract.

19. PLANT HIRED ON A DAILY BASIS WITHOUT QUALIFICATION AS TO HOURS

The full daily rate will be charged on a daily basis irrespective of the hours worked except in the case of breakdown for which the Owner is responsible, when the actual hours worked will be charged pro rata to the average working day. No hire charge shall be made for Saturday and/or Sunday unless the plant is actually worked.

20. PLANT HIRED BY THE WEEK OR MONTH WITHOUT QUALIFICATION AS TO HOURS

The weekly or monthly rate shall be charged irrespective of the number of hours worked, except in the case of breakdown for which the Owner is responsible when an allowance at the rate of one-fifth of the agreed weekly rate or one-twentieth of the agreed monthly rate will be made for each full working day broken down calculated to the nearest half working day. No allowance will be made for breakdowns on Saturdays or Sundays.

21. PLANT HIRED BY THE WEEK OR THE HOUR FOR A MINIMUM OF 40 HOURS PER WEEK OR A DAY OF 8 HOURS

If no breakdown occurs, the full hire for the minimum period in the Contract will be charged and an additional pro rata charge will be made for hours worked in excess of such minimum period. The stipulated minimum number of hours can be worked at any time during the minimum period of a week. Allowance will be made for breakdowns up to 8 hours providing always that where the actual hours worked are in excess of the minimum period less breakdown time, the actual hours worked shall be chargeable. Idle time for this purpose shall be treated as actual working time. The minimum week of 40 hours shall be reduced by 8 hours Monday to Friday for each day's statutory holiday occurring in such week, provided that the plant does not work on the holiday.

22. "ALL-IN" RATES

Where "All-In" rates are charged by agreement the minimum period shall be as defined in the Contract and in accordance with the hire rates and terms contained therein, subject to the provisions of Clause 26.

23. COMMENCEMENT AND TERMINATION OF HIRE (Transport of Plant)

(a) The hire period shall commence from the time when the plant leaves the Owner's depot or place where last employed and shall continue until the plant is received back at the Owner's named depot or equal, but an allowance shall be made of not more than one day's hire charge each way for travelling time. If the plant be used on day of travelling, full hire rates shall be paid for the period of use on that day. If more than one day be properly and unavoidably occupied in transporting the plant, a hire charge at idle time rates shall be payable for such extra time, provided that where plant is hired for a total period of less than one week, the full hire rate shall be paid from the date of despatch to the date of return to the Owner's named depot or equal.

(b) An allowance of not more than one day's travelling time shall be allowed when the plant is travelling to a site other than that specified in the Contract provided that:

(i) consent to such transfer has been given by the Owner under Clause 16, and,

(ii) the plant is moved by means other than under its own power, and,

(iii) the plant shall have been on the site specified in the Contract or on any other site to which consent to transfer has been given under Clause 16 for a period of at least 14 days.

Copyright C.P.A.

24. NOTICE OF TERMINATION OF CONTRACT

Where the period of hire is indeterminate or having been defined becomes indeterminate the Contract shall be determinable by seven days' notice in writing given by either party to the other (except in cases where the plant has been lost or damaged). In the event of the Hirer desiring to terminate the Contract and failing to give such notice, hire for the period of the seven days' notice shall be chargeable at the idle time rates in lieu. Notice given by the Hirer to the Owner's driver or operator shall not be deemed to constitute compliance with the provisions of this Clause.

25. IDLE TIME

When plant works for any time during a guaranteed minimum period, then the whole of that guaranteed minimum period shall be charged as working time. If the plant is idle for the whole of a guaranteed minimum period, the charge shall be two thirds of the hire rate. In any case no period less than one day shall be reckoned as idle time. Where an "All-In" rate is charged, idle time is charged on the machine element only. Full rate will be charged for the operator.

26. WAGES AND OTHER CHARGEABLE ITEMS RELATING TO DRIVERS AND OPERATORS OF PLANT

All chargeable items shall be paid by the Hirer at the rates contracted save that any subsequent increases before and/or during the hire period arising from awards under national wage agreements and/or from increases in the employer's statutory contribution shall be charged as additions at cost by the Owner and shall be admitted and paid by the Hirer.

27. TRAVELLING TIME AND FARES

Travelling time and fares for operators, similar expenses incurred at the beginning and end of the hire period and where appropriate the operator's return fare to his home at periods in accordance with the appropriate national agreement will be chargeable at cost. No charge shall be made by the Owner for any such expenses incurred by other employees of the Owner for the purpose of servicing, repair or maintenance of plant, unless necessitated by the Hirer's negligence, misdirection or misuse of the plant.

28. FUEL, OIL AND GREASE

Fuel, oil and grease shall, when supplied by the Owner, be charged at net cost or an agreed estimate of net cost, and when supplied by the Hirer, shall be of a grade or type specified by the Owner.

29. SHARPENING OF DRILLS/STEELS, ETC.

Where appropriate, the cost of re-sharpening shall be borne by the Hirer.

30. OWNER'S NAME PLATES

The Hirer shall not remove, deface or cover up the Owner's name plate or mark on the plant indicating that it is his property.

31. TRANSPORT

The Hirer shall pay the cost of and if required by the Owner, arrange transport of, the plant from the Owner's depot or equal to the site and return to named depot or equal on completion of the hire period.

32. GOVERNMENT REGULATIONS

The Hirer will be responsible for compliance with relevant regulations issued by the Government or Local Authorities, including Regulations under the Factories Acts, Health and Safety at Work etc. Act and observance of the Road Traffic Acts should they apply, including the cost of Road Fund Licences and any insurances made necessary thereby, save that if and during such time as the plant is travelling, whether for full or part journey from Owner to site and site to Owner under its own power with a driver supplied by the Owner, the Owner and not the Hirer shall be responsible as aforesaid.

33. PROTECTION OF OWNER'S RIGHTS

(a) The Hirer shall not re-hire, sell, mortgage, charge, pledge, part with possession of or otherwise deal with the plant except as provided under Clause 15 and shall protect the same against distress, execution or seizure and shall indemnify the Owner against all losses, damage, costs, charges and expenses arising as a direct result of any failure to observe and perform this condition except in the event of Government requisition.

(b) If the Hirer make default in punctual payment of all sums due to the Owner for hire of plant or other charges or shall fail to observe and perform the terms and conditions of this Contract, or if the Hirer shall suffer any distress or execution to be levied against him or make or propose to make any arrangement with his creditors or being a Company, shall go into liquidation (other than a member's voluntary liquidation) or shall do or shall cause to be done or permit or suffer any act or thing whereby the Owner's rights in the plant may be prejudiced or put into jeopardy, this Agreement shall forthwith be terminated (without any notice or other act on the part of the Owner and notwithstanding that the Owner may have waived some previous default or matter of the same or a like nature), and it shall thereupon be lawful for the Owner to retake possession of the said plant and for that purpose enter into or upon any premises where the same may be and the determination of the hiring under this Condition shall not affect the right of the Owner to recover from the Hirer any monies due to the Owner under the Contract or damages for breach thereof.

34. CHANGES IN NORMAL WORKING WEEK

The foregoing provisions have been framed upon the basis of the Hirer working a 5-day week of 40 hours; it is hereby agreed that in the event of

(a) there being any change in the normal weekly hours in the industry in which the Hirer is engaged or

(b) the Contract being made with reference to a 5-day week being worked by the Hirer (either of 40 hours or of such number of hours as may constitute the normal working week in the said industry)

Clauses 1(d) and (f), 18(c) and (d), 20 and (in regard to breakdown allowance and reduction for statutory holidays) 21 shall be deemed to be modified conformably and in the event of an alteration in the normal weekly working hours in the said industry the "Hire Rates and Terms" of plant hired for a minimum weekly or daily period shall be varied pro rata.

35. ENFORCED TRANSFERENCE OF CONTRACT

In the event of any item or items of the plant comprised in this hire Contract being used by the Hirer on or in connection with a contract for the construction of works or buildings and of a forfeiture of such contract being made by the Employer thereunder, the Owner will upon request in writing made by the Employer within seven days after the date when such forfeiture has become effective and on such Employer undertaking to pay all hire charges therefore from such last mentioned date, hire such item or items to such Employer for the remainder of the period during which such item or items were hired to the Hirer upon the same terms in all respects as are herein contained save that notwithstanding the provisions of Clause 33 hereof such Employer shall be entitled to permit the use thereof by any other contractor employed by him for the purpose of completing the works or buildings comprised in such contract.

36. ARBITRATION

If during the continuance of the Contract or at any time thereafter any dispute, difference or question shall arise between the Owner and the Hirer in regard to the Contract or the construction of these Conditions or anything therein contained or the rights or liabilities of the Owner or the Hirer such dispute, difference or question shall be referred pursuant to the Arbitration Act 1950, or the Arbitration (Scotland) Act 1894 as the case may be or any Statutory modification thereof, to a Sole Arbitrator to be agreed upon by the Owner and the Hirer and failing agreement to be appointed at the request of either the Owner or the Hirer by the President for the time being of the Institution of Mechanical Engineers.

Printed by
Deverell, Gibson & Hoare Ltd., 47/51 Gt. Suffolk Street, London SE1 0PA.

NOTES ON CONDITIONS FOR THE HIRING OF PLANT

1. This form of contract reflects the normal pattern in straightforward contracts of hire, that the owner is responsible for providing a machine that works at the beginning of the hire period (see cl 5) and for keeping the machine working: if the machine breaks down, the hirer is given an allowance for the time lost (cl 9(b) and cll 19–21). Note, however, that the hirer may be responsible for notifying the owner of breakdowns (9(a)), and except for punctures may not effect repairs himself without permission (9(c)). Moreover, the owner may not be responsible for consequential losses of time, etc, caused by the breakdown (cl 12).

2. If the owner finds it necessary to remove the plant for repairs, and he cannot provide a replacement, he may determine the contract (cl 17).

3. The hirer is responsible for damage to the plant, unless the damage was caused by an initial defect, a breakdown for which the owner is responsible or an incompetent driver supplied by the owner (cl 13(b), as qualified by cll 5, 8, 9 and 13(a)). The hirer is also responsible for most cases of loss or injury caused to third parties, promising that if the owner is made liable to the third party the hirer will indemnify the owner (cll 8 and 13(b)).

4. Where the contract is not for a fixed period of time, either party may determine it on seven days' notice (cl 24). The owner also has the right to terminate the contract if the hirer defaults in paying, commits any breach or becomes insolvent (cl 33(b)). For the effect of such a clause, see below, p 428.

5. For cases involving similar terms, see below, pp 274, 718 and 723.

Bill of Lading (see fold-out)

NOTES ON BILL OF LOADING

1. A very large proportion of the world's shipping contracts are arranged in London and are subject to English law. This makes law a considerable 'export industry', and explains in part why so many of the reported contract cases involve shipping contracts of various types.
2. A 'bill of lading contract' is a contract made between a person who ships goods by sea and (usually—see note 12 below) the owner of the vessel on which the goods are shipped.
3. The bill of lading itself serves three functions. Firstly, it contains the terms of the contract (though occasionally the shipper and carrier will have agreed different terms to those in the bill, which is only issued after the goods have been shipped: in that case, it is the terms agreed which will apply, and therefore it is often said that the bill is only evidence of the terms).
4. Secondly, the bill acts as a receipt for the goods, showing the quantity shipped, their apparent condition when shipped and any leading (identifying) marks. Note the headings to be filled in on the face of the bill, and the first clause also on the face (starting 'SHIPPED . . .'). For the effect of a statement that the goods were shipped in good order and condition, see below, p 433.
5. Thirdly, the bill operates as a document of title: the shipper can transfer his ownership of the goods while they are afloat by indorsing the bill of lading to the transferee. (Note that the bill reproduced is simply the copy retained by the master of the ship, and is stamped 'not negotiable', so that it does not act as a document of title. The other copies of the bill will not bear these words.) The bill may be taken to the order of the consignee (see the second box on the face), or to the order of the shipper himself.
6. When the bill is indorsed to the consignee or buyer, the latter acquires the right to sue the shipper on the bill of lading contract, and at the same time becomes liable on that contract. This is the effect of the Bills of Lading Act 1855, s 1. (In some circumstances the bill may be indorsed to a bank by way of pledge—in other words, as security for a loan, rather as you might pledge your watch to a pawnbroker. A common example of the bill being pledged to a bank occurs when the buyer pays via a documentary credit in favour of the seller, see below, p 112. In this case the rights and liabilities are not transferred to the pledgee.) Thus the buyer can sue the shipowner if the goods are damaged, and is liable to pay the freight if it has not been paid already. As between the shipowner and the indorsee of the bill, the terms of the bill are the contract: any different arrangement made between the shipowner and the original shipper is irrelevant.
7. All bill of lading contracts for goods being shipped from the UK are subject to the 'Hague-Visby Rules', by virtue of the Carriage of Goods by Sea Act 1971, s 1(3): these rules are referred to in cl 1 on the back of the bill. The rules, and their predecessors the Hague Rules, are part of an International Convention designed to strike a fair balance between shippers and carriers, by on the one hand limiting the carrier's liability for loss of or damage to the goods (see cl 11) and, on the other, control-ling the 'exceptions' from liability which the carrier is allowed to insert

into the bill. Examples of exceptions will be found in cl 2: these particular clauses relate to deck cargo and livestock, to which the rules do not apply. An account of the background to the Hague Rules will be found below, p 736.

8. The bill also purports to limit the liability of contractors ('stevedores' and others) employed by the carrier in discharging his contractual obligations: see cl 1 on the back. These independent contractors are not parties to the contract between shipper and carrier, and the attempt to protect them has given rise to great legal difficulty: see the cases on pp 814–820.

9. The carrier is at common law obliged to proceed directly to the port of destination by the normal route. Clause 3(a) permits the ship to deviate from this route: for the interpretation of this clause, see below, p 686.

10. The carrier is also obliged to deliver the goods at the port of destination. The first clause on the face and cl 3(e) permit discharge elsewhere in certain circumstances (see p. 687).

11. The bill contemplates the freight (the price of the carriage) being paid either in advance by the shipper or by the consignee at the destination (see second clause on face). In the latter event, cl 8 gives the carrier a lien over the goods (ie the right to retain them until the freight is paid) and a power to sell them.

12. Occasionally goods will be carried for a shipper in a ship which is under charter to another person. Usually the shipper's contract will still be with the owner of the ship, unless the charterer has taken over complete control of the ship and its crew under what is called a 'demise' charter. Clause 15 expressly states that this is how the bill of lading contract is to take effect.

'Baltime 1939' time charter (see pp 46–47)

1. Shipbroker	THE BALTIC AND INTERNATIONAL MARITIME CONFERENCE UNIFORM TIME-CHARTER (Box Layout 1974) CODE NAME: "BALTIME 1939"
	PART I
	2. Place and date
3. Owners/Place of business	4. Charterers/Place of business
5. Vessel's name	6. GRT/NRT
7. Class	8. Indicated horse power
9. Total tons d.w. (abt.) on Board of Trade summer freeboard	10. Cubic feet grain/bale capacity
11. Permanent bunkers (abt.)	
12. Speed capability in knots (abt.) on a consumption in tons (abt.) of	
13. Present position	
14. Period of hire (Cl. 1)	15. Port of delivery (Cl. 1)
	16. Time of delivery (Cl. 1)
17. (a) Trade limits (Cl. 2)	
(b) Cargo exclusions specially agreed	
18. Bunkers on re-delivery (state min. and max. quantity) (Cl. 5)	
19. Charter hire (Cl. 6)	20. Hire payment (state currency, method and place of payment: also beneficiary and bank account) (Cl. 6)
21. Place or range of re-delivery (Cl. 7)	22. War (only to be filled in if Section (C) agreed) (Cl. 21)
23. Cancelling date (Cl. 22)	24. Place of arbitration (only to be filled in if place other than London agreed) (Cl. 23)
25. Brokerage commission and to whom payable (Cl. 25)	
	26. Numbers of additional clauses covering special provisions, if agreed

It is mutually agreed that this Contract shall be performed subject to the conditions contained in this Charter which shall include Part I as well as Part II. In the event of a conflict of conditions, the provisions of Part I shall prevail over those of Part II to the extent of such conflict.

| Signature (Owners) | Signature (Charterers) |

PART II
"BALTIME 1939" Uniform Time-Charter (Box Layout 1974)

It is agreed between the party mentioned in Box 3 1
as Owners of the Vessel named in Box 5 of the 2
gross/net Register tonnage indicated in Box 6, 3
classed as stated in Box 7 and of indicated horse 4
power as stated in Box 8, carrying about the 5
number of tons deadweight indicated in Box 9 on 6
Board of Trade summer freeboard inclusive of bun- 7
kers stores, provisions and boiler water, having as 8
per builder's plan a cubic feet grain bale capacity 9
as stated in Box 10, exclusive of permanent bun- 10
kers, which contain about the number of tons 11
stated in Box 11, and fully loaded capable of 12
steaming about the number of knots indicated in 13
Box 12 in good weather and smooth water on a 14
consumption of about the number of tons best 15
Welsh coal or oil-fuel stated in Box 12, now in 16
position as stated in Box 13 and the party men- 17
tioned as Charterers in Box 4, as follows 18

1. Period-Port of Delivery/Time of Delivery 19
The Owners let, and the Charterers hire the Ves- 20
sel for a period of the number of calendar months 21
indicated in Box 14 from the time (not a Sunday 22
or a legal Holiday unless taken over) the Vessel 23
is delivered and placed at the disposal of the 24
Charterers between 9 a.m. and 6 p.m., or between 25
9 a.m. and 2 p.m. if on Saturday, at the port 26
stated in Box 15 in such suitable berth where 27
she can safely lie always afloat, as the Charterers 28
may direct, she being in every way fitted for or- 29
dinary cargo service. 30
The Vessel to be delivered at the time indicated 31
in Box 16. 32

2. Trade 33
The Vessel to be employed in lawful trades for 34
the carriage of lawful merchandise only between 35
good and safe ports or places where she can 36
safely lie always afloat within the limits stated in 37
Box 17. 38
No live stock nor injurious, inflammable or dan- 39
gerous goods (such as acids, explosives, calcium 40
carbide, ferro silicon, naphtha, motor spirit, tar, 41
or any of their products) to be shipped 42

3. Owners to Provide 43
The Owners to provide and pay for all provisions 44
and wages, for insurance of the Vessel, for all 45
deck and engine-room stores and maintain her in 46
a thoroughly efficient state in hull and machinery 47
during service. 48
The Owners to provide one winchman per hatch. 49
If further winchmen are required, or if the steve- 50
dores refuse or are not permitted to work with 51
the Crew, the Charterers to provide and pay 52
qualified shore-winchmen. 53

4. Charterers to Provide 54
The Charterers to provide and pay for all coals, 55
including galley coal, oil-fuel, water for boilers, 56
port charges, pilotages (whether compulsory or 57
not), canal steersman, boatage, lights, tug-assist- 58
ance, consular charges (except those pertaining 59
to the Master, Officers and Crew), canal, dock and 60
other dues and charges, including any foreign 61
general municipality or state taxes, also all dock, 62
harbour and tonnage dues at the ports of de- 63
livery and re-delivery (unless incurred through 64
cargo carried before delivery or after re-delivery), 65
agencies, commissions, also to arrange and pay 66
for loading, trimming, stowing (including dunnage 67
and shifting boards, excepting any already on 68
board), unloading, weighing, tallying and delivery 69
of cargoes, surveys on hatches, meals supplied to 70
officials and men in their service and all other 71
charges and expenses whatsoever including de- 72
tention and expenses through quarantine (includ- 73
ing cost of fumigation and disinfection). 74
All ropes, slings and special runners actually 75
used for loading and discharging and any special 76
gear, including special ropes, hawsers and chains 77
required by the custom of the port for mooring 78
to be for the Charterers' account. The Vessel to 79
be fitted with winches, derricks, wheels and or- 80
dinary runners capable of handling lifts up to 2 81
tons. 82

5. Bunkers 83
The Charterers at port of delivery and the Ow- 84
ners at port of re-delivery to take over and pay 85
for all coal or oil-fuel remaining in the Vessel's 86
bunkers at current price at the respective ports. 87
The Vessel to be re-delivered with not less than 88
the number of tons and not exceeding the num- 89
ber of tons of coal or oil-fuel in the Vessel's 90
bunkers stated in Box 5. 91

6. Hire 92
The Charterers to pay as hire the rate stated in 93
Box 19 per 30 days, commencing in accordance 94
with Clause 1 until her re-delivery to the Owners. 95
Payment 96
Payment of hire to be made in cash, in the cur- 97
rency stated in Box 20, without discount, every 98
30 days, in advance, and in the manner prescribed 99
in Box 20. 100
In default of payment the Owners to have the 101
right of withdrawing the Vessel from the service 102
of the Charterers, without noting any protest and 103
without interference by any court or any other 104
formality whatsoever and to any other prejudice 105
any claim the Owners may otherwise have on the 106
Charterers under the Charter. 107

7. Re-delivery 108
The Vessel to be re-delivered on the expiration 109
of the Charter in the same good order as when 110
delivered to the Charterers (fair wear and tear 111
excepted) at an ice-free port in the Charterers' 112
option at the place or within the range stated in 113
Box 21, between 9 a.m. and 6 p.m., and 9 a.m. 114
and 2 p.m. on Saturday, but the day of re-delivery 115
shall not be a Sunday or legal Holiday. 116
Notice 117
The Charterers to give the Owners not less than 118
ten days' notice at which port and on about 119
which day the Vessel will be re-delivered. 120
Should the Vessel be ordered on a voyage by 121
which the Charter period will be exceeded the 122
Charterers to have the use of the Vessel to 123
enable them to complete the voyage, provided it 124
could be reasonably calculated that the voyage 125
would allow re-delivery about the time fixed for 126
the termination of the Charter, but for any time 127
exceeding the termination date the Charterers to 128
pay the market rate if higher than the rate stipu- 129
lated herein. 130

8. Cargo Space 131
The whole reach and burthen of the Vessel, in- 132
cluding lawful deck-capacity to be at the Char- 133
terers' disposal, reserving proper and sufficient 134
space for the Vessel's Master, Officers, Crew, 135
tackle, apparel, furniture, provisions and stores. 136

9. Master 137
The Master to prosecute all voyages with the ut- 138
most despatch and to render customary assist- 139
ance with the Vessel's Crew. The Master to be 140
under the orders of the Charterers as regards 141
employment, agency, or other arrangements. The 142
Charterers to indemnify the Owners against all 143
consequences or liabilities arising from the Ma- 144
ster, Officers or Agents signing Bills of Lading 145
or other documents or otherwise complying with 146
such orders, as well as from any irregularity in 147
the Vessel's papers or for overcarrying goods. 148
The Owners not to be responsible for shortage, 149
mixture, marks, nor for number of pieces or 150
packages, nor for damage to or claims on cargo 151
caused by bad stowage or otherwise. 152
If the Charterers have reason to be dissatisfied 153
with the conduct of the Master, Officers, or En- 154
gineers, the Owners on receiving particulars of 155
the complaint, promptly to investigate the matter, 156
and, if necessary and practicable, to make a 157
change in the appointments. 158

10. Directions and Logs 159
The Charterers to furnish the Master with all in- 160
structions and sailing directions and the Master 161
and Engineer to keep full and correct logs ac- 162
cessible to the Charterers or their Agents. 163

11. Suspension of Hire etc. 164
(A) In the event of drydocking or other necessary 165
measures to maintain the efficiency of the Ves- 166
sel, deficiency of men or Owners' stores, break- 167
down of machinery, damage to hull or other ac- 168
cident, either hindering or preventing the work- 169
ing of the Vessel and continuing for more than 170
twenty-four consecutive hours, no hire to be paid 171
in respect of any time lost thereby during the 172
period in which the Vessel is unable to perform 173
the service immediately required. Any hire paid 174
in advance to be adjusted accordingly. 175
(B) In the event of the Vessel being driven into 176
port or to anchorage through stress of weather, 177
trading to shallow harbours or to rivers or ports 178
with bars or suffering an accident to her cargo, 179
any detention of the Vessel and/or expenses re- 180
sulting from such detention to be for the Char- 181
terers' account even if such detention and/or ex- 182
penses, or the cause by reason of which either 183
is incurred, be due to, or be contributed to 184
by, the negligence of the Owners' servants. 185

12. Cleaning Boilers 186
Cleaning of boilers whenever possible to be done 187
during service, but if impossible the Charterers 188
to give the Owners necessary time for cleaning, 189
Should the Vessel be detained beyond 48 hours 190
hire to cease until again ready. 191

13. Responsibility and Exemption 192
The Owners only to be responsible for delay in 193
delivery of the Vessel or for delay during the 194
currency of the Charter and for loss or damage 195
to goods onboard, if such delay or loss has been 196
caused by want of due diligence on the part of 197
the Owners or their Manager in making the Ves- 198
sel seaworthy and fitted for the voyage or any 199
other personal act or omission or default of the 200
Owners or their Manager. The Owners not to be 201
responsible in any other case nor for damage or 202
delay whatsoever and howsoever caused even if 203
caused by the neglect or default of their ser- 204
vants. The Owners not to be liable for loss or 205
damage arising or resulting from strikes, lock- 206
outs or stoppage or restraint of labour (including 207
the Master, Officers or Crew) whether partial or 208
general. 209
The Charterers to be responsible for loss or dam- 210
age caused to the Vessel or to the Owners by 211
goods being loaded contrary to the terms of the 212
Charter or by improper or careless bunkering or 213
loading, stowing or discharging of goods or any 214
other improper or negligent act on their part or 215
that of their servants. 216

14. Advances 217
The Charterers or their Agents to advance to the 218
Master, if required, necessary funds for ordinary 219
disbursements for the Vessel's account at any 220
port charging only interest at 6 per cent. p.a., 221
such advances to be deducted from hire. 222

15. Excluded Ports 223
The Vessel not to be ordered to nor bound to 224
enter: a) any place where fever or epidemics are 225
prevalent or to which the Master, Officers and 226
Crew by law are not bound to follow the Vessel. 227
Ice 228
b) any ice-bound place or any place where lights, 229
lightships, marks and buoys are or likely to 230
be withdrawn by reason of ice on the Vessel's 231
arrival or where there is risk that ordinarily the 232
Vessel will not be able on account of ice to 233
reach the place or to get out after having com- 234
pleted loading or discharging. The Vessel not to 235
be obliged to force ice. If on account of ice the 236
Master considers it dangerous to remain at the 237
loading or discharging place for fear of the Ves- 238
sel being frozen in and/or damaged, he has 239
liberty to sail to a convenient open place and 240
await the Charterers' fresh instructions. 241
Unforeseen detention through any of above cau- 242
ses to be for the Charterers' account. 243

16. Loss of Vessel 244
Should the Vessel be lost or missing, hire to 245
cease from the date when she was lost. If the 246
date of loss cannot be ascertained half hire to 247
be paid from the date the Vessel was last re- 248
ported until the calculated date of arrival at the 249
destination. Any hire paid in advance to be ad- 250
justed accordingly. 251

17. Overtime 252
The Vessel to work day and night if required. The 253
Charterers to refund the Owners their out- 254
lays for all overtime paid to Officers and Crew 255
according to the hours and rates stated in the 256
Vessel's articles. 257

18. Lien 258
The Owners to have a lien upon all cargoes and 259
sub-freights belonging to the Time-Charterers and 260
any Bill of Lading freight for all claims under 261
this Charter, and the Charterers to have a lien 262
on the Vessel for all moneys paid in advance 263
and not earned 264

19. Salvage 265
All salvage and assistance to other vessels to be 266
for the Owners and the Charterers' equal benefit 267
after deducting the Master's and Crew's propor- 268
tion and all legal and other expenses including 269
hire paid under the charter for time lost in the 270
salvage, also repairs of damage and coal or oil- 271
fuel consumed. The Charterers to be bound by 272
all measures taken by the Owners in order to 273
secure payment of salvage and to fix its amount. 274

20. Sublet 275
The Charterers to have the option of subletting 276
the Vessel, giving due notice to the Owners, but 277
the original Charterers always to remain respon- 278
sible to the Owners for due performance of the 279
Charter. 280

21. War 281
(A) The Vessel unless the consent of the Owners 282
be first obtained not to be ordered nor continue 283
any Bill of Lading freight for all claims under 284
any service which will bring her within a zone 285
which is dangerous as the result of any actual 286
or threatened act of war, war hostilities, warlike 287
operations, acts of piracy or of hostility or ma- 288
licious damage against this or any other vessel 289
soever, revolution, civil war, civil commotion or 290
the operation of international law, nor be ex- 291
posed in any way to any risks or penalties whatso- 292
ever consequent upon the imposition of Sanc- 293
tions, nor carry any goods that may in any way 294
expose her to any risks of seizure, capture, pe- 295
nalties or any other interference of any kind 296
whatsoever by the belligerent or fighting powers 297
or parties or by any Government or Ruler. 298
(B) Should the Vessel approach or be brought or 299
ordered within such zone, or be exposed in any 300
way to the said risks, (1) the Owners to be en- 301
titled from time to time to insure their interests 302
in the Vessel and/or hire against any of the risks 303
likely to be involved thereby on such terms as 304
they shall think fit, the Charterers to make a re- 305
fund to the Owners of the premium on demand, 306
and (2) notwithstanding the terms of Clause 11 307
hire to be paid for all time lost including any 308
lost owing to loss of or injury to the Master, 309
Officers, or Crew or to the action of the Crew in 310
refusing to proceed to such zone or to be ex- 311
posed to such risks. 312
(C) In the event of the wages of the Master, Of- 313
ficers and/or Crew or the cost of provisions and 314
or stores for deck and/or engine room and or 315
insurance premiums being increased by reason 316
of or during the existence of any of the matters 317
mentioned in section (A) the amount of any in- 318
crease to be added to the hire and paid by the 319
Charterers on production of the vouchers 320
therefor, such account being rendered monthly. 322
(D) The Vessel to have liberty to comply with 323
any orders or directions as to departure, arrival, 324
routes, ports of call, stoppages, destination, de- 325
livery or in any other way whatsoever given by 326
the Government of the nation under whose flag 327
the Vessel sails or any other Government or any 328
person (or body) acting or purporting to act with 329
the authority of such Government or by any com- 330
mittee or person having under the terms of the 331
war risks insurance on the Vessel the right to 332
give any such orders or directions. 333
(E) In the event of the nation under whose flag 334
the Vessel sails becoming involved in war, ho- 335
stilities, warlike operations, revolution, or civil 336
commotion, both the Owners and the Charterers 337
may cancel the Charter and, unless otherwise 338
agreed, the Vessel to be re-delivered to the Ow- 339
ners at the port of destination or, if prevented 340
through the provisions of section (A) from reach- 341
ing or entering it, then at a near open and safe 342
port at the Owners' option, after discharge of any 343
cargo on board. 344
(F) If in compliance with the provisions of this 345
clause anything is done or is not done, such not 346
to be deemed a deviation. 347
Section (C) is optional and should be considered 348
deleted unless agreed according to Box 22. 349

22. Cancelling 350
Should the Vessel not be delivered by the date 351
indicated in Box 23; the Charterers to have the 352
option of cancelling. 353
If the Vessel cannot be delivered by the cancel- 354
ling date, the Charterers if required, to declare 355
within 48 hours after receiving notice thereof 356
whether they cancel or will take delivery of the 357
Vessel. 358

23. Arbitration 359
Any dispute arising under the Charter to be re- 360
ferred to arbitration in London (or such other 361
place as may be agreed according to Box 24) 362
one Arbitrator to be nominated by the Owners 363
and the other by the Charterers, and in case the 364
Arbitrators shall not agree then to the decision 365
of an Umpire to be appointed by them, the award 366
of the Arbitrators or the Umpire to be final and 367
binding upon both parties. 368

24. General Average 369
General Average to be settled according to York/ 370
Antwerp Rules, 1974. Hire not to contribute to 371
General Average. 372

25. Commission 373
The Owners to pay a commission at the rate 374
stated in Box 25 to the party mentioned in Box 375
26 on any hire paid under the Charter, but in no 376
case less than is necessary to cover the actual 377
expenses of the Brokers and a reasonable fee 378
for their work. If the full hire is not paid owing 379
to breach of Charter by either of the parties the 380
party liable therefor to indemnify the Brokers 381
against their loss of commission. 382
Should the parties agree to cancel the Charter, 383
the Owners to indemnify the Charterers against the 384
loss of commission but in such case the com- 385
mission not to exceed the brokerage on one 386
year's hire. 387

NOTES TO BALTIME 1939 TIME CHARTER

1. A time charter is a contract by which the charterer obtains the services of a ship and its crew for a specified period of time (see face, box 14). He can then use the ship to carry any cargo which is not excluded (see box 17(b) and cl 2 on back) between any safe ports within the trading limits (see box 17(a) and cll 2 and 15).

2. The feature which distinguishes a time charter from a voyage charter (see next specimen) is that the owner is paid hire on a time basis (usually monthly or semi-monthly) by the charterer: see box 20 and cl 6. Note particularly the second part of cl 6 allowing the owner to 'withdraw' the vessel in default of payment (and see below, p 452). The charterer does not have to pay for the ship if it is unavailable because it needs repairs, etc: see cl 11 (the 'off-hire' clause, see below, p 430).

3. The vessel is to be delivered at a specified port at a specified time (see boxes 15 and 16). If the vessel is not delivered within an agreed time after this date the charterer may cancel the charter: see box 23 and cl 22.

4. At the end of the charter, the ship must be redelivered (see cl 7 and below, p 547).

'Gencon' voyage charter (see pp 49–51)

1. Shipbroker	RECOMMENDED THE BALTIC AND INTERNATIONAL MARITIME CONFERENCE UNIFORM GENERAL CHARTER (AS REVISED 1922 and 1976) INCLUDING "F.I.O." ALTERNATIVE, ETC. (To be used for trades for which no approved form is in force) CODE NAME: "GENCON" **Part I**
	2. Place and date
3. Owners/Place of business (Cl. 1)	4. Charterers/Place of business (Cl. 1)
5. Vessel's name (Cl. 1)	6. GRT/NRT (Cl. 1)
7. Deadweight cargo carrying capacity in tons (abt.) (Cl. 1)	8. Present position (Cl. 1)
9. Expected ready to load (abt.) (Cl. 1)	
10. Loading port or place (Cl. 1)	11. Discharging port or place (Cl. 1)
12. Cargo (also state quantity and margin in Owners' option, if agreed; if full and complete cargo not agreed state "part cargo") (Cl. 1)	
13. Freight rate (also state if payable on delivered or intaken quantity) (Cl. 1)	14. Freight payment (state currency and method of payment; also beneficiary and bank account) (Cl. 4)
15. Loading and discharging costs (state alternative (a) or (b) of Cl. 5; also indicate if vessel is gearless)	16. Laytime (if separate laytime for load. and disch. is agreed, fill in a) and b). If total laytime for load. and disch., fill in c) only) (Cl. 6) a) Laytime for loading
17. Shippers (state name and address) (Cl. 6)	b) Laytime for discharging
	c) Total laytime for loading and discharging
18. Demurrage rate (loading and discharging) (Cl. 7)	19. Cancelling date (Cl. 10)
20. Brokerage commission and to whom payable (Cl. 14)	
21. Additional clauses covering special provisions, if agreed.	

It is mutually agreed that this Contract shall be performed subject to the conditions contained in this Charter which shall include Part I as well as Part II. In the event of a conflict of conditions, the provisions of Part I shall prevail over those of Part II to the extent of such conflict.

Signature (Owners)	Signature (Charterers)

PART II
"Gencon" Charter (As Revised 1922 and 1976)
Including "F.I.O." Alternative, etc.

1. It is agreed between the party mentioned in Box 3 as Owners of the　1
steamer or motor-vessel named in Box 5, of the gross/nett Register　2
tons indicated in Box 6 and carrying about the number of tons of　3
deadweight cargo stated in Box 7, now in position as stated in Box 8　4
and expected ready to load under this Charter about the date in-　5
dicated in Box 9, and the party mentioned as Charterers in Box 4　6
that:　7
The said vessel shall proceed to the loading port or place stated　8
in Box 10 or so near thereto as she may safely get and lie always　9
afloat, and there load a full and complete cargo (if shipment of deck　10
cargo agreed same to be at Charterers' risk) as stated in Box 12　11
(Charterers to provide all mats and/or wood for dunnage and any　12
separations required, the Owners allowing the use of any dunnage　13
wood on board if required) which the Charterers bind themselves to　14
ship, and being so loaded the vessel shall proceed to the discharg-　15
ing port or place stated in Box 11 as ordered on signing Bills of　16
Lading or so near thereto as she may safely get and lie always　17
afloat and there deliver the cargo on being paid freight on delivered　18
or intaken quantity as indicated in Box 13 at the rate stated in　19
Box 13.　20

2.　Owners' Responsibility Clause　21
Owners are to be responsible for loss of or damage to the goods　22
or for delay in delivery of the goods only in case the loss, damage　23
or delay has been caused by the improper or negligent stowage of　24
the goods (unless stowage performed by shippers/Charterers or their　25
stevedores or servants) or by personal want of due diligence on the　26
part of the Owners or their Manager to make the vessel in all respects　27
seaworthy and to secure that she is properly manned, equipped and　28
supplied or by the personal act or default of the Owners or their　29
Manager.　30
And the Owners are responsible for no loss or damage or delay　31
arising from any other cause whatsoever, even from the neglect or　32
default of the Captain or crew or some other person employed by the　33
Owners on board or ashore for whose acts they would, but for this　34
clause, be responsible, or from unseaworthiness of the vessel on　35
loading or commencement of the voyage or at any time whatsoever.　36
Damage caused by contact with or leakage, smell or evaporation　37
from other goods or by the inflammable or explosive nature or in-　38
sufficient package of other goods not to be considered as caused　39
by improper or negligent stowage, even if in fact so caused.　40

3.　Deviation Clause　41
The vessel has liberty to call at any port or ports in any order, for　42
any purpose, to sail without pilots, to tow and/or assist vessels in　43
all situations, and also to deviate for the purpose of saving life and/　44
or property.　45

4.　Payment of Freight　46
The freight to be paid in the manner prescribed in Box 14 in cash　47
without discount on delivery of the cargo at mean rate of exchange　48
ruling on day or days of payment, the receivers of the cargo being　49
bound to pay freight on account during delivery, if required by Cap-　50
tain or Owners.　51
Cash for vessel's ordinary disbursements at port of loading to be　52
advanced by Charterers if required at highest current rate of ex-　53
change, subject to two per cent. to cover insurance and other ex-　54
penses.　55

5.　Loading/Discharging Costs　56
* (a) Gross Terms　57
The cargo to be brought alongside in such a manner as to enable　58
vessel to take the goods with her own tackle. Charterers to procure　59
and pay the necessary men on shore or on board the lighters to do　60
the work there, vessel only heaving the cargo on board.　61
If the loading takes place by elevator, cargo to be put free in vessel's　62
holds, Owners only paying trimming expenses.　63
Any pieces and/or packages of cargo over two tons weight, shall be　64
loaded, stowed and discharged by Charterers at their risk and expense.　65
The cargo to be received by Merchants at their risk and expense　66
alongside the vessel not beyond the reach of her tackle.　67

* (b) F.i.o. and free stowed/trimmed　68
The cargo shall be brought into the holds, loaded, stowed and/or trim-　69
med and taken from the holds and discharged by the Charterers or　70
their Agents, free of any risk, liability and expense whatsoever to the　71
Owners.　72
The Owners shall provide winches, motive power and winchmen from　73
the Crew if requested and permitted; if not, the Charterers shall　74
provide and pay for winchmen from shore and/or cranes, if any. (This　75
provision shall not apply if vessel is gearless and stated as such in　76
Box 15).　77
* indicate alternative (a) or (b), as agreed, in Box 15　78

6.　Laytime　79
* (a) Separate laytime for loading and discharging　80
The cargo shall be loaded within the number of running hours as　81
indicated in Box 16, weather permitting, Sundays and holidays ex-　82
cepted, unless used, in which event time actually used shall count.　83
The cargo shall be discharged within the number of running hours　84
as indicated in Box 16, weather permitting, Sundays and holidays ex-　85
cepted, unless used, in which event time actually used shall count.　86
* (b) Total laytime for loading and discharging　87
The cargo shall be loaded and discharged within the number of total　88
running hours as indicated in Box 16, weather permitting, Sundays and　89
holidays excepted, unless used, in which event time actually used　90
shall count.　91
(c) Commencement of laytime (loading and discharging)　92
Laytime for loading and discharging shall commence at 1 p.m. if　93
notice of readiness is given before noon, and at 6 a.m. next working　94
day if notice given during office hours after noon. Notice at loading　95
port to be given to the Shippers named in Box 17.　96
Time actually used before commencement of laytime shall count.　97
Time lost in waiting for berth to count as loading or discharging　98
time, as the case may be　99
* indicate alternative (a) or (b) as agreed, in Box 16.　100

7.　Demurrage　101
Ten running days on demurrage at the rate stated in Box 18 per　102
day or pro rata for any part of a day, payable day by day, to be　103
allowed Merchants altogether at ports of loading and discharging.　104

8.　Lien Clause　105
Owners shall have a lien on the cargo for freight, dead-freight,　106
demurrage and damages for detention. Charterers shall remain re-　107
sponsible for dead-freight and demurrage (including damages for　108
detention), incurred at port of loading. Charterers shall also remain　109
responsible for freight and demurrage (including damages for deten-　110
tion) incurred at port of discharge, but only to such extent as the　111
Owners have been unable to obtain payment thereof by exercising　112
the lien on the cargo.　113

9.　Bills of Lading　114
The Captain to sign Bills of Lading at such rate of freight as　115
presented without prejudice to this Charterparty, but should the　116
freight by Bills of Lading amount to less than the total chartered　117
freight the difference to be paid to the Captain in cash on signing　118
Bills of Lading.　119

10.　Cancelling Clause　120
Should the vessel not be ready to load (whether in berth or not) on　121
or before the date indicated in Box 19, Charterers have the option　122
of cancelling this contract, such option to be declared, if demanded,　123
at least 48 hours before vessel's expected arrival at port of loading.　124
Should the vessel be delayed on account of average or otherwise,　125
Charterers to be informed as soon as possible, and if the vessel is　126
delayed for more than 10 days after the day she is stated to be　127
expected ready to load, Charterers have the option of cancelling this　128
contract, unless a cancelling date has been agreed upon.　129

11.　General Average　130
General average to be settled according to York-Antwerp Rules,　131
1974. Proprietors of cargo to pay the cargo's share in the general　132
expenses even if same have been necessitated through neglect or　133
default of the Owners' servants (see clause 2).　134

12.　Indemnity　135
Indemnity for non-performance of this Charterparty, proved damages,　136
not exceeding estimated amount of freight.　137

13.　Agency　138
In every case the Owners shall appoint his own Broker or Agent both　139
at the port of loading and the port of discharge.　140

14.　Brokerage　141
A brokerage commission at the rate stated in Box 20 on the freight　142
earned is due to the party mentioned in Box 20.　143
In case of non-execution at least ⅓ of the brokerage on the estimated　144
amount of freight and dead-freight to be paid by the Owners to the　145
Brokers as indemnity for the latter's expenses and work. In case of　146
more voyages the amount of indemnity to be mutually agreed.　147

15.　GENERAL STRIKE CLAUSE　148
Neither Charterers nor Owners shall be responsible for the con-　149
sequences of any strikes or lock-outs preventing or delaying the　150
fulfilment of any obligations under this contract　151
If there is a strike or lock-out affecting the loading of the cargo,　152
or any part of it, when vessel is ready to proceed from her last port　153
or at any time during the voyage to the port or ports of loading or　154
after her arrival there, Captain or Owners may ask Charterers to　155
declare, that they agree to reckon the laydays as if there were no　156
strike or lock-out. Unless Charterers have given such declaration in　157
writing (by telegram, if necessary) within 24 hours, Owners shall　158
have the option of cancelling this contract. If part cargo has already　159
been loaded, Owners must proceed with same, (freight payable on　160
loaded quantity only) having liberty to complete with other cargo　161
on the way for their own account.　162
If there is a strike or lock-out affecting the discharge of the cargo　163
on or after vessel's arrival at or off port of discharge and same has　164
not been settled within 48 hours, Receivers shall have the option of　165
keeping vessel waiting until such strike or lock-out is at an end　166
against paying half demurrage after expiration of the time provided　167
for discharging, or of ordering the vessel to a safe port where she　168
can safely discharge without risk of being detained by strike or lock-　169
out. Such orders to be given within 48 hours after Captain or Owners　170
have given notice to Charterers of the strike or lock-out affecting　171
the discharge. On delivery of the cargo at such port, all conditions　172
of this Charterparty and of the Bill of Lading shall apply and vessel　173
shall receive the same freight as if she had discharged at the　174
original port of destination, except that if the distance of the sub-　175
stituted port exceeds 100 nautical miles, the freight on the cargo　176
delivered at the substituted port to be increased in proportion.　177

16.　War Risks ("Voywar 1950")　178
(1) In these clauses "War Risks" shall include any blockade or any　179
action which is announced as a blockade by any Government or by any　180
belligerent or by any organized body, sabotage, piracy, and any actual　181
or threatened war, hostilities, warlike operations, civil war, civil com-　182
motion, or revolution.　183
(2) If at any time before the Vessel commences loading, it appears that　184
performance of the contract will subject the Vessel or her Master and　185
crew or her cargo to war risks at any stage of the adventure, the Owners　186
shall be entitled by letter or telegram despatched to the Charterers, to　187
cancel this Charter.　188
(3) The Master shall not be required to load cargo or to continue　189
loading or to proceed on or to sign Bill(s) of Lading for any adventure　190
on which or any port at which it appears that the Vessel, her Master　191
and crew or her cargo will be subjected to war risks. In the event of　192
the exercise by the Master of his right under this Clause after part or　193
full cargo has been loaded, the Master shall be at liberty either to　194
discharge such cargo at the loading port or to proceed therewith. In　195
the latter case the Vessel shall have liberty to carry other cargo for　196
Owners' benefit and accordingly to proceed to and load or　197
discharge such other cargo at any other port or ports whatsoever,　198
backwards or forwards although in a contrary direction to or out of or　199
beyond the ordinary route. In the event of the Master electing to　200
proceed with part cargo under this Clause freight shall in any case　201
be payable on the quantity delivered.　202
(4) If at the time the Master elects to proceed with part or full cargo　203
under Clause 3, or after the Vessel has left the loading port, or the　204

PART II
"Gencon" Charter (As Revised 1922 and 1976)
Including "F.I.O." Alternative, etc.

last of the loading ports, if more than one, it appears that further 205
performance of the contract will subject the Vessel, her Master and 206
crew or her cargo, to war risks, the cargo shall be discharged, or if 207
the discharge has been commenced shall be completed, at any safe 208
port in vicinity of the port of discharge as may be ordered by the 209
Charterers. If no such orders shall be received from the Charterers 210
within 48 hours after the Owners have despatched a request by 211
telegram to the Charterers for the nomination of a substitute discharg- 212
ing port, the Owners shall be at liberty to discharge the cargo at 213
any safe port which they may, in their discretion, decide on and such 214
discharge shall be deemed to be due fulfilment of the contract of 215
affreightment. In the event of cargo being discharged at any such 216
other port, the Owners shall be entitled to freight as if the discharge 217
had been effected at the port or ports named in the Bill(s) of Lading 218
or to which the Vessel may have been ordered pursuant thereto. 219

(5) (a) The Vessel shall have liberty to comply with any directions 220
or recommendations as to loading, departure, arrival, routes, ports 221
of call, stoppages, destination, zones, waters, discharge, delivery or 222
in any other wise whatsoever (including any direction or recom- 223
mendation not to go to the port of destination or to delay proceeding 224
thereto or to proceed to some other port) given by any Government or 225
by any belligerent or by any organized body engaged in civil war, 226
hostilities or warlike operations or by any person or body acting or 227
purporting to act as or with the authority of any Government or 228
belligerent or of any such organized body or by any committee or 229
person having under the terms of the war risks insurance on the 230
Vessel, the right to give any such directions or recommendations. If, 231
by reason of or in compliance with any such direction or recom- 232
mendation, anything is done or is not done, such shall not be deemed 233
a deviation. 234

(b) If, by reason of or in compliance with any such directions or re- 235
commendations, the Vessel does not proceed to the port or ports 236
named in the Bill(s) of Lading or to which she may have been 237
ordered pursuant thereto, the Vessel may proceed to any port as 238
directed or recommended or to any safe port which the Owners or 239
their discretion may decide on and there discharge the cargo. Such 240
discharge shall be deemed to be due fulfilment of the contract of 241
affreightment and the Owners shall be entitled to freight as if 242
discharge had been effected at the port or ports named in the Bill(s) 243
of Lading or to which the Vessel may have been ordered pursuant 244
thereto. 245

(6) All extra expenses (including insurance costs) involved in discharg- 246
ing cargo at the loading port or in reaching or discharging the cargo 247
at any port as provided in Clauses 4 and 5 (b) hereof shall be paid 248
by the Charterers and/or cargo owners, and the Owners shall have 249
a lien on the cargo for all moneys due under these Clauses. 250

17. **GENERAL ICE CLAUSE** 251
Port of loading 252

(a) In the event of the loading port being inaccessible by reason of 253
ice when vessel is ready to proceed from her last port or at any 254
time during the voyage or on vessel's arrival or in case frost sets in 255
after vessel's arrival, the Captain for fear of being frozen in is at 256
liberty to leave without cargo, and this Charter shall be null and 257
void. 258

(b) If during loading the Captain, for fear of vessel being frozen in, 259
deems it advisable to leave, he has liberty to do so with what cargo 260
he has on board and to proceed to any other port or ports with 261
option of completing cargo for Owners' benefit for any port or ports 262
including port of discharge. Any part cargo thus loaded under this 263
Charter to be forwarded to destination at vessel's expense but 264
against payment of freight, provided that no extra expenses be 265
delivered (in proportion if lumpsum), all other conditions as per 266
thereby caused to the Receivers, freight being paid on quantity 267
Charter. 268

(c) In case of more than one loading port, and if one or more of 269
the ports are closed by ice, the Captain or Owners to be at liberty 270
either to load the part cargo at the open port and fill up elsewhere 271
for their own account as under section (b) or to declare the Charter 272
null and void unless Charterers agree to load full cargo at the open 273
port. 274

(d) This Ice Clause not to apply in the Spring. 275

Port of discharge 276

(a) Should ice (except in the Spring) prevent vessel from reaching 277
port of discharge Receivers shall have the option of keeping vessel 278
waiting until the re-opening of navigation and paying demurrage, or 279
of ordering the vessel to a safe and immediately accessible port 280
where she can safely discharge without risk of detention by ice. 281
Such orders to be given within 48 hours after Captain or Owners 282
have given notice to Charterers of the impossibility of reaching port 283
of destination. 284

(b) If during discharging the Captain for fear of vessel being frozen 285
in deems it advisable to leave, he has liberty to do so with what 286
cargo he has on board and to proceed to the nearest accessible 287
port where she can safely discharge. 288

(c) On delivery of the cargo at such port, all conditions of the Bill 289
of Lading shall apply and vessel shall receive the same freight as 290
if she had discharged at the original port of destination, except that if 291
the distance of the substituted port exceeds 100 nautical miles, the 292
freight on the cargo delivered at the substituted port to be increased 293
in proportion. 294

NOTES TO GENCON VOYAGE CHARTER

1. A voyage charter is a contract between a shipowner and the charterer to carry a stated cargo (see box 12: the charterer may be given an option as to the cargo) from the loading port (box 10) to the port of discharge (box 11).

2. The distinguishing feature of a voyage charter is that the owner is paid freight on the quantity of cargo carried rather than on a time basis. This payment basis is reflected in a number of other clauses in the contract.

3. Firstly, the charterer agrees to load a full and complete cargo (see cl 1). If he loads less than this, so that the freight is less than it might have been, the charterer will be liable for the difference in damages, often called 'dead freight'.

4. Secondly, the shipowner will obviously be concerned to make as many voyages as possible, and to have the ship kept in port loading and discharging for as short a time as he can. The charter therefore allows a fixed number of days, the 'lay days', for these operations (box 16 and cl 6). The lay days start running once the ship has arrived and the charterer has been notified, and if (because of congestion in the port or because of some order given by the charterer) the ship is kept in port for longer than the lay days, the charterer has to pay liquidated damages, called 'demurrage' (see box 18 and cl 7). For a case involving the demurrage clause, see below, p 692.

5. Instead of a straightforward time or voyage charter, the parties may adopt a hybrid form. So a ship may be chartered on a time basis but the trading limits be fixed so that the ship can only be used between a small number of ports, eg Rotterdam and the US Gulf ports. Alternatively, sometimes the charter is for a whole series of consecutive voyages between the two ports. In the *Suisse Atlantique* case (below, p 692) the charter was for as many consecutive voyages as could be performed within two years. This looks rather like a time charter, but the shipowner is being paid on a freight, not a time, basis, so it is still a form of voyage charter, and the allocation of risks of delays in port is the same as for other voyage charters.

6. The shipowner can seldom undertake that the ship will be ready to load the cargo by a fixed date; instead, the charter states the current position of the ship (box 8) and the date at which the ship is 'expected ready to load' (box 9), and gives the charterer a right to cancel if the ship is not ready by an agreed date thereafter (box 19 and cl 10). For the operation of these clauses, see below, p 435.

'GAFTA No 119' F.O.B. sales contract (see fold-out)

NOTES ON F.O.B. SALES CONTRACT

1. The two most common types of international sale of goods contract are the f.o.b. (free on board) and the c.i.f. (cost, insurance and freight) contracts. Under a classic f.o.b. contract the seller's obligation is to deliver the goods by having them loaded onto a ship nominated by the buyer, which is responsible for arranging the contract of carriage. (This might be under a bill of lading or a charter of the whole ship.)
2. The description of the goods is entered in cl 1 and the quantity in cl 3. Note that the quantity is flexible at the buyer's option, to enable the buyer to arrange economical use of the available shipping space.
3. The port at which the goods are to be loaded is entered in the blank in cl 4. Sometimes the form is amended so that the goods are to be loaded at one of several ports which are near each other, eg 'one US Gulf port' and the seller is given the right to choose which one later on.
4. Under cl 7 the buyer has to tender the vessel ready to load within certain dates. The seller must be given an agreed number of days' notice of the date at which the ship is expected to be ready, and, if the contract quantity is too large for one ship so that the buyer will have to nominate several, of the estimated tonnage that will be required for each. If the seller is to choose the port of loading (see note 3) it may have to select one within a set number of days of receiving the notice of expected readiness. (For a case involving Form 119 amended in this way see below, p 438).
5. Under some f.o.b. contracts the seller agrees to arrange shipment to a particular destination and insurance; if so, this will be charged as an extra on top of the f.o.b. price.
6. Under a c.i.f. contract many of the clauses will be similar, but the seller's fundamental delivery obligation is different: it is to have the goods on board a ship bound for a named port (the goods are often already afloat by the time the contract is made), properly insured and with the freight paid. The c.i.f. price includes insurance and freight. If, as sometimes is agreed, the freight is only payable on arrival, the buyer may deduct what it has to pay from the c.i.f. price. The seller must ship the goods, or have had them shipped already, between stated dates.
7. After shipment under a c.i.f. contract, the seller will present the shipping documents (an invoice for the goods, a bill of lading or a ship's delivery order and the insurance policy) to the buyer, or if payment is to be by documentary credit (see below, p 112) to the bank at which the credit has been opened, and will be paid the contract price.
8. Even if the goods are totally lost before the documents have been presented, the buyer must 'take up' the documents and pay the price; it will have to claim on the insurance policy or sue the carrier. (Provided that the buyer has received a bill of lading, and the goods are sufficiently identified, it will have a contractual right of action against the carrier, see above, p 44. If it has accepted a delivery order there may be severe problems about recovering from the carrier: see *The Aliakmon* [1986] AC 785, which held that the buyer has no action in tort if the goods had not become its property when they were destroyed. Even though the goods are at the buyer's risk, its loss is purely economic.)

Hire-purchase agreement

HPC **Hire-Purchase Agreement** *regulated by the Consumer Credit Act 1974*   **Original**
(d)   With right of cancellation

Agreement No. _____

This Hire-Purchase Agreement sets out below and overleaf the terms on which we (the owners) agree to let and you (the customer) agree to hire the goods described below:

The Owners _____
Name and address

_____

The Customer _____
Full names please

Address _____

SPECIMEN

Particulars of Goods		Cash Price Incl. VAT	
Qty.	Description	£	p
	Identification Nos:		
	Total Cash Price (incl. VAT)		

Financial Details and Payments	£	p	
Total Cash Price			
Less Deposit: Cash £_____ Pt Ex £_____			(a)
= Credit Extended			
Add: Charges			
= Balance Payable			(b)
Total Amount Payable (a) + (b)			
A.P.R.		_____%	
Number of monthly payments			
Date of first payment _____			
Subsequent payments on same day of each succeeding month			
Amount of each payment			
Amount of final payment (if different)			

TERMINATION: YOUR RIGHTS
You have a right to end this agreement. If you wish to do so, you should write to the person authorised to receive your payments. We will then be entitled to the return of the goods and to half the total amount payable under this agreement, that is £ _____.[1] If you have already paid at least this amount plus any overdue instalments, you will not have to pay any more, provided you have taken reasonable care of the goods.

[1] Insert one-half of the total amount payable.

REPOSSESSION: YOUR RIGHTS
If you fail to keep to your side of this agreement but you have paid at least one third of the total amount payable under this agreement, that is £ _____,[2] we may not take back the goods against your wishes unless we get a court order. (In Scotland, we may need to get a court order at any time.) If we do take them without your consent or a court order, you have the right to get back all the money you have paid under the agreement.

[2] Insert one third of the total amount payable.

Witness: Signature _____

Name _____
Block letters please

Address _____

_____

Witness: Signature _____
Second witness required in Scotland only

Name _____
Block letters please

Address _____

_____

Signature of (or on behalf of) Owners

_____

Date of Owners' Signature (Date of Agreement)

_____

DECLARATION BY CUSTOMER
By signing this agreement you are declaring that:

★ The information given by you before entering into this agreement is correct. You realise that we will rely on that information in deciding whether to enter into this agreement.

★ You are aware that we may register information about this agreement with any licensed credit reference agency.

This is a Hire-Purchase Agreement regulated by the Consumer Credit Act 1974. Sign it only if you want to be legally bound by its terms.

Signature(s)
of Customer(s) _____

Date(s) of Signature(s) _____

The goods will not become your property until you have made all the payments. You must not sell them before then.

✂ --

CANCELLATION FORM
(Complete and return this form ONLY IF YOU WISH TO CANCEL THE AGREEMENT).

To: _____[1]

_____

I/We* hereby give notice that I/we* wish to cancel

agreement _____[2].

Signed _____

Date _____

Name _____

Address _____

_____

YOUR RIGHT TO CANCEL
Once you have signed this agreement, you will have for a short time a right to cancel it. Exact details of how and when you can do this will be sent to you by post by us.

Notes for cancellation form:
[1] Owners to insert name and address.
[2] Owners to insert reference number, code or other identification details.
* Delete inapplicable pronoun.

HPC
(d)
Original

TERMS OF THE AGREEMENT

1 Payment

Before signing this agreement you must have paid the deposit shown overleaf. By signing this agreement you agree to pay the Balance Payable by making the payments set out overleaf, by their specified dates, to us at the address stated overleaf or to any person or address notified by us in writing. Punctual payment is essential. If you pay by post you do so at your own risk.

2 Failure to pay on time

We have the right to charge interest at the annual percentage rate shown overleaf on all overdue amounts. This interest will be calculated on a daily basis from the date the amount falls due until it is received and will run both before and after any judgment.

3 Ownership of the goods

You will become the owner of the goods only after we have received payment of all amounts payable under this agreement, including under Clauses 2 and 11. Until then the goods remain our property and your rights are solely those of a hirer.

4 Selling or disposing of the goods

You must keep the goods safely at your address and you may not sell or dispose of them or transfer your rights under this agreement. You may only part with the goods to have them repaired. You may not use the goods as security for any of your obligations.

5 Repair of the goods

You must keep the goods in good condition and repair at your own expense. You are responsible for all loss of or damage to them (except fair wear and tear) even if caused by acts or events outside your control. You must not allow a repairer or any other person to obtain a lien on or a right to retain the goods.

6 Change of address

You must immediately notify us in writing of any change of your address.

7 Inspection

You must allow us or our representative to inspect and test the goods at all reasonable times.

8 Insurance

You must keep the goods insured under a fully comprehensive policy of insurance at your own expense. You must notify us of any loss of or damage to the goods and hold any monies payable under the policy in trust for us. You irrevocably authorise us to collect the monies from the insurers. If a claim is made against the insurers we may at our absolute discretion conduct any negotiations and effect any settlement of the claim with the insurers. You agree to abide by such settlement and to pay us any shortfall under the agreement. Subject to the provisions of Clause 12 any loss of or damage to the goods shall not affect the continuance of this agreement.

9 Your right to end the agreement

You have the right to end this agreement as set out in the notice 'Termination: Your Rights' overleaf. You must then at your own expense return to us the goods, together with in the case of a motor vehicle, the registration document, road fund licence and test certificate.

10 Our right to end the agreement

We may end this agreement, after giving you written notice, if:

(a) you fail to keep to any of the terms of this agreement;

(b) you commit any act of bankruptcy or have a receiving, interim or bankruptcy order made against you or you petition for your own bankruptcy, or are served with a creditor's demand under the Insolvency Act 1986 or the Bankruptcy (Scotland) Act 1985, or make a formal composition or scheme with your creditors, or call a meeting of them.

(c) you make a formal composition with or call a meeting of your creditors;

(d) execution is levied or attempted against any of your assets or income or, in Scotland, your possessions are poinded or your wages arrested;

(e) the landlord of the premises where the goods are kept threatens or takes any step to distrain on the goods or, in Scotland exercises his right of hypothec over them;

(f) where you are a partnership, the partnership is dissolved;

(g) you have given false information in connection with your entry into this agreement;

(h) the goods are destroyed or the insurers treat a claim under the above policy on a total loss basis.

If we end this agreement then, subject to your rights as set out in the Form 'Repossession: Your Rights' overleaf, we may retake the goods. You will also then have to pay to us all overdue payments and the balance of the Total Amount Payable under the agreement less:

(i) a rebate for early payment required by law and

(ii) the net proceeds of sale of the goods (if any) after deduction of the cost of recovery, insurance, storage and sale.

You must also return to us the documents listed in Clause 9.

11 Expenses

You must repay on demand our expenses and legal costs for:

(a) finding your address if you change address without first informing us or finding the goods if they are not at the address given by you;

(b) taking steps, including court action, to recover the goods or to obtain payment for them.

12 Exclusion

(a) If you are dealing as consumer (as defined in the Unfair Contract Terms Act 1977) nothing in this agreement will affect your rights under the Supply of Goods (Implied Terms) Act 1973.

(b) In all other cases:

(i) you rely on your own skill and judgement as to the quality of the goods and their fitness for their intended purpose:

(ii) we will not be responsible for their quality, their fitness for any purpose or their correspondence with any description or specification.

13 General provisions

(a) The word 'goods' includes replacements, renewals and additions which we or you may make to them.

(b) No relaxation or indulgence which we may extend to you shall affect our strict rights under this agreement.

(c) Where two or more persons are named as the customer, you jointly and severally accept the obligations under this agreement. This means that each of you can be held fully responsible under this agreement.

(d) We may transfer our rights under this agreement.

14 When this agreement takes effect

This agreement will only take effect if and when it is signed by us or our authorised representative.

IMPORTANT — YOU SHOULD READ THIS CAREFULLY YOUR RIGHTS

The Consumer Credit Act 1974 covers this agreement and lays down certain requirements for your protection which must be satisfied when the agreement is made. If they are not, we cannot enforce the agreement against you without a court order.

The Act also gives you a number of rights. You have a right to settle this agreement at any time by giving notice in writing and paying off all amounts payable under the agreement which may be reduced by a rebate.

If you would like to know more about the protection and remedies provided under the Act, you should contact either your local Trading Standards Department or your nearest Citizens' Advice Bureau.

NOTES ON HIRE-PURCHASE AGREEMENT

1. Buying goods on HP normally involves three parties. The retailer or dealer from whom the customer wishes to obtain the goods sells them to a finance company, which becomes the 'Owner'. This company then hires the goods out to the customer, who is often referred to as the 'hirer'. The customer agrees to pay the price of the goods and the credit charges (cl 1). When he has made all the payments, the ownership of the goods passes to him; until then, it remains with the Owners as 'security' (cl 3). The point of making the contract one of hire, rather than a 'conditional sale' with the passing of property deferred until the price has been paid was originally to evade the rule that a buyer of goods who is given possession of them has the power to sell the goods to a third party, who will get good title to the goods, even though the first buyer had not yet become owner. In respect of conditional sales to consumers the rule has in any event been reversed by statute.

2. The distorted nature of an HP agreement is reflected in the imposition on the customer of the obligation to repair the goods (cl 5): compare the simple contract of hire, above pp 39–42.

3. If the customer defaults, the Owner is entitled to terminate the agreement and repossess the goods (cl 10). The customer will have to pay the costs of so doing (cl 11). Note, however, the statutory restriction on the owner's right of repossession once the customer has paid one-third of the price (see the notice headed 'REPOSSESSION: YOUR RIGHTS' on the face of the agreement).

4. The customer may also opt to terminate the agreement at any time (cl 9), but if he does so he must return the goods, and may have to make his payments up to half the amount of the price (see the notice headed 'TERMINATION: YOUR RIGHTS').

5. This form is designed for use where the agreement is signed by the customer away from the business premises of the dealer or finance company—on his own doorstep, for instance. In such circumstances the customer may have a 'cooling-off period' during which he may cancel the agreement (see below, p 664). This is referred to in the boxes at the foot of the page

Guarantee and indemnity covering a conditional sale debt

GUARANTEE AND INDEMNITY SUBJECT TO THE CONSUMER CREDIT ACT 1974

The Creditor:	The Surety:
....	Name ....
1 Lyonsdown Road,	Address ....
New Barnet,	....
Herts. EN5 1HU	....
The Debtor:	**The Subject Matter:**
Name	Conditional Sale Agreement between the Creditor and the
Address	Debtor relating to ....
....	....
....	Ref. No. ....

In consideration of the Creditor entering into the Conditional Sale Agreement with the Debtor, the Surety:

1. guarantees the due performance and observance by the Debtor of all the terms and conditions of the Conditional Sale Agreement and the due prompt and punctual payment of each and every sum of money payable by the Debtor thereunder, and agrees that should the Debtor fail to pay any such sums the Surety will pay them immediately on demand;

2. independently of the Guarantee above and as a separate independent and severable provision indemnifies the Creditor against and holds the Creditor harmless from all or any loss or damage suffered or sustained and all claims costs and expenses made against or incurred by the Creditor as a consequence of or arising out of (in either event whether directly or indirectly) the Creditor having entered into the Conditional Sale Agreement provided always that the Surety's liability hereunder shall not exceed any liability the Debtor may have or, in the event that the Debtor is a minor or otherwise not of full contractual capacity, the liability the Debtor would have had if the Debtor had been of full contractual capacity;

3. agrees that neither the Guarantee nor the Indemnity herein contained shall be affected, prejudiced or vitiated by any time or indulgence the Creditor may grant or allow the Debtor and that if more than one person or body corporate is shown as the Surety the obligations of the Surety hereunder shall be several as well as joint.

IMPORTANT — YOU SHOULD READ THIS CAREFULLY   YOUR RIGHTS

The Consumer Credit Act 1974 covers this guarantee and indemnity and lays down certain requirements for your protection. If they are not carried out, the Creditor cannot enforce the guarantee and indemnity against you without a court order.

Until the agreement between the Creditor and the Debtor has been made, you can change your mind about giving the guarantee and indemnity. If you wish to withdraw, you must give **WRITTEN** notice to the Creditor which must reach him **BEFORE** the main Agreement is made. Once it has been made you can no longer change your mind.

Under this guarantee and indemnity **YOU MAY HAVE TO PAY INSTEAD** of the Debtor and fulfil any other obligations under the guarantee and indemnity.(But you cannot be made to pay more than he could have been made to pay unless he is under 18.) However, if the Debtor fails to keep to his side of the Agreement, the Creditor must send him a default notice (and a copy to you) giving him a chance to put things right before any claim is made on you.

If you would like to know more about your rights under the Act, you should contact either your local Trading Standards Department or your nearest Citizens' Advice Bureau.

This is a guarantee and indemnity subject to the Consumer Credit Act 1974. If the Debtor fails to keep to his Agreement with the Creditor, **YOU MAY HAVE TO PAY INSTEAD** and fulfil any other obligations under the guarantee and indemnity. Sign only if you want to be legally bound by its terms.

Signature(s) of
Indemnifier(s) ....

Witness(es) to Indemnifer(s) signatures

Signature of Witness ....
Name ....
Address ....
....

*Signature of Witness ....
Name ....
Address ....
....

*Second witness required only in Scotland.

Date of Guarantee and Indemnity ....

D255 (Gen) C/S (9/88)

NOTES ON GUARANTEE AND INDEMNITY

1. This specimen is of a guarantee of specific obligation, in this example a buyer's obligation under a conditional sale agreement.
2. Note the opening words emphasizing that the guarantee is given in exchange for the finance company ('the Creditor') entering the conditional sale agreement with the buyer. If the guarantee were not given in exchange for this or some other consideration (for instance, if the guarantee were only asked for and obtained *after* the sale agreement had been made, and before there had been any default or any question of giving any extra time to pay or other concession to the buyer) the guarantee would be unenforceable for want of consideration (see below, p 116).
3. The probable intention of the words used is not to put the finance company under any obligation *to the guarantor* to enter the main agreement with the buyer. Guarantees of consumer debts at least are more usually in the form, 'you agree that *if* we lend money to the debtor, you will guarantee repayment . . .'.
4. This form contains not only a guarantee but also an indemnity—a device which is very similar but subject to a number of different rules. One of the differences is that a guarantor is not liable if for some reason the debtor is not liable (eg because the debtor is under 18: see below, p 666), but a promise to indemnify is independent and will be enforceable even if the creditor has no enforceable rights under the main contract: see Treitel, p 137.
5. The purpose of the third paragraph is to avoid the effect of the common law rule that the granting of any concession by the creditor (the finance company) to the debtor (the buyer) releases the guarantor.

The Carbolic Smoke Ball Company's advertisement (p 59, and see Carlill v Carbolic Smoke Ball Co Ltd, above, p 12, and below, p 184)

JAN. 23, 1892   THE ILLUSTRATED LONDON NEWS   119

CARBOLIC SMOKE BALL

WILL POSITIVELY CURE

COUGHS	CATARRH	HOARSENESS	THROAT DEAFNESS	INFLUENZA	CROUP
Cured in 1 week	Cured in 1 to 3 months.	Cured in 12 hours.	Cured 1 to 3 months.	Cured in 24 hours.	Relieved in 5 minutes.
COLD IN THE HEAD	ASTHMA	LOSS OF VOICE	SNORING	HAY FEVER	WHOOPING COUGH
Cured in 12 hours.	Relieved in 10 minutes.	Fully restored.	Cured in 1 week.	Cured in every case.	Relieved the first application.
COLD ON THE CHEST	BRONCHITIS	SORE THROAT	SORE EYES	HEADACHE	NEURALGIA
Cured in 12 hours.	Cured in every case.	Cured in 12 hours.	Cured in 2 weeks.	Cured in 10 minutes.	Cured in 10 minutes.

As all the Diseases mentioned above proceed from one cause, they can be Cured by this Remedy

£100 REWARD

WILL BE PAID BY THE

CARBOLIC SMOKE BALL CO.

to any Person who contracts the Increasing Epidemic,

INFLUENZA,

Colds, or any Diseases caused by taking Cold, after having used the **CARBOLIC SMOKE BALL** according to the printed directions supplied with each Ball.

£1000 IS DEPOSITED

with the ALLIANCE BANK, Regent Street, showing our sincerity in the matter.

During the last epidemic of **INFLUENZA** many thousand **CARBOLIC SMOKE BALLS** were sold as preventives against this disease, and in no ascertained case was the disease contracted by those using the **CARBOLIC SMOKE BALL.**

THE CARBOLIC SMOKE BALL,

TESTIMONIALS.

The DUKE OF PORTLAND writes : "I am much obliged for the Carbolic Smoke Ball which you have sent me, and which I find most efficacious."

Sir FREDERICK MILNER, Bart., M.P., writes from Nice, March 7, 1890 : "Lady Milner and my children have derived much benefit from the Carbolic Smoke Ball."

Lady MOSTYN writes from Carshalton, Cary Crescent, Torquay, Jan. 10, 1890 : "Lady Mostyn believes the Carbolic Smoke Ball to be a certain check and a cure for a cold, and will have great pleasure in recommending it to her friends. Lady Mostyn hopes the Carbolic Smoke Ball will have all the success its merits deserve."

Lady ERSKINE writes from Spratton Hall, Northampton, Jan. 1, 1890 : "Lady Erskine is pleased to say that the Carbolic Smoke Ball has given every satisfaction ; she considers it a very good invention."

Mrs. GLADSTONE writes : "She finds the Carbolic Smoke Ball has done her a great deal of good."

Madame ADELINA PATTI writes : "Madame Patti has found the Carbolic Smoke Ball very beneficial, and the only thing that would enable her to rest well at night when having a severe cold."

AS PRESCRIBED BY

SIR MORELL MACKENZIE, M.D.,

HAS BEEN SUPPLIED TO

H.I.M. THE GERMAN EMPRESS.

H.R.H. The Duke of Edinburgh, K.G.
H.R.H. The Duke of Connaught, K.G.
The Duke of Fife, K.T.
The Marquis of Salisbury, K.G.
The Duke of Argyll, K.T.
The Duke of Westminster, K.G.
The Duke of Richmond and Gordon, K.G.
The Duke of Manchester.
The Duke of Newcastle.
The Duke of Norfolk.
The Duke of Rutland, K.G..
The Duke of Wellington.
The Marquis of Ripon, K.G.
The Earl of Derby, K.G.
Earl Spencer, K.G.
The Lord Chancellor.
The Lord Chief Justice.
Lord Tennyson.

TESTIMONIALS.

The BISHOP OF LONDON writes : "The Carbolic Smoke Ball has benefited me greatly."

The MARCHIONESS DE SAIN writes from Padworth House, Reading, Jan. 13, 1890 : "The Marchioness de Sain has daily used the Smoke Ball since the commencement of the epidemic of Influenza, and has not taken the Influenza, although surrounded by those suffering from it."

Dr. J. RUSSELL HARRIS, M.D., writes from 6, Adam Street, Adelphi, Sept. 24, 1891 : "Many obstinate cases of post-nasal catarrh, which have resisted other treatment, have yielded to your Carbolic Smoke Ball."

A. GUINNESS, Esq., Editor of the *Lady's Pictorial*, writes from 172, Strand, W.C., Feb. 14, 1890 : "During a recent sharp attack of the prevailing epidemic I had none of the unpleasant and dangerous catarrh and bronchial symptoms. I attribute this entirely to the use of the Carbolic Smoke Ball."

The Rev. Dr. CHICHESTER A. W. READE, LL.D., D.C.L., writes from Bustead Downs, Surrey, May 1890 : "My duties in a large public institution have brought me daily, during the recent epidemic of influenza, in close contact with the disease. I have been perfectly free from any symptom by having the Smoke Ball always handy. It has also wonderfully improved my voice for speaking and singing."

The Originals of these Testimonials may be seen at our Consulting Rooms, with hundreds of others.

One **CARBOLIC SMOKE BALL** will last a family several months, making it the cheapest remedy in the world at the price—10s., post free.

The **CARBOLIC SMOKE BALL** can be refilled, when empty, at a cost of 5s., post free. Address:

CARBOLIC SMOKE BALL CO., 27, PRINCES ST., HANOVER SQ., LONDON, W.

The functions of contract law

'Elements of Politics' by Sidgwick (1879), p 82

In a summary view of the civil order of society, as constituted in accordance with the individualistic ideal, performance of contract presents itself as the chief positive element, protection of life and property being the chief negative element. Withdraw contract—suppose that no one can count upon the fulfilment of any engagement—and the members of a human community are atoms that cannot effectively combine; the complex cooperation and division of employments that are the essential characteristics of modern industry cannot be introduced among such beings. Suppose contracts freely made and effectively sanctioned, and the most elaborate social organization becomes possible, at least in a society of such human beings as the individualistic theory contemplates: gifted with mature reason, and governed by enlightened self-interest. Of such beings it is *prima facie* plausible to say that, when once their respective relations to the surrounding material world have been determined so as to prevent mutual encroachment and secure to each the fruits of his industry, the remainder of their positive mutual rights and obligations ought to depend entirely on that coincidence of their free choices, which we call contract.

NOTE

Commenting on this passage, Kessler and Sharp say:

The representatives of this school of thought were firmly convinced, to state it somewhat roughly, of the existence of a natural law according to which, if not in the short run then at least in the long run, the individual serving his own interest was also serving the interest of the community. Profits, under this system, could only be earned by supplying wanted commodities, and freedom of competition would prevent profits from rising unduly. The play of the market, if left to itself, would, therefore, maximize net satisfactions and afford the ideal conditions for the distribution of wealth. Justice within this context has a very definite meaning. It means freedom of property and of contract, of profitmaking and of trade. The 'pre-established harmony' of a social system based on freedom of enterprise and perfect competition sees to it that the private autonomy of contracting parties will be kept within bounds and will work out to the benefit of society as a whole. Freedom of contract, within this cultural framework, like all freedom, is not an end in itself; it is only valuable as a means to an end: 'the liberation of the powers of all men equally for contributions to a common good'.

Small wonder, that freedom of contract, as evolved in the spirit of *laissez faire*, has found repeated expression in Anglo-American case law. '(If) there is one thing which more than another public policy requires,' Sir George Jessel, MR, assures us, 'it is that men of full age and competent understanding shall have the utmost liberty of contracting, and that their contracts entered into freely and voluntarily shall be held sacred and shall be enforced by Courts of Justice.' [*Printing & Numerical Registering Co v Sampson.*] True, fraud and force must be ruled out by the courts in the exercise of their function of making sure that the 'rules of the game' will be adhered to. But this qualification was thought to be of no great moment, owing to the policing force of the competitive market. Except for according protection against force and fraud, it is not the function of courts to make contracts for the parties or to strike down or tamper with improvident bargains. Courts have only to interpret contracts made by the parties; they do not make them. This attitude is in keeping with liberal social and moral philosophy, according to which it pertains to the dignity of man to lead his own life as a reasonable person and to accept responsibility for his own mistakes.

('Contract as a Principle of Order', from *Contracts: Cases and Materials*, 1953).

'The Control of Contract Power' by Reiter (1981) 1 Oxford J of Legal Studies 347, 348–350, 356, 358–361

(NB: do not worry about the details of the rules mentioned by Reiter; concentrate on his general arguments.)

. . . [T]he view presented as a fact by Jessel MR is simply wrong. We never did have, we do not have, and we never could have a total and unthinking delegation of contract power in society. . . .

My thesis applies at two levels. It applies at what I shall call a 'macro' level. Here, I suggest that contract as an organizing principle in society—the society—the market—has a limited role. The thesis also applies at what I shall call a 'micro' level. Within the area nominally delegated to private individuals' law-making, I assert that 'contract law' contains principles for limiting the ability to exercise contract power. I shall attempt to describe the controls, to assert their legitimacy and necessity, and to examine the institutions fit to impose them.

II. A SOCIETY ORGANIZED ON MARKET PRINCIPLES?

The more important level of the thesis is the macro level, which considers the extent to which society should be organized by the market as opposed to other, and historically more venerable principles. These principles, around which many other societies have been organized, include custom, kinship, authoritarianism, religion, feudalism, and the more modern varieties of socialized power ranging from communism through democracy. It is important to appreciate at the outset the implausibility of a claim that society should be organized on the basis of private contracting behaviour. The claim advocates apparent anarchy and amoralism. Never before the birth of faith in markets had gain been advanced as an inherently worthy motive. Nor had economic structures ever been sharply differentiated from social structures and relations. But in an effort to throw off feudal and religious shackles, to release energy and to give vent to new theories of social justice, a broad coalition was forged over the sixteenth through the nineteenth century. The coalition, including economic liberals, utilitarians, and classes rising in power politically and intellectually, adduced powerful arguments in support of the market. The central benefits they attributed to organization in this form included the following. First, the market would provide powerful incentives motivating individuals to work and to produce wealth in society. The resultant gain would improve the lot of all (or of most, depending on the economist) individuals in society. The notion of incentives could be, and indeed was, pushed to the point of urging the necessity of a substantial level of poverty in society and of starvation as a sharp stick to keep the incentive structure keen. Second, market organization offered promises of efficiency. The consumer would determine what society produced: the cheapest mode of production of the right quantities of goods and an efficient distribution network were explicit outcomes of the model. Third, market organization would allow for innovation. This was a particularly critical attribute given the substantial barriers to innovation that had been erected by the guilds and other local protective arrangements. Fourth, the market meant freedom from imposition by governmental or religious authorities. This freedom offered a consent basis to society, a basis seen both as good in itself and as a legitimating force. Finally, the market promised justice. The entire notion of market rewards and failures could be and was linked to a personal merit principle.

The case was powerful, but it was never wholly accepted. Instead, strange and shifting alliances of intellectual and political power combined to prevent the excesses of the market through the assertion of political power. Society reacted in a 'spontaneous outburst' to assert its primacy over economics. The details of the social reaction and the proof of what I assert about its success are provided in Polanyi's class study, *The Great Transformation* and in Atiyah's interesting and extensive recent work, *The Rise and Fall of Freedom of Contract*. It may suffice to describe the nature of the rejection of market principles in one critical sector only, that of 'the supply of labour'. The commodification of labour was a critical step necessary to establish a market-based economy. Older feudal notions of the relationship between workers and those responsible for them had to give way if mobile labour was to be available to be bought and sold as supply and demand dictated. The commodification of labour was not really achieved even in theory until the repeal of the Poor Laws in 1834. However, as the momentum to turn labour into a commodity grew, the social reaction was already taking shape. It appeared in the form of the reassertion and the continued assertion of values limiting market values in respect of human labour. The force of the social reaction demonstrates that the nineteenth century was anything but an era of *laissez-faire*. The best known reactions involve those associated with the various Factory Acts, dating from 1833. The Acts dealt with employment of children, hours of work and safety matters. Similar legislation regulated other important industrial sectors. A bureaucracy was created, industrial inspection Commissions were established. Reports were issued and legislation followed frequently. Combination laws were enacted early in the nineteenth century and Truck Acts were passed frequently thereafter.

All of this social reaction occurred early in the 'era of market economy'. Today the dimensions of the reaction are even more apparent . . .

III. CONTRACT AT THE GRASS ROOTS

[At the micro level] . . . I ask, 'What is the current "law of contract"?', and more specifically, 'Where is that law to be found?' Two competing expressions and sources of the law appear. First, one could refer to the views of Jessel MR and of textwriters who have based their opinions on what he said. Or, alternatively, one could refer to the 'mine run' of cases, to legislation in *pari materia*, to philosophical and other social scientific writing, and to community expectations revealed through sources that may be referred to legitimately by common law judges.

There is little doubt about what Jessel and the textwriters would say. Expressions to the effect that 'the courts enforce contracts as written', that they 'mend no man's bargain', and that 'inadequacy of consideration is of no concern to the law', abound. But are such expressions accurate as descriptions or predictions of what courts do, or will do? Do they state 'the law' correctly?

. . . [O]ne must appreciate the extent to which the courts have overridden 'contract principles' and have established limits on the exercise of contract power. They have achieved this in a direct and consistent manner through the use of doctrines of public policy and illegality. For instance, well before the classical theory of contract was evolved, and ever since, the courts have exercised control over contracts in restraint of trade in an endeavour to assure their reasonableness. The courts have always asserted a power to find common law illegality or to deny enforcement to contracts found repulsive . . .

The courts have also asserted limits to contract power in less open and direct ways. In large areas where judges have felt that contract principles are unsuitable, but that it would be inadvisable to admit the fact, the courts have created 'exceptions', or special bodies of law that are regarded as 'not contract'. More suitable treatment can then be accorded to the 'exceptional cases' without risk to 'contract' generally. Consider, for instance, aspects of the 'law of' mortgages, sureties, insurance, fiduciaries, bailment, or admiralty. Though what may often be involved in each of these fields is a consensual arrangement between two individuals, it is quite clear that the courts pay no attention to what the contract says where judicially ordained limits have been exceeded. In many cases the written contract is neglected completely, and the parties' rights are determined wholly by the court. It would be interesting and, I believe, informative to establish empirically the proportion of the nineteenth century or even of the twentieth century 'contracts docket' represented by these 'exceptional cases'. As well, and even within 'contract' itself, a number of unique spheres have been created where judicial control of contract power is regarded as quite legitimate because the areas are somehow regarded as 'special', rather than as reflective of general principle. Consider, for instance, the 'law of' penalties, forfeitures, expectant heirs, or the various forms of duress (ranging from duress of the person, through duress *colore officii*, practical duress and economic duress). It is only by ignoring the existence of all these various 'pockets' of law that a theory devoid of a notion of limits to contract power could be constructed. Gilmore has argued that the isolation of 'pockets' reflecting such conflicting values was the result of conscious efforts by the classical theory builders.

Courts have asserted limits to contract power in an even more subtle but practically more important manner. Through a great variety of techniques, the courts have paid lip service to contract law in theory, and have ignored it in practice. Consider, for instance, the various interpretation, or more realistically non-interpretation, techniques they have employed in an attempt to make contracts read 'fairly' (from the courts' point of view) rather than as one of the parties undoubtedly intended them to read. Or consider the use of implied terms. While one view of the law is that courts can imply terms only when it is absolutely necessary to do so, it is quite clear that courts have implied terms frequently in an effort to make the parties' obligations appear as the courts think they should. The courts have used notions of 'repugnancy' to exclude undesirable terms. For many years, they manipulated a concept of fundamental breach so that exclusion clauses could not operate to the grave disadvantage of a weaker or a surprised party. (Now, and more realistically, that line is being pursued through notions of unreasonableness and unconscionability.) Courts have found collateral contracts that either serve to import warranties not available in the 'main contract', or that introduce different terms that the court considers preferable to those contained in the 'main contract'. They have limited the scope of contracts through various devices in order to keep undesirable terms at bay. For instance, they have used techniques of characterization to achieve such ends, characterizing an offer and acceptance so that a harsh clause is excluded. The use of these concepts can always be defended as other than manipulative: it *really was* necessary to imply a term in this case; the offer *really was* made before the ticket came out of the machine; it *really was* the intention of one of the parties to give a collateral warranty. However, I would submit that any but the most biased and blind observer can appreciate the policy orientations lying behind the manipulations of the various techniques. To my mind, the manipulations show what Friedman concluded about what happened to doctrine in the Wisconsin Supreme Court over about 150 years. While the stated doctrine remained the same, there was a fundamental transformation in its role and functions: the effects of its use changed dramatically. I suggest that we in England and in Canada have witnessed a similar transformation in the use of doctrine and that the different devices (varying in availability depending on the legal climate) have been employed in pursuit of values oft-unexpressed but nonetheless readily apparent.

NOTE

The reference to Friedman is to Friedman, *Contract Law in America* (1965); an extract from this will be found below, p 82.

'The ideologies of contract law' by Adams and Brownsword (1987) 7 Legal Studies 205, 205–214, 217–222

Our sketch elaborates two central contentions. First, we contend that it is illuminating to interpret the materials which comprise the contract rule-book (ie the rules and principles which are traditionally taken to represent the law of contract) in the light of two underpinning 'ideologies', which we will term 'Market-Individualism' and 'Consumer-Welfarism'. Secondly, we contend that decisions of the higher courts in contract disputes (or in any tribunal where the dispute hinges on a point of contract law) should be interpreted within a framework in which general judicial ideologies (ie general understandings of the judicial role) are combined with the specifically contractual market-individualist and consumer-welfarist ideologies. At the price of some over-simplification, we employ just two such general judicial ideologies, which we term 'Formalism' and 'Realism'. . . .

[T]hese terms are employed stipulatively: they simply mean what we say they mean. . . .

[These ideologies are] a resource for interpreting the actions of others, or for organising our understanding of some phenomenon. Accordingly, our proposed ideological framework should be read as a resource which enables us both to reinterpret the materials in the contract rule-book and to understand more clearly what is going on when judges resolve contract disputes. . . .

I. Market-Individualism
The ideology of Market-Individualism has both market and individualistic strands. The strands are mutually supportive, but it aids exposition to separate them. We can look first at the market side of this ideology and then at its individualistic aspect.

(1) The market ideology
According to Market-Individualism, the market place is a site for competitive exchange. The function of contract is not simply to facilitate exchange, it is to facilitate *competitive* exchange. Contract establishes the ground rules within which competitive commerce can be conducted. Thus, subject to fraud, mistake, coercion and the like, bargains made in the market must be kept. In many ways, the line drawn between (actionable) misrepresentation and mere non-disclosure, epitomises this view. There are minimal restraints on contractors: the law of the market is not the law of the jungle, and this rules out misrepresentations. However, non-disclosure of some informational advantage is simply prudent bargaining—contractors are involved in a competitive situation and cannot be expected to disclose their hands. In line with these assumptions, the market-individualist philosophy attaches importance to the following considerations.

First, security of transactions is to be promoted. This means that where a party, having entered the market, reasonably assumes that he has concluded a bargain, then that assumption should be protected. . . .

Secondly, it is important for those who enter into the market to know where they stand. This means that the ground rules of contract should be clear. Hence, the restrictions on contracting must not only be minimal (in line with the competitive nature of the market), but also must be clearly defined (in line with the market demand for predictability, calculability etc). . . .

Thirdly, since contract is concerned essentially with the facilitation of market operations, the law should accommodate commercial practice, rather than the other way round. . . .

(2) The Individualistic Ideology

A persistent theme in Market-Individualism is that judges should play a non-interventionist role with respect to contracts. This distinctive non-interventionism derives from the individualistic side of the ideology. The essential idea is that parties should enter the market, choose their fellow-contractors, set their own terms, strike their bargains and stick to them. The linchpins of this individualistic philosophy are the doctrines of 'freedom of contract' and 'sanctity of contract'.

The emphasis of freedom of contract is on the parties' freedom of choice. First, the parties should be free to choose one another as contractual partners (ie partner-freedom). Like the tango, contract takes two. And, ideally the two should consensually choose one another. Secondly, the parties should be free to choose their own terms (ie term-freedom). Contract is competitive, but the exchange should be consensual. Contract is about unforced choice. . . .

Although the principle of partner-freedom still has some life in it (eg in defending the shopkeeper's choice of customer), it is the principle of term-freedom which is the more vital. Term-freedom can be seen as having two limbs:
(i) The free area within which the parties are permitted, in principle, to set their own terms should be maximised; and,
(ii) Parties should be held to their bargains, ie to their agreed terms (provided that the terms fall within the free area). . . .

The second limb of term-freedom is none other than the principle of sanctity of contract. By providing that parties should be held to their bargains, the principle of sanctity of contract has a double emphasis. First, if parties must be held to *their* bargains, they should be treated as masters of their own bargains, and the courts should not indulge in *ad hoc* adjustment of terms which strike them as unreasonable or imprudent. Secondly, if parties must be *held* to their bargains, then the courts should not lightly relieve contractors from performance of their agreements. It will be appreciated that, while freedom of contract is the broader of the two principles, it is sanctity of contract which accounts for the distinctive market-individualistic stand against paternalistic intervention in particular cases.

2. Consumer-Welfarism

The consumer-welfarist ideology stands for a policy of consumer-protection, and for principles of fairness and reasonableness in contract. It does not start with the market-individualist premise that all contracts should be minimally regulated. Rather, it presupposes that consumer contracts are to be closely regulated, and that commercial contracts, although still ordinarily to be viewed as competitive transactions, are to be subject to rather more regulation than Market-Individualism would allow. The difficulties with Consumer-Welfarism appear as soon as one attempts to identify its particular guiding principles (ie its operative principles and conceptions of fairness and reasonableness).

Without attempting to draw up an exhaustive list of the particular principles of Consumer-Welfarism, we suggest that the following number amongst its leading ideas:

(1) The principle of constancy: parties should not 'blow hot and cold' in their dealings with one another, even in the absence of a bargain. A person should not encourage another to act in a particular way or to form a particular expectation (or acquiesce in another's so acting or forming an expectation) only then to act inconsistently with that encouragement (or acquiescence). . .

(2) The principle of proportionality: an innocent party's remedies for breach should be proportionate to the seriousness of the consequences of the breach. . .

(3) The principle of bad faith: a party who cites a good legal principle in bad faith should not be allowed to rely on that principle. . .

(4) The principle that no man should profit from his own wrong. . .

(5) The principle of unjust enrichment: no party, even though innocent, should be allowed unfairly to enrich himself at the expense of another. . .

(6) The better loss-bearer principle: where a loss has to be allocated to one of two innocent parties, it is reasonable to allocate it to the party who is better able to carry the loss. As a rule of thumb, commercial parties are deemed to be better loss-bearers than consumers. . .

(7) The principle of exploitation: a stronger party should not be allowed to exploit the weakness of another's bargaining situation; but parties of equal bargaining strength should be assumed to have a non-exploitative relationship. . .

(8) The principle of a fair deal for consumers: consumers should be afforded protection against sharp advertising practice, against misleading statements, against false representations, and against restrictions on their ordinary rights. Moreover, consumer disappointment should be properly compensated.

(9) The principle of informational advantage: representors who have special informational advantage must stand by their representations; but representees who have equal informational opportunity present no special case for protection. The positive aspect of the principle of informational advantage is protective, but its negative aspect offers no succour to representees who are judged able to check out statements for themselves.

(10) The principle of responsibility for fault: contractors who are at fault should not be able to avoid responsibility for their fault. . .

(11) The paternalistic principle: contractors who enter into imprudent agreements may be relieved from their bargains where justice so requires. The case for paternalistic relief is at its most compelling where the party is weak or naïve. . .

II JUDICIAL DECISIONS IN CONTRACT CASES

Our second contention is that if we are to understand contract decisions we must construct an interpretive framework which links general judicial ideologies with the specifically contractual ideologies.

1. The general judicial ideologies

Although there are no doubt many starting points for constructing a scheme of general judicial ideologies, the black-letter assumption of judicial fidelity to the rule-book give us an obvious cue. Therefore, we take the decisive question to be the judicial attitude towards the materials in the rule-book. Accordingly, in this section, we outline the characteristics of two general judicial ideologies. At one extreme, which we call the ideology of Formalism, the judicial role is defined in terms of applying the materials in the rule-book, irrespective of the result. At the other extreme, which we call the ideology of Realism, the judicial role is defined in terms of handing down acceptable decisions, irrespective of the dictates of the rule-book. In other words, the formalist approach is rule-book-orientated, the realist approach result-orientated. In between these extremes, of course, there will be many graduations, and to do justice to the complexity of judicial reasoning, it would be essential to construct other categories. However, for our purposes, the crude dichotomy between Formalism and Realism will suffice, for it dramatises the standing tension between rules and results. . .

2. Completing the interpretive framework: the ideological field

The specifically contractual ideologies of Market-Individualism and Consumer-Welfarism feed into the general framework of judicial ideologies at two points. On the one hand, they are fed in by the formalist approach (the particular configuration of the rule-book largely determining which of the contractual ideologies will actually be applied by a judge employing a formalist approach). On the other hand, judges adopting a realist approach will be guided by considerations drawn from the contractual ideologies. Thus, while one brand of realist approach measures the desirability of results by reference to the market-individualist ideology, another takes the consumer-welfarist ideology as its yardstick. This entails that judicial decisions in contract cases should be interpreted against the backcloth of three basic approaches, namely: formalist, realist guided by Market-Individualism, and realist guided by Consumer-Welfarism. Overall, therefore, our interpretive framework can be represented thus:

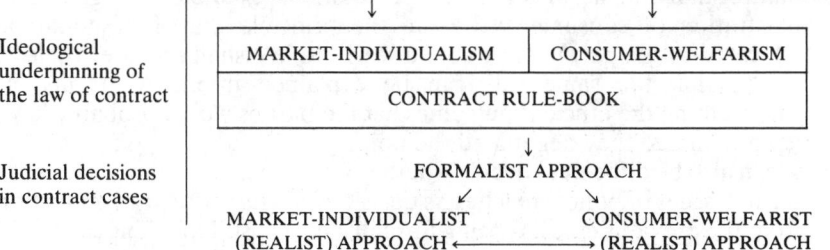

Ideological underpinning of the law of contract	MARKET-INDIVIDUALISM	CONSUMER-WELFARISM
	CONTRACT RULE-BOOK	

Judicial decisions in contract cases

FORMALIST APPROACH

MARKET-INDIVIDUALIST (REALIST) APPROACH ←——————→ CONSUMER-WELFARIST (REALIST) APPROACH

Put rather crudely, this entails that the interpreter must decide whether a judge is concerned in a particular case to apply the rule-book (ie to follow the formalist approach) or to generate desired results (ie to follow a realist approach). In the latter eventuality, the interpreter must consider whether the realist approach followed by the judge is inspired by the ideas of Market-Individualism or Consumer-Welfarism.

Now it is tempting to treat our model as a basis for classifying particular judges as eg formalists, market-individualist realists, and consumer-welfarist realists—schools of judges as it were. Moreover, readers may already believe that they can identify modern leaders of these schools in the persons of, say, Lord Diplock (for Formalism), Lord Wilberforce (for market-individualist Realism), and Lord Denning (for consumer-welfarist Realism). Our intention, however, is not to pigeonhole judges in this way. Our contention, rather, is that judges are caught within the ideological tensions represented by our model, and that their decisions in particular cases will necessarily reflect one of the basic approaches. However, this does not imply that any one judge must necessarily adopt the same approach in every case, although, no doubt, some judges are more consistent than others in this respect. Just how consistent judges are is a matter about which readers must form their own views if and when they attempt to apply our interpretive framework.

The significance of our remark that judges are 'caught within the ideological tensions' should not be lost. It means, that there is no escape for judges, who are necessarily drawn towards one or other opposing ideology, and are likely to be criticised whichever it is. . . .

It is possible, however, to discern certain features of the ideologies which create a natural affinity, on the one hand, between Formalism and Market-Individualism, and, on the other, between Realism and Consumer-Welfarism.

Consider, first, Formalism and Market-Individualism. Market-individualist realists will not shrink from putting the rule-book to one side where it obstructs commercial convenience (see eg in *The Eurymedon*). Nevertheless, they cannot encourage unbridled Realism, for this would be to invite the destruction of certainty and predictability so essential to Market-Individualism. Market-individualist realists, therefore, must exercise their Realism with restraint, departing from the rule-book only where it is judged that the market needs change more than it needs continuity. Now, formalist judges seek a rule-book which has just the sort of clear rules generally favoured by market-individualists. It follows that formalists must find it easier to work with Market-Individualism than with Consumer-Welfarism. There is, therefore, a natural affinity between Formalism and Market-Individualism for, irrespective of the content of the rule-book, both ideologies favour a particular form of rule-book (comprising clear, general, non-discretionary rules) and a particular style of judging (basically directed towards the routine application of general rules).

Converse considerations suggest a natural affinity between Realism and Consumer-Welfarism. Both ideologies favour a flexible rule-book giving judges discretion to accommodate the particular circumstances surrounding a dispute. Naturally, this militates against setting down rules which will settle disputes irrespective of their particular characteristics. In a sense, the whole thrust of Consumer-Welfarism is to point judges in a realist direction, by insisting that decisions should be fair and reasonable in the particular circumstances. . . .

NOTES

1. Adams and Brownsword have developed their approach more fully in their book *Understanding Contract Law* (1987), which is a useful introduction to the subject.
2. Their analysis does have to be handled with care. It is not always possible to label the approach the court takes to a contract problem as either market-individualist or consumer-welfarist. For example, they give as an illustration of consumer-welfarism the principle that loss should be allocated to the party better able to carry it. We shall see later (below, p 305) that the same rule can be explained in market terms, as representing the efficient outcome that the parties would probably have agreed on had they negotiated the point.
3. It can also be difficult to decide whether a court which, without comment on any issues of policy, reaches its decision by straightforward deduction from the previous cases, is being formalist or realist. Does it not consider

the practical outcome important, or does it think that the caselaw embodies the most appropriate solution? See generally, Whightman (1989) 52 MLR 115.

4. Nonetheless Adams and Brownsword provide a helpful framework within which to begin to ask, 'what is going on?' There are writers who make much stronger claims, that since the nineteenth century consumerist notions have transformed the law.

'The law of contract' by Hugh Collins (1986) pp 1–2, 8–15

This book identifies the purpose of the law of contract as the channelling and regulation of market transactions according to ideals of social justice. These ideals embody the communitarian values comprising assistance to the weak and handicapped, fairness in the distribution of wealth, and altruistic concern for the interests of others which gave birth to the Welfare State. Guided by this vision of social justice, the law of contract prescribes the terms on which commonplace market transactions such as transfers of property, hiring, and lending may take place.

A more conventional classification of the law of contract, which has dominated legal discourse during the last century, views the purpose of contract law as the creation of a facility for individuals to pursue their voluntary choices. Its latent social ideal embodies a liberal state in which the law maximizes the liberty of individual citizens, encourages self-reliance, and adopts a more or less neutral stance with regard to permissible patterns of social life. It secures these goals by facilitating the creation of legal obligations on any terms which individuals freely choose. This familiar textbook picture unites the law of contract by deriving its principal doctrines from the concept of voluntary choice. The event which triggers and moulds liability is an individual's choice to enter a legal obligation, signified in practice by promises or agreements. As a corollary this conventional classification insists upon a sharp distinction between the imposed obligations found in tort and unjust enrichment and the voluntary obligations of contract. This book differs from this popular image of the law of contract both in its description of the social ideal which motivates the law and in its mapping of the boundaries of the subject.

By emphasizing how communitarian values channel market transactions into approved patterns, the book removes the assumption that the law provides an open-ended facility for making binding commitments. Although the permissible types of transaction can be renegotiated, this freedom is merely a privilege granted on stringent conditions rather than a general licence to enter contractual obligations of one's choice. This perspective reduces the facilitative role of the law of contract to a mere rump, leaving the detailed regulations which define the model contracts as the core of the subject. As a consequence, the contrast between imposed and voluntary obligations ceases to provide a useful distinguishing characteristic of contractual obligations. . . .

1. Two Ideals of Justice

In the nineteenth century the common law defined its conception of a just market order in a remarkably rigorous set of doctrines. Its architecture was so elegant that it merits the title of the classical law of contract. We shall call the dominant ideal behind the classical law 'the justice of exchange'. Often the governing ideal is described as 'freedom of contract' but, though this terminology captures part of the spirit of the classical model, it is incomplete and ultimately misses the principal virtues of the justice of the market order as they were conceived. The theory of legal obligations represented by the ideal of the justice of exchange comprises two parts: a conception of individual responsibility and a restrictive definition of the role of the state.

Its conception of individual responsibility holds that all adult persons of sound mind may enter binding transactions by consent, usually express, but also by conduct designed to signify agreement. In a few cases, aberrational threats of violence vitiate consent because they remove a person's freedom of choice, but normally apparent consent to a transaction engenders legal responsibility. Mirroring this relaxed test of individual responsibility, the ideal of the justice of exchange ascribes a meagre role to the state. The judges eschew examination of the fairness or social utility of the transaction. Apart from shunning any transaction which involves criminal or grossly immoral behaviour and ensuring that the arrangement includes an exchange of resources, including labour, the court looks no further. The phrase 'freedom of contract' summarizes well some of the consequences of these two parts of the classical law's ideal: each person enjoys a broad discretion to make contracts; the law routinely respects their choice of terms; and the voluntariness of their choices is protected against coercion. Yet liberty is not the governing ideal of the classical law of contract. It plays second fiddle to a deeper faith in the justice of an order of wealth and power established through exchange relations. This faith stems from the belief that the market order establishes equality in place of social hierarchy and reciprocity instead of exploitation.

The justice of this market order compares favourably with earlier social orders which assigned wealth and power to persons according to their social status. . . . however, [this ideal of the justice of exchange] has long since lost its moral force and explanatory power. The advent of the Welfare State signals a loss of faith in the justice of exchange. A legislative framework supplants the market order with compulsory obligations of social insurance in order to relieve hardship and poverty. But even in the sphere of social interaction left to market transactions, this disenchantment with the classical ideal pervades the detailed rules of the law of contract. We cannot pretend that society's adoption of communitarian values has left untouched the fundamental rules governing ordinary market transactions. Texts which ignore this transformation of the law of contract hamper our understanding and impede the realization of the new market order of power and wealth defined by the ideals of the Welfare State.

To a limited extent the communitarian ideals which infuse the modern law of contract should be regarded as a response to a change in the types of market relation. As a result of the increasing division of labour, the simple model of a brief exchange transaction envisaged by the classical law rarely corresponds to modern business transactions. These days, a business deal often involves multiple parties with varying degrees of interdependence over a period of time. Though at first sight a consumer's purchase of a car from a dealer conforms to a simple exchange model, in practice many other parties are intimately connected with the transaction. The manufacturer of the car usually guarantees replacement of defective parts as an inducement to the purchaser to select that make. The manufacturer, dealer, or both make arrangements with a financial institution so that potential purchasers will find it easy to raise a loan to buy the car. Indeed, technically, the purchaser often buys the car not from the dealer but from the financial institution as an intermediary. . .

Whilst many authors recognize the impact of this alteration in the relations of production and exchange upon the classical law, most seek to accommodate these developments in a reconstituted liberal theory of contract law. Their conception of individual responsibility changes from the identification of voluntary consent to the imposition of a duty of care to prevent harm to the interests of others. The role of the state becomes the enforcement of this duty of care to protect the rights and liberty of individuals from unjustified interference by others. These important reformulations of the purpose of law of contract illuminate the path of the modern law, yet they fail to grasp the full force of the impact of communitarian values on the law. The role of the state remains confined to the purposes of prevention of harm to others and compensation for damage to their interests, rather than the prescription of fair market relations. . . . A further vital impetus toward a more interventionist role for the state stems from three major criticisms voiced against the injustice of the market order established by the classical law.

The first criticism of the justice of exchange results from an awareness of the oppressive nature of the power relations permitted by the classical law of contract. Under this regime, the potentialities of ownership and knowledge can be realized into oppressive forms of domination to the extent that lawyers can devise complex organizational structures in the form of exchange relations. The main constraint upon the facility for domination lies in the limits of one's ability to persuade others to bind themselves by way of contract. But here the discipline of economic necessity operates to provide compelling inducements to contract. Since the principal source of wealth lies in the market in the form of wages and profits, few can afford to remain aloof. Consequently, the law of contract lies at the intersection of the market and state power, and it uses the coercion of the latter to reinforce the discipline of the former.

This order of power etablished by the classical law was legitimized in two distinct ways. First, the association between liberty and the classical law, encapsulated in the slogan 'freedom of contract', emphasized the relative absence of coercion and the fulfilment of liberty. . . . Under this analysis, for example, an employer's right to give orders to his employees rests upon consent at the moment of hiring and is restricted to the scope of the duties envisaged in the contract. Such a limited obligation apparently runs little risk of establishing unjustifiable domination.

The classical law legitimizes the order of power which it creates in a second, more subtle way. It suppresses questions about the origins of ownership of capital and other resouces, and thereby ignores the ability, concomitant with ownership, to transform these potentialities into power through contracts. These questions about the effects of inequality of bargaining power can be evaded because they are irrelevant to the justice of exchange relations, where all that matters is free consent and observance of the limits of the transaction. . . .

But in modern society, we have begun to question the legitimacy of the order of power established by the uninhibited exploitation of the potentialities of ownership and knowledge. We no longer think that contracts of employment or sales of goods are automatically justifiable on the ground that there was an agreement and an exchange between the parties. In the modern law we look more closely at the comparative wealth and knowledge of the parties before we judge the legitimacy of the relation of power established between them. . . .

[The] modern law of contracts enlists a number of doctrines to place limits upon the creation of relations of domination through contracts. The test of responsibility broadens its scope of inquiry to take into account all the disparities of resources which sustain inequality of bargaining power. In effect, the law moulds market power so that fair conditions of trading prevail before bargains are struck. In addition, the modern law persistently imposes duties upon stronger parties to a contract through such devices as implied terms and the restructuring of remedies in order to counter unjustifiable relations of domination. In short, paternalism exercised by the state replaces the broad discretion to enter contracts of one's choice.

A second major criticism of the ideal of the justice of exchange challenges the fairness of the distributive scheme established under the classical law. We have noted already that the market provides the principal distributive mechanism of wealth in our society. Since the law of contract constitutes this market order, we cannot ignore the distributive consequences of rival doctrinal schemes. Under the ideal of the justice of exchange the courts insisted upon reciprocity of obligations, but not upon equivalence in value. The role of the state was the minimal one of checking that some degree of reciprocity existed, but not to question the parties' own valuation of the deal. This makes good sense in many cases, for the parties normally judge their own interests best. Provided that some exchange of values has taken place, then the transaction is likely to be fair in its distributive consequences. Yet in the twentieth century, we have become less sanguine in our estimation of many people's ability to fend for themselves. Furthermore, we have come to recognize that the 'laissez-faire' attitude leaves open the real possibility that many members of society will fail to achieve the economic conditions under which individual liberty can be a worthwhile experience. The Welfare States tries to satisfy everyone's basic needs, such as food, clothing, and shelter, in order to establish the basic conditions for human dignity and flourishing. In place of a negative concept of liberty which requires the state to minimize its regulation of social life to protect individual freedom, modern societies place greater emphasis upon fairness in the distribution of wealth out of respect for the dignity of individuals.

The impact upon the law of contract of this challenge to the fairness of the distribution of wealth established by the ideal of the justice of exchange emerges in numerous legal doctrines designed to invalidate unfair contracts and further provisions governing the character of remedies for breach of contract. Together these rules introduce a criterion of fairness into the question of the legal validity of contractual obligations which indirectly prescribes models of fair market transactions. But since distributive fairness is not an end in itself, but rather a condition of flourishing of human dignity, the modern law still respects to some extent the choices and aspirations of individuals by restricting contractual responsibility according to the negative concept of liberty. In other words, though voluntary consent is not essential to the ascription of contractual obligations, nevertheless the modern law requires strong reasons before it attaches liability without a person's consent.

The third major criticism of the ideal of the justice of exchange insists that its underlying image of social and economic relations as ones between antagonistic individuals who transact solely for the sake of their own interests propagates estranged social relations at the expense of more important bonds of solidarity. In modern society, contracting parties accept the virtues of accommodation and co-operation instead of standing on their rights, weaselling out of obligations by pointing to exemption clauses inserted in small print, refusing to do more than is absolutely necessary, and insisting upon their pound of flesh. Whilst this flexible attitude differs from pure altruism, because often long-term self-interest and self-esteem inspire steps to preserve friendly relations with others, it nevertheless introduces a new value of co-operation into the modern law, which contradicts the strict measures of duty counted out by the ideal of the justice of exchange. During performance of the obligations, subsequent modifications of the duties, and termination of the contract, the modern law insists that strict entitlements be mellowed by ancillary principles which require co-operation. Moreover, modern law recognizes the existence of contractual relations outside the strict confines of self-interested exchange, where mutual reliance should be buttressed by obligations requiring concern for the interests of others. . . .

When we gather together the themes of paternalism, fairness, and co-operation which infuse the modern law of contract, we notice that a quiet revolution has occurred. Whilst the commitment to the egalitarian quality of the market division of labour has been preserved, in place of a broad discretion to make enforceable contracts of one's choice the modern law directly imposes patterns of responsibilities and closely regulates the fairness of the distributive consequences of the operation of the market. Instead of the priority afforded to freedom of contract as the natural corollary of respect for individual liberty, the law of contract now rests upon the perception that in order to ensure respect for individual dignity a citizen must be permitted to satisfy his wants through the market, whilst at the same time the market must be controlled in order to prevent abuses of power resulting in domination and unfairness and to ensure that others take account of the citizen's interests. The underlying significance of this change in social policy concerns the legitimacy of the market order. Whereas the ideal of the justice of exchange perceived the virtue of the market order in its respect for the values of liberty, equality, and reciprocity, the modern law insists that the market order can be legitimate only when it achieves a proper balance between, on the one hand, a respect for individual dignity and equality and, on the other, a fair distribution of wealth, the avoidance of unjustifiable domination, and a duty to respect the interests of others.

NOTES

1. In the space available it is only possible to give a quick taste of Collins' approach. His attempt at restating the law in terms of the promotion of paternalism, fairness and co-operation is extremely challenging and controversial. His book is one which is well worth reading, particularly after you have studied rather more contract law, but one which must be treated with even more caution than Adams and Brownsword. His claim of a transformation is a stronger one than they make and is not wholly made out (compare, for instance, what Reiter says about the nineteenth century, above, p 61). Many of his points are open to the same kind of objection as were noted to theirs, see note 2 on p 66 above; and there is some doubt about his concepts of paternalism, fairness and co-operation: see Whightman (1989) 52 MLR 115.
2. In addition the beginning student must be very careful of Collins' statements as to the law, which are apt to jump from English to American law without much warning.

CHAPTER 5
Economic analysis of contract law

'Economics of Contract Law' by Kronman and Posner (1979), pp 1–4

The fundamental economic principle with which we begin is that if voluntary exchanges are permitted—if, in other words, a market is allowed to operate—resources will gravitate toward their most valuable uses. If A owns a good that is worth only $100 to him but $150 to B, both will be made better off by an exchange of A's good for B's money at any price between $100 and $150; and if they realize this, they will make the exchange. By making both of them better off, the exchange will also increase the wealth of the society (of which they are members), assuming the exchange does not reduce the welfare of nonparties more than it increases A's and B's welfare. Before the exchange—which, let us say, takes place at a price of $125—A had a good worth $100 in cash and B had $125 in cash, a total of $225. After the exchange, A has $125 in cash and B has a good worth $150 to him, a total of $275. The exchange has increased the wealth of society by $50 (ignoring, as we have done, any possible third-party effects).

The principle is the same whether we are speaking of the purchase of a string of pearls, a lawyer's time, a machine for making shoes, or an ingot of aluminium. The existence of a market—a locus of opportunities for mutually advantageous exchanges—facilitates the allocation of the good or service in question to the use in which it is most valuable, thereby maximizing the wealth of society.

This conclusion may be questioned on various grounds. For example, it may be argued that since 'value' in this analysis is measured by willingness to pay, which in turn is affected by the distribution of income and wealth (one cannot offer to buy a good without having money or the means to obtain it), the maximization of value cannot be regarded as an uncontroversially proper goal for society to pursue. An introductory chapter is not the place to explore the philosophical basis of the economist's concept of value. For our purposes it is enough that the reader understand the technical meaning of the concept. The reader can then decide whether there is any 'value', in an ultimate social sense, to the *economic* concept of value which the system of free exchanges promotes.

The principle that voluntary exchange should be freely permitted in order to maximize value is frequently summarized in the concept (or slogan) of 'freedom of contract'. This is something of a misnomer, for the concept of *contract* typically plays an insignificant role in elucidations and critiques of the principle of voluntary exchange. Many value-maximizing exchanges occur without contracts, or with contracts so rudimentary or transitory as to have little interest for economists studying the phenomenon of voluntary exchange. If A buys the *Chicago Tribune* from B, a news vendor, paying 20¢ for it on the spot, this is a value-maximizing exchange; but it would be pretentious to speak of a contract between A and B, though technically there is one (if a section of the paper is missing. A can probably rescind the contract and get his 20¢ back). One can talk about the principle or system of voluntary exchange for quite some time before it becomes necessary to consider the role of contracts and contract law in facilitating the process.

In the newspaper example, the exchange is virtually (though not completely) instantaneous; and this provides a clue to the role of contracts in the process of voluntary exchange. It is true that, although money and good cross at the same moment, the actual *use* of the good—the reading of the newspaper—occurs after the exchange and takes some time; so really the process of exchange is not complete until the paper has been opened and inspected. Only then can the buyer be satisfied that he got what he paid for (that no pages are missing or illegible, etc). Still, the time required to complete the exchange in the newspaper example is quite short. Where the time is long, contracts and contract law become important.

Suppose that A promises to build a house for B, construction to take six months to complete and B to pay either periodically or on completion. With construction so time-consuming, there is a significant likelihood that something will occur to frustrate the exchange—insolvency, changes in the price inputs, labour troubles, etc. Nor is A's performance complete when construction of the house is finished. A durable good like a house by definition yields services to the purchaser over a period of time, a long one in the case of a house; and it is these services rather than the physical structure itself that the purchaser is hoping to acquire. If the house wears out long before the purchaser reasonably believed it would, the exchange will be effectively thwarted long after nominal completion of performance by the promisor.

Economists have pointed out that the cost of an undertaking tends to be inversely related to the time allowed for completion. Stated differently, it is costly to accelerate completion of a time-consuming task. It would also be costly to make goods less durable in order to compress the period in which the full exchange of the goods could be completed. These observations suggest that a system of contract rights, and not merely one of property rights, may be necessary to minimize the cost of production in a market system.

Thus far we have been attempting to elucidate the concept of a contract and explain its economic significance. We have said nothing about the economic function of contract *law*. Its basic function is to provide a sanction for reneging, which, in the absence of sanctions, is sometimes tempting where the parties' performance is not simultaneous. During the process of an extended exchange, a point may be reached where it is in the interest (though perhaps only the very narrow, short-run interest) of one of the parties to terminate performance. If A agrees to build a house for B and B pays him in advance. A can make himself better off, at least if loss of reputation (which, depending on A's particular situation, may be unimportant to him) is ignored, by pocketing B's money and not building the house. The problem arises because the nonsimultaneous character of the exchange offers one of the parties a strategic advantage which he can use to obtain a transfer payment that utterly vitiates the advantages of the contract to the other party. Clearly, if such conduct were permitted, people would be reluctant to enter into contracts and the process of economic exchange would be retarded.

A noninstantaneous or extended exchange creates not only strategic opportunities that parties might try to exploit in the absence of legal sanction, but also uncertainty with regard to the conditions under which performance will occur. This uncertainty exposes the parties to the risk that the costs and benefits of their exchange will turn out to be different from what they expected. An important function of contract law is to enforce the parties' agreed-upon allocation of risk.

A related function is to reduce the costs of the exchange process by supplying a standard set of risk-allocation terms for use by contracting parties. Many substantive rules of contract law are simply specifications of the consequences of some contingency for which the contract makes no express provision. If the parties are satisfied with the way in which the rules allocate the risk of that contingency, they have no need to incur the expense of writing their own risk-allocation rule into the contract.

Besides (1) imposing costs on people who try to exploit the other party to the contract by refusing to abide by its terms and (2) providing a stock of standard contractual provisions, the law of contracts (3) imposes costs on, and thereby discourages, *careless* behaviour in the contracting process—behaviour that unnecessarily increases the costs of the process itself. Suppose A promise to give B a boat if B stops smoking, B complies with this condition (at some cost to himself), but A refuses to give him the boat. A proves that B misunderstood him—he never meant to promise him a boat. B in turn proves that he was reasonably induced by A's words and conduct to believe that A had indeed promised him the boat. If we believe that A did not in fact intend such a promise, then enforcement of the promise cannot be justified as necessary to prevent frustration of a value-maximizing exchange; there is no basis for presuming that an exchange will make the parties better off if one of them never intended to make it. But we may still want to enforce the contract in order to give people in A's position an incentive to avoid carelessly inducing others to incur costs in reliance on the existence of a contract. This problem may seem to belong to the law of torts rather than contracts, since enforcement serves not to promote a mutually beneficial exchange but instead to deter careless behaviour. But enforcement does promote the contractual process by discouraging a costly form of carelessness that would tend to impede it.

The foregoing discussion suggests a resolution along economic lines of the old dispute in contract law over whether the basis of contract formation is a 'subjective' or 'objective' one—whether the law requires an actual meeting of minds or whether it is enough that the parties use words or conduct that would signify agreement to an impartial observer. Only a contract that involves an actual meeting of minds satisfies the economist's definition of a value-maximizing exchange; but the economist allows a place for rules designed to prevent people from misleading others into thinking they have a contract with them; hence both the subjective and objective theories have a place in contract law.

NOTES

1. It is worth considering some of the concepts and assumptions which Kronman and Posner use in this piece, together with some of the really quite simple ideas upon which economic analysis is based. These notes should form a sufficient introduction to all the economic analysis contained in the book.

2. The first is that individuals are rational maximisers of their own self-interest—that is, they will respond to other people and to events in a way that increases their own utility. It is this which lies behind the notion that individuals will trade resources until the resources reach the people who value them most highly.

3. Economists express the idea that something may be worth more to one person than to another by saying that the first will be prepared to pay more for it than the other. However, they use the word 'utility' rather than 'wealth' because the theory does not assume that every one is selfishly pursuing greater personal wealth. Individuals may well like to see other individuals made better off and be prepared to give some of their own wealth to achieve that. An economist fits this into his general theory by saying that the donor's 'utility' is increased by seeing the donee made better off. (See further below, p 124.)

4. Exchanges which increase the utility of both the parties increase 'efficiency', in the special sense in which economists use that term. Efficiency will also be increased even if one of the parties is left worse off, provided that the other party is made so much better off that she could compensate the first party for his loss and still gain herself—in other words, if the benefits exceed the costs. A state of affairs will be fully efficient (or 'optimal') if it is not possible to make any further change without finding that the aggregate losses to the losers equal or exceed the aggregate gains to the gainers. When this state has been achieved, wealth has been maximised.

5. In economics, cost also has a special meaning: it is measured by the value of opportunities foregone. Economics is all about understanding what happens when people who are subject to constraints and to incentives make choices, such as the choice between the various ways in which they could use resources. What matters is the value of the resource in its next best alternative use, not the amount which was spent to acquire or produce it. So if A has spent £3m on a factory to produce CFC's but the Government has now banned production of CFC's on environmental grounds, and A now has to decide whether to use it to produce other gases or to knock it down and sell the land, the choice will be between the revenue each of those activities will produce; the £3m spent already is irrelevant. Bygones are always bygones in economics.

6. On the other hand, cost will include normal profit. The cost of using capital will always include the amount that the capital could earn in alternative risk-free investments such as government stocks—and if a firm does not offer at least such a return to investors it will not attract the capital it needs, any more than it would be able to employ workers if it didn't offer them wages. (In fact it will have to offer something extra, a 'risk premium'.)

7. Kronman and Posner say that the increase in the wealth of the two individuals who trade will increase the overall wealth of society

provided that the exchange does not make third parties worse off. The effect on the third party is known as an 'externality'—though there is also an externality if a third party is made better off. The externality problem is not relevant to most contract law problems, which will involve only the parties to the contract. There is one important exception: illegal contracts. Suppose Beale concludes that the only thing standing between him and a highly prestigious chair at the University of Bristol is Furmston. He might be tempted to hire an assassin to poison Furmston for £10,000—which, if the crime were not detected, might leave both Beale and the assassin better off, but would not be value-maximising for Furmston or society at large. Where parties enter into a contract to do something illegal the general task of the law may be to frustrate their intentions—the exact opposite of the usual purpose of contract law. (We shall see later that the economist's normal assumption that most contracts have no external effects may be made much too easily: see below, p 576.)

8. The question the authors raise about whether the maximisation of value is a proper goal to pursue given the unequal distribution of income and wealth is taken up below, pp 576 and 582.

9. Kronman and Posner point out that the provision of legal remedies reduces the likelihood of default in an exchange which extends over a period of time. Without legal remedies, some such exchanges might not take place because they would seem too costly—the risk of default would outweigh the gains to be made. This would discourage what would otherwise be a value-maximizing exchange. Posner in his *Economic Analysis of Law* (2nd edn, p 66) gives other examples:

> . . . [T]he absence of legally enforceable rights would, among other consequences, bias investment toward economic activities where the interval in which the contemplated economic activity could be completed was short, and this would reduce the efficiency of resource use. Suppose A wants to sell his cow, and there are two bidders, B and C. The cow is worth $50 to B and $60 to C (and only $30 to A), so efficiency requires that the cow be sold to C rather than to B. However, B has $50 cash in hand while C cannot obtain any cash for a week. C promises to pay $55 to A in a week, and let us assume that the $5 difference would more than compensate A for the costs, in the event of default, of bringing suit for damages or for return of the cow, discounted by the risk of default—if the law made C's promise to A enforceable. But if the law does not enforce such promises A may decide that, since C may fail to raise the money and B in the interim lose interest in the transaction, he is better off selling to B now. If so, the failure of the law to provide a remedy if C breaks his promise will, by discouraging parties from entering into exchanges in which performance by one party is deferred, have induced a suboptimum allocation of resources.
>
> Now suppose that A offers a shirt for sale at $5 and B offers one for $6 which he claims (truthfully) will last three times as long as A's shirt and is therefore better value. But the difference in shirts is not apparent on casual inspection or handling, so while B may be willing to guarantee the superior durability of this shirt, if his promise is not legally enforceable consumers may doubt the honesty of his claim and buy A's shirt instead, again a suboptimum result.

In broad terms, this is an example of how contract law can reduce 'transaction costs'.

10. The idea that if exchanges were riskier or more costly in other ways, fewer of them would take place, is simply an application of a basic economic idea often expressed as 'demand curves slope down'. Anything desirable will be demanded, purchased and consumed more as its price falls and less as its price rises relative to other prices. In elementary textbooks the idea is captured by a diagram which relates

price (on the vertical axis) to quantity demanded (on the horizontal): the demand curve falls as the eye moves from left to right.

11. Not all parties will stop entering a particular type of transaction because it becomes more costly or start entering it because it becomes cheaper. Every important quantity of economics is decided at the margin. Some people value certain resources so much that they would be prepared to pay much more to get them than others. The first group will continue to purchase even though the price rises, but some of the others will find it no longer 'just worthwhile'. Conversely, if the price of an item falls, some people for whom it was previously not worthwhile will start to buy it, but it will remain too expensive for others. The people whose behaviour alters in response to the price change are at the margin.

12. The risk of the other party defaulting and leaving you out of pocket is just one example of a 'transaction cost'. In the real world all contracting involves some transactions costs. People need to acquire information, to negotiate terms and conditions, and to monitor the other party's performance as well to enforce the agreement if there is a breach—and usually all of these are costly. All are examples of transactions costs. As we shall see, economists often start an analysis by assuming that there are no transaction costs, but this 'modelling' should never be assumed to represent the real world. (For an example, see notes 9 and 10.)

13. Kronman and Posner point out that a second way in which the law can reduce transactions costs is by 'supplying a standard set of risk-allocation terms'. If negotiation cost nothing, parties would presumably make sure that whatever future events affected the contract, they had agreed a set of terms which would leave them both as well off as possible. They would continue to negotiate, in other words, until they had reached an optimal arrangement under which any further change could only make one of them better off by making the other one equally worse off. The result would be that the parties had what economists call a 'complete contingent claims contract'—one in which every eventuality was provided for.

14. If all contracts were complete in this sense, the whole law of contract could be reduced to a single sentence: 'whatever the parties have agreed shall be enforced.' But although some contracts are very detailed none is complete. Nonetheless the idea is useful, because to an economist the question, 'what should the law be now that such and such has happened' should be answered by asking what the parties would probably have agreed had they negotiated on it (though see below p 305). If the court can decide what terms the parties would have negotiated in a hypothetical world in which negotiation was costless, and then 'mimic' this solution by applying it as a rule of law, that rule can be described as efficient: the parties could not negotiate to any other solution which would leave them jointly better off, so there is no need for them to negotiate (see Coase, 'The Problem of Social Cost' (1960) 3 J Law & Econ 1, 15–16). Thus transactions costs are reduced and more exchanges are encouraged. Of course, if the court chooses a solution that is less than optimal for parties making that type of contract, the law will then be inefficient: the parties will either have to make an express agreement excluding the legal rule and substituting their own preferred solution, or put up with the sub-optimal result.

15. Analysis of legal rules from an economic point of view often leads to

what is called 'the economics of the second best'. A simple economic model sometimes suggests a legal rule which in the real world would be impracticable, because it would be too difficult to apply. Kronman and Posner's example of misleading the other party into thinking you are contracting provides an example. If you made a mistake and did not mean what you said, the resulting exchange is not a value-maximizing exchange, and they suggest that there ought in this case to be tort-like liability to deter such careless behaviour. But we shall see that the law does not distinguish between the person who means what he says and the person who does not: subject to some qualifications (see below, chapter 11) the law judges contracting parties objectively, by their words and actions not their thoughts. This decision not to distinguish between genuine bargains and merely misleading conduct can be justified on the basis that to try to distinguish them would be just too costly. Judges and arbitrators do not have privileged access to the workings of the minds of the parties; they cannot always easily discern who is telling the truth. To ask them to do so would increase the length (and therefore the cost) of trials—and also the difficulties of reaching a settlement out of court. Thus it may be sensible to adopt a rule that does not require them to distinguish, as being the best compromise between theoretical efficiency and administrative cost. Such costs are often termed 'adjudication costs'. The converse, of course, is that the law may end up with a solution that is not really appropriate on the facts of the case: this may be termed 'error cost'. The choice of which rule of law to adopt is frequently influenced by the balance between adjudication and error costs.

16. The assumption that parties will bargain in ways that leaves each of them better off assumes that they have information about each other. Information is extremely important to the operation of markets and to contract law, even though the economics of information have been studied only during the last 30 years. Information is often very valuable; it can also be very costly to acquire or produce. If the parties do not have adequate information they may well misjudge the costs or benefits of the transactions they are contemplating, with inefficient results: see for example the discussion of the 'small print' in consumer contracts, below, p 700. There are a number of rules which place contractual liability in such a way as to encourage the use of existing information by the party who has access to it (eg the rule in *Hadley v Baxendale*, below, p 475).

17. However, information is a peculiar commodity; once it has been produced, it can be reproduced and passed on to others at very little cost. Thus it is hard for the producer to capture the full benefit of what he produces: he cannot 'sell' the information without revealing it to all and sundry, so that even information of great social benefit may not be produced without special incentives to the producer. It is not worth going to the expense of designing a better mousetrap if, as soon as you put it on the market, your design can be copied by your competitors. It is for this reason that the law creates intellectual property rights in the form of patents and copyright. We shall see that there are also rules of contract law apparently aimed at encouraging the production of information (eg the rules allowing parties to make contracts without disclosing some types of relevant information to the other party, below, p 398).

18. You will notice that analysis in terms of efficiency looks to see whether a transaction or change will increase the aggregate or joint wealth of the parties, but it is not concerned with how the increase is distributed between them. Thus to use the example in Kronman and Posner's first paragraph, the exchange would still be efficient if B agreed to buy the good from A at $149.99. Normally the maximum amount that A can charge B (and conversely the minimum amount that B can get A to accept) will be constrained by competition, the presence of other sellers (or buyers) in the market. It is easier to explain this if we first introduce the notion of 'marginal cost'.

19. Marginal cost is the cost of producing an extra unit of what is on offer. Every producer has limited capacity. If it is operating at below capacity, it will be eager to sell more; but at some point to produce extra units may cost the producer more on average than it has been spending up to that point. For instance a solicitor handling 30 conveyances a month might well like to see more business come through her door if her staff are not fully occupied. But if the number got to 60 a month she might be rushed and at 90 a month she might find that the extra business was costing more in overtime, temps and so on than it was bringing in. In other words, the marginal cost would have risen until it exceeded the 'marginal revenue', the extra income brought in by each conveyance. A producer will not normally want marginal cost to exceed marginal revenue.

20. Under competition, market price will normally equal marginal cost. If it rises above that, some firms will see a profit opportunity. They will hire more resources and produce more. But eventually this will lead to a significant rise in supply in the total market. Assuming demand does not change, the rise in supply will lead to a lower price, and this will go on until price equals marginal cost again. At that point no firm sees any further profit opportunity. (Remember that in economics cost includes normal profit.) The market has reached a point of stability, an equilibrium, in which P = MC. Conversely, if market price goes below MC some firms will drop out of this now unprofitable line of business, and a parallel process will bring the market back to the point of equilibrium P = MC. This is an attractive destination, because at this point, and at no other, the cost of resources (eg the *labour*, earning normal wages, and the *capital*, earning normal profit) needed to produce the good exactly equals its value to the marginal consumer.

21. Under monopoly, however, price exceeds marginal cost. A monopolist is someone with significant control over the price of a good and the total quantity supplied to the market—eg the sole producer of the product. Such a person will maximise his own profit by putting the price above marginal cost. Then he can make a greater profit than competing businesspeople can normally make. Of course, because demand curves slope down, he will sell less than he would sell at the competitive price P = MC. Therein lies the problem of monopoly. Some marginal consumers would be willing to buy if the price were a little lower than the monopoly price. They are willing to pay enough to 'hire' the resources (eg labour and capital) needed to produce the good, but they cannot because the monopolist stands between them and the hiring of the resources. Thus monopoly leads to a misallocation of resources, ie too few resources flow into the production of the monopolised good.

Note that it is *not* the extra profit made by the monopolist which worries economists. That is a distributional question, a 'mere transfer of wealth'. Customers lose but shareholders in the monopolist firm (the majority of shares nowadays are held by pension funds, which are in turn owned by the individuals in the pension scheme) benefit; nothing to get excited about. But misallocation of resources all economists are happy to condemn. Thus economists and the person in the street both dislike monopoly, but their reasons differ sharply. (Note that economists may accept that temporary monopolies are necessary in order to encourage the development of new products (see note 17 above). A patent is nothing more than a grant of a temporary monopoly.)

CHAPTER 6
Empirical work

Kronman and Posner envisage contracts involving a short time frame being made and performed without reference to the law, but say: 'Where the time is long, contracts and contract law become important.' Their statement contains a vital insight, but it is an oversimplification.

'Contracts between Businessmen' by Beale and Dugdale (1975) 2 Brit J Law & Society, 45, pp 45–48

Contract law may be 'used' in at least two ways. First, use may be made of the remedies which the law provides in the event of something going wrong: for instance, the victim of a breach of contract may be able to bring the contract to an end or to recover damages. . . .

But much more 'use' of contract law is made in a second way . . . The parties may . . . 'use' contract law to regulate their relationship, to plan what is to happen in the future. They may plan their primary obligations, for instance in a contract sale the item, the price and the delivery date, and also mechanisms by which these primary obligations may be adjusted; for instance, what is to happen if the cost of materials increases or an unavoidable delay occurs. The agreement may proceed further and set out the rights of the parties in the event of something going seriously wrong. In other words the parties may plan their own remedies. Examples would be an express right to terminate or a 'liquidated damages' clause fixing in advance the amount payable by a party who breaks the contract. At this point the planning use of contract merges with the remedial use, at least if the parties make use of the planned remedies.

. . . Professor Stewart Macaulay has published the results of some research into this topic done in Wisconsin, where he interviewed representatives of 48 companies and six law firms. [For extracts from Macaulay's article, see below, p 301.] He described contract as involving '. . . two distinct elements: (a) rational planning of the transaction with careful provision for as many future contingencies as can be foreseen, and (b) the existence or use of actual or potential legal sanctions to induce performance of the exchange or to compensate for non-performance'. He divided the types of issue which might be planned into four—description of the primary obligations, contingencies, defective performances and legal sanctions—and concluded that while many business exchanges will involve a high degree of planning about each category, equally many at least 'reflect no planning, or only a minimal amount of it, especially concerning legal sanctions and the effect of defective performances'. He found little use of 'contractual practices' in the later adjustment of relationships, though there was some evidence of tacit reliance on contractual rights; and very little use of the formal dispute-settlement procedures available through the courts.

The picture which emerges from our research is, as will be seen, broadly similar to that drawn by Macaulay, and many of the general explanations of why contract law may or may not be used are the same as his . . .

We interviewed representatives of nineteen firms of engineering manufacturers, mainly in Bristol, about their firm's contracts of purchase and sale. We talked to 33 persons: five of these were legal staff, and in other cases we normally spoke to at least one senior member of the firm. In some cases we spoke to sales personnel and in other cases to purchasing officers: we have tried where appropriate to contrast the attitudes of the 'two sides'. The interviews varied in length according to the time that could be spared us, from twenty minutes to several hours: in some cases we made more than one visit to a firm. It was therefore not possible to ask the same questions of each representative, and regrettably we obtained no information on some topics from a few firms. We did endeavour to find out however not only what each firm did but what was generally done in the trade. Contracts of sale and purchase by engineering manufacturers were chosen because of their relative simplicity and our findings may have no validity outside that area.

We realize that our sample was small (about half the size of Macaulay's), but we hope it is sufficiently large to show general trends and to confirm Macaulay's picture. On the more detailed issues it will clearly not indicate accurately how common particular practices are, but we think it worthwhile to indicate their existence so that they can be studied in more depth if that is thought worthwhile.

Before dealing with the particular issues on which we concentrated it may be useful to indicate some of the more general factors which may influence engineering manufacturers in their decision on whether to plan a contract in detail, whether to adhere to their contractual rights and duties and whether to employ contractual remedies. For instance the reason why in most exchanges the parties agree expressly only on their primary obligations, and not on the effect of, say, late or defective performances may be that on each of the issues studied there appeared to be a certain amount of 'tacit' planning: within the trade certain terms and certain customs or 'unwritten laws' were widely accepted. For instance it was generally accepted that the seller would not compensate the buyer for certain losses. Thus, although firms would sometimes claim 'unusual' rights the trade custom might provide a basis for settling any dispute. Moreover, most firms traded regularly with the other party, and would know what attitude the other was likely to take. Firms frequently stated that they would take much greater care when contracting with relatively unknown parties, especially those outside the engineering trade.

A second general reason for not planning a transaction in much detail is that such planning is expensive, while the risk of a serious dispute or loss may be low; for instance if orders of low value are sold on credit to a diversity of customers the loss likely to be caused by customers failing to pay may not be great, and may not justify the cost of planning security arrangements. Conversely a high degree of planning was often explained by a high risk—perhaps a customer who would lose heavily if delivery were late or a machine which would cause great loss of life if it were defective. Even then there might be reluctance to do any more than was strictly necessary: there seemed to be a feeling that a carefully negotiated contract might be insufficiently flexible to meet even foreseeable events, and too much negotiation might sour a peaceful relationship.

Even if plans had been made to cover possible disruptions, there was usually thought to be no need to fall back on legal rights if the disruption materialized. It was made very clear to us that, besides there being a common acceptance of certain norms within the trade, there was a considerable degree of trust among firms. This was particularly so among smaller firms who obtained most of their orders locally and who frequently placed great trust in the fairness of one or two very large firms. No doubt belief in mutual fairness was reinforced by the considerable degree of personal contact between officers, usually in the business context but sometimes on social occasions. The firm's general reputation was also at stake. Not only did salesmen stress the need to have a good product and to stand behind it, buyers also emphasized the need to maintain a reputation for the firm as fair and efficient, and both said that any attempt to shelter behind contractual provisions or even frequent citation of contractual terms would destroy the firm's reputation very quickly. But even more important than the general reputation of the firm was the desire to do business again with the other party, or with other firms in the same group of companies. Each side had to be prepared to make concessions and to do so in a spirit of co-operation. The importance of the 'on-going' nature of the relationship will become clear when the individual issues are discussed.

With this need to avoid 'taking sides' and thereby souring the relationship and the time and expense involved in taking legal advice and remedies, it was not surprising to find relatively little use of contractual remedies and almost none of formal dispute-settlement procedures such as a court hearing or an arbitration. It would be a mistake however to assume that contract law has very little relevance. Firstly, it is always in the background: contract law may not be mentioned but the parties probably know in general what the legal position is and may adjust their attitudes accordingly. As one sales manager put it: 'it is an umbrella under which we operate'. But secondly we hope to show that while non-legal factors and extra-contractual devices do commonly reduce the need to use contract law, there are certain problems which for one reason or another are not infrequently dealt with by contract planning and sometimes by the use of contractual remedies . . .

NOTES

1. Although this study suggests that some businesses make only limited use of contract law, it must be remembered that it was studying only a small sample from one industry. Other trades may well demonstrate a much

more 'legalistic' approach: for instance, a glance into Lloyd's Reports, which concentrate on commercial cases, suggests that businesses in some commodity trades and in the charter markets litigate much more regularly—frequently taking points that lack any real merit in order to escape unprofitable contracts (see below, p 452). The contracts seem to have been planned in quite some detail, using forms similar to those reproduced in chapter 3. (Possible explanations for this are explored below, p 627.)

2. There does not seem to have been any systematic study of what contract cases the courts in this country are actually handling. Indeed the only figures in which the cases are broken down by subject matter relate to the House of Lords. These show an interesting contrast to the Australian High Court.

'An Australian Contract Law?' by Ellinghaus (1989) 1 J of Contract Law 13, 19–20

The *important* differences between one country's law and another's, particularly in a field as ancient as contract law, are not the divergencies of doctrine. Rather, the autonomous quality of a nation's case-law lies in the 'shape' in which it is cast by the particular situations brought before its courts. It will cause no surprise to Australian contract lawyers to learn that by far the most litigated contract before the High Court from its inception to 1986 has been that of sale of land.[1] The most litigated contract before the House of Lords in the same period (1904–86) although by a much smaller margin, was the charterparty.[2] These contracts both continue respectively to lead the field before each tribunal.[3] It must be the case that a law of contract devised by a court most often confronted with one type of contract will differ from that devised by a court most often confronted with another type of contract. A court of ultimate appeal which draws on its own precedents in the development of a particular body of doctrine will naturally be influenced by the data most often placed before it. The recurrence of certain issues and contexts results in corresponding accumulations of doctrine at certain points, the disposition of which determines the 'shape' of the whole. Thus the suggestion has been plausibly made that the Australian High Court has been more inclined to grant equitable relief in contracts than the House of Lords because 'we are not an international commercial or maritime centre'. But the difference in shape between Australian and English contract law can as yet be perceived only dimly, precisely because of the veiling effect of constant reference to English decisions.

Footnotes

1 Of 718 reported High Court cases arising from contract disputes (forming nearly 12% of a total of about 6100 reported cases) an astonishing 493, or 68%, concerned the sale of land. The next most litigated contracts were (percentage of total in brackets): sale of goods (11.5%); construction (6.8%); insurance (6.4%) [marine insurance in 13% of these cases]; employment (4.6%); sale of business (3.9%). Only 2% of High Court cases concerned charterparties; only 2.4% contracts of carriage.

2 Of 593 reported House of Lords cases arising from contract disputes (forming nearly 20% of a total of about 3000 reported cases) 46, or nearly 8% concerned charterparties. The next most litigated contracts were: carriage (7.3%); insurance (6.6%) [marine insurance in 56% of these cases]; sale of goods (5.2%); construction (5.2%); employment (4.4%). Only 1.5% of House of Lords cases concerned the sale of land.

3 In the decade 1975–85 the most litigated contracts were: High Court, sale of land (34%); construction (10%); rent (7.5%); mortgages (7%); insurance (6%); restraints (6%); House of Lords, charterparties (20%); carriage (14%); sale of goods (14%); sale of land (12%); rent (12%).

NOTES

1. There can be little doubt that the nature of the cases coming before the House of Lords and the other superior courts has done much to 'shape'

English law (see eg below, p 430). The famous American commercial lawyer Karl Llewellyn said that he never understood English contract law until he opened Lloyd's Reports.

2. The study of the work of the Wisconsin Supreme Court by Friedman has already been mentioned (above, p. 63). He shows how the cases changed in nature over the three periods he studied.

'Contract Law in America' by Friedman (1965), pp 11–12, 186–187, 189–190, 217

This study explores contract law and contract behavior as revealed in the opinions of the Wisconsin Supreme Court and the work of some other agencies of Wisconsin government, especially the Wisconsin legislature. . . .

The decisions of the Wisconsin Supreme Court on contract questions form the basic material of the study. These cases have been drawn from three periods. Period I covers the time between the organization of Wisconsin Territory (1836) and the outbreak of the Civil War (1861); the study embraces all reported contract decisions during this span of years. This period is significant in that it marks the beginning of Wisconsin's functioning legal system; it also coincides with the 'frontier' period in the state, a period which had just about ended at the time of the Civil War. For Period II, 1905–1915, the cases were drawn from the years 1905–1907, and 1913. This period is equidistant in time between Periods I and III; more important, it provides a sample of legal materials drawn from the age of the Progressives in Wisconsin. This was a time in which the consequences of a maturing economic system and the effects of the post-Civil War industrialization and urbanization of the state had been strongly felt, and had called forth a set of major legal and social responses which reached a kind of climax during the days of the La Follette Progressives. For Period III (the decade of the 1950's), the cases were drawn from the years 1955–1958. The major characteristics of this period, on the threshold of the present, will be known to most readers: the post-World War II economic boom, the growth of the metropolitan areas, the cold war, the continuance of the big government of wartime and depression, and an ever increasing unification of the country through mass communications and transport. In Periods II and III, the volume of decisions of the Court was heavier than in Period I, and reporting was more complete. For these two periods, it was necessary to use a sample (large but limited) in order to examine the materials with the necessary intensity.

Within each period the cases were analyzed and tabulated according to their underlying fact-situations and their use of legal doctrines. The total number of tabulated cases comes to 553. Intensive use was made of the briefs and records of the cases as well. Unfortunately, for Period I most of these have been lost; for Periods II and III the records were full and invaluable. Within each period some examination was also made of non-contract cases, which shed incidental light on major topics and helped place the contract cases in perspective, ie, in relation to the general flow of appellate court business. . . .

In Period I, economic theory was valued as a statement of appropriate means to ends grounded in general notions of the common good. The end which enlisted widest loyalty in nineteenth-century Wisconsin was economic growth. People felt that this end would be best served by legal arrangements which legitimized and encouraged the maximum exercise of private will. But economic growth was the end, rather than some abstract ideal of freedom of private enterprise from public interference. Positive use of law in the economy—land grants to subsidize the building of canals and railroads are a good example—was widely approved where this use of law seemed likely to promote economic development. Abstraction, then, had to give way whenever it interfered with a greater goal.

In general, however, Period I was the age of abstraction. Abstraction was not simply a tool of the law; it also reflected the actual state of the economy. It was fact, not theory, that land was often bought and sold as a colorless commodity. It was fact, not theory, that the residents of Wisconsin were mobile men, not rooted to a particular community or to ancient customs which fixed persons from birth with a given social status. It was fact, not theory, that the economy was in a state of rapid growth. Opportunities were not limited by all the built-in and conservative values which inhere in a locality of age-old settlement, whose cultural shape has been decisively molded by existing social patterns.

As the economy matured, these factual underpinnings of abstraction weakened; and the weakness of abstraction as a theory was reflected in the work of both the court and the legislature. The decay of the abstract rules of the law of contract has as one of its sources the decay of those conditions which lent strong support to abstraction in pioneer Wisconsin. But the weakening of abstraction cannot be attributed only to the differences within the state between its first age of growth and a more economically mature generation. Nor can the argument be pressed too far that the many derogations from contract abstraction (particularly the legislative derogations) were necessary to maintain the social system presupposed by abstraction. In Period II, the revolt against the full sweep of the competitive system was strong enough to indicate that it must have had broad roots in contemporary ideas and attitudes. It affected all classes of society. The urban workers expressed their opinions through unions, strikes, and boycotts. Big businesses formed 'trusts'. The farmers joined co-operative movements and raised hell along with corn. The middle-class tradesmen, the retailers, and the wholesalers spawned great numbers of national, state, and local 'associations' of one form or another, responding to the same hunger for unity and standardized strength. . . .

The economic struggle, so far as it was viewed by the unsophisticated, now centered not over position in the race to develop the economy, but over the status quo—a struggle to exact a greater share in existing product, existing wealth. If conservatives decided that freedom of contract and laissez faire were God-given rights, it was in order to stave off the urban poor who would storm the citadels of prosperity. The worker and the farmer tended to deny the truth of the free market altogether; it did not give them the fair share they deserved. . . .

The effect of these grand movements of public opinion and of the critical facts of economic life—the interdependence of human relationships, the growth of technology, the increasing industrial cast of economic life—was deeply felt by the law of contract. On the legislative side, the ambit within which the law of contract was allowed to operate was increasingly narrowed. Occupational licensing was only one symptom. Commodity legislation, for example, reflected technological advance, judgments concerning inequality of bargaining power (between producer and consumer), humanitarian impulses toward state action of a kind which presupposed an economically mature community, and not least of all, the attempt of 'reputable' producers forcefully to insure a rationalized and standardized market through invocation of the power of the state. . . .

The number of cases which arose out of personal, non-business situations rather than in pure market transactions also illustrated the increasing use of contract law, not for purposes of policing an abstract system, but for solving disputes of unique particularity. The docket affected deeply the court's mode of handling its cases. The heavy use of such malleable concepts as waiver and estoppel shows how the court, faced with inherited rules, but with facts which looked the other way, was inclined to use these formulae of escape from the rigors of abstraction. Concepts such as fraud and mistake, the doctrine of specific performance, the permutation of the rule of *Hadley v Baxendale*—all these illustrate the court's retreat from abstraction, its growing interest in the precise and particular facts of the immediate case.

The court's interest in the unique situation before it was only heightened in Period III. . . .

TABLE III. Wisconsin Contract Cases by Fact-Category

	Period I No.	Period II No.	Period III No.	Total
1. Land	54	46	22	122
2. Labor	31	61	34	126
3. Sales	30	32	12	74
4. Merchandise	12	15	4	31
5. Insurance	8	15	9	32
6. Business ventures	11	16	10	37
7. Credit	31	14	8	53
8. Government	15	12	6	33
9. Public utilities	4	5	1	10
10. Arbitration	8	5	3	16
11. Miscellaneous	2	6	3	11
12. Testamentary	—	—	8	8
	206	227	120	553

NOTES

1. The docket of the Wisconsin Supreme Court is very different to that of the House of Lords, and one would not necessarily expect contract litigation to be performing even broadly similar functions in two legal

systems which have developed in very different cultures. But the move that Friedman notes from abstraction to particularity has also been noted in this country: see Atiyah, *From Principles to Pragmatism* (1978).

2. Friedman and Ellinghaus look only at the cases in the highest courts. These, of course, are responsible for much of the doctrinal developments in the law, but to get anything like an accurate picture of the ways in which contract disputes are adjudicated it would be necessary to look at all courts—and, of course, at all the cases, whether reported or not. The cases which are selected for reporting because they raise some interesting point of legal principle are not an accurate guide to what the courts are actually handling. In addition, in this country it would also be essential to look at a mass of 'third party adjudication' that is hidden from public view because it is conducted before arbitrators.

'The adjudication of commercial disputes and the legal system in modern England' by Ferguson (1980) 7 Brit J Law & Society 141, 142–148, 151–154

The legal system offers participants in commerce a mechanism for the determination of commercial disputes, namely trial. In the mid-nineteenth century that still meant trial by jury.

The most extensive evidence of the commercial community's attitude to jury trial is to be found in the traces left by the tribunals of commerce movement, whose grievances and goals were articulated by the Tribunals of Commerce Association, chambers of commerce and individual businessmen before a House of Commons Select Committee in 1871 and the Judicature Commission in 1874. The movement was an amalgam of businessmen's demands for three things:

(*i*)   A quicker and cheaper administration of justice.

(*ii*) A less capricious decision-making procedure.

(*iii*) The ascription of priority in adjudication to norms based on commercial usage. [Discussion of this point is omitted—eds]

Quicker and cheaper justice. A leading complaint was that litigation for sums just beyond the scope of the County Courts' jurisdiction was not worth the candle, the expenditure risked being disproportionate to the prospective gain. Even in more or less straightforward cases of default the uncertainties of legal process were said to be such that one could not be sure of recouping one's outlay. According to Jacob Behrens, a Bradford export merchant, if a defaulter was pressed

> . . . the rogue has a very ready answer. He says, 'Bring an action.' I have myself been dared to bring actions, and my solicitor has said, 'It is not worth your while or expense; submit to it.'

Less capricious decision-making. In the hearings before the Judicature Commission in 1874 witness after witness complained about the extreme uncertainty of the jury system. The gist of it was: 'The verdict of a jury in commercial cases is as fair a subject for gambling as horse-racing.' The trouble with juries, according to the proponents of tribunals of commerce, was that they tended to lack the commercial acumen and experience which would enable them to understand the evidence: as a result, verdicts contrary to the weight of the evidence were not unusual. . . .

[I]n the decades after the passage of the Judicature Acts of the mid-1870s the option of doing without the jury was more and more often taken by commercial litigants so that by 1913 their cases were largely tried by judges alone. . . . So commercial litigants solved the jury problem by voting with their feet.

In some sections of the commercial community however, particularly in the commodity trades, the primary response to the problems which actuated the tribunals of commerce movement has been a resort to non-forensic decision-making procedures—that is, arbitration.

The present-day position is that arbitration is firmly established as the most adjudicative mechanism. Overall it has been estimated that London arbitration bodies handle about 10,000 disputes *per annum*. All the commodity associations have 'long-established arbitration tribunals, both first instance and appellate, to which disputes under commodity contracts are referred.' Such arbitrations are predominantly international in character, reflecting the worldwide currency of the English standard contract forms with their arbitration clauses. The arbitration machinery of the London commodity associations handles about three or four thousand cases annually. In some trades, however, for example, grain, quality disputes no longer predominate. This change reflects modern market conditions: 'the hazards involved in postwar trading, such as the sudden imposition of export restrictions and duties, and violent fluctuations of price, have occasioned . . . a considerable increase in the number of "technical" arbitrations.' Currency fluctuations and the involvement of state trading companies whose governments are sometimes short of foreign exchange have also played their part.

Arbitration in London is also the usual adjudicative procedure for disputes arising on charterparties made on the Baltic Exchange, the world's leading freight market. Some 70% or 80% of the world's maritime arbitrations, involving shipbroking and chartering disputes, are held in London. The members of the London Maritime Arbitrator's Association thus account for perhaps 4,000 arbitrations each year.

This can be contrasted with the volume of business handled by the forensic alternative to commercial arbitration, the Commercial Court, with its abbreviated procedure and manning by judges whose experience lies on the commercial law side. In the 1950s a couple of dozen or so cases were tried annually in the Commercial Court. In the later 1970s there was a marked increase in its caseload, over 200 actions being brought in 1976 and over 100 annually being tried. Even so, it is clear that in purely quantitative terms the Commercial Court plays a relatively small part in commercial dispute adjudication.

The commercial preference for arbitration over trial in a court of law is obviously attributable to some extent to its speed and cheapness. On the whole arbitration is still quicker and less expensive, although a typical maritime arbitration now costs over £2,000 and takes about a year. But its *decisive* virtue is that arbitrators are chosen for their personal knowledge and experience of the trade in which the dispute has arisen so that they have the requisite technical expertise and a detailed grasp of commercial practice. This point is borne out by the reception given to section 4 of the Administration of Justice Act 1970. The 1970 Act authorised Commercial Court judges to accept appointment as arbitrators in commercial disputes. The idea was that commercial disputants would appreciate the opportunity to dispense with the formality and publicity of an ordinary trial while nevertheless securing the juridical expertise of a judge. The scheme has not proved attractive, having scarcely been used at all. And yet it is inexpensive to use, the statutory fees being lower than those usual in many ordinary arbitrations. The best explanation is that judge-arbitrators cannot be relied upon to have the intimate familiarity with the trade or the market which characterises the professional or semi-professional arbitrator . . .

Notwithstanding the developments sketched in previous sections, the English courts occupy ground of strategic importance in the process of commercial dispute adjudication by virtue of their powers of judicial review in relation to arbitrations. Questions of fact are within the exclusive domain of the arbitrators but the Arbitration Act, 1889 and its successor in effect enabled either 'arbitrant' to appeal against the arbitrators' decision on a point of law, by means of the special case procedure. In *Czarnikow v Roth, Schmidt* (1922), a contract incorporating the rules of the Refined Sugar Association came before the Court of Appeal. The Association's rules expressly purported to negate the Courts' power of review. But the judges held that this was legally impossible: their power to review was entrenched.

. . . The virtue of judicial review for a company like Tradax, one of the world's leading dry-cargo charterers, was recently put thus:

> [It has been] the essential factor in developing English law into the most sophisticated and highly developed maritime and commercial law in the world. We further consider that the existence of this right of appeal has ensured that English arbitrators decide cases in accordance with law and not in accordance with the necessarily subjective notions of *ex aequo et bono*; [and] that this has led to the certainty and . . . predictability which is essential to a trading company like our own which must have a solid foundation of clearly fixed rules on which to base its everyday trading decisions and assessment of risks.

Some businesses at least, therefore, value the exegetical function of judicial review. . . .

Nonetheless the circumstances whose conjunction eventuated in the passage of the Arbitration Act 1979 show that judicial review—at any rate while undertaken by means of the special case procedure—cannot be regarded as an unalloyed benefit to commerce. The Act was passed as a response to apprehensions that London's standing as leading centre of international commercial arbitration was endangered by certain modern developments. On the one hand the economic climate of the seventies—high inflation, high interest rates and unstable exchange rates—had made it worthwhile to some companies to mobilise the special case procedure, not to raise *bona fide* points of law, but to postpone the evil day of payment. In the words of one judge, 'success in litigation is no longer measured simply by the decision whether or not a party is liable to pay. The problems of liquidity are such that an immediate judgment, or the ability to stave off the day of reckoning, can make the difference between survival and insolvency.' The point was reached where some major companies began to delete English arbitration clauses.

On the other hand there was the fact that the arbitration work from supranational development contracts was not on the whole finding its way to London. One reason was that governments or government agencies are often party to these contracts, and 'their desire to avoid submitting to the jurisdiction of foreign courts is equalled by the private parties' unwillingness to litigate in local courts, in which the local governments may be given a friendlier reception.' But arbitration in London on the basis of English law would have entailed submission to the review jurisidiction of the English courts.

. . . [A] compromise was enacted in the Arbitration Act 1979. By the Act the special case procedure is abolished, and in its place is substituted a streamlined system of appeals from reasoned awards, which is expected to place 'very grave obstacles in the way of those seeking unmeritoriously to avoid meeting their just obligations.' At the same time, contracting out of judicial review by means of an 'exclusion agreement' is authorised in respect of supranational contracts, but not, broadly speaking in respect of maritime, insurance and commodity contracts. . . .

The emphasis so far has been on the use of contracts and contract law by business and commercial interests. Contract law may also be used by employees and by consumers. Although we shall see examples of each succeeding in contract litigation, it is likely that the 'litigation rates' for each category are very low. In 1982–1983 the National Consumer Council conducted a survey which concluded:

> In formal terms, the courts exist to resolve disputes of fact or law or to enable legal rights to be enforced. In real life, however, it is rare for consumers to go to court with disputes about goods. In our Consumer Concerns survey [1979–1980] amongst the population at large, there was not a single case of court action. Our latest survey confirms that very few consumers take this option. The strongest influence appeared to be the policy or resources of the individual advice centre. Out of nine questionnaires returned by clients of one centre, no fewer than three told us they had started proceedings. But this level of activity was quite exceptional . . .
>
> (*Buying problems* (1984), para 3.12.)

'Consumer redress mechanisms for poor-quality and defective products' by Ramsay (1981) 31 U of Toronto LJ 117, 134–136

Recent literature provides depressing reading for those consumers interested in mobilizing the legal system. The reactive nature of legal institutions means that consumers must expend significant transaction costs if they wish to use the court system. It is not surprising to find either that few consumers are willing or able to take their disputes to court or that the great majority of product-quality cases involve automobiles or mobile homes.

Law reformers have concentrated much of their effort on changes within the structure of the existing court system. Greater access to small claims courts and more extensive and effective private law remedies have been advocated and in some cases legislated. The focus has been primarily on dispute resolution and case-by-case adjudication of individual claims. Yet reformers have not adequately solved the fundamental problem of the difference between the competence of one-shotters and repeat-player organizations in effectively using the legal system.

The majority of civil litigation in Canada and the United States involves organizations suing individuals, primarily for default on debts. These cases are part of the bureaucratic process of debt collection, and the judgment (usually by default) of the court provides formal validity to a creditor's claims. Few of these cases could be classified as disputes about legal rules. Many of these organizations use the court system on a continuing basis. They are repeat players and thus have many strategic advantages over the one-shotter. An individual consumer, unless he is a lawyer or a self-appointed consumer advocate, is a one-shotter. Individuals suing organizations account for only 5% of civil litigation in Canada. Among the advantages of the repeat player are the ability to use 'advance intelligence' and 'structure transactions in advance' (the form contract), to develop 'expertise and access to specialists' such as lawyers, and to 'develop continuing relations with institutional incumbents' such as court personnel. They have 'the ability to play for rules as well as for immediate gain. It pays a recurrent litigant to expend resources in influencing the making of the relevant rules and avoiding unfavourable litigation outcomes through settlements.'

There is also a clear dichotomy between legal services provided to organizations and to individuals. This is reflected in the division within the legal profession between those who provide a limited range of services to individuals on an occasional basis and those who provide a far wider range of preventive and counselling services to organizations on a continuing basis.

It is becoming clear, therefore, that the disparity in the use of legal services and recourse to litigation is not simply a question of individual social status or income or of rich and poor individuals but is rather a disparity between organizations and individuals. For example, statistics indicate that organizations as plaintiffs tend to be represented more often by counsel than are individual defendants.

One conclusion from these studies, therefore, is the importance of organization as a strategy for reform if consumers are to become 'effective players of the law game'. Changing the rules either at the legislative or the judicial level may have little effect if there are not competent parties capable of fully taking advantage of the benefit of the rules. . . .

Section 2
Enforceable types of promise

CHAPTER 7
Consideration

In the first chapter we saw that contractual liability is based on the breach of a promise, but that not every promise will be enforced even if it was meant as a binding commitment: in particular, the law of contract appears to be concerned with enforcing promised exchanges, and unless the promise is made by deed (see below, pp 119–127), the promise must be supported by consideration if it is to be enforceable.

(a) Definitions of consideration

A valuable consideration, in the sense of the law, may consist either in some right, interest, profit or benefit accruing to one party or some forbearance, detriment, loss or responsibility, given, suffered or undertaken by the other.

(*Currie v Misa* (1875) LR 10 Exch 153, 162.)

Consideration means something which is of some value in the eye of the law, moving from the plaintiff; it may be some detriment to the plaintiff or some benefit to the defendant, but at all events it must be moving from the plaintiff.

(Patteson J in *Thomas v Thomas* (1842) (below, p 114).)

An act or forbearance of the one party, or the promise thereof, is the price for which the promise of the other is bought, and the promise thus given for value is enforceable.

(Pollock, *Principles of Contract* (13th edn) p 133, approved by Lord Dunedin in *Dunlop v Selfridge* (1915) (below, p 804).)

(1) To constitute consideration, a performance or a return promise must be bargained for.
(2) A performance or return promise is bargained for if it is sought by the promisor in exchange for his promise and is given by the promisee in exchange for that promise.
(3) The performance may consist of
    (a) an act other than a promise, or
    (b) a forbearance, or
    (c) the creation, modification or destruction of a legal relation.

(Restatement, *Contracts 2d*, s 71. The Restatement of contract is one of nine Restatements produced by the American Law Institute. In the US, contracts are governed by state law, so that there is not one law but fifty laws. The Institute was founded in 1923 'to promote the clarification and simplification of the law . . .'; its membership includes judges, practitioners and law professors. The final draft of the first Restatement of contracts was approved in 1932. The Reporter, Williston, stated that 'the endeavour in the Restatement is to restate the law as it is, not as new law' (3 ALI Proceedings 159), but several of its sections were remarkable innovations, as we shall see later. As a statement of law it has no binding force, but it has been extremely influential, many of its sections being adopted by state courts as representing the law. A revised version was begun in 1962 and was published in final form

in 1981 as the Restatement Second; its Reporters were Braucher and later
Farnsworth.)

NOTES

1. The descriptions of consideration given in *Currie v Misa* and *Thomas v Thomas* are often quoted but were almost certainly not meant as complete definitions, merely as sufficient to decide the points before the court. The newer definitions, Pollock and Restatement 2d, are more complete. It will be seen that they differ from the older ones in three ways. Firstly they do not speak of benefit and detriment but of an act or a return promise. Why this change in the formulation? In some types of contract the promise is not exchanged for any return undertaking by the promisee, but is to operate *if* the promisee performs a certain act which he may or may not do. For example a person selling his house usually promises his estate agent that if the agent introduces a person who buys the house, the seller will pay the agent a commission, but the agent does not (for obvious reasons) promise that he will find a buyer, nor does he necessarily promise that he will even look for one. If there is a promise only on one side, this is called a *unilateral* contract. The consideration for the seller's promise is the agent's act of introducing the purchaser (see further below, pp 187–188), and here there is no difficulty over describing the act as a benefit to the promisor and a detriment to the promisee. More commonly, however, each party makes promises to perform in the future, and the contract is *bilateral*. The consideration for each promise is said to be the promise received in return: thus in a contract to sell a book for £10, the seller's promise to deliver the book is consideration for the buyer's promise to pay the money, and vice versa. The contract is enforceable even if it is wholly 'executory' (ie neither party has yet performed), but is there any benefit or detriment to either party at that stage? See Atiyah, *Essays on Contract*, pp 191–192.

2. Secondly the newer definitions stress the act or the return promise, rather than whether this benefits the person making the promise which it is sought to enforce (the promisor) or is detrimental to the person seeking to enforce it (the promisee). The reasons for this change are less easy to explain. It is well established that there may be consideration even though the promisor appears to derive no benefit from the act or the performance of the promise. For instance, if Furmston promises in writing to guarantee a loan that Bishop intends to make to Beale, and on the strength of that promise Bishop lends money to Beale who fails to repay it, Furmston is liable even though he derived no benefit from the arrangement. (The Statute of Frauds 1677, s 4 makes Furmston's promise unenforceable unless evidenced in writing. See below, pp 131–133. Do you see why there might be thought a need to protect the promisor in this situation?) Whether there must always be some detriment to the promisee is more controversial and we shall consider the question in more detail later (below, pp 126–127). The newer definitions avoid these difficulties by speaking of act or promise.

3. Thirdly, the newer definitions stress that the promise must be exchanged for the act or return promise. As we shall see, this reflects the language of the English decisions, at least in this century, but whether it reflects the actual outcomes is more controversial.

(b) Sufficient consideration

Neither Pollock's definition nor Restatement 2d specify what act or forbearance, actual or promised, will suffice. The older definitions' use of 'benefit' and 'detriment' may seem more helpful, but everything depends on what has 'value in the eye of the law'. It is often said that consideration need not be adequate (ie there will be consideration even if the values of the things exchanged are in no way equivalent) but it must have some economic value (eg Treitel, p 67. See further below, p 113).

It is worth stressing that in the vast majority of commercial contracts there is no problem over consideration when the contract is made. This is because the parties will have agreed on an exchange, say of goods or services for money. In the normal course of events the things to be exchanged will be more or less equivalent in value, but even if they are not—for instance if goods are sold at much more or much less than their normal price—the doctrine of consideration will be satisfied. Because the consideration does not have to 'adequate', a marginal financial advantage can be good consideration for a promise. Thus in *Charnock v Liverpool Corpn* [1968] 3 All ER 473, [1968] 1 WLR 1498, CA the owner of a car which had been damaged in an accident took it to the defendants for repairs, which were to be paid for by his insurers. The defendants were dilatory in carrying out the repairs. The Court of Appeal held that the defendants had impliedly promised to carry out the repairs in a reasonable time: the consideration for this promise was 'leaving his car with the repairers'. Occasionally, of course, promises are made even in the commercial world with nothing being asked for in return: for an example see the tax case of *Dickinson v Abel* [1969] 1 All ER 484, [1969] 1 WLR 295. Here the promise will be without consideration and therefore unenforceable unless made by deed. There are also a number of commercial situations which give rise to difficulties over consideration, and we shall examine these shortly. The other great source of difficulties over consideration is cases which are 'marginal' in relation to normal contracts.

(i) Intangible returns

The promisor may feel natural love and affection toward the promisee, which will be fulfilled to some extent by the promise. It is firmly established that this is not sufficient consideration: *Bret v JS* (1600) Cro Eliz 756. Nor is the fact that the promisee will feel some moral obligation to the promisor in return.

In *The Atlantic Baron* (see below, p 639) the builders of a tanker, faced with increased costs because of a currency devaluation, demanded a price increase from the purchasers. The latter were concerned to have the tanker delivered on time and agreed to pay the increase 'in order to maintain an amicable relationship'. Mocatta J held that this could not be consideration.

White v Bluett (1853) 23 LJ Ex 36, Court of Exchequer

Bluett had given his father a promissory note (see note 1 below) for money his father had lent him. When sued on the note by his father's executor he pleaded that he had had just grounds to complain about his father's distribution of property among his children; and that his father, admitting this, had promised that if Bluett stopped complaining he would discharge Bluett from liability on the note.

Pollock CB. . . . Looking at the words merely, there is some foundation for the argument, and, following the words only, the conclusion may be arrived at. It is said, the son had a right to an equal distribution of his father's property, and did complain to his father because he had not an equal share, and said to him, I will cease to complain if you will not sue upon this note. Whereupon the father said, if you will promise me not to complain I will give up the note. In reality, there was no consideration whatever. . . . The son had no right to complain, for the father might make what distribution of his property he liked; and the son's abstaining from doing what he had no right to do can be no consideration.

[Parke and Alderson BB also held the plea bad and Platt B concurred.]

Judgment for the plaintiff.

NOTES

1. A promissory note is a promise to pay contained in a written document: an example, and a description of its legal characteristics, will be found below, p 837. The main point is that a promissory note is a 'negotiable instrument', that is, it can be passed to a third party by endorsement, and the third party can then sue on the note. If the note is payable to bearer, delivery to the third party is sufficient: the commonest example of a promissory note payable to bearer is a bank note.
2. *White v Bluett* involves the alleged discharge of an existing obligation, rather than the creation of a new contract, but the traditional rule is that a promise to discharge a debt must equally be supported by consideration. See further below, Chapter 27.
3. The point that it cannot be consideration to promise not to do that which you have no right to do seems sensible enough (and compare the converse, promising to do what you already have a duty to do, see below, pp 102–107). It would be undesirable to say there was consideration if Furmston promised Beale £10 if Beale would stop stealing Furmston's goats. But when Pollock says the son had no right to complain, is he using right in this sense? See Hohfeld, *Fundamental Legal Conceptions* (1946).

Hamer v Sidway 124 NY 538, 27 NE 256 (Court of Appeals, New York, 1891)

Parker J. The question which provoked the most discussion by counsel on this appeal, and which lies at the foundation of plaintiff's asserted right of recovery, is whether by virtue of a contract defendant's testator, William E. Story, became indebted to his nephew, William E. Story, 2d, on his twenty-first birhday in the sum of $5,000. The trial court found as a fact that 'on the 20th day of March, 1869, . . . William E. Story agreed to and with William E. Story, 2d, that if he would refrain from drinking liquor using tobacco, swearing, and playing cards or billiards for money until [he] should become twenty-one years of age, then he, the said William E. Story, would at that time pay him, the said William E. Story, 2d, the sum of $5,000 for such refraining, to which the said William E. Story, 2d, agreed', and that he 'in all things fully performed his part of said agreement'.

[The nephew assigned any right of action he might have to the plaintiff. The defendant was William E. Story's executor.]

The defendant contends that the contract was without consideration to support it, and therefore invalid. He asserts that the promisee, by refraining from the use of liquor and tobacco, was not harmed, but benefited; that that which he did was best for him to do, independently of his uncle's promise,—and insists that it follows that, unless the promisor was benefited, the contract was without consideration,—a contention which, if well founded, would seem to leave open for controversy in many cases whether that which the promisee did or omitted to do was in fact of such benefit to him as to leave no consideration to support the enforcement of the promisor's agreement. Such a rule could not be tolerated, and is without foundation in the law.

. . . [T]he promisee used tobacco, occasionally drank liquor, and he had a legal right to do so. That right he abandoned for a period of years upon the strength of the promise of the testator that for such forbearance he would give him $5,000. We need not speculate on the effort which may have been required to give up the use of those stimulants. It is sufficient that he restricted his lawful freedom of action within certain prescribed limits upon the faith of his uncle's agreement, and now, having fully performed the conditions imposed, it is of no moment whether such performance actually proved a benefit to the promisor, and the court will not inquire into it; but, were it a proper subject of inquiry, we see nothing in this record that would permit a determination that the uncle was not benefited in a legal sense.

Judgment for the plaintiff.

NOTES

1. This American case is not of course binding in this country, but it is usually assumed to represent English law (eg Atiyah, *Essays on Contract*, p 195).
2. Did the nephew suffer any detriment, or the uncle gain any benefit, in *Hamer v Sidway*?
3. Suppose the nephew in *Hamer* already had religious beliefs which prevented him from indulging in any of the things he agreed to forego, would the outcome be different? Compare the judgment with *Arrale v Costain Civil Engineering Ltd* [1976] 1 Lloyd's Rep 98, 106: 'It is no consideration to refrain from a course of conduct which it was never intended to pursue.' (This case involved the validity of a 'release' of a claim for compensation for personal injuries signed by a workman. The majority of the Court of Appeal decided that the release did not affect the workman's claim to damages at common law as a matter of construction of the document, but all three judges appear to have agreed on this consideration point. Whether it was fully argued is not clear. How often will it be possible to prove that the relevant course of conduct would not be pursued under any circumstances whatever?)
4. Of what economic value were the actions in *Hamer*? If the nephew in *Hamer* could not sue, how could uncles persuade their nephews to live lives free of vice?
5. If there was an action of economic value in *Hamer*, why did the claim in *White v Bluett* fail? Could the court's perception of whether the nephew's or son's forbearance constituted adequate consideration have been influenced by the nature of the conduct foregone?
6. Suppose that performance of a contract between A Ltd and B Ltd unexpectedly becomes much more expensive for A to perform, but B refuses to increase the payment although it is now making a very large profit. A complains publicly that B is a harsh employer and to protect its reputation B agrees to pay A 10% extra if A will stop. Is there consideration?

(ii) Compromise of a claim

If I agree to compromise a valid claim for an uncertain amount, or a genuinely doubtful claim, there is no doubt that the promise to drop the claim is consideration for the promise to pay the sum offered in settlement (see *Haigh v Brooks* (1839) 10 Ad & El 309, and *Horton v Horton (No 2)* [1961] 1 QB 215). What if my claim was demonstrably bound to fail?

Wade v Simeon (1846) 2 CB 548, 135 ER 1061, Court of Common Pleas

Tindal CJ. The only question now remaining is upon the demurrer [see note below] to the fourth plea. I am of opinion that the fourth plea is a good and valid plea, on general demurrer. The declaration alleges that the plaintiff had commenced an action against the defendant in the Exchequer, to recover two sums of 1300*l* and 700*l* respectively, which action was about to be tried, and that, in consideration that the plaintiff would forbear proceeding in that action, until the 14th of December then next, the defendant promised the plaintiff that he would on that day pay the money, with interest, and costs; that the plaintiff, confiding in the defendant's promise, forbore prosecuting the action, and stayed the proceedings until the day named; but that the defendant did not pay the money or the costs. The fourth plea states that the plaintiff never had any cause of action against the defendant in respect of the subject-matter of the action in the court of Exchequer, which he, the plaintiff, at the time of the commencement of the said action, and thence until the time of the making of the promise in the first count mentioned, well knew. By demurring to that plea, the plaintiff admits that he had no cause of action against the defendant in the action therein mentioned, and that he knew it. It appears to me, therefore, that he is estopped from saying that there was any valid consideration for the defendant's promise. It is almost contra bonos mores, and certainly contrary to all the principles of natural justice, that a man should institute proceedings against another, when he is conscious that he has no good cause of action. In order to constitute a binding promise, the plaintiff must shew a good consideration, something beneficial to the defendant, or detrimental to the plaintiff. Detrimental to the plaintiff it cannot be, if he has no cause of action: and beneficial to the defendant it cannot be; for, in contemplation of law, the defence upon such an admitted state of facts must be successful, and the defendant will recover costs, which must be assumed to be a full compensation for all the legal damage he may sustain. The consideration, therefore, altogether fails. On the part of the plaintiff it has been urged, that the cases cited for the defendant were not cases where actions had already been brought, but only cases of promises to forbear commencing proceedings. I must, however, confess, that, if that were so, I do not see that it would make any substantial difference . . .

Here, . . . there was no uncertainty: the defendant asserts, and the plaintiff admits, that there never was any cause of action in the original suit, and that the plaintiff knew it. I therefore think the fourth plea affords a very good answer, and that the defendant is entitled to judgment thereon.

[Maule, Cresswell and Erle JJ also held that the defendant was entitled to judgment on the fourth plea.]

NOTE

A demurrer is a plea which accepts the truth of the facts alleged by the other party, but objects that they do not disclose a cause of action, or have the legal effect contended for.

Cook v Wright (1861) 1 B & S 559, 121 ER 822, Queen's Bench

After a verdict for the defendant in an action on three promissory notes, the plaintiffs moved that the evidence did not show want of consideration for the notes, and that they were entitled to a verdict.

Blackburn J delivered the judgment of Cockburn CJ, Wightman J and himself. . . .

In this case it appeared on the trial that the defendant was agent for a Mrs Bennett, who was non-resident owner of houses in a district subject to a local Act. Works had been done in the adjoining street by the Commissioners for executing the Act, the expenses of which, under the provisions of their Act, they charged on the owners of the adjoining houses. Notice had been given to the defendant, as if he had himself been owner of the houses, calling on him to pay the proportion chargeable in respect of them. He attended at a Board meeting of the Commissioners, and objected both to the amount and nature of the charge, and also stated that he was not the owner of the houses, and that Mrs Bennett was. He was told that, if he did not pay, he would be treated as one Goble had been. It appeared that Goble had refused to pay a sum charged against him as owner of some houses, and the Commissioners had taken legal proceedings against him, and he had then submitted and paid, with costs. In the result it was agreed between the Commissioners and the defendant that the amount charged upon him should be reduced, and that time should be given to pay it in three instalments; he gave three promissory notes for the three instalments; the first was duly honoured; the others were not, and were the subject of the present action. At the trial it appeared that the defendant was not in fact owner of the houses. As agent for the owner he was not personally liable under the Act. In point of law, therefore, the Commissioners were not entitled to claim the money from him; but no case of deceit was alleged against them. It must be taken that the Commissioners honestly believed that the defendant was personally liable, and really intended to take legal proceedings against him, as they had done against Goble. The defendant, according to his own evidence, never believed that he was liable in law, but signed the notes in order to avoid being sued as Goble was. Under these circumstances the substantial question reserved . . . was whether there was any consideration for the notes. We are of opinion that there was.

. . . Here there was no mistake on the part of the defendant either of law or fact. What he did was not merely the making an erroneous account stated, or promising to pay a debt for which he mistakenly believed himself liable. It appeared on the evidence that he believed himself not to be liable; but he knew that the plaintiffs thought him liable, and would sue him if he did not pay, and in order to avoid the expence and trouble of legal proceedings against himself he agreed to a compromise; and the question is, whether a person who has given a note as a compromise of a claim honestly made on him, and which but for that compromise would have been at once brought to a legal decision, can resist the payment of the note on the ground that the original claim thus compromised might have been successfully resisted. . . . it was argued before us that . . . though where the plaintiff has actually issued a writ against a defendant, a compromise honestly made is binding, yet the same compromise, if made before the writ actually issues, though the litigation is impending, is void.

We agree that unless there was a reasonable claim on the one side, which it was bona fide intended to pursue, there would be no ground for a compromise; but we cannot agree that (except as a test of the reality of the claim in fact) the issuing of a writ is essential to the validity of the compromise. The position of the parties must necessarily be altered in every case of compromise, so that, if the question is afterwards opened up, they cannot be replaced as they were before the compromise. The plaintiff may be in a less favourable position for renewing his litigation, he must be at an additional trouble and expence in again getting up his case, and he may no longer be able to produce the evidence which would have proved it originally. Besides, though he may not in point of law be bound to refrain from enforcing his rights against third persons during the continuance of the compromise, to which they are not parties, yet practically the effect of the compromise must be to prevent his doing so. For instance, in the present case, there can be no doubt that the practical effect of the compromise must have been to induce the Commissioners to refrain from taking proceedings against Mrs Bennett, the real owner of the houses, while the notes given by the defendant, her agent, were running; though the compromise might have afforded no ground of defence had such proceedings been resorted to. It is this detriment to the party consenting to a compromise arising from the necessary alteration in his position which, in our opinion, forms the real consideration for the promise, and not the technical and almost illusory consideration arising from the extra costs of litigation. The real consideration therefore depends, not on the actual commencement of a suit, but on the reality of the claim made and the bona fides of the compromise.

In the present case we think that there was sufficient consideration for the notes in the compromise made as it was.

NOTES

1. What distinction is there between these two cases? Isn't the defendant saved the trouble of legal proceedings irrespective of the good faith of the plaintiff? Is the court's perception again swayed by some policy consideration? What policy?
2. If a person brings a claim which he knows to be false against another who for some reason cannot wait for the action to be heard but pays up, the

latter may be able to recover the money under the doctrine of duress, see below, pp 638–647.

3. Should the test be the honesty of the plaintiff's claim, or its reasonableness?

(iii) Performance of a duty imposed by law

If the defendant promises to pay the plaintiff for performing an act which the plaintiff is already obliged to do as a matter of general law, it is hard to see that the defendant gets any additional benefit or that the plaintiff suffers any additional detriment. In the US this approach has often been applied quite rigidly: for example, in *Denney v Reppert* 432 SW2d 647 (Kentucky, 1968) employees of a bank which had been robbed gave information leading to the capture of the robbers, but they could not recover a promised reward.

In England there are some cases taking this line. One example is *Collins v Godefroy* (1831) 1 B&Ad 950, where it was held that a promise to pay a witness who had been subpoenaed six guineas for his trouble was without consideration. (Nowadays a subpoenaed witness must be given 'conduct money'). In *Glasbrook Bros Ltd v Glamorgan County Council* [1925] AC 270 it was assumed that this was the law; the actual decision was that the police had gone beyond the duty imposed on them by law when at a colliery owner's request they provided him with a garrison, and his promise to pay was binding. (See also *Harris v Sheffield United Football Club Ltd* [1988] QB 77, in which it was held that providing police at a football match was 'special police services', within section 15(1) of the Police Act 1964, for which the Club was required to pay.)

Other cases take a more flexible line, holding that performance of an existing public duty may be consideration if that would encourage performance of the duty. In *England v Davidson* (1840) 11 Ad&El 856, a police constable was held to be entitled to claim the reward offered for information he had given. Lord Denman CJ said: 'I think there may be services which the constable is not bound to render, and which he may therefore make the ground of a contract. We should not hold a contract to be against the policy of the law unless the grounds for so deciding were very clear.'

What do you think Denman's view would have been if the constable had flatly refused to give the information unless paid the reward—might that have been 'against the policy of the law'? Money which has been paid to an official who, without authority, has refused to perform his duty unless paid is recoverable in restitution, see Goff and Jones, *Law of Restitution* (3rd ed), pp 216–222.

Williams v Williams [1957] 1 All ER 305, Court of Appeal

Denning LJ. In the present case a wife claims sums due to her under a maintenance agreement. No evidence was called in the court below because the facts are agreed. The parties were married on Apr 25, 1945. They have no children. On Jan 24, 1952, the wife deserted the husband. On Mar 26, 1952, they signed the agreement now sued on, which has three clauses:

'(1) The husband will pay to the wife for her support and maintenance a weekly sum of £1 10s to be paid every four weeks during the joint lives of the parties so long as the wife shall lead a chaste life the first payment hereunder to be made on Apr 15, 1952. (2) The wife will out of the said weekly sum or otherwise support and maintain herself and will indemnify the husband against all debts to be incurred by her and will not in any way at any time hereafter pledge the husband's credit. (3) The wife shall not so long as the husband shall punctually make the payments hereby agreed to be commence or prosecute against the husband any matrimonial proceedings other than proceedings for dissolution of marriage but upon the failure of the husband to make the said weekly payments as and when the same become due the wife shall be at full liberty on her election to pursue all and every remedy in this regard either by enforcement of the provisions hereof or as if this agreement had not been made.'

So far as we know, the parties have remained apart ever since. On June 1, 1955, the husband petitioned for divorce, on the ground of his wife's desertion, and so on Oct 12, 1955, a decree nisi was made against her. On Dec 2, 1955, the decree was made absolute. In this action the wife claims maintenance at the rate of £1 10s a week under the agreement for a period from October, 1954, to October, 1955. The sum claimed is £30 5s 9d, which is the appropriate sum after the deduction of tax. The husband disputes the claim, on the ground that there was no consideration for his promise. Clause 2, he says, is worthless and cl 3 is unenforceable.

Let me first deal with cl 3. It is settled law that a wife, despite such a clause as cl 3, can make application to the magistrates or to the High Court for maintenance. If this wife had made such an application, the husband could have set up the fact of desertion as an answer to the claim, but he could not have set up cl 3 as a bar to the proceedings. The clause is void, and as such is no consideration to support the agreement: see *Bennett v Bennett*. Now let me deal with cl 2. The husband relies on the fact that his wife deserted him. If there had been a separation by consent, he agrees that the agreement would have been enforceable. In that case the husband would still be under a duty to maintain, and the sum of 30s a week would be assumed to be a quantification of a reasonable sum for her maintenance having regard to her own earning capacity. The ascertainment of a specific sum in place of an unascertained sum has always been held to be good consideration. So long as circumstances remained unchanged, it would be treated by the courts as binding on her and she could not recover more from him: see *National Assistance Board v Parkes*. In the present case the husband says that, as the wife deserted him, he was under no obligation to maintain her and she was not entitled to pledge his credit in any way. Clause 2 therefore gives him nothing and is valueless to him. The husband says that *Goodinson v Goodinson* is distinguishable because there was no finding in that case that the wife was in desertion, and, moreover, the wife promised to maintain the child as well as herself.

Now I agree that, in promising to maintain herself whilst she was in desertion, the wife was only promising to do that which she was already bound to do. Nevertheless, a promise to perform an existing duty is, I think, sufficient consideration to support a promise, so long as there is nothing in the transaction which is contrary to the public interest. Suppose that this agreement had never been made, and the wife had made no promise to maintain herself and did not do so. She might then have sought and received public assistance or have pledged her husband's credit with tradesmen; in which case the National Assistance Board might have summoned him before the magistrates, or the tradesmen might have sued him in the county court. It is true that he would have an answer to those claims because she was in desertion, but nevertheless he would be put to all the trouble, worry and expense of defending himself against them. By paying her 30s a week and taking this promise from her that she will maintain herself and will not pledge his credit, he has an added safeguard to protect himself from all this worry, trouble and expense. That is a benefit to him which is good consideration for his promise to pay maintenance. That was the view which appealed to the county court judge, and I must say that it appeals to me also.

There is another ground on which good consideration can be found. Although the wife was in desertion, nevertheless it must be remembered that desertion is never irrevocable. It was open to her to come back at any time. Her right to maintenance was not lost by the desertion. It was only suspended. If she made a genuine offer to return which he rejected, she would have been entitled to maintenance from him. She could apply to the magistrates or the High Court for an order in her favour. If she did so, however, whilst this agreement was in force, the 30s would be regarded as prima facie the correct figure. It is a benefit to the husband for it to be so regarded, and that is sufficient consideration to support his promise.

I construe this agreement as a promise by the husband to pay his wife 30s a week in consideration of her promise to maintain herself during the time she is living separate from him, whether due to her own fault or not.

Hodson LJ. [It was argued that, as the wife was in desertion,] she had forfeited all right to be maintained by her husband and so she was giving no consideration at all when she said she would maintain herself, because that is what she would have to do anyway. The short answer to that is, I think, that she had not forfeited her right to be maintained by her husband by being in desertion. She had only suspended her right and not destroyed it. . . .

The wife had deserted the husband and was temporarily wrongfully away from home; but she might at any time return. In those circumstances, if she returned or offered to return her husband's liability to maintain her would revive. So that there was good consideration there to meet that contingency, which was a real contingency and not a fanciful one at that time. It is not affected by the fact that (as we now know, as a matter of history) the parties never have come together again but have been divorced.

It was urged by counsel for the wife that, whether the point which I have just put was or was not good, nevertheless it was a valid consideration even if the wife was in desertion, because it was some benefit to the husband to be protected from the embarrassment of invalid claims against him. For my part, I would prefer not to rest my judgment on that, because, once it is conceded that there is no basis for a claim by a wife, no consideration for giving an indemnity by the wife appears to me to emerge. It is unnecessary to express any concluded opinion on that matter.

[Morris LJ delivered a judgment in similar terms to that of Hodson LJ.]

Appeal dismissed.

NOTES

1. *Bennett v Bennett* was reversed by the Matrimonial Causes Act 1973, s 34.
2. If the wife had returned to the husband, what would have happened to the agreement?
3. What would have been the position if she had offered to return but he had refused her offer?
4. Denning expressed similar views in *Ward v Byham* [1956] 2 All ER 318, which also involved the performance of an existing duty, in this case the maintenance of an illegitimate child by her mother. Again the other members of the court found consideration: in return for the father's promise to pay £1 a week, the mother had to keep the child well looked after and happy, and to allow her to decide for herself whether she wished to live with the mother.
5. Do you think the outcome of *Williams v Williams* and *Ward v Byham* was influenced by policy? If so, by what policy?

(iv) Performance of a duty imposed by contract with a third party

In *Shadwell v Shadwell* (1860) 9 CBNS 159, 30 LJCP 145 (below, p 115) an uncle promised his nephew an annual sum if the nephew married his fiancée. Although an engagement to marry was a binding contract (and remained legally enforceable until 1971) the Common Bench held that there was consideration for the uncle's promise. In *Scotson v Pegg* (1861) 6 H&N 295, 30 LJ Ex 225 the defendant agreed to unload a cargo of coal in consideration of the plaintiff delivering it to him, which the plaintiff was already obliged to do under a contract with a third party. The plaintiff sued the defendant for delay in unloading and succeeded. In neither case does the point seem to have been argued fully. However, the general rule that performance of an existing contractual obligation to a third party may be good consideration was approved by the Privy Council in *New Zealand Shipping Co Ltd v A M Satterthwaite & Co Ltd* (below, p 818) and again in *Pao On v Lau Yiu Long* (below, p 117).

The *New Zealand Shipping* case illustrates the complex commercial context in which the 'contractual duty owed to a third party' point is likely to arise. The owners of goods (to keep the parties straight, let us call them A) had contracted with carriers (B) for the goods to be transported by ship to New Zealand under a bill of lading contract. The goods were negligently damaged by stevedores (C) who had been employed (it was assumed) by B to unload them. By this time the plaintiffs had become holders of the bill and thus stood in A's shoes (see above, p 44). In the bill of lading (see above, p 44) which contained the terms of the contract, the owners (A) purported to promise the stevedores (C) the benefit of various exemptions and limitations of liability (in fact the main dispute in the case was whether the terms of the bill of lading were clear enough to constitute such a promise: the majority held they were, see below, p 818). The Privy Council held that by unloading the goods the stevedores (C) had provided consideration for this promise. Lord Wilberforce said:

> If the choice, and the antithesis, is between a gratuitous promise, and a promise for consideration, as it must be, in the absence of a tertium quid, there can be little doubt which, in commercial reality, this is. The whole contract is of a commercial character, involving service on one side, rates of payment on the other, and qualifying stipulations as to both. The relations of all parties to each other are commercial relations entered into for business reasons of ultimate profit. To describe one set of promises, in this context, as gratuitous, or nudum pactum, seems paradoxical and is prima facie implausible. It is only the precise analysis of this complex of relations into the classical offer and acceptance, with identifiable consideration, that seems to present difficulty, but this same difficulty exists in many situations of daily life, eg sales at auction; supermarket purchases; boarding an omnibus; purchasing a train ticket; tenders for the supply of goods; offers of rewards; acceptance by post; warranties of authority by agents; manufacturers' guarantees; gratuitous bailments; bankers' commercial credits. These are all examples which show that English law, having committed itself to a rather technical and schematic doctrine of contract, in application takes a practical approach, often at the cost of forcing the facts to fit uneasily into the marked slots of offer, acceptance and consideration.
>
> In their Lordships' opinion the present contract presents much less difficulty than many of those above referred to. It is one of carriage from Liverpool to Wellington. The carrier assumes an obligation to transport the goods and to discharge at the port of arrival. The goods are to be carried and discharged, so the transaction is inherently contractual. It is contemplated that a part of this contract, viz discharge, may be performed by independent contractors—viz the stevedore. By cl 1 of the bill of lading the shipper agrees to exempt from liability the carrier, his servants and independent contractors in respect of the performance of this contract of carriage. Thus, if the carriage including the discharge, is wholly carried out by the carrier, he is exempt. If part is carried out by him, and part by his servants, he and they are exempt. If part is carried out by him and part by an independent contractor, he and the independent contractor are exempt. The exemption is designed to cover the whole carriage from loading to discharge, by whomsoever it is performed: the performance attracts the exemption or immunity in favour of whoever the performer turns out to be.
>
> There is possibly more than one way of analysing this business transaction into the necessary components; that which their Lordships would accept is to say that the bill of lading brought into existence a bargain initially unilateral but capable of becoming mutual, between the shippers and the stevedore, made through the carrier as agent. This became a full contract when the stevedore performed services by discharging the goods. The performance of these services for the benefit of the shipper was the consideration for the agreement by the shipper that the stevedore should have the benefit of the exemptions and limitations contained in the bill of lading. The conception of a 'unilateral contract' of this kind was recognised in *Great Northern Railway Co v Witham* and is well established. This way of regarding the matter is very close to, if not identical to, that accepted by Beattie J in the Supreme Court: he analysed the transaction as one of an offer open to acceptance by action such as was found in *Carlill v Carbolic Smoke Ball Co*.
>
> . . . In their Lordships' opinion, consideration may quite well be provided by the stevedore, as suggested, even though (or if) it was already under an obligation to discharge to the carrier. (There is no direct evidence of the existence or nature of this obligation, but

their Lordships are prepared to assume it.) An agreement to do an act which the promisor is under an existing obligation to a third party to do, may quite well amount to valid consideration and does so in the present case: the promisee obtains the benefit of a direct obligation which he can enforce. This proposition is illustrated and supported by *Scotson v Pegg* . . . which their Lordships consider to be good law.

[Further extracts from this case will be found below, p 818.]

What exactly is the extra benefit to A which constitutes the consideration for its return promise to C? Is making a second promise to perform, or actually performing, the contract with B an additional detriment to C? Remember that if for some reason C does not perform its contract with B, A may suffer a loss, and if C is liable only to B, A may have no remedy.

(v) Performance of a contractual duty owed to the promisor

Harris v Watson (1791) Peake 102, 170 ER 94, King's Bench

In this case the declaration stated, that the plaintiff being a seaman on board the ship 'Alexander', of which the defendant was master and commander, and which was bound on a voyage to Lisbon: whilst the ship was on her voyage, the defendant, in consideration that the plaintiff would perform some extra work, in navigating the ship, promised to pay him five guineas over and above his common wages. . . .

The plaintiff proved that the ship being in danger, the defendant, to induce the seamen to exert themselves, made the promise stated in the first count.

Lord Kenyon. If this action was to be supported, it would materially affect the navigation of this kingdom. It has been long since determined, that when the freight is lost, the wages are also lost. This rule was founded on a principle of policy, for if sailors were in all events to have their wages, and in times of danger entitled to insist on an extra charge on such a promise as this, they would in many cases suffer a ship to sink, unless the captain would pay any extra extravagant demand they might think proper to make.

The plaintiff was nonsuited.

Stilk v Myrick (1809) 2 Camp 317, 170 ER 1168; 6 Esp 129, 170 ER 851, King's Bench

The Espinasse report:

This was an action brought by the plaintiff, a private sailor, to recover the amount of his wages, on a voyage from London to the Baltick and back.

The sum claimed was partly for monthly wages, according to articles which he had signed, and a further sum claimed under these circumstances.

Two sailors, part of the crew, had deserted the ship, and the master (the defendant), not being able to supply their places at Cronstadt, promised to divide among the crew, in addition to their wages, the wages due to the two men who had deserted.

Upon this being claimed, it was objected, That any engagement by the master for a larger sum than was stipulated for by the articles was void, and the case of *Harris v Watson*, cited.

It was answered, that this case was very different from the case cited: that this engagement was made before the ship sailed on her voyage home; it was made under no coercion, from the apprehension of danger, nor extorted from the captain; but a voluntary offer on his part for extraordinary service.

Lord Ellenborough ruled, That the plaintiff could not recover this part of his demand. His Lordship said, That he recognized the principle of the case of *Harris v Watson* as founded on just and proper policy. When the defendant entered on board the ship, he stipulated to do all the work his situation called upon him to do. Here the voyage was to the Baltick and back, not to Cronstadt only; if the voyage had then terminated, the sailors might have made what terms they pleased. If any part of the crew had died, would not the remainder have been forced to work the ship home? If that accident would have left them liable to do the whole work without any extraordinary remuneration, why should not desertion or casualty equally demand it?

Campbell's report:

Lord Ellenborough. I think *Harris v Watson* was rightly decided; but I doubt whether the ground of public policy, upon which Lord Kenyon is stated to have proceeded, be the true principle on which the decision is to be supported. Here, I say, the agreement is void for want of consideration. There was no consideration for the ulterior pay promised to the mariners who remained with the ship. Before they sailed from London they had undertaken to do all that they could under all the emergencies of the voyage. They had sold all their services till the voyage should be completed. If they had been at liberty to quit the vessel at Cronstadt, the case would have been quite different; or if the captain had capriciously discharged the two men who were wanting, the others might not have been compellable to take the whole duty upon themselves, and their agreeing to do so might have been a sufficient consideration for the promise of an advance of wages. But the desertion of a part of the crew is to be considered an emergency of the voyage as much as their death; and those who remain are bound by the terms of their original contract to exert themselves to the utmost to bring the ship in safety to her destined port. Therefore, without looking to the policy of this agreement, I think it is void for want of consideration, and that the plaintiff can only recover at the rate of £5 a month.

Verdict accordingly.

NOTES

1. On what ground was this case decided according to Espinasse? according to Campbell? Campbell's explanation is the one now generally accepted. See Gilmore, *The Death of Contract* (1974), pp 22–28.
2. Although one might have expected Espinasse to report accurately the judgment given in a case in which he had appeared as counsel, his reputation as a reporter is poor. Pollock CB is quoted as having said: 'Mr Espinasse was deaf. He heard one half of a case and reported the other.' (See Megarry, *A Second Miscellany-at-law* (1973), p 118.)

More recently, however, the courts have developed a separate doctrine to deal with cases in which one party has pressurised the other into giving a promise to pay extra. This is the doctrine of economic duress, which is considered in detail below, p 639ff. Its existence seems to be encouraging a more flexible attitude towards consideration in cases in which, without there having been any coercion, one party has promised the other an extra payment to encourage the other to perform its existing contractual duty. In *Woodhouse AC Israel Cocoa Ltd SA v Nigerian Produce Marketing Co Ltd* [1972] AC 741 (see below, p 614) Lord Hailsham said:

> . . . I imagine that a modern court would have found no difficulty in discovering consideration for such a promise. Businessmen know their own business best, even when they appear to grant an indulgence . . .

Williams v Roffey Bros & Nicholls (Contractors) Ltd [1990] 1 All ER 512, Court of Appeal

The defendants were building contractors who had agreed to refurbish 27 flats for a housing association under a contract which contained a 'penalty clause' for late completion (ie a clause stating that the defendants would pay so much for every week that they were late: see below, p 508ff.) The defendants employed the plaintiff, a carpenter, as a subcontractor to do the necessary carpentry for £20,000. There was nothing in the contract about how the plaintiff was to be paid, but in fact he was paid as the work progressed. By April 1986 he had been paid some £16,000 and he had done some work on all the flats, but he had completed only nine of them and he was in financial difficulties. These were caused partly by his failure to supervise his workmen properly but largely because, as the defendants agreed, the original price for the work was too low. The defendants therefore promised to pay him an extra amount of £10,300, to be paid at the rate of £575 per completed flat. The plaintiff completed work on eight further flats but the defendants paid only £1,500 more and the plaintiff stopped work and brought this action for payment. The Recorder awarded him £3,500 (8 × £575 plus a proportion of the original £20,000 less the £1,500 paid and various deductions for defects). The defendants appealed.

Glidewell LJ. . . The Judge quoted and accepted the evidence of [the defendant's surveyor] to the effect that a main contractor who agrees too low a price with a sub-contractor is acting contrary to his own interests. He will never get the job finished without paying more money.

The Judge therefore concluded:

'In my view where the original sub-contract price is too low, and the parties subsequently agree that the additional monies shall be paid to the sub-contractor, this agreement is in the interests of both parties. This is what happened in the present case, and in my opinion the agreement of 9 April 1986 does not fail for lack of consideration.'

In his address to us, counsel for the defendants outlined the benefits to his clients the defendant which arose from their agreement to pay the additional £10,300 as:

    (i) seeking to ensure that the plaintiff continued work and did not stop in breach of the sub-contract;

    (ii) avoiding the penalty for delay;

    (iii) avoiding the trouble and expense of engaging other people to complete the carpentry work.

However, counsel submits that, though his clients may have derived, or hoped to derive, practical benefits from their agreement to pay the 'bonus', they derived no benefit in law, since the plaintiff was promising to do no more than he was already bound to do by his sub-contract, ie continue with the carpentry work and complete it on time. Thus there was no consideration for the agreement.

Counsel relies on the principle of law which, traditionally, is based on the decision in *Stilk v Myrick*. . . .

In *North Ocean Shipping Co Ltd v Hyundai Construction Co Ltd* Mocatta J regarded the general principle of the decision in *Stilk v Myrick* as still being good law. He referred to two earlier decisions of this court, dealing with wholly different subjects, in which Denning LJ, as he then was, sought to escape from the confines of the rule, but was not accompanied in his attempt by the other members of the court.

[Glidewell LJ referred to *Ward v Byham* and *Williams v Williams* and continued:]

There is, however, another legal concept of relatively recent development which is relevant, namely, that of economic duress. Clearly if a sub-contractor has agreed to undertake work at a fixed price, and before he has completed the work declines to continue with it unless the contractor agrees to pay an increased price, the sub-contractor may be held guilty of securing the contractor's promise by taking unfair advantage of the difficulties he will cause if he does not complete the work. In such a case an agreement to pay an increased price may well be voidable because entered into under duress. Thus this concept may provide another answer in law to the question of policy which has troubled the courts since before *Stilk v Myrick*, and no doubt led at the date of that decision to a rigid adherence to the doctrine of consideration.

This possible application of the concept of economic duress was referred to by Lord Scarman, delivering the judgment of the Judicial Committee of the Privy Council in *Pao On v Lau Yiu Long*. . . .

It is true that *Pao On* is a case of a tripartite relationship, ie a promise by A to perform a pre-existing contractual obligation owed to B, in return for a promise of payment by C. But Lord Scarman's words [below, p 644] seem to me to be of general application, equally applicable to a promise made by one of the original two parties to a contract.

Accordingly, following the view of the majority in *Ward v Byham* and of the whole court in *Williams v Williams* and that of the Privy Council in *Pao On* the present state of the law on this subject can be expressed in the following proposition:

    (i) if A has entered into a contract with B to do work for, or to supply goods or services to, B in return for payment by B, and

    (ii) at some stage before A has completely performed his obligations under the contract B has reason to doubt whether A will, or will be able to, complete his side of the bargain; and

    (iii) B thereupon promises A an additional payment in return for A's promise to perform his contractual obligations on time; and

    (iv) as a result of giving his promise, B obtains in practice a benefit, or obviates a disbenefit; and

(v) B's promise is not given as the result of economic duress or fraud on the part of A; then

(vi) the benefit to B is capable of being consideration for B's promise, so that the promise will be legally binding.

As I have said, counsel for the defendants accepted that in the present case by promising to pay the extra £10,300 his client secured benefits. There is no finding, and no suggestion, that in this case the promise was given as a result of fraud or duress.

If it be objected that the propositions above contravene the principle in *Stilk v Myrick*, I answer that in my view they do not; they refine, and limit the application of, that principle, but they leave the principle unscathed, eg where B secures no benefit by his promise. It is not in my view surprising that a principle enunciated in relation to the rigours of seafaring life during the Napoleonic wars should be subjected during the succeeding 180 years to a process of refinement and limitation in its application in the present day.

It is therefore my opinion that on his findings of fact in the present case, the Judge was entitled to hold, as he did, that the defendants' promise to pay the extra £10,300 was supported by valuable consideration, and thus constituted an enforceable agreement.

As a subsidiary argument, Mr Evans submits that on the facts of the present case the consideration, even if otherwise good, did not 'move from the promisee.' This submission is based on the principle illustrated in the decision in *Tweddle v Atkinson*.

My understanding of the meaning of the requirement that 'consideration must move from the promisee' is that such consideration must be provided by the promisee, or arise out of his contractual relationship with the promisor. It is consideration provided by somebody else, not a party to the contract, which does not 'move from the promisee'. This was the situation in *Tweddle v Atkinson*, but it is, of course, not the situation in the present case. Here the benefits to the defendants arose out of their agreement of 9 April 1986 with the plaintiff, the promisee. In this respect I would adopt the following passage from Chitty on Contracts, 25th edition, para 173, and refer to the authorities there cited:

'The requirement that consideration must move from the promisee is most generally satisfied where some detriment is suffered by him, eg where he parts with money or goods, or renders services, in exchange for the promise. But the requirement may be equally well satisfied where the promisee confers a benefit on the promisor without *in fact* suffering any detriment.' (*Chitty's* emphasis.)

That is the situation in this case. . . For these reasons I would dismiss this appeal,

Russell LJ. I find [the] argument relating to consideration much more difficult . . . whilst consideration remains a fundamental requirement before a contract not under seal can be enforced, the policy of the law in its search to do justice between the parties has developed considerably since the early nineteenth century when *Stilk v Myrick* was decided by Lord Ellenborough CJ. In the late twentieth century I do not believe that the rigid approach to the concept of consideration to be found in *Stilk v Myrick* is either necessary or desirable. Consideration there must still be but in my judgment the courts nowadays should be more ready to find its existence so as to reflect the intention of the parties to the contract where the bargaining powers are not unequal and where the finding of consideration reflects the true intention of the parties.

What was the true intention of the parties when they arrived at the agreement pleaded by the defendants in paragraph 5 of the amended defence. The defendants, through their [surveyor], recognised the price that had been agreed originally with the plaintiff was less than what [the surveyor] himself regarded as a reasonable price. There was a desire on [the surveyor's] part to retain the services of the plaintiff so that the work could be completed without the need to employ another sub-contractor. There was further a need to replace what had hitherto been a haphazard method of payment by a more formalised scheme involving the payment of a specified sum on the completion of each flat. These were all advantages accruing to the defendants which can fairly be said to have been in consideration of their undertaking to pay the additional £10,300. True it was that the plaintiff did not undertake to do any work additional to that which he had originally undertaken to do but the terms upon which he was to carry out the work were varied and, in my judgment, that variation was supported by consideration which a pragmatic approach to the true relationship between the parties readily demonstrates.

For my part I wish to make it plain that I do not base my judgment upon any reservation as to the correctness of the law long ago enunciated in *Stilk v Myrick*. A gratuitous promise, pure and simple, remains unenforceable unless given under seal. But where, as in this case a party undertakes to make a payment because by so doing it will gain an advantage arising out of the continuing relationship with the promisee the new bargain will not fail for want of consideration. As I read the judgment of the assistant recorder this was his true ratio upon that part of the case wherein the absence of consideration was raised in argument. For the reasons that I have endeavoured to outline I think that the assistant recorder came to a correct conclusion and I too would dismiss this appeal.

Purchas LJ. . . [T]here were clearly incentives to both parties to make a further arrangement in order to relieve the plaintiff of his financial difficulties and also to ensure that the plaintiff was in a position, or alternatively was willing, to continue with the sub-contract works to a reasonable and timely completion. Against this context the judge found that on the 9th April 1986 a meeting took place between the plaintiff and a man called Hooper, on the one hand, and [the surveyor] and Mr Roffey on the other hand. The arrangement was that the defendants would pay the plaintiff an extra £10,300 by way of increasing the lump sum for the total work. It was further agreed that the sum of £10,300 was to be paid at the rate of £575 per flat on the completion of each flat. This arrangement was beneficial to both sides. By completing one flat at a time rather than half completing all the flats the plaintiff was able to receive moneys on account and the defendants were able to direct their other trades to do work in the completed flats which otherwise would have been held up until the plaintiff had completed his work . . .

In my judgment, the rule in *Stilk v Myrick* remains valid as a matter of principle, namely that a contract not under seal must be supported by consideration. Thus, where the agreement upon which reliance is placed provides that an extra payment is to be made for work to be done by the payee which he is already obliged to perform then unless some other consideration is detected to support the agreement to pay the extra sum that agreement will not be enforceable. The two cases *Harris v Watson* and *Stilk v Myrick* involved circumstances of a very special nature, namely the extraordinary conditions existing at the turn of the eighteenth century under which seamen had to serve their contracts of employment on the high seas. There were strong public policy grounds at that time to protect the master and owners of a ship from being held to ransom by disaffected crews. Thus, the decision that the promise to pay extra wages even in the circumstances established in those cases, was not supported by consideration is readily understandable. Of course, conditions today on the high seas have changed dramatically and it is at least questionable, as Mr Makey submitted, whether these cases might not well have been decided differently if they were tried today. The modern cases tend to depend more upon the defence of duress in a commercial context rather than lack of consideration for the second agreement. In the present case the question of duress does not arise. The initiative in coming to the agreement of the 9th April came from [the surveyor] and not from the plaintiff. It would not, therefore, lie in the defendants' mouth to assert a defence of duress. Nevertheless the court is more ready in the presence of this defence being available in the commercial context to look for mutual advantages which would amount to sufficient consideration to support the second agreement under which the extra money is paid.

[Purchas LJ referred to Lord Hailsham's speech in *Woodhouse Cocoa* and continued:]

The question must be posed: What consideration has moved from the plaintiff to support the promise to pay the extra £10,300 added to the lump sum provision? In the particular circumstances, which I have outlined above, there was clearly a commercial advantage to both sides from a pragmatic point of view in reaching the agreement of 9 April. The defendants were on risk that as a result of the bargain they had struck the plaintiff would not or indeed possibly could not comply with his existing obligations without further finance. As a result of the agreement the defendants secured their position commercially. There was, however, no obligation added to the contractual duties imposed upon the plaintiff under the original contract. Prima facie this would appear to be a classic *Stilk v Myrick* case. It was, however, open to the plaintiff to be in deliberate breach of the contract in order to 'cut his losses' commercially. In normal circumstances the suggestion that a contracting party can rely upon his own breach to establish consideration is distinctly unattractive. In many cases it obviously would be and if there was any element of duress brought upon the other contracting party under the modern development of this branch of the law the proposed breaker of the contract would not benefit. With some hesitation and comforted by the passage from the speech of Lord Hailsham, to which I have referred, I consider that the modern approach to the question of consideration would be that where there were benefits derived by each party to a contract of variation even though one party did not suffer a detriment this would not be fatal to establishing sufficient consideration to support the agreement. If both parties benefit from an agreement it is not necessary that each also suffers a detriment. In my judgment, on the facts as found by the judge, he was entitled to reach the conclusion that consideration existed and in those circumstances I would not disturb that finding. This is sufficient to determine the appeal. . .

Appeal dismissed.

NOTES

1. These cases are about purported changes to the terms of existing contracts and we will return to them in section 7.
2. In all the 'existing duty' cases the promisee has done something which he might not otherwise have done, and the promisor has had the benefit of this performance which he might not otherwise have got. Isn't the problem the law's reluctance to acknowledge that, but for the extra payment, the promisee might not have performed his legal duty? Or is the courts' main concern that the promisee might refuse to perform as a way of extorting additional payment from the promisor?
3. *Williams v Roffey Bros* seems to suggest that if the promisor in fact gets a benefit out of the promisee's actions, it doesn't matter that there was no real detriment to the promisee. But wasn't there a benefit in fact to the promisor in *Wade v Simeon* (above, p 96)? Is the point that only some 'benefits' and only some 'detriments' are recognised by the law? And if so, which ones? Does the existence of a benefit or detriment really tell us anything at all, or is it all a matter of policy? If so, what policy?
4. We return to the question of whether the consideration must 'move from the promisee' below, p 126.

(vi) Requirements contracts

As we suggested earlier, even in the commercial context there are occasional situations where there is difficulty about the sufficiency of consideration.

Great Northern Railway Co v Witham (1873) LR 9 CP 16, Common Pleas

Keating J. In this case Mr Digby Seymour moved to enter a nonsuit. The circumstances were these:—The Great Northern Railway Company advertised for tenders for the supply of stores. The defendant made a tender in these words,—'I hereby undertake to supply the Great Northern Railway Company, for twelve months, from &c to &c, with such quantities of each or any of the several articles named in the attached specifications as the company's store-keeper may order from time to time, at the price set opposite each article respectively,' &c. Some orders were given by the company, which were duly executed. But the order now in question was not executed; the defendant seeking to excuse himself from the performance of his agreement, because it was unilateral, the company not being bound to give the order. The ground upon which it was put by Mr Seymour was, that there was no consideration for the defendant's promise to supply the goods; in other words, that, inasmuch as there was no obligation on the company to give an order, there was no consideration moving from the company, and therefore no obligation on the defendant to supply the goods. . . . If before the order was given the defendant had given notice to the company that he would not perform the agreement, it might be that he would have been justified in so doing. But here the company had given the order, and had consequently done something which amounted to a consideration for the defendant's promise. I see no ground for doubting that the verdict for the plaintiffs ought to stand.

[Brett J delivered a judgment to the same effect. Grove J concurred.]

NOTES

1. What do you think the position would have been if the defendant had notified the company that he would not accept any further orders? The traditional view is that non-exclusive requirements contracts (ones that do not require the buyer to take all his requirements from the seller) are

unenforceable, because there is no consideration for the seller's promise to supply at the stated price if the buyer is not promising to buy from the seller (though for a different view see Adams, 'Consideration for Requirements Contracts' (1978) 94 LQR 73). The same is true of the converse 'output' contract whereby a buyer agrees to take a seller's output.

2. If, on the other hand, the contract is 'exclusive', in the sense that the buyer is promising that if he has any requirements for the goods in question he will buy from the seller (or in an output contract, the seller will sell any output to the buyer), there is consideration.

3. What is the purpose of entering into a requirements contract whereby the buyer agrees to take all his requirements of a particular item from the seller? What advantage does either party get out of the arrangement?

4. Why enter a non-exclusive contract that does not oblige the buyer to take all his requirements from the seller? Although the latter type of contract is probably unenforceable, it appears that it is not uncommon: but if it is unenforceable, what is the point of it?

'The Standardized Contracts of United States Automobile Manufacturers' by Macaulay (International Encyclopedia of Comparative Law, VII, paras 3.21–29)

CONTRACTS TO BUILD AND SELL CARS

The manufacturers and their suppliers

Description of the relationship
Although the manufacturers can and do make in their own plants some of almost all of the parts which go into an assembled automobile, they also buy many of these parts from suppliers. There are a number of reasons why they purchase from outside suppliers. First, the manufacturer gets a product without investing additional capital in buildings, machines and a trained work force. Second, the manufacturer gets a yardstick which can be used to measure the efficiency of its own division making the same item. If a division making grease seals can produce them at 2 cents each, but an outsider can make them for 1½ cents each, the manufacturer knows he must re-examine the efficiency of his internal operation. Third, the manufacturer increases the chance that he may benefit from technological innovation. The supplier's designers and engineers may be able to suggest a different design or an improved manufacturing process. On the other side, most businesses, but not all, that can produce parts for automobiles want to sell their output to the automobile manufacturers because of the possibilities for extremely high volume production which, in an efficiently managed firm, can be highly profitable.

There are three additional factors influencing the course a manufacturer-supplier relationship takes: First, the mass production techniques of American automobile manufacturing require that the assembly line not be stopped. When, for example, a particular Ford sedan arrives at a certain point on the assembly line four hubcaps must be there ready to be installed. It would be extremely costly to the manufacturer if the line had to be stopped because the supplier's machines that stamp out hubcaps broke down, because a supplier's inventory was not great enough to meet the demand or because the parts were lost in shipment. However, demand for automobiles and even for particular types of automobiles fluctuates. To a great extent, this second factor offsets the first. The easiest way to avoid stopping assembly lines would be to produce large quantities of parts far in advance of need. Yet this approach increases costs because of the possibility of waste and the loss of the use of funds thus devoted to inventories. If, for example, the demand for station wagons declines during the year, exhaust pipes that fit only station wagons that will never be produced are mere scrap metal. Third, component parts can be defective, the defect can cause injury to property or person, and in United States law the injured party in such cases has increasingly been gaining rights against manufacturers. Not surprisingly, one finds that manufacturers wish to hold suppliers responsible for such claims, and the suppliers must defend themselves against the costly results of seemingly minor defects in the parts they make.

The blanket order system

The system described

The *manufacturers* have accommodated all of these economic and legal factors in an imaginative piece of transaction architecture which is usually called a 'blanket order'. Coupled with the suppliers' great desire to do business with the automobile manufacturers, the blanket order system almost always insures that parts will arrive at the assembly plants at the right time, that the suppliers will take the risk of scrapped parts caused by fluctuations in demand, and that the suppliers will be responsible for claims caused by defects. Moreover, the system gives the manufacturers great leverage to ward off price increases caused by the suppliers' increased costs.

This is how it works: Some time before the beginning of the model year, the manufacturer will issue a blanket order to a supplier of, for example, tail pipes designed specifically for one of the manufacturer's station wagons. The blanket order states a number of 'agreements'. One of the most important is the price per unit. This price is computed on the basis of an estimated number of units to be ordered, and it will not be increased if fewer are actually ordered. Thus, the manufacturer has made the supplier run the risk that he will not even recover his cost of producing the items actually shipped to the manufacturer in the event that the manufacturer uses substantially fewer than the estimated number. And the blanket order does not oblige the manufacturer to take and pay for *any* of the parts described in it. That obligation comes only when the manufacturer sends the supplier documents called 'releases'. The idea seems to be that the blanket order creates a force which is held back until released little by little.

Each month, sometimes more often, the manufacturer sends the supplier a release, ordering him to manufacture and ship a specified number of the parts each week. On the release form, the manufacturer also will estimate the number of parts he will require for the next two or three months, but this estimate, to quote one manufacturer's form, 'is for planning purposes only and does not constitute a commitment'. Typically, manufacturers do not send releases calling for more parts than they will need in a month since their monthly estimates of sales are fairly accurate. However, sometimes they do order too few or too many parts. If there is an increase in public demand for a particular model, the blanket order allows the manufacturer to send another release form to the supplier calling for increased deliveries. Such sudden increases may be a great strain on the supplier if he does not have unused capacity for production. Moreover, a supplier must always guard against a break-down of his machinery, which temporarily destroys his ability to meet the manufacturer's demands. As a result, the supplier usually makes more than the number of parts ordered by the manufacturer so that the supplier will have an inventory to cover anticipated future demands. He builds this inventory at his own risk since the blanket order clearly provides that 'Seller shall not fabricate any articles covered by this order, or procure materials required therefor, or ship any articles to Purchaser, except to the extent authorized by . . . written releases . . . Purchaser will make no payment for finished work, work in process or raw material fabricated or produced by Seller in excess of Purchaser's written releases'.

If a manufacturer has 'released' too many parts in light of a sudden decrease in demand, the blanket order gives it the right to cancel the amount ordered in whole or in part. It then is obligated to pay the contract price for each part finished and 'the cost to Seller (excluding profit or losses) of work in process and raw material based on any audit Purchaser may conduct and generally accepted accounting principles . . .'

Blanket orders and American contract law

Legal enforceability

. . . . In effect at the manufacturer's request, the supplier makes an offer—a promise to supply certain goods if they are ordered—which the manufacturer accepts every time it sends a release. . . The large automobile manufacturers try to avoid placing total reliance on any one supplier, and other suppliers usually can increase production so that a manufacturer's assembly line is not stopped for lack of an item. Thus manufacturers tend to avoid injury rather than litigate for compensation. On the other hand, no automobile parts supplier is likely to bring a case against a manufacturer; the loss on any one order is very unlikely to be large enough to justify jeopardizing future business. Of course, the trustee of a bankrupt supplier would be free of this constraint. However, in light of the uncertainty of the supplier's legal position, many trustees would think it unwise to risk the cost of legal action against a manufacturer.

What are the consequences of the legal situation? If we assume that the developing reliance and fairness doctrines would not apply, the parties get legal rights only after the manufacturer has issued a release and only as to the goods ordered in that release. This means that there can be a great deal of reliance by the supplier which is unprotected by contract rights. On the other hand, legally the supplier would be free to refuse to continue the relationship by revoking his outstanding offer to supply the parts as ordered by the release forms. As we have said previously, few suppliers who were not going out of business could afford to exercise such a right; very few situations short of bankruptcy would justify losing the good will of General Motors, Ford, Chrysler or American Motors. Most importantly for the manufacturer, it does get legal rights once a release is issued. As a result, it manages to avoid any question that the supplier will bear liability for injuries caused by defective parts which it ships. Once the parts are ordered by a relese there is a contract which the manufacturer has written, and the disclaimers and limitations of remedy so typically found in documents drafted by sellers are thus avoided. As between Chrysler and its suppliers, the responsibility for compliance with federal safety and air pollution regulations is also clearly placed on the supplier.

Remedies
The standard blanket order documents drastically limit the remedies to which a supplier would otherwise be entitled under American contract law once a legally binding contract is created by the issuance of a release. Typically, the manufacturer reserves a right to cancel the goods ordered by its release, either in whole or in part. Under American contract law such a cancellation would be a breach if not authorized by the agreement, and, absent a contract provision to the contrary, the seller would be entitled to recover what he had spent in performance before the buyer's notice of cancellation plus the profit he would have made had he been allowed to complete his performance. Most blanket order cancellation clauses, however, exclude a right to profit except as to those parts which have been completed before cancellation. Thus even when a contract is formed by a release, the supplier's rights in most situations will be minimal. The manufacturer gains a practical commitment from the supplier to meet the demands of its assembly line. It retains maximum flexibility by making no commitment to buy any parts until a release is given and making only a very limited payment if it wishes to cancel after one is sent.

The absence of a reform movement
There are no statutes attempting to regulate this relationship, and no movement seeking such legislation has been discovered. Insofar as statutes in the United States are the result of pluralistic struggle and compromise, one essential element of pluralism seems lacking. It would be hard to form a group of suppliers to seek legislation. Supplying the manufacturers is very profitable for a firm that can accept all the risks allocated to it by the blanket order system . . .

In summary, the manufacturers have tailored a relationship whereby they get most of the advantages of producing parts in a division of their own firms while preserving most of the advantages of dealing with an outside organization. The suppliers are offered a chance to make high profits in exchange for assuming great risks. Most suppliers are eager for the chance to play the blanket order game. The public may get better automobiles at a lower price as a result of the system, but one cannot be sure.

[This paper is based on Macaulay, *Law and the Balance of Power* (New York 1966); Whitford, *Strict Products Liability and the Automobile Industry—Much Ado About Nothing*: 1968 Wis L Rev 83, cited Strict Products Liability; idem, *Law and the Consumer Transaction— A Case Study of the Automobile Warranty*: 1968 Wis L Rev 1006, cited Law; and an unpublished study of the 'blanket order' system by the author.]

NOTE

This is not the only study suggesting that businessmen set considerable store by contracts which they know are legally unenforceable. See below, p 191.

Wood v Lucy, Lady Duff-Gordon 222 NY 88, 118 NE 214 (Court of Appeals, New York, 1917)

Cardozo J. The defendant styles herself 'a creator of fashions'. Her favour helps a sale. Manufacturers of dresses, millinery and like articles are glad to pay for a certificate of her approval. The things which she designs, fabrics, parasols, and what not, have a new value in the public mind when issued in her name. She employed the plaintiff to help her turn this vogue into money. He was to have the exclusive right, subject always to her approval, to place her indorsements on the designs of others. He was also to have the exclusive right to place her own designs on sale, or to license others to market them. In return, she was to have one-half of 'all profits and revenues' derived from any contracts he might make. The exclusive right was to last at least one year from April 1, 1915, and thereafter from year to year unless terminated by notice of ninety days. The plaintiff says that he kept the contract on his part, and that the defendant broke it. She placed her indorsement on fabrics, dresses and millinery without his knowledge, and withheld the profits. He sues her for the damages, and the case comes here on demurrer.

The agreement of employment is signed by both parties. It has a wealth of recitals. The defendant insists, however, that it lacks the elements of a contract. She says that the plaintiff does not bind himself to anything. It is true that he does not promise in so many words that he will use reasonable efforts to place the defendant's indorsements and market her designs. We think, however, that such a promise is fairly to be implied . . .

The implication of a promise here finds support in many circumstances. The defendant gave an exclusive privilege. She was to have no right for at least a year to place her own indorsements or market her own designs except through the agency of the plaintiff. The acceptance of the exclusive agency was an assumption of its duties. . . . We are not to suppose that one party was to be placed at the mercy of the other. . . . Many other terms of the agreement point the same way. We are told at the outset by way of recital that 'the said Otis F. Wood possesses a business organization adapted to the placing of such indorsements as the said Lucy, Lady Duff-Gordon has approved'. The implication is that the plaintiff's business organization will be used for the purpose for which it is adapted. But the terms of the defendant's compensation are even more significant. Her sole compensation for the grant of an exclusive agency is to be one-half of all the profits resulting from the plaintiff's efforts. Unless he gave his efforts, she could never get anything. Without an implied promise, the transaction cannot have such business 'efficacy as both parties must have intended that at all events it should have' (Bowen LJ, in *The Moorcock*). But the contract does not stop there. The plaintiff goes on to promise that he will account monthly for all moneys received by him, and that he will take out all such patents and copyrights and trademarks as may in his judgment be necessary to protect the rights and articles affected by the agreement. It is true, of course, as the Appellate Division has said, that if he was under no duty to try to market designs or to place certificates of indorsement, his promise to account for profits or take out copyrights would be valueless. But in determining the intention of the parties, the promise has a value. It helps to enforce the conclusion that the plaintiff had some duties. His promise to pay the defendant one-half of the profits and revenues resulting from the exclusive agency and to render accounts monthly, was a promise to use reasonable efforts to bring profits and revenues into existence. For this conclusion, the authorities are ample. . . .

The judgment of the Appellate Division should be reversed, and the order of the Special Term affirmed, with costs in the Appellate Division and in this court.

Cuddeback, McLaughlin and Andrews JJ, concur; Hiscock CJ, Chase and Crane JJ, dissent.

Judgment reversed.

NOTES

1. In this case Cardozo was prepared to imply an obligation on the part of the plaintiff, whereas with non-exclusive requirements contracts the courts have not implied an obligation on the buyer (for example, to take a reasonable proportion of its requirements from the seller). Is there anything in the nature of the arrangements which justifies this difference in treatment?
2. In *A Schroeder Music Publishing Co Ltd v Macaulay* (see below, p 785) the House of Lords held an agreement between a young composer and a music publisher, under which the publisher obtained copyright of any compositions of the composer during the contract period and the composer would be paid royalties on sales, contrary to public policy as being in unreasonable restraint of trade and therefore void. One of the reasons given by Lord Reid was that the publisher was not obliged to publish the songs. It was argued that the publishers had an implied obligation to act in good faith, so that they could not maliciously refrain

from publishing. Lord Reith doubted this but said it would make no difference. Why do you think it was not argued that the publisher was under an implied obligation to use its best efforts to earn royalties for the composer? (You may like to return to this question after you have read the chapter on implied terms.)

(vii) Irrevocable commercial credits

'The Sale of Goods' (7th ed, 1985) by Atiyah, 329–330

Where a person carrying on business in one country buys goods from a seller in another country, it is common practice nowadays for the price to be paid by means of a banker's commercial credit. The normal procedure is more or less as follows, although there may frequently be variations of detail.

The buyer instructs his own bank (the issuing bank) to open a credit in favour of the seller with a bank in the seller's country (the 'intermediary' or 'correspondent' or 'confirming' banker). Almost invariably, the buyer instructs the issuing bank that the seller is only to be allowed to draw on the credit on presentation to the paying bank of documents showing that the goods have been shipped and are on their way to the buyer. The shipping documents will comprise the seller's invoice for the goods, the bill of lading and, frequently (always in c.i.f. contracts), an insurance policy or certificate. The intermediary banker will then notify the seller that instructions have been received to open a credit in his favour and will inform him of the precise terms on which he will be allowed to avail himself of the credit. As soon as the goods are shipped, the seller will present these documents to the intermediary banker. The bank will check the documents with the terms of the credit to ensure that the goods shipped are (so far as can be seen from the documents) the contract goods and that everything appears to be in order and, if satisfied that this is the case, will permit the seller to draw against the credit. This may be done by accepting a bill of exchange, or discounting a bill drawn on the buyer, or by making funds available in cash.

The intermediary bank will then transmit the documents to the issuing bank, which will inform the buyer that they have been received. The buyer will also satisfy himself that the documents are in order and will, in due course, pay the issuing bank an amount corresponding to the price paid to the seller, together with the bank's own charges. The issuing bank will, of course, pay the intermediary bank and will release the documents to the buyer, sometimes even before it has been paid. Armed with these, the buyer will then be in a position to resell the goods and transfer the documents to a sub-buyer or, alternatively, to take delivery as soon as the goods arrive.

Virtually all bankers' credits are today granted on the terms that they are to be governed by the Uniform Customs and Practice for Documentary Credits (5th edition, 1983) prepared by the International Chamber of Commerce. The banks of nearly all the countries in the world use this document (hereafter referred to as the Uniform Customs) which is, therefore, to all intents and purposes a part of the law of bankers' commercial credits.

There are many variations in the forms of commercial credits, the principal distinctions being between revocable and irrevocable credits, and confirmed and unconfirmed credits. Under the Uniform Customs, an irrevocable credit constitutes a definite undertaking by the issuing bank that the credit will be made available if the seller complies with the stipulated conditions. A revocable credit does not constitute a definite undertaking by the issuing bank and may be cancelled or modified without notice until payment is made or documents accepted under the credit. The distinction between a confirmed and unconfirmed credit turns upon whether or not the intermediary bank accepts a direct obligation to the seller to honour the credit. In the former event, the intermediary bank 'confirms' the credit, that is, undertakes (sometimes for an extra commission payable directly by the seller) to pay whether or not it is put in funds by the issuing bank; in the latter event, the credit is unconfirmed, the intermediary bank merely informs the seller that the credit has been opened in his favour, and the seller will have no right of recourse against the bank in the event of its refusing to pay.

In the past, doubts have even existed as to whether the seller could sue the bank if it refused to honour a confirmed credit, on the ground that there is no contract between seller and bank, owing to the absence of consideration. But, in practice, banks never take this technical point and judicial pronouncements now seem to have put their liability beyond doubt.*

* See especially *per* Jenkins, LJ, in *Hamzeh Malas & Sons v British Imex Industries Ltd* [1958] 2 QB 127, at 129; *Urquhart Lindsay & Co v Eastern Bank Ltd* [1922] 1 KB 318; *per* Lord Diplock in *United City Merchants (Investments) Ltd v Royal Bank of Canada* [1982] 2 All ER 720.

NOTE

It is, as Atiyah says, generally considered that an irrevocable confirmed credit becomes binding on the bank as soon as it has notified the seller that the credit has been opened. Unless the seller has paid the bank an extra commission for the confirmation, what consideration has the seller provided? Suppose (i) the bank only refuses to pay when the seller presents the documents; (ii) the bank revokes the credit when the seller has got the goods ready for shipment but has not yet shipped them; and (iii) the bank revokes the credit soon after it has notified the seller of its opening and before the seller has taken any steps in response?

(viii) Why need not consideration be adequate?

'Economic Analysis of Law' by Posner, pp 70–71

. . . [C]ourts have no comparative advantage in determining at what price goods should be sold. On the contrary, in all but very exceptional cases negotiation between buyer and seller is the more reliable method of determining a reasonable price, ie one at which exchange is mutually beneficial.

Courts inquire only as to the existence, not as to the adequacy, of the consideration for a contract. The distinction is important and economically sound. To ask whether there is consideration is simply to enquire whether the situation is one of exchange and a bargain has been struck. To go further and ask whether the consideration is adequate would require the court to do what we have just said it is less well equipped to do than the parties—decide whether the price (and other essential terms) specified in the contract are reasonable. It does not follow that a court is bound to enforce every contract. We shall see that there are cases where the presumption that the contemplated exchange increases value can be rebutted without inquiry into the reasonableness of particular terms; in such cases enforcement is appropriately refused even though the promise sought to be enforced is supported by consideration.

NOTE

In fact the rule that consideration need not be adequate can be seriously misleading. It is quite true that a contract in which the consideration is inadequate will not fail for lack of consideration, but as we shall see (in section 8 especially) there are many situations in which inadequacy of consideration combined with other factors is a ground for relief. Moreover it can be argued that many rules of contract law that do not explicitly refer to the adequacy of consideration are nonetheless concerned with the fairness of exchanges: see Atiyah, 'Contract and Fair Exchange' in *Essays on Contract* (1986). We will note some of them as we come to them.

(c) Exchange

(i) Consideration or conditional gift?

If I promise you an outright gift there is no consideration for my promise. What if my promise is conditional on some event, and the event is your doing something—for instance I promise you a wedding present if you marry? Is your marriage consideration for my promise, or is my promise merely a conditional gift promise?

It is clear that a promise that is essentially gratuitous may be made enforceable by casting it into the form of a bargain. A case which is probably an example of this is *Thomas v Thomas* (1842) 2 QB 851. The plaintiff, Eleanor Thomas, was the widow of John Thomas. On the eve of his death, John stated that he wished to make further provision for his wife, and the next morning said he wished her to have the house and all that it contained, or £100 instead. His will made no mention of this, but his executors and residuary legatees, hearing of the testator's wishes, executed with the plaintiff an agreement which provided that 'in consideration of such desire', they would convey the premises to her for her life,

> provided nevertheless, and it is hereby further agreed and declared, that the said Eleanor Thomas, or her assigns, shall and will, at all times during which she shall have possession of the said dwelling house, &c, pay to the said Samuel Thomas and Benjamin Thomas, their executors, &c, the sum of 1*l* yearly towards the ground rent payable in respect of the said dwelling house and other premises thereto adjoining, and shall and will keep the said dwelling house and premises in good and tenantable repair.

The plaintiff was allowed possession for some time, but after the death of his fellow executor, the defendant refused to convey the house to her and had her ejected. The plaintiff brought an action, alleging that the defendant had made the promise in consideration of her undertaking to pay the £1 per year and keep the premises in repair. Williams, for the defendant, argued that there was no consideration, or that if there was, that it was the fulfilment of the testator's wishes, and as the plaintiff had not alleged this as the consideration in her declaration, she must fail. The Court of Queen's Bench held that fulfilling the testator's wishes could not be consideration, being merely the motive behind the transaction. Patteson J remarked:

> It would be giving to causa too large a construction if we were to adopt the view urged for the defendant: it would be confounding consideration with motive. Motive is not the same thing with consideration. Consideration means something which is of some value in the eye of the law, moving from the plaintiff: it may be some benefit to the plaintiff, or some detriment to the defendant; but at all events it must be moving from the plaintiff. Now that which is suggested as the consideration here, a pious respect for the wishes of the testator, does not in any way move from the plaintiff; it moves from the testator; therefore, legally speaking, it forms no part of the consideration.

However, the undertaking to pay £1 towards the ground rent and to keep the house in repair were consideration. In the words of Denman CJ:

> . . . the stipulation for the payment of it is not a mere proviso, but an express agreement. (His Lordship here read the proviso.) This is in terms an express agreement, and shews a sufficient legal consideration quite independent of the moral feeling which disposed the executors to enter into such a contract

Would the result have been different if the proviso had merely stated 'provided that the said ET shall . . . pay . . .'?

Shadwell v Shadwell (1860) 9 CBNS 159, 142 ER 62, Common Bench

After his engagement, the plaintiff received the following letter:

> 11th August, 1838. Gray's Inn. My dear Lancey,—I am glad to hear of your intended marriage with Ellen Nicholl; and, as I promised to assist you at starting, I am happy to tell you that I will pay to you 150*l* yearly during my life and until your annual income derived from your profession of a Chancery barrister shall amount to 600 guineas; of which your own admission will be the only evidence that I shall receive or require. Your ever affectionate uncle, Charles Shadwell.

His uncle, now deceased, had paid thirteen yearly sums: the plaintiff claimed the remaining five from his uncle's executors. The plaintiff alleged that this promise was made in consideration of his marriage, and that as his income as a barrister never amounted to 600 guineas he was now entitled to the money. The executors demurred.

Erle CJ. The question raised by the demurrer . . . is, whether there is a consideration which will support the action on the promise to pay the annuity of 150*l* per annum . . .

The circumstances are, that the plaintiff had made an engagement to marry one Ellen Nicholl, that his uncle had promised to assist him at starting,—by which, as I understand the words, he meant on commencing his married life. Then the letter containing the promise declared on is sent, to specify what that assistance would be, namely, 150*l* per annum during the uncle's life, and until the plaintiff's professional income should be acknowledged by him to exceed 600 guineas per annum; and the declaration avers, that the plaintiff, relying on this promise, without any revocation on the part of the uncle, did marry Ellen Nicholl.

Now, do these facts shew that the promise was in consideration either of a loss to be sustained by the plaintiff or a benefit to be derived from the plaintiff to the uncle, at his, the uncle's, request? My answer is in the affirmative.

First, do these facts shew a loss sustained by the plaintiff at his uncle's request? When I answer this in the affirmative, I am aware that a man's marriage with the woman of his choice is in one sense a boon, and in that sense the reverse of a loss: yet, as between the plaintiff and the party promising to supply an income to support the marriage, it may well be also a loss. The plaintiff may have made a most material change in his position, and induced the object of his affection to do the same, and may have incurred pecuniary liabilities resulting in embarrassments which would be in every sense a loss if the income which had been promised should be withheld; and, if the promise was made in order to induce the parties to marry, the promise so made would be in legal effect a request to marry.

Secondly, do these facts shew a benefit derived from the plaintiff to the uncle, at his request? In answering again in the affirmative, I am at liberty to consider the relation in which the parties stood and the interest in the settlement of his nephew which the uncle declares. The marriage primarily affects the parties thereto; but in a secondary degree it may be an object of interest to a near relative, and in that sense a benefit to him. This benefit is also derived from the plaintiff at the uncle's request. If the promise of the annuity was intended as an inducement to the marriage, and the averment that the plaintiff, relying on the promise, married, is an averment that the promise was one inducement to the marriage, this is the consideration averred in the declaration; and it appears to me to be expressed in the letter, construed with the surrounding circumstances . . . My judgment is for the plaintiff.

[Keating J agreed with Erle CJ.]

Byles J (dissenting). I am of opinion that the defendant is entitled to the judgment of the court on the demurrer . . .

The inquiry . . . narrows itself to this question,—Does the letter disclose any consideration for the promise? the consideration relied on by the plaintiff's counsel being the subsequent marriage of the plaintiff. I think the letter discloses no consideration . . .

It is by no means clear that the words 'at starting' mean 'on marriage with Ellen Nicholl', or with any one else. The more natural meaning seems to me to be, 'at starting in the profession;' for, it will be observed that these words are used by testator in reciting a prior promise made when the testator had not heard of the proposed marriage with Ellen Nicholl, or, so far as appears, heard of any proposed marriage. This construction is fortified by the consideration that the annuity is not in terms made to begin from the marriage, but, as it should seem, from the date of the letter: neither is it in terms made defeasible if Ellen Nicholl should die before marriage.

But, even on the assumption that the words 'at starting' mean on marriage, I still think that no consideration appears, sufficient to sustain the promise . . .

Marriage of the plaintiff at the testator's express request would be no doubt an ample consideration. But marriage of the plaintiff without the testator's request is no consideration to the testator. It is true that marriage is or may be a detriment to the plaintiff: but detriment to the plaintiff is not enough, unless it either be a benefit to the testator, or be treated by the testator as such by having been suffered at his request. Suppose a defendant to promise a plaintiff,—'I will give you 500*l* if you break your leg',—would that detriment to the plaintiff, should it happen, be any consideration? If it be said that such an accident is an involuntary mischief, would it have been a binding promise if the testator had said,—'I will give you 100*l* a year while you continue in your present chambers?' I conceive that the promise would not be binding, for want of a previous request by the testator.

Now, the testator in the case before the court derived, so far as appears, no personal benefit from the marriage. The question, therefore, is still further narrowed to this point,—Was the marriage at the testator's request? Express request there was none. Can any request be implied? The only words from which it can be contended that it is to be implied, are the words 'I am glad to hear of your intended marriage with Ellen Nicholl.' But it appears . . . that the marriage had already been agreed on, and that the testator knew it. These words, therefore, seem to me to import no more than the satisfaction of the testator at the engagement,—an accomplished fact. No request can, as it seems to me, be inferred from them.

Judgment for the plaintiff.

NOTE

A similar problem of whether an act was consideration or merely a condition occurred in *Chappell & Co Ltd v Nestlé Co Ltd* [1960] AC 87, [1959] 2 All ER 701, HL. The defendants offered records, including 'Rockin' Shoes', to anyone sending in a postal order for 1s 6d together with three wrappers from 6d bars of Nestlé's milk chocolate. Section 8 of the Copyright Act 1956 permitted the making of records of a musical work for selling retail, provided the maker gave the owner of the copyright prior notice and paid a royalty of 6¼% of the 'ordinary retail selling price'. The plaintiffs, who were exclusive licensees of the copyright of 'Rockin' Shoes', were given notice that the ordinary retail selling price was 1s 6d. They sought an injunction to restrain a breach of copyright, contending that 1s 6d was not the 'ordinary retail selling price' and that the defendants could not avail themselves of s 8, which applied only where the price was solely money. Upjohn J granted the injunction, but it was reversed by the Court of Appeal. The plaintiffs appealed, and the House of Lords held by a majority that the injunction should be granted. Sending in the wrappers was not just a condition which had to be fulfilled before the record could be obtained; the wrappers formed part of the consideration. Perhaps the determining factor was that having to send in the wrappers would increase the sales of chocolate, and so would benefit the sellers. Compare Williston, *Contracts* (3rd edn, 1953), s 112:

> It is often difficult to decide whether words of condition in a promise indicate a request for consideration or state a mere condition in a gratuitous promise. An aid, though not a conclusive test in determining which interpretation of the promise is more reasonable, is an inquiry whether the happening of the condition will be a benefit to the promisor. If so, it is a fair inference that the happening was requested as a consideration.

(ii) Past consideration

Suppose Beale misses his train from Oxford back to Warwick, so Bishop takes him there by car. As he gets out of the car Beale promises to pay Bishop £15 for his trouble. Is there any consideration for the promise?

Pao On v Lau Yiu Long [1979] 3 All ER 65, Privy Council

The plaintiffs owned all the shares in a private company, Shing On, whose principal asset was a building. The defendants, 'the Laus', were the majority shareholders in a public company, Fu Chip, which wanted to acquire the building. Rather than SO simply selling the building to FC, the parties agreed in February 1973 that the plaintiffs would transfer their shares in SO to FC and receive in exchange shares in FC. The plaintiffs could then sell these shares, but to avoid depressing the market in FC shares, the plaintiffs also agreed that they would retain 60% of these shares for one year. The plaintiffs wanted some form of guarantee in case the price of the shares fell during the year, so the Laus and the plaintiffs simultaneously entered a subsidiary agreement that the Laus were to buy back 60% of the shares at or before the end of the year at $2.50 each.

The plaintiffs then realized that if the FC shares *rose* in value during the year, the defendants and not they would benefit. They therefore refused to perform the main agreement unless the subsidiary agreement was cancelled and replaced by a guarantee by way of indemnity. The Laus, fearing delays and loss of public confidence in FC, acceded, and signed a written contract stating that '. . . in consideration of your having at our request agreed to sell all your shares' in SO, they would indemnify the plaintiffs if at the end of the year the 60% of the shares retained by the plaintiffs were worth less than $2.50 each. When this occurred the Laus refused to indemnify the plaintiffs. The plaintiffs brought an action which succeeded in the High Court, but the decision was reversed on appeal. They then appealed to the Privy Council.

The opinion of their Lordships was delivered by Lord Scarman:

The first question
The first question is whether on its true construction the written guarantee of 4th May 1973 states a consideration sufficient in law to support the Laus' promise of indemnity against a fall in value of the Fu Chip shares . . .

Counsel for the plaintiffs before their Lordships' Board but not below contends that the consideration stated in the agreement is not in reality a past one. It is to be noted that the consideration was not on 4th May 1973 a matter of history only. The instrument by its reference to the main agreement with Fu Chip incorporates as part of the stated consideration the Paos' three promises to Fu Chip: to complete the sale of Shing On, to accept shares as the price for the sale, and not to sell 60% of the shares so accepted before 30th April 1974. Thus, on 4th May 1973 the performance of the main agreement still lay in the future. Performance of these promises was of great importance to the Laus, and it is undeniable that, as the instrument declares, the promises were made to Fu Chip at the request of the Laus. It is equally clear that the instrument also includes a promise by the Paos to the Laus to fulfil their earlier promises given to Fu Chip.

The Board agrees with the submission of counsel for the plaintiffs that the consideration expressly stated in the written guarantee is sufficient in law to support the Laus' promise of indemnity. An act done before the giving of a promise to make a payment or to confer some other benefit can sometimes be consideration for the promise. The act must have been done at the promisor's request, the parties must have understood that the act was to be remunerated either by a payment or the conferment of some other benefit, and payment, or the conferment of a benefit, must have been legally enforceable had it been promised in advance. All three features are present in this case. The promise given to Fu Chip under the main agreement not to sell the shares for a year was at Lau's request. The parties understood at the time of the main agreement that the restriction on selling must be compensated for by the benefit of a guarantee against a drop in price: and such a guarantee would be legally enforceable. The agreed cancellation of the subsidiary agreement left, as the parties knew, the Paos unprotected in a respect in which at the time of the main agreement all were agreed they should be protected.

Counsel's submission for the plaintiffs is based on *Lampleigh v Brathwait*. In that case the judges said:

'First . . . a mere voluntary curtesie will not have a consideration to uphold an assumpsit. But if that curtesie were moved by a suit or request of the party that gives the assumpsit, it will bind, for the promise, though it follows, yet it is not naked, but couples it self with the suit before, and the merits of the party procured by that suit, which is the difference.'

The modern statement of the law is in the judgment of Bowen LJ in *Re Casey's Patents, Stewart v Casey*. Bowen LJ said:

'Even if it were true, as some scientific students of law believe, that a past service cannot support a future promise, you must look at the document and see if the promise cannot receive a proper effect in some other way. Now, the fact of a past service raises an implication that at the time it was rendered it was to be paid for, and, if it was a service which was to be paid for, when you get in the subsequent document a promise to pay, that promise may be treated either as an admission which evidences or as a positive bargain which fixes the amount of that reasonable remuneration on the faith of which the service was originally rendered. So that here for past services there is ample justification for the promise to give the third share.'

Conferring a benefit is, of course, an equivalent to payment: . . .

Counsel for the defendants does not dispute the existence of the rule but challenges its application to the facts of this case. He submits that it is not a necessary inference or implication from the terms of the written guarantee that any benefit or protection was to be given to the Paos for their acceptance of the restriction on selling their shares. Their Lordships agree that the mere existence or recital of a prior request is not sufficient in itself to convert what is prima facie past consideration into sufficient consideration in law to support a promise: as they have indicated, it is only the first of three necessary preconditions. As for the second of those preconditions, whether the act done at the request of the promisor raises an implication of promised remuneration or other return is simply one of the construction of the words of the contract in the circumstances of its making. Once it is recognised, as the Board considers it inevitably must be, that the expressed consideration includes a reference to the Paos' promise not to sell the shares before 30th April 1974, a promise to be performed in the future, though given in the past, it is not possible to treat the Laus' promise of indemnity as independent of the Paos' antecedent promise, given at Lau's request, not to sell. The promise of indemnity was given because at the time of the main agreement the parties intended that Lau should confer on the Paos the benefit of his protection against a fall in price. When the subsidiary agreement was cancelled, all were well aware that the Paos were still to have the benefit of his protection as consideration for the restriction on selling. It matters not whether the indemnity thus given be regarded as the best evidence of the benefit intended to be conferred in return for the promise not to sell, or as the positive bargain which fixes the benefit on the faith of which the promise was given, though where, as here, the subject is a written contract, the better analysis is probably that of the 'positive bargain.' Their Lordships, therefore, accept the submission that the contract itself states a valid consideration for the promise of indemnity.

This being their Lordships' conclusion, it is unnecessary to consider the further submission of counsel for the plaintiffs (also raised for the first time before the Board) that the option given the Laus, if called on to fulfil their indemnity, to buy back the shares at $2.50 a share was itself a sufficient consideration for the promise of indemnity. But their Lordships see great force in the contention. The Laus promised to indemnify the plaintiffs if the market price of Fu Chip shares fell below $2.50. However, in the event of the Laus being called on to implement this promise they were given an option to take up the shares themselves at $2.50. This on the face of it imposes on the plaintiffs in the circumstances envisaged, an obligation to transfer the shares to the Laus at the price of $2.50 if called on to do so. The concomitant benefit to the Laus could be a real one, for example, if they thought that the market, after a temporary set-back, would recover to a price above $2.50. The fact that the option is stated in the form of a proviso does not preclude it being a contractual term or one under which consideration moves.

[His Lordship went on to hold that there was good consideration for the promise of indemnity despite the fact that the primary consideration was the promise given by the plaintiffs to the Laus to perform their contract with FC: a promise to perform, or the performance of, a pre-existing contractual obligation to a third party can be valid consideration. See above, p 100.]

[Further extracts from this case will be found on p 642.]

NOTES

1. In what circumstances will it be inferred that the party who later made the promise was originally requesting the service on the understanding that it would be remunerated? To revert to the example of Bishop driving Beale home, suppose that Beale asks for the lift. Do you think the result might differ according to whether Bishop lives in Oxford or just outside Warwick?
2. Suppose the service is provided on the understanding that it is to be paid for, but Beale never makes any promise to pay. Can Bishop recover, and if so, how much?
3. In *Gilbert & Partners v Knight* [1968] 2 All ER 248 the parties agreed that the plaintiff surveyors would plan and supervise some alterations estimated to cost some £600, for a fee of £30. Later the defendant decided to make the alterations more extensive and the total cost was £2,238. The surveyors supervised the work and claimed an additional fee (in effect a scale fee) of £105. The Court of Appeal held that given that the defendant knew nothing of scale fees and had not been warned by the plaintiffs that an extra fee would be charged, there was no necessary implication that the defendant was going to pay extra, and she was not liable.
4. What would have been the outcome in *Gilbert v Knight* if the defendant had equally not realized that she would be asked to pay, but when the plaintiffs broached the matter she had said she would pay them £50 extra and had then failed to pay it?

(d) Gratuitous promises

Why are informal gratuitous promises, however seriously made, not enforceable in English law? Reasons for enforcing bargains but not gift promises fall into two broad categories, the substantive and the formal.

(i) Substantive reasons

> A truly gratuitous, nonreciprocal promise to confer a benefit is not part of the process by which resources are moved, through a series of exchanges, into successively more valuable uses.

(Posner, *Economic Analysis of Law*, p 69.)

> From an economic point of view onerous contracts tend to promote an increase in the public wealth. A gift, on the other hand, is a sterile transmission . . . Gifts are furthermore transactions in which there may be reason to fear that the donor is activated by motives that are not always honorable; so that from this point of view the protection of the family should be drawn into consideration, especially since gifts expose the giver to improper influences and intrigues against which he should be defended.

(Bufnoir, *Propriété et Contrat* (2nd edn, 1924), pp 487–488.)

NOTE

A has promised to pay B for goods which B has now delivered to A, and £50 to C as a gift. He cannot pay both B and C. Should their claims rank equally?

Despite these points, gift promises are enforceable in two circumstances.

Firstly, a gift promise is enforceable if it is made by deed. Traditionally the deed had to bear a seal, though this came to mean no more than that the document bore some reference to a seal or 'being sealed' (see the example shown opposite). In its Working Paper No 93, *Transfer of Land: Formalities for Deeds and Escrows* (1985) the Law Commission said:

> 4.2 In practice, sealing today is for most individuals a meaningless exercise involving sticking a small circle of red adhesive paper onto the document. It is probably not fixed to the document by the grantor himself, but by his solicitor. As long ago as 1937 it was said that ". . . a seal nowadays is very much in the nature of a legal fiction . . . It is the party's signature, and not his seal, which in fact authenticates the document . . ." More recently Lord Wilberforce has suggested the removal of "this medieval doctrine of the seal." He continued ". . . sealing is now a completely fictitious matter . . . I would have hoped that we might have got rid of that mumbo-jumbo and aligned ourselves with most other civilised countries."
>
> 4.3 Quite apart from the lack of any reason of substance for requiring a seal, the law as to what constitutes a valid seal is still unclear. The Court of Appeal in *First National Securities Ltd v Jones* held that a document which had no wax or wafer seal but which had a circle with the letters "L.S." printed on it was capable of being a deed. It was sufficient that the document purported to be a deed and indicated where the seal should be.

It proposed instead that deeds should have to be witnessed. Its final recommendations (Report No 163, *Deeds and Escrows*, HC1, 1987) led to legislation.

Law of Property (Miscellaneous Provisions) Act 1989

Section 1: Deeds and their execution

(1) Any rule of law which
  (a) restricts the substances on which a deed may be written;
  (b) requires a seal for the valid execution of an instrument as a deed by an individual; or
  (c) requires authority by one person to another to deliver an instrument as a deed on his behalf to be given by deed,
is abolished.

(2) An instrument shall not be a deed unless
  (a) it makes it clear on its face that it is intended to be a deed by the person making it or, as the case may be, by the parties to it (whether by describing itself as a deed or expressing itself to be executed or signed as a deed or otherwise); and
  (b) it is validly executed as a deed by that person or, as the case may be, one or more of those parties.

(3) An instrument is validly executed as a deed by an individual if, and only if
  (a) it is signed
    (i) by him in the presence of a witness who attests the signature; or
    (ii) at his direction and in his presence and the presence of two witnesses who each attest the signature; and
  (b) it is delivered as a deed by him or a person authorised to do so on his behalf.

(4) In subsections (2) and (3) above 'sign', in relation to an instrument, includes making one's mark on the instrument and 'signature' is to be construed accordingly.

. . . .

(11) Nothing in this section applies in relation to instruments delivered as deeds before this section comes into force.

It is quite likely that seals will continue to be used; their presence will not invalidate deeds. You will find that some of the readings which follow refer to sealed documents.

Secondly, a gift promise can be made enforceable by employing the device of nominal consideration, so that the promise is ostensibly exchanged for £1 or a peppercorn. The enforcement of promises made for merely nominal consideration may seem to follow from the law's (supposed) refusal to

FORM 2

To be returned with
Form 1

University of Bristol

Alumni Foundation

ANNUAL GIFTS

DEED OF COVENANT

**Please insert full
name and address**

I (Professor/Dr/Mr/Mrs/Miss) ....

of ....

....

hereby covenant with the University of Bristol that for four years from the date hereof or
during my life if shorter, I will pay to the University of Bristol on the ..... *day

of .... in each year such sum as after deduction of income tax at the

standard rate for the time being in force will amount to £. ......†

Signed, sealed and delivered

....
Donor's signature

Date ....

**in the presence of
Signature of witness** ....

Address of witness ....

Notes: *This date must be the same as or later than the date on which this deed is signed.
†Enter here the actual amount which you wish to give annually.

investigate the adequacy of consideration, but it is not a necessary consequence. It would be possible for the law to differentiate between exchanges which were bargains, even though the items exchanged were not apparently of equal value, and 'sham' bargains, gift promises merely cast into the form of bargains. Such distinctions could be very difficult, but just this sort of distinction has to be made frequently in tax cases. This is also the approach taken by Restatement 2d s 75 comment (b): '. . . a mere pretence of bargain does not suffice, as where there is a false recital of consideration or where the consideration is purely nominal'. It remains to be seen whether this lead will be followed by the US courts.

Why are gift promises by deed and promises for merely nominal consideration treated differently from gift promises made without such formalities?

(ii) Formal reasons

'Consideration and Form' by Fuller (1941) 31 Col LR 799 at 800–806, 822–823

THE FUNCTIONS PERFORMED BY LEGAL FORMALITIES

The evidentiary function. The most obvious function of a legal formality is, to use Austin's words, that of providing 'evidence of the existence and purport of the contract, in case of controversy'. The need for evidentiary security may be satisfied in a variety of ways: by requiring a writing, or attestation, or the certification of a notary. It may even be satisfied, to some extent, by such a device as the Roman *stipulatio*, which compelled an oral spelling out of the promise in a manner sufficiently ceremonious to impress its terms on participants and possible bystanders.

The cautionary function. A formality may also perform a cautionary or deterrent function by acting as a check against inconsiderate action. The seal in its original form fulfilled this purpose remarkably well. The affixing and impressing of a wax wafer—symbol in the popular mind of legalism and weightiness—was an excellent device for inducing the circumspective frame of mind appropriate in one pledging his future. To a less extent any requirement of a writing, of course, serves the same purpose, as do requirements of attestation, notarization, etc.

The channeling function. Though most discussions of the purposes served by formalities go no further than the analysis just presented, this analysis stops short of recognizing one of the most important functions of form. That a legal formality may perform a function not yet described can be shown by the seal. The seal not only insures a satisfactory memorial of the promise and induces deliberation in the making of it. It serves also to mark or signalize the enforceable promise; it furnishes a simple and external test of enforceability. This function of form Ihering described as 'the facilitation of judicial diagnosis', and he employed the analogy of coinage in explaining it.

Form is for a legal transaction what the stamp is for a coin. Just as the stamp of the coin relieves us from the necessity of testing the metallic content and weight—in short, the value of the coin (a test which we could not avoid if uncoined metal were offered to us in payment), in the same way legal formalities relieve the judge of an inquiry *whether* a legal transaction was intended, and—in case different forms are fixed for different legal transactions—*which* was intended.

In this passage it is apparent that Ihering has placed an undue emphasis on the utility of form for the judge, to the neglect of its significance for those transacting business out of court . . . To the business man who wishes to make his own or another's promise binding, the seal was at common law available as a device for the accomplishment of his objective. In this aspect form offers a legal framework into which the party may fit his actions, or, to change the figure, it offers channels for the legally effective expression of intention. It is with this aspect of form in mind that I have described the third function of legal formalities, as 'the channeling function'. . . .

Interrelations of the three functions. Though I have stated the three functions of legal form separately, it is obvious that there is an intimate connection between them. Generally speaking, whatever tends to accomplish one of these purposes will also tend to accomplish the other two. He who is compelled to do something which will furnish a satisfactory memorial of his intention will be induced to deliberate. Conversely, devices which induce deliberation will usually have an evidentiary value. Devices which insure evidence or prevent inconsiderateness will normally advance the desideratum of channeling, in two different ways. In the first place, he who is compelled to formulate his intention carefully will tend to fit it into legal and business categories. In this way the party is induced to canalize his own intention. In the second place, wherever the requirement of a formality is backed by the sanction of the invalidity of the informal transaction (and this is the means by which requirements of form are normally made effective), a degree of channeling results automatically. Whatever may be its legislative motive, the formality in such a case tends to effect a categorization of transactions into legal and non-legal.

Just as channeling may result unintentionally from formalities directed toward other ends, so these other ends tend to be satisfied by any device which accomplishes a channeling of expression. There is an evidentiary value in the clarity and definiteness of contour which such a device accomplishes. Anything which effects a neat division between the legal and the non-legal, or between different kinds of legal transactions, will tend also to make apparent to the party the consequences of his action and will suggest deliberation where deliberation is needed. . . .

Despite the close interrelationship of the three functions of form, it is necessary to keep the distinctions between them in mind since the disposition of borderline cases of compliance may turn on our assumptions as to the end primarily sought by a particular formality. . . .

When are formalities needed? The effect of an informal satisfaction of the desiderata underlying the use of formalities. The analysis of the functions of legal form which has just been presented is useful in answering a question which will assume importance in the later portion of this discussion when a detailed treatment of consideration is undertaken. That question is: In what situations does good legislative policy demand the use of a legal formality? One part of the answer to the question is clear at the outset. Forms must be reserved for relatively important transactions. We must preserve a proportion between means and end; it will scarcely do to require a sealed and witnessed document for the effective sale of a loaf of bread.

But assuming that the transaction in question is of sufficient importance to support the use of a form if a form is needed, how is the existence of this need to be determined? A general answer would run somewhat as follows: *The need for investing a particular transaction with some legal formality will depend upon the extent to which the guaranties that the formality would afford are rendered superfluous by forces native to the situation out of which the transaction arises—* including in these 'forces' the habits and conceptions of the transacting parties.

Whether there is any need, for example, to set up a formality designed to induce deliberation will depend upon the degree to which the factual situation, innocent of any legal remolding, tends to bring about the desired circumspective frame of mind. An example from the law of gifts will make this point clear. To accomplish an effective gift of a chattel without resort to the use of documents, delivery of the chattel is ordinarily required and mere donative words are ineffective. It is thought, among other things, that mere words do not sufficiently impress on the donor the significance and seriousness of his act. In an Oregon case, however, the donor declared his intention to give a sum of money to the donee and at the same time disclosed to the donee the secret hiding place where he had placed the money. Though the whole donative act consisted merely of words, the court held the gift to be effective. The words which gave access to the money which the donor had so carefully concealed would presumably be accomplished by the same sense of present deprivation which the act of handing over the money would have produced. The situation contained its own guaranty against inconsiderateness.

So far as the channeling function of a formality is concerned it has no place where men's activities are already divided into definite, clear-cut business categories. Where life has already organized itself effectively, there is no need for the law to intervene. It is for this reason that important transactions on the stock and produce markets can safely be carried on in the most 'informal' manner. At the other extreme we may cite the negotiations between a house-to-house book salesman and the housewife. Here the situation may be such that the housewife is not certain whether she is being presented with a set of books as a gift, whether she is being asked to trade her letter of recommendation for the books, whether the books are being offered to her on approval, or whether—what is, alas, the fact—a simple sale of the books is being proposed. The ambiguity of the situation is, of course, carefully cultivated and exploited by the canvasser. Some 'channeling' here would be highly desirable, though whether a legal form is the most practicable means of bringing it about is, of course, another question.

NOTES

1. How far are Fuller's three functions fulfilled in the case of:
   (1) a witnessed deed promising to pay £100?
   (2) a promise in a letter written in the promisor's own handwriting and signed by her?
   (3) a promise by a company to sell some used office equipment to a charitable organisation for £1 when both sides know the equipment is worth at least £1,000?
2. Fuller argues that sometimes the inherent nature or circumstances of the transaction will ensure that the three functions are adequately fulfilled without need for formalities. To what extent is this the case with:
   (1) a bargain which has been performed on one side, for example a contract for the sale of goods where the goods have been delivered but not paid for?
   (2) a bargain which is wholly executory, neither party having performed yet?
   (3) a promise by a woman to a bank to guarantee her son-in-law's overdraft?
3. For further reading, see Dawson, *Gifts and Promises* (1980), especially chapter 4; Hamson, 'The Reform of Consideration' (1938) 54 LQR 233.

Even if problems of proof, intention and rashness are taken care of by requiring a deed or nominal consideration, is there any good reason for enforcing even these gratuitous promises?

'Gratuitous promises in economics and law' by Posner (1977) 6 JLS 411 at 411–415, 419–420

THE ECONOMICS OF 'GRATUITOUS' PROMISES

Why would 'economic man' ever make a promise without receiving in exchange something of value from the promisee, whether it be money, a promise of future performance beneficial to the promisor, or something else of value to him? It is tempting to answer this question simply by invoking 'interdependent utilities'. Since people may indeed derive utility or welfare from increases in the utility or welfare of family members, or for that matter of strangers, interdependence may explain why (some) gifts or transfers are made. But it cannot explain why a *promise* to make a transfer in the future is made. . . .

[I]f A wanted merely to transfer $25,000 to B (his favourite charity), why would he *promise* B to make the transfer in the future? Why not wait until he is ready to make the transfer and just do it? The purpose of a promise seems to be to induce performance of some sort by the promisee; if reciprocal performance is not desired, there seems no reason to make a promise.

The approach taken here is that a gratuitous promise, to the extent it actually commits the promisor to the promised course of action (an essential qualification), creates utility for the promisor over and above the utility to him of the promised performance. At one level this proposition is a tautology: a promise would not be made unless it conferred utility on the promisor. The interesting question is how it does so. I shall argue that it does so by increasing the present value of an uncertain future stream of transfer payments.

To illustrate, suppose A promises to give $1000 a year for the next 20 years to the B symphony orchestra. The value of the gift to B is the discounted present value of $1000 to be paid yearly over a 20-year period in the future. Among the factors that will be used by B in discounting these expected future receipts to present value is the likelihood that at some time during the 20-year period A will discontinue the annual payments. Depending on B's estimation of A's fickleness, income prospects, etc, the present value of the gift of $1000 a year may be quite small; it may not be much more than $1000. But suppose the gift is actually worth more to B because A is certain to continue the payments throughout the entire period, though this fact is not known to B. If A can make a binding promise to continue the payments in accordance with his intention, B will revalue the gift at its true present worth. The size of the gift (in present-value terms) will be increased at no cost to A. Here is a clear case where the enforcement of a gratuitous promise would increase net social welfare.

This can be seen even more clearly by considering A's alternatives if his promise is not enforceable. One possibility would be for A to promise a larger gift, the discounted value of which to B would be equal to the true value as known to A. The higher cost of the gift to A would be a measure of the social cost of the unenforceability of his promise. Another possibility would be for A to substitute for the promised series of future transfers a one-time transfer the present value of which would be the same as that of the series of enforceable future transfers. However, the fact that A preferred making a future gift to a present one suggests that they are not perfect substitutes; there are many reasons (including tax and liquidity considerations) why they might not be. Consequently, if A cannot bind himself to make a series of future gifts, he may be led to substitute a one-time transfer, the present value of which is less than that of the series of future gifts, although greater than that of a declared but unenforceable intention to make a series of future gifts. Thus, nonenforceability of gratuitous promises could tend to bias transfers excessively toward immediacy.

The above analysis rests on the assumption of a symmetry of information between promisor and promisee. Such an assumption may seem implausible: why would not the asymmetry be corrected by a simple communication from A to B, which would make both parties better off? However, because the relevant information concerns A's subjective intentions, the asymmetry is both plausible and difficult to eliminate. A can state his true intentions to B, but how is he to convince B that the statement is correct? One way of making his statement credible is for A to make it costly for himself to lie; embodying the statement in a promise that is legally enforceable does this.

. . . Suppose that A really is fickle and B assesses his fickleness accurately. There is then no asymmetry in the information possessed by the parties. But A may still want to make a gift having a present value that is larger than it would be if B's future receipts had to be discounted by the probability that A would actually make each payment when the time came to do so. A will balance the utility to him of making a larger (in present-value terms) gift now against the disutility of losing the freedom to change his mind in the future. He may decide that the utility of the larger gift now is greater, in which event it will be in his self-interest to make a promise that commits him irrevocably. Once again, enforcement of a gratuitous promise will lead to a net increase in social welfare.

The economic case for enforcing the gratuitous promise, it should be noted, is similar to that for enforcing bilateral promises. The failure to enforce bilateral promises would bias exchanges toward those that take place instantaneously, as distinct from those that are completed only over a period of time, even though the former may often be less valuable (as in our examples), or more costly, than the deferred exchange. But the symmetry between gratuitous and bilateral promises has been obscured in conventional legal analysis by a tendency to view a promise as a pure cost to the promisor, a limitation on his freedom of action and nothing more.

. . . [T]his analysis ignores the fact that being legally bound to make an intended transfer may enhance ex ante the value of the transfer to A and thereby increase the social product, just as in the case of bilateral promises.

One may doubt in light of the foregoing analysis whether the term 'gratuitous' promise is useful or even meaningful. To make a binding promise may, as we have seen, be rational maximizing behavior even in the absence of consideration flowing from the promisee. The *source* of the benefit to the promisor would seem a detail from the standpoint of whether particular promises should be enforced by the law.

OPTIMAL RULES FOR ENFORCING 'GRATUITOUS' PROMISES

The analysis in Part I may seem to imply that *all* promises, whether compensated or 'gratuitous', should be enforced; or at least that enforceability should not depend on whether the promise is one or the other. The second implication has, as we shall see, appeal; but the first is questionable because it ignores the costs to the legal system of enforcing promises. The design of optimal rules of substantive law must always take into account the costs of enforcement. Promises should not be enforced where the enforcement cost—to the extent not borne by the promisor—exceeds the gain from enforcement. The qualification is, of course, essential; if the promisor bore the full costs of enforcement, it would be a matter of indifference to society whether he chose to make enforceable a promise that seemed to confer on him but trivial utility relative to enforcement costs. But it is in fact unlikely—quite apart from the public subsidy of the court system—that such a promisor would bear those costs fully: if he reneged on his promise, and the promisee brought suit against him, the promisor would not be required to defray the promisee's costs of suit. Another category of enforcement costs that are not fully internalized consists of the costs of legal error. Here the focus is not on the promisor but on the mistaken or dishonest 'promisee' who imposes on his 'promisor' the costs of defending a groundless suit, at the same time incurring litigation costs of his own which have no social value either.

The question whether it is economical for society to recognize a promise as legally enforceable thus requires a comparison of the utility of the promise to the promisor with the social cost of enforcing the promise.

. . . The social costs of enforcing the promise depend first of all on the administrative costs of enforcement. These in turn are a function in part of the size of the promised transfer, for expenditures on litigation are an investment in its outcome and therefore tend to be larger, the greater the stakes in the litigation. The social costs of enforcement also depend on the likelihood of an error—eg of finding a promise where none in fact was made. . . .

Promises under seal
Promises under seal are a traditional and, again, an economically appropriate exception to the requirement that an enforceable promise must be supported by consideration. The requirement of the seal eliminates the major administrative costs associated with the enforcement of unilateral promises. The formalities and written character of the promise reduce both the costs of determining the content of the promise and the probability that the promise was not made or was not intended to be binding.

NOTES

1. Posner is writing of American law, and his point that the promisor who is successfully sued by a promisee does not have to pay the latter's costs of suit refers to the American practice of not awarding costs. Even in England, however, it is rare that the winning party recovers his or her full costs.
2. If a person covenants to pay a sum of money to a charity but then defaults, how likely is it that the charity will sue? If the answer is, not at all likely, does that affect Posner's analysis?
3. Posner's analysis suggests that a person who makes a purely gratuitous promise may well derive a benefit thereby. If this is correct, and if the older definitions of consideration which say that a benefit to the promisor is sufficient are also correct, are gratuitous promises made for good consideration? Something must be wrong somewhere. One possibility is that the older definitions are misleading, that benefit to the promisor alone is *not* sufficient, and that the essence of consideration doctrine is that the promisee should be doing something (suffering a 'detriment') in exchange for the promise. But there is another possibility which seems to be more consistent with both the older definitions and the recent case of *William v Roffey Bros* (above, p 103). Remember that in *Thomas v Thomas* (above, p 114) Patteson J said that some benefit accruing to the promisor but not moving from the promisee (in that case, the benefit was the satisfaction of having carried out the testator's wishes) was mere 'motive'. Thus a benefit to the promisor by itself can be consideration but only if it results from something done by the promisee (or something the promisee has forborne from doing) in exchange for the promise, even if the promisee doesn't suffer any real detriment. Or to put it another way, the 'detriment' may be purely 'legal'—something recognised by the law as a detriment—even if *in fact* there is no real detriment. Thus promising not to smoke until you are 21 can provide consideration, even if you don't smoke anyway: but receiving a gift, though in a sense it 'benefits' the promisor, doesn't amount to consideration because it doesn't result from anything the promisee has done. (Even when the promisee has 'done something' in exchange for the promise, the difficulty of deciding

whether it is the kind of detriment the law recognises remains: see above, p 93.)

Are there other promises which should be enforced without consideration? Suppose a bankrupt who has been discharged promises one of his erstwhile creditors that he will pay the discharged debt; a minor who obtained goods on credit and was not liable for them because they were not 'necessaries' (see below, p 666) on coming of age promises to pay the supplier; or a debtor whose liability is barred under the Limitation Act promises to pay his creditor after all?

At one time each of these three promises would have been binding in English law. Lord Mansfield held that in such cases of a liability which was unenforceable because of a technical rule of law the existence of a moral obligation to pay was sufficient.

> Where a man is under a moral obligation, which no Court of Law of Equity can inforce, and promises, the honesty and rectitude of the thing is a consideration. As if a man promises to pay a just debt, the recovery of which is barred by the Statute of Limitations: or if a man, after he comes of age, promises to pay a meritorious debt contracted during his minority, but not for necessaries; or if a bankrupt, in affluent circumstances after his certificate, promises to pay the whole of his debts . . . In such and many other instances, though the promise gives a compulsory remedy, where there was none before either in law or equity; yet as the promise is only to do what an honest man ought to do, the ties of conscience upon an upright mind are a sufficient consideration.

(*Hawkes v Saunders* (1782) 1 Cowp 289, at 290.)

Historically there was support for this doctrine (see Simpson, *History of the Common Law of Contract* (1975), p 323). In *Sharp v Ellis, Re Edward Love & Co Pty Ltd* [1972] VR 137 an Australian judge refused to extend it to a case where a company subsequently promised to pay a debt which when it was contracted was void by statute because it was ultra vires, but the doctrine enunciated by Mansfield has never formally been overruled. In many of the United States it is still in force (see Farnsworth, *Contracts*, pp 53–54), and as the next reading suggests, there is something to be said for it.

'Gratuitous Promises in Economics and Law', by Posner at 418

Past consideration
Among the exceptions to the general principle that gratutitous promises will not be enforced are several which are grouped under the rubric of 'past consideration'. A subsequent promise to pay a debt barred by the statute of limitations, or to pay a debt discharged in bankruptcy, or to pay a debt that is uncollectable because the debtor was a minor at the time the debt was contracted, is legally enforceable even though there is no fresh consideration for the promise. These are classes of promise in which the utility of the promise to the promisor is often great and the costs of enforcement low. First, as regards utility, it should be noted not only that the stakes are often substantial (these are formal debts after all) but that the *incremental* gain in utility from the enforceable character of the promise may be great. The legal promise conveys information (which a mere stated intention to pay would not) about the promisor's attitude toward the payment of debts barred by a technicality. The information conveyed enhances the promisor's reputation for credit-worthiness and may induce people—not necessarily the promisee himself, which is why the promise itself may not be bilateral—to extend credit to him in the future. And enforcement costs are likely to be low or at least no higher than in conventional bilateral-contract cases because the underlying obligation—the original debt—is fully bilateral. The original debt is not directly enforceable only because of a condition which in the case of the statute of limitations slightly, and in the case of discharge in bankruptcy or voidability by reason of minority not at all, increases the likelihood of error compared to what it would have been in a suit on the original bilateral contract that gave rise to the debt.

However, in English law the rule has been changed by a statute in two of the three situations (Bankruptcy Act 1869, s 4, and see *Heather & Son v Webb* (1876) 2 CPD 1; Limitation Act 1980, s 29(7).) Now the promisor will only be liable if there is fresh consideration for the promise. Why have these changes been made? Since the changes are statutory they are unlikely to be the result of a quest for doctrinal purity. What policies underlie the statutes? You may like to consider *Wild v Tucker* [1914] 3 KB 36; Law Reform Committee, 21st Report, *Final Report on Limitation of Actions*, (Cmnd 6923 (1977)) paras 2.68–2.71.

For many years promises to perform obligations incurred in infancy were also invalidated by the Infants Relief Act 1874, s 2. This may have given young adults some protection against being pressured into promising to perform; but the restrictions were easily evaded as they did not apply to 'fresh contracts' to perform the previously unenforceable bargains (except for fresh contracts to repay loans incurred in infancy, which were invalidated by the Betting and Loans (Infants) Act 1892, s 5). Thus if the creditor gave some fresh consideration, however small, to the young adult, the latter's promise would be binding. The Law Commission thought it illogical to distinguish between fresh promises and fresh contracts (see Report No 184, *Law of Contract: Minors' Contracts*, 1984) and both the Infants Relief Act 1874, s 2, and the Betting and Loans (Infants) Act 1892, s 5, were repealed by the Minors' Contracts Act 1987, s 1. Thus the old common law, whereby a promise made to perform an obligation incurred in infancy is binding without fresh consideration, was revived.

Could the moral obligation doctrine be broadened to cover the case of a benefit which the promisee has earlier conferred gratuitously on the promisor?

In *Webb v McGowin* 27 Ala App 82, 168 So 196 (1935) Webb was in the act of dropping a pine block from the upper floor of a sawmill (this being the accepted procedure) when McGowin stepped where the block would have fallen. Webb kept hold of the block and fell with it, preventing it hitting McGowin but receiving injuries that crippled him for life. A month later McGowin promised to support Webb for the rest of Webb's life at a rate of $15 every two weeks, but after McGowin's death eight years later the payments were discontinued. The Court of Appeals of Alabama held that the benefit received by McGowin was sufficient consideration. In contrast, in *Harrington v Taylor* 225 NC 690, 36 SE 2d 227 (1945) the defendant had assaulted his wife, who took refuge in the plaintiff's house. The next day the defendant gained access to the house and began another assault on his wife. The wife knocked down the defendant with an axe and was on the point of cutting his head open or decapitating him while he lay on the floor when the plaintiff intervened, catching the axe as it descended. The defendant's life was saved but the plaintiff's hand was badly mutilated. The defendant subsequently promised to pay the plaintiff her loss, but after paying a small sum failed to pay any more. The Supreme Court of North Carolina held that the promise was without consideration.

At present English courts could not achieve the result in *Webb v McGowin* without overruling venerable authority.

Eastwood v Kenyon (1840) 11 Ad&El 438, 113 ER 482, Queen's Bench

John Sutcliffe had died leaving his infant daughter Sarah as his sole heiress. The plaintiff, Sutcliffe's executor, acted as her guardian and spent money on her education and improving her estate, borrowing £140 for these purposes. When she came of age, Sarah promised to pay the plaintiff the amount of the loan, and when she married, her husband, the defendant, made a similar promise. The plaintiff sued on the husband's promise. The Court of Queen's Bench held the promise to be unenforceable. Lord Denman CJ said:

Most of the older cases on this subject are collected in a learned note to the case of *Wennall v Adney*, and the conclusion there arrived at seems to be correct in general, 'that an express promise can only revive a good consideration, which might have been enforced at law through the medium of an implied promise, had it not been suspended by some positive rule of law; but can give no original cause of action, if the obligation, on which it is founded, never could have been enforced at law, though not barred by any legal maxim or statute provision'. Instances are given of voidable contracts, as those of infants ratified by an express promise after age, and distinguished from void contracts, as of married women, not capable of ratification by them when widows; *Loyd v Lee*; debts of bankrupts revived by subsequent promise after certificate; and similar cases. . . .

The eminent counsel who argued for the plaintiff in *Lee v Muggeridge*, spoke of Lord Mansfield as having considered the rule of nudum pactum as too narrow, and maintained that all promises deliberately made ought to be held binding. I do not find this language ascribed to him by any reporter, and do not know whether we are to receive it as a traditional report, or as a deduction from what he does appear to have laid down. If the latter, the note to *Wennall v Adney*, shews the deduction to be erroneous. If the former, Lord Tenterden and this Court declared that they could not adopt it in *Littlefield v Shee*. Indeed the doctrine would annihilate the necessity for any consideration at all, inasmuch as the mere fact of giving a promise creates a moral obligation to perform it.

The enforcement of such promises by law, however plausibly reconciled by the desire to effect all conscientious engagements, might be attended with mischievous consequences to society; one of which would be the frequent preference of voluntary undertakings to claims for just debts. Suits would thereby be multiplied, and voluntary undertakings would also be multiplied, to the prejudice of real creditors. The temptations of executors would be much increased by the prevalence of such a doctrine, and the faithful discharge of their duty be rendered more difficult.

NOTE

Why is this kind of voluntary undertaking less deserving than a 'just debt'? Compare p 119 above.

'Gratuitous Promises', by Posner at pp 418–419

Another class of 'past consideration' cases, however, is best understood on the premise of the law's (implicit) recognition of the existence of interdependent utility functions. These are cases involving promises to compensate rescuers or others who have rendered an unbargained but valuable service to the promisor. The existence of a promise in such a case is strongly attested by the presence of circumstances likely to induce an act of altruism by the promisor toward the promisee. A sees B about to be run down by a speeding car and pushes him out of the way. He saves him but sustains a serious injury in the process. In economic terms, A rescued B because at the moment of danger B's expected utility or wealth was very low; the rescue was like a gift to a starving man. But after the rescue the wealth positions of the parties are dramatically reversed: now A's wealth is low relative to B's since B is whole and A is injured. Hence it is to be expected that B would promise to reward A. The presence of altruistic motivation makes the promise a more plausible one—ie, one less likely to be a figment of the promisee's imagination—than in the standard unilateral promise case. Stated otherwise, the legal-error costs of enforcing the promise are lower in the rescue case.

The facts of a leading rescue past consideration case, *Webb v McGowin*, illustrate the benefits that may accrue to the promisor in such cases if the promise is legally enforceable, over and above the benefits of the transfer itself. The rescued person promised to pay his rescuer $15 every two weeks for the rest of the rescuer's life. This was a generous gift to the extent that the promise was enforceable but a much less generous one to the extent it was not. Had the promisor believed that such a promise was unenforceable, he might have decided instead to make a one-time transfer that might have had a much lower present value than that of the annuity which he in fact promised. Both parties would have been made worse off by this alternative. Hence, it is not surprising that the court held the promise to be enforceable.

NOTES

1. Posner presents apparently persuasive reasons for enforcing the promise in *Webb v McGowin*, but can you see any reasons against enforcing the promise as if it had been made for consideration? Firstly, suppose McGowin had immediately after the accident promised Webb a sum which McGowin could pay only by making himself destitute? Were the circumstances in which McGowin made his promise such that the 'cautionary function' was automatically fulfilled?
2. Secondly, suppose that after McGowin had paid Webb for some months, circumstances changed—perhaps McGowin himself had to stop work because of ill-health, or the State introduced a scheme of industrial injury benefits that covered Webb. Should McGowin's promise still be enforced? If it ranked as a normal contract, would it still be enforceable?
3. In the light of the last question, do you think that it may have been significant that in *Webb v McGowin* the defendant was McGowin's executor, whereas in *Harrington v Taylor* the defendant had made the promise himself?
4. If you think it may not be appropriate to impose normal contractual liability in a case like *Webb v McGowin*, is there some other basis on which it could be done? Sometimes the rescued person was negligent in putting himself into a dangerous situation and should have foreseen that someone might try to rescue him and get injured in the process. Then the rescuer may recover for her injuries in tort, quite irrespective of whether the rescued person has promised her anything (see *Horsley v Maclaren* [1971] 2 Lloyds Rep 410, Sup Ct of Canada; and *Ogwo v Taylor* [1988] AC 431).
5. If the rescued person has not been negligent, no tort action will lie. Could the plaintiff recover in restitution? Compare this type of case to the restitution cases considered earlier (pp 28–32). It may well be correct to deny restitution to the 'officious intermeddler' when the defendant has never indicated any willingness to pay for the benefit conferred on him; but if he does indicate that he is willing to pay by promising to pay the rescuer something, even if only subsequently, why deny recovery?

You may like to consider Restatement 2d s 86:

Promise for benefit received
(1) A promise made in recognition of a benefit previously received by the promisor from the promisee is binding to the extent necessary to prevent injustice.
(2) A promise is not binding under subsection (1)
   (a) if the promisee conferred the benefit as a gift or for other reasons the promisor has not been unjustly enriched; or
   (b) to the extent that its value is disproportionate to the benefit.

The reporter, the late Professor Robert Braucher, conceded that the section 'bristles with non-specific concepts' (42 ALI Procs 273–274, 1965).

(e) Formal requirements

Fuller's three functions of form are, as we have seen, fulfilled to some extent in the case of even a wholly executory bilateral contract, but the safeguards may not be adequate. Many businessmen seem to believe that no contract is binding unless it is in writing, or at least that without writing it is practicably unenforceable—witness Samuel Goldwyn's famous aphorism, 'a verbal contract isn't worth the paper it's written on'.

As a matter of law, the general rule is that oral contracts are fully enforceable, but there are certain types of contract which must either be in writing or be evidenced in writing. For example:

(i) *Contracts which must be in writing.* The Law of Property (Miscellaneous Provisions) Act 1989, s 2(1) provides:

'A contract for the sale or other disposition of an interest in land can only be made in writing and only by incorporating all the terms which the parties have expressly agreed . . .'.

Under the Consumer Credit Act 1974 various types of agreement must be in a particular written form if they are to be 'properly executed' and thus fully enforceable (see below, p 665). Bills of exchange, promissory notes and bills of sale must also be in writing (Bills of Exchange Act 1882, ss 3(1), 17(2); Bills of Sale Act (1878) Amendment Act 1882.)

(ii) *Contracts which must be evidenced in writing.* The Statute of Frauds 1677 imposed this requirement on several types of contract.

Section 4
No action shall be brought whereby to charge any executor or administrator upon any special promise to answer damages out of his own estate; or whereby to charge the defendant upon any special promise to answer for the debt, default or miscarriage of another person; or to charge any person upon any agreement made upon consideration of marriage; or upon any contract or sale of lands, tenements or hereditaments, or any interest in or concerning them; or upon any agreement that is not to be performed within the space of one year from the making thereof; unless the agreement upon which such action shall be brought, or some memorandum or note thereof, shall be in writing and signed by the party to be charged therewith or some other person thereunto by him lawfully authorised.

Section 17
No contract for the sale of goods, wares or merchandises for the price of £10 sterling or upwards shall be allowed to be good except the buyer shall accept part of the goods so sold and actually receive the same, or give something in earnest to bind the bargain or in part payment, or that some note or memorandum in writing of the said bargain be made and signed by the parties to be charged by such contract or their agents thereunto lawfully authorised.

(s 17 was later replaced by s 4, Sale of Goods Act 1893).

The part of s 4 relating to land was replaced by the Law of Property Act 1925, s 40(1); this in turn was repealed by the Law of Property (Miscellaneous Provisions) Act 1989, see above. The rest of the list, including the Sale of Goods Act 1893, s 4, was gradually whittled away until now only promises 'to answer for the debt, default or miscarriage of another person' remain. This book will not cover the law on this topic, nor consider why the requirements for contracts for the sale of land were changed recently—that is a complex topic involving the doctrine of 'part performance' which the courts had developed as a qualification to the statutory requirements. (See Law Commission Report No 164, *Formalities for contracts for sale etc of land*, HC2, 1987). However it is worth considering why the remainder of sections 4 and 17 of the Statute of Frauds has been repealed, and why it was seen fit to leave the existing requirements.

Sixth Interim Report (Statute of Frauds and the Doctrine of Consideration) of the Law Revision Committee, Cmd 5449 (1937)

. . . [I]n 1851 so experienced a common lawyer as Lord Campbell could record the opinion that the Act promotes more frauds than it prevents'. Lord Nottingham (who, since the Act was his offspring, may well have felt for it some parental partiality) used to claim that 'every line of it was worth a subsidy'; upon which claim a learned lawyer, nearly two centuries later, commented that 'every line has cost one'.

Contemporary opinion is almost unanimous in condemning the Statute and favouring its amendment or repeal.

The main criticisms directed against Section 4 may be summarised under the following heads:—

(1) First and foremost, it is urged that the Act is a product of conditions which have long passed away. At the time when it was passed, essential kinds of evidence were excluded (eg, the parties themselves could not give evidence), and objectionable types of evidence were admitted (eg juries were still in theory entitled to act on their own knowledge of the facts in dispute). It was an improvement on this state of affairs to admit the evidence of the parties, even though only to the extent that such evidence was in signed writing. To-day, when the parties can freely testify, the provisions of Section 4 are an anachronism. A condition of things which was advanced in relation to 1677 is backward in relation to 1937.

(2) 'The Act', in the words of Lord Campbell already cited 'promotes more frauds than it prevents'. True, it shuts out perjury; but it also more frequently shuts out the truth. It strikes impartially at the perjurer and at the honest man who has omitted a precaution, sealing the lips of both. Mr Justice FitzJames Stephen (writing of Section 17, but his observation applies equally to Section 4) went so far as to assert that 'in the vast majority of cases its operation is simply to enable a man to break a promise with impunity, because he did not write it down with sufficient formality'.

(3) The classes of contracts to which Section 4 applies seem to be arbitrarily selected and to exhibit no relevant common quality. There is no apparent reason why the requirement of signed writing should apply to these contracts, and to all of them, and to no others.

(4) The Section is out of accord with the way in which business is normally done. Where actual practice and legal requirement diverge, there is always an opening for knaves to exploit the divergence.

(5) The operation of the Section is often lopsided and partial. A and B contract: A has signed a sufficient note or memorandum, but B has not. In these circumstances B can enforce the contract against A, but A cannot enforce it against B.

(6) The Section does not reduce contracts which do not comply with it to mere nullities, but merely makes them unenforceable by action. For other purposes they preserve their efficacy (for *what* other purposes precisely, is doubtful). Anomalous results flow from this: eg in *Morris v Baron* . . . a contract which complied with the Section was superseded by a second contract which did not so comply. It was held that neither contract could be enforced: the first, because it was validly rescinded by the second, the second because, owing to its purely oral character, no action could be brought on it. This was a result which the parties could not possibly have intended.

(7) Apart from its policy the Statute is in point of language obscure and ill-drafted. 'It is universally admitted', observed the original editor of Smith's Leading Cases, 'that no Enactment of the Legislature has become the subject of so much litigation'. This could hardly have been so if its terms had been reasonably lucid.

Most of the above criticisms apply, both to Section 4 and to Section 17 of the Statute of Frauds, and therefore to Section 4 of the Sale of Goods Act, 1893, so far as it reproduces that Section. . . .

RECOMMENDATION BY A MINORITY AS TO GUARANTEES

. . . [I]f oral contracts of guarantee are allowed, we feel that there is a real danger of inexperienced people being led into undertaking obligations that they do not fully understand, and that opportunities will be given to the unscrupulous to assert that credit was given on the faith of a guarantee which in fact the alleged surety had no intention of giving. A guarantee is in any case a special class of contract; it is generally one-sided and disinterested as far as the surety is concerned, and the necessity of writing would at least give the proposed surety an opportunity of pausing and considering, not only the nature of the obligation he is undertaking, but also its terms. The contract often gives rise to many questions, eg whether it is to apply to the whole of the debt or to a portion only, and, if the former, whether it is to be limited in amount or to a certain period. We think these questions ought to be definitely settled and recorded before the contract becomes binding on the surety. Parliament has in the Law of Property Act, 1925, re-enacted the requirement of a signed note or memorandum in writing in the case of contracts for the sale of land, and has quite recently enacted that a money-lending contract is invalid unless the exact terms are embodied in a document which must be given to the proposing borrower so that he may see exactly to what he is agreeing, and, while it may be doubted if a needy borrower has ever been deterred from taking a loan by this provision, at least he cannot say that he did not know to what he was consenting. We see nothing unreasonable in putting sureties in a like position and giving them the same opportunity.

It is the 'small man' we desire to protect, the father or father-in-law of the small tradesman who may be pressed to guarantee the account for goods supplied to stock the shop of his son or son-in-law. Moreover, we believe that guarantees are a class of contract that at present most people know quite definitely must be in writing. The lay public know nothing about the Statute of Frauds; but they do, we believe, appreciate that writing is necessary for a guarantee; so our proposal only perpetuates that to which they are accustomed.

Legislation did not follow this report. In 1952 the Law Reform Committee in its First Report (Cmnd 8809) adopted the Interim Report with the revision that contracts of guarantee should remain subject to the old requirement. The Law Reform (Enforcement of Contracts) Act 1954 put these recommendations into effect.

The requirements of the Consumer Credit Act 1974 also serve evidentiary, cautionary and channelling functions. However some of the requirements are aimed at more specific problems and they will be considered later (below, p 664).

(f) Reliance on non-bargain promises

In the American case of *Ricketts v Scothorn* 57 Neb 51, 77 NW 365 (1898) Katie Scothorn was at work when her grandfather entered and gave her a promissory note which read:

> May 1st 1891. I promise to pay to Katie Scothorn on demand, $2,000, to be at 6 per cent per annum. J C. Ricketts.

He said: 'I have fixed something that you have not got to work any more. None of my grandchildren work and you don't have to.' Miss Scothorn gave notice to her employer and left her job, though a year and a half later, with her grandfather's consent, she did go back to work. Her grandfather paid her some interest but died without paying all the interest due or any of the principal sum. Miss Scothorn sued his executor.

Is it possible to say that Miss Scothorn's leaving work was consideration for her grandfather's promise? The Supreme Court of Nebraska held not: 'her right to the money promised in the note was not made to depend on an abandonment of her employment . . . Mr Ricketts made no condition, requirement or request'. The same decision might be reached in English law—indeed, this seems inevitable if, as Pollock and Restatement 2d (above, p 91) suggest, the only test of consideration is bargain. Even in more recent years, some commentators have taken this view, for instance Hamson (1938) 54 LQR 233 and Odgers (1970) 86 LQR 69, 79. On this view Miss Scothorn's act could not be consideration unless it were requested, or at least specified by her grandfather as the price of his promise (see Smith

(1953) 60 LQR 99; Goodhart, ibid 106; Atiyah, *Essays on Contract*, pp 213–214). There is also judicial support for this view. In *Combe v Combe* (below, p 139) the wife argued that her husband's promise in a separation agreement to pay her £100 a year was supported by consideration in that she never applied to the divorce court for maintenance. The Court of Appeal held that this forbearance could not be consideration as the husband had never requested it, even impliedly.

Other decisions do not seem to fit so easily with the requirement of the bargain. The promisee has done something which is to his or her detriment, and it *could* be inferred that the promisor requested it, but this interpretation seems a bit strained.

In *Shadwell v Shadwell* (above, p 115) did Charles bargain for Lancey's marriage to Ellen?

In *De La Bere v Pearson Ltd* [1908] 1 KB 280, CA a newspaper offered financial advice to readers who wrote asking for it. The advice given to the plaintiff was negligent and he lost money. It was held that the newspaper had a contractual duty to use care, the consideration being that the defendants had the right to publish the reader's letter. Was this bargained for? (Note that tortious liability for negligent advice was not recognized in this type of case until *Hedley Byrne & Co Ltd v Heller & Partners Ltd* [1964] AC 465. In that case Lord Devlin said (at p 528) that 'today the result [in *De la Bere v Pearson*] can and should be reached by application of the law of negligence and . . . it is unnecessary and undesirable to construct an artificial consideration'.)

In *Wells (Merstham) Ltd v Buckland Sand and Silica Co Ltd* (above, p 16) D told P that D's sand would conform to a certain chemical analysis, which would make it suitable for propagating chrysanthemum cuttings. P later bought some of this sand from a third party, but the sand did not conform to the analysis and P's cuttings died. It was held that D had given a warranty and buying the sand from a third party in reliance on D's statement was consideration. Was this bargained for?

In *Warlow v Harrison* (below, p 177) an auction was advertised as being 'without reserve', but the auctioneer allowed the owner to bid when the goods seemed to be going for a low price. It was held that the auctioneer was in breach of a contract with the highest bona fide bidder; the consideration was presumably the act of bidding, or perhaps attending the auction. Did the auctioneer bargain for this act?

Returning to *Ricketts v Scothorn*, the court found that there was no consideration, but nonetheless held that Miss Scothorn could enforce the note. Because she had changed her position for the worse in reliance on her grandfather's promise, just as he had intended, he was 'estopped' from 'denying the consideration'.

Would an English court enforce Rickett's promise? The question must be answered in two parts. Firstly, would it employ estoppel as a substitute for consideration? Or, secondly, would it be prepared to find that there was consideration after all?

(i) Estoppel as a substitute for consideration

What is estoppel? The essentials of the traditional version of estoppel were stated by Lord Birkenhead in *Maclaine v Gatty* [1921] 1 AC 376, at 386:

> Where A has by his words or conduct justified B in believing that a certain state of facts exists, and B has acted upon such belief to his prejudice, A is not permitted to affirm against B that a different state of facts existed at the same time.

A classic example of estoppel is if one party represents to another that A has authority to contract on his behalf, when in fact he has not so authorized A. If in reliance on this representation the other party enters a contract with A as agent, the first party (the principal) is estopped from denying that A had authority to act as his agent, and the contract made through A will be binding on him.

The estoppel is said to arise when B acts on the facts he has assumed to be true to his 'prejudice' or 'detriment'. This appears to mean that B must have acted in such a way that, were A now permitted to assert the true facts, B would be left worse off than before A misled him. In *Grundt v Great Boulder Pty Gold Mines Ltd* (1937) 59 CLR 641 at 674–675, Dixon J explained the point as follows:

> . . . [T]he real detriment or harm from which the law seeks to give protection is that which would flow from the change of position if the assumption were deserted that led to it. So long as the assumption is adhered to, the party who altered his situation upon the faith of it cannot complain. His complaint is that when afterwards the other party makes a different state of affairs the basis of an assertion of right against him then, if it is allowed, his own original change of position will operate as a detriment. His action or inaction must be such that, if the assumption upon which he proceeded were shown to be wrong and an inconsistent state of affairs were accepted as the foundation of the rights and duties of himself and the opposite party, the consequence would be to make his original act or failure to act a source of prejudice.

The traditional doctrine of estoppel is limited in two ways. Firstly, it is usually said that estoppel will not create a cause of action; it can be used as a shield but not as a sword. This is apt to be misleading; in the example just given, if an action is brought against the principal, the estoppel plays a crucial role, because without the estoppel the contract would not be binding on him. What seems to be meant is this. If there would be a cause of action against the person who made the statement if only the statement were true, estoppel will operate to provide the missing element; but if there would not be an action against the representor even if the fact stated were true, then estoppel will not create one.

The point may be illustrated by considering an estoppel created by statute, the Bills of Lading Act 1855, s 3. This provides that if the master of a ship or any other person signs a bill of lading stating that goods have been loaded on board, this shall be conclusive evidence against the signor that the goods were loaded, unless the holder of the bill of lading knew when he took it that the goods had not actually been loaded. The effect of the section depends on who it is who signs.

(a) If the owner of the ship which was to carry the goods were to sign in person for goods which had never been loaded, the section might make him liable. If the goods had actually been loaded, but subsequently disappeared, and he could not show that they had been lost through some peril for which he was not responsible, he would be liable to the holder for the value of the goods. The result of s 3 is to make him similarly liable even though the goods were never loaded at all.

(b) If, however, the bill were signed by a loading broker (a person who acts as agent for the shipowner, arranging the loading of goods, etc), the section will not make the loading broker liable to the holder, because the loading broker would not be liable even if the goods *had* been loaded and subsequently lost in some unexplained manner. He is not a party to the contract of carriage, nor would the goods ever be in his possession or custody. See *Rasnoimport V/O v Guthrie & Co Ltd* [1966] 1 Lloyd's Rep 1 at 18.

It is presumably with the point that estoppel does not itself create a cause of action in mind that the Supreme Court of Nebraska formulated its judgment in *Ricketts v Scothorn* in terms that the promisor was estopped from denying the consideration—if there had been consideration, he would have been bound.

Secondly, the representation must be one of fact. In a number of situations the law draws a distinction between a statement of existing fact, such as '*x* is the case' or 'I have done *y*', and a promise for the future, such as 'I will do *z*'. (For a further example of this distinction see below, p 288.) A promise can only be binding if there is consideration or if it is in a deed, but a statement of fact can give rise to an estoppel.

Jorden v Money (1854) 5 HL Cas 185, 10 ER 868, House of Lords

Money had given Charles Marnell a bond and warrant of attorney to secure repayment of a debt of £1,200 that Money owed to Charles' brother. On Charles' death, the defendant Mrs Jorden (then Miss Marnell) took the bond as Charles' executrix. She felt that Money had been badly treated, and frequently stated that she would never enforce the bond, repeating this particularly when Money's prospective parents-in-law expressed concern about Money's position. In reliance on her statements Money married, and then sought a declaration that the debt had been abandoned, and a release from the bond. The Master of the Rolls granted an injunction to prevent enforcement and this was upheld by the Court of the Lord Justices. Jorden appealed.

Lord Cranworth LC. There are two grounds upon which it is said that the parties have lost their right to enforce the bond. The one is, that previously to William Money's marriage Mrs Jorden, then Miss Marnell, represented that the bond had been abandoned, that she had given up her right upon it, and upon the faith of that representation the marriage was contracted. And then it is said that upon a principle well known in the law, founded upon good faith and equity, a principle equally of law and of equity, if a person makes any false representation to another, and that other acts upon that false representation, the person who has made it shall not afterwards be allowed to set up that what he said was false, and to assert the real truth in place of the falsehood which has so misled the other. That is a principle of universal application, and has been particularly applied to cases where representations have been made as to the state of the property of persons about to contract marriage, and where, upon the faith of such representations, marriage has been contracted. There the person who has made the false representations has in a great many cases been held bound to make his representations good. . . .

I am bound to state my view of the case; I think that that doctrine does not apply to a case where the representation is not a representation of a fact, but a statement of something which the party intends or does not intend to do. In the former case it is a contract, in the latter it is not; what is here contended for, is this, that Mrs Jorden, then Miss Marnell, over and over again represented that she abandoned the debt. Clothe that in any words you please, it means no more than this, that she would never enforce the debt; she does not mean, in saying that she had abandoned it, to say that she had executed a release of the debt so as to preclude her legal right to sue. All that she could mean, was that she positively promised that she never would enforce it. My opinion is, that if all the evidence had come up to the mark, which, for reasons I shall presently state, I do not think it did, that if upon the very eve of the marriage she had said, 'William Money, I never will enforce the bond against you', that would not bring it within these cases. It might be, if all statutable requisites, so far as there are statutable requisites, had been complied with, that it would have been a very good contract whereby she might have bound herself not to enforce the payment. That, however, is not the way in which it is put here; in short, it could not have been, because it must have been a contract reduced into writing and signed; but that is not the way in which this case is put; it is put entirely upon the ground of representation. Now, my Lords, I think that the not adhering to this statement, call it contract or call it representation, is no more a fraud than it would be not adhering to her engagement, if she had said, 'Mr William Money, you may marry; do not be in fear, you will not be in want; I promise to settle £10,000 Consols upon you.' If she does not perform that promise, she is guilty of a breach of contract, in respect of which she may be sued, if it is put into a valid form, but not otherwise; so if she had said, as she did to William Money, 'I mean to give you everything I am worth in the world; I promise to do so' her not doing so, is no fraud in the sense in which these cases speak of fraud; it is no misrepresentation of a fact which the party is afterwards held bound to make good as true; it seems to me that the distinction is founded upon perfectly good sense, and that in truth in the case of what is something future, there is no reason for the application of the rule, because the parties have only to say, 'Enter into a contract', and then all difficulty is removed. It appears to me, therefore, that this which is the ground upon which the Master of the Rolls proceeded, and upon which he thought that the Plaintiff Money had the right to restrain the Jordens from enforcing this bond, fails, for the reasons which I have stated.

[Lord Brougham concurred and Lord St Leonards dissented.]

Appeal allowed.

NOTES

1. In practice the distinction between a statement of fact and a promise may be a narrow one. What would have been the outcome had Mrs Jorden stated that she *had* released the debt (by release under seal)?
2. In *Ricketts v Scothorn*, did Mr Ricketts make any false statement of fact?

Central London Property Trust Ltd v High Trees House Ltd [1947] KB 130, Denning J

In 1937 the plaintiff had granted the defendant, a subsidiary of the plaintiff, a ninety-nine year lease of a block of flats at a rent of £2,500 per year. The flats had not been fully sub-let at the beginning of the war, and the tenant company could not pay the rent out of the profits of the flats that had been sub-let. After discussions, the landlord company agreed that the rent should be reduced to £1,250 per year as from the beginning of the lease, and the tenant company paid accordingly. By the beginning of 1945 the flats were fully let, and the receiver of the landlord company wrote claiming the full arrears. Later, however, he instituted a friendly action to test the legal position, merely claiming the difference between the rent paid and the original full rent as from the third quarter of 1945.

Denning J stated the facts and continued: If I were to consider this matter without regard to recent developments in the law, there is no doubt that had the plaintiffs claimed it, they would have been entitled to recover ground rent at the rate of 2,500*l* a year from the beginning of the term, since the lease under which it was payable was a lease under seal which, according to the old common law, could not be varied by an agreement by parol (whether in writing or not), but only by deed. Equity, however stepped in, and said that if there has been a variation of a deed by a simple contract (which in the case of a lease required to be in writing would have to be evidenced by writing), the courts may give effect to it as is shown in *Berry v Berry*. That equitable doctrine, however, could hardly apply in the present case because the variation here might be said to have been made without consideration. With regard to estoppel, the representation made in relation to reducing the rent, was not a representation of an existing fact. It was a representation, in effect, as to the future, namely, that payment of the rent would not be enforced at the full rate but only at the reduced rate. Such a representation would not give rise to an estoppel, because, as was said in *Jorden v Money*, a representation as to the future must be embodied as a contract or be nothing.

But what is the position in view of developments in the law in recent years? The law has not been standing still since *Jorden v Money*. There has been a series of decisions over the last fifty years which, although they are said to be cases of estoppel are not really such. They are cases in which a promise was made which was intended to create legal relations and which, to the knowledge of the person making the promise, was going to be acted on by the person to whom it was made, and which was in fact so acted on. In such cases the courts have said that the promise must be honoured. The cases to which I particularly desire to refer are: *Fenner v Blake*, *In re Wickham*, *Re William Porter & Co Ld*, and *Buttery v Pickard*. As I have said they are not cases of estoppel in the strict sense. They are really promises—promises intended to be binding, intended to be acted on, and in fact acted on. *Jorden v Money* can be distinguished, because there the promisor made it clear that she did not intend to be legally bound, whereas in the cases to which I refer the proper inference was that the promisor did intend to be bound. In each case the court held the promise to be binding on the party making it, even though under the old common law it might be difficult to find any consideration for it. The courts have not gone so far as to give a cause of action in damages for the breach of such a promise, but they have refused to allow the party making it to act inconsistently with it. It is in that sense, and that sense only, that such a promise gives rise to an estoppel. The decisions are a natural result of the fusion of law and equity: for the cases of *Hughes v Metropolitan Rly Co*, *Birmingham and District Land Co v London & North Western Rly Co* and *Salisbury (Marquess) v Gilmore*, afford a sufficient basis for saying that a party would not be allowed in equity to go back on such a promise. In my opinion, the time has now come for the validity of such a promise to be recognized. The logical consequence, no doubt is that a promise to accept a smaller sum in discharge of a larger sum, if acted upon, is binding notwithstanding the absence of consideration: and if the fusion of law and equity leads to this result, so much the better. That aspect was not considered in *Foakes v Beer*. At this time of day, however, when law and equity have been joined together for over seventy years, principles must be reconsidered in the light of their combined effect. It is to be noticed that in the Sixth Interim Report of the Law Revision Committee, it is recommended that such a promise as that to which I have referred, should be enforceable in law even though no consideration for it has been given by the promisee. It seems to me that, to the extent I have mentioned, that result has now been achieved by the decisions of the courts.

I am satisfied that a promise such as that to which I have referred is binding and the only question remaining for my consideration is the scope of the promise in the present case. I am satisfied on all the evidence that the promise here was that the ground rent should be reduced to 1,250*l* a year as a temporary expedient while the block of flats was not fully, or substantially fully let, owing to the conditions prevailing. That means that the reduction in the rent applied throughout the years down to the end of 1944, but early in 1945 it is plain that the flats were fully let, and, indeed the rents received from them (many of them not being affected by the Rent Restrictions Acts), were increased beyond the figure at which it was originally contemplated that they would be let. At all events the rent from them must have been very considerable. I find that the conditions prevailing at the time when the reduction in rent was made, had completely passed away by the early months of 1945. I am satisfied that the promise was understood by all parties only to apply under the conditions prevailing at the time when it was made, namely, when the flats were only partially let, and that it did not extend any further than that. When the flats became fully let, early in 1945, the reduction ceased to apply.

In those circumstances, under the law as I hold it, it seems to me that rent is payable at the full rate for the quarters ending September 29 and December 25, 1945.

If the case had been one of estoppel, it might be said that in any event the estoppel would cease when the conditions to which the representation applied came to an end, or it also might be said that it would only come to an end on notice. In either case it is only a way of ascertaining what is the scope of the representation. I prefer to apply the principle that a promise intended to be binding, intended to be acted on and in fact acted on, is binding so far as its terms properly apply. Here it was binding as covering the period down to the early part of 1945, and as from that time full rent is payable.

I therefore give judgment for the plaintiff company for the amount claimed.

Judgment for plaintiffs.

NOTES

1. The landlords did not claim the unpaid rent for the war years, but Denning J clearly indicates that such a claim would have failed. Was there any consideration for the promise not to exact this rent?

2. It is not clear that the tenants had acted to their detriment in the case. See below, p 612.
3. In support of his dicta, Denning J cited a number of cases including *Hughes v Metropolitan Rly Co*. Whether these cases actually support him will be examined in Section 7, Changing the Bargain.

Combe v Combe [1951] 1 All ER 767, Court of Appeal

After they had been divorced, the husband promised to pay the wife £100 per year maintenance, but he failed to pay. She pressed him for payment, but she did not make any application to the divorce court. Her income was in fact greater than his. Nearly seven years after the decree absolute of divorce had been given she brought an action for £675, being arrears for six and three-quarter years.

Denning LJ. . . . Byrne J held that the first three quarterly instalments of £25 were barred by the Limitation Act, 1939, but he gave judgment for £600 in respect of the instalments which accrued within the six years before the action was brought. He held, on the authority of *Gaisberg v Storr*, that there was no consideration for the husband's promise to pay his wife £100, but, nevertheless, he held that the promise was enforceable on the principle stated in *Central London Property Trust Ltd v High Trees House Ltd* and *Robertson v Minister of Pensions*, because it was an unequivocal acceptance of liability, intended to be binding, intended to be acted on, and, in fact, acted on.

Much as I am inclined to favour the principle of the *High Trees* case, it is important that it should not be stretched too far lest it should be endangered. It does not create new causes of action where none existed before. It only prevents a party from insisting on his strict legal rights when it would be unjust to allow him to do so, having regard to the dealings which have taken place between the parties. That is the way it was put in the case in the House of Lords which first stated the principle—*Hughes v Metropolitan Rly Co*—and in the case in the Court of Appeal which enlarged it—*Birmingham and District Land Co v London & North Western Rly Co*. It is also implicit in all the modern cases in which the principle has been developed.

It may be part of a cause of action, but not a cause of action in itself. The principle, as I understand it, is that where one party has, by his words or conduct, made to the other a promise or assurance which was intended to affect the legal relations between them and to be acted on accordingly, then, once the other party has taken him at his word and acted on it, the one who gave the promise or assurance cannot afterwards be allowed to revert to the previous legal relations as if no such promise or assurance had been made by him, but he must accept their legal relations subject to the qualification which he himself has so introduced, even though it is not supported in point of law by any consideration, but only by his word.

Seeing that the principle never stands alone as giving a cause of action in itself, it can never do away with the neecessity of consideration when that is an essential part of the cause of action. The doctrine of consideration is too firmly fixed to be overthrown by a side-wind. Its ill effects have been largely mitigated of late, but it still remains a cardinal necessity of the formation of a contract, although not of its modification or discharge. I fear that it was my failure to make this clear in *Central London Property Trust Ltd v High Trees House Ltd* which misled Byrne J in the present case. He held that the wife could sue on the husband's promise as a separate and independent cause of action by itself, although, as he held, there was no consideration for it. That is not correct. The wife can only enforce the promise if there was consideration for it. That is, therefore, the real question in the case: Was there sufficient consideration to support the promise?

If it were suggested that, in return for the husband's promise, the wife expressly or impliedly promised to forbear from applying to the court for maintenance—that is, a promise in return for a promise—there would clearly be no consideration because the wife's promise would not be binding on her and, therefore, would be worth nothing. Notwithstanding her promise, she could always apply to the divorce court for maintenance—perhaps, only with leave—but nevertheless she could apply. No agreement by her could take away that right: *Hyman v Hyman*, as interpreted by this court in *Gaisberg v Storr*. There was, however, clearly no promise by the wife, express or implied, to forbear from applying to the court. All that happened was that she did, in fact, forbear—that is, she did an act in return for a promise. Is that sufficient consideration? Unilateral promises of this kind have long been enforced so long as the act or forbearance is done on the faith of the promise and at the request of the promisor, express or implied. The act done is then in itself sufficient consideration for the promise, even though it arises *ex post facto*, as Parker J pointed out in *Wigan v English and Scottish Law Life Assurance Assocn*. If the findings of Byrne J are accepted, they are sufficient to bring this principle into play. His finding that the husband's promise was intended to be binding, intended to be acted on, and was, in fact, acted on—although expressed to be a finding on the principle of the *High Trees House* case—is equivalent to a finding that there was consideration within this long-settled rule, because it comes to the same thing expressed in different words: see *Oliver v Davis*. My difficulty, however, is to accept the findings of Byrne J that the promise was 'intended to be acted on'. I cannot find any evidence of any intention by the husband that the wife should forbear from applying to the court for maintenance, or, in other words, any request by the husband, express or implied, that the wife should so forbear.

Birkett LJ. . . . There does not appear any evidence of a request by the husband that the wife should refrain from going to the court, or a promise by the wife that she would not go to the court, or any matter of that kind. It appears simply to have been that after some talk in February, 1943, an agreement was arrived at that the husband would pay £100 a year free of tax. It seems on the first point, therefore, that there was no consideration for this agreement.

With regard to the second point, we have had the great advantage of hearing Denning LJ deal with *Central London Property Trust Ltd v High Trees House Ltd* and *Robertson v Minister of Pensions* which formed such a prominent part of the judgment of the court below. I am bound to say that reading them for myself I think the description which was given by counsel for the husband in this court, namely, that the doctrine there enunciated was, so to speak, a doctrine which would enable a person to use it as a shield and not as a sword, is a very vivid way of stating what, I think, is the principle underlying both those cases.

Asquith LJ. I agree. The learned judge decided that while the husband's promise was unsupported by any valid consideration, yet the principle in *Central London Property Trust Ltd v High Trees House Ltd* entitled the wife to succeed. It is unnecessary to express any view as to the correctness of the decision in the *High Trees* case, although I certainly must not be taken to be questioning it. I would, however, remark in passing that it seems to me a complete misconception to suppose that it struck at the roots of the doctrine of consideration. Assuming, without deciding, that it is good law, I do not think it helps the wife at all. What that case decides is that when a promise is given which (i) is intended to create legal relations, (ii) is intended to be acted on by the promisee, and (iii) is, in fact, so acted on, the promisor cannot bring an action against the promisee which involves the repudiation of his promise or is inconsistent with it. It does not, as I read it, decide that a promisee can sue on the promise. Denning J expressly states the contrary. Neither in the *High Trees* case nor in *Robertson v Minister of Pensions* (another decision of my Lord which is relied on by the plaintiff) was an action brought by the promisee on the promise. In the first of those two cases the plaintiff was, in effect, the promisor or a person standing in the shoes of the promisor, while in the second the action, although brought by the promisee, was brought on a cause of action which was not the promise, but was an alleged statutory right. . . .

Finally, I do not think an actual forbearance, as opposed to an agreement to forbear to approach the court, is a good consideration unless it proceeds from a request, express or implied, on the part of the promisor. If not moved by such a request, the forbearance is not in respect of the promise. For these reasons and the others given by my Lords, I agree that the appeal should be allowed.

Appeal allowed.

The doctrine propounded by Denning, often known as the *High Trees* doctrine or the doctrine of promissory estoppel, has been applied in a number of cases where one party has promised to forgo, or has waived, his rights under an existing contract: these will be examined in the section on Changing the Bargain. The limitation imposed or confirmed by *Combe v Combe*, that the doctrine applies only to such a situation, and cannot be used as a substitute for consideration to create a fresh contractual right, remains good law: see *Argy Trading Development Co Ltd v Lapid Developments Co Ltd* [1977] 3 All ER 785, at 796, and *Syros Shipping Co SA v Elaghill Trading Co, The Proodos C* [1981] 3 All ER 189.

There is one class of case, however, where estoppel has come to be used despite the absence of a representation of fact, with a result that looks very much like making estoppel into a cause of action. These cases are often referred to as 'acquiescence' or 'proprietary estoppel'. In *Dillwyn v Llewelyn* (1862) 4 De GF&J 517 a father and son signed a written memorandum by which the father purported to present the son with a farm. There was no consideration for the father's promise, so the memorandum conferred no interest in the land on the son. The son took possession and, with his father's knowledge, built a residence on it at a cost of some £14,000; but no conveyance of the land to the son was ever executed. After the father's death the son sought a declaration of his rights and a conveyance to him. Lord Westbury LC held that the son's expenditure had given him an equitable right to have the incomplete gift completed, and he was entitled to a conveyance in fee simple.

> . . . [T]he subsequent expenditure by the son, with the approbation of the father, supplied a valuable consideration originally wanting . . .

It is possible to look at this case as one where the testator represented that he *had* given the land. In *Plimmer v Wellington Corpn* (1884) 9 Ap Cas 699, 53 LJ PC 105 it was held that where the representor had encouraged the building, a representation that the land *would* be conveyed was sufficient. See also the statement of the principle by Lord Kingsdown in *Ramsden v Dyson* (quoted below, p 143) and the more modern case of *Inwards v Baker* [1965] 2 QB 29.

If the person to whom the promise has been made builds on the promisor's land, to allow the promisor to turn the promisee off might result in the promisor getting a house for nothing at the expense of the promisee. What if the element of unjust enrichment is taken away because the plaintiff has not built on the defendant's land, but he has relied on the defendant's representation in some other way and will suffer loss if the defendant does not act as he had indicated he would?

Crabb v Arun District Council [1975] 3 All ER 865, Court of Appeal

The plaintiff owned a plot of land adjoining an existing road. Next to the land was a plot owned by the defendants, on which the defendants were to build houses. The defendants built a new road running down the boundary between their property and the plaintiff's. They granted him access onto this road through a gateway (point A) in the front portion of his property, and a right of way over the road. Subsequently the plaintiff decided to divide his property into two and sell the front portion. He discussed the matter with representatives of the defendants, and was given the impression that he would be given a right of access at a second point (point B), serving the back portion of his property. The defendants later erected a boundary fence, with apparently permanent gates at both access points, but no right of access or easement for the back access point was ever granted. Believing he nonetheless had a right of access to the back portion, the plaintiff sold the front portion without reserving to himself any right of way to either the front access point or the old road. The defendants later blocked the rear access point (B) and offered to grant the plaintiff a right of access for £3,000. The plaintiff refused this offer and was unable to obtain access to his land. He sought a declaration that he was entitled to a right of way from the back part of the land along the new road, and an injunction to restrain the defendants from interfering with this right of way. Pennycuick V-C dismissed the action on the ground that the defendants' representative had given no definite assurance, so no question of estoppel could arise. The plaintiff appealed.

Lord Denning MR. . . . In June 1971 Mr Crabb brought this action claiming a right of access at point B and a right of way along the estate road. He had no such right by any deed or conveyance or written agreement. So, in strict law, on the conveyance, the council were entitled to their land, subject only to an easement at point A, but none at point B. To overcome this strict law, Mr Crabb claimed a right of access at B on the ground of equitable estoppel, promissory or proprietary. The judge held that he could not avail himself of any estoppel. He said: 'In the absence of a definite assurance by the representative of the Council, no question of estoppel can arise, and that really concludes the action.' Mr Crabb appeals to this court.

When counsel for Mr Crabb said that he put his case on an estoppel, it shook me a little, because it is commonly supposed that estoppel is not itself a cause of action. But that is because there are estoppels and estoppels. Some do give rise to a cause of action. Some do not. In the species of estoppel called proprietary estoppel, it does give rise to a cause of action . . . The new rights and interests, so created by estoppel, in or over land, will be protected by the courts and in this way give rise to a cause of action. This was pointed out in Spencer Bower and Turner on Estoppel by Representation.

The basis of this proprietary estoppel—as indeed of promissory estoppel—is the interposition of equity. Equity comes in, true to form, to mitigate the rigours of strict law. The early cases did not speak of it as 'estoppel'. They spoke of it as 'raising an equity' . . . What then are the dealings which will preclude him from insisting on his strict legal rights? If he makes a binding contract that he will not insist on the strict legal position, a court of equity will hold him to his contract. Short of a binding contract, if he makes a promise that he will not insist on his strict legal rights—even though that promise may be unenforceable in point of law for want of consideration or want of writing—and if he makes the promise knowing or intending that the other will act on it, and he does act on it, then again a court of equity wil not allow him to go back on that promise: see *Central London Property Trust v High Trees House, Charles Rickards v Oppenheim*. Short of an actual promise, if he, by his words or conduct, so behaves as to lead another to believe that he will not insist on his strict legal rights—knowing or intending that the other will act on that belief— and he does so act, that again will raise an equity in favour of the other, and it is for a court of equity to say in what way the equity may be satisfied. The cases show that this equity does not depend on agreement but on words or conduct. In *Ramsden v Dyson* Lord Kingsdown spoke of a verbal agreement 'or what amounts to the same thing, an expectation, created or encouraged'. In *Birmingham Land Co v London and North Western Railway* Cotton LJ said that '. . . what passed did not make a new agreement but what took place . . . raised an equity against him'. And it was the Privy Council who said that 'the Court must look at the circumstances in each case to decide in what way the equity can be satisfied', giving instances: see *Plimmer v Mayor of Wellington* . . .

The question then is: were the circumstances here such as to raise an equity in favour of Mr Crabb? True the council on the deeds had the title to their land, free of any access at point B. But they led Mr Crabb to believe that he had or would be granted a right of access at point B. At the meeting of 26th July 1967, Mr Alford and Mr Crabb told the council's representative that Mr Crabb intended to split the two acres into two portions and wanted to have an access at point B for the back portion, and the council's representative agreed that he should have this access. I do not think the council can avoid responsibility by saying that their representative had no authority to agree this. They entrusted him with the task of setting out the line of the fence and the gates; and they must be answerable for his conduct in the course of it: see *Attorney-General to His Royal Highness the Prince of Wales v Collom; Moorgate Mercantile Co Ltd v Twitchings*.

The judge found that there was 'no definite assurance' by the council's representative, and 'no firm commitment', but only an 'agreement in principle', meaning I suppose that, as Mr Alford said, there were 'some further processes' to be gone through before it would become binding. But if there were any such processes in the minds of the parties, the subsequent conduct of the council was such as to dispense with them. The council actually put up the gates at point B at considerable expense. That certainly led Mr Crabb to believe that they had agreed that he should have the right of access through point B without more ado.

The judge also said that, to establish this equity or estoppel, the council must have known that Mr Crabb was selling the front portion without reserving a right of access for the back portion. I do not think this was necessary. The council knew that Mr Crabb *intended* to sell the two portions separately and that he would need an access at point B as well as point A. Seeing that they knew of his intention—and they did nothing to disabuse him, but rather confirmed it by erecting gates at point B—it was their conduct which led him to act as he did; and this raised an equity in favour against them.

In the circumstances it seems to me inequitable that the council should insist on their strict title as they did; and to take the high-handed action of pulling down the gates without a word of warning; and to demand of Mr Crabb £3,000 as the price for the easement. If he had moved at once for an injunction in aid of his equity—to prevent them removing the gates—I think he should have been granted it. But he did not do so. He tried to negotiate terms, but these failing, the action has come for trial. And we have the question: in what way now should the equity be satisfied?

Here equity is displayed at its most flexible: see Snell's Equity and the illustrations there given. If the matter had been finally settled in 1967, I should have thought that, although nothing was said at the meeting in July 1967, nevertheless it would be quite reasonable for the council to ask Mr Crabb to pay something for the access at point B, perhaps—and I am guessing—some hundreds of pounds. But, as counsel for the plaintiff pointed out in the course of the argument, because of the council's conduct, the back land has been landlocked. It has been sterile and rendered useless for five or six years; and Mr Crabb has been unable to deal with it during that time. This loss to him can be taken into account. And at the present time, it seems to me, in order to satisfy the equity, Mr Crabb should have the right of access at point B free of charge without paying anything for it.

I would, therefore, hold that Mr Crabb, as the owner of the back portion, has a right of access at point B over the verge on to Mill Park Road and a right of way along that road to Hook Lane without paying compensation. I would allow the appeal and declare that he has an easement, accordingly.

Scarman LJ. I agree that the appeal should be allowed. . . .

I think it is now well-settled law that the court, having analysed and assessed the conduct and relationship of the parties, has to answer three questions. First, is there an equity established? Secondly, what is the extent of the equity, if one is established? And, thirdly, what is the relief appropriate to satisfy the equity? See *Duke of Beaufort v Patrick, Plimmer v Mayor of Wellington* and *Inwards v Baker*, a decision of this court, and particularly the observations of Lord Denning MR. Such therefore I believe to be the nature of the enquiry that the courts have to conduct in a case of this sort. In pursuit of that enquiry I do not find helpful the distinction between promissory and proprietary estoppel. This distinction may indeed be valuable to those who have to teach or expound the law, but I do not think that, in solving the particular problem raised by a particular case, putting the law into categories is of the slightest assistance.

I come now to consider the first of the three questions which I think in a case such as this the court has to consider. What is needed to establish an equity? In the course of an interesting addition to his submissions this morning, counsel for the defendants cited *Ramsden v Dyson* to support his proposition that in order to establish an equity by estoppel, there must be a belief by the plaintiff in the existence of a right created or encouraged by the words or actions of the defendant. With respect, I do not think that that is today a correct statement of the law. I think the law has developed so that today it is to be considered as correctly stated by Lord Kingsdown in his dissenting speech in *Ramsden v Dyson*. Like Lord Denning MR, I think that the point of dissent in *Ramsden v Dyson* was not on the law but on the facts. Lord Kingsdown's speech, insofar as it dealt with propositions of law, has been often considered, and recently followed, by this court in *Inwards v Baker*. Lord Kingsdown said:

> 'The rule of law applicable to the case appears to me to be this: If a man, under a verbal agreement with a landlord for a certain interest in land, or what amounts to the same thing, *under an expectation, created or encouraged by the landlord* [my italics], that he shall have a certain interest, takes possession of such land, with the consent of the landlord, and upon the faith of such promise or expectation, with the knowledge of the landlord, and without objection by him, lays out money upon the land, a Court of equity will compel the landlord to give effect to such promise or expectation.'

. . . I turn now to the other two questions—the extent of the equity and the relief needed to satisfy it. There being no grant, no enforceable contract, no licence, I would analyse the minimum equity to do justice to the plaintiff as a right either to an easement or to a licence on terms to be agreed. I do not think it is necessary to go further than that. Of course, going that far would support the equitable remedy of injunction which is sought in this action. If there is no agreement as to terms, if agreement fails to be obtained, the court can, in my judgment, and must, determine in these proceedings on what terms the plaintiff should be put to enable him to have the benefit of the equitable right which he is held to have. . . .

I am not disposed to consider whether or not the defendants are to be blamed in moral terms for what they did. I just do not know. But the effect of their action has been to sterilise the plaintiff's land; and for the reasons which I have endeavoured to give, such action was an infringement of an equitable right possessed by the plaintiff. It has involved him in loss, which has not been measured; but, since it amounted to sterilisation of an industrial estate for a very considerable period of time, it must surpass any sort of sum of money which the plaintiff ought reasonably, before it was done, to have paid the defendants in order to obtain an enforceable legal right. I think therefore that nothing should now be paid by the plaintiff and that he should receive at the hands of the court the belated protection of the equity that he has established. Reasonable terms, other than money payment, should be agreed: or, if not agreed, determined by the court. For those reasons I also would allow the appeal.

[Lawson LJ delivered a concurring judgment.]

Appeal allowed.

NOTES

1. It thus seems that English law sometimes comes close to enforcing gratuitous promises that have been relied on under the guise of estoppel, but only in the context of property. Is this enforcement 'contractual'? Atiyah (1976) 92 LQR 174 argued that in *Crabb* there was a contract which the Court of Appeal in effect enforced. But as Millett (1976) 92 LQR 342 pointed out in a riposte, the parties had not reached a concluded agreement. Thus one difference between proprietary estoppel and 'contract' is that contract requires a promise, even if only implicit, which has been accepted by the other party; whereas proprietary estoppel can give rise to liability on the basis of less definite representations, provided that these have created a 'belief or expectation' that the proprietary interest has been or will be granted: *A-G of Hong Kong v Humphreys Estate (Queens Gardens) Ltd* [1987] 2 All ER 387.

2. A second difference appears to be the nature of the remedies available. If there is a contract, the court will normally protect the plaintiff's expectation by granting specific performance (if the contract is for land) or full damages. The proprietary estoppel cases envisage something more flexible—'the minimum equity to do justice to the plaintiff', as Scarman put it. In *Pascoe v Turner* [1979] 2 All ER 945 the plaintiff told the defendant, with whom he had been living, that a house was hers, but no conveyance was ever drawn up. With his encouragement she spent some of her money on improving the house. When the plaintiff tried to regain possession, the Court of Appeal held that he was estopped. In determining the remedy, it took into account the ruthlessness with which the plaintiff had tried to evict the defendant, and concluded that the defendant could only be properly protected if she were given the fee simple of the house as she had been promised. While this approach suggests that if the plaintiff had been less demanding the defendant might have got less, it amounts to enforcing the promise the plaintiff had made to her. As Cumming-Bruce LJ put it:

   Weighing such considerations this court concludes that the equity to which the facts in this case give rise can only be satisfied by compelling the plaintiff to give effect to his promise and her expectations.

   Moriarty (1984) 100 LQR 376 persuasively argues that in fact the courts have consistently used proprietary estoppel to protect the expectations engendered by the party estopped:

> Normally . . . a remedy will be chosen which gives the party precisely what he has been led to expect, but occasionally, where joint rights to land have been represented, he may get money instead.

(p 100). Thus the difference between the remedies for contract and proprietary estoppel may be more apparent than real.

3. Proprietary estoppel is confined to rights in or over land or other property: *Western Fish Products Ltd v Penwith Ditrict Council* [1981] 2 All ER 204 at 217–218. On the other hand the belief or expectation created by the defendant does not have to relate to any specific piece of property; in *Re Basham (deceased)* [1987] 1 All ER 405 the plaintiff was held to be entitled to the residue of an estate. The principle is thus very wide.

4. Proprietary estoppel will arise when the plaintiff has acted to her detriment on the defendant's representation, but what she did does not have to have been requested or even known to the defendant (see Denning's judgment in *Crabb's* case above, at p 142.). At least on the traditional 'bargain' analysis of consideration, an act done by the plaintiff to her detriment will only be consideration if it was requested by the defendant: see *Combe v Combe*, above p 139. You may remember that this point also came up in *Re Hudson* (above, p 19); the risks and liabilities assumed by the committee formed to distribute the fund were not consideration for Hudson's promise. In argument Pearson J had made the point even more clearly:

> If A says 'I will give you, B, £1,000,' and B in reliance on that promise spends £1,000 in buying a house, B cannot recover the £1,000 from A. (54 LJCh at p 813.)

But whether the bargain analysis is an accurate description of consideration is fiercely contested. We will explore this in the next subsection (below, p 146ff.).

5. To summarize, it seems that there are two situations in which a gratuitous promise which has been relied on to his detriment by the promisee may become binding by virtue of 'estoppel' acting as a substitute for consideration. One is the 'proprietary estoppel' cases just described; the other is where the promise is that the promisor will not enforce some contractual right against the promisee, a subject which will be dealt with in detail in Section 7. In other cases a gratuitous promise will be unenforceable unless contained in a deed.

A full discussion of the 'cause of action' point will be found in the judgment at first instance by Robert Goff J in *Amalgamated Investment and Propety Co Ltd v Texas Commerce International Bank Ltd* [1982] QB 84. He points out that while, with the two exceptions mentioned, estoppel cannot be used as a substitute for consideration, estoppel can provide an essential element in a cause of action that would otherwise fail. Thus in a case where a principal has held out an agent as having authority which in fact has not been given to the agent, an action by a third party with whom the agent contracts in the principal's name would fail without the estoppel: the unauthorized action by the agent would not be binding on the principal. The estoppel prevents the principal denying that the agent *did* have authority, so the third party's action can succeed. The estoppel is not being used as a substitute for consideration. He held that estoppel had a similar effect in the case before him. The plaintiff AIP had arranged with the defendant bank that the bank should make a loan (the 'Nassau loan') to a subsidiary of the plaintiffs, ANPP, based in the Bahamas, the loan being guaranteed by the plaintiffs. To avoid Bahamian restrictions on foreign banks trading in the Bahamas, the defendants purchased an 'off-the-shelf' subsidiary company, Portsoken, and lent the money to it: Portsoken then lent the money to the plaintiffs' subsidiary. The guarantee read as follows:

> The Guarantor will pay to you on demand all moneys which now are or shall at any time or times hereafter be due or owing or payable to you on any account whatsoever by [ANPP] . . .

In the course of dealings between them, both plaintiff and defendant treated the guarantee as covering the loan by Portsoken to the plaintiff's subsidiary. However, after the plaintiffs got into financial difficulties and were ordered to be compulsorily wound up, the liquidator sought a declaration that the plaintiff was under no liability under the guarantee in respect of the outstanding amount of the loan. Robert Goff J held that, on its wording, the guarantee did not apply to the loan made; but that as both parties had treated the guarantee as covering the loan and had acted on that assumption, they were estopped from denying that the guarantee covered the loan. In the Court of Appeal [1981] 3 All ER 577 it was held that the judge was wrong on the question of construction: viewed in its factual circumstances, the proper meaning of the guaranee was that it covered loans originating from the defendant bank even if made through a subsidiary (extracts from the Court of Appeal judgment will be found below, p 315). However, the judge's decision on estoppel was affirmed. The estoppel was not based on a representation by one party to the other, but on an agreed assumption, and should be termed 'estoppel by convention'. Again, the estoppel was not used in this case as a substitute for consideration: the problem was that AIP's promise did not cover the loan. If, as was held, AIP was estopped from raising that point, there was ample consideration for the promise through the bank lending the money to ANPP.

(ii) An act done in reliance on the promise as consideration

As we saw, the court in *Ricketts v Scothorn* held that there was no consideration for the grandfather's promise because he did not ask anything of Miss Scothorn in return; in other words, there was no bargain. Would the same result be reached in English law? Certainly cases such as *Combe v Combe* seem to suggest so. On the other hand Atiyah in his *Consideration in Contracts: A Fundamental Restatement* (1971) has denied the validity of most of the 'conventional' statement of the doctrine of consideration. In particular he denies that benefit to the promisor or detriment to the promisee are either sufficient or necessary, and that the law of contract enforces only bargains. The piece deserves reading in full: the following extracts, which are taken from a revised version published in 1986, are chosen to show his approach, and his views on gratuitous promises which have been relied on.

'Consideration: A Restatement' in Essays on Contract by Atiyah (1986), pp 184–187, 226–230, 232–235, 238–239, 241

At a relatively early date it was established that the courts would enforce a promise if another promise or an act was given in return for it; and also that they would not normally enforce a promise if it was merely intended as a gift with no return of any kind. In the first class of case it came therefore to be said that there was good consideration; there were good reasons for enforcing the promise. In the second class there was no such reason, and therefore no consideration. But it also became clear from a very early time that the whole law could not be reduced to such very simple terms. There were some cases in which a promise was given in return for another promise or an act, in which for one reason or another it was felt unjust or inexpedient that the promise should be enforced. Such cases could be, and sometimes were explained by saying that there was no consideration for the promise; but as the nineteenth century wore on, an alternative approach began to manifest itself. This was to say that there was good consideration (though perhaps the word 'good' would more usually be omitted) but that nevertheless the promise was unenforceable for other reasons, for example, because it had been extorted by duress, or fraud, or because it was illegal. The last type of case was often dealt with by saying that the consideration was unlawful; a judge who formulated his reasons in this way would perhaps, if pressed, have said that there was no 'good' consideration.

More recently still, this alternative approach has hardened so that courts now find nothing inconsistent in holding that there is consideration for a promise, but nevertheless refusing to enforce it because the transaction is illegal. This approach also manifests itself in the relatively modern device of refusing to enforce a promise on the ground that the promisor did not 'intend' to create legal relations by his promise. Where this is done (as it usually is) in a case where there is no express disavowal of the intent to create legal relations, it appears to be merely a legal justification for refusing to enforce a promise which the courts think, for one reason or another, it is unjust or impolitic to enforce. There seems no doubt that a hundred years ago the courts would have dealt with these problems in terms of consideration. Indeed, the comparison between *Shadwell v Shadwell* and *Jones v Padavatton* [below, p 156] is striking. . . .

This change of approach is symptomatic of the change which has developed in the way lawyers think about consideration. It is no longer thought that consideration is a compendious word simply indicating whether there are good reasons for enforcing a promise; it is widely assumed that consideration is a technical requirement of the law which has little or nothing to do with the justice or desirability of enforcing a promise. Modern lawyers thus see nothing incongruous in asserting that a promise made for good consideration should nevertheless not be enforced.

Exactly the same development has taken place with regard to those promises which are not normally enforced, that is the promise to make a gift with no return of any kind. Since the courts first decided that such promises were not enforceable, it came to be asserted that gratuitous promises were promises given without consideration. But in course of time, occasions arose when the courts found that there were sometimes very good reasons for enforcing gratuitous promises in certain cases, and they accordingly enforced them. When cases of this kind arose during the first part of the nineteenth century the natural approach of the courts was to say that there *was* consideration—which at that time seems merely to have meant that there were good reasons for enforcing the promise. But here again, as lawyers began to treat consideration as a 'doctrine' whose content was a set of fixed and rigid rules tailored to the typical case, these cases came to seem anomalous. It therefore became fashionable to deny that there was consideration; and yet such promises were and still are quite often enforced. Modern lawyers are thus forced to say that some promises may be enforceable even though there is no consideration for them.

As will be apparent from the above discussion, there has gradually been a hardening of the attitude of the English common lawyer to the whole notion of consideration. . . . Because most contracts are bargains, lawyers have steadfastly refused to recognize the evidence under their very eyes, that courts often enforce promises which are not bargains, and that they do so for reasons of justice and good policy. Because a promise to make a gift is not usually recognized as a sufficient reason for its enforcement, lawyers have refused to acknowledge that in some circumstances it is particularly desirable to enforce a gratuitous promise and that the courts in fact do so. . . .

As we shall see below, the restatement of the law which the actual decisons compel us to adopt, differs from the conventional view principally in recognising the importance of the untypical and marginal cases. It is not, however, merely a question of recognising that there are exceptions to the ordinary rules to which adequate attention has not always been paid. If that were all, there would be little need, or justification, for a fundamental restatement of the law. A restatement will require rather more than that; it will require in particular that lawyers start to think of consideration once again in terms of reasons for enforcing a promise; it will require lawyers to recognise that the presence of factors like benefit, detriment, and bargain is taken into account not because they fit some preconceived plan or definition, but because they are often very material factors in determining whether it is just or desirable to enforce a promise;

and this necessarily involves recognition that these are not the only factors to which attention must be, and is in practice paid by the Courts.

The frontier between promissory estoppel and unilateral contracts

Orthodox theory draws a firm line between a promise given for consideration, and a promise enforceable on the ground of promissory estoppel. In the case of a promise for an act, the distinction comes down to a very fine point. If the act is stated or specified (or possibly if it is requested) by the promisor, then the promise is enforceable in the ordinary way; the performance of the act is a good consideration. If the act is done by the promisee in reliance on the promise, but it has not been requested or stated or specified by the promisor, then orthodoxy asserts that there is no consideration, though there is a sufficient reason for giving the promise the limited validity recognised by promissory estoppel. It may help to see this distinction in perspective if the following fact situations are differentiated. . . .

5. The promisor does not state any act which is to be performed by the promisee but it is reasonably implicit that such an act is requested or desired by him, eg A promises additional payment to his creditor without stating that he asks for more time to pay, but it is reasonably implicit in the circumstances that this is what he wants. This promise is enforceable.

6. The promisor does not state any act which is to be performed by the promisee but the promisee does act in reliance on the promise in a way which was the natural and foreseeable result of the promise. This promise is said to be not enforceable as a contract, but enforceable to the limited extent recognised by promissory estoppel.

7. The promisor states the act to be performed by the promisee, and the promisee performs some other act which is a necessary step towards the performance of the act stated by the promisor, but he does not perform the act stated. The promisee cannot enforce the principal promise but may in some circumstances be able to enforce an implied subsidiary promise.

8. The promisor does not state any act which is to be performed by the promisee, but the promisee acts in reliance on the promise in a way which the promisor had no reason to anticipate.

The factual difficulty of defining the frontier

If the law of consideration had been recognised for what I suggest it to be, namely a set of guides for deciding whether there is good reason for the enforcement of a promise, the answer would surely have been clear. There is no natural frontier between Case 5 and Case 6. Indeed, there are frequently great difficulties in drawing the factual distinction between Case 5 and Case 6. . . .

The fineness of this distinction in fact is illustrated by the situation in *Hohler v Aston*. In this case the defendant, Mrs A, promised to give a London house to Mr and Mrs R, her niece and husband. She contracted to acquire the property and Mr and Mrs R gave up the lease of their country property and moved into the London house. The defendant then died before the property had been transferred to her or to Mr and Mrs R. Sargant J was able to decide the case in favour of the plaintiffs without having to consider whether the facts already stated were sufficient to enable Mr and Mrs R to enforce the aunt's promise. But he expressed the view that the promise would probably not have been enforceable, although he acknowledged the hardship which this would have entailed for Mr and Mrs R. If they had given up their country house at Mrs A's request, this would have rendered the promise enforceable, but because this was not actually stated as an act to be performed by them, the promise was (he thought) unenforceable. This distinction is exactly the orthodox doctrine, but the distinction seems so fine as to be virtually unintelligible. It seems most undesirable to decide a case of this kind on such a point because the whole issue would turn on oral evidence as to whether the aunt ever said to Mr and Mrs R that they must give up their country property and come and live in the London house. It is probable that recollection of oral discussions to this degree of accuracy would be impossible, and that the decision would actually turn on findings of fact which are bound to be unreliable. Perhaps if the decision had actually turned on this issue Sargant J would have been prepared to imply a request. It could not be said that this was a *necessary* implication of the defendant's conduct; doubtless Mr and Mrs R could have retained the lease of their country house while going to live in the London house. But the possibility of implying a request where the Court feels it necessary to do justice is another confirmation of the unreality of the factual distinction between Case 5 and Case 6.

Policy arguments for maintaining the frontier

But even if these arguments are not felt to be convincing, it remains to inquire whether there can be any rational ground for distinguishing between Case 5 and Case 6. I have already indicated that this seems to me an impossible line to maintain. So long as it is believed that all contracts are bargains, there is some rational ground for requiring that the act to be performed by the promisee must be stated, if not actually requested, by the promisor; but once it is agreed that many promises are enforced though they are not bargains, it is hard to see what rational purpose is intended to be served by the insistence that the act must be stated. The natural place to draw a line in the above listed cases is not between Case 5 and Case 6 but between Case 7 and Case 8. The difference between an act done by the promisee which is impliedly stated by the promisor, and an act done in natural and foreseeable reliance on the promise seems much less substantial than the distinction between the latter case and an act in reliance which could not have been anticipated by the promisor. That is not to say that even this last case may not, in certain circumstances, be thought to be a promise worthy of enforcement. . .

Once again I feel obliged to depart from orthodox doctrine. I would suggest that, on the contrary, [*Combe v Combe*] decided nothing more than this: that an act (or forbearance) which naturally and forseeably follows from and in reliance on a promise is not a consideration for the enforcement of the promise *where the justice of the case does not require that it should be.* So viewed the decision is perfectly in line with older cases. Among these cases are the ones to which I have already made reference, namely *Dillwyn v Llewellyn*, and the line of authorities following it, and culminating in *Inwards v Baker*. There is no doubt that the principle stated in these cases is flatly inconsistent with orthodox doctrine; for these cases stand for the principle that if a man promises to give another some land, and permits the other to build a property on his land, then even though he has not requested or stated that such building, is the act on which his promise becomes enforceable, the promise will be enforceable.

I do not rely solely on *Dillwyn v Llewellyn* and the cases following it for my view that an act done in reliance on a promise may be a good consideration even though it is not stated or requested by the promisor as an act to be performed by the promisee. These particular cases may be explained away as anomalous or exceptional. I therefore turn to an examination of the House of Lords' decision in *Jorden v Money* which lies at the heart of this whole question. The treatment of this case by lawyers during the past thirty-five years is one of the most extraordinary chapters in the whole law of consideration, and must make one wonder whether lawyers actually read the cases which form the pillars of orthodoxy. . . .

The truth is that there is a very much simpler explanation of *Jorden v Money* which seems to stare in the face anyone who actually reads the report. Discussions of the case all start with the assumption that the plaintiff could not enforce the defendant's promise in contract because he could show no consideration; and it is for this reason that (it is assumed) the plaintiff relied on estoppel. The truth is precisely the opposite. The plaintiff could have proved a good contract; in fact he *did* show a good contract, and that is precisely why he failed. To understand this paradoxical statement it must be recalled that the Statute of Frauds required at this time that a promise in consideration of marriage must be proved in writing. The only act in reliance on the promise which the plaintiff could show was his marriage; *but he had no written note or memorandum signed by the defendant.* His counsel, therefore, deliberately refrained from arguing his case in contract but relied on estoppel. The whole point of the case (at all events as it developed in the House of Lords) was whether the plaintiff was entitled to do this. Could he evade the Statute of Frauds by calling his cause of action estoppel instead of contract? Had this stratagem succeeded, a blow would have been dealt to the Statute of Frauds greater than anything that had gone before; for it would have meant that any plaintiff who could show that he had altered his position in reliance on the defendant's promise could ignore the Statute and rely on estoppel. And since at this time the distinction between estoppel as a cause of action and as a ground of defence was not established, the threatened evasion of the Statute would have seemed even wider than it might today. It is, therefore, quite understandable that the House of Lords should not have sanctioned the plaintiff's claim.

The true view; an unnecessary frontier
It will be seen, therefore, that virtually all modern academic (and much judicial) discussion of promissory estoppel has been entirely beside the point. This discussion invariably takes as its starting point the assumption that the performance of an act in reliance on a promise, not requested or stated by the promisor, cannot be a good consideration. If this assumption is unfounded then there is not, and never has been, any need for promissory estoppel. *Jorden v Money*, far from being (as the new orthodoxy would have it) a difficult obstacle in the way of recognition of promissory estoppel, is a clear indication that promissory estoppel was never necessary at all. The facts of *Jorden v Money* are the clearest possible example of my Case 6 that I have been able to find. The plaintiff undoubtedly married in reliance on the defendant's promise but the defendant never requested the marriage nor did she promise to release the debt if and when the plaintiff married. Her promise was, indeed, originally made before any question of marriage was in contemplation; it was repeated time and again and the plaintiff acted upon it by his marriage. I have myself no doubt that, as the law was then understood, this was a good consideration for the enforcement of the promise which would (apart from the Statute of Frauds) have been enforced by the House of Lords in 1854.

I do not of course, mean to say that nineteenth-century Courts would have held that a promise always becomes enforceable whenever the promisee acts in reliance on it (even though the act is not requested or stated by the promisor). But what I suggest is that the Courts were at that time prepared to enforce such a promise where they felt that the justice of the case required it. If this was so, then there was good reason (or consideration) for enforcement in the promisee's actions in reliance on the promise. Alas, the new orthodoxy has now itself grown so strong and vigorous that it seems too late for the courts to recognize what they have actually done. In *Crabb v Arun District Council* the Court of Appeal actually 'enforced' (by appropriate equitable decrees) an arrangement (to use a neutral term) in a case where one judge insisted that the whole question was whether there was an agreement between the parties. But this 'agreement' though 'enforced' by court decrees was not regarded as a contract, but merely as a set of representations of intention which were enforceable because they had been relied upon to the plaintiff's prejudice. When I protested that if there was an agreement and it was enforced, this must have been a contract, I was rebuked for failing to understand that contracts are designed to enforce agreements, while estoppel is designed to protect reliance. The reader will (I trust) by now know enough of my views to appreciate that I do not assume that because there was (as I think) a 'contract' in this case, it should have been enforceable without any reliance by the plaintiff. I merely protest at the absurdity of a conceptual analysis which states that the agreement in *Crabb v Arun District Council* was not enforceable because the detrimental reliance was not requested, and therefore failed to comply with the requirements of consideration; and then proceeds to add that the 'agreement' was nevertheless enforceable because the element of reliance did satisfy the doctrine of promissory estoppel. Surely, it would be simpler and more sensible if the law made up its mind what kind of detrimental reliance was sufficient to justify the imposition of some kind of obligation without regard to whether the case should be classified as involving consideration or promissory estoppel.

The present position—which I have called the new orthodoxy—might be more defensible if estoppel, or promissory estoppel, was only called upon to protect reliance. . . .

Consideration *means* a reason for the enforcement of a promise.

NOTE

Atiyah's views have not gone unchallenged, in particular his opinion about *Jorden v Money* (though you might like to consider the language used in *Dillwyn v Llewelyn* in this context) and his assertion that there is no doctrine of consideration. See in particular Treitel, *Consideration: A Critical Analysis of Professor Atiyah's Fundamental Restatement* (1976) 50 Austr LJ 439. Moreover we have seen that it is doubtful whether *Dillwyn* and the other cases of proprietary estoppel are cases of contractual liability at all—the basis and the remedies available seem different. On the other hand Treitel says that the English doctrine of consideration does not just enforce bargains: the rule adopted in many of the United States that 'Nothing is consideration which is not regarded as such by both parties' (Holmes) 'quite clearly does not represent English law' (p 440). He cites a number of cases to support this, including some of those we noted earlier (p 134) as being hard to reconcile with a requirement of bargain. Atiyah's riposte (Essays on Contract, pp 182–183) is worth noting:

Professor Treitel's critique of my original essay (and his textbook on the *Law of Contract*) insists that the courts have power to 'invent' consideration, and that this ability is an important phenomenon which I have overlooked and which explains many otherwise puzzling things about the doctrine. I find this a difficult concept to grasp. Is an 'invented' consideration something different from a 'real' consideration or is it the same thing? If it is the same thing, then it is hard to see in what sense it is invented; and if it is not the same thing, then it either violates the rules of law, or it modifies them. Presumably Professor Treitel does not mean to suggest that when judges invent consideration they are defying the law and violating their judicial oaths, but if an invented consideration modifies the rules governing ordinary consideration, then an invented consideration becomes again an ordinary consideration, though the legal significance of the doctrine has now changed. The only other possibility that occurs to me is that the courts might use the concept of 'invented consideration' rather like an equitable or merciful dispensation from the ordinary law, but it is unthinkable that judges should behave in this way. They have no power to invent a consideration in one case and refuse to do so in a relevantly identical case. Thus an invented consideration must in the end be the same thing as an ordinary consideration. I fear that Professor Treitel has himself invented the concept of an invented consideration because he finds it the only way in which he is able to reconcile many decisions with what he takes to be the 'true' or 'real' doctrine.

Thus the outcome of a case with the same facts as *Ricketts* is somewhat doubtful in English law; although the courts ostensibly enforce only bargains, so that an act done in reliance on a promise but not requested by the promisor cannot be consideration, they sometimes infer a request even though the inference seems a bit strained. Clearly it would not take much of a reinterpretation of the facts of *Ricketts* to say that the grandfather was impliedly requesting that Miss Scothorn give up her job. Cases like *Combe v Combe* in which the court refused to imply a request may, as Atiyah says, be explicable on the ground that there were good reasons for not enforcing the promise. It is noteworthy that in *Re Hudson* (above p 19) Pearson J followed his decision that there was no consideration with the words:

> I do not know to what extent a contrary decision might open a new form of posthumous charity. Posthumous charity is already bad enough. . . .

A similar 'flexibility' has been shown in some of the United States, not all of which were or are firmly wedded to the bargain principle. However in the majority of states the problem of the gratuitous but relied-on promise is now taken care of not under the guise of consideration, but under a new and separate principle included in the Restatement of Contracts (1932) as a response to dubious bargain cases and cases like *Ricketts* adopting an estoppel approach. The Restatement 2d version is as follows:

s 90 Promise Reasonably Inducing Action or Forbearance

(1) A promise which the promisor should reasonably expect to induce action or forbearance on the part of the promisee . . . and which does induce such action or forbearance is binding if injustice can be avoided only by enforcement of the promise. The remedy granted for breach may be limited as justice requires.

An account of the events leading up to adoption of s 90 alongside a strict bargain definition of consideration (see Rest 2d s 71, above p 91) will be found in Gilmore, *The Death of Contract* (1974) pp 62–65; and see Henderson, 'Promissory Estoppel and Traditional Contract Doctrine' (1969) 78 Yale LJ 343. The High Court of Australia has also recognised that promissory estoppel can create new rights: *Walton's Stores (Interstate) Ltd v Maher* (1988) 62 ALJR 110. Should a similar principle be adopted by English law? The Law Reform Committee recommended so in 1937 (see Sixth Interim Report, Cmd 5449). On the merits, consider the following extract.

'Economic Analysis of Law' by Posner (2nd edn, 1977), pp 67–70

Holding people to their promises is not, however, the only economic function of contract law, as [an] example will illustrate. A wealthy man in an expansive moment promises to pay my way through college. I give up my part-time job, but he then breaks his promise and I am unable to get a new job.

. . . There is no exchange in [this] case: giving up my part-time job confers no advantage on the wealthy promisor. Indeed, he may not even have known that I gave it up. . . .

Yet . . . there is an economic argument for imposing sanctions on the party who fails to perform. The wealthy man's idle promise induced reliance that cost the promisee heavily when it was broken. Such a cost can be avoided for the future by holding such a promisor liable for the promisee's reliance costs. It is, of course, necessary to distinguish the sort of donative promise that is likely to induce reliance from the sort that is not. I promise you a trivial gift and the next day withdraw my promise. I had no reason to expect you to rely, so whether or not you do rely the law will not hold me to my promise. . . .

§4.2 CONSIDERATION

The principle that a promise, to be enforceable, must be supported by 'consideration' is used to deny liability for breach of a promise mainly in two types of cases. The first is where there is no exchange and where, therefore, enforcement of the promise would not advance the economic purpose of the law of contracts, which is to facilitate exchange. A truly gratuitous, nonreciprocal promise to confer a benefit is not a part of the process by which resources are moved, through a series of exchanges, into successively more valuable uses. This justification of the doctrine of consideration has been obscured by the characterization of 'detrimental reliance' (my giving up my part-time job, in the first example of the preceding section) as consideration sufficient to support a wholly one-sided promise. There is, as we have seen, a good economic reason for awarding damages to one who has reasonably relied, to his detriment, on another's promise. But it obscures analysis to equate reliance with consideration in circumstances where no exchange is contemplated. A better approach would be to treat the breach of a promise likely to induce reliance as a form of negligence actionable under tort law.

If gratuitous promises were always enforced, however, people would be very cautious about making any statement that could possibly be construed as promissory; they might go to considerable lengths to disclaim promissory intentions whenever there was the slightest ambiguity. Such elaborate forbearance would involve costs not offset by benefits in the form of a more efficient system of exchange. It is uneconomical to require people to be too careful.

NOTES

1. If 'reliance' were to be recognized as creating liability, what would be the appropriate measure of damages? This was debated in a famous exchange between Williston and Coudert during the drafting of the first Restatement. Johnny is promised $1,000 by his uncle and on the strength of the promise buys a car for $500. Williston argued that the uncle should be liable for $1,000 (4 ALI Proceedings 98–99; reprinted in (1936) 46 Yale LJ at p 64 n 14). Do you agree?

2. Goetz and Scott, 'Enforcing Promises: An Examination of the Basis of Contract' (1980) 89 Yale LJ 1261 (extracted in Ogus and Veljanovski (eds), *Readings in the Economics of Law and Regulation*, 1984), have propounded a theory of the reasons behind the enforcement of promises, including a more developed theory of promissory estoppel. Goetz and Scott begin by noting that a promise gives information about the promisor's future action. The promisee may, and frequently will, adapt his behaviour in accordance with this new information (cf Posner, 'Gratuitous Promises', above, p 124). If the promisor does act as promised, this reliance by the promisee will normally have beneficial effects. If, on the other hand, the promise is broken, the promisee's reliance will normally prove detrimental. The aim of the law is to encourage beneficial reliance as well as to discourage detrimental reliance (which is the justification put forward by Posner in the last extract).

    There is always some possibility that, when the time comes to perform, the promised action will have become unattractive to the promisor. Where the promisor and promisee are in a trading relationship (exchanging resources), the price the promisee is willing to pay for the promisor's promise can be adjusted to reflect the fact that, the greater the likelihood that the promisor will not perform, the less valuable his promise is to the promisee. The promisor thus has an incentive to find an appropriate balance between making his promise reliable (for instance, not hedging it about with conditions), and preserving himself some freedom to choose whether or not to perform if, when the time comes, he finds that performance would be very burdensome. But where the promise is gratuitous, no such adjustment can be made. If liability is imposed on the promisor, he will adjust in a quite different way: he will make fewer and vaguer promises, thus conveying less valuable information to the promisee. If liability for the gratuitous promise is *not* imposed, the promisee will adopt 'self protective' measures—perhaps simply passing up the opportunity to change his expenditure pattern as he would have done if he could have been sure of receiving the promised benefit. What is needed is a rule which makes the gratuitous promise binding, and thus encourages reliance by the promisee, when the benefits to be gained from the reliance outweigh the costs imposed on the promisor. This theory, the authors suggest, can give content to the notion of 'reasonable reliance' required by s 90. It also suggests, however, that neither a full expectation measure of damages, nor a measure based on the actual detriment incurred by the promisee, is wholly appropriate. The former would encourage too great a degree of reliance by the promisee, the latter too little. At least in an ideal world, the measure of damages should be based on the degree of reliance that would be optimal, rather than that which has in fact occurred. However, such a measure would be too difficult to apply, and use of the traditional 'reliance' measure is a reasonable second-best (see above, pp 75–76).

Intention to create legal relations

Balfour v Balfour [1918–19] All ER Rep 860, Court of Appeal

In 1915 the parties came to England from Ceylon, where the husband had a Government post, during the husband's leave. He returned when his leave expired, but the wife remained in England on her doctor's advice, intending to follow when she could. She alleged that just before the husband sailed, they entered an oral contract whereby the husband agreed to pay the wife an allowance of £30 a month. Subsequently they agreed to live apart. The wife brought an action to recover the money she claimed was due under the agreement. Sargant J gave judgment for the wife, and the husband appealed.

Atkin LJ. The defence to this action on the alleged contract is that the husband says he entered into no contract with his wife, and for the determination of that it is necessary to remember that there are agreements between parties which do not result in contracts within the meaning of that term in our law. The ordinary example is where two parties agree to take a walk together, or where there is an offer and an acceptance of hospitality. Nobody would suggest in ordinary circumstances that those agreements result in what we know as a contract, and one of the most usual forms of agreement which does not constitute a contract appears to me to be the arrangements which are made between husband and wife. It is quite common, and it is the natural and inevitable result of the relationship of husband and wife, that the two spouses should make agreements between themselves, agreements such as are in dispute in this action, agreements for allowances by which the husband agrees that he will pay to his wife a certain sum of money per week or per month or per year to cover either her own expenses or the necessary expenses of the household and of the children, and in which the wife promises either expressly or impliedly to apply the allowance for the purpose for which it is given.

To my mind those agreements, or many of them, do not result in contracts at all, and they do not result in contracts even though there may be what as between other parties would constitute consideration for the agreement. The consideration, as we know, may consist either in some right, interest, profit, or benefit accruing to one party, or some forbearance, detriment, loss, or responsibility given, suffered, or undertaken by the other. That is a well-known definition, and it constantly happens. I think, that such arrangements made between husband and wife are arrangements in which there are mutual promises, or in which there is consideration in form within the definition that I have mentioned. Nevertheless they are not contracts, and they are not contracts because the parties did not intend that they should be attended by legal consequences. It would be the worst possible example to hold that agreements such as this resulted in legal obligations which could be enforced in the courts. It would mean that when a husband made his wife a promise to give her an allowance of 30s or £2 per week, whatever he could afford to give her for the maintenance of the household and children, and she promised so to apply it, not only could she sue him for his failure in any week to supply the allowance, but he could sue her for non-performance of the obligation, express or implied, which she had undertaken upon her part. The small courts of this country would have to be multiplied one hundredfold if these arrangements did result in fact in legal obligations. They are not sued upon, and the reason that they are not sued upon is not because the parties are reluctant to enforce their legal rights when the agreement is broken, but they are not sued upon because the parties in the inception of the arrangement never intended that they should be sued upon. Agreements such as these, as I say, are outside the realm of contracts altogether. The common law does not regulate the form of agreements between spouses. Their promises are not sealed with seals and sealing wax. The consideration that really obtains for them is that natural love and affection which counts for so little in these cold courts. The terms may be repudiated, varied, or renewed as performance proceeds, or as the disagreements develop, and the principles of the common law as to exoneration and discharge and accord and satisfaction are such as find no place in the domestic code. The parties themselves are advocates, judges, courts, sheriff's officer and reporter. In respect of these promises each house is a domain into which the king's writ does not seek to run, and to which his officers do not seek to be admitted.

The only question in the present case is whether or not this promise was of such a class or not. For the reasons given by my brethren it appears to me to be plain. I think it is plainly established that the promise here was not intended by either party to be attended by legal consequences. I think the onus was upon the wife, and that the wife has not established any contract.

[Warrington and Duke LJJ delivered judgments to the same effect.]

Appeal allowed.

Merritt v Merritt [1970] 2 All ER 760, Court of Appeal

The husband left the matrimonial home, which was in the joint names of husband and wife. Later he met the wife to discuss financial arrangements, and they agreed that he would pay the wife £40 a month, out of which she must pay the outstanding mortgage payments. He gave her the building society book, and at the wife's insistence, signed an agreement which stated:

> In consideration of the fact that you will pay all charges in connection with the house . . . until such time as the mortgage repayment has been completed I will agree to transfer the property into your sole ownership.

The wife paid off the mortgage, but the husband refused to transfer the house to the wife.

Lord Denning MR. . . . The first point taken on his behalf by counsel for the husband was that the agreement was not intended to create legal relations. It was, he says, a family arrangement such as was considered by the court in *Balfour v Balfour* and in *Jones v Padavatton*. So the wife could not sue on it. I do not think that those cases have any application here. The parties there were living together in amity. In such cases their domestic arrangements are ordinarily not intended to create legal relations. It is altogether different when the parties are not living in amity but are separated, or about to separate. They then bargain keenly. They do not rely on honourable understandings. They want everything cut and dried. It may safely be presumed that they intend to create legal relations. . . .

[Widgery and Karminski LJJ delivered judgments to the same effect.]

NOTES

1. Is the presumption stated by Atkin LJ based on (i) the parties' actual intentions, (ii) what as reasonable people they probably would have agreed had they considered the question or (iii) a policy of non-intervention? If the last, why should there be such a policy?
2. In *Pettitt v Pettitt* [1970] AC 777, a case where one spouse had improved the matrimonial home which was in the other's name, Lord Diplock said (at p 822):

> Where the acquisition or improvement is made as a result of contributions in money or money's worth by both spouses acting in concert the proprietary interests in the family asset resulting from their respective contributions depend upon their common intention as to what those interests should be.
>
> I have used the neutral expression 'acting in concert' because many of the ordinary domestic arrangements between man and wife do not possess the legal characteristics of a contract. So long as they are executory they do not give rise to any chose in action, for neither

party intended that non-performance of their mutual promises should be the subject of sanctions in any court (see *Balfour v Balfour*). But this is relevant to non-performance only. If spouses do perform their mutual promises the fact that they could not have been compelled to do so while the promises were executory cannot deprive the acts done by them of all legal consequences upon proprietary rights; for these are within the field of the law of property rather than of the law of contract. It would, in my view, be erroneous to extend the presumption accepted in *Balfour v Balfour* that mutual promises between man and wife in relation to their domestic arrangements are prima facie not intended by either to be legally enforceable to a presumption of a common intention of both spouses that *no* legal consequences should flow from acts done by them in performance of mutual promises with respect to the acquisition, improvement or addition to real or personal property—for this would be to intend what is impossible in law.

3. The decision whether legal relations were intended seems to depend on the circumstances. What factors are relevant? Consider the next case.

Jones v Padavatton [1969] 2 All ER 616, Court of Appeal

The daughter, who had a good job in Washington DC, was offered by her mother, who lived in Trinidad, an allowance of $200 a month if she would go to England to study for the Bar, with a view to practising in Trinidad. Although she did not want to leave Washington, the daughter accepted; she also accepted $200 West Indian dollars, which was what the mother had meant, though the daughter had expected $200 US dollars, which were worth considerably more. No written contract was entered, nor was there any agreement as to the duration of the arrangement. The daughter came to England in 1962. In 1964 it was arranged that the mother would buy a house in London for the daughter to live in: she was to rent out some of the rooms and use the income to maintain herself in place of the $200 a month. In 1967 the mother claimed possession of the house; the daughter had not yet passed the Bar examinations.

Danckwerts LJ delivered judgment to the same effect as Fenton Atkinson LJ below.

Salmon LJ. I agree with the conclusion at which Dankwerts LJ has arrived, but I have reached it by a different route. . . .

In the present case the learned county court judge, having had the advantage of seeing the mother and the daughter in the witness box, entirely accepted the daughter's version of the facts. He came to the conclusion that on these very special facts the true inference must be that the arrangements between the parties prior to the daughter's leaving Washington were intended by both to have contractual force. On the facts as found by the learned county court judge this was entirely different from the ordinary case of a mother promising her daughter an allowance whilst the daughter read for the Bar, or a father promising his son an allowance at university if the son passed the necessary examinations to gain admission.

I cannot think that either intended that if, after the daughter had been in London, say, for six months, the mother dishonoured her promise and left her daughter destitute, the daughter would have no legal redress. . . .

The agreement was to last for a reasonable time. The parties cannot have contemplated that the daughter should go on studying for the Bar and draw the allowance until she was seventy, nor on the other hand that the mother could have discontinued the allowance if the daughter did not pass her examinations within, say, 18 months. The promise was to pay the allowance until the daughter's studies were completed, and to my mind there was a clear implication that they were to be completed within a reasonable time. Studies are completed either by the student being called to the Bar or giving up the unequal struggle against the examiners. I cannot think that a reasonable time could possibly exceed five years from November 1962, the date when she began her studies.

It follows, therefore, that on no view can she now in November 1968 be entitled to anything further under the contract which the learned county court judge, rightly I think, held that she made with the mother in 1962. She has some of Part I of the Bar examination still to pass, and necessarily the final has not yet even been attemped.

Fenton Atkinson LJ. . . . In my judgment it is the subsequent history which gives the best guide to the parties' intention at the material time. There are three matters which seem to me important: (i) The daughter thought that her mother was promising her $(U.S.) 200, or £70 a month, which she regarded as the minimum necessary for her support. The mother promised $200 but she had in mind $(West Indian) 200, £42 a month, and that was what she in fact paid from November 1962 to December 1964. Those payments were accepted by the daughter without any sort of suggestion at any stage that the mother had legally contracted for the larger sum. (ii) When the arrangements for the purchase of no 181, Highbury Quadrant were being discussed, and the new arrangement was made for maintenance to come out of the rents, many material matters were left open: How much accommodation was the daughter to occupy; how much money was she to have out of the rents; if the rents fell below expectation, was the mother to make up the difference below £42, or £42 less the sum saved by the daughter in rent; for how long was the arrangement to continue, and so on. The whole arrangement was, in my view, far too vague and uncertain to be itself enforceable as a contract; but at no stage did the daughter bring into the discussions her alleged legal right of £42 per month until her studies were completed, and how that right was to be affected by the new arrangement. (iii) It is perhaps not without relevance to look at the daughter's evidence in cross-examination. She was asked about the occasion when the mother visited the house, and she, knowing perfectly well that the mother was there, refused for some hours to open the door. She said:

'I didn't open the door because a normal mother doesn't sue her daughter in court. Anybody with normal feelings would feel upset by what was happening.'

Those answers and the daughter's conduct on that occasion provided a strong indication that she had never for a moment contemplated the possibility of the mother or herself going to court to enforce legal obligations, and that she felt it quite intolerable that a purely family arrangement should become the subject of proceedings in a court of law.

At the time when the first arrangement was made, the mother and the daughter were, and always had been, to use the daughter's own words, 'very close'. I am satisfied that neither party at that time intended to enter into a legally binding contract, either then or later when the house was bought. The daughter was prepared to trust the mother to honour her promise of support, just as the mother no doubt trusted the daughter to study for the Bar with diligence, and to get through her examinations as early as she could. It follows that in my view the mother's claim for possession succeeds. . . .

Coward v Motor Insurers' Bureau [1962] 1 All ER 531, Court of Appeal

Coward was killed in an accident caused by the negligence of Cole, on whose motorbike Coward was a pillion passenger. Cole was also killed. Coward's widow brought an action against Cole's personal representatives and was given judgment, but the judgment was unsatisfied as Cole's insurance did not cover pillion passengers and his estate had no other assets. The widow then sued the MIB, which had an obligation to pay unsatisfied judgments in respect of a 'liability which is required to be covered by a policy . . .' under the Road Traffic Act 1930, claiming that Cole was bound to insure as he was carrying Coward for 'hire or reward'. The Court of Appeal thought it was necessary to decide whether there was a contract between Cole and Coward (in *Albert v Motor Insurers' Bureau*, below, the House of Lords held by a majority that this question need not be answered after all).

Upjohn LJ, delivering the judgment of the court, said:

On this point, the fact that both parties are dead, we believe matters little, for if the question had been posed to Coward or Cole: 'Did you intend to enter into a legal relationship?' each would probably have answered 'I never gave it a thought'. The practice whereby workmen go to their place of business in the motor car or on the motor cycle of a fellow-workman on the terms of making a contribution to the costs of transport is well known and widespread. In the absence of evidence that the parties intended to be bound contractually, we should be reluctant to conclude that the daily carriage by one of another to work on payment of some weekly (or it may be daily) sum involved them in a legal contractual relationship. The hazards of everyday life, such as temporary indisposition, the incidence of holidays, the possibility of a change of shift or different hours of overtime, or incompatibility arising, make it most unlikely that either contemplated that the one was legally bound to carry and the other to be carried to work. It is made all the more improbable in this case by reason of the fact that alternative means of transport seem to have been available to Coward.

Albert v Motor Insurers' Bureau [1971] 2 All ER 1345, House of Lords

Quirk had regularly carried other dockers to work in his car, on the understanding that they should pay five to ten shillings each per week. Sometimes he received beer or cigarettes in lieu, and he sometimes did not charge friends who were short of money.

The majority held that a vehicle was used to carry passengers for hire or reward if the carriage was on a systematic basis going beyond acts of social kindness, even if there was no contract between the owner and the passengers: Quirk's vehicle had been so used. Lord Cross, differing from the majority, held it *was* necessary to determine whether there was a contract, and continued:

I think that the judge was wrong in holding that the facts which he found warranted the inference that there were no legally binding agreements between Mr Quirk and any of his passengers. It is not necessary in order that a legally binding contract should arise that the parties should direct their minds to the question and decide in favour of the creation of a legally binding relationship. If I get into a taxi and ask the driver to drive me to Victoria Station it is extremely unlikely that either of us directs his mind to the question whether we are entering into a contract. We enter into a contract not because we form any intention to enter into one but because if our minds were directed to the point we should as reasonable people both agree that we were in fact entering into one. When one passes from the field of transactions of an obviously business character between strangers to arrangements between friends or acquaintances for the payment by the passenger of a contribution towards expenses the fact that the arrangement is not made purely as a matter of business and that if the anticipated payment is not made it would probably never enter into the head of the driver to sue for it disposes one to say that there is no contract; but in fact the answer to the question 'contract' or 'no contract' does not depend on the likelihood of an action being brought to enforce it in case of default.

Suppose that when one of Mr Quirk's fellow workers got in touch with him and asked him whether he could travel in his car to Tilbury and back next day, an 'officious bystander' had asked 'Will you be paying anything for your transport?' the prospective passenger would have answered at once 'Of course I will pay'. If the 'officious bystander'. had gone on to ask Mr Quirk whether, if he was not paid, he would sue the the man in the county court, Mr Quirk might well have answered in the words used by the driver in *Connell's* case—'Not bloody likely'. But the fact that if default was made Mr Quirk would not have started legal proceedings but would have resorted to extra-judicial remedies does not mean that an action could not in theory have been brought to recover payment for the carriage. If one imagines such proceedings being brought a plea on the part of the passenger that he never meant to enter into a contract would have received short shrift and so, too, would a plea that the contract was void for uncertainty because no precise sum was mentioned. If the evidence did not establish a regular charge for the Tilbury trip the judge would have fixed the appropriate sum.

NOTE

Are these statements by Upjohn LJ and Lord Cross reconcilable? Could it be that there is no contract for the future, yet there is liability to pay for lifts received (compare *Pettitt v Pettitt*, above, p 155)? Query, however, whether the liability to pay for the lifts received would be contractual or restitutionary: see *BSC v Cleveland Bridge Engineering* (below, p 224).

Rose & Frank Co v JR Crompton Bros [1924] All ER Rep 245, Court of Appeal; [1925] AC 445, House of Lords

In 1913 the plaintiffs and defendants signed a document expressing their willingness that the existing arrangements between them for goods made by the defendants to be supplied to the plaintiffs should be continued for a specified period, at prices quoted for periods of six months. The document concluded:

> This arrangement is not entered into, nor is this memorandum written, as a formal or legal agreement, and shall not be subject to legal jurisdiction in the law courts either of the United States or England, but it is only a definite expression and record of the purpose and intention of the three parties concerned, to which they each honourably pledge themselves with the fullest confidence—based on past business with each other—that it will be carried through by each of the three parties with mutual loyalty and friendly co-operation.

The defendants terminated the agreement without notice, and the plaintiffs sued for breach of the agreement and also for failure to deliver goods they had ordered in accordance with the agreement in 1919, before the termination.

Scrutton LJ. In 1913 the parties concurred in signing a document which gives rise to the present dispute. I agree that if the clause beginning 'This arrangement' were omitted, the courts would treat the rest of the agreement as giving rise to legal relations, though of great vagueness. But the clause in question beginning 'This arrangement' is not omitted. Bailhache J thought that by itself this clause 'plain as it is' means that the parties shall not be under any legal obligation to each other at all, but, coming to the conclusion that without this clause the agreement would create legal obligations, he takes the view that the clause must be rejected as repugnant to the rest of the agreement. He also holds that, if the clause merely means to exclude recourse to the law courts as a means of settling disputes, it is contrary to public policy as ousting the jurisdiction of the King's courts.

In my view, the learned judge adopts a wrong canon of construction. He should seek the intention of the parties as shown by the language they use, not in part of that language only, but in the whole of that language. It is true that in deeds and wills where it is impossible from the whole of the contradictory language used to ascertain the true intention of the framers, resort may be had, but only as a last expedient, to what Jessell MR called 'the rule of thumb' in *Re Bywater*, of rejecting clauses as repugnant according to their place in the document, the later clause being rejected in deeds and the earlier in wills. But before this heroic method is adopted of finding out what the parties meant by assuming that they did not mean part of what they have said, it must be clearly impossible to harmonise the whole of the language they have used. It is quite possible for parties to come to an agreement by accepting a proposal with the result that the agreement concluded does not give rise to legal relations. The reason of this is that the parties do not intend that their agreement shall give rise to legal relations. This intention may be implied from the subject-matter of the agreement, but it may also be expressed by the parties. In social and family relations such an intention is readily implied, while in business matters the opposite result would ordinarily follow. But I can see no reason why, even in business matters, the parties should not intend to rely on each other's good faith and honour, and to exclude all idea of settling disputes by any outside intervention with the accompanying necessity of expressing themselves so precisely that outsiders may have no difficulty in understanding what they mean. If they clearly express such an intention I can see no reason in public policy why effect should not be given to their intention. . . .

The remaining question is the claim in the statement of claim for damage for the non-delivery of the whole of the undelivered part of the goods said to be legally due under some thirty-two specified orders. . . .

Messrs Crompton, on Feb 12, 1919, write a letter which appears to me fully to carry out the vague arrangements in honour which I have held to be constituted by the arrangements of 1913, but, as made under that arrangement in honour, to give rise to no legal obligation. It runs as follows:

> 'We beg to acknowledge receipt of your favour of the 24th ult, contents of which are duly noted. We also thank you for the twenty-four orders for 286 cases of Messrs Brittains' papers, and eight orders for sixty-four cases of our paper, to all of which we will give our best attention, and Messrs Brittain write us with regard to the orders for their papers that they are

endeavouring to let you have deliveries this year up to at least the full 100 per cent for the standard year ending Feb 28, 1918, but that at the moment conditions are particularly uncertain. Nevertheless, they would like us to assure you that they would give their most careful attention to your requirements, and endeavour to let you have the fullest output they possibly can, and they add that time will make the position clearer.'

This I cannot construe as a binding acceptance of a legal proposal. It is, in my opinion, an assurance that the suppliers will do their best to comply with the probable requirements of the agents, but do not bind themselves.

[**Atkin LJ** agreed in relation to the alleged contract of 1913, but in relation to the specific orders said:]

In this case the defendants by the honourable understanding entered into the vague engagement contained in the document which had as a basis the average turnover for the last three years before the agreement. But whatever the terms of the agreement or understanding, it contemplated, as nearly all such agreements do, that the actual business done under it should be done by particular contracts of purchase and sale upon the terms of the general agreement so far as applicable. The actual business was done in this case, as in countless others, by orders for specific goods given by the 'agent' and accepted by the manufacturer or merchant. To see whether the orders given were accepted the terms of the alleged acceptance have to be regarded. . . .

'We . . . thank you for the twenty-four orders for 286 cases of Messrs Brittains' papers and eight orders for sixty-four cases of our paper, to all of which we will give our best attention.'

Pausing there, this is the common formula of acceptance in the business world which has been treated as acceptance in countless cases since merchants first wrote to one another. It would be understood as an acceptance passing between two merchants while there was no obligation at all on the part of the vendor to accept. Why it should bear a different meaning in a case where there is an honourable understanding by the merchant to accept up to some vague limit, I am unable to understand. The letter continues.

'and Messrs Brittains write us with regard to the orders for their papers that they are endeavouring to let you have deliveries this year up to at least the full 100 per cent for the standard year ending Feb 28, 1918, but that at the moment conditions are particularly uncertain.'

This seems to me to relate to the business likely to be done over the whole year, and particularly to the plaintiff's statement in the letter of Jan 24, 1919, under reply that they had not yet determined the full quantity of paper that they would require, and that they would send on further orders later. I read the whole letter as saying: 'We definitely accept these orders and as to further orders for Brittains' paper we expect to be able to execute them up to the 1918 quantity, but this is not certain.'

[The House of Lords agreed with Atkin LJ.]

NOTES

1. Compare the cases on whether the defendant made a promise (above, pp 11–19). Aren't those cases and many of the 'intention to create legal relations' cases asking the same question?

2. In *Ford Motor Co Ltd v Amalgamated Union of Engineering and Foundry Workers* [1969] 2 All ER 481 the question arose whether a series of collective agreements between Ford and the Union were legally enforceable contracts. Geoffrey Lane J held that they were not intended to create legal relations. Firstly, in determining the parties' intentions, it was proper to look at the general opinion on the point in industrial circles at the time the agreements were made. The Report of the Royal Commission on Trade Unions (the Donovan Report, Cmd 3623, 1968), and the evidence given to the Commission, showed clearly that collective agreements were generally regarded as legally unenforceable. Both Ford and the Union would have known that. Secondly, many of the clauses were very vague. The judge concluded:

If one applies the subjective test and asks what the intentions of the various parties were, the answer is that, so far as they had any express intentions, they were certainly not to make the agreement enforceable at law. If one applies an objective test and asks what intention must be imputed from all the circumstances of the case, the answer is the same. The fact that the agreements prima facie deal with commercial relationships is outweighed by the other considerations, by the wording of the agreements, by the nature of the agreements, and by the climate of opinion voiced and evidenced by the extra-judicial authorities. Agreements such as these, composed largely of optimistic aspirations, presenting grave practical problems of enforcement and reached against a background of opinion adverse to enforceability, are, in my judgment, not contracts in the legal sense and are not enforceable at law. Without clear and express provisions making them amenable to legal action, they remain in the realm of undertakings binding in honour. None of the authorities cited by counsel for Fords dissuades me from this view. In my judgment, the parties, neither of them, had the intention to make these agreements binding at law.

See on this case and the general doctrine, Hepple, 'Intention to create Legal Relations' [1970] CLJ 122.

Esso Petroleum Ltd v Commissioners of Customs and Excise [1976] 1 All ER 117, House of Lords

In 1970 Esso devised a sales promotions scheme under which garage owners offered a 'free' 'World Cup Coin' with every four gallons of petrol. The coins had little intrinsic value. The Commissioners claimed that the coins were chargeable to purchase tax under s 2(1) of the Purchase Tax Act 1963, on the ground that they were 'produced in quantity for general sale'.

The House of Lords held, by a majority, that the coins were not being 'sold'. They differed on whether there was any intention to create legal relations.

Lord Simon of Glaisdale. My Lords, I have had the advantage of reading in draft the speech prepared by my noble and learned friend, Lord Russell of Killowen. I beg to take advantage of his explanation of the facts that have led to the appeal and the statutory provisions by which they are to be judged.

I am, however, my Lords, not prepared to accept that the promotion material put out by Esso was not envisaged by them as creating legal relations between the garage proprietors who adopted it and the motorists who yielded to its blandishments. In the first place, Esso and the garage proprietors put the material out for their commercial advantage, and designed it to attract the custom of motorists. The whole transaction took place in a setting of business relations. In the second place, it seems to me in general undesirable to allow a commercial promoter to claim that what he has done is a mere puff, not intended to create legal relations (cf *Carlill v Carbolic Smoke Ball Co*). The coins may have been themselves of little intrinsic value; but all the evidence suggests that Esso contemplated that they would be attractive to motorists and that there would be a large commercial advantage to themselves from the scheme, an advantage in which the garage proprietors also would share. Thirdly, I think that authority supports the view that legal relations were envisaged.

[I]t begs the questions to assert that no motorist who bought petrol in consequence of seeing the promotion material prominently displayed in the garage forecourt would be likely to bring an action in the county court if he were refused a coin. He might be a suburb Hampden who was not prepared to forego what he conceived to be his rights or to allow a tradesman to go back on his word.

Believing as I do that Esso envisaged a bargain of some sort between the garage proprietor and the motorist, I must try to analyse the transaction. The analysis that most appeals to me is one of the ways in which Lord Denning MR considered the case, namely a collateral contract of the sort described by Lord Moulton in *Heilbut, Symons & Co v Buckleton*:

'. . . there may be a contract the consideration for which is the making of some other contract. "If you will make such and such a contract I will give you one hundred pounds", is in every sense of the word a complete legal contract. It is collateral to the main contract . . .'

So here. The law happily matches the reality. The garage proprietor is saying, 'If you will buy four gallons of my petrol, I will give you one of these coins'. None of the reasons which have caused the law to consider advertising or display material as an invitation to treat, rather than an offer, applies here. What the garage proprietor says by his placards is in fact and in law an offer of consideration to the motorist to enter into a contract of sale of petrol. Of course, not every motorist will notice the placard, but nor will every potential offeree of many offers be necessarily conscious that they have been made. However, the motorist who does notice the placard, and in reliance thereon drives in and orders the petrol, is in law doing two things at the same time. First, he is accepting the offer of a coin if he buys four gallons of petrol. Secondly, he is himself offering to buy four gallons of petrol: this offer is accepted by the filling of his tank.

Here the coins were not transferred for a money consideration. They were transferred in consideration of the motorist entering into a contract for the sale of petrol. The coins were therefore not produced for sale, and do not fall within the schedule. They are exempt from purchase tax.

I would therefore dismiss the appeal.

[Lord Wilberforce agreed with Lord Simon's analysis. Lord Fraser of Tullybelton also held that there was intention to create legal relations.]

Lord Russell of Killowen. . . . My Lords, it is not in dispute that unless the medals were produced at the instance of Esso for the purpose of, ie with a view to, their being sold by garage proprietors to motorists there cannot be the suggested charge of purchase tax. The first question accordingly is whether, notwithstanding the liberal references in the documents attending the promotion scheme to 'giving', 'gifts', and 'free', that which would and did take place gave rise to a contract, enforceable by a motorist who bought four gallons from a participating proprietor, that he should receive one of these medals. It is to be borne in mind in this connection that the mere facts that Esso and the garage proprietors undoubtedly had a commercial aim in promoting the scheme does not deprive the delivery of a medal of the quality of a gift as distinct from a sale; for benevolence it is not a necessary feature of a gift which may well be motivated by self interest. On the other hand it is trite law that if on analysis a transaction has in law one character, the fact that the parties either accidentally or deliberately frame the transaction in language appropriate to a transaction of a different character will not deny to it its true character.

We have here, my Lords, a promotion scheme initiated by Esso, who procured the production of the medals. Each medal was of negligible intrinsic value, though the incentive to soccer enthusiasts to collect all 30 may have been strong. Plainly it was never in Esso's mind that this negligible intrinsic value should be reflected in an increase in the pump price of petrol, and it never was; indeed the price of a gallon could not be increased by $\frac{3}{16}$ of a penny. In my opinion it would have been thought by Esso, and rightly, that there could have been no occasion, in order to ensure success of the scheme, for an outlet proprietor to subject himself to a contractual liability to deliver a coin to a motorist who had bought four gallons. The subject-matter was trivial: the proprietor was directly interested in the success of the scheme and would be in the highest degree unlikely to renege on the free gift offer, and indeed there is no suggestion that a motorist who qualified and wanted a medal ever failed to get one; from the motorist's viewpoint, if this had ever happened, I cannot think that he would have considered that he had a legal grievance, though he might have said that he would not patronise that outlet again; similarly in my opinion if a garage advertised 'Free Air' and after buying petrol or oil the motorist was told that the machine was out of order that day. In my opinion, the incentive for the garage proprietor to carry out the scheme was such as to make it quite unnecessary to invest, or for Esso to intend to invest, the transaction with the additional compulsion of a contractual obligation, and in all the circumstances of the case I am unable to regard that which under the scheme was intended by Esso to take place in relation to the medals, and did take place, as something which would be intended to or regarded as creating a legal contractual relationship. In forming that opinion I regard the mimimal intrinsic value of a medal as important. I would not wish it to be thought that my opinion, if correct, would, in other cases in which a sales promotion scheme involves substantial benefits, give carte blanche to participants to renege on 'free' offers. I am simply of opinion, in agreement with the Court of Appeal, though not I fear with the majority of your Lordships, that in the instant case, because of the absence of any contractual element, it should not be said that any medal was produced for general sale.

Suppose however that there was a contractual obligation on the proprietor to deliver a medal to the motorist who had bought four gallons of petrol, the further question arises whether there was a contract of sale of the medal for a price in money.

[Lord Russell went on to hold that the coins were not being 'sold': there was an offer to give a coin to any motorist who purchased four gallons of petrol.]

[Viscount Dilhorne gave judgment to the same effect as Lord Russell.]

Appeal dismissed.

J Evans & Son (Portsmouth) Ltd v Andrea Merzario Ltd [1976] 2 All ER 930

The plaintiffs, who were importers of machinery, regularly used the defendant forwarding agents to arrange the carriage of the goods to England. The contracts were on the standard conditions of the forwarding trade. The machinery was liable to rust if carried on deck, and before 1967 the defendants had always arranged for the crates or trailers containing it to be carried below decks. In 1967, in the course of a 'courtsey call' to the plaintiffs, the defendants' representative proposed that in future the plaintiffs' machinery should be carried by container transport. When the plaintiffs expressed concern about rusting, the representative gave an oral assurance that any container used for the plaintiffs' goods would be shipped below decks (many container ships are designed to carry large numbers of containers stacked on the decks). On that basis the plaintiffs agreed to the change in method. Subsequently the defendants arranged for the transport in a container of an injection moulding machine for the plaintiffs, and by an oversight it was placed on deck. The container was not properly fastened down, and when the ship left port the container fell overboard and the machine was lost. . . .

At first instance Kerr J held that the oral assurance made during the courtsey call was not intended to be legally binding. The Court of Appeal disagreed. Roskill LJ said:

I unreservedly accept counsel for the defendants' submission that one must not look at one or two isolated answers given in evidence; one should look at the totality of the evidence. When one does that, one finds first, as I have already mentioned, that these parties had been doing business in transporting goods from Milan to England for some time before; secondly, that transportation of goods from Milan to England was always done on trailers which were always under deck; thirdly, that the defendants wanted a change in the practice—they wanted containers used instead of trailers; fourthly, that the plaintiffs were only willing to agree to that change if they were promised by the defendant that those containers would be shipped under deck, and would not have agreed to the change but for that promise. The defendants gave such a promise which to my mind against this background plainly amounted to an enforceable contractual promise. In those circumstances it seems to me that the contract was this: 'If we continue to give you our business, you will ensure that those goods in containers are shipped under deck'; and the defendants agreed that this would be so. Thus there was a breach of that contract by the defendants when this container was shipped on deck; and it seems to me to be plain that the damage which the plaintiffs suffered resulted from that breach.

[Lord Denning MR and Geoffrey Lane LJ delivered concurring judgments.]

Appeal allowed.

[Further extracts from this case will be found on p 685.]

NOTE

In contrast, in *Independent Broadcasting Authority v EMI Electronics Ltd and BICC Construction Ltd* (1980) 14 BLR 1 EMI were employed as main contractors by the IBA to put up the Elmley Moor television mast, which at 1,250 feet was the highest mast erected on this side of the Atlantic. It was understood that the design of the mast and its construction would be carried out by BIC (now BICC), who were employed as sub-contractors: there was no direct contract between IBA and BIC.

The mast was erected, but it collapsed on a day when there was only a light wind but it was very cold. The trial judge found that the collapse was caused by a combination of oscillations set up in the mast by 'vortex shedding' as the light wind blew past the cylindrical part of the mast, and asymmetric icing on the stays of the mast. It appeared that no-one had foreseen the dangerous combination of oscillations and icing at wind speeds low enough that the ice was not blown off the stays. The judge held that this failure on BIC's part constituted negligence.

During the course of construction, IBA had questioned the safety of the mast after another, similar mast being built had started to oscillate. However, on 11 November 1964 BIC wrote to EMI that 'we are well satisfied that the structure will not oscillate dangerously', and relying on this IBA permitted work to go ahead without further investigation of the design.

The House of Lords held that as EMI had tendered for the 'design, supply and erection' of the mast, they were contractually liable for the defective design. However, they also considered whether BIC were liable to IBA.

The House of Lords, differing from the courts below, held that BIC were not liable in contract to IBA: the letter did not show any intention to contract. BIC were, however, held liable in tort for giving the assurance negligently.

Section 3
Has an agreement been reached?

CHAPTER 9
Offer and acceptance

The traditional method of determining whether the parties have in fact agreed to be bound by a contract is to ask whether one party has made an 'offer' and the other has 'accepted' that offer.

Throughout the materials which follow, it will be seen that the courts are faced with striking a balance between conflicting interests. On the one hand, it is important to preserve the freedom of action of a party seeking to make an exchange. He must be able to disseminate information about his willingness to contract without the risk of being subjected to obligations he cannot meet, and without having to hedge his words so carefully that the process becomes too costly and the information appears too unreliable to the recipient (who may not understand the need for the hedging phrases and be suspicious of them). On the other hand, the recipient may need to be able to rely on the information given him, without being at a stage where he can sensibly commit himself to a contract, at least without elaborate and therefore costly safeguards. To take an example of these points, a person with goods to sell needs to be able to advertise them widely, but does not want to become committed to more buyers than he can supply; and he may need the freedom to negotiate with a number of buyers until he obtains the best price. Potential buyers, on the other hand, whether buying for use or for resale, may need to be able to count on a supply of the goods at a certain maximum price in planning their own ventures, without as yet being able to commit themselves to buying. Clearly the seller could protect himself by stating that he was reserving the right to refuse any order, and the buyer could make contracts for the goods with elaborate cancellation clauses, but this is an expensive approach which is seldom adopted unless the risks are very high. Instead, the courts have to construe the facts of what happened during negotiations in a way that seems fair to the parties and workable for the future.

To some extent the courts' ability to do this has been limited by the tools available; in particular, by the fact that the analysis has traditionally been 'contract or no contract', with no intermediate position. This is not always the case even in English law, as the courts have sometimes been able to provide a solution through restitutionary or even tortious remedies (see p 224 below); but English law has not yet followed the US example of manipulating reliance doctrine (see above, p 151) to impose liability without subjecting the parties to a contract. Whether this is a sensible approach will be discussed later (p 227).

See generally Winfield, 'Some Aspects of Offer and Acceptance' (1939) 55 LQR 499; Kahn (1955) 72 SALJ 246.

(a) The objective principle

As mentioned earlier (above, p 14), it is normally what you say or do which matters in contract, not what you meant. The objective principle is particularly important in cases of mistake about what the proposed terms are (see below, Chapter 11) and a classic formulation of the principle is found in one of these, *Smith v Hughes* (see below, p 244). Blackburn J said:

> If, whatever a man's real intention may be, he so conducts himself that a reasonable man would believe that he was assenting to the terms proposed by the other party, and that other party upon that belief enters into the contract with him, the man thus conducting himself would be equally bound as if he had intended to agree to the other party's terms.

However, exactly the same principle applies to determine whether an offer has been made or accepted.

The Hannah Blumenthal [1983] 1 All ER 34, House of Lords

A contract for the sale of a ship provided that any dispute arising out of the sale should be settled by arbitration in London. In 1972 the buyers commenced arbitration proceedings. There followed a long delay, with letters being exchanged intermittently, until 1980, when the buyers proposed fixing a date for arbitration. The sellers then issued a writ seeking a declaration that the arbitration agreement had been discharged by the buyers' repudiation of it, or by frustration or by mutual rescission arising out of an agreement to abandon the arbitration. The House of Lords held firstly that as there were mutual obligations to avoid delay, neither party could rely on the other's conduct as amounting to a repudiation; and secondly, that the agreement was not frustrated, as there had been no external change of events affecting the performance of the arbitration agreement, nor had the delay occurred without the fault of either party. On the abandonment point:

Lord Brandon: . . . I pass now to the further question raised by the cross-appeal. That question is, as I indicated earlier, whether, assuming (contrary to the decisions of the courts below) that the agreement to refer in the present case was not frustrated, the conduct of the parties was nevertheless of such a character as to lead to the inference that they impliedly consented with each other to abandon that agreement.

The question whether a contract has been abandoned or not is one of fact. That being so, it would, I think, be sufficient, for the purposes of the present case, to say that there are concurrent findings of fact by both the courts below against the sellers on that question, that it is not the practice of your Lordships' House to interfere with such concurrent findings of fact save in exceptional circumstances which are not here present, and that the cross-appeal fails on that ground alone.

Because the question of the abandonment of a contract is, however, of some general importance, I consider that it may be helpful to examine the matter, as it arises in the present case, somewhat further. For this purpose it is, I think, necessary to make some additions to the history of the parties' conduct in relation to the reference which I set out earlier. The additional facts which I regard, for reasons which will become apparent later, as necessary to state are these. According to the affidavit of Mr Fitzpatrick, a solicitor employed by Sinclairs, sworn on 16 December 1980, that firm was still seeking to trace, and obtain evidence from, witnesses whom it might be necessary to call on the hearing of the arbitration as late as November 1979, February 1980 and November 1980.

The concept of the implied abandonment of a contract as a result of the conduct of the parties to it is well established in law: see *Chitty on Contracts* (23rd edn, 1968) vol 1, para 1231 and cases there cited. Where A seeks to prove that he and B have abandoned a contract in this way, there are two ways in which A can put his case. The first way is by showing that the conduct of each party, as evinced to the other party and acted on by him, leads necessarily to the inference of an implied agreement between them to abandon the contract. The second method is by showing that the conduct of B, as evinced towards A, has been such as to lead A reasonably to believe that B has abandoned the contract, even though it has not in fact been B's intention to do so, and that A has significantly altered his position in reliance on that belief. The first method involves actual abandonment by both A and B. The second method involves the creation by B of a situation in which he is estopped from asserting, as against A, that he, B, has not abandoned the contract (see *Pearl Mill Co Ltd v Ivy Tannery Co Ltd*).

On whichever of the two bases of abandonment discussed above the sellers seek to reply in the present case, it seems to me that they are bound to fail. As I indicated above, Sinclairs, as the sellers' solicitors, were still, in November 1979, February 1980 and even as late as November 1980, trying to trace, and obtain evidence from witnesses who might be called at the hearing of the arbitration. Even if it could fairly be said (which I do not think that it can) that the buyers' prolonged delays from 1974 onwards were such as to induce in the minds of the sellers or their solicitors a reasonable belief that the buyers had abandoned the agreement to refer, Sinclairs' continuing conduct with regard to tracing, and obtaining evidence from, witnesses referred to above makes it impossible for the sellers to say that they acted on any such belief, or that they altered their position significantly in reliance on it.

For the reasons which I have given I would allow the buyer's original appeal and dismiss the sellers' cross-appeal, with costs against the sellers in either case.

Lord Diplock: . . . Abandonment of a contract (the former contract) which is still executory, ie one in which at least one primary obligation of one or other of the parties remains unperformed, is effected by the parties entering into a new contract (the contract of abandonment) . . .

To the formation of the contract of abandonment, the ordinary principles of the English law of contract apply. To create a contract by exchange of promises between two parties where the promise of each party constitutes the consideration for the promise of the other what is necessary is that the intention of each *as it has been communicated to and understood by the other* (even though that which has been communicated does not represent the actual state of mind of the communicator) should coincide. That is what English lawyers mean when they resort to the latin phrase consensus ad idem and the words that I have italicised are essential to the concept of consensus ad idem, the lack of which prevents the formation of a binding contract in English law.

Thus if A (the offeror) makes a communication to B (the offeree), whether in writing, orally or by conduct, which, in the circumstances at the time the communication was received, (1) B, if he were a reasonable man, would understand as stating A's intention to act or refrain from acting in some specified manner if B will promise on his part to act or refrain from acting in some manner also specified in the offer, and (2) B does in fact understand A's communication to mean this, and in his turn makes to A a communication conveying his willingness so to act or to refrain from acting which mutatis mutandis satisfies the same two conditions as respects A, the consensus ad idem essential to the formation of a contract in English law is complete.

The rule that neither party can rely on his own failure to communicate accurately to the other party his own real intention by what he wrote or said or did, as negativing the consensus ad idem, is an example of a general principle of English law that injurious reliance on what another person did may be a source of legal rights against him. I use the broader expression 'injurious reliance' in preference to 'estoppel' so as to embrace all circumstances in which A can say to B, 'You led me reasonably to believe that you were assuming particular legally enforceable obligations to me', of which promissory or *High Trees* estoppel (see *Central London Property Trust Ltd v High Trees House Ltd* [above, p 137]. . .) affords another example, whereas 'estoppel', in the strict sense of the term, is an exclusionary rule of evidence, though it may operate so as to affect substantive legal rights inter partes. . . .

Lord Brightman: The basis of 'tacit abandonment by both parties', to use the phraseology of the sellers' case, is that the primary facts are such that it ought to be inferred that the contract to arbitrate the particular dispute was rescinded by the mutual agreement of the parties. To entitle the sellers to rely on abandonment, they must show that the buyers so conducted themselves as to entitle the sellers to assume, *and that the sellers did assume*, that the contract was agreed to be abandoned sub silentio. The evidence which is relevant to that inquiry will consist of or include: (1) what the buyers did or omitted to do *to the knowledge of the sellers*. Excluded from consideration will be the acts of the buyers of which the sellers were ignorant, because those acts will have signalled nothing to the sellers and cannot have founded or fortified any assumption on the part of the sellers; (2) what the sellers did or omitted to do, *whether or not to the knowledge of the buyers*. These facts evidence the state of mind of the sellers, and therefore the validity of the assertion by the sellers that they assumed that the contract was agreed to be abandoned. The state of mind of the buyers is irrelevant to a consideration of what the sellers were entitled to assume. The state of mind of the sellers is vital to what the sellers in fact assumed.

[Lords Roskill and Keith concurred.]

Appeal allowed. Cross-appeal dismissed.

NOTES

1. Some commentators have seen significant differences in the way the three members of the House of Lords formulated the objective test. On the one hand, Lord Diplock's words have been interpreted as meaning that the parties (A and B) must actually be in agreement (B must actually think A was making an offer to him and accept in such a way that A actually understands that B is accepting.) On the other, Lord Brandon's formulation seems to suggest that it is not enough that one party reasonably understood the other to be making an offer and accepted that apparent offer; he seems to suggest that the first party must have acted in reliance on the apparent offer. If this means he must have changed his position (as is required for estoppel, see above, p 135), this is inconsistent with the normal understanding that it is enough simply to accept the apparent offer (see the *Centrovincial* case, below, p 233). In *The Leonidas D* (see below, p 593) Robert Goff LJ said:

   > Three distinct views were however expressed by their Lordships as to how an implied abandonment of a contract might come about. Lord Brandon, who delivered the leading speech, considered that it could be established 'by showing that the conduct of each party, as evinced to the other party and acted on by him, leads necessarily to the inference of an implied agreement between them to abandon the contract' (see [1983] 1 All ER 34 at 47, [1983] 1 AC 854 at 914). Lord Diplock's formulation appears to us to involve the requirement that the actual intentions of both parties should in fact coincide (see [1983] 1 All ER 34 at 48–49, [1983] 1 AC 854 at 915–916). Lord Brightman, on the other hand, thought that, to enable one party (the sellers) to rely on abandonment, it was enough for them to show 'that the buyers so conducted themselves as to entitle the sellers to assume, *and that the sellers did assume*, that the contract was agreed to be abandoned sub silentio' (see [1983] 1 All ER 34 at 55, [1983] 1 AC 854 at 924) (Lord Brightman's emphasis).
   >   It is apparent that these three approaches are not identical. However, if we have to choose between them, we would respectfully prefer to follow the approach of Lord Brightman. In his speech Lord Brightman was, as we understand it, asserting that if one party (O) so acts that his conduct, objectively considered, constitutes an offer, and the other party (A), believing that the conduct of O represents his actual intention, accepts O's offer, then a contract will come into existence, and on those facts it will make no difference if O did not in fact intend to make an offer, or if he misunderstood A's acceptance, so that O's state of mind is, in such circumstances, irrelevant. With that proposition we very respectfully agree and so, if it is necessary for us to choose, we would prefer to follow the reasoning of Lord Brightman in so far as it differs from the reasoning of Lord Brandon and Lord Diplock.

   For further discussion of these points see Atiyah (1986) 102 LQR 363; Vorster (1987) 103 LQR 274.

2. Why do the courts apply the objective principle, when that may mean parties become bound by contracts when they didn't intend to?

(b) Offer or preliminary negotiations

(i) Correspondence

Gibson v Manchester City Council [1979] 1 All ER 972

In 1970 the city council, then in the control of the Conservative party, adopted a policy of selling council houses to its tenants. It circulated printed forms which tenants could send in to obtain details; the form read in part:

> Please inform me of the price of buying my council house. I am interested in obtaining a mortgage from the Corporation to buy the house. Please send me the details.

Gibson sent in a form and received a letter from the city treasurer stating (in part):

> The Corporation may be prepared to sell the house to you at the purchase price of £2,725 less 20% = £2,180 (freehold).
>
> Maximum mortgage the Corporation may grant: £2,177 repayable over 20 years.
>
> . . .
>
> This letter should not be regarded as a firm offer of a mortgage.
> *If you would like to make a formal application to buy your council house, please complete the enclosed application form and return it to me as soon as possible.*

(Emphasis supplied.)
Gibson completed the application form except for the price and returned it; after being told that the Corporation would not lower the price as he had requested, he wrote:

> I would be obliged if you will carry on with the purchase as per my application already in your possession.

Thereafter the house was removed from the council's maintenance list and placed on their house purchase list; but before the contracts had been exchanged, control of the council passed to the Labour party and it was resolved to discontinue sales of council houses except in cases where there was a binding contract to sell. Gibson was notified that the council would not be proceeding with the sale to him, and he brought an action seeking specific performance of the agreement he alleged had been made. The county court judge and, on appeal, the Court of Appeal, held that there was a concluded contract and ordered specific performance. The Council appealed.

Lord Diplock. My Lords, this is an action for specific performance of what is claimed to be a contract for the sale of land. The only question in the appeal is of a kind with which the courts are very familiar. It is whether in the correspondence between the parties there can be found a legally enforceable contract for the sale by the Manchester Corporation to Mr Gibson of the dwelling-house of which he was the occupying tenant at the relevant time in 1971. That question is one that, in my view, can be answered by applying to the particular documents relied on by Mr Gibson as constituting the contract, well settled, indeed elementary, principles of English law. This being so, it is not the sort of case in which leave would have been likely to be granted to appeal to your Lordships' House, but for the fact that it is a test case.

. . . Lord Denning MR rejected what I have described as the conventional approach of looking to see whether on the true construction of the documents relied on there can be discerned an offer and acceptance. One ought, he said, to 'look at the correspondence as a whole and at the conduct of the parties and see therefrom whether the parties have come to an agreement on everything that was material'. This approach, which in referring to the conduct of the parties where there is no allegation of part performance appears to me to overlook the provisions of s 40 of the Law of Property Act 1925 [see above, p 131], led him however to the conclusion that there should be imported into the agreement to be specifically performed additional conditions, against use except as a private dwelling-house and against advertising and a restriction not to sell or lease the property for five years. These are conditions which would not be implied by law in an open contract for the sale of land. The reason for so varying the county court judge's order was that clauses in these terms were included in the standard form of 'Agreement for Sale of a Council House' which, as appears from the earlier case of *Storer v Manchester City Council*, was entered into by the council and council tenants whose applications to purchase the freehold of their council house reached the stage at which contracts were exchanged. There was, however, no reference to this standard form of agreement in any of the documents said to constitute the contract relied on in the instant case, nor was there any evidence that Mr Gibson had knowledge of its terms at or before the time that the alleged contract was concluded. . . .

My Lords, the words italicised seem to me, as they seemed to Geoffrey Lane LJ, to make it quite impossible to construe this letter as a contractual offer capable of being converted into a legally enforceable open contract for the sale of land by Mr Gibson's written acceptance of it. The words 'may be prepared to sell' are fatal to this; so is the invitation, not, be it noted, to accept the offer, but 'to make formal application to buy' on the enclosed application form. It is, to quote Geoffrey Lane LJ, a letter setting out the financial terms on which it may be the council would be prepared to consider a sale and purchase in due course.

Both Ormrod LJ and the county court judge, in reaching the conclusion that this letter was a firm offer to sell the freehold interest in the house for £2,180, attached importance to the fact that the second paragraph, dealing with the financial details of the mortgage of which Mr Gibson had asked for particulars, stated expressly, 'This letter should not be regarded as a firm offer of a mortgage'. The necessary implication from this, it is suggested, is that the first paragraph of the letter *is* to be regarded as a firm offer to sell despite the fact that this is plainly inconsistent with the express language of that paragraph. My Lords, with great respect, this surely must be fallacious. If the final sentence had been omitted the wording of the second paragraph, unlike that of the first, with its use of the indicative mood in such expressions as 'the interest rate *will* change', might have been understood by council tenants to whom it was addressed as indicating a firm offer of a mortgage of the amount and on the terms for repayment stated if the council were prepared to sell the house at the stated price. But, whether or not this be the explanation of the presence of the last sentence in the second paragraph, it cannot possibly affect the plain meaning of the words used in the first paragraph.

My Lords, the application form and letter of 18th March 1971 were relied on by Mr Gibson as an unconditional acceptance of the council's offer to sell the house; but this cannot be so unless there was a contractual offer by the council available for acceptance; and, for the reason already given I am of opinion that there was none. It is unnecessary to consider whether the application form and Mr Gibson's letters of 5th and 18th March 1971 are capable of amounting to a contractual offer by him to purchase the freehold interest in the house at a price of £2,180 on the terms of an open contract, for there is no suggestion that, even if it were, it was ever accepted by the council. Nor would it ever have been even if there had been no change in the political control of the council, as the policy of the council before the change required the incorporation in all agreements for sale of council houses to tenants of the conditions referred by Lord Denning MR in his judgment and other conditions inconsistent with an open contract. I therefore feel compelled to allow the appeal.

[Lords Edmund-Davies and Russell made speeches allowing the appeal and Lords Fraser and Keith agreed with Lord Diplock.]

Appeal allowed.

NOTES

1. Suppose that the city treasurer's letter had stated that the sale would be on the 'Standard Form of Agreement for Sale of a Council House' referred to. It might then have been said that the parties had agreed what all the material terms should be. Would there then have been a contract, or is something else required?
2. In *Storer v Manchester City Council* [1974] 3 All ER 824, another case arising from the same change of policy, the town clerk had written to the tenant:

I understand you wish to purchase your council house and enclose the Agreement for Sale. If you will sign the agreement and return it to me I will send you the agreement signed on behalf of the Corporation in exchange. From the enclosed list of solicitors, who are prepared to act for you and advise you on the purchase, please let me know the name of the firm that you select, as soon as possible.

The letter enclosed an Agreement for Sale in which were set out details of the mortgage. The date at which the tenancy was to cease and mortgage payments commence was left blank. The form continued:

... *Warning.* As from the date mentioned ... the property is at your risk. If you are taking a mortgage from the Corporation it will be insured for you but the cost recharged to you. *If you are not taking a Mortgage insure it at once* ...

The plaintiff signed and returned the Agreement, but before it had been signed by the town clerk the council changed hands. The Court of Appeal held that there was a contract. What distinguishes the two cases? (Note that it was held that the council were, by the language of the town clerk's letter, dispensing with the 'exchange of contracts' by which contracts for the sale of land are usually made. See below, p 204.)

3. Apart from the words of the letter from the City Treasurer italicized, do you see any other words which suggest the letter did not contain an offer? Remember that if it were an offer which Mr Gibson could accept by completing and sending in the application, the resulting contract would be binding on both parties.
4. Would it be sensible for the City Council to commit itself to selling to an applicant without first deciding on the mortgage? Was the difference in language in the letters to Gibson and to Storer, from whom the Council had already received an 'application', fortuitous?
5. Gibson had already made some alterations to the property. If he had done this in the expectation that he would be buying the house, should this make a difference? Should the law protect (and thus encourage) such a form of reliance in this type of case? See further below, p 227.

In *Harvey v Facey* [1893] AC 552 appellants sent a telegram from Kingston to the respondent 'on the train to Porus', asking 'will you sell us Bumper Hall Pen? Telegraph lowest cash price'. The respondent telegraphed in reply: 'Lowest price for Bumper Hall Pen £900'. Assuming this to be an offer, the appellants wired an acceptance, but the Privy Council held that no offer had been made which they could accept: the respondent had merely replied to the second of the two questions contained in the appellants' telegram. In *Canadian Dyers Association Ltd v Burton* (1920) 47 OLR 259 the plaintiff company had for some time been negotiating to buy the house next door to its factory from the defendant, who had been a director of the company. In response to an enquiry the defendant wrote: 'the last price I gave you is the lowest I am prepared to accept. In fact I feel that under present conditions this is exceptionally low and if it were to any other party I would ask more'. The plaintiff accepted. The letter was held to be an offer, especially as the defendant had his solicitor send a draft deed. Are the cases distinguishable? What if the defendant's subsequent conduct is left out of account?

(ii) Advertisements and displays of goods

Grainger & Son v Gough [1896] AC 325, House of Lords

The question was whether a foreign merchant who canvassed for orders through agents in the United Kingdom was exercising a trade in the United Kingdom within the meaning of the Income Tax Acts.

Lord Herschell said in the course of his judgment:

The learned Solicitor-General, in his argument for the Crown, did not contend that any contracts were made in this country by M Roederer either personally or through his agents; indeed, he admitted the contrary. Mr Danckwerts did argue that there were such contracts. His argument was an ingenious one. He called attention to certain price-lists which were distributed by the appellants amongst persons likely to give orders, and contended that as soon as an order was given to them by a person receiving one of those lists a contract to supply the specified quantity at the price named in the list was complete, subject only to a right on the part of Roederer to disavow it. I think it impossible to accede to this contention. In my opinion, this would not be understood by any one in the trade to be the effect of giving an order for goods specified in such a price-list. The transmission of such a price-list does not amount to an offer to supply an unlimited quantity of the wine described at the price named, so that as soon as an order is given there is a binding contract to supply that quantity. If it were so, the merchant might find himself involved in any number of contractual obligations to supply wine of a particular description which he would be quite unable to carry out, his stock of wine of that description being necessarily limited. I entertain, I confess, a very clear opinion that the Solicitor-General was quite right in arguing the case on the assumption that no sales were made in this country.

NOTE

A competitive market requires a full and free flow of information. What might be the effect if advertisements *were* treated as offers—how would potential sellers react (assuming they knew the law)?

Carlill v Carbolic Smoke Ball Co [1893] 1 QB 256, Court of Appeal (above, p 12)

NOTE

If this advertisement had been held not to constitute an offer, what would have been the practical problem facing parties wishing to offer rewards to persons giving information, or coming forward to do some other specified act?

Pharmaceutical Society of GB v Boots Cash Chemists (Southern) Ltd [1953] 1 QB 401, Court of Appeal

The defendant's 'self-service' shop comprised one room around whose walls were shelves on which were laid out certain drugs and medicines specified in Part I of the Poisons List compiled under s 17(1) of the Pharmacy and Poisons Act 1933. These preparations were wrapped in packages and containers with the prices marked on them. A customer entering the shop took a wire basket, selected any articles he required from the shelves, placed them in the basket, and carried them to a cashier at one of the two exits. The cashier then examined the articles the customer wished to purchase, stated the total price, and accepted payment. At this stage a registered pharmacist, who was authorised by the chemist to prevent the customer from buying any article if he thought fit, supervised the transaction.

[Section 18(1) of the Act provided:]

'Subject to the provisions of this Part of this Act, it shall not be lawful—(a) for a person to sell any poison included in Part I of the Poisons List, unless . . . (iii) the sale is effected by, or under the supervision of, a registered pharmacist.'

Somervell LJ. . . . The point taken by the plaintiffs is this: it is said that the purchase is complete if and when a customer going round the shelves takes an article and puts it in the receptacle which he or she is carrying, and that therefore, if that is right, when the customer comes to the pay desk, having completed the tour of the premises, the registered pharmacist, if so minded, has no power to say: 'This drug ought not to be sold to this customer.' Whether and in what circumstances he would have that power we need not inquire, but one can, of course, see that there is a difference if supervision can only be exercised at a time when the contract is completed.

I agree with the Lord Chief Justice in everything that he said, but I will put the matter shortly in my own words. Whether the view contended for by the plaintiffs is a right view depends on what are the legal implications of this layout—the invitation to the customer. Is a contract to be regarded as being completed when the article is put into the receptacle, or is this to be regarded as a more organized way of doing what is done already in many types of shops—and a bookseller is perhaps the best example—namely, enabling customers to have free access to what is in the shop, to look at the different articles, and then, ultimately, having got the ones which they wish to buy, to come up to the assistant saying 'I want this'? The assistant in 999 times out of 1,000 says 'That is all right', and the money passes and the transaction is completed. I agree with what the Lord Chief Justice has said, and with the reasons which he has given for his conclusion, that in the case of an ordinary shop, although goods are displayed and it is intended that customers should go and choose what they want, the contract is not completed until, the customer having indicated the articles which he needs, the shopkeeper, or someone on his behalf, accepts that offer. Then the contract is completed. I can see no reason at all, that being clearly the normal position, for drawing any different implication as a result of this layout.

The Lord Chief Justice, I think, expressed one of the most formidable difficulties in the way of the plaintiffs' contention when he pointed out that, if the plaintiffs are right, once an article has been placed in the receptacle the customer himself is bound and would have no right, without paying for the first article, to substitute an article which he saw later of a similar kind and which he perhaps preferred. I can see no reason for implying from this self-service arrangement any implication other than that which the Lord Chief Justice found in it, namely, that it is a convenient method of enabling customers to see what there is and choose, and possibly put back and substitute, articles which they wish to have, and then to go up to the cashier and offer to buy what they have so far chosen. On that conclusion the case fails, because it is admitted that there was supervision in the sense required by the Act and at the appropriate moment of time. For these reasons, in my opinion, the appeal should be dismissed.

[Birkett and Romer LJJ delivered concurring judgments.]

Appeal dismissed.

NOTES

1. If the display had been treated as an offer, would it necessarily have followed that the customer could not change his mind after putting the goods in his basket? Why not say there is no acceptance until he presents the goods to the cashier? See generally Montrose, 'Contract of Sale in Self-Service Stores' 4 Am J Comp Law 235.
2. Furmston picks up a bottle of tonic water from the shelves of Beale's Supermarket Ltd, and the bottle bursts injuring his hand. He could attempt to sue Beale or Bishop Ltd, the manufacturer, but as there is no evidence as to whether the defect (a cracked bottle) was caused by the carelessness of Bishop, Beale or another customer who might have dropped the bottle and then put it back onto the shelf, he wishes to know whether he can recover from Beale in contract (on the basis of strict liability for goods not of merchantable quality). Advise him on the basis that the explosion occurred:
   (a) as he first placed the bottle in his trolley;
   (b) as he took it out of the trolley and placed it on the checkout desk; and
   (c) as he put it into his shopping bag after the assistant had rung it up, but before all the other items he had selected had been rung up?

3. Suppose that when all the items Furmston has selected have been rung up, the total is more than he has the cash to pay for?
4. The 'rules' that advertisements and displays of goods in shops do not amount to offers are so firmly established that it has been held that advertising bramblefinch hens and displaying flickknives do not amount to the crimes of 'offering for sale' those articles (*Partridge v Crittenden* [1968] 2 All ER 421; *Fisher v Bell* [1961] 1 QB 394). But do such advertisements and displays *never* amount to offers? And what problems arise if they are not treated as offers? Consider the American case of *Lefkowitz v Great Minneapolis Surplus Store* 251 Minn 188, 86 NW 2d 689 (1957). The defendants on 6 April published the following in a newspaper:

> Saturday 9 am sharp; 3 Brand new fur coats, worth to $100, First come first served, $1 each.

On 13 April they published another similarly worded advertisement in the same newspaper. On each of the Saturdays concerned the plaintiff was the first to present himself at the appropriate counter of the defendants' store, and demanded the coat, offering to pay the $1. On each occasion the defendants refused to sell to him, stating on the first occasion that under their house rules the offer was open only to women, and on the second occasion that the plaintiff knew the rules. The Supreme Court of Minnesota held that each of the advertisements amounted to an offer. How do you think an English court would decide this case? You may like to compare it to *Carlill's* case, above, p 12. (If you think it would hold there to be an offer, could the plaintiff have demanded all three coats?)

Trade Descriptions Act 1968

Section 11
(2) If any person offering to supply any goods gives, by whatever means, any indication likely to be taken as an indication that the goods are being offered at a price less than that at which they are in fact being offered he shall, subject to the provisions of this Act, be guilty of an offence.

(iii) Auctions

Sale of Goods Act 1979

Section 57
(1) Where goods are put up for sale by auction in lots, each lot is prima facie deemed to be the subject of a separate contract of sale.
(2) A sale by auction is complete when the auctioneer announces its completion by the fall of the hammer, or in other customary manner; and until the announcement is made any bidder may retract his bid.
(3) A sale by auction may be notified to be subject to a reserve or upset price, and a right to bid may also be reserved expressly by or on behalf of the seller.
(4) Where a sale by auction is not notified to be subject to a right to bid by or on behalf of the seller, it is not lawful for the seller to bid himself or to employ any person to bid at the sale, or for the auctioneer knowingly to take any bid from the seller or any such person.
(5) A sale contravening subsection (4) above may be treated as fraudulent by the buyer.
(6) Where, in respect of a sale by auction, a right to bid is expressly reserved (but not otherwise) the seller or any one person on his behalf may bid at the auction.

NOTES

1. Under s 57(2) who makes the offer, who the acceptance?
2. Auctioneer holds an auction of Beale's horse, and the bidding is between Bishop and Furmston. Bishop outbids Furmston and the horse is knocked down to him. He then discovers that Furmston was employed by Beale as a 'puffer' to drive up the bidding. What rights does Bishop have?

Warlow v Harrison (1859) 1 E&E 309, 120 ER 925, Exchequer Chamber

The defendant auctioneer advertised the sale of a horse as 'without reserve' but allowed the owner to bid. The plaintiff, the next highest bidder, was informed of this and refused to bid further, and the horse was knocked down to its owner. The plaintiff claimed it as the highest bona fide bidder. It was held that the plaintiff could not succeed on the pleadings he had entered, but Martin B, delivering the judgment of the court, said:

Upon the facts of the case, it seems to us that the plaintiff is entitled to recover. In a sale by auction there are three parties, viz the owner of the property to be sold, the auctioneer, and the portion of the public who attend to bid, which of course includes the highest bidder. In this, as in most cases of sales by auction, the owner's name was not disclosed: he was a concealed principal. The name of the auctioneers, of whom the defendant was one, alone was published; and the sale was announced by them to be 'without reserve'. This, according to all the cases both at law and equity, means that neither the vendor nor any person on his behalf shall bid at the auction, and that the property shall be sold to the highest bidder, whether the sum bid be equivalent to the real value or not; *Thornett v Haines* . . . We cannot distinguish the case of an auctioneer putting up property for sale upon such a condition from the case of the loser of property offering a reward, or that of a railway company publishing a time table stating the times when, and the places to which, the trains run. It has been decided that the person giving the information advertised for, or a passenger taking a ticket, may sue as upon a contract with him; *Denton v Great Northern Railway Company* . . . Upon the same principle, it seems to us that the highest bona fide bidder at an auction may sue the auctioneer as upon a contract that the sale shall be without reserve. We think the auctioneer who puts the property up for sale upon such a condition pledges himself that the sale shall be without reserve; or, in other words, contracts that it shall be so; and that this contract is made with the highest bona fide bidder; and, in case of a breach of it, that he has a right of action against the auctioneer . . . Neither does it seem to us material whether the owner, or person on his behalf, bid with the knowledge or privity of the auctioneer . . . For these reasons, if the plaintiff think fit to amend his declaration, he, in our opinion, is entitled to the judgment of the Court.

Willes J. My brother Bramwell and myself do not dissent from the judgment which has been pronounced. But we prefer to rest our decision, as to the amendment, upon the ground that the defendant undertook to have, and yet there was evidence that he had not, authority to sell without reserve. The result is the same.

Judgment of Court of Queen's Bench to be affirmed; unless the parties elect to enter a stet processus, or the plaintiff amend his declaration; in which latter case, a new trial to be had.

NOTES

1. The difficulties involved in the case of goods advertised as being sold without reserve simply being withdrawn are discussed in Slade, 68 LQR 238; Gower, 68 LQR 457; Slade, 69 LQR 21.
2. In *Harris v Nickerson* (1873) LR 8 QB 286 the defendant, acting in good faith, advertised that certain furniture would be auctioned on a particular day. The plaintiff travelled to the auction with a commission to buy the furniture, but it was withdrawn from the sale. The judge at first instance

allowed the plaintiff's action to recover his loss of time, but the Court of Queen's Bench reversed the decision: *Warlow v Harrison* was no authority for saying that the advertisement of an auction amounted to a contract with everyone attending the sale. What is the distinction between the two cases? Would the potential liability in the case of a cancelled auction be much greater? What difficulties of proof can you envisage?

3. In *Denton v Great Northern Rly Co* (1856) 4 E&B 860 the plaintiff arrived at the station to catch a train which he had seen advertised in the company's timetable as providing a connecting service to Hull, but discovered that the connecting service (operated by another company) had been withdrawn some time before the timetable had been published. As a result the plaintiff missed an appointment in Hull and suffered damage amounting to £5 10s. The Queen's Bench held he could recover on the ground of fraud, and (Crompton J dissenting) breach of contract. Lord Campbell CJ remarked:

> . . . It seems to me that the representations made by railway companies in their time tables cannot be treated as mere waste paper; and in the present case I think the plaintiff is entitled to recover, on the ground that there was a contract with him . . . The consideration is one which is a prejudice to the person who makes his arrangements with a view to the fulfilment of the contract, and comes to the station on the faith of it . . . '

Crompton J disagreed because he doubted 'whether the promise here in fact was in consideration of coming to the station.' How do British Rail prevent themselves becoming liable for trains that are cancelled?

(c) Acceptance in bilateral contracts

The question of whether an offer has been made is one of fact, to be decided in the light of what was said or written and the circumstances. The question of acceptance is similar; the next case is included to give some idea of the practical difficulties.

(i) Acceptance by words

Tomlin v Standard Telephones and Cables Ltd [1969] 3 All ER 201, Court of Appeal

The plaintiff suffered a back injury during the course of his employment. His solicitor and his employer's insurers negotiated, all the insurer's letters being headed 'without prejudice'. An arrangement was reached that the insurers would accept liability on a 50/50 basis, and on 20 December 1966 the plaintiff's solicitor wrote:

> . . . [the plaintiff] has instructed me to say that he will agree to settle his case on a 50/50 basis as you propose and accordingly this leaves only the question of quantum [ie amount of the loss] to be disposed of.

The insurer never contradicted this and several of its subsequent letters referred to the 'agreement' on liability. On 21 July 1967 the insurers offered to settle for £625. The plaintiff rejected this and commenced proceedings, in which the defendants tried to raise the question of liability. Fisher J held that there was a concluded agreement on liability.

Danckwerts LJ. . . . A point that arises is that all the letters written by the agent of the insurance company bore the words 'Without Prejudice'. The point is taken that, by reason of those words, there could not be any binding agreement between the parties and it was said, indeed, on behalf of the defendants that the letters were not admissible . . .

But in the course of his judgment [in *Walker v Wilsher*], Lindley LJ said:

'What is the meaning of the words "without prejudice"? I think they mean without prejudice to the position of the writer of the letter if the terms he proposes are not accepted. If the terms proposed in the letter are accepted a complete contract is established and the letter, although written without prejudice, operates to alter the old state of things and to establish a new one.'

The statement of Lindley LJ is of great authority and seems to me to apply exactly to the present case if in fact there was a binding agreement, or an agreement intended to be binding, reached between the parties; and, accordingly, it seems to me that not only was the court entitled to look at the letters although they were nearly all described as 'Without Prejudice', but it is quite possible (and in fact the intention of the parties was) that there was a binding agreement contained in that correspondence. That disposes of the first point.

When, however, it comes to the letters there is another and more difficult point, I think, and that is: was there (as Fisher J held) an agreement which was effective and binding between the parties that the rights of the plaintiff should be 50 per cent of any liability and, therefore, he would be entitled to recover 50 per cent of whatever was the proper amount of damages, which was the construction put on the matter by the learned judge; or is there the alternative construction (which other people may possibly view as being the right one) that the agreement as to 50/50 liability was merely a step in the negotiations which were still in progress and which were intended to reach a final settlement between the parties of the amount of damages and of the liability of the defendants in respect of those damages, as was contended on behalf of the defendants? It seems to me quite possible that that might be the proper result, but when the correspondence that I have read is looked at, and in particular the letter of 20th December 1966 from the plaintiff's solicitor, which states that a 50/50 basis has been agreed as proposed by the insurance company on behalf of the defendants 'and accordingly this leaves only the question of quantum to be disposed of', that was never contradicted or rejected on behalf of the defendants. In four letters at least the defendants' representative, the insurance company's claims manager, had referred to the agreement for 50/50 as an 'agreement', and there is no suggestion that it was merely a step in an eventual settlement to be reached. The correspondence proceeds on the basis that there is an agreement for sharing the liability 50/50, and that the plaintiff should be entitled to recover 50 per cent of whatever was the proper amount of damages. In the face of the letters written by the representatives of the defendants, I come to the conclusion that the proper construction is that there was a definite and binding agreement on a 50/50 basis and that, although certain negotiations were entered into for the purpose of trying to agree the amount of the damages, the agreement as to the 50/50 basis stands and the plaintiff is entitled to hold on to that agreement which was reached. Accordingly, I would dismiss the appeal.

Ormrod J. I have the misfortune to differ from Danckwerts LJ as to his conclusion on this appeal . . . [T]he court will protect, and ought to protect so far as it can, in the public interest, 'without prejudice' negotiations because they are very helpful to the disposal of claims without the necessity for litigating in court and, therefore, nothing should be done to make more difficult or more hazardous negotiations under the umbrella of 'without prejudice'. I am well aware, coming from the Divison which I do, that letters get headed 'without prejudice' in the most absurd circumstances, but these letters, in my judgment, are not letters headed 'without prejudice' unnecessarily or meaninglessly. They are plainly 'without prejudice' letters and, therefore, the court, in my judgment, should be very slow to lift the umbrella of 'without prejudice' unless the case is absolutely plain. . . .

I ask myself, looking at this correspondence: is there here a complete contract and, more importantly perhaps, did both parties intend there to be here a complete contract? The contract which counsel for the plaintiff argues for is a contract to settle this litigation on the basis that the parties are equally to blame for the accident and, therefore, should share the damages in equal proportions, which means of necessity that it is an implied term of the agreement that the court will assess the damages in the event the parties cannot agree. In my judgment, that is not what this correspondence meant or was intended to mean. I think that it was an attempt to settle this case for a sum of money and that the 'without prejudice' umbrella remains up and protects the parties negotiating up to the point when they agree on a figure. It might well have been otherwise if they had set out quite separately to negotiate the issue of liability; then I think that it might be different.

[Sir Gordon Willmer delivered a judgment agreeing with Danckwerts LJ.]

Appeal dismissed.

NOTE

Was Ormrod J striking a different balance from the other members of the court between the interests of the parties as described on p 167? Whose approach do you favour?

(ii) Acceptance by conduct

Brogden v Metropolitan Railway Co (1877) 2 App Cas 666, House of Lords

The defendants (the appellants) had for some years supplied coal to the plaintiffs. The plaintiffs' agent sent the defendants a draft agreement for 220 tons or, at the plaintiffs' option, up to 350 tons, per week from 1 January 1872, at 20s per ton. The defendants filled in some blanks, wrote 'approved' on the contract, signed it and returned it to the plaintiffs' manager, who put it in his desk. The manager then ordered 250 tons per week from 1 January and these were supplied at 20s per ton; but there were delays in delivery, and after some correspondence the defendants declined to supply further coal.

Lord Blackburn. . . . I have always believed the law to be this, that when an offer is made to another party, and in that offer there is a request express or implied that he must signify his acceptance by doing some particular thing, then as soon as he does that thing, he is bound. If a man sent an offer abroad saying: I wish to know whether you will supply me with goods at such and such a price, and, if you agree to that, you must ship the first cargo as soon as you get this letter, there can be no doubt that as soon as the cargo was shipped the contract would be complete, and if the cargo went to the bottom of the sea, it would go to the bottom of the sea at the risk of the orderer. So again, where, as in the case of *Ex parte Harris*, a person writes a letter and says, I offer to take an allotment of shares, and he expressly or impliedly says, If you agree with me send an answer by the post, there, as soon as he has sent that answer by the post, and put it out of his control, and done an extraneous act which clenches the matter, and shews beyond all doubt that each side is bound, I agree the contract is perfectly plain and clear.

But when you come to the general proposition which [the judge at first instance] seems to have laid down, that a simple acceptance in your own mind without any intimation to the other party, and expressed by a mere private act, such as putting a letter into a drawer, completes a contract, I must say I differ from that. . . .

But my Lords, while, as I say, this is so upon the question of law, it is still necessary to consider this case farther upon the question of fact. I agree, and I think every Judge who has considered the case does agree, certainly Lord Chief Justice Cockburn does, that though the parties may have gone no farther than an offer on the one side, saying, Here is the draft,—(for that I think is really what this case comes to,)—and the draft so offered by the one side is approved by the other, everything being agreed to except the name of the arbitrator, which the one side has filled in and the other has not yet assented to, if both parties have acted upon that draft and treated it as binding, they will be bound by it.

[His Lordship went on to hold that the subsequent order for and supply of coal at 20s per ton, which was higher than the price had been before, showed that the offer was accepted.]

[The Lord Chancellor and Lords Hatherley, Selborne and Gordon gave judgment to the same effect.]

Suppose that Arts Magazine Ltd, without having been asked to do so, sends Beale a copy of its magazine every week for six weeks. Each copy has printed on the front cover, price £1. There is nothing to indicate that it has been sent as a free sample. Beale reads part of the first copy, decides he is not interested and throws it and all the subsequent copies straight into the dustbin. He then receives a bill from Arts Magazine Ltd for £6 for the copies sent to him. Does he have to pay? At common law, see *Weatherby v Banham* (1832) 5 C&P 228; now see:

Unsolicited Goods and Services Act 1971

Section 1
(1) In the circumstances specified in the following subsection, a person who after the commencement of this Act receives unsolicited goods, may as between himself and the sender, use, deal with or dispose of them as if they were an unconditional gift to him, and any right of the sender to the goods shall be extinguished.
(2) The circumstances referred to in the preceding subsection are that the goods were sent to the recipient with a view to his acquiring them, that the recipient has no reasonable cause to believe that they were sent with a view to their being acquired for the purposes of a trade or business and has neither agreed to acquire nor agreed to return them, and either—
  (a) that during the period of six months beginning with the day on which the receipient received the goods the sender did not take possession of them and the receipient did not unreasonably refuse to permit the sender to do so; or
  (b) that not less than thirty days before the expiration of the period aforesaid the recipient gave notice to the sender in accordance with the following subsection, and that during the period of thirty days beginning with the day on which the notice was given the sender did not take possession of the goods and the recipient did not unreasonably refuse to permit the sender to do so.
(3) A notice in pursuance of the preceding subsection shall be in writing and shall—
  (a) state the recipient's name and address and, if possession of the goods in question may not be taken by the sender at that address, the address at which it may be so taken;
  (b) contain a statement, however expressed, that the goods are unsolicited, and may be sent by post.
(4) In this section 'sender', in relation to any goods, includes any person on whose behalf or with whose consent the goods are sent, and any other person claiming through or under the sender or any such person.

Section 2
(1) A person who, not having reasonable cause to believe there is a right to payment, in the course of any trade or business makes a demand for payment, or asserts a present or prospective right to payment, for what he knows are unsolicited goods sent (after the commencement of this Act) to another person with a view to his acquiring them, shall be guilty of an offence and on summary conviction shall be liable to a fine . . .
(2) A person who, not having reasonable cause to believe there is a right to payment, in the course of any trade or business and with a view to obtaining any payment for what he knows are unsolicited goods sent as aforesaid—
  (a) threatens to bring any legal proceedings; or
  (b) places or causes to be placed the name of any person on a list of defaulters or debtors or threatens to do so; or
  (c) invokes or causes to be invoked any other collection procedure or threatens to do so, shall be guilty of an offence and shall be liable on summary conviction to a fine . . .

(iii) Communication of acceptance

It is common for large organizations selling on credit to ask would-be buyers to sign an agreement, but not to commit the organization until they have taken up credit references on the buyer. The form signed by the buyer usually contains a clause such as:

This agreement shall only become binding on the Owners upon acceptance by signature on their behalf and shall be deemed to be made on the date on which it is so signed.

(Taken from a hire-purchase agreement)

If the agreement is signed by the owners, but before they have communicated this to the other party the latter notifies them that he is withdrawing, what is the position? Consider the *Brogden* case and *Carlill's* case (below, p 184). In *Robophone Facilities Ltd v Blank* [1963] 3 All ER 128 a form for the hire of an answering machine provided: 'This agreement shall become binding upon the [owners] only upon acceptance thereof on their behalf'. The hirer cancelled before the fact of the owner's signature had been communicated to him, but it was held that his offer had been accepted earlier when he was asked by the owners to fill in an application to the Post Office for permission to use the machine. Lord Denning MR said an uncommunicated signature would not suffice, but Diplock LJ refused to express an opinion and Harman LJ did not do so.

It is generally said that silence is not acceptance, even if the offeror told the offeree that the offeree need not reply. The authority cited is *Felthouse v Bindley* (1862) 11 CBNS 869. Paul Felthouse and his nephew John had been negotiating for Paul to buy one of John's horses, but confusion had arisen over the price. Paul wrote:

Dear Nephew,—Your price, I admit, was 30 guineas. I offered £30—never offered more: and you said the horse was mine. However as there may be a mistake about him, I will split the difference—£30 15s . . . If I hear no more about him, I consider the horse mine at £30 15s . . .

John did not reply, but on 25 February instructed Bindley, an auctioneer who was selling John's stock, to keep back the horse as it was already sold. Bindley forgot and sold it. On 27 February John wrote to Paul explaining what had happened. Paul sued Bindley in conversion, and obtained a verdict for £33, but the verdict was set aside. One ground for the decision, and the ground on which it was upheld in the Court of Exchequer Chamber (1863) 1 New Rep 401, was that Paul had no title to the horse because there was no written evidence of the contract to satisfy the Statute of Frauds (see above, p 131); but in his judgment Willes J also said:

. . . the uncle had no right to impose upon the nephew a sale of his horse for £30.15s unless he chose to comply with the condition of writing to repudiate the offer . . . It is clear . . . that the nephew in his own mind intended his uncle to have the horse at the price which he (the uncle) had named,—£30.15s: but he had not communicated such his intention to his uncle or done anything to bind himself. Nothing therefore had been done to vest the property in the horse in the plaintiff. . . .

The Leonidas D [1985] 2 All ER 796 was another case (see *The Hannah Blumenthal,* above p 168) on whether a claim in arbitration had implicitly been abandoned. Mustill J held that the charterers, by commencing arbitration but then totally stopping, tacitly represented that they did not intend to pursue the claim, and the owners, whose response (with one exception, which the judge held was neutral) had been a 'complete blank', had accepted the tacit offer of abandonment. The Court of Appeal disagreed. Robert Goff LJ said (at p 805):

. . . We have here to consider an appeal from a decision that a binding agreement should be inferred from silence and inaction. Silence and inaction by both parties are apparently here considered to be capable of giving rise to an offer by one, and to an acceptance by the other communicated in response to that offer. This is most surprising. We have all been brought up to believe it to be axiomatic that acceptance of an offer cannot be inferred from silence, save in the most exceptional circumstances (as to which see, for example, G H Treitel *The Law of Contract* (6th edn, 1983) p 27). Yet it is here suggested that silence and inaction can give rise both to an offer and to an acceptance; and there do not appear to be any special circumstances, in the silent abandonment of this reference to arbitration, which could justify any departure from general principle. In the absence of special circumstances, silence and inaction by a party to a reference are, objectively considered, just as consistent with his having inadvertently forgotten about the matter; or with his simply hoping that the matter will die a natural death if he does not stir up the other party; or with his office staff, or his agents, or his insurers, or his solicitors, being appallingly slow. If so, there should, on ordinary principles, be no basis for the inference of an offer. Exactly the same comment can be made of the silence and inaction of the other party, for the same reasons, there appears to be no basis for drawing the inference of an acceptance in response to the supposed offer, still less of the communication of that acceptance of the offeror.

We should add that we see the same difficulty in invoking the principle of equitable estoppel in such circumstances. It is well settled that that principle requires that one party should have made an unequivocal representation that he does not intend to enforce his strict legal rights against the other; yet it is difficult to imagine how silence and inaction can be anything but equivocal.

NOTES

1. Is it correct that in *Felthouse v Bindley* there was no contract—why was John's instruction to Bindley not acceptance by conduct?

2. Suppose John had simply put the horse on one side himself, and, relying on what Paul had written, had not replied to Paul. Can John hold Paul to a contract if the latter subsequently tries to withdraw?

Miller, '*Felthouse v Bindley* Revisited' (1972) 35 MLR 489 argues that if the offeror has waived the need for communication of the acceptance, the offeree who remains silent intending to accept should be able to hold the offeror to a contract. However in *Fairline Shipping Corpn v Adamson* [1975] QB 180, Kerr J disagreed:

It seems to me . . . that such a result can only flow from an estoppel operating against the offeror and that such facts cannot give rise to any contract or fit into the settled law governing offer and acceptance. The plaintiff's cause of action cannot be founded on an estoppel . . .

But is it correct that the offeree would be founding an action on an estoppel? Wouldn't he be founding it on a contract, the estoppel merely preventing the offeror from denying communication of any acceptance? (Cf above, p 145).

3. Suppose an offer is made to which the offeree does not reply. If he sees the offeror starting to perform, thinking there is a contract, and he does nothing to correct the offeror's misunderstanding, might he be estopped from denying acceptance? See Restatement 2d s 69 (next note) and *St John Tugboat Co Ltd v Irving Refinery Ltd* [1964] SCR 614 (offeree knew tug being kept 'standing by' for offeree's use and that offeror expected to be paid, but did nothing to dispense with service or complain: held, offer accepted). Compare using unsolicited goods, above p 181.

4. In many circumstances it is obviously sensible to have a rule that silence on the part of an offeree who does not want to enter a contract will not amount to acceptance, even if the offeror says he will treat it as acceptance. But is it always sensible? Consider Restatement 2d s 69:

Acceptance by Silence or Exercise of Dominion
(1) Where an offeree fails to reply to an offer, his silence and inaction operate as an acceptance in the following cases only:
(a) Where an offeree takes the benefit of offered services with reasonable opportunity to reject them and reason to know that they were offered with the expectation of compensation.

(b) Where the offeror has stated or given the offeree reason to understand that assent may be manifested by silence or inaction, and the offeree in remaining silent or inactive intends to accept the offer.

(c) Where because of previous dealings or otherwise, it is reasonable that the offeree should notify the offeror if he does not intend to accept.

The First Restatement version of s 69(1)(c) was applied in the case of *Ammons v Wilson* 176 Miss 645, 170 So 227 (1936). The offeror had regularly ordered shortening from the offeree: he would give the order to the offeree's traveller, who would give him a tentative booking (without legal effect), and transmit the order to head office. Every order had been accepted. On the occasion in question he was given the booking, but not told until twelve days later (when he enquired when shipment would be made) that his order was not accepted. Meanwhile the price of shortening had risen from seven-and-a-half to nine cents a pound. The Supreme Court of Mississippi held a contract had been created.

(d) Acceptance in unilateral contracts

In *Carlill v Carbolic Smoke Ball Co* (above, p 12) the defendants argued that Mrs Carlill had never accepted any offer they might have made. Bowen LJ said:

> Then it was said that there was no notification of the acceptance of the contract. One cannot doubt that, as an ordinary rule of law, an acceptance of an offer made ought to be notified to the person who makes the offer, in order that the two minds may come together. Unless this is done the two minds may be apart, and there is not that consensus which is necessary according to the English law—I say nothing about the laws of other countries—to make a contract. But there is this clear gloss to be made upon that doctrine, that as notification of acceptance is required for the benefit of the person who makes the offer, the person who makes the offer may dispense with notice to himself if he thinks it desirable to do so, and I suppose there can be no doubt that where a person in an offer made by him to another person, expressly or impliedly intimates a particular mode of acceptance as sufficient to make the bargain binding, it is only necessary for the other person to whom such offer is made to follow the indicated method of acceptance; and if the person making the offer, expressly or impliedly intimates in his offer that it will be sufficient to act on the proposal without communicating acceptance of it to himself, performance of the condition is a sufficient acceptance without notification. . . .
>
> Now, if that is the law, how are we to find out whether the person who makes the offer does intimate that notification of acceptance will not be necessary in order to constitute a binding bargain? In many cases you look to the offer itself. In many cases you extract from the character of the transaction that notification is not required, and in the advertisement cases it seems to me to follow as an inference to be drawn from the transaction itself that a person is not to notify his acceptance of the offer before he performs the condition, but that if he performs the condition notification is dispensed with. It seems to me that from the point of view of common sense no other idea could be entertained. If I advertise to the world that my dog is lost, and that anybody who brings the dog to a particular place will be paid some money, are all the police or other persons whose business is to find lost dogs to be expected to sit down and write me a note saying that they have accepted my proposal? Why, of course, they at once look after the dog, and as soon as they find the dog they have performed the condition. The essence of the transaction is that the dog should be found, and it is not necessary under such circumstances, as it seems to me, that in order to make the contract binding there should be any notification of acceptance. It follows from the nature of the thing that the performance of the condition is sufficient acceptance without the notification of it, and a person who makes an offer in an advertisement of that kind makes an offer which must be read by the light of that common sense reflection. He does, therefore, in his offer impliedly indicate that he does not require notification of the acceptance of the offer.

The first point to note is that it is now established that an offer of a unilateral contract is not 'accepted' by doing the required act in ignorance of the offer (see *R v Clarke* (1927) 40 CLR 227; *Taylor v Allon* [1965] 1 QB 304). It is not necessary that the offer is the main motivation for the offeree acting, provided he or she is aware of the offer (*Williams v Carwardine* (1833) 5 C & P 566).

The second and more difficult point concerns the point at which there is an effective acceptance and the offeror becomes bound. Look again at the facts of *Carlill's* case (above, p 12). Could the company have revoked their offer at any time before Mrs Carlill had completed the required performance, ie using the ball for three weeks? In *Petterson v Pattberg* 248 NY 86, 161 NE 428 (1928) Pattberg, who held a mortgage on Petterson's property, told Petterson that he would 'allow' Petterson $780 if the latter paid off the mortgage by 31 May 1924. Before that date Petterson knocked at Pattberg's door, and when the latter demanded the name of his caller, replied: 'It is Mr Petterson. I have come to pay off the mortgage.' Pattberg replied that he had sold the mortgage. He then partly opened the door but refused to take the cash exhibited by Petterson. The Court of Appeals (Kellogg J, Cardozo CJ, Pound, Crane and O'Brien JJ concurring) held that even though the offeree had approached with the intention of performing, the offer could be withdrawn at any time before an actual tender had been made, and that Pattberg's statement was effective to withdraw it. Lehman J dissented on the ground that the offer of payment was a sufficient tender.

Errington v Errington [1952] 1 All ER 149, Court of Appeal

The plaintiff appealed from a refusal to make an order for possession of a house occupied by her daughter-in-law.

Denning LJ. The facts are reasonably clear. In 1936 the father bought the house for his son and daughter-in-law to live in. The father put down £250 in cash and borrowed £500 from a building society on the security of the house, repayable with interest by instalments of 15s a week. He took the house in his own name and made himself responsible for the instalments. The father told the daughter-in-law that the £250 was a present for them, but he left them to pay the building society instalments of 15s a week themselves. He handed the building society book to the daughter-in-law and said to her: 'Don't part with this book. The house will be your property when the mortgage is paid.' He said that when he retired he would transfer it into their names. She has, in fact, paid the building society instalments regularly from that day to this with the result that much of the mortgage has been repaid, but there is a good deal yet to be paid. The rates on the house came to 10s a week. The couple found that they could not pay those as well as the building society instalments so the father said he would pay them and he did so.

It is to be noted that the couple never bound themselves to pay the instalments to the building society, and I see no reason why any such obligation should be implied. It is clear law that the court is not to imply a term unless it is necessary, and I do not see that it is necessary here. Ample content is given to the whole arrangement by holding that the father promised that the house should belong to the couple as soon as they had paid off the mortgage. The parties did not discuss what was to happen if the couple failed to pay the instalments to the building society, but I should have thought it clear that, if they did fail to pay the instalments, the father would not be bound to transfer the house to them. The father's promise was a unilateral contract—a promise of the house in return for their act of paying the instalments. It could not be revoked by him once the couple entered on performance of the act, but it would cease to bind him if they left it incomplete and unperformed, which they have not done. If that was the position during the father's lifetime, so it must be after his death. If the daughter-in-law continues to pay all the building society instalments, the couple will be entitled to have the property transferred to them as soon as the mortgage is paid off, but if she does not do so, then the building society will claim the instalments from the father's estate and the estate will have to pay them. I cannot think that in those circumstances the estate would be bound to transfer the house to them, any more than the father himself would have been. . . .

In the present case it is clear that the father expressly promised the couple that the property should belong to them as soon as the mortgage was paid, and impliedly promised that, so long as they paid the instalments to the building society, they should be allowed to remain in possession. They were not purchasers because they never bound themselves to pay the instalments, but nevertheless they were in a position analogous to purchasers. They have acted on the promise and neither the father nor his widow, his successor in title, can eject them in disregard of it. The result is that, in my opinion, the appeal should be dismissed and no order for possession should be made.

[Somervell and Hodson LJJ delivered concurring judgments.]

Appeal dismissed.

Daulia v Four Millbank Nominees Ltd [1978] 2 All ER 557, Court of Appeal

The plaintiffs were keen to buy a portfolio of properties from the defendants, who were mortgagees entitled to sell because the mortgagor was in default. The plaintiffs alleged that on 21 December an agent of the defendants had orally promised the plaintiffs that if the latter attended the defendants' offices at ten o'clock the next morning, and tendered the plaintiffs' part of the contract engrossed and signed together with a banker's draft for the deposit, the defendants would enter a written contract of sale of the properties to the plaintiffs. The plaintiffs duly attended and tendered the documents, but the defendants refused to go ahead (they had the evening before received a substantially higher offer and had been advised that their duty as mortgagees required them to accept this and refuse the plaintiffs' offer). The plaintiffs' action was struck out as disclosing no cause of action, and they appealed.

Goff LJ. . . . The facts pleaded . . . give rise to three questions of law: (a) Do they establish a valid unilateral contract? If they do, then there is no question but that they disclose a breach. (b) If the answer to (a) is 'Yes' then is that contract unenforceable for want of a written note or memorandum to satisfy s 40 of the Law of Property Act 1925, unless there be sufficient acts of part performance to take the case out of the statute? (c) If s 40 applies are there such acts? . . . Was there a concluded unilateral contract by the defendants to enter into a contract for sale on the agreed terms?

The concept of a unilateral or 'if' contract is somewhat anomalous, because it is clear that, at all events until the offeree starts to perform the conditon, there is no contract at all, but merely an offer which the offeror is free to revoke. Doubts have been expressed whether the offeror becomes bound so soon as the offeree starts to perform or satisfy the condition, or only when he has fully done so. In my judgment, however, we are not concerned in this case with any such problem, because in my view the plaintiffs had fully performed or satisfied the condition when they presented themselves at the time and place appointed with a banker's draft for the deposit and their part of the written contract for sale duly engrossed and signed, and the retendered the same, which I understand to mean proferred it for exchange. Actual exchange, which never took place, would not in my view have been part of the satisfaction of the condition but something additional which was inherently necessary to be done by the plaintiffs to enable, not to bind, the defendants to perform the unilateral contract.

Accordingly in my judgment, the answer to the first question must be in the affirmative.

Even if my reasoning so far be wrong the conclusion in my view is still the same for the following reasons. Whilst I think the true view of a unilateral contract must in general be that the offeror is entitled to require full performance of the condition which he has imposed and short of that he is not bound, that must be subject to one important qualification, which stems from the fact that there must be an implied obligation on the part of the offeror not to prevent the condition becoming satisfied, which obligation it seems to me must arise as soon as the offeree starts to perform. Until then the offeror can revoke the whole thing, but once the offeree has embarked on performance it is too late for the offeror to revoke his offer.

[His Lordship went on to hold that the contract was one for the disposition of an interest in land and was unenforceable as there was no memorandum or sufficient act of part performance.]

[Buckley and Orr LJJ delivered judgments agreeing with Goff LJ, Buckley LJ specifically agreeing with the last excerpt.]

Appeal dismissed.

NOTE

1. Another suggested way of reaching a similar result is to say that the offer of a unilateral contract is accepted, and thus can no longer be withdrawn, once the offeree starts performing, though the offeror is not bound to perform his part until the offeree has performed completely (Pollock, *Principles of Contract* (13th edn) p 19).
2. Is it always appropriate to prevent the offeror revoking once the offeree has begun to perform? What does 'perform' mean in this context? Consider the next case.

Luxor (Eastbourne) Ltd v Cooper [1941] AC 108, House of Lords

The two appellant companies (the owners) orally agreed with the respondent (the agent) that if he introduced a party who should buy the appellants' two cinemas for at least £185,000, each of the appellants would pay the respondent £5,000 on the completion of the sale. The respondent introduced a party who agreed to pay that price subject to contract and remained willing to pay it, but the appellants did not proceed. The respondent claimed £10,000 commission, or £10,000 damages for breach of an implied term that the appellants would not without just cause so act as to prevent the respondent earning his commission. The Court of Appeal, reversing Branson J, had awarded the respondent damages of £8,000.

Lord Russell of Killowen. . . . . A few preliminary observations occur to me. (1) Commission contracts are subject to no peculiar rules or principles of their own. The law which governs them is the law which governs all contracts and all questions of agency. (2) No general rule can be laid down by which the rights of the agent or the liabilities of the principal under commission contracts are to be determined. In each case, these must depend upon the exact terms of the contract in question, and upon the true construction of those terms. (3) Contracts by which owners of property, desiring to dispose of it, put it in the hands of agents on commission terms are not (in default of specific provisions) contracts of employment in the ordinary meaning of those words. No obligation is imposed on the agent to do anything. The contracts are merely promises binding on the principal to pay a sum of money upon the happening of a specified event, which involves the rendering of some service by the agent. There is no real analogy between such contracts and contracts of employment by which one party binds himself to do certain work and the other binds himself to pay remuneration for the doing of it.

I do not assent to the view, which I think, was the view of the majority in *Trollope (George) & Sons v Martyn Bros*, that a mere promise by a property owner to an agent to pay him a commission if he introduces a purchaser for the property at a specified price, or at a minimum price, ties the owner's hands and compels him, as between himself and the agent, to bind himself contractually to sell to the agent's client who offers that price, with the result that, if he refuses the offer, he is liable to pay the agent a sum equal to, or less than, the amount of the commission, either (a) on a *quantum meruit*, or (b) as damages for breach of a term to be implied in the commission contract. As to the claim on a *quantum meruit*, I do not see how this can be justified in the face of the express provision for remuneration which the contract contains. This must necessarily exclude such a claim, unless it can (upon the facts of a particular case) be based upon a contract subsequent to the original contract, and arising from some conduct on the part of the principal. As to the claim for damages, this rests upon the implication of some provision in the commission contract, the exact terms of which were variously stated in the course of the argument, the object always being to bind the principal not to refuse to complete the sale to the client whom the agent has introduced. I can find no safe ground on which to base the introduction of any such implied term. Implied terms, as we all know, can be justified only under the compulsion of some necessity. No such compulsion or necessity exists in the case under consideration. The agent is promised a commission if he introduces a purchaser at a specified or minimum price. The owner is desirous of selling. The chances are largely in favour of the deal going through if a purchaser is introduced. The agent takes the risk in the hope of a substantial remuneration for comparatively small exertion. In the case of the plaintiff, his contract was made on Sept 23, 1935, and his client's offer was made on Oct 2, 1935. A sum of £10,000, the equivalent of the remuneration of a year's work by a Lord Chancellor, for work done within a period of 8 or 9 days is no mean reward, and is one well worth a risk. There is no lack of business efficacy in such a contract, even though the principal is free to refuse to sell to the agent's client. The position will no doubt be different if the matter has proceeded to the stage of a binding contract having been made between the principal and the agent's client. In that case, it can be said with truth that a 'purchaser' has been introduced by the agent. In other words, the event has happened upon the occurrence of which a right to the promised commission has become vested in the agent. From that moment, no act or commission by the principal can deprive the agent of that vested right. . . .

[Lord Thankerton agreed with Lord Russell, and Viscount Simon LC and Lords Wright and Romer delivered speeches in favour of allowing the appeal.]

Appeal allowed.

NOTES

1. At what point does an estate agent earn the commission? In *Christie Owen & Davies Ltd v Rapacioli* [1974] QB 781 the Court of Appeal applied Lord Russell's dictum that it depends on the terms of the contract and held that as the contract provided for a commission in the event of the plaintiffs 'Effecting an introduction . . . of a person . . . ready, able and willing to purchase' at an agreed price, and they had done this, the commission was payable even though the vendor later refused to complete. No commission would have been payable had the purchaser withdrawn.
2. Even if it were appropriate to imply into estate agents' contracts a term that the vendors would not unreasonably withdraw once the agent had started to perform, what would count as starting? Does advertising the property count as starting performance, or is the performance actually introducing a buyer, the advertising being merely preparatory? See Murdoch, 'The Nature of Estate Agency' (1975) 91 LQR 357, at 371–373.
3. Murdoch also points out that, if the restriction on the offeror's power to revoke an offer of a unilateral contract is based on an implied term, the case for implying the term is weaker than in some other types of unilateral contract: in many of the unilateral contract cases the offeror will get no greater personal benefit from complete performance than from partial performance, but a vendor who withdraws a property from the hands of his agent thereby deprives himself of the benefit of a suitable introduction. Presumably most vendors expect to pay the agent out of the proceeds of sale.
4. Suppose an estate agent is promised a commission of £500 if she 'introduces a party who buys the property'. She incurs expenditure of £100 on advertising and expenditure of time, and introduces a buyer who is ready to complete, but the vendor refuses to go ahead. If the agent were protected on the *Daulia* principle, would she recover £500 or £100? Which would be more appropriate?
5. An estate agent is approached by a vendor wishing to sell an unusual house which is unlikely to find a ready buyer without widespread and expensive advertising. What form of agreement would you advise the agent to make with the vendor?
6. It may be that much of the foregoing discussion is misconceived, because even in the normal case the contract with the agent is bilateral. It might

surprise many clients to discover that the agent is not liable if she does nothing at all to attempt to find a buyer, which seems to be the result of the unilateral contract analysis. Compare *Wood v Duff-Gordon*, above, p 110. In the light of *Luxor v Cooper*, however, it might take a bold court to adopt a bilateral contract approach.

(e) Bilateral or unilateral?

An offer of a bilateral contract may be accepted by an acceptance communicated to the offeror, or by an 'extraneous' act; an offer of a unilateral contract by commencing, or perhaps completing, performance. It is not always clear which type of contract is involved.

Suppose Ace Manufacturing Ltd telexes Bends Ltd: 'Urgent. Please make us and dispatch as soon as possible by express 100 bends as per previous special order'. Bends Ltd starts manufacturing these bends, which are of a special design, during the night shift that same evening, and next morning a letter is written accepting Ace's order. However, before the letter has been sent, Ace telexes: 'Cancel order of yesterday'. Has Bends accepted Ace's order (i) if the contract was bilateral, (ii) if it was unilateral? A decision that the offer was for a unilateral contract would protect the offeree, but equally might hamper the offeror, who might be trying to obtain goods from other suppliers at the same time. (For a case involving a choice between unilateral and bilateral, see *Dawson v Helicopter Exploration Co Ltd* [1955] 5 DLR 404.)

Some commentators think the distinction between unilateral and bilateral contracts is too rigid: the offeror may be indifferent as to whether the offeree accepts verbally or starts performing. Restatement 2d provides:

§54. Acceptance by performance; necessity of notification to offeror
(1) Where an offer invites an offeree to accept by rendering a performance, no notification is necessary to make such an acceptance effective unless the offer requests such a notification.
(2) If an offeree who accepts by rendering a performance has reason to know that the offeror has no adequate means of learning of the performance with reasonable promptness and certainty, the contractual duty of the offeror is discharged unless
  (a) the offeree exercises reasonable diligence to notify the offeror of acceptance, or
  (b) the offeror learns of the performance within a reasonable time, or
  (c) the offer indicates that notification of acceptance is not required.

§62. Effect of performance by offeree where offer invites either performance or promise
(1) Where an offer invites an offeree to choose between acceptance by promise and acceptance by performance, the tender or beginning of the invited performance or a tender of a beginning of it is an acceptance by performance.
(2) Such an acceptance operates as a promise to render complete performance.

Comment:
a. The offeree's power to choose. The offeror normally invites a promise by the offeree for the purpose of obtaining performance of the promise. Full performance fulfills that purpose more directly than the promise invited, and hence constitutes a reasonable mode of acceptance. The offeror can insist on any mode of acceptance, but ordinarily he invites acceptance in any reasonable manner; in case of doubt, an offer is interpreted as inviting the offeree to choose between acceptance by promise and acceptance by performance. See §§30, 32, 58.

Illustrations:
1. A, a merchant, mails B, a carpenter in the same city, an offer to employ B to fit up A's office in accordance with A's specifications and B's estimate previously submitted, the work to be

completed in two weeks. The offer says, 'you may begin at once', and B immediately buys lumber and begins to work on it in his own shop. The next day, before B has sent a notice of acceptance or begun work at A's office or rendered the lumber unfit for other jobs, A revokes the offer. The revocation is timely, since B has not begun to perform.

2. A, a regular customer of B, orders fragile goods from B which B carries in stock and ships in his own trucks. Following his usual practice, B selects the goods ordered, tags them as A's, crates them and loads them on a truck at substantial expense. Performance has begun, and A's offer is irrevocable. See Uniform Commercial Code §2–206 and Comment 2.

The result in our problem would be that there is a contract, as Bends has begun the stipulated performance, though s 54 would also require him to notify the offeror within a reasonable time of starting, or 'the contractual duty of the offeror is discharged'. Do you think this is a worthwhile approach, or might it be better to treat this type of problem not by holding that there is a contract, but by imposing liability on some other basis? Compare the cases discussed below, p 224

(f) Differing proposals

Hyde v Wrench (1840) 3 Beav 334, 49 ER 132, Rolls Court

The defendant offered to sell a farm to the plaintiff for £1,000, to which the plaintiff responded by offering (through his agent) £950 for it. The defendant rejected this offer, and the plaintiff then purported to accept the defendant's original offer of £1,000. The plaintiff brought an action for specific performance, and the defendant filed a general demurrer.

The Master of the Rolls [Lord Langdale]. Under the circumstances stated in this bill, I think there exists no valid binding contract between the parties for the purchase of the property. The Defendant offered to sell it for £1,000, and if that had been at once unconditionally accepted, there would undoubtedly have been a perfect binding contract; instead of that, the Plaintiff made an offer of his own, to purchase the property for £950, and he thereby rejected the offer previously made by the Defendant. I think that it was not afterwards competent for him to revive the proposal of the Defendant, by tendering an acceptance of it; and that, therefore, there exists no obligation of any sort between the parties; the demurrer must be allowed.

Stevenson, Jaques & Co v McLean (1880) 5 QBD 346, Lush J

The defendant wrote to the plaintiffs offering to sell them some iron, represented by a number of delivery warrants, at 40s net cash, and stating that he would hold the offer open until the following Monday. At 9.42 am on the Monday morning the plaintiffs telegraphed the defendant:

> Please wire whether you would accept forty for delivery over two months, or if not, longest limit you could give.

The defendant did not answer this telegram but sold the warrants, and at 1.25 pm telegraphed the plaintiffs to inform them. Meanwhile the plaintiffs had found a buyer for the iron and at 1.34 pm (before the defendant's telegram had reached them), they sent a telegram accepting his offer. The plaintiffs sued for breach of contract.

Lush J. . . . Two objections were relied on by the defendant: first, it was contended that the telegram sent by the plaintiffs on the Monday morning was a rejection of the defendant's offer and a new proposal on the plaintiffs' part, and that the defendant had therefore a right to regard it as putting an end to the original negotiation.

Looking at the form of the telegram, the time when it was sent, and the state of the iron market, I cannot think this is its fair meaning. The plaintiff Stevenson said he meant it only as an inquiry, expecting an answer for his guidance, and this, I think, is the sense in which the defendant ought to have regarded it.

It is apparent throughout the correspondence, that the plaintiffs did not contemplate buying the iron on speculation, but that their acceptance of the defendant's offer depended on their finding some one to take the warrants off their hands. All parties knew that the market was in an unsettled state, and that no one could predict at the early hour when the telegram was sent how the prices would range during the day. It was reasonable that, under these circumstances, they should desire to know before business began whether they were to be at liberty in case of need to make any and what concession as to the time or times of delivery, which would be the time or times of payment, or whether the defendant was determined to adhere to the terms of his letter; and it was highly unreasonable that the plaintiffs should have intended to close the negotiation while it was uncertain whether they could find a buyer or not, having the whole of the business hours of the day to look for one. Then, again, the form of the telegram is one of inquiry. It is not 'I offer forty for delivery over two months', which would have likened the case to *Hyde v Wrench* . . .

Here there is no counter proposal. The words are, 'Please wire whether you would accept forty for delivery over two months, or, if not, the longest limit you would give.' There is nothing specific by way of offer or rejection, but a mere inquiry, which should have been answered and not treated as a rejection of the offer. This ground of objection therefore fails.

(The second objection was that the offer had been revoked before it had been accepted: this also failed, see below, p 197.)

Judgment for the plaintiffs.

NOTE

Why is a counter offer, but not a mere enquiry, treated as revoking the original offer? Would it be reasonable in either case for the offeree to assume the original offer was still good?

'Contracts between Businessmen' by Beale and Dugdale (1975) 2 Br J Law&Soc 45, at 48–51

(for another extract from this piece, describing the research upon which it was based, see above, pp 79–80)

Formation

The attitudes of firms towards problems of formation provide an indication of their awareness of and concern about the process of contract law, and illustrate the conscious nature of the decision whether or not to plan in detail. The degree of planning is in part likely to be determined by the process of formation adopted. Contracts formed as a result of detailed negotiation were comparatively rare. They were usually to be found only where the goods to be supplied were expensive and complex, for instance complete aircraft, aero engines or machinery worth more than £50,000, and the risks were thus sufficient to justify the time and trouble, particularly as the sale of a finished product of this type would often be to a customer outside the trade who would not know or accept the usual practices. The negotiated contracts were often many pages in length and contained detailed planning of both the primary obligations and the mechanisms for adjustment. However even in such contracts planning might not be complete. Some details might be left vague, either consciously because the parties had decided that it was not worth negotiating certain areas of conflict, or unconsciously: managing directors might draw up 'heads of agreement' unwittingly leaving many areas vague. Research and development contracts provided a special problem for by their very nature they required some areas to be left unnegotiated in order to provide for future eventualities.

At the other extreme were contracts made informally by telephone or simple exchange of letters. Here only the primary obligations would be planned expressly but the parties to such contracts often held unexpressed assumptions about the way in which obligations would be adjusted or enforced, relying either upon trade custom or a 'gentlemen's agreement' with the other contracting party. The informal formation process was deliberately adopted only by a minority of firms who either were not prepared to create sufficient office capacity to deal with much paper work or who felt able to place faith in the other contracting party because of the market conditions. Often such firms were doing nearly all their business locally and there was close and continuous personal contact with their customers and suppliers; this would be more important to them than safeguarding an individual exchange which was usually of low value anyway.

The majority of firms intended to make their contracts by the use of forms containing standard conditions of sale or purchase. Usually these forms would have the primary obligations (item, price, delivery date and perhaps terms of payment) typed on the front, while terms providing for adjustment, contingencies and so on would be printed on the back—hence they were commonly referred to as 'back of order' conditions.

When one set of conditions has been accepted by both seller and buyer as governing their exchange then in law a contract on the basis of those conditions has been formed. It was common for buyers of component parts or raw materials to accept sellers' conditions; occasionally sellers would accept the buyer's terms. It was clear that this was not done, however, with any conscious aim of ensuring that there would be a legally enforceable, fully-planned contract. It was partly the product of market power: a buyer faced with short supply might be forced to accept the seller's terms while we found sellers accepting buyers' terms only when selling to very powerful concerns such as a nationalized industry. But it may also be explained by the difficulty in drafting uniform purchase conditions to suit a wide variety of different purchases, and the generally greater prestige and time given to sales, for the firm will be known by its product.

More usually each party attempted to get its 'back of order' conditions accepted by the other. Under commercial pressure this system might break down—salesmen trying to meet targets might enter informal contracts without bothering with their terms or engineers more concerned about production than purchasing arrangements might unthinkingly accept the other party's terms. The significance of what was being done was not always appreciated by the officer concerned despite occasional lectures complete with instructive cartoons provided by purchasing officers. Firms seemed to consider that it was difficult to prevent this sort of breakdown but the majority of contracts were made by each party using his 'back of order' conditions.

This meant that in many cases one party's conditions would not be fully accepted by the other, but the parties would instead exchange conditions. Typically the seller would issue to the purchaser a quotation form backed with his standard conditions, the buyer would reply with an order form with his conditions, and the seller would then acknowledge the order and in doing so refer again to his conditions. This stage would normally complete the exchange. Inevitably the seller's and buyer's conditions would conflict and indeed this was contemplated for most forms contained a condition to the effect that in the case of a conflict that set of conditions would override the other.

The legal effect of such an exchange of conflicting forms is not entirely clear but it seems most likely that no enforceable contract results: each communication, providing it refers clearly to the standard conditions, is an offer which is refused and replaced by another on different terms, the last one (the sellers' 'acknowledgment') remaining an unaccepted offer. If however the other party later does something recognizing the existence of a contract, such as telephoning the seller to press for delivery, he may be held to have accepted that offer, so that the last set of conditions sent may win the day.

There was considerable awareness of the fact that in many cases an exchange of conditions would not necessarily lead to an enforceable contract, and some that the last set of conditions might prevail: one legal adviser had prepared a 'confirmation of order' form to be used to 'get his firm's conditions in last' when buying as well as when selling. But most firms seemed unconcerned about the failure to make a contract. They usually tried to ensure that they referred to their conditions in any written communications, which would prevent the letter 'accepting' the other party's terms, but no more, and some were not even concerned with that.

What did concern all the firms who contracted by this method was to reach a clear understanding on particular important points or ones on which any difficulty was anticipated. Of course in every exchange certain items would be agreed expressly, if only the item and the price, and in some cases the 'back of order' would never be looked at. In others however almost every major difference would be followed up and settled, and in the majority of cases at least a few of the more important items dealt with in the standard conditions would be discussed and agreed. Usually these were the same items that would be the subject of detailed discussion if a contract were specifically negotiated, or at the other extreme which would be mentioned if a contract were made formally by 'phone or letter; for instance payment terms or warranty periods, and whether the price was fixed or open.

In commercial terms therefore the result of an exchange of 'back of order' conditions did not offer a complete contrast to a negotiated contract on the one hand or an informal exchange of letters on the other: the number of issues planned would vary enormously, but there would be definite agreement on certain of them. Legal enforceability seemed secondary to reaching a common understanding. But even this was not always considered necessary. Frequently we were told that the other party's 'back of order' conditions would be scrutinized but no objection would be raised unless some unusual term was found: for instance, many sellers did not mind what the buyer's order contained on the question of delay provided it did not attempt to impose liquidated damages. The implication seems to be that provided the two sets of conditions contained terms commonly found in the trade a sufficient basis would exist to enable any dispute to be settled without difficulty; even common understanding did not have to be very precise.

As far as the legal enforceability of agreement is concerned, two qualifications should be made to what has been said. First it is possible that enforceable contracts were created by the exchange of standard conditions more frequently than our analysis above suggests. A court faced with a clearly unresolved conflict of terms on the one hand but a clear intention to contract on the other *might* decide that there was a contract containing those terms which had been agreed, and dismiss the remainder of the conditions. Therefore positive planning on particular issues even while using standard terms may have legal as well as commercial significance. Secondly we were told of and saw signs of a gradual change in attitude towards tightening up procedures and creating legally enforceable agreements. For instance we came across several examples of purchasing departments who for years had bought from their main suppliers on 'back of order' conditions now negotiating standing supply contracts to govern future orders. This may be entirely explicable by the recent inflation and economic troubles which make it desirable to have clear agreement on such matters as price increases and delays, but we were told by several representatives that it was the result of a new professionalism among young managers, many of whom have studied contract law.

Butler Machine Tool Co Ltd v Ex-Cell-O Corpn (England) Ltd [1979] 1 All ER 965, Court of Appeal

On 23rd May 1969, in response to an enquiry by the buyers, the sellers made a quotation offering to sell a machine tool to the buyers for £75,535, delivery to be in ten months' time. The offer was stated to be subject to certain terms and conditions which 'shall prevail over any terms and conditions in the Buyer's order'. The conditions included a price variation clause providing for the goods to be charged at the price ruling on the date of delivery. On 27th May the buyers replied by placing an order for the machine. The order was stated to be subject to certain terms and conditions, which were materially different from those put forward by the sellers and which, in particular, made no provision for a variation in price. At the foot of the buyers' order there was a tear-off acknowledgment of receipt of the order stating that 'We accept your order on the Terms and Conditions stated thereon'. On 5th June the sellers completed and signed the acknowledgment and returned it to the buyers with a letter stating that the buyers' order was being entered in accordance with the sellers' quotation of 23rd May. When the sellers came to deliver the machine they claimed that the price had increased by £2,892. The buyers refused to pay the increase in price and the sellers brought an action claiming that they were entitled to increase the price under the price variation clause contained in their offer.

[The judge upheld the sellers' claim and the buyers appealed.]

Lord Denning MR. This case is a 'battle of forms'. The suppliers of a machine, Butler Machine Tool Co Ltd ('the sellers'), on 23rd May 1969 quoted a price for a machine tool of £75,535. Delivery was to be given in ten months. On the back of the quotation there were terms and conditions. One of them was a price variation clause. It provided for an increase in the price if there was an increase in the costs and so forth. The machine tool was not delivered until November 1970. By that time costs had increased so much that the sellers claimed an additional sum of £2,892 as due to them under the price variation clause.

The buyers, Ex-Cell-O Corpn, rejected the excess charge. They relied on their own terms and conditions. They said: 'We did not accept the sellers' quotation as it was. We gave an order for the self-same machine at the self-same price, but on the back of our order we had our own terms and conditions. Our terms and conditions did not contain any price variation clause.'

. . . If [the] documents are analysed in our traditional method, the result would seem to me to be this: the quotation of 23rd May 1969 was an offer by the sellers to the buyers containing the terms and conditions on the back. The order of 27th May 1969 purported to be an acceptance of that offer in that it was for the same machine at the same price but it contained such additions as to cost of installation, date of delivery and so forth, that it was in law a rejection of the offer and

constituted a counter-offer. That is clear from *Hyde v Wrench*. As Megaw J said in *Trollope &
Colls Ltd v Atomic Power Constructions Ltd:* '. . . the counter-offer kills the original offer'. The
letter of the sellers of 5th June 1969 was an acceptance of .nat counter-offer, as is shown by the
acknowledgement which the sellers signed and returned to the buyers. The reference to the
quotation of 23rd May 1969 referred only to the price and identity of the machine . . .

The judge held that the sellers were entitled to the sum of £2,892 under the price variation
clause. He did not apply the traditional method of an analysis by way of offer and counter-offer.
He said that in the quotation of 23rd May 1969 'one finds the price variation clause appearing
under a most emphatic heading stating that it is a term or condition that is to prevail'. So he held
that it did prevail.

I have much sympathy with the judge's approach to this case. In many of these cases our
traditional analysis of offer, counter-offer, rejection, acceptance and so forth is out-of-date.
This was observed by Lord Wilberforce in *New Zealand Shipping Co Ltd v A M Satterthwaite*.
The better way is to look at all the documents passing between the parties and glean from them,
or from the conduct of the parties, whether they have reached agreement on all material points,
even though there may be differences between the forms and conditions printed on the back of
them . . . Applying this guide, it will be found that in most cases when there is a 'battle of forms'
there is a contract as soon as the last of the forms is sent and received without objection being
taken to it. That is well observed in Benjamin on Sale. The difficulty is to decide which form, or
which part of which form, is a term or condition of the contract. In some cases the battle is won
by the man who fires the last shot. He is the man who puts forward the latest terms and
conditions: and, if they are not objected to by the other party, he may be taken to have agreed to
them. Such was *British Road Services Ltd v Arthur V Crutchley & Co Ltd* per Lord Pearson; and
the illustration given by Professor Guest in Anson's Law of Contract where he says that 'the
terms of the contract consist of the terms of the offer subject to the modifications contained in
the acceptance'. That may however go too far. In some cases, however, the battle is won by the
man who gets the blow in first. If he offers to sell at a named price on the terms and conditions
stated on the back and the buyer orders the goods purporting to accept the offer on an order
form with his own different terms and conditions on the back, then, if the difference is so
material that it would affect the price, the buyer ought not to be allowed to take advantage of
the difference unless he draws it specifically to the attention of the seller. There are yet other
cases where the battle depends on the shots fired on both sides. There is a concluded contract
but the forms vary. The terms and conditions of both parties are to be construed together. If
they can be reconciled so as to give a harmonious result, all well and good. If differences are
irreconcilable, so that they are mutually contradictory, then the conflicting terms may have to
be scrapped and replaced by a reasonable implication.

In the present case the judge thought that the sellers in their original quotation got their blow
in first; especially by the provision that 'These terms and conditions shall prevail over any terms
and conditions in the Buyer's order'. It was so emphatic that the price variation clause
continued through all the subsequent dealings and that the buyer must be taken to have agreed
to it. I can understand that point of view. But I think that the documents have to be considered
as a whole. And, as a matter of construction, I think the acknowledgment of 5th June 1969 is the
decisive document. It makes it clear that the contract was on the buyers' terms and not on the
sellers' terms: and the buyers' terms did not include a price variation clause.

I would therefore allow the appeal and enter judgment for the buyers.

Lawton LJ. The modern commercial practice of making quotations and placing orders with
conditions attached, usually in small print, is indeed likely, as in this case, to produce a battle of
forms. The problem is how should that battle be conducted? The view taken by the judge was
that the battle should extend over a wide area and the court should do its best to look into the
minds of the parties and make certain assumptions. In my judgment, the battle has to be
conducted in accordance with set rules. It is a battle more on classical 18th century lines when
convention decided who had the right to open fire first rather than in accordance with the
modern concept of attrition.

The rules relating to a battle of this kind have been known for the past 130-odd years. They
were set out by the then Master of the Rolls, Lord Langdale, in *Hyde v Wrench*, and Lord
Denning MR has already referred to them; and, if anyone should have thought they were
obsolescent, Megaw J in *Trollope & Colls Ltd v Atomic Power Constructions Ltd* called
attention to the fact that those rules are still in force.

When those rules are applied to this case, in my judgement, the answer is obvious. . . . the
[sellers] completed that tear-off slip and sent it back to the buyers . . . It is true, as counsel for
the sellers has reminded us, that the return of that printed slip was accompanied by a letter
which had this sentence in it: 'This is being entered in accordance with our revised quotation of

23rd May for delivery in 10/11 months'. I agree with Lord Denning MR that, in a business sense, that refers to the quotation as to the price and the identity of the machine, and it does not bring into the contract the small print conditions on the back of the quotation. Those small print conditions had disappeared from the story. That was when the contract was made. At that date it was a fixed price contract without a price escalation clause. . . .

I agree with Lord Denning MR that this appeal should be allowed.

[Bridge LJ also delivered judgment allowing the appeal on the basis of 'the classical doctrine'.]

NOTES

1. Why treat the tear-off slip as the crucial document, and the accompanying letter as merely identifying the relevant papers, rather than the other way round?
2. Subsequent cases where there was no tear-off slip have followed Lawton's approach, holding that the last document was a counter-offer only accepted by conduct when the contract was performed: eg *Sauter Automation Ltd v Goodman (Mechanical Services) Ltd* (1986) 34 BLR 81.
3. Can you draft a clause which, if included in your client's standard conditions, will ensure that any contract he purports to make using those conditions will in fact be on his terms, not the other party's? Was the 'clause paramount' in the sellers' conditions in the *Butler Machine Tool* case of any effect?
4. If you cannot devise an effective clause paramount, what advice would you give him about buying and selling the routine items he now buys and sells 'on' his standard conditions?
5. Could the law be improved? Consider Uniform Commercial Code s 2–207*:

2–207. Additional Terms in Acceptance or Confirmation
(1) A definite and seasonable expression of acceptance or a written confirmation which is sent within a reasonable time operates as an acceptance even though it states terms additional to or different from those offered or agreed upon, unless acceptance is expressly made conditional on assent to the additional or different terms.
(2) The additional terms are to be construed as proposals for addition to the contract. Between merchants such terms become part of the contract unless:

  (a) the offer expressly limits acceptance to the terms of the offer;
  (b) they materially alter it; or
  (c) notification of objection to them has already been given or is given within a reasonable time after notice of them is received.

(3) Conduct by both parties which recognizes the existence of a contract is sufficient to establish a contract for sale although the writings of the parties do not otherwise establish a contract. In such case the terms of the particular contract consist of those terms on which the writings of the parties agree, together with any supplementary terms incorporated under any other provisions of this Act.

*The Uniform Commercial Code is a model statute produced under the joint sponsorship of the American Law Institute and the National Conference of Commissioners on Uniform State Laws. Work began on it in the 1940s, and the first edition was approved in 1952. It covers a wide range of commercial transactions; in this book, we shall examine sections from articles one (general) and two (sale of goods). The UCC has been adopted in full by all the United States except Louisiana (which was originally a civil law jurisdiction, and has adopted only certain articles of the UCC), and by the District of Columbia. Its stated purpose, 'to simplify, clarify and modernize the law governing commercial transactions; to permit the continued expansion of commercial practices through custom, usage and agreement of the parties; to make uniform the law among the various jurisdictions' (s 1–102(2)), does not reveal the many innovations contained in the code; many of these reflect the ideas of the professor considered to be the code's chief architect, Karl Llewellyn. See Danzig, 'A Comment on the Jurisprudence of the UCC' (1975) 27 Stan LR 621.

If you like the look of 2–207, try answering the following questions:

B orders goods by a purchase order which describes the goods and states the price on its face and states 'subject to the terms overleaf', one of which is that all contracts are fixed price. S sends back an acknowledgement, 'accepting your order subject to our terms overleaf', one of which is that all prices are subject to cost increases between the date of order and the date of delivery (let us assume, quite unrealistically, that this is the only difference).

(i) Has there been 'a definite and seasonable expression of acceptance' within 2–207(1)?

(ii) Is S's 'acceptance' 'expressly made conditional upon an assent to the additional or different terms'?

(iii) If there is a contract, is it fixed price or variable price? Would your answer differ if B's forms were silent on price?

(iv) Suppose S starts manufacturing the goods, which are to be made to B's special design. Is there a contract under 2–207(3)?

(v) Suppose the goods are delivered by S and accepted by B before the discrepancy is noticed. Whose terms apply? Is the solution provided by 2–207(3) any better than the common law solution?

6. Having gone through those questions, how important or worthwhile do you think law reform on these lines is?

See further Ontario Law Reform Commission, *Sale of Goods Report* (1979) and Scottish Law Commission, Consultation Paper: '*Contract Law—Exchange of Standard Forms in Contract Formation*' (1981).

(g) Postal communications

Adams v Lindsell (1818) 1 B & Ald 681, 106 ER 250, King's Bench

Action for non-delivery of wool according to agreement. At the trial at the last Lent Assizes for the county of Worcester, before Burrough J it appeared that the defendants, who were dealers in wool, at St Ives, in the county of Huntingdon, had, on Tuesday the 2nd of September 1817, written the following letter to the plaintiffs, who were woollen manufacturers residing in Bromsgrove, Worcestershire. 'We now offer you eight hundred tods of wether fleeces, of a good fair quality of our country wool at 35s 6d per tod, to be delivered at Leicester, and to be paid for by two months' bill in two months, and to be weighed up by your agent within fourteen days, receiving your answer in course of post.'

This letter was misdirected by the defendants, to Bromsgrove, Leicestershire, in consequence of which it was not received by the plaintiffs in Worcestershire till 7 pm on Friday, September 5th. On that evening the plaintiffs wrote an answer, agreeing to accept the wool on the terms proposed. The course of the post between St Ives and Bromsgrove is through London, and consequently this answer was not received by the defendants till Tuesday, September 9th. On the Monday September 8th, the defendants not having, as they expected, received an answer on Sunday September 7th, (which in case their letter had not been misdirected, would have been in the usual course of the post,) sold the wool in question to another person. Under these circumstances, the learned Judge held, that the delay having been occasioned by the neglect of the defendants, the jury must take it, that the answer did come back in due course of post; and that then the defendants were liable for the loss that had been sustained: and the plaintiffs accordingly recovered a verdict.

[The defendants sought a new trial, arguing that there was no contract until the plaintiffs' acceptance was received.]

The Court said, that if that were so, no contract could ever be completed by the post. For if the defendants were not bound by their offer when accepted by the plaintiffs till the answer was received, then the plaintiffs ought not to be bound till after they had received the notification that the defendants had received their answer and assented to it. And so it might go on ad infinitum. The defendants must be considered in law as making, during every instant of the time their letter was travelling, the same identical offer to the plaintiffs; and then the contract is completed by the acceptance of it by the latter. Then as to the delay in notifying the acceptance, that arises entirely from the mistake of the defendants, and it therefore must be taken as against them, that the plaintiffs' answer was received in course of post.

Rule discharged.

NOTE

On what ground was this case decided, according to the report? Can you see any other ground upon which the same result could have been reached?

Henthorn v Fraser [1892] 2 Ch 27, Court of Appeal

The secretary of a land society in Liverpool had handed to Henthorn a written option to purchase some houses belonging to the society at £750. About mid-day the next day the secretary of the society posted a withdrawal of the offer; it did not reach Henthorn's home in Birkenhead until after 5 pm. Meanwhile at 3.50 pm Henthorn had posted an acceptance of the offer; this was delivered to the society's office after it had closed and was opened by the secretary the next day. Henthorn's action for specific performance was dismissed and he appealed.

Lord Herschell. . . . If the acceptance by the Plaintiff of the Defendants' offer is to be treated as complete at the time the letter containing it was posted, I can entertain no doubt that the society's attempted revocation of the offer was wholly ineffectual. I think that a person who has made an offer must be considered as continuously making it until he has brought to the knowledge of the person to whom it was made that it is withdrawn . . .

The grounds upon which it has been held that the acceptance of an offer is complete when it is posted have, I think, no application to the revocation or modification of an offer. These can be no more effectual than the offer itself, unless brought to the mind of the person to whom the offer is made. But it is contended on behalf of the Defendants that the acceptance was complete only when received by them and not on the letter being posted. It cannot, of course, be denied, after the decision in *Dunlop v Higgins* in the House of Lords, that, where an offer has been made through the medium of the post, the contract is complete as soon as the acceptance of the offer is posted, but that decision is said to be inapplicable here, inasmuch as the letter containing the offer was not sent by post to *Birkenhead*, but handed to the Plaintiff in the Defendants' office at *Liverpool*. The question therefore arises in what circumstances the acceptance of an offer is to be regarded as complete as soon as it is posted. . . .

I am not sure that I should myself have regarded the doctrine that an acceptance is complete as soon as the letter containing it is posted as resting upon an implied authority by the person making the offer to the person receiving it to accept by those means. It strikes me as somewhat artificial to speak of the person to whom the offer is made as having the implied authority of the other party to send his acceptance by post. He needs no authority to transmit the acceptance through any particular channel; he may select what means he pleases, the Post Office no less than any other. The only effect of the supposed authority is to make the acceptance complete so soon as it is posted, and authority will obviously be implied only when the tribunal considers that it is a case in which this result ought to be reached. I should prefer to state the rule thus: Where the circumstances are such that it must have been within the contemplation of the parties that, according to the ordinary usages of mankind, the post might be used as a means of communicating the acceptance of an offer, the acceptance is complete as soon as it is posted. It matters not in which way the proposition be stated, the present case is in either view within it . . .

[Lindley and Kay LJJ delivered concurring judgments.]

Appeal allowed.

NOTES

1. See Evans, 'The Anglo-American Mailing Rule' 15 ICLQ 553.
2. Is the 'postal rule' a logical deduction from the rules of offer and acceptance, or a rule of commercial convenience? In *Household Fire and Carriage Accident Insurance Co Ltd v Grant* (1879) 4 Ex D 216, where it was held that the letter of acceptance was effective even though it never arrived at all, Thesiger LJ said (at pp 223–224):

> There is no doubt that the implication of a complete, final, and absolutely binding contract being formed, as soon as the acceptance of an offer is posted, may in some cases lead to inconvenience and hardship. But such there must be at times in every view of the law. It is impossible in transactions which pass between parties at a distance, and have to be carried on through the medium of correspondence, to adjust conflicting rights between innocent parties, so as to make the consequences of mistake on the part of a mutual agent fall equally upon the shoulders of both. At the same time I am not prepared to admit that the implication in question will lead to any great or general inconvenience or hardship. An offerer, if he chooses, may always make the formation of the contract which he proposes dependent upon the actual communication to himself of the acceptance. If he trusts to the post he trusts to a means of communication which, as a rule, does not fail, and if no answer to his offer is received by him, and the matter is of importance to him, he can make inquiries of the person to whom his offer was addressed. On the other hand, if the contract is not finally concluded, except in the event of the acceptance actually reaching the offerer, the door would be opened to the perpetration of much fraud, and, putting aside this consideration, considerable delay in commercial transactions, in which despatch is, as a rule, of the greatest consequence, would be occasioned; for the acceptor would never be entirely safe in acting upon his acceptance until he had received notice that his letter of acceptance had reached its destination.

Does the rule enable reliance by one party or the other? Would it cause practical difficulty if the letter of acceptance did have to arrive to be effective? Or if the rule were reversed, so that acceptances had to be communicated but revocations were effective on posting?

3. What if the offeree posts an acceptance but then changes his mind and sends a rejection of the offer by telex, which arrives before the letter? Should he be allowed to play 'fast and loose' in this manner? Can you see any practical difficulty which might arise if it were held that the acceptance was effective despite the overtaking telex?
4. What if the offeree carelessly puts the wrong address on the envelope? Should the offeror still have to bear the risk of loss or delay in the post? Compare *Adams v Lindsell*.
5. In what circumstances will acceptance by post *not* be impliedly authorized?

Holwell Securities Ltd v Hughes [1974] 1 All ER 161, Court of Appeal

By cl 1 of an agreement dated 19th October 1971 made between the defendant of the one part and the plaintiffs of the other, the plaintiffs were granted an option to purchase certain freehold property from the defendant. Clause 2 of the agreement provided: 'The said option shall be exercisable by notice in writing to the [defendant] at any time within six months from the date hereof . . .' On 14th April 1972 the plaintiffs' solicitors wrote a letter to the defendant giving notice of the exercise of the option. The letter was posted, properly addressed and prepaid, on 14th April, but it was never in fact delivered to the defendant or to his address. No other written communication of the exercise of the option was given or sent to the defendant before the expiry of the time limit on 19th April. In an action against the defendant seeking specific performance of the option agreement, the plaintiffs contended that, since a contractual offer could be accepted by posting a letter of acceptance, the time of acceptance being the moment of posting, the option had been validly exercised when their letter of 14th April was posted.

Russell LJ. . . . It is the law in the first place that prima facie acceptance of an offer must be communicated to the offeror. On this principle the law has engrafted a doctrine that, if in any given case the true view is that the parties contemplated that the postal service might be used for the purpose of forwarding an acceptance of the offer, committal of the acceptance in a regular manner to the postal service will be acceptance of the offer so as to constitute a contract, even if the letter goes astray and is lost. Nor, as was once suggested, are such cases limited to cases in which the offer has been made by post. It suffices I think at this stage to refer to *Henthorn v Fraser*. In the present case, as I read a passage in the judgment below, Templeman J concluded that the parties here contemplated that the postal service might be used to communicate acceptance of the offer (by exercise of the option); and I agree with that.

But that is not and cannot be the end of the matter. In any case, before one can find that the basic principle of the need for communication of acceptance to the offeror is displaced by this artificial concept of communication by the act of posting, it is necessary that the offer is in its terms consistent with such displacement and not one which by its terms points rather in the direction of actual communication. . .

The relevant language here is, 'The said option shall be exercisable by notice in writing to the Intending Vendor . . .'. a very common phrase in an option agreement. There is, of course, nothing in that phrase to suggest that the notification to the defendant could not be made by post. But the requirement of 'notice . . . to', in my judgment, is language which should be taken expressly to assert the ordinary situation in law that acceptance requires to be communicated or notified to the offeror, and is inconsistent with the theory that acceptance can be constituted by the act of posting, referred to by Anson as 'acceptance *without notification*'.

It is of course true that the instrument could have been differently worded. An option to purchase within a period given for value has the characteristic of an offer that cannot be withdrawn. The instrument might have said 'The offer constituted by this option may be accepted in writing within six months': in which case no doubt the posting would have sufficed to form the contract. But that language was not used, and, as indicated, in my judgment the language used prevents that legal outcome. Under this head of the case hypothetical problems were canvassed to suggest difficulties in the way of that conclusion. What if the letter had been delivered through the letterbox of the house in due time, but the defendant had either deliberately or fortuitously not been there to receive it before the option period expired? This does not persuade me that the artificial posting rule is here applicable. The answer might well be that in the circumstances the defendant had impliedly invited communication by use of an orifice in his front door designed to receive communications. . . .

Accordingly I would dismiss the appeal; and Buckley LJ authorises me to say that he agrees with the judgment I have delivered.

Lawton LJ delivered a concurring judgment. He commented:

A notice is a means of making something known. The Shorter Oxford English Dictionary gives as the primary meanings of the word: 'Intimation, information, intelligence, warning . . . formal intimation or warning of something.' If a notice is to be of any value it must be an intimation to someone. A notice which cannot impinge on anyone's mind is not functioning as such.

Entores Ltd v Miles Far East Corpn [1955] 2 All ER 493, Court of Appeal

An English company in London was in communication by telex with a Dutch company in Amsterdam; the Dutch company was acting as agent for an American company in New York. Messages typed in on one telex machine were simultaneously printed out by the other. The English company received an offer of goods from the Dutch company via telex, and made a counter-offer which the Dutch company accepted by telex. The English company applied for leave to service notice of a writ on the American principal in New York; service out of the jurisdiction is allowed under RSC Ord 11, rule 1 if the contract to be enforced was made within the jurisdiction.

Denning LJ. . . . The question for our determination is: Where was the contract made?

When a contract is made by post it is clear law throughout the common law countries that the acceptance is complete as soon as the letter of acceptance is put into the post box, and that is the place where the contract is made. But there is no clear rule about contracts made by telephone or by Telex. Communications by these means are virtually instantaneous and stand on a different footing.

The problem can only be solved by going in stages. Let me first consider a case where two people make a contract by word of mouth in the presence of one another. Suppose, for instance, that I shout an offer to a man across a river or a courtyard but I do not hear his reply because it is drowned by an aircraft flying overhead. There is no contract at that moment. If he wishes to make a contract, he must wait till the aircraft is gone and then shout back his acceptance so that I can hear what he says. Not until I have his answer am I bound. I do not agree with the observations of Hill J in *Newcomb v De Roos* (2 E & E at p 275).

Now take a case where two people make a contract by telephone. Suppose, for instance, that I make an offer to a man by telephone and, in the middle of his reply, the line goes 'dead' so that I do not hear his words of acceptance. There is no contract at that moment. The other man may not know the precise moment when the line failed. But he will know that the telephone conversation was abruptly broken off, because people usually say something to signify the end of the conversation. If he wishes to make a contract, he must therefore get through again so as to make sure that I heard. Suppose next that the line does not go dead, but it is nevertheless so indistinct that I do not catch what he says and I ask him to repeat it. He then repeats it and I hear his acceptance. The contract is made, not on the first time when I do not hear, but only the second time when I do hear. If he does not repeat it, there is no contract. The contract is only complete when I have his answer accepting the offer.

Lastly take the Telex. Suppose a clerk in a London office taps out on the teleprinter an offer which is immediately recorded on a teleprinter in a Manchester office, and a clerk at that end taps out an acceptance. If the line goes dead in the middle of the sentence of acceptance, the teleprinter motor will stop. There is then obviously no contract. The clerk, at Manchester must get through again and send his complete sentence. But it may happen that the line does not go dead, yet the message does not get through to London. Thus the clerk at Manchester may tap out his message of acceptance and it will not be recorded in London because the ink at the London end fails or something of that kind. In that case the Manchester clerk will not know of the failure but the London clerk will know of it and will immediately send back a message 'not receiving'. Then, when the fault is rectified, the Manchester clerk will repeat his message. Only then is there a contract. If he does not repeat it, there is no contract. It is not until his message is received that the contract is complete.

In all the instances I have taken so far, the man who sends the message of acceptance knows that it has not been received or he has reason to know it. So he must repeat it. But suppose that he does not know that his message did not get home. He thinks it has. This may happen if the listener on the telephone does not catch the words of acceptance, but nevertheless does not trouble to ask for them to be repeated: or if the ink on the teleprinter fails at the receiving end, but the clerk does not ask for the message to be repeated: so that the man who sends an acceptance reasonably believes that his message has been received. The offeror in such circumstances is clearly bound, because he will be estopped from saying that he did not receive the message of acceptance. It is his own fault that he did not get it. But if there should be a case where the offeror without any fault on his part does not receive the message of acceptance—yet the sender of it reasonably believes it has got home when it has not—then I think there is no contract.

My conclusion is that the rule about instantaneous communications between the parties is different from the rule about the post. The contract is only complete when the acceptance is received by the offeror: and the contract is made at the place where the acceptance is received.

Applying the principles which I have stated, I think that the contract in this case was made in London where the acceptance was received. It was therefore a proper case for service out of the jurisdiction.

[Birkett and Parker LJJ gave judgments to the same effect.]

Appeal dismissed.

NOTES

1. In *The Brimnes* [1975] QB 929 a charterparty gave the shipowner the right to withdraw the vessel if the hire was not paid punctually. The trial judge held that a notice of withdrawal that had been sent during office hours was 'received' then although it was apparently not seen by the charterers' staff until the following morning. The Court of Appeal agreed with his conclusion.

2. *Entores Ltd v Miles Far East Corpn* was approved and applied by the House of Lords in *Brinkibon Ltd v Stahag Stahl* [1983] 2 AC 34, though Lord Wilberforce remarked:

> Since 1955 the use of telex communications has been greatly expanded, and there are many variants on it. The senders and recipients may not be the principals to the contemplated contract. They may be servants or agents with limited authority. The message may not reach, or be intended to reach, the designated recipient immediately: messages may be sent out of office hours, or at night, with the intention, or on the assumption, that they will be read at a later time. There may be some error or fault at the recipient's end which prevents receipt at the time contemplated and believed in by the sender. The message may have been sent and/or received through machines operated by third persons. And many other variations may occur. No universal rule can cover all such cases: they must be resolved by reference to the intentions of the parties, by sound business practice and in some cases by a judgment where the risks should lie.

3. What rule should apply to acceptance sent by fax?

Manchester Diocesan Council for Education v Commercial and General Investments Ltd [1969] 3 All ER 1593, Buckley J

Late in 1963 the plaintiff decided to sell property by tender. Particulars and conditions of sale were prepared and these incorporated a form of tender. The conditions required, inter alia, that tenders be sent to the plaintiff's surveyor by 27th August 1964 and stipulated that the sale was subject to the approval of the purchase price by the Secretary of State. Clause 4 provided: 'The person whose tender is accepted shall be the purchaser and shall be informed of the acceptance of his tender by letter sent to him by post addressed to the address given in the tender . . .' On 25th August 1964 the defendant company completed the form of tender and stated thereon: 'and we agree that in the event of this offer being accepted in accordance with the above conditions . . . we will pay the said purchase price and carry out and complete the purchase in accordance with the said conditions . . .' This was sent on the following day to the plaintiff's surveyor. On 1st September the plaintiff's surveyor informed the defendant company's surveyor that he would recommend acceptance of the defendant company's offer and that he would write again as soon as he had formal instructions. On 14th September the defendant company's surveyor replied to the effect that he looked forward to receiving formal acceptance of the offer and he named the solicitors acting for the defendant company. This letter was acknowledged by the plaintiff's solicitor on 15th September when he also stated that the 'sale has now been approved' by the plaintiff and that instructions had been given to obtain the approval of the Secretary of State. The approval of the Secretary of State (in relation to that part of the property in respect of which approval was necessary) was obtained on 18th November. On 23rd December the plaintiff's solicitors wrote to the defendant company's solicitors and, after reciting that the offer by tender had been accepted by the plaintiff subject to the consent of the Secretary of State, added that the consent had been forthcoming and they concluded therefore that the contract was binding on both parties. The defendant company's solicitors replied that they did not agree that there was any subsisting binding contract. On 7th January 1965 the plaintiff's solicitors wrote to the defendant company at the address given by it in the form of tender giving formal notification of acceptance of its offer.

Buckley J. . . . . The offer contained in the tender was to the effect that in the event of its being accepted in accordance with the conditions of sale on or before the day named therein for that purpose (and none was so named) the defendant company would pay the price and complete the purchase. An offerer may by the terms of his offer indicate that it may be accepted in a particular manner. In the present case the conditions included condition 4 which I have read. It is said on the defendant company's behalf that that condition was not complied with until 7th

January 1965; that until that date the offer was never accepted in accordance with its terms; and that consequently nothing earlier than that date can be relied on as an acceptance resulting in a binding contract. If an offeror stipulates by the terms of his offer that it may, or that it shall, be accepted in a particular manner a contract results as soon as the offeree does the stipulated act, whether it has come to the notice of the offeror or not. In such a case the offeror conditionally waives either expressly or by implication the normal requirement that acceptance must be communicated to the offeror to conclude a contract. There can be no doubt that in the present case, if the plaintiff or its authorised agent had posted a letter addressed to the defendant company at no. 15, Berkeley Street, on or about 15th September informing the defendant company of the acceptance of its tender, the contract would have been complete at the moment when such letter was posted, but that course was not taken. Condition 4, however, does not say that that shall be the sole permitted method of communicating an acceptance. It may be that an offeror, who by the terms of his offer insists on acceptance in a particular manner, is entitled to insist that he is not bound unless acceptance is effected or communicated in that precise way, although it seems probable that, even so, if the other party communicates his acceptance in some other way, the offeror may by conduct or otherwise waive his right to insist on the prescribed method of acceptance. Where, however, the offeror has prescribed a particular method of acceptance, but not in terms insisting that only acceptance in that mode shall be binding, I am of opinion that acceptance communicated to the offeror by any other mode which is no less advantageous to him will conclude the contract. . . . If an offeror intends that he shall be bound only if his offer is accepted in some particular manner, it must be for him to make this clear. Condition 4 in the present case had not, in my judgment, this effect.

Moreover, the inclusion of condition 4 in the defendant company's offer was at the instance of the plaintiff, who framed the conditions and the form of tender. It should not, I think, be regarded as a condition or stipulation imposed by the defendant company as offeror on the plaintiff as offeree, but as a term introduced into the bargain by the plaintiff and presumably considered by the plaintiff as being in some way for the protection or benefit of the plaintiff. It would consequently be a term strict compliance with which the plaintiff could waive, provided the defendant company was not adversely affected. The plaintiff did not take advantage of the condition which would have resulted in a contract being formed as soon as a letter of acceptance complying with the condition was posted, but adopted another course, which could only result in a contract when the plaintiff's acceptance was actually communicated to the defendant company.

For these reasons, I have reached the conclusion that in accordance with the terms of the tender it was open to the plaintiff to conclude a contract by acceptance actually communicated to the defendant company in any way; and, in my judgment, the letter of 15th September constituted such an acceptance. It follows that, in my judgment . . . the parties thereupon became contractually bound. . . .

If I am right in thinking that there was a contract on 15th September 1964 that disposes of the case but, in case I should be held to be wrong in that view, I will now consider the other point in the case and will for this purpose assume that no contract was made at that date. On this basis no contract can have been concluded before 7th January 1965. The defendant company contend that, as the tender stipulated no time within which it must be accepted, it was an implied term of the offer that it must be accepted, if at all, within a reasonable time. It is said that acceptance on 7th January was not within a reasonable time.

It has long been recognised as being the law that, where an offer is made in terms which fix no time limit for acceptance, the offer must be accepted within a reasonable time to make a contract . . . There seems, however, to be no reported case in which the reason for this is explained.

There appear to me to be two possible views on methods of approaching the problem. First, it may be said that by implication the offer is made on terms that, if it is not accepted within a reasonable time, it must be treated as withdrawn. Alternatively, it may be said that, if the offeree does not accept the offer within a reasonable time, he must be treated as having refused it. On either view the offer would cease to be a live one on the expiration of what in the circumstances of the particular case should be regarded as a reasonable time for acceptance. The first of these alternatives involves implying a term that if the offer is not accepted within a reasonable time, it shall be treated as withdrawn or lapsing at the end of that period if it has not then been accepted; the second is based on an inference to be drawn from the conduct of the offeree, that is, that having failed to accept the offer within a reasonable time he has manifested an intention to refuse it. If, in the first alternative, the time which the offeror is to be treated as having set for acceptance is to be such a time as is reasonable at the date of the offer, what is reasonable must depend on circumstances then existing and reasonably likely to arise during the continuance of the offer; but it would be not unlikely that the offeror and offeree would make different assessments of what would be reasonable even if, as might quite possibly not be the case, they based those judgments on identical known and anticipated circumstances. No doubt a court could resolve any dispute about this, but this approach clearly involves a certain degree of uncertainty about the precise terms of the offer. If on the other hand the time which the offeror is to be treated as having set for acceptance is to be such as turns out to be reasonable in the light of circumstances then existing and of circumstances arising thereafter during the continuance of the offer, whether foreseeable or not, an additional element of uncertainty is introduced. The second alternative on the other hand involves simply an objective assessment of facts and the determination of the question whether on the facts the offeree should in fairness to both parties be regarded as having refused the offer.

It does not seem to me that either party is in greater need of protection by the law in this respect than the other. Until his offer has been accepted it is open to the offeror at any time to withdraw it or to put a limit on the time for acceptance. On the other hand, the offeree can at any time refuse the offer or, unless he has been guilty of unreasonable delay, accept it. Neither party is at a disadvantage. Unless authority constrains me to do otherwise, I am strongly disposed to prefer the second alternative to the first.

[Buckley J examined the cases, finding them inconclusive.]

. . . I have dealt with this part of the case at some length because, if the first alternative were the correct view of the law and if what is reasonable had to be ascertained as at the time of the offer, the subsequent conduct of the parties would be irrelevant to the question how long the offer should be treated as remaining open. In my opinion, however, the subsequent conduct of the parties is relevant to the question, which I think is the right test, whether the offeree should be held to have refused the offer by his conduct.

In my judgment the letter of 15th September 1964 excludes the possibility of imputing to the plaintiff a refusal of the offer. If that letter does not itself constitute an effective acceptance, it clearly discloses an intention to accept from which there is nothing to suggest a departure before 7th January 1965. Accordingly, if no contract was formed earlier, I am of opinion that it was open to the plaintiff to accept it on 7th January and that the plaintiff's letter of that date was effectual to bind the defendant company contractually.

Order for specific performance.

Dickinson v Dodds (1876) 2 Ch D 463, Court of Appeal

On Wednesday 10 June 1874 Dodds gave Dickinson a note which read, in part,

'I hereby agree to sell to Mr George Dickinson the whole of the dwelling-houses, garden ground, stabling, and outbuildings thereto belonging, situate at *Croft*, belonging to me, for the sum of £800. As witness my hand this tenth day of June, 1874.

£800   (Signed)   John Dodds.'

P.S.—This offer to be left over until Friday, 9 o'clock, am. J.D. (the twelfth), 12th June, 1874.

                                              '(Signed)   J. Dodds.'

[It was] alleged that Dodds understood and intended that the Plaintiff should have until Friday 9 am within which to determine whether he would or would not purchase, and that he should absolutely have until that time the refusal of the property at the price of £800, and that the Plaintiff in fact determined to accept the offer on the morning of Thursday, the 11th of June, but did not at once signify his acceptance to Dodds, believing that he had the power to accept it until 9 am on the Friday.

In the afternoon of the Thursday the Plaintiff was informed by a Mr Berry that Dodds had been offering or agreeing to sell the property to Thomas Allan, the other Defendant. Thereupon the Plaintiff, at about half-past seven in the evening, went to the house of Mrs Burgess, the mother-in-law of Dodds, where he was then staying, and left with her a formal acceptance in writing of the offer to sell the property. According to the evidence of Mrs Burgess this document never in fact reached Dodds, she having forgotten to give it to him.

On the following (Friday) morning, at about seven o'clock, Berry, who was acting as agent for Dickinson, found Dodds at the Darlington railway station, and handed to him a duplicate of the acceptance by Dickinson, and explained to Dodds its purport. He replied that it was too late, as he had sold the property. A few minutes later Dickinson himself found Dodds entering a railway carriage, and handed him another duplicate of the notice of acceptance, but Dodds declined to receive it, saying, 'You are too late. I have sold the property.'

It appeared that on the day before, Thursday, the 11th of June, Dodds had signed a formal contract for the sale of the property to the Defendant Allan for £800, and had received from him a deposit of £40. Dickinson brought a bill for specific performance.

James LJ. . . . 'This offer to be left over until Friday, 9 o'clock am, 12th June, 1874.' That shews it was only an offer. There was no consideration given for the undertaking or promise, to whatever extent it may be considered binding, to keep the property unsold until 9 o'clock on Friday morning; but apparently Dickinson was of opinion, and probably Dodds was of the same opinion, that he (Dodds) was bound by that promise, and could not in any way withdraw from it, or retract it, until 9 o'clock on Friday morning, and this probably explains a good deal of what afterwards took place. But it is clear settled law, on one of the clearest principles of law, that this promise, being a mere *nudum pactum* was not binding, and that at any moment before a complete acceptance by Dickinson of the offer, Dodds was as free as Dickinson himself. Well, that being the state of things, it is said that the only mode in which Dodds could assert that freedom was by actually and distinctly saying to Dickinson, 'Now I withdraw my offer.' It appears to me that there is neither principle nor authority for the proposition that there must be an express and actual withdrawal of the offer, or what is called a retraction. It must, to constitute a contract, appear that the two minds were at one, at the same moment of time, that is, that there was an offer continuing up to the time of the acceptance. If there was not such a continuing offer, then the acceptance comes to nothing. Of course it may well be that the one man is bound in some way or other to let the other man know that his mind with regard to the offer has been changed; but in this case, beyond all question, the Plaintiff knew that Dodds was no longer minded to sell the property to him as plainly and clearly as if Dodds had told him in so many words, 'I withdraw the offer.' This is evident from the Plaintiff's own statements in the bill . . .

Mellish LJ delivered a judgment to the same effect and Baggallay JA concurred.

Bill dismissed.

(h) Exchange of contracts

In contracts for the sale of land it is very common for the parties to negotiate over the price, and then to hand the matter over to their solicitors, leaving the agreement 'subject to contract'. Though it depends on the circumstances, this expression is nearly always taken to mean that the parties do not intend to be legally bound until formal contracts have been completed, signed and exchanged. Although contracts for the sale of land must be in writing (above, p 131), this requirement can be satisfied by a quite informal writing. Delaying the point at which the contract is binding until formal contracts are exchanged is useful to buyers because it gives them time for pre-contract investigations, surveys of the property and mortgage negotiation; but in times when house prices are rising it gives sellers the chance to withdraw unless the price is increased (called 'gazumping'). This practice is widely disapproved of, but the Law Commission concluded in its report on 'Subject to Contract' (No 65, 1975) that any change in the law would cause more difficulties than it was worth. A purchaser who is particularly afraid of being gazumped can make a conditional contract (see below, p 228) or take an option. Parties who want additional protection against default by the other but who don't want to enter even a conditionally binding contract to buy and sell can use a device recommended by the Conveyancing Standing Committee (*Pre-contract Deposits: A Practice Recommendation*, 1987). This involves each side depositing a small sum, say ½% of the purchase price, with a stakeholder; if either party backs out unjustifiably, his deposit will be forfeited and paid to the other party.

Eccles v Bryant [1947] 2 All ER 865, Court of Appeal

The vendors had agreed to sell the purchaser a house by correspondence which was expressly stated to be 'subject to contract'. The vendors' solicitors wrote to the purchaser's solicitors: 'Our clients have now signed their part of the contract herein and we are ready to exchange and shall be glad to hear from you.' A week later the purchaser's solicitors wrote back: 'We accordingly enclose herewith the contract signed by our client and shall be glad to receive in exchange the part signed by your client.' The vendors changed their minds and did not send their part in exchange. A decree of specific performance was granted to the purchaser, and the vendors appealed.

Lord Greene MR. . . . It is clear that both firms of solicitors, when they were instructed to carry this matter through by their clients, intended to do so in the customary way which is familiar to every firm of solicitors in the country, namely, by preparing the engrossment of the draft contract when agreed in duplicate and exchanging the two parts when signed by their clients. Anyone, I think, would have understood from the language of the earlier correspondence and the words 'subject to contract' that the contract would be brought about by an exchange of the two parts signed by the parties. Vaisey J pointed out that what he called the ceremonial form of exchange, namely, the meeting of solicitors in the offices of one of them—usually the vendor's solicitor's office—and the passing of the two engrossments signed over the table may be taken to have fallen, and, indeed, no doubt it has, into disuse to a certain extent, particularly when the solicitors are in different parts of the country. He recognised that an exchange by post would in many cases take the place of the old more ceremonial exchange, but that an exchange was contemplated by both firms of solicitors appears to me to be clear. I am prepared to assume that their intention was that the exchange should take place by post. When an exchange takes place by post and a contract comes into existence through the act of exchange, the earliest date at which such a contract can come into existence would be the date when the later of the two documents to be put in the post is actually put in the post. Another view might be that the exchange takes place and the contract thereby comes into existence when, and not before, the parties or their solicitors receive from their opposite numbers their parts of the contract. It is not necessary here to choose between those two views. I mention them particularly because counsel for the purchaser tried to suggest an intermediate stage, that where the parties contemplate an exchange by post the contract is completed, not when an exchange takes place, but when one of the parties puts his part into the post. I am afraid I cannot accept that. It seems to me to be a contradiction in terms to speak of that as an exchange . . .

It is said that a contract took place when, in response to an alleged invitation on behalf of the vendors, the purchaser signed his part of the contract and communicated the fact to the vendors. It was argued that there is no necessity in this class of case for an exchange of documents, and that the references which have been made in many judgments in this court and other courts to an exchange are either inaccurate or wrong. The answer to that seems to me to be simple. When parties are proposing to enter into a contract, the manner in which the contract is to be created so as to bind them must be gathered from the intentions of the parties, express or implied. In such a contract as this, there is a well-known common and customary method of dealing, namely, by exchange, and anyone who contemplates that method cannot contemplate the coming into existence of a binding contract before the exchange takes place. It was argued that exchange is a mere matter of machinery, having in itself no particular importance or significance. So far as significance is concerned, it appears to me that not only is it not right to say of exchange that it has no significance, but it is the crucial and vital fact which brings the contract into existence. As for importance, it is of the greatest importance, and that is why in past ages this procedure came to be adopted by everybody as the proper procedure. In dealing with contracts for the sale of land, it is of the greatest importance to the vendor that he should have a document signed by the purchaser and to the purchaser that he should have a document signed by the vendor. It is of the greatest importance that there should be no dispute whether a contract has or has not been made, and that there should be no dispute as to the terms of it. This procedure of exchange ensures that none of those difficulties will arise. Each party has got a document of title, because directly a contract is entered into and that contract is in writing relating to land, it is a document of title. That can be illustrated by the simple case where a purchaser makes a sub-sale. The contract is a vital document for the purpose of the sub-sale. If he had not got the vendor's part, signed by the vendors, to show to the sub-purchaser, the purchaser would not be able to make a good title.

[Cohen and Asquith LJJ delivered judgments to the same effect.]

Appeal allowed.

NOTE

In *Storer v Manchester City Council* (see above, p 172) the Court of Appeal held that there was a contract despite the fact that contracts had not been exchanged. The instructions given by the council to the town clerk to devise a simple procedure for selling the houses, coupled with the language of the clerk's letter ('If you will sign the Agreement and return it to me, I will send you the Agreement signed on behalf of the [council] in exchange') showed that the parties intended to be bound without an exchange of contracts.

If there is a 'chain' transaction, for example Furmston selling his cottage to Beale, Beale selling his house to Bishop and Bishop selling his flat to Bentham, exchanging contracts will be too slow and uncertain. Neither Beale nor Bishop will normally be prepared to sell his old property until he has secured his new one or vice versa. One individual in the chain can safeguard himself, by getting possession of signed contracts from both people he is dealing with before accepting either contract by sending off his own parts; but as Beale and Bishop have to deal with each other, they cannot both do this: one will have to commit himself in one direction not knowing whether he has a contract in the other. A way of reducing the risks to a minimum is for their solicitors to agree to 'exchange by telephone'. The solicitors on each side get their clients to sign their parts of the contracts but hold on to them. When all the solicitors for everyone in the chain are ready to exchange on behalf of their clients, they agree by telephone (which will only take a matter of minutes) to hold the signed documents not for their own clients any longer but as agents for the solicitors representing the other party to each transaction. This means that each seller's part of the contract is now in the constructive possession of the buyer's solicitor and vice versa. In *Domb v Isoz* [1980] Ch 548 the Court of Appeal held that this was effective to make the contracts binding.

(i) Tenders

If tenders are invited for the construction of a project or the purchase of property, what is the process of offer and acceptance?

Spencer v Harding (1870) LR 5 CP 561, Common Pleas

Willes J. I am of opinion that the defendants are entitled to judgment. The action is brought against persons who issued a circular offering a stock for sale by tender, to be sold at a discount in one lot. The plaintiffs sent in a tender which turned out to be the highest, but which was not accepted. They now insist that the circular amounts to a contract or promise to sell the goods to the highest bidder, that is, in this case, to the person who should tender for them at the smallest rate of discount; and reliance is placed on the cases as to rewards offered for the discovery of an offender. In those cases, however, there never was any doubt that the advertisement amounted to a promise to pay the money to the person who first gave information. The difficulty suggested was that it was a contract with all the world. But that, of course, was soon overruled. It was an offer to become liable to any person who before the offer should be retracted should happen to be the person to fulfil the contract of which the advertisement was an offer or tender. That is not the sort of difficulty which presents itself here. If the circular had gone on, 'and we undertake to sell to the highest bidder', the reward cases would have applied, and there would have been a good contract in respect of the persons. But the question is, whether there is here any offer to enter into a contract at all, or whether the circular amounts to anything more than a mere proclamation that the defendants are ready to chaffer for the sale of the goods, and to receive offers for the purchase of them. In advertisements for tenders for buildings it is not usual to say that the contract will be given to the lowest bidder, and it is not always that the contract is made with the lowest bidder. Here there is a total absence of any words to intimate that the highest bidder is to be the purchaser. It is a mere attempt to ascertain whether an offer can be obtained within such a margin as the sellers are willing to adopt.

Keating and Montague Smith JJ concurred.

Judgment for the defendants.

NOTE

In *Harvela Investments Ltd v Royal Trust Co of Canada (CI) Ltd* [1984] 2 All ER 65, trustees of a settlement invited two parties to submit sealed offers or confidential telexes for a parcel of shares which formed part of the settlement property, and they stated in the invitation that 'we bind ourselves to accept the [highest] offer'. Peter Gibson J held that this constituted an offer which was accepted by the highest genuine bid, the consideration for the promise to accept the highest bid being the act of bidding. He also held that one of the bids was invalid because it was a referential bid ('C$2,100,000 or C$101,000 in excess of any other offer'): he held that it was an implied term of the offer that such bids were excluded. Thus the trustees were bound to accept the other bid, which was for C$2,175,000. The Court of Appeal reversed this part of the decision, holding that there was nothing to exclude referential bids, so that there was a contract with the referential bidder [1985] 1 All ER 261; but the House of Lords restored the first instance judgment [1987] 2 All ER 966.

Institution of Civil Engineers Form of Tender (5th edn)

To ....

....

....

GENTLEMEN,

Having examined the Drawings, Conditions of Contract, Specification and Bill of Quantities for the construction of the above-mentioned Works (and the matters set out in the Appendix hereto), we offer to construct and complete the whole of the said Works and maintain the Permanent Works in conformity with the said Drawings, Conditions of Contract, Specification and Bill of Quantities for such sum as may be ascertained in accordance with the said Conditions of Contract.

We undertake to complete and deliver the whole of the Permanent Works comprised in the Contract within the time stated in the Appendix hereto.

If our tender is accepted we will, when required, provide two good and sufficient sureties or obtain the guarantee of a Bank or Insurance Company (to be approved in either case by you) to be jointly and severally bound with us in a sum equal to the percentage of the Tender Total as defined in the said Conditions of Contract for the due performance of the Contract under the terms of a Bond in the form annexed to the Conditions of Contract.

Unless and until a formal Agreement is prepared and executed this Tender, together with your written acceptance thereof, shall constitute a binding Contract between us.

We understand that you are not bound to accept the lowest or any tender you may receive.

†To the best of our knowledge and belief we have complied with the general conditions required by the Fair Wages Resolution for the three months immediately preceding the date of this tender.

We are, Gentlemen,

Yours faithfully,

Signature ....

Address ....

Date..

†Delete if not required

A general contractor, wishing to put in a tender for a large project, himself invites tenders from subcontractors for parts of the work. He uses a low bid put in by a subcontractor in calculating his own tender price, and he is awarded the main contract. What if before he has had time to notify the subcontractor, the latter withdraws his bid, perhaps even though he had agreed to keep it open (see *Dickinson v Dodds*, above p 203)? In the United States, Learned Hand J held there was no remedy: *James Baird Co v Gimbel Bros, Inc* 64 F 2d 344 (2d Cir 1933). However, in *Drennan v Star Paving Company* 51 Cal 2d 409, 333 P 2d 757 (1958) the plaintiff general contractor put in a bid for the 'Monte Vista School Job' calculated on the basis of a bid by the defendant subcontractor to do the paving work for $7,132, and naming the defendant as the subcontractor. The plaintiff was awarded the contract, but when he called at the defendant's office, he was immediately told that a mistake had been made and the defendant could not do the work at that price. Ultimately the plaintiff employed another subcontractor who charged $10,949. The Supreme Court of California affirmed a judgment for the plaintiff.
Traynor J said:

There is no evidence that defendant offered to make its bid irrevocable in exchange for plaintiff's use of its figures in computing his bid. Nor is there evidence that would warrant interpreting plaintiff's use of defendant's bid as the acceptance thereof, binding plaintiff, on condition he received the main contract, to award the subcontract to defendant. In sum, there was neither an option supported by consideration nor a bilateral contract binding on both parties.
    Plaintiff contends, however, that he relied to his detriment on defendant's offer and that defendant must therefore answer in damages for its refusal to perform. Thus the question is squarely presented: Did plaintiff's reliance make defendant's offer irrevocable?
    . . . Section 90 of the Restatement . . . [above, p 151] applies in this state. . . .
    Had defendant's bid expressly stated or clearly implied that it was revocable at any time before acceptance we would treat it accordingly. It was silent on revocation, however, and we must therefore determine whether there are conditions to the right of revocation imposed by law or reasonably inferable in fact. In the analogous problem of an offer for a unilateral contract, the theory is now obsolete that the offer is revocable at any time before complete

performance. Thus section 45 of the Restatement of Contracts provides: 'If an offer for a unilateral contract is made, and part of the consideration requested in the offer is given or tendered by the offeree in response thereto, the offeror is bound by a contract, the duty of immediate performance of which is conditional on the full consideration being given or tendered within the time stated in the offer, or, if no time stated therein, within a reasonable time'. In explanation, comment b states that the 'main offer includes as a subsidiary promise, necessarily implied, that if part of the requested performance is given, the offeror will not revoke his offer, and that if tender is made it will be accepted. Part performance or tender may thus furnish consideration for the subsidiary promise. Moreover, merely acting in justifiable reliance on an offer may in some cases serve as sufficient reason for making a promise binding (see s 90).'

Whether implied in fact or law, the subsidiary promise serves to preclude the injustice that would result if the offer could be revoked after the offeree had acted in detrimental reliance thereon. Reasonable reliance resulting in a foreseeable prejudical change in position affords a compelling basis also for implying a subsidiary promise not to revoke an offer for a bilateral contract . . .

When plaintiff used defendant's offer in computing his own bid, he bound himself to perform in reliance on defendant's terms. Though defendant did not bargain for this use of its bid neither did defendant make it idly, indifferent to whether it would be used or not . . .

It bears noting that a general contractor is not free to delay acceptance after he has been awarded the general contract in the hope of getting a better price. Nor can he reopen bargaining with the subcontractor and at the same time claim a continuing right to accept the original offer.

Law Commission Working Paper No 60, 'Firm Offers' (1975)

Provisional recommendations
55. We have formulated five provisional recommendations on which comments are invited. They will of course only apply to firm offers that are not made under seal and for which no consideration has been given by the offeree:
(a) An offeror who has promised that he will not revoke his offer for a definite time should be bound by the terms of that promise for a period not exceeding six years, *provided that* the promise has been made 'in the course of a business' as that expression is explained in paragraph 31 above (paras 30–34).
(b) Such a promise need not be evidenced in writing (paras 35–38).
(c) It should be capable of applying to land or interests in land (paras 39–40).
(d) A firm offer to which (a) applies should be capable of acceptance by the offeree during the time that the offeror is bound by his promise, notwithstanding his purported revocation of it (paras 41–47).
(e) An offeror who breaks a promise by which he is bound under (a) should be liable in damages to the offeree (paras 48–50).
56. We should, in addition, welcome information on business practices in relation to firm offers and comments on the relevance to those practices of our provisional recommendations.

'Contracts between Businessmen: Reform of the Law of Firm Offers' by Lewis (1982) 9 Brit J Law & Society 153, at 153, 158–160, 162–165, 166, 168–171

This article examines the role of a particular area of the law of contract in a specific commercial context involving the relationship of a general building contractor and a sub-contractor. The focus is upon the formation of agreement through the submission of bids to carry out work put out to tender. An empirical examination of the attitudes of these builders to the tendering procedure has been carried out and is related to a Law Commission proposal to change the law on 'firm offers'. To what extent do those in business rely on legal sanction as a method of guaranteeing the expectations to which a promise may give rise? The aim of the article is to provide a case study for Weber's discussion of the extent the law of contract is required to support the development of commercial relations in a market economy. The article forms a part of but a limited literature empirically examining the use and non-use of law by the business community. It also reflects upon the legitimising force of the general principles of classical contract law and considers the difficulties of those, such as the Law Commission, who continue to refine these principles when faced with the specific circumstances of a particular relationship. . . .

As Macaulay puts it:

'A rough sketch of the classical model of the contract process in western capitalist societies would stress its formal and normative aspects. Formally, it assumes that the rules of contract law will be invoked by the parties and applied by the courts; normatively, it holds that they ought to be.'

. . . Classical theory has continued to dominate the analysis of the exchange relationship despite studies exposing the non-use of its general principles and their attendant sanctions in certain areas. . . .

The classical model is thus the orthodox picture of contract which has influenced, among others, those whose direct task it is to reform the law . . .

The . . . example [of a subcontract bid being revoked] given by the Law Commission carries with it several implications concerning the importance and effectiveness of the general principles of contract and of business attitudes towards legal remedies. In investigating the reform proposals questions such as the following could be asked: What is the overall relationship of the general to the sub-contractor and how do they both view the tendering procedure? Do general contractors find withdrawal by sub-contractors a problem and if so do they do anything about it? To what extent are the parties already influenced by the general principles of law embodied in offer and acceptance? Would general contractors resort to any legal solution to withdrawal rather than more informal and flexible techniques of control found in other business relationships? Are the views of contractors sufficiently cohesive and their practices sufficiently uniform to provide some basis for establishing a rule to affect all bids made? Is the unequal balance in the bidding procedure as illustrated by the Commission the whole story or does the sub-contractor have a tale to tell?

To answer these and other questions this article relies upon two particular sources. The first is the evidence submitted to the Law Commission in response to its appeal for the views of business men upon withdrawal. . . .

The second source of information was a survey by questionnaire of the views of a small number of contractors operating in the Cardiff area. . . .

Withdrawal by a sub and the action a general may take
How common is the problem of withdrawal by the sub after the general has used his bid? Most of the generals noted that at some time they had encountered the problem, and one small firm even remarked that withdrawal 'is the great difficulty with sub-contracting today'. The others, however, doubted whether the problem was very common, one of them commenting 'we have never (in 30 years) known a sub-contractor withdrawing his bid before an award' [of the main contract to the general. This does not exclude withdrawal after the award.]

There are certain precautions that could be taken by generals in advance of submitting their own bids to ensure that a sub's bid is reliable. Firstly a general could create an option contract and threaten the use of legal sanction in order to bind the sub to his bid. This would necessitate the general obtaining the sub's agreement that in exchange for a nominal fee the sub's bid would be kept firm for a set period. In the survey this had been considered only by one general, being the exceptional firm which had stated that it had found withdrawal of bids a common practice. Even this small firm had only considered and not actually attempted to use option contracts. Its failure to do so may be related to the inconvenience of building into the tendering system an option procedure, especially when bids are received late. But the difficulties of employing such a technique are not insuperable, especially with regard to those subs from whom it is usual to expect tenders. The reason for the failure of generals to establish a legal sanction to prevent withdrawal of a bid before acceptance must lie elsewhere.

A second method of protection for the general is for him to demand from the sub a sum of money as a guarantee or 'bid bond'. In large international contracts it is common to find a requirement that the tenderer should submit together with his bid a deposit of around one per cent of the contract sum. 'The purpose inherent in this machinery is the protection of the employer against default by the contractor, whom it would be difficult to sue owing to his being outside the jurisdiction of the employer's country. The "bid bond" is forfeit if, upon being offered a contract on the basis of his tender, the tenderer refuses to enter upon the contract.' However the survey revealed that such precautions were not adopted by generals for those domestic contracts with subs which form the basis of the present investigation.

Although withdrawal was uncommon, what would be the attitude of a general towards a sub who did try to revoke his bid? Five of the nine generals believed that before the award of the main contract the sub was free to do as he liked; after all, within certain limits the general was also free to change his bid at this time. However, after the award six generals considered that a sub should be bound to his bid, and only three felt he was free to withdraw. A similar majority of subs agreed that they felt bound to their bid. Eight of the eleven said that after the award they were committed to performing the work at the price quoted. However, their commitment was not influenced by the legal position: they would keep to their bid either because they felt morally bound not to revoke, or because they feared loss of their business reputation. Only two subs considered themselves legally bound to perform, although one of these had gone so far as to ensure that liability would not arise by stating that his bid was only an estimate and did not form a legally binding undertaking to keep his price firm.

What action would a general take against a sub who withdrew his bid? As found in the previous studies in the USA no general mentioned threat of legal action, but nearly all considered that if they had a continuing relationship with a sub they could bring pressure to bear. Persuasion 'might well pay dividends if he is already doing work for you or hopes to in the future'. If the sub could not be persuaded to change his mind 'we would have serious reservations about inviting him to tender for future work', or ultimately, 'we would strike him off our list'. Other action 'would depend a lot upon the size of job, size of subcontractor relative to the size of job, and the difference between the price of the lowest sub's tender and the next lowest. If the financial implications were not much relatively, we would accept the second lowest tender. If they were serious we would approach the clients' Quantity Surveyors and try to reach an agreement with them on a revised tender'. . . .

The use made by generals of the bidding procedure
Withdrawal of a bid by a sub reveals only one side of the problem for the general similarly may be guilty of what some consider unethical or improper practice which in turn can injure the sub. In evidence to the Law Commission it was said of the Commission's example: 'No mention is made of the fact that just as the sub is not bound to the general, neither is the general bound to the sub.' The general can take advantage of the open nature of the tendering procedure and the fact that a contract with a sub is not formed until some time after the award of the main contract. As a result of this delay in the formation of contract the general has the opportunity after receiving a bid to disclose it to other subs and thus put pressure upon them to undercut the price quoted ('bid shopping'). Alternatively the initiative may be taken by the other subs themselves in inquiring of the general as to the lowest bid submitted. If the general provides the information he may be encouraging the subs to make a lower offer ('bid peddling'). Both practices reveal that a general in fact may not rely upon employing the sub whose bid he has used in computing his tender, and it is then more difficult for him to claim that in justice the sub should be bound to his bid whilst he remains free to do as he pleases. To what extent does the general fail to use the sub on whose bid he has relied or to what extent does he try to change that bid? Several questions in the survey were aimed at investigating this aspect of the problem.

After receiving a sub's tender all the generals agreed that sometimes the lack of detail in the bid led to further negotiations taking place and these could continue even after the general had been awarded the main contract. They dealt with such matters as 'work content, extent, areas, sequence of work, timing, phasing, agreement concerning the extent of assistance or services to be provided.' But there could also be discussion of the specifications for the job and of the quality of materials to be used, and in particular, the price to be paid could be re-negotiated. Six of the nine generals admitted that occasionally they had been involved in further negotiations about the price and that this happened both before and after they had been awarded the main contract. This may simply reflect that there were indeed matters which had been left vague in the subs' original bids, but it could also indicate that generals were shopping around for a lower price. The subs confirmed that such shopping was taking place, one of them stating that '[i]t is almost common practice for a large number of general contractors to request further negotiations regarding the price prior to their placing an order. They are usually trying to obtain a reduction.'

Further evidence of the generals not always relying upon sub's bids came from their admission that even after using a bid they were quite willing to switch subs if necessary. . . .

Further possible 'abuse' of the bidding procedure was admitted by five of the generals. They agreed that sometimes they used a sub's tender to estimate what a part of their job should cost with an eye to doing that part of the work themselves. One of them remarked, 'Why not? The tendering subcontractor is fully aware that this is a general practice and can always decine to submit a quotation if he so desires.' Somewhat less forcefully another said that it was only an occasional practice employed 'if we are not sure if our own men will be free to do the work. We would only ask for a tender if there was some chance that the tenderer would get the work'. The subs, again with the one exception, condemned the practice for, as one said, 'we cannot afford to be a free estimating service'. . . .

The survey's final question to both generals and subs sought their reaction to [binding the general to the sub whose bid he had used] combined with . . . the proposal to make the sub's bid irrevocable for the time it stated it was to be firm. In the survey of generals the form of the question was as follows:

'Would you support a proposal that a contract between you and the sub is formed when you used a sub's tender in submitting your own bid? This contract would only come into operation if you were successful in being awarded the main contract. It would then bind you to employ the subcontractor, but equally, once you have used his tender he could not withdraw.'

The question produced a divided response from both subs and generals, with about half of each group rejecting the proposal and the rest, with varying degrees of enthusiasm, accepting it subject to serious qualifications. . . .

Summary

In a private construction contract withdrawal of a firm bid by a sub is less of a problem than the Law Commission's example implies. It cannot occur where there is direct nomination of a sub, nor where a sub's bid is not stated to be firm as in a third of the cases in the survey. Even where there are firm bids generals do not necessarily rely upon the figures supplied by the lowest tendering sub when computing their own bid. Instead of being troubled by an enforced change of sub resulting from withdrawal, generals are as likely to initiate such a change themselves by encouraging undercutting of original tenders.

The infrequency of the problem of withdrawal undoubtedly influences attitudes towards the introduction of legal sanctions to control it. But it may also be that the informal control methods that already exist make formal legal regulation unnecessary. At least it is important to observe that the potential which exists for making use of the legal system has not been exploited. Generals have either not devised standard tender forms or allow subs to ignore them. They do not use option contracts or bid bonds and they do not close a deal as soon as possible so as to create a contract and threaten legal sanction to prevent withdrawal. Resort to a court to determine rights and liabilities was not mentioned as a possible remedy. Instead the sanctions discussed were informal: re-negotiation and applying economic pressure; arbitration by a third party such as a quantity surveyor or architect; and, as an ultimate deterrent, the severing of trade relations between the respective firms. The same pattern emerged with regard to the sub's attitudes to generals 'misusing' the bidding procedure, although the subs were generally thought to be in a weaker economic position. The final question in the survey was biased in favour of relying upon formal remedies based upon legal rights and it carried with it a balance and appearance of justice which might be thought superficially to appeal to the contractors surveyed. Despite this its legal solutions were rejected either as impractical, easily avoided and difficult to enforce, or as unfair and too inflexible in not making allowance for the several excuses which contractors recognised as good reasons for non-performance. The informal remedies which already existed, whether cost cutting by subs or the use of economic 'muscle' by generals, emerged as more important methods of regulating the commercial relationship. . . .

Conclusion

. . . [I]t may be suggested, for example, that in bringing about reform it may be advisable at times to examine a specific commercial relationship *in toto*, for to change the legal position in relation to certain aspects of a transaction without considering the bargaining strength occasioned by the legal framework as a whole may produce unintended results. To focus upon the potential abuse of power by only one of the parties, as the Law Commission example does, can lead to a mistaken impression as to the nature and extent of reform required. By taking the broader view it is possible to conclude, as Schultz did, that either both general and sub should be bound or neither. However, the present study reveals how difficult it is to decide whether both parties should be bound.

. . . [T]he Law Commission might also wish to reflect upon the attitude of the parties towards legal remedies. The contractors' need of and desire for litigation must be contrasted with their use of other, more informal methods of regulating their relationship as summarised above.

Such a law reform perspective, however, is but incidental to a second level upon which this article may be read. It is intended as a case study of the extent to which commercial people rely on or are interested in legal sanction as a method of guaranteeing the expectations which arise from a promise made in the course of a business. . . .

In addition to the above study this article has suggested that the work of the Law Commission in relation to the general principles of the law of contract may be explained in part as being the product of a particular ideology. The refinement of the general principles of contract has been the concern of lawyers steeped in classical contract theory. The working paper on firm offers rests on an assumption of classical theory that formally available legal opportunities will be exploited in practice. This article together with earlier empirical studies has suggested that in the particular areas investigated such an assumption is not warranted.

CHAPTER 10
Uncertainty and incompleteness

The parties may leave even fundamental obligations under a contract vague or 'to be agreed'. What is the legal effect?

Sale of Goods Act 1979

Section 8
(1) The price in a contract of sale may be fixed by the contract, or may be left to be fixed in a manner agreed by the contract, or may be determined by the course of dealing between the parties.
(2) Where the price is not determined as mentioned in subsection (1) above the buyer must pay a reasonable price.
(3) What is a reasonable price is a question of fact dependent on the circumstances of each particular case.

May & Butcher Ltd v R [1934] 2 KB 17n, House of Lords 1929

The plaintiffs (suppliants) alleged that the Controller of the Disposals Board had agreed to sell them tentage on terms contained in a letter, as follows:

(1) The Commission agrees to sell and [the suppliants] agree to purchase the total stock of old tentage . . .

. . .

(3) The price or prices to be paid, and the date or dates on which payment is to be made by the purchasers to the Commission for such old tentage shall be agreed upon from time to time between the Commission and the purchasers as the quantities of the said old tentage become available for disposal, and are offered to the purchasers by the Commission.

. . .

(10) It is understood that all disputes with reference to or arising out of this agreement will be submitted to arbitration in accordance with the provisions of the Arbitration Act 1889.

The Disposals Board contended that there was no binding contract, and the House of Lords upheld this view. Viscount Dunedin said:

To be a good contract there must be a concluded bargain, and a concluded contract is one which settles everything that is necessary to be settled and leaves nothing to be settled by agreement between the parties. Of course it may leave something which still has to be determined, but then that determination must be a determination which does not depend upon the agreement between the parties. . . . [T]he Sale of Goods Act, 1893, says that if the price is not mentioned and settled in the contract it is to be a reasonable price. The simple answer in this case is that the Sale of Goods Act provides for silence on the point and here there is no silence, because there is a provision that the two parties are to agree. . . . Here there was clearly no contract. There would have been a perfectly good settlement of price if the contract had said that it was to be settled by arbitration by a certain man, or it might have been quite good if it was said that it was to be settled by arbitration under the Arbitration Act so as to bring in a material plan by which a certain person could be put in action. The question then arises, has anything of that sort been done? I think clearly not. The general arbitration clause is one in very common form as to disputes arising out of the arrangements. In no proper meaning of the word can this be described as a dispute arising between the parties; it is a failure to agree, which is a very different thing from a dispute.

213

NOTES

1. Beale rings up Bishop and orders 100 widgets to be delivered in a month's time; they agree that 'we will fix the price when we meet next week.' Bishop, who is a distributor, rings up Furmston, a manufacturer of widgets, and places an order for 100 widgets for delivery in three weeks: Furmston accepts the order without any discussion about the price. If widgets are a standard item of commerce for which there is an established market, is there a contract between Bishop and Furmston? Is there one between Bishop and Beale before they have met again? If you think there is a contract in one case but not in the other, why do you think the courts treat the two situations differently? Does doing so accord with business reality? (See further below, p 221).

2. A comparison of s 8(2) and *May & Butcher v The King* suggests that there are two categories: terms left vague or unstated will not prevent the formation of a contract but there will be no contract if something is left 'to be agreed'. Is it quite so simple?

(a) Uncertainty

If the parties leave something uncertain, does it matter that in practice they would normally negotiate over it? How far can the courts go in filling in the gaps?

Hillas & Co Ltd v Arcos Ltd (1932) 147 LT 503, House of Lords

Arcos were business representatives of the Russian Government which in 1930 was very anxious to defeat the 'English ring' who were refusing to buy. Hillas, who had left the ring, were therefore given very favourable terms.

The timber was of various kinds, mainly redwood and whitewood, and was cut into many different lengths and scantlings. A price list was issued each year giving prices for wood of each type, length, etc. The wood was shipped at First Open Water (May in Leningrad, June in the White Sea) until the ice closed the ports again (in January and November respectively).

In the 1930 season Hillas agreed to buy 22,000 standards of 'fair specification' at agreed prices with certain agreed discounts. Clause 6 of the agreement provided: 'Buyers to arrange shipping dates and loading instructions according to the readiness of the goods purchased'. Clause 9 provided: 'Buyers shall also have the option of entering into a contract with sellers for the purchase of 100,000 standards for delivery in 1931. Such contract to stipulate that, whatever the conditions are, buyers shall obtain the goods on conditions and at prices which show to them a reduction of 5% on the f.o.b. value of the official price list at any time ruling during 1931. Such option to be declared before 1st January, 1931.'

Hillas purported to exercise this option on 22nd December, 1930, but Arcos had already sold their entire production to the British Isles. Hillas sued for damages for breach of contract.

During cross-examination Mr Hillas was asked how a specification for the actual parcel of timber would be arrived at. He replied that he would give the sellers a specification; they would never accept it in its entirety but would make a counter-proposal, and so on until a specification was arrived at.

The Court of Appeal held that there was no contract and Hillas appealed.

Lord Tomlin. . . . In the present case one or two preliminary observations fall to be made.

First, the parties were both intimately acquainted with the course of business in the Russian softwood timber trade and had without difficulty carried out the sale and purchase of 22,000 standards under the first part of the document of the 21st May 1930;

Secondly, although the question here is whether clause 9 of the document of the 21st May 1930, with the letter of the 22nd Dec. 1930, constitutes a contract, the validity of the whole of the document of the 21st May 1930 is really in question so far as the matter depends upon the meaning of the phrase 'of fair specification'; and

Thirdly, it is indisputable, having regard to clause 11, which provides that 'this agreement cancels all previous agreements,' that the parties intended by the document of the 21st May 1930 to make, and believed that they had made, some concluded bargain. . . . it is said that there is in clause 9 no sufficient description of the goods to be sold. . . . it is plain that something must necessarily be implied in clause 9. The words '100,000 standards' without more do not even indicate that timber is the subject-matter of the clause. The implication at the least of the words 'of softwood goods' is, in my opinion, inevitable, and if this is so I see no reason to separate the words 'of fair specification' from the words 'of softwood goods'. In my opinion there is a necessary implication of the words 'of softwood goods of fair specification' after the words '100,000 standards' in clause 9.

What then is the meaning of '100,000 standards of softwood goods of fair specification for delivery during 1931'?

If the words 'of fair specification' have no meaning which is certain or capable of being made certain, then not only can there be no contract under clause 9 but there cannot have been a contract with regard to the 22,000 standards mentioned at the beginning of the document of the 21st May 1930. This may be the proper conclusion; but before it is reached it is, I think, necessary to exclude as impossible all reasonable meanings which would give certainty to the words. In my opinion this cannot be done.

The parties undoubtedly attributed to the words in connection with the 22,000 standards, some meaning which was precise or capable of being made precise. Scrutton LJ laid stress upon the evidence of Mr Hillas as indicating a different view on the part of the parties. I am unable to think that upon a question of construction such evidence if directed to the intention of the parties was admissible at all. In fact, I think, Mr Hillas's evidence was misunderstood. It really amounted, in my opinion, to nothing more than a statement as to how the parties would in the first instance proceed, just as on a purchase of property at its fair value the parties would no doubt first endeavour to reach agreement as to the fair value.

Reading the document of the 21st May 1930 as a whole, and having regard to the admissible evidence as to the course of the trade, I think that upon their true construction the words 'of fair specification over the season, 1930', used in connection with the 22,000 standards, means that the 22,000 standards are to be satisfied in goods distributed over kinds, qualities, and sizes in the fair proportions having regard to the output of the season 1930, and the classifications of that output in respect of kinds, qualities, and sizes. That is something which if the parties fail to agree can be ascertained just as much as the fair value of a property.

I have already expressed the view that clause 9 must be read as '100,000 standards of fair specification for delivery during 1931' and these words, I think, have the same meaning, *mutatis mutandis*, as the words relating to the 22,000 standards. Thus, there is a description of the goods which if not immediately yet ultimately is capable of being rendered certain . . .

It was also urged as a minor point that there was no provision as to shipment and that this was an essential of such a contract.

. . .[U]pon the true construction of the document the sale conditions in relation to the 22,000 standards are so far as applicable imported into the option for the sale of the 100,000 standards, and in particular that clause 6 relating to shipping dates and loading instructions is so imported.

[Lords Warrington and Macmillan concurred with Lord Tomlin: Lords Thankerton and Wright delivered judgments to similar effect.]

Appeal allowed.

Scammell v Ouston [1941] 1 All ER 14, House of Lords

The parties agreed that the respondents should buy a new lorry from the appellants, trading in an old lorry and paying the balance of the agreed purchase price 'on hire-purchase terms' over two years. The precise terms of the hire-purchase agreement were not settled. The appellants subsequently refused to go ahead, alleging that there was no contract.

Viscount Maugham. . . . It is a regrettable fact that there are few, if any, topics on which there seems to be a greater difference of judicial opinion than those which relate to the question whether, as the result of informal letters or like documents, a binding contract has been arrived at. Many well-known instances are to be found in the books, the latest being that of *Hillas & Co, Ltd v Arcos, Ltd.* The reason for these different conclusions is that laymen unassisted by persons with a legal training are not always accustomed to use words or phrases with a precise or definite meaning. In order to constitute a valid contract, the parties must so express themselves that their meaning can be determined with a reasonable degree of certainty. It is plain that, unless this can be done, it would be impossible to hold that the contracting parties had the same intention. In other words the *consensus ad idem* would be a matter of mere conjecture. This general rule, however, applies somewhat differently in different cases. In commercial documents connected with dealings in a trade with which the parties are perfectly familiar, the court is very willing, if satisfied that the parties thought that they made a binding contract, to imply terms, and, in particular, terms as to the method of carrying out the contract, which it would be impossible to supply in other kinds of contract: *Hillas & Co, Ltd v Arcos, Ltd.* . . .

We come, then, to the question as to the effect of the so-called purchase being on 'hire-purchase terms', and here we are confronted with a strange and confusing circumstance. The term 'hire-purchase' for a good many years past has been understood to mean a contract of hire by the owner of a chattel conferring on the hirer an option to purchase on the performance of certain conditions: *Helby v Matthews.* There is in these contracts—and this is, from a business standpoint, a most important matter—no agreement to buy within the Factors Act, 1889, or the Sale of Goods Act, 1893. There is only an option, and the hirer can confer on a purchaser from him no better title than he himself has, except in the case of sale in market overt. It is inaccurate and misleading to add to an order for goods, as if given by a purchaser, a clause that hire-purchase terms are to apply, without something to explain the apparent contradiction. Moreover, a hire-purchase agreement may assume many forms, and some of the variations in those forms are of the most important character—eg those which relate to termination of the agreement, warranty of fitness, duties as to repair, interest, and so forth.

Bearing these facts in mind, what do the words 'hire-purchase terms' mean in the present case? They may indicate that the hire-purchase agreement was to be granted by the appellants, or, on the other hand, by some finance company acting in collaboration with the appellants. They may contemplate that the appellants were to receive by instalments a sum of £168 spread over a period of 2 years upon delivering the new van and receiving the old car, or, on the other hand, that the appellants were to receive from a third party a lump sum of £168, and that the third party, presumably a finance company, was to receive from the respondents a larger sum than £168, to include interest and profit spread over a period of 2 years. Moreover, nothing is said (except as to the 2-years' period) as to the terms of the hire-purchase agreement—for instance, as to the interest payable, and as to the rights of the letter, whoever he may be, in the event of default by the respondents in payment of the instalments at the due dates. As regards the last matters, there was no evidence to suggest that there are any well-known 'usual terms' in such a contract, and I think that it is common knowledge that in fact many letters, though by no means all of them, insist on terms which the legislature regards as so unfair and unconscionable that it was recently found necessary to deal with the matter in the Hire-Purchase Act, 1938. These, my Lords, are very serious difficulties, and, when we find, as we do, in this curious case, that the trial judge and the three Lords Justices, and even the two counsel who addressed your Lordships for the respondents, were unable to agree upon the true construction of the alleged agreement, it seems to me that it is impossible to conclude that a binding agreement has been established by the respondents.

[Viscount Simon LC and Lords Wright and Russell of Killowen made speeches to the same effect.]

Appeal allowed.

NOTES

1. It is possible that since this case was decided, hire-purchase contracts have become more standardized, and that if it were clear that the supplier

was going to grant the hire-purchase agreement in its own name, the case might be decided the other way: there is, however, no certainty about this!

2. In *Bushwall Properties Ltd v Vortex Properties Ltd* [1976] 1 WLR 591 an agreement for the sale of land by instalments provided for 'a proportionate part' of the land to be conveyed as each instalment was paid. The Court of Appeal rejected suggestions that one party should be allowed to select which parts should be conveyed each time and held the agreement void for uncertainty.

Nicolene Ltd v Simmonds [1953] 1 All ER 822, Court of Appeal

Denning LJ. This case raises a short, but important, point which can be stated quite simply. There was a contract for the sale of three thousand tons of steel reinforcing bars; the seller broke his contract, and when the buyer claimed damages the seller set up the defence that, owing to a sentence in one of the letters which were alleged to constitute the contract, there was no contract at all. The material words are: 'We are in agreement that the usual conditions of acceptance apply'. There were no usual conditions of acceptance and so it is said that those words are meaningless, that there is nothing to which they can apply, and that, therefore, there was never any contract between the parties.

In my opinion, a distinction must be drawn between a clause which is meaningless and a clause which is yet to be agreed. A clause which is meaningless can often be ignored, while still leaving the contract good, whereas a clause which has yet to be agreed may mean that there is no contract at all, because the parties have not agreed on all the essential terms. I take it to be clear law that, if one of the parties to a contract inserts into it an exempting condition in his own favour which the other side agrees and it afterwards appears that that condition is meaningless or is so ambiguous that no ascertainable meaning can be given to it, that does not render the whole contract a nullity. The only result is that the exempting condition is a nullity and must be rejected. It would be strange, indeed, if a party could escape every one of his obligations by inserting a meaningless exemption from some of them.

. . . The sentence is meaningless and must be ignored, but the contract, nevertheless, remains good. I agree that the appeal should be dismissed.

[Singleton and Hodson LJJ delivered judgments to the same effect.]

(b) Incompleteness

Sale of Goods Act 1979

Section 9

(1) Where there is an agreement to sell goods on the terms that the price is to be fixed by the valuation of a third party, and he cannot or does not make the valuation, the agreement is avoided; but if the goods or any part of them have been delivered to and appropriated by the buyer he must pay a reasonable price for them.

(2) Where the third party is prevented from making the valuation by the fault of the seller or buyer, the party not at fault may maintain an action for damages against the party at fault.

Courtney and Fairbairn Ltd v Tolaini Brothers (Hotels) Ltd [1975] 1 All ER 716, Court of Appeal

Lord Denning MR. The question in this case is whether two letters give rise to a concluded contract.

Mr Tolaini wanted to develop a site in Hertfordshire. It was The Thatched Barn Hotel together with five acres of land. He got in touch with a property developer, a Mr Courtney. It appears that Mr Courtney was well placed to obtain finance for building development. He was also a building contractor himself. The two met and discussed ways and means at the office of Mr Sacks, an architect. The proposal was that Mr Courtney should introduce someone to provide the money and lend it to Mr Tolaini. Mr Tolaini was to develop the site by building a motel and other things. But he was to employ Mr Courtney or his company to do the construction work. After the meeting, on 10th April 1969, Mr Courtney wrote to Mr Tolaini this letter:

. . . I would be very happy to know that, if my discussions and arrangements with interested parties lead to an introductory meeting, which in turn leads to a financial arrangement acceptable to both parties you will be prepared to instruct your Quantity Surveyor to negotiate fair and reasonable contract sums in respect of each of the three projects as they arise. (These would, incidentally be based upon agreed estimates of the net cost of work and general overheads with a margin for profit of 5%) which, I am sure you will agree, is indeed reasonable.'

. . . Mr Tolaini [replied] on 28th April 1969, in the terms:

'In reply to your letter of the 10th April, I agree to the terms specified therein, and I look forward to meeting the interested party regarding finance.'

Those are the two letters on which the issue depends. But I will tell the subsequent events quite shortly. Mr Courtney did his best. He found a person interested who provided finance of £200,000 or more for the projects. Mr Tolaini on his side appointed his quantity surveyor with a view to negotiating with Mr Courtney the price for the construction work. But there were differences of opinion about the price. And nothing was agreed. In the end Mr Tolaini did not employ Mr Courtney or his company to do the construction work. Mr Tolaini instructed other contractors and they completed the motel and other works. But then Mr Tolaini took advantage of the finance which Mr Courtney had made possible, but he did not employ Mr Courtney's company to do the work. Naturally enough, Mr Courtney was very upset. He has brought this action in which he says that there was a contract by which his company were to be employed as builders for the work, and it was a breach of contract by Mr Tolaini or his company to go elsewhere and employ somebody else. Mr Courtney's company claimed the loss of profits which they would have made if they had been employed as builders for this motel. . . .

I am afraid that I have come to a different view from the judge. The reason is because I can find no agreement on the price or on any method by which the price was to be calculated. The agreement was only an agreement to 'negotiate' fair and reasonable contract sums. The words of the letter are 'your Quantity Surveyor to *negotiate* fair and reasonable contract sums in respect of each of the three projects as they arise.' Then there are words which show that estimates had not yet been agreed, but were yet to be agreed. The words are: 'These [the contract sums] would, incidentally be based upon agreed estimates of the net cost of work and general overheads with a margin for profit of 5%.' Those words show that there were no estimates agreed and no contract sums agreed. All was left to be agreed in the future. It was to be agreed between the parties themselves. If they had left the price to be agreed by a third person such as an arbitrator, it would have been different. But here it was to be agreed between the parties themselves.

Now the price in a building contract is of fundamental importance. It is so essential a term that there is no contract unless the price is agreed or there is an agreed method of ascertaining it, not dependent on the negotiations of the two parties themselves. In a building contract both parties must know at the outset, before the work is started, what the price is to be, or, at all events, what agreed estimates are. No builder and no employer would ever dream of entering into a building contract for over £200,000 without there being an estimate of the cost and an agreed means of ascertaining the price.

In the ordinary course of things the architects and the quantity surveyors get out the specification and the bills of quantities. They are submitted to the contractors. They work out the figures and tender for the work at a named price; and there is a specified means of altering it up or down for extras or omissions and so forth, usually by means of an architect's certificate. In the absence of some such machinery, the only contract which you might find is a contract to do the work for a reasonable sum or for a sum to be fixed by a third party. But here there is no such contract at all. There is no machinery for ascertaining the price except by negotiation. In other words, the price is still to be agreed. Seeing that there is no agreement on so fundamental a matter as the price, there is no contract.

But then this point was raised. Even if there was not a contract actually to build, was not there a contract to negotiate? In this case Mr Toliani did instruct his quantity surveyor to negotiate, but the negotiations broke down. It may be suggested that the quantity surveyor was to blame for the failure of the negotiations. But does that give rise to a cause of action? There is very little guidance in the book about a contract to negotiate. It was touched on by Lord Wright in *Hillas & Co Ltd v Arcos Ltd* where he said: 'There is then no bargain except to negotiate, and negotiations may be fruitless and end without any contract ensuing.' Then he went on:

'. . . yet even then, in strict theory, there is a contract (if there is good consideration) to negotiate, though in the event of repudiation by one party the damages may be nominal, unless a jury think that the opportunity to negotiate was of some appreciable value to the injured party.'

That tentative opinion by Lord Wright does not seem to me to be well founded. If the law does not recognise a contract to enter a contract (when there is a fundamental term yet to be agreed) it seems to me it cannot recognise a contract to negotiate. The reason is because it is too uncertain to have any binding force. No court could estimate the damages because no one can tell whether the negotiations would be successful or would fall through; or if successful, what the result would be. It seems to me that a contract to negotiate, like a contract to enter into a contract, is not a contract known to the law. We were referred to the recent decision of Brightman J about an option, *Mountford v Scott*, but that does not seem to me to touch this point. I think we must apply the general principle that when there is a fundamental matter left undecided and to be the subject of negotiation, there is no contract. So I would hold that there was not any enforceable agreement in the letters between the plaintiff and the defendants. I would allow the appeal accordingly.

Lord Diplock: I agree and would only add my agreement that the dictum—for it is no more—of Lord Wright in *Hillas & Co Ltd v Arcos Ltd* to which Lord Denning MR has referred, though an attractive theory, should in my view be regarded as bad law.

Lawton LJ: I agree with both the judgments which have been delivered.

Appeal allowed. Action dismissed.

NOTE

Is there some method by which Courtney could have ensured that Tolaini was committed to him? You may like to return to this question when you have read the rest of the cases in the chapter.

British Bank for Foreign Trade Ltd v Novinex Ltd [1949] 1 All ER 155, Court of Appeal

The plaintiffs had arranged for P to supply a consignment of oilskins to the defendants, who had not had any previous contact with P, and the defendants wrote confirming that they had agreed to pay the plaintiffs a commission for this. The letter continued:

We also undertake to cover you with an agreed commission on any other business transacted with your friends [P]. In return for this, you are to put us in direct touch with your friends.

The plaintiffs put the defendants in direct contact with P, and the defendants entered into further transactions with P, but they refused to pay the plaintiffs any commission on them. The plaintiffs' action was dismissed by Denning J, and they appealed.

Cohen LJ. . . . . Is this an enforceable agreement? A number of authorities have been cited to us, to which I do not propose to refer in detail, because, in my view, the effect of the authorities is stated correctly in the learned judge's judgment where he said:

'The principle to be deduced from the cases is that, if there is an essential term which has yet to be agreed and there is no express or implied provision for its solution, the result in point of law is that there is no binding contract. In seeing whether there is an implied provision for its solution, however, there is a difference between an arrangement which is wholly executory on both sides, and one which has been executed on one side or the other. In the ordinary way, if there is an arrangement to supply goods at a price "to be agreed", or to perform services on terms "to be agreed", then, although, while the matter is still executory there may be no binding contract, nevertheless, if it is executed on one side, that is, if the one does his part without having come to an agreement as to the price or the terms, then the law will say that there is necessarily implied from the conduct of the parties a contract that, in default of agreement, a reasonable sum is to be paid.'

With that statement of the principle of law I respectfully agree. My difference with the learned judge is only on the question whether he has correctly applied that statement of principle to the facts of this case. . . . Denning J goes on to say that this shows that the agreement is too vague, but this argument involves the proposition that the agreement had not said in terms: 'We also undertake to cover you with a reasonable commission on any other business transacted with your friends.' Denning J regarded that condition as being too vague to be enforceable. I cannot agree with his view. I think that the court should take the view that a jury properly directed would be able to arrive at a proper conclusion as to what in the circumstances of this case is a reasonable commission.

[His Lordship then considered what would be a reasonable commission in respect of the transactions and concluded that it would not exceed ¼d per skin.]

[Bucknill and Singleton LJJ agreed.]

NOTE

Suppose Bishop agrees to sell Beale 200 widgets 'at a price to be agreed', delivery to be in two instalments. Bishop delivers and Beale accepts the first instalment without there being any further negotiation on the price. How much does Beale have to pay for the first instalment? Is there a binding contract for the second instalment?

Foley v Classique Coaches Ltd [1934] 2 KB 1, Court of Appeal

The defendants agreed to buy from the plaintiff a piece of land adjoining the plaintiff's garage. The defendants intended to use the land for their motor coach business, and the sale was made subject to the defendants entering a second agreement, which was executed on the same day, to purchase all the petrol they required for their business from the plaintiff 'at a price to be agreed by the parties in writing and from time to time'. Clause 8 provided that 'If any dispute or difference shall arise on the subject matter or construction of this agreement the same shall be submitted to arbitration . . .'. For three years after the conveyance of the land the defendants obtained all their petrol from the plaintiff, but a dispute arose and they repudiated the second agreement, alleging that it was not binding (i) because no written agreement on the price of petrol had been made and (ii) because the obligation to take all the petrol they required from the plaintiff was in unreasonable restraint of trade. The Court of Appeal held that there was a binding agreement and that it was not an unreasonable restraint of trade. On the first point Scrutton LJ said:

In the present case the parties obviously believed they had a contract and they acted for three years as if they had; they had an arbitration clause which relates to the subject-matter of the agreement as to the supply of petrol, and it seems to me that this arbitration clause applies to any failure to agree as to the price. By analogy to the case of a tied house there is to be implied in this contract a term that the petrol shall be supplied at a reasonable price and shall be of reasonable quality. For these reasons I think the Lord Chief Justice was right in holding that there was an effective and enforceable contract, although as to the future no definite price had been agreed with regard to the petrol.

NOTES

1. The price of a standard commodity like petrol is easy to fix once it has been determined that the parties originally intended, or in the light of their performance must be taken to intend, that the price shall be a reasonable one. What about other obligations? In *F & G Sykes (Wessex) Ltd v Fine Fare Ltd* [1967] 1 Lloyd's Rep 53 the plaintiffs had agreed with the defendants that the plaintiffs would produce large numbers of day-old chicks, which would then be sold to growers to be reared to a size fit for eating. The growers would then supply the birds to the defendants, who planned to build a new plant to process them. The agreement was to last five years or more. The defendants were to give at least 26 weeks' notice of the number of fowls they would require in each week, and it was agreed that the number would be not less than 30,000 and not more than 80,000 per week for the first year, 'and thereafter such other figures as may be agreed between the parties hereto . . .'. The defendants then discovered that there were problems over water supplies to the proposed site of their new plant, and, after the agreement had run for over a year, they cancelled the arrangements. In an action for damages by the plaintiffs, the Court of Appeal held that the contract was still binding: given that the parties clearly intended a five-year agreement and had commenced implementing it, the court should strive to uphold it. Lord Denning MR pointed out that, in default of agreement, the number of chicks should be treated as a reasonable one which could be ascertained under the arbitration clause. Danckwerts and Winn LJJ agreed with this approach, pointing out that the reasonable maximum and minimum figures would be the maximum throughput of the factories and the minimum throughput for efficient operation respectively. What if the defendants had shown that the numbers of chicks for the first year were not related to those criteria, but were, for instance, a much narrower band? How would an arbitrator go about determining a reasonable figure for chicks?

2. If a dispute about the price of petrol or the number of chicks to be supplied could go to arbitration, why couldn't a dispute as to the price of tentage in *May & Butcher*'s case?

3. A price 'to be agreed', with no mechanism for valuation or arbitration, can be treated as an agreement to pay a reasonable price when it forms just a subsidiary part of an agreement that has been partially performed. Why cannot the same be done when it is a major element, but the court thinks the parties nonetheless intended to be bound? In other words, should phrases such as 'price to be negotiated' always be taken literally? In *Hillas v Arcos* Scrutton LJ in the Court of Appeal said of the case of *May & Butcher v The King:*

> I took the view, for the reasons stated in my judgment, that there was a contract; that if no price was agreed, the price under sect. 8 of the Sale of Goods Act 1893 would be a reasonable price, or there would be a dispute arising out of the agreement, which should be settled under the arbitration clause. My brothers Sargant LJ and Eve J took Lord Parker's view that there could not be a contract to make a contract, and that in spite of the language of absolute sale used in the document, there was no enforceable contract. The three members of the House of Lords who heard the appeal thought there was no need to call on the respondents. They said that the price should be agreed and was not agreed, and when the arbitration clause spoke of disputes arising out of the contract, its framers forgot that there was no contract. I refer to the judgment for its terms. I am afraid I remain quite impenitent. I think I was right and that nine out of ten business men would agree with me. But of course I recognise that I am bound as a judge to follow the principles laid down by the House of Lords. But I regret that in many commercial matters the English law and the practice of commercial men are getting wider apart, with the result that commercial business is leaving the courts and is being decided by commercial arbitrators with infrequent reference to the courts.

Sudbrook Trading Estate Ltd v Eggleton [1982] 3 All ER 1, House of Lords

Lord Fraser of Tullybelton. My Lords, the appellants (the lessees) are the tenants in four leases, by each of which they were granted an option to purchase the freehold reversion of the leased premises at a valuation. The lessees have exercised the options, but the respondents (the lessors), who are the landlords, contend that the options are unenforceable. The questions now to be determined, therefore, are whether the options are valid and enforceable, and, if so, how they should be enforced.

The leases relate to adjacent industrial premises in Gloucester. . . . The clause in the [earliest] lease, cl 11, has been taken as typical of them all. It entitled the lessees to purchase the reversion in fee simple, on certain conditions which were all satisfied—

> 'at such price not being less than Seventy five thousand pounds as may be agreed upon by two valuers one to be nominated by the Lessor and the other by the Lessee or in default of such agreement by an Umpire appointed by the said Valuers . . .'

The lessors contend that the options are void for uncertainty on the ground that they contain no formula by which the price can be fixed in the event of no agreement being reached, and that they are no more than agreements to agree. The lessors have therefore declined to appoint their valuer. The machinery provided in the leases has accordingly become inoperable.

In these proceedings the lessees seek a declaration that the options are valid, that they have been validly and effectively exercised, and that the contents constituted by the exercise ought to be specifically performed. As regards the mode of performance, the main argument for the lessees is that the court should order such inquiries as are necessary to ascertain the value of each of the properties. Lawson J decided the question of principle in favour of the lessees, but his decision was reversed by the Court of Appeal which held that the options were unenforceable. Templeman LJ, who delivered the judgment of the Court of Appeal, made a full review of the English authorities and the conclusion which he drew from them was, in my opinion inevitably, adverse to the lessees' contentions. The fundamental proposition on which he relied was, in his own words—

> 'that where the agreement on the face of it is incomplete until something else has been done, whether by further agreement between the parties or by the decision of an arbitrator or valuer, the court is powerless, because there is no complete agreement to enforce . . .'

I agree that that is the effect of the earlier decisions but, with the greatest respect, I am of opinion that it is wrong. It appears to me that, on the exercise of the option, the necessary preconditions having been satisfied, as they were in this case, a complete contract of sale and purchase of the freehold reversion was constituted. The price, which was of course an essential term of the contract, was, for reasons which I shall explain, capable of being ascertained and was therefore certain. Certum est quod certum reddi potest: see *May & Butcher Ltd v The King*, per Viscount Dunedin.

The courts have applied clauses such as those in the present case in a strictly literal way and have treated them as making the completion of a contract of sale conditional on agreement between the valuers either on the value of the property or, failing that, on the choice of an umpire. They have further laid down the principle that where parties have agreed on a particular method of ascertaining the price, and that method has for any reason proved ineffective, the court will neither grant an order for specific performance to compel parties to operate the agreed machinery nor substitute its own machinery to ascertain the price, because either of these clauses would be to impose on parties an agreement that they had not made. . . .

While that is the general principle it is equally well established that, where parties have agreed to sell 'at a fair valuation' or 'at a reasonable price' or according to some similar formula, without specifying any machinery for ascertaining the price, the position is different. . . .

I recognise the logic of the reasoning which has led to the courts refusing to substitute their own machinery for the machinery which has been agreed on by the parties. But the result to which it leads is so remote from that which parties normally intend and expect, and is so inconvenient in practice, that there must in my opinion be some defect in the reasoning. I think the defect lies in construing the provisions for the mode of ascertaining the value as an essential part of the agreement. That may have been perfectly true early in the nineteenth century, when the valuer's profession and the rules of valuation were less well established than they are now. But at the present day these provisions are only subsidiary to the main purpose of the agreement, which is for sale and purchase of the property at a fair or reasonable value. In the ordinary case parties do not make any substantial distinction between an agreement to sell at a fair value, without specifying the mode of ascertaining the value, and an agreement to sell at a value to be ascertained by valuers appointed in the way provided in these leases. The true distinction is between those cases where the mode of ascertaining the price is an essential term of the contract and those cases where the mode of ascertainment, though indicated in the contract, is subsidiary and non-essential. . . . The present case falls, in my opinion, into the latter category. Accordingly, when the option was exercised, there was constituted a complete contract for sale, and the clause should be construed as meaning that the price was to be a fair price. On the other hand, where an agreement is made to sell at a price to be fixed by a valuer who is named, or who, by reason of holding some office such as auditor of a company whose shares are to be valued, will have special knowledge relevant to the question of value, the prescribed mode may well be regarded as essential. Where, as here, the machinery consists of valuers and an umpire, none of whom is named or identified, it is in my opinion unrealistic to regard it as an essential term. If it breaks down there is no reason why the court should not substitute other machinery to carry out the main purpose of ascertaining the price in order that the agreement may be carried out.

[Lords Diplock, Scarman and Bridge delivered concurring judgments.]

Lord Russell of Killowen [dissenting]: My Lords, it appears to be generally accepted that the law as previously understood since at least the early nineteenth century is in favour of the respondents (the lessors) and of the decision of the Court of Appeal. It is proposed by the majority of your Lordships to assert that that previous understanding was erroneous. I cannot agree.

Basically the assumption is made that the parties intended that the exercise of the option should involve payment of a 'fair price' or a 'fair value'. Of course parties to such a contract could in terms so agree, and I am not concerned to deny that in such a case a court could enforce the contract by ascertainment of a fair price or fair value, treating specific provisions in the contract for methods (which proved to be unworkable) of ascertaining that fair price or valuation as being inessential. But that is not this case. Why should it be thought that potential vendor and purchaser intended the price to be 'fair'? The former would intend the price to be high, even though 'unfairly' so. And the latter vice versa. Vendors and purchasers are normally greedy. . . .

Appeal allowed.

NOTES

1. The option to purchase the freehold in this case was, of course, part of a contract which had been partly performed: but not a lot of stress seems to have been laid on this.
2. The House of Lords relied on the fact that the price of the reversion was to be fixed by *valuers* as indicating that a fair or reasonable price was to be paid. Arbitrators, on the other hand, are supposed to decide cases in the same way as judges. Was Scrutton correct to lay stress on the arbitration clause in *Foley v Classique Coaches*? Would the case have to be decided the other way if there were no arbitration clause? What about *F & G Sykes (Wessex) Ltd v Fine Fare Ltd*?

You may like to compare English law to the Uniform Commercial Code:

§2–204. Formation in general
(3) Even though one or more terms are left open a contract for sale does not fail for indefiniteness if the parties have intended to make a contract and there is a reasonably certain basis for giving an appropriate remedy.

§2–305. Open price term
(1) The parties if they so intend can conclude a contract for sale even though the price is not settled. In such a case the price is a reasonable price at the time for delivery if
    (a) nothing is said as to price; or
    (b) the price is left to be agreed by the parties and they fail to agree; or
    (c) the price is to be fixed in terms of some agreed market or other standard as set or recorded by a third person or agency and it is not so set or recorded.
(2) A price to be fixed by the seller or by the buyer means a price for him to fix in good faith.
(3) When a price left to be fixed otherwise than by agreement of the parties fails to be fixed

through fault of one party the other may at his option treat the contract as cancelled or himself fix a reasonable price.

(4) Where, however, the parties intend not to be bound unless the price be fixed or agreed and it is not fixed or agreed there is no contract. In such a case the buyer must return any goods already received or if unable so to do must pay their reasonable value at the time of delivery and the seller must return any portion of the price paid on account.

NOTE

Do you think these provisions are an improvement on English law? Or do you think the test of whether the parties 'intended' there to be a contract causes more problems than it solves? What sort of evidence do you think a court might appropriately consider when trying to decide what the parties intended? Should it, for instance, consider evidence as to whether the seller had instructed its delivery department to package some goods and label them for the buyer? Whether the buyer had filed away the seller's acknowledgment form in its 'completed contracts' file? Compare *Brogden v Metropolitan Rly Co* (above, p 180), and see the note on adjudication and error costs in the Introduction (above, pp 75–76).

(c) Work done and steps taken before a contract has been agreed

It is quite common for the parties to start work before the contract has been fully negotiated or signed. When the contract is ultimately signed, it will (unless otherwise agreed) 'relate back' so as to apply to what has been done: *Trollope & Colls Ltd v Atomic Power Constructions Ltd* [1962] 3 All ER 1035. What if agreement is never reached?

British Steel Corpn v Cleveland Bridge and Engineering Co Ltd [1984] 1 All ER 504, Robert Goff J

The plaintiffs (BSC) were approached by the defendants (CBE) to supply a number of steel nodes to be used in the construction of a steel framed building which CBE were building under another contract. There were extensive discussions as to the specification and the terms on which the nodes were to be supplied, and while the discussion over terms was still continuing, CBE issued a letter of intent requesting BSC to start work, 'pending the preparation and issuing to you of the official form of sub-contract'. By 28 December all but one of the nodes had been delivered but the parties were still negotiating over the terms, including the question of liability for loss caused by late delivery. As they had not been paid for any of the nodes delivered so far, BSC withheld delivery of the last node; there was then a steel strike, and the node could not be delivered until 11 April. BSC, claiming that no contract had been made, brought an action for the reasonable value of the nodes, and CBE counterclaimed for damages of a higher amount for late delivery.

Robert Goff J. . . . I now turn to the first issue in the case, which is concerned with the legal basis for BSC's claim for payment, and in particular whether there was any binding contract between BSC and CBE and, if so, what were its terms. As I have already indicated, it is the contention of CBE that there was such a contract; whereas BSC contends that they are entitled to payment in quasi contract. . . .

Now the question whether in a case such as the present any contract has come into existence must depend on a true construction of the relevant communications which have passed between the parties and the effect (if any) of their actions pursuant to those communications. There can be no hard and fast answer to the question whether a letter of intent will give rise to a binding agreement: everything must depend on the circumstances of the particular case. In most cases, where work is done pursuant to a request contained in a letter of intent, it will not matter whether a contract did or did not come into existence, because, if the party who has acted on the request is simply claiming payment, his claim will usually be based on a quantum meruit, and it will make no difference whether that claim is contractual or quasi-contractual. Of course, a quantum meruit claim (like the old actions for money had and received and for money paid) straddles the boundaries of what we now call contract and restitution, so the mere framing of a claim as a quantum meruit claim, or a claim for a reasonable sum, does not assist in classifying the claim as contractual or quasi contractual. But where, as here, one party is seeking to claim damages for breach of contract, the question whether any contract came into existence is of crucial importance.

As a matter of analysis the contract (if any) which may come into existence following a letter of intent may take one of two forms: either there may be an ordinary executory contract, under which each party assumes reciprocal obligations to the other; or there may be what is sometimes called an 'if' contract, ie a contract under which A requests B to carry out a certain performance and promises B that, if he does so, he will receive a certain performance in return, usually remuneration for his performance. The latter transaction is really no more than a standing offer which, if acted on before it lapses or is lawfully withdrawn, will result in a binding contract.

The former type of contract was held to exist by Mr Edgar Fay QC, the official Referee, in *Turriff Construction Ltd v Regalia Knitting Mills Ltd*, and it is the type of contract for which counsel for CBE contended in the present case. Of course, as I have already said, everything must depend on the facts of the particular case; but certainly, on the facts of the present case (and, as I imagine, on the facts of most cases), this must be a very difficult submission to maintain. It is only necessary to look at the terms of CBE's letter of intent in the present case to appreciate the difficulties. In that letter, the request to BSC to proceed immediately with the work was stated to be 'pending the preparation and issuing to you of the official form of sub-contract', being a sub-contract which was plainly in a state of negotiation, not least on the issues of price, delivery dates, and the applicable terms and conditions. In these circumstances, it is very difficult to see how BSC, by starting work, bound themselves to any contractual performance. No doubt it was envisaged by CBE at the time they sent the letter that negotiations had reached an advanced stage, and that a formal contract would soon be signed; but, since the parties were still in a stage of negotiation, it is impossible to say with any degree of certainty what the material terms of that contract would be. I find myself quite unable to conclude that, by starting work in these circumstances, BSC bound themselves to complete the work. In the course of argument, I put to counsel for CBE the question whether BSC were free at any time, after starting work, to cease work. His submission was that they were not free to do so, even if negotiations on the terms of the formal contract broke down completely. I find this submission to be so repugnant to common sense and the commercial realities that I am unable to accept it. It is perhaps revealing that, on 4 April 1979, BSC did indeed state that they were not prepared to proceed with the contract until they had an agreed specification, a reaction which, in my judgment, reflected not only the commercial, but also the legal, realities of the situation.

I therefore, reject CBE's submission that a binding executory contract came into existence in this case. There remains the question whether, by reason of BSC carrying out work pursuant to the request contained in CBE's letter of intent, there came into existence a contract by virtue of which BSC were entitled to claim reasonable remuneration; ie whether there was an 'if' contract of the kind I have described. In the course of argument, I was attracted by this alternative (really on the basis that, not only was it analytically possible, but also that it could provide a vehicle for certain contractual obligations of BSC concerning their performance, eg implied terms as to the quality of goods supplied by them). But the more I have considered the case, the less attractive I have found this alternative. The real difficulty is to be found in the factual matrix of the transaction, and in particular the fact that the work was being done *pending* a formal sub-contract the terms of which were still in a state of negotiation. It is, of course, a notorious fact that, when a contract is made for the supply of goods on a scale and in circumstances such as the present, it will in all probability be subject to standard terms, usually the standard terms of the supplier. Such standard terms will frequently legislate, not only for the liability of the seller for defects, but also for the damages (if any) for which the seller will be liable in the event not only of defects in the goods but also of late delivery. It is a commonplace that a seller of goods may exclude liability for consequential loss, and may agree liquidated damages for delay. In the present case, an unresolved dispute broke out between the parties on the question whether CBE's or BSC's standard terms were to apply, the former providing no limit to the seller's liability for delay and the latter excluding such liability altogether. Accordingly, when, in a case such as the present, the parties are still in a state of negotiation, it is impossible to predicate what liability (if any) will be assumed by the seller for, eg defective goods or late delivery, if a formal contract should be entered into. In these circumstances, if the buyer asks the seller to commence work 'pending' the parties entering into a formal contract, it is difficult to infer from the buyer acting on that request that he is assuming any responsibility for his performance, except such responsibility as will rest on him under the terms of the contract which both parties confidently anticipate they will shortly enter into. It would be an extraordinary result if, by acting on such a request in such circumstances, the buyer were to assume an unlimited liability for his contractual performance, when he would never assume such liability under any contract which he entered into.

For these reasons, I reject the solution of the 'if' contract. In my judgment, the true analysis of the situation is simply this. Both parties confidently expected a formal contract to eventuate. In these circumstances, to expedite performance under that anticipated contract, one requested the other to commence the contract work, and the other complied with that request. If thereafter, as anticipated, a contract was entered into, the work done as requested will be treated as having been performed under that contract; if, contrary to their expectation, no contract was entered into, then the performance of the work is not referable to any contract the terms of which can be ascertained, and the law simply imposes an obligation on the party who made the request, such an obligation sounding in quasi contract or, as we now say, in restitution. Consistently with that solution, the party making the request may find himself liable to pay for work which he would not have had to pay for as such if the anticipated contract had come into existence, eg preparatory work which will, if the contract is made, be allowed for in the price of the finished work (cf *William Lacey (Hounslow) Ltd v Davis*). This solution moreover accords with authority: see the decision in *Lacey v Davis*, the decision of the Court of Appeal in *Sanders & Forster Ltd v A Monk & Co Ltd*, though that decision rested in part on a concession, and the crisp dictum of Parker J in *OTM Ltd v Hydranautics*, when he said of a letter of intent that 'its only effect would be to enable the defendants to recover on a quantum meruit for work done pursuant to the direction' contained in the letter. I only wish to add to this part of my judgment the footnote that, even if I had concluded that in the circumstances of the present case there was a contract between the parties and that that contract was of the kind I have described as an 'if' contract, then I would still have concluded that there was no obligation under that contract on the part of BSC to continue with or complete the contract work, and therefore no obligation on their part to complete the work within a reasonable time. However, my conclusion in the present case is that the parties never entered into any contract at all.

Judgment for the plaintiffs.

NOTES

1. As Robert Goff points out, a *quantum meruit* claim may be a restitutionary claim or a contractual claim. A plaintiff who claims in restitution for the value of services rendered to the defendant when there was no contract between them (eg p 28 above) will bring a *quantum meruit* claim; but where there is a contract to pay a reasonable sum, the sum payable is often also referred to as a *quantum meruit*.

2. There may still be liability on a *quantum meruit* even if the work done at the defendant's request is ultimately of no use to him, such as the preparation of detailed estimates, as required by the licensing authority of the cost of converting a building which ultimately the defendant sells without converting: *William Lacey (Hounslow) Ltd v Davis* [1957] 2 All ER 712.

3. A full survey of the cases may be found in Jones, 'Claims Arising out of Anticipated Contracts which do not Materialise' (1980) 18 Univ of W Ontario LR 447.

4. Suppose one of the steel nodes supplied had failed because of a defect in manufacture not due to negligence on BSC's part. Would a 'contractual' rather than a 'restitutionary' analysis then seem more appropriate?

What if one party, to the knowledge of the other and perhaps encouraged by him, takes some steps other than beginning to perform in anticipation of a contract which never materializes? Should he have some remedy, or should he be regarded as having proceeded at his own risk? If there should sometimes be a remedy, under what circumstances should it be available and what form should it take? A problem of this type arose in *Hoffman v Red Owl Stores Inc* 26 Wis 2d 683, 133 NW 2d 267 (1965). Hoffman wanted to obtain a franchise to operate a Red Owl store, and the Red Owl agent encouraged him to take several steps in preparation, such as selling his existing business, moving house and buying a site for the new store. The franchise never materialized. The jury found that Red Owl had represented to Hoffman that if he fulfilled certain conditions he would get a franchise, and that he had fulfilled these conditions when the negotiations broke down because Red Owl unexpectedly increased the amount of capital that Hoffman was required to put into the store to be the subject of the franchise. Hoffman was awarded his reliance loss. Currie CJ said:

There remains for consideration the question of law raised by defendants that agreement was never reached on essential factors necessary to establish a contract between Hoffman and Red Owl. Among these were the size, cost, design, and layout of the store building; and the terms of the lease with respect to rent, maintenance, renewal, and purchase options. This poses the question of whether the promise necessary to sustain a cause of action for promissory estoppel must embrace all essential details of a proposed transaction between promisor and promisee so as to be the equivalent of an offer that would result in a binding contract between the parties if the promisee were to accept the same.

Originally the doctrine of promissory estoppel was invoked as a substitute for consideration rendering a gratuitous promise enforceable as a contract. See Williston, Contracts (1st ed) p 307, sec 139. In other words, the acts of reliance by the promisee to his detriment provided a substitute for consideration. If promissory estoppel were to be limited to only those situations where the promise giving rise to the cause of action must be so definite with respect to all details that a contract would result were the promise supported by consideration, then the defendants' instant promises to Hoffman would not meet this test. However, sec. 90 of Restatement, 1 Contracts, does not impose the requirement that the promise giving rise to the cause of action must be so comprehensive in scope as to meet the requirements of an offer that would ripen into a contract if accepted by the promisee. Rather the conditions imposed are:

(1) Was the promise one which the promisor should reasonably expect to induce action or forbearance of a definite and substantial character on the part of the promisee?

(2) Did the promise induce such action or forbearance?

(3) Can injustice be avoided only by enforcement of the promise?

We deem it would be a mistake to regard an action grounded on promissory estoppel as the equivalent of a breach of contract action. As Dean Boyer points out, it is desirable that fluidity in the application of the concept be maintained, 98 University of Pennsylvania Law Review (1950), 459, at page 497. While the first two of the above listed three requirements of promissory estoppel present issues of fact which ordinarily will be resolved by a jury, the third requirement, that the remedy can only be invoked where necessary to avoid injustice, is one that involves a policy decision by the court. Such a policy decision necessarily embraces an element of discretion.

We conclude that injustice would result here if plaintiffs were not granted some relief because of the failure of defendants to keep their promises which induced plaintiffs to act to their detriment.

See also *Wheeler v White* 398 SW2d 93 (Sup Ct of Texas, 1966), where one party, encouraged by the other, had taken steps in reliance on a contract which the court held was void for uncertainty, and was held to be entitled to recover his reliance loss. The majority said:

. . . [W]here there is actually no contract the promissory estoppel theory may be invoked, thereby supplying a remedy which will enable the injured party to be compensated for his foreseeable, definite and substantial reliance. Where the promisee has failed to bind the promisor to a legally sufficient contract, but where the promisee has acted in reliance upon a promise to his detriment, the promisee is to be allowed to recover no more than reliance damages measured by the detriment sustained.

Could such a result be reached in English law in a case not involving land? Note that in one way, *Crabb v Arun District Council* went beyond the US cases: the council did not actively encourage Crabb to sell his front plot. The only other reported case which comes close to the US authorities is *Box v Midland Bank Ltd* [1979] 2 Lloyd's Rep 391, where a bank was held liable for a negligent misrepresentation by one of its employees. The employee had told the plaintiff that his request for a loan was certain to be approved if the plaintiff obtained an ECGD policy. In fact the type of policy referred to was of a different type to the one that might have satisfied the Bank, and there was no chance of the loan being approved. Meanwhile, however, the plaintiff suffered loss in that he continued to draw on his account, thinking the loan would come through. It will be noted that neither of the US cases was decided on the basis of negligent misstatement.

(d) Conditional contracts

The parties may have reached a broad measure of agreement, but wish to take further steps or make further investigations before a complete agreement is reached. Different attempts to bridge the gap, for example, by issuing a letter of intent (see *BSC v Cleveland Bridge and Engineering Ltd*, above, p 224), or by providing that certain matters are to be agreed later (*May & Butcher v R*, above, p 213), have already been encountered.

If the further step can be defined with sufficient certainty, a useful device in this context is the conditional contract.

Ee v Kakar (1979) 40 P&CR 223, Walton J

The defendant agreed to sell his house to the plaintiff for £14,250 'subject to survey of the property', but later repudiated the agreement. The plaintiff brought an action for specific performance, claiming that as the condition was in his favour, he could waive it.

Walton J. . . . . [A]t the end of the day there is one and only one crucial question in the case, namely, what is the effect of the words "subject to survey". I therefore now turn to that crucial question, which is whether the document of April 1, 1978, is or is not a contract.

It is said that the words 'subject to survey' are in law equivalent to the words 'subject to contract' and produce the same result.

[Walton J referred to *Marks v Board*, in which Rowlatt J had held that an agreement 'subject to surveyor's report' was not binding, and continued:]

The nub of the judgment is contained in the few words "there was no contract because the buyer was not yet bound and, therefore, the seller was not bound either."

It appears to me to be well settled that, in order to constitute a contract, there must be consideration on both sides. Consideration consists in the suffering of detriment by the person furnishing the consideration, not necessarily in a benefit to the other party to the contract. I need do no more than refer to *Currie v Misa*.

The oddity of the decision, as I see it, in *Marks v Board* [is that] Rowlatt J recognised, as I should in any event have thought would have been obvious, that as a result of the—I shall use the neutral word—document in question, the purchaser became bound to obtain a surveyor's report. In other words, he was not free simply to say, "I am not going on with the transaction," although, doubtless subject to a qualification I shall pose hereafter, he was free when he had received the report to come to his own conclusion as to whether he was satisfied with it or not. Looking further ahead, if the purchaser had not obtained such a report within a reasonable time, it would then, I should have thought, have been too late for him to resile from the document. He would have waived this condition completely.

If that be correct, then the purchaser does furnish consideration. He has to obtain a surveyor's report, and that will cost him money, and money which will not be *de minimis* either. He has therefore suffered detriment, and so given consideration. Hence, it appears to me that the inevitable conclusion is that, the document being otherwise on its face intended to take effect as a contract, it will do so.

I can myself see no reason why, although of course retaining the right to be satisfied with any kind of report, a purchaser should not be bound, if presented with a report which is basically a satisfactory one, to have to act bona fide, just as he must, as I take it, in any event, proceed with due diligence. Although the two tests are quite clearly not the same, if a reasonable man would be satisfied with the report, I should have thought that a purchaser would experience some difficulty in persuading a court that his failure to proceed with the contract was bona fide. . . .

There is also another possible analysis of the legal situation which can be made, which leads to the same result. In *Lee-Parker v Izzet (No 2)* the contract for sale contained the clause, 'Subject to the purchaser obtaining a satisfactory mortgage.' This clause was, indeed and obviously, held to be void for uncertainty, but it was first analysed as constituting a condition precedent.

Now it is well settled that a contract may be made subject to conditions precedent, for example, *Aberfoyle Plantations Ltd v Cheng, Smallman v Smallman* in both of which cases the condition precedent—in one case fulfilled and the other not—was contained in the contract.

So far as I am aware, it has never been suggested that, provided the condition is not void for uncertainty, its form or any question of consideration is of any materiality. So here, provided that it is a real condition, I see no reason why the condition 'subject to survey' should not represent a simple suspensory condition, suspensory of a contract as to which there can be no question as to the consideration furnished by each side.

Of course I would readily agree that, if the condition was an illusory one, that is to say, the fulfilment of which was wholly at the whim of one party, the case would be different. But the condition as to survey is not, because, at the least, the purchaser must obtain the survey and consider it and, in my judgment, also act bona fide.

So, looked at from this slightly different point of view, it also appears to me that the document of April 1, 1978, was a perfectly valid and binding contract.

I think the only other point in the case which arises, arises from the fact that the statement of claim, somewhat oddly, pleads waiver of the condition rather than fulfilment, which, I gather is what in fact happened. It is of course well settled that a party to a contract can waive a condition wholly in his favour; see, for example, *Heron Garage Properties Ltd v Moss*. This form of the pleadings afford Mr Raffety an opportunity of arguing that the condition in the present case was not one exclusively in favour of the plaintiff, but that, as the defendant was also clearly interested in the condition of the property, it was one in favour of both parties, and hence one which could not be unilaterally waived in this manner. I cannot, I am afraid, accept this submission.

To test it, suppose that the plaintiff had obtained a surveyor's report, which, let us suppose, had stated that the property was in a deplorable condition, but that, as a result of some wholly extraneous factor, plans to build a swimming pool nearby, the property had become an absolute bargain at the contract price. What would there be in the contract to prevent the plaintiff notifying the defendant that the survey was acceptable to him and he was proceeding to go ahead with the transaction? So far as I can see, nothing. There is no provision for disclosure of the report to the defendant under any circumstances at all.

It follows, in my judgment, that the plaintiff in the present action succeeds on all counts.

NOTES

1. What is the vendor's position if the purchaser (i) fails to get a survey or (ii) refuses to go ahead on the ground that he is dissatisfied with the report even though the report is largely a favourable one?
2. Walton J referred to *Lee-Parker v Izzet (No 2)* [1972] 2 All ER 800, where an agreement to buy and sell land 'subject to the purchaser obtaining a satisfactory mortgage' was held invalid for uncertainty. There is no doubt that conditions must be sufficiently certain, but whether a condition in such terms passes the test has provoked widespread differences of judicial opinion. See *Meehan v Jones* (1982) 42 ALR 463 (High Court of Australia); Furmston (1983) 3 Oxford J of Legal Studies 438.

3. In *Heron Garage Properties Ltd v Moss* [1974] 1 All ER 421 land had been sold subject to the purchasers obtaining planning permission for use as a filling station. The vendor had retained adjoining land on which he planned to build a car showroom. Brightman J held that, as having a filling station on the land sold might benefit both the parties, the condition was for the benefit of both, and the purchasers could not waive it and insist on the land being conveyed to them when they failed to get the permission.

The fulfilment of the condition is quite often outside the control of either party, for example, sale of Blackacre 'subject to planning permission being obtained for use as a hotel'. In such a case, one party will commonly be under a subsidiary obligation to make a serious application for permission: see *Hargreaves Transport Ltd v Lynch* [1969] 1 All ER 455.

CHAPTER 11
Communication mistakes

(a) Mistakes as to the terms

Tamplin v James (1880) 15 ChD 215, Baggallay LJ (for the V-C) and Court of Appeal

The Ship inn and an adjoining saddler's shop were put up for auction. Behind the property there were two pieces of garden, which for many years had been occupied with the inn and the shop and were hardly fenced off from them. The gardens did not belong to the vendors, and the area of land stated in the particulars as being for sale did not include them; nor were the gardens included in the plans showing the property to be sold. At the auction the property remained unsold but immediately afterwards the defendant offered £750 for it and his offer was accepted. The defendant, who knew the property and that the gardens were occupied along with the inn and shop, had not looked at the plans and bought the property in the belief that he was buying the gardens as well as the inn and shop. When the defendant discovered his mistake he refused to complete. The vendors sought specific performance.

Baggallay LJ, after stating the leading facts, continued:
The Defendant insists in his statement of defence that he signed the memorandum in the reasonable belief that the property comprised therein included the whole of the premises in the occupation of Mrs Knowles and of Mr Samuel Merrick, and not merely the messuages and hereditaments which the Plaintiffs allege to be the only property comprised therein, and that such his belief was induced and confirmed by the acts and words of the auctioneer at the sale. The Defendant has sworn positively that he had such a belief at the time he signed the memorandum, and I see no reason to doubt the statement so made by him; but was such a belief a reasonable belief?
It is doubtless well established that a Court of Equity will refuse specific performance of an agreement when the Defendant has entered into it under a mistake, and where injustice would be done to him were performance to be enforced. The most common instances of such refusal on the ground of mistake are cases in which there has been some unintentional misrepresentation on the part of the Plaintiff (I am not now referring to cases of intentional misrepresentation which would fall rather under the category of fraud), or where from the ambiguity of the agreement different meanings have been given to it by the different parties. . . . But where there has been no misrepresentation, and where there is no ambiguity in the terms of the contract, the Defendant cannot be allowed to evade the performance of it by the simple statement that he has made a mistake. Were such to be the law the performance of a contract could rarely be enforced upon an unwilling party who was also unscrupulous.

[A decree for specific performance was therefore made.]

The defendant appealed but the Court of Appeal dismissed the appeal.

James LJ. . . . The defence on the ground of mistake cannot be sustained. It is not enough for a purchaser to swear, 'I thought the farm sold contained twelve fields which I knew, and I find it does not include them all', or, 'I thought it contained 100 acres and it only contains eighty.' It would open the door to fraud if such a defence was to be allowed. Perhaps some of the cases on this subject go too far, but for the most part the cases where a Defendant has escaped on the ground of a mistake not contributed to by the Plaintiff, have been cases where a hardship amounting to injustice would have been inflicted upon him by holding him to his bargain, and it was unreasonable to hold him to it. *Webster v Cecil* is a good instance of that, being a case where a person snapped at an offer which he must have perfectly well-known to be made by mistake, and the only fault I find with the case is that, in my opinion, the bill ought to have been dismissed with costs. It is said that it is hard to hold a man to a bargain entered into under a mistake, but we must consider the hardship on the other side. Here are trustees realizing their testator's estate, and the reckless conduct of the Defendant may have prevented their selling to somebody else. If a man makes a mistake of this kind without any reasonable excuse he ought to be held to his bargain.

[Brett and Cotton LJJ delivered concurring judgments.]

NOTES

1. If there had been any misrepresentation by the plaintiff, even an unintentional one, the defendant would have been entitled to rescind the contract: see below, p 285ff.
2. It was explained earlier that granting specific performance involves forcing the defendant to take the land and pay the agreed price for it. In contrast, if the defendant is made liable in damages he will not have to go through with the purchase but will have to reimburse the plaintiff's loss, typically the cost of arranging a resale plus the difference between the price the defendant had agreed to pay and the price obtained on the resale. The remedy of specific performance is discretionary, and is sometimes refused on the ground of hardship to the defendant, even though the contract is valid at common law and so the defendant will be liable in damages if he does not perform. An example is *Wood v Scarth*: a landlord intended to take a premium when he let a public house, but failed to make this clear to the lessee. The lessee's action for specific performance (without premium) was refused (1855) 2 K&J 33, 3 Eq Rep 385 but an action against the landlord for damages succeeded (1858) 1 F&F 293. The grounds on which specific performance may be refused were described by Lord Macnaghten in *Steward v Kennedy* (1890) 15 App Cas 75, 105, thus:

   It cannot be disputed that the Court of Chancery has refused specific performance in cases of mistake when the mistake has been on one side only; and even when the mistake on the part of the defendant resisting specific performance has not been induced or contributed to by any act or omission on the part of the plaintiff. But I do not think it is going too far to say that in all those cases—certainly in all that have occurred in recent times—the Court has thought, rightly or wrongly, that the circumstances of the particular case under consideration were such that (to use a well-known phrase) it would be 'highly unreasonable' to enforce the agreement specifically. The Court will not be active in assisting one party to an agreement who has always his remedy in damages to take advantage of the mistake of the other so as to involve him in serious and unforeseen consequences . . . the remedy of specific performance is an extraordinary remedy. It is a matter of discretion . . .

   For a recent example of specific performance being refused on the ground of hardship, see *Patel v Ali* (below, p 539).
3. What is the purpose of making the defendant perform a contract which he would not have entered had he realized the truth? Is the exchange value-maximizing? Or is the point that the defendant has behaved carelessly and should bear the consequences, so as to provide an incentive to others to exercise more care (see Kronman and Posner's

comment, above, p 72)? If the point is the latter, is it right to force actual performance by the defendant?
4. James LJ referred to *Webster v Cecil*. In that case the defendant wrote to the plaintiff offering to sell a piece of land for £1,250. He meant £2,250, and it must have been obvious to the plaintiff that there had been some mistake because the defendant had recently refused the plaintiff's offer of £2,000. The plaintiff wrote accepting, but the court refused his action for specific performance, saying he might 'bring such action at law as he might be advised'. Read the next case and consider how you would advise him.

Hartog v Colin & Shields [1939] 3 All ER 566, Singleton J

The defendants offered to sell the plaintiff a quantity of Argentine Hare skins at 10¼d per lb. This was an error for 10¼d per piece. In the trade, such skins were always sold by the piece; and there are about three pieces to the pound, so that the defendants' offer was the equivalent of 3¾d per piece, whereas three weeks earlier the quoted price had been 10¾d per piece. The plaintiff purported to accept the offer and, when the defendants refused to deliver, brought this action.

Singleton J. In this case, the plaintiff, a Belgian subject, claims damages against the defendants because he says they broke a contract into which they entered with him for the sale of Argentine hare skins. The defendants' answer to that claim is: 'There really was no contract, because you knew that the document which went forward to you, in the form of an offer, contained a material mistake. You realised that, and you sought to take advantage of it.'

Counsel for the defendants took upon himself the onus of satisfying me that the plaintiff knew that there was a mistake and sought to take advantage of that mistake. In other words, realising that there was a mistake, the plaintiff did that which James LJ in *Tamplin v James* described as 'snapping up the offer'. It is important, I think, to realise that in the verbal negotiations which took place in this country, and in all the discussions there had ever been, the prices of Argentine hare skins had been discussed per piece, and later, when correspondence took place, the matter was always discussed at the price per piece, and never at a price per pound. . . .

I am satisfied however, from the evidence given to me, that the plaintiff must have realised, and did in fact know, that a mistake had occurred. . . .

There was an absolute difference from anything which had gone before—a difference in the manner of quotation, in that the skins are offered per pound instead of per piece.

I am satisfied that it was a mistake on the part of the defendants or their servants which caused the offer to go forward in that way, and I am satisfied that anyone with any knowledge of the trade must have realised that there was a mistake. . . .

The offer was wrongly expressed, and the defendants by their evidence, and by the correspondence, have satisfied me that the plaintiff could not reasonably have supposed that that offer contained the offerers' real intention. Indeed, I am satisfied to the contrary. That means that there must be judgment for the defendants.

NOTE

Did the plaintiff actually know of the defendants' mistake, or was it that he should have known of it? In *McMaster University v Wilchar Construction Ltd* (1971) 22 DLR (3d) 9 (affd (1973) 69 DLR (3d) 400n), Thompson J said:

In this context, it should be stressed that one is taken to have known that which would have been obvious to a reasonable person in the light of the surrounding circumstances: see *Hartog v Colin & Shields*.

In *Centrovincial Estates plc v Merchant Investors Assurance Co Ltd* [1983] Com LR 158 the English Court of Appeal seemed to imply that this is the correct approach. Slade LJ said:

. . . [I]t is contrary to the well established principles of contract law to suggest that the offeror under a bilateral contract can withdraw an unambiguous offer, after it has been accepted in the manner contemplated by the offeror, merely because he made a mistake which the offeree neither knew nor could reasonably have known at the time he accepted it.

However, we shall see later that in cases on the rectification of mistakes in written contracts the same court said that relief should not be granted unless one party's mistake was actually known to the other party. (See below, p 241.)

Scriven Bros & Co v Hindley & Co [1913] 3 KB 564, A. T. Lawrence J

The plaintiffs instructed an auctioneer, Northcott, to sell a number of bales of hemp and tow. The auctioneer's catalogue described the goods as so many bales in different lots, all bearing the same shipping marks (S.L.), which was unusual for two different commodities, and the catalogue did not show the difference between the lots bearing the same marks. Samples of the hemp and tow were on view before the auction, marked with the catalogue numbers for the relevant lots: the defendant's manager, Gill, examined the hemp, but not the tow as he did not intend to bid for tow. He was not warned by the auctioneer's foreman, Calman, that the hemp and tow bore the same marks. When the lots which were in fact tow were put up for sale, the defendant's buyer, Macgregor, bid on them at a price which was extravagant for tow and they were immediately knocked down to him.

The jury in answer to questions found: (1) That hemp and tow are different commodities in commerce. (2) That the auctioneer intended to sell 176 bales of tow. (3) That Macgregor intended to bid for 176 bales of hemp. (4) That the auctioneer believed that the bid was made under a mistake when he knocked down the lot. (5) That the auctioneer had reasonable ground for believing that the mistake was merely one as to value. (6) That the form of the catalogue and the conduct of Calman, or one of them, contributed to cause the mistake that occurred. (7) That Mr Gill's 'negligence' in not taking his catalogue to Cutler Street and more closely examining and identifying the bales with the lots contributed to cause Macgregor's mistake.

A. T. Lawrence J. . . . The jury have found that hemp and tow are different commodities in commerce. I should suppose that no one can doubt the correctness of this finding. The second and third findings of the jury shew that the parties were never ad idem as to the subject-matter of the proposed sale; there was therefore in fact no contract of bargain and sale. The plaintiffs can recover from the defendants only if they can shew that the defendants are estopped from relying upon what is now admittedly the truth. Mr Hume Williams for the plaintiffs argued very ingeniously that the defendants were estopped; for this he relied upon findings 5 and 7, and upon the fact that the defendants had failed to prove the allegation in paragraph 4 of the defence to the effect that Northcott knew at the time he knocked down the lot that Macgregor was bidding for hemp and not for tow.

I must, of course, accept for the purpose of this judgment the findings of the jury, but I do not think they create any estoppel. Question No 7 was put to the jury as a supplementary question, after they had returned into Court with their answers to the other questions, upon the urgent insistence of the learned junior counsel for the plaintiffs. It begs an essential question by using the word 'negligence' and assuming that the purchaser has a duty towards the seller to examine goods that he does not wish to buy, and to correct any latent defect there may be in the sellers' catalogue.

Once it was admitted that Russian hemp was never before known to be consigned or sold with the same shipping marks as Russian tow from the same cargo, it was natural for the person inspecting the 'S.L.' goods and being shewn hemp to suppose that the 'S.L.' bales represented the commodity hemp. Inasmuch as it is admitted that some one had perpetrated a swindle upon the bank which made advances in rspect of this shipment of goods it was peculiarly the duty of the auctioneer to make it clear to the bidder either upon the fact of his catalogue or in some other way which lots were hemp and which lots were tow.

. . . In my view it is clear that the findings of the jury upon the sixth question prevents the plaintiffs from being able to insist upon a contract by estoppel. Such a contract cannot arise when the person seeking to enforce it has by his own negligence or by that of those for whom he is responsible caused, or contributed to cause, the mistake.

I am therefore of opinion that judgment should be entered for the defendants.

Judgment for defendants.

NOTES

1. Did the auctioneer know that the buyer was under a mistake as to what was being sold? If not, why was the buyer not held to the contract he had appeared to agree to, when he bid and allowed his bid to be accepted?

2. Do you think the result would have been different if the jury had concluded that there had been some carelessness on the auctioneer's part, but that the predominant fault had been the buyer's, because he should have realized that the bales were tow?

3. If, as in these cases, one party has made some mistake about the terms on which he is prepared to contract, why is he not held bound to what he appeared to agree to, even if the other party knew of the mistake, should have known of it or had caused it by his own misleading conduct? Where the second party has *actual knowledge* of the mistake, does it seem fair to allow him to take advantage of it? He will not have been misled, and he could easily correct the mistaken party's error by pointing it out. Where he *caused* it, it seems equally unfair to allow him to benefit by it, and moreover, of the two parties, it seems sensible to put the loss caused on the party whose negligence was responsible—he is the 'least cost avoider' (see below, p 305, and compare liability in tort for negligence). What of the case where the mistaken party causes his own mistake (by careless typing, for instance), but the other *should have known* of it? Is the point that here also the party who should have realized the mistake on the other's part has become the least cost avoider?

4. We suggested earlier that the reason for holding a party to a contract which he would not have made but for a mistake which was not known to the other party may be that he has misled the other, and that of the two it is right that the mistaken party should bear the consequences (unless the other should have realized the mistake). We also suggested that such a case may be an appropriate one for refusing specific performance and leaving the non-mistaken party to his remedy in damages. Normally the damages will include loss of expectation, ie loss of profit (see above, p 201). In a case where the defendant can show that he only entered the contract under a mistake, is it right to make him pay expectation damages? It is likely that his mistake will have led him to pay more than the market value of the property, although it does not have this extra value to him. Where the land is sold at auction, the mistaken party is unlikely to be paying much 'over the odds'—he will normally have bid up the price just 'one notch' higher than other bidders were prepared to pay (though note what happened in *Tamplin v James* and in *Scriven v Hindley*, where Macgregor seems to have been the only bidder). But if the sale had been by private treaty the mistaken party might make an offer at much more than the market value. Wouldn't the plaintiff be justly compensated if he were given the cost of arranging another sale—or at most the value of some other offer for the land which he passed up because he thought he had a contract with the defendant? Consider the following extract from the judgment of Frank J in *Ricketts v Pennsylvania Railroad* 153 F2d 757, 766–767 (1946):

Two approaches have been suggested which diverge from that of Williston and the Restatement but which perhaps come closer to the realities of business experience. The first utilizes the concept of an 'assumption of risk': The parties to a contract, it is said, are presumed to undertake the risk that the facts upon the basis of which they entered into the contract might, within a certain margin, prove to be non-existent; accordingly, one who is mistaken about any such fact should not, absent a deliberate assumption by him of that risk, be held for more than the actual expenses caused by his conduct. Otherwise, the other party will receive a windfall to which he is not entitled. The second suggestion runs thus: Business is conducted on the assumption that men who bargain are fully informed as to all vital facts about the transactions in which they engage; a contract based upon a mistake as to any such fact as would have deterred either of the parties from making it, had he known that fact, should therefore be set aside in order to prevent unjust enrichment to him who made the mistake; the other party, on this suggestion also, is entitled to no more than his actual expenses. Each of those suggestions may result in unfairness, if the other party reasonably believing that he has made a binding contract, has lost the benefit of other specific bargains available at that time but no longer open to him.

5. Is there also a case for allowing the mistaken party to escape the contract if the non-mistaken party has not yet relied on it in any way? The Court of Appeal in *Centrovincial* rejected this approach. After the passage quoted above (p 234) Slade LJ went on to say:

> . . . [I]t is nothing to the point that the offeree may not have changed his position beyond giving the promise requested of him.

6. In *Hartog v Colin & Shields* and *Scriven & Co v Hindley & Co* the mistake was used as a defence to an action to enforce the contract, and all that the courts had to decide was that the defendant was not liable to perform on the terms which he had mistakenly given his apparent consent to. What would have been the position if he had wanted to enforce the contract, either on those terms, or (more realistically) on the terms that he actually intended? To put the same question another way, in a case like *Hartog v Colin & Shields* is there, as counsel for the defendants argued, no contract? There are at least two other possibilities:
   (i) There is a contract on the terms stated by the seller (ie 10¼d per lb), but it is voidable at the seller's option;
   (ii) There is a contract on the terms actually intended by the seller (ie 10¼d per piece).
   There is no clear answer to this question on the present authorities, but cases on rectification suggest that at least where it is obvious what the terms are meant to be, the correct solution is that there is a contract on the terms the mistaken party intended and the other party should have known he intended.
7. It may be helpful at this point to note the distinction between void and voidable contracts. If, for instance, you have entered a contract as the result of a misrepresentation of fact by the other party, you may set the contract aside, or 'rescind' it, if you wish to do so and act quickly enough (see note 1 on p 232, above and chapter 14 below). The contract is thus 'voidable' at your option; but until you rescind it, the contract remains in force. If on the other hand you never reach any effective agreement at all (eg what you agree is too uncertain to be enforceable, see chapter 10 above), the supposed contract is 'void'—ie there is no contract at all. This was what counsel for the defendants in *Hartog v Colin & Shields* argued was the effect of the mistake. As the last note suggested, it is not completely clear that this is correct. There are certainly some cases in which the existence of a mistake makes the supposed contract void (see the mistaken identity cases, below, p 249 ff); but where the mistake is not about who the parties are but about the other terms of the contract, there are as suggested in the last note two other possibilities. One is that there is a contract which is voidable at the seller's option (but there is

little if any authority for this: see below, p 256). The other is that there is a contract which is neither void nor voidable, but which is on the terms intended by the mistaken party and which the other party knew (or perhaps should have known) the mistaken party meant.

(b) Rectification

Joscelyne v Nissen [1970] 1 All ER 1213, Court of Appeal

The father lived in a house called Martindale from where he carried on a car hire business. In 1960, the father received a notice to quit. The daughter in order to help her parents bought Martindale with the help of a mortgage and let her husband's house furnished to pay off the mortgage instalments and moved to Martindale. The parents occupied the ground floor and the daughter and her husband the first floor. In 1963, the daughter's mother became very ill with two successive strokes and was unable to look after herself. The father had to devote a good deal of his time to looking after her with the result that his business was adversely affected. The father and the daughter discussed a scheme, which culminated in the signing by them of a contract dated 18th June 1964. By this contract the father agreed to transfer his motor car hire business to the daughter on certain terms and conditions, one of which was that in consideration of the transfer, the daughter would permit the father during his life to have the uncontrolled right to occupy and reside in the ground floor of Martindale 'free of all rent and outgoings of every kind in any event'. In pursuance of this term in the contract the daughter for a time paid the gas, electricity and coal bills and the cost of home help for the father. Trouble then arose between the daughter and her parents, and the father commenced proceedings in the county court against the daughter. The daughter was apparently advised that the wording of the contract did not require her to pay for the items previously mentioned and she accordingly stopped further payments of those items. The father amended his particulars of claim to raise the point either as a matter of construction or by way of rectification.

The first instance judge rectified the contract.

Russell LJ: For the daughter it is argued that the law is that the father cannot get rectification of the written instrument save to accord with a complete antecedent concluded oral contract with the daughter, and, as was found by the judge, there was none. For the father it is argued that if in the course of negotiation a firm accord has been expressly reached on a particular term of the proposed contract, and both parties continue minded that the contract should contain appropriate language to embrace that term, it matters not that the accord was not part of a complete antecedent concluded oral contract.

The point of law has a curious judicial history.

[His Lordship considered a number of authorities including *Lovell and Christmas Ltd v Wall* (below, p 309), *Frederick E. Rose (London) Ltd v W. H. Pim Jnr & Co* (below, p 246).]

In *Crane v Hegeman-Harris Co Inc* . . . Simonds J said:

'Before I consider the facts and come to a conclusion whether the defendants are right in their contention, it is necessary to say a few words upon the principles which must guide me in this matter. I am clear that I must follow the decision of Clauson J as he then was, in *Shipley Urban District Council v Bradford Corpn.*, the point of which is that, in order that this court may exercise its jurisdiction to rectify a written instrument, it is not necessary to find a concluded and binding contract between the parties antecedent to the agreement which it is sought to rectify. The judge held, and I respectfully concur with his reasoning and his conclusion, that it is sufficient to find a common continuing intention in regard to a particular provision or aspect of the agreements. If one finds that, in regard to a particular point, the parties were in agreement up to the moment when they executed their formal instrument, and the formal instrument does not conform with that common agreement, then this court has jurisdiction to rectify, although it may be that there was, until the formal instrument was executed, no concluded and binding contract between the parties. That is what the judge decided, and, as I say, with his reasoning I wholly concur, and I can add nothing to his authority in the matter, except that I would say that, if it were not so, it would be a strange thing, for the result would be that two parties binding themselves by a mistake to which each had equally contributed, by an instrument which did not express their real intention, would yet be bound by it. That is a state of affairs which I hold is not the law, and, until a higher court tells me it is the law, I shall continue to exercise the jurisdiction which Clauson J as I think rightly, held might be entertained by this court. Secondly, I want to say this upon the principle of the jurisdiction. It is a jurisdiction which is to be exercised only upon convincing proof that the concluded instrument does not represent the common intention of the parties. That is particularly the case where one finds prolonged negotiations between the parties eventually assuming the shape of a formal instrument in which they have been advised by their respective skilled legal advisers. The assumption is very strong in such a case that the instrument does represent their real intention, and it must be only upon proof which Lord Eldon, I think, in a somewhat picturesque phrase described as 'irrefragable.' that the court can act. I would rather, I think, say that the court can only act if it is satisfied beyond all reasonable doubt that the instrument does not represent their common intention, and is further satisfied as to what their common intention was. For let it be clear that it is not sufficient to show that the written instrument does not represent their common intention unless positively also one can show what their common intention was. It is in the light of those principles that I must examine the facts of this somewhat complicated case.'

In our judgment the law is as expounded by Simonds J in *Crane's* case with the qualification that some outward expression of accord is required. We do not wish to attempt to state in any different phrases that with which we entirely agree, except to say that it is in our view better to use only the phrase 'convincing proof' without echoing an old fashioned word such as 'irrefragable' and without importing from the criminal law the phrase 'beyond all reasonable doubt'. Remembering always the strong burden of proof that lies on the shoulders of those seeking rectification, and that the requisite accord and continuance of accord of intention may be the more difficult to establish if a complete antecedent concluded contract be not shown, it would be a sorry state of affairs if when that burden is discharged a party to a written contract could, on discovery that the written language chosen for the document did not on its true construction reflect the accord of the parties on a particular point, take advantage of the fact.

The contention in law for the daughter would, we apprehend, involve this proposition, that if all the important terms of an agreement were set out in correspondence with clarity, but expressly 'subject to contract', and the contract by a slip of the copyist unnoticed by either party, departed from what had been 'agreed', there could not be rectification.

Appeal dismissed.

Rectification can be also obtained however, where the document does not record correctly the intentions of just one of the parties, provided the other knew of this and took advantage of it.

Riverlate Properties Ltd v Paul [1974] 2 All ER 656, Court of Appeal

The lessor, the owner of a maisonette on the first and second floors of a building, sent the lessee's solicitor a draft lease which provided by cl 5(iii) that the lessee covenanted to pay half of the reasonable costs, expenses, outgoings and matters for which the lessor was responsible by virtue of the provisions of cl 6(b), (c) and (d), namely insurance, decoration of the exterior of the building and water rates. This was a drafting error: the lessor intended the reference to be to cl 6(a), (b) and (c), so that the lessee would be responsible for part of the expense of exterior and structural repairs. Neither the lessee nor her solicitor appreciated that a mistake had been made or intended that she should undertake this responsibility. Contracts were exchanged and the lease was executed in the form of the draft. Later the lessor commenced an action to have the lease set aside or, at the lessee's option, rectified to substitute in cl 5(iii) a reference to cl 6(a), (b) and (c). Templeman J dismissed the action and the lessor appealed.

Russell LJ read the judgment of the court, in which Stamp and Lawton LJJ concurred.

. . . Finally, the proposition is put forward for the plaintiff that there was unilateral mistake by the plaintiff of a character which entitles the plaintiff to rescission or annulment of the lease, subject only to this, that the defendant can escape rescission or annulment by agreeing to retain the lease subject to variation in the manner suggested as appropriate to correct the plaintiff's unilateral mistake—here, for example, by variation substituting in cl 5(iii) reference to cl 6(a), (b) and (c) for 6(b), (c) and (d). It is to be observed that this contention does not depend in any way on the knowledge or state of mind of the other party at the time of the transaction in question. It is further to be observed that we are not concerned with a case in which a party is seeking an equitable remedy under a contract such as specific performance, where in an appropriate case the court may refuse specific performance if the defendant has made a unilateral mistake. Here the lessee seeks no equitable remedy: she is in possession under a lease.

Is the plaintiff entitled to rescission of the lease on the mere ground that it made a serious mistake in the drafting of the lease which it put forward and subsequently executed, when (a) the defendant did not share the mistake, (b) the defendant did not know that the document did not give effect to the plaintiff's intention, and (c) the mistake of the plaintiff was in no way attributable to anything said or done by the defendant? What is there in principle, or in authority binding on this court, which requires a person who has acquired a leasehold interest on terms on which he intended to obtain it, and who thought when he obtained it that the lessor intended him to obtain it on those terms, either to lose the leasehold interest, or, if he wish to keep it, to submit to keep it only on the terms which the lessor meant to impose but did not? In point of principle, we cannot find that this should be so. If reference be made to principles of equity, it operates on conscience. If conscience is clear at the time of the transaction, why should equity disrupt the transaction? If a man may be said to have been fortunate in obtaining a property at a bargain price, or on terms that make it a good bargain, because the other party unknown to him has made a miscalculation or other mistake, some high-minded men might consider it appropriate that he should agree to a fresh bargain to cure the miscalculation or mistake, abandoning his good fortune. But if equity were to enforce the views of those high-minded men, we have no doubt that it would run counter to the attitudes of much the greater part of ordinary mankind (not least the world of commerce), and would be venturing on the field of moral philosophy in which it would soon be in difficulties.

What then of authority? There are a number of authorities at first instance, of some antiquity, to which our attention was drawn, which it was said decided that in cases of mere unilateral mistake rescission could be ordered, but with the opportunity being given to the defendant to retain the benefit of the transaction if he consent to a variation (that is to say, rectification) which will mend the plaintiff's mistake.

[His Lordship then referred to a number of cases, including *Garrard v Frankel, Harris v Pepperell, Paget v Marshall and May v Platt.*]

It follows from this review of the authorities cited to us that there is no authority binding on this court which requires us to arrive at a conclusion for which, as we have indicated, there is no justification in principle.

Consequently, since the defendant neither directly nor through her solicitor, Mr Mills, knew of the plaintiff's mistake, and was not guilty of anything approaching sharp practice in relation thereto, it is a case of mere unilateral mistake which cannot entitle the plaintiff to rescission of the lease either with or without the option to the defendant to accept rectification to cure the plaintiff's mistake.

Appeal dismissed.

Thomas Bates & Son Ltd v Wyndham's (Lingerie) Ltd [1981] 1 All ER 1077, Court of Appeal

In 1957 the tenants took an assignment of an existing lease which gave the tenants the option, on the expiration of the lease, to take a further seven or fourteen years' lease 'at a rent to be agreed between the landlords and the tenants but in default of such agreement at a rent to be fixed by [an] arbitrator'. The tenants exercised the option and in 1963 were granted a new seven-year lease containing a similar option for a renewal for seven further years. In 1970 the tenants gave notice exercising that option and negotiations followed. Ultimately the tenants accepted the landlords' offer of a fourteen-year lease at £2,350 pa for the first five years and subject to review every five years thereafter. By an oversight the landlords failed to include a provision for the fixing of the rent by arbitration in the default of agreement. It had not been agreed that this should be omitted; the tenants noticed the omission but did not point it out before executing the new lease. The landlords sought rectification, and the trial judge ordered it. The tenants appealed.

Buckley LJ. . . . The landlords claim rectification in the present case on the basis of a principle enunciated by Pennycuick J in *A Roberts & Co, Ltd v Leicestershire County Council.* . . .

> 'The second ground rests on the principle that a party is entitled to rectification of a contract on proof that he believed a particular term to be included in the contract and that the other party concluded the contract with the omission or a variation of that term in the knowledge that the first party believed the term to be included . . . The principle is stated in Snell's Principles of Equity (25th edn, 1960, p 569) as follows: "By what appears to be a species of equitable estoppel, if one party to a transaction knows that the instrument contains a mistake in his favour but does nothing to correct it, he (and those claiming under him) will be precluded from resisting rectification on the ground that the mistake is unilateral and not common".'

Of course if a document is executed in circumstances in which one party realises that in some respect it does not accurately reflect what down to that moment had been the common intention of the parties, it cannot be said that the document is executed under a common mistake, because the party who has realised the mistake is no longer labouring under the mistake.

For this doctrine (that is to say the doctrine of *A Roberts v Leicestershire County Council*) to apply I think it must be shown: first, that one party, A, erroneously believed that the document sought to be rectified contained a particular term or provision, or possibly did not contain a particular term or provision which, mistakenly, it did contain; second, that the other party, B, was aware of the omission or the inclusion and that it was due to a mistake on the part of A; third, that B has omitted to draw the mistake to the notice of A. And I think there must be a fourth element involved, namely that the mistake must be one calculated to benefit B. If these requirements are satisfied, the court may regard it as inequitable to allow B to resist rectification to give effect to A's intention on the ground that the mistake was not, at the time of execution of the document, a common mistake.

[Buckley LJ went on to hold that, on the facts as found by the trial judge, rectification was properly ordered.]

[Eveleigh and Brightman LJJ delivered concurring judgments.]

Appeal dismissed.

NOTES

1. Is there any essential difference between this case and *Hartog v Colin & Shields*? If not, doesn't that suggest that in *Hartog's* case there must have been a contract at 10¼d per piece and, if necessary, the sellers could have had the documents rectified to reflect this?

2. What will be the position if it is obvious to the offeree that the offeror has made a mistake, for instance because the price offered is far too low, but it is not apparent what the offeror did intend?

3. In *The Nai Genova* [1984] 1 Lloyd's Rep 353 the Court of Appeal pointed out that in none of the cases was it suggested that rectification could properly be granted on account of unilateral mistake unless the defendant had actual knowledge of the existence of the plaintiff's mistake at the time when the contract was signed. Slade LJ said (at p 365):

> While it is not necessary to go so far for the purpose of this present decision, I might perhaps add that I strongly incline to the view that in the absence of estoppel, fraud, undue influence or a fiduciary relationship between the parties, the authorities do not in any circumstances permit the rectification of a contract on the grounds of unilateral mistake, unless the defendant had actual knowledge of the existence of the relevant mistaken belief at the time when the mistaken plaintiff signed the contract. In view of the drastic nature of such an order, so far as the non-mistaken defendant is concerned, the consequences of any such conclusion may not appear unduly harsh.

See also *The Ypatia Halcoussi* [1985] 2 Lloyd's Rep 364 at 371 (not enough that defendant may have suspected a mistake).

4. Why limit relief to cases where the defendant actually knew of the plaintiff's mistake? Particularly if he suspects that a mistake has been made, is it too much to ask that he check with the plaintiff?

5. In *Riverlate Properties Ltd v Paul* (above, p 238) the Court of Appeal seemed to reject the idea of giving the defendant an option between rectification and rescission of the contract. However this might be an appropriate remedy when the defendant did not actually know of the mistake but should have known of it. See *Stepps Investments Ltd v Security Capital Corpn Ltd* (1976) 73 DLR (3d) 351 (High Court of Ontario).

6. In the extract in note 3 above, Slade refers to estoppel. An estoppel might arise if the parties had earlier reached an accord including the terms the plaintiff intended, the defendant had represented to the plaintiff that the document gave effect to that accord, and the plaintiff, foreseeably, did not check the document: [1984] 1 Lloyd's Rep 353, 365. For undue influence and fiduciary relationships see below, pp 395 and 648.

(c) Misunderstanding as to terms

Raffles v Wichelhaus (1864) 2 H & C 906, 159 ER 375, Exchequer

Declaration. For that it was agreed between the plaintiff and the defendants to wit, at Liverpool, that the plaintiff should sell to the defendants, and the defendants buy of the plaintiff, certain goods, to wit, 125 bales of Surat cotton, guaranteed middling fair merchant's Dhollorah, to arrive ex 'Peerless' from Bombay; and that the cotton should be taken from the quay, and that the defendants would pay the plaintiff for the same at a certain rate, to wit, at the rate of 17¼d per pound, within a certain time then agreed upon the arrival of the said goods in England. Averments: that the said goods did arrive by the said ship from Bombay in England to wit, at Liverpool, and the plaintiff was then and there ready, and willing and offered to deliver the said goods to the defendants, &c. Breach: that the defendants refused to accept the said goods or pay the plaintiff for them.

Plea. That the said ship mentioned in the said agreement was meant and intended by the defendants to be the ship called the 'Peerless', which sailed from Bombay, to wit, in October; and that the plaintiff was not ready and willing and did not offer to deliver to the defendants any bales of cotton which arrived by the last mentioned ship, but instead thereof was only ready and willing and offered to deliver to the defendants 125 bales of Surat cotton which arrived by another and different ship, which was also called the 'Peerless', and which sailed from Bombay, to wit in December.

Demurrer, and joinder therein.

Milward, in support of the demurrer. The contract was for the sale of a number of bales of cotton of a particular description, which the plaintiff was ready to deliver. It is immaterial by what ship the cotton was to arrive, so that it was a ship called the 'Peerless'. The words 'to arrive ex "Peerless"', only mean that if the vessel is lost on the voyage, the contract is to be at an end. [Pollock CB. It would be a question for the jury whether both parties meant the same ship called the 'Peerless'.] That would be so if the contract was for the sale of a ship called the 'Peerless'; but it is for the sale of cotton on board a ship of that name. [Pollock CB. The defendant only bought that cotton which was to arrive by a particular ship. It may as well be said, that if there is a contract for the purchase of certain goods in warehouse A, that is satisfied by the delivery of goods of the same description in warehouse B.] In that case there would be goods in both warehouses; here it does not appear that the plaintiff had any goods on board the other 'Peerless'. [Martin B. It is imposing on the defendant a contract different from that which he entered into. Pollock CB. It is like a contract for the purchase of wine coming from a particular estate in France or Spain, where there are two estates of that name.] The defendant has no right to contradict by parol evidence a written contract good upon the face of it. He does not impute misrepresentation or fraud, but only says that he fancied the ship was a different one. Intention is of no avail, unless stated at the time of the contract. [Pollock CB. One vessel sailed in October and the other in December.] The time of sailing is no part of the contract.

Mellish (Cohen with him), in support of the plea. There is nothing on the face of the contract to shew that any particular ship called the 'Peerless' was meant; but the moment it appears that two ships called the 'Peerless' were about to sail from Bombay there is a latent ambiguity, and parol evidence may be given for the purpose of shewing that the defendant meant one 'Peerless' and the plaintiff another. That being so, there was no consensus ad idem, and therefore no binding contract. He was then stopped by the Court.

Per Curiam. There must be judgment for the defendants.

Judgment for the defendants.

[Pollock CB, Martin and Pigott BB.]

NOTES

1. It is far from clear on what ground the court actually decided this case. Clearly the court did not accept that the ship was immaterial; but it is not clear whether there was a contract to deliver from the earlier ship, or whether, as was argued for the defendants, there was no contract because there was no actual agreement, no *consensus ad idem*. During the nineteenth century actual agreement was often thought of as an essential ingredient of a contract, though there were competing theories.

'Innovation in Nineteenth Century Contract Law' by Simpson (1975) 91 LQR 247, 268

This case [*Raffles v Wichelhaus*] seems doomed to being misunderstood. The plaintiff sued for failure to accept delivery of goods 'to arrive ex *Peerless* from Bombay'. The defendants had refused to accept goods arriving on a ship 'Peerless' leaving Bombay in December; they pleaded that the ship *they* had intended was another vessel of the same name. The plaintiffs demurred to this plea and there was joinder in demurrer. The plaintiffs argued that so long as the goods arrived on any ship 'Peerless' from Bombay the express terms of a written contract had been complied with; hence the plea was no answer to the action. The court took the view that the plea was good, and the ground for this view (there being no judgments given) must be gleaned from the arguments and interjections of the judges. From these it seems plain that it was good because the court took the view that it was open to the defendants, once a latent ambiguity appeared, to adduce parol evidence to show what the intention was; the jury would then have to determine whether the parties meant one ship (if so which) or different ships. In the latter case, *counsel* suggested, there would be no *consensus* and no contract, but the decision on the demurrer does not enable one to say whether the court agreed with this or not and no judicial interjection deals with the suggestion. On the concept of latent ambiguity see *Smith v Jeffryes*.

For another account of *Raffles v Wichelhaus*, claiming that it was decided on a *consensus ad idem* basis and later 'objectivized', see Gilmore, *The Death of Contract* (1974), pp 35–44.

Whatever the original basis of *Raffles v Wichelhaus*, it now seems to be the law that actual agreement is not needed to create a contract: if one party reasonably appears to the other to assent, and the resulting agreement is not hopelessly ambiguous, there will be a contract. Occasionally the parties will sign a contract conscious that they are not agreed on its meaning, in effect leaving it to the court to establish the proper meaning of the words if necessary: see below, p 313.

2. When a court is called upon to interpret a contract, it will normally look only at the words of the contract, and not at external ('parol') evidence of what was meant. This case establishes an exception to the rule, namely that external evidence can be considered to resolve a latent ambiguity—though here it is not at all clear that the parol evidence helped. On interpretation and the parol evidence rule see below, p 308–316.

3. The cases in subsection (a) above are often referred to as cases of unilateral mistake, whereas *Raffles v Wichelhaus* is referred to as mutual mistake. What is the difference?

4. Cases of mutual mistake—ie cases where there is a misunderstanding which cannot be resolved on the ground that one party knew or should have known what the other meant, so that the contract is void—are rare in the reports, but see *Falck v Williams* [1900] AC 176 and *London Holeproof Hosiery Co Ltd v Padmore* (1928) 44 TLR 499. It is possible that *Scriven Bros & Co v Hindley & Co* is better looked at as a case of mutual mistake than as one of unilateral mistake: it is not clear that there was any reason to prefer one party's version of the transaction to the other's. On the facts the category did not matter; if the buyers had sued the sellers for failing to deliver hemp it might have been crucial.

(d) Mistaken expectations

Anson's Law of Contract (26th ed., ed. Guest), pp 268–269)

A sells *X* a piece of china.

(α) *X* thinks that it is Dresden china. *A* thinks it is not. Each takes his chance. *X* may get a better thing than *A* intended to sell, or a worse thing than he himself intended to buy; in neither case is the validity of the contract affected.

(β) *X* thinks that it is Dresden china. *A* knows that *X* thinks so, and knows that it is not.

The contract holds. *A* must do nothing to deceive *X*, but he is not bound to prevent *X* from deceiving himself as to the *quality* of the thing sold. *X*'s error is one of motive alone, and although it is known to *A*, it is insufficient.

(γ) *X* thinks that it is Dresden china and thinks that *A* intends to contract to sell it as Dresden china; and *A* knows that it is not Dresden china, but does not know that X thinks that he is contracting to sell it as Dresden china. *A* reasonably believes that *X* is assenting to a sale of china in general terms.

The contract holds. The misapprehension by *X* of the extent of *A*'s promise, *if unknown to A*, has no effect, unless, as in *Scriven Bros & Co v Hindley & Co*, *A* has caused or contributed to *X*'s misapprehension.

(δ) *X* thinks it is Dresden china, and thinks that *A* intends to contract to sell it as Dresden china. *A* knows that *X thinks he is contracting to sell it as Dresden china*, but does not mean to, and in fact does not, offer more than china in general terms.

The contract is void. *X*'s error was not one of judgment as to the quality of the china, as in (β), but was an error as to the nature of *A*'s promise, and *A*, knowing that his promise was misunderstood, nevertheless allowed the mistake to continue. There can be no contract if *A* knows that *X* has accepted his offer in terms different from those in which it was in fact made.

This rule is sometimes known as the rule in *Smith v Hughes*. . . .

Smith v Hughes (1871) LR 6 QB 597, Queen's Bench

The plaintiff, a farmer, offered the defendant, a race horse trainer, a quantity of oats. The defendant's manager inspected a sample of the oats and the defendant agreed to take the whole quantity. When the first parcel was delivered, the defendant discovered that they were 'green', ie that season's oats, and he refused to pay for them or accept further deliveries, saying that he had been under the impression that the oats were 'old', ie oats of the previous season; he had no use for green oats. The plaintiff brought an action to recover the price of the oats delivered and for damages for the defendant's refusal to take the remainder. At the trial the plaintiff alleged that he did not know the defendant did not want green oats: the plaintiff had no old oats to sell. On what had been said there was a conflict of evidence. The plaintiff said he had told the defendant that he 'had some good oats for sale', and the defendant had replied that he was always a buyer of good oats; whereas the defendant claimed the plaintiff had said 'good *old* oats', and he had replied that he was always a buyer of good *old* oats.

In summing up, the judge told the jury that the first question for their consideration was, whether the word 'old' had been used by the plaintiff or defendant in making the contract, and that the inclination of his opinion was that the word 'old' had not been so used; but that was a question entirely for their consideration. If they were of opinion that the word 'old' had been so used, they would return a verdict for the defendant. If, however, they thought that the word 'old' had not been used, the second question would be, whether they were of opinion, on the state of the evidence, that the plaintiff believed the defendant to believe, or to be under the impression, that he was contracting for the purchase of old oats. If so, there would be a verdict for the defendant. But if the jury were of opinion that nothing was said as to the oats being old or new, and if they were of opinion that the plaintiff did not believe that the defendant believed or was under the impression that he was contracting for old oats, then they would find for the plaintiff.

The jury found a verdict for the defendant.

The question for the opinion of the Court was, whether the direction to the jury as above is or is not correct.

Cockburn CJ. . . . It is to be regretted that the jury were not required to give specific answers to the questions so left to them. For, it is quite possible that their verdict may have been given for the defendant on the first ground; in which case there could, I think, be no doubt as to the propriety of the judge's direction; whereas now, as it is possible that the verdict of the jury—or at all events of some of them—may have proceeded on the second ground, we are called upon to consider and decide whether the ruling of the learned judge with reference to the second question was right.

For this purpose we must assume that nothing was said on the subject of the defendant's manager desiring to buy *old* oats, nor of the oats having been said to be old; while, on the other hand, we must assume that the defendant's manager believed the oats to be old oats, and that the plaintiff was conscious of the existence of such belief, but did nothing, directly or indirectly, to bring it about, simply offering his oats and exhibiting his sample, remaining perfectly passive as to what was passing in the mind of the other party. The question is whether, under such circumstances, the passive acquiescence of the seller in the self-deception of the buyer will entitle the latter to avoid the contract. I am of opinion that it will not. . . .

I take the true rule to be, that where a specific article is offered for sale, without express warranty, or without circumstances from which the law will imply a warranty—as where, for instance, an article is ordered for a specific purpose—and the buyer has full opportunity of inspecting and forming his own judgment, if he chooses to act on his own judgment, the rule caveat emptor applies. If he gets the article he contracted to buy, and that article corresponds with what it was sold as, he gets all he is entitled to, and is bound by the contract. Here the defendant agreed to buy a specific parcel of oats. The oats were what they were sold as, namely, good oats according to the sample. The buyer persuaded himself they were old oats, when they were not so; but the seller neither said nor did anything to contribute to his deception. He has himself to blame. The question is not what a man of scrupulous morality or nice honour would do under such circumstances. The case put of the purchase of an estate, in which there is a mine under the surface, but the fact is unknown to the seller, is one in which a man of tender conscience or high honour would be unwilling to take advantage of the ignorance of the seller; but there can be no doubt that the contract for the sale of the estate would be binding. . . .

Now, in this case, there was plainly no legal obligation in the plaintiff in the first instance to state whether the oats were new or old. He offered them for sale according to the sample, as he had a perfect right to do, and gave the buyer the fullest opportunity of inspecting the sample, which practically, was equivalent to an inspection of the oats themselves. What, then, was there to create any trust or confidence between the parties, so as to make it incumbent on the plaintiff to communicate the fact that the oats were not, as the defendant assumed them to be, old oats? If, indeed, the buyer, instead of acting on his own opinion, had asked the question whether the oats were old or new, or had said anything which intimated his understanding that the seller was selling the oats as old oats, the case would have been wholly different; or even if he had said anything which shewed that he was not acting on his own inspection and judgment, but assumed as the foundation of the contract that the oats were old, the silence of the seller, as a means of misleading him, might have amounted to a fraudulent concealment, such as would have entitled the buyer to avoid the contract. Here, however, nothing of the sort occurs. The buyer in no way refers to the seller, but acts entirely on his own judgment. . . .

It only remains to deal with an argument which was pressed upon us, that the defendant in the present case intended to buy old oats, and the plaintiff to sell new, so the two minds were not ad idem; and that consequently there was no contract. This argument proceeds on the fallacy of confounding what was merely a motive operating on the buyer to induce him to buy with one of the essential conditions of the contract. Both parties were agreed as to the sale and purchase of this particular parcel of oats. The defendant believed the oats to be old, and was thus induced to agree to buy them, but he omitted to make their age a condition of the contract. All that can be said is, that the two minds were not ad idem as to the age of the oats; they certainly were ad idem as to the sale and purchase of them. Suppose a person to buy a horse without a warranty, believing him to be sound, and the horse turns out unsound, could it be contended that it would be open to him to say that, as he had intended to buy a sound horse, and the seller to sell an unsound one, the contract was void, because the seller must have known from the price the buyer was willing to give, or from his general habits as a buyer of horses, that he thought the horse was sound? The cases are exactly parallel.

The result is that, in my opinion, the learned judge of the county court was wrong in leaving the second question to the jury, and that, consequently, the case must go down to a new trial.

Blackburn J. . . . . I have more difficulty about the second point raised in the case. I apprehend that if one of the parties intends to make a contract on one set of terms, and the other intends to make a contract on another set of terms, or, as it is sometimes expressed, if the parties are not ad idem, there is no contract, unless the circumstances are such as to preclude one of the parties from denying that he has agreed to the terms of the other. The rule of law is that stated in *Freeman v Cooke*. If, whatever a man's real intention may be, he so conducts himself that a reasonable man would believe that he was assenting to the terms proposed by the other party, and that other party upon that belief enters into the contract with him, the man thus conducting himself would be equally bound as if he had intended to agree to the other party's terms.

The jury were directed that, if they believed the word 'old' was used, they should find for the defendant—and this was right; for if that was the case, it is obvious that neither did the defendant intend to enter into a contract on the plaintiff's terms, that is, to buy this parcel of oats without any stipulation as to their quality; nor could the plaintiff have been led to believe he was intending to do so.

But the second direction raises the difficulty. I think that, if from that direction the jury would understand that they were first to consider whether they were satisfied that the defendant intended to buy this parcel of oats on the terms that it was part of his contract with the plaintiff that they were old oats, so as to have the warranty of the plaintiff to that effect, they were properly told that, if that was so, the defendant could not be bound to a contract without any such warranty unless the plaintiff was misled. But I doubt whether the direction would bring to the minds of the jury the distinction between agreeing to take the oats under the belief that they were old, and agreeing to take the oats under the belief that the plaintiff contracted that they were old.

The difference is the same as that between buying a horse believed to be sound, and buying one believed to be warranted sound; but I doubt if it was made obvious to the jury, and I doubt this the more because I do not see much evidence to justify a finding for the defendant on this latter ground if the word 'old' was not used. There may have been more evidence than is stated in the case; and the demeanour of the witnesses may have strengthened the impression produced by the evidence there was; but it does not seem a very satisfactory verdict if it proceeded on this latter ground. I agree, therefore, in the result that there should be a new trial.

Hannen J. . . . . In order to relieve the defendant it was necessary that the jury should find not merely that the plaintiff believed the defendant to believe that he was buying old oats, but that he believed the defendant to believe that he, the plaintiff, was contracting to sell old oats. . . .

Judgment accordingly.

NOTES

1. If the word 'old' was used, on what grounds should judgment be given for the defendant? One ground would be that there was a warranty by the seller that the oats were old, another that he had misrepresented the age of the oats (see below, pp 259 and 285).
2. Even if the sale is in what Anson calls 'general terms' (ie of that piece of China or those oats, rather than of 'a piece of Dresden' or 'so many old oats'), does it seem fair that A should be able to hold *X* to the contract for the china even if A knows that *X* thinks it is a piece of Dresden? See further below, chapter 20.
3. In *Scriven Bros & Co v Hindley & Co* was the contract meant to be for 'lots *x* and *y*', or was it that the sellers were trying to sell what they were promising was tow and the buyers were trying to buy what they thought was promised to be hemp?
4. In the Canadian case of *Imperial Glass Ltd v Consolidated Supplies Ltd* (1960) 22 DLR (2d) 759 (BC, CA) a glazing subcontractor put in a bid for a job at far too low a figure because an assistant had misplaced a decimal point in calculating the square footage of glass involved. The court held that this was not a mistake about the terms of the contract, but only about the motives for it, so that the offeree could accept the bid even though he knew of the mistake. Do you agree with this reasoning? Do you think the outcome should have been different if the bid had set out the method of calculation, so that the error was 'on the face' of the bid? (Compare *McMaster University v Wilchar Construction Ltd* (1971) 22 DLR (3d) 9 (Ont), where it was held that an employer could not hold a contractor to a bid which, to the employer's knowledge, omitted an escalation clause.)
5. The same requirement, that the mistake must be about the terms of the contract, seems to apply to rectification as well: see the next case.

Frederick E Rose (London) Ltd v William H Pim Jnr & Co Ltd [1953] 2 All ER 739, Court of Appeal

The plaintiffs were asked by an English firm in Egypt if they could supply 'up to five hundred tons Moroccan horsebeans described here as feveroles', which a customer had asked them for. The plaintiffs did not know what feveroles were, and consulted the defendants, who replied 'feveroles means just horsebeans'. The plaintiffs then agreed to buy five hundred tons of Tunisian horsebeans from the defendants; they also entered a contract with the firm in Egypt in similar terms, and the defendants agreed to buy a like quantity of horsebeans from an Algerian company. When the customer in Egypt ultimately received the beans, he complained that they were not feveroles. There are three sizes of bean, 'feves', 'feveroles' and 'fevettes', all of which in English are known generically as horsebeans, and the beans supplied were the larger and less valuable feves, not feveroles. The customer took the beans but claimed damages. In order to cover themselves against a claim against them by the firm in Egypt, the plaintiffs sought to have their agreement with the defendants rectified to read 'feveroles', so that they would be able to claim damages from the defendants for having delivered the wrong article.

Denning LJ. . . . The buyers now, after accepting the goods, seek to rectify the contract. Instead of its being a contract for 'horsebeans' simpliciter, they seek to make it a contract of 'horsebeans described in Egypt as feveroles' or, in short, a contract for 'feveroles'. The judge has granted their request. He has found that there was 'a mutual and fundamental mistake' and that the sellers and the buyers, through their respective market clerks, 'intended to deal in horsebeans of the feverole type'. And he has held that, because that was their intention—their continuing common intention—the court could rectify their contract to give effect to it. In this I think he was wrong. Rectification is concerned with contracts and documents, not with intentions. In order to get rectification, it is necessary to show that the parties were in complete agreement on the terms of their contract, but by an error wrote them down wrongly. And in this regard, in order to ascertain the terms of their contract, you do not look into the inner minds of the parties—into their intentions—any more than you do in the formation of any other contract. You look at their outward acts, ie, at what they said or wrote to one another in coming to their agreement, and then compare it with the document which they have signed. If you can predicate with certainty what their contract was, and that it is, by a common mistake, wrongly expressed in the document, then you rectify the document. But nothing less will suffice. It is not necessary that all the formalities of the contract should have been executed so as to make it enforceable at law: see *Shipley Urban District Council v Bradford Corpn*; but, formalities apart, there must have been a concluded contract. There is a passage in *Crane v Hegeman-Harris Co Inc*, which suggests that a continuing common intention alone will suffice, but I am clearly of the opinion that a continuing common intention is not sufficient unless it has found expression in outward agreement. There could be no certainty at all in business transactions if a party who had entered into a firm contract could afterwards turn round and claim to have it rectified on the ground that the parties intended something different. He is allowed to prove, if he can, that they *agreed something different*: see *Lovell & Christmas, Ltd v Wall* . . ., per Lord Cozens-Hardy MR and per Buckley LJ; but not that they *intended* something different.

The present case is a good illustration of the distinction. The parties, no doubt, intended that the goods should satisfy the inquiry of the Egyptian buyers, namely, 'horsebeans described in Egypt as feveroles'. They assumed that they would do so, but they made no contract to that effect. Their agreement, as outwardly expressed, both orally and in writing, was for 'horsebeans'. That is all that the sellers ever committed themselves to supply, and all they should be bound to. There was, no doubt, an erroneous assumption underlying the contract— an assumption for which it might have been set aside on the ground of misrepresentation or mistake—but that is very different from an erroneous expression of the contract, such as to give rise to rectification. The matter can best be tested by asking what would have been the position if the contract between the sellers and the buyers had been for 'feveroles'. Surely, then, the sellers on their side would have stipulated with their Algerian suppliers for the delivery of 'feveroles', and the buyers on their side would have agreed with their sub-buyers to deliver 'feveroles'. It would not be fair to rectify one of the contracts without rectifying all three, a thing which is obviously impossible.

There is one other matter I must mention. In the statement of claim the buyers originally claimed damages for breach of a collateral warranty—a warranty that the horsebeans would be a compliance with a demand for 'feveroles'—but that claim was formally abandoned at the trial. I do not myself quite see why it was abandoned. Section 4 of the Sale of Goods Act 1893, was no bar to it. Nor was such a warranty in any way in contradiction of the written contract. (*Smith v Jeffryes* was not an action on a collateral warranty.) The only difficulty might be whether it was a contractual warranty or merely an innocent misrepresentation. I should myself have thought that it had a better chance of success than the claim for rectification. It was put forward by the buyers very forcibly in their letter on Mar 12, 1951, but its abandonment at the trial makes it impossible for us to consider it. We have only to consider the question of rectification, and on that I think that the buyers fail. I agree that the appeal should be allowed and judgment entered for the sellers.

Morris LJ. . . . It seems to me clear beyond doubt that both parties proceeded on the basis that 'feveroles' and 'horsebeans' were the same. Mr Hampson expressed the matter succinctly when he said:

> 'I had agreed to buy because feveroles were horsebeans and horsebeans were feveroles.'

In that belief the parties came to agreement, and the formal written contracts were prepared and signed. The parties had throughout a clear common intention and purpose of buying and selling horsebeans, and their written agreements faithfully embodied and exactly recorded what they had agreed. In these circumstances it seems to me that no claim for rectification can succeed.

[Singleton LJ delivered a concurring judgment.]

Appeal allowed.

'The Rule in L'Estrange v Graucob' by Spencer [1973] CLJ 104, 108–113

A rival theory of agreement

The notion behind what has been said so far is that A's words must be judged as they appeared to B, the person to whom they were directed. There is nothing new or original in this: in fact, it has been repeated so often in the past that some readers may wonder why it has been necessary to labour the point. The reason is that in recent years an even more objective theory of agreement has emerged, according to which A's words must be judged, not as they appeared to B, but as they would have appeared to C, a reasonable man eavesdropping on the negotiations. The test is not what the other party would have thought, but how things would have appeared to the reasonable fly on the wall. This rival theory has begun to gain ground at the expense of the more orthodox theory which we have just examined, and it is time we examined it closely to see what its implications are.

In some cases, the two theories produce the same results. Thus according to either theory, the unobservant A will usually be bound to buy the bull he bid for thinking it was a cow; if the *Smith v Hughes* theory is used, this is because A led B to believe A was contracting to buy a bull; if the later theory is used, it is because a reasonable bystander would have thought A was contracting to buy a bull. On these facts, it makes no difference which theory is used—'you pays your money and you takes your choice'. . . .

The dissemination of the 'fly on the wall' theory of agreement appears to be largely the work of Lord Denning MR. In *Solle v Butcher* he said

> 'once a contract has been made, that is to say, once the parties, whatever their inmost states of mind, have to all outward appearances agreed with sufficient certainty in the same terms on the same subject-matter, then the contract is good unless and until it is set aside for failure of some condition on which the existence of the contract depends, or for fraud, or on some equitable ground. Neither party can rely on his own mistake to say it was a nullity from the beginning, no matter that it was a mistake which to his mind was fundamental, *and no matter that the other party knew that he was under a mistake.*'

. . . The 'fly on the wall' theory is . . . open to the objection that it leads to absurd results. What happens if the parties are *inwardly* agreed, but *outwardly* at variance, or agreed on something else? Suppose, for example, that Ali and Benedetto, two immigrants with little knowledge of English, agree on the purchase and sale of a 'bull' both of them intending to deal with a cow, and in the belief that the word 'bull' means the female of the species. According to the 'fly on the wall' theory of agreement, they have made a contract to buy and sell a bull, although A does not want one and B has not got one to sell. This is ridiculous. Yet this is the result reached in the Court of Appeal by Denning LJ in *Rose v Pim*. The facts as interpreted by Denning LJ were that A and B made a written agreement for the purchase and sale of 'horsebeans', by which both A and B meant 'feveroles', which, again according to Denning LJ, are something 'essentially different'. Denning LJ held that although both parties meant to deal with feveroles, they were contractually bound to buy and sell horsebeans, because their agreement as outwardly expressed, both orally and in writing, was for 'horsebeans'. It is a platitude to say that the law of contract exists to enforce agreements, and that agreements are what people have agreed to do, not what officious people with no interest in the matter would think they had agreed to do. It may be acceptable for the law occasionally to force upon *one* of the parties an agreement he did not want; but surely there is something wrong with a theory which forces upon *both* of the parties an agreement which *neither* of them wants. If the 'fly on the wall' theory does this, that is an excellent reason for rejecting it.

NOTE

Is Spencer's analysis of *Rose v Pim* correct? Did the parties mean to deal in feveroles, or did they mean to deal in horsebeans which they thought were the same thing as feveroles? What would have been the outcome of the case if the parties had known the differences between the various sizes of beans, but had both mistakenly thought the middle-sized beans were called 'feves' and had concluded their contract in these terms; if the buyers had later refused to accept anything but the middle-sized beans properly called feveroles, could the sellers not have obtained rectification? This situation is akin to Spencer's example about the cow and the bull. See Glanville Williams (1954) 17 MLR 154, 155.

(e) Mistakes as to identity

Boulton v Jones (1857) 27 LJ Ex 117, Exchequer

The defendant sent a written order for some goods to Brocklehurst, against whom the defendant had a set-off. Unknown to the defendant, Brocklehurst had that day sold his stock-in-trade and assigned his business to the plaintiff. The plaintiff sent the goods to the defendant and only later sent him an invoice showing the change in the business. The defendant refused to pay. At the trial it was objected that the contract was with Brocklehurst, not the plaintiff, and the Assessor reserved the point.

Pollock CB. . . . Now the rule of law is clear, that if you propose to make a contract with A, then B cannot substitute himself for A without your consent and to your disadvantage, securing to himself all the benefit of the contract. . . .

Martin B. . . . Where the facts prove that the defendant never meant to contract with A alone, B can never force a contract upon him; he has dealt with A, and a contract with no one else can be set up against him.

Bramwell, B. It is an admitted fact, that the defendant supposed he was dealing with Brocklehurst; and the plaintiff misled him by executing the order unknown to him. It is clear also, that if the plaintiff were at liberty to sue, it would be a prejudice to the defendant, because it would deprive him of a set-off, which he would have had if the action had been brought by the party with whom he supposed he was dealing. And upon that my judgment proceeds. . . .

As to the difficulty suggested, that if the plaintiff cannot sue for the price of goods, no one else can, I do not feel pressed by it any more than I did in such a case as I may suppose, of work being done to my house, for instance, by a party different from the one with whom I had contracted to do it. The defendant has, it is true, had the goods; but it is also true that he has consumed them and cannot return them. And that is no reason why he should pay money to the plaintiff which he never contracted to pay, but upon some contract which he never made, and the substitution of which for that which he did make would be to his prejudice, and involve a pecuniary loss by depriving him of a set-off.

[Channell B delivered a concurring judgment.]

Rule absolute for a nonsuit.

NOTES

1. The plaintiff had been Brocklehurst's foreman and may have known of the set-off. If he had been a newcomer, would he have had any reason to think that the offer was not addressed to the current owner of the business?
2. The goods were supplied and appear to have been used by the defendant. Even if there was no contract to sell them to him, shouldn't he still have to pay their value, either in an action for conversion of someone else's property, or by way of restitution? Bramwell 'disliked the whole law of quasi-contract, for he could not understand how a man could be forced to pay for a benefit which he had received but which he had not agreed to pay for': Atiyah, *Rise and Fall of Freedom of Contract* (1979), p 376.
3. Without accepting Bramwell's extreme view, it can be argued that Jones was not unjustly enriched as he expected to receive the goods without further payment to anyone. If Boulton acted 'officiously' in supplying goods under an order which he should have known was not meant for him, there seems some merit in this argument, particularly if Jones could not recover the credit balance on his running account with Brocklehurst, for instance because the latter had subsequently become insolvent. See *Continental Forest Products Inc v Chandler Supply Co* 95 Idaho 739, 518 P2d 121 (1974). A neat solution would be to require Jones to assign to Boulton the debt owed him by Brocklehurst: if Boulton manages to enforce the debt, he gets paid without Jones being put at risk.

Most of the reported cases of contracts involving mistaken identity have a different and distinctive fact pattern. A would-be seller of goods is tricked by a rogue into believing that the rogue is someone else, and on the strength of that the seller allows the rogue to buy the goods and take them away on credit or against a cheque. Before the seller discovers the fraud or that the cheque is worthless, the rogue resells or pledges the goods to an innocent party (for cash) and disappears. In an attempt to recover the goods (or their value) from the third party, the original seller brings an action of conversion against him. Whether this action will succeed depends on whether the 'property' in the goods has passed to the third party via the rogue. There is no doubt that if there is any contract between the seller and the rogue, it will be voidable for fraud, and if the seller acts quickly enough he may be able to rescind and revest the property in himself (this normally entails the victim of the fraud giving notice of rescission to the fraudulent party, but it has been held that giving notice to the police and other authorities may suffice if the rogue is deliberately hiding: *Car and Universal Finance Co Ltd v Caldwell* [1965] 1 QB 525); but in the cases to be considered here, the right to rescind was lost when the innocent third party acquired rights over the goods, ie before the seller discovered that he had been tricked. If, on the other hand, the original seller can show that there was no contract with the rogue, then the rogue never acquired any property in the goods and could not pass any to the innocent third party, so the owner's action in conversion will succeed.

In these cases, therefore, the original seller relies on his mistake about the rogue's identity as preventing the formation of a contract. There are many cases, and not all of them are easy to reconcile. Some of the older ones may have been influenced by the theory mentioned earlier that actual agreement, consensus ad idem, is necessary for the formation of a contract. Thus in

Cundy v Lindsay (1878) 3 App Cas 459 the rogue was named Blenkarn and had an address at 37, Wood Street. A highly respectable firm called Blenkiron & Co carried on business at 123, Wood Street. Blenkarn ordered large numbers of handkerchiefs from the plaintiffs, signing his name so as to look like Blenkiron. The plaintiffs despatched the goods on credit to 'Blenkiron & Co' but at 37, Wood Street; they were received by Blankarn and some were resold to the defendants before the fraud was discovered. Queen's Bench held that there was a contract: 'the intention of the plaintiffs was to contract with the person carrying on business at 37, Wood Street'. (See *Lindsay v Cundy* (1876) 1 QBD 348, 355). The Court of Appeal and the House of Lords disagreed, the Lord Chancellor (Lord Cairns) saying (at p 465):

> . . . [H]ow is it possible to imagine that in that state of things any contract could have arisen between the Respondents and Blenkarn the dishonest man? Of him they knew nothing, and of him they never thought. With him they never intended to deal. Their minds never even for an instant of time rested on him, and as between him and them there was no *consensus* of mind which could lead to any agreement or any contract whatsoever.

In *King's Norton Metal Co Ltd v Edridge, Merrett & Co* (1897) 14 TLR 98, CA the rogue set up business as Hallam & Co and had notepaper printed which suggested that Hallam & Co was a substantial concern with agencies and depots overseas. The plaintiffs supplied goods on credit and the rogue sold them to the defendants. The Court of Appeal held that there was a contract between the plaintiffs and the rogue: *Cundy v Lindsay* was distinguished on the ground that there a confusion of two distinct entities was involved, whereas the plaintiffs had not confused Hallam & Co with anyone else.

In *Phillips v Brooks Ltd* [1919] 2 KB 243, 88 LJKB 953 a man named North entered the plaintiff's jewellery shop and selected some pearls and a ring. As he made out a cheque to pay for them he said 'You see who I am, I am Sir George Bullough', and gave an address in St James' Square. After checking that Sir George, of whom he had heard, did live at the address given, the plaintiff allowed the rogue to take the ring. The rogue pledged the ring to the defendant, who had no notice of the fraud. Horridge J held that the plaintiff intended to contract with the person present, although he thought that person was Sir George.

Ingram v Little [1960] 3 All ER 332, Court of Appeal

The Ingram sisters were joint owners of a car which they advertised for sale. The rogue called on them and agreed with one of the sisters to buy the car for £717. When, however, he offered a cheque in payment, she categorically refused to accept it. He then said he was a P. G. M. Hutchinson of Stanstead House, Stanstead Road, Caterham. While the discussion was going on the other sister went to the post office and checked this name and address in the telephone directory. The sisters then agreed to let him buy the car and pay by cheque. The cheque was dishonoured and the rogue, who was not P. G. M. Hutchinson, disappeared after having sold it to the defendant, who bought in good faith. The plaintiffs' action for conversion succeeded and the defendant appealed.

Sellers LJ. . . . It does not seem to me to matter whether the right view of the facts is, as the judge has held and as I would agree, that there was no concluded contract before the cheque book was produced and before the vital fraudulent statements were made or that there was a concluded contract which Hutchinson at once repudiated by refusing to pay cash and that this repudiation was accepted by the plaintiffs and the transaction was then and there at an end. The property would not have passed until cash had been paid and it never was paid or intended to be paid.

Was there a contract of sale subsequently made which led to the plaintiffs' taking Hutchinson's cheque and in exchange for it handing over the car and its log book? The judgment holds that there never was a concluded contract, applying, as I understand it, the elementary factors required by law to establish a contract. The learned judge, treating the plaintiffs as the offerors and the rogue Hutchinson as the offeree, finds that the plaintiffs in making their offer to sell the car not for cash but for a cheque (which in the circumstances of the Bank Holiday week-end could not be banked before the following Tuesday, Aug 6) were under the belief that they were dealing with, and therefore making their offer to, the honest Mr P. G. M. Hutchinson, of Caterham, who they had reason to believe was a man of substance and standing. Hutchinson, the offeree, knew precisely what was in the minds of the two ladies, for he had put it there and he knew that their offer was intended for Mr P. G. M. Hutchinson, of Caterham, and that they were making no offer to and had no intention to contract with him, as he was. There was no offer which he, Hutchinson, could accept and therefore there was no contract. The judge pointed out that the offer which the plaintiffs made was one which was capable of being accepted only by the honest Mr P. G. M. Hutchinson, of Caterham, and was incapable of acceptance by the rogue Hutchinson. In all the circumstances of this case I would accept the learned judge's findings. Indeed the conclusion so reached seems self-evident.

Is the conclusion to be held wrong in law? If it is, then, as I see it, it must be on the sole ground that as Hutchinson was present, albeit making fraudulent statements to induce the plaintiffs to part with their car to him in exchange for his worthless cheque and was successful in so doing, then a bargain must have been struck with him personally, however much he deceived the plaintiffs into thinking they were dealing with someone else.

Where two parties are negotiating together and there is no question of one or the other purporting to act as agent for another and an agreement is reached, the normal and obvious conclusion would no doubt be that they are the contracting parties. A contrary finding would not be justified unless very clear evidence demanded it. The unfortunate position of the defendant in this case illustrates how third parties who deal in good faith with the fraudulent person may be prejudiced. The mere presence of an individual cannot, however, be conclusive that an apparent bargain which he may make is made with him. If he were disguised in appearance and in dress to represent someone else and the other party, deceived by the disguise, dealt with him on the basis that he was that person and would not have contracted had he known the truth, then, it seems clear, there would be no contract established. If words are substituted for outward disguise so as to depict a different person from the one physically present, in what circumstances would the result be different?

Whether the person portrayed, by disguise or words, is known to the other party or not is important in considering whether the identity of the person is of any moment or whether it is a matter of indifference. . . .

The question in each case should be solved in my opinion by applying the test which Slade J applied: 'How ought the promisee to have interpreted the promise?' in order to find whether a contract has been entered into. I am in agreement with the learned judge when he quotes, accepts and applies the following passage from Dr Goodhart's article (Law Quarterly Review (1941), Vol 57, at p 231):

> 'It is the interpretation of the *promise* which is the essential thing. This is usually based on the interpretation which a reasonable man, in the promisee's position, would place on it, but in those cases where the promisor knows that the promisee has placed a peculiar interpretation on his words, then this is the binding one. The English law is not concerned with the motives of the parties nor with the reasons which influenced their actions. For practical reasons it has limited itself to the simple questions: what did the promisor promise, and how should this be interpreted?'

. . . The legal position is, I think, well illustrated by Dr Goodhart in the article already referred to. There is a difference between the case where A makes an offer to B in the belief that B is not B but is someone else and the case where A makes an offer to B in the belief that B is X. In the first case B does in fact receive an offer, even though the offeror does not know that it is to B to whom he is making it, since he believes B to be someone else. In the second case A does not in truth make any offer to B at all; he thinks that B is X, for whom alone the offer is meant.

There was an offer intended for and available only to X. B cannot accept it, if he knew or ought to have known that it was not addressed to him. . . .

If it is the formation of a contract which calls for consideration, as it is here, 'How ought the promisee to have interpreted the promise?' is in my opinion the correct approach, as the judge has held; but I recognise that the correct answer may not always prove as ascertainable as I believe it to be in the present case. I would dismiss the appeal.

Pearce LJ. I agree. The question here is whether there was any contract, whether offer and acceptance met. . . .

An apparent contract made orally inter praesentes raises particular difficulties. The offer is apparently addressed to the physical person present. Prima facie, he, by whatever name he is called, is the person to whom the offer is made. His physical presence identified by sight and hearing preponderates over vagaries of nomenclature. 'Praesentia corporis tollit errorem nominis' said Lord Bacon. Yet clearly, though difficult, it is not impossible to rebut the prima facie presumption that the offer can be accepted by the person to whom it is physically addressed. To take two extreme instances. If a man orally commissions a portrait from some unknown artist who had deliberately passed himself off, whether by disguise or merely by verbal cosmetics, as a famous painter, the imposter could not accept the offer. For, though the offer is made to him physically, it is obviously, as he knows, addressed to the famous painter. The mistake in identity on such facts is clear and the nature of the contract makes it obvious that identity was of vital importance to the offeror. At the other end of the scale, if a shopkeeper sells goods in a normal cash transaction to a man who misrepresents himself as being some well known figure, the transaction will normally be valid. For the shopkeeper was ready to sell goods for cash to the world at large, and the particular identity of the purchaser in such a contract was not of sufficient importance to override the physical presence identified by sight and hearing. Thus the nature of the proposed contract must have a strong bearing on the question whether the intention of the offeror (as understood by his offeree) was to make his offer to some other particular identity rather than to the physical person to whom it was orally offered.

In our case the facts lie in the debatable area between the two extremes . . . I should hesitate long before interfering with [the learned judge's] finding of fact and I would only do so if compelled by the evidence or by the view that the judge drew some erroneous inference . . . I am not persuaded that on the evidence he should have found otherwise.

[Devlin LJ dissented on the ground that Hutchinson's identity was immaterial to Miss Ingram. She was concerned only with his creditworthiness.]

Appeal dismissed.

NOTE

Is an explanation of the test laid down in this case that, in order to prevent a contract coming into existence, the mistake must be one about a term—ie one of the terms of the offer must be that the offer is open only to the person the rogue is thought to be?

Lewis v Averay [1971] 3 All ER 907, Court of Appeal

L was the owner of a car which he wanted to sell. He advertised it in a newspaper. In reply a man rang up; he gave no name but said that he was interested in buying the car at the price advertised. Arrangements were made for him to come to L's flat that evening. He was there shown the car which was parked outside. The man, who turned out to be a rogue, tested the car and said that he liked it. L and the rogue then went to the flat of L's financée, Miss K. There the rogue introduced himself as 'Richard Green' and made L and Miss K believe that he was the well-known film actor Richard Greene. He said that he would like to buy the car and they agreed a price of £450. The rogue wrote out a cheque for that amount, signing it 'R.

A. Green'. He wanted to take the car at once. L was hesitant and asked for proof of identity. He was shown a special pass of admission to Pinewood Studios with an official stamp on it. It bore the name 'Richard A. Green', an address, and a photograph which was plainly that of the rogue. On seeing this L was satisfied and let the rogue have the car and log book. A few days later the bank told L that the cheque was worthless. Meanwhile the rogue had sold the car to A, who bought it in good faith and without knowledge of the fraud.

L brought an action against A for conversion of the car, and was successful at first instance. On appeal:

Lord Denning MR. . . . . This case therefore raises the question: what is the effect of a mistake by one party as to the identity of the other? It has sometimes been said that, if a party makes a mistake as to the identity of the person with whom he is contracting, there is no contract, or, if there is a contract, it is a nullity and void, so that no property can pass under it. This has been supported by a reference to the French jurist Pothier but I have said before, and I repeat now, his statement is no part of English law. I know that it was quoted by Viscount Haldane in *Lake v Simmons* and, as such, misled Tucker J in *Sowler v Potter* into holding that a lease was void whereas it was really voidable. But the statement by Pothier has given rise to such refinements that it is time it was dead and buried altogether.

For instance, in *Ingram v Little* the majority of the court suggested that the difference between *Phillips v Brooks* and *Ingram v Little* was that in *Phillips v Brooks* the contract of sale was concluded (so as to pass the property to the rogue) before the rogue made the fraudulent misrepresentation, whereas in *Ingram v Little* the rogue made the fraudulent misrepresentation before the contract was concluded. My own view is that in each case the property in the goods did not pass until the seller let the rogue have the goods.

Again it has been suggested that a mistake as to the identity of a person is one thing; and a mistake as to his attributes is another. A mistake as to identity, it is said, avoids a contract; whereas a mistake as to attributes does not. But this is a distinction without a difference. A man's very name is one of his attributes. It is also a key to his identity. If then, he gives a false name, is it a mistake as to his identity? or a mistake as to his attributes? These fine distinctions do no good to the law.

As I listened to the argument in this case, I felt it wrong that an innocent purchaser (who knew nothing of what passed between the seller and the rogue) should have his title depend on such refinements. After all, he has acted with complete circumspection and in entire good faith; whereas it was the seller who let the rogue have the goods and thus enabled him to commit the fraud. I do not, therefore, accept the theory that a mistake as to identity renders a contract void.

I think the true principle is that which underlies the decision of this court in *King's Norton Metal Co Ltd v Eldridge, Merrett & Co Ltd* and of Horridge J in *Phillips v Brooks Ltd*, which has stood for these last 50 years. It is this: when two parties have come to a contract—or rather what appears, on the face of it, to be a contract—the fact that one party is mistaken as to the identity of the other does not mean that there is no contract, or that the contract is a nullity and void from the beginning. It only means that the contract is voidable, that is, liable to be set aside at the instance of the mistaken person, so long as he does so before third parties have in good faith acquired rights under it.

Applied to the cases such as the present, this principle is in full accord with the presumption stated by Pearce LJ and also by Devlin LJ in *Ingram v Little*. When a dealing is had between a seller like Mr Lewis and a person who is actually there present before him, then the presumption in law is that there is a contract, even though there is a fraudulent impersonation by the buyer representing himself as a different man than he is. There is a contract made with the very person there, who is present in person. It is liable no doubt to be avoided for fraud but it is still a good contract under which title will pass unless and until it is avoided. . . .

Megaw LJ. For myself, with very great respect, I find it difficult to understand the basis, either in logic or in practical considerations, of the test laid down by the majority of the court in *Ingram v Little*. That test is I think accurately recorded in the headnote:

'. . . where a person physically present and negotiating to buy a chattel fraudulently assumed the identity of an existing third person, the test to determine to whom the offer was addressed was how ought the promisee to have interpreted the promise . . .'

The promisee, be it noted, is the rogue. The question of the existence of a contract and therefore the passing of property, and therefore the right of third parties, if the test is correct, is made to depend on the view which some rogue should have formed, presumably knowing that he is a rogue, as to the state of mind of the opposite party, to the negotiation, who does not know that he is dealing with a rogue.

However that may be, and assuming that the test as so stated is indeed valid, in my view this appeal can be decided on a short and simple point. It is the point which was put at the outset of his argument by counsel for the defendant. The well-known textbook on the Law of Contract, *Cheshire and Fifoot*, deals with the question of invalidity of a contract by virtue of unilateral mistake, and in particular unilateral mistake relating to mistaken identity. The learned editors describe what in their submission are certain facts that must be established in order to enable one to avoid contract on the basis of unilateral mistake by him as to the identity of the opposite party. The first of those facts is that at the time when he made the offer he regarded the identity of the offeree as a matter of vital importance. To translate that into the facts of the present case, it must be established that at the time of offering to sell his car to the rogue, Mr Lewis regarded the identity of the rogue as a matter of vital importance. In my view, counsel for the defendant is abundantly justified, on the notes of the evidence and on the findings of the learned judge, in his submission that the mistake of Mr Lewis went no further than a mistake as to the attributes of the rogue. It was simply a mistake as to the creditworthiness of the man who was there present and who described himself as Mr Green. . . .

[Phillimore LJ also held that a contract had come into existence.]

Appeal allowed.

NOTE

Is this case reconcilable with *Ingram v Little*? It is hard to see much of a distinction between the cases on the facts relating to what happened between the sellers and the rogues. Were the courts taking different views on the importance of protecting the third party? Might the courts' perceptions of the need to protect the third party have been influenced by the fact that the defendant in *Lewis v Averay* was a private buyer (a student), whereas the defendant in *Ingram v Little* appears to have been a car dealer?

(f) Non est factum

If one party is induced to sign a contract by the other's misrepresenting what the document signed contains, the resulting 'contract' is at least voidable for misrepresentation (see Chapter 14). As we have seen, even between the contracting parties the right to rescind for fraud will be lost once an innocent third party's rights have intervened. In many cases, however, the fraud is committed not by the other party to the contract but by a third party. For instance, in *United Dominions Trust Ltd v Western* [1976] QB 513 the defendant signed a hire-purchase proposal in blank and left it with the car dealer, who filled in incorrect figures and forwarded it to the finance company. In such a case no question of mistake can arise if the other party does not know what has happened.

Equally no question of mistake can arise if the document signed is not a contract with the fraudulent party but a conveyance to him: the conveyance may be voidable for fraud, but it cannot be void for mistake as offer and acceptance are not required for such a conveyance to be valid (see Russell LJ in *Gallie v Lee* [1969] 2 Ch 17, 41). If a third party has acquired rights over the property conveyed, the right to rescind will have been lost.

In these cases, therefore, the mistaken party's only hope will be to show that the document was totally invalid under the old defence of non est factum. This was originally available to illiterate people who signed deeds which had been read over to them incorrectly: at least if they had not been negligent, they could claim that the deed 'was not their deed'. The law of non est factum was comprehensively reviewed by the House of Lords in *Gallie v Lee (sub nom Saunders v Anglia Building Society)* [1971] AC 1004. A distinction which had grown up between mistakes as to the 'character' and as to the 'contents' of the document was rejected and it was held that the defence is available to a party who signed under a fundamental misapprehension as to the substance of the document in terms of its practical result, provided that the party also proves that he or she took all due care. It was pointed out that the defence will very seldom be available to literate people who are in full possession of their faculties and who sign documents in a language they can understand. On the facts of the case, a widow of 78 wanted to help her nephew raise money on the security of her house provided that she could continue to live there. She signed what she was told was a deed of gift of her house to her nephew, but which was actually an assignment on sale to a third party for £3,000 (which was never paid). This scheme had been arranged by the nephew, who did not wish to raise the money in his own name in case this enabled his wife, from whom he was separated, to enforce maintenance payments against him. The third party mortgaged the house to the building society but failed to pay the money over to the nephew. The widow had not read the document because her glasses were broken. It was held that the widow's mistake was not sufficiently serious; the document enabled the nephew to raise the money though not in the way she had envisaged.

NOTES

1. Why is this defence so restricted? For a full discussion, see Stone, 'The Limits of Non est Factum after *Gallie v Lee*' (1972) 88 LQR 190.
2. Should the defence not be abolished altogether?
3. Can it be argued that where a person signs a contract after a fraudulent misrepresentation by the other party as to the contents, no contract results at all, since the misrepresentor knows that the apparent offer made by the signer is not what the signer intends? It was suggested earlier that where the other party (as here, ex hypothesi) knows what the signing party thinks the terms of the document to be, the preferable view is that there is a contract on the latter terms and the document can be rectified accordingly, as in *Bates v Wyndham's*. Rectification is however an equitable remedy which will be refused if third party rights have intervened, so that the mistake will not help the signer. The result seems to be that the law of mistake affects written contracts rather differently to oral ones: if there is an operative unilateral mistake in an oral contract, either there will be no contract or there will be one on the terms actually intended by the mistaken party, whereas if the contract is written it will in *effect* be voidable only, since a third party's reliance on it may defeat the right of the mistaken party to have it rectified. Lord Denning has often said that, in his view, a mistake only makes a contract voidable, not void (eg above, p 254). Most lawyers regard this as heresy, but perhaps there is something to be said for Lord Denning's view.

Section 4
Obligations and risks

Express terms in oral agreements

When the parties have reached a binding oral agreement, the express terms of that agreement will normally consist of any promises made by either party during the course of negotiations and not withdrawn before final agreement. At least three questions may arise: Firstly, did a particular statement amount to a promise? Secondly, if the statement was a promise, what was being promised? Thirdly, did the oral contract incorporate a set of written terms, printed perhaps on a notice or ticket?

(a) Terms, representations and puffs

A promise made by one party, and not withdrawn before final agreement, will be treated as a term of the oral contract (for an example see *Evans v Merzario*, above, p 163). At the other extreme there are the vague commendatory statements known as puffs, to which no legal liability attaches—statements which are regarded as unsafe to rely on because they are obviously not to be taken literally ('This car goes like a bomb') or because they are merely vague commendations ('This washing powder washes whiter than white'). In between clear promises and puffs is a 'grey area' of statements which are not on their face promissory, but which are not just puffs either, because the statement is one of fact. The statement of fact may be explicit, or it may be implicit in a statement of opinion. A statement of opinion which turns out to be incorrect does not normally give rise to liability, but it may do so where it carries with it an implication that the opinion expressed is a genuine one, or that the speaker has some facts to justify the opinion and this is not true (see below, p 288ff).

If such an assertion of fact is made and turns out to be untrue, there will usually be a remedy in misrepresentation (see below, chapter 14); but even today this will often be less effective than if it can be shown that the maker of the statement was promising that what he asserted was true, 'guaranteeing' the truth of his statement.

Whether a statement contains a promise that it is true depends on the parties' 'intentions'. This contractual intention is judged objectively. A critical question is what factors a court will take into account in deciding whether a statement was 'intended' to be contractual.

One factor is the importance of the statement. If the statement is about something which is critical to the other party it is likely to be treated as a term of the contract. Thus in *Bannerman v White* (1861) 10 CB NS 844 the buyer asked the seller during the negotiations if the hops had been treated with sulphur, adding that if they had, he would not even trouble to ask the price. The seller said they had not been treated with sulphur, which he believed to be the case. It was held that the seller's statement was a term of the contract. If, on the other hand, the statement seems to be about some incidental characteristic of the goods being sold—something which at most affects the price to be paid rather than whether the buyer will buy the goods at all—the statement is probably less likely to be treated as a term: see the next case and below, p 263.

Oscar Chess Ltd v Williams [1957] 1 All ER 325, Court of Appeal

In June, 1955, the defendant sold to the plaintiffs, who were motor dealers, a second-hand Morris motor car for £290, this sum being credited to the defendant on the purchase of a new car through the dealers. The car sold to the dealers had been obtained by the defendant's mother in 1954 under a hire-purchase contract, and was shown in the registration book to have been first registered in 1948. There had been five changes of ownership between 1948 and 1954. The defendant, who honestly believed that the car was a 1948 model, described it as such to L, the salesman who acted for the plaintiffs in the matter, and showed L the registration book. L, who had frequently been given lifts in the car, also believed that it was a 1948 model, and the purchase price of £290 was calculated on this basis. In January, 1956, the plaintiffs sent the chassis and engine numbers of the car to the manufacturers and were informed by them that the car was a 1939 model. If the plaintiffs had known at the time of the purchase that the car was a 1939 model, they would have paid only £175 for it. In an action brought by them against the defendant eight months after the sale the plaintiffs claimed the sum of £115 as damages for breach of warranty.

[The trial judge held that the assumption that the car was a 1948 model was fundamental and gave judgment for the plaintiffs.]

Denning LJ . . . I entirely agree with the judge that both parties assumed that the Morris car was a 1948 model and that this assumption was fundamental to the contract. This does not prove, however, that the representation was a term of the contract. The assumption was based by both of them on the date given in the registration book as the date of first registration. They both believed that the car was a 1948 model, whereas it was only a 1939 one. They were both mistaken and their mistake was of fundamental importance.

The effect of such a mistake is this: It does not make the contract a nullity from the beginning, but it does in some circumstances enable the contract to be set aside in equity. If the buyer had come promptly, he might have succeeded in getting the whole transaction set aside in equity on the ground of this mistake (see *Solle v Butcher*), but he did not do so and it is now too late for him to do it (see *Leaf v International Galleries*). His only remedy is in damages, and to recover these he must prove a warranty.

In saying that he must prove a warranty, I use the word 'warranty' in its ordinary English meaning to denote a binding promise. Everyone knows what a man means when he says, 'I guarantee it', or 'I warrant it', or 'I give you my word on it'. He means that he binds himself to it. That is the meaning which it has borne in English law for three hundred years from the leading case of *Chandelor v Lopus* onwards. During the last hundred years, however, the lawyers have come to use the word 'warranty' in another sense. They use it to denote a subsidiary term in a contract as distinct from a vital term which they call a 'condition'. In so doing they depart from the ordinary meaning, not only of the word 'warranty', but also of the word 'condition'. There is no harm in their doing this, so long as they confine this technical use to its proper sphere, namely to distinguish between a vital term, the breach of which gives the right to treat the contract as at an end, and a subsidiary term which does not.

 . . . The material distinction here is between a statement which is a term of the contract and a statement which is only an innocent misrepresentation. This distinction is best expressed by the ruling of Holt CJ, 'Was it intended as a warranty or not?', using the word 'warranty' there in its ordinary English meaning: because it gives the exact shade of meaning that is required. It is something to which a man must be taken to bind himself.

In applying this test, however, some misunderstanding has arisen by the use of the word 'intended'. It is sometimes supposed that the tribunal must look into the minds of the parties to see what they themselves intended. That is a mistake . . . The question whether a warranty was intended depends on the conduct of the parties, on their words and behaviour, rather than on their thoughts. If an intelligent bystander would reasonably infer that a warranty was intended, that will suffice. And this, when the facts are not in dispute, is a question of law. . . .

It is instructive to take some recent instances to show how the courts have approached this question. When the seller states a fact which is or should be within his own knowledge and of which the buyer is ignorant, intending that the buyer should act on it and he does so, it is easy to infer a warranty; see *Couchman v Hill*, where a farmer stated that a heifer was unserved, and *Harling v Eddy*, where he stated that there was nothing wrong with her. So also if the seller makes a promise about something which is or should be within his own control; see *Birch v Paramount Estates, Ltd*, decided on Oct 2, 1956, in this court, where the seller stated that the house would be as good as the show house. If, however, the seller, when he states a fact, makes it clear that he has no knowledge of his own but has got his information elsewhere, and is merely passing it on, it is not so easy to imply a warranty. Such a case was *Routledge v McKay*, where the seller stated that a motor cycle combination was a 1942 model, and pointed to the corroboration of that statement to be found in the registration book, and it was held that there was no warranty.

Turning now to the present case, much depends on the precise words that were used. If the seller says: 'I believe the car is a 1948 Morris. Here is the registration book to prove it', there is clearly no warranty. It is a statement of belief, not a contractual promise. If however, the seller says: 'I guarantee that it is a 1948 Morris. This is borne out by the registration book, but you need not rely solely on that. I give you my own guarantee that it is', there is clearly a warranty. The seller is making himself contractually responsible, even though the registration book is wrong.

In this case much reliance was placed by the judge on the fact that the buyer looked up 'Glass's Guide' and paid £290 on the footing that the car was a 1948 model, but that fact seems to me to be neutral. Both sides believed the car to have been made in 1948 and in that belief the buyer paid £290. That belief can be just as firmly based on the buyer's own inspection of the log-book as on a contractual warranty by the seller.

Once that fact is put on one side, I ask myself: What is the proper inference from the known facts? It must have been obvious to both that the seller had himself no personal knowledge of the year when the car was made. He only became owner after a great number of changes. He must have been relying on the registration book. It is unlikely that such a person would warrant the year of manufacture. The most that he would do would be to state his belief, and then produce the registration book in verification of it. In these circumstances the intelligent bystander would, I suggest, say that the seller did not intend to bind himself so as to warrant that the car was a 1948 model. If the seller was asked to pledge himself to it, he would at once have said 'I cannot do that. I have only the log-book to go by, the same as you.'

The judge seems to have thought that there was a difference between written contracts and oral contracts. He thought that the reason why the buyer failed in *Heilbut, Symons & Co v Buckleton* and *Routledge v McKay* was because the sales were afterwards recorded in writing, and the written contracts contained no reference to the representation. I agree that that was an important factor in those cases. If an oral representation is afterwards recorded in writing, it is good evidence that it was intended as a warranty. If it is not put into writing, it is evidence against a warranty being intended; but it is by no means decisive. There have been many cases, such as *Birch v Paramount Estates, Ltd*, where the courts have found an oral warranty collateral to a written contract. When, however, the purchase is not recorded in writing at all, it must not be supposed that every representation made in the course of the dealing is to be treated as a warranty. The question then is still: Was it intended as a warranty? In the leading case of *Chandelor v Lopus* in 1603 a man by word of mouth sold a precious stone for £100 affirming it to be a bezoar stone whereas it was not. The declaration averred that the seller *affirmed* it to be a bezoar stone, but did not aver that he *warranted* it to be so. The declaration was held to be ill because (Cro Jac 4): '. . . the bare affirmation that it was a bezoar stone, without warranting it to be so, is no cause of action . . .' That has been the law from that day to this and it was emphatically re-affirmed by the House of Lords in *Heilbut, Symons & Co v Buckleton* . . .

[Hodson LJ delivered a judgment to the same effect.]

Morris LJ (dissenting). . . . In the present case, on a consideration of the evidence which he heard, the learned judge came to the conclusion that the statement which he held to have been made by the defendant at the time of the making of the contract was a statement made contractually. It seems to me that the totality of the evidence points to that view. The statement related to a vitally important matter: it described the subject-matter of the contract then being made and directed the parties to, and was the basis of, their agreement as to the price to be paid or credited to the defendant. In the language of Scott LJ, it seems to me that the statement made by the defendant was 'an item in [the] description' of what was being sold and that it constituted a substantial ingredient in the identity of the thing sold. It is with diffidence that I arrive at a conclusion differing from that of my Lords, but I cannot see that the learned judge in any way misdirected himself or misapplied any principle of law, and I see no reason for disturbing his conclusion.

Appeal allowed.

NOTE

Denning LJ's statement that had the buyer acted promptly, he could have had the transaction set aside for *mistake*, must be doubted (see below pp 380–387). However, if he had acted promptly he could have rescinded for *misrepresentation* (see below, pp 286–292). On the facts he had lost this right and, as the seller had not been fraudulent, as the law stood then, the buyer had no remedy unless he could prove a warranty. As the court held that the seller had not even been negligent, the same would apply today (see below, pp 297–300).

Dick Bentley Productions Ltd v Harold Smith (Motors) Ltd [1965] 2 All ER 65, Court of Appeal

The plaintiff asked the defendant car dealer to find him a 'well vetted' Bentley car. The defendant found a car and told the plaintiff that it had been fitted with a replacement engine and gearbox, and that it had since done only twenty thousand miles (the mileage shown on the odometer). The plaintiff bought the car but it turned out to be unsatisfactory, and he brought an action against the defendant. The trial judge held that the statement as to the mileage was untrue though not dishonest, and awarded the plaintiff £400 damages for breach of warranty. The defendant appealed.

Lord Denning MR. . . . The first point is whether this representation, namely that the car had done twenty thousand miles only since it had been fitted with a replacement engine and gearbox, was an innocent misrepresentation (which does not give rise to damages), or whether it was a warranty. It was said by Holt CJ and repeated in *Heilbut, Symons & Co v Buckleton*:

> 'An affirmation at the time of the sale is a warranty, provided it appear on evidence to be so intended.'

But that word 'intended' has given rise to difficulties. I endeavoured to explain in *Oscar Chess, Ltd v Williams* that the question whether a warranty was intended depends on the conduct of the parties, on their words and behaviour, rather than on their thoughts. If an intelligent bystander would reasonably infer that a warranty was intended, that will suffice. What conduct, then? What words and behaviour, lead to the inference of a warranty?

Looking at the cases once more, as we have done so often, it seems to me that if a representation is made in the course of dealings for a contract for the very purpose of inducing the other party to act on it, and it actually induces him to act on it by entering into the contract, that is prima facie ground for inferring that the representation was intended as a warranty. It is not necessary to speak of it as being collateral. Suffice it that the representation was intended to be acted on and was in fact acted on. But the maker of the representation can rebut this inference if he can show that it really was an innocent misrepresentation, in that he was in fact innocent of fault in making it, and that it would not be reasonable in the circumstances for him to be bound by it. In the *Oscar Chess* case the inference was rebutted. There a man had bought a second-hand car and received with it a log-book, which stated the year of the car, 1948. He afterwards resold the car. When he resold it he simply repeated what was in the log-book and passed it on to the buyer. He honestly believed on reasonable grounds that it was true. He was completely innocent of any fault. There was no warranty by him but only an innocent misrepresentation. Whereas in the present case it is very different. The inference is not rebutted. Here we have a dealer, Mr Smith, who was in a position to know, or at least to find out, the history of the car. He could get it by writing to the makers. He did not do so. Indeed it was done later. When the history of this car was examined, his statement turned out to be quite wrong. He ought to have known better. There was no reasonable foundation for it. . . .

Danckwerts LJ. I agree with the judgment of Lord Denning MR.

Salmon LJ. I agree. I have no doubt at all that the learned county court judge reached a correct conclusion when he decided that Mr Smith gave a warranty to the second plaintiff Mr Bentley, and that that warranty was broken. Was what Mr Smith said intended and understood as a legally binding promise? If so, it was a warranty and as such may be part of the contract of sale or collateral to it. In effect, Mr Smith said: 'If you will enter into a contract to buy this motor car from me for £1,850, I undertake that you will be getting a motor car which has done no more than twenty thousand miles since it was fitted with a new engine and a new gearbox.' I have no doubt at all that what was said by Mr Smith was so understood and was intended to be so understood by Mr Bentley.

I accordingly agree that the appeal should be dismissed.

Appeal dismissed.

NOTES

1. Normally when a seller gives a warranty his liability is strict (though for an exception see *Esso v Mardon*, below). Denning suggests that the test is whether the seller was actually at fault, but a more suitable test is whether he was in a better position to discover the truth. Suppose he *had* contacted the car's makers but they had misinformed him: should the outcome be different?
2. Placing the risk that the facts will turn out to be different from what was stated upon the party best able to discover the truth (the 'least cost avoider') has a clear economic rationale. See below, p 305.
3. In these two cases the test of which party was in the better position to discover the truth and the test of whether the statement was critical to the other party seem to have pointed in the same direction: it seems unlikely that Bentley would have bought the car had he known the truth, whereas Oscar Chess Ltd would presumably have bought the Morris for £175. What if the tests point in opposite directions?
4. Nowadays the question whether the statement was contractual or merely a representation is of less practical importance because, as we shall see (below, pp 297–300), since 1967 even a misrepresentation will give rise to damages provided it was negligent. However there is still no liability in damages in the absence of negligence and the measure of damages is less generous than for breach of contract.

(b) What was being promised?

Esso Petroleum Co Ltd v Mardon [1976] 2 All ER 5, Court of Appeal

The plaintiffs ('Esso') were a company engaged in the production and distribution of petroleum. In 1961 Esso acquired a site on a busy main street of a town for development as a petrol filling station. The site was acquired on the basis of calculations which showed that the estimated annual consumption of petrol at the station would be 200,000 gallons from the third year of operation. After the site had been acquired the local planning authority required the forecourt and petrol pumps to be placed at the back of the site which was accessible only from side streets and which was not visible from the busy main road. The station was constructed in compliance with that requirement. The result of that change of plan was to falsify the basis on which Esso had calculated the annual consumption of petrol, but through lack of care Esso failed to revise their original estimate of 200,000 gallons. Subsequently Esso opened negotiations with the defendant for the grant to him of a tenancy of the station. During the negotiations L, an Esso representative who had had 40 years' experience in the petrol trade, told the defendant in good faith that Esso had estimated that the throughput of petrol would reach 200,000 gallons a year in the third year of operation of the station. The defendant was aware of the deficiencies of the station and suggested that a lower estimate would be more realistic, but L's greater expertise quelled his doubts, and on the basis of L's representation as to the potential throughput the defendant was induced to enter into a tenancy agreement in April 1963. That agreement was for three years at a rent assessed by Esso in accordance with their estimate of the potential throughput of petrol. The defendant put capital into the station and incurred a bank overdraft to operate it but, despite his hard work, at the end of the first 15 months only 78,000 gallons of petrol had been consumed at the station and the defendant had incurred a loss in running it. In July 1964 he tendered notice to quit the tenancy but Esso wished to retain him as the tenant and granted him a new tenancy agreement, dated 1st September 1964, at a reduced rent. The defendant accepted the new tenancy in an attempt to mitigate the loss already incurred, but continued to lose money in the business, since the site with the pumps situated at the back was only capable of an annual throughput of some 70,000 gallons of petrol. By August 1966 the defendant was unable to pay Esso for petrol supplied to the station and in December 1966 Esso issued a writ against him claiming possession of the station, money due for petrol and mesne profits. The defendant continued trading at the station until March 1967 when he gave up possession. He had lost all the capital he had put into the station and had incurred a substantial overdraft. By his defence and counterclaim the defendant claimed damages in respect of the representation made by L as to the potential throughput of petrol, alleging (i) that it amounted to a warranty for breach of which the defendant was entitled to damages, and (ii) that it also amounted to negligent misrepresentation in breach of Esso's duty of care to the defendant in advising him as to the potential throughput. The trial judge rejected the claim for breach of warranty, but held that Esso were liable in damages for breach of their duty of care to the defendant. In assessing those damages the judge limited the recoverable loss to that suffered between April 1963 and September 1964 on the ground that the misrepresentation made in 1963 had not induced the defendant to enter into the tenancy agreement of September 1964. The defendant appealed.

Lord Denning MR: . . .

Collateral warranty

Ever since *Heilbut Symons & Co v Buckleton* we have had to contend with the law as laid down by the House of Lords that an innocent misrepresentation gives no right to damages. In order to escape from that rule, the pleader used to allege—I often did it myself—that the misrepresentation was fraudulent, or alternatively a collateral warranty. At the trial we nearly always succeeded on collateral warranty. We had to reckon, of course, with the dictum of Lord Moulton that 'such collateral contracts must from their very nature be rare'. But more often than not the court elevated the innocent misrepresentation into a collateral warranty; and thereby did justice—in advance of the Misrepresentation Act 1967. I remember scores of cases of that kind, especially on the sale of a business. A representation as to the profits that had been made in the past was invariably held to be a warranty. Besides that experience, there have been many cases since I have sat in this court where we have readily held a representation—which induces a person to enter into a contract—to be a warranty sounding in damages. I summarised them in *Dick Bentley Productions Ltd v Harold Smith (Motors) Ltd.*

Counsel for Esso retaliated, however, by citing *Bisset v Wilkinson* where the Privy Council said that a statement by a New Zealand farmer that an area of land 'would carry 2,000 sheep' was only an expression of opinion. He submitted that the forecast here of 200,000 gallons was an expression of opinion and not a statement of fact; and that it could not be interpreted as a warranty or promise.

Now, I would quite agree with counsel for Esso, that it was not a warranty—in this sense—that it did not *guarantee* that the throughput *would be* 200,000 gallons. But, nevertheless, it was a forecast made by a party, Esso, who had special knowledge and skill. It was the yardstick (the 'e a c') by which they measured the worth of a filling station. They knew the facts. They knew the traffic in the town. They knew the throughput of comparable stations. They had much experience and expertise at their disposal. They were in a much better position than Mr Mardon to make a forecast. It seems to me that if such a person makes a forecast—intending that the other should act on it and he does act on it—it can well be interpreted as a warranty that the forecast is sound and reliable in this sense that they made it with reasonable care and skill. It is just as if Esso said to Mr Mardon: 'Our forecast of throughput is 200,000 gallons. You can rely on it as being a sound forecast of what the service station should do. The rent is calculated on that footing.' If the forecast turned out to be an unsound forecast, such as no person of skill or experience should have made, there is a breach of warranty. Just as there is a breach of warranty when a forecast is made 'expected to load' by a certain date if the maker has no reasonable grounds for it: see *Samuel Sanday v Keighley Maxted & Co*: or bunkers 'expected 600/700 tons': see *The Pantanassa* by Diplock J. It is very different from the New Zealand case where the land had never been used as a sheep farm and both parties were equally able to form an opinion as to its carrying capacity.

In the present case it seems to me that there was a warranty that the forecast was sound, that is that Esso had made it with reasonable care and skill. That warranty was broken. Most negligently Esso made a 'fatal step' in the forecast they stated to Mr Mardon, and on which he took the tenancy. For this they are liable in damages. . . .

Ormrod LJ. . . . A representation of fact is much more likely to be intended to have contractual effect than a statement of opinion; so it is much easier to infer that in the former case it was so intended, and more difficult in the latter. Similarly, where statements of future fact or forecasts are under consideration, it will require much more cogent evidence to justify the conclusion that such statements were intended to be contractual in character. It is, therefore, with respect to counsel for Esso's argument, not an answer to say, simply, that the statement relied on was an expression of opinion or a forecast and therefore cannot be a warranty. In my view, following Lord Moulton in the *Heilbut Symons* case, the test is whether on the totality of the evidence the parties intended or must be taken to have intended that the representation was to form part of the basis of the contractual relations between them. . . .

I think that Mr Mardon has established the warranty alleged in para 6 of the defence and counterclaim and is entitled to damages for breach of contract. . . .

Shaw LJ. . . . Mr Mardon complained that 'he had been sold a pup'. I think he had; but it was a warranted pup so that Esso are in breach of warranty and liable in damages accordingly. . . .

Appeal allowed.

[Further extracts from this case will be found below, p 298.]

NOTES

1. In *Esso v Mardon* the court held that Esso had given a warranty, but it was not a warranty that the station would sell 200,000 gallons a year: that was outside Esso's control (though there is no doubt that Esso could have given Mardon such a warranty if they had used clear enough language). The warranty was only that they had made the forecast with reasonable care and skill.
2. A point which *Esso v Mardon* did not have to decide was whether Esso's liability was one for negligence only, or a strict one that reasonable care and skill had been taken. If, for instance, unknown to Mardon, the e a c had been prepared by an independent firm of specialists employed by Esso (ie by a third party for whom Esso would not normally be responsible), would Esso still have been liable?

In *Thake v Maurice* the plaintiffs, who were husband and wife, arranged for the defendant to carry out a vasectomy to sterilise the husband. The defendant made it clear that the operation was irreversible, demonstrating with his arms how the vas is cut and the ends tied back, and the plaintiffs signed forms stating that they understood the nature of the operation. Apparently the defendant did not give them his normal warning that there was a small chance that after the normal sperm tests the operation might reverse itself naturally, or at least he failed to ensure that this risk was conveyed to the plaintiffs. The operation was carried out with all due care and skill and the sperm tests were satisfactory, but the vasectomy reversed itself and the wife became pregnant. She did not realise this until it was too late to have an abortion and she gave birth to a healthy child. At first instance [1984] 2 All ER 513 Peter Pain J held that the contract was not merely one to carry out a vasectomy but one to render the husband irreversibly sterile. Alternatively he held the defendant's failure to give an adequate warning was a breach of a contractual duty of care. He awarded damages for the cost of a layette for the baby, the cost of her upkeep to 17 and loss of earnings for the wife, but nothing for pain and distress. The defendant appealed and the plaintiffs cross-appealed on damages. The Court of Appeal [1986] 1 All ER 497 upheld the finding of negligence and increased the damages to include an element for pain and suffering. Kerr LJ agreed that on the facts the plaintiffs could not reasonably have concluded anything other than that the defendant had undertaken to make the husband permanently sterile, but the majority disagreed. Nourse LJ said (at p 511):

> Would the words and visual demonstrations of the defendant have led a reasonable person standing in the position of the plaintiffs to understand that, come what may, Mr Thake would be rendered sterile and incapable of parenthood?
>
> The function of the court in ascertaining, objectively, the meaning of words used by contracting parties is one of everyday occurrence. But it is often exceedingly difficult to discharge it where the subjective understandings and intentions of the parties are clear and opposed. Here the plaintiffs understood that Mr Thake would be permanently sterile. The defendant himself recognised that they would have been left with that impression. On the other hand, he did not intend, and on the state of his knowledge he could not have intended, to guarantee that that would be the case. Both the understanding and the intention appear to them, as individuals, to have been entirely reasonable, but an objective interpretation must choose between them. In the end the question seems to be reduced to one of determining the extent of the knowledge which is to be attributed to the reasonable person standing in the position of the plaintiffs. Would he have known that the success of the operation, either because it depended on the healing of human tissue, or because in medical science all things, or nearly all things, are uncertain, could not be guaranteed? If he would, the defendant's words could only have been reasonably understood as forecasts of an almost certain, but nevertheless uncertain, outcome and his visual demonstrations as no more than explanations of how the operation would be done. He could not be taken to have given a guarantee of its success.
>
> I do not suppose that a reasonable person standing in the position of the plaintiffs would have known that a vasectomy is an operation whose success depends on a healing of human tissue which cannot be guaranteed. To suppose that would be to credit him with an omniscience beyond all reason. But it does seem to me to be reasonable to credit him with the more general knowledge that in medical science all things, or nearly all things, are uncertain. That knowledge is part of the general experience of mankind, and in my view it makes no difference whether what has to be considered is some form of medical or surgical treatment or the excision, apparently final, of a section of the vas. Doubtless the general experience of mankind will acknowledge the certainty that a limb, once amputated, has gone forever. Such has been the observation from time immemorial of a species to whom the spectacle of war and suffering is commonplace. But where an operation is of modern origin, its effects untried over several generations, would a reasonable person, confronted even with the words and demonstrations of the defendant in this case, believe that there was not one chance in ten thousand that the object would not be achieved? I do not think that he would.

On the measure of damages, Kerr LJ said (at p 509):

> In the event of the plaintiffs succeeding in contract, the damages for pain and suffering were agreed in the sum of £2,500 . . . without the need for any division between the two plaintiffs. However, in the event of the plaintiffs only succeeding in tort, it was agreed that there should be a reduction of £1,000 for this sum, because credit would have to be given for the fact that Mrs. Thake did not have to undergo the distress and suffering of an abortion. Although surprising at first sight, I agree that this must logically follow. If the plaintiffs are only entitled to complain of the defendant's failure to warn them that Mrs. Thake might become pregnant again, as she did, then her renewed pregnancy did not in itself amount to a breach on his part, with the result that, but for the events which in fact happened after she had again become pregnant, she would have had to undergo an abortion . . . Since my brethren take the view that the plaintiff's claim in contract fails, the additional award on the cross-appeal will only be £1,500.

See also *Eyre v Measday* [1986] 1 All ER 488 (no implied term that sterilisation operation would render woman absolutely sterile.)

(c) Incorporation of written terms into an oral contract

If a set of conditions is contained in a document which has been signed by the parties, the conditions form part of the contract: see below, p 277. The problem comes with unsigned documents such as tickets or notices which purport to state some or all of the terms of the contract. Most of the cases in which there is a dispute about whether a contract which has been concluded orally incorporates a set of written terms seem to involve exemption clauses (see below, Section 8, chapter 34). However, the rules on this point seem equally applicable to other types of clause, and we consider them here.

(i) Reasonable notice

Parker v South Eastern Railway (1877) 2 CPD 416, Court of Appeal

The plaintiff deposited his bag in the cloakroom at the defendants' station. He paid 2d and was given a ticket, on the face of which was printed the times at which the cloakroom was open and the words 'see back'. On the back was a clause stating that the company would not be responsible for any package exceeding the value of £10, and a placard to the same effect hung in the cloakroom. The bag, which was worth more than £10, was lost or stolen, and the plaintiff claimed its value. The trial judge left two questions to the jury: (1) Did the plaintiff read or was he aware of the special condition upon which the article was deposited? (2) Was the plaintiff, under the circumstances, under any obligation, in the exercise of reasonable and proper caution, to read or make himself aware of the condition? The jury answered both questions in the negative, and judgment was directed for the plaintiff.

Mellish LJ. . . . The question then is, whether the plaintiff was bound by the conditions contained in the ticket. In an ordinary case, where an action is brought on a written agreement which is signed by the defendant, the agreement is proved by proving his signature, and, in the absence of fraud, it is wholly immaterial that he has not read the agreement and does not know its contents. The parties may, however, reduce their agreement into writing, so that the writing constitutes the sole evidence of the agreement, without signing it; but in that case there must be evidence independently of the agreement itself to prove that the defendant has assented to it. In that case, also, if it is proved that the defendant has assented to the writing constituting the agreement between the parties, it is, in the absence of fraud, immaterial that the defendant had not read the agreement and did not know its contents. Now if in the course of making a contract one party delivers to another a paper containing writing, and the party receiving the paper knows that the paper contains conditions which the party delivering it intends to constitute the contract, I have no doubt that the party receiving the paper does, by receiving and keeping it, assent to the conditions contained in it, although he does not read them, and does not know what they are . . . [I]f the person receiving the ticket does not know that there is any writing upon the back of the ticket, he is not bound by a condition printed on the back . . . the plaintiffs admitted that they knew there was writing on the back of the ticket, [but] they swore not only that they did not read it, but that they did not know or believe that the writing contained conditions . . .

Now, I am of opinion that we cannot lay down, as a matter of law, either that the plaintiff was bound or that he was not bound by the conditions printed on the ticket, from the mere fact that he knew there was writing on the ticket, but did not know that the writing contained conditions. I think there may be cases in which a paper containing writing is delivered by one party to another in the course of a business transaction, where it would be quite reasonable that the party receiving it should assume that the writing contained in it no condition, and should put it in his pocket unread. For instance, if a person driving through a turnpike-gate received a ticket upon paying the toll, he might reasonably assume that the object of the ticket was that by producing it he might be free from paying toll at some other turnpike-gate, and might put it in his pocket unread. On the other hand, if a person who ships goods to be carried on a voyage by sea receives a bill of lading signed by the master, he would plainly be bound by it, although afterwards in an action against the shipowner for the loss of the goods, he might swear that he had never read the bill of lading, and that he did not know that it contained the terms of the contract of carriage, and that the shipowner was protected by the exceptions contained in it. Now the reason why the person receiving the bill of lading would be bound seems to me to be that in the great majority of cases persons shipping goods do know that the bill of lading contains the terms of the contract of carriage; and the shipowner, or the master delivering the bill of lading, is entitled to assume that the person shipping goods has that knowledge. It is, however, quite possible to suppose that a person who is neither a man of business nor a lawyer might on some particular occasion ship goods without the least knowledge of what a bill of lading was, but in my opinion such a person must bear the consequences of his own exceptional ignorance, it being plainly impossible that business could be carried on if every person who delivers a bill of lading had to stop to explain what a bill of lading was.

Now the question we have to consider is whether the railway company were entitled to assume that a person depositing luggage, and receiving a ticket in such a way that he could see that some writing was printed on it, would understand that the writing contained the conditions of contract, and this seems to me to depend upon whether people in general would in fact, and naturally, draw that inference. The railway company, as it seems to me, must be entitled to make some assumptions respecting the person who deposits luggage with them: I think they are entitled to assume that he can read, and that he understands the English language, and that he pays such attention to what he is about as may be reasonably expected from a person in such a transaction as that of depositing luggage in a cloak-room. The railway company must, however, take mankind as they find them, and if what they do is sufficient to inform people in general that the ticket contains conditions, I think that a particular plaintiff ought not to be in a better position than other persons on account of his exceptional ignorance or stupidity or carelessness. But if what the railway company do is not sufficient to convey to the minds of people in general that the ticket contains conditions, then they have received goods on deposit without obtaining the consent of the persons depositing them to the conditions limiting their liability. I am of opinion, therefore, that the proper direction to leave to the jury in these cases is, that if the person receiving the ticket did not see or know that there was any writing on the ticket, he is not bound by the conditions; that if he knew there was writing, and knew or believed that the writing contained conditions, then he is bound by the conditions; that if he knew there was writing on the ticket, but did not know or believe that the writing contained conditions, nevertheless he would be bound, if the delivering of the ticket to him in such a manner that he could see there was writing upon it, was, in the opinion of the jury, reasonable notice that the writing contained conditions.

[Baggallay LJ delivered a judgment to the same effect.]

Bramwell LJ. . . . The plaintiffs have sworn that they did not know that the printing was the contract, and we must act as though that was true and we believed it, a least as far as entering the verdict for the defendants is concerned. Does this make any difference? The plaintiffs knew of the printed matter. Both admit they knew it concerned them in some way, though they said they did not know what it was; yet neither pretends that he knew or believed it was not the contract. Neither pretends he thought it had nothing to do with the business in hand; that he thought it was an advertisement or other matter unconnected with his deposit of a parcel at the defendants' cloak-room. They admit that, for anything they knew or believed, it might be, only they did not know or believe it was, the contract. Their evidence is very much that they did not think, or, thinking, did not care about it. Now they claim to charge the company, and to have the benefit of their own indifference. Is this just? Is it reasonable? Is it the way in which any other business is allowed to be conducted? Is it even allowed to a man to 'think', 'judge', 'guess', 'chance' a matter, without informing himself when he can, and then when his 'thought', 'judgment', 'guess' or 'chance' turns out wrong or unsuccessful, claim to impose a burthen or duty on another which he could not have done had he informed himself as he might?
. . . Has not the giver of the paper a right to suppose that the receiver is content to deal on the terms in the paper? What more can be done? Must he say, 'Read that?' As I have said, he does so in effect when he puts it into the other's hands. The truth is, people are content to take these

things on trust. They know that there is a form which is always used—they are satisfied it is not unreasonable, because people do not usually put unreasonable terms into their contracts. If they did, then dealing would soon be stopped. Besides, unreasonable practices would be known. The very fact of not looking at the paper shews that this confidence exists. It is asked: What if there was some unreasonable condition, as for instance to forfeit 1000*l* if the goods were not removed in forty-eight hours? Would the depositor be bound? I might content myself by asking: Would he be, if he were told 'our conditions are on this ticket', and he did not read them? In my judgment, he would not be bound in either case. I think there is an implied understanding that there is no condition unreasonable to the knowledge of the party tendering the document and not insisting on its being read—no condition not relevant to the matter in hand. I am of opinion, therefore, that the plaintiffs, having notice of the printing, were in the same situation as though the porter had said, 'Read that, it concerns the matter in hand;' that if the plaintiffs did not read it, they were as much bound as if they had read it and had not objected.

Order for a new trial.

NOTES

1. Bramwell was well-known for his strong ideas on self-reliance. See Atiyah, *Rise and Fall of Freedom of Contract* (1979), pp 374–380.
2. Mellish's point that some tickets might reasonably be regarded as mere receipts was applied in *Chapelton v Barry UDC* [1940] 1 KB 532. The plaintiff visited a seaside resort and wished to sit in a deck chair on the beach. The defendant Council had left a pile of deck chairs near to a notice which indicated that they could be hired for 2d per session of three hours. The notice contained no exempting conditions, but requested the hirer to obtain a ticket from the attendant. The plaintiff took two chairs and gave 4d to the attendant, receiving two tickets in return. The ticket stated:

   The council will not be liable for any accident or damage arising from the hire of the chair.

   The plaintiff's chair collapsed when he sat on it owing to the negligence of the defendants. The Court of Appeal held that the clause did not protect the defendants; the ticket was 'a mere voucher or receipt'. In the normal case the person hiring a chair would not receive a ticket until after he had sat on the chair, so it was reasonable to regard the notice as an offer of the terms on which the chairs were to be hired, and the ticket as a mere receipt to show the person had paid; it made no difference that in this case the plaintiff had received his ticket at the outset. The 'mere voucher or receipt' point is sometimes treated as an independent principle, but seems really to be an application of the reasonable notice requirement.
3. Unless the plaintiff actually knew of the terms, a notice which is given only after the contract has been concluded is of no effect. Thus in *Olley v Marlborough Court Ltd* [1949] 1 KB 532 the plaintiff was not affected by clauses in a notice in her hotel bedroom when she had made the contract earlier at the reception desk. A graphic illustration of this rule came in *Thornton v Shoe Lane Parking Ltd* [1971] 1 All ER 686.

   The plaintiff went to park his car at a multi-storey car park owned and operated by the defendants. At the entry to the car park there was a sign stating the charges and that parking was 'at owner's risk'; the motorist then drove in past a machine which dispensed tickets. The ticket bore the time of entry and, in small print, the words:

   This ticket is issued subject to the conditions of issue as displayed on the premises.

Inside the premises were notices displaying the conditions, which purported to exclude liability to customers, not only for damage to cars but for personal injuries. On his return to collect his car, the plaintiff was injured, due partly to his own negligence and partly to that of the defendants. The defendants argued that the conditions excluded their liability, but the Court of Appeal held that the ticket came too late, as by that stage the plaintiff had driven up the entrance ramp and, as Megaw LJ put it, 'it was practically impossible for him to withdraw from his intended entry.' Lord Denning MR said of ticket machines generally (at p 689):

> The customer pays his money and gets a ticket. He cannot refuse it. He cannot get his money back. He may protest to the machine, even swear at it; but it will remain unmoved. He is committed beyond recall. He was committed at the very moment when he put his money into the machine. The contract was concluded at that time. It can be translated into offer and acceptance in this way. The offer is made when the proprietor of the machine holds it out as being ready to receive the money. The acceptance takes place when the customer puts his money into the slot. The terms of the offer are contained in the notice placed on or near the machine stating what is offered for the money. The customer is bound by those terms as long as they are sufficiently brought to his notice beforehand, but not otherwise. He is not bound by the terms printed on the ticket if they differ from the notice, because the ticket comes too late. In the present case the offer was contained in the notice at the entrance giving the charges for garaging and saying 'at owner's risk', ie at the risk of the owner so far as damage to the car was concerned. The offer was accepted when the plaintiff drove up to the entrance and, by the movement of his car, turned the light from red to green, and the ticket was thrust at him. The contract was then concluded, and it could not be altered by any words printed on the ticket itself.

4. It is treated as common knowledge that some types of ticket, eg railway tickets, are issued subject to conditions (see *Thompson v London, Midland and Scottish Rly Co* [1930] 1 KB 41). Suppose an intending traveller asks for a ticket for London and pays the price demanded by the booking clerk. The clerk then hands her a ticket which has printed on it that it is subject to some condition (eg a restriction on trains she can take) that she did not know of and does not like. Can she demand her money back? Who makes the offer and when does acceptance take place? See *Nunan v Southern Rly Co* [1923] 2 KB 703 at 707. Does it make any difference whether the railway timetables or advertising refer to the restriction?

5. Beale owns a multi-storey car park which has its entrance on a very busy street where waiting is not permitted and its exit on the other side of the building onto another street. How can he effectively incorporate a set of conditions into the contracts with his customers?

6. In *Thornton's* case Denning seemed to suggest that an unreasonable condition might be void. He made the same suggestion in other cases, but it is generally accepted that at common law there is no rule that an unreasonable condition is for that reason invalid. Unreasonable conditions may, however, be ineffective under the Unfair Contract Terms Act 1977 (see below, pp 705–731).

Interfoto Picture Library Ltd v Stiletto Visual Programmes Ltd [1988] 1 All ER 348, Court of Appeal

The defendant advertising agency required photographs of the 1950s for a presentation for a client. On 5 March 1984 they telephoned the plaintiffs, who ran a library of photographic transparencies and with whom they had not dealt before, inquiring whether the plaintiffs had any photographs of that period which might be suitable for the presentation. On the same day the plaintiffs dispatched to the defendants 47 transparencies packed in a bag with a delivery note which clearly specified that the transparencies were to be returned by 19 March and which under the heading 'Conditions' printed prominently in capitals, set out nine printed conditions in four columns. Condition 2 stated that all transparencies were to be returned within 14 days from the date of delivery and that 'A holding fee of £5.00 plus VAT per day will be charged for each transparency which is retained by you longer than the said period of 14 days'. The defendants accepted delivery of the transparencies but it was unlikely that they read any of the conditions. The defendants did not use the transparencies for their presentation but instead put them to one side and forgot about them. The transparencies were not returned to the plaintiffs until 2 April. The plaintiffs sent the defendants an invoice for £3,783.50 being the holding charge calculated at £5 per transparency per day from 19 March to 2 April. The defendants refused to pay and the plaintiffs brought an action against them claiming the amount of the invoice. The trial judge gave judgment for the plaintiffs and the defendants appealed.

Dillon LJ: . . . The primary point taken in the court below was that condition 2 was not part of the contract between the parties because the delivery note was never supplied to the defendants at all. That the judge rejected on the facts; he found that the delivery note was supplied in the same Jiffy bag with the transparencies, and that finding is not challenged in this court. He made no finding however that Mr Beeching or any other representative of the defendants read condition 2 or any of the other printed conditions, and it is overwhelmingly probable that they did not.

An alternative argument for the defendants, in this court as below, was to the effect that any contract between the parties was made before the defendants knew of the existence of the delivery note, viz either in the course of the preliminary telephone conversation between Mr Beeching and Miss Fraser or when the Jiffy bag containing the transparencies was received in the defendants' premises but before the bag was opened. I regard these submissions as unrealistic and unarguable. The original telephone call was merely a preliminary inquiry and did not give rise to any contract. But the contract came into existence when the plaintiffs sent the transparencies to the defendants and the defendants, after opening the bag, accepted them by Mr Beeching's phone call to the plaintiffs at 3.10 on 5 March. The question is whether condition 2 was a term of that contract.

There was never any oral discussion of terms between the parties before the contract was made. In particular there was no discussion whatever of terms in the original telephone conversation when Mr Beeching made his preliminary inquiry. The question is therefore whether condition 2 was sufficiently brought to the defendant's attention to make it a term of the contract which was only concluded after the defendants had received, and must have known that they had received the transparencies *and* the delivery note.

This sort of question was posed in relation to printed conditions, in the ticket cases, such [as] *Parker v South Eastern Rly Co*, in the last century. At that stage the printed conditions were looked at as a whole and the question considered by the courts was whether the printed conditions as a whole had been sufficiently drawn to a customer's attention to make the whole set of conditions part of the contract; if so the customer was bound by the printed conditions even though he never read them.

More recently the question has been discussed whether it is enough to look at a set of printed conditions as a whole. When for instance one condition in a set is particularly onerous does something special need to be done to draw customer's attention to that particular condition? In an obiter dictum in *J Spurling Ltd v Bradshaw* [1956] 2 All ER 121 at 125, [1956] 1 WLR 461 at 466 (cited in *Chitty on Contracts* (25th edn, 1983) vol 1, para 742, p 408) Denning LJ stated:

'Some clauses which I have seen would need to be printed in red ink on the face of the document with a red hand pointing to it before the notice could be held to be sufficient.'

Then in *Thornton v Shoe Lane Parking Ltd*, both Lord Denning MR and Megaw LJ held as one of their grounds of decision, as I read their judgments, that where a condition is particularly onerous or unusual the party seeking to enforce it must show that that condition, or an unusual condition of that particular nature, was fairly brought to the notice of the other party. . . .

Counsel for the plaintiffs submits that *Thornton v Shoe Lane Parking Ltd* was a case of an exemption clause and that what their Lordships said must be read as limited to exemption clauses and in particular exemption clauses which would deprive the party on whom they are imposed of statutory rights. But what their Lordships said was said by way of interpretation and application of the general statement of the law by Mellish LJ in *Parker v South Eastern Rly Co* and the logic of it is applicable to any particularly onerous clause in a printed set of conditions of the one contracting party which would not be generally known to the other party.

Condition 2 of these plaintiffs' conditions is in my judgment a very onerous clause. The defendants could not conceivably have known, if their attention was not drawn to the clause, that the plaintiffs were proposing to charge a 'holding fee' for the retention of the transparencies at such a very high and exorbitant rate.

At the time of the ticket cases in the last century it was notorious that people hardly ever troubled to read printed conditions on a ticket or delivery note or similar document. That remains the case now. In the intervening years the printed conditions have tended to become more and more complicated and more and more one-sided in favour of the party who is imposing them, but the other parties, if they notice that there are printed conditions at all, generally still tend to assume that such conditions are only concerned with ancillary matters of form and are not of importance. In the ticket cases the courts held that the common law required that reasonable steps be taken to draw the other parties' attention to the printed conditions or they would not be part of the contract. It is in my judgment a logical development of the common law into modern conditions that it should be held, as it was in *Thornton v Shoe Lane Parking Ltd*, that, if one condition in a set of printed conditions is particularly onerous or unusual, the party seeking to enforce it must show that that particular condition was fairly brought to the attention of the other party.

In the present case, nothing whatever was done by the plaintiffs to draw the defendants' attention particularly to condition 2; it was merely one of four columns' width of conditions printed across the foot of the delivery note. Consequently condition 2 never, in my judgment, became part of the contract between the parties. . . .

Bingham LJ: . . . In many civil law systems, and perhaps in most legal systems outside the common law world, the law of obligations recognises and enforces an overriding principle that in making and carrying out contracts parties should act in good faith. This does not simply mean that they should not deceive each other, a principle which any legal system must recognise; its effect is perhaps most aptly conveyed by such metaphorical colloquialisms as 'playing fair', 'coming clean' or 'putting one's cards face upwards on the table'. It is in essence a principle of fair and open dealing. In such a forum it might, I think, be held on the facts of this case that the plaintiffs were under a duty in all fairness to draw the defendants' attention specifically to the high price payable if the transparencies were not returned in time and, when the 14 days had expired, to point out to the defendants the high cost of continued failure to return them.

English law has, characteristically, committed itself to no such overriding principle but has developed piecemeal solutions in response to demonstrated problems of unfairness. Many examples could be given. Thus equity has intervened to strike down unconscionable bargains. Parliament has stepped in to regulate the imposition of exemption clauses and the form of certain hire-purchase agreements. The common law also has made its contribution, by holding that certain classes of contract require the utmost good faith, by treating as irrecoverable what purport to be agreed estimates of damage but are in truth a disguised penalty for breach, and in many other ways.

The well-known cases on sufficiency of notice are in my view properly to be read in this context. At one level they are concerned with a question of pure contractual analysis, whether one party has done enough to give the other notice of the incorporation of a term in the contract. At another level they are concerned with a somewhat different question, whether it would in all the circumstances be fair (or reasonable) to hold a party bound by any conditions or by a particular condition of an unusual and stringent nature. . . .

Turning to the present case, I am satisfied for reasons which Dillon LJ has given that no contract was made on the telephone when the defendants made their initial request. I am equally satisfied that no contract was made on delivery of the transparencies to the defendants before the opening of the Jiffy bag in which they were contained. Once the Jiffy bag was opened and the transparencies taken out with the delivery note, it is in my judgment an inescapable inference that the defendants would have recognised the delivery note as a document of a kind likely to contain contractual terms and would have seen that there were conditions printed in small but visible lettering on the face of the document. To the extent that the conditions so displayed were common form or usual terms regularly encountered in this business, I do not think the defendants could successfully contend that they were not incorporated into the contract.

The crucial question in the case is whether the plaintiffs can be said fairly and reasonably to have brought condition 2 to the notice of the defendants. The judge made no finding on the point, but I think that it is open to this court to draw an inference from the primary findings which he did make. In my opinion the plaintiffs did not do so. They delivered 47 transparencies, which was a number the defendant had not specifically asked for. Condition 2 contained a daily rate per transparency after the initial period of 14 days many times greater than was usual or (so far as the evidence shows) heard of. For these 47 transparencies there was to be a charge for each day of delay of £235 plus value added tax. The result would be that a venial period of delay, as here, would lead to an inordinate liability. The defendants are not to be relieved of that liability because they did not read the condition, although doubtless they did not; but in my judgment they are to be relieved because the plaintiffs did not do what was necessary to draw this unreasonable and extortionate clause fairly to their attention. I would accordingly allow the defendants' appeal and substitute for the judge's award the sum which he assessed on the alternative basis of quantum meruit.

In reaching the conclusion I have expressed I would not wish to be taken as deciding that condition 2 was not challengeable as a disguised penalty clause. This point was not argued before the judge nor raised in the notice of appeal. It was accordingly not argued before us. I have accordingly felt bound to assume, somewhat reluctantly, that condition 2 would be enforceable if fully and fairly brought to the defendant's attention.

Appeal allowed.

NOTES

1. By what criteria is it to be decided if conditions are 'unusual'?

2. For the rules on penalty clauses, see below, p 508.

(ii) Course of dealing

In *Henry Kendall & Sons v William Lillico & Sons Ltd* (appeals from *Hardwick Game Farm v Suffolk Agricultural and Poultry Producers Association*) [1969] 2 AC 31 there had been three or four contracts a month between two of the parties, Grimsdale and SAPPA. The practice had been that when an oral contract had been made, Grimsdale would send a contract note to SAPPA, either later on the same day or on the following day. On the back of the notes were conditions, including one that 'the buyer . . . takes the responsibility for latent defects'. The House of Lords held that it was

> . . . reasonable to hold that when SAPPA placed an order to buy, they did so on the basis and with the knowledge that an acceptance of the order by Grimsdale and their agreement to sell would be on the terms and conditions set out on their contract notes.

In this case the course of dealings was long, continuous and consistent. In *McCutcheon v David MacBrayne Ltd* [1964] 1 All ER 430 the plaintiff had shipped his car several times on the defendants' ship between Islay and the mainland of Scotland. The evidence was that sometimes he was asked to sign a risk note, containing exempting conditions, and sometimes not. On the relevant voyage, on which the ship sank owing to the defendant's negligence, the plaintiff's brother had arranged the shipment and had not been asked to sign a risk note. It was held by the House of Lords that there was no consistent course of dealings. See MacDonald (1988) 8 Legal Studies 48.

In *Hollier v Rambler Motors (AMC) Ltd* (below, p 683) the plaintiff had taken his car for servicing to the defendants' garage three or four times over a five year period. On previous occasions he had been asked to sign a service 'invoice' containing conditions, but on the relevant occasion this step was omitted. The Court of Appeal held that the previous contracts did not amount to a course of dealings incorporating the defendants' conditions into the oral contract.

(iii) Common understanding

British Crane Hire Corporation Ltd v Ipswich Plant Hire Ltd [1974] 1 All ER 1059, Court of Appeal

The plaintiffs and the defendants were companies engaged in the business of hiring out heavy earth moving equipment. The defendants were themselves carrying out drainage and other work of a civil engineering nature on marshy ground. They urgently required a dragline crane and so got in touch with the plaintiffs who agreed to supply one on hire. The agreement was made by telephone. The hiring and transport charges were agreed but nothing was said about the conditions of hire. Soon after the crane had been delivered, the plaintiffs, in accordance with their normal practice, sent the defendants a printed form to be signed by them which set out the conditions of hire. Before the defendants had signed it, however, an accident occurred in consequence of which the crane sank into the marshy ground. The accident was not caused by any negligence on the part of the defendants. Under the printed conditions the defendants were liable to indemnify the owner against all expense in connection with the use of the crane. The plaintiffs' conditions were in similar terms to those used by all firms in the plant-hiring business including the defendants themselves. In an action by the plaintiffs for the cost of recovering the crane the defendants claimed that they were not liable under the plaintiffs' conditions since they had not been incorporated into the oral contract of hire.

Lord Denning MR. . . . . [H]ere the parties were both in the trade and were of equal bargaining power. Each was a firm of plant hirers who hired out plant. The defendants themselves knew that firms in the plant-hiring trade always imposed conditions in regard to the hiring of plant; and that their conditions were on much the same lines. The defendants' manager, Mr Turner (who knew the crane), was asked about it. He agreed that he had seen these conditions or similar ones in regard to the hiring of plant. He said that most of them were, to one extent or another, variations of a form which he called 'the Contractors' Plant Association form'. The defendants themselves (when they let out cranes) used the conditions of that form. The conditions on the plaintiffs' form were in rather different words, but neverthless to much the same effect. . . .

From [the] evidence it is clear that both parties knew quite well that conditions were habitually imposed by the supplier of these machines: and both parties knew the substance of those conditions. In particular that, if the crane sank in soft ground, it was the hirer's job to recover it; and that there was an indemnity clause. In these circumstances, I think the conditions on the form should be regarded as incorporated into the contract. I would not put it so much on the course of dealing, but rather on the common understanding which is to be derived from the conduct of the parties, namely, that the hiring was to be on the terms of the plaintiffs' usual conditions.

As Lord Reid said in *McCutcheon v David MacBrayne Ltd*, quoting from the Scottish textbook Gloag on Contract:

'The judicial task is not to discover the actual intentions of each party: it is to decide what each was reasonably entitled to conclude from the attitude of the other.'

It seems to me that, in view of the relationship of the parties, when the defendants requested this crane urgently and it was supplied at once—before the usual form was received—the plaintiffs were entitled to conclude that the defendants were accepting it on the terms of the plaintiffs' own printed conditions—which would follow in a day or two. It is just as if the plaintiffs had said, 'We will supply it on our usual conditions', and the defendants said, 'Of course, that is quite understood'.

Applying the conditions, it is quite clear that conditions 6 and 8 cover the second mishap. The defendants are liable for the costs of recovering the crane from the soft ground.

[Megaw LJ and Sir Eric Sachs agreed.]

NOTES

1. Was the clause incorporated on the basis of a custom in the trade, or on some other basis? For a trade custom to form an implied term of a contract, the custom must be generally accepted by those doing business in the particular trade in the particular place, and be so generally known that an outsider making reasonable enquiries could not fail to disover it (*Kum v Wah Tat Bank Ltd* [1971] 1 Lloyd's Rep 439, 444, PC). It will thus become binding on a newcomer to the trade. Had the hirers in this case been newcomers (eg a building firm which had not hired plant before), do you think the court would have decided the case the same way? If not, what was the basis of the decision?
2. There was evidence of the terms each company used when hiring *to* other people; but was there any evidence of the terms either used when hiring *from* others?
3. How is the equality or otherwise of bargaining power relevant to this point? Should the outcome of the case be different if the owners were a large, prosperous company and the hirers a small, struggling one?
4. Suppose A Ltd and B Ltd are engineering firms: A makes castings, B builds machinery using castings made by other firms. B has ordered castings from A three or four times in the last two years and has previously agreed to A's standard conditions of trading, which provide for a price increase or decrease if the market price of copper rises or falls. A similar clause is used by all firms making copper castings. B has its own set of purchasing conditions which provide for a fixed price.

    B makes a contract over the telephone to buy from A 1,000 castings at £1.00 each for delivery in six months' time. No letters are exchanged and no reference is made to A's conditions. After three months the price of copper doubles and A tells B that he will not deliver unless he is paid the price increase which would be appropriate if A's 'rise and fall' clause applies. Advise B.

(iv) Negation by circumstances

Couchman v Hill [1947] 1 All ER 103, Court of Appeal

The plaintiff bought at an auction sale a heifer belonging to the defendant and described in the sale catalogue as a 'red and white stirk heifer, unserved'. The catalogue contained the following words: 'All lots must be taken subject to all faults or errors of description (if any), and no compensation will be paid for the same'. By No 3 of the conditions of sale: 'The lots are sold with all faults, imperfections, and errors of description, the auctioneers not being responsible for the correct description, genuineness, or authenticity of, or any defect in, any lot, and giving no warranty whatever'. Before the sale and when the heifers were in the ring the plaintiff asked the defendant and the auctioneer: 'Can you confirm heifers unserved?' and received from both the answer: 'Yes.' Between 7 and 8 weeks after the purchase the heifer suffered a miscarriage and three weeks later died as a result of the strain of carrying a calf at too young an age for breeding. [The plaintiff brought an action] for damages for breach of warranty . . .

Scott LJ. . . . The real question is.: What did the parties understand by the question addressed to and the answer received from both the defendant and the auctioneer? It is contended by the defendant that the question meant 'having regard to the onerous stipulations which I know I shall have to put up with if I bid and the lot is knocked down to me, can you give me your honourable assurance that the heifers have in fact not been served? If so, I will risk the penalties of the catalogue'. The alternative meaning is: 'I am frightened of contracting on your published terms, but I will bid if you will tell me by word of mouth that you accept full responsibility for the statement in the catalogue that the heifers have not been served, or, in other words, give me a clean warranty. That is the only condition on which I will bid'. If that was the meaning there was clearly an oral offer of a warranty which over-rode the stultifying condition in the printed terms, that offer was accepted by the plaintiff when he bid, and the contract was made on that basis when the lot was knocked down to him. In some circumstances I concede that such a question might on its face be somewhat ambiguous, but I think in the present case the only inference that could properly be drawn by the judge or jury charged with the duty of finding the facts—and this is a question of fact as to the intention of the parties—is that the question was asked and answered with the alternative meaning indicated. That this is so follows, I think, conclusively from the plaintiff's evidence which was accepted by the judge, taken in conjunction with the admissions of the defendant that the words if used—which he denied—would have bound him. It is obvious that it was the stipulations that prompted the question. The plaintiff was not a lawyer, but he knew what he wanted. So did the defendant, and he got it. What the plaintiff wanted was to know where he stood before he made an offer which the fall of the hammer would turn into a contract.

The county court judge in a careful reserved judgment has found that this oral statement was made, and he refers to it as a warranty, but holds that its value was destroyed by the qualifying stipulations. He has not in terms put the question to himself: 'Did the parties by this question and answer intend to exclude the stipulations from the contract that resulted on the fall of the hammer?' I have, accordingly, felt some doubt whether or not the proper course was to order a new trial. On reading his judgment as a whole I have, however, arrived at the conclusion that it is implicit therein that it was not the intention of the parties to exclude the stipulation. As we are of opinion that on the facts found by him he could not properly arrive at this conclusion, I think we are not compelled to put the parties to the expense of a further trial.

There was a good deal of discussion whether the description 'unserved' constituted a warranty or a condition. I have, in what I have said so far deliberately refrained from expressing a view thereon, but as a matter of law I think every item in a description which constitutes a substantial ingredient in the 'identity' of the thing sold is a condition, although every such condition can be waived by the purchaser who thereon becomes entitled to treat it as a warranty and recover damages.

I think there was here an unqualified condition which, on its breach, the plaintiff was entitled to treat as a warranty and recover the damages claimed. One final word. The printed condition that the vendor will take no responsibility for errors of description of things or animals specifically offered for sale on inspection is reasonable for visible defects, but for qualities or attributes which are invisible it is not reasonable. It may well become a mere trap for the unwary. The point deserves consideration by the Auctioneers' Associations.

The appeal should, therefore, in my opinion be allowed with costs here and below, the latter on Scale B.

[Tucker and Bucknill LJJ agreed.]

Appeal allowed.

NOTES

1. For the distinction between 'condition' and 'warranty', see below, p 326.
2. A party which has misrepresented the effect of a clause may not be permitted to rely on it: see below, p 278.

CHAPTER 13
Contents of written contracts

(a) Effect of signature

L'Estrange v Graucob Ltd [1934] 2 KB 394, Divisional Court

The plaintiff bought an automatic slot machine from the defendants, signing an order form which contained, in small print, a number of conditions, one of which was that 'any express or implied condition, statement, or warranty, statutory or otherwise not stated herein is hereby excluded'. She received in exchange a printed confirmation order. The machine did not work satisfactorily and the plaintiff brought an action in the county court in which she claimed that the machine was not fit for the purpose for which it was sold. The county court judge held that the sellers could not rely on the printed condition, and the defendant appealed. The plaintiff claimed that she had not read the form and did not know what it contained.

Scrutton LJ. . . . A clause of [this] sort has been before the Courts for some time. The first reported case in which it made its appearance seems to be *Wallis, Son & Wells v Pratt & Haynes*, where the exclusion clause mentioned only 'warranty' and it was held that it did not exclude conditions. In the more recent case of *Andrews Bros (Bournemouth), Ltd v Singer & Co Ltd* where the draftsman had put into the contract of sale a clause which excluded only implied conditions, warranties and liabilities, it was held that the clause did not apply to an express term describing the article, and did not exempt the seller from liability where he delivered an article of a different description. The clause here in question would seem to have been intended to go further than any of the previous clauses and to include all terms denoting collateral stipulations, in order to avoid the result of these decisions.

The main question raised in the present case is whether that clause formed part of the contract. If it did, it clearly excluded any condition or warranty.

In the course of the argument in the county court reference was made to the railway passenger and cloak-room ticket cases . . .

These cases have no application when the document has been signed. When a document containing contractual terms is signed, then, in the absence of fraud, or, I will add, misrepresentation, the party signing it is bound, and it is wholly immaterial whether he has read the document or not.

[Maugham LJ agreed.]

Appeal allowed.

NOTES

1. This decision must now be read in the light of the Unfair Contract Terms Act 1977, s 6(3) and Schedule 2, para (c): see below, pp 705 and 718.
2. When Scrutton says that a party will not be bound when there has been fraud or misrepresentation, he may be referring to the rule that a misrepresentation, whether fraudulent or innocent, may entitle the

misrepresentee to rescind the contract (see below, chapter 14), or to a misrepresentation about the meaning of the clause itself. In *Curtis v Chemical Cleaning and Dyeing Co Ltd* [1951] 1 All ER 631 the plaintiff took a wedding dress to the defendants for cleaning and was asked to sign a document exempting the defendants from liability 'for any damage howsoever arising'. She asked why she had to sign and was told that it was because the defendants would not accept liability for damage to beads or sequins on the dress. The plaintiff then signed. The dress was returned with a stain on it that had not been there before. The defendants denied liability, relying on the clause. The Court of Appeal held that the statement made to the plaintiff misrepresented the effect of the clause and prevented the defendants from relying on it. Somervell LJ said that the clause 'never became part of the contract', but probably this goes too far: what if the only damage had been to the sequins? Compare estoppel, above p 134.

3. Suppose Graucob Ltd knew that the plaintiff thought she was being given a full and unrestricted warranty?

'Signature, Consent and the Rule in L'Estrange v Graucob' by Spencer [1973] CLJ 103 at 114–116

Was this right? When Miss L'Estrange signed the order form on which were written various terms, she gave the appearance of agreeing to everything that was written on the document. To borrow the words from *Smith v Hughes* itself, she so conducted herself 'that a reasonable man would believe that she was assenting to the terms proposed by the other party'. It would usually follow from this that she was bound by her apparent consent to all those terms. However, a person is not bound by apparent consent where the other party knew that his mind did not go with his apparent consent, or where the other party is responsible for the mistake which has been made. Didn't the facts of the case bring Miss L'Estrange within the scope of these exceptions to apparent consent?

The order form which Graucob Ltd provided seems to have been drawn up in a most confusing way. Maugham LJ said '. . . I could wish that the contract had been in a simpler and more usual form. It is unfortunate that the important clause excluding conditions and warranties is in such small print'. Not only was this clause printed in small print, but it was also printed on brown paper, which must have made the small print even harder to read. The general layout of the form also appears to have been confusing, too, the exemption clause being in a part of the document where it easily escaped notice. Then was this not one of those cases where although A apparently consented to B's terms, he did so because B had earlier confused him as to what those terms should be? In principle, the case is surely the same as *Scriven v Hindley*, where A was allowed to deny his apparent consent to a contract to buy tow, because the auction catalogue had been confusing, and had contributed to form A's belief that he was offering to buy, not tow, but hemp.

Perhaps Miss L'Estrange could have gone even further than this, and also denied her apparent consent to the exemption clause on the ground that the company either knew or ought to have known that her mind did not go with her apparent consent. Why did Graucob Ltd use order forms printed on brown paper containing obscure exemption clauses in minute print in unexpected places? Was it because it knew that if it said what it meant more plainly, its customers would understand the document they were being asked to sign, and would refuse to do so? . . .

The truth is that whatever may have been Graucob Ltd's intentions disreputable companies put harsh exemption clauses in minute print in order to 'put one over' people like Miss L'Estrange. Then why should people in her position not be allowed to deny their apparent consent to the clause because the company either *knew* or *ought to have known* that their mind did not go with their apparent consent?

NOTES

1. Compare Samek, 'The Objective Theory of Contract and the Rule in *L'Estrange v Graucob*' (1974) 52 Can BR 351; Howarth, 'The Meaning

of Objectivity in Contract' (1984) 100 LQR 252; Vorster (1987) 103 LQR 274.

2. If it was clear to Graucob Ltd that Miss L'Estrange thought she was getting a full warranty, one can see Spencer's argument succeeding; but what if she simply 'didn't know what she was signing'?

3. In *Tilden Rent-a-Car Co v Clendenning* (1978) 83 DLR(3d) 400 the Ontario Court of Appeal cited Spencer's article. Clendenning rented a car from the defendant's office at Vancouver airport, as he had often done before. He was asked whether he required additional insurance coverage, and he replied that he did. In fact the contractual document which he received and signed, while excluding the whole of the driver's liability for damage to the rented car, limited this exclusion to cases where there was no breach of the conditions of the rental agreement. On the back of the contract, in very small print, there was a clause by which the customer undertook not to drive in violation of any traffic law or ordinance, or after consuming any quantity of intoxicating liquor. Clendenning had an accident while driving after having had a drink, but not so as to be incapable of driving. The majority of the court held that Clendenning was not bound by this 'onerous' provision, as Tilden had not taken steps to alert him to its presence.

Tilden Rent-a-Car cannot rely on provisions of the contract which it had no reason to believe were being assented to by the other contracting party . . .

4. It may be hard to reconcile this approach with more traditional attitudes to mistake, which at least recently have denied relief unless one party actually knew of the other's mistake: see above, pp 233 and 241. Is there anything to be said for it in policy terms? Would denying that a customer's signature on a standard form is conclusive evidence of her consent to all the terms of the document be an improper interference with freedom of contract?

'Freedom of Contract and the New Right' by Atiyah (1988) 20 Skriftserien, Juridiska Fakulteten i Stockholm, pp 11–13

The whole point of Freedom of Contract is to reject paternalism and leave the parties to their own bargain. Yet, as all lawyers know, there are many types of circumstances in which for fifty years and more the law has been busy interfering with express contractual terms on grounds of unfairness.

Furthermore, most lawyers brought up in the atmosphere prevailing after the second World War have shown considerable sympathy with these legislative interferences with Freedom of Contract. I myself have often argued (for example in my Cecil Wright Memorial Lecture [see *Essays on Contract*, chap. 11]) that it is impossible to ignore the idea of a fair exchange in contract law. In that lecture I pointed out that there are all sorts of legal doctrines which enable the common law courts to pursue normative criteria of fairness in handling contractual disputes, and I rejected the idea that the express terms of the contract can always be treated as a conclusive and definite decision on what is fair. On the other hand, I must admit to a good deal of sympathy with the ideology of the New Right, so a major problem for those who think as I do is to reconcile much traditional and apparently paternalistic interference with free contract with this new ideology. . . .

To what extent can this sort of interference with contractual freedom be reconciled with the ideology of the New Right?

First, there is surely nothing seriously objectionable about the provisions requiring information to be given to the consumer, nor even about the cooling-off provisions. It is true that even these may seem unnecessarily fussy and over-protective in the more robust market favoured by the New Right, but the main purpose here is to ensure that the contracts do indeed have the full consent and understanding of the consumer. There is nothing contrary to Freedom of Contract ideology in that. In fact, the giving of information about true rates of interest available from suppliers of credit can be justified as an aid to the competitive market.

But I would go much further, and suggest that there is nothing in Freedom of Contract ideology which requires us to accept without question the binding validity of pages of small print, simply because they are signed by contracting parties, whether they are consumers or even commercial organisations. The truth perhaps is that the practical convenience of treating signed printed forms as binding on the parties is so great that we have far too readily accepted these forms as conclusive evidence of what the parties really intended. This may well have been a wrong turning from the beginning, and if modern protective legislation is ever to be challenged by the New Right, some fundamental rethinking on this question will surely be in order. This could be a major gain, because much of our protective legislation, like the Consumer Credit Act itself draws no distinction between the consumer who truly understands the nature and essential terms of the contract he is entering into, and the consumer who does not. Nor will it suffice today to insist blandly that no consumers can understand the essential elements of a credit transaction. Some consumers are well informed, and others may have independent advice.

In this connection it is interesting to note that there are at least some recent judicial decisions which do seem more willing to treat consumers as rational adults, at least where they have been advised by their own lawyers. Of course this is not likely to happen with the purchase of consumer goods, but in two recent cases dealing with mortgage loan transactions, in which consumers were advised by their own lawyers, and fully understood the nature and essential elements of the transactions, the contracts were upheld by the courts even though the terms were arguably harsh or unfair [see below, p 658]. So here perhaps is a small pointer suggesting that the message of the New Right is being heard in the law courts as well as in the City of London. . . .

NOTES

1. Questions of the provision of information to consumers are explored in more detail below, p 700 ff.
2. Compare the *Interfoto* case, above p 270.
3. As so often seems to be the case, the courts in an indirect fashion evade the rule in *L'Estrange v Graucob* by using other doctrines. See in particular the rules on interpretation of exclusion clauses, below, p 682 ff.

(b) Parol evidence rule

Suppose the parties have signed a written contract (this may be a single document, or the part signed may refer expressly to another document, in which case the contract will include both documents read together). One party then alleges that the writings do not contain the whole contract: there is some other term which was expressly agreed, either orally or in a separate writing, but which is not stated or referred to in the signed writings.

Two points arise. Firstly, if the term was agreed to, why was it left out? Doesn't leaving it out show that it was not 'part of the final deal'? (Compare Fuller's 'channelling function', above, p 122.) Secondly, to allow the party to rely on the unstated term may produce costly uncertainty—uncertainty in court, where it will be more difficult to determine what the contract really was; uncertainty for third parties who may rely on the written contract (eg a bank which, after seeing a written contract its client has made, lends him money on the strength of it); and uncertainty for the parties, who later may not recollect just what was agreed. The last is particularly a problem when a party is a company, as the contract may be made by one officer but administered by another; this may explain why it is common in commercial contracts to find 'merger' or 'integration' clauses, such as:

The parties have negotiated this Agreement and shall enter into any Contract made subject hereto on the basis that the provisions of this Agreement and such Contract represent their entire agreement relating to the matters contained in this Agreement and such Contract.

An example of the problem is *Jacobs v Batavia and General Plantations Trust Ltd* [1924] 1 Ch 287, affd [1924] 2 Ch 329. The plaintiff applied for and was allotted four £100 deposit notes of the defendant company. He relied on the prospectus issued by the defendants. This stated that in the event of the sale of the Rio Bravo estates owned by the Trust, the Trust would set aside out of the proceeds of sale a sum sufficient to redeem all the notes then outstanding, and the holders would be given the option of being paid off then in cash at 105%, or of retaining their notes until the normal date for redemption. The notes themselves (which were in the same form as a specimen contained in the prospectus) made no reference to this undertaking. The estates in question were sold and the plaintiff brought an action for an injunction to restrain the Trust from dealing with the proceeds of sale without first setting aside a sum sufficient to pay off the outstanding notes. Was the contract simply what was contained in the notes or what was in the prospectus as well?

At one time the courts appeared to apply a strict rule, known as the 'parol evidence rule', to this sort of case: 'parol evidence cannot be admitted to add to, vary or contradict a deed or other written instrument'. The rule applied not just to oral promises but also to written promises which were not in or referred to by the written and signed contract (in the strict legal sense, parol means 'not under seal'; here it is used to mean 'extrinsic to the written and signed contract'). When the rule was applied it prevented the party who would otherwise have relied on the extrinsic promise from adducing any evidence on the point. It was thus not a rule of evidence at all, as it did not govern *how* the extrinsic promise might be proved; it was a rule of substantive law.

Some contracts, particularly contracts for the sale of land, were enforceable only if there was written evidence of their terms (see above, p 131). A complex body of rules was developed to deal with cases in which this requirement was not complied with, but generally speaking the contract could only be enforced in the terms set out in the writing—indeed, in some situations, if it were proved that the writing did not contain all the terms, the whole contract might turn out to be unenforceable (eg *Beckett v Nurse* [1948] 1 KB 535). Dicta often seem to suggest that the parol evidence rule applied to other kinds of contract as well. At least by the turn of the century this was misleading. The rule did not apply to contracts which were partly written and partly oral. Thus it was open to the court to find that on the facts the contract was not a 'written contract' within the meaning of the rule, but only partly written, and thus the parol evidence could be admitted. (It is not wholly clear whether this was always implicit in the rule or was a later development.) Although statements of the rule in a strict form continued (eg in *Jacobs*' case), it was openly acknowledged that the rule was really no more than a presumption.

Although when the parties arrive at a definite written contract the implication or presumption is very strong that such contract is intended to contain all the terms of their bargain, it is a presumption only, and it is open to either of the parties to allege that there was, in addition to what appears in the written agreement, an antecedent express stipulation not intended by the parties to be excluded, but intended to continue in force with the express written agreement.

(Lord Russell of Killowen CJ in *Gillespie Bros & Co v Cheney, Eggar & Co* [1896] 2 QB 59, 62.)

In the *Jacobs* case itself P O Lawrence J held that the deposit notes did not contain the whole contract, but must be read with the prospectus. As Wedderburn put it in 1959:

> What the parol evidence rule has bequeathed to modern law is a presumption—namely that a document which *looks* like a contract is to be treated as the whole contract. ([1959] CLJ 58, 62.)

Alternatively, the courts would sometimes give effect to the oral promise as an independent or collateral contract, for which the consideration was entering the main contract. In *De Lassalle v Guildford* [1901] 2 KB 215, for example, the tenant had refused to sign the lease until the landlord gave an assurance that the drains were in good order. This assurance was held to be a collateral contract. The majority in the Court of Appeal in the *Jacobs* case upheld the first instance decision on this ground (Pollock MR held that the notes and the prospectus should be read together). A collateral contract has even been found when its terms directly contradict the written contract. In *City and Westminster Properties (1934) Ltd v Mudd* [1959] Ch 129 the defendant had in 1941 become tenant of premises which included a lock-up shop and a back room in which he slept. In 1947 he was offered a new lease which contained covenants against using the premises for dwelling or sleeping. He objected to this and only signed after being told that if he would sign the lease in its original form the landlords would make no objection to his residing on the premises. Ten years later the landlords attempted to forfeit the lease for breach of the convenant but Harman J held that there was 'a clear contract acted upon by the defendant to his detriment and from which the plaintiffs cannot be allowed to resile.' The landlords' action therefore failed.

In 1976 the Law Commission provisionally proposed that what remained of the parol evidence rule should be abolished (Working Paper No 70). However in 1986 it issued a report stating that legislation is not required because the rule no longer exists.

'Law of Contract: The Parol Evidence Rule' (No 154), Law Commission (Cmnd 9700, 1986), paras. 2.7, 2.10–13, 2.15, 2.17, 2.22–24

2.7. We have now concluded that although a proposition of law can be stated which can be described as the 'parol evidence rule' it is not a rule of law which, correctly applied, could lead to evidence being unjustly excluded. Rather, it is a proposition of law which is no more than a circular statement: *when it is proved or admitted that the parties to a contract intended that all the express terms of their agreement should be as recorded in a particular document or documents, evidence will be inadmissible (because irrelevant) if it is tendered only for the purpose of adding to, varying, subtracting from or contradicting the express terms of that contract.* We have considerable doubts whether such a proposition should properly be characterised as a 'rule' at all, but several leading textbook writers and judges have referred to it as a 'rule' and we are content to adopt their terminology for the purposes of this report. . . .

2.10. The two principal reasons which have led us to our conclusion on the nature of the parol evidence rule are, in substance, two aspects of the same process of reasoning. The first relates to the circumstances in which the rule is to be applied. In our view, some statements of the rule may have given rise to misunderstandings because they have concentrated on the *effect* of the rule rather than *when it is to be applied*. The effect of the rule is to exclude evidence or to cause the judge to ignore the evidence if given. As to the application of the rule, Lord Morris' statement in *Bank of Australasia v Palmer* refers to the inadmissibility of parol evidence to 'contradict, vary, add to or subtract from the terms of a *written contract*' (emphasis added).

Thus, the rule can only be applied where the parties have entered into a 'written contract'. Parties can only be said to have entered into a written contract when 'the writing is intended by the parties as a contractual document which is to contain all the terms of their agreement'. When the parties have set down *all* the terms of their contract in writing, extrinsic evidence of other terms must be ignored. If the contract is not entirely in writing, it is not a written contract. There are many authorities and dicta to support this view. . . . If it is proved or admitted that all the terms of the contract have been set out in a particular document or documents, then evidence of other terms must be irrelevant and therefore inadmissible, because inconsistent with the finding that the parties have entered into a written contract.

2.11. The second reason for our conclusion as to the nature of the parol evidence rule is exemplified by the concept of the contract which is made partly orally and partly in writing. . . .

2.12. Because a contract can be made partly orally and partly in writing, the mere production of a contractual document, however complete it may look, cannot as a matter of law exclude evidence of oral terms if the other party asserts that such terms were agreed. If that assertion is proved, evidence of the oral terms cannot be excluded because the court will, by definition, have found that the contractual terms are partly to be found in what was agreed orally as well as in the document in question. No parol evidence rule could apply. On the other hand, if that assertion is not proved, there can be no place for a parol evidence rule because the court will have found that all the terms of the contract were set out in the document in question and, by implication, will thereby have excluded evidence of terms being found elsewhere. The pleadings in the action should normally reveal whether there is an issue as to where the contractual terms are to be found and what those terms are. If there is an issue, it will be an issue of fact for resolution on the balance of probabilities. If there is no issue, neither party will be permitted to adduce evidence of the contractual terms being found elsewhere than as admitted in the pleadings.

2.13. Of course, the more the parties have done to create what appears to be a written contract, the greater are the probabilities that the court will conclude that they did indeed make such a contract.

[The Law Commission referred to Wedderburn's statement above]. . . .

[W]e do not think that in this context it is strictly correct to refer to a 'presumption'. In reaching a conclusion as to whether a document which looks like a complete contract was the whole contract, the court does not apply any presumption of law. Rather, it will reach its conclusion on the evidence tendered, applying to its judgment the prima facie probability derived from its experience of how people normally behave in a given situation. For example, if the plaintiff proves that the parties signed a document, such as a complicated lease of a commercial chattel, which document appears to be a complete contract and which is in a form generally adopted for setting out all the contractual terms, it may be difficult in practice for the defendant to prove, on the balance of probabilities, that terms were orally agreed in addition to those set out in the document.

2.15. Sometimes parties may include in their contracts a clause to the effect that the whole contract is contained in the document and that nothing was agreed outside it (sometimes called a 'merger' or 'integration' clause). In particular, it may be provided that nothing said during negotiations is intended to be of any contractual effect unless recorded in the document. Without legislative provision such a clause cannot, we think, have conclusive effect. It may have a very strong persuasive effect but if it were proved that, notwithstanding the clause, the parties actually intended some additional term to be of contractual effect, the court would give effect to that term because such was the intention of the parties. . . .

2.17. The conclusion which emerges from the discussion above is that there is no *rule of law* that evidence is rendered inadmissible or is to be ignored solely because a document exists which looks like a complete contract. Whether it is a complete contract depends upon the intention of the parties, objectively judged, and not on any rule of law.

Rectification

2.22. It is the very essence of the parol evidence rule that the parties wrote down all that they had agreed, at least in relation to a particular subject-matter. It is in these circumstances that evidence of anything else which it is alleged they agreed is excluded. However, having agreed orally what had to be written down, the parties might mistakenly have written down something else or mistakenly have omitted something which they intended should be in the contractual document. The writing would not then accurately record their agreement. In these circumstances the party who alleges and is able to prove the error in the written contract can obtain from the court an order of rectification. The effect of the order is retrospectively to amend the document so that it states what it should have stated all the time. Parol evidence is, of course, admissible in support of an application to rectify.

2.23.   Rectification may be sought of any written contract or the written part of a contract which is partly oral and partly in writing. The essence of the remedy is that the written agreement does not accurately state what it was intended it should state. If, therefore, the parties agreed a term but also agreed that it should not appear in the written contract, rectification could not be ordered so as to include that term in the document. It is important to note that the factual basis for rectification must be very clearly proved.

2.24.   In one sense rectification may be seen as complementary to the parol evidence rule: if the parties made a contract and they intended that all they had agreed should be recorded in writing, effect can be given to omitted terms by rectifying the agreement so as to include them. If the parties did not intend their agreement to be wholly in writing, the parol evidence rule does not exclude evidence of oral terms. The terms would be enforced as terms of a contract made partly orally and partly in writing. Alternatively, they could be enforced as a collateral contract.

NOTES

1. Not all commentators agree completely with the Law Commission's analysis of the rule, eg Treitel, pp 151–152, who argues that the presumption that a written document is the exclusive record of the terms of the contract goes beyond the normal objective test of the parties' intentions.

2. If it was always open to the courts to find that a contract was partly oral, partly written, why go to the trouble of treating the oral promise as a collateral contract? There seem to be two answers. One is that if the main contract has to be in writing, or evidenced in writing, treating the oral promise as a separate contract may allow both 'parts' of the contract to be given effect without rendering the whole thing unenforceable because the statutory requirement of writing is not fulfilled. Another is that sometimes the 'two contract analysis' reflects the intentions of the parties. In *Mudd's* case the landlords had specifically refused to alter the lease itself to allow the tenant to sleep there for fear that the tenancy would then fall under the Rent Restriction Acts; and the concession that the tenant might sleep on the premises was intended to be personal to him, not assignable to future tenants. Treating it as a separate collateral contract achieved these aims. In other cases, it simply did not matter which analysis is used—witness the judgments in the Court of Appeal in the *Jacobs* case.

CHAPTER 14

Inaccurate information and misrepresentation

In this chapter we will deal with the problems of one party being under a misapprehension as to the facts because he has been misled by the other (we call this the problem of 'inaccurate information'), and we look at the remedies for misrepresentation. We have already seen that as a rule, a party who is under a self-induced misapprehension as to the facts cannot complain that the other failed to put him right (*Smith v Hughes*, above, p 244). We shall consider later cases where there is an obligation to disclose relevant information; in particular we shall concentrate on this problem in chapter 19 of this section, which we have entitled 'Duties of Disclosure'. In fact, however, there are a number of other doctrines which in effect impose duties of disclosure, and we shall return to this theme frequently in this section of the book.

What makes it so difficult to mark out boundaries is that the problems caused by one or both parties entering a contract under a misapprehension as to the facts are dealt with by a broad array of doctrines. Some of these have been explained already; the cases on when a representation amounts to a term of the contract clearly involved one party giving the other inaccurate information. Equally many of the cases in later chapters—those on implied terms, the common mistake cases and most of the frustration cases—involve situations where the parties had inadequate information about present facts or future developments. We shall have to consider in turn each of these doctrines, and examine its relationship to the others; but the case where one party has actively misled the other is perhaps the easiest to visualise and thus the best place to start.

In one way this chapter is separate from the rest of the section. The doctrine of misrepresentation involves a different legal technique to the cases in the previous chapters and the chapters that follow. The statement is often treated as being something 'outside' the contract. The victim of the misrepresentation, 'the misrepresentee', may be entitled to rescind the contract even though the contract itself has not been broken. In addition or instead, the misrepresentee may be able to recover damages; but they will be damages for fraud or negligence in tort, or damages under statute, not damages for breach of contract.

Before we turn to misrepresentation itself, please look again at chapter 12 of this section (pp 259–263). If one party makes a statement of fact to the other, and the statement is crucial or he is in a better position to know the truth, he is likely to be treated as promising that the fact stated is true. The cases that follow largely involve situations where a statement was made which did *not* amount to a promise.

(a) Rescission for misrepresentation

Redgrave v Hurd (1881) 20 Ch D 1, Court of Appeal

The plaintiff, an elderly solicitor, advertised for a younger partner, who would not object to buying the plaintiff's suburban residence. The defendant had two interviews with the plaintiff, who told him that the practice brought in about £300 a year. The plaintiff produced summaries for three years showing business of about £200 a year and said the rest was made up by other business not included in the summaries; he showed the defendant a bundle of papers relating to this other business. The defendant did not examine these papers; they in fact showed that there was almost no other business. The defendant signed an agreement to purchase the house; at the plaintiff's insistence, this agreement made no reference to the agreement to buy the practice. The defendant discovered the truth and refused to complete. The plaintiff sought specific performance, and the defendant counter-claimed for rescission of the agreement and damages. Fry J held that the defendant, having had the opportunity to check the truth of the representations but not having taken it, must be taken not to have relied on them. The Court of Appeal held that the defendant's counterclaim for damages for fraud must fail because he had not pleaded that the plaintiff knew that the statements he was making were untrue; but it reversed Fry J's decision and rescinded the contract on the grounds of innocent misrepresentation.

Jessel MR. . . . As regards the rescission of a contract, there was no doubt a difference between the rules of Courts of Equity and the rules of Courts of Common Law—a difference which of course has now disappeared by the operation of the *Judicature Act*, which makes the rules of equity prevail. According to the decisions of Courts of Equity it was not necessary, in order to set aside a contract obtained by material false representation, to prove that the party who obtained it knew at the time when the representation was made that it was false. It was put in two ways, either of which was sufficient. One way of putting the case was, 'A man is not allowed to get a benefit from a statement which he now admits to be false. He is not allowed to say, for the purpose of civil jurisdiction, that when he made it he did not know it to be false; he ought to have found that out before he made it.' The other way of putting it was this: 'Even assuming that moral fraud must be shewn in order to set aside a contract, you have it where a man, having obtained a beneficial contract by a statement which he now knows to be false, insists upon keeping that contract. To do so is a moral delinquency: no man ought to seek to take advantage of his own false statements.' The rule in equity was settled, and it does not matter on which of the two grounds it was rested. As regards the rule of Common Law there is no doubt it was not quite so wide. There were, indeed, cases in which, even at Common Law, a contract could be rescinded for misrepresentation, although it could not be shewn that the person making it knew the representation to be false. They are variously stated, but I think, according to the later decisions, the statement must have been made recklessly and without care, whether it was true or false, and not with the belief that it was true . . .

There is another proposition of law of very great importance which I think it is necessary for me to state, because, with great deference to the very learned Judge from whom this appeal comes, I think it is not quite accurately stated in his judgment. If a man is induced to enter into a contract by a false representation it is not a sufficient answer to him to say, 'If you had used due diligence you would have found out that the statement was untrue. You had the means afforded you of discovering its falsity, and did not choose to avail yourself of them.' I take it to be a settled doctrine of equity, not only as regards specific performance but also as regards rescission, that this is not an answer unless there is such delay as constitutes a defence under the *Statute of Limitations*. That, of course, is quite a different thing. Under the statute delay deprives a man of his right to rescind on the ground of fraud, and the only question to be considered is from what time the delay is to be reckoned. It had been decided, and the rule was adopted by the statute, that the delay counts from the time when by due diligence the fraud might have been discovered. Nothing can be plainer, I take it, on the authorities in equity than that the effect of false representation is not got rid of on the ground that the person to whom it was made has been guilty of negligence. One of the most familiar instances in modern times is where men issue a prospectus in which they make false statements of the contracts made before the formation of a company, and then say that the contracts themselves may be inspected at the offices of the solicitors. It has always been held that those who accepted those false statements as true were not deprived of their remedy merely because they neglected to go and look at the contracts. Another instance with which we are familiar is where a vendor makes a false statement as to the contents of a lease, as, for instance, that it contains no covenant preventing the carrying on of the trade which the purchaser is known by the vendor to be desirous of carrying on upon the property. Although the lease itself might be produced at the sale, or might have been open to the inspection of the purchaser long previously to the sale, it has been repeatedly held that the vendor cannot be allowed to say, 'You were not entitled to give credit to my statement'. It is not sufficient, therefore, to say that the purchaser had the opportunity of investigating the real state of the case, but did not avail himself of that opportunity.

. . . [T]he learned Judge came to the conclusion either that the Defendant did not rely on the statement, or that if he did rely upon it he had shewn such negligence as to deprive him of his title to relief from this Court. As I have already said, the latter proposition is in my opinion not founded in law, and the former part is not founded in fact; I think also it is not founded in law, for when a person makes a material representation to another to induce him to enter into a contract, and the other enters into that contract, it is not sufficient to say that the party to whom the representation is made does not prove that he entered into the contract, relying upon the representation. If it is a material representation calculated to induce him to enter into the contract, it is an inference of law that he was induced by the representation to enter into it, and in order to take away his title to be relieved from the contract on the ground that the representation was untrue, it must be shewn either that he had knowledge of the facts contrary to the representation or that he stated in terms, or shewed clearly by his conduct, that he did not rely on the representation. . . .

[Baggallay and Lush LJJ concurred.]

NOTES

1. It appears that even at common law, rescission was available to the victim of a fraudulent misrepresentation. Fraud, however, requires proof that the misrepresentor either knew that his statement was false, or was reckless as to whether or not it was false: *Derry v Peek* (1889) 14 App Cas 337.

2. What justification does Jessel MR offer for the rule that a contract entered in reliance on an innocent (ie non-fraudulent) misrepresentation should be rescinded?

3. Why is it no answer that the misrepresentee could have discovered the truth for himself?

4. Suppose that in *Redgrave v Hurd* it had been possible to ascertain the true position from the books, and the defendant had examined them, but he had not noticed that the figures in the books did not correspond to those given by the plaintiff? (cf *Attwood v Small* (1838) 6 Cl & Fin 232).

5. If the misrepresentation had been fraudulent, the misrepresentee would have been entitled to claim damages as well as to rescind. The damages would not have been for breach of contract but for the tort of deceit. The measure of damages in tort does not include compensation for 'loss of expectation', see above, p 28, and below, p 299.

6. Jessel MR states that an innocent misrepresentation must be 'material' if it is to be a ground for relief. This presumably excludes incorrect statements of facts which would not influence the reasonable person. Cf Marine Insurance Act 1906, s 18(2): 'every circumstance is material which would influence the judgment of a prudent insurer in fixing the premium, or determining whether he will take the risk'.

7. The contract for the house in *Redgrave v Hurd* deliberately made no reference to the business, and thus the defendant could not recover for breach of contract. What if it had done? As we saw earlier, some statements of fact do amount to contractual terms, for example the dealer's statement about the car's mileage in *Dick Bentley Productions Ltd v Harold Smith Motors Ltd* (above, p 262). Could the buyer in that case have elected to treat the statement as a representation, so as to seek rescission? In *Pennsylvania Shipping Co v Compagnie Nationale de Navigation* [1936] 2 All ER 1167 the plaintiffs had time-chartered the defendants' tanker. During lengthy negotiations the defendants had made statements which turned out to be inaccurate about the pipe lines and heating coils. These statements were embodied as 'Guaranteed' in the charterparty. Branson J held that the pre-contract representations had become merged with the contract terms, so that there could be no question of rescission. This view was reversed by the Misrepresentation Act 1967, s 1, which states that rescission is available even though the representation has *become* a term of the contract (for the text of s 1, see below, p 296). It is not quite clear whether this applies to a statement such as that in the *Dick Bentley* case, which has been made only once and which is held to constitute a contractual promise. Probably even in this case the representee has the choice of remedies for breach or for misrepresentation. Needless to say, he cannot opt for inconsistent alternatives, such as both rescinding the contract for misrepresentation and recovering damages for breach.

Bisset v Wilkinson [1927] AC 177, Privy Council

The respondents had agreed to buy from the plaintiff (the appellant) two blocks of land, called 'Homestead' and 'Hogan's', at Avondale in New Zealand. During the negotations the plaintiff had said that the land would carry two thousand sheep, but he had never run sheep on anything but a small part of it and that only for a short time. The respondents alleged that the plaintiff's statement was a misrepresentation and refused to proceed.

Lord Merrivale. . . . Sheep-farming was the purpose for which the respondents purchased the lands of the plaintiff. One of them had no experience of farming. The other had been before the war in charge of sheep on an extensive sheep-farm carried on by his father, who had accompanied and advised him in his negotiation with the appellant and had carefully inspected the lands at Avondale. In the course of coming to his agreement with the respondents the appellant made statements as to the property which, in their defence and counterclaim, the respondents alleged to be misrepresentations . . .

In an action for rescission, as in an action for specific performance of an executory contract, when misrepresentation is the alleged ground of relief of the party who repudiates the contract, it is, of course, essential to ascertain whether that which is relied upon is a representation of a specific fact, or a statement of opinion, since an erroneous opinion stated by the party affirming the contract, though it may have been relied upon and have induced the contract on the part of the party who seeks rescission, gives no title to relief unless fraud is established. The application of this rule, however, is not always easy, as is illustrated in a good many reported cases, as well as in this. A representation of fact may be inherent in a statement of opinion and, at any rate, the existence of the opinion in the person stating it is a question of fact. In *Karberg's* case Lindley LJ, in course of testing a representation which might have been, as it was said to be by interested parties, one of opinion or belief, used this inquiry: 'Was the statement of expectation a statement of things not really expected?' The Court of Appeal applied this test and rescinded the contract which was in question. In *Smith v Land and House Property Corporation* there came in question a vendor's description of the tenant of the property sold as 'a most desirable tenant'—a statement of his opinion, as was argued on his behalf in an action to enforce the contract of sale. This description was held by the Court of Appeal to be a misrepresentation of fact, which, without proof of fraud, disentitled the vendor to specific performance of the contract of purchase. 'It is often fallaciously assumed', said Bowen LJ 'that a statement of opinion cannot involve the statement of fact. In a case where the facts are equally well known to both parties, what one of them says to the other is frequently nothing but an expression of opinion. The statement of such opinion is in a sense a statement of fact about the condition of the man's own mind, but only of an irrelevant fact, for it is of no consequence what the opinion is. But if the facts are not equally well known to both sides, then a statement of opinion by one who knows the facts best involves very often a statement of a material fact, for he impliedly states that he knows facts which justify his opinion'. The kind of distinction which is in question is illustrated again in the well known case of *Smith v Chadwick*. There the words under consideration involved the inquiry in relation to the sale of an industrial concern whether a statement of 'the present value of the turnover or output' was of necessity a statement of fact that the produce of the works was of the amount mentioned, or might be, and was a statement that the productive power of the works was estimated at so much. The words were held to be capable of the second of these meanings. The decisive enquiries came to be: what meaning was actually conveyed to the party complaining; was he deceived, and, as the action was based on a charge of fraud, was the statement in question made fraudulently?

In the present case, as in those cited, the material facts of the transaction, the knowledge of the parties respectively, and their relative positions, the words of representation used, and the actual condition of the subject-matter spoken of, are relevant to the two inquiries necessary to be made: What was the meaning of the representation? Was it true?

In ascertaining what meaning was conveyed to the minds of the now respondents by the appellant's statement as to the two thousand sheep, the most material fact to be remembered is that, as both parties were aware, the appellant had not and, so far as appears, no other person had at any time carried on sheep-farming upon the unit of land in question. That land as a distinct holding had never constituted a sheep-farm. The two blocks comprised in it differed substantially in character. Hogan's block was described by one of the respondents' witnesses as 'better land'. 'It might carry', he said, 'one sheep or perhaps two or even three sheep to the acre'. He estimated the carrying capacity of the land generally as little more than half a sheep to the acre. And Hogan's land had been allowed to deteriorate during several years before the respondents purchased. As was said by Sim J: 'In ordinary circumstances, any statement made by an owner who has been occupying his own farm as to its carrying capacity would be regarded as a statement of fact. . . . This, however, is not such a case. The defendants knew all about Hogan's block and knew also what sheep the farm was carrying when they inspected it. In these circumstances . . . the defendants were not justified in regarding anything said by the plaintiff as to the carrying capacity as being anything more than an expression of his opinion on the subject.' In this view of the matter their Lordships concur.

Whether the appellant honestly and in fact held the opinion which he stated remained to be considered. This involved examination of the history and condition of the property. If a reasonable man with the appellant's knowledge could not have come to the conclusion he stated, the description of that conclusion as an opinion would not necessarily protect him against rescission for misrepresentation. But what was actually the capacity in competent hands of the land the respondents purchased had never been, and never was, practically ascertained. The respondents, after two years' trial of sheep-farming, under difficulties caused in part by their inexperience, found themselves confronted by a fall in the values of sheep and wool which would have left them losers if they could have carried three thousand sheep. As is said in the judgment of Ostler J: 'Owing to sheep becoming practically valueless, they reduced their flock and went in for cropping and dairy-farming in order to make a living'.

Appeal allowed. Judgment of Sim J restored.

Edgington v Fitzmaurice (1885) 29 Ch D 459, Court of Appeal

The directors of a company issued a prospectus which invited subscriptions for debentures, and which stated that the objects for which the money was being raised were to complete some alterations and additions to the buildings, to purchase horses and vans and to develop the supply of fish. The plaintiff advanced money on the strength of this and other statements. In fact the money was being raised to meet pressing liabilities. Denman J held the directors liable for deceit.

Bowen LJ. This is an action for deceit, in which the Plaintiff complains that he was induced to take certain debentures by the misrepresentations of the Defendants, and that he sustained damage thereby. The loss which the Plaintiff sustained is not disputed. In order to sustain his action he must first prove that there was a statement as to facts which was false; and secondly, that it was false to the knowledge of the Defendants, or that they made it not caring whether it was true or false . . .

But when we come to the third alleged misstatement I feel that the Plaintiff's case is made out. I mean the statement of the objects for which the money was to be raised. These were stated to be to complete the alterations and additions to the buildings, to purchase horses and vans, and to develop the supply of fish. A mere suggestion of possible purposes to which a portion of the money might be applied would not have formed a basis for an action of deceit. There must be a misstatement of an existing fact: but the state of a man's mind is as much a fact as the state of his digestion. It is true that it is very difficult to prove what the state of a man's mind at a particular time is, but if it can be ascertained it is as much a fact as anything else. A misrepresentation as to the state of a man's mind is, therefore, a misstatement of fact. Having applied as careful consideration to the evidence as I could, I have reluctantly come to the conclusion that the true objects of the Defendants in raising the money were not those stated in the circular.

[Fry and Cotton LJJ were of the same opinion.]

Appeal dismissed.

NOTES

1. Suppose the defendant makes a statement as to his intention which is true when he speaks, and it is only after the contract is made that he changes his mind? For instance, a vendor sells a plot of land, telling the purchaser that he intends to keep an adjoining plot (which he is retaining) as an open field, but he later changes his mind and builds on the field. Will the purchaser have any remedy if he does not have one for misrepresentation? (If you do not see the answer, look again at chapter 12 of this section.)

2. In *British Airways Board v Taylor* [1976] 1 All ER 65 BOAC had informed a passenger that his reservation on a flight from London to Bermuda was 'confirmed'. BOAC operated a policy of 'overbooking' seats, and though when the confirmation was given there were sufficient seats for the passenger to travel on that flight, it was subsequently overbooked and the passenger was refused a seat on it. An information was laid against British Airways Board (which had subsequently taken over the rights and liabilities of BOAC pursuant to the Air Corporations (Dissolution) Order 1973) that the confirmation had contravened the Trade Descriptions Act 1968, s 14(1)(b), in that it had recklessly made a false statement about the provision of services. The House of Lords held that British Airways Board were not responsible for offences committed by BOAC, but held that there was evidence to entitle the justices in finding that there had been a false statement of fact. Lord Wilberforce said:

My Lords, the distinction in law between a promise as to future action, which may be broken or kept, and a statement as to existing fact, which may be true or false, is clear enough. There may be inherent in a promise an implied statement as to a fact, and where this is really the case, the court can attach appropriate consequences to any falsity in, or recklessness in the making of, that statement. Everyone is familiar with the proposition that a statement of intention may itself be a statement of fact and so capable of being true or false. But this proposition should not be used as a general solvent to transform the one type of assurance with another: the distinction is a real one and requires to be respected particularly where the effect of treating an assurance as a statement is to attract criminal consequences, as in the present case. As Lord Widgery CJ said in *Beckett v Cohen* it was never intended that the 1968 Act should be used so as to make a criminal statement out of what is really a breach of warranty.

Which character—promise or statement—should be attributed to the letter, seems on the face of it to be debatable.

[In the present case the justices made the following relevant findings:]

'. . . (c) The statement contained in the letter was false and made recklessly since in view of the [Board's] admitted policy a reservation on the flight could not be confirmed at the date of the letter as it was always possible that Mr Edmunds would be off-loaded. It followed that no reservation had been made in the sense that an ordinary person would take it to mean ie a certain booking. This was especially so in view of the circumstances in which the letter was written.'

In my opinion these were findings which the justices were entitled to make. And the essence of them is that the letter, taken together with the ticket and the Earlybird Certificate, would be taken as a statement that Mr Edmunds had a certain booking, which statement, in view of the overbooking policy, was untrue, since his booking though very likely to be a firm one was exposed to a risk—small but, as events proved, real—that it might not give him a seat on the aircraft. I think that the justices were entitled to find that this would be taken as a statement of a fact, rather than as a mere promise that Mr Edmunds would be flown on the day and at the time specified, and that they did so find.

Turner v Green [1895] 2 Ch 205, Chitty J

The plaintiff's solicitor, Fowler, met the defendant and his solicitor, and the parties negotiated the compromise of an action, without Fowler revealing that shortly beforehand he had received a telegram to the effect that other proceedings in the action, before the chief clerk in London, had gone in the defendant's favour.

Chitty J. . . . Ought the Court to decline to enforce this agreement because Fowler, being aware of the circumstance that the chief clerk has expressed his opinion—which however did not amount to a decision—did not disclose that circumstance to the defendant and his solicitors when the terms of this compromise were being settled?

The question thus raised is not one of fraud, but one as to the doctrine of the Court in granting relief against a claim for specific performance, where the Court has a discretion; but that is, of course, a judicial discretion, which cannot be exercised arbitrarily, but only according to settled principles laid down for it by the authorities. I will take the proposition laid down by Sir Edward Fry in his book (3rd ed p 325, para 705) as a good exposition of the law; there he says: 'Mere silence as regards a material fact which the one party is not under an obligation to disclose to the other cannot be a ground for rescission or a defence to specific performance.'

It cannot be contended that Fowler was under any obligation to disclose the result of the telegram: therefore Mr Butcher, who argued his case with skill and ingenuity, was driven to say that it was a shabby trick on Fowler's part not to disclose the information he had received, and that such conduct was not consistent with the usual practice of solicitors of high standing in their dealing with one another, who would ordinarily have disclosed any such circumstance; therefore, he argued that specific performance ought to be refused, because the course adopted in this case would be generally condemned by high-minded men. I find myself unable to act judicially on any such ground. Had there been any overreaching by Fowler, or any misleading conversation with reference to the proceedings in London before the chief clerk, at the time the terms of the compromise were settled, a very different case might have been presented on behalf of the defendant, and in such a case an obligation might have arisen binding Fowler at law or in equity to make a disclosure of all he knew; but I am satisfied on the evidence that no conversation on the subject took place.

With v O'Flanagan [1936] Ch 575, Court of Appeal

In January 1934 the vendor of a medical practice had truthfully told the purchasers that the practice took in £200 a year. Before the contract was signed on 1 May, the practice had fallen away to almost nothing because the vendor had been ill, but the change of circumstances was not revealed to the purchasers.

Romer LJ. The only principle invoked by the appellants in this case is as follows. If A with a view to inducing B to enter into a contract makes a representation as to a material fact, then if at a later date and before the contract is actually entered into, owing to a change of circumstances, the representation then made would to the knowledge of A be untrue and B subsequently enters into the contract in ignorance of that change of circumstances and relying upon that representation, A cannot hold B to the bargain. There is ample authority for that statement and, indeed, I doubt myself whether any authority is necessary, it being, it seems to me, so obviously consistent with the plainest principles of equity.

[Lord Wright MR and Clauson J delivered judgments to the same effect.]

Appeal allowed.

NOTE

For a discussion of the reasons for the duty to disclose being so limited, see below, p 396.

(b) Limits to rescission for misrepresentation

(i) Bars to rescission

To rescind a contract may be rather a drastic step, particularly where the contract has been performed. Equity therefore took the view that the right to rescind could be lost, or 'barred'. So rescission is barred if an innocent third party has in the meantime acquired rights over the property which is the subject of the contract, eg *Lewis v Averay* (above, p 253).

Other bars are illustrated by the next three cases. It should be noted that in the first two the Court of Appeal was also considering a possible bar now removed by the Misrepresentation Act 1967, s 1 (below, p 296).

Leaf v International Galleries [1950] 2 KB 86, Court of Appeal

The plaintiff, on March 8, 1944, purchased from the defendants, International Galleries . . . a picture called 'Salisbury Cathedral' for 85*l*. At the time of the purchase the defendants represented that the picture was painted by John Constable, but when five years later the plaintiff tried to sell it he was informed that it was not by Constable. Thereupon he returned it to the defendants and asked them to refund the 85*l* which he had paid for it. The defendants having refused to do so, the plaintiff by this action claimed to rescind the contract and to have repayment of the 85*l*.

When the hearing began in the county court, the judge suggested that the plaintiff's proper remedy was a claim for damages, and asked if he wished to amend his claim. It was then stated that no such amendment was desired. At the end of the hearing, however, the plaintiff applied for leave to amend and add a claim for damages, but this was refused on the ground that the application had been made too late. The county court judge found that the defendants had made an innocent misrepresentation and that the picture had not been painted by Constable. He gave judgment for them, however, holding, on the authority of *Angel v Jay*, that the equitable remedy of rescission was not available in the case of an executed contract.

The plaintiff appealed.

[The Court of Appeal doubted the existence of the rule applied by the Judge, at least in contracts for the sale of goods, but declined to decide the point as the case could be decided on another ground.]

Jenkins LJ. . . . In those circumstances, it seems to me to be quite out of the question that a court of equity should grant relief by way of rescission. It is perfectly true that the county court judge held that there had been no laches, and, of course, it may be said that the plaintiff had no occasion to obtain any further evidence as to the authorship of the picture until he wanted to sell; but in my judgment contracts such as this cannot be kept open and subject to the possibility of rescission indefinitely. Assuming that completion is not fatal to his claim, I think that, at all events, it behoves the purchaser either to verify or, as the case may be, to disprove the representation within a reasonable time, or else stand or fall by it. If he is allowed to wait five, ten, or twenty years and then re-open the bargain, there can be no finality at all. I, for my part, do not think that equity will intervene in such a case, more especially as in the present case it cannot be said that, apart from rescission, the plaintiff would have been without remedy. The county court judge was of opinion, and it seems to me that he was clearly right, that the representation that the picture was a Constable amounted to a warranty. If it amounted to a warranty, and that was broken, as on the findings of the county court judge it was, then the plaintiff had a right at law in the shape of damages for breach of warranty. That remedy he did not choose to exercise, and, although he was invited at the hearing to amend his claim so as to include a claim for breach of warranty, he declined that opportunity. That being so, it seems to me that he has no justification at all for now coming to equity five years after the event and claiming rescission. Accordingly, it seems to me that this is not a case in which the equitable remedy of rescission, assuming it to be available in the absence of fraud in respect of a completed sale of chattels, should be allowed to the plaintiff. For these reasons. I agree that the appeal fails and should be dismissed.

Denning LJ: . . . There was a term in the contract as to the quality of the subject-matter: namely, as to the person by whom the picture was painted—that it was by Constable. That term of the contract was, according to our terminology, either a condition or a warranty. If it was a condition, the buyer could reject the picture for breach of the condition at any time before he accepted it, or is deemed to have accepted it; whereas, if it was only a warranty, he could not reject it at all but was confined to a claim for damages.

I think it right to assume in the buyer's favour that this term was a condition, and that, if he had come in proper time he could have rejected the picture; but the right to reject for breach of condition has always been limited by the rule that, once the buyer has accepted, or is deemed to have accepted, the goods in performance of the contract, then he cannot thereafter reject, but is relegated to his claim for damages: see Sale of Goods Act, 1893, s 11(1)(c) and *Wallis, Son & Wells v Pratt & Haynes.*

The circumstances in which a buyer is deemed to have accepted goods in performance of the contract are set out in s 35 of the Act, which says that the buyer is deemed to have accepted the goods, amongst other things, 'when, after the lapse of a reasonable time, he retains the goods without intimating to the seller that he has rejected them.' In this case the buyer took the picture into his house and, apparently, hung it there, and five years passed before he intimated any rejection at all. That, I need hardly say, is much more than a reasonable time. It is far too late for him at the end of five years to reject this picture for breach of any condition. His remedy after that length of time is for damages only, a claim which he has not brought before the court.

Is it to be said that the buyer is in any better position by relying on the representation, not as a condition, but as an innocent misrepresentation?. . .

Although rescission may in some cases be a proper remedy, it is to be remembered that an innocent misrepresentation is much less potent than a breach of condition; and a claim to rescission for innocent misrepresentation must at any rate be barred when a right to reject for breach of condition is barred. A condition is a term of the contract of a most material character, and if a claim to reject on that account is barred, it seems to me a fortiori that a claim to rescission on the ground of innocent misrepresentation is also barred.

So, assuming that a contract for the sale of goods may be rescinded in a proper case for innocent misrepresentation, the claim is barred in this case for the self-same reason as a right to reject is barred. The buyer has accepted the picture. He had ample opportunity for examination in the first few days after he had bought it. Then was the time to see if the condition or representation was fulfilled. Yet he kept it all this time. Five years have elapsed without any notice of rejection. In my judgment he cannot now claim to rescind. His only claim, if any, as the county court judge said, was one for damages, which he has not made in this action. In my judgment, therefore, the appeal should be dismissed.

Lord Evershed MR delivered a judgment to the same effect.

Appeal dismissed.

Long v Lloyd [1958] 2 All ER 402, Court of Appeal

The defendant, a haulage contractor, advertised for sale at £850 a 1947 motor lorry which he described as in 'exceptional condition'. The plaintiff, also a haulage contractor, saw the lorry at the defendant's premises on a Saturday; the defendant said that it was capable of a speed of forty miles per hour. During a trial run on the following Monday, the plaintiff found that the speedometer was not working, that the spring was missing from the accelerator pedal, and that he had difficulty with the top gear. The defendant said that the lorry did eleven miles to the gallon and assured the plaintiff that he had told him all that was wrong with the vehicle. The plaintiff thereupon purchased the lorry for £750, paying £375 and agreeing to pay the balance at a later date. On the following Wednesday the plaintiff drove from Sevenoaks to Rochester to pick up a load. During the journey the dynamo ceased to function, and the plaintiff also noticed that an oil seal was leaking, that there was a crack in a wheel and that he had used eight gallons of petrol on the journey of about forty miles. That evening the plaintiff told the defendant of these defects and the defendant offered to pay half the cost of a reconstructed dynamo but denied any knowledge of a broken oil seal. The plaintiff accepted the offer. He had a dynamo fitted and on the next day, Thursday, the lorry was driven by the plaintiff's brother on a journey to Middlesbrough. On Friday night the plaintiff, having heard that the lorry had broken down on its journey, wrote to the defendant pointing out the various defects in the lorry and asking for the return of his money. The lorry was subsequently examined by an expert who was of the opinion that the lorry was not in roadworthy condition. The lorry had in fact the defects alleged but the defendant's representations concerning it, though untrue, were honestly made. The plaintiff's action for rescission of the contract on the ground of the defendant's innocent misrepresentations was dismissed and he appealed.

Pearce LJ. . . . Nevertheless, a strict application to the facts of the present case of Denning LJ's view to the effect that the right (if any) to rescind after completion on the ground of innocent misrepresentation is barred by acceptance of the goods must necessarily prove fatal to the plaintiff's case. Apart from special circumstances, the place of delivery is the proper place for examination and for acceptance. It was open to the plaintiff to have the lorry examined by an expert before driving it away, but he chose not to do so. It is true, however, that the truth of certain of the representations, for example, that the lorry would do 11 miles to the gallon—could not be ascertained except by user and, therefore—the plaintiff should have a reasonable time to test it. Until he had had such an opportunity it might well be said that he had not accepted the lorry, always assuming, of course, that he did nothing inconsistent with the ownership of the seller. An examination of the facts, however, shows that on any view he must have accepted the lorry before he purported to reject it.

Thus, to recapitulate the facts, after the trial run the plaintiff drove the lorry home from Hampton Court to Sevenoaks, a not inconsiderable distance. After that experience he took it into use in his business by driving it on the following day to Rochester and back to Sevenoaks with a load. By the time he returned from Rochester he knew that the dynamo was not charging, that there was an oil seal leaking, that he had used 8 gallons of fuel for a journey of 40 miles, and that a wheel was cracked. He must also, as we think, have known by this time that the vehicle was not capable of 40 miles per hour. As to oil consumption, we should have thought that, if it was so excessive that the sump was practically dry after 300 miles, the plaintiff could have reasonably been expected to discover that the rate of consumption was unduly high by the time he had made the journey from Hampton Court to Sevenoaks and thence to Rochester and back.

On his return from Rochester the plaintiff telephoned to the defendant and complained about the dynamo, the excessive fuel consumption, the leaking oil seal and the cracked wheel. The defendant then offered to pay half the cost of the reconstructed dynamo which the plaintiff had been advised to fit, and the plaintiff accepted the defendant's offer. We find this difficult to reconcile with the continuance of any right of rescission which the plaintiff might have had down to that time.

But the matter does not rest there. On the following day the plaintiff, knowing all that he did about the condition and performance of the lorry, dispatched it, driven by his brother, on a business trip to Middlesbrough. That step, at all events, appears to us to have amounted, in all the circumstances of the case, to a final acceptance of the lorry by the plaintiff for better or for worse, and to have conclusively extinguished any right of rescission remaining to the plaintiff after completion of the sale.

Appeal dismissed.

NOTE

Pearce suggests that the right to rescind may have been lost as soon as the plaintiff accepted the defendant's offer to repair the defects. Doesn't it seem rather draconian to expect the plaintiff to reject any such compromise out of hand? A possible way out is to treat the plaintiff's acceptance of repair as merely conditional upon there being no further defects: see *Farnworth Finance Facilities Ltd v Attryde* [1970] 1 WLR 1053. The rules in the Sale of Goods Act 1979 on loss of the right to reject do not always seem very appropriate in the consumer context: see further below, p 461.

Clarke v Dickson (1858) EB & E 148, Queen's Bench

On the trial, before Lord Campbell CJ, at the London Sittings after last Michaelmas Term, the statements made by the plaintiff's counsel, in opening his case, were: that, in 1853, the plaintiff was induced, by representations made by the three defendants, to take shares in a Company called The Welsh Potosi Lead and Copper Mining Company, which was then formed for working a mine on the cost book principle, and of which the defendants were directors; and to pay deposits for those shares. The mine was worked by the Company during the years 1854, 1855 and 1856; and dividends were declared in each of those years. The plaintiff was induced to accept fresh allotments of shares in lieu of the dividends declared. In 1857 the Company was in bad circumstances: it was, with the plaintiff's assent, registered as a Company with limited liability, and was afterwards wound up under the Winding-up Act. During the process of winding up, the plaintiff for the first time discovered that the representations by which he was induced to make the purchase were false and fraudulent on the part of the defendants, and that the dividends declared were fraudulent dividends. He therefore brought this action to recover back the deposits which he had paid for the shares.

Crompton J. When once it is settled that a contract induced by fraud is not void, but voidable at the option of the party defrauded, it seems to me to follow that, when that party exercises his option to rescind the contract, he must be in a state to rescind; that is, he must be in such a situation as to be able to put the parties into their original state before the contract. Now here I will assume, what is not clear to me, that the plaintiff bought his shares from the defendants and not from the Company, and that he might at one time have had a right to restore the shares to the defendants if he could, and demand the price from them. But then what did he buy? Shares in a partnership with others. He cannot return those; he has become bound to those others. Still stronger, he has changed their nature: what he now has and offers to restore are shares in a quasi corporation now in process of being wound up. That is quite enough to decide this case. The plaintiff must rescind in toto or not at all: he cannot both keep the shares and recover the whole price. That is founded on the plainest principles of justice. If he cannot return the article he must keep it, and sue for his real damage in an action on the deceit. Take the case I put in the argument, of a butcher buying live cattle, killing them, and even selling the meat to his customers. If the rule of law were as the plaintiff contends, that butcher might, upon discovering a fraud on the part of the grazier who sold him the cattle, rescind the contract and get back the whole price: but how could that be consistent with justice? The true doctrine is, that a party can never repudiate a contract after, by his own act, it has become out of his power to restore the parties to their original condition.

[Erle J and Lord Campell CJ delivered concurring judgments.]

(ii) The court's discretion

Originally, rescission was available if there had been any misrepresentation of fact, provided the misrepresentee had relied on it and it was material. As we saw above (p 287), the latter requirement probably means only that the misrepresentation must not be trivial; it does not mean that the misrepresentation needs to be a very serious one. Thus while the misrepresentee could only get damages if he could prove fraud, rescission for misrepresentation was more readily available than is termination when there has been a breach of contract: as we shall see (below, p 423ff), termination is often only permitted where the breach deprives the innocent party of the substance of what he was contracting for.

Thus the rather draconian remedy of rescission might be available, and be the only remedy, for a rather slight misrepresentation—eg a statement that the drains in a house were in good order when in fact one drain was broken and needed replacement. No doubt the parties in such a case could bargain their way to a settlement under which the vendor paid the cost of repairs if the purchaser would refrain from rescinding, but the law itself permitted rescission. On the other hand, in cases of the sale or lease of land, the remedy was severely curtailed by a rule that the right to rescind for innocent misrepresentation was lost once the contract had been executed by the conveyance of the land or the grant of the lease (see *Wilde v Gibson* (1848) 1 HL Cas 605; *Angel v Jay* [1911] 1 KB 666). This had the effect of preventing rescission in the most inconvenient case, where the vendor has already moved in before discovering the untruth, and the vendor has spent the purchase money on another property. On the other hand, the rule deprived the misrepresentee of any remedy unless fraud could be proved, and in other contexts where the rule applied (eg the sale of shares: *Seddon v North Eastern Salt Co Ltd* [1905] 1 Ch 326) it was hard to see any justification for it. It was not clear whether the rule applied to sale of goods (see *Leaf v International Galleries*, above). Despite a recommendation of the Law Reform Committee (Tenth Report (Innocent Misrepresentation), Cmnd 1782, (1962)) that the rule should be retained for sale of land and leases for over three years, it was abolished by the Misrepresentation Act 1967, s 1. At the same time, however, power was given to the court to refuse to permit rescission, or to reinstate a contract already rescinded by the misrepresentee, and give damages in lieu of rescission where rescission did not seem an appropriate remedy.

Misrepresentation Act 1967

Section 1
Where a person has entered into a contract after a misrepresentation has been made to him, and—
(a) the misrepresentation has become a term of the contract; or
(b) the contract has been performed
or both, then, if otherwise he would be entitled to rescind the contract without alleging fraud, he shall be so entitled, subject to the provisions of this Act, notwithstanding the matters mentioned in paragraphs (a) and (b) of this section.

Section 2
(2) Where a person has entered into a contract after a misrepresentation has been made to him otherwise than fraudulently, and he would be entitled, by reason of the misrepresentation, to rescind the contract, then, if it is claimed, in any proceedings arising out of the contract, that the contract ought to be or has been rescinded, the court or arbitrator may declare the contract subsisting and award damages in lieu of rescission, if of opinion that it would be equitable to do so, having regard to the nature of the misrepresentation and the loss that would be caused by it if the contract were upheld, as well as to the loss that rescission would cause to the other party.

NOTES

1. Section 2(2) refers to the case where the misrepresentee 'would be entitled . . . to rescind'. Can the court award damages under this subsection if the misrepresentee has already lost the right to rescind under one of the 'bars'? See further below, p 403.

2. If the court exercises its discretion under s 2(2) to declare the contract subsisting, it may (or perhaps must—it is not clear on the wording of the section) 'award damages in lieu of rescission'. How these damages might be assessed is discussed below, pp 299–300.

(c) Rescission and consequential loss

If there has been an innocent misrepresentation, and the misrepresentee rescinds, he will recover any money paid to the other party; but (unless there has been negligence, see below, p 298) he will not recover damages. What if the contract required the misrepresentee to make some payment to a third party, or to incur liabilities to third parties, and he has done so before discovering the misrepresentation and seeking rescission?

Suppose a student takes a flat under a lease which puts the obligation to pay the rates on her, and she has paid the rates before she discovers that the landlord has made a misrepresentation. If when she rescinded she simply got back the rent, the misrepresentor would not have 'given back' all that he received, because the obligation to pay the rates would otherwise have fallen on him; the student's obligation to pay rates is really part of the price the landlord was paid.

To correct this, the court will give the misrepresentee an indemnity against payments made and liabilities incurred as obligations under the contract. Thus in *Newbigging v Adam* (1886) 34 Ch D 582 the plaintiff had been induced to join a partnership by false representations. He obtained dissolution of the partnership, the return of the money he had paid to it and an indemnity against the liabilities he had incurred while a partner.

Payments which the misrepresentee made in reliance on the contract but which were not required by it can only be recovered by way of damages. In *Whittington v Seale-Hayne* (1900) 82 LT 49, the plaintiffs, who were breeders of prize poultry, leased premises from the defendant, relying on his statement that the premises were in a sanitary condition. Under the lease the plaintiffs covenanted to execute all such works as might be required by the local or public authority. The water supply was contaminated due to the insanitary condition of the premises. The plaintiffs' manager and his family became ill, the poultry died or became valueless for breeding, and the local authority required the drains to be put in good order and the house to be made fit for human habitation. The plaintiffs claimed the value of the stock lost, the loss of a breeding season and removal expenses. Farwell J, following *Newbigging v Adam*, held that the plaintiffs were entitled to an indemnity in respect of the repairs they had done under the covenant, but that they could not recover for the other items, which were 'really damages pure and simple'.

(d) Damages for misrepresentation

(i) When damages are available

At common law before 1963 damages were recoverable for misrepresentation only if it had been made fraudulently—ie made in the knowledge of its falsity or recklessly, not caring whether it was true or false—or if a fiduciary relationship existed between the parties (*Derry v Peek* (1889) 14 App Cas 337; *Nocton v Ashburton* [1914] AC 932). The Law Reform Committee recommended in its Report of 1962 (above, p 296) that damages should be recoverable from the misrepresentor unless he could show that he believed the representation to be true and had reasonable grounds for his belief.

The following year the House of Lords held in the *Hedley Byrne* case (above, p 23) that there could be liability in tort for negligent mis-representation; but until 1976 it was not clear whether there could be a 'relationship equivalent to contract' between the parties when there actually was a contract between them.

Esso Petroleum Co Ltd v Mardon [1976] 2 All ER 5 at 14–16, Court of Appeal

(For the facts of this case, see above, p 263. Note that the events occurred before the Misrepresentation Act 1967 had come into force.)

[Lord Denning MR:]

Negligent misrepresentation
Assuming that there was no warranty, the question arises whether Esso are liable for negligent mis-statement under the doctrine of *Hedley Byrne & Co Ltd v Heller & Partners Ltd*. It has been suggested that *Hedley Byrne* cannot be used so as to impose liability for negligent pre-contractual statements; and that, in a pre-contract situation, the remedy (at any rate before the 1967 Act) was only in warranty or nothing. Thus in *Hedley Byrne* itself Lord Reid said: 'Where there is a contract there is no difficulty as regards the contracting parties: the question is whether there is a warranty.' . . .

In arguing this point, counsel for Esso took his stand in this way. He submitted that, when the negotiations between two parties resulted in a contract between them, their rights and duties were governed by the law of contract and not by the law of tort. There was, therefore, no place in their relationship for *Hedley Byrne*, which was solely a case of liability in tort. He relied particularly on *Clark v Kirby Smith* where Plowman J held that the liability of a solicitor for negligence was a liability in contract and not in tort, following the observations of Greene MR in *Groom v Crocker*. Counsel for Esso might also have cited *Bagot v Stevens, Scanlon & Co* about an architect, and other cases, too. But I venture to suggest that those cases are in conflict with other decisions of high authority which were not cited in them. These decisions show that, in the case of a professional man, the duty to use reasonable care arises not only in contract, but is also imposed by the law apart from contract, and is therefore actionable in tort. . . .

To this there is to be added the high authority of Viscount Haldane LC in *Nocton v Lord Ashburton*: '. . . the solicitor contracts with his client to be skilful and careful. For failure to perform his obligation he may be made liable at law in contract or even in tort, for negligence in breach of a duty imposed on him.'

That seems to me right. A professional man may give advice under a contract for reward; or without a contract, in pursuance of a voluntary assumption of responsibility, gratuitously without reward. In either case he is under one and the same duty to use reasonable care: see *Cassidy v Ministry of Health*. In the one case it is by reason of a term implied by law. In the other, it is by reason of a duty imposed by law. For a breach of that duty, he is liable in damages; and those damages should be, and are, the same, whether he is sued in contract or in tort.

It follows that I cannot accept counsel for Esso's proposition. It seems to me that *Hedley Byrne* properly understood, covers this particular proposiiton: if a man, who has or professes to have special knowledge or skill, makes a representation by virtue thereof to another—be it advice, information or opinion—with the intention of inducing him to enter into a contract with him, he is under a duty to use reasonable care to see that the representation is correct, and that the advice, information or opinion is reliable. If he negligently gives unsound advice or misleading information or expresses an erroneous opinion, and thereby induces the other side into a contract with him, he is liable in damages. This proposition is in line with what I said in *Candler v Crane Christmas & Co*, which was approved by the majority of the Privy Council in *Mutual Life and Citizens' Assurance Ltd v Evatt*. And the judges of the Commonwealth have shown themselves quite ready to apply *Hedley Byrne* between contracting parties: see, in Canada, *Sealand of the Pacific Ltd v Ocean Cement Ltd* and, in New Zealand, *Capital Motors Ltd v Beecham*.

Applying this principle, it is plain that Esso professed to have—and did in fact have—special knowledge or skill in estimating the throughput of a filling station. They made the representation—they forecast a throughput of 200,000 gallons—intending to induce Mr Mardon to enter into a tenancy on the faith of it. They made it negligently. It was a 'fatal error'.

And thereby induced Mr Mardon to enter into a contract of tenancy that was disastrous to him. For this misrepresentation they are liable in damages.

[Ormrod and Shaw LJJ agreed.]

Misrepresentation Act 1967

Section 2
(1) Where a person has entered into a contract after a misrepresentation has been made to him by another party thereto and as a result thereof he has suffered loss, then, if the person making the misrepresentation would be liable to damages in respect thereof had the misrepresentation been made fraudulently, that person shall be so liable notwithstanding that the misrepresentation was not made fraudulently, unless he proves that he had reasonable grounds to believe and did believe up to the time the contract was made that the facts represented were true.

(ii) The measure of damages for misrepresentation

In *Doyle v Olby* [1969] 2 QB 158, a case of fraudulent misrepresentation, the Court of Appeal confirmed that in fraud the damages will compensate the plaintiff for 'out of pocket' or reliance loss, but will not give the plaintiff the loss of profit which would be available if there had been a breach of contract (see above, p 28).

The difference between the contract and tort measures of damages is that tort damages will return the plaintiff to the pre-contractual position, while contract damages will put the plaintiff into the same position as if the promise had been performed (see above, p 20). The point may be illustrated thus: suppose the seller of a car tells the buyer that it is a 1982 model, when in fact it is a 1980 model. They agree on a price of £1,000, when the value of a 1980 model is £800 and the value of a 1982 model is £1,250. If the buyer decides to keep the car and claim damages, if he can only show that the seller committed a misrepresentation, he will recover the difference between what he paid out and what he received, £200; if he can show that the seller's statement amounted to a contractual promise (see above, p 259), he will recover the difference between the actual value of the car and the value it would have had, had it been a 1982 model, here £450.

On the other hand, damages in contract are limited by a rule that prevents recovery of losses which were not foreseeable as substantially likely at the time the contract was made (the 'remoteness' rule, below, p 475). In *Doyle v Olby* the Court of Appeal held that there was no such limitation in cases of fraud (this is a general rule for intentional torts.)

It is probable that damages under s 2(1) of the Misrepresentation Act are also to be assessed on the tortious basis: see *André et Cie SA v Ets Michel Blanc & Fils* [1977] 2 Lloyd's Rep 166, 181 (affirmed without reference to this point [1979] 2 Lloyd's Rep 427, CA) and *Chesneau v Interhome Ltd* (1983) Times, 9 June, CA.

Presumably damages under s 2(2) would also be on the tortious basis rather than the contractual; but it may be that s 2(2) damages are to be awarded on a yet more limited basis. Firstly, s 2(3) seems to contemplate that damages under s 2(2) will be more limited than under s 2(1). Secondly, the damages are stated to be 'in lieu of rescission'. The effect of rescission is to permit the representee to recapture the difference in value between what he gave up and what he received. It is certainly possible, and it might be appropriate, to say that damages under s 2(2) should be assessed by the same measure—a restitution measure, to adopt the terminology used in the Introduction (above, p 32), with no compensation for consequential loss.

(iii) Contributory negligence

We saw earlier (p 286) that if a misrepresentee is claiming rescission, it is no answer that he could with reasonable diligence have discovered the truth for himself. Does the same apply if he is claiming damages for negligence at common law or under s 2(1), or should his damages be reduced? Perhaps the case falls within the Law Reform (Contributory Negligence) Act 1945, s 1(1):

> 'Where any person suffers damage as the result partly of his own fault and partly of the fault of any other person or persons, a claim in respect of that damage shall not be defeated by reason of the fault of the person suffering the damage, but the damages recoverable in respect thereof shall be reduced to such extent as the court thinks just and equitable having regard to the claimant's share in the responsibility for the damage . . .'

(e) Attempts to exclude or restrict liability for misrepresentation

Any clause purporting to exclude or restrict liability for fraudulent misrepresentation is probably ineffective at common law (see *S Pearson & Son Ltd v Dublin Corpn* [1907] AC 351, 353–354). Clauses attempting to do the same for non-fraudulent misrepresentations are now governed by the Misrepresentation Act 1967, s 3 (as amended by the Unfair Contract Terms Act 1977, s 8):

Misrepresentation Act 1967

Section 3
If a contract contains a term which would exclude or restrict—
(a) any liability to which a party to a contract may be subject by reason of any misrepresentation made by him before the contract was made; or
(b) any remedy available to another party to the contract by reason of such a misrepresentation;
that term shall be of no effect except in so far as it satisfies the requirement of reasonableness as stated in section 11(1) of the Unfair Contract Terms Act 1977; and it is for those claiming that the term satisfies that requirement to show that it does.

The application of this section will be considered below, p 718.

CHAPTER 15
Gapfilling by interpretation

(a) Introduction

The last two chapters dealt with the question of what had expressly been agreed between the parties. This is only the beginning of the process of deciding what the parties' contractual obligations are in a given situation. The terms expressly agreed may not provide a clear answer, or may not cover the situation at all. This frequently happens with even the basic performance obligations: for instance, there may be no express agreement on price or the time for performance. It is even more common for there to be no express agreement on the effect of events which may occur before the contract has been performed and which disrupt it in some way ('contingencies').

'Non-contractual Relations in Business' by Macaulay (1963) 28 American Sociological Review 55, 55–60

What good is contract law? who uses it? when and how? Complete answers would require an investigation of almost every type of transaction between individuals and organizations. In this report, research has been confined to exchanges between businesses, and primarily to manufacturers. Furthermore, this report will be limited to a presentation of the findings concerning when contract is and is not used and to a tentative explanation of these findings.

This research is only the first phase in a scientific study. The primary research technique involved interviewing 68 businessmen and lawyers representing 43 companies and six law firms. The interviews ranged from a 30-minute brush-off where not all questions could be asked of a busy and uninterested sales manager to a six-hour discussion with the general counsel of a large corporation. Detailed notes of the interviews were taken and a complete report of each interview was dictated, usually no later than the evening after the interview. All but two of the companies had plants in Wisconsin; 17 were manufacturers of machinery but none made such items as food products, scientific instruments, textiles or petroleum products. Thus the likelihood of error because of sampling bias may be considerable. However, to a great extent, existing knowledge has been inadequate to permit more rigorous procedures—as yet one cannot formulate many precise questions to be asked of a systematically selected sample of 'right people'. Much time has been spent fishing for relevant questions or answers, or both. . . .

Tentative findings

It is difficult to generalize about the use and nonuse of contract by manufacturing industry. However, a number of observations can be made with reasonable accuracy at this time. The use and nonuse of contract in creating exchange relations and in dispute settling will be taken up in turn.

The creation of exchange relationships

In creating exchange relationships, businessmen may plan to a greater or lesser degree in relation to several types of issues. Before reporting the findings as to practices in creating such relationships, it is necessary to describe what one can plan about in a bargain and the degrees of planning which are possible.

People negotiating a contract can make plans concerning several types of issues: (1) They can plan what each is to do or refrain from doing; eg, S might agree to deliver ten 1963 Studebaker four-door sedan automobiles to B on a certain date in exchange for a specified amount of money. (2) They can plan what effect certain contingencies are to have on their duties; eg, what is to happen to S and B's obligations if S cannot deliver the cars because of a strike at the Studebaker factory? (3) They can plan what is to happen if either of them fails to perform; eg, what is to happen if S delivers nine of the cars two weeks late? (4) They can plan their agreement so that it is a legally enforceable contract—that is, so that a legal sanction would be available to provide compensation for injury suffered by B as a result of S's failure to deliver the cars on time.

As to each of these issues, there may be a different degree of planning by the parties. (1) They may carefully and explicitly plan; eg S may agree to deliver ten 1963 Studebaker four-door sedans which have six cylinder engines, automatic transmissions and other specified items of optional equipment and which will perform to a specified standard for a certain time. (2) They may have a mutual but tacit understanding about an issue; eg, although the subject was never mentioned in their negotiations, both S and B may assume that B may cancel his order for the cars before they are delivered if B's taxi-cab business is so curtailed that B can no longer use ten additional cabs. (3) They may have two inconsistent unexpressed assumptions about an issue; eg, S may assume that if any of the cabs fails to perform to the specified standard for a certain time, all S must do is repair or replace it. B may assume S must also compensate B for the profits B would have made if the cab had been in operation. (4) They may never have thought of the issue; eg, neither S nor B planned their agreement so that it would be a legally enforceable contract. Of course, the first and fourth degrees of planning listed are the extreme cases and the second and third are intermediate points. Clearly other intermediate points are possible: eg, S and B neglect to specify whether the cabs should have automatic or conventional transmissions. Their planning is not as careful and explicit as that in the example previously given.

The following diagram represents the dimensions of creating an exchange relationship just discussed with 'X's' representing the example of S and B's contract for ten taxi-cabs.

	Definition of Performances	Effect of Contingencies	Effect of Defective Performances	Legal Sanctions
Explicit and careful	X			
Tacit agreement		X		
Unilateral assumptions			X	
Unawareness of the issue				X

Most larger companies, and many smaller ones, attempt to plan carefully and completely. Important transactions not in the ordinary course of business are handled by a detailed contract. For example, recently the Empire State Building was sold for $65 million. More than 100 attorneys, representing 34 parties, produced a 400 page contract. Another example is found in the agreement of a major rubber company in the United States to give technical assistance to a Japanese firm. Several million dollars were involved and the contract consisted of 88 provisions on 17 pages. The 12 house counsel—lawyers who work for one corporation rather than many clients—interviewed said that all but the smallest business carefully planned most transactions of any significance. Corporations have procedures so that particular types of exchanges will be reviewed by their legal and financial departments.

More routine transactions commonly are handled by what can be called standardized planning. A firm will have a set of terms and conditions for purchases, sales, or both printed on the business documents used in these exchanges. Thus the things to be sold and the price may be planned particularly for each transaction, but standard provisions will further elaborate the performances and cover the other subjects of planning. Typically, these terms and conditions are lengthy and printed in small type on the back of the forms. . . .

While businessmen can and often do carefully and completely plan, it is clear that not all exchanges are neatly rationalized. Although most businessmen think that a clear description of both the seller's and buyer's performances is obvious common sense, they do not always live up to this ideal. The house counsel and the purchasing agent of a medium size manufacturer of automobile parts reported that several times their engineers had committed the company to buy expensive machines without adequate specifications. The engineers had drawn careful specifications as to the type of machine and how it was to be made but had neglected to require that the machine produce specified results. An attorney and an auditor both stated that most contract disputes arise because of ambiguity in the specifications.

Businessmen often prefer to rely on 'a man's word' in a brief letter, a handshake, or 'common honesty and decency'—even when the transaction involves exposure to serious risks. Seven lawyers from law firms with business practices were interviewed. Five thought that businessmen often entered contracts with only a minimal degree of advance planning. They complained that businessmen desire to 'keep it simple and avoid red tape' even where large amounts of money and significant risks are involved. One stated that he was 'sick of being told, "We can trust old Max", when the problem is not one of honesty but one of reaching an agreement that both sides understand'. Another said that businessmen when bargaining often talk only in pleasant generalities, think they have a contract, but fail to reach agreement on any of the hard, unpleasant questions until forced to do so by a lawyer. Two outside lawyers had different views. One thought that large firms usually planned important exchanges, although he conceded that occasionally matters might be left in a fairly vague state. The other dissenter represents a large utility that commonly buys heavy equipment and buildings. The supplier's employees come on the utility's property to install the equipment or construct the buildings, and they may be injured while there. The utility has been sued by such employees so often that it carefully plans purchases with the assistance of a lawyer so that suppliers take this burden. . . .

It is likely that businessmen pay more attention to describing the performances in an exchange than to planning for contingencies or defective performances or to obtaining legal enforceability of their contracts. Even when a purchase order and acknowledgment have conflicting provisions printed on the back, almost always the buyer and seller will be in agreement on what is to be sold and how much is to be paid for it. The lawyers who said businessmen often commit their firms to significant exchanges too casually, stated that the performances would be defined in the brief letter or telephone call; the lawyers objected that nothing else would be covered. Moreover, it is likely that businessmen are least concerned about planning their transactions so that they are legally enforceable contracts. For example, in Wisconsin requirements contracts—contracts to supply a firm's requirements of an item rather than a definite quantity—probably are not legally enforceable. Seven people interviewed reported that their firms regularly used requirements contracts in dealings with Wisconsin. None thought that the lack of legal sanction made any difference. Three of these people were house counsel who knew the Wisconsin law before being interviewed. Another example of a lack of desire for legal sanctions is found in the relationship between automobile manufacturers and their suppliers of parts. The manufacturers draft a carefully planned agreement, but one which is so designed that the supplier will have only minimal, if any, legal rights against the manufacturers. The standard contract used by manufacturers of paper to sell to magazine publishers has a pricing clause which is probably sufficiently vague to make the contract legally unenforceable. The house counsel of one of the largest paper producers said that everyone in the industry is aware of this because of a leading New York case concerning the contract, but that no one cares. Finally, it seems likely that planning for contingencies and defective performances are in-between cases—more likely to occur than planning for a legal sanction, but less likely than a description of performance.

Thus one can conclude that (1) many business exchanges reflect a high degree of planning about the four categories—description, contingencies, defective performances and legal sanction—but (2) many, if not most, exchanges reflect no planning, or only a minimal amount of it, especially concerning legal sanctions and the effect of defective performances. As a result, the opportunity for good faith disputes during the life of the exchange relationship often is present.

NOTE

This study by Macaulay is the one referred to earlier (above, p 79). If you would like to read more of it but do not have access to the American Sociological Review, you will find a slightly abridged version in *Sociology of Law*, ed Aubert.

In a case where there is a gap in the terms, the court has to fulfil two functions at once. One is to decide what was the obligation or risk allocation in the present case; the other is by deciding what the terms mean or what the parties' implied obligations are, to supply a standard set of risk-allocation terms for use by contracting parties in the future (see above, p 75). This will save the cost of negotiating over the point in the future, as parties making similar contracts in future will be able to rely on the standard set of terms—provided, of course the obligations imposed by the court fit the parties' needs. If they do not, the parties will then have to agree expressly on a different solution, thus increasing the cost of contracting once more.

There are a number of techniques by which the court may 'fill' the gap in the express terms; this chapter and the next concentrate on the two most obvious, the interpretation of the words expressly agreed and the implication of terms. There are other doctrines, however, which are on their face very different but in fact involve very similar issues—in particular the doctrines of common mistake (under which a contract entered under a shared and fundamental mistake as to the facts may be void, or voidable in equity) and frustration (under which a contract may be discharged if without the fault of either party a subsequent event makes it impossible to perform).

The solutions that the doctrines provide are different in their theoretical effect and sometimes in their practical outcome. When the court interprets an express term as applying to the contingency which has occurred, or implies a term covering it, it is normally thought of as 'enforcing' the contract, and the usual outcome will be that one or other of the parties is held to have borne the risk of the loss which the contingency caused. Thus a party may have to perform his part of the contract, even though the contingency has seriously impaired the value to him of the performance he is to receive in exchange; or a party may have to pay compensation because he is held in default, even though his default was unintentional and sometimes without blame on his part. In contrast, if the doctrine of the common mistake or frustration is applied the contract is not enforced: it is void (or perhaps voidable) for mistake or it is discharged by frustration and neither party will be liable in damages to the other for failing to perform. The result thus appears to be that the loss is divided between the parties, though we shall see that the division is sometimes pretty rough and ready. Occasionally a similar result (which we shall refer to as 'the discharge solution') is reached via interpretation or the implication of terms (see below, chapter 19).

Despite these differences the various techniques are clearly interrelated. Firstly, when considering one approach the court will always have to bear in mind the outcome that would be reached under another: thus interpretation of the express terms will be carried out in the light of what implied term would otherwise apply; the question of what terms should be implied will depend in part on the express terms of the contract; the question of whether the contract is discharged by frustration will depend on the express and implied terms; and so on. Secondly, whichever doctrine is applied, it has been traditional to justify the outcome in terms of the presumed intentions of the parties. In recent years this has often been decried as a mere pretence. For instance, the implication of terms into a contract has often been explained as giving effect to the presumed intention of the parties. This is clearly no longer an acceptable rationale, as some of the terms implied by statute are now compulsory, and will thus apply even when the parties both consciously intend to exclude them (see below, p 705ff). Even before the advent of such compulsory terms the explanation seemed inadequate: many of the implied terms were so complex and so uniformly applied that it was more accurate to say that each type of contract carried with it a set of 'normal' obligations, which would govern unless it was the intention to exclude them. Similarly with frustration: the older cases explained the discharge of the contract as based on a term implied 'in order to fulfil the intention of those who entered into the contract' (below, p 347). Later courts have baulked at implying a term to cover something the parties 'neither expected nor foresaw', and have preferred to rest the doctrine on so-called construction; the contract does not apply to the new situation (below, p 350).

There is no doubt that in many cases of implied terms or frustration the parties did not have any actual intention on what was to happen in the circumstances, or certainly no common intentions; and reference to their intentions was partly a polite fiction by which the court justified its decision. But the fictitious nature of the 'intention' should not be allowed to obscure the fact that the courts were in a sense using the right approach. If we turn to the question of what outcome the court should aim for in a particular situation that the parties have not provided for, the single most important guide is, what would the parties have agreed on if they *had* negotiated a clause on this question? The following extract explores this point further. It is discussing the doctrine of discharge by frustration, but the criteria suggested are equally relevant to what terms should be implied, to cases of mistake and even as a guide to interpretation.

'Impossibility and Related Doctrines in Contract Law: An Economic Analysis' by Posner and Rosenfield (1977) 6 JLS 83, 87–92

There is . . . in the literature some recognition that the problem of discharge is one of allocating risk, since the effect of granting discharge is to place the risk of the event preventing performance on the promisee, while the effect of denying discharge is to place it on the promisor. But thus far the insight has been a sterile one because of a failure to develop any criteria for assigning the risk to one party or the other. Corbin is typical in suggesting both that it is a matter of indifference who bears the risk and that risk allocation is arbitrary: 'Where neither custom nor agreement determines the allocation of risk, the court must exercise its equity powers and pray for the wisdom of Solomon.'

We shall try to give content to the concept of risk allocation as applied to the discharge question, first by sketching a theoretical framework that demonstrates why and when it is economically sensible to discharge a contract because of some unexpected event, and then by subjecting the theory to preliminary verification by comparing its implication with prevailing doctrinal positions and typical case holdings.

B. Economic principles

1. *Of contract law in general.* The process by which goods and services are shifted into their most valuable uses is one of voluntary exchange. The distinctive problems of contract law arises when the agreed-upon exchange does not take place instantaneously (for example, A agrees to build a house for B and construction will take several months). The fact that performance is to extend into the future introduces uncertainty, which in turn creates risks. A fundamental purpose of contracts is to allocate these risks between the parties to the exchange.

One purpose of contract *law*, but not a particularly interesting one here, is to assure compliance with the allocation of risks that the parties have agreed upon (that is, to prevent bad faith). A second purpose, central to our subject, is to reduce the costs of contract negotiation by supplying contract terms that the parties would probably have adopted explicitly had they negotiated over them. This purpose has been understood since Bentham's day:

'. . . [O]bligations may be distinguished into original and adjective. I call those original, of which express mention is made in the contract itself: I call those adjective, which the law thinks proper to add to the first. The first turn upon events which the contracting parties have foreseen; the others upon events which they could not foresee.

It is thus that in every country the law has supplied[?] the shortsightedness of individuals, by doing for them what they would have done for themselves, if their imagination had anticipated the march of nature.'

This function of contract *law* is analogous to that performed by standard or form *contracts*. The form contract economizes on the costs of contract negotiation by providing a set of terms to govern in the absence of explicit negotiations. The parties can of course vary the terms of the form contract, but to the extent that they do not, finding the terms suitable for their needs, contracting costs are reduced. It is much the same with the law of contracts. Judicial decisions, the Uniform Commercial Code, and other sources of contract law operate to define the parties' contractual obligations in the absence of express provisions in the contract. Every contract automatically incorporates a host of (generally) appropriate terms, over which the parties do not have to negotiate explicitly unless they want to vary the standard terms supplied by the law. Incidentally, the role of contract law in supplying contract terms, like the role of the standard or form contract, is less important the larger the stakes in the contract and hence the smaller the ratio of the costs of transacting to the value of the exchange. The larger the stakes, the more it will pay the parties to negotiate contract terms finely adapted to the particular circumstances of their contract.

If the purpose of the law of contracts is to effectuate the desires of the contracting parties, then the proper criterion for evaluating the rules of contract law is surely that of economic efficiency. Since the object of most voluntary exchanges is to increase value or efficiency, contracting parties may be assumed to desire a set of contract terms that will maximize the value of the exchange. It is true that each party is interested only in the value of the contract to it. However, the more efficiently the exchange is structured, the larger is the potential profit of the contract for the parties to divide between them.

The use of economic efficiency as a criterion for legal decision-making is of course controversial. In the area of contract, however, the criterion is well-nigh inevitable once it is conceded that the parties to a contract have the right to vary the terms at will. If the rules of contract law are inefficient, the parties will (save as transaction costs may sometimes outweigh the gains from a more efficient rule) contract around them. A law of contract not based on efficiency considerations will therefore be largely futile. This is a powerful reason for expecting that the law of contract has, in fact, been informed by efficiency considerations, even if judges and lawyers may have found it difficult to articulate the underlying economic premises of the law.

Moreover, the spirit of our analysis is severely positive. We are interested not in whether a contract law based on efficiency is ultimately a good law, but in whether the assumption that contract law has been shaped by a concern with economic efficiency is a fruitful one in explaining the doctrinal positions and typical case outcomes of that law.

2. *The economics of impossibility.* The typical case in which impossibility or some related doctrine is invoked is one where, by reason of an unforeseen or at least unprovided-for event, performance by one of the parties of his obligations under the contract has become so much more costly than he foresaw at the time the contract was made as to be uneconomical (that is, the costs of performance would be greater than the benefits). The performance promised may have been delivery of a particular cargo by a specified delivery date—but the ship is trapped in the Suez Canal because of a war between Israel and Egypt. Or it may have been a piano recital by Gina Bachauer—and she dies between the signing of the contract and the date of the recital. The law could in each case treat the failure to perform as a breach of contract, thereby in effect assigning to the promisor the risk that war, or death, would prevent performance (or render it uneconomical). Alternatively, invoking impossibility or some related notion, the law could treat the failure to perform as excusable and discharge the contract, thereby in effect assigning the risk to the promisee.

From the standpoint of economics—and disregarding, but only momentarily, administrative costs—discharge should be allowed where the promisee is the superior risk bearer; if the promisor is the superior risk bearer, nonperformance should be treated as a breach of contract. 'Superior risk bearer' is to be understood here as the party that is the more efficient bearer of the particular risk in question, in the particular circumstances of the transaction. Of course, if the parties have expressly assigned the risk to one of them, there is no occasion to inquire which is the superior risk bearer. The inquiry is merely an aid to interpretation.

A party can be a superior risk bearer for one of two reasons. First, he may be in a better position to prevent the risk from materializing. This resembles the economic criterion for assigning liability in tort cases. It is an important criterion in many contract settings, too, but not in this one. Discharge would be inefficient in any case where the promisor could prevent the risk from materializing at a lower cost than the expected cost of the risky event. In such a case efficiency would require that the promisor bear the loss resulting from the occurrence of the event, and hence that occurrence should be treated as precipitating a breach of contract.

But the converse is not necessarily true. It does not necessarily follow from the fact that the promisor could not at any reasonable cost have prevented the risk from materializing that he should be discharged from his contractual obligations. Prevention is only one way of dealing with risk; the other is insurance. The promisor may be the superior insurer. If so, his inability to prevent the risk from materializing should not operate to discharge him from the contract, any more than an insurance company's inability to prevent a fire on the premises of the insured should excuse it from its liability to make good the damage caused by the fire.

To understand how it is that one party to a contract may be the superior (more efficient) risk bearer even though he cannot prevent the risk from materializing, it is necessary to understand the fundamental concept of risk aversion. Compare a 100 percent chance of having to pay $10 with a one percent chance of having to pay $1,000. The expected cost is the same in both cases, yet not everyone would be indifferent as between the two alternatives. Many people would be willing to pay a substantial sum to avoid the uncertain alternative—for example, $15 to avoid having to take a one percent chance of having to pay $1,000. Such people are risk averse. The prevalence of insurance is powerful evidence that risk aversion is extremely common, for insurance is simply trading an uncertain for a certain cost. Because of the administrative expenses of insurance, the certain cost (that is, the insurance premium) is always higher, often much higher, than the uncertain cost that it avoids—the expected cost of the fire, of the automobile accident, or whatever. Only a risk-averse individual would pay more to avoid bearing risk than the expected cost of the risk.

The fact that people are willing to pay to avoid risk shows that risk is a cost. Accordingly, insurance is a method (alternative to prevention) of reducing the costs associated with the risk that performance of a contract may be more costly than anticipated. It is a particularly important method of cost avoidance in the impossibility context because the risks with which that doctrine is concerned are generally not preventable by the party charged with nonperformance. As mentioned, if they were, that would normally afford a compelling reason for treating nonperformance as a breach of contract. (Stated otherwise, a 'moral hazard' problem would be created if the promisor were insured against a hazard that he could have prevented at reasonable cost.)

The factors relevant to determining which party to the contract is the cheaper insurer are (1) risk-appraisal costs and (2) transaction costs. The former comprise the costs of determining (a) the probability that the risk will materialize and (b) the magnitude of the loss if it does materialize. The amount of risk is the product of the probability loss and of the magnitude of the loss if it occurs. Both elements—probability and magnitude—must be known in order for the insurer to know how much to ask from the other party to the contract as compensation for bearing the risk in question.

The relevant transaction costs are the costs involved in eliminating or minimizing the risk through pooling it with other uncertain events, that is, diversifying away the risk. This can be done either through self-insurance or through the purchase of an insurance policy (market insurance). To illustrate, a corporation's shareholders might eliminate the risk associated with some contract the corporation had made by holding a portfolio of securities in which their shares in the corporation were combined with shares in many other corporations whose earnings would not be (adversely) affected if this particular corporation were to default on the contract. This would be an example of self-insurance. Alternatively, the corporation might purchase business-loss or some other form of insurance that would protect it (and, more important, its shareholders) from the consequence of a default on the contract; this would be an example of market insurance. Where good opportunities for diversification exist, self-insurance will often be cheaper than market insurance.

The foregoing discussion indicates the factors that courts and legislatures might consider in devising efficient rules for the discharge of contracts. An easy case for discharge would be one where (1) the promisor asking to be discharged could not reasonably have prevented the event rendering his performance uneconomical, and (2) the promisee could have insured against the occurrence of the event at lower cost than the promisor because the promisee (a) was in a better position to estimate both (i) the probability of the event's occurrence and (ii) the magnitude of the loss if it did occur, and (b) could have self-insured, whereas the promisor would have had to buy more costly market insurance. As we shall see, not all cases are this easy.

NOTE

Posner gives the following explanation of risk aversion (*Economic Analysis of Law*, 2nd edition, pp 75–77):

The theoretical explanation is the principle of diminishing marginal utility of money income. If a person who has one chair buys a second, and then a third, and then a fourth, he will probably derive less utility from the second than from the first, and from the third than from the second, and so on; this illustrates the principle of diminishing marginal utility (notice that his *total* utility increases with every additional purchase, since he would not make a purchase that did not add to his net utility). Although money is a more versatile commodity than chairs, it is plausible to suppose that as an individual acquires more and more money the contribution of each dollar to his total utility or well being diminishes. His last $100 will be worth less than his next-to-last $100, etc, and therefore a $100 insurance premium (or indeed, a substantially larger one) will represent a lesser cost to him than 1 percent of the sum of 99 intramarginal $100 wealth units.

Clearly, then, to the risk-averse risk is a cost, and its elimination a gain. But, it may be asked, how does shifting a risk from the insured to the insurance company reduce or eliminate the risk and thus enhance welfare? The answer is that the insurance company, by pooling the insured's fire risk with many other risks with which the insured's is uncorrelated, is able to transform a risky into a (nearly) certain cost and thus eliminate risk—which is why it is able to charge an insurance premium that covers all its own costs yet is still attractive to the insured, ie, that is lower than his costs including the disutility he attaches to risk. For example, the insurance company might insure 1,000 buildings, each with a 1 percent probability of sustaining $10,000 damage. If these probabilities are independent (can you guess the meaning and significance of this qualification?), then the company can be reasonably certain that it will have to pay out close to $100,000 in insurance claims; the probability that it will have to make good the total loss insured against—$10,000,000—is infinitesimal. In contrast, the probability that, in the absence of insurance, the individual building owner would sustain his maximum loss is, as we know, a nonnegligible 1 percent. Stated otherwise, an expected cost, when incurred repeatedly, becomes a more or less certain average cost.

The purchase of an explicit insurance policy is referred to as 'market insurance'. In some cases 'self-insurance' is possible. A real estate company may own the 1,000 buildings in the previous example; if so, its 'risk' of fire loss is a nearly certain prospect of incurring a $100,000 cost. We shall see . . . that an investor can reduce the risks associated with a particular security by holding a diversified portfolio, ie, a set of securities whose risks are (at least partially) uncorrelated with one another; it is the same principle as illustrated by our fire self-insurance example.

(b) Interpretation

When there is a dispute about the obligations of the parties in a given situation, the first task of the court will normally be to apply the express terms of the contract, if any are relevant. It is at this point that interpretation is necessary.

Extract from Evening Times and Echo, Saturday 8 May 1920

Is a Dog a Workman?

A Problem which Remains Unsolved

Is a dog a workman?

The question has arisen at Bath in consequence of the revision of the tramcar fares owing to the increased running costs. Hitherto dogs have travelled free, but now a fare is charged.

A workman who boarded a car accompanied by his dog tendered the money for two workmen's tickets (says the Daily Express correspondent) whereupon the following dialogue took place:

Conductor: Where is the dog's ticket?
Workman: Oh, the second ticket is for the dog.
Conductor: But he is not a workman.
Workman: Oh, yes he is. I take him to look after my kit.
The problem remains unresolved.

Despite the obvious importance of interpretation, it is very difficult to give a description of the process. There are a few 'rules', but for the most part the courts proceed case by case. Some of the cases which follow state rules; others are put in simply as examples. The only area in which many 'rules' have developed is in the interpretation of exemption clauses. The interpretation of exemption clauses raises rather different issues, relating to the policing of bargains, and it will be dealt with later (below, p 682ff).

Lovell & Christmas Ltd v Wall (1911) 104 LT 85, Court of Appeal

The defendant had been a director of a company of provision merchants, which had made a substantial part of its profit from the manufacture and sale of margarine by two subsidiaries. When the company amalgamated with the plaintiff company, the defendant agreed to become a director of the plaintiff company, and that for five years he would not, at any time, solely or jointly, directly or indirectly, carry on or be engaged or concerned or interested in the business of a 'provision merchant', within a certain area, save on behalf of the plaintiff company. Before five years had elapsed, the defendant ceased to be a director and threatened to carry on a business of making margarine and selling it wholesale within the prohibited area. The plaintiff company sought an injunction to restrain him.

Cozens-Hardy MR. In this action the plaintiffs claim an injunction against the defendant Charles Tomlinson Wall to restrain him from carrying on a business as a manufacturer of margarine at Liverpool. Their right to such an injunction depends upon the true construction of an agreement under seal dated the 16 June 1906, to the terms of which I must presently refer more particularly. If, however, the document does not bear the construction contended for by the plaintiffs, they claim to have it rectified so as to make it prohibit the defendant from doing the act complained of. Now, it is of the utmost importance to keep those two heads of relief perfectly distinct. The question of construction logically comes first. The question of rectification only arises if and when the plaintiffs have failed on the question of construction. If there is one principle more clearly established than another in English law it is surely this: It is for the court to construe a written document. It is irrelevant and improper to ask what the parties, prior to the execution of the instrument, intended or understood. What is the meaning of the language that they have used therein? That is the problem, and the only problem. In saying that, I do not mean to assert that no evidence can be admitted. Indeed, the contrary is clear. If a deed relates to Black Acre, you may have evidence to show what are the parcels. If a document is in a foreign language, you may have an intepreter. If it contains technical terms, an expert may explain them. If, according to the custom of a trade or the usage of the market, a word has acquired a secondary meaning, evidence may be given to prove it. A well-known instance is where in a particular trade 1,000 rabbits meant 1,200. But unless the case can be brought within some or one of these exceptions, it is the duty of the court, which is presumed to understand the English language, to construe the document according to the ordinary grammatical meaning of the words used therein, and without reference to anything which has previously passed between the parties to it. When we come to the question of rectification, wholly different considerations apply. The essence of rectification is to bring the document which was expressed and intended to be in pursuance of a prior agreement into harmony with that prior agreement.

. . . in considering clause 13, I am entitled to receive evidence that in the term 'provision merchant' there is a secondary meaning attached to the word 'provision' so as to exclude many articles which in its primary sense would be included, such as bread, fruit, and vegetables, but to include margarine. Such evidence was rightly admitted by Eve J. Enlightened by that evidence, I ask myself whether a margarine manufacturer—as distinguished from a dealer in margarine—falls within the meaning of the words 'provision merchant', and I hold that he does not. Certain evidence was tendered to show that some people in the trade might consider or call a margarine manufacturerer a 'provision merchant'. But when it was admitted—as it was deliberately admitted by the appellant's counsel—that there is no special or secondary meaning attached to the words 'provision mechant', it seems to me to follow that the evidence tendered was properly rejected.

[The discussion of rectification is omitted; it was held that there were no grounds for rectification.]

Appeal dismissed.

NOTE

Many courts treat the rule that, when construing a contract, it is not proper to consider what the parties intended, as an aspect of the parol evidence rule (see above, p 280). The same rule applies, however, to construing the words of a purely oral contract, to which the parol evidence rule proper (if, indeed, there is such a thing) would not apply, and it is probably better to treat them as separate rules.

Prenn v Simmonds [1971] 3 All ER 237, House of Lords

P wished to procure the services of S, the managing director and leading technician of A Ltd, a wholly-owned subsidiary of RTT Ltd, which did not itself trade. For this purpose P agreed, in 1959 to purchase from CP Ltd its holding of 94 per cent of the ordinary capital of RTT Ltd and the whole of an issue of redeemable preference stock, the amount required to redeem it being £294,716. For this P paid £160,000 in cash, and further agreed to pay the balance of £94,716 in four equal annual instalments, the final instalment being payable on 19th August 1963. The agreement provided that any money applied by RTT Ltd in redeeming preference stock was to go in reduction of the balance of the purchase price. By cl 1 of a separate agreement made in July 1960 between P and S, which specifically referred to the contract between P and CP Ltd, provision was made, inter alia, for the sale of shares in RTT Ltd to S for a specified sum. By cl 2 however it was provided that cl 1 should not take effect unless either (a) the sum of £294,716 payable by P to CP Ltd had been satisfied out of moneys 'provided by RTT Ltd redeeming its Preference Stock Units out of profits which would otherwise be available for dividend' or (b) in the event of the stock being redeemed otherwise than out of the profits of RTT Ltd or the balance of £294,716 being satisfied from another source, the 'aggregate profits of RTT earned during the four years ending 19th August 1963 and available for dividend on the Ordinary Stock Units for the time being issued whether declared or not shall have amounted to £300,000 after payment of provision for income tax and profits tax'. Although in the relevant period the profits of the group, ie RTT Ltd and A Ltd, greatly exceeded £300,000 the separate profits of RTT Ltd fell short of this figure. It was contended by P that the reference to 'profits' in paras (a) and (b) of cl 2 of the agreement was to the separate profits of RTT Ltd and that since these had not reached the target figure under cl 2 (b) S was not entitled to exercise his right under cl 1 to purchase the shares in RTT Ltd.

Lord Wilberforce. My Lords, Dr Simmonds's claim in this action is that, under the terms of an agreement under seal dated 6th July 1960, he is entitled to acquire from Mr Prenn, for a consideration of £6,000, a 4 per cent interest in the ordinary capital of a company controlled by Mr Prenn called now Controls & Communications Ltd, but at the relevant date Radio & Television Trust Ltd ('RTT'). This interest was worth at the date of the trial about £200,000. Mr Prenn disputes the claim on the ground that a necessary condition set by the agreement has not been satisfied because less than £300,000 profits available for dividend on the ordinary stock of RTT over the relevant period has been earned. Dr Simmonds maintains that the condition has been fulfilled. The dispute relates not to the figures, which are agreed, but to the definition of profits of RTT available for dividend on its ordinary stock. If this means the separate profits of RTT alone, the amount over the period fell just short of the target, by less than £10,000. If it means the consolidated profits of the group consisting of RTT and subsidiaries, the amount was largely exceeded. The small margin of deficiency, although capable of arousing sympathy for Dr Simmonds, is not an argument for one or other side. A similar situation might arise on either interpretation and is inherent in the nature of 'target' agreements. . . .

In order for the agreement of 6th July 1960 to be understood, it must be placed in its context. The time has long passed when agreements, even those under seal, were isolated from the matrix of facts in which they were set and interpreted purely on internal linguistic considerations. There is no need to appeal here to any modern, anti-literal, tendencies, for Lord Blackburn's well-known judgment in *River Wear Comrs v Adamson* provides ample warrant for a liberal approach. We must, as he said, enquire beyond the language and see what the circumstances were with reference to which the words were used, and the object, appearing from those circumstances, which the person using them had in view. Moreover, at any rate since 1859 (*Macdonald v Longbottom*) it has been clear enough that evidence of mutually known facts may be admitted to identify the meaning of a descriptive term.

Counsel for Dr Simmonds, however, contended for even greater extension of the court's interpretative power. They argued that later authorities have gone further and allow prior negotiations to be looked at in aid of the construction of a written document. In my opinion, they did not make good their contention. . . .

I may refer to one other case to dispel the idea that English law is left behind in some island of literal interpretation. In *Utica City National Bank v Gunn* the New York Court of Appeals followed precisely the English line. Cardozo J in his judgment refers to 'the genesis and aim of the transaction' citing Stephen's Digest of the Law of Evidence, and Wigmore on Evidence. Surrounding circumstances may, he says, 'stamp upon a contract a popular or looser meaning' than the strict legal meaning, certainly when to follow the latter would make the transaction futile. 'It is easier to give a new shade of meaning to a word than to give no meaning to a whole transaction.' The whole judgment, as one may expect, combines classicism with intelligent realism.

So I think that Dr Simmonds gains little support from authority. On principle, the matter is worth pursuing a little, because the present case illustrates very well the disadvantages and danger of departing from established doctrine and the virtue of the latter. There were prolonged negotiations between solicitors, with exchanges of draft clauses, ultimately emerging in cl 2 of the agreement. The reason for not admitting evidence of these exchanges is not a technical one or even mainly one of convenience (although the attempt to admit it did greatly prolong the case and add to its expense). It is simply that such evidence is unhelpful. By the nature of things, where negotiations are difficult, the parties' positions, with each passing letter, are changing and until the final agreement, although converging, still divergent. It is only the final document which records a consensus. If the previous documents use different expressions, how does construction of those expressions, itself a doubtful process, help on the construction of the contractual words? If the same expressions are used, nothing is gained by looking back; indeed, something may be lost since the relevant surrounding circumstances may be different. And at this stage there is no consensus of the parties to appeal to. It may be said that previous documents may be looked at to explain the aims of the parties. In a limited sense this is true; the commercial, or business object, of the transaction, objectively ascertained, may be a surrounding fact. Cardozo J thought so in the *Utica Bank* case. And if it can be shown that one interpretation completely frustrates that object, to the extent of rendering the contract futile, that may be a strong argument for an alternative interpretation, if that can reasonably be found. But beyond that it may be difficult to go; it may be a matter of degree, or of judgment, how far one interpretation, or another, gives effect to a common intention; the parties, indeed, may be pursuing that intention with differing emphasis, and hoping to achieve it to an extent which may differ, and in different ways. The words used may, and often do, represent a formula which means different things to each side, yet may be accepted because that is the only way to get 'agreement' and in the hope that disputes will not arise. The only course then can be to try to ascertain the 'natural' meaning. Far more, and indeed totally, dangerous is it to admit evidence of one party's objective—even if this is known to the other party. However strongly pursued this may be, the other party may only be willing to give it partial recognition, and in a world of give and take, men often have to be satisfied with less than they want. So, again, it would be a matter of speculation how far the common intention was that the particular objective should be realised. In the present case, Lord Denning MR seems to have taken into account Dr Simmonds's anxiety (as testified by a witness) to protect himself against unilateral decisions by Mr Prenn; and an argument pressed on us was that, if Mr Prenn's interpretation (ie that only the holding company's profits were relevant) was correct, Dr Simmonds would, in this matter on which he felt so anxious, in some respect at least, be completely in Mr Prenn's hands, for Mr Prenn could decide just how much, or how little, of the subsidiaries' profits were to be passed to the holding company. I cannot see how any of this can be admissible because, I repeat, I cannot see how it is helpful. Given the fact of Dr Simmonds's anxiety, the whole question is how far does the agreement meet it; how can we know, except by interpreting the agreement, how far Mr Penn was willing to meet him or how far Dr Simmonds decided to take what he could get? Even the argument that Mr Prenn's interpretation would put Dr Simmonds in his hands, although apparently attractive, I find to be dangerous; a man in Dr Simmonds's position—a professional man—entering into relations with the source of finance and benefits to come, might decide, in his own interest, that if he could not get all the protection he wanted, the risk of partial protection was one to accept; that Mr Prenn had to be trusted to act fairly. To say that the clause had this result is not to say that it was futile or frustratory: it is to say that a better clause could, with hindsight, in Dr Simmonds's interest have been drawn. But the court cannot construct such a clause out of the material given.

In my opinion, then, evidence of negotiations, or of the parties' intentions, and a fortiori of Dr Simmonds's intentions, ought not to be received, and evidence should be restricted to evidence of the factual background known to the parties at or before the date of the contract, including evidence of the 'genesis' and objectively the 'aim' of the transaction. . . .

What profits, then, are contemplated by this clause? The profits of the RTT group, including Airmec, or only such separate profits as reach RTT as holding company? This is the whole question in the case.

As a final preliminary matter, before answering this question, it is necessary to state a few more matters of fact which must have been present to the minds of both parties. First, it must have been known to those businessmen, at least in general terms, that under the Companies Act 1948 there had to be placed before the shareholders of RTT in general meeting a consolidated profit and loss account giving a true and fair view of the profits of RTT and its subsidiaries combined just as if it was an account of a single company. No doubt there would also be separate profit and loss accounts of each individual company, including RTT itself, but I have no hesitation in asserting that both under the scheme of the Act and in accepted business practice, the significant document is the consolidated account which alone would show whether the enterprise represented by the group was making profit or not.

Secondly, as one would expect, accounts in this form had been prepared by RTT. There are among the documents consolidated profit and loss accounts of RTT and subsidiaries for the year ended 31st March 1958, the fifteen months ended 30th June 1959, the nine months ended 31st March 1960, the three relevant periods immediately before the agreement. Each of these shows the consolidated profit on trading (ie of the group), the dividend paid (ie on the preference and ordinary capital of RTT) and the balance on profit and loss account (of RTT and the subsidiaries). Thirdly, there are minutes showing how the decisions as to dividends (on RTT capital) out of the profits (of the group) were made. Minutes of 11th August 1959 and 10th June 1960 show, as one would expect, that these were made by the board of the holding company, which then instructed the subsidiaries to declare the appropriate amount by way of dividend, in favour of the holding company.

In the light of this, the meaning of cl 2 of the agreement seems to me clear. The references to 'profits' in para (a) and in para (b) can only, in my opinion, be to the consolidated profits of the group consisting of RTT and its subsidiaries. It is only these profits which could provide an incentive to Dr Simmonds to remain and work with the group and which could be a measure of his success. On the other hand, no purpose can be discerned why the reference should be to the separate profits of RTT, which in fact means such part of the group profits as the board of that company, effectively Mr Prenn, decided to pass up to the parent company.

Linguistically, the arguments point decidedly the same way. The reference to profits 'earned', and that to income and profits tax, point strongly to consolidated profits. The use of the words 'R.T.T.' even coupled with the definition appears to me perfectly neutral, since other usages of 'R.T.T.' in the agreement (definition of 'the Contract' and cl 3) dispel any idea that the draftsman had in mind any segregation of RTT (qua parent) from the rest of its group. The reference (in para (b)) to profits 'available for dividend on the Ordinary Stock Units', so far from pointing towards the limited construction, points, for me, the other way. For both commercially and on the established accounting practice, all profits of the group are available for these dividends. It is true that a large part of the profits was ploughed back into the business of the subsidiaries, and that both parties must have contemplated that this would be done, but this is not to the point. To say so is to confuse the earning of profits with their appropriation; all profits earned are available for dividend; what is done with them is a matter of choice which rests with those who control the company. Even if they decide to 'plough them back' they still remain 'available for dividend', so long as they remain in the balance sheet as 'balance on profit and loss account'. . . .

To sum up, Mr Prenn's construction does not fit in any way the aim of the agreement, or correspond with commercial good sense, nor is it, even linguistically, acceptable. The converse of each of these propositions applies to Dr Simmonds's interpretation. I would accept it. It follows, in consequence, that the alternative claim for rectification does not arise.

[Lords Reid, Donovan, Diplock and Pearson concurred in dismissing the appeal.]

NOTES

1. In *Prenn v Simmonds* Lord Wilberforce claimed that English law was not 'left behind in some island of literal interpretation'. A modern transatlantic exposition of the problems can be found in the judgment of Traynor J in *Pacific Gas and Electric Co v G W Thomas Drayage and*

Rigging Co 69 Cal 2d 33, 69 Cal Rptr 561, 442 P 2d 641 (1968), Supreme Court of California, where he said:

> Although extrinsic evidence is not admissible to add to, detract from, or vary the terms of a written contract, these terms must first be determined before it can be decided whether or not extrinsic evidence is being offered for a prohibited purpose. The fact that the terms of an instrument appear clear to a judge does not preclude the possibility that the parties chose the language of the instrument to express different terms. That possibility is not limited to contracts whose terms have acquired a particular meaning by trade usage, but exists whenever the parties' understanding of the words used may have differed from the judge's understanding.

You may like to return to this statement after you have read the remaining cases in this chapter, and consider whether it reflects English law. For an instructive extra-judicial discussion, see Goff, 'The Commercial Court and Commercial Contracts' [1984] Lloyd's MCLQ 382.

2. In *Prenn v Simmonds* Wilberforce says that the parties may adopt a formula which they realise means different things to each side because that is the only way to get 'agreement'. In *Henry Boot & Sons Ltd v LCC* [1959] 1 All ER 77, the question was whether a 'rise-and-fall' clause in a building contract allowing for an adjustment in the price if the 'rates of wages' changed, covered an increase in the amount of 'holiday credits' payable to the contractor's workmen. ('Holiday credits' were sums set aside by employers for each employee and which could be drawn out as a lump sum when the employee went on holiday.) The parties had corresponded on the point before entering the contract, the employer maintaining that holiday credits were not within the clause and the contractor maintaining that they were. The dispute was not resolved. In the Court of Appeal Lord Somervell said of the employers' letter:

> The letter is on the face of it saying: 'This is what we say these words mean'; I think that the contractor was entitled to reply: 'We do not agree with that; we accept your contract, and let the court decide whether you are right, or we are.'

The court held that 'rates of wages' did include holiday credits. This decision was reversed on appeal to the House of Lords [1959] 3 All ER 636, but Lord Somervell's statement on the effect of the pre-contractual discussions was approved. Presumably if the court found that the phrase adopted was hopelessly ambiguous it would have either to ignore it as redundant (cf *Nicolene Ltd v Simmonds*, above, p 217) or hold the whole contract void for uncertainty (cf *Scammel v Ouston*, above, p 215, and *Raffles v Wichelhaus*, above, p 241.)

The Karen Oltmann [1976] 2 Lloyd's Rep 708, Kerr J

The owners of the *Karen Oltmann* let her on a timecharter to the charterers 'for a period of 2 years 14 days more or less'. Clause 26 of the charter provided that:

> Charterers to have the option to redeliver the vessel after 12 months trading subject to giving three months' notice.

After the vessel had been in the charterers' service for 19 months, the charterers (on 30 July 1971) gave three months' notice of their intention to redeliver the vessel. The owners protested on the ground that 'after 12 months trading' meant 'on the expiry of 12 months trading', so that notice should have been given about nine months after the vessel had entered the charterers' service; and they pleaded an estoppel to the effect that in a telex sent before the conclusion of the contract, the charterers had represented that 'after 12 months trading'

> involved that the charter would be a period of two years with an option in favour of [the charterers] to keep the vessel for twelve months only instead of the full two years.

The owners sought a declaration that the charterers were not entitled to give notice under cl 26 after 19 months.

Kerr J. . . . The first question which arose at this point was whether this plea and the submissions founded on it entitled the Court to look at the exchange of telex messages. In my view they do. Take *Prenn v Simmonds*, as an example. The issue in that case was whether the reference to 'profits' in the contract meant the profits of the holding company only or the consolidated profits of the whole group. If in the course of the negotiations one party had made anything in the nature of a representation to the other to the effect that references to 'profits' were to be taken in one of these senses and not in the other, and the other party had thereupon negotiated on this basis, then extrinsic evidence to establish this representation would in my view clearly be admissible. Similarly, if it had been contended that the parties had conducted their negotiations on an agreed basis that the word 'profits' was used in one sense only, although in the contract it was capable of having two senses, and that the contract had been executed on this basis, then I do not think that the Court would be precluded by authority from admitting extrinsic evidence to see whether or not this agreed basis could be established. Both these situations would be a long way from the attempts made in *Prenn v Simmonds* and *Arrale v Costain*, to adduce extrinsic evidence to try to persuade the Court that one interpretation of the contract was in all the circumstances to be preferred to the other.

I think that in such cases the principle can be stated as follows. If a contract contains words which, in their context, are fairly capable of bearing more than one meaning, and it is alleged that the parties have in effect negotiated on an agreed basis that the words bore only one of the two possible meanings, then it is permissible for the Court to examine the extrinsic evidence relied upon to see whether the parties have in fact used the words in question in one sense only, so that they have in effect given their own dictionary meaning to the words as the result of their common intention. Such cases would not support a claim for rectification of the contract, because the choice of words in the contract would not result from any mistake. The words used in the contract would ex hypothesi reflect the meaning which both parties intended.

In the present case, after some argument about these principles and the limits of the parole evidence rule, I decided to look at the pleaded telex messages, though Counsel for the charterers rightly submitted that I could only do so de bene esse. He was right about this, because if they did not support the owners' arguments on the lines discussed above, then I would have to put them out of mind and fall back on my construction as a matter of first impression.

I therefore turn to consider the pleaded telex exchanges. Although I do not consider that they support the allegation of an estoppel, I think that they clearly show that the words 'after 12 months trading' were used in an agreed sense. From start to finish the owners wanted maximum duration and certainty whereas the charterers wanted minimum duration and maximum flexibility. It is clear that both parties throughout used the word 'after' in the sense of 'on the expiry of' and not 'at any time after the expiry of'.

Judgment for the owners.

NOTES

1. Suppose a buyer contacts a seller saying he needs 'feveroles'. The seller asks what these are and the buyer says he thinks they are just horsebeans. The seller says he thinks so too, and they enter a contract for 'feveroles'. The seller supplies horsebeans. The buyer then discovers that the technical meaning of 'feverole' is a particular kind of bean different to those supplied. Is the seller in breach?
2. Would your answer differ if there had been no discussion between the parties about the meaning of 'feverole', but it can be proved from each party's internal memoranda that neither realised that 'feverole' had this narrower meaning?

Amalgamated Investment & Property Co Ltd v Texas Commerce International Bank Ltd [1981] 3 All ER 577, Court of Appeal

(For the facts of this case, see above, p 145.) Robert Goff J held that the guarantee given by AIP to the bank, covering 'moneys . . . payable to you' by the plaintiffs' subsidiary ANPP, did not apply to the loan which had been made, as the loan had been made not by the defendants directly but by the defendants to a Bahamian subsidiary called Portsoken and then by Portsoken to ANPP. He held, however, that AIP was estopped from denying that the guarantee covered the loan. The Court of Appeal agreed with this, but also held that as a matter of construction the guarantee did cover the loan.

Eveleigh LJ. . . . Ignoring the existence of the guarantee form, in my opinion the agreement reached between the parties orally and evidenced by or contained in (it matters not) the correspondence was clearly to the effect that Amalgamated would be responsible for seeing that the bank was repaid. The subsequent negotiations between Amalgamated and the bank after the money was made available on 31st December 1970 and up to 1976 in which Amalgamated clearly recognised this obligation provides admissible and strong evidence of this. Are we driven to arrive at a different conclusion because of the existence of the standard guarantee form containing the name of ANPP?

It might have been possible to have approached this case on the basis that the form was not introduced into the final contract. In that case the position would be as I have stated above. However, this case has been argued on the basis that it formed part of the final agreement. In that case the undertaking by the guarantor must be construed in the general setting of the transaction. It was a document that had been used by the bank to secure its own position in relation to the facilities it was affording. I think that the reference to 'all monies . . . payable to you . . . by the Principal' (ie ANPP) can only refer to the facility which the bank was affording. In the context of the whole transaction, it can in my opinion have no other meaning. The fact that the money could be legally demanded in the first instance by Portsoken does not rob it of its character of moneys payable to the bank, and the fact that Portsoken would first receive it and hand it over to the bank does not rob it of the description of moneys payable by ANPP. To deny this result by an analytical examination of the different legal liabilities engendered by the form which the transaction ultimately took is to deprive the words of the guarantee of a wider meaning which they are fully capable of bearing. It runs counter to all principles of construction to give the words a meaning that would defeat the clear intention of the parties as revealed by the rest of the relevant evidence of the agreement. I too am of the opinion that Amalgamated's claim fails on this ground. . . .

Brandon LJ. . . . The contract between the bank and AIP did not reach its final form until the fourth stage in the negotiations in December 1970, when it was agreed that the loan should be channelled from the bank to ANPP through Portsoken. It follows from this that the guarantee, which formed part of the contract, falls to be interpreted by reference to the situation which then existed, rather than the situation which existed earlier when the guarantee was signed on behalf of AIP at the third stage on 28th September 1970.

What then was the situation which existed when the contract between the bank and AIP relating to the Nassau loan was at last finalised in December 1970? It was that it had been decided that the bank should not make the loan available directly to ANPP as originally arranged, but indirectly through the medium of its wholly-owned subsidiary Portsoken, in such a manner that any indebtedness of ANPP to Portsoken was accompanied by an exactly corresponding indebtedness of Portsoken to the bank. It is by reference to that situation that the words in para 1 of the guarantee, 'moneys due or owing or payable to you on any count whatsoever by the Principal', fall to be construed. In my opinion, when those words are construed by reference to the situation which I have just described, they are wide enough to include moneys due or owing or payable by ANPP to Portsoken, which Portsoken are then immediately required to pass on, without deduction of any kind, to the bank.

Schuler AG v Wickman Machine Tool Sales Ltd [1973] 2 All ER 39, House of Lords

This case involved the allegedly wrongful termination of a distributorship agreement. Whether the termination was wrongful depended on the meaning of the word 'condition' in cl 7 of the agreement (a full account of the case will be found below at p 424). During argument the question was raised whether in deciding the meaning of the word, the court was entitled to take into account the conduct of the parties subsequent to the making of the contract. Lord Wilberforce said:

> . . . In my opinion, subsequent actions ought not to have been taken into account. The general rule is that extrinsic evidence is not admissible for the construction of a written contract; the parties' intentions must be ascertained, on legal principles of construction, from the words they have used. It is one and the same principle which excludes evidence of statements, or actions, during negotiations, at the time of the contract, or subsequent to the contract, any of which to the lay mind might at first sight seem to be proper to receive. As to statements during negotiations this House has affirmed the rule of exclusion in *Prenn v Simmonds*, and as to subsequent actions (unless evidencing a new agreement or as the basis of an estoppel) in *James Miller and Partners Ltd v Whitworth Street Estates (Manchester) Ltd.*
>
> There are of course exceptions. I attempt no exhaustive list of them. In the case of ancient documents, contemporaneous or subsequent action may be adduced in order to explain words whose contemporary meaning may have become obscure. And evidence may be admitted of surrounding circumstances or in order to explain technical expressions or to identify the subject-matter of an agreement: or (an overlapping exception) to resolve a latent ambiguity. But ambiguity in this context is not to be equated with difficulty of construction, even difficulty to a point where judicial opinion as to meaning has differed. This is, I venture to think, elementary law. On this test there is certainly no ambiguity here. . . .
>
> In my opinion, therefore, the subsequent actings relied on should have been left entirely out of account: in saying this I must not be taken to agree that the particular actings relied on are of any assistance whatever towards one or other construction of the contract. Indeed if one were to pursue the matter, the facts of the present case would be found to illustrate, rather vividly, the dangers inherent in entertaining this class of evidence at all.

NOTE

Subsequent conduct may not be taken into account in interpreting the meaning of the words of a contract. It may, however, amount to a *variation* of the terms or give rise to a waiver or an estoppel: see below, Chapter 27.

CHAPTER 16
Implied terms

Terms may be implied in a contract as a matter of custom, by statute or by common law. In this chapter we will consider these three sources of implied terms before looking briefly at three types of contract—contracts for the supply of goods, contracts for services and contracts of employment—to see how the terms which the law implies give a characteristic shape to each one.

(a) Terms implied by custom

Hutton v Warren (1836) 1 M & W 466, Exchequer

By a lease under seal, dated Jan 2, 1811, the plaintiff became tenant to the defendant's father, the rector of the parish, of a farm consisting of the parsonage house and glebe land for a term of six years, if the lessor continued as incumbent, from the following Lady Day. The lease contained a stipulation that the plaintiff should consume three-fourths of the hay and straw on the farm spread the manure arising therefrom, and have such of it as was not so spread for the use of the landlord on receiving a reasonable price for it. In October, 1832, his father having resigned the living, the defendant became landlord, and, in October, 1833, served a notice to quit on the plaintiff who had continued to occupy the farm, paying the same rent. Having first sown the arable land, the plaintiff quitted the farm on Lady Day, 1834. In an action in which the plaintiff, as outgoing tenant, claimed compensation for the sowing of the arable land, it was proved that, by the custom of the country, the tenant of a farm, cultivating it according to the course of good husbandry, was entitled, on quitting, to receive from the landlord a reasonable allowance for seeds and labour bestowed on the arable land in the last year of the tenancy and was bound to leave the manure for the landlord if he would purchase it. The defendant contended that the stipulation in the lease excluded the custom of the country as to allowances.

[The judgment of the court (Parke and Alderson BB) was delivered by **Parke B**

. . . The second question requires some consideration. The custom of the country as to cultivation and the term of quitting with respect to allowances for seed and labour, is clearly applicable to a tenancy from year to year, and, therefore, if this custom was, by implication, imported into the lease, the plaintiff and defendant were bound by it after the lease expired. We are of opinion that this custom was, by implication, imported into the lease. It has long been settled that, in commercial transactions, extrinsic evidence of custom and usage is admissible to annex incidents to written contracts in matters with respect to which they are silent. The same rule has also been applied to contracts in other transactions of life, in which known usages have been established and parties did not mean to express in writing the whole of the contract by which they intended to be bound, but a contract with reference to those known usages. Whether such a relaxation of the strictness of the common law was wisely applied where formal instruments have been entered into, and particularly leases under the seal, may well be doubted; but the contrary has been established by such authority, and the relations between landlord and tenant have been so long regulated on the supposition that all customary obligations not altered by the contract, are to remain in force, that it is too late to pursue a contrary course; and it would be productive of much inconvenience if this practice were now to be disturbed. . . .
We are therefore of opinion that the plaintiff is entitled to recover. . . .

NOTES

1. For the legal definition of a custom, see above, p 275.
2. A customary term will not be implied if this would be inconsistent with the express terms of the agreement, but it is possible to rely on custom to show that a particular express term has a meaning different to its normal one. See the reference in *Lovell & Christmas Ltd v Wall* (above, p 309) to the case where '1,000 rabbits' was held to mean by custom, '1,200 rabbits': *Smith v Wilson* (1832) 3 B & Ad 728, 1 LJKB 194.

(b) Terms implied by statute

A contract for the sale of goods is an example of a contract in which the main implied terms are statutory, as the result of the codification of the common law by the Sale of Goods Act 1893. The 1893 Act has been replaced by the Sale of Goods Act 1979 but the basic structure and many of the sections remain unchanged.

For example, under the Sale of Goods Act 1979 the following terms will normally be implied: that the seller has the right to sell the goods (s 12); that the goods will correspond to their description (s 13); that, if the seller sells in the course of a business, the goods will be of merchantable quality and, subject to certain conditions, will be reasonably fit for the particular purpose for which the buyer requires them (s 14); and that, if the goods were sold by sample, the goods will correspond to the sample (s 15). We will consider these implied terms in more detail later (below, p 325ff).

Curiously, not all the obligations which the Act imposes are described as implied terms. It seems to make little practical difference, but frequently the Act simply lays down rules which are to apply to the point in question. The rules on who bears the risk of accidental damage to or destruction of the goods (s 20; see below, p 349) and on the time for delivery when no date has been agreed (s 29(3), see below, p 333) are examples.

Determining what terms are implied in any particular sale of goods contract is not, however, a simple matter of reading the statute. Firstly, a complex body of caselaw developed around some sections of the Act. Secondly, the Sale of Goods Act adopts the same theoretical basis as the common law, that implied terms rest on the 'intentions' of the parties. To a large extent this is a fiction: it would be idle to pretend that each seller intends, or reasonably appears to intend, the elaborate implied undertakings set out in the Act. But the parties' 'intentions' are still relevant under the Sale of Goods Act in that the terms will not be implied if the contract specifically excludes them or if the terms would be inappropriate in the circumstances of the contract. The Act provides:

Section 55: Exclusion of implied terms
(1) Where a right, duty or liability would arise under a contract for the sale of goods by implication of law, it may (subject to the Unfair Contract Terms Act 1977) be negatived or varied by express agreement, or by the course of dealing between the parties, or by such usage as binds both parties to the contract.

For an example of the normal implied term being excluded by the circumstances, see below, p 335.

However the words 'subject to the Unfair Contract Terms Act 1977' are critical. In 1973 the Supply of Goods (Implied Terms) Act, the relevant sections of which were later incorporated into Unfair Contract Terms Act 1977, radically changed the law on sale of goods by making the regime of implied terms in ss 12–15 at least partly mandatory. The details of the Act will be considered in section 8, but broadly speaking the Act distinguished between consumer sales (in which a business sells goods of a type ordinarily supplied for private use or consumption to a private purchaser) and non-consumer sales (eg sales by one business to another). In consumer sales the seller cannot rely on a term of the contract to exclude or restrict its obligations under ss 12–15 of the Sale of Goods Act. In non-consumer sales the terms implied by ss 13–15 may be excluded or restricted but only in so far as the clause excluding or restricting them was a fair and reasonable one (see now UCTA 1977, ss 6 and 11(1)).

Even in a consumer sale the intentions of the parties still seem to have some residual relevance. It is probably the case (though the matter is debated—see below, pp 707–708) that the usual implied terms will not apply in the first place (and thus the ban on excluding them by a contract term will not bite) if the circumstances of the contract show that, quite apart from the contract term, the normal implied term would not be appropriate. For instance, while a car dealer selling a used car cannot exclude its obligation to deliver a merchantable car, is it possible for it to sell an old banger 'as is' or 'for parts' without any obligation as to merchantability? (See further below, p 338.)

(c) Terms implied at common law

There is considerable debate about the conditions which must exist before the court may imply a term adding to or qualifying the express terms of the contract.

The Moorcock [1886–90] All ER Rep 530, Court of Appeal

The plaintiffs had agreed with the defendant wharfingers that the plaintiffs' vessel should discharge and load cargo at the defendants' wharf, where both parties knew that the vessel would take the ground at low tide. The vessel was damaged by the unevenness of the river bed, which was not within the defendants' control but the state of which they could have ascertained. The plaintiffs brought an action for damages.

Lord Esher MR held the defendants liable.

Bowen LJ. The defendants in this case are the owners of a wharf and jetty attached in the river Thames, and the only use to which it is put is holding out to ships facilities for loading and unloading alongside of it. There is only one berth where the ships can lie, and that is close alongside the jetty. The question which arises in this case is whether, when a contract is made to let the use of this jetty to a ship which can only use it, as is known to both parties, by her taking the ground, there is any implied warranty on the part of the wharfingers, and if so what is the extent of that warranty.

An implied warranty, or as it is called a covenant in law, as distinguished from an express contract or express warranty, really is in every instance founded on the presumed intention of the parties and upon reason. It is the implication which the law draws from what must obviously have been the intention of the parties, an implication which the law draws with the object of giving efficacy to the transaction and preventing such a failure of consideration as cannot have been within the contemplation of either of the parties. I believe that if one were to take all the instances, which are many, of implied warranties and covenants in law which occur in the earlier cases which deal with real property, passing through the instances which relate to the warranties of title and of quality, and the cases of executory contracts of sale and other classes of implied warranties like the implied authority of an agent to make contracts, it will be seen that in all these cases the law is raising an implication from the presumed intention of the parties with the object of giving to the transaction such efficacy as both parties must have intended it should have. If that is so, the reasonable implication which the law draws must differ according to the circumstances of the various transactions, and in business transactions what the law desires to effect by the implication is to give such business efficacy to the transaction as must have been intended by both parties; not to impose on one side all the perils of the transaction, or to emancipate one side from all the burdens, but to make each party promise in law as much, at all events, as it must have been in the contemplation of both parties that he should be responsible for.

What did each party in the present case know? because, if we are examining into their presumed intention, we must examine into their minds as to what the transaction was. Both parties knew that the jetty was let for the purpose of profit, and knew that it could only be used by the ship taking the ground and lying on the ground. They must have known that it was by grounding that she would use the jetty. They must have known, both of them, that unless the ground was safe the ship would be simply buying an opportunity of danger and buying no convenience at all, and that all consideration would fail unless the ground was safe. In fact, the business of the jetty could not be carried on unless, I do not say the ground was safe, it was supposed to be safe. The master and crew of the ship could know nothing, whereas the defendants or their servants might, by exercising reasonable care, know everything. The defendants or their servants were on the spot at high and low tide, morning and evening. They must know what had happened to the ships that had used the jetty before, and with the slightest trouble they could satisfy themselves in case of doubt whether the berth was or not safe. The ship's officers, on the other hand, had no means of verifying the state of the berth, because, for aught I know, it might be occupied by another ship at the time the *Moorcock* got there.

The question is how much of the peril or the safety of this berth is it necessary to assume in order to get the minimum of efficacy to the business consideration of the transaction which the ship consented to bear, and which the defendants took upon themselves. Supposing that the berth had been actually under the control of the defendants, they could, of course, have repaired it and made it fit for the purpose of loading and unloading. It seems to me that *Mersey Docks Trustees v Gibbs* shows that those who own a jetty, who take money for its use, and who have under their control the locus in quo, are bound to take all reasonable care to prevent danger to those using the jetty, either to make the berth good or else not to invite ships to go to the jetty, ie either to make it safe or to advise ships not to go there. But there is a distinction between that case and the present. The berth here was not under the actual control of the defendants. . . .

Applying that modification, which is a reasonable modification, to this case, it may well be said that the law will not imply that the defendants, who had not control of the place, ought to have taken reasonable care to make the berth good, but it does not follow that they are relieved from all responsibility, a responsibility which depends not merely on the control of the place, which is one element as to which the law implies a duty, but on other circumstances. The defendants are on the spot. They must know the jetty cannot be safely used unless reasonable care is taken. No one can tell whether reasonable safety has been secured except themselves, and I think that, if they let out their jetty for use, they at all events imply that they have taken reasonable care to see that the berth, which is the essential part of the use of the jetty, is safe, and, if it is not safe, and if they have not taken such reasonable care, it is their duty to warn persons with whom they have dealings that they have not done so. . . .

[Fry LJ agreed.]

Appeal dismissed.

NOTE

Since *The Moorcock* there have been a number of judicial attempts to describe the test for implying terms. One which is often quoted is that of MacKinnon LJ in *Shirlaw v Southern Foundries (1926) Ltd* [1939] 2 KB 206, 227:

> '*Prima facie* that which in any contract is left to be implied and need not be expressed is something so obvious that it goes without saying.'

Thus, if, while the parties were making their bargain, an officious bystander were to suggest some express provision for it in their agreement, they would testily suppress him with a common: 'Oh, of course.'

A very similar test had earlier been suggested by Scrutton LJ in *Reigate v Union Manufacturing Co (Ramsbottom) Ltd* [1918] 1 KB 592, 605.

Liverpool City Council v Irwin [1976] 2 All ER 39, House of Lords

A local corporation was the owner of a tower block which contained some 70 dwelling units. Access to the various units was provided by a common staircase together with two electrically operated lifts. The tenants were provided with an internal chute into which they could discharge rubbish and garbage. In July 1966 the appellants, who were husband and wife, became the tenants of a maisonette on two floors of the block. The tenancy agreement incorporated a list of obligations imposed on tenants but contained nothing concerning the obligations of the corporation. Over the course of years the condition of the block deteriorated very badly, partly in consequence of the activities of vandals and the lack of co-operation on the part of tenants. The defects in the common parts of the block including the following: (a) continual failure of the lifts, (b) lack of proper lighting on the stairs and (c) blockage of the rubbish chutes. In addition, the lavatory cisterns in the block had been designed and constructed so badly that they overflowed causing damage to the property. The appellants together with other tenants protested against the condition of the block by refusing to pay rent to the corporation. The corporation sought an order for possession of the appellants' premises and the appellants counterclaimed against the corporation alleging, inter alia, a breach on the part of the corporation of its implied covenant for the appellants' quiet enjoyment of the property. The trial judge granted the corporation an order for possession against the appellants but held (a) that the corporation was under an implied covenant to keep the common parts in repair and properly lighted, (b) that the corporation had been in breach of that implied covenant together with the covenant implied under s 32(1) of the Housing Act 1961 and (c) that accordingly the appellants were entitled to £10 damages on their counterclaim. The Court of Appeal allowed an appeal by the corporation, holding, by a majority, that there was no implied covenant on the part of the corporation to repair the common parts of the block and, unanimously, that the corporation was not in breach of the covenant implied under s 32(1) of the 1961 Act. On appeal to the House of Lords, it was contended, inter alia, for the appellants that there was an implied obligation on the corporation to keep the staircase and corridors of the block in repair and the lights in working order, and that the corporation was in breach of the obligation. . . .

Lord Wilberforce. . . . I consider first the appellants' claim insofar as it is based on contract. The first step must be to ascertain what the contract is. This may look elementary, even naive, but it seems to me to be the essential step and to involve, from the start, an approach different, if simpler, from that taken by the members of the Court of Appeal. We look first at documentary material. As is common with council lettings there is no formal demise or lease or tenancy agreement. There is a document headed 'Liverpool Corporation, Liverpool City Housing Department' and described as 'Conditions of Tenancy'. This contains a list of obligations on the tenant—he shall do this, he shall not do that, or he shall not do that without the corporation's consent. This is an amalgam of obligations added to from time to time, no doubt, to meet complaints, emerging situations, or problems as they appear to the council's officers. In particular there have been added special provisions relating to multi-storey flats which are supposed to make the conditions suitable to such dwellings. We may note under 'Further special notes' some obligations not to obstruct staircases and passages, and not to permit children under ten to operate any lifts. I mention these as a recognition of the existence and relevance of these facilities. At the end there is a form for signature by the tenant stating that he accepts the tenancy. On the landlords' side there is nothing, no signature, no demise, no covenant; the contract takes effect as soon as the tenants sign the form and are let into possession.

We have then a contract which is partly, but not wholly, stated in writing. In order to complete it, in particular to give it a bilateral character, it is necessary to take account of the actions of the parties and the circumstances. As actions of the parties, we must note the granting of possession by the corporation and reservation by it of the 'common parts'—stairs, lifts, chutes etc. As circumstances we must include the nature of the premises, viz a maisonette for family use on the ninth floor of a high block, one which is occupied by a large number of other tenants, all using the common parts and dependent on them, none of them having any expressed obligation to maintain or repair them.

To say that the construction of a complete contract out of these elements involves a process of 'implication' may be correct: it would be so if implication means the supplying of what is not expressed. But there are varieties of implications which the courts think fit to make and they do not necessarily involve the same process. Where there is, on the face of it, a complete, bilateral contract, the courts are sometimes willing to add terms to it, as implied terms; this is very common in mercantile contracts where there is an established usage; in that case the courts are spelling out what both parties know and would, if asked, unhesitatingly agree to be part of the bargain. In other cases, where there is an apparently complete bargain, the courts are willing to add a term on the ground that without it the contract will not work—this is the case, if not of *The Moorcock* itself on its facts, at least of the doctrine of *The Moorcock* as usually applied. This is, as was pointed out by the majority in the Court of Appeal, a strict test—though the degree of strictness seems to vary with the current legal trend, and I think that they were right not to accept it as applicable here. There is a third variety of implication, that which I think Lord Denning MR favours, or at least did favour in this case, and that is the implication of reasonable terms. But though I agree with many of his instances, which in fact fall under one or other of the preceding heads, I cannot go so far as to endorse his principle; indeed, it seems to me, with respect, to extend a long, and undesirable, way beyond sound authority.

The present case, in my opinion, represents a fourth category or, I would rather say, a fourth shade on a continuous spectrum. The court here is simply concerned to establish what the contract is, the parties not having themselves fully stated the terms. In this sense, the court is searching for what must be implied.

What then should this contract be held to be? There must first be implied a letting, ie a grant of the right of exclusive possession to the tenants. With this there must, I suppose, be implied a covenant for quiet enjoyment, as a necessary incident of the letting. The difficulty begins when we consider the common parts. We start with the fact that the demise is useless unless access is obtained by the staircase; we can add that, having regard to the height of the block, and the family nature of the dwellings, the demise would be useless without a lift service; we can continue that there being rubbish chutes built in to the structures and no other means of disposing of light rubbish there must be a right to use the chutes. The question to be answered—and it is the only question in this case—is what is to be the legal relationship between landlord and tenant as regards these matters.

There can be no doubt that there must be implied (i) an easement for the tenants and their licensees to use the stairs, (ii) a right in the nature of an easement to use the lifts and (iii) an easement to use the rubbish chutes.

But are these easements to be accompanied by any obligation on the landlord, and what obligation? There seem to be two alternatives. The first, for which the corporation contends, is for an easement coupled with no legal obligation, except such as may arise under the Occupiers' Liability Act 1957 as regards the safety of those using the facilities, and possibly such other liability as might exist under the ordinary law of tort. The alternative is for easements coupled with some obligation on the part of the landlords as regards the maintenance of the subject of them, so that they are available for use.

My Lords, in order to be able to choose between these, it is necessary to define what test is to be applied, and I do not find this difficult. In my opinion such obligation should be read into the contract as the nature of the contract itself implicitly requires, no more, no less; a test in other words of necessity. The relationship accepted by the corporation is that of landlord and tenant; the tenant accepts obligations accordingly, in relation, inter alia, to the stairs, the lifts and the chutes. All these are not just facilities, or conveniences provided at discretion; they are essentials of the tenancy without which life in the dwellings, as a tenant, is not possible. To leave the landlord free of contractual obligation as regards these matters, and subject only to administrative or political pressure, is, in my opinion, totally inconsistent with the nature of this relationship. The subject-matter of the lease (high-rise blocks) and the relationship created by the tenancy demands, of its nature, some contractual obligation on the landlord.

I do not think that this approach involves any innovation as regards the law of contract. The necessity to have regard to the inherent nature of a contract and of the relationship thereby established was stated in this House in *Lister v Romford Ice and Cold Storage Co Ltd*. That was a case between master and servant and of a search for an 'implied term'. Viscount Simonds made a clear distinction between a search for an implied term such as might be necessary to give 'business efficacy' to the particular contract and a search, based on wider considerations, for such a term as the nature of the contract might call for, or as a legal incident of this kind of contract. If the search were for the former, he said: 'I should lose myself in the attempt to formulate it with the necessary precision'. We see an echo of this in the present case, when the majority in the Court of Appeal, considering a 'business efficacy term'. ie *'Moorcock'* term, found themselves faced with five alternative terms and therefore rejected all of them. But that is not, in my opinion, the end, or indeed, the object, of the search. . . .

It remains to define the standard. My Lords, if, as I think, the test of the existence of the term is necessity the standard must surely not exceed what is necessary having regard to the circumstances. To imply an absolute obligation to repair would go beyond what is a necessary legal incident and would indeed be unreasonable. An obligation to take reasonable care to keep in reasonable repair and usability is what fits the requirements of the case. Such a definition involves—and I think rightly—recognition that the tenants themselves have their responsibilities. What it is reasonable to expect of a landlord has a clear relation to what a reasonable set of tenants should do for themselves. . . .

. . . . [I]t has not been shown that there was any breach of [the corporation's] obligation . . .

Lord Cross of Chelsea. . . . When it implies a term in a contract the court is sometimes laying down a general rule that in all contracts of a certain type—sale of goods, master and servant, landlord and tenant, and so on—some provision is to be implied unless the parties have expressly excluded it. In deciding whether or not to lay down such a prima facie rule the court will naturally ask itself whether in the general run of such cases the term in question would be one which it would be reasonable to insert. Sometimes, however, there is no question of laying down any prima facie rule applicable to all cases of a defined type but what the court is being in effect asked to do is to rectify a particular—often a very detailed—contract by inserting in it a term which the parties have not expressed. Here it is not enough for the court to say that the suggested term is a reasonable one the presence of which would make the contract a better or fairer one; it must be able to say that the insertion of the term is necessary to give—as it is put—'business efficacy' to the contract and that if its absence had been pointed out at the time both parties—assuming them to have been reasonable men—would have agreed without hesitation to its insertion. The distinction between the two types of case was pointed out by Viscount Simonds and Lord Tucker in their speeches in *Lister v Romford Ice and Cold Storage Co Ltd*, but I think that Lord Denning MR in proceeding—albeit with some trepidation—to 'kill off' Mackinnon LJ's 'officious bystander' must have overlooked it . . .

[Lord Salmon, Lord Edmund-Davies and Lord Fraser of Tullybelton delivered speeches to the same effect.]

Appeal dismissed.

NOTES

1. In *Shell UK Ltd v Lostock Garage Ltd* [1977] 1 All ER 481, 487–488, Lord Denning MR summarised the effect of *Liverpool City Council v Irwin* as follows:

As I read the speeches, there are two broad categories of implied terms.

(i) *The first category*
The first category comprehends all those relationships which are of common occurrence, such as the relationship of seller and buyer, owner and hirer, master and servant, landlord and tenant, carrier by land or by sea, contractor for building works, and so forth. In all those relationships the courts have imposed obligations on one party or the other, saying they are

implied terms. These obligations are not founded on the intention of the parties, actual or presumed, but on more general considerations . . . In such relationships the problem is not solved by asking: what did the parties intend? or, would they have unhesitatingly agreed to it, if asked? It is to be solved by asking: has the law already defined the obligation or the extent of it? If so, let it be followed. If not, look to see what would be reasonable in the general run of such cases (see per Lord Cross of Chelsea) and then say what the obligation shall be. The House in *Liverpool City Council v Irwin* went through that very process. They examined the existing law of landlord and tenant, in particular that relating to easements, to see if it contained the solution to the problem; and, having found that it did not, they imposed an obligation on the landlord to use reasonable care. In these relationships the parties can exclude or modify the obligation by express words, but unless they do so, the obligation is a legal incident of the relationship which is attached by the law itself and not by reason of any implied term. . . .

(ii) *The second category*

The second category comprehends those cases which are not within the first category. These are cases, not of common occurrence, in which from the particular circumstances a term is to be implied. In these cases the implication is based on an intention imputed to the parties from their actual circumstances: see *Luxor (Eastbourne) Ltd v Cooper* per Lord Wright. Such an imputation is only to be made when it is necessary to imply a term to give efficacy to the contract and make it a workable agreement in such manner as the parties would clearly have done if they had applied their mind to the contingency which has arisen. These are the 'officious bystander' type of case: see *Lister v Romford Ice and Cold Storage Co* per Lord Tucker. In such cases a term is not to be implied on the ground that it would be reasonable, but only when it is necessary and can be formulated with a sufficient degree of precision. This was the test applied by the majority of this court in *Liverpool City Council v Irwin*; and they were emphatically upheld by the House on this point; see per Lord Cross of Chelsea and Lord Edmund-Davies.

There is this point to be noted about *Liverpool City Council v Irwin*. In this court the argument was only about an implication in the second category. In the House of Lords that argument was not pursued. It was only the first category.

2. Those terms which are normally implied in all contracts of a particular type are sometimes called 'terms implied in law', while those implied on a 'one-off' basis in order to give business efficacy to the individual contract are called 'terms implied in fact'.

3. Within the first category, it is fairly clear that the 'officious bystander' test does not have to be satisfied; yet some judges like Lord Wilberforce insist that, in the absence of previous authority, a term will only be implied on the basis of necessity; reasonableness is not sufficient. Is this anything more than judicial reluctance to abandon the pretence that judges will not make a contract for the parties? Doesn't it overlook the point that a decision *not* to imply a maintenance obligation is just as much an allocation of responsibility as the decision to do so?

4. Into which category would you put *The Moorcock*?

5. As Denning suggests, the courts are reluctant to imply 'one-off' terms and will do so only if both parties would clearly have agreed to the term and the term is capable of precise formulation. A recent illustration is *Trollope and Colls Ltd v North West Metropolitan Regional Hospital Board* [1973] 2 All ER 260. A building contract which was to be completed in three phases provided that phase I was to be completed by 30 April 1969; phase III was to be commenced six months after the completion of phase I, and was to be completed by 30 April 1972. Phase I was completed 59 weeks late, leaving only 16 months in which to build phase III by the stated date. The respondent board was unable to nominate sub-contractors who could perform the work which was to be done by nominated sub-contractors within the remaining time, and the appellants claimed that they were released from the contract. The respondents argued that a term should be implied that the completion date for phase III should be put back. The House of Lords held that no term could be implied. Two factors were particularly important in the decision. The first was that the terms of the contract were clear and unambiguous. The possibility that phase I might be late was easily apparent, but the parties had chosen a fixed completion date for phase III which was independent of the starting point for that phase: it might even be the case that this had been done deliberately to limit the contractor's obligations if phase I were so late that sub-contractors could not be nominated for phase III. A second consideration was that, if a term were to be implied to cover the overrun of phase I, it was difficult to say what that term should be. For instance, should the completion date for phase III be set back by the whole period of delay, or only by that part of the delay for which the contractor was not responsible?

(d) Contracts for the sale or supply of goods

In this and the next two subsections we look at the implied terms in three common types of contract. The aim is not to give a complete account of them, but to give some idea of the general nature of the implied obligations under each one.

A contract of sale is one under which the seller transfers, or agrees to transfer, the ownership of goods to the buyer in exchange for money (SGA 1979, s 2(1)). The Sale of Goods Act applies only to such transactions. There are several other types of contract under which goods are supplied. The implied terms in contracts of hire (in which the owner transfers possession but not ownership), contracts of barter (in which goods are exchanged for goods) and contracts for work and materials (in which the element of work is predominant but goods are also supplied, eg a building contract) are governed by the Supply of Goods and Services Act 1982. The implied terms about title and quality in hire-purchase contracts (see above, p 54) are governed by Supply of Goods (Implied Terms) Act 1973.

(i) Implied terms as to title

Sale of Goods Act 1979, s 12: Implied terms about title, etc

Section 12: Implied terms about title, etc
(1) In a contract of sale, other than one to which subsection (3) below applies, there is an implied condition on the part of the seller that in the case of a sale he has a right to sell the goods, and in the case of an agreement to sell he will have such a right at the time when the property is to pass.
(2) In a contract of sale, other than one to which subsection (3) below applies, there is also an implied warranty that
    (a) the goods are free, and will remain free until the time when the property is to pass, from any charge or encumbrance not disclosed or known to the buyer before the contract is made, and
    (b) the buyer will enjoy quiet possession of the goods except so far as it may be disturbed by the owner or other person entitled to the benefit of any charge or encumbrance so disclosed or known.
(3) This subsection applies to a contract of sale in the case of which there appears from the contract or is to be inferred from its circumstances an intention that the seller should transfer only such title as he or a third person may have.
(4) In a contract to which subsection (3) above applies there is an implied warranty that all

charges or encumbrances known to the seller and not known to the buyer have been disclosed to the buyer before the contract is made.

(5) In a contract to which subsection (3) above applies there is also an implied warranty that none of the following will disturb the buyer's quiet possession of the goods, namely

   (a) the seller;
   (b) in a case where the parties to the contract intend that the seller should transfer only such title as a third person may have, that person;
   (c) anyone claiming through or under the seller or that third person otherwise than under a charge or encumbrance disclosed or known to the buyer before the contract is made. . . .

(Section 8 of the Supply of Goods (Implied Terms) Act provides very similar terms for hire-purchase. Section 2 of Supply of Goods and Services Act 1982 provides similar terms for other contracts under which the ownership of goods is to be transferred.)

NOTES

1. It is an implied *condition* that the seller has the right to sell but only an implied *warranty* that the goods are free from encumbrances etc. Here the word condition is being used in its technical sense, meaning not just 'a term of the contract' (as in the phrase 'conditions of sale') but a term which is so important that if it is not complied with the other party may refuse to perform its side of the contract. Equally warranty here has a technical meaning, a term of the contract which is not sufficiently important that breach of it will justify a refusal to perform; the remedy for a breach of warranty will only be damages. This should be contrasted with the use of 'warranty' to mean an undertaking relating to the quality of goods sold (as in the *Dick Bentley* case, above, p 262). See further below, pp 423–429. If the seller has no right to sell the goods, the buyer might be dispossessed by the true owner at any time, and so needs the right to reject the goods and recover the money paid. If the goods are found to be encumbered (eg they are subject to a charge in favour of a third party), damages should be a sufficient remedy, as the damages can be used to pay off the charge.

2. Although many goods are bought for the purpose of use for a limited period of time, the seller's obligation to pass title is regarded as so essential in a contract of sale that if the buyer has not received title the whole of the price is recoverable (on the grounds of 'total failure of consideration': see below, p 365) even though the buyer has had some use from the goods: *Rowland v Divall* [1923] 2 KB 500. In that case, in which the seller had in good faith sold the buyer a car which later turned out to have been stolen, Atkin LJ (at p 506) said:

   It seems to me that in this case there has been a total failure of consideration, that is to say that the buyer has not got any part of that for which he paid the purchase money. He paid the money in order that he might get the property, and he has not got it. . . .

   In *Butterworth v Kingsway Motors Ltd* [1954] 1 WLR 1286 the buyer was allowed to recover the whole price even after having used the car for a considerable period and even though shortly after he had demanded his money the sellers had obtained the title. Pearson J described the plaintiff's case as somewhat without merit, and several proposals were made to require the buyer to pay for the use that he or she had had (see Law Reform Committee, Twelfth Report (Cmnd 2958, 1966), para 36 ff.; Law Commission Working Paper no 65, part IV and

Working Paper No 85, paras 6.11–6.21). Ultimately, however, the Law Commission recommended that the law be left unchanged. The benefit to the buyer would be hard to value and in any event it was gained at the expense of the true owner rather than that of the seller.

3. In a contract of hire-purchase the ultimate object of the buyer is to become owner, so the same rule applies. In a contract of simple hire the hirer does not normally care about the ownership of the thing provided that the firm that hires it out has the right to do so, so that the hirer can be sure of getting uninterrupted use. Supply of Goods and Services Act 1982 provides:

> 7.(1) In a contract for the hire of goods there is an implied condition on the part of the bailor that in the case of a bailment he has a right to transfer possession of the goods by way of hire for the period of bailment and in the case of an agreement to bail he will have such a right at the time of bailment.

(A bailment is the relationship created when goods possessed by one person, the 'bailor', are temporarily in the possession of another, the 'bailee'.)

(ii) Implied terms as to description and quality of goods

Section 13: Sale by description
(1) Where there is a contract for the sale of goods by description, there is an implied condition that the goods will correspond with the description.
(2) If the sale is by sample as well as by description it is not sufficient that the bulk of the goods corresponds with the sample if the goods do not also correspond with the description.
(3) A sale of goods is not prevented from being a sale by description by reason only that, being exposed for sale or hire, they are selected by the buyer. . . .

Section 14: Implied terms about quality or fitness
(1) Except as provided by this section and section 15 below and subject to any other enactment, there is no implied condition or warranty about the quality or fitness for any particular purpose of goods supplied under a contract of sale.
(2) Where the seller sells goods in the course of a business, there is an implied condition that the goods supplied under the contract are of merchantable quality, except that there is no such condition—
  (a) as regards defects specifically drawn to the buyer's attention before the contract is made; or
  (b) if the buyer examines the goods before the contract is made, as regards defects which that examination ought to reveal.
(3) Where the seller sells goods in the course of a business and the buyer, expressly or by implication, makes known—
  (a) to the seller, or
  (b) where the purchase price or part of it is payable by instalments and the goods were previously sold by a credit-broker to the seller, to that credit-broker,
any particular purpose for which the goods are being bought, there is an implied condition that the goods supplied under the contract are reasonably fit for that purpose, whether or not that is a purpose for which such goods are commonly supplied, except where the circumstances show that the buyer does not rely, or that it is unreasonable for him to rely, on the skill or judgment of the seller or credit-broker.
(4) An implied condition or warranty about quality or fitness for a particular purpose may be annexed to a contract of sale by usage.
(5) The preceding provisions of this section apply to a sale by a person who in the course of a business is acting as agent for another as they apply to a sale by a principal in the course of a business, except where that other is not selling in the course of a business and either the buyer knows that fact or reasonable steps are taken to bring it to the notice of the buyer before the contract is made.
(6) Goods of any kind are of merchantable quality within the meaning of subsection (2) above if they are as fit for the purpose or purposes for which goods of that kind are commonly bought

as it is reasonable to expect having regard to any description applied to them, the price (if relevant) and all the other relevant circumstances . . .

Section 15: Sale by sample
(1) A contract of sale is a contract for sale by sample where there is an express or implied term to that effect in the contract.
(2) In the case of a contract for sale by sample there is an implied condition—
   (a) that the bulk will correspond with the sample in quality;
   (b) that the buyer will have a reasonable opportunity of comparing the bulk with the sample;
   (c) that the goods will be free from any defect, rendering them unmerchantable, which would not be apparent on reasonable examination of the sample.
(3) In subsection (2)(c) above 'unmerchantable' is to be construed in accordance with section 14(6) above . . .

NOTES

1. Similar terms are implied into hire-purchase contracts by Supply of Goods (Implied Terms) Act 1973, ss 9–11 and into other supply of goods contracts by Supply of Goods and Services Act 1982, ss 3–5.
2. The requirement under s 13 that goods correspond with their description is treated strictly, and apparently trifling non-conformities have been held to entitle the buyer to reject the goods even when the buyer did not appear to be prejudiced by them and was rejecting the goods for other reasons. For example in *Arcos Ltd v E A Ronaasen & Son* [1933] AC 470 a buyer was permitted to reject barrel staves that did not correspond to the contractual description of half an inch thick, even though they were only one sixteenth of an inch out and were perfectly suitable for the buyer's purpose of making barrels. The probable reason for this strict approach is that in many of the contracts which have come before the courts on this topic the goods were being bought for resale and the exact description might be important to some other buyer further down the 'chain'.
3. On the other hand, not every statement about the goods amounts to the 'description' of them within s 13; the description for this purpose only covers those characteristics of the goods which 'identify' what is being sold. Thus if the parties are negotiating for the sale of two specific ships and the seller states their capacity is 460 tons, but this is not a characteristic in which the buyer appeared particularly interested, the statement does not form part of the description and is only a misrepresentation: *T & J Harrison v Knowles & Foster* [1910] 1 KB 608. It would be different if the buyer had asked for ships of that capacity.
4. Even words which in one sense identify the goods do not form part of the description if their purpose is merely to indicate which goods are being sold. In *Reardon Smith Line Ltd v Hansen-Tangen* [1929] 1 WLR 989 a charterparty described the ship to be chartered as 'called Yard no 354 at Osaka', Osaka being the name of the yard responsible for building it; but in fact the building was subcontracted to another yard, Oshima, because the Osaka yard could not handle a tankship of that size. Both parties knew this but the buyers argued that the ship did not correspond with the description. It was held that the words were merely labelling which vessel was involved and there was no breach of s 13: the words either did not form part of the description or were not promissory at all. (If you have difficulty following this, think of this example: if Furmston were to sell his cottage, 'known as Denning's Orchard' to Beale, would

Beale be able to get out of the contract on the grounds that the cottage had never belonged to anyone called Denning and didn't have a single fruit tree in the grounds?)

5. The implied term that the goods should correspond with their description applies to all sales, but the implied terms as to merchantability under s 14(2) and fitness for purpose under s 14(3) apply only where the seller sells in the course of a business. Thus if you buy a 1961 Triumph Herald from a private seller and later discover that it is actually the front and back ends of two cars of different years welded together, you may have a remedy for breach of s 13 (*Beale v Taylor* [1967] 1 WLR 1193), but if the engine blows up after five miles you won't have any remedy, unless you can prove misrepresentation or breach of an express warranty.

6. The seller is not responsible for defects drawn to the buyer's attention nor for defects which the buyer's examination ought to have revealed. What if the buyer doesn't bother to examine the goods and so doesn't spot the defect?

7. Before 1973 the Act did not define merchantable quality. The courts had developed two tests of whether goods were merchantable. One, perhaps most suited to cases where the goods are of generally lower quality than expected, is whether the goods would be commercially resaleable under the description applied to them to buyers who knew all the facts, without a substantial reduction in price. The other is that the goods must be fit for the purpose for which goods of that description are commonly used; but if such goods are commonly used for more than one purpose, they need only be fit for one of the common purposes. A full discussion will be found in the judgment of Lloyd LJ in *Aswan Engineering Establishment Co v Lupdine Ltd* [1987] 1 WLR 1. At page 12 Lloyd LJ summarised the position thus:

> . . . the goods did not have to be suitable for every purpose for which goods were normally bought under that description. It was sufficient that they were suitable for one or more of such purposes without abatement of price since, if they were, they were commercially saleable under that description.

The Court of Appeal held that the new definition of merchantability in s 14(6) had not changed the law in this respect. Thus even if goods have clearly been damaged or are unfit for one of the common purposes for which they are bought, provided that they are suitable for another common purpose and are saleable without a substantial price reduction, the buyer may have no remedy under s 14(2).

8. If the buyer wishes to be sure that the goods will be suitable for its particular purpose, it must make the purpose known to the seller and rely on the seller's judgment. Unless it is unreasonable for the buyer to rely on the seller, for instance because the seller makes it clear that there may be problems in using the goods for that purpose, the seller is then responsible.

9. If the buyer indicates a purpose in very general terms, and reasonably relies on the seller, the latter is responsible for the goods being fit for all normal applications within the general purpose indicated. So if the buyer indicates that herring meal is required for making into animal foodstuffs (as opposed to fertiliser) without specifying which animals are to be given it, the meal must be fit for feeding to all animals to which

it might normally be fed: *Ashington Piggeries Ltd v Christopher Hill Ltd* [1972] AC 441.

10. Section 14(3)(b) is dealing with the case where the retailer arranges for the buyer to buy the goods on credit—normally under a conditional sale, see above p 56—not from the retailer but from a finance company, to which the retailer sells the goods. Then it is sufficient that the buyer's purpose is made known to the retailer, who is termed the 'credit-broker'.

11. Why shouldn't the buyer take responsibility for deciding whether the goods are fit for some unusual purpose for which he requires them? Is it really right to make the seller liable for some bland assertion by an enthusiastic salesperson, who may not have had a chance to assess properly how the goods will function in the unusual application? Consider this clause from a contract for the sale of axles:

> WARRANTY. Except where the buyer has completed an 'Application Recommendation' form and this has been accepted in writing by the seller, the seller does not warrant that the goods are fit for any particular purpose.

12. We have suggested already that the courts' interpretation of the implied terms under the Sale of Goods Act has been influenced by the nature of the cases that come before it. Thus the interpretation of s 13, and perhaps of s 12, seems affected by cases in which the goods are being bought for resale. Commercial cases have also had a strong influence on the interpretation of s 14(2); the notions of 'useable for the common purpose' and 'resaleable' do not seem appropriate to consumer goods such as cars, where the customer will legitimately be concerned with the finish of the vehicle as well as whether it is useable for the common purpose of transportation. This caused considerable concern to consumer organisations, and the matter was referred to the Law Commission. (Subsequently the Court of Appeal in *Rogers v Parish (Scarborough) Ltd* [1987] QB 933 suggested that the common purposes for which cars are bought include comfort, convenience, ease of handling, reliability and appearance.)

Law Commission Report No 160, Sale and Supply of Goods (Cmnd 137, 1987), paras 3.5–3.12 and p 70

2. Should the implied term as to quality be altered at all?

3.5 In the Consultative Document we suggested that the present implied term is not satisfactory. The reasons we gave for this view are set out in Part 2 above, but it may be helpful to summarise them here:

(i) The word 'merchantable' refers to transactions between merchants and is not suitable for consumer transactions, even in its dictionary meaning. In any event it is also a word of uncertain meaning which is largely obsolete.

(ii) The present definition relies on the fitness of goods for their purpose and not on their other characteristics. Despite the recent Court of Appeal decision in *Rogers v Parish (Scarborough) Ltd*, the exact extent to which minor defects and defects of appearance and finish fall within the definition remains unclear.

(iii) The present definition does not expressly say that the goods must be reasonably durable. There is no doubt that if goods are to be 'merchantable' they must be reasonably durable, but this important point is found only in cases.

3.6 Almost all of those who commented on our proposals in the Consultative Document agreed that the implied term as to merchantable quality needed alteration. While in theory it would be possible to return to the pre-1973 situation and leave the word 'merchantable' (or any replacement word) undefined, we suggested in the Consultative Document that the required quality should continue to be defined. The arguments which led our predecessors to recommend that the required standard of quality be defined still remain and we agreed with them. It would not, we thought, be helpful to ask sellers and buyers to rely once again upon a single word to express the required standard of quality, whatever that word might be. After consultation we are confirmed in that view. It is therefore necessary to consider what new definition of the implied term as to quality is needed. In seeking to answer this question we have had to consider what is the primary function of the implied term itself.

3. In what way should the implied term be re-defined?

(a) *The function of the implied term*

3.7 The implied term as to quality has to play a very subtle role. As we have seen, the word 'merchantable' was derived from Victorian cases where (putting the matter at its simplest) the question was, 'were the goods of such a quality that one merchant buying them from another, would have regarded them as suitable?' But, as so often happens, although the word had been perfectly apt on the facts of the cases in which it was first used by the judges, when the word became of universal application in the 1893 Act, it was gradually seen not to be suitable for *all* cases. On its face the word is not suitable for non-mercantile transactions. It became necessary for judges to explain what the word meant. In some cases it was said to mean that the goods had to be fit for their purpose. In other cases it was said that the goods had to be acceptable. In all of these cases what was really at issue was whether the goods were 'up to scratch' in the particular circumstances. But sale transactions may take an almost infinite variety of forms. A sale may be of a new jet aircraft from the manufacturers to a major international carrier, of a washing machine still in its packaging from a department store to a young married couple, of a catapult to a child, of an old motor car from a back-street garage to a student, of a breeding ewe from one farmer to another, of thousands of tons of a primary product, such as wheat, from one trader to another (neither of whom will ever see the goods), or a newspaper or box of matches from a street-vendor to a passer-by. The possible circumstances are so varied that a single formula to describe the required quality is hard to define.

3.8 One way out of this difficulty might be to define the standard differently for, say, different types of goods or different types of transaction. Could there be a different standard for new goods from that applicable to second-hand goods? Could there be a different standard applicable to transactions where one party deals as a consumer? We said in the Consultative Document that we did not think it practical to provide different standards of quality for different types of goods, different types of transaction, or different types of buyer and seller. On consultation there was very little, if any, support for having different quality standards, at least within the framework of existing legislation. The creation of different categories of transaction is likely to give rise to many disputes on the question which side of any given line a particular transaction falls. Further, although it might (for example) seem obvious that 'new' goods should be of a different standard from 'second-hand' goods, is this really always so? A 'second-hand' Rolls Royce motor car, sold after only 300 miles driving, should probably have all the qualities of a brand new car of that marque. On the other hand, 'new' goods may be sold as 'seconds' or their sub-standard quality otherwise indicated. Some 'new' crockery is very cheap and of poor quality. Certainly it is (and would be expected to be) of lower quality than some expensive 'second-hand' crockery. Defining different types of sale for the purposes of implying a different quality for each type of sale did not seem to us in the Consultative Document a promising way out of the difficulties; those we consulted overwhelmingly supported this conclusion and, although we have reconsidered it, we maintain our view that different implied terms for different types of transaction would not be satisfactory.

3.9 It may be suggested that there should, at least, be a special implied quality term for transactions in which the buyer acts as a consumer. As will be seen below, we are suggesting that if the implied term has been broken the buyer's rights should differ according to whether he dealt as a consumer or not. However, our proposals regarding the consumer buyer's rights on a breach of contract by the seller are justified only by an overriding policy consideration that he needs a regime which favours him if he is not to be disadvantaged in his dealings with a seller who has broken the contract. In the case of the implied term as to quality, we can see no special justification for putting the consumer buyer in a different position from other buyers. To do so would carry with it the obvious danger that the shopkeeper would buy from his wholesaler under a contract containing a different implied term from that under which he sells to his customer. The shopkeeper might find that there has been no breach of contract by the wholesaler but that he himself is in breach of contract as against the consumer who bought from him. This is a situation which we wish to avoid as far as possible. We propose below what the *remedies* available to a consumer on a breach by the seller may differ from those available to a shopkeeper, but we think that the question whether there was a breach of contract at all should be answered in the same way for both.

3.10 A further ground which leads us not to recommend that there should be a special implied term for a buyer who deals as a consumer is that the circumstances in which consumers buy goods vary enormously, just as do the circumstances in which buyers generally buy goods. They can buy low quality as well as high quality goods, new or second-hand, from the manufacturer or from the shop round the corner. Consumer transactions, such as the purchase of a motor car, may involve large sums of money and complicated objects with hundreds of parts which may go wrong. No particular term seemed especially appropriate for consumer transactions, and organisations which represented consumers' interests did not press us for a special implied term relating to consumers. We have decided not to recommend such a term.

3.11 The decision to recommend a single implied term as to the quality of goods to be supplied under all types of contract brings with it certain consequences. There is no one word which we have found or which has been suggested to us by which the appropriate standard can be defined. The term must be sufficiently flexible to be able to apply to all the many types of sale which can take place. Above all, there is no 'magic' formula which will provide an instant answer in every case to the question whether goods meet the standard of quality which they should have. (Even if there were, this would not resolve most disputes about defective goods, since most disputes are not about the law but about the facts.)

3.12 In the Consultative Document we suggested that the new definition of quality should consist of two elements:

(i) a basic principle formulated in language sufficiently general to apply to all kinds of goods and all kinds of transaction; this principle would also refer, as at present, to the description of the goods, their price, and any other relevant circumstances, which are factors which would be taken into account in determining how stringent the quality requirement should be in any particular case; and

(ii) a list of aspects of quality, any of which could be important in a particular case; the list would, however, not be exhaustive.

This approach was generally supported on consultation and is the one which we now recommend. The definition which we shall propose is longer and more complex than the existing one. For the reasons which we have set out, we do not believe this is avoidable. . . .

The Law Commission Report concluded by recommending that s 14(2) be replaced by the following:

(2) Where the seller sells goods in the course of a business, there is an implied term that the goods supplied under the contract are of acceptable quality.

(2A) For the purposes of this Act, goods are of acceptable quality if they meet the standard that a reasonable person would regard as acceptable, taking account of any description of the goods, the price (if relevant) and all the other relevant circumstances.

(2B) For the purposes of this Act, the quality of goods includes their state and condition and the following (among others) are in appropriate cases aspects of the quality of goods—

(a) fitness for all the purposes for which goods of the kind in question are commonly supplied,
(b) appearance and finish,
(c) freedom from minor defects,
(d) safety, and
(e) durability.

(2C) The term implied by subsection (2) above does not extend to any matter making the quality of goods unacceptable—

(a) which is specifically drawn to the buyer's attention before the contract is made,
(b) where the buyer examines the goods before the contract is made, which that examination ought to reveal, or
(c) in the case of a contract for sale by sample, which would have been apparent on a reasonable examination of the sample.

(iii) Time and place for delivery

Sale of Goods Act 1979, s 29: Rules about delivery

(1) Whether it is for the buyer to take possession of the goods or for the seller to send them to the buyer is a question depending in each case on the contract, express or implied, between the parties.

(2) Apart from any such contract, express or implied, the place of delivery is the seller's place of business if he has one, and if not, his residence; except that, if the contract is for the sale of specific goods, which to the knowledge of the parties when the contract is made are in some other place, then that place is the place of delivery.

(3) Where under the contract of sale the seller is bound to send the goods to the buyer, but no time for sending them is fixed, the seller is bound to send them within a reasonable time.

(4) Where the goods at the time of sale are in the possession of a third person, there is no delivery by seller to buyer unless and until the third person acknowledges to the buyer that he holds the goods on his behalf; but nothing in this section affects the operation of the issue or transfer of any document of title to goods.

(5) Demand or tender of delivery may be treated as ineffectual unless made at a reasonable hour; and what is a reasonable hour is a question of fact.

(6) Unless otherwise agreed, the expenses of and incidental to putting the goods into a deliverable state must be borne by the seller.

NOTE

If a party undertakes to perform by a particular date, but is delayed by some event, he is liable whether it was his fault or not. If, on the other hand, no date was set for the performance, he must perform within a reasonable time, and unavoidable delays caused by events outside his control may be taken into account. This is so even though the events could not have been anticipated at the time the contract was made (*Hick v Raymond and Reid* [1893] AC 22). Why the difference? Is it just that courts tend to enforce express promises literally, or is there some other factor at work?

In practice the strict obligation to perform on time is often qualified by a Force Majeure clause, such as:

If it becomes apparent that the Works will not be completed by the date for completion . . . (or any extended date . . . in accordance with this sub-clause) for reasons beyond the control of the Contractor, then the Contractor shall so notify the Architect/Supervising Officer who shall extend the time for completion by a reasonable period.

(JCT Minor Works.) Another example is the following:

We shall not be held responsible or liable for any loss, damage, retention or delay caused by fire, strike, civil or military authority, insurrection or riot, earthquake, transportation embargo or by any other means beyond our control.

(Bendix Westinghouse Ltd.) (See also the specimen conditions of sale in the Introduction, cl 5).

Why should the parties agree to such a term? Is either party in a better position to prevent such delays? If not, is either in a better position than the other to estimate their likelihood, or to insure against them?

(iv) Standard of liability for quality

Young and Marten Ltd v McManus Childs Ltd [1969] 1 AC 454

The respondents, the employers, engaged a contractor to build a number of houses for sale. The contractor subcontracted the roofing to the appellants; the appellants were instructed to use a rather expensive type of tile called a 'Somerset 13', manufactured only by Browne of Bridgwater. The appellants in turn subcontracted the work to Acme, who bought the tiles from Browne. The titles were defective in a way that could not have been detected by any reasonable examination and the buyers of the houses recovered the cost of reroofing them from the respondents. The respondents then brought in the appellants, arguing that the appellants were liable to them on an implied warranty of quality. (For reasons which are not explained, the case was argued on the basis that the contractor had merely acted as agent for the employers in making the contract with the appellants, so that there was a direct contract between appellant and respondents, and the judgments discuss the situation as if the appellants were the contractors.) The appellants were unable to bring in Acme in turn, as they would normally have done, because the limitation period for their claim against Acme had expired.

Lord Reid: This is a contract for the supply of work and materials and this case raises a general question as to the nature and extent of the warranties which the law implies in such a contract. As regards the contractor's liability for the work done there is no dispute in this case: admittedly it must be done with all proper skill and care. The question at issue relates to his liability in respect of material supplied by him under the contract. The appellants maintain that the warranty in respect of materials is similar to that in respect of work, so that, if the selection of material and of the person to supply it is left to the contractor, he must exercise due skill and care in choosing the material and the person to supply it. But where, as in this case, the material and the supplier were chosen by the respondents, the appellants maintain that there was no warranty as to the fitness or quality of the tiles. The respondents admit that, if it is held that the choice of this type of tile was theirs and theirs alone, there can be no implied warranty that this type of tile was fit for the contract purpose. But they say that there still was a warranty that the tiles would be of good quality and that that warranty must be implied, notwithstanding the fact that they left no choice to the appellants in selecting the person who was to supply the tiles. If that is right, then the respondents must succeed. The loss was not caused by Somerset 13 tiles being unsuitable for the contract purpose: it was caused by the tiles which were supplied being of defective quality.

There is not very much authority on this matter, so it may be well first to consider it as a question of principle.

I take first the general question of the contractor's liability where the material which he is required to use can be obtained from any one of several suppliers and the choice of suppliers is left to him. There is no doubt that in every case he is bound to make a proper inspection of the material before using it, and he will be liable if the loss is caused by the use of material which reasonable inspection would have shown to be defective. The question is whether he warrants the material against latent defects.

There are, in my view, good reasons for implying such a warranty if it is not excluded by the terms of the contract. If the contractor's employer suffers loss by reason of the emergence of the latent defect, he will generally have no redress if he cannot recover damages from the contractor. But, if he can recover damages, the contractor will generally not have to bear the loss: he will have bought the defective material from a seller who will be liable under section 14 (2) of the Sale of Goods Act, 1893, because the material was not of merchantable quality. And, if that seller had in turn bought from someone else, there will again be liability, so that there will be a chain of liability from the employer who suffers the damage back to the author of the defect. Of course, the chain may be broken because the contractor (or an earlier buyer) may have agreed to enter into a contract under which his supplier excluded or limited his ordinary liability under the Sale of Goods Act. But in general that has nothing to with the employer and should not deprive him of his remedy. If the contractor chooses to buy on such terms, he takes the risk of having to bear the loss himself if the goods prove to be defective.

Moreover, many contracts for work and materials closely resemble contracts of sale: where the employer contracts for the supply and installation of a machine or other article, the supply of the machine may be the main element and the work of installation be a comparatively small matter. If the employer had bought the article and installed it himself, he would have had a warranty under section 14 (2), and it would be strange that the fact that the seller also agreed to instal it should make all the difference.

The specialty in the present case is that these tiles were only made by one manufacturer. So the contractor had to buy them from him or from someone who bought from him. Why should that make any difference? It would make a difference if that manufacturer was only willing to sell on terms which excluded or limited his ordinary liability under the Sale of Goods Act, and that fact was known to the employer and the contractor when they made their contract. For it would be unreasonable to put on the contractor a liability for latent defects when the employer had chosen the supplier with knowledge that the contractor could not have recourse against him. If the manufacturer's disclaimer of liability caused him to supply the goods at a cheaper price, as in theory at least it should, the employer ought not to get the benefit of a cheap price as well as a warranty from the contractor.

A more difficult case would be where the employer and contractor had no reason to suppose, when they made their contract, that the manufacturer would refuse to sell subject to a seller's ordinary liabilities in respect of the goods which he sells. But I need not consider that case now because there is no suggestion that Brownes had refused to sell except on terms which limited their ordinary liability in respect of latent defects in their tiles. No doubt there will be some cases where, although the contractor had a right of recourse against the manufacturer, he cannot in fact operate that right. The supplier may have become insolvent, or, as in the present case, the action against the contractor may be so delayed that he has no time left in which to sue his supplier. But these cases must be relatively few and it would seem better that the contractor should occasionally have to suffer than that the employer should very seldom have any remedy at all. It therefore seems to me that general principles point strongly to there being an implied warranty of quality in this case.

There is little assistance to be got from the earlier authorities. . . .

In the present case one must sympathise with the appellants because, through no fault of their own, they have lost their right of ultimate recourse against the makers of these tiles. But, putting that aside, because the existence or non-existence of the warranty must be determined as at the date of the contract, this appears to me to be a clear case in which a warranty of quality must be implied. I would therefore dismiss this appeal.

Lord Pearce: . . . . If the appellants' argument is correct, an employer has no redress for loss arising out of the use of material with latent defects, if he has ordered a particular kind of material. For it was not the employer but the contractor who bought from the manufacturer. The employer therefore cannot sue the manufacturer, unless it is possible to extend *Donoghue v Stevenson* further than it has gone up to the present.

I see great difficulty in extending to an ultimate consumer a right to sue the manufacturer in tort in respect of goods which create no peril or accident but simply result in substandard work under a contract which is unknown to the original manufacturer. And if originally, as a term of his contract, the manufacturer limited his liability for defects, there seems no reason (where there is no peril or accident) why a third party should have better rights than the original purchaser. And, if his rights are the same, there is no need to introduce a rule which would cause various confusions and difficulties, since the same result can be achieved in the normal case by the third party procedure.

If, however, the employer can sue the contractor in respect of the faulty materials, then the contractor can in turn recover from the manufacturer, with whom the ultimate blame lies. This would follow the normal chain of liability which attaches to sales and sub-sales of goods. . . .

Appeal dismissed.

(v) Exclusion of the usual implied terms as to quality

Gloucestershire CC v Richardson [1968] 2 All ER 1181, House of Lords

A contractor contracted with employers to erect an extension to a technical college. The agreement incorporated the RIBA form of contract. The tender allowed a prime cost of £7,000 for concrete columns to be supplied by nominated suppliers. In accepting the contractor's tender the employers nominated, by their architect, suppliers (not those named in the tender) at a price of about £4,941. The authorised quotation of the suppliers, which the contractor was thus bound to accept, included a term limiting liability for defective goods and excluding liability for consequential loss or damage. The columns had defects which were undetectable when they were supplied, but which appeared after some columns had been used in the construction. . . . Clause 21 of the conditions of the building contract dealt with nominated sub-contractors, and provided that no nominated sub-contractor should be employed against whom the contractor made reasonable objection or who would not contract to indemnify the contractor; but cl 22, which dealt with nominated suppliers, contained no such provision for the protection of the contractor. Clause 22 provided that all specialists who had been nominated to supply materials or goods were suppliers to the contractor . . .

The question was whether the contractor was liable.

Lord Reid. My Lords, I agree with the majority of your lordships that this appeal should be dismissed.

Lord Pearce. My Lords, the contractor in any particular field of business, when he engages to do certain work and supply materials, impliedly warrants that the materials will be of good quality, unless the particular circumstances of the case show that the parties intended otherwise. To find the intention one must consider the express terms of the contract and any admissible surrounding circumstances.

Here the parties entered into a Royal Institute of British Architects contract, a complicated and sophisticated document. There is no express acceptance by either party of liability for the quality of the nominated materials. The contractor must comply with the instructions of the architect. He must accept the architect's nomination in respect of certain sub-contractors and nominated suppliers. No nominated sub-contractor, however, can be employed (cl 21) if the contractor makes reasonable objection to him or if, inter alia, the sub-contractor will not enter into a sub-contract indemnifying the contractor against claims for negligence of the sub-contractor and 'against the same obligations in respect of the sub-contract as those for which the contractor is liable in respect of this contract'. These words seem to make it clear that the contractor is accepting liability in respect of work done by the nominated sub-contractor.

The situation with regard to nominated suppliers, however, is noticeably different. The clause (22) which deals with nominated suppliers follows directly on that which deals with nominated sub-contractors. It provides no veto on the ground of the contractor's reasonable objection, nor on the ground of the nominated supplier refusing to indemnify the contractor. This omission cannot, I think, be unintentional. It seems, in contrast to cl 21, to point to an intention that the contractor is not undertaking liability for materials provided by a nominated supplier; otherwise he must surely have been given, in the case of a nominated sub-contractor, an opportunity of making reasonable objections, and a right to insist on an indemnity from the supplier.

It would not be unreasonable for the parties to intend that an employer should take the responsibility for materials provided by nominated suppliers. They have been selected, without giving the contractor any right to express views, by the employer's own expert architect, who has decided that the nominated goods are suitable for the purpose and who has made the preliminary arrangements with the suppliers either before or during the main contract. The contractor is simply instructed to obtain his supplies from the nominated supplier. It is the employer who, through his architect, alone arranges the price, which is liable to be reflected in the quality and who alone can insist on tests and checks of quality. All the circumstances of the nomination appear actually to exclude any reliance on the contractor's skill and judgment; and though the contractor receives a profit on the nominated supply, it is a controlled profit and he has certain duties to perform such as co-ordinating the delivery with the work and doing his best to see that there are no delays (see cl 18 (vii)).

On the other hand, if the contractor is not liable for materials provided by nominated suppliers, the employer is left without a remedy for faulty materials; for the contract, by cl 22 indicates clearly that the nominated supplier is in contractual relation with the contractor only and, although the employer is paying for the nominated materials, he pays the contractor for them and the contractor pays the nominated supplier. Thus to hold that the contractor is not liable for nominated supplies is to go against one of the important reasons for the general rule that there is a warranty of good quality in materials supplied under a contract for labour and materials, namely that the employer should have a remedy against the contractor who can in turn enforce it against the supplier with whom the fault lies.

Yet in spite of this important fact I think that the contrast between the wording of cl 21 and that of cl 22 persuades one to the view that the contract shows an intention to exclude a warranty by the contractor in respect of nominated supplies. And the particular circumstances of the case fortify this view. The employers (or their architect) employed a skilled engineer to advise in respect of the columns in question. The engineer, without any consultation with the contractor, prepared detailed designs of the columns, chose out Cawood Wharton & Co, Ltd ('Cawoods') as suitable suppliers, and gave them such instructions as he considered were necessary to specify the composition of the columns. The architects obtained a quotation from Cawoods which was lower than the amount quoted by another firm and also substantially lower than the prime cost item, and which contained a substantial limitation of the purchaser's right of recourse in the event of the columns being defective. The architect presumably was satisfied with this and, without discussing the matter with the contractor, instructed him to accept the quotation.

The employers, through their architect, having directed the contractor to buy from a manufacturer who had substantially limited his own liability, it would not be reasonable to suppose that the parties were intending the contractor to accept an unlimited liability, which might have been very great, for these columns over whose manufacture he had no control whatsoever. It is suggested in argument by the appellants that one should assume some implied intention that there will be liability on the contractor limited to the curtailed right of recourse provided under Cawoods' quotation. If so, one would have to imply in respect of each nominated supplier that there is a liability limited to the right of recourse provided in each particular subcontract of supply; but I see no ground for such a complicated implication which, if it existed, must surely have been embodied in express terms in cl 22. In my opinion, the limitation of recourse against the nominated supplier and the other particular circumstances in respect of the supply of the columns provide confirmation of the intention indicated by the contract itself, namely, that any warranty by the contractor in respect of the quality of the nominated supplies was to be excluded.

The defect in the columns was not, therefore, a matter for which the contractor was liable or at fault.

Lord Upjohn. . . . [W]as the contractor debarred from giving an effective notice because at law he can be held responsible for Cawoods' defective manufacture?—in other words, does the term normally implied in a contract for work and materials, as your lordships have just held in *Young and Marten, Ltd v McManus Childs, Ltd*, apply or is it excluded having regard to the circumstances of the case? Rightly or wrongly it has been conceded throughout that if the contractor was in law responsible for Cawoods' defective work he could not rely on cl 18 of the conditions. . . . . The general rule . . . is not in doubt; the contractor who performs work and supplies materials warrants that the goods which he supplies will be of good quality and reasonably fit for the purpose for which he is using them, unless the circumstances of the contract are such as to exclude any such warranty.

Your lordships heard some argument on the question whether having regard to the great contrast between condition 21 of the RIBA contract making provision for the contractor's dealings with 'nominated sub-contractors' and condition 22 making provision for the contractor's dealings with 'nominated suppliers' the contract showed an intention to exclude the implied warranty in regard to 'nominated suppliers'. With all respect to those of your lordships who take a different view, I cannot accept this. The truth is that this complex agreement, in my opinion, made no provision for the parties' intentions in this matter at all. It was quite unnecessary that the contract should do so, for this was not a matter that had to be dealt with once and for all at that stage unless the parties chose to do so. If the point ever occurred to them, which is unlikely, they did not provide for it in their contract. That contract provided for the nomination of sub-contractors and for suppliers by the architect. The precise terms and conditions as between the employers and the contractor on which each such person is nominated must depend on the terms of the nomination at the time, whether expressed or properly to be implied in the circumstances of the case. Normally it seems to me that the usual rule of implied warranty must apply to the goods to be supplied by the contractor through the nominated supplier. Thus if the architect merely nominated Cawoods to provide the forty columns without more, for my part I can see no reason why there should not be implied in that nomination the usual obligation that the contractor warrants the quality and fitness of the columns. But if the architect nominated Cawoods to provide the columns on the terms, which he instructed the contractor to accept, that Cawoods should not be liable for any delays, defects or deficiencies whatever (no doubt a fanciful and purely theoretical example), it is difficult to see how in law or as a matter of common sense or justice the contractor could be held liable on some implied obligation for the failure of Cawoods to deliver the goods.

[Lord Wilberforce delivered a concurring judgment. Lord Pearson dissented.]

Appeal dismissed.

NOTES

1. The question in this case was whether the Contractor was liable for the quality, or merchantability, of the concrete beams—just as in the *Young & Martens* case the question was whether the subcontractor was liable for the quality of the tiles. In neither case could they be liable for the fitness for purpose of the materials because these had been selected by the employer (ie there was no reliance on the skill and judgment of the contractor or subcontractor.) If before finalising the specification the employer consults the contractor about materials, and the contractor agrees that a particular item can be used, the contractor will be responsible if it turns out not to be fit for the purpose: *Steel Co of Canada v Willand Management* (1966) 58 DLR (2d) 595.
2. The *Gloucestershire CC* case was heard by the House of Lords between the dates of the hearing and of the judgment in the *Young & Marten* case. In each case the party on whom it was sought to impose liability had been given no choice about which materials to use. Why was there liability in one case but not in the other? Look again at the sixth paragraph of Lord Reid's judgment in *Young & Marten* (above, p 335).
3. The *Gloucestershire CC* case is an example of a situation in which, even if there were to be a clause stating that the contractor is not liable for the quality of goods from the nominated supplier, the provisions of the Unfair Contract Terms Act 1977 restricting the exclusion of the implied terms as to quality (see above, p 319) might not 'bite', because the contractor would not be liable even apart from the clause.
4. The RIBA form of contract has been replaced by the Joint Contract Tribunal form (currently JCT 80). This gives the contractor a right of objection to nominated suppliers as well as to nominated subcontractors. If the contractor does not object it is responsible for the quality of the goods supplied.

(e) Contracts for services

Supply of Goods and Services Act 1982

Section 12: The contracts concerned
(1) In this Act a 'contract for the supply of a service' means, subject to subsection (2) below, a contract under which a person ('the supplier') agrees to carry out a service.
(2) For the purposes of this Act, a contract of service or apprenticeship is not a contract for the supply of a service.
(3) Subject to subsection (2) above, a contract is a contract for the supply of a service for the purposes of this Act whether or not goods are also—
    (a) transferred or to be transferred, or
    (b) bailed or to be bailed by way of hire,
under the contract, and whatever is the nature of the consideration for which the service is to be carried out.
(4) The Secretary of State may by order provide that one or more of sections 13 or 15 below shall not apply to services of a description specified in the order, and such an order may make different provision for different circumstances.
(5) The power to make an order under subsection (4) above shall be exercisable by statutory instrument subject to annulment in pursuance of a resolution of either House of Parliament.

Section 13: Implied term about care and skill
In a contract for the supply of a service where the supplier is acting in the course of a business, there is an implied term that the supplier will carry out the service with reasonable care and skill.

Section 14: Implied term about time for performance
(1) Where, under a contract for the supply of a service by a supplier acting in the course of a business, the time for the service to be carried out is not fixed by the contract, left to be fixed in a manner agreed by the contract or determined by the course of dealing between the parties, there is an implied term that the supplier will carry out the service within a reasonable time.
(2) What is a reasonable time is a question of fact.

Section 15: Implied terms about consideration
(1) Where, under a contract for the supply of a service, the consideration for the service is not determined by the contract, left to be determined in a manner agreed by the contract or determined by the course of dealing between the parties, there is an implied term that the party contracting with the supplier will pay a reasonable charge.
(2) What is a reasonable charge is a question of fact.

Greaves & Co (Contractors) Ltd v Baynham Meikle & Partners [1975] 3 All ER 99, Court of Appeal

The plaintiffs, who were building contractors, were employed by a company to construct a warehouse under a 'package deal' whereby, in addition to providing the labour and materials, the plaintiffs were to employ the architects and engineers as sub-contractors. The warehouse was required by the company as a store for oil drums which were to be kept on the first floor of the warehouse and, when required for despatch, were to be moved into position by fork-lift stacker trucks. The plaintiffs knew the purpose for which the warehouse was required and therefore were under a duty to the company to see that the building when finished was reasonably fit for that purpose. The plaintiffs employed the defendants, a firm of consultant structural engineers, to design the structure of the warehouse. It was to be built according to a new system of construction which was governed by a British Standards code of practice. A circular had been issued by the British Standards Institution warning designers of the effect of vibrations caused by imposed loadings in such constructions. The plaintiffs made known to the defendants the purpose for which the warehouse was required and in particular that the first floor would have to take the weight of loaded fork-lift trucks moving to and fro. Although the defendants were aware of the circular they did not read it as a warning against vibrations in general and so did not take measures to deal with the random impulses of fork-lift trucks. There was evidence that other designers might have taken the same view of the circular. The warehouse was built in accordance with the defendants' design, and the first floor was put into use for storing oil drums and moving them about by fork-lift trucks. After a time the floor cracked and became dangerous, and it was found that remedial works costing some £100,000 would have to be carried out to cure structural damage. The plaintiffs became liable to the company to remedy that damage. They brought an action against the defendants for damages for breach of the agreement to design the structure and claimed a declaration of the defendants' liability for the cost of all work necessary to rectify the damage caused by breach of the agreement and an indemnity against all sums payable by the plaintiffs to the company by reason of breach of the agreement. At the trial of the action the defendants gave evidence admitting that they had been engaged by the plaintiffs to produce a building the first floor of which would be fit for use as a store for oil drums and for moving the drums by fork-lift truck. Further, by the original defence to the statement of claim the defendants admitted that it was an implied term of the agreement that the defendants' design should be such that the building would be structurally sound, although on the second day of the trial the defence was amended to strike out that admission. The trial judge found that the cracks in the floor had been caused by vibration produced by movement of loaded fork-lift trucks, and that the floor had not been designed with sufficient strength to withstand that vibration. He held that as the design was inadequate for its intended purpose the defendants were in breach of duty and in breach of an implied term of the agreement that the design would be fit for its purpose; the plaintiffs were therefore entitled to the declaration and indemnity claimed. The defendants appealed.

Lord Denning MR. . . . The law does not usually imply a warranty that [a professional man] will achieve the desired result, but only a term that he will use reasonable care and skill. The surgeon does not warrant that he will cure the patient. Nor does the solicitor warrant that he will win the case. But, when a dentist agrees to make a set of false teeth for a patient, there is an implied warranty that they will fit his gums: see *Samuels v Davis*.

What then is the position when an architect or an engineer is employed to design a house or a bridge? Is he under an implied warranty that, if the work is carried out to his design, it will be reasonably fit for the purpose? Or is he only under a duty to use reasonable care and skill? This question may require to be answered some day as a matter of law. But in the present case I do not think we need answer it. For the evidence shows that both parties were of one mind on the matter. Their common intention was that the engineer should design a warehouse which would be fit for the purpose for which it was required. That common intention gives rise to a term implied *in fact*. . . .

[Browne LJ and Geoffrey Lane LJ delivered judgments to the same effect.]

NOTES

1. Furmston employs Bishop to design a house for him. Bishop's design specifies Beale's tiles, which are of apparently high quality. After a year, however, the tiles disintegrate because of a latent defect. Both Beale and the building contractor are insolvent. Is Bishop liable? Wasn't it the common intention that the house should be watertight?

2. Although this case seemed to suggest that professionals who are given a specification of what is required might now be strictly liable, it has been interpreted as depending on its special facts, in particular that the contractors who had employed the engineer were themselves employed under a 'package deal' contract under which they may have been obliged to produce a building that was fit for the employers' purposes: see *Hawkins v Chrysler (UK) Ltd and Burne Associates* (1986) 38 BLR 36.

3. Why are suppliers of goods, builders and other such tradesmen strictly liable, but professional people liable only for negligence? Or is that the wrong question?

4. Perhaps one explanation for the difference is that suppliers are much more likely to be involved in a 'chain'—ie to have obtained the goods from someone else to whom the liability can be passed back: see the *Young & Marten* case, above p 334. Professionals are more likely to be doing the work themselves. However, professionals may also subcontract—and the 'oddball result' in the *Greaves* case cannot be explained on this ground: there was a chain in that case but the engineer was at the end of it.

5. Are there any circumstances in which it will be inferred that a professional was undertaking to achieve a particular result? Furmston, who already has a fine Roman nose, employs Beale, a plastic surgeon, to give him a 'nose job'. Beale tells Furmston, 'I will turn your nose into a real Sherlock Holmser.' Without any negligence on Beale's part the operation is a failure and Furmston's nose ends up resembling a squashed tomato. Is Beale liable? (Consider *Thake v Maurice*, above p 265 and *Sullivan v O'Connor* (363 Mass 579, 296 NE 2d 183 (1973).) (The measure of damages, if any, will be considered below, p 501).

(f) Contracts of employment

'The contract of employment' by Napier, in Labour Law in Britain (ed R. Lewis, 1986), pp 327–331, 337–339, 347–348.

The content of individual employment law has altered dramatically in the last twenty years, mainly as a result of changes which occurred in the 1970s, the decade in which legislation brought a new framework of rights for employees, and created specialised labour courts—the industrial tribunals—before which these rights can be claimed. Important though these rights are, however, it remains true—and this is perhaps one of the leading paradoxes of the contemporary employment law—that they complement rather than oust the common law of the contract. Today the common law fulfils a dual function. It operates as a backcloth, providing a set of rules important in the many situations left unregulated by specific statutory measures, or where the legislative remedies that do exist are either inadequate or restricted in their application. It also has a crucial role to play in the operation of the statutory rights themselves, however, for Parliament has typically incorporated contractual terms and concepts in defining these. Thus, for example, there can be no proper understanding of what amounts to a 'dismissal' for the purposes of unfair dismissal without a knowledge of the common law rules regarding repudiation of contract, and no real grasp of redundancy law without an appreciation of the limits placed on job mobility by the implied terms of the contract of employment.

It follows that the history of the common law of the contract deserves attention too. For, through the system of binding precedent, the response of the courts to problems arising today is conditioned by what their predecessors had to say about similar problems in the past. This account of the modern contract thus begins with an examination of the historical antecedents of the present law.

DEVELOPMENT OF THE CONTRACT OF EMPLOYMENT

Status and Contract

Although there has been systematic legal regulation of the employment relationship since the fourteenth century, it has only been in the last hundred and fifty years or so that this regulation has taken contract as its primary model. Before then the relationship was shaped in part by the criminal law, operating through a line of statutes which imposed compulsory labour and gave magistrates the power to fix wages, in part by the civil law regulating the status of different categories of persons. The great jurist Blackstone, writing in 1795, analysed the relationship of master and servant in ways which, to modern eyes, are both revealing and deficient. For Blackstone, employment was akin to the relationships of husband and wife, parent and child and guardian and ward, and was classed by him alongside these as one of the 'great relations in private life'. Moreover, his world of servants was peopled almost exclusively by workers in domestic service and engaged in agricultural labour. As Kahn-Freund (1977:508–13) has shown, Blackstone's concept of employment was seriously out of date even against the social conditions of late eighteenth century England. His treatment of the topic tells us not only that the understanding of employment as the product of a free bargain between individuals had not yet been achieved, but also that the leading jurist of the age was little concerned with explaining and classifying the diverse forms of engagement of labour which, from other sources, we know existed in English society of the time. Why did Blackstone ignore the position of the factory labourer, the office clerk, indeed the urban worker in general? Probably for two reasons: the conditions of employment of the new working classes took them outside the terms of the disused but still-venerated Elizabethan and Jacobean criminal statutes, and there was no incentive for lawyers of his time to concern themselves with the details of such employment. The workers did not have the resources to go to law to ascertain the dimensions of their employment obligations, and, if their employers did, they lacked the inclination to do so.

The nineteenth century saw fundamental changes in the legal attitude towards the employment relationship, changes which still underpin many of the assumptions found in the law. To begin with there was, in the first half of the century, a transformation in the basic legal model. Instead of being part of the law dealing with personal status, employment was brought within the fold of the expanding law of contract. Most famously expressed in Maine's dictum that the movement of civilised society was from status to contract and that the status of the slave was superseded by the contractual relations of the servant to his master (cf. Kahn-Freund, 1977:512), the view that the key to understanding the history of employment in the nineteenth century lies in an appreciation of how contract replaced status has recently been attacked by writers who rightly warn against over-simple explanations of complex phenomena (Merritt, 1982; Foster, 1983). None the less, it would be a mistake to underestimate the impact of the shift towards contract at both theoretical and practical levels. On a theoretical level, the embracing of contractual notions was seen as an important part of the general liberal trend in labour law which, in the second half of the century, led in 1875 to the repeal of the Master and Servant Acts and gave a measure of protection to those engaged in certain trade union activities (Ruegg, 1901:277–9). To explain the employment relationship as a bargain, the terms of which lay entirely within the control of two independent parties, was to stress the even-handedness of the law, and was a view which accorded well with Benthamite thinking on individualism which, as Dicey (1962:63–4) noted, exercised such a potent intellectual force in the middle years of the century. But the influence of contract was also felt in the content of specific legal rules with practical consequences.

In the shape of the doctrine of common employment, for example, it was used as a means of developing a particular legal doctrine which had dramatic and disastrous effects for many thousands of working people and their families (Bartrip and Burman, 1983:103–25). The legal rule that an employee, injured at work by the negligence of a fellow employee, could not hold the common employer liable for the tort originated in the case of *Priestley v Fowler* in 1837. At first the rule was expressed as turning on what, in modern terminology, would be seen as the employer's 'duty of care' to his employees. But, as it was refined and enthusiastically developed by the English courts (in Scotland the courts were far more cautious), it was explained in contractual terms. The employee (or his successors) could not sue because he had bargained away his right to do so as a term (albeit implied) of the contract he had entered into with his employer: 'the negligence of a fellow servant is taken to be one of the risks, which a servant as between himself and his master undertakes, when he enters into the service.' The convenience and plausibility of the contractual analysis was a potent factor in the spread of a doctrine which became one of the most controversial aspects of the law of tort, and which was eventually to provide the impetus for the introduction of workmen's compensation legislation in 1897.

As the example of common employment illustrates, the transition from status to contract was far from being the unqualified improvement it seemed to many Victorian and Edwardian jurists. As the form of the relationship of master and servant changed, so too did its content. The transition from what Fox (1974:181–90) has called a 'high-trust' to a 'low-trust' relationship brought with it the abandonment of some of the rules which had existed in the earlier law for the protection of the weaker party. In the case of *Limland v Stephen* at the beginning of the century, Lord Kenyon could say there were 'reciprocal duties between masters and servants. From the servant is due obedience and respect; from the master protection and good treatment.' While the principle of employer's control remained largely unaffected under the changing law, except in so far as the duty to obey was now explained as an implied term of the contract and not as an essential part of the relationship of master and servant (Selznick, 1969:136), the master's obligations in respect of welfare were watered-down in several important respects. For example, the obligation to pay wages and to provide medical assistance to sick servants was cut back by a judiciary increasingly aware of the phenomenon of industrial employment and the appropriateness of linking payment of wages directly with productive effort.

Judges had the opportunity of developing the law in this and other ways because, to an unprecedented extent, cases on the master and servant relationship were coming before them. This was not just due to a change in attitudes as to the desirability of recourse to law as a means of settling disputes, although no doubt the rise of a commercial middle-class did have some influence here, but also to the workings of the poor law. Parish fought parish in the courts over who had the burden of looking after the poor, and often the answer was given by where the unfortunate pauper had previously acquired a 'settlement' of a year's duration. This in turn was largely dependent on the terms of the employment over the period, and thus the courts were brought to consider the terms of service of even the most menial workers.

A range of other developments in the detail of the master and servant relationship are also associated with judicial activity in the nineteenth century (Haines, 1980:271–84). As tort liability became more important, so too it was increasingly important to distinguish between the acts of servants (for whom the employer was vicariously liable) and those of independent contractors (for whom he was not). So detailed case law also emerged to decide what acts were carried out 'in the scope of employment', and which were not. Gradually, the courts recognised that employment relationships were not governed by rules appropriate to an agricultural economy; periods of hiring, it was accepted, might be terminated by the giving of notice, although the presumption that, unless the contrary was indicated, a hiring was to last for the rotation of the year was not abandoned by English law until 1969. More generally, the nineteenth century saw the development and, in some instances, creation of many of the basic principles within the contract of employment relating to the payment of wages and dismissal which still apply today.

But no account of the many changes in individual employment law in this period should neglect the tension which arose between the standards tolerated by the common law and those laid down by statute. For although the judges, by and large, embraced contractualism and laissez-faire ideas of economic behaviour with energy and enthusiasm—except, it should be noted, in developing the notion of contractual terms unenforceable because they were incompatible with the fundamental principles of freedom of trade—the nineteenth century also saw legislative intervention to maintain minimum standards of civilised conditions of labour. One commentator (Friedmann, 1959:99) has concluded from this and other evidence that the judges are incapable of effecting major social adjustment by using the common law device of contract as a social equaliser. The most notable example of statutory intervention is to be found in the history of factory legislation. But mention can also be made of the Truck Acts, which sought to protect the worker's right to payment of wages, and lesser measures such as the Merchant Shipping Acts of 1844 and 1854 which gave close regulation of the terms of employment of sailors (Atiyah, 1979:543–4). Thus the significance of the nineteenth century from the point of view of the history of employment law is not simply the displacement of status by contract; it is also that during this period English law accepted the propriety of imposing, by legislation, certain protections for workers outside the realm of contract (Hepple, 1982:399). In so doing, some of the worst effects of unbridled individualism were mitigated, and a pattern for legal intervention was set which was to have profound consequences for the subsequent development of the law.

Characteristics of the Modern Law

The story of the contract of employment during the present century can be more briefly told, notwithstanding the many fundamental changes in society and industrial relations which have taken place in this period. There has been no truly radical alteration in the conception of the individual employment relationship similar to that which occurred in Victorian England. By 1914 most of the great legislative and judicial battles in this field had been fought, and the foundations of social and industrial legislation had been well and truly laid. Thus, in particular, the doctrine of freedom of contract has remained central to the common law's understanding of employment throughout this century, although this understanding has had to be modified in various ways in order to accommodate new phenomena such as the growth in collective bargaining, and different forms of statutory intervention in the employment relationship . . .

THE CONTRACT AS AN AUTHORITATIVE SOURCE OF RULES

Although the parties are free (within the limits imposed by the general law and particular statutory rules) to contract on their own terms, the great majority of contracts of employment share certain common features. The employee undertakes, in exchange for the payment of remuneration, to obey the lawful and reasonable orders of the employer, and to take reasonable care in the carrying out of his employment duties. There is also a duty of fidelity towards the employer, which is translated into particular obligations not to enter into competition with him during working time, not to divulge or improperly use confidential information acquired in the course of his employment, and, within certain limits, to disclose to the employer information harmful to the employer's interests. The employee is, however, under no general duty to disclose personal misconduct, although he may be required to inform the employer of the misbehaviour of fellow employees.

The employer is bound by a duty to take reasonable care for the safety of the employee, to pay wages, and to exercise due respect and consideration in dealings with the employee. This duty of respect may be seen as the counterpart of the employee's duty of fidelity. It is not of recent creation, but it is a duty which, through the operation of the law of unfair dismissal and, in particular, that part of it concerned with 'constructive' dismissal (see below), has acquired a much-increased significance in recent years.

Express and Implied Terms

Although the parties are free to make the bargain of their choice, in practice many of the key features of their relationship are left undefined, and are settled by the courts through the device of the implied term. Implied terms are, in legal theory, of secondary significance in defining the contract, in the sense that they will not override express terms which state the contrary, nor can they be used as a basis for an interpretation having this effect. In reality, however, it would be hard to overemphasise either the contribution made by such terms in building up the content of the contract, or the flexibility and power this operation gives to the judges whose job it is to construe the contract. The importance is only enhanced by the closer link (explained below) between implied contractual terms and the legal effect of collective bargaining.

Implied terms are often divided by lawyers into those implied in fact, and those implied in law. The difference between the two is not as clear in practice as it appears on paper, but its basis is that, in relation to the former category, the courts will seek to justify their findings by reference to the presumed but unexpressed wishes of the parties. As an aid in so doing they will, among other things, have regard to what is established practice in the trade or industry in question, and to what they are sure must have been in the parties' contemplation. In the past, the standards to be met before such a power of implication was exercised were high, and imposed, in theory at least, a limit on judicial creativity. Judges were supposed to imply terms only where it was necessary to do so to give business efficacy to the contract, or where the term was one which would immediately have been accepted by both parties when their attention was drawn to it. Today, although it is going too far to say openly that the judges have power to imply all terms which they think reasonable, the case law has developed in that direction. It has recently been said judicially that 'we can treat as an agreed term a term which would not have been at once assented to by both parties at the time when they made the contract, for example where one party would at once have assented to it and the other would have done so after it had been made clear to him that unless he did so there would be no contract', and it has also been held that the conduct of the parties under the contract is highly relevant to deciding the content of any implied terms which may be contained in it.

In relation to terms implied in law, as opposed to fact, the basis for judicial intervention is a legal requirement that the employment relationship contains a term dealing with a particular matter. Sometimes this will be as a result of statute, but, more often, the legal requirement will arise as a result of judicial interpretation of the rules of the common law. There the judges obviously enjoy a great measure of discretion. The term implied by law is seen as a necessary incident of the constitution of the employment relationship.

One of the best illustrations is to be found in the *ASLEF* case, where the Court of Appeal in an important judgment (Napier, 1972) held that a 'work to rule' on the railways amounted to breach of an implied duty of co-operation, which was a part of the contract of employment. Such a finding could in no sense be justified by reference to the common intentions of the parties, since it was so contrary to the interests of the workers concerned. Nevertheless, the term in question was held, as a matter of law, to form part of the contract. The case provides the clearest evidence of what the judges think are the proper dimensions of the employment bargain, and an object lesson in the discovery and application of one of the most significant implied terms to be found in the contract. . . .

SUBSTANCE OF THE CONTRACT

The following discussion, which is in no sense exhaustive, is intended to illustrate the duties arising in three important areas: the employee's duty of obedience, . . .

Duty of Obedience

As noted above the employee's duty to obey the reasonable orders of his employer constitutes one of the traditional distinguishing features of the contract of employment. In the modern law, the legal basis for this feature is a term implied into the contract as a matter of law. In the past, breach of this duty left the employee open to the sanction of summary dismissal, and this remains true today, although the standards of behaviour expected of employees have been somewhat relaxed in line with changing social attitudes. Some of the most interesting developments, however, have taken place elsewhere. In the past, the ambit of the duty of obedience was explored by the courts only in the context of allegedly wrongful dismissals; not so today, when the existence of the range of statutory employment protection rights directs attention on to what may legitimately or reasonably be required by an employer of his employee. Examples may be drawn from the law of unfair dismissal and redundancy, topics which are discussed in detail in Chapter 15.

In unfair dismissal law the question whether an order falls within the scope of the powers of command given by the contract to the employer may be relevant at the stage of deciding either the reasonableness of a dismissal, or whether or not a dismissal took place. With regard to the former, while the issue whether the employee was contractually bound to obey is not decisive one way or the other as to fairness, this test allows the courts to evaluate and criticise the exercise of managerial prerogative. The cases show, for example, the courts' readiness to express views on such diverse matters as the scope of the employer's right to specify the details of his employee's dress, and to implement badly thought-out systems for assessing work performance. By contrast, in proving a constructive dismissal—where the employer's improper conduct has allegedly justified the employee in leaving—the test is based on contract. A tribunal will often have to decide whether the giving of orders which the employee has found unacceptable amounts to a serious breach of the employer's implied duty of good and reasonable conduct, and as such warranted the employee's departure.

Another example may be taken from the law of redundancy, where the concept of job mobility has become of fundamental importance. An employee who is dismissed because of refusal to comply with a lawful order to take up another job with the same employer in another part of the country is dismissed for misconduct, not redundancy, and accordingly it is often vital to know the extent to which such a right on the part of the employer to direct movement forms part of the contract.

As these particular examples demonstrate, under the influence of the framework of individual statutory rights, the courts have, to a much greater extent than in the past, been given opportunities of passing judgment on the orders given by an employer to his employees. Under the influence of these rights, the prevailing view which has emerged favours a much more restrictive interpretation of the right to command than was previously found acceptable. The right to command is seen as more limited in scope and is itself subject to the employer's contractual duty to maintain the employee's trust and confidence. Some (for example, Napier, 1977; Elias, 1981) have seen in these changes a movement among the judiciary towards a more pluralistic analysis of the employment relationship, although this argument has not gone unchallenged (Collins, 1982; Glasbeek, 1984).

REFERENCES

Atiyah, P.S. 1979. *The Rise and Fall of Freedom of Contract*. Oxford: Clarendon Press.

Bartrip, P.W.J., and S.B. Burman. 1983. *The Wounded Soldiers of Industry*. Oxford: Clarendon Press.

Collins, H. 1982. 'Capitalist Discipline and Corporatist Law'. *Industrial Law Journal*, 11 June (June and September), 78–93, 170–77.

Dicey, A.V. 1914. *Lectures on the Relation between Law and Public Opinion in England During the Nineteenth Century*. 2nd edn. London: Macmillan. Reissued 1962. London: Macmillan.

Elias, P. 1981. 'Fairness in Unfair Dismissal: Trends and Tensions'. *Industrial Law Journal*, 10 (December), 201–17.

Foster, K. 1983. 'The Legal Form of Work in the 19th Century: The Myth of Contract?' Paper presented to conference on 'The History of Law, Labour and Crime', University of Warwick, September. (Unpublished).

Fox, A. 1974. *Beyond Contract: Work, Power and Trust Relations*. London: Faber.

Friedmann, W. 1959. *Law in a Changing Society*. London: Stevens.

Glasbeek, H.J. 1984. 'The Utility of Model Building—Collins' Capitalist Discipline and Corporatist Law'. *Industrial Law Journal*, 13 (September), 133–52.

Haines, B.W. 1980. 'English Labour Law and the Separation from Contract'. *Journal of Legal History*, 1 (December), 262–96.

Hepple, B.A. 1982. 'Labour Law and Public Employees in Great Britain'. *Labour Law and the Community: Perspectives for the 1980s*. Eds. Lord Wedderburn and W.T. Murphy. London: Institute of Advanced Legal Studies, 67, 83.

Kahn-Freund, O. 1977. 'Blackstone's Neglected Child: The Contract of Employment'. *Law Quarterly Review*, 93 (October), 508–28.

Merritt, A. 1982. 'The Historical Role of Law in the Regulation of Employment—Abstentionist or Interventionist?'. *Australian Journal of Law and Society*, 1 (1), 56–82.

Napier, B.W. 1972. 'Working to Rule—A Breach of the Contract of Employment?' *Industrial Law Journal*, 1 (September), 125–34.

——. 1977. 'Judicial Attitudes towards the Employment Relationship—Some Recent Developments'. *Industrial Law Journal*, 6 (March), 1–18.

Ruegg, A.H. 1901. 'Changes in the Law of England Affecting Labour'. *A Century of Law Reform. Twelve Lectures on the Changes in the Law of England During the Nineteenth Century*. London: Macmillan, 241–79.

Selznick, P. 1969. *Law, Society and Industrial Justice*. New York: Russell Sage Foundation.

NOTES

1. The current judicial attitude towards contracts of employment—for instance the extent to which the judges adopt a pluralist approach by recognising that employers and employees have divergent interests and the need for some sort of partnership between them—is clearly a matter of debate. No attempt to resolve the question need be made here. What is important for our purposes is to realise that neither judge-made law nor statute is 'neutral'—it is premissed on particular, though changing, views of the proper relationship between employer and employee.

2. An employment contract is an example of a 'relational' contract—it will normally last some time and it is usually not possible to specify at the outset exactly what the employee will be required to do. The 'management prerogative' to give orders to the employee is a response to this. Without suggesting that the current approach is in any way wrong, it

is interesting to contrast it with the contract of partnership. This shares many of the employment contract's relational characteristics, but the common law and the Partnership Act 1890 which codified it take the view that the relationship between parties is not hierarchical but equal. Thus the Partnership Act 1890 s 24 provides:

> (8) Any difference arising as to ordinary matters connected with the partnership business may be decided by a majority of the partners, but no change may be made in the nature of the partnership business without the consent of all existing partners.

Under the Act partners owe each other a series of fiduciary duties, derived from the earlier common law. In *Dean v MacDowell* (1878) 8 Ch D 345, 350–351 James LJ said:

> It is quite clear . . . that in partnership matters there must be the utmost good faith, and that there is to that extent a fiduciary relation between the parties. That is to say, one partner must not directly or indirectly use the partnership assets for his own private benefit. He must not, in anything connected with the partnership, take any profit clandestinely for himself. . . .

As we shall see, this goes further than the obligations imposed upon employees (below, p 376); it is completely different to the obligations of an employer.

CHAPTER 17
Discharge by frustration

In this chapter we examine the doctrine of frustration, under which a contract may be discharged by some subsequent change of circumstance. As we shall see, the doctrine is dealing with events which are outside the control of either party and which the contract does not provide for—it is perhaps even confined to events which the parties had not foreseen (see below, p 363). As we noted earlier (p 304), the doctrine is thus concerned with allocating risks, but rather than put the risk wholly on one or other of the parties, the doctrine achieves a very rough-and-ready division of the risks between them. Often this can be justified in terms of efficiency: the parties would probably have agreed something similar had they made a 'complete contingent contract' (see above, p 75). Often the result can also be justified as promoting fairness.

'Impossibility in Contract Law' by Posner and Rosenfield (above, p 305)

Taylor v Caldwell (1863) 3 B & S 826, 122 ER 826, Queen's Bench

Blackburn J. In this case the plaintiffs and defendants had, on the 27th May, 1862, entered into a contract by which the defendants agreed to let the plaintiffs have the use of The Surrey Gardens and Music Hall on four days then to come, viz, the 17th June, 15th July, 5th August and 19th August, for the purpose of giving a series of four grand concerts, and day and night fêtes at the Gardens and Hall on those days respectively; and the plaintiffs agreed to take the Gardens and Hall on those days, and pay 100*l* for each day.

The parties inaccurately call this a 'letting', and the money to be paid a 'rent'; but the whole agreement is such as to shew that the defendants were to retain the possession of the Hall and Gardens so that there was to be no demise of them, and that the contract was merely to give the plaintiffs the use of them on those days. Nothing however, in our opinion, depends on this. The agreement then proceeds to set out various stipulations between the parties as to what each was to supply for these concerts and entertainments, and as to the manner in which they should be carried on. The effect of the whole is to shew that the existence of the Music Hall in the Surrey Gardens in a state fit for a concert was essential for the fulfilment of the contract,—such entertainments as the parties contemplated in their agreement could not be given without it.

After the making of the agreement, and before the first day on which a concert was to be given, the Hall was destroyed by fire. This destruction, we must take it on the evidence, was without the fault of either party, and was so complete that in consequence the concerts could not be given as intended. And the question we have to decide is whether, under these circumstances, the loss which the plaintiffs have sustained is to fall upon the defendants. The parties when framing their agreement evidently had not present to their minds the possibility of such a disaster, and have made no express stipulation with reference to it, so that the answer to the question must depend upon the general rules of law applicable to such a contract.

There seems no doubt that where there is a positive contract to do a thing, not in itself unlawful, the contractor must perform it or pay damages for not doing it, although in consequence of unforeseen accidents, the performance of his contract has become unexpectedly burthensome or even impossible. The law is so laid down in 1 Roll Abr 450, Condition (G), and in the note to *Walton v Waterhouse*, and is recognised as the general rule by all the Judges in the much discussed case of *Hall v Wright*. But this rule is only applicable when the contract is positive and absolute, and not subject to any condition either express or implied: and there are authorities which, as we think, establish the principle that where, from the nature of the contract, it appears that the parties must from the beginning have known that it could not be fulfilled unless when the time for the fulfilment of the contract arrived some particular specified thing continued to exist, so that, when entering into the contract, they must have contemplated such continuing existence as the foundation of what was to be done; there, in the absence of any express or implied warranty that the thing shall exist, the contract is not to be construed as a positive contract, but as subject to an implied condition that the parties shall be excused in case, before breach, performance becomes impossible from the perishing of the thing without default of the contractor.

There seems little doubt that this implication tends to further the great object of making the legal construction such as to fulfil the intention of those who entered into the contract. For in the course of affairs men in making such contracts in general would, if it were brought to their minds, say that there should be such a condition. . . . There is a class of contracts in which a person binds himself to do something which requires to be performed by him in person; and such promises, eg promises to marry, or promises to serve for a certain time, are never in practice qualified by an express exception of the death of the party; and therefore in such cases the contract is in terms broken if the promisor dies before fulfilment. Yet it was very early determined that, if the performance is personal, the executors are not liable; *Hyde v The Dean of Windsor*. See 2 Wms Exors 1560 5th edn, where a very apt illustration is given. 'Thus', says the learned author, 'if an author undertakes to compose a work, and dies before completing it, his executors are discharged from this contract: for the undertaking is merely personal in its nature, and, by the intervention of the contractor's death, has become impossible to be performed.' For this he cites a dictum of Lord Lyndhurst in *Marshall v Broadhurst*, and a case mentioned by Patteson J in *Wentworth v Cock*. In *Hall v Wright*, Crompton J, in his judgment, puts another case. 'Where a contract depends upon personal skill, and the act of God renders it impossible, as, for instance, in the case of a painter employed to paint a picture who is struck blind, it may be that the performances might be excused.'

It seems that in those cases the only ground on which the parties or their executors, can be excused from the consequences of the breach of the contract is, that from the nature of the contract there is an implied condition of the continued existence of the life of the contractor, and, perhaps in the case of the painter of his eyesight. In the instances just given, the person, the continued existence of whose life is necessary to the fulfilment of the contract, is himself the contractor, but that does not seem in itself to be necessary to the application of the principle; as is illustrated by the following example. In the ordinary form of an apprentice deed the apprentice binds himself in unqualified terms to 'serve until the full end and term of seven years to be fully complete and ended', during which term it is covenanted that the apprentice his master 'faithfully shall serve', and the father of the apprentice in equally unqualified terms binds himself for the performance by the apprentice of all and every covenant on his part. (See the form, 2 Chitty on Pleading, 370, 7th ed by Greening.) It is undeniable that if the apprentice dies within the seven years, the covenant of the father that he shall perform his covenant to serve for seven years is not fulfilled, yet surely it cannot be that an action would lie against the father? Yet the only reason why it would not is that he is excused because of the apprentice's death.

These are instances where the implied condition is of the life of a human being, but there are others in which the same implication is made as to the continued existence of a thing. For example, where a contract of sale is made amounting to a bargain and sale, transferring presently the property in specific chattels, which are to be delivered by the vendor at a future day; there, if the chattels, without the fault of the vendor, perish in the interval, the purchaser must pay the price and the vendor is excused from performing his contract to deliver, which has thus become impossible . . .

That this is the rule of the English law is established by the case of *Rugg v Minett*, where the article that perished before delivery was turpentine, and it was decided that the vendor was bound to refund the price of all those lots in which the property had not passed; but was entitled to retain without deduction the price of those lots in which the property had passed, though they were not delivered, and though in the conditions of sale, which are set out in the report, there was no express qualification of the promise to deliver on payment. It seems in that case rather to have been taken for granted than decided that the destruction of the thing sold before delivery excused the vendor from fulfilling his contract to deliver on payment.

This also is the rule in the Civil law, and it is worth noticing that Pothier, in his celebrated Traité du Contrat de Vente (see Part 4, ss 307 et seq; and Part 2, ch 1, s 1, art 4, s 1), treats this as merely an example of the more general rule that every obligation de certo corpore is extinguished when the thing ceases to exist. See Blackburn on the Contract of Sale, p 173.

It may, we think, be safely asserted to be now English law, that in all contracts of loan of chattels or bailments if the performance of the promise of the borrower or bailee to return the things lent or bailed, becomes impossible because it has perished, this impossibility (if not arising from the fault of the borrower or bailee from some risk which he has taken upon himself) excuses the borrower or bailee from the performance of his promise to redeliver the chattel.

. . . The principle seems to us to be that, in contracts in which the performance depends on the continued existence of a given person or thing, a condition is implied that the impossibility of performance arising from the perishing of the person or thing shall excuse the performance.

In none of these cases is the promise in words other than positive, nor is there any express stipulation that the destruction of the person or thing shall excuse the performance; but that excuse is by law implied, because from the nature of the contract it is apparent that the parties contracted on the basis of the continued existence of the particular person or chattel. In the present case, looking at the whole contract, we find that the parties contracted on the basis of the continued existence of the Music Hall at the time when the concerts were to be given; that being essential to their performance.

We think, therefore, that the Music Hall having ceased to exist, without fault of either party, both parties are excused, the plaintiffs from taking the gardens and paying the money, the defendants from performing their promise to give the use of the Hall and Gardens and other things. Consequently the rule must be absolute to enter the verdict for the defendants.

Rule absolute.

NOTES

1. In theory there were three possible outcomes to this case:
   (a) the licensees should pay even though they could not use the Hall (risk on licensee);
   (b) the licensors should be liable for failing to provide the hall even though they were not at fault (risk on licensor);
   (c) both parties were released by discharge of the contract (risk divided).

   In the event (a) was not argued: the contest was between (b) and (c).

2. Blackburn uses as an example of a party being excused by impossibility the case of goods which are destroyed after they have become the buyer's property but before they have been delivered. What he says is still the law but it would probably be analysed rather differently nowadays. Under the Sale of Goods Act the risk of accidental destruction of or damage to the goods normally passes to the buyer with the property, s 20; and once the risk has passed the buyer will have to pay the price even if there is nothing left for the seller to deliver. Although to that extent the seller is excused, this outcome is usually explained in terms that the seller has performed its side of the contract, rather than the contract being discharged. The other situation mentioned by Blackburn, the destruction of the turpentine *before* property has passed, *is* considered to be a case of discharge of the contract. The Sale of Goods Act 1979 provides:

   7. Where there is an agreement to sell specific goods and subsequently the goods, without any fault on the part of the seller or buyer, perish before the risk passes to the buyer, the agreement is avoided.

   the result is that the buyer can recover the price paid, but the seller is not liable for non-delivery. (Note that in some contracts by express agreement or by implication, the risk passes before the property: thus in f.o.b. and c.i.f. contracts, risk passes as from shipment, above, p 53.)

3. The doctrine which originated in *Taylor v Caldwell* and which has come to be known as the doctrine of frustration may apply not only where the subject-matter of the contract has been destroyed but also in other cases

where one party's obligation has, without either party's fault, become impossible to perform; where the contract has become illegal; and, but only in very extreme cases, where the commercial purpose of the contract has been destroyed (see below, section (d)).

4. Although it is usual to think of there being a single doctrine of frustration, in practice it applies rather differently in the various situations. This is particularly clear with contracts which have become illegal. As we shall see, normally there will be no frustration if the parties foresaw the event or provided for it; but neither restriction applies when the contract is frustrated by illegality. This is because whereas the other rules about frustration are primarily concerned with the allocation of risks of unexpected events, the rules on contracts frustrated by illegality are primarily concerned with matters of 'public policy', see section 9 below. We shall see however that the rules do not fit terribly easily into some other contexts, particularly employment contracts (below, p 353).

(a) The juristic basis of frustration

Davis Contractors Ltd v Fareham UDC [1956] 2 All ER 145, House of Lords

The appellants agreed to build 78 council houses for the respondent council within a period of eight months. In fact the work took twenty-two months. The respondents paid the contract price. The appellants argued that the contract has been frustrated by the long delay, which was due mainly to a shortage of skilled labour. Since the houses had been completed, the purpose of the contention was to argue for payment on a quantum meruit basis. The House of Lords held that the contract had not been frustrated.

Lord Reid. . . . . Frustration has often been said to depend on adding a term to the contract by implication. . . .

I may be allowed to note an example of the artificiality of the theory of an implied term given by Lord Sands in *Scott & Sons v Del Sel* . . .

'A tiger has escaped from a travelling menagerie. The milkgirl fails to deliver the milk. Possibly the milkman may be exonerated from any breach of contract; but, even so, it would seem hardly reasonable to base that exoneration on the ground that "tiger days excepted" must be held as if written into the milk contract.'

I think that there is much force in Lord Wright's criticism in *Denny, Mott & Dickson, Ltd v James B. Fraser & Co, Ltd*:

'The parties did not anticipate fully and completely, if at all, or provide for what actually happened. It is not possible to my mind to say that, if they had thought of it, they would have said, "Well, if that happens, all is over between us." On the contrary, they would almost certainly on the one side or the other have sought to introduce reservations or qualifications or compensations.'

It appears to me that frustration depends, at least in most cases, not on adding any implied term but on the true construction of the terms which are, in the contract, read in light of the nature of the contract and of the relevant surrounding circumstances when the contract was made. . . .

Lord Radcliffe. . . . . Before I refer to the facts, I must say briefly what I understand to be the legal principle of frustration. It is not always expressed in the same way, but I think that the points which are relevant to the decision of this case are really beyond dispute. The theory of frustration belongs to the law of contract and it is represented by a rule which the courts will apply in certain limited circumstances for the purpose of deciding that contractual obligations, ex facie binding, are no longer enforceable against the parties. The description of the circumstances that justify the application of the rule and, consequently, the decision whether, in a particular case, those circumstances exist are, I think, necessarily questions of law. It has often been pointed out that the descriptions vary from one case of high authority to another. Even as long ago as 1918, Lord Sumner was able to offer an anthology of different tests directed to the factor of delay alone, and delay, though itself a frequent cause of the principle of frustration being invoked, is only one instance of the kind of circumstance to which the law attends (see *Bank Line, Ltd v A. Capel & Co*). A full current anthology would need to be longer yet. But the variety of description is not of any importance, so long as it is recognised that each is only a description and that all are intended to express the same general idea. I do not think that there has been a better expression of that idea than the one offered by Earl Loreburn in *F A Tamplin SS Co, Ltd v Anglo-Mexican Petroleum Products Co, Ltd*. It is shorter to quote than to try to paraphrase it:

> ' . . . a court can and ought to examine the contract and the circumstances in which it was made, not of course to vary, but only to explain it, in order to see whether or not from the nature of it the parties must have made their bargain on the footing that a particular thing or state of things would continue to exist. And if they must have done so, then a term to that effect will be implied, though it be not expressed in the contract . . . no court has an absolving power, but it can infer from the nature of the contract and the surrounding circumstances that a condition which is not expressed was a foundation on which the parties contracted.'

So expressed, the principle of frustration, the origin of which seems to lie in the development of commercial law, is seen to be a branch of a wider principle which forms part of the English law of contract as a whole. But, in my opinion, full weight ought to be given to the requirement that the parties 'must have made' their bargain on the particular footing. Frustration is not to be lightly invoked as the dissolvent of a contract.

Lord Loreburn ascribes the dissolution to an implied term of the contract that was actually made. This approach is in line with the tendency of English courts to refer all the consequences of a contract to the will of those who made it. But there is something of a logical difficulty in seeing how the parties could even impliedly have provided for something which, ex hypothesi, they neither expected nor foresaw; and the ascription of frustration to an implied term of the contract has been criticised as obscuring the true action of the court which consists in applying an objective rule of the law of contract to the contractual obligations that the parties have imposed on themselves. So long as each theory produces the same result as the other, as normally it does, it matters little which theory is avowed (see *British Movietonews, Ltd v London & District Cinemas, Ltd* per Viscount Simon). But it may still be of some importance to recall that, if the matter is to be approached by way of implied term, the solution of any particular case is not to be found by inquiring what the parties themselves would have agreed on had they been, as they were not, forewarned. It is not merely that no one can answer that hypothetical question; it is also that the decision must be given 'irrespective of the individuals concerned, their temperaments and failings, their interest and circumstances' (*Hirji Mulji v Cheong Yue SS Co*). The legal effect of frustration 'does not depend on their intention or their opinions, or even knowledge, as to the event'. On the contrary, it seems that, when the event occurs, the

> 'meaning of the contract must be taken to be, not what the parties did intend (for they had neither thought nor intention regarding it), but that which the parties, as fair and reasonable men, would presumably have agreed upon if, having such possibility in view, they had made express provision as to their several rights and liabilities in the event of its occurrence'

(*Dahl v Nelson, Donkin & Co*, per Lord Watson).

By this time, it might seem that the parties themselves have become so far disembodied spirits that their actual persons should be allowed to rest in peace. In their place there rises the figure of the fair and reasonable man. And the spokesman of the fair and reasonable man, who represents after all no more than the anthropomorphic conception of justice, is, and must be, the court itself. So, perhaps, it would be simpler to say at the outset that frustration occurs whenever the law recognises that, without default of either party, a contractual obligation has become incapable of being performed because the circumstances in which performance is called for would render it a thing radically different from that which was undertaken by the contract. Non haec in foedera veni. It was not this that I promised to do. There is, however, no uncertainty as to the materials on which the court must proceed.

> 'The data for decision are, on the one hand, the terms and construction of the contract, read in the light of the surrounding circumstances, and, on the other hand, the events which have occurred.'

(*Denny, Mott & Dickson Ltd v James B Fraser & Co Ltd*, per Lord Wright).

In the nature of things there is often no room for any elaborate inquiry. The court must act on a general impression of what its rule requires. It is for that reason that special importance is necessarily attached to the occurrence of any unexpected event that, as it were, changes the face of things. But, even so, it is not hardship or inconvenience or material loss itself which calls the principle of frustration into play. There must be as well such a change in the significance of the obligation that the thing undertaken would, if performed, be a different thing from that contracted for.

I am bound to say that, if this is the law, the appellants' case seems to be a long way from a case of frustration. . . .

NOTES

1. Isn't Radcliffe's objection to the implied term theory almost equally applicable to any of the 'usual' implied terms? Doesn't Lord Watson's formulation of the implied term test come closest to what is going on? (Perhaps 'technique' would be a more appropriate word than theory: see Atiyah, *Essays on Contract* (1986), p 273.)

2. Why does the doctrine require such a fundamental change of circumstances before the contract is discharged? Why not permit discharge whenever one party satisfies the court that he would never have agreed to the contract on these terms had he foreseen the risk? (Compare force majeure clauses, above, p 333.) Should it be sufficient for the contract to be frustrated that businessmen in the relevant trade would consider the contract to be at an end in the circumstances which have occurred? Although the rule is that a contract will only be frustrated if events have rendered performance fundamentally different, it is recognised that the decision may follow closely

   > . . . from a commercial arbitrator's findings as to mercantile usage and the understanding of mercantile men about the significance of the commercial differences between what was promised and what in the changed circumstances would now fall to be performed.

   (Lord Diplock in *Pioneer Shipping Ltd v BTP Tioxide Ltd, The Nema* [1981] 2 All ER 1030 at 1036.) In that case arbitrators had found that a charter was frustrated when strikes at the loading port would probably prevent more than three out of the seven voyages originally contemplated. The House of Lords refused to upset this finding, saying that this should be done only if the arbitrator had not applied the right legal test or had reached a conclusion no reasonable person could have reached (ibid, p 1047).

3. If a contract is frustrated, the discharge is automatic, rather than depending on a choice by one of the parties: *Hirji Mulji v Cheong Yue SS Co Ltd* [1926] AC 497. The parties may think it is still in force when it has been frustrated, and vice versa. When it is clear what the effect of the supervening event is, this may not cause too much uncertainty: one may take the line that they should have realized. But what if the effect of the event is hard to gauge, for instance if a strike or the illness of one of the parties is preventing performance, but the parties cannot tell how long it will last? In *The Nema* at p 1047 Lord Roskill said:

   > . . . where the effect of [the] event is to cause delay in the performance of contractual obligations, it is often necessary to wait on events in order to see whether the delay already suffered and the prospects of further delay from that cause will make the ultimate performance of the relevant contractual obligations 'radically different', to borrow Lord Radcliffe's phrase, from that which was undertaken by the contract.

As frustration is automatic, it would seem that the parties' conduct should not be taken into account in determining the date of frustration, if any. In the context of employment contracts this rule does not sit easily. Frequently when an employee falls ill it is not clear how long the illness will be nor what permanent effects it will have and often the parties leave matters unresolved. As Phillips J said in *Hart v AR Marshall & Sons (Bulwell) Ltd* [1978] 2 All ER 413:

> . . . if the employer has not dismissed the employee on the ground that he cannot reasonably be expected to wait any longer for his return, why should the court declare that the contract of employment has terminated by operation of law?
>
> It seems to us that considerable importance attaches to the failure of an employer in such circumstances to dismiss the employee. We have wondered whether in truth the doctrine of frustration has anything much to do with short-term periodic contracts of employment, for there is no doubt that the concept is alien to both employers and employees, and is often not matched by the reality of the situation as they see it. The automatic ending of a contract by operation of law in a case where the subject-matter is destroyed is easily understood and matches experience. So is the case where a sudden calamity overtakes an employee which there and then renders any future service by him impossible. But in the case of an illness of uncertain duration the situation is quite different and neither employer nor employee thinks in terms approaching those underlying the concept of frustration.
>
> However, experience shows that in a surprisingly large area of industry formal contracts of employment, and standard terms and conditions, still do not exist or if they do, make no provision for the rights of the parties during a prolonged period of illness of an employee. Very often, as in the present case, no wages are paid during sickness nor are any other formal arrangements made. In such cases the employee is in a sort of limbo. It seems that from the employer's point of view there is a reluctance to dismiss an employee when he is away sick because to do so may seem harsh. From the employee's point of view it may seem preferable not to be dismissed, albeit that no wages are being paid, because there is a hope that one day he will be able to return to work, though not necessarily to the same job. Experience in such cases shows that the parties very often drift along in this situation for long periods of time during which the employee has ceased to do any work, or to be able to do any work, but has not been formally dismissed. The legal position seems to be that the employee is still employed although he is not in receipt of wages, and that his employment continues until he is dismissed or the contract is frustrated and comes to an end by operation of law. In these circumstances, while we think it right to attach considerable importance in a case of this kind to the failure by the employer to dismiss the employee, it is, we think, impossible to say that unless the employee is dismissed the contract must always be taken to continue. To do so would be tantamount to saying that frustration cannot occur in the case of short-term periodic contracts of employment. . . .
>
> In our judgment it comes to this. The failure of the employer to dismiss the employee is a factor, and an important factor, to take into account when considering whether the contract of employment has been frustrated. But it is not conclusive.

(b) Least cost avoider

Even if there is a radical change the contract is not necessarily discharged.

Maritime National Fish Ltd v Ocean Trawlers Ltd [1935] AC 524, Privy Council

By s 69a of the Canadian Fisheries Act it was a punishable offence to leave any port in Canada with intent to fish with a vessel that used an otter trawl, except under licence from the Minster. The appellants were charterers of the *St C*, a steam trawler belonging to the respondents, which was fitted with, and could only operate as a trawler with, an otter trawl. It was expressly agreed that the trawler should be employed in the fishing industry only. The charter-party was dated Oct 23, 1928, and was to continue from year to year. It was renewed on Oct 25, 1932, for one year. On March 11, 1933, the appellants applied to the Minister of Fisheries for licenses for the five trawlers they were operating. The Minister in his reply stated that only three licenses would be granted, and he requested the appellants to state for which of the five trawlers they desired to have licenses. The appellants gave the names of three trawlers other than the *St C* and licenses were issued for those three trawlers. The appellants thereupon claimed that the charter-party had thereby been frustrated and that they were no longer bound by it. In an action brought by the respondents for hire due under the charter, the appellants pleaded that the contract had become impossible of performance, and that they were wholly discharged from it.

The opinion of the Privy Council (Lords Atkin, Tomlin, Macmillan and Wright) was delivered by Lord Wright:]

In a case such as the present it may be questioned whether the Court should imply a condition resolutive of the contract (which is what is involved in frustration) when the parties might have inserted an express condition to that effect but did not do so, though the possibility that things might happen as they did, was present in their minds when they made the contract.

This was one of the grounds on which the judges of the Supreme Court were prepared to decide this case. Their Lordships did not indicate any dissent from the reasoning of the Supreme Court on this point, but they did not consider it necessary to hear a full argument, or to express any final opinion about it, because in their judgment the case could be properly decided on the simple conclusion that it was the act and election of the appellants which prevented the *St Cuthbert* from being licensed for fishing with an otter trawl. It is clear that the appellants were free to select any three of the five trawlers they were operating and could, had they willed, have selected the *St Cuthbert* as one, in which event a licence would have been granted to her. It is immaterial to speculate why they preferred to put forward for licences the three trawlers which they actually selected. Nor is it material, as between the appellants and the respondents, that the appellants were operating other trawlers to three of which they gave the preference. What matters is that they could have got a licence for the *St Cuthbert* if they had so minded. If the case be figured as one in which the *St Cuthbert* was removed from the category of privileged trawlers, it was by the appellants' hand that she was so removed, because it was their hand that guided the hand of the Minister in placing the licences where he did and thereby excluding the *St Cuthbert*. The essence of 'frustration' is that it should not be due to the act or election of the party. There does not appear to be any authority which has been decided directly on this point. There is, however, a reference to the question in the speech of Lord Sumner in *Bank Line, Ltd v Arthur Capel & Co*. What he says is: 'One matter I mention only to get rid of it. When the shipowners were first applied to by the Admiralty for a ship they named three, of which the *Quitto* was one and intimated that she was the one they preferred to give up. I think it is now well settled that the principle of frustration of an adventure assumes that the frustration arises without blame or fault on either side. Reliance cannot be placed on a self-induced frustration; indeed, such conduct might give the other party the option to treat the contract as repudiated. Nothing, however, was made of this in the courts below, and I will not now pursue it.' . . . their Lordships are of opinion that the loss of the *St Cuthbert's* licence can correctly be described, quoad the appellants, as 'a self induced frustration'.

NOTES

1. The appellants nominated for licences ships they owned themselves. What would have been the outcome if the five ships they operated had all been chartered to them, so that the only choice was which of the chartered ships should go without licences? See *Lauritzen AS v Wijsmuller BV, The Super Servant Two* [1990] 1 Lloyd's Rep 1.
2. The respondents' act was deliberate. Presumably a contract would equally not be frustrated if performance was prevented by the negligence of one of the parties—at least in some cases. Thus it seems likely that the defendants in *Taylor v Caldwell* would have been liable had the fire been their fault (see the end of the fourth paragraph of Blackburn's judgment, above, p 348); but will any act of negligence, even completely unconnected to the contract, prevent a party from relying on frustration? Would a concert pianist be allowed to plead frustration if she could not play because of injuries received in a road accident for which she was to blame?

3. If an event occurs which would normally frustrate the contract, but one party alleges that it was caused by the other's fault so that the doctrine does not apply, it is for the party alleging fault to prove it: *Joseph Constantine SS Line Ltd v Imperial Smelting Corpn Ltd* [1942] AC 154.

Blackburn Bobbin Company Ltd v TW Allen & Sons Ltd [1918] 2 KB 467, Court of Appeal

Pickford LJ. This is an appeal from a decision of McCardie J, and the point raised is whether an implication is to be read into the contract the performance of which has been interfered with or prevented by matters arising out of the war. The contract, which contained no exceptions, was for the sale by the defendants to the plaintiffs of 70 standards of Finland birch timber at the price of 10*l* 15*s* per standard free on rail at Hull. Before the war it was the regular practice to load the timber on vessels at ports in Finland for direct sea carriage to English ports, and not to send it by rail across Scandinavia and ship it from a Scandinavian port to England. When war broke out the Germans declared timber to be contraband, but, even before that declaration, sailings from Finnish ports had entirely ceased, and therefore the ordinary and normal method of supplying Finland timber came to an end. I will assume that it was not possible, at first at any rate, to get Finland birch timber to England at all, although it is true that in 1916 a certain amount was sent across Scandinavia and shipped from ports there. In August, 1914, and the following months some correspondence took place between the plaintiffs and the defendants as to the timber, the former asking for supplies, and the defendants taking up the position that all pre-war contracts had been cancelled by the war.

The defendants contend that the contract was at an end because it was in the contemplation of both parties that the defendants should be able to supply the timber according to the ordinary method of supplying it in the trade, and that when that became impossible both parties were discharged from their obligations.

. . . In my opinion McCardie J was right in saying that the principle of [frustration] did not apply to discharge the defendants in this case. He has found that the plaintiffs were unaware at the time of the contract of the circumstance that the timber from Finland was shipped direct from a Finnish port to Hull, and that they did not know whether the transport was or was not partly by rail across Scandinavia, nor did they know that timber merchants in this country did not hold stocks of Finnish birch. I accept the finding that in fact the method of dispatching this timber was not known to the plaintiffs. But there remains the question, Must they be deemed to have contracted on the basis of the continuance of that method although they did not in fact know of it? I see no reason for saying so. Why should a purchaser of goods, not specific goods, be deemed to concern himself with the way in which the seller is going to fulfil his contract by providing the goods he has agreed to sell? The sellers in this case agreed to deliver the timber free on rail at Hull, and it was no concern of the buyers as to how the sellers intended to get the timber there. I can see no reason for saying—and to free the defendants from liability this would have to be said—that the continuance of the normal mode of shipping the timber from Finland was a matter which both parties contemplated as necessary for the fulfilment of the contract. To dissolve the contract the matter relied on must be something which both parties had in their minds when then entered into the contract, such for instance as the existence of the music hall in *Taylor v Caldwell*, or the continuance of the vessel in readiness to perform the contract, as in *Jackson v Union Marine Insurance Co*. Here there is nothing to show that the plaintiffs contemplated, and there is no reason why they should be deemed to have contemplated, that the sellers should continue to have the ordinary facilities for dispatching the timber from Finland. As I have said, that was a matter which to the plaintiffs was wholly immaterial. It was not a matter forming the basis of the contract they entered into. . . . For the reasons I have given the defendants have failed on the facts to make out their case that the contract was dissolved. The appeal will be dismissed. . . .

[Warrington and Bankes LJJ delivered concurring judgments.]

Appeal dismissed.

NOTES

1. Suppose the contract had been for 10,000 standards of Finnish birch *ex Peerless* from Helsinki, and the Peerless had been trapped in Helsinki by the enemy ships. Would the result have been different?
2. In *Davis Contractors Ltd v Fareham UDC* which party was the least cost avoider?

(c) Best insurer

It is less easy to spot cases in which the question of whether or not the contract should be frustrated has been decided on the grounds of which party was the better insurer. In fact, however, some common instances of frustration are at least consistent with the notion of 'best insurer'. Firstly, as Blackburn J pointed out in *Taylor v Caldwell*, it is well established that a contract of employment is frustrated by the death of the employee, at least where the death is unconnected to the employment. Yet occasionally the employer may suffer considerable loss if a key employee dies. Why should the employee's estate not be liable for this loss? Conversely, why should the employer not be liable to continue paying the employee's salary at least for the period of notice it would normally be required to give to terminate the employment?

Secondly, in *Taylor v Caldwell* itself, who was in the better position to insure against (a) the licensor's loss of rent; (b) the waste of advertising expenditure by the licensee?

Similar notions of who should bear the risk also appear at the end of the case that is thought to typify the rule of 'absolute contract' generally applied before *Taylor v Caldwell* was decided:

Paradine v Jane (1647) [1558–1774] All ER Rep 172, Aleyn 26, 82 ER 897, King's Bench

. . . Action of debt for rent due for lands let to the defendant, Jane. The plaintiff declared upon a lease rendering rent quarterly, and for rent in arrears for three years ending Lady Day, 1646.

The defendant pleased that a German prince, Prince Rupert, an alien born, enemy to the King and kingdom, had invaded the realm with an army of men, and with the same force had entered upon the lands let by the plaintiff to the defendant and had expelled him therefrom, and held him out of possession from July, 1642, until Lady Day, 1646, whereby he could not take the profits. To this plea the plaintiff demurred.

Per curiam: The plea was resolved insufficient on the following grounds: first, because the defendant had not answered to one quarter's rent; secondly, he had not averred that the army were aliens, which shall not be intended, and then he has his remedy against them; and Bacon J, cited YB 33 Hen 6, f, fo 1, pl 3, where the gaoler in bar of an escape pleaded that alien enemies broke [into] the prison, etc, and an exception was taken to it, for that he ought to show of what country they were, ie, Scots.

Thirdly, it was resolved that the matter of the plea was insufficient, for although the whole army had been alien enemies, yet the defendant ought to pay the rent. This difference was taken, that where the law creates a duty or charge, and the party is disabled from performing it without any default in him, and has no remedy over, there the law will excuse him. As in the case of waste, if a house be destroyed by tempest or by enemies, the lessee is excused.

. . . But when the party by his own contract creates a duty or charge upon himself he is bound to make it good, if he may, notwithstanding any accident by inevitable necessity because he might have provided against it by his contract. Therefore, if the lessee covenants to repair a house, although it is burnt by lightning or thrown down by enemies yet he ought to repair it: *Anon* YB 40 Edw 3, fo 6.

The rent is a duty created by the parties upon the reservation, and had there been a covenant to pay it there would have been no question but the lessee must have made it good, notwithstanding the interruption by enemies, for the law would not protect him beyond his own agreement, no more than in the case of reparations. This reservation, then, being a covenant in law and whereupon an action of covenant has been maintained (as Rolle J, has said) it is all one as if there had been an actual covenant. Another reason was added, that as the lessee is to have the advantage of casual profits, so he must run the hazard of casual losses and not lay the whole burden of them upon his lessor. *Richards le Taverner's Case* was cited for this purpose, that though the land be surrounded or gained by the sea or made barren by wildfire, yet the lessor shall have his whole rent.

Judgment for plaintiff.

NOTES

1. A useful discussion of *Paradine v Jane* will be found in Corbin, *Contracts*, Vol 7, ss 1320, 1322.
2. For many years it was unclear whether the doctrine of frustration could ever apply to a lease, the argument being that the grant of the lease conveyed an estate in land to the lessee, so that the lessee got what he had bargained for even if subsequent events prevented him enjoying the property. In *National Carriers Ltd v Panalpina (Northern) Ltd* [1981] AC 675 the House of Lords rejected that view, saying that in extreme cases there could be frustration of a lease if the joint purpose of the parties was that the lessee should have the use of the property and this had become impossible. Lord Wilberforce said (at pp 694–695):

   . . . if the argument is to have any reality, it must be possible to say that frustration of leases cannot occur because in any event the tenant will have that which he bargained for, namely, the leasehold estate. Certainly this may be so in many cases, let us say most cases. . . . But there may also be cases where this is not so. A man may desire possession and use of land or buildings for, and only for, some purpose in view and mutually contemplated. Why is it an answer, when he claims that this purpose is 'frustrated' to say that he has an estate if that estate is unusable and unsaleable? In such a case the lease, or the conferring of an estate, is a subsidiary means to an end, not an aim or end of itself.

   But both he and the other Lords stressed that frustration of a lease would be very rare. As Lord Hailsham put it (at pp 688 and 692):

   The point, though one of principle, is a narrow one. It is the difference immortalised in HMS Pinafore between 'never' and 'hardly ever'. . .
   In the result, I come down on the side of the 'hardly ever' school of thought. No doubt the circumstances in which the doctrine can apply to leases are, to quote Viscount Simon LC in the *Cricklewood* case, 'exceedingly rare'. Lord Wright appears to have thought the same, whilst adhering to the view that there are cases in which frustration can apply. But, as he said in the same passage: 'The doctrine of frustration is modern and flexible and is not subject to being constricted by an arbitrary formula.' To this school of thought I respectfully adhere. Like Lord Wright, I am struck by the fact that there appears to be no reported English case where a lease has ever been held to have been frustrated. I hope this fact will act as a suitable deterrent to the litigious, eager to make legal history by being first in this field. But I am comforted by the reflexion of the authority referred to in the Compleat Angler (pt i, ch 5) on the subject of strawberries: 'Doubtless God could have made a better berry, but doubtless God never did.' I only append to this observation of nature the comment that it does not follow from these premises that He never will, and, if it does not follow, an assumption that He never will becomes exceedingly rash.

   On the facts—because of a street closure order, the leased warehouse had been unuseable for about eighteen months out of four and a half years remaining under the lease—there was no question of the lease being frustrated.

(d) Frustration of purpose

It is very rare for a contract to be held to have been frustrated by an event which leaves it possible to perform, but which makes it much more burdensome to one party. Thus increased costs in performing did not excuse the contractors in *Davis Contractors Ltd v Fareham UDC* (above, p 350); and in *Tsakiroglou & Co Ltd v Noblee Thorl GmbH* [1962] AC 93 it was held that a contract to sell groundnuts cif Hamburg was not frustrated by the blockage of the Suez Canal, even though the nuts were to be loaded at Port Sudan and would normally have been carried through the Canal. The seller could have performed by shipping them via the Cape of Good Hope, even though that would have been more expensive and taken longer. Lord Reid pointed out that it was not a case where the longer voyage would damage the goods, or one where the buyers would suffer extraordinary losses as a result of the goods arriving later than anticipated. Similarly, it is rare for the contract to be frustrated by some event which makes the transaction pointless as far as one party is concerned.

Krell v Henry [1900–03] All ER Rep 20, Court of Appeal

. . . The plaintiff, Paul Krell, sued the defendant, C. S. Henry, to recover £50, being the balance of a sum of £75, at which price the defendant had agreed to hire from the plaintiff some rooms at 56A, Pall Mall, London, of which the plaintiff was tenant, on June 26 and 27, 1902, to view the processions which it had been intended to hold on those days in connection with the coronation of His Majesty King Edward VII. The defendant denied that he was liable to pay the £50, and counterclaimed for the return of £25 which he had paid as a deposit, on the ground that, the processions not having taken place owing to the illness of the King, there had been a total failure of consideration for the contract entered into by him. On August 11, 1902, the action came on for trial before Darling J, sitting without a jury, when the learned judge gave judgment for the defendant on both claim and counterclaim. The plaintiff appealed.

Vaughan Williams LJ read the following judgment. The real question in this case is the extent of the application in English law of the principle of the Roman law which has been adopted and acted on in many English decisions, and notably in *Taylor v Caldwell*.
. . . English law applies the principle not only to cases where the performance of the contract becomes impossible by the cessation of existence of the thing which is the subject-matter of the contract, but also to cases where the event which renders the contract incapable of performance is the cessation or non-existence of an express condition or state of things, going to the root of the contract, and essential to its performance. It is said, on the one side, that the specified thing, state of things, or condition the continued existence of which is necessary for the fulfilment of the contract, so that the parties entering into the contract must have contemplated the continued existence of that thing, condition, or state of things as the foundation of what was to be done under the contract, is limited to things which are either the subject-matter of the contract, or a condition or state of things, present or anticipated, which are expressly mentioned in the contract. But, on the other side, it is said that the condition or state of things clearly appears by extrinsic evidence to have been assumed by the parties to be the foundation or basis of the contract and the event which causes the impossibility is of such a character that it cannot reasonably be supposed to have been in the contemplation of the contracting parties when the contract was made. In such a case the contracting parties will not be held bound by general words which, though large enough to include, were not used with reference to a possibility of a particular event rendering performance of the contract impossible.
I do not think that the principle of the civil law as introduced into the English law is limited to cases in which the event causing the impossibility of performance is the destruction or non-existence of some thing which is the subject-matter of the contract or of some condition or state

of things expressly specified as a condition of it. I think that you first have to ascertain, not necessarily from the terms of the contract, but if necessary from necessary inferences, drawn from surrounding circumstances recognised by both contracting parties, what is the substance of the contract, and then to ask the question whether that substantial contract needs for its foundation the assumption of the existence of a particular state of things. If it does, this will limit the operation of the general words, and in such case if the contract becomes impossible of performance by reason of the non-existence of the state of things assumed by both contracting parties, as the foundation of the contract, there will be no breach of the contract thus limited.

What are the facts of the present case? The contract is contained in two letters of June 20, 1902, which passed between the defendant and the plaintiff's agent, Mr Cecil Bisgood. These letters do not mention the coronation, but speak merely of the taking of Mr Krell's chambers, or, rather, of the use of them, in the daytime of June 26 and 27, 1902, for the sum of £75, £25 then paid, balance £50 to be paid on the 24th. But the affidavits, which by agreement between the parties are to be taken as stating the facts of the case, show that the plaintiff exhibited on his premises, third floor, 56A, Pall Mall, an announcement to the effect that windows to view the royal coronation processions were to be let, and that the defendant was induced by that announcement to apply to the housekeeper on the premises, who said that the owner was willing to let the suite of rooms for the purpose of seeing the royal procession for both days, but not nights, of June 26 and 27. In my judgment, the use of the rooms was let and taken for the purpose of seeing the royal processions. It was not a demise of the rooms or even an agreement to let and take the rooms. It was a licence to use rooms for a particular purpose and none other. And in my judgment the taking place of those processions on the days proclaimed along the proclaimed route, which passed 56A, Pall Mall, was regarded by both contracting parties as the foundation of the contract. I think that it cannot reasonably be supposed to have been in the contemplation of the contracting parties, when the contract was made, that the coronation would not be held on the proclaimed days, or the processions not take place on those days along the proclaimed route; and I think that the words imposing on the defendant the obligation to accept and pay for the use of the rooms for the named days, although general and unconditional, were not used with reference to the possibility of the particular contingency which afterwards occurred.

It was suggested in the course of the argument that if the occurrence, on the proclaimed days, of the coronation and the processions in this case were the foundation of the contract, and if the general words are thereby limited or qualified, so that in the event of the non-occurrence of the coronation and processions along the proclaimed route they would discharge both parties from further performance of the contract, it would follow that if a cabman was engaged to take someone to Epsom on Derby-day at a suitable enhanced price for such a journey, both parties to the contract would be discharged in the contingency of the race at Epsom for some reason becoming impossible, but I do not think this follows, for I do not think that in the cab case the happening of the race would be the foundation of the contract. No doubt the purpose of the engager was to go to see the Derby, and that the price was proportionately high; but the cab had no special qualifications for the purpose which led to the selection of the cab for this particular occasion. Any other cab would have done as well. Moreover, I think that, under the cab contract, the hirer, even if the race went off, could have said: 'Drive me to Epsom, I will pay you the agreed sum, you have nothing to do with the purpose for which I hired the cab'—and that if the cabman refused he would have been guilty of a breach of contract, there being nothing to qualify his promise to drive the hirer to Epsom on a particular day, whereas, in the case of the coronation, there is not merely the purpose of the hirer to see the coronation processions, but it is the coronation procession and the relative position of the rooms which is the basis of the contract as much for the lessor as the hirer; and I think that if the King, before the coronation days and after the contract had died, the hirer could not have insisted on having the rooms on the days named. It could not in the cab case be reasonably said that seeing the Derby race was the foundation of the contract, as viewing the processions was of the licence in this case, whereas, in the present case, where the rooms were offered and taken, by reason of their peculiar suitability from the position of the rooms for a view of the coronation processions, surely the view of the coronation processions was the foundation of the contract, which is a very different thing from the purpose of the man who engaged the cab—viz, to see the race—being held to be the foundation of the contract.

Each case must be judged by its own circumstances. In each case one must ask oneself, first: What having regard to all the circumstances, was the foundation of the contract?; secondly: Was the performance of the contract prevented?; and thirdly: Was the event which prevented the performance of the contract of such a character that it cannot reasonably be said to have been in the contemplation of the parties at the date of the contract? I think both parties are discharged from further performance of the contract. I think that the coronation processions were the foundation of this contract, and that the non-happening of them prevented the performance of the contract; and, secondly, I think that the non-happening of the processions, to use the words of Sir James Hannen in *Baily v De Crespigny*, was an event

'of such a character that it cannot reasonably be supposed to have been in the contemplation of the contracting parties when the contract was made, and that they are not to be held bound by general words which, though large enough to include, were not used with reference to the possibility of the particular contingency which afterwards happened'.

The test seems to be, whether the event which causes the impossibility was or might have been anticipated and guarded against. It seems difficult to say, in a case where both parties anticipate the happening of an event, which anticipation is the foundation of the contract, that either party must be taken to have anticipated, and ought to have guarded against, the event which prevented the performance of the contract. In both *Jackson v Union Marine Insurance Co* and *Nickoll and Knight v Ashton, Edridge & Co* the parties might have anticipated as a possibility that perils of the sea might delay the ship and frustrate the commercial venture, in the former case the carriage of the goods to effect which the charter-party was entered into, and in the latter case the sale of the goods which were to be shipped on the steamship which was delayed. But the court held in the former case that the basis of the contract was that the ship would arrive in time to carry out the contemplated commercial venture, and in the latter that the steamship would arrive in time for the loading of the goods the subject of the sale.

I wish to observe that cases of this sort are very different from cases where a contract or warranty or representation is implied, such as was implied in *The Moorcock*, and refused to be implied in *Hamlyn & Co v Wood & Co*. But *The Moorcock* is of importance in the present case as showing that, whatever is the suggested implication—be it condition, as in this case, or warranty or representation—one must, in judging whether the implication ought to be made, look not only at the words of the contract, but also at the surrounding facts and the knowledge of the parties of those facts. There seems to me to be ample authority for this proposition. Thus, in *Jackson v Union Marine Insurance Co* in the Common Pleas, the question whether the object of the voyage had been frustrated by the delay of the ship was left as a question of fact to the jury, although there was nothing in the charterparty defining the time within which the charterers were to supply the cargo of iron rails for San Francisco, and nothing on the face of the charterparty to indicate the importance of time in the venture. That was a case in which, as Bramwell, B, points out in his judgment, *Taylor v Caldwell* was a strong authority to support the conclusion arrived at—that not arriving in time for the voyage contemplated, but at such time that it frustrated the commercial venture, was not only a breach of the contract, but discharged the charterer, though he had such an excuse that no action would lie.

. . . I myself am clearly of opinion that in this case, where we have to ask ourselves whether the object of the contract was frustrated by the non-happening of the coronation and its processions on the days proclaimed, parol evidence is admissible to show that the subject of the contract was seats to view the coronation processions, and was so to the knowledge of both parties.

When once this is established, I see no difficulty whatever in the case. It is not essential to the application of the principle of *Taylor v Caldwell* that the direct subject of the contract should perish or fail to be in existence at the date of performance of the contract. It is sufficient if a state of things or condition expressed in the contract and essential to its performance perishes or fails to be in existence at that time. In the present case the condition which fails and prevents the achievement of that which was, in the contemplation of both parties, the foundation of the contract, is not expressly mentioned either as a condition of the contract or the purpose of it, but I think for the reasons which I have given that the principle of *Taylor v Caldwell* ought to be applied. This disposes of the plaintiff's claim for £50 unpaid balance of the price agreed to be paid for the use of the rooms. The defendant at one time set up a cross-claim for the return of the £25 he paid at the date of the contract. As that claim is now withdrawn it is unnecessary to say anything about it. I have only to add that the facts of this case do not bring it within the principle laid down in *Stubbs v Holywell Rail. Co*, that in the case of contracts falling directly within the rule of *Taylor v Caldwell* the subsequent impossibility does not affect rights already acquired, because the defendant had the whole of June 24 to pay the balance, and the public announcement that the coronation and processions would not take place on the proclaimed days was made early on the morning of the 24th, and no cause of action could accrue till the end of that day. I think this appeal ought to be dismissed.

[Romer and Stirling LJJ concurred.]

Appeal dismissed.

Herne Bay Steam Boat Co v Hutton [1900–03] All ER Rep 627, Court of Appeal

The defendant had chartered the steamboat *Cynthia* from the plaintiffs for 28 and 29 June 1902, 'to take out a party . . . for the purpose of viewing the naval review and for a day's cruise around the fleet'. The naval review was cancelled because of the King's illness, but the fleet remained anchored at Spithead. The defendant, who had paid £50 in advance, did not use the *Cynthia*, and the plaintiffs sued for the balance of the price. Grantham J held that they could not recover.

Vaughan Williams LJ. . . . The defendant when hiring this boat had the object in view of taking people to see the Naval Review, and on the next day of taking them round the fleet and also round the Isle of Wight. But it does not seem to me that, because those purposes of the defendant became impossible, it is a legitimate inference that the happening of the Naval Review was contemplated by both parties as the foundation of the contract, so as to bring the case within the doctrine of *Taylor v Caldwell*. On the contrary, when the contract is properly considered, I think that the purposes of the defendant, whether of going to the review or going round the fleet or the Isle of Wight with a party of paying guests, do not make those purposes the foundation of the contract within the meaning of *Taylor v Caldwell*.

Having expressed this view, I do not know that there is any advantage to be gained by in any way defining what are the circumstances which might or might not constitute the happening of a particular contingency the foundation of the contract. I will only say I see nothing to differentiate this contract from a contract by which some person engaged a cab to take him on each of three days to Epsom to see the race, and for some reason, such as the spread of an infectious disease or an anticipation of a riot, the races are prohibited. In such a case it could not be said that he would be relieved of his bargain. So in the present case it is sufficient to say that the happening of the Naval Review was not the foundation of this contract.

Romer LJ. . . . It is really a contract for hiring the ship by the defendant for a certain voyage, though the object of the hirer is stated—viz., to see the Naval Review and the fleet. But that object was one with which the defendant as hirer of the ship was alone concerned, and not the plaintiffs, the owners. This contract cannot, in my opinion, be distinguished from many common cases of the hiring of vessels in which the object of the hiring is stated; very often the contract states the details of the voyage and the nature and details of the cargo to be carried. If the voyage is a pleasure trip it might also state the object in view, which is a matter which concerns the passengers, but this statement of the objects of the hirer would not, in my opinion, make the owner of the ship as much concerned with these objects as the hirer himself. The shipowner would say: 'I am concerned with the ship only as a passenger or cargo carrying machine. It is for the hirer to concern himself with the objects'. In the present case it is suggested that the provision that the plaintiffs were to have the right of having ten persons on board besides the crew changed the nature of the hiring; but there is nothing in that provision to prevent the court treating the transaction as a hiring of the vessel by the defendant. It does not make it in any sense a joint speculation. It only amounts to this, that the defendant, being the hirer, gives the owners a licence to put ten men on board. This view of the general effect of the contract is borne out by this consideration. The ship itself had nothing to do with the review or the fleet. It was only a carrier of passengers to see it, and many other ships would have done just as well. It is similar to the hiring of a cab or other vehicle, on which, though the object of the hirer was stated, that statement would not make the object any less a matter for the hirer alone, and would not affect the person who was letting the vehicle for hire. There was not here, by reason of the review not taking place, a total failure of the consideration, nor anything like a total destruction of the subject-matter of the contract. Nor can I on this contract imply any condition which would relieve the defendant from liability to carry out the contract. Conditions are only implied to carry out the presumed intentions of the parties, and I cannot find any such presumed intention here. It follows that in my opinion, so far as the plaintiffs are concerned, the objects of the passengers on this voyage with regard to sightseeing do not form the subject-matter or essence of the contract. . . .

Stirling LJ. . . . It seems to me that the reference in the contract to the review is explained by the object of the voyage, and I am quite unable to treat the reference to the voyage as the foundation of the contract so as to entitle either party to the benefit of the doctrine in *Taylor v Caldwell*. I come to that conclusion more readily as the object of the voyage was not to see the review only, but included a cruise round the fleet. The fleet was there, and the passengers might have been willing to go round it. It seems to me that that was the business of the defendant, whose venture it was. I am therefore unable to agree with the decision of Grantham J, and I think the defendant was not discharged from the performance of the contract. . . .

Appeal allowed.

NOTES

1. These cases may be seen as inconsistent, though they were decided at the same time by the same judges in the Court of Appeal. Certainly the suitability of the particular ship or room does not seem a relevant distinction. In the *Herne Bay* case it was still possible to view the fleet at anchor, but only Stirling LJ makes that point. Does the distinction perhaps lie in what it seems likely the parties would have agreed on had they foreseen the problem? The steamboat company, like the driver of the cab to Epsom, were presumably prepared to carry passengers on any day, but is it likely that Krell would have agreed in advance to suffering a crowd of strangers in his flat if there were no procession? It has to be remembered that if Henry had to take the room 'procession or no procession', he would almost certainly not have been prepared to pay as much for it as he would have been if the contract provided that he need not pay at all in the event of cancellation. It is a reasonable guess that Krell would have preferred the higher payment, given the inconvenience of having to move out. (This explanation rests to some extent on the fact that Krell was a private property owner, whereas the Herne Bay Steam Boat Company was a business. Contrast Brownsword (1985) 129 SJ 860, who argues that the distinction is that Henry was a consumer whereas Hutton, who intended to sell tickets for the trip on the *Cynthia*, was not.)
2. A second possible distinction is this. If the coronation procession were cancelled, it would be very likely that it would be re-arranged (as indeed happened). If the contract in *Krell v Henry* had not been frustrated, Krell would have been able to profit from his flat all over again, while Henry would have to pay twice to see the procession. Making the reasonable assumption that they were equally risk-averse, it seems unlikely that the parties would have chosen such a result had they foreseen the problem. More probably they would have provided what some of the other contracts related to the coronation did, namely that Henry should have the use of the room on the re-arranged date. The court could not solve the problem by implying that into the agreement—it hardly 'goes without saying'—but by holding the contract frustrated it permitted the negotiation of a fresh agreement without leaving Krell enriched at Henry's expense. There was no certainty that the naval review would be re-arranged, however.

Occasionally the change in circumstances may make the contract much *more* profitable to one party and the other may claim frustration in an attempt to capture the profit, eg: *FA Tamplin SS Co Ltd v Anglo-Mexican Petroleum Products Co Ltd* [1916] 2 AC 397, where the owner of a chartered ship unsuccessfully claimed frustration when the vessel was requisitioned for a few months, hoping thereby to receive the compensation.

(e) Foreseen events

If the parties had foreseen an event but did not provide for it, a possible interpretation is that they intended the contract to continue regardless, with the risk lying where it falls. There are many dicta to the effect that the event must be one which could not have been 'anticipated or guarded against' (Vaughan Williams LJ in *Krell v Henry*) if it is to frustrate a contract. On the other hand there are a number of situations where a foreseen event may still frustrate a contract—where the contract becomes illegal because of the outbreak of war, or where an employee dies in service; and it is not clear what the general position is.

Ocean Tramp Tankers Corpn v V O Sovracht, The Eugenia [1964] 1 All ER 161, Court of Appeal

By a charterparty dated 8 September 1956, the *Eugenia*, which was then in Genoa, was let to the charterers 'for a trip out to India via the Black Sea'. Both parties realized at the time of the negotiations that there was a danger of the Suez Canal being closed, but they came to no agreement on that eventuality. On 25 October the *Eugenia*, having loaded, sailed from Odessa. At that time the customary route to India was still via Suez. By the time the vessel reached the vicinity of the canal it had become a 'dangerous' zone, but in breach of contract the charterers failed to take steps to prevent the ship entering Port Said. The ship entered the canal on 31 October, and became trapped when the canal was closed. The charterers claimed that the contract had been frustrated by the closure of the canal.

Lord Denning MR. . . . . The second question is whether the charterparty was frustrated by what took place. The arbitrator has held that it was not. The judge has held that it was. Which is right? One thing that is obvious is that the charterers cannot rely on the fact that the *Eugenia* was trapped in the canal; for that was their own fault. They were in breach of the war clause in entering it. They cannot rely on a self-induced frustration; see *Maritime National Fish, Ltd v Ocean Trawlers, Ltd*. But they seek to rely on the fact that the canal itself was blocked. They assert that, even if the *Eugenia* had never gone into the canal but had stayed outside (in which case she would not have been in breach of the war clause) nevertheless she would still have had to go round by the Cape; and that, they say, brings about a frustration, for it makes the venture fundamentally different from what they contracted for. The judge has accepted this view. . . .

This means that, once again, we have had to consider the authorities on this vexed topic of frustration. But I think that the position is now reasonably clear. It is simply this: If it should happen, in the course of carrying out a contract, that a fundamentally different situation arises for which the parties made no provision—so much so that it would not be just in the new situation to hold them bound to its terms—then the contract is at an end.

It was originally said that the doctrine of frustration was based on an implied term. In short, that the parties, if they had foreseen the new situation, would have said to one another: 'If that happens, of course, it is all over between us'. But the theory of an implied term has now been discarded by everyone, or nearly everyone, for the simple reason that it does not represent the truth. The parties would not have said: 'It is all over between us'. They would have differed about what was to happen. Each would have sought to insert reservations or qualifications of one kind or another. Take this very case. The parties realised that the canal might become impassable. They tried to agree on a clause to provide for the contingency. But they failed to agree. So there is no room for an implied term.

It has frequently been said that the doctrine of frustration only applies when the new situation is 'unforeseen' or 'unexpected' or 'uncontemplated', as if that were an essential feature. But it is not so. It is not so much that it is 'unexpected', but rather that the parties have made no provision for it in their contract. The point about it, however, is this: If the parties did not foresee anything of the kind happening, you can readily infer that they have made no provision for it. Whereas, if they did foresee it, you would expect them to make provision for it. But cases have occurred where the parties have foreseen the danger ahead, and yet made no provision for it in the contract. Such was the case in the Spanish Civil War when a ship was let on charter to the Republican Government. The purpose was to evacuate refugees. The parties foresaw that she might be seized by the Nationalists. But they made no provision for it in their contract. Yet, when she was seized, the contract was frustrated: see *W. J. Tatem, Ltd v Gamboa*. So, here, the parties foresaw that the canal might become impassable. It was the very thing that they feared. But they made no provision for it. So the doctrine may still apply, if it be a proper case for it.

We are thus left with the simple test that a situation must arise which renders performance of the contract 'a thing radically different from that which was undertaken by the contract': see *Davis Contractors, Ltd v Fareham UDC*, per Lord Radcliffe. To see if the doctrine applies, you have first to construe the contract and see whether the parties have themselves provided for the situation that has arisen. If they have provided for it, the contract must govern. There is no frustration. If they have not provided for it, then you have to compare the new situation with the old situation for which they did provide. Then you must see how different it is. The fact that it has become more onerous or more expensive for one party than he thought is not sufficient to bring about a frustration. It must be more than merely more onerous or more expensive. It must be positively unjust to hold the parties bound. It is often difficult to draw the line. But it must be done, and it is for the courts to do it as a matter of law: see *Tsakiroglou & Co, Ltd v Noblee & Thorl GmbH*, per Viscount Simonds and per Lord Reid.

Applying these principles to this case, I have come to the conclusion that the blockage of the canal did not bring about a 'fundamentally different situation' such as to frustrate the venture. My reasons are these: (i) The venture was the *whole* trip from delivery at Genoa, out to the Black Sea, there load cargo, thence to India, unload cargo, and re-delivery. The time for this vessel from Odessa to Vizagapatam via the Suez Canal would be twenty-six days, and via the Cape fifty-six days. But that is not the right comparison. You have to take the whole venture from delivery at Genoa to re-delivery at Madras. We were told that the time for the whole venture via the Suez Canal would be 108 days, and via the Cape 138 days. The difference over the whole voyage is not so radical as to produce a frustration. (ii) The cargo was iron and steel goods which would not be adversely affected by the longer voyage, and there was no special reason for early arrival. The vessel and crew were at all times fit and sufficient to proceed via the Cape. (iii) The cargo was loaded on board at the time of the blockage of the canal. If the contract was frustrated, it would mean, I suppose, that the ship could throw up the charter and unload the cargo wherever she was, without any breach of contract. (iv) The voyage round the Cape made no great difference except that it took a good deal longer and was more expensive for the charterers than a voyage through the canal. . . .

Donovan LJ. . . . There is clearly no room here for holding that the parties agreed by implication that the blocking of the Suez Canal should end the contract, or that they would have so agreed had they considered this contingency. In fact, they did consider it, and, through their agents, made rival suggestions what should happen in that event. But they came to no conclusion, except to leave the terms of the contract as they were. Should the canal be blocked before the vessel passed through it, the parties were content to have their rights and duties settled on the basis of the terms of the contract which they were signing. In other words, the problem, should it arise, would be left to the lawyers. . .

[Danckwerts LJ concurred in the judgments above.]

Appeal allowed.

NOTES

1. In *W J Tatem Ltd v Gamboa* [1939] 1 KB 132 Goddard J also said that a contract might be frustrated by an event which had been foreseen.
2. Many events are foreseeable, but only as such remote possibilities that it is reasonable to assume that even if the parties foresaw them, they did not take them into account when they made the contract. The more likely the event, the more probable that the parties took it into account and intended that the contract should continue to apply. See Treitel, pp 696–699.

(f) Effect of frustration

If a contract is frustrated, each party is released from any further obligation to perform. Accrued rights to damages for any breach which may have occurred before the date of frustration are not affected, but neither can be liable in damages to the other for non-performance of the rest of the contract.

What is the position if a party has performed part or all of its contractual obligations before frustration occurs? Firstly, a party may have made an advance payment, eg for goods which were to have been delivered after the date of frustration. Secondly, a party may have delivered some of the goods due or have partially performed some service. Sometimes parts of the performance are to be paid for separately (see below, p 415 ff.). Accrued claims for any parts of the price that have been earned by partial performance will not be affected by the subsequent frustration. Often, however, none of the price may be due until all the goods have been delivered or the whole of the services have been performed.

Let us take advance payments first. At one time the rule at common law was that payments made before the date of frustration were not repayable, on the ground that the contract was discharged only from the moment of frustration and accrued rights were not affected: *Chandler v Webster* [1904] 1 KB 493. However *Chandler's* case was overruled by the House of Lords in *Fibrosa Spolka Akcyjna v Fairbairn Lawson Combe Barbour Ltd* [1943] AC 32. The Lords pointed out that, even under a contract which has not been frustrated, a party who has received no part of the promised performance is entitled to claim in restitution for return of the money paid for total failure of consideration. (Thus the victim of a breach of contract may have a choice between claiming damages and simply reclaiming any money paid: see below, p 551.) Unless the parties have agreed otherwise, this rule applies also when the contract has been frustrated: the claim in restitution is not affected by the discharge of the contractual obligations. Thus in the *Fibrosa* case the plaintiff buyers had made an advance payment of £1,000 for a machine that was to be delivered c.i.f. Gydnia. Before the machine had been shipped the contract was frustrated by the German occupation of Poland. The buyers were entitled to recover the £1,000.

However, as Viscount Simon LC pointed out, neither this rule nor the one it replaced were satisfactory.

> While this result obviates the harshness with which the previous view in some instances treated the party who had made a prepayment, it cannot be regarded as dealing fairly between the parties in all cases, and must sometimes have the result of leaving the recipient who has to return the money at a grave disadvantage. He may have incurred expenses in connection with the partial carrying out of the contract which are equivalent, or more than equivalent, to the money which he prudently stipulated should be prepaid, but which he now has to return for reasons which are no fault of his. He may have to repay the money, though he has executed almost the whole of the contractual work, which will be left on his hands. These results follow from the fact that the English common law does not undertake to apportion a prepaid sum in such circumstances—contrast the provision, now contained in the Partnership Act, 1890, s 40, for apportioning a premium if a partnership is prematurely dissolved. It must be for the legislature to decide whether provision should be made for an equitable apportionment of prepaid monies which have to be returned by the recipient in view of the frustration of the contract in respect of which they were paid.

In 1943 the rule was changed by the Law Reform (Frustrated Contracts) Act, see below.

In the *Fibrosa* case the buyers could recover their advance payment because there had been a total failure of consideration: they had not received anything from the sellers. If the sellers had delivered part of the goods, the failure would have been only partial, and at common law none of the advance payment would be recoverable: *Whincup v Hughes* (below, p 551). The only exceptions to this would be if the contract were severable into distinct units, and an advance payment had been made in respect of a unit which remained completely unperformed; or perhaps if the price was clearly apportionable among the units even though the contract was entire (ie the buyer could insist on delivery in full as a condition of his having to accept any of the goods). Thus in *Ebrahim Dawood Ltd v Heath (Est 1927) Ltd* [1961] 2 Lloyd's Rep 512 (a case of breach by the seller, not frustration, but the same rule applied at common law, see below, p 551) the buyer paid in advance for the steel sheets he was buying at a price per ton, but justifiably rejected four-fifths of them as not conforming to the contract. He was allowed to recover four-fifths of the money he had paid. The basic rule that money can be recovered only if the failure of consideration was total seemed unsatisfactory and was also changed by the Law Reform (Frustrated Contracts) Act 1943, s 1(2) (below).

Turning now to the case where a party has partly performed in some other way than by paying money, the position at common law depends upon the nature of the performance. If the party has delivered goods to the other party, the latter will have either to return them or to pay for them at the contract rate if the contract is frustrated. In contrast, if the party has performed services so that there is nothing to return, the other party need pay nothing. Thus in *Appleby v Myers* (1867) LR 2 CP 651 a contract to instal machinery in a factory with payment due upon completion was frustrated when the factory was destroyed by fire after only some of the machinery was in place. The contractor was held not to be entitled to any payment—the price had not yet been earned and recovery would not be given on a restitutionary basis either. To do so would be inconsistent with the express terms of the contract stipulating for payment only on completion. (See also *Sumpter v Hedges*, below, p 418, which applies a similar rule when the contract has been terminated because of a breach by the contractor.) This rule was also altered by the Law Reform (Frustrated Contracts) Act 1943, s 1(3), (below).

Law Reform (Frustrated Contracts) Act 1943

Section 1
(1) Where a contract governed by English law has become impossible of performance or been otherwise frustrated, and the parties thereto have for that reason been discharged from the further performance of the contract, the following provisions of this section shall, subject to the provisions of section two of this Act, have effect in relation thereto.
(2) All sums paid or payable to any party in pursuance of the contract before the time when the parties were so discharged (in this Act referred to as 'the time of discharge') shall, in the case of sums so paid, be recoverable from him as money received by him for the use of the party by whom the sums were paid, and, in the case of sums so payable, cease to be so payable:
Provided that, if the party to whom the sums were so paid or payable incurred expenses before the time of discharge in, or for the purpose of, the performance of the contract, the court may, if it considers it just to do so having regard to all the circumstances of the case, allow him to retain or, as the case may be, recover the whole or any part of the sums so paid or payable, not being an amount in excess of the expenses so incurred.
(3) Where any party to the contract has, by reason of anything done by any other party thereto in, or for the purpose of, the performance of the contract, obtained a valuable benefit (other than a payment of money to which the last foregoing subsection applies) before the time of discharge, there shall be recoverable from him by the said other party such sum (if any), not

exceeding the value of the said benefit to the party obtaining it, as the court considers just, having regard to all the circumstances of the case and, in particular,—

    (a) the amount of any expenses incurred before the time of discharge by the benefited party in, or for the purpose of, the performance of the contract, including any sums paid or payable by him to any other party in pursuance of the contract and retained or recoverable by that party under the last foregoing subsection, and

    (b) the effect, in relation to the said benefit, of the circumstances giving rise to the frustration of the contract.

(4) In estimating, for the purposes of the foregoing provisions of this section, the amount of any expenses incurred by any party to the contract, the court may, without prejudice to the generality of the said provisions, include such sum as appears to be reasonable in respect of overhead expenses and in respect of any work or services performed personally by the said party.

(5) In considering whether any sum ought to be recovered or retained under the foregoing provisions of this section by any party to the contract, the court shall not take into account any sums which have, by reason of the circumstances giving rise to the frustration of the contract, become payable to that party under any contract of insurance unless there was an obligation to insure imposed by any express term of the frustrated contract or by or under any enactment.

(6) Where any person has assumed obligations under the contract in consideration of the conferring of a benefit by any other party to the contract upon any other person, whether a party to the contract or not, the court may, if in all the circumstances of the case it considers it just to do so, treat for the purposes of sub-section (3) of this section any benefit so conferred as a benefit obtained by the person who has assumed the obligations as aforesaid.

Section 2

(1) This Act shall apply to contracts, whether made before or after the commencement of this Act, as respects which the time of discharge is on or after the first day of July, nineteen hundred and forty-three, but not to contracts as respects which the time of discharge is before the said date.

(2) This Act shall apply to contracts to which the Crown is a party in like manner as to contracts between subjects.

(3) Where any contract to which this Act applies contains any provision which, upon the true construction of the contract, is intended to have effect in the event of circumstances arising which operate, or would but for the said provision operate, to frustrate the contract, or is intended to have effect whether such circumstances arise or not, the court shall give effect to the said provision and shall only give effect to the foregoing section of this Act to such extent, if any, as appears to the court to be consistent with the said provision.

(4) Where it appears to the court that a part of any contract to which this Act applies can properly be severed from the remainder of the contract, being a part wholly performed before the time of discharge, or so performed except for the payment in respect of that part of the contract of sums which are or can be ascertained under the contract, the court shall treat that part of the contract as if it were a separate contract and had not been frustrated and shall treat the foregoing section of this Act as only applicable to the remainder of that contract.

(5) This Act shall not apply—

    (a) to any charterparty, except a time charterparty or a charterparty by way of demise, or to any contract (other than a charterparty) for the carriage of goods by sea; or

    (b) to any contract of insurance, save as is provided by subsection (5) of the foregoing section; or

    (c) to any contract to which section seven of the Sale of Goods Act, 1893 (which avoids contracts for the sale of specific goods which perish before the risk has passed to the buyer) applies, or to any other contract for the sale, or for the sale and delivery, of specific goods, where the contract is frustrated by reason of the fact that the goods have perished.

NOTES

1. For a detailed account of the Act and the common law which it was intended to change, see Glanville Williams, *Law Reform (Frustrated Contracts) Act 1943* (Stevens, 1944).

2. How would the *Fibrosa* case be decided under the Act? Suppose the sellers had incurred expenses of £600 in starting work on the machine: what would be the maximum and minimum amounts the court could have ordered the sellers to return to the buyers?

3. Suppose the sellers had been paid £1,000 in advance, and had delivered some accessories for the machine that cost £750. In addition, the sellers had spent £600 on starting to build the machine itself. What is the maximum amount that the court could have awarded the seller under the Act? (NB. s 1(3)(a).)

4. The Act does not cover the case where the seller has incurred expenditure before the time of discharge if the expenditure is not covered by an advance payment not results in any benefit to the buyer. Why is no recovery provided for in this case? The Law Revision Committee, on whose Seventh Interim Report (Cmd 6009 of 1939), the Act was based, considered that the seller who does not stipulate for an advance payment must be taken to be incurring such expense at his own risk. Given that frustration occurs only when there is some event which was unforeseen or at least not 'covered' by the contract, how realistic is the Committee's approach?

5. Section 2(5) preserves the common law rules in certain cases in which it was felt that the rules were well known and accepted. Williams argues convincingly that cases falling within Sale of Goods Act 1893 (now 1979), s 7 should have been covered by the new rules.

6. Go back to the facts in note 2: how much should the court allow the sellers to retain in respect of their expenditure: the full £600, nothing, or some amount in between? The Law Revision Committee seemed to think the seller should be reimbursed in full, but Williams favoured an equal distribution of the loss (see Williams, pp 35–39).

7. If the plaintiff has conferred some benefit on the defendant and makes a claim under s 1(3), how should the court value the benefit and determine the 'just sum' to award the plaintiff? See the next case.

BP Exploration Co (Libya) Ltd v Hunt (No 2) [1982] 1 All ER 925, Robert Goff J

In December 1957 the then Libyan government granted the defendant a concession to explore for oil and extract oil from a specified area of the Libyan desert. The defendant did not have the resources to exploit the concession himself and in 1960 entered into what was called a 'farm-in agreement' with the plaintiffs. Essentially the contract involved a transfer by the defendant to the plaintiffs of a half share in the concession, in return for which the plaintiffs agreed to explore, develop and operate the whole of the concession entirely from their own resources and to make down payments to the defendant in cash and oil. This put the risk of failure to find oil in commercial quantities on the plaintiffs. However, if oil were discovered, the agreement provided for the repayment of the plaintiffs' expenditure out of the defendant's share of the oil (the precise details were very complex). Oil was discovered in large quantities and the field came on stream on 1967.

In 1971 the then Libyan government expropriated the plaintiffs' share of the concession, and in 1973 the defendant's share. The plaintiffs brought an action claiming that the contract had been frustrated and seeking such sums as the court considered just under s 1(3) of the 1943 Act in respect of benefits obtained by the defendant prior to the frustration by reason of the plaintiffs' performance of the contract.

The whole judgment repays careful study, but for reasons of space the extracts are limited to three crucial questions:

(a) definition of the defendant's benefit under s 1(3);
(b) valuation of the benefit;
(c) assessment of the just sum.

Robert Goff J: . . . *Identification of the defendant's benefit.* In the course of the argument before me, there was much dispute whether, in the case of services, the benefit should be identified as the services themselves, or as the end product of the services. One example canvassed (because it bore some relationship to the facts of the present case) was the example of prospecting for minerals. If minerals are discovered, should the benefit be regarded (as counsel for Mr Hunt contended) simply as the services of prospecting, or (as counsel for BP contended) as the minerals themselves being the end product of the successful exercise? Now, I am satisfied that it was the intention of the legislature, to be derived from s 1(3) as a matter of construction, that the benefit should in an appropriate case be identified as the end product of the services. This appears, in my judgment, not only from the fact that s 1(3) distinguishes between the plaintiff's performance and the defendant's benefit, but also from s 1(3)(b) which clearly relates to the product of the plaintiff's performance. Let me take the example of a building contract. Suppose that a contract for work on a building is frustrated by a fire which destroys the building and which, therefore, also destroys a substantial amount of work already done by the plaintiff. Although it might be thought just to award the plaintiff a sum assessed on a quantum meruit basis, probably a rateable part of the contract price, in respect of the work he has done, the effect of s 1(3)(b) will be to reduce the award to nil, because of the effect, in relation to the defendant's benefit, of the circumstances giving rise to the frustration of the contract. It is quite plain that, in s 1(3)(b), the word 'benefit' is intended to refer, in the example I have given, to the actual improvement to the building, because that is what will be affected by the frustrating event; the subsection therefore contemplates that, in such a case, the benefit is the end product of the plaintiff's services, not the services themselves. This will not be so in every case, since in some cases the services will have no end product; for example, where the services consist of doing such work as surveying, or transporting goods. In each case it is necessary to ask the question: what benefit has the defendant obtained by reason of the plaintiff's contractual performance? But it must not be forgotten that in s 1(3) the relevance of the value of the benefit is to fix a ceiling to the award. If, for example, in a building contract, the building is only partially completed, the value of the partially completed building (ie the product of the services) will fix a ceiling for the award; but the stage of the work may be such that the uncompleted building may be worth less than the value of the work and materials that have gone into it, particularly as completion by another builder may cost more than completion by the original builder would have cost. In other cases, however, the actual benefit to the defendant may be considerably more than the appropriate or just sum to be awarded to the plaintiff, in which event the value of the benefit will not in fact determine the quantum of the award. I should add, however, that, in a case of prospecting, it would usually be wrong to identify the discovered mineral as the benefit. In such a case there is always (whether the prospecting is successful or not) the benefit of the prospecting itself, ie of knowing whether or not the land contains any deposit of the relevant minerals; if the prospecting is successful, the benefit may include also the enhanced value of the land by reason of the discovery; if the prospector's contractual task goes beyond discovery and includes development and production, the benefit will include the further enhancement of the land by reason of the installation of the facilities, and also the benefit of in part transforming a valuable mineral deposit into a marketable commodity.

I add by way of footnote that all these difficulties would have been avoided if the legislature had thought it right to treat the services themselves as the benefit. In the opinion of many commentators, it would be more just to do so; after all, the services in question have been requested by the defendant, who normally takes the risk that they may prove worthless, from whatever cause. In the example I have given of the building destroyed by fire, there is much to be said for the view that the builder should be paid for the work he has done, unless he has (for example by agreeing to insure the works) taken on himself the risk of destruction by fire. But my task is to construe the Act as it stands. On the true construction of the Act, it is in my judgment clear that the defendant's benefit must, in an appropriate case, be identifed as the end product of the plaintiff's services, despite the difficulties which this construction creates, difficulties which are met again when one comes to value the benefit. . . .

Valuing the benefit. Since the benefit may be identified with the product of the plaintiff's performance, great problems arise in the valuation of the benefit. First, how does one solve the problem which arises from the fact that a small service may confer an enormous benefit, and conversely, a very substantial service may confer only a very small benefit? The answer presumably is that at the stage of valuation of the benefit (as opposed to assessment of the just sum) the task of the court is simply to assess the value of the benefit to the defendant. For example, if a prospector after some very simple prospecting discovers a large and unexpected deposit of a valuable mineral, the benefit to the defendant (namely, the enhancement in the value of the land) may be enormous; it must be valued as such, always bearing in mind that the assessment of a just sum may very well lead to a much smaller amount being awarded to the plaintiff. But conversely, the plaintiff may have undertaken building work for a substantial sum which is, objectively speaking, of little or no value, for example, he may commence the redecoration, to the defendant's execrable taste, of rooms which are in good decorative order. If the contract is frustrated before the work is complete, and the work is unaffected by the frustrating event, it can be argued that the defendant has obtained no benefit, because the defendant's property has been reduced in value by the plaintiff's work; but the partial work must be treated as a benefit to the defendant, since he requested it, and valued as such.

Assessment of the just sum. The principle underlying the Act is prevention of the unjust enrichment of the defendant at the plaintiff's expense. Where, as in cases under s 1(2), the benefit conferred on the defendant consists of payment of a sum of money, the plaintiff's expense and the defendant's enrichment are generally equal; and, subject to other relevant factors, the award of restitution will consist simply of an order for repayment of a like sum of money. But where the benefit does not consist of money, then the defendant's enrichment will rarely be equal to the plaintiff's expense. In such cases, where (as in the case of a benefit conferred under a contract thereafter frustrated) the benefit has been requested by the defendant, the basic measure of recovery in restitution is the reasonable value of the plaintiff's performance: in a case of services, a quantum meruit or reasonable remuneration, and in a case of goods, a quantum valebat or reasonable price. Such cases are to be contrasted with cases where such a benefit has not been requested by the defendant. In the latter class of case, recovery is rare in restitution; but if the sole basis of recovery was that the defendant had been incontrovertibly benefited, it might be legitimate to limit recovery to the defendant's actual benefit, a limit which has (perhaps inappropriately) been imported by the legislature into s 1(3) of the Act. However, under s 1(3) as it stands, if the defendant's actual benefit is less than the just or reasonable sum which would otherwise be awarded to the plaintiff, the award must be reduced to a sum equal to the amount of the defendant's benefit.

Applying s 1(3), Robert Goff J awarded the plaintiffs some $15 million in US dollars and some £9 million in sterling. Subject to a minor variation, his decision was affirmed by the Court of Appeal and the House of Lords, [1982] 1 All ER 925. Delivering the judgment of the Court of Appeal, Lawton LJ noted that Robert Goff J had thought the concept behind the Act was the prevention of unjust enrichment, and remarked, 'We get no help from the use of words which are not in the statute', but he went on to point out that there were various possible approaches to the assessment of a 'just sum' and the Court of Appeal would not be justified in setting aside the judge's method 'merely because we thought there were better ways'.

NOTES

1. The judge held that the effect of the frustrating circumstances must be taken into account in assessing the value of the benefit received. Is this what the Act provides, or does it say that the relevant benefit is that received *before* the frustration, and the effect of the frustrating event is to be taken into account when assessing the 'just sum'? It might make a considerable difference. If the contract had been frustrated by expropriation without compensation before any oil had been obtained, it would seem on the judge's approach that Hunt would have received no benefit, so BP could not be awarded anything for its work; whereas on the other approach, the benefit would be the value of the work done before the frustration, and the expropriation without compensation would merely be a factor tending to reduce the just sum. See Treitel, p 707.

2. Robert Goff J notes various things the Act is *not* intended to achieve.

> . . . The Act is *not* designed to do certain things. (i) It is not designed to apportion the loss between the parties. There is no general power under either s 1(2) or s 1(3) to make any allowance for expenses incurred by the plaintiff (except, under the proviso to s 1(2), to enable him to enforce pro tanto payment of a sum payable but unpaid before frustration); and expenses incurred by the defendant are only relevant in so far as they go to reduce the net benefit obtained by him and thereby limit any award to the plaintiff. (ii) It is not concerned to put the parties in the position in which they would have been if the contract had been performed. (iii) It is not concerned to restore the parties to the position they were in before the contract was made. A remedy designed to prevent unjust enrichment may not achieve that result; for expenditure may be incurred by either party under the contract which confers no benefit on the other, and in respect of which no remedy is available under the Act. . . .

In the introduction in Chapter 15 (pp 303–308, above) we noted that the doctrine of frustration seems to enable the court to allocate losses which it feels the contract itself had not allocated between the two parties. How far do its powers under the Act enable it to achieve that end? We have seen one problem already, the wasted expenditure incurred by one party in preparing to perform, when the expenditure does not produce a benefit to the other party and is not covered by an advance payment. Are there other examples? As Robert Goff J points out, the Act does not enable the court to put the parties into the position they would have been in if the contract had been performed (eg, no recovery of lost profit), nor to restore them to their pre-contractual position. Thus the licensees in *Taylor v Caldwell* would still get nothing for the wasted advertising, Krell nothing for the cost of arranging to store his valuables away while Henry and company were in his flat, etc. Perhaps this is right: the court has already determined that neither party was better able to prevent the frustrating event, and maybe each is the best insurer of his own expenses, since he alone knows the amount of them.

CHAPTER 18
Expectation mistakes

In the last chapter we saw that in some cases the courts divide the losses caused by an event not covered by the contract, by holding the contract discharged by frustration. A similar solution is achieved in cases where the risk in question is not one of a subsequent contingency, but of the facts existing when the contract was made turning out to be different to what the parties believed. In this case of common mistake, however, technically the contract is not discharged: if the mistake operates it renders the contract either void ab initio or voidable in equity.

Suppose that A has agreed to sell to B a particular machine which B is to collect from a disused factory. Unknown to either party there has just been a fire at the factory, and the machine has been rendered valueless except as scrap. Just as in the case of frustration, three solutions are possible:

(a) A is liable to B for failing to deliver, and will have to compensate B for any consequential loss (eg wasted transport costs);
(b) B must take the remains of the machine and pay the full price;
(c) The contract is void or voidable, so that B does not have to pay but cannot recover damages.

In cases of alleged frustration the court normally had to choose between holding the contract discharged and holding that its express and implied terms were still enforceable, so that the parties must perform or, if that was impossible, pay damages. In cases of common mistake the same choice applies, but the position is complicated by the possibility that during the negotiations one party will have stated his understanding of the facts. This may have two effects. First, the courts may treat the statement as a warranty that the facts stated are true (see above, p 259). This will automatically lead to the risk of their being untrue being placed on the speaker. Secondly, even if the statement is not a warranty, it may give rise to remedies for misrepresentation if the other party relied on it, and the contract may be avoided on that ground, without the need to argue mistake. As a result the doctrine of common mistake has a narrow field of practical operation, as it will not normally be needed if one party has stated his version of the facts. It will only apply if the parties were mistaken about unstated assumptions, or each relied on his own understandings rather than on what the other said. This no doubt explains why there are so few cases.

The doctrine of common mistake appears to have been a nineteenth century importation from civil law (see Simpson (1975) 91 LQR 247, 269). During the first half of the century various cases which are now seen as involving common mistake were decided without invoking any such doctrine. Perhaps the best known is *Couturier v Hastie* (1856) 5 HL Cas 673. A c. & f. contract (rather like the c.i.f. contract described above, p 53, but without the insurance element) had been made for a cargo of corn that both parties assumed was in existence. In fact the corn had begun overheating and the captain of the ship had unloaded and sold it (the normal practice). The sellers argued that the buyers must still take up the shipping documents and pay the price. If it had been the case that the goods had been damaged or lost after the contract had been made, then at least in modern law the buyer would indeed have been obliged to pay—the risk (see above, pp 53 and 349) would have passed as from shipment and the buyer would be expected to claim on the insurance, if any. But the House of Lords affirmed the decision of Exchequer Chamber that on the actual facts the buyer did not have to pay. The contract was one 'for the sale of a cargo supposed to exist', not 'for goods lost or not lost'. The word mistake does not occur in the judgments, nor is there any discussion of whether the contract was void—the only point decided was that the sellers could not require the buyer to perform.

The most obvious source for the doctrine of mistake is *Kennedy v Panama, New Zealand and Australian Royal Mail Co Ltd* (1867) LR 2 QB 580. The plaintiff had bought some shares relying on a statement that the Company had obtained a valuable contract to carry mail for the New Zealand government. This was an innocent misrepresentation, but the case was argued and decided on purely common law grounds, and the question was simply whether there had been a total failure of consideration so that the plaintiff could get his money back (see above, p 365). Again, this is something different from mistake, but in deciding that there had not been a total failure of consideration Blackburn J drew on Roman law principles (cf. his judgment in *Taylor v Caldwell*, above, p 347). He referred to the Roman doctrine of *error*, under which a mistake as to substance would invalidate a contract but a mistake merely as to quality would not; and said that the misunderstanding about the shares went only to quality, so that there was no total failure of consideration. It is easy to see how this could be interpreted as saying that a mistake as to substance will make the contract void for mistake, as it did in Roman law. At any rate, by the end of the century *Couturier v Hastie* was considered to have been decided on the ground that the contract was *void*, and this solution was adopted by Sale of Goods Act 1893.

Sale of Goods Act 1979

Section 6
Where there is a contract for the sale of specific goods, and the goods without the knowledge of the seller have perished at the time when the contract is made, the contract is void.

McRae v Commonwealth Disposals Commission (1950) 84 CLR 377, High Court of Australia

The Commonwealth Disposals Commission, which was authorized to make contracts on behalf of the Commonwealth, invited tenders 'for the purchase of an oil tanker lying on Jourmaund Reef, which is approximately 100 miles north of Samarai. The vessel is said to contain oil'. The Commission notified the plaintiff by letter that his tender had been accepted and that a 'sales advice note' would be sent him within a few days. The plaintiff subsequently received the sales advice note, which described what was sold as 'one (1) oil tanker including contents wrecked on Jourmaund Reef approximately 100 miles north of Samarai. Price £285', and referred to conditions, one of which was that the goods 'are sold as and where they lie with all faults' and no warranty was given as to 'condition description quality or otherwise'. The plaintiff was unable to locate Jourmaund Reef on a map and, on inquiry, was supplied by the Commission with the latitude and longitude at which the tanker was alleged to be lying. At considerable expense the plaintiff fitted out a salvage expedition and proceeded to the locality given but found no tanker there; and in fact there was none in the locality at any material time. . . .

Dixon and Fullagar JJ.

. . . The first question to be determined is whether a contract was made between the plaintiffs and the Commission. The argument that the contract was void, or, in other words, that there was no contract, was based, as has been observed, on *Couturier v Hastie*. It is true that *Couturier v Hastie* has been commonly treated in the text-books as a case of a contract avoided by mutual mistake, and it is found cited in the company of such cases as *Gompertz v Bartlett* and *Strickland v Turner*. Section 7 [sic] of the English Sale of Goods Act 1893 is generally regarded as expressing the effect of the case. The case has not, however, been universally regarded as resting on mistake. . .

In considering *Couturier v Hastie* it is necessary to remember that it was, in substance, a case in which a vendor was suing for the price of goods which he was unable to deliver. If there had been nothing more in the case, it would probably never have been reported: indeed the action would probably never have been brought. But the vendor founded his claim on the provision for 'payment upon handing over shipping documents'. He was not called upon to prove a tender of the documents, because the defendant had 'repudiated' the contract, but he was able and willing to hand them over, and his argument was, in effect, that by handing them over he would be doing all that the contract required of him. The question thus raised would seem to depend entirely on the construction of the contract, and it appears really to have been so treated throughout . . .

The judgment of the Exchequer Chamber was delivered by Coleridge J. The view that the contract was void is probably derived from certain expressions which were used in the course of this judgment. But it does seem clear that again the question of construction was regarded as the fundamental question in the case. In stating the question for decision Coleridge J refers first to the direction of Martin B to the jury, and says that the Lord Chief Baron had agreed with the opinion of Martin B whereas the other learned Barons had differed from him. The judgment below, he says 'turned entirely on the meaning of the contract' and he proceeds to set out its terms in full. 'The question', he says, 'turns entirely upon the terms of the contract'. The argument for the defendant is then put as including the proposition 'that a vendor of goods undertakes that they exist', and the argument for the plaintiff as being 'that this was not a mere contract for the sale of an ascertained cargo, but that the purchaser bought the adventure, and took upon himself all risks from the shipment of the cargo'. The final conclusion reached is expressed at the end of the judgment by saying that 'the basis of the contract in this case was the sale and purchase of goods, and all the other terms in the bought note were dependent upon that, and we cannot give to it the effect of a contract for goods lost or not lost'. In the light of these passages it seems impossible to regard the expressions 'If the contract for the sale of the cargo was valid' and 'the contract failed as to the principal subject-matter of it' as meaning that the contract was treated as being void. All that the passages in which those expressions occur seem in their context to mean is that the principal subject matter of the contract was a cargo of goods, that the purchaser did not buy shipping documents representing non-existent goods, that the consideration to the purchaser had failed, and that he could not therefore be liable to pay the contract price. . .

The observation of Lord *Atkin* in *Bell v Lever Bros Ltd* [below, p 377] seems entirely appropriate to *Couturier v Hastie*. In that case there was a failure of consideration, and the purchaser was not bound to pay the price: if he had paid it before the truth was discovered, he could have recovered it back as money had and received. The construction of the contract was the vital thing in the case because, and only because, on the construction of the contract depended the question whether the consideration had really failed, the vendor maintaining that, since he was able to hand over the shipping documents, it had not failed. The truth is that the question whether the contract was void, or the vendor excused from performance by reason of the non-esistence of the supposed subject matter, did not arise in *Couturier v Hastie*. It would have arisen if the purchaser had suffered loss through non-delivery of the corn and had sued the vendor for damages. If it had so arisen, we think that the real question would have been whether the contract was subject to an implied condition precedent that the goods were in existence. Prima facie, one would think, there would be no such implied condition precedent, the position being simply that the vendor *promised* that the goods *were* in existence. That is the real meaning of the direction of Martin B to the jury, and so the argument for the defendant, as has already been pointed out, included the proposition that 'a vendor of goods undertakes that they exist and that they are capable of being transferred, although he may not stipulate for their condition'. . . .

If the view so far indicated be correct, as we believe it to be, it seems clear that the case of *Couturier v Hastie* does not compel one to say that the contract in the present case was void. But, even if the view that *Couturier v Hastie* was a case of a void contract be correct, we would still think that it could not govern the present case. . . . [I]t must be true to say that a party cannot rely on mutual mistake where the mistake consists of a belief which is, on the one hand, entertained by him without any reasonable ground, and, on the other hand, deliberately induced by him in the mind of the other party. It does not seem possible on the evidence to say that Bowser or Sheehan was guilty of fraud in the sense that either knew at the date of the contract that the Commission had no tanker to sell. And even at the later stage, after the receipt of the message from Misima, it is difficult to impute to them actual knowledge that there was no tanker at Jomard Entrance. The message should have conveyed to them the fact that the only vessel lying in the vicinity was almost certainly worthless, and ordinary commonsense and decency would have suggested that the contents of the message ought to be communicated to the plaintiffs. But the message referred to a 'barge type tanker', and it is quite possible that this description would fail to bring home to their minds that there was no tanker. A finding of actual knowledge that they had nothing to sell does not seem justified by the evidence, though it is difficult to credit them at the time of the publication of the advertisements with any honest affirmative belief that a tanker existed. The confusion as to locality in the description advertised is almost enough to exclude the inference of any such affirmative belief. But, even if they be credited with a real belief in the existence of a tanker, they were guilty of the grossest negligence. It is impossible to say that they had any reasonable ground for such a belief. Having no reasonable grounds for such a belief, they asserted by their advertisement to the world at large, and by their later specification of locality to the plaintiffs, that they had a tanker to sell. They must have known that any tenderer would rely implicitly on their assertion of the existence of a tanker, and they must have known that the plaintiffs would rely implictly on their later assertion of the existence of a tanker in the latitude and longitude given. They took no steps to verify what they were asserting, and any 'mistake' that existed was induced by their own culpable conduct. In these circumstances it seems out of the question that they should be able to assert that no contract was concluded. It is not unfair or inaccurate to say that the only 'mistake' the plaintiffs made was that they believed what the Commission told them.

The position so far, then, may be summed up as follows. It was not decided in *Couturier v Hastie* that the contract in that case was void. The question whether it was void or not did not arise. If it had arisen, as in an action by the purchaser for damages, it would have turned on the ulterior question whether the contract was subject to an implied condition precedent. Whatever might then have been held on the facts of *Couturier v Hastie*, it is impossible in this case to imply any such term. The terms of the contract and the surrounding circumstances clearly exclude any such implication. The buyers relied upon, and acted upon, the assertion of the seller that there was a tanker in existence. It is not a case in which the parties can be seen to have proceeded on the basis of a common assumption of fact so as to justify the conclusion that the correctness of the assumption was intended by both parties to be a condition precedent to the creation of contractual obligations. The officers of the Commission made an assumption, but the plaintiffs did not make an assumption in the same sense. They knew nothing except what the Commission had told them. If they had been asked, they would certainly not have said: 'Of course, if there is no tanker, there is no contract'. They would have said: 'We shall have to go and take possession of the tanker. We simply accept the Commission's assurance that there is a tanker and the Commission's promise to give us that tanker.' The only proper construction of the contract is that it included a promise by the Commission that there was a tanker in the position specified. The Commission contracted that there was a tanker there. 'The sale in this case of a ship implies a contract that the subject of the transfer did exist in the character of a ship' (*Barr v Gibson*). If, on the other hand, the case of *Couturier v Hastie* and this case ought to be treated as cases raising a question of 'mistake', then the Commission cannot in this case rely on any mistake as avoiding the contract, because any mistake was induced by the serious fault of their own servants, who asserted the existence of a tanker recklessly and without any reasonable ground. There *was* a contract, and the Commission contracted that a tanker existed in the position specified. Since there was no such tanker, there has been a breach of contract, and the plaintiffs are entitled to damages for that breach.

Before proceeding to consider the measure of damages, one other matter should be briefly mentioned. The contract was made in Melbourne, and it would seem that its proper law is Victorian law. Section 11 of the Victorian Goods Act 1928 corresponds to s 6 of the English Sale of Goods Act 1893, and provides that 'where there is a contract for the sale of specific goods, and the goods without the knowledge of the seller have perished at the time when the contract is made the contract is void'. This has been generally supposed to represent the legislature's view of the effect of *Couturier v Hastie*. Whether it correctly represents the effect of the decision in that case or not, it seems clear that the section has no application to the facts of the present case. Here the goods never existed, and the seller ought to have known that they did not exist. . . .

[McTiernan J delivered a concurring judgment.]

Appeal allowed.

NOTES

1. Suppose that the tanker had been on the reef at one stage but had disintegrated long before the contract was made, and that the Commission should have known this. Could the court have reached the same result, or would s 6 have forced them to hold that the contract was void and so the Commission was not liable? Unlike many sections of the Sale of Goods Act, s 6 seems to impose an absolute rule rather than a rule which applies only in the absence of contrary intention (see Treitel, pp 222–223). Probably the Commission could nowadays be found liable under *Hedley Byrne v Heller* (above, p 23); or perhaps the court would discover a collateral contract that the tanker existed. (What could be the consideration for a collateral contract?)
2. Was one of the parties in *McRae's* case able to avoid the loss at less cost than the other? Isn't there a close parallel to self-induced frustration (see above, p 353)?

Bell v Lever Bros [1931] All ER Rep 1, House of Lords

. . . By agreements dated Aug 9, 1923, Oct 9, 1923, and July 1, 1926, made between the respondents (plaintiffs in the action) and Bell and Snelling, the appellants (defendants), it was agreed that the appellants should act as chairman and vice-chairman respectively of the Niger Co, Ltd, for five years, devoting the whole of their time to the business of the company. The assets of the Niger Co were afterwards transferred to a new company called the United Africa Co, Ltd, and in March, 1929, the respondents entered into a further agreement with the appellants under which they paid them £50,000 as compensation for the termination of the agreement of July 1, 1926, and in full satisfaction of all claims against the respondents or the Niger Co. Subsequent to this agreement it was discovered that the appellants had entered into certain dealings on their own account which they had kept secret from the respondents. The respondents then demanded a return of the £50,000. The appellants admitted they were liable to account for profits on the private dealings, but denied liability to repay the £50,000. The respondents then brought this action claiming damages for fraudulent misrepresentation and breach of contract. The jury by their findings negatived the allegation of fraudulent misrepresentation or concealment, but found that the appellants had committed a breach of contract owing to the private transactions, and that the respondents were entitled on this account to terminate the service contract of 1926 and would have elected to do so had they known of the breach in question. . . . The Court of Appeal held (i) that the cancellation agreement was invalidated on the ground of mutual [more usually nowadays termed 'common' —eds] mistake. . . .

Lord Atkin. . . . In the view that I take of the whole case it becomes unnecessary to deal finally with the appellants' complaint that the points upon which the plaintiffs succeeded were not open to them. I content myself with saying that much may be said for that contention.

Two points present themselves for decision. (i) Was the agreement of March 19, 1929, void by reason of a mutual mistake of Mr D'Arcy Cooper and Mr Bell? (ii) . . . The rules of law dealing with the effect of mistake on contract appear to be established with reasonable clearness. If mistake operates at all it operates so as to negative or in some cases to nullify consent. The parties may be mistaken in the identity of the contracting parties, or in the existence of the subject-matter of the contract at the date of the contract, or in the quality of the subject-matter of the contract. These mistakes may be by one party, or by both, and the legal effect may depend upon the class of mistake above mentioned. Thus a mistaken belief by A that he is contracting with B, whereas in fact he is contracting with C, will negative consent where it is clear that the intention of A was to contract only with B. So the agreement of A and B for the purchase of a specific article is void if in fact the article had perished before the date of sale. In this case, though the parties in fact were agreed about the subject-matter, yet a consent to transfer or take delivery of something not existent is deemed useless, the consent is nullified. As codified in the Sale of Goods Act, 1893, the contract is expressed to be void if the seller was in ignorance of the destruction of the specific chattel. I apprehend that if the seller with knowledge that a chattel was destroyed purported to sell it to a purchaser, the latter might sue for damages for non-delivery though the former could not sue for non-acceptance, but I know of no case where a seller has so committed himself. This is a case where mutual mistake certainly and unilateral mistake by the seller of goods will prevent a contract from arising. Corresponding to mistake as to the existence of the subject-matter is mistake as to title in cases where unknown to the parties the buyer is already the owner of that which the seller purports to sell him. The parties intended to effectuate a transfer of ownership; such a transfer is impossible; the stipulation is naturali ratione inutilis. This is the case of *Cooper v Phibbs*, where A agreed to take a lease of a fishery from B, though, contrary to the belief of both parties at the time, A was tenant for life of the fishery and B appears to have had no title at all. To such a case Lord Westbury applied the principle that, if parties contract under a mutual mistake and misapprehension as to their relative and respective rights, the result is that the agreement is liable to be set aside as having proceded upon a common mistake. Applied to the context the statement is only subject to the criticism that the agreement would appear to be void rather than voidable. Applied to mistake as to rights generally it would appear to be too wide. Even where the vendor has no title, though both parties think he has, the correct view would appear to be that there is a contract, but that the vendor has either committed a breach of a stipulation as to title or is not able to perform his contract. The contract is unenforceable by him, but is not void. Mistake as to quality of the thing contracted for raises more difficult questions. In such a case a mistake will not affect assent unless it is the mistake of both parties and is as to the existence of some quality which makes the thing without the quality essentially different from the thing as it was believed to be. Of course it may appear that the parties contracted that the article should possess the quality which one or other or both mistakenly believed it to possess. But in such a case there is a contract and the inquiry is a different one, being whether the contract as to quality amounts to a condition or a warranty, a different branch of the law. The principles to be applied are to be found in two cases which, so far as my knowledge goes, have always been treated as authoritative expositions of the law.

The first is *Kennedy v Panama, New Zealand and Australian Royal Mail Co*. In that case the plaintiff had applied for shares in the defendant company on the faith of a prospectus which stated falsely but innocently that the company had a binding contract with the government of New Zealand for the carriage of mails. On discovering the true facts the plaintiff brought an action for the recovery of the sums that he had paid on calls. The defendants brought a cross-section for further calls . . . The court came to the conclusion in that case that, through there was a misapprehension as to that which was a material part of the motive inducing the applicant to ask for the shares, it did not prevent the shares from being in substance those he applied for.

The next case is *Smith v Hughes*, the well-known case as to new and old oats. . . .

The court ordered a new trial. It is not quite clear whether they considered that if the defendant's contention was correct the parties were not ad idem or there was a contractual condition that the oats sold were old oats. In either case the defendant would succeed in defeating the claim.

In these cases I am inclined to think that the true analysis is that there is a contract, but that the one party is not able to supply the very thing, whether goods or services, that the other party contracted to take, and, therefore, the contract is unenforceable by the one if executory, while, if executed, the other can recover back money paid on the ground of failure of the consideration.

We are now in a position to apply to the facts of this case the law as to mistake so far as it has been stated. The agreement which is said to be void is the agreement contained in the letter of March 19, 1929, that Bell would retire from the board of the Niger Co and its subsidiaries, and that in consideration of his doing so Levers would pay him as compensation for the termination of his agreements and consequent loss of office the sum of £30,000 in full satisfaction and discharge of all claims and demands of any kind against Lever Bros, the Niger Co, or its subsidiaries. The agreement which, as part of the contract, was terminated, had been broken so that it could be repudiated. Is an agreement to terminate a broken contract different in kind from an agreement to terminate an unbroken contract, assuming that the breach has given the one party the right to declare the contract at an end? I feel the weight of the respondents' contention that a contract immediately determinable is a different thing from a contract for an unexpired term and that the difference in kind can be illustrated by the immense price of release from the longer contract as compared with the shorter. And I agree that an agreement to take an assignment of a lease for five years is not the same thing as to take an assignment of a lease for three years, still less a term for a few months. But on the whole I have come to the conclusion that it would be wrong to decide that an agreement to terminate a definite specified contract is void if it turns out that the contract had already been broken and could have been terminated otherwise. The contract released is the identical contract in both cases; and the party paying for release gets exactly what he bargains for. It seems immaterial that he could have got the same result in another way: or that, if he had known the true facts, he would not have entered into the bargain. A buys B's horse: he thinks the horse is sound, and he pays the price of a sound horse: he would certainly not have bought the horse if he had known as the fact is that the horse is unsound. If B has made no representation as to soundness and has not contracted that the horse is sound A is bound, and cannot recover back the price. A buys a picture from B: both A and B believe it to be the work of an old master, and a high price is paid. It turns out to be a modern copy. A has no remedy in the absence of representation or warranty. A agrees to take on lease or to buy from B an unfurnished dwelling-house. The house is in fact uninhabitable. A would never have entered into the bargain if he had known the fact. A has no remedy: and the position is the same whether B knew the fact or not, so long as he made no representation or gave no warranty. A buys a roadside garage business from B abutting on a public thoroughfare: unknown to A, but known to B, it has already been decided to construct a by-pass road which will divert substantially the whole of the traffic from passing A's garage. Again A has no remedy. All these cases involve hardship on A, and benefit B, as most people would say, unjustly. They can be supported on the ground that it is of paramount importance that contracts should be observed: and that if parties honestly comply with the essentials of the formation of contracts, ie, agree in the same terms on the same subject-matter they are bound: and must rely on the stipulations of the contract for protection from the effect of facts unknown to them.

This brings the discussion to the alternative mode of expressing the result of a mutual mistake. It is said that in such a case as the present there is to be implied a stipulation in the contract that a condition of its efficacy is that the facts should be as understood by both parties, namely, that the contract would not be terminated till the end of the current term. The question of the existence of conditions express or implied is obviously one that affects not the formation of contract, but the investigation of the terms of the contract when made. A condition derives its efficacy from the consent of the parties express or implied. They have agreed, but on what terms? One term may be that unless the facts are or are not of a particular nature, or unless an event has or has not happened, the contract is not to take effect. With regard to future facts such a condition is obviously contractual. Till the event occurs the parties are bound. Thus the condition (the exact terms of which need not here be investigated) that is generally accepted as underlying the principle of the frustration cases is contractual: an implied condition. Counsel for the respondents formulated for the assistance of your Lordships a proposition which should be recorded: 'Whenever it is to be inferred from the terms of a contract or its surrounding circumstances that the consensus has been reached upon the basis of a particular contractual assumption, and that assumption is not true, the contract is avoided; ie, it is void ab initio if the assumption is of present fact and it ceases to bind if the assumption is of future fact.' I think few would demur to this statement, but its value depends upon the meaning of 'a contractual assumption' and also upon the true meaning to be attached to 'basis', a metaphor which may mislead. When used expressly in contracts—for instance, in policies of insurance which state that the truth of the statements in the proposal is to be the basis of the contract of insurance— the meaning is clear. The truth of the statements is made a condition of the contract which, failing the condition, is void unless the condition is waived. The proposition does not amount to more than this, that, if the contract expressly or impliedly contains a term that a particular assumption is a condition of the contract, the contract is avoided if the assumption is not true. But we have not advanced far on the inquiry how to ascertain whether the contract does contain such a condition. Various words are to be found to define the state of things which makes a condition. 'In the contemplation of both parties fundamental to the continued validity of the contract', 'a foundation essential to its existence', and 'a fundamental reason for making it', are phrases found in the important judgment of Scrutton LJ in the present case. The first two phrases appear to me to be unexceptionable. They cover the case of a contract to serve in a particular place, the existence of which is fundamental to the service, or to procure the services of a professional vocalist whose continued health is essential to performance. But 'a fundamental reason for making a contract' may with respect be misleading. The reason of one party only is presumably not intended, but in the cases that I have above suggested of the sale of a horse or of a picture, it might be said that the fundamental reason for making the contract was the belief of both parties that the horse was sound or the picture an old master, yet in neither case would the condition as I think exist. Nothing is more dangerous than to allow oneself liberty to construct for the parties contracts which they have not in terms made by importing implications which would appear to make the contract more business-like or more just. The implications to be made are to be no more than are 'necessary' for giving business efficacy to the transaction; and it appears to me that as to both existing facts and future facts a condition should not be implied unless the new state of facts makes the contract something different in kind from the contract in the original state of facts. . . . We, therefore, get a common standard for mutual mistake, and implied conditions whether as to existing or as to future facts. Does the state of the new facts destroy the identity of the subject-matter as it was in the original state of facts? To apply the principle to the infinite combinations of facts that arise in actual experience will continue to be difficult; but if this case results in establishing order in what has been a somewhat confused and difficult branch of the law it will have served a useful purpose. I have already stated my reasons for deciding that in the present case the identity of the subject-matter was not destroyed by the mutual mistake, if any, and I need not repeat them. . . .

[Lord Blanesburgh and Thankerton agreed that the plea of mistake must fail; Viscount Hailsham and Lord Warrington of Clyffe dissented.]

Order of the Court of Appeal reversed.

NOTES

1. Bishop sells Furmston a picture of Salisbury Cathedral which they both believe to be by Constable. It is in fact a modern painting after the style of Constable. Is the identity of the subject matter destroyed? Was the bargain essentially for a picture of Salisbury Cathedral, or for a Constable? See Treitel pp 218–219.

2. If the answer to the last question is 'a Constable', the contract might be void. But what if:

   (a) the seller was an art dealer who had told the buyer the picture was a Constable? (see above, p 259, and *Leaf v International Galleries*, above, p 292);

   (b) the sale was made by an auctioneer selling off the contents of a country house at an informal auction held at the house, and it was quite obvious that the auctioneer knew nothing about pictures? Cf *Bisset v Wilkinson*, above, p 288.)

3. In the Canadian case of *Diamond v British Columbia Thoroughbred Breeders' Society and Boyd* (1965) 52 DLR(2d) 146 (BC) the plaintiff attended an auction and successfully bid on a horse numbered 'Hip No 16'. The sale catalogue identified this horse as Pennate, a full brother of the winner of the Canadian Derby in Alberta in 1961. In fact the horse had been mislabelled, and was not Pennate but Palloffair, a half-brother to the winner. When the plaintiff discovered the mistake, he sought the return of his purchase money and damages. Aikins J held that the contract was not void for mistake because it was for the horse displayed in the ring. He went on to hold that the plaintiff could have rescinded for misrepresentation had he acted more promptly (see above, p 292); but that the plaintiff could also recover damages for breach of contract that the horse had the stated lineage. This case illustrates the possible solutions to the problem in note 2, above; but, with respect, it seems that the judge was trying to adopt inconsistent solutions at the same time. Either the contract was one to sell Pennate, in which case the seller is

liable for breach; or the contract was for the horse in the ring. If it was the latter, then there might still be a remedy for misrepresentation, if there had been one; or, if the mistake was sufficiently fundamental, the contract might be void for mistake. It is hard to see that the mistake in this case was fundamental, but it might have been if the horse were being sold and bought for breeding and turned out to be a nag of no pedigree whatever. If neither mistake nor misrepresentation will assist the buyer, he must accept the horse and cannot claim compensation.

4. It has been argued that a contract will only be void for common mistake in cases where goods have perished or the buyer buys his own property; but see below, p 385.

Solle v Butcher [1949] 2 All ER 1107, Court of Appeal

In 1947 the landlord acquired a long lease of a war-damaged house which in 1939 had been let in flats subject to the Rent Restrictions Acts. The landlord carried out repairs and alterations to the house, in the course of which he re-constructed the flat the subject of the present proceedings. The alterations left the outside and cubic capacity of the house and of the flat in question unchanged, the only substantial change made to the flat being the removal of inner walls so as to subtract from a bedroom a space which was then incorporated into the dining-room. During the course of the work the parties discussed whether the flat when rebuilt would be subject to the standard rent fixed by the 1939 letting, and they came to the conclusion that it would not, the tenant expressing that opinion. The standard rent of the flat in 1939 was £140 a year, and if the reconstructed flat were the same dwelling it would have been possible to increase the rent in respect of expenditure on improvements, in accordance with s 2(1) of the Increase of Rent and Mortgage Interest (Restrictions) Act, 1920, as amended by the Rent and Mortgage Interest Restrictions Act, 1939, Sch 1, to approximately £250, by serving the necessary notices of increase. On Sept 29, 1947, on completion of the work, the landlord let the flat, including a garage which had not formed part of the 1939 demise, to the tenant on a lease for seven years at a rent of £250 a year, but, being under the impression that the rent fixed by the 1939 letting had no application to the reconstructed flat, he served no notice of increase. The tenant paid rent at £250 a year for some time and then took proceedings in the county court for a declaration that the standard rent of the flat was £140 a year and that he was entitled to recover from the landlord the amount overpaid since the commencement of the tenancy. The landlord contended that the alterations were such that the flat had become a new and separate dwelling by reason of change of identity, but the county court judge found as a fact that the flat was not a new and separate dwelling. The landlord further contended that the lease should be rescinded as it had been entered into under a mutual mistake of fact.

Denning LJ. . . . In this plight the landlord seeks to set aside the lease. He says with truth that it is unfair that the tenant should have the benefit of the lease for the outstanding five years of the term at £140 a year when the proper rent is £250 a year. If he cannot give a notice of increase now, can he not avoid the lease? The only ground on which he can avoid it is on the ground of mistake. It is quite plain that the parties were under a mistake. They thought that the flat was not tied down to a controlled rent, whereas in fact it was. In order to see whether the lease can be avoided for this mistake it is necessary to remember that mistake is of two kinds: first, mistake which renders the contract void, that is, a nullity from the beginning, which is the kind of mistake which was dealt with by the courts of common law, and secondly, mistake which renders the contract not void, but voidable, that is, liable to be set aside on such terms as the court thinks fit, which is the kind of mistake which was dealt with by the courts of equity. Much of the difficulty which has attended this subject has arisen because, before the fusion of law and equity, the courts of common law, in order to do justice in the case in hand, extended this doctrine of mistake beyond its proper limits and held contracts to be void which were really only voidable, a process which was capable of being attended with much injustice to third persons who had bought goods or otherwise committed themselves on the faith that there was a contract. Since the fusion of law and equity there is no reason to continue this process, and it will be found that only those contracts are now held void where the mistake was such as to prevent the formation of any contract at all.

Let me first consider mistakes which render a contract a nullity. All previous decisions on this subject must now be read in the light of *Bell v Lever Bros Ltd.* The correct interpretation of that case, to my mind, is that once a contract has been made, that is to say, once the parties, whatever their inmost states of mind, have to all outward appearances agreed with sufficient certainty in the same terms on the same subject-matter, then the contract is good unless and until it is set aside for breach of some condition expressed or implied in it, or for fraud, or on some equitable ground. Neither party can rely on his own mistake to say it was a nullity from the beginning, no matter that it was a mistake which to his mind was fundamental, and no matter that the other party knew he was under a mistake. *A fortiori* if the other party did not know of the mistake, but shared it. The cases where goods have perished at the time of sale, or belong to the buyer, are not really contracts which are void for mistake, but are void by reason of an implied condition to that effect, and even cases like *Smith v Hughes* turn at law on whether there was a contractual condition or not. So far as cases later than *Bell v Lever Bros Ltd* are concerned, I do not think that *Sowler v Potter* can stand with *King's Norton Metal Co Ltd v Edridge, Merrett & Co Ltd*, which shows that the doctine of French law as enunciated by Pothier is no part of English law. Nor do I think that the contract in *Nicholson and Venn v Smith-Marriott* was void from the beginning. Applying these principles it is clear that here there was a contract. The parties agreed in the same terms on the same subject-matter. It is true that the landlord was under a mistake which was to him fundamental. He would not for one moment have considered letting the flat for seven years if it meant that he could only charge £140 a year for it. He made the fundamental mistake of believing that the rent he could charge was not limited to a controlled rent, but, whether it was his own mistake or a mistake common to both him and the tenant, it is not a ground for saying that the lease was from the beginning a nullity. Any other view would lead to remarkable results, for it would mean that in the many cases where the parties mistakenly think the house is outside the Rent Acts when it is really within them, the tenancy would be a nullity, and the tenant would have to go, with the result that tenants would not dare to seek to have their rents reduced to the permitted amounts lest they should be turned out.

Let me next consider mistakes which render a contract voidable, that is, liable to be set aside on some equitable ground. While presupposing that a contract was good at law, or at any rate not void, the court of equity would often relieve a party from the consequences of his own mistake, so long as it could do so without injustice to third parties. The court had power to set aside the contract whenever it was of opinion that it was unconscientious for the other party to avail himself of the legal advantage which he had obtained: *Torrance v Bolton*. This branch of equity has shown a progressive development. It is now clear that a contract will be set aside if the mistake of the one party has been induced by a material misrepresentation of the other, even though it was not fraudulent or fundamental, or if one party, knowing that the other is mistaken about the terms of an offer, or the identity of the person by whom it is made, lets him remain under his delusion and conclude a contract on the mistaken terms instead of pointing out the mistake, which is, I venture to think, the ground on which the defendant in *Smith v Hughes* would be exempted nowadays, and on which, according to Blackburn J's view of the facts, the contract in *Lindsay v Cundy* was voidable and not void, and on which the lease in *Sowler v Potter* was, in my opinion, voidable and not void. A contract is also liable in equity to be set aside if the parties were under a common misapprehension either as to facts or as to their relative and respective rights, provided that the misapprehension was fundamental and that the party seeking to set it aside was not himself at fault. . . . [T]he House of Lords in 1867 in the great case of *Cooper v Phibbs* affirmed the doctine then acted on as perfectly correct doctrine. In that case an uncle had told his nephew, not intending to misrepresent anything but being in fact in error, that he (the uncle) was entitled to a fishery, and the nephew, after the uncle's death, acting in the belief of the truth of what the uncle had told him, entered into an agreement to rent the fishery from the uncle's daughters, whereas it actually belonged to the nephew himself. The mistake there as to the title to the fishery did not render the tendancy agreement a nullity. If it had done so, the contract would have been void at law from the beginning and equity would have had to follow the law. There would have been no contract to set aside and no terms to impose. The House of Lords, however, held that the mistake was only such as to make it voidable, or, in Lord Westbury's words (LR 2 HL 170) 'liable to be set aside' on such terms as the court thought fit to impose, and it was so set aside.

The principle so established by *Cooper v Phibbs* has been repeatedly acted on: see, for instance, *Earl Beauchamp v Winn*; *Huddersfield Banking Co, Ltd v Lister (Henry) & Son Ltd*. It is in no way impaired by *Bell v Lever Bros Ltd* which was treated in the House of Lords as a case at law depending on whether the contract was a nullity or not. If it had been considered on equitable grounds, the result might have been different. In any case the principle of *Cooper v Phibbs* has been fully restored by *Norwich Union Fire Insurance Society v Price Ltd* . . . On the landlord's evidence, which the judge preferred, I should have thought there was a good deal to be said for the view that the lease was induced by an innocent material misrepresentation by the tenant. It seems to me that the tenant was not merely expressing an opinion on the law. He was making an unambiguous statement as to private rights and a misrepresentation as to private rights is equivalent to a misrepresentation of fact for this purpose: *MacKenzie v Royal Bank of Canada*. But it is unnecessary to come to a firm conclusion on this point, because, as Bucknill LJ has said, there was clearly a mutual mistake, or, as I would prefer to describe it, a common misapprehension, which was fundamental and in no way due to any fault of the landlord, and *Cooper v Phibbs* affords ample authority for saying that, by reason of the common misapprehension, this lease can be set aside on such terms as the court thinks fit. . . .

What terms then should be imposed here? If the lease were set aside without any terms being imposed, it would mean that the tenant would have to go out and would have to pay a reasonable sum for his use and occupation. That would, however, not be just to the tenant. It is similar to a case where a long lease is made at the full permitted rent in the common belief that notices of increase have previously been served, whereas in fact they have not. In *Cooper v Phibbs*, as in this, when the lease is set aside, terms must be imposed so as to see that the tenant is not unjustly evicted. . . . If the mistake here had not happened a proper notice of increase would have been given and the lease would have been executed at the full permitted rent. I think this court should follow these examples and should impose terms which will enable the tenant to choose either to stay on at the proper rent or to go out.

In my opinion, therefore, the appeal should be allowed. The declaration that the standard rent of the flat is £140 per annum should stand. An order should be made on the counter-claim that, on the landlord giving the undertakings which I have mentioned, the lease be set aside. An account should be had to determine the sum payable for use and occupation. The tenant's claim for repayment of rent and for breach of covenant should be dismissed. In respect of the tenant's occupation during the rescinded lease and subsequent licence, he will be liable to pay a reasonable sum for use and occupation. That sum should, *prima facie*, be assessed at the full amount permitted by the Acts, not, however, exceeding £250 a year. Mesne profits as against a trespasser are assessed at the full amount permitted by the Acts, even though notices of increase have not been served, because that is the amount lost by the landlord. The same assessment should be made here because the sums payable for use and occupation are not rent, and the statutory provisions about notices of increase do not apply to them. All necessary credits must, of course, be given in respect of past payments, and so forth.

[Bucknill LJ delivered a concurring judgment.]

Jenkins LJ (dissenting). . . . The learned county court judge in the passage I have just quoted said that 'both parties for some obscure reason imagined that the Rent Acts did not apply', and that he did not think 'they ever addressed their minds to the material question of identity'. This was criticised as contrary to the evidence. I do not agree. I think the learned county court judge, who had himself formed a clear opinion to the effect that the re-constructed flat was in substance the same dwelling-house as the original flat, described the reason why the parties did not appreciate this and the consequent continued application of the standard rent of £140 as 'obscure', but accounted for it by concluding that the parties formed the view that the alterations and improvements prevented the old standard rent from applying without really directing their minds to the material question whether, notwithstanding all the alterations and improvements, the flat proposed to be let to the tenant was not, after all, substantially the same dwelling-house as the flat formerly let to Mr Howard Taylor. I see nothing in the evidence inconsistent with this explanation of the mistake, but, whether the parties failed to ask themselves the right question or, having asked it, answered it wrongly, I find it impossible to hold that a mutual mistake of the character here involved affords a good ground for rescission. The landlord meant to grant and the tenant meant to take a lease in the terms in which the lease was actually granted of the premises which the lease as granted actually comprised. They knew all the material facts bearing on the effect of the Rent Restrictions Acts on a lease of these premises, but they mutually misapprehended the effect which in that state of facts those Acts would have on such a lease. That is a mistake of law of a kind which, so far as I am aware, has never yet been held to afford good ground for rescission. It is a mistake, not as to the subject-matter, nature or purport of the contract entered into, nor as to any question of private right affecting the basis of the contract entered into: see *Cooper v Phibbs*; but simply a mistake as to the effect of certain public statutes on the contract made, being in all respects precisely the contract the parties intended to make. . . .

NOTES

1. Do you think that Denning LJ's statement of the law laid down in *Bell v Lever Bros Ltd* is accurate? See below, p 385.
2. In *Svanosio v McNamara* (1956) 96 CLR 186 at 196, Dixon CJ and Fullagar J of the High Court of Australia said:

> 'Mistake' might, of course, afford a ground on which equity would refuse specific performance of a contract, and there may be cases of 'mistake' in which it would be so inequitable that a party should be held to his contract that equity would set it aside. No rule can be laid down *a priori* as to such cases: see an article by Professor *R. A. Blackburn* in *Res Judicatae* (1955), vol 7, p 43. But we would agree with Professor *Shatwell* [(1955) 33 Can BR 164, at 186–187] that it is difficult to conceive any circumstances in which equity could properly give relief by setting aside the contract unless there has been fraud or misrepresentation or a condition can be found expressed or implied in the contract.

3. If there is an equitable jurisdiction to set aside a contract because of a common mistake, even though the contract is not void at common law, is it not strange that this was not discussed, let alone applied, in *Bell v Lever Bros*? In *Magee v Pennine Insurance Co Ltd* [1969] 2 QB 507 the plaintiff had entered an agreement with the defendants settling a claim under a policy the plaintiff had with them. The defendants then discovered that the original policy was voidable because of an innocent misrepresentation made by the plaintiff in his proposal form and refused to pay the sum agreed in settlement. In the Court of Appeal Lord Denning MR applied his own words in *Solle v Butcher* and held that the settlement agreement was voidable for common mistake. Fenton Atkinson LJ agreed, apparently for the same reasons. Winn LJ dissented: the case was indistinguishable from *Bell v Lever Bros*. The equitable doctrine was also applied in *Grist v Bailey* [1967] Ch 532; see below, p 393.
4. Under the equitable doctrine a contract which is valid at law may be set aside if the mistake is 'fundamental'. If the mistake 'destroys the identity of the subject matter' there will be no contract at all. What does 'fundamental' mean then?
5. Suppose the parties are both acting under a common mistake which might make the situation fundamentally different, but one party (only) should have realized, or has contributed to, the mistake. What result would be reached under (a) the common law rule, (b) the equitable rule?

Associated Japanese Bank (International) Ltd v Crédit du Nord SA [1988] 3 All ER 902, Steyn J

Under a sale and leaseback transaction the plaintiff bank purchased four specified precision engineering machines from B and then leased them back to him. B received £1,021,000 from the plaintiff bank under the transaction. As a condition of the transaction, B's obligations under the leaseback agreement were guaranteed by the defendant bank. At all times both banks believed that the four machines existed and were in B's possession. After B failed to keep up payments under the lease it was discovered that the machines did not in fact exist and that the transaction was a fraud perpetrated by B. The plaintiff claimed the outstanding balance due under the lease from B but he went bankrupt and the plaintiff then sued the defendant on the guarantee. The defendant refused to pay, contending, inter alia, that the guarantee was subject to an express or implied condition precedent that the machines in fact existed and therefore the guarantee was void ab initio for common mistake.

Steyn J. . . . THE CONSTRUCTION POINT

The first question to be considered is whether the guarantee was expressly made subject to a condition precedent that the four machines existed. The factual matrix, which is relevant to this question of construction, is that both parties, the creditor and the guarantor, were induced to commit themselves by information supplied by the lease brokers employed by Mr Bennett. That information included the statement, which was made expressly or by necessary implication, that the four machines existed. . . . Against that contextual scene, CDN provided a guarantee to AJB—

> in consideration of your leasing 4 Textile Compression Packaging machines to British Consolidated Engineering Company . . . pursuant to a Leasing Contract dated 29th February 1984 . . .

The only other provision of the guarantee which is relevant to this question of construction is cl 6 of the guarantee. It reads as follows:

> *This Guarantee and your rights under it shall not be affected or prejudiced* by your holding or taking any other or further securities or by your varying releasing or omitting or neglecting to enforce any such securities or by your giving time for payment or granting any other indulgence to or making any other arrangements with or accepting any composition from the Lessee or *subject to our prior consent to any such variation by your varying the terms of the Leasing Contract made between yourselves and the Lessee or by the substitution of any other goods comprised in such contract.* (My emphasis.)

On behalf of AJB it was submitted that the words 'subject to our prior consent' govern only variations of the lease other than variations entailing a substitution of goods. In other words, it was submitted that consent of the guarantor was required for any variation except one of the most important of all variations, viz substitution of goods. That interpretation is not justified by the language of cl 6, and it is a wholly unreasonable interpretation. I reject it. Clause 6 of the guarantee therefore contemplated the existence of the machines, and made provision for a right of substitution only if the guarantor granted consent. Against that background the question is whether it was *expressly* agreed that the guarantee would only become effective if there was a lease of four existing machines. The point is not capable of elaborate analysis. It is a matter of first impression. On balance, my conclusion is that, sensibly construed against its objective setting, the guarantee was subject to an express condition precedent that there was a lease in respect of four existing machines. If this conclusion is right, AJB's claim against CDN as guarantor or as sole or principal debtor under cl 11 fails.

If my conclusion about the construction of the guarantee is wrong, it remains to be considered whether there was an *implied* condition precedent that the lease related to four existing machines. . . . It is possible to imply a term if the court is satisfied that reasonable men, faced with the suggested term which was ex hypothesi not expressed in the contract, would without hesitation say, 'Yes, of course, that is so obvious that it goes without saying': see *Shirlaw v Southern Foundries (1926) Ltd*, per Mackinnon LJ [see above, p 320]. . . . [A]gainst the contextual background of the fact that both parties were informed that the machines existed, and the express terms of the guarantee, I have come to the firm conclusion that the guarantee contained an implied condition precedent that the lease related to existing machines. Again, if this conclusion is right, AJB's claim against CDN as guarantor or as sole or principal debtor under cl 11 fails. . . .

Notwithstanding these conclusions, which are determinative of the case, I will now consider the arguments as to common or mutual mistake which played such a large part at the hearing of this case.

MISTAKE

The common law regarding mutual or common mistake

There was a lively debate about the common law rules governing a mutual or common mistake of the parties as to some essential quality of the subject matter of the contract. Counsel for CDN submitted that *Bell v Lever Bros Ltd* authoritatively established that a mistake by both parties as to the existence of some quality of the subject matter of the contract, which makes the subject matter of the contract without the quality essentially different from the subject matter as it was believed to be, renders the contract void ab initio. Counsel for AJB contested this proposition. He submitted that at common law a mistake even as to an essential quality of the subject matter of the contract will not affect the contract unless it resulted in a total failure of consideration. It was not clear to me that this formulation left any meaningful and independent scope for the application of common law rules in this area of the law. In any event, it is necessary to examine the legal position in some detail.

The landmark decision is undoubtedly *Bell v Lever Bros Ltd*. . . .

[Steyn J considered the history of common mistake and continued:]

Lord Atkin held:

> . . . a mistake will not affect assent unless it is the mistake of both parties, and is as to the existence of some quality which makes the thing without the quality essentially different from the thing as it was believed to be.

In my view none of the other passages in Lord Atkin's speech detract from that statement of the law. Lord Thankerton came to a similar conclusion. He held that common mistake 'can only properly relate to something which both must necessarily have accepted in their minds as an essential and integral part of the subject-matter'.

That seems to me exactly the same test as Lord Atkin enunciated. . . .

It seems to me that the better view is that the majority in *Bell v Lever Bros Ltd* had in mind only mistake at common law. That appears to be indicated by the shape of the argument, the proposed amendment placed before the House of Lords (see [1932] AC 161 at 191, [1931] All ER Rep 1 at 15) and the speeches of Lord Atkin and Lord Thankerton. But, if I am wrong on this point, it is nevertheless clear that mistake at common law was in the forefront of the analysis in the speeches of the majority.

The law has not stood still in relation to mistake in equity. Today, it is clear that mistake in equity is not circumscribed by common law definitions. A contract affected by mistake in equity is not void but may be set aside on terms: see *Solle v Butcher*; *Magee v Pennine Insurance Co Ltd*; *Grist v Bailey*. It does not follow, however, that *Bell v Lever Bros Ltd* is no longer an authoritative statement of mistake at common law. On the contrary, in my view the principles enunciated in that case clearly still govern mistake at common law. It is true that in *Solle v Butcher* Denning LJ interpreted *Bell v Lever Bros Ltd* differently. He said that a common mistake, even on a most fundamental matter, does not make the contract void at law. That was an individual opinion. . . . With the profoundest respect to the former Master of the Rolls, I am constrained to say that in my view his interpretation of *Bell v Lever Bros* does not do justice to the speeches of the majority.

When Lord Denning MR referred in *Magee v Pennine Insurance Co Ltd* to the views of commentators he may have had in mind comments in Cheshire and Fifoot *Law of Contract* (6th edn, 1964) p 196. In substance the argument was that the actual decision in *Bell v Lever Bros Ltd* contradicts the language of the speeches. If the test was not satisfied there, so the argument runs, it is difficult to see how it could ever be satisfied: see the latest edition of this valuable textbook for the same argument (Cheshire, Fifoot and Furmston *Law of Contract* (11th edn, 1986) pp 225–226). This is a point worth examining because at first glance it may seem persuasive. *Bell v Lever Bros Ltd* was a quite exceptional case; all their Lordships were agreed that common mistake had not been pleaded and would have required an amendment in the House of Lords if it were to succeed. The speeches do not suggest that the employees were entitled to keep both the gains secretly made and the golden handshakes. The former were clearly recoverable from them. Nevertheless, the golden handshakes were very substantial. But there are indications in the speeches that the so-called 'merits' were not all in favour of Lever Bros. The company was most anxious, because of a corporate merger, to terminate the two service agreements. There was apparently a doubt whether voidability of the service agreements if revealed to the company *at the time of the severance contract* would have affected the company's decision. . . .

. . . With due deference to the distinguished authors who have argued that the actual decision in *Bell v Lever Bros Ltd* contradicts the principle enunciated in the speeches it seems to me that their analysis is altogether too simplistic, and that the actual decision was rooted in the particular facts of the case. In my judgment there is no reason to doubt the substantive reasons emerging from the speeches of the majority.

No one could fairly suggest that in this difficult area of the law there is only one correct approach or solution. But a narrow doctrine of common law mistake (as enunciated in *Bell v Lever Bros Ltd*), supplemented by the more flexible doctrine of mistake in equity (as developed in *Solle v Butcher* and later cases), seems to me to be an entirely sensible and satisfactory state of the law: see *Sheikh Bros Ltd v Ochsner* [1957] AC 136. And there ought to be no reason to struggle to avoid its application by artificial interpretations of *Bell v Lever Bros Ltd*.

It might be useful if I now summarised what appears to me to be a satisfactory way of approaching this subject. Logically, before one can turn to the rules as to mistake, whether at common law or in equity, one must first determine whether the contract itself, by express or implied condition precedent or otherwise, provides who bears the risk of the relevant mistake. It is at this hurdle that many pleas of mistake will either fail or prove to have been unnecessary. Only if the contract is silent on the point is there scope for invoking mistake. That brings me to the relationship between common law mistake and mistake in equity. Where common law mistake has been pleaded, the court must first consider this plea. If the contract is held to be void, no question of mistake in equity arises. But, if the contract is held to be valid, a plea of mistake in equity may still have to be considered: see *Grist v Bailey* and the analysis in *Anson's Law of Contract* (26th edn, 1984) pp 290–291. Turning now to the approach to common law mistake, it seems to me that the following propositions are valid although not necessarily all entitled to be dignified as propositions of law.

The first imperative must be that the law ought to uphold rather than destroy apparent contracts. Second, the common law rules as to a mistake regarding the quality of the subject matter, like the common law rules regarding commercial frustration, are designed to cope with the impact of unexpected and wholly exceptional circumstances on apparent contracts. Third, such a mistake in order to attract legal consequences must substantially be shared by both parties, and must relate to facts as they existed at the time the contract was made. Fourth, and this is the point established by *Bell v Lever Bros Ltd*, the mistake must render the subject matter of the contract essentially and radically different from the subject matter which the parties believed to exist. While the civilian distinction between the substance and attributes of the subject matter of a contract has played a role in the development of our law (and was cited in the speeches in *Bell v Lever Bros Ltd*), the principle enunciated in *Bell v Lever Bros Ltd* is markedly narrower in scope than the civilian doctrine. It is therefore no longer useful to invoke the civilian distinction. The principles enunciated by Lord Atkin and Lord Thankerton represent the ratio decidendi of *Bell v Lever Bros Ltd*. Fifth, there is a requirement which was not specifically discussed in *Bell v Lever Bros Ltd*. What happens if the party who is seeking to rely on the mistake had no reasonable grounds for his belief? An extreme example is that of the man who makes a contract with minimal knowledge of the facts to which the mistake relates but is content that it is a good speculative risk. In my judgment a party cannot be allowed to rely on a common mistake where the mistake consists of a belief which is entertained by him without any reasonable gounds for such belief: cf *McRae v Commonwealth Disposals Commission*. That is not because principles such as estoppel or negligence require it, but simply because policy and good sense dictate that the positive rules regarding common mistake should be so qualified. Curiously enough this qualification is similar to the civilian concept where the doctrine of error in substantia is tempered by the principles governing culpa in contrahendo. More importantly, a recognition of this qualification is consistent with the approach in equity where fault on the part of the party adversely affected by the mistake will generally preclude the granting of equitable relief: see *Solle v Butcher*.

Applying the law to the facts

It is clear, of course, that in this case both parties, the creditor and the guarantor, acted on the assumption that the lease related to existing machines. If they had been informed that the machines might not exist, neither AJB nor CDN would for one moment have contemplated entering into the transaction. That, by itself, I accept, is not enough to sustain the plea of common law mistake. I am also satisfied that CDN had reasonable grounds for believing that the machines existed. That belief was based on CDN's discussions with Mr Bennett, information supplied by National Leasing, a respectable firm of lease brokers, and the confidence created by the fact that AJB were the lessors.

The real question is whether the subject matter *of the guarantee* (as opposed to the sale and lease) was essentially different from what it was reasonably believed to be. The real security of the guarantor was the machines. The existence of the machines, being profit-earning chattels, made it more likely that the debtor would be able to service the debt. More importantly, if the debtor defaulted and the creditor repossessed the machines, the creditor had to give credit for 97½% of the value of the machines. If the creditor sued the guarantor first, and the guarantor paid, the guarantor was entitled to be subrogated to the creditor's rights in respect of recovery against the debtor: see Goff and Jones *Law of Restitution* (3rd edn, 1986) pp 533–536. No doubt the guarantor relied to some extent on the creditworthiness of Mr Bennett. But I find that the prime security to which the guarantor looked was the existence of the four machines as described to both parties. For both parties the guarantee of obligations under a lease with non-existent machines was essentially different from a guarantee of a lease with four machines which both parties at the time of the contract believed to exist. The guarantee is an accessory contract. The non-existence of the subject matter of the principal contract is therefore of fundamental importance. Indeed the analogy of the classic res extincta cases, so much discussed in the authorities, is fairly close. In my judgment, the stringent test of common law mistake is satisfied; the guarantee is void ab initio. . . .

Equitable mistake

Having concluded that the guarantee is void ab initio at common law, it is strictly unnecessary to examine the question of equitable mistake. Equity will give relief against common mistake in cases where the common law will not, and it provides more flexible remedies, including the power to set aside the contract on terms. It is not necessary to repeat my findings of fact save to record again the fundamental nature of the common mistake, and that CDN was not at fault in any way. If I had not decided in favour of CDN on construction and common law mistake, I would have held that the guarantee must be set aside on equitable principles. Unfortunately, and counsel are not to blame for that, the question of the terms (if any) to be imposed (having regard particularly to sums deposited by Mr Bennett with CDN) were not adequately explored in argument. If it becomes necessary to rule on this aspect, I will require further argument. . . .

Claim dismissed.

NOTES

1. The first ground for the decision in this case was that the guarantee was void as a matter of construction. We shall see in the next chapter a number of cases in which the courts have used the 'construction technique' to find contracts void or discharged without ever mentioning mistake or frustration.
2. If, as we have suggested, common law cases on mistake are really exercises in deciding how, given the terms and circumstances of the contract, the risk of what has happened should be allocated, how much difference is there between the 'construction technique' and the 'mistake technique' at common law? In other words, when Steyn J considered first construction and then whether the contract was void for mistake, was he really considering two different questions or the same question twice but dressed up in different language?
3. The equitable doctrine does seem conceptually different because of the apparent discretion to impose terms when setting aside the contract. Could it be argued that much the same results could be reached by elaborate use of the construction technique?

CHAPTER 19
Discharge by construction

There are a number of cases where the court has held that the occurrence of a contingency has the effect of discharging the contract, without relying specifically on either frustration or mistake.

Staffordshire Area Health Authority v South Staffordshire Waterworks Co [1978] 3 All ER 769, Court of Appeal

In 1908 a water company proposed to pump water from a well about a mile away from a hospital which had its own well. By the South Staffordshire Waterworks Act 1909 the water company was given statutory authority to pump water from its well subject to providing the hospital with such water as it required, at the rate it would cost the hospital to operate its own well, if the supply from the hospital's own well was diminished by reason of the water company's operations. Any disputes were to be settled by arbitration. In 1915 the water company began pumping water from its well and by 1918 this had an adverse effect on the supply from the hospital's well. The water company agreed to make up the deficiency from their mains. In 1927 the hospital authorities decided to abandon their well and commenced taking all the hospital's water from the company's mains. In 1929 the hospital authorities and the water company entered into an agreement under seal whereby 'at all times hereafter' the hospital was to receive 5,000 gallons of water per day free and all the additional water it required at the rate of 7d per 1,000 gallons. When decimal currency was introduced the rate was changed to 2.9p per 1,000 gallons. By 1975 the normal rate charged by the water company was 45p, and on 30th September 1975 the water company wrote to the hospital authorities giving notice that they intended to terminate the 1929 agreement in six months' time, and that thereafter they would supply 5,000 gallons per day free and any excess at normal rates. The hospital authorities refused to accept the notice as valid and took out an originating summons to establish that it was not. The judge upheld their claim on the ground that the 1929 agreement, being expressed to apply 'at all times hereafter', had been made forever or in perpetuity and therefore the water company could not resile from it.

Lord Denning MR. . . . I think that the rule of strict construction is now quite out of date. It has been supplanted by the rule that written instruments are to be construed in relation to the circumstances as they were known to or contemplated by the parties; and that even the plainest words may fall to be modified if events occur which the parties never had in mind and in which they cannot have intended the agreement to operate. . . .

As I understand this modern rule, we are no longer to go by the strict construction of the words as judges did in the 19th century. We are to put ourselves in the same situation as the parties were in at the time they drew up the instrument, to sit in their chairs with our minds endowed with the same facts as theirs were, and envisage the future with the same degree of foresight as they did. So placed we have to ask ourselves: what were the circumstances in which the contract was made? Does it apply in the least to the new situation which has developed? If events occur for which they have made no provision, and which were outside the realm of their speculations altogether, or of any reasonable persons sitting in their chairs, then the court itself must take a hand and hold that the contract ceases to bind. Such was the rule which I suggested long ago in *British Movietonews Ltd v London and District Cinemas Ltd* without success at that time: but which seems to have come into its own now. . . .

We were taken through six cases which considered contracts which contained no provision for determination. On going through them, they seem to show that, when a person agrees to supply goods or services continuously over an unlimited period of time in return for a fixed monthly or yearly payment, the courts shrink from holding it to be an agreement in perpetuity. The reason is because it is so unequal. The cost of supply of goods and services goes up with inflation through the rooftops: and the fixed payment goes down to the bottom of the well so that it is worth little or nothing. Rather than tolerate such inequality, the courts will construe the contract so as to hold that it is determinable by reasonable notice. They do this by reference to the modern rule of construction. They say that in the circumstances as they have developed, which the parties never had in mind, the contract ceases to bind the parties forever. It can be determined on reasonable notice.

[His Lordship considered the cases and continued.]

[From these cases] it is possible to detect a new principle emerging as to the effect of inflation and the fall in the value of money. In the ordinary way this does not affect the bargain between the parties. As I said in *Treseder-Griffin v Co-operative Insurance Society*:

'. . . in England we have always looked on a pound as a pound whatever its international value . . . Creditors and debtors have arranged for payment in our sterling currency in the sure knowledge that the sum they fix will be upheld by the law. A man who stipulates for a pound must take a pound, whenever payment is made, whatever the pound is worth at that time.'

But times have changed. We have since had mountainous inflation and the pound dropping to cavernous depths. In the recent case of *Multiservice Bookbinding Ltd v Marden* Browne-Wilkinson J departed from some of the things I said in *Treseder-Griffin* for that very reason, because of 20 years' experience of continuing inflation. The time has come when we may have to revise our views about the principle of nominalism, as it is called. Dr F A Mann in his book, The Legal Aspect of Money, said: 'If the trend of inflation which has clouded the last few decades continues some relief in the case of long-term obligations will become unavoidable.' That was written in 1971. Inflation has been more rampant than ever since that time. Here we have in the present case a striking of a long term obligation entered into 50 years ago. It provided for yearly payments for water supplied at seven old pence a 1,000 gallons. In these 50 years, and especially in the last 10 years, the cost of supplying the water has increased twentyfold. It is likely to increase with every year that passes. Is it right that the hospital should go on forever only paying the old rate of 50 years ago? It seems to me that we have reached the point which Viscount Simon contemplated in *British Movietonews Ltd v London and District Cinemas Ltd*. Speaking apropos of a depreciation of currency, he envisaged a situation where:

' . . . a consideration of the terms of the contract, in the light of circumstances existing when it was made, shows that they never agreed to be bound in a fundamentally different situation which has now unexpectedly emerged, [and he went on to say that when such a situation emerges] the contract ceases to bind at that point – not because the court in its discretion thinks it just and reasonable to qualify the terms of the contract, but because on its true construction it does not apply in that situation.'

That is the forerunner of the modern rule of construction.

So here the situation has changed so radically since the contract was made 50 years ago that the term of the contract 'at all times hereafter' ceases to bind: and it is open to the court to hold that the contract is determined by reasonable notice.

I do not think that the water company could have determined the agreement immediately after it was made. That cannot have been intended by the parties. No rule of construction could sensibly permit such a result. But, in the past 50 years, the whole situation has changed so radically that one can say with confidence: 'The parties never intended that the supply should be continued in these days at that price.' Rather than force such unequal terms on the parties, the court should hold that the agreement could be and was properly determined in 1975 by the reasonable notice of six months.

Cumming-Bruce LJ. . . . I have come to the conclusion that the words do not carry the meaning that the judge decided but that the words 'at all times hereafter' mean that the obligations granted and accepted by the agreement were only intended to persist during the continuance of the agreement; and the agreement, in my view, was determinable on reasonable notice at any time, so that had there been a change of circumstances which would have afforded either party an opportunity for arbitration under s 23 the agreement could then have been determined on reasonable notice.

Having regard to the cases which were helpfully cited in argument, I agree with the analysis of those cases proposed by Goff LJ and cannot usefully add anything. With all respect to Lord

Denning MR, I do not found my decision on the existence of an implied term that the agreement should not continue to bind the parties on the emergence of circumstances which the parties did not then foresee. I find it unnecessary on the view which I have formed about the intention of the parties to be collected from the circumstances to consider that. I am not attracted against the history of fact in this case either by the argument founded on frustration or on an implied term akin to frustration, and I can find no authority which leads me to the view that the changing value of money has the effect in relation to domestic as compared to international contracts of giving rise to the operation of an implied term that the contract should only persist while money maintained the value or more or less the value that it had at the date of the formation of the agreement.

[Goff LJ also held that the agreement was determinable by reasonable notice.]

Appeal allowed.

NOTES

1. Is it correct that the majority's analysis would have permitted determination for any reason whatever after one or two years? Is that a sensible outcome?
2. Are Denning's dicta reconcilable with *Davis Contractors Ltd v Fareham UDC*?
3. What can the parties do to cope with the uncertainties of inflation? One possibility is to agree that the price will be the seller's list price for the item at the date of delivery (see *Butler Machine Tool Co Ltd v Ex-Cell-O Corpn (England) Ltd*, above. p 193); another, to link the price directly to indices which give the prices of the materials and labour involved. It is also permissible, it seems, to link the price to an 'unrelated' index such as the value of the Swiss franc: see *Multiservice Bookbinding Ltd v Marden*, below, p 658.
4. England has suffered serious inflation, but not hyperinflation. Should hyperinflation occur, should the risk be allocated in the same way as that of 'normal' inflation? You may find it interesting to look at Horn, Kotz and Leser, *German Private and Commercial Law* (1982), pp 140–143. French law has also developed a doctrine ('imprévision') to permit adjustment of long-term contracts with public authorities which have become too burdensome for the contractor to perform, so that the public interest in performance is at risk: see Nicholas, *French Law of Contract* (1982), pp 202–204.
5. Quite different problems are posed by a sharp price increase in just the commodity sold, or just the class from which the commodity comes (eg fuels). A very interesting discussion of the recent difficulties faced by Westinghouse when uranium increased dramatically in price will be found in Joskow, 'Commercial Impossibility, The Uranium Market and the Westinghouse Case' (1977) 6 JLS 119. Note that Joskow is discussing American law under UCC 2-615, which is in theory markedly different to English law in allowing a defence of commercial impracticability.

In *HR & S Sainsbury Ltd v Street* [1972] 3 All ER 1127 there was a contract between the plaintiffs and the defendant for the purchase of 275 tons of feed barley to be grown on the defendant's land at East Knoyle in Wiltshire. The harvest was a very poor one and the land produced only 140 tons, which the defendant sold to another corn merchant at a higher price per ton. The plaintiffs claimed damages for failure to deliver the 140 tons produced.

MacKenna J decided in favour of the plaintiffs; he was prepared to assume that there was an implied condition that the defendant would be excused if through no fault of his the land did not produce the contract quantity, but that did not release him from the obligation to deliver the barley actually produced. Since there was an obligation to deliver the barley grown, the contract was not frustrated (unless there can be frustration pro rata, as to which see Hudson, 'Prorating in the English Law of Frustrated Contracts' (1968) 31 MLR 535). Presumably the buyer was equally bound to take the 140 tons? Yet the seller was excused from his obligation to deliver the ungrown portion. For other cases of partial excuse, see *Minnevitch v Café de Paris (Londres) Ltd* [1936] 1 All ER 884, 52 TLR 413; *Poussard v Spiers and Pond* (1876) 1 QBD 410.

Financings Ltd v Stimson [1962] 3 All ER 386, Court of Appeal

On Mar 16, 1961, the defendant saw a motor car on the premises of a dealer and signed a hire purchase form provided by the plaintiff finance company and produced by the dealer. The form contained, amongst others, clauses that the agreement should be binding on the finance company only on acceptance by their signature, that the hirer acknowledged that before he signed the agreement he had examined the goods and satisfied himself that they were in good order and condition, and that the goods should be at the risk of the hirer from the time of purchase by the owner. On Mar 18 the defendant paid the first instalment due and was allowed to take possession of the motor car, but, on Mar 20, being dissatisfied with it, he returned it to the dealer, saying that he did not want it and offering to forfeit the instalment which he had paid. Neither the defendant nor the dealer informed the finance company of the return of the car. On the night of Mar 24–25 the car was stolen from the dealer's premises and recovered severely damaged. On Mar 25 the finance company signed the agreement. Subsequently the finance company sold the damaged car and claimed damages from the defendant for breach of the hire-purchase agreement or as bailee on the terms of the agreement.

[The majority (Lord Denning MR and Donovan LJ, Pearson LJ dissenting) held that the plaintiffs' claim should be dismissed, and the defendant's counter-claim for the return of his deposit be allowed, on two grounds. Firstly:]

. . . the return of the motor car by the defendant to the dealer on Mar. 20 amounted to revocation of the offer by the defendant, since, on the facts of the case, the dealer had ostensible authority to accept the revocation of the offer on behalf of the finance company . . .

[On the second point:]

Lord Denning MR. [T]here is the second point to be considered which appealed to the county court judge: He said:

'When this offer was made, it was made on the basis that the car was in good condition, or at all events in the condition in which the defendant had seen it, but, before the offer was accepted (it was accepted on Mar 25), on the night of Mar 24/25 it suffered this extra damage which cost £44 to repair, having been scratched and dented by the thieves who stole it. Can a man accept an offer when the condition of the goods has deteriorated in a material respect since the date of the offer?

It seems to me that, on the facts of this case, the offer made by the defendant was a conditional offer. It was conditional on the car remaining in substantially the same condition until the moment of acceptance. Take the case put by Donovan LJ in the course of the argument: Suppose an offer is made to buy a Rolls-Royce car at a high price on one day and, before it is accepted, it suffers the next day severe damage. Can it be accepted and the offeror bound? My answer to that is: No, because the offer is conditional on the goods at the moment of acceptance remaining in substantially the same condition as at the time of the offer. Counsel for the plaintiffs argued that there was an express clause here saying that the goods were to be 'at the risk of the hirer from the time of purchase by the owner'. The time of purchase by the owner, he said, was Mar 18, when the plaintiffs told the dealer orally that they accepted the transaction.

Thence-forward, he said, the goods were at the risk of the defendant. This shows, says counsel, that the condition which I have suggested is inconsistent with the express terms, or, at all events, is not to be implied. In my judgment, however, this clause on which counsel relies only comes into operation when a contract is concluded and accepted. Meanwhile the offer is made on the understanding that, so long as it remains an offer, it is conditional on the goods being in substantially the same condition as at the time when the offer was made. I agree, therefore, with the county court judge in thinking that, in view of the damage which occurred to this car before the acceptance was given, the plaintiffs were not in a position to accept the offer, because the condition on which it was made had not been fulfilled. So on that ground also there was no contract.

NOTES

1. Technically, this decision again meant that a contract had never come into existence, but it is included in this chapter because the court achieves a just result by holding that neither party is bound.
2. For a discussion of this case and others using a 'construction' technique to solve a variety of problems, see Atiyah, 'Judicial Techniques and the Law of Contract' in *Essays on Contract* (1986), Chap 9.

'The Law of Contract' by Collins, pp 151–153, 156–158

During the performance of a contract, the classical rule holds the parties strictly liable for failure to fulfil their obligations. No matter that unexpected events have dramatically altered the costs of one party's performance, the courts have generally insisted upon strict enforcement of the contract. . . .

Judicial revision of contracts on grounds of fairness in the circumstances which have arisen represents the opposite of strict liability. Instead of holding the parties to their contract come fair weather or foul, judicial revision involves a termination of the existing contract and, where appropriate, the formation of a new contractual relation between the parties on terms which are fair. . . .

By stating the implications of judicial revision of contracts in this stark fashion, we can appreciate immediately why most judges and commentators fervently reject it. . . .

[T]he courts are unwilling to contemplate exceptions to the principle of strict liability, let alone indulge in the practice of revising the price of contracts. Indeed, it remains uncertain in the modern law whether any exceptions to strict liability exist. In many treatises the writers suggest that two doctrines—frustration and, to a lesser extent, mistake—afford occasional relief from the rigours of strict liability. But the courts have hesitated to acknowledge these exceptions, preferring to decide cases through construction of the terms of the contract. In effect, the courts in these cases of changed circumstances interpret the contract in such a way as to exculpate the party who is disadvantaged. . . .

The fundamental policy behind judicial revision through techniques of construction is to preserve the balance of advantage throughout the life of the contract. Although many judges deny that fairness is relevant to the question of whether or not a contract is frustrated or can be rescinded for mistake, in increasing numbers they have been admitting that a notion of fairness underlies their decisions. The courts usually avoid the terminology of fairness, however, preferring the concepts of justice and injustice to express the scope of the doctrine. In a representative dictum, Lord Denning MR states his interpretation of the doctrine of frustration thus:

> if it should happen, in the course of carrying out a contract, that a fundamentally different situation arises for which the parties made no provision—so much so that it would not be just in the new situation to hold the bound to its terms—then the contract is at an end.

Of course, these references to injustice or, as we prefer to say, unfairness, fail to specify the concept of justice which lies behind the courts' decisions. In the remaining pages of the chapter we will examine the concept of fairness employed in the modern law.

Many considerations influence courts in their decision to revise the contract, but in the modern law the two key factors which prompt intervention are the values of paternalism and co-operation. Paternalism leads courts to adjust the contract when the person seeking relief lacks commercial skills, but to refrain from revision in ordinary commercial contracts. The contrast between *Amalgamated Investment and Property Co. Ltd v John Walker & Sons Ltd* [1977] 1 WLR 164 and *Grist v Bailey* [above, p 383] illustrates this differential treatment. In the former case the plaintiffs sought to avoid a contract for the purchase of a building intended for redevelopment when shortly after signing the agreement it emerged that the government had designated the building one of special architectural or historical interest which immediately reduced the market value of the property. In *Grist v Bailey* the vendor of a house claimed rescission of the contract on the ground that the parties had mistakenly believed that it was occupied by a tenant with statutorily protected tenure which reduced the price. Whereas the English Court of Appeal in the former case gave short shrift to the plaintiffs' argument that they should be relieved from their calamitous contract on the ground that the government order was just one of those risks which purchasers of property take, the High Court in *Grist v Bailey* bent over backwards to permit the vendor, who was an ordinary house-owner with no special skills, to rescind the contract because of her mistake about vacant possession. These cases may be distinguished on a number of other grounds which potentially subvert the argument that paternalist motives affect the application of judicial revision . . . [For instance it could be argued] that the mistake in one case was more fundamental than in the other, though in monetary terms this is a tough argument to present since the drop in value in *Amalgamated Investment and Property Co Ltd v John Walker & Sons Ltd* was from £1,710,000 to approximately £200,000. It is more realistic, however, to acknowledge that paternalist considerations determined the divergent results. Whereas the parties in one case were commercial enterprises, aware of the risks of property development, the parties in the other were ordinary householders and relatively naive about the risks associated with their transaction. The courts adopt a criterion of fairness which discriminates between types of contractors, forcing commercial enterprises to shoulder more risks of misadventure than ordinary individuals.

Yet courts do revise a few commercial contracts on the ground of fairness, especially in contracts calling for successive performances over a long period. The value of co-operation explains this differential treatment of long-term contracts. In *Aluminium Co of America v Essex Group* 499 F. Supp. 53 (WDPa. 1980), under a 16-year contract with an option to renew for an additional five years, ALCOA agreed to convert alumina supplied by Essex into molten aluminium. The contract contained detailed provisions designed to raise the price in line with the wholesale price index, but this index failed to account for the sharp rise in the cost of energy to ALCOA, so the contract became increasingly unprofitable to them. The Federal District Court declared that the contract had gone awry because of a mistake in formulating the pricing mechanism to account for inflation. So the court set aside the contract and imposed a new pricing formula. The distinction between the willingness to adopt a criterion of fairness in this case and the insistence on strict liability in *Amalgamated Investment and Property Co Ltd v John Walker & Sons Ltd* is justified because a long-term contract presents special problems of ensuring the equilibrium of the obligations, which leads naturally to a duty to co-operate during performance even to the extent of adjusting the price.

NOTES

1. *Grist v Bailey* was a case in which the vendor was given relief under the equitable doctrine of mistake. It can be argued that it was wrongly decided, as it effectively placed the 'risk' that the tenant would unexpectedly turn out not to be protected on the purchaser, who was in a less good position to discover the truth beforehand. The case may even be said to pay insufficient regard to the requirement that the party seeking relief should not be at fault. Although neither the plaintiff nor her solicitor were personally at fault, there had clearly been a slip-up somewhere on their side. But as Collins shows, there may be other views of the case.

2. The ALCOA case is very controversial even in the U.S.; it seems most unlikely that any English court would openly engage in judicial revision of the terms. But what would you expect the parties in the South Staffordshire case to have done after the decision was announced? Wasn't the decision tantamount to telling the parties to negotiate a new contract?

3. How far do you agree with Collins' analysis of what is going on in frustration, mistake and discharge by construction cases? Is it possible to prove that either his explanation or the efficiency explanation put forward earlier is the 'right' one?

CHAPTER 20
Duties of disclosure

Smith v Hughes (1871) LR 6 QB 597 (above, p 244)

There is no doubt that Cockburn CJ's judgment represents the general law. There are, however, a number of important exceptions. As far as goods are concerned, the most important is the duty to disclose known defects that would render the goods unmerchantable, which is in effect imposed by the implied condition of merchantability (above, p 327). The main difficulties arise in other contexts where there is no equivalent implied term, or the defect does not go to merchantability.

Moody v Cox & Hatt [1917] 2 Ch 71, Court of Appeal

Hatt, a solicitor, and Cox, his managing clerk, were trustees of some property which they agreed to sell to Moody. Hatt, through Cox, acted as solicitor for both vendors and purchaser. Cox failed to reveal to Moody that the property was worth much less than Moody was paying for it.

Scrutton LJ. . . . First of all as to the law. Generally when you have made a legal contract and correctly expressed it in writing, and it has not been obtained by any misstatement of fact, innocent or fraudulent, the contract stands, and the fact that one party or the other knows facts about which he says nothing, which make the contract an unprofitable one to the other party, is of no legal importance. But there are certain relations and certain contracts in which a higher duty is imposed upon the parties, and they must not only tell the truth, but they must tell the whole truth so far as it is material, and they must not only not misrepresent by words, but they must not misrepresent by silence if they know of something that is material. Some of those cases depend on the relation between the parties, and, generally speaking, are cases where the relation is such that you have confidence reposed by one party and influence exercised by the other. In that class of relation of parties you may get the duty, first of all, that the party who has influence must make a full disclosure of everything that he knows material to the contract; secondly, that the party who has the influence must not make a contract with the party over whom he has the influence unless he can satisfy the Court that that contract is an advantageous one to the other party. The second class of cases is one not depending on the relation of the parties, but depending on the nature of the contract; and a typical case of that kind is the contract of insurance, where to an underwriter who knows nothing comes an assured, a man who wants to be insured and who knows everything, and on him is imposed the duty of telling the man who knows nothing all that he knows, so that the underwriter may fix the premium. In the first class of relations that of solicitor and client is one of the obviously and constantly recognized examples. If a man who is in the position of solicitor to a client so that the client has presumably confidence in him, and the solicitor has presumably influence over the client, desires to contract with his client, he must make a full disclosure of every material fact that he knows, and must take upon himself the burden of satisfying the Court that the contract is one of full advantage to his client. . . .

(a) Undue influence

In *Tate v Williamson* (1866) 2 Ch App 55, Tate, an extravagant undergraduate hard pressed by his Oxford creditors and anxious to extricate himself from his financial embarrassment, sought the advice of Williamson. Having recommended the sale of Tate's Staffordshire estate, Williamson offered to buy it himself without disclosing that it was worth at least double the amount offered because of minerals under the land. Tate accepted Williamson's offer and conveyed the land, but some years later, after Tate had drunk himself to death, the sale was set aside at the instance of Tate's heir. Similar cases of undue influence will be dealt with in Chapter 30.

(b) Contracts uberrimae fidei

Lambert v Co-operative Insurance Society Ltd [1975] 2 Lloyd's Rep 485, Court of Appeal

In 1963 the plaintiff signed a proposal form for one of the defendants' 'All Risks' insurance policies to cover her own and her husband's jewellery. She did not mention that her husband had been convicted some years earlier of receiving 1,730 cigarettes knowing them to have been stolen and had been fined £25. The defendants issued a policy. In December 1971 Mr Lambert was convicted of two further offences of dishonesty and was sentenced to 15 months' imprisonment. At the next renewal date in March 1972 Mrs Lambert did not reveal this conviction. In April 1972 a number of items, valued at £311, were lost or stolen. The defendants refused to meet the plaintiff's claim on the ground of her failure to disclose her husband's convictions. The trial judge held for the defendants and the plaintiff appealed.

Mackenna J. . . . . Everyone agrees that the assured is under a duty of disclosure and that the duty is the same when he is applying for a renewal as it is when he is applying for the original policy. The extent of that duty is the matter in controversy. There are, at least in theory, four possible rules or tests which I shall state. (1) The duty is to disclose such facts only as the particular assured believes to be material. (2) It is to disclose such facts as a reasonable man would believe to be material. (3) It is to disclose such facts as the particular insurer would regard as material. (4) It is to disclose such facts as a reasonable or prudent insurer might have treated as material.

Section 18 of the Marine Insurance Act, 1906, chooses the fourth . . .

There is no obvious reason why there should be a rule in marine insurance different from the rules in other forms of insurance and in my opinion, there is no difference . . . The present case shows the unsatisfactory state of the law. Mrs Lambert is unlikely to have thought that it was necessary to disclose the distressing fact of her husband's recent conviction when she was renewing the policy on her little store of jewellery. She is not an underwriter and has presumably no experience in these matters. The defendant company would act decently if, having established the point of principle, they were to pay her. It might be thought a heartless thing if they did not, but that is their business, not mine. I would dismiss the appeal.

NOTE

The duty to disclose material facts applies to the insurer as well as to the insured. The duty is not founded on an implied term of the contract or on tort but on 'the jurisdiction originally exercised by the Courts of Equity to prevent imposition.' As a result, the remedy for a breach of it is rescission of the contract, and not damages: *Banque Financière de la Cité SA v Westgate Insurance Co Ltd* [1989] 2 All ER 952. (For more on this case see below, p 400.)

Family arrangements form another category of contracts uberrimae fidei. In *Gordon v Gordon* (1821) 3 Swan 400 a settlement, agreed on the basis that the elder son was probably illegitimate, was set aside upon proof that the younger son had concealed his knowledge of a private ceremony solemnized between his parents in America before the birth of the elder brother. Lord Eldon said:

> I think myself justified by the authority of *Cann v Cann* and other decisions, in holding that if a dispute arises relative to the legitimacy of children, and the members of the family, to maintain their character in the world, arrange their rights among themselves, if the matter is fully before them, their arrangement will not be disturbed, because it is founded on a supposition, which imputes the character of legitimacy to the illegitimate, or illegitimacy to the legitimate; but then there must be not only good faith and honest intention, but full disclosure; and without full disclosure honest intention is not sufficient.

(c) Information wrongfully obtained

In *Phillips v Homfray* (1871) 6 Ch App 770 the owners of a colliery entered into a contract with an adjoining landowner to buy his land, without disclosing that they had wrongfully extracted a considerable quantity of coal from under it. It was held by the Lord Chancellor, on appeal from Stuart V-C, that the contract was not enforceable by the purchasers, even though it was not shown to be at an undervalue.

> **Lord Hatherley LC.** . . . I apprehend that in such a case the Court, whatever it might do as to cancelling the contract, certainly would decline to enforce it. The case would, I think, be something analogous to this: Suppose a picture-dealer, employed to clean a picture, scrapes off a part of the picture to see if he can discover a mark which will tell him who is the artist, and thus finds a mark shewing it to be the work of a great artist; that would not be a legitimate mode of acquiring knowledge for the purpose of enabling him to buy the picture at a lower price than the owner would have sold it for had he known it to be the work of that artist. I do not, however, dwell on that point, as it is not satisfactorily established in my mind that the price was inadequate. The ground of my decision is, that the Appellants suppressed the fact of their having wrongfully got a large quantity of the Respondents' coal, and so given the Respondents a heavy pecuniary claim against them.

(d) Statutory duties of disclosure

There are many statutory duties of disclosure relating to information to which the other party is unlikely to have access. See the Companies Act 1985, ss 56, 57, 66 and 67; Medicines Act 1968; Food Labelling Regulations 1984; Hallmarking Act 1973; etc. Of the statutes listed, only the Companies Act gives rise to civil liability if there is a breach, but nonetheless the buyer is given more information about the product than he might otherwise receive.

(e) A general duty of disclosure?

Should English law recognize a general duty to disclose facts which one party knows that the other party is ignorant of, and which would influence the other in his decision whether or not to enter the contract? In the US different courts have reached different solutions in different contexts. Parties who have (without acting wrongfully) discovered minerals under another's land have usually been permitted to take advantage of their knowledge, by being permitted to buy the land without disclosing their information. In contrast, read the next case.

Obde v Schlemeyer 56 Wash 2d 449, 353 P2d 672 (Supreme Court of Washington, 1960)

The plaintiffs bought a house from the defendants. The house was infested with termites. The trial court found that the defendants knew of the termite infestation and had not revealed it to the plaintiffs. The plaintiffs had asked no question about termites. The plaintiffs claimed damages for fraudulent concealment and the trial court awarded them $3,950. The defendants appealed.

Finley J. . . . . The Schlemeyers urge that, in any event, as sellers, they had no duty to inform the Obdes of the termite condition. They emphasize that it is undisputed that the purchasers asked no questions respecting the possibility of termites. They rely on a Massachusetts case involving a substantially similar factual situation, *Swinton v Whitinsville Savings Bank* (1942) . . . Applying the traditional doctrine of *caveat emptor*—namely, that, as between parties dealing at arms length (as vendor and purchaser), there is no duty to speak, in the absence of a request for information—the Massachusetts court held that a vendor of real property has no duty to disclose to a prospective purchaser the fact of a latent termite condition in the premises.

Without doubt, the parties in the instant case were dealing at arms length. Nevertheless, and notwithstanding the reasoning of the Massachusetts court above noted, we are convinced that the defendants had a duty to inform the plaintiffs of the termite condition. In *Perkins v Marsh* (1934) a case involving parties dealing at arms length as landlord and tenant, we held that,

'Where there are concealed defects in demised premises, dangerous to the property, health, or life of the tenant, which defects are known to the landlord when the lease is made, but unknown to the tenant, and which a careful examination on his part would not disclose, it is the landlord's duty to disclose them to the tenant before leasing, and his failure to do so amounts to a fraud.'

We deem this rule to be equally applicable to the vendor-purchaser relationship. See 15 TexLaw Review (December, 1936) 1, 14–16, Keeton: 'Fraud—Concealment and Non-Disclosure'. In this article Professor Keeton also aptly summarized the modern judicial trend away from a strict application of *caveat emptor* by saying:

'It is of course apparent that the content of the maxim 'caveat emptor', used in its broader meaning of imposing risks on both parties to a transaction, has been greatly limited since its origin. When Lord Cairns stated in *Peek v Gurney* that there was no duty to disclose facts, however morally censurable their non-disclosure may be, he was stating the law as shaped by an individualistic philosophy based upon freedom of contract. It was not concerned with morals. In the present stage of the law, the decisions show a drawing away from this idea, and there can be seen an attempt by many courts to reach a just result in so far as possible, but yet maintaining the degree of certainty which the law must have. The statement may often be found that if either party to a contract of sale conceals or suppresses a material fact which he is in good faith bound to disclose then his silence is fraudulent.

The attitude of the courts toward non-disclosure is undergoing a change and contrary to Lord Cairns' famous remark it would seem that the object of the law in these cases should be to impose on parties to the transaction a duty to speak whenever justice, equity, and fair dealing demand it'. (page 31.)

A termite infestation of a frame building, such as that involved in the instant case, is manifestly a serious and dangerous condition. . . . Further, at the time of the sale of the premises, the condition was clearly latent—not readily observable upon reasonable inspection. As we have noted, all superficial or surface evidence of the condition had been removed by reason of the efforts of Senske, the pest control specialist. Under the circumstances, we are satisfied that 'justice, equity, and fair dealing', to use Professor Keeton's language, demanded that the Schlemeyers speak—that they inform prospective purchasers, such as the Obdes, of the condition, regardless of the latter's failure to ask any questions relative to the possibility of termites.

[Weaver CJ, Rosellini, Foster and Hill JJ concurred.]

Judgment affirmed.

NOTE

To some extent the opposing results reflect different attitudes to self-reliance, but it has been suggested that there is an underlying economic rationale.

'Mistake, Disclosure, Information and the Law of Contracts' by Kronman (1978) 7 JLS 1, 2–5, 13–15, 25

Every contractual agreement is predicated upon a number of factual assumptions about the world. Some of these assumptions are shared by the parties to the contract and some are not. It is always possible that a particular factual assumption is mistaken. From an economic point of view, the risk of such a mistake (whether it be the mistake of only one party or both) represents a cost. It is a cost to the contracting parties themselves and to society as a whole since the actual occurrence of a mistake always (potentially) increases the resources which must be devoted to the process of allocating goods to their highest-valuing users.

There are basically two ways in which this particular cost can be reduced on an optimal level. First, one or both of the parties can take steps to prevent the mistake from occurring. Second, to the extent a mistake cannot be prevented, either party (or both) can insure against the risk of its occurrence.

Information is the antidote to mistake. Although information is costly to produce, one individual may be able to obtain relevant information more cheaply than another. If the parties to a contract are acting rationally, they will minimize the joint costs of a potential mistake by assigning the risk of its occurrence to the party who is the better (cheaper) information-gatherer. Where the parties have actually assigned the risk—whether explicitly, or implicitly through their adherence to trade custom and past patterns of dealing—their own allocation must be respected. Where they have not—and there is a resulting gap in the contract—a court concerned with economic efficiency should impose the risk on the better information-gatherer. This is so for familiar reasons: by allocating the risk in this way, an efficiency-minded court reduces the transaction costs of the contracting process itself.'

The most important doctrinal distinction in the law of mistake is the one drawn between 'mutual' and 'unilateral' mistakes. Traditionally, courts have been more reluctant to excuse a mistaken promisor where he alone is mistaken than where the other party is mistaken as to the same fact. Although relief for unilateral mistake has been liberalized during the last half-century (to the point where some commentators have questioned the utility of the distinction between unilateral and mutual mistake and a few have even urged its abolition), it is still 'black-letter' law that a promisor whose mistake is not shared by the other party is less likely to be relieved of his duty to perform than a promisor whose mistake happens to be mutual.

Viewed broadly, the distinction between mutual and unilateral mistake makes sense from an economic point of view. Where both parties to a contract are mistaken about the same fact or state of affairs, deciding which of them would have been better able to prevent the mistake may well require a detailed inquiry regarding the nature of the mistake and the (economic) role or position of each of the parties involved. But where only one party is mistaken, it is reasonable to assume that he is in a better position than the other party to prevent his own error. As we shall see, this is not true in every case, but it provides a useful beginning point for analysis and helps to explain the generic difference between mutual and unilateral mistakes.

Allocative efficiency is promoted by getting information of changed circumstances to the market as quickly as possible. Of course, the information doesn't just 'get' there. Like everything else, it is supplied by individuals (either directly, by being publicized, or indirectly, when it is signalled by an individual's market behavior).

In some cases, the individuals who supply information have obtained it by a deliberate search; in other cases, their information has been acquired casually. A securities analyst, for example, acquires information about a particular corporation in a deliberate fashion by carefully studying evidence of its economic performance. By contrast, a businessman who acquires a valuable piece of information when he accidentally overhears a conversation on a bus acquires the information casually.

As it is used here, the term 'deliberately acquired information' means information whose acquisition entails costs which would not have been incurred but for the likelihood, however great, that the information in question would acually be produced. These costs may include, of course, not only direct search costs (the cost of examining the corporation's annual statement) but the costs of developing an initial expertise as well (for example, the cost of attending business school). If the costs incurred in acquiring the information (the cost of the bus ticket in the second example) would have been incurred in any case—that is, whether or not the information was forthcoming—the information may be said to have been casually acquired. The distinction between deliberately and casually acquired information is a shorthand way of expressing this economic difference. Although in reality it may be difficult to determine whether any particular item of information has been acquired in one way or the other, the distinction between these two types of information has—as I hope to show—considerable analytical usefulness.

If information has been deliberately acquired (in the sense defined above), and its possessor is denied the benefits of having and using it, he will have an incentive to reduce (or curtail entirely) his production of such information in the future. This is in fact merely a consequence of defining deliberately acquired information in the way that I have, since one who acquires information of this sort will by definition have incurred costs which he would have avoided had it not been for the prospect of the benefits he has now been denied. By being denied the same benefits, one who has casually acquired information will not be discouraged from doing what—for independent reasons—he would have done in any case. . . .

One (seldom noticed) way in which the legal system can establish property rights in information is by permitting an informed party to enter—and enforce—contracts which his information suggests are profitable, without disclosing the information to the other party. Imposing a duty to disclose upon the knowledgeable party deprives him of a private advantage which the information would otherwise afford. A duty to disclose is tantamount to a requirement that the benefit of the information be publicly shared and is thus antithetical to the notion of a property right which—whatever else it may entail—always requires the legal protection of private appropriation. . . .

Where the seller actually knows of the defect, and the buyer does not, the seller is clearly the party best able to avoid the buyer's mistake at least cost—unless the seller has made a deliberate investment in acquiring his knowledge which he would not have made had he known he would be required to disclose to purchasers of the property any defects he discovered. A seller, of course, may make a substantial investment in acquiring information concerning a particular defect: for example, he may hire exterminators to check his property for termites. But even so, it is unlikely that his principal aim in acquiring such information is to obtain an advantage over potential purchasers. Typically, homeowners conduct investigations of this sort in order to protect their own investments. In most cases, a homeowner will have an adequate incentive to check for termites even if the law requires him to disclose what he discovers; furthermore, many termite infestations are discovered by simply living in the house—something the owner will do in any event. A disclosure requirement is unlikely to have a substantial effect on the level of investment by homeowners in the detection of termites: the point is not that information regarding termites is costless (it isn't), but that a disclosure requirement would not be likely to reduce the production of such information. This represents an important distinction between cases like *Obde*, on the one hand, and [cases where it was held that relevant information need not be disclosed] . . .

NOTE

Is encouraging parties to invest in acquiring information a sufficient justification for allowing, for instance, companies which have discovered minerals under the other party's land to buy the land without disclosing anything and thereby to capture the whole of the increased value of the land? (See further below, p 582).

There is no sign of any move in English case law towards recognition of a general duty of disclosure—if anything, the indications are negative. Thus we will see below (p 651 ff.) that the grounds on which relief will be given after there have been other forms of advantage-taking seem to have been narrowed in the last few years. Moreover in *Banque Financière de la Cité SA v Westgate Insurance Co Ltd* [1989] 2 All ER 952 the Court of Appeal, having held that a breach of the duty to disclose in an insurance contract does not give any right to damages (see above, p 396), went on to hold that it did not give a right to damages under s 2(1) of the Misrepresentation Act or under the common law of tort. Section 2(1) did not apply because it refers to a 'misrepresentation' having been 'made', which does not cover mere non-disclosure; and the fact that the parties to an insurance contract are under mutual obligations to disclose material facts does not put them into a special relationship within *Hedley Byrne v Heller* (above, p 23). In the *Banque de la Cité* case a Mr Dungate, who was an employee of the insurers, had become aware that an employee of the insurance brokers, a Mr Lee, was issuing false cover notes on the strength of which the plaintiff banks were advancing loans, but Dungate did not tell either the brokers or the banks of the deception. As a result the banks could not recover on the insurance itself, but they argued that the insurers were liable to them in damages for failure to disclose Lee's dishonesty. Slade LJ said (at pp 1007–1012):

> Can a mere failure to speak ever give rise to liability in negligence under *Hedley Byrne* principles? On our view it can, but subject to the all-important proviso that there has been on the facts a voluntary assumption of responsibility in the relevant sense and reliance on that assumption. These features may be much more difficult to infer in a case of mere silence than in a case of misrepresentation . . .
>
> [However we] can see no sufficient reason on principle or authority why a failure to speak should not be capable of giving rise to liability under *Hedley Byrne* principles, provided that the two essential conditions are satisfied.
>
> A hypothetical example may illustrate the point. Suppose that a father employs an estate agent for a fee to advise his son on the proposed purchase of a house and the estate agent negligently fails to inform the son that a motorway is shortly to be constructed within a few hundred yards of the property. We would not doubt that in such a case the son, knowing of the estate agent's duty and relying on it, would have a claim in negligence . . .
>
> . . . Did Mr Dungate in fact assume responsibility towards the banks? If so, did the banks rely on that assumption of responsibility? The answer to each part of the question must surely be no.
>
> We can see no justification for holding that Mr Dungate, who made no representation, assumed any responsibility at all in relation to Mr Lee's honesty or dishonesty. Counsel for the banks other [than] Chemical Bank argued that a voluntary assumption of responsibility is to be found in Mr Dungate's voluntary conduct in continuing to deal with Mr Lee. We do not agree. The phrase 'voluntary assumption of responsibility' in this context means what it says: conduct by the party signifying that he assumes responsibility for taking due care in respect of the statement or action. No doubt, in deciding whether there has been such an assumption of responsibility the conduct of the party may be objectively construed. To deal in the ordinary way with an agent without any relevant communication to his principal cannot, we think, be held to be an assumption of responsibility because the party has done nothing which signifies assumption of responsibility in the relevant sense.
>
> Nor is there any evidence that the banks relied on any assumption of responsibility by the insurers in respect of Mr Lee's honesty. . . .
>
> But counsel for the banks other than Chemical Bank had an alternative submission. He argued that, although voluntary assumption of responsibility, coupled with reliance, is a condition for the existence of a duty of care in some cases of pure economic loss, it is not a condition of every such case; a duty of care not to cause economic loss may be owed without it.
>
> . . . [w]e are prepared to accept, for the purposes of this judgment, that in some cases (if rare) of pure economic loss the court may be willing to find the existence of a duty of care owed by a defendant to a plaintiff even in the absence of evidence of any actual voluntary assumption by the defendant of such duty and/or of any reliance on such assumption. We shall accordingly proceed on the basis that, on appropriate facts, the court may be willing to hold that, having regard to the special circumstances and the relationship between the parties, a defendant should be treated *in law* (even though not in fact) as having assumed a

responsibility to the plaintiff which is capable of giving rise to a claim for damages for pure economic loss. The remaining question, therefore, is whether Hodge should be so treated in this case.

In this context we attach importance to the distinction to which the judge in our view gave insufficient weight. For better or worse, our law of tort draws a fundamental distinction between the legal effects of acts on the one hand and omissions on the other . . .

The example given by Lord Keith is of a failure to prevent physical harm. But the same reluctance on the part of the courts to give a remedy in tort for pure omission applies, perhaps even more so, when the omission is a failure to prevent economic harm. As will appear below, a corresponding distinction is drawn by the law of contract which in general imposes no liability by virtue of a failure to speak as opposed to a misrepresentation.

In an important passage of his judgment the judge said that he did not regard the present case as 'a case of pure omission.' He gave two reasons (see [1987] 2 All ER 923 at 951, [1987] 2 WLR 1300 at 1338–1339):

> The relationship between the parties involved obligations of good faith and fair dealing. Moreover, the alleged duty arises in the context of insurers who had an established business relationship with the banks, and continued to transact further with the banks (and to make profits) in the knowledge that a risk, viz further dishonesty by Mr Lee, which was obvious to the insurers, was not appreciated by the banks and could not be discovered by them. It is a situation essentially different from pure omission cases. In my judgment the fact that the duty relied on by the banks required affirmative action on the part of the insurers (unless they simply decided in the circumstances not to insure) does not preclude a ruling that such a duty existed.

We take first his point that there was here an established business relationship with the banks, and the insurers continued to do business with the banks, even though they knew of the risk resulting from Mr Lee's dishonesty, while the banks did not.

In our judgment, to hold that these factors by themselves gave rise to a duty on the part of Mr Dungate to report Mr Lee's dishonesty to the banks, capable of exposing him or his employers to a liability in tort, would undermine basic principles of our law of contract.

Throughout this case it has to be borne in mind that the period in June 1980 in which it is said that Mr Dungate's duty to report arose and continued was one during which he was in the course of conducting contractual negotiations with the banks on behalf of his employers.

The general principle that there is no obligation to speak within the context of negotiations for an ordinary commercial contract (though qualified by the well-known special principles relating to contracts uberrimae fidei, fraud, undue influence, fiduciary duty etc) is one of the foundations of our law of contract, and must have been the basis of many decisions over the years. There are countless cases in which one party to a contract has in the course of negotiations failed to disclose a fact known to him which the other party would have regarded as highly material, if it had been revealed. However, ordinarily in the absence of misrepresentation, our law leaves that other party entirely without remedy. Lord Atkin gave some striking examples in *Bell v Lever Bros Ltd* . . .

. . . [I]n our judgment, it would be wholly contrary to principle to suggest, at least in the case of an ordinary contract made between persons in an ordinary relationship, that B, having undertaken no relevant contractual obligation to A, should be treated as having assumed a responsibility which could give rise to a liability to A in tort. To reach such a decision as to the effect of a non-disclosure in the course of contractual negotiations would run counter to the general principle of caveat emptor on which our law of contract is founded. . . .

By the same token we would hold that no legal obligation on the part of Mr Dungate to inform the banks of Mr Lee's dishonesty arose, either in contract or in tort, merely because there was an 'established business relationship' between the parties, and because the insurers continued to transact further business with the banks. That factor does not turn a pure omission into a misrepresentation, in tort any more than in contract. It would not justify the court treating Mr Dungate as having assumed a duty or responsibility to speak, in tort, which was not imposed on him by the law of contract.

This brings us to what was, in our view, the most forceful submission made on behalf of the banks. It ran on the following lines. As is common ground the negotiations between Hodge and the banks which resulted in the contract of insurance of 24 June 1980 imported mutual obligations of disclosure . . .

Why on those facts should the court not treat Hodge as having in law voluntarily assumed responsibility to make full disclosure of all material facts to the banks, not only for the purpose of the principles of *Carter v Boehm*, but also for the purpose of the law of negligence in tort? The very nature of the contract which was being negotiated, it is said, gives rise to a special relationship between the negotiating parties which justifies the imposition of a duty of care. . . .

We do not think that the nature of the contract as one of the utmost good faith can be used as a platform to establish a common law duty of care. Parliament has provided that in the case of marine insurance the consequence of a failure to disclose a material fact, and by inference the *only* consequence, is that the contract may be avoided. It is not suggested that the consequences in non-marine insurance should be different. In those circumstances it is not, we think, open to the court to assist the banks by providing a supplementary remedy in tort. No doubt, on the very unusual facts of the present case, the statutory remedy of rescission seems inadequate. This is unfortunate for the banks. But the banks' misfortune is of the same kind as the misfortune suffered by the injured party in the various instances given by Lord Atkin in *Bell v Lever Bros Ltd* [see p 378 above], where the law affords no remedy at all. What the banks cannot do in our judgment is to invoke the nature of the contract as one of good faith, with its limited contractual remedy, to bridge the gap so as to give them cause of action in tort.

In 1988 the Conveyancing Standing Committee of the Law Commission provisionally recommended that:

A vendor of land should be under a positive duty to disclose all material facts about the property he is selling, providing he is aware of those facts or ought reasonably to be aware of them. (*Caveat Emptor in Sale of Land*, para 4.1)

It appears that this proposal did not meet with favour: the Committee's report, *Let the Buyer be Well Informed* (1990) made much more limited recommendations.

Summary of the rules on inaccurate and inadequate information

At this point it may be helpful to summarize the various forms of relief and remedies available when one party has entered the contract on the basis of inaccurate or inadequate information.

Basis of relief	Effect on contract	Damages
Breach of express promissory statement	Termination if serious	Contract measure
Breach, undisclosed defect renders goods not in accordance with description or unmerchantable	Termination	Contract measure
Fraudulent misrepresentation	Rescission	Tort measure
Negligent misrepresentation	Rescission, subject to court's discretion	Tort measure
Innocent misrepresentation	Rescission, subject to court's discretion	(only in lieu of rescission, ?restitutionary measure)
Non-disclosure (if applicable)	Rescission	—
Common mistake at common law	Void	—
Common mistake in equity	Rescission on terms	—

Bishop mentions to Beale that he wants to buy an antique ring for his (Bishop's) wife's birthday. Beale has in his desk an antique ring which belonged to his mother and he shows it to Bishop. Bishop offers to buy it at a price which clearly indicates that he thinks it is gold. Beale knows that the ring is made of base metal and is worth much less, but he does nothing to point out Bishop's mistake and accepts Bishop's offer. Bishop later discovers the truth and wants to get his money back. Is he entitled to recover? Would it make any difference if Beale were a dealer in antique jewellery? If Bishop were a dealer? What if Bishop had resold the ring as gold and had incurred liability to his buyer when the truth was discovered? What is the least alteration in the facts that would give Bishop the right to recover the price? To recover damages?

What, if anything, justifies the many subtle distinctions in this area?

QUESTIONS

1. Why is relief given so much more readily when one party has given the other inaccurate information, even if the party giving the information was in no way to blame, than when he knows that the other is acting under some misapprehension?
2. If one party makes an inaccurate statement, why is it sometimes treated as a promise, carrying (normally) strict liability for loss-of-bargain damages, but at other times only as a representation, leading to out-of-pocket damages and then only if the misrepresentor was at fault? A possible explanation is that when the court holds that a statement amounts to a warranty, it does so because the statement relates to some crucial characteristic of the subject-matter, something the buyer was 'bargaining for'. If the characteristic is lacking, the buyer should get at least the cost of purchasing a substitute that does have it—ie expectation damages. If, on the other hand, the statement is about something which is only incidental and merely affects the price paid, for instance, it is sufficient to allow the buyer to rescind or recover her out-of-pocket loss.
3. Why is there no liability for damages where a misrepresentation is purely innocent? Is it because neither party is then the least cost avoider, and each is perhaps the best insurer of his own losses? (Compare Posner and Rosenfield, above, p 305.) (We leave damages under s 2(2) for the moment.)
4. Why then allow rescission for innocent misrepresentation? Is it because of the unjust enrichment that might otherwise occur, or for some other reason?
5. In some situations rescission will be a costly and inappropriate remedy (on this see above, p 296). The court is therefore given power to refuse to permit it when the representation was not fraudulent, and in addition the right to rescission is easily lost under the 'bars'. If the court refuses to permit rescission which would otherwise be justified, it can award damages to remove the unjust enrichment element. Why has it no similar power when the right to rescind has been lost under one of the bars?
6. Turning to cases of inadequate information, why is relief granted more readily (in theory, at least) when both parties have made the same mistake than when only one has made the mistake? Kronman argues that if only one party is mistaken, it is reasonable to assume that he was in a better position to prevent his own error than the other party. Do you agree? What if the other party actually knows of the first party's error? (Compare communication mistakes, above, p 235.)

7. He also argues that when the parties share the mistake it is costly to inquire who was the least cost avoider. What does English law do in such a case? (See above, p 386.)

8. If one party carelessly makes a false statement to the other, the misrepresentee may recover damages in addition to rescinding. If the parties enter the contract sharing a fundamental false assumption, but they make no statements to each other (or do not rely on what the other said), the party prejudiced may be able to rescind, or the contract may be void, but no damages will be available to compensate for any consequential loss she may have suffered. Do you think a mistaken party should be allowed to recover her consequential loss? (Compare p 371, above.)

Section 5
Remedies

Some preliminary questions

In this section we shall be considering the remedies available when one party has broken the contract, or has not yet performed his obligations. It may be helpful to list the main remedies available. Refusing to perform until the other has done so, called here 'withholding performance', and termination of the contract are considered in Chapter 22. Chapter 23 covers damages. Chapter 24 considers the action for sums due under the contract, specific performance and injunction. Chapter 25 deals with an alternative way of claiming money, by way of restitution.

(a) The distinction between rights and remedies

In some areas of law there is a clear distinction between right and remedy. In the field of administrative law, for instance, it commonly happens that it can be shown that the defendant may have breached some duty imposed by the law or otherwise have acted illegally, yet the complainant cannot bring an action because he has no sufficient interest in the case (see *IRC v National Federation of Self-Employed and Small Businesses Ltd* [1982] AC 617). In contract law this problem does not arise, at least in this form. If one party to a contract has committed a breach of it, the other party (or parties) will have a remedy in every case. Persons who are not party to the contract will (subject to some exceptions) not have a remedy if the contract is broken (this problem is examined in detail in Section 10), but any party will be entitled to at least nominal damages if the contract has been broken. In addition the court may in an appropriate case grant a declaration that the other party's action, or threatened action, is in breach of contract.

A declaration or nominal damages may seem an insubstantial remedy, but frequently nothing more can be obtained unless the complaining party has suffered or is likely to suffer some loss as the result of the other party's breach. This follows from the nature of the remedies available for breach of contract. The first point is that although it is common to speak of enforcing the contract, it is only in certain types of case that the court will actually compel the defaulting party to carry out his obligation. Before 1854 different remedies were available in respect of contracts in the common law courts and in Chancery. At common law only money judgments could be recovered. Where the defendant had simply failed to pay a sum of money due under the contract (eg the price of the goods sold to him) judgment could be given for the sum due, thus effectively enforcing the contract in a literal sense; but where the default was of some other kind, the judgment would have to be for compensation, normally damages. The Court of Chancery would in certain circumstances order specific performance, that is, order the defendant to perform the contract on pain of being committed for contempt of court; or it would grant an injunction restraining him from actions which would be a breach of contract. These equitable remedies were seen as extraordinary, not generally available. For instance the rule was developed that specific performance would not be granted unless for some reason damages at common law would not be an adequate remedy. Nowadays specific performance and injunction can be awarded in any division of the High Court, but the distinction between common law and equitable remedies is maintained, and the latter remain restricted in their availability: as we shall see, specific performance is commonly granted for sales of land, as each piece of land is regarded as unique, but it is not usually available where the contract is for the sale of goods, as substitute goods can normally be obtained by a disappointed buyer. (There are also some restrictions on the action for the price, as we shall see.) Thus remedies may be divided into primary (those actually enforcing the primary obligations under the contract) and secondary (those leading to other relief as a substitute for performance).

Even when primary enforcement is concerned, it is relatively unusual for a party to have a substantial remedy unless he has suffered a loss. Thus he will not be able to get a common law judgment for payments due under the contract unless they were to be paid to him (see below, p 806), and save in exceptional circumstances he will not be able to get specific performance unless he has suffered a loss which would not be adequately compensated by damages. We shall see that there are also other restrictions on the equitable remedies: for instance, specific performance will not usually be granted of a contract for personal services. The result may be that the wronged party who cannot show any particular loss flowing from the other's breach may have no effective remedy despite a clear infringement of his rights. Thus if a university professor of economics were to depart two days before the beginning of term to take up a post with the World Bank in Washington DC, and the university could not show that his departure had not caused it to lose more than it saved in not having to pay his salary, it would at most get a declaration that his conduct was in breach, or nominal damages.

Withholding performance and termination do not fit easily into the distinction between primary and secondary, though clearly the former is aimed at encouraging actual performance, whereas the latter involves giving up the right to actual performance. In theory, at least, neither is available as a matter of general law (as opposed to available under the express terms of the agreement) unless the default on account of which the complaining party is threatening withholding or termination is a critical one, or is likely to cause him serious loss. We shall see that in practice this is not always the case.

(b) Self-help and judicial remedies

It is also useful to distinguish between remedies that require the complainant to enlist the aid of a court and those that he can use on his own. Just as in tort you are permitted to use reasonable force to eject a trespasser from your land, so in contract there are some actions which can be taken without resort to litigation. Orders of specific performance, injunctions and judgments for sums due under the contract are judicial remedies, whereas withholding performance and termination may (if justified) be exercised as a form of self-help. Damages do not fall clearly into either category; if the claimant owes money to the other party under the contract he may generally deduct the damages he claims from the money owed; if not, he will have to sue for damages which the other party refuses to pay.

(c) Off-the-shelf remedies and expressly planned remedies

The remedies discussed so far are all ones made available by the general law of contract, and the general law also lays down the conditions under which they may be employed. Many contracting parties are content to rely on these standard remedies should a dispute arise, but in contracts of any sophistication it is common to provide additional or different remedies by express agreement. Thus there may be express provision about the damages that may be recovered, either providing for the recovery of some item that might not be compensable at common law, or more commonly restricting the damages more narrowly than is done by the common law, by means of a limitation clause. Express planning is particularly common in relation to self-help remedies: as we shall see, contracts often make the remedies of withholding and termination more readily available than they would be at common law. There are a number of important remedies that are permitted only if the agreement expressly provides for them, for example the forfeiture of money paid or the repossession of property under a contract of sale. One of the vital questions in this area is the extent to which the law permits the parties to alter the remedies available to them. We shall see that there are explicit rules controlling some of these remedies (this is particularly so of limitation clauses, and this topic will be kept for a separate detailed treatment in Section 8). Other expressly planned remedies may be permitted in theory, but in practice are treated with such hostility by the courts that it is difficult to employ them successfully.

CHAPTER 22
Withholding performance and termination for default

In this chapter we look at the two remedies of withholding performance (refusing to perform part or all of your contractual obligations until the other party has performed, or is ready to perform, some obligation of his) and termination for default (refusing to perform your further obligations at all, and refusing to accept further performance by the other party, on the grounds of his failure to perform some part of his obligations).

The two remedies are closely connected. Both depend on the notion that A may not be under any obligation to render his performance until B has done something or is ready to do it. Withholding performance depends on this alone. It is such a direct result of the terms of the contract that some commentators do not view it as a 'remedy' at all. As Lord Oliver put it in a case involving an employment contract:

> The question to be asked . . . is not so much: has the employer a *right* to withhold from an employee who voluntarily absents himself from work wages for the period he is absent? but: is the employee entitled to sue for and recover from his employer wages in respect of a period during which he has made it perfectly clear he is not ready and willing to perform his own contractual obligations?

(*Miles v Wakefield Metropolitan District Council* [1987] 1 All ER 1089 at 1104.) But in practical terms withholding performance operates as a form of remedy by protecting the employer from having to perform and giving the employee an incentive to work.

Termination depends also on additional factors: A must show that his obligation to perform was conditional on B rendering his performance within a certain period of time, and that either the time has expired, or B has in advance repudiated his obligations. In this section we shall refer to the former as 'default termination', and to the latter as termination for 'anticipatory repudiation'.

Although we treat withholding and termination as remedies, it is worth remembering that much of the law in this area is just a continuation of the process of gapfilling by interpretation and implication that we looked at in section 4. In other words, the starting point is still, what does the contract provide? The contract may state expressly that until B has done x, A need not do y, or that if B does not do x by a certain date, A may terminate. What the parties have agreed will normally govern, though we shall see that on occasions, when what the parties seem to have agreed strikes the court as unreasonable, effect will only be given to it if the language is very clear.

In this chapter we present the material in a way which will help you grasp the technical rules. After introducing the concept of conditions, we look at how it is determined in what order the parties are to perform. We then deal with whether A's obligation to perform is conditional on B doing everything the contract requires, or only on B performing the more important

410

obligations, and, if the latter, the difficult question of determining which of B's obligations are the crucial ones. These points are all relevant to both withholding and termination. The law on when withholding and termination are permitted depends upon the concept of conditions in the contract. Thus cases on one topic are usually relevant to the other, and as in practice litigation will not be resorted to until a fairly late stage, most of the cases are ones in which one party claims that he has justifiably terminated the contract. The chapter then concludes by looking at the rules on default termination and termination for anticipatory repudiation.

'Some problems of breach of contract' by Treitel (1967) 30 MLR 139, 149–150

[J]ust what practical interest is at stake when a party seeks 'rescission' [termination] of a contract? A buyer who has undertaken to pay cash on delivery will obviously not want to pay for defective goods and be left to pursue his claim for damages. Rejection combines, for him, all the advantages of a specific remedy and self-help; it enables him to avoid the delays of litigation as well as the risk that the seller's credit may fail. If the sale is on credit, the buyer's interest in rejection is less strong, since the damages can be set off against the price. But even here an innocent party who wants to determine his precise liability without recourse to legal proceedings runs the risk of quantifying his damages wrongly; and he may also be prejudiced if some of the loss he suffers as a result of having to accept defective performance is regarded as too remote.

On the other hand, the party in breach may have equally strong interests in acceptance: for example if the market has fallen, if he has incurred expenses in making the defective performance, or if the result of that performance has been to enrich the other party. The first of these interests will be more fully discussed below; but at this stage it is worth stressing the distinction between the last two. The expense of making a defective tender (eg, at a distant place) may be considerable but may not enrich the other contracting party at all. It is obvious, also, that these two interests grow in importance the further performance has gone.

(a) The notion of conditions

The idea that a party's obligation to perform might be conditional upon some event outside the control of the parties was introduced in Section 3 (above, p 228). Here we are dealing with what are often called 'promissory' conditions.

Trans Trust SPRL v Danubian Trading Co Ltd [1952] 1 All ER 970, Court of Appeal

On Sept 10, 1950, a Belgian company offered to A Co one thousand tons of rolled steel, fob Antwerp, delivery in December, payment to be against an irrevocable and confirmed letter of credit. A Co, who were unable to produce the letter of credit themselves, offered the steel to the sellers who in turn offered it to the buyers. On Sept 20, 1950, the buyers, subject to the requirements as to the provision of a letter of credit, offered the steel to an American company. Both the sellers and the buyers knew that neither of them was in a position to fulfil their contractual obligations unless the American company made the money available through a letter of credit. On Sept 25 the American company accepted the buyers' offer, and on the same day the buyers agreed with the sellers that they would purchase the steel, stating: 'A credit will be opened forthwith'. Thereupon the sellers gave a written order to A Co. The American company failed to open the credit, and, the buyers being unable to do so, the sellers claimed against the buyers for breach of contract and a declaration that the sellers were entitled to be indemnified against any damages payable by them to A Co. At all material times the market value of the steel was higher than the contract price.

Denning LJ. This is another case concerned with the modern practice whereby a buyer agrees to provide a banker's confirmed credit in favour of the seller. This credit is an irrevocable promise by a banker to pay money to the seller in return for the shipping documents. One reason for this practice is because the seller wishes to be assured in advance, not only that the buyer is in earnest, but also that he, the seller, will get his money when he delivers the goods. Another reason is because the seller often has expenses to pay in connection with the goods and he wishes to use the credit to pay those expenses. He may, for instance, be himself a merchant, who is buying the goods from the growers or the manufacturers and has to pay for them before he can get delivery, and his own bank may only grant him facilities for the purpose if he has the backing of a letter of credit. The ability of the seller to carry out the transaction is, therefore, dependent on the buyer's providing the letter of credit, and for this reason the seller stipulates that the credit should be provided at a specified time well in advance of the time for delivery of the goods.

What is the legal position of such a stipulation? Sometimes it is a condition precedent to the formation of a contract, that is, it is a condition which must be fulfilled before any contract is concluded at all. In those cases the stipulation 'subject to the opening of a letter of credit' is rather like a stipulation 'subject to contract'. If no credit is provided, there is no contract between the parties. In other cases a contract is concluded and the stipulation for a credit is a condition which is an essential term of the contract. In those cases the provision of the credit is a condition precedent, not to the formation of a contract, but to the obligation of the seller to deliver the goods. If the buyer fails to provide the credit, the seller can treat himself as discharged from any further performance of the contract and can sue the buyer for damages for not providing the credit.

The first question is: What was the nature of the stipulation in this case? When the buyers sent their order, they stated in writing on Sept 25, 1950, that 'a credit will be opened forthwith'. It was suggested that the buyers were not making any firm promise on their own account, but were only passing on information which had been given to them by their American buyers. The judge did not accept that suggestion and I agree with him. The statement was a firm promise by the buyers by which they gave their personal assurance that a credit would be opened forthwith. At that time there were some discrepancies about gauges and dates of delivery which had to be cleared up, but these were all resolved at the meetings in Brussels, and there was then, as the judge found, a concluded contract by the sellers to sell, and the buyers to buy, the steel for December/January delivery, and it was a part of that contract that the buyers would be personally responsible for seeing that a credit should be opened forthwith. Of those findings it is clear that the stipulation for a credit was not a condition precedent to the formation of any contract at all. It was a condition which was an essential term of a contract actually made. That conditon was not fulfilled. The sellers extended the time for the credit, but it never came, not even after reasonable notice. The sellers were, therefore, discharged from any further performance on their side, and are entitled to claim damages.

[Denning LJ went on to hold that, as the buyers knew that the sellers would not be able to obtain the goods unless the credit were opened, the sellers were entitled to damages for loss of profit. Somervell and Romer LJJ delivered concurring judgments.]

Appeal allowed in part.

NOTES

1. Observe the distinction implicit in Denning's analysis between withholding performance and termination. The sellers did not have to deliver until the credit was opened, and once the (extended) time for opening had expired, they were 'discharged from any further performance'—ie they were entitled to terminate the contract.

2. Denning contrasts the promissory condition found in this case with a 'condition precedent to the formation of a contract'. It will be remembered that in fact even non-promissory conditions, such as 'subject to satisfactory survey', are not usually construed as preventing the *existence* of a contract: both parties are bound, but the main obligations of the contract only come into play if the condition is fulfilled. See above, p 228 ff.

(b) Conditions and the order of performance

Kingston v Preston (1773) cited in 2 Doug KB at 689–91

The plaintiff agreed to serve the defendant for a year and a quarter in the defendant's business as silk-mercer, and the defendant agreed that at the end of the period he would convey the business and the stock in trade to the plaintiff and the defendant's nephew. The stock in trade was to be paid for over a period of time, and the plaintiff agreed to provide security for these payments. The plaintiff claimed that the defendant had failed to convey the business; the defendant pleaded that the plaintiff had failed to provide the promised security.

In delivering the judgment of the Court, **Lord Mansfield** expressed himself to the following effect: There are three kinds of covenants: 1. Such as are called mutual and independant, where either party may recover damages from the other, for the injury he may have received by a breach of the covenants in his favour, and where it is no excuse for the defendant, to allege a breach of the covenants on the part of the plaintiff. 2. There are covenants which are conditions and dependant, in which the performance of one depends on the prior performance of another, and, therefore, till this prior condition is performed, the other party is not liable to an action on his covenant. 3. There is also a third sort of covenants, which are mutual conditions to be performed at the same time; and, in these, if one party is ready, and offered, to perform his part, and the other neglected, or refused, to perform his, he who was ready, and offered, has fulfilled his engagement, and may maintain an action for the default of the other; though it is not certain that either is obliged to do the first act.—His Lordship then proceeded to say, that the dependance, or independance, of covenants, was to be collected from the evident sense and meaning of the parties, and, that, however transposed they might be in the deed, their precedency must depend on the order of time in which the intent of the transaction requires their performance. That, in the case before the Court, it would be the greatest injustice if the plaintiff should prevail: the essence of the agreement was, that the defendant should not trust to the personal security of the plaintiff, but, before he delivered up his stock and business, should have good security for the payment of the money. The giving of such security, therefore, must necessarily be a condition precedent.—Judgment was accordingly given for the defendant, because the part to be performed by the plaintiff was clearly a condition precedent.

NOTES

1. Examples of Lord Mansfield's first category are relatively rare, at least where the basic obligations under the contract are concerned. However, under a lease the tenant's obligation to pay the rent and the landlord's obligation to repair have been held to be independent, so that the tenant could not withhold the rent because of non-repair: *Taylor v Webb* [1937] 2 KB 283. Occasionally unimportant terms of a contract are referred to as 'independent covenants', but this is a misnomer: see below, p 424.
2. An example of performances which the law treats as due simultaneously and as concurrently conditional on each other are delivery and payment in a sale of goods contract which does not expressly provide when the price is to be paid:

Sale of Goods Act 1979

Section 28
Unless otherwise agreed, delivery of the goods and payment of the price are concurrent conditions, that is to say, the seller must be ready and willing to give possession of the goods to the buyer in exchange for the price and the buyer must be ready and willing to pay the price in exchange for possession of the goods.

An example of how this section might work is provided by *Total Oil (Great Britain) Ltd v Thompson Garages (Biggin Hill) Ltd* [1972] 1 QB 318, where the garage owner agreed to pay for petrol 'cash upon delivery'. The petrol company insisted on receiving a banker's draft before it would dispatch the petrol (which was to be 'delivered' at the filling station). This gave the garage owner the right to refuse to go on with the agreement. For a case where the seller argued that he was not bound to deliver until the buyer provided a credit for the full price, see *W J Alan & Co Ltd v El Nasr Export and Import Co* (below, p 609).

3. The order in which the two performances are due, if not stated in the contract, seems to be determined in the light of common sense considerations. If simultaneous exchange is feasible, they will be treated as due simultaneously; if one performance will take a period of time but the other will be more or less instantaneous, the former will be treated as due first—thus 'work first, payment later' (see Restatement 2d s 234). Why is there this preference for treating them as simultaneous?

4. Enabling A to say that he is not obliged to perform until B has done so clearly protects A. Does it have any other function? See the next reading.

5. When the agreement does not expressly state that A is to do *x* as a condition of B's having to perform, but the court construes the obligations in this way, it is common to call the condition a 'constructive' condition.

'Constructive Conditions in Contracts' by Patterson (1942) 42 Col LR 903 at 917–920, 925–926

4. *Order of time of performance.* The order of the time of performance of the several promises has long been regarded as determining which promises are dependent and which are independent, and is the subject of many of the rules relating to dependency. Obviously if A performs promptly his promise to convey land to B on July 1st, and B has promised to pay the price on August 1st, A will credit B for one month. Then if A does not convey on July 1st, B's action commenced on July 2nd may be maintained without B's having tendered the price before suing. Yet even this mechanical test of dependency is controlled and supplemented, it is submitted, by a principle of policy which favors the construction of concurrent conditions and thus minimizes the credit burden of the transaction . . .

Where one party's promise requires a substantial time for performance, some extension of credit is practically unavoidable. The rule laid down for all such promises, where the other party's performance does not require a substantial time, is that the latter's duty is conditional on performance by the former, the party whose performance requires time is to extend credit to the latter. This is not the only solution of the difficulty. The extension of credit might be reversed (as where a student pays tuition in advance) . . . [O]ne may ask, why should the party whose promised performance takes time be required to extend credit to the one whose performance does not? The typical case falling under this rule—of which it is a kind of extrapolation—is the contract to do work for money. The usual practice in the community to which the rule was applicable was to pay for the work after it was completed. This 'belief as to the practice of a community or a class' is empirically verified, but it does not settle the questions of justice or policy with which the law is concerned. The practice may be ascribed to the influence of employers as a dominant class, and to judicial inertia which allows an outmoded rule to continue unchanged. The dominance of employers as a class is not what it used to be, yet no demand has appeared to require that employees generally be paid their wages or salaries in advance. There may be sufficient reasons for the survival of the rule. Professor Williston suggests two: 1. The normally greater responsibility of the employer; and 2. The fact that the employee cannot be compelled to perform specifically.

The policy of the law, here as in the tendency to construct concurrent conditions, is to minimize credit risks. If employers usually present less credit risks than employees, the rule of construction effectuates this end. That colleges and theatres ordinarily require payment in advance for the services which they furnish merely exemplifies the operation of the principle. A further justification may be found in the belief that a moderate postponement of reward stimulates productivity of social goods; such a belief is operative as a part of the mores of a particular culture. This justification, like the second reason given by Professor Williston, must be limited in scope of application, if it is not to conflict with the prohibition of involuntary servitude; that is, it may become a too-effective means of coercing the employee to work. The rule which makes performance by the employee a condition precedent of the duty of payment by the employer and which thus places the credit risk and the credit strain on the employee, has been mitigated in its severity by statutes requiring that wages be paid at short intervals (weekly or bi-weekly) to certain classes of employees (in the lower income brackets), by provisions making wage claims preferred in the case of bankruptcy of the employer and by a limited relief for unjust enrichment. The order-of-performance test of credit burdens is thus supplemented by custom and by policy.

. . .

6. *The coercive function of constructive conditions.* The construction of conditions of exchange not only protects a contracting party against impairment of his expectations and enhancement of his credit burden, but also gives him a method of coercing performance. The coercive effect on the employee was pointed out above. So, in *Kingston v Preston*, the refusal of the defendant to turn over his business was a more effective way of inducing the clerk to give security than would have been an action for damages. The constructive condition thus supplements the limited remedies for specific performance by a kind of legalized self-help. The promisor's privilege of refusing performance until a condition is fulfilled is a continuation of the coercive power which he had before he contracted, the power which any man has to refuse to relinquish his property or to perform his services unless paid or promised such return as he chooses to exact. This coercive power is preserved after the making of the contract, in so far as is compatible with the terms of the bargain.

(c) Entire and severable obligations

Cutter v Powell (1795) 6 Term Rep 320

To assumpsit for work and labour done by the intestate, the defendant pleaded the general issue. And at the trial at Lancaster the jury found a verdict for the plaintiff for 31*l* 10s subject to the opinion of this Court on the following case.

The defendant being at Jamaica subscribed and delivered to T. Cutter the intestate a note, whereof the following is a copy; 'Ten days after the ship "Governor Parry", myself master, arrives at Liverpool, I promise to pay to Mr T. Cutter the sum of thirty guineas, provided he proceeds, continues and does his duty as second mate in the said ship from hence to the port of Liverpool. Kingston, July 31st, 1793.' The ship 'Governor Parry' sailed from Kingston on the 2d of August 1793, and arrived in the port of Liverpool on the 9th of October following. T. Cutter went on board the ship on the 31st of July, 1793, and sailed in her on the 2d day of August, and proceeded, continued and did his duty as second mate in her from Kingston until his death, which happened on the 20th of September following, and before the ship's arrival in the port of Liverpool. The usual wages of a second mate of a ship on such a voyage, when shipped by the month out and home is four pounds per month: but when seamen are shipped by the run from Jamaica to England, a gross sum is usually given. The usual length of a voyage from Jamaica to Liverpool is about eight weeks.

This was argued last term by J. Haywood for the plaintiff: but the Court desired the case to stand over, that inquiries might be made relative to the usage in the commercial world on these kinds of agreements. It now appeared that there was no fixed settled usage one way or the other: but several instances were mentioned as having happened within these two years, in some of which the merchants had paid the whole wages under circumstances similar to the present, and in others a proportionable part. . . .

Lord Kenyon CJ. I should be extremely sorry that in the decision of this case we should determine against what had been the received opinion in the mercantile world on contracts of this kind, because it is of great importance that the laws by which the contracts of so numerous and so useful a body of men as the sailors are supposed to be guided should not be overturned. Whether these kind of notes are much in use among the seamen, we are not sufficiently informed; and the instances now stated to us from Liverpool are too recent to form any thing like usage. But it seems to me at present that the decision of this case may proceed on the particular words of this contract and the precise facts here stated, without touching marine contracts in general. That where the parties have come to an express contract none can be implied has prevailed so long as to be reduced to an axiom in the law. Here the defendant expressly promised to pay the intestate thirty guineas, provided he proceeded, continued and did his duty as second mate in the ship from Jamaica to Liverpool; and the accompanying circumstances disclosed in the case are that the common rate of wages is four pounds per month, when the party is paid in proportion to the time he serves: and that this voyage is generally performed in two months. Therefore if there had been no contract between these parties, all that the intestate could have recovered on a quantum meruit for the voyage would have been eight pounds; whereas here the defendant contracted to pay thirty guineas provided the mate continued to do his duty as mate during the whole voyage, in which case the latter would have received nearly four times as much as if he were paid for the number of months he served. He stipulated to receive the larger sum if the whole duty were performed, and nothing unless the whole of that duty were performed: it was a kind of insurance. On this particular contract my opinion is formed at present; at the same time I must say that if we were assured that these notes are in universal use, and that the commercial world have received and acted upon them in a different sense, I should give up my own opinion.

Ashhurst J. We cannot collect that there is any custom prevailing among merchants on these contracts; and therefore we have nothing to guide us but the terms of the contract itself. This is a written contract, and it speaks for itself. And as it is entire, and as the defendant's promise depends on a condition precedent to be performed by the other party, the condition must be performed before the other party is entitled to receive any thing under it. It has been argued however that the plaintiff may now recover on a quantum meruit: but she has no right to desert the agreement; for wherever there is an express contract the parties must be guided by it; and one party cannot relinquish or abide by it as it may suit his advantage. Here the intestate was by the terms of his contract to perform a given duty before he could call upon the defendant to pay him any thing; it was a condition precedent, without performing which the defendant is not liable. And that seems to me to conclude the question: the intestate did not perform the contract on his part; he was not indeed to blame for not doing it; but still as this was a condition precedent, and as he did not perform it, his representative is not entitled to recover.

[Grose and Lawrence JJ delivered concurring judgments.]

NOTES

1. Constructive conditions are just as much 'standard terms' as the risk allocations discussed in the last section, and it is just as pertinent to ask, what would the parties have agreed if their minds had been directed to the question?
2. Normally a contract of employment will be treated as severable, so that the employee earns payment for the period served. It seems that at common law the contract would be severable into units corresponding to the intervals at which the employee was to be paid. Thus in *Taylor v Laird* (1856) 1 H & N 266, 25 LJ Ex 329 the plaintiff was employed to command a steamer 'for an exploring and trading voyage up the river Niger . . . at the rate of £50 per month'. The plaintiff took the vessel up as far as Dagbo, but refused to go further and abandoned the command. It was held that this was not a contract for the entire voyage: the phrase 'per month' showed that he was

entitled to be paid for each month he served. Pollock CB said that the parties could not have intended the plaintiff to have received no payment if the voyage had not been completed for reasons outside his control. See now Apportionment Act 1870 (below). Why was the contract in *Cutter v Powell* not treated as one under which Cutter earned so much a day or a month?

Apportionment Act 1870

Section 2
All rents, annuities, dividends, and other periodical payments in the nature of income . . . shall, like interest on money lent, be considered as accruing from day to day, and shall be apportionable in respect of time accordingly.

Section 5
The word annuities includes salaries and pensions.

NOTES

1. Does this statute affect the decision in *Cutter v Powell*? Was there any 'periodical payment' in that case?
2. In *Cutter v Powell* the contract was, in modern parlance, frustrated by Cutter's death. Would his estate recover anything under the Law Reform (Frustrated Contracts) Act 1943?

Sale of Goods Act 1979

Section 30
(1) Where the seller delivers to the buyer a quantity of goods less than he contracted to sell, the buyer may reject them, but if the buyer accepts the goods so delivered he must pay for them at the contract rate.
(2) Where the seller delivers to the buyer a quantity of goods larger than he contracted to sell, the buyer may accept the goods included in the contract and reject the rest, or he may reject the whole.
(3) Where the seller delivers to the buyer a quantity of goods larger than he contracted to sell and the buyer accepts the whole of the goods so delivered he must pay for them at the contract rate.
(4) Where the seller delivers to the buyer the goods he contracted to sell mixed with goods of a different description not included in the contract, the buyer may accept the goods which are in accordance with the contract and reject the rest, or he may reject the whole.
(5) This section is subject to any usage of trade, special agreement, or course of dealing between the parties.

Section 31
(1) Unless otherwise agreed, the buyer of goods is not bound to accept delivery of them by instalments.
(2) Where there is a contract for the sale of goods to be delivered by stated instalments, which are to be separately paid for, and the seller makes defective deliveries in respect of one or more instalments, or the buyer neglects or refuses to take delivery of or pay for one or more instalments, it is a question in each case depending on the terms of the contract and the circumstances of the case whether the breach of contract is a repudiation of the whole contract or whether it is a severable breach giving rise to a claim for compensation but not to a right to treat the whole contract as repudiated.

NOTE

The effect of s 30 is that unless the parties have agreed to delivery by instalments, a contract for the sale of goods is 'entire as to quantity', so that if the seller delivers too little or too much the buyer need not perform its side. If the time for performance has not yet expired the seller may make a fresh tender, and meanwhile the buyer only has the right to withhold until a proper tender is made. If the time for performance has expired the buyer may refuse any further tender and terminate the contract.

(d) Effect of partial performance of an entire obligation

Sumpter v Hedges [1898] 1 QB 673, Court of Appeal

(Note that a lump sum building contract is normally construed as entire, so that no part of the contract price is due until completion.)

Appeal from the judgment of Bruce J at the trial before him without a jury.

The action was for work done and materials provided. The plaintiff, a builder, had contracted with the defendant to build upon the defendant's land two houses and stables for the sum of 565*l*. The plaintiff did part of the work, amounting in value to about 333*l*, and had received payment of part of the price. He then informed the defendant that he had no money, and could not go on with the work. The learned judge found that he had abandoned the contract. The defendant thereupon finished the buildings on his own account, using for that purpose certain building materials which the plaintiff had left on the ground. The judge gave judgment for the plaintiff for the value of the materials so used, but allowed him nothing in respect of the work which he had done upon the buildings.

Collins LJ. . . . . I think the case is really concluded by the finding of the learned judge to the effect that the plaintiff had abandoned the contract. If the plaintiff had merely broken his contract in some way so as not to give the defendant the right to treat him as having abandoned the contract, and the defendant had then proceeded to finish the work himself, the plaintiff might perhaps have been entitled to sue on a quantum meruit on the ground that the defendant had taken the benefit of the work done. But that is not the present case. There are cases in which, though the plaintiff has abandoned the performance of a contract, it is possible for him to raise the inference of a new contract to pay for the work done on a quantum meruit from the defendant's having taken the benefit of that work, but, in order that that may be done, the circumstances must be such as to give an option to the defendant to take or not to take the benefit of the work done. It is only where the circumstances are such as to give that option that there is any evidence on which to ground the inference of a new contract. Where, as in the case of work done on land, the circumstances are such as to give the defendant no option whether he will take the benefit of the work or not, then one must look to other facts than the mere taking the benefit of the work in order to ground the inference of a new contract. In this case I see no other facts on which such an inference can be founded. The mere fact that a defendant is in possession of what he cannot help keeping, or even has done work upon it, affords no ground for such an inference. He is not bound to keep unfinished a building which in an incomplete state would be a nuisance on his land. I am therefore of opinion that the plaintiff was not entitled to recover for the work which he had done.

[A. L. Smith and Chitty LJJ delivered concurring judgments.]

Appeal dismissed.

NOTES

1. The judgment for the cost of the materials was not appealed against. Why was the defendant liable for this?
2. In *Sumpter v Hedges* the builder had in fact received some payment (though he had no right to it), but the reasoning would be exactly the same if he had received nothing. You may have noticed exactly this result, and the same reasoning being used, in *Cutter v Powell* (above p 415). To mitigate this harsh rule the courts will try to find the contract severable (see *Appleby v Myers* (1867) LR 2 CP 651, 660), but in a lump sum building contract this will normally be impossible as there is no way of apportioning the price over the various items of work. (Some sophisticated building contracts do contain 'bills of quantities', which are lists of the items to be done, with unit prices inserted: but these prices will not represent accurately the cost of doing each unit when the contract is only partly performed. They are intended primarly for valuing 'variations', eg additions to the work originally specified (see below, p 620), and may represent only the marginal cost of performing one additional unit.) Instead the doctrine of 'substantial performance' has been developed.

Hoenig v Isaacs [1952] 2 All ER 176, Court of Appeal

The defendant employed the plaintiff to decorate and furnish the defendant's flat for £750. The work was finished bar some defects in a bookcase and a wardrobe, which would cost about £55 to rectify, and the defendant moved into the flat, but he refused to pay the outstanding balance of the contract price.

Somervell LJ. . . . Each case turns on the construction of the contract. In *Cutter v Powell* the condition for the promissory note sued on was that the sailor should proceed to continue and do his duty as second mate in the ship from Jamaica to the port of Liverpool. The sailor died before the ship reached Liverpool and it was held his estate could not recover either on the contract or on a quantum meruit. It clearly decided that his continuing as mate during the whole voyage was a condition precedent to payment. It did not decide that if he had completed the main purpose of the contract, namely, serving as mate for the whole voyage, the defendant could have repudiated his liability by establishing that in the course of the voyage the sailor had, possibly through inadvertence, failed on some occasion in his duty as mate whereby some damage had been caused. . . .

The learned official referee regarded *H Dakin & Co Ltd v Lee* laying down that the price must be paid subject to set-off or counterclaim if there was a substantial compliance with the contract. I think on the facts of this case where the work was finished in the ordinary sense, though in part defective, this is right. It expresses in a convenient epithet what is put from another angle in the Sale of Goods Act, 1893. The buyer cannot reject if he proves only the breach of a term collateral to the main purpose. I have, therefore, come to the conclusion that the first point of counsel for the defendant fails.

The learned official referee found that there was substantial compliance. Bearing in mind that there is no appeal on fact, was there evidence on which he could so find? The learned official referee having, as I hold, properly directed himself, this becomes, I think, a question of fact. The case on this point was, I think, near the border line, and if the finding had been the other way I do not think we could have interfered. Even if I had felt we could interfere, the defendant would be in a further difficulty. The contract included a number of chattels. If the defendant wished to repudiate his liability under the contract he should not, I think, have used those articles which he could have avoided using. On this view, though it is not necessary to decide it, I think he put himself in the same position as a buyer of goods who by accepting them elects to treat a breach of condition as a breach of warranty.

Denning LJ. This case raises the familiar question: Was entire performance a condition precedent to payment? That depends on the true construction of the contract. In this case the contract was made over a period of time and was partly oral and partly in writing, but I agree with the official referee that the essential terms were set down in the letter of Apr 25, 1950. It describes the work which was to be done and concludes with these words:

'The foregoing, complete, for the sum of £750 net. Terms of payment are net cash, as the work proceeds; and balance on completion.'

The question of law that was debated before us was whether the plaintiff was entitled in this action to sue for the £350 balance of the contract price as he had done. The defendant said that he was only entitled to sue on a quantum meruit. The defendant was anxious to insist on a quantum meruit, because he said that the contract price was unreasonably high. He wished, therefore, to reject that price altogether and simply to pay a reasonable price for all the work that was done. This would obviously mean an inquiry into the value of every item, including all the many items which were in compliance with the contract as well as the three which fell short of it. That is what the defendant wanted. The plaintiff resisted this course and refused to claim on a quantum meruit. He said that he was entitled to the balance of £350 less a deduction for the defects.

In determining this issue the first question is whether, on the true construction of the contract, entire performance was a condition precedent to payment. It was a lump sum contract, but that does not mean that entire performance was a condition precedent to payment. When a contract provides for a specific sum to be paid on completion of specified work, the courts lean against a construction of the contract which would deprive the contractor of any payment at all simply because there are some defects or omissions. The promise to complete the work is, therefore, construed as a term of the contract, but not as a condition. It is not every breach of that term which absolves the employer from his promise to pay the price, but only a breach which goes to the root of the contract, such as an abandonment of the work when it is only half done. Unless the breach does go to the root of the matter, the employer cannot resist payment of the price. He must pay it and bring a cross-claim for the defects and omissions, or, alternatively, set them up in diminution of the price. The measure is the amount which the work is worth less by reason of the defects and omissions, and is usually calculated by the cost of making them good: see *Mondel v Steel; H Dakin & Co, Ltd v Lee* and the notes to *Cutter v Powell* in *Smith's Leading Cases*, 13th edn, vol 2, pp 19–21. It is, of course, always open to the parties by express words to make entire performance a condition precedent. A familiar instance is when the contract provides for progress payments to be made as the work proceeds, but for retention money to be held until completion. Then entire performance is usually a condition precedent to payment of the retention money, but not, of course, to the progress payments. The contractor is entitled to payment pro rata as the work proceeds, less a deduction for retention money. But he is not entitled to the retention money until the work is entirely finished, without defects or omissions. . . . But . . . I think this contract should be regarded as an ordinary lump sum contract. It was substantially performed. The contractor is entitled, therefore, to the contract price, less a deduction for the defects.

Even if entire performance was a condition precedent, nevertheless the result would be the same, because I think the condition was waived . . . [The defendant] did not refuse to accept the work. On the contrary, he entered into possession of the flat and used the furniture as his own, including the defective items. That was a clear waiver of the condition precedent. Just as in a sale of goods the buyer who accepts the goods can no longer treat a breach of condition as giving a right to reject but only a right to damages, so also in a contract for work and labour an employer who takes the benefit of the work can no longer treat entire performance as a condition precedent, but only as a term giving rise to damages.

Romer LJ. . . . The position is, I think, in some respects analogous to a case where a man agrees to sell land and, before completion, finds that he is unable to make title to a small part of it which is of no great significance in relation to the whole. In such a case the vendor can substantially perform what he has agreed to do but cannot perform it wholly, and the Court of Chancery has never hesitated to grant specific performance at this instance against the purchaser subject to a proper and reasonable deduction being made in the purchase price. It would not, however, make such an order if it resulted in the purchaser getting something substantially less than or different from what he had bargained for. . . . . I am, accordingly, of the opinion, as already indicated, that the learned official referee fell into no error of law and that this appeal fails. If, however, I had come to a different conclusion on the point which I have been considering I should, nevertheless, be inclined to the view (for the reasons stated by Denning LJ in his judgment) that the appeal must fail on the ground of the defendant's waiver.

Appeal dismissed.

NOTES

1. Which is the better way of expressing the substantial performance rule: that the builder is entitled to the price once he has done almost all the work, or that he is entitled to it once he has done all the work, even though some of it is defective?

2. Corbin, 'Conditions in the Law of Contract' (1919) 28 Yale LJ 739, 759 explains the doctrine of substantial performance thus:

> It is never correct to say that substantial performance *of a condition* is sufficient; but it is frequently correct to say that absolutely exact and complete performance by the plaintiff as promised is not a condition precedent to the duty of the defendant. If substantial performance by the plaintiff was sufficient to charge the defendant, then such substantial performance was the only condition and the requirement has been exactly fulfilled. The question of the plaintiff's duty to pay damages for his own partial non-performance is a different question altogether. Substantial performance of A's promise may be sufficient to enable him to maintain action against B, and yet at the same time be insufficient to prevent B from having an action against A.

3. Two members of the court considered that the defendant had waived any condition precedent. Given that the work was being done in the plaintiff's flat, is that consistent with *Sumpter v Hedges*? Would it be more accurate to say that he had waived the right to refuse payment for the furniture?

4. Romer LJ refers to cases where a vendor of land can obtain specific performance although he cannot make title to a small part of the land. An example is *Re Fawcett and Holmes' Contract* (1889) 42 Ch D 150.

5. Denning LJ refers to a scheme of interim payments with retention money. The following is an example of such a scheme:

> 30. (3) (a) In respect of any Interim Certificate issued before the issue of the Certificate of Practical Completion the Employer may, subject to paragraph (c) of this sub-clause, retain a percentage (in these Conditions called 'the Retention Percentage') of the total value of the work, materials and goods referred to. . . . The Retention Percentage shall be 5 per cent, unless a lower rate shall be agreed between the parties and specified in the Appendix to these Conditions as the Retention Percentage. . . .
>   (4) (b) On the issue of the Certificate of Practical Completion the Architect shall issue a certificate for one moiety of the total amounts then so retained and the Contractor shall, on presenting any such certificate to the Employer, be entitled to payment of the said moiety within 14 days from the presentation of that certificate.
>   (4) (c) On the expiration of the Defects Liability Period named in the Appendix to these Conditions, or on the issue of the Certificate of Completion of Making Good Defects, whichever is the later, the Architect shall issue a Certificate for the residue of the amounts then so retained and the Contractor shall, on presenting any such certificate to the Employer, be entitled to payment of the said residue within 14 days from the presentation of that certificate.

(Joint Contracts Tribunal Form of Building Contract, 1963)

6. In *Hoenig v Issacs* you can see a subplot emerging: it is not fair to allow the defendant to use some minor failure or imperfection as an excuse for

not paying the price. Note, however, that the substantial performance rule only allows the builder to recover the price if the defects or shortcomings are pretty slight. The employer doesn't have to pay if the work isn't substantially complete, even if a lot of it has been done. In *Bolton v Mahadeva* [1972] 1 WLR 1009, CA the plaintiff agreed to install central heating in the defendant's house for a lump sum of £560. The system gave off insufficient and uneven heat, and also gave off fumes. The plaintiff refused to correct the defects, which could be put right for about £174. The defendant refused to pay anything, and the Court of Appeal held that the plaintiff was not entitled to recover, as there had been no substantial performance. Sachs LJ remarked (at p 1015):

> It is not merely that so very much of the work was shoddy, but it is the general ineffectiveness of it for its primary purpose that leads me to that conclusion.

7. The Law Commission, in its Report No 121, 'Pecuniary Restitution for Breach of Contract' (1983), criticised the result of cases such as *Bolton v Mahadeva*:

> . . . [T]he mischief which we have identified is not that the parties can require complete performance before any counter-performance is due, but that under the present law they may, and usually will, be held to have done so merely by providing for postponement of payment. In our view the present law leads to a result which was not necessarily the one which the parties in all cases would have contemplated as flowing from their agreement solely by reason of the postponement of payment.

(para 2.32). The Commission recommended that the law should be changed, so that a party who in breach of contract fails to complete an entire contract, but who by part performance has conferred a net benefit on the innocent party, should be entitled to some payment, unless the contract expressly stipulated otherwise. However, Brian Davenport QC wrote a note of dissent.

Note of dissent
I have the misfortune to differ from my colleagues both as regards the principal policy conclusion reached in this report and as to the manner of its implementation. In almost all contracts of any substance today under which one party promises to carry out certain work in return for a consideration to be given by the other, the contract will make provision for stage payments of one sort or another. The facts of modern economic life have demonstrated that payments on account while the work proceeds are a necessity. Both printed and specially prepared contracts will therefore, in almost every case, provide for such payments. Where a written contract does not provide for such payments, the reason may well be that the parties intended that payment would be due if, but only if, the contractor finished the work. The so-called mischief which the report is intended to correct is therefore likely only to exist in relation to small, informal contracts of which the normal example will be a contract between a householder and a jobbing builder to carry out a particular item of work. Experience has shown that it is all too common for such builders not to complete one job of work before moving on to the next. The effect of the report is to remove from the householder almost the only effective sanction he has against the builder not completing the job. In short, he is prevented from saying with any legal effect, 'Unless you come back and finish the job, I shan't pay you a penny'. In my view, the disadvantages in practice of the recommendations contained in the report outweigh the advantages to be gained from the search for theoretically perfect justice between the parties. If the report's recommendations are implemented, the jobbing builder can leave the site and, when the irate and exasperated householder finally brings the contract to an end, send in a bill for the work done up to the time when he abandoned the site. It will then be for the householder to dispute the amount and calculate his counter-claim for damages. To put the burden on the householder in this manner is, in my view, to put him in a disadvantageous position where he negotiates from a position of weakness. It must not be forgotten that it is the builder who

has broken the contract, not the householder, and that the contract is one under which the parties agreed that payment would be by lump-sum only when the work was done. . . .

It is understood that the recommendation in the Report has not been accepted.

(e) Conditions and warranties

In all the cases so far, the obligation which had to be performed as a condition of the other party's performance being due was clearly basic to the contract, and if there was not at least substantial performance, the result would be that the other party would not get the substance of what he contracted for. Clearly not every non-performance of a contractual term would have this result. What if the obligation left unperformed was not so obviously basic? During the first half of this century it became customary to deal with this problem by asking whether the term which had not been performed was a condition or merely a warranty. The distinction was explained by Fletcher Moulton LJ in his dissenting judgment in *Wallis, Son & Wells v Pratt and Haynes* [1910] 2 KB 1003 in the following terms:

A party to a contract who has performed or is ready and willing to perform his obligations under that contract is entitled to the performance by the other contracting party of all the obligations which rest upon him. But from a very early period of our law it has been recognised that such obligations are not all of equal importance. There are some which go so directly to the substance of the contract, or, in other words, are so essential to its very nature, that their non-performance may fairly be considered by the other party as a substantial failure to perform the contract at all. On the other hand, there are other obligations which, though they must be performed, are not so vital that a failure to perform them goes to the substance of the contract. Both clauses are equally obligations under the contract, and the breach of any one of them entitles the other party to damages. But in the case of the former class he has the alternative of treating the contract as being completely broken by the non-performance, and (if he takes proper steps) he can refuse to perform any of the obligations resting upon himself and sue the other party for a total failure to perform the contract . . .

This usage has been followed in the codification of the law of the contract of sale in the Sale of Goods Act. . . .

Fletcher Moulton's judgment was approved by the House of Lords [1911] AC 394.

Sale of Goods Act 1979

Section 11 . . .
(2) Where a contract of sale is subject to a condition to be fulfilled by the seller, the buyer may waive the condition, or may elect to treat the breach of the condition as a breach of warranty and not as a ground for treating the contract as repudiated.
(3) Whether a stipulation in a contract of sale is a condition, the breach of which may give rise to a right to treat the contract as repudiated, or a warranty, the breach of which may give rise to a claim for damages but not to a right to reject the goods and treat the contract as repudiated, depends in each case on the construction of the contract; and a stipulation may be a condition, though called a warranty in the contract.
(4) Where a contract of sale is not severable and the buyer has accepted the goods or part of them, the breach of a condition to be fulfilled by the seller can only be treated as a breach of warranty, and not as a ground for rejecting the goods and treating the contract as repudiated, unless there is an express or implied term of the contract to that effect.

NOTES

1. The terms 'condition' and 'warranty' can be confusing. Firstly (as noted earlier, p 326) both have more general meanings: 'condition' is often used to mean just a term of a contract, as in the phrase 'conditions of contract', while 'warranty' is often used to denote a promise as to the quality of goods, as in the 'term or representation?' cases (above, p 259). Some of the promises were so crucial that they almost certainly were conditions in the technical sense, so that the buyer could refuse to accept goods which did not have the promised quality.

2. Secondly, as Reynolds, 'Warranty, condition and fundamental term' (1963) 79 LQR 534, 539, remarks:

> The terminology [of 'condition' and 'warranty'] confuses . . . formation with performance: what is referred to as a condition is actually a promise the performance of which is a condition of the other party's liability. And, as Diplock LJ points out in the *Hong Kong Fir* case, it is the situation which ensues when one party fails to perform that entitles the other party to repudiate: whereas this terminology attracts attention away from that situation and focuses it upon the promise instead. In this respect it is misleading.

3. A further confusion can be caused by the not uncommon habit of referring to a warranty (in the technical sense) as an 'independent covenant'. What is meant is that a failure to perform the warranty does not justify the refusal to perform the rest of the contract. Thus if you order a new car, and one of the terms is that the seller is to fit the car with a radio, but the seller delivers the car without the radio, you would not be justified in refusing to accept the car. The obligation to fit the radio is probably only a warranty: you can get one fitted easily at some other garage, so damages will be adequate compensation. If the word 'independent' is to be used at all, it might be better to say that the rest of the contract is independent of the warranty. In contrast, if the car turned out not to be new (it is a 'demonstrator', for instance), there is a breach of condition and you can refuse to accept the car: see *Andrews Bros Ltd v Singer & Co Ltd*, noted below, p 682. Your obligation to accept the car is dependent on its being new.

A term may be a condition because the contract expressly says so, because statute so provides or because the court construes it as one.

(i) Express conditions

We have already noted that in theory the courts will enforce any express provision in the contract stating that in certain circumstances A may withhold performance or terminate if B doesn't do something. There is no difficulty where the obligation which B has to do is fundamental to the contract. But what if the obligation, or at least the failure to perform it which has actually occurred, doesn't seem important?

L Schuler AG v Wickman Machine Tools Sales Ltd [1973] 2 All ER 39, House of Lords

Wickman was appointed sole distributor of Schuler's panel presses in the UK for a period of four-and-a-half years. Clause 7(b) of the agreement provided that:

> It shall be condition of this agreement that (i) [Wickman] shall send its representatives to visit [the six large UK motor manufacturers] at least once in every week for the purpose of soliciting orders for panel presses . . .

Clause 11(a) provided that either party might determine the agreement by notice in writing if:

> (i) the other shall have committed a material breach of its obligations hereunder and shall have failed to remedy the same within sixty days of being required in writing so to do . . .

Wickman's representatives failed to make the weekly visit on a few occasions, and Schuler terminated the agreement immediately, claiming that Wickman was in breach of a condition under cl 7(b).

The dispute went to arbitration, and, on a case stated, Mocatta J held that Schuler's contention was correct, but the decision was reversed by the Court of Appeal. Schuler appealed.

Lord Reid. . . . I think it right first to consider the meaning of cl 11 because, if Wickman's contention with regard to this is right, then cl 7 must be construed in light of the provisions of cl 11. Clause 11 expressly provides that the agreement 'shall continue in force (unless previously determined as hereinafter provided) until' 31st December 1967. That appears to imply the corollary that the agreement shall not be determined before that date in any other way than as provided in cl 11. It is argued for Schuler that those words cannot have been intended to have that implication. In the first place Schuler say that anticipatory breach cannot be brought within the scope of cl 11 and the parties cannot have intended to exclude any remedy for an anticipatory breach. And, secondly, they say that cl 11 fails to provide any remedy for an irremediable breach however fundamental such breach might be.

There is much force in this criticism. But on any view the interrelation and consequences of the various provisions of this agreement are so ill-thought out that I am not disposed to discard the natural meaning of the words which I have quoted merely because giving to them their natural meaning implies that the draftsman has forgotten something which a better draftsman would have remembered. If the terms of cl 11 are wide enough to apply to breaches of cl 7 then I am inclined to hold that cl 7 must be read subject to the provisions of cl 11.

It appears to me that cl 11(a)(i) is intended to apply to all material breaches of the agreement which are capable of being remedied. The question then is what is meant in this context by the word 'remedy'. It could mean obviate or nullify the effect of a breach so that any damage already done is in some way made good. Or it could mean cure so that matters are put right for the future. I think that the latter is the more natural meaning. The word is commonly used in connection with diseases or ailments and they would normally be said to be remedied if they were cured although no cure can remove the past effect or result of the disease before the cure took place. And in general it can only be in a rare case that any remedy of something that has gone wrong in the performance of a continuing positive obligation will, in addition to putting it right for the future, remove or nullify damage already incurred before the remedy was applied. To restrict the meaning of remedy to cases where all damage past and future can be put right would leave hardly any scope at all for this clause. On the other hand, there are cases where it would seem a misuse of language to say that a breach can be remedied. For example, a breach of cl 14 by disclosure of confidential information could not be said to be remedied by a promise not to do it again.

So the question is whether a breach of Wickman's obligation under cl 7(b)(i) is capable of being remedied within the meaning of this agreement. On the other hand, failure to make one particular visit might have irremediable consequences, eg a valuable order might have been lost when making that visit would have obtained it. But looking at the position broadly I incline to the view that breaches of this obligation should be held to be capable of remedy within the meaning of cl 11. Each firm had to be visited more than 200 times. If one visit is missed I think that one would normally say that making arrangements to prevent a recurrence of that breach would remedy the breach. If that is right and if cl 11 is intended to have general application than cl 7 must be read so that a breach of cl 7(b)(i) does not give to Schuler a right to rescind but only to require the breach to be remedied within 60 days under cl 11(a)(i). I do not feel at all confident that this is the true view but I would adopt it unless the provisions of cl 7 point strongly in the opposite direction; so I turn to cl 7.

Clause 7 begins with the general requirement that Wickman shall 'use its best endeavours' to promote sales of Schuler products. Then there is in cl 7(b)(i) specification of those best endeavours with regard to panel presses, and in cl 12(b) a much more general statement of what Wickman must do with regard to other Schuler products. This intention to impose a stricter obligation with regard to panel presses is borne out by the use of the word 'condition' in cl 7(b). I cannot accept Wickman's argument that condition here merely means term. It must be intended to emphasise the importance of the obligations in sub-cll (b)(i) and (b)(ii). But what is the extent of that emphasis?

Schuler maintain that the word 'condition' has now acquired a precise legal meaning; that, particularly since the enactment of the Sale of Goods Act 1893, its recognised meaning in English law is a term of a contract any breach of which by one party gives to the other party an immediate right to rescind the whole contract. Undoubtedly the word is frequently used in that sense. There may, indeed, be some presumption that in a formal legal document it has that meaning. But it is frequently used with a less stringent meaning. One is familiar with printed 'conditions of sale' incorporated into a contract, and with the words 'for conditions see back' printed on a ticket. There it simply means that the 'conditions' are terms of the contract.

In the ordinary use of the English language 'condition' has many meanings, some of which have nothing to do with agreements. In connection with an agreement it may mean a pre-condition: something which must happen or be done before the agreement can take effect. Or it may mean some state of affairs which must continue to exist if the agreement is to remain in force. The legal meaning on which Schuler rely is, I think, one which would not occur to a layman; a condition in that sense is not something which has an automatic effect. It is a term the breach of which by one party gives to the other an option either to terminate the contract or to let the contract proceed and, if he so desires, sue for damages for the breach.

Sometimes a breach of a term gives that option to the aggrieved party because it is of a fundamental character going to the root of the contract, sometimes it gives that option because the parties have chosen to stipulate that it shall have that effect. Blackburn J said in *Bettini v Gye*: 'Parties may think some matter, apparently of very little importance, essential; and if they sufficiently express an intention to make the literal fulfilment of such a thing a condition precedent, it will be one.'

In the present case it is not contended that Wickman's failures to make visits amounted in themselves to fundamental breaches. What is contended is that the terms of cl 7 'sufficiently express an intention' to make any breach, however small, of the obligation to make visits a condition so that any such breach shall entitle Schuler to rescind the whole contract if they so desire.

Schuler maintain that the use of the word 'condition' is in itself enough to establish this intention. No doubt some words used by lawyers do have a rigid inflexible meaning. But we must remember that we are seeking to discover intention as disclosed by the contract as a whole. Use of the word 'condition' is an indication—even a strong indication—of such an intention but it is by no means conclusive. The fact that a particular construction leads to a very unreasonable result must be a relevant consideration. The more unreasonable the result the more unlikely it is that the parties can have intended it, and if they do intend it the more necessary it is that they shall make that intention abundantly clear.

Clause 7(b) requires that over a long period each of the six firms shall be visited every week by one or other of two named representatives. It makes no provision for Wickman being entitled to substitute others even on the death or retirement of one of the named representatives. Even if one could imply some right to do this, it makes no provision for both representatives being ill during a particular week. And it makes no provision for the possibility that one or other of the firms may tell Wickman that they cannot receive Wickman's representative during a particular week. So if the parties gave any thought to the matter at all they must have realised the probability that in a few cases out of the 1,400 required visits a visit as stipulated would be impossible. But if Schuler's contention is right failure to make even one visit entitles them to terminate the contract however blameless Wickman might be. This is so unreasonable that it must make me search for some other possible meaning of the contract. If none can be found then Wickman must suffer the consequences. But only if that is the only possible interpretation.

If I have to construe cl 7 standing by itself then I do find difficulty in reaching any other interpretation. But if cl 7 must be read with cl 11 the difficulty disappears. The word 'condition' would make any breach of cl 7(b), however excusable, a material breach. That would then entitle Schuler to give notice under cl 11(a)(i) requiring the breach to be remedied. There would be no point in giving such a notice if Wickman were clearly not in fault but if it were given Wickman would have no difficulty in shewing that the breach had been remedied. If Wickman were at fault then on receiving such a notice they would have to amend their system so that they could shew that the breach had been remedied. If they did not do that within the period of the notice then Schuler would be entitled to rescind.

In my view, that is a possible and reasonable construction of the contract and I would therefore adopt it. The contract is so obscure that I can have no confidence that this is its true meaning but for the reasons which I have given I think that it is the preferable construction. It follows that Schuler were not entitled to rescind the contract as they purported to do. So I would dismiss this appeal.

Lord Wilberforce. . . . Does cl 7(b) amount to a 'condition' or a 'term'? (to call it an important or material term adds, with all respect, nothing but some intellectual assuagement). My Lords, I am clear in my own mind that it is a condition, but your Lordships take the contrary view. On a matter of construction of a particular document, to develop the reasons for a minority opinion serves no purpose. I am all the more happy to refrain from so doing because the judgments of Mocatta J, Stephenson LJ, and indeed of Edmund Davies LJ on construction, give me complete satisfaction and I could in any case add little of value to their reasons. I would only add that, for my part, to call the clause arbitrary, capricious or fantastic, or to introduce as a test of its validity the ubiquitous reasonable man (I do not know whether he is English or German) is to assume, contrary to the evidence, that both parties to this contract adopted a standard of easygoing tolerance rather than one of aggressive, insistent punctuality and efficiency. This is not an assumption I am prepared to make, nor do I think myself entitled to impose the former standard on the parties if their words indicate, as they plainly do, the latter. I note finally, that the result of treating the clause, so careful and specific in its requirements, as a term is, in effect, to deprive the appellants of any remedy in respect of admitted and by no means minimal breaches. The arbitrator's finding that these breaches were not 'material' was not, in my opinion, justified in law in the face of the parties' own characterisation of them in their document: indeed the fact that he was able to do so, and so leave the appellants without remedy, argues strongly that the legal basis of his finding—that cl 7(b) was merely a term—is unsound.

I would allow this appeal.

[Lords Morris of Borth-y-Gest, Simon of Glaisdale and Kilbrandon delivered speeches dismissing the appeal.]

Appeal dismissed.

NOTES

1. If the purpose of visiting every week is to keep in close touch with every development at a potential purchaser's factory, how can a missed visit be 'remedied'?
2. Why was the result of treating cl 7(b) as a condition in the strict sense so unreasonable? Suppose Schulers had asked you to draft the contract for them, and had stressed that even though they might not be able to show that any particular visit missed had led to the loss of a sale (a point referred to by Mocatta J at first instance), they nonetheless wanted to be sure that Wickmans would not miss any; how would you have drafted the contract? (Of course, Wickmans might not have been prepared to sign your version, as Lord Kilbrandon remarked at p 63.)
3. The House of Lords seems recently to have changed its attitude towards conditions in contracts, favouring certainty over a 'just' result on the facts of the case. Consider this statement by Lord Bridge in *Awilco A/S v Fulvia SpA di Navigazione, The Chikuma* [1981] 1 All ER 652 at 658–659:

It has often been pointed out that shipowners and charterers bargain at arm's length. Neither class has such a preponderance of bargaining power as to be in a position to oppress the other. They should be in a position to look after themselves by contracting only on terms which are acceptable to them. Where, as here, they embody in their contracts common form clauses, it is, to my mind, of overriding importance that their meaning and legal effect should be certain and well understood. The ideal at which the courts should aim, in construing such clauses, is to produce a result such that in any given situation both parties seeking legal advice as to their rights and obligations can expect the same clear and confident answer from their advisers and neither will be tempted to embark on long and expensive litigation in the belief that victory depends on winning the sympathy of the court. This ideal may never be fully attainable, but we shall certainly never even approximate to it unless we strive to follow clear and consistent principles and steadfastly refuse to be blown off course by the supposed merits of individual cases.

(See also *Bunge v Tradax*, below, p 438.) That is not to say that *Schuler v Wickman* would be decided differently today, but who knows . . .?

Suppose you decide that Schulers do need the right to terminate the contract for even a single visit missed. What language would you employ to achieve this result? One solution might seem to be to spell out that Schulers could terminate, but the clause must be very carefully drafted to achieve the right effect. In *Financings Ltd v Baldock* [1963] 2 QB 104 a hire-purchase agreement provided:

> 8. Should the hirer fail to pay the initial instalment . . . or any subsequent instalment . . . within ten days after the same shall have become due or if he shall die . . . the owner may . . . by written notice . . . forthwith and for all purposes terminate the hiring.

Clause 11 provided that if the agreement were terminated under cl 8, the hirer would pay to the owner 'such further sum as with the total amount of any instalments previously paid hereunder will equal two-thirds of the total hiring cost . . .'.

The hirer failed to pay the second and third instalments, and the owners gave notice of termination under cl 8 and repossessed the vehicle. Clause 11 was invalid as a penalty clause (for the reasons explained in *Bridge v Campbell Discount Co Ltd*, below, p 521), so the owners claimed damages from the hirer for their full loss. The Court of Appeal held that they were entitled to the overdue instalments up to the date of repossession, but no more. The failure to pay one or two instalments on time would not justify termination of the contract under the general law (see below, p 436), and cl 8 merely conferred a right to terminate the agreement without making the failure to pay a breach of condition. If the hirer's failure to pay had amounted to a repudiation, as in *Overstone v Shipway* [1962] 1 All ER 52, CA, the hirer would have been liable in damages, but here the owners could only claim money due at the date of termination and any payments required under the termination clause itself (none in this case). On the effect of cl 8 Diplock LJ said:

> . . . [The hirer] was clearly in breach of his obligation to pay two instalments on the due dates but, in the absence of any express provision to the contrary in the contract, these breaches of a contract of hire expressed to be for a duration of 24 months would not of themselves go to the root of the contract or evince an intention on the part of the hirer no longer to be bound by the contract. The owners' only remedy would have been to sue for the two instalments overdue and their measure of damages would have been the amount of these instalments, together with interest at the agreed rate of 10 per cent. per annum. They would also have continued to be liable to perform their own obligations under the contract, viz., to continue to hire the van to the hirer; for again, in the absence of express provision to the contrary, the non-payment of two instalments would not be an event which relieved the owners from their undertaking to do what they had agreed to do but had not yet done . . . [P]arties to a contract may incorporate in it provisions which expressly define the events, whether or not they amount to breaches of contract, which are to have this result. But such a provision of itself may do no more than define an event which of itself, or at the option of one or other of the parties, brings the contract to an end and thus relieves both parties from their undertakings further to perform their obligations thereunder. Whether it does more than this and confers any other rights or remedies on either party on the termination of the contract, depends upon the true construction of the relevant provision. If it does not, then each party is left with such causes of action, if any, as had already accrued to him at the date that the contract came to an end, but acquires no fresh cause of action as a result of the termination.

In *Thomas Feather & Co (Bradford) Ltd v Keighley Corpn* (1953) 52 LGR 30 the same approach was taken to a clause in a building contract which gave the employer the right to determine the contract if the contractor sub-contracted any of the work without consent. The contractor failed to obtain consent and the employer exercised its right to terminate. The employer then employed another contractor to finish the work at an extra cost of

£21,000, but it was held that the employer could not recover this sum from the original contractor.

Thus merely giving Schulers the right to terminate if Wickmans miss a visit might leave Schulers with no right to damages. As with so many 'rules' of contract law, however, it is a question of construction of the contract and the trick is to use very clear language. For instance, if each visit had been made a 'condition precedent to the continuation of the contract' Schulers could have terminated: see *Lombard North Central plc v Butterworth* [1987] QB 527 (below, p 510).

(ii) Statute

Sale of Goods Act 1979, ss 13–15 (see above, pp 327–328), 28 (above, p 413) and 30 (above, p 417)

(iii) Constructive conditions

Bentsen v Taylor, Sons & Co (No 2) [1893] 2 QB 274, Court of Appeal

A charterparty described the ship as 'now sailed or about to sail from a pitch pine port to the UK'. She did not in fact sail until over three weeks after the date of the charter. The charterers discovered what had occurred and entered into correspondence with the owner's brokers; ultimately, when the ship arrived they refused to load.

Bowen LJ. . . . Of course it is often very difficult to decide as a matter of construction whether a representation which contains a promise, and which can only be explained on the ground that it is in itself a substantive part of the contract, amounts to a condition precedent, or is only a warranty. There is no way of deciding that question except by looking at the contract in the light of the surrounding circumstances, and then making up one's mind whether the intention of the parties, as gathered from the instrument itself, will best be carried out by treating the promise as a warranty sounding only in damages, or as a condition precedent by the failure to perform which the other party is relieved of his liability. In order to decide this question of construction, one of the first things you would look to is, to what extent the accuracy of the statement—the truth of what is promised—would be likely to affect the substance and foundation of the adventure which the contract is intended to carry out. There, again, it might be necessary to have recourse to the jury. In the case of a charterparty it may well be that such a test could only be applied after getting the jury to say what the effect of a breach of such a condition would be on the substance and foundation of the adventure; not the effect of the breach which has in fact taken place, but the effect likely to be produced on the foundation of the adventure by any such breach of that portion of the contract.

[Applying this test, Bowen LJ held that the statement that the ship had sailed or was about to sail amounted to a condition precedent. He went on to hold, however, that the charterers had waived their right to terminate. Lord Esher MR and Kay LJ gave judgment to the same effect.]

(f) A more flexible approach

Any failure to perform a condition will give the other party the right to refuse to perform. The only qualification is a de minimis rule: in *Shipton, Anderson & Co v Weil Bros & Co* [1912] 1 KB 574 it was held that a buyer could not refuse to accept delivery under a contract for 4,950 tons of wheat on the ground that the sellers had tendered 55 lbs too much. The result is that a party may use a technical breach which actually does him no harm as an excuse for getting out of a contract which has turned out unfavourably to him because of a fall in the market; see, for example, *Arcos Ltd v EA Ronaasen & Son* (above, p 328).

Hong Kong Fir Shipping Co Ltd v Kawasaki Kisen Kaisha Ltd [1962] 1 All ER 474, Court of Appeal

A twenty-four month time charter provided that the vessel was to be delivered to the charterers at Liverpool, 'she being in every way fitted for ordinary cargo service'. The 'off-hire' clause provided that the charterers need not pay hire in respect of periods over 24 hours lost in carrying out repairs, and that such off-hire periods might, at the charterers' option, be added to the hire period. (The charter was on the Baltime 1939 form, see above, p 46). The vessel left for Newport News, to load a cargo of coal for carriage to Osaka. At the date of her delivery, the ship was unseaworthy because she had old engines which required careful supervision, whereas her engine room staff was undermanned and inefficient. As a result, repairs had to be carried out on the way to Osaka and after her arrival there, and it took a total of 18 weeks to make her seaworthy. This left a period of 17 months during which she could be available to the charterers. There had been a steep fall in freight rates since the date of the charter, and the charterers purported to terminate. Salmon J held that they had no right to do so, and they appealed.

[Sellers LJ held that there had been only a breach of warranty.]

Upjohn LJ. . . . . Why is this apparently basic and underlying condition of seaworthiness not, in fact, treated as a condition? It is for the simple reason that the seaworthiness clause is breached by the slightest failure to be fitted 'in every way' for service. Thus, to take examples from the judgments in some of the cases I have mentioned above, if a nail is missing from one of the timbers of a wooden vessel, or if proper medical supplies or two anchors are not on board at the time of sailing, the owners are in breach of the seaworthiness stipulation. It is contrary to common sense to suppose that, in such circumstances, the parties contemplated that the charterer should at once be entitled to treat the contract as at an end for such trifling breaches. . . .

. . . It is open to the parties to a contract to make it clear either expressly or by necessary implication that a particular stipulation is to be regarded as a condition which goes to the root of the contract, so that it is clear that the parties contemplate that *any* breach of it entitles the other party at once to treat the contract as at an end. That matter is to be determined as a question of the proper interpretation of the contract. Where . . . on the true construction of the contract, the parties have not made a particular stipulation a condition, it would be unsound and misleading to conclude that, being a warranty, damages is a sufficient remedy.

In my judgment, the remedies open to the innocent party for breach of a stipulation which is not a condition strictly so called, depend entirely on the nature of the breach and its foreseeable consequences. Breaches of stipulation fall, naturally, into two classes. First, there is the case where the owner by his conduct indicates that he considers himself no longer bound to perform his part of the contract; in that case, of course, the charterer may accept the repudiation and treat the contract as at an end. The second class of case is, of course, the more usual one, and that is where, due to misfortune such as the perils of the sea, engine failures, incompetence of the crew and so on, the owner is unable to perform a particular stipulation precisely in accordance with the terms of the contract try he never so hard to remedy it. In that case, the question to be answered is, does the breach of the stipulation go so much to the root of the contract that it makes further commercial performance of the contract impossible, or, in other words, is the whole contract frustrated? If yea, the innocent party may treat the contract as at an end. If nay, his claim sounds in damages only.

If I have correctly stated the principles, then, as the stipulation as to seaworthiness is not a condition in the strict sense, the question to be answered is, did the initial unseaworthiness as found by the learned judge, from which finding there has been no appeal, go so much to the root of the contract that the charterers were then and there entitled to treat the charterparty as at an end? The only unseaworthiness alleged, serious though it was, was the insufficiency and incompetence of the crew, but that surely cannot be treated as going to the root of the contract for the parties must have contemplated that, in such an event, the crew could be changed and augmented. In my judgment, on this part of his case counsel for the charterers necessarily fails.

I turn, therefore, to his second point: Where there have been serious and repeated delays due to the inability of the owner to perform his part of the contract, is the charterer entitled to treat the contract as repudiated after a reasonable time, or can he do so only if delays are such as to amount to a frustration of the contract? Some of my earlier observations on the remedy available for breach of contract are relevant here, but I do not repeat them. I agree with the conclusions reached by the learned judge and by Sellers LJ . . . Accordingly, I agree that this appeal must be dismissed.

Diplock LJ. . . . Every synallagmatic contract contains in it the seeds of the problem: in what event will a party be relieved of his undertaking to do that which he has agreed to do but has not yet done? The contract may itself expressly define some of these events, as in the cancellation clause in a charterparty, but, human prescience being limited, it seldom does so exhaustively and often fails to do so at all. In some classes of contracts, such as sale of goods, marine insurance, contracts of affreightment evidenced by bills of lading and those between parties to bills of exchange, Parliament has defined by statute some of the events not provided for expressly in individual contracts of that class; but, where an event occurs the occurrence of which neither the parties nor Parliament have expressly stated will discharge one of the parties from further performance of his undertakings, it is for the court to determine whether the event has this effect or not. The test whether an event has this effect or not has been stated in a number of metaphors all of which I think amount to the same thing: does the occurrence of the event deprive the party who has further undertakings still to perform of substantially the whole benefit which it was the intention of the parties as expressed in the contract that he should obtain as the consideration for performing those undertakings? This test is applicable whether or not the event occurs as a result of the default of one of the parties to the contract, but the consequences of the event are different in the two cases. Where the event occurs as a result of the default of one party, the party in default cannot rely on it as relieving himself of the performance of any further undertakings on his part and the innocent party, although entitled to, need not treat the event as relieving him of the performance of his own undertakings. This is only a specific application of the fundamental legal and moral rule that a man should not be allowed to take advantage of his own wrong. Where the event occurs as a result of the default of neither party, each is relieved of the further performance of his own undertakings, and their rights in respect of undertakings previously performed are now regulated by the Law Reform (Frustrated Contracts) Act, 1943.

This branch of the common law has reached its present stage by the normal process of historical growth, and the fallacy in counsel for the charterers' contention that a different test is applicable when the event occurs as a result of the default of one party from that applicable in cases of frustration where the event occurs as a result of the default of neither party arises, in my view, from a failure to view the cases in their historical context. The problem: in what event will a party to a contract be relieved of his undertaking to do that which he has agreed to do but has not yet done? has exercised the English courts for centuries, probably ever since assumpsit emerged as a form of action distinct from covenant and debt, and long before even the earliest cases which we have been invited to examine; but, until the rigour of the rule in *Paradine v Jane* was mitigated in the middle of the last century by the classic judgments of Blackburn J in *Taylor v Caldwell* and Bramwell B in *Jackson v Union Marine Insurance Co*, it was in general only events resulting from one party's failure to perform his contractual obligations which were regarded as capable of relieving the other party from continuing to perform that which he had undertaken to do. . . .

Once it is appreciated that it is the event and not the fact that the event is a result of a breach of contract which relieves the party not in default of further performance of his obligations, two consequences follow: (i) The test whether the event relied on has this consequence is the same whether the event is the result of the other party's breach of contract or not, as Devlin J pointed out in *Universal Cargo Carriers Corpn v Citati*. (ii) The question whether an event which is the result of the other party's breach of contract has this consequence cannot be answered by treating all contractual undertakings as falling into one of two separate categories: 'conditions', the breach of which gives rise to an event which relieves the party not in default of further performance of his obligations, and 'warranties', the breach of which does not give rise to such an event. Lawyers tend to speak of this classification as if it were comprehensive, partly for the historical reasons which I have already mentioned, and partly because Parliament itself adopted it in the Sale of Goods Act, 1893, as respects a number of implied terms in contracts for the sale of goods and has in that Act used the expressions 'condition' and 'warranty' in that meaning. But it is by no means true of contractual undertakings in general at common law.

No doubt there are many simple contractual undertakings, sometimes express, but more often because of their very simplicity ('It goes without saying') to be implied, of which it can be predicated that every breach of such an undertaking must give rise to an event which will deprive the party not in default of substantially the whole benefit which it was intended that he should obtain from the contract. And such a stipulation, unless the parties have agreed that breach of it shall not entitle the non-defaulting party to treat the contract as repudiated, is a 'condition'. So, too, there may be other simple contractual undertakings of which it can be predicated that *no* breach can give rise to an event which will deprive the party not in default of substantially the whole benefit which it was intended that he should obtain from the contract; and such a stipulation, unless the parties have agreed that breach of it shall entitle the non-defaulting party to treat the contract as repudiated, is a 'warranty'. There are, however, many contractual undertakings of a more complex character which cannot be categorised as being 'conditions' or 'warranties' if the late nineteenth century meaning adopted in the Sale of Goods Act, 1893, and used by Bowen LJ in *Bentsen v Taylor, Sons & Co*, be given to those terms. Of such undertakings, all that can be predicated is that some breaches will, and others will not, give rise to an event which will deprive the party not in default of substantially the whole benefit which it was intended that he should obtain from the contract; and the legal consequences of a breach of such an undertaking, unless provided for expressly in the contract, depend on the nature of the event to which the breach gives rise and do not follow automatically from a prior classification of the undertaking as a 'condition' or a 'warranty'. For instance, to take the example of Bramwell B in *Jackson v Union Marine Insurance Co*, by itself breach of an undertaking by a shipowner to sail with all possible despatch to a named port does not necessarily relieve the charterer of further performance of his obligation under the charterparty, but, if the breach is so prolonged that the contemplated voyage is frustrated, it does have this effect.

As my brethren have already pointed out, the shipowner's undertaking to tender a seaworthy ship has, as a result of numerous decisions as to what can amount to 'unseaworthiness', become one of the most complex of contractual undertakings. It embraces obligations with respect to every part of the hull and machinery, stores and equipment and the crew itself. It can be broken by the presence of trivial defects easily and rapidly remediable as well as by defects which must inevitably result in a total loss of the vessel. Consequently, the problem in this case is, in my view, neither solved nor soluble by debating whether the owners' express or implied undertaking to tender a seaworthy ship is a 'condition' or a 'warranty'. It is, like so many other contractual terms, an undertaking one breach of which may give rise to an event which relieves the charterer of further performance of his undertakings if he so elects, and another breach of which may not give rise to such an event but entitle him only to monetary compensation in the form of damages. It is, with all deference to counsel for the charterers' skilful argument, by no means surprising that, among the many hundreds of previous cases about the shipowner's undertaking to deliver a seaworthy ship, there is none where it was found profitable to discuss in the judgments the question whether that undertaking is a 'condition' or a 'warranty'; for the true answer, as I have already indicated, is that it is neither, but one of that large class of contractual undertakings, one breach of which may have the same effect as that ascribed to a breach of 'condition' under the Sale of Goods Act, 1893, and a different breach of which may have only the same effect as that ascribed to a breach of 'warranty' under that Act. . . .

What the learned judge had to do in the present case as in any other case where one party to a contract relies on a breach by the other party as giving him a right to elect to rescind the contract, was to look at the events which had occurred as a result of the breach at the time at which the charterers purported to rescind the charterparty, and to decide whether the occurrence of those events deprived the charterers of substantially the whole benefit which it was the intention of the parties as expressed in the charterparty that the charterers should obtain from the further performance of their own contractual undertakings. One turns, therefore, to the contract, the Baltime 1939 Charter. Clause 13, the 'due diligence' clause, which exempts the shipowners from responsibility for delay or loss or damage to goods on board due to unseaworthiness unless such delay or loss or damage has been caused by want of due diligence of the owners in making the vessel seaworthy and fitted for the voyage, is in itself sufficient to show that the mere occurrence of the events that the vessel was in some respect unseaworthy when tendered or that such unseaworthiness had caused some delay in performance of the charterparty would not deprive the charterer of the whole benefit which it was the intention of the parties he should obtain from the performance of his obligations under the contract—for he undertakes to continue to perform his obligations notwithstanding the occurrence of such events if they fall short of frustration of the contract and even deprives himself of any remedy in damages unless such events are the consequence of want of due diligence on the part of the shipowner.

The question which the learned judge had to ask himself was, as he rightly decided, whether or not, at the date when the charterers purported to rescind the contract, namely June 6, 1957, or when the owners purported to accept such rescission, namely Aug 8, 1957, the delay which had already occurred as a result of the incompetence of the engine-room staff, and the delay which was likely to occur in repairing the engines of the vessel and the conduct of the owners by that date in taking steps to remedy these two matters, were, when taken together, such as to deprive the charterers of substantially the whole benefit which it was the intention of the parties they should obtain from further use of the vessel under the charterparty. In my view, in his judgment—on which I would not seek to improve—the learned judge took into account and gave due weight to all the relevant considerations and arrived at the right answer for the right reasons.

Appeal dismissed.

NOTES

1. Diplock LJ seems to suggest that a term will be a condition only if the agreement so provides, or if 'it can be predicated that every breach of such an undertaking must give rise to an event which will deprive the party not in default of substantially the whole benefit . . .' Upjohn LJ, in contrast, recognizes that a term may be a condition *by implication*, without such serious consequences necessarily being entailed. The House of Lords has recently held that the latter is the correct position: *Bunge v Tradax*, below, p 438.

2. The more flexible approach, of not classifying a term as a condition or a warranty but as an 'intermediate' or (for want of a better name) 'innominate' term, was applied to a sale of goods contract in *Cehave NV v Bremer Handelsgesellschaft mbH, The Hansa Nord* [1975] 3 All ER 739. Two contracts were made, each for 6,000 tons citrus pulp pellets cif Rotterdam, on the Grain and Feed Trade Association (GAFTA) terms. Clause 7 provided that 'Shipment to be made in good condition'. The buyers paid the price, some £100,000, and obtained the shipping documents, but when the goods (which had been shipped as a single, undifferentiated cargo) were discharged at Rotterdam, it was found that part of the shipment had been damaged by overheating. The buyers rejected the whole shipment, and when the sellers refused to refund the price, the buyers applied to the court at Rotterdam, which ordered the shipment to be sold. The shipment was then bought for £30,000 by B, who sold it back to the buyers at the same price, and the buyers used it for their original purpose, making cattle feed. The dispute was referred to arbitration, and the umpire held that the buyers were not entitled to reject the goods, but on appeal to the Board of GAFTA it was held that the buyers were entitled to reject on the grounds that (i) the goods, though merchantable in a commercial sense, were not merchantable within the meaning of the Sale of Goods Act, and (ii) the goods were not shipped in good condition. Mocatta J upheld the Board's findings. On the latter point, Mocatta J held that under the Sale of Goods Act, terms in

contracts for the sale of goods must be either conditions or warranties, and that, as a breach of the 'shipped in good condition' clause might have serious consequences, it must be a condition. The Court of Appeal allowed the sellers' appeal. It held that the goods were merchantable, as they were still fit for the purpose for which such goods are commonly sold, ie for making cattle food, even if they were only saleable at a reduced price (on the possible repercussions of this approach, see above, p 330). The Court went on to hold that the Sale of Goods Act did not exclude the rules of common law, under which the 'shipped in good condition' clause was not a condition. The Sale of Goods Act did not exclude the common law rules on termination and, as Roskill LJ put it, 'It is desirable that the same legal principles should apply to the law of contract as a whole and that different legal principles should not apply to different branches of that law.' The buyer's right to reject depended on the seriousness of the consequences of the breach, and on the facts rejection was not justified. Ormrod LJ said (at 766–767):

If this view is correct it is bound to have important repercussions on the way in which courts in future will approach the construction of stipulations in contracts for the sale of goods. It will no longer be necessary to place so much emphasis on the *potential* effects of a breach on the buyer, and to feel obliged, as Mocatta J did in this case, to construe a stipulation as a condition because in other cases or in other circumstances the buyer ought to be entitled to reject. Consequently, the court will be freer to regard stipulations, as a matter of construction, as warranties, if what might be called the 'back-up' rule of the common law is available to protect buyers who ought to be able to reject in proper circumstances. I doubt whether, strictly speaking, this involves the creation of a third category of stipulations; rather, it recognises another ground for holding that a buyer is entitled to reject, namely that, de facto, the consideration for his promise has been wholly destroyed.

The result may be summarised in this way. When a breach of contract has taken place the question arises: is the party who is not in breach entitled in law to treat the contract as repudiated or, in the case of a buyer, to reject the goods? The answer depends on the answers to a series of other questions. Adopting Upjohn LJ's judgment in the *Hong Kong Fir Shipping* case the first question is: does the contract expressly provided that in the event of the breach of the term in question the other party is entitled to terminate the contract or reject the goods? If the answer is No, the next question is: does the contract when correctly construed so provide? The relevant term, for example, may be described as a 'condition'. The question then arises whether this word is used as a code word for the phrase 'shall be entitled to repudiate the contract or reject the goods', or in some other sense as in *Wickman Machine Tool Sales Ltd v Schuler AG*. The next question is whether the breach of the relevant term creates a right to repudiate or reject. This may arise either from statute or as a result of judicial decision on particular contractual terms. For example, if the requirements of s 14(1) or (2) of the Sale of Goods Act 1893 are fulfilled, the buyer will be entitled to reject the goods, as a result of this section read with s 11(1). In fact, in all those sections of the 1893 Act which create implied conditions the word 'condition' is by definition a code word for 'breach of this term will entitle the buyer to reject the goods', subject to any other relevant provision of the Act. In other cases, the courts have decided that breach of some specific terms, such as, for example, an 'expected ready to load' stipulation, will ipso facto give rise to a right in the other party to repudiate the contract (*The Mihalis Angelos* per Lord Denning MR). In these two classes of case the consequences of the breach are irrelevant or, more accurately, are assumed to go to the root of the contract, and to justify repudiation. There remains the non-specific class where the events produced by the breach are such that it is reasonable to describe the breach as going to the root of the contract and so justifying repudiation.

If this approach is permissible in the present case I would unhesitatingly hold that the stipulation in cl 7 that the goods were to be shipped in good condition was not a condition, and that on the facts of this case the breach did not go to the root of the contract, and that, consequently, the buyers were not entitled to reject the goods.

If, on the contrary, I have to make an exclusive choice between condition and warranty I would categorise the relevant part of cl 7 as a warranty, mainly because I find it unrealistic to hold that parties who have expressly stipulated in cl 5 that terms as to quality shall be treated, in effect, as warranties, except in the special circumstances defined by the clause itself, should have intended the general stipulation as to condition of the goods on shipment to have any greater effect.

I would therefore allow the appeal, and hold that the buyers were not entitled to reject the goods but are entitled to such damages as may be appropriate.

3. In contrast, in *Maredelanto Compania Naviera SA v Bergbau-Handel GmbH, The Mihalis Angelos* [1970] 3 All ER 125 a clause in a charterparty stating that the vessel was 'expected ready to load under this charter about 1 July 1965' was held to be a condition in the strict sense, so that the charterers could terminate the contract without having to prove that the breach had serious consequences. Megaw LJ said (at pp 138–139):

I reach that conclusion for four interrelated reasons. First, it tends towards certainty in the law. One of the essential elements of law is some measure of uniformity. One of the important elements of the law is predictability. At any rate in commercial law, there are obvious and substantial advantages in having, where possible, a firm and definite rule for a particular class of legal relationship, eg as here, the legal categorisation of a particular, definable type of contractual clause in common use. It is surely much better, both for shipowners and charterers (and, incidentally, for their advisers) when a contractual obligation of this nature is under consideration, and still more when they are faced with the necessity for an urgent decision as to the effects of a suspected breach of it, to be able to say categorically: 'If a breach is proved, then the charterer can put an end to the contract', rather than that they should be left to ponder whether or not the courts would be likely, in the particular case, when the evidence had been heard, to decide that in the particular circumstances the breach was or was not such as to go to the root of the contract. Where justice does not require greater flexibility, there is everything to be said for, and nothing against, a degree of rigidity in legal principle.

4. Further cases on the question whether a particular breach of contract justifies the innocent party in terminating the contract will be found in the next section. Note particularly the House of Lords decision in *Bunge Corpn v Tradax SA*, below, p 438.

5. In both the *Hong Kong Fir* case and the *Hansa Nord* the Court of Appeal held that there had been no breach of condition. This does not mean that the charterers' or buyers' obligations were *un*conditional. Their obligations were conditional upon the other party performing in such a way that they would receive the substance of what they were contracting for, but were *not* conditional on absolute compliance with the seaworthiness or 'shipped in good condition' clauses. If the breaches had been sufficiently serious in effect, the charterers or buyers would still have been entitled to refuse to perform.

6. Terminology in this area is confused because differing terms are used to describe conditions and breaches which are sufficiently serious to justify the innocent party in terminating. In the *Suisse Atlantique* case Lord Upjohn said ([1967] 1 AC 361 at 422):

There was much discussion during the argument about the phrases 'fundamental breach' and 'breach of a fundamental term' and I think it is true that in some of the cases these terms have been used interchangeably; but in fact they are quite different. I believe that all of your Lordships are agreed and, indeed, it has not seriously been disputed before us that there is no magic in the words 'fundamental breach'; this expression is no more than a convenient shorthand expression for saying that a particular breach or breaches of contract by one party is or are such as to go to the root of the contract which entitles the other party to treat such breach or breaches as a repudiation of the whole contract. Whether such breach or breaches do constitute a fundamental breach depends on the construction of the contract and on all the facts and circumstances of the case. The innocent party may accept that breach or those breaches as a repudiation and treat the whole contract at an end and sue for damages generally or he may at his option prefer to affirm the contract and treat it as continuing on foot in which case he can sue only for damages for breach or breaches of the particular stipulation or stipulations in the contract which has or have been broken.

But the expression 'fundamental term' has a different meaning. A fundamental term of a contract is a stipulation which the parties have agreed either expressly or by necessary implication or which the general law regards as a condition which goes to the root of the contract so that *any breach* of that term may at once and without further reference to the facts and circumstances be regarded by the innocent party as a fundamental breach and thus is conferred on him the alternative remedies at his option that I have just mentioned.

7. Compare the *Hong Kong Fir* test ('does the breach deprive the innocent party of substantially the whole benefit of the contract?') to the doctrine of substantial performance. The two rules reflect similar ideas but isn't the emphasis different? It seems that defects or deficiencies in performance might prevent there being substantial performance even though they are not so serious as to deprive the innocent party of substantially the whole benefit of the contract. See below, p 456.

8. Note that if a party purports to terminate on an insufficient ground, it is normally permitted to justify its action later on some quite different ground, even if it was not aware of the other ground at the date of termination. In recent years there has been an attempt to restrict this rule, but the exact limits (if any) which have been imposed on it are very unclear: see below, p 618.

(g) Time stipulations

As we saw earlier, one party may be able to withhold his performance until the other is ready to perform or has done so, but in the absence of an anticipatory repudiation he will not be entitled to terminate until the time for performance has expired (see the note on *Trans-Trust v Danubian Trading* above, p 412). Meanwhile the other party can perform. Thus in *Borrowman, Phillips & Co v Free & Hollis* (1878) 4 QBD 500 a seller who had tendered goods that did not conform to the contract, and which were rejected by the buyers, was permitted to retender within the contract period. For a recent case where the assessment of damages depended on the same point, see *Berger & Co Inc v Gill & Duffus SA* [1948] AC 382.

Once the date set in the contract for performance has passed, the party who has unjustifiably failed to perform will normally be in breach and thus liable for damages even if he does later perform (for exceptional cases where he may not be liable, see above, p 391). In addition, the other party may be able to terminate for default, but he will only be entitled to do this immediately if 'time was of the essence'.

(i) Time of the essence

In ordinary commercial contracts for the sale of goods, the rule clearly is, that time is prima facie of the essence with respect to delivery.

(McCardie J in *Hartley v Hymans* [1920] 3 KB 475 at 484.)

(ii) Time not of the essence

Sale of Goods Act 1979

Section 10
(1) Unless a different intention appears from the terms of the contract, stipulations as to time of payment are not of the essence of a contract of sale.

For a case in which the parties had agreed expressly that time of payment should be of the essence, see below, p 510.

The time for performance of many obligations is not of the essence, unless the contract provides otherwise. Sometimes the reason is fairly obvious. For instance, if time for building work were of the essence, the employer would be able to terminate if by the date for completion the builder was a day behind and, under the rule in *Sumpter v Hedges* (above, p 418), the employer could avoid paying anything for what the builder had done.

If time is not of the essence, how long does the innocent party have to wait? In *Universal Cargo Carriers Corpn v Citati* [1957] 2 QB 401 the charterer had failed to provide a cargo within the laydays (the time permitted for loading—see above, p 52), and the owners refused to keep the vessel at the charterer's disposal any longer. Devlin J held that time was not of the essence and that the owners could terminate only if the delay went to the root of the contract. What yardstick should be used to determine whether it went to the root? The arbitrator had held that the delay must have been for a reasonable time. Devlin J rejected this and held that the delay must 'frustrate' the charterparty. This was not frustration in the sense of the 'doctrine of frustration' considered in section 4—it couldn't be a case of frustration in that sense because the delay was the charterer's fault—but in the older sense of defeating the object of the venture (compare Diplock's judgment in the *Hong Kong Fir* case, above, p 431.). If the delay had become that serious, the owners could have terminated. (They could also have terminated before the delay had become that bad if it was clear that the charterer would not be able to load within a frustrating time. In the *Citati* case Devlin explains this as depending on the doctrine of anticipatory repudiation, see below, p 443 ff. Other explanations may be possible.)

At first sight, the distinction between a 'frustrating time' and a 'reasonable time' may seem semantic, but the point is that they involve different factors. 'Frustrating time' is determined by the effect on the innocent party: does the delay deprive him of substantially the whole benefit of the contract? 'Reasonable time' is governed by what remains to be done by the party in breach, how hard he has been pressed by the innocent party previously, and other such factors: see the judgment of Denning LJ in *Charles Rickards Ltd v Oppenhaim* below, p 603.

Since 1957, however, it seems that the law may have changed so that the innocent party need not wait so long. Once the date for performance has passed he may serve notice on the other party to complete performance within a reasonable time; and if the other fails to perform within this period, the innocent party may then terminate.

This had been the rule in contracts for the sale of land for a long time. The position was complicated because common law and equity took different views as to when time was of the essence. Originally at common law, the time for the performance of both the vendor's and the purchaser's obligations was of the essence, but (with certain exceptions, for instance if the contract *expressly* provided that time was to be of the essence) equity took a different view. If the innocent party purported to determine the contract, and to forfeit or recover a deposit, the court of equity could declare his action ineffective or stay it, and grant specific performance to the party guilty of the delay. The equitable rule now prevails (Law of Property Act

1925, s 41, re-enacting Judicature Act 1873, s 25(1)). Note that it was only termination of the contract, and the accompanying forfeiture or recovery of a deposit, that would be restrained: the party guilty of the delay would still be liable in damages to the other (*Raineri v Miles* [1981] AC 1050).

However, equity would not grant specific performance, or restrain termination by the innocent party, if either the party in breach had delayed an unreasonably long time, or the innocent party had 'made time of the essence' by serving a notice to complete within a reasonable time, and this notice had not been complied with (see *Stickney v Keeble* [1915] AC 386).

These rules appeared to depend upon the availability of specific performance, so that it did not seem that there was any general rule that time could be 'made' of the essence in contracts in which specific performance would not be granted. But *Halsbury's Laws of England* (4th edn, Vol 9, para 481) had stated that there was a general rule:

> The modern law, in the case of contracts of all types, may be summarised as follows. Time will not be considered to be of the essence unless: (1) the parties expressly stipulate that conditions as to time must be strictly complied with: or (2) the nature of the subject matter of the contract or the surrounding circumstances show that time should be considered to be of the essence: or (3) a party who has been subjected to unreasonable delay gives notice to the party in default making time of the essence.

This statement of the law has now been accepted in dicta in two recent cases in the House of Lords. The first is *United Scientific Holdings Ltd v Burnley Borough Council* [1978] AC 904, where the question was whether time was of the essence in a timetable of steps to be taken under a rent review clause in a lease. The House of Lords held that it was not, so that the landlords could still claim rent review despite the fact that they had allowed the prescribed time limits to expire. Viscount Dilhorne and Lord Simon explicitly approved the statement of law contained in the first two sections of the passage from *Halsbury's Laws of England*. Lord Fraser went further and approved the whole passage (at p 958). He thus appears to accept that time can be made of the essence in any type of contract, irrespective of specific performance, and it may be that the same thought lay behind the rather delphic remarks of Lord Diplock (p 925) that 'the waters of the confluent streams of law and equity have surely mingled by now' (see Baker (1977) 93 LQR 529). Whether the owner in a case like *Citati* can now make time of the essence by serving the charterer with reasonable notice is not wholly clear.

The second case is the one that follows.

Bunge Corpn v Tradax SA [1981] 2 All ER 513, Court of Appeal and House of Lords

Under a contract which incorporated GAFTA form 119 [see above, p 53] the buyers agreed to purchase from the sellers 15,000 tons of soya bean meal, 5% more or less, for shipment from the United States. It was the practice in the trade for a string of contracts to be made in which the shipment contract was merely an intermediate contract made in the course of the passage of the goods from the supplier to the eventual receiver. The terms of the parties' contract required three shipments of 5,000 tons fob from an American port in the Gulf of Mexico nominated by the sellers. By agreement between the parties one of the shipments was to be during June 1975. The buyers were to provide a vessel at the nominated port and by virtue of cl 7 of form 119 as completed by the parties they were required to 'give at least 15 consecutive days' notice' of the probable readiness of the vessel. If the goods were to be shipped during June the buyers were therefore required to give notice of their vessel's readiness by 13th June. In fact the buyers did not give notice until 17th June. The sellers claimed that the late notice was a breach of contract amounting to a repudiation and claimed damages from the buyers on the basis that by then the market price had fallen by over $US60 a ton. The dispute was referred to arbitration where the sellers were awarded $US317,500 damages . . . On appeal to the Commercial Court the judge reversed that award on the ground that the term as to time when notice was required to be given was not a condition but an intermediate term and the lateness of the notice did not amount to a breach of contract. [The sellers appealed.]

Megaw LJ. . . . I come to the second main issue: is the term of the contract which has been broken by the buyers a condition or an intermediate term? The sellers have, before us, made it clear that if the term is not a condition, but is an intermediate term, they will not seek to contend that they can discharge the burden of showing that they were entitled to treat the contract as having been repudiated by the buyers.

The contract is, by its express terms, governed by English law. That is the effect of cl 25 of GAFTA 119.

It is an accepted principle of English law that in a mercantile contract for the sale of goods 'prima facie a stipulated time of delivery is of the essence'. This long-standing principle has recently been re-stated by Lord Diplock in *United Scientific Holdings Ltd v Burnley Borough Council* . . .

In the present case, then, there can be no doubt but that the obligation of the sellers to deliver the soya bean meal not later than 30th June 1975 was a condition of the contract. They had an obligation to tender the contractual quantity of the goods at the ship's rail so that they could be loaded in accordance with the contractual provision as to rate of loading, on or before that date. If they failed, in breach of contract, to carry out that obligation, and if the buyers thereupon were to treat the contract as having been wrongfully repudiated by the sellers, it would be no answer for the sellers to say that the buyers had not proved that they, the buyers, had suffered any loss or would suffer any loss, if loading were to take place on 1st July. It would be unreal to suggest that one day's lateness in delivery would necessarily be a matter of serious consequence to the buyers. The lateness might or might not have such consequences. But the buyers' right to treat the contract as repudiated, and to treat themselves as freed from the performance of any further contractual obligations which they would otherwise have been required to perform under the contact, does not depend on the buyers being able to prove any such thing. . . .

In para 5 of the award the board of appeal, having said that the term means 'Buyers were to give at least 15 consecutive days' notice of probable readiness of vessel(s)', went on: 'Such a provision is customarily treated in the trade as being for the purpose of giving to sellers sufficient time to make necessary arrangements to get the goods to the port for loading on board the nominated vessel.' In other words, the parties have agreed, by acceptance of this term, that 15 days is the time which is reasonably required by the sellers for the purpose of this particular contract, to enable them to make the arrangements necessary for the fulfilment by them of their contractual duty to deliver the goods by the due time. It would, in my view, be impossible for a court to hold that that was not the parties' intention in agreeing this term. There is no question here of the parties not being in an equal bargaining position. It would, in my opinion, be arrogant and unjustifiable for a court to substitute any view of its own for the view of the parties themselves as to what was a reasonable time for this purpose.

Unless there is some principle of law, or some authority binding on us, which leads necessarily to a contrary conclusion, it appears to me to follow that, just as the contractual time for delivery of the goods is a condition binding on the sellers, so that the contractual time by which the notice has to be given for the purpose of enabling the sellers to perform that condition should be regarded as a condition binding on the buyers. There is no more, and no less, reason to suppose that a breach of the time provision in the sellers' obligation will necessarily or probably lead to serious loss to the buyers than there is to suppose that a breach of the notice of readiness provision will necessarily or probably lead to serious loss to the sellers. . . .

I come back to the purpose of the notice of probable readiness term in the present contract. The commercial reasons why advance notice is required are, I think, obvious. The sellers have to nominate the loading port. Is loading going to be possible, and if possible convenient, at port A, or port B, or port C? Until the probable date of readiness is known, it may be impossible to answer those questions. Until they are answered, the sellers cannot perform their contractual duty of nominating the port. When the port is decided, arrangements have to be made to have the contract quantity (to be defined by the buyers by reference to '5% more or less') of the contract goods available when the vessel is ready. What is involved in making such arrangements? It may involve, or include, buying goods, arranging for them to be moved by road, rail or water from wherever they may be; for warehousing them or moving them from one warehouse to another. Of course, in any given case, some or all of these tasks may be simply achieved, or their achievement may be possible in less than 15 days, in order to have the goods ready for loading where and when the vessel is ready for loading. It obviously cannot be predicated that 14 days' notice, instead of 15 days', would necessarily and in all circumstances cause sellers serious difficulties in respect of a contract containing these terms. What can and should be accepted is that the parties have agreed that, for the purpose of this contract, the reasonable time required to enable the sellers to perform their contractual obligations as to delivery of the goods is 15 days' notice of the probable readiness of the vessel to load. . . .

Apart from [a] particular reason, relating to the extension of shipment clause, Parker J was of the opinion that the term could not be a condition because of what he regarded as being 'the principles established in the *Hong Kong Fir* case' . . . and *Cehave NV v Bremer Handelsgesellschaft mbH, The Hansa Nord*. In the latter case, Roskill LJ, while recognising that some terms of a contract of sale may be conditions, expressed the view that 'a court should not be over ready, unless required by statute or authority so to do, to construe a term in a contract as a "condition" . . .'

The passage in the *Hong Kong Fir* case, to which Parker J referred, was that where Diplock LJ said this . . :

'No doubt there are many simple contractual undertakings, sometimes express, but more often because of their very simplicity ("It goes without saying") to be implied, of which it can be predicated that every breach of such an undertaking must give rise to an event which will deprive the party not in default of substantially the whole benefit which it was intended that he should obtain from the contract. And such a stipulation, unless the parties have agreed that breach of it shall not entitle the non-defaulting party to treat the contract as repudiated, is a "condition".'

If that statement is intended to be a definition of the requirements which must always be satisfied, in all types of contract and all types of clauses, in order that a term may qualify as a condition, I would very respectfully express the view that it is not a correct statement of the law. I am confirmed in the view that it was not so intended because of what was recently said by Lord Diplock in a passage . . . from his speech in *United Scientific Holdings Ltd v Burnley Borough Council* in relation to time being 'of the essence' in certain commercial contracts. . . .

In the light of what was said by their Lordships in that case, I think it can fairly be said that in mercantile contracts stipulations as to time not only may be, but usually are, to be treated as being 'of the essence of the contract', even though this is not expressly stated in the words of the contract. It would follow that in a mercantile contract it cannot be predicated that, for time to be of the essence, any and every breach of the term as to time must necessarily cause the innocent party to be deprived of substantially the whole of the benefit which it was intended that he should have. . . .

In my opinion in the term with which we are concerned the provision as to time is of the essence of the contract. The term is a condition.

It is, I believe, a factor which is not without weight in that conclusion that, at least, it tends towards certainty in the law . . . The parties, where time is of the essence, will at least know where they stand when the contractually agreed time has passed and the contract has been broken. They will not be forced to make critical decisions by trying to anticipate how serious, in the view of arbitrators or courts, in later years, the consequences of the breach will retrospectively be seen to have been, in the light, it may be, of hindsight.

I must, however, return to the *Hong Kong Fir* case . . . No one now doubts the correctness of that decision: that there are 'intermediate' terms, breach of which may or may not entitle the innocent party to treat himself as discharged from the further performance of his contractual obligation. No one now doubts that a term as to seaworthiness in a charterparty, in the absence of express provision to the opposite effect, is not a condition, but is an 'intermediate' term. The question arising on that case which I think we are compelled to examine in the present case is the test by which it falls to be decided whether a term is a condition.

I have previously quoted a passage from the judgment of Diplock LJ. In its literal sense, the words there used would mean that the test whether a term is a condition is whether *every* breach of such an undertaking *must* give rise to an event which will deprive the party not in default of *substantially the whole benefit which it was intended that he should obtain from the contract*. If this is a definition of the requirements which, in English law, must always be fulfilled before any contractual term (in the absence, of course, of express words) can achieve the legal status of a condition, then the term with which we are here concerned would not pass the test. The view which I have expressed that it is a condition would necessarily be wrong.

There are various reasons why I do not think that this was intended to be a literal, definitive and comprehensive statement of the requirements of a condition; and also, if it were, why, with great respect, I do not think that it represents the law as it stands today.

First, if it were intended to cover terms as to time in mercantile contracts, how could the requirements be said to be met in respect of stipulations in contracts of types in which, as Lord Diplock has recently said, time may be of the essence: for example, in respect of a stipulated time for delivery? It could never be said, as I see it, in any real sense, that *any* breach of such a stipulation *must necessarily cause the innocent* party to be deprived of *substantially all the benefit*.

Second, and following on what I have just said, I do not see how any contractual term, whether as to time or otherwise, could ever pass the test. Conditions would no longer exist in the English law of contract. For it is always possible to suggest hypothetically some minor breach or breaches of any contractual term which might, without undue use of the imagination, be wholly insufficient to produce serious effects for the innocent party, let alone the loss of substantially all the benefit.

Third, English law does recognise as conditions contractual terms which do not pass that test. For example, *Bowes v Shand* and, I think a substantial number of other cases which are binding, at least on this court.

Fourth, it is clear law, reaffirmed by the House of Lords since *Hong Kong Fir* was decided, that where there has been a breach of a condition the innocent party is entitled to elect whether or not to treat the contracts as repudiated. . . .

. . . How could this right of election be anything other than a legal fiction, a chimera, if the election can arise only in circumstances in which, as a result of the breach, an event has happened which will deprive the innocent party of substantially the whole benefit which it was intended that he should receive? This test, it is to be observed, is regarded (*Hong Kong Fir*) . . . as applying also where the term is an intermediate term, except that you then look to what has actually happened in order to see if the innocent party has lost substantially all the benefit. So, again, if the test be right, the former principle of English law that the innocent party has the right to elect is no longer anything but an empty shadow. For a right to elect to continue a contract, with the result that the innocent party will be bound to continue to perform his own contractual obligations, when he will, by definition, have lost substantially all his benefit under the contract, does not appear to me to make sense.

Fifth, the same considerations as I have set out in the previous paragraph apply if the test be that a breach of contract gives a right to the innocent party to treat it as a repudiation only if the events which in fact have flowed from the breach would, if they had come about otherwise than by a breach of contract, amount to frustration of the contract. . . .

I would allow the appeal and, subject to any questions of detail which may arise as to the form of the order, I would restore the decision of the board of appeal.

Browne LJ. I agree that this appeal should be allowed, for the reasons given by Megaw LJ, with which I entirely agree. . . .

[Brightman LJ concurred.]

The House of Lords affirmed the judgment of the Court of Appeal. Lord Wilberforce said:

. . . The fundamental fallacy of the appellants' argument lies in attempting to apply this analysis to a time clause such as the present in a mercantile contract, which is totally different in character. As to such a clause there is only one kind of breach possible, namely to be late, and the questions which have to be asked are: first, what importance have the parties expressly ascribed to this consequence? and, second, in the absence of expressed agreement, what consequences ought to be attached to it having regard to the contract as a whole?

The test suggested by the appellants was a different one. One must consider, they said, the breach actually committed and then decide whether that default would deprive the party not in default of substantially the whole benefit of the contract. They even invoked certain passages in the judgment of Diplock LJ in *Hong Kong Fir* to support it. One may observe in the first place that the introduction of a test of this kind would be commercially most undesirable. It would expose the parties, after a breach of one, two, three, seven and other numbers of days, to an argument whether this delay would have left time for the seller to provide the goods. It would make it, at the time, at least difficult, and sometimes impossible, for the supplier to know whether he could do so. It would fatally remove from a vital provision in the contract that certainty which is the most indispensable quality of mercantile contracts, and lead to a large increase in arbitrations. It would confine the seller, perhaps after arbitration and reference through the courts, to a remedy in damages which might be extremely difficult to quantify. These are all serious objections in practice. But I am clear that the submission is unacceptable in law. The judgment of Diplock LJ does not give any support and ought not to give any encouragement to any such proposition; for beyond doubt it recognises that it is open to the parties to agree that, as regards a particular obligation, any breach shall entitle the party not in default to treat the contract as repudiated. Indeed, if he were not doing so he would, in a passage which does not profess to be more than clarificatory, be discrediting a long and uniform series of cases, at least from *Bowes v Shand* onwards.

Lord Wilberforce also approved the paragraph from *Halsbury* extracted above, p 438. Lords Fraser, Scarman and Lowry agreed with his speech. It is interesting to contrast this case with the House's attitude towards giving relief against forfeiture, below, p 449 ff.

We saw earlier (p 436) that if a party can cure a defective performance before the date set for performance, he can normally prevent the other from terminating. A parallel rule applies if time is not of the essence: the passing of the date for performance does not prevent the party in default from performing, or from curing an originally defective performance, providing that he can do so within a frustrating time (or, perhaps, within a reasonable time of being given notice to perform). Thus in *Stanton v Richardson* (1872) LR 7 CP 421; affirmed (1874) LR 9 CP 390 a ship chartered to carry a cargo of wet sugar was unseaworthy, because her pumps could not cope with the liquid flowing from the sugar. The Court of Common Pleas held that the charterer was entitled to reject the ship at once, as the jury found that the defect could not be put right within a frustrating time. It did not decide the point, but it seems to follow that, if the defect *could* have been corrected within such a time, the charterer would at most have had an action for damages.

Stanton v Richardson again shows the distinction between withholding performance and termination: had the owner been able to adjust the pumps to make the ship suitable for the cargo, the charterer would not have been able to throw up the charter; but he would not have had to load the goods until the pumps had been put right.

Before leaving the question of time stipulations, it is perhaps worth reflecting for a moment on the *Hong Kong Fir* case. A ship is not seaworthy if it has any defect which a prudent shipowner would put right before allowing the ship to go to sea on the voyage and with the cargo in question (*McFadden v Blue Star Line* [1905] 1 KB 697 at 706). Can a charterer be expected to load his goods aboard a ship which is known to be unseaworthy at the time, even if the matter is a relatively trivial one? In the *Hong Kong Fir* case the majority of the Court of Appeal seemed to say that seaworthiness itself is not a condition, which must mean that sometimes the charterer *will* have to load on to an unseaworthy ship. Perhaps a better analysis would be that seaworthiness *is* a condition in terms of *substance*, but that the owner does not have to make it seaworthy immediately—in other words, time is not of the essence. Thus, if the owner fails to make the ship seaworthy within a frustrating time, the charterer can refuse to load (if he has not done so) or can terminate the charter. See further Devlin, 'The Treatment of Breach of Contract' [1966] CLJ 192, 194–195.

(h) Conditions in unilateral contracts and options

In *United Dominions Trust (Commercial) Ltd v Eagle Aircraft Services Ltd* [1968] 1 All ER 104 the Court of Appeal held that the 'flexible' approach is not applicable to conditions forming a unilateral contract: these are conditions in the strict sense, so that if they are not complied with exactly, the promisor need not perform his part of the bargain. In that case Eagle had sold aircraft to UDT, who had let them on hire-purchase to Orion Airways. A 'recourse' agreement between UDT and Eagle provided that if for any reason the hire-purchase agreement was terminated before the full amount had been paid, Eagle would re-purchase the aircraft from UDT when called upon to do so, at a price equal to the unpaid balance plus certain expenses. A compulsory winding up order was made against Orion, and the aircraft were repossessed, in December 1960, but UDT did not call upon Eagle to repurchase until the following May. The Court of Appeal held that it was an implied condition of the agreement that the call for repurchase must be made within a reasonable time of the repossession, and that as a reasonable time was three months, Eagle were no longer obliged to repurchase, whether or not they were prejudiced by the delay. Diplock LJ said (at p 109) that two consequences followed from the fact that the contract was unilateral rather than bilateral:

The first is that there is no room for any inquiry whether any act done by the promisee in purported performance of a unilateral contract amounts to a breach of warranty or a breach of condition on his part, for he is under no obligation to do or to refrain from doing any act at all. The second is that, as respects the promisor, the initial inquiry is whether the event, which under the unilateral contract gives rise to obligations on the part of the promisor, has occurred. To that inquiry the answer can only be a simple 'Yes' or 'No'.

(i) Anticipatory breach

Hochster v De La Tour (1853) [1843–60] All ER Rep 12

Lord Campbell CJ read the following judgment of the Court.—On this motion in arrest of judgment, the question arises, whether, if there be an agreement between A and B, whereby B engages to employ A on and from a future day for a given period of time, to travel with him into a foreign country as a courier and to start with him in that capacity on that day, A being to receive a monthly salary during the continuance of such service, B may, before the day, refuse to perform the agreement and break and renounce it so as to entitle A, before the day, to commence an action against B to recover damages for breach of the agreement, A having been ready and willing to perform it till it was broken and renounced by B.

The defendant's counsel very powerfully contended that, if the plaintiff was not contented to dissolve the contract and to abandon all remedy upon it, he was bound to remain ready and willing to perform it till the day when the actual employment as courier in the service of the defendant was to begin, and that there could be no breach of the agreement, before that day, to give a right of action. But it cannot be laid down as a universal rule that, where by agreement an act is to be done on a future day, no action can be brought for a breach of the agreement till the day for doing the act has arrived. If a man promises to marry a woman on a future day and before that day marries another woman, he is instantly liable to an action for breach of promise of marriage: *Short v Stone*. If a man contracts to execute a lease on and from a future day for a certain term, and, before that day, executes a lease to another for the same term, he may be immediately sued for breaking the contract: *Ford v Tiley*. So, if a man contracts to sell and deliver specific goods on a future day, and before the day he sells and delivers them to another, he is immediately liable to an action at the suit of the person with whom he first contracted to sell and deliver them: *Bowdell v Parsons*. One reason alleged in support of such an action is that the defendant has, before the day, rendered it impossible for the plaintiff to perform the contract at the day, but this does not necessarily follow, for, prior to the day fixed for doing the act, the first wife may have died, a surrender of the lease executed might be obtained, and the defendant might have re-purchased the goods so as to be in a situation to sell and deliver them to the plaintiff. Another reason may be that where there is a contract to do an act on a future day there is a relation constituted between the parties in the meantime by the contract, and that they impliedly promise that in the meantime neither will do any thing to the prejudice of the other inconsistent with that relation. As an example, a man and woman engaged to marry are affianced to one another during the period between the time of the engagement and the celebration of the marriage.

In the present case, of traveller and courier, from the day of the hiring till the day when the employment was to begin, the parties were engaged to each other, and it seems to be a breach of an implied contract if either of them renounces the engagement. This reasoning seems in accordance with the unanimous decision of the Exchequer Chamber in *Elderton v Emmens* which we have followed in subsequent cases in this court. The declaration in the present case, in alleging a breach, states a great deal more than a passing intention on the part of the defendant which he may repent of, and could only be proved by evidence that he had utterly renounced the contract or done some act which rendered it impossible for him to perform it. If the plaintiff has no remedy for breach of the contract unless he treats the contract as in force, and acts upon it down to June 1, 1852, it follows that, till then, he must enter into no employment which will interfere with his promise 'to start with the defendant on such travels on the day and year', and that he must then be properly equipped in all respects as a courier for a three months' tour on the continent of Europe.

But it is surely much more rational, and more for the benefit of both parties, that, after the renunciation of the agreement by the defendant, the plaintiff should be at liberty to consider himself absolved from any future performance of it, retaining his right to sue for any damage he has suffered from the breach of it. Thus, instead of remaining idle and laying out money in preparations which must be useless, he is at liberty to seek service under another employer, which would go in mitigation of the damages to which he would otherwise be entitled for a breach of the contract. It seems strange that the defendant, after renouncing the contract, and absolutely declaring that he will never act under it, should be permitted to object that faith is given to his assertion, and that an opportunity is not left to him of changing his mind. If the plaintiff is barred of any remedy by entering into an engagement inconsistent with starting as a courier with the defendant on June 1, he is prejudiced by putting faith in the defendant's assertion, and it would be more consonant with principle, if the defendant were precluded from saying that he had not broken the contract when he declared that he entirely renounced it.

Suppose that the defendant, at the time of his renunciation, had embarked on a voyage for Australia, so as to render it physically impossible for him to employ the plaintiff as a courier on the continent of Europe in the months of June, July and August, 1852. According to decided cases the action might have been brought before June 1, but the renunciation may have been founded on other facts, to be given in evidence, which would equally have rendered the defendant's performance of the contract impossible. The man who wrongfully renounces a contract into which he has deliberately entered cannot justly complain if he is immediately sued for a compensation in damages by the man whom he has injured: and it seems reasonable to allow an option to the injured party, either to sue immediately or to wait till the time when the act was to be done, still holding it as prospectively binding for the exercise of this option, which may be advantageous to the innocent party, and cannot be prejudicial to the wrongdoer.

An argument against the action before June 1 is urged from the difficulty of calculating the damages, but this argument is equally strong against an action before Sep 1, when the three months would expire. In either case, the jury in assessing the damages would be justified in looking to all that had happened, or was likely to happen, to increase or mitigate the loss of the plaintiff down to the day of trial.

We do not find any decision contrary to the view we are taking of this case. . . .

If it should be held that, upon a contract to do an act on a future day, a renunciation of the contract by one party dispenses with a condition to be performed in the meantime by the other, there seems no reason for requiring that other to wait till the day arrives before seeking his remedy by action, and the only ground on which the condition can be dispensed with seems to be that the renunciation may be treated as a breach of the contract. Upon the whole, we think that the declaration in this case is sufficient. It gives us great satisfaction to reflect that, the question being on the record, our opinion may be reviewed in a court of error. In the meantime we must give judgment for the plaintiff.

Judgment for plaintiff.

NOTES

1. What did counsel for the defendant argue was the effect of the plaintiff's acceptance of the repudiation?
2. There will also be a repudiation if it is clear that the defendant will be unable to perform when the time comes: *Citati's* case (above, p 437).

3. The victim of an anticipatory repudiation does not have to 'accept the repudiation' by terminating the contract: he or she can wait and see whether the repudiating party will perform when the time comes (see further below, pp 483 and 544). If, however, the contract is left in force, the fact that there has been a repudiation is for many purposes ignored. Thus, firstly, the victim must normally tender his performance as usual, and if he does not he will himself be in breach of contract when the time comes, giving the party who repudiated the right to terminate. The only exception is if the repudiating party made it clear that it has no interest in receiving performance and the victim accordingly doesn't tender it: then the repudiating party would be estopped from complaining: *Fercometal SARL v Mediterranean Shipping Co SA* [1988] 2 All ER 742, HL.

4. A second consequence of leaving the contract in force is that the repudiating party can take advantage of any subsequent circumstances that may arise to excuse him. In *Avery v Bowden* (1855) 5 E & B 714; affirmed (1856) 6 E & B 953 a ship was chartered to carry a cargo from Odessa. The master was told before the end of the lay days that no cargo was available, but he remained in port and urged the charterers to perform. The contract was then frustrated by the outbreak of the Crimean War.

5. The test of whether a party has repudiated is whether there has been 'an intimation of an intention to abandon and altogether to refuse performance of the contract . . . [or of] an intention no longer to be bound by the contract' (Lord Coleridge CJ in *Freeth v Burr* (1874) LR 9 CP 208 at 213). How is this to be applied if a party refuses to perform the contract but claims that this is because the terms of the contract allow him to do so in the circumstances? If a party terminates the contract alleging that some breach by the other party gives him the right to do so, but the court disagrees, the terminating party will himself normally be guilty of a wrongful repudiation and be liable to the other for damages: the *Hong Kong Fir* case is an example. Similarly if a party announces that he is going to perform in some way which the court decides is wholly inconsistent with the contract, even if his legal advisers have (wrongly) told him that what he plans is permissible, and he in fact wants to go on with his own version of the contract. Thus in *Federal Commerce and Navigation Ltd v Molena Alpha Inc, The Nanfri, The Benfri and The Lorfri* [1979] AC 757 the owners and the charterers were in dispute about some deductions the charterers were making from the hire payments. After taking legal advice, the owners announced that they were instructing the masters of the ships to issue bills of lading marked 'subject to lien for freight' instead of 'freight prepaid', and they refused to withdraw these instructions unless the disputed deductions from hire were paid. The issue of 'claused bills' would have very serious consequences for the charterers. The House of Lords held that ordering the masters to issue claused bills was a breach of contract, and that the owners' action amounted to a wrongful repudiation, even though the owners clearly wanted to continue with the charters, which were very profitable to them, and were simultaneously seeking resolution of the dispute about deductions through arbitration.

In contrast, in *Woodar Investment Development Ltd v Wimpey Construction (UK) Ltd* [1980] 1 All ER 571 a contract for the sale of land provided that the purchasers (Wimpey) could rescind the contract if prior to completion a statutory authority 'shall have commenced' to acquire the property by compulsory purchase. In fact at the date the contract was signed the authority had already commenced compulsory purchase proceedings in respect of part of the land. Meanwhile Wimpey wished to escape from the contract because land prices had fallen, and, after taking legal advice, they discussed the situation with Mr Cornwell of Woodar, the vendors. Wimpey proposed renegotiation, failing which they would serve notice of rescission under the clause, Mr Cornwell disputed Wimpey's right to do this and indicated that Woodar would take the matter to court. Wimpy then wrote purporting to rescind because of the authority's action, stating that 'the contract is now discharged'. Woodar did not accept this, and Mr Cornwell said the matter 'must now await the decision of the court' and 'I am sure you will abide by the result as I will'. Woodar then sought a declaration that the purchasers, Wimpey, were not entitled to rescind, and when Wimpey counterclaimed for a declaration that they had rescinded, Woodar brought a second action claiming that the purchasers had repudiated, that the repudiation was accepted and that they were entitled to damages. The majority of the House of Lords held that Wimpey had not repudiated the contract. Lord Wilberforce said:

So far from repudiating the contract, Wimpey were relying on it and invoking one of its provisions, to which both parties had given their consent. And unless the invocation of that provision were totally abusive, or lacking in good faith, (neither of which is contended for), the fact that it has proved to be wrong in law cannot turn it into a repudiation. At the lowest, the notice of rescission was a neutral document consistent either with an intention to preserve, or with an intention to abandon, the contract, and I will deal with it on this basis, more favourable to Woodar. In order to decide which is correct Wimpey's conduct has to be examined. . . .

In my opinion . . . Wimpey are entitled to succeed on the repudiation issue, and I would only add that it would be a regrettable development of the law of contract to hold that a party who bona fide relies on an express stipulation in a contract in order to rescind or terminate a contract should, by that fact alone, be treated as having repudiated his contractual obligations if he turns out to be mistaken as to his rights. Repudiation is a drastic conclusion which should only be held to arise in clear cases of a refusal, in a matter going to the root of the contract, to perform contractual obligations. To uphold Woodar's contentions in this case would represent an undesirable [extension] of the doctrine.

Lord Scarman added:

. . . [T]he notice of rescission, which Wimpey gave, was not, in the circumstances which existed when it was given, one which Wimpey had any contractual right to give. But they honestly believed the contract did give them the right. When one examines the totality of their conduct and its impact on Mr Cornwell it is plain, as shown by my noble and learned friend Lord Wilberforce's analysis of the facts, that Wimpey, though claiming mistakenly to exercise a power given them by the contract to bring it to an end, were not evincing an intention not to be bound by the contract. On the contrary, they believed they were acting pursuant to the contract. And Mr Cornwell well understood the situation. As he put it in his final letter to Sir Godfrey Mitchell, the president of Wimpey: '. . . all I need say now is that we will retire to our battle stations and it goes without saying I am sure that you will abide by the result as I will.' It never occurred to Mr Cornwell that Wimpey, if held not to have been entitled to give notice of rescission, would refuse to perform the contract. In fact, it would seem that he believed exactly the contrary. Such was the impact on him of Wimpey's conduct.

Woodar, in an effort to mitigate loss, had sold the land to a third party. Was this action itself a breach of contract? See Nicol and Rawlings (1980) 43 MLR 696.

In *Hochster v De La Tour* the defendant had repudiated all his obligations. What if a party indicates that it is unwilling or unable to perform a part of the contract but will perform the rest? The test is the same as in cases of actual breach. In *Decro-Wall International SA v Practitioners in Marketing Ltd* [1971] 2 All ER 216 Buckley LJ said:

> . . . To constitute repudiation, the threatened breach must be such as to deprive the injured party of a substantial part of the benefit to which he is entitled under the contract. The measure of the necessary degree of substantiality has been expressed in a variety of ways in the cases. It has been said that the breach must be of an essential term, or of a fundamental term of the contract, or that it must go to the root of the contract. Various tests have been suggested: see eg *Freeth v Burr* per Lord Coleridge CJ and Keating J; *Mersey Steel and Iron Co Ltd v Naylor, Benzon & Co* per the Earl of Selborne LC and per Lord Blackburn and *Hong Kong Fir Shipping Co Ltd v Kawasaki Kisen Kaisha Ltd* per Diplock LJ. I venture to put the test in my own words as follows: will the consequences of the breach be such that it would be unfair to the injured party to hold him to the contract and leave him to the remedy in damages as and when a breach or breaches may occur? If this would be so, then a repudiation has taken place.

In that case the defendants, who had been appointed sole dealers in the UK for the plaintiffs, were short of working capital and were persistently slightly late in paying for goods received. This cost the plaintiffs a small amount in bank interest each month, but there was never any doubt that the payments would be made in the end. Even though this situation appeared likely to continue, it was not a repudiation of the contract. Time for payment was not a condition (see above, p 436) and the consequences of the late payments were not serious; they would be adequately compensated by recovering the extra interest.

As the *Decro-Wall* case suggests, the concept of anticipatory repudiation is very important in relation to contracts which are to be performed in stages or instalments. A breach relating to one stage may justify termination of the whole contract, but only if it amounts to a repudiation of the whole contract (Sale of Goods Act 1979, s 31(2), above, p 418). In *Millar's Karri and Jarrah Co v Weddel, Turner & Co* (1908) 14 Com Cas 25, at p 29, Bigham J said:

> Thus, if the breach is of such a kind, or takes place in such circumstances as reasonably to lead to the inference that similar breaches will be committed in relation to subsequent deliveries, the whole contract may there and then be regarded as repudiated and may be rescinded. If, for instance, a buyer fails to pay for one delivery in such circumstances as to lead to the inference that he will not be able to pay for subsequent deliveries; or if a seller delivers goods differing from the requirements of the contract, and does so in such circumstances as to lead to the inference that he cannot, or will not, deliver any other kind of goods in the future, the other contracting party will be under no obligation to wait to see what may happen; he can at once cancel the contract and rid himself of the difficulty.

In that case the first of two deliveries was so defective that it justified termination. In contrast, in *Maple Flock Co Ltd v Universal Furniture Products (Wembley) Ltd* [1934] 1 KB 148 one delivery out of twenty was defective. Lord Hewart CJ, delivering the judgment of the Court of Appeal said (at p 157):

> . . . [T]he main tests to be considered in applying the sub-section to the present case are, first, the ratio quantitatively which the breach bears to the contract as a whole, and secondly the degree of probability or improbability that such a breach will be repeated. On the first point, the delivery complained of amounts to no more than 1½ tons out of a contract for 100 tons. On the second point, our conclusion is that the chance of the breach being repeated is practically negligible.

Therefore the defective delivery did not justify termination.

In a contract for a large building or engineering project, the completion date is likely to be months or years after the start of the project. Supposing the contract said nothing about time except that the work was to be done by a certain date, what would the employer's rights be if the contractor (i) failed to start work when expected? (ii) worked extremely slowly? (iii) did some work defectively at an early stage?

Institution of Civil Engineers Conditions (5th edn), cl 63(1)

Clause 63

(1) If the Contractor shall become bankrupt or have a receiving order made against him or shall present his petition in bankruptcy or shall make an arrangement with or assignment in favour of his creditors or shall agree to carry out the Contract under a committee of inspection of his creditors or (being a corporation) shall go into liquidation (other than a voluntary liquidation for the purposes of amalgamation or reconstruction) or if the Contractor shall assign the Contract without the consent in writing of the Employer first obtained or shall have an execution levied on his goods or if the Engineer shall certify in writing to the Employer that in his opinion the Contractor:—

    (a) has abandoned the Contract; or

    (b) without reasonable excuse has failed to commence the Works in accordance with Clause 41 or has suspended the progress of the Works for 14 days after receiving from the Engineer written notice to proceed; or

    (c) has failed to remove goods or materials from the Site or to pull down and replace work for 14 days after receiving from the Engineer written notice that the said goods materials or work have been condemned and rejected by the Engineer; or

    (d) despite previous warning by the Engineer in writing is failing to proceed with the Works with due diligence or is otherwise persistently or fundamentally in breach of his obligations under the Contract; or

    (e) has to the detriment of good workmanship or in defiance of the Engineer's instruction to the contrary sub-let any part of the Contract;

then the Employer may after giving 7 days' notice in writing to the Contractor enter upon the Site and the Works and expel the Contractor therefrom without thereby avoiding the Contract or releasing the Contractor from any of his obligations or liabilities under the Contract or affecting the rights and powers conferred on the Employer or the Engineer by the Contract and may himself complete the Works or may employ any other contractor to complete the Works. . . .

NOTES

1. In what ways does this clause attempt to improve on the position of the Employer at common law? To put the same question another way, would the Employer be entitled to terminate the contract at common law in the situations listed in (a) to (e)?

2. Insolvency on the part of the Contractor is not *itself* a ground for termination at common law: the liquidator could opt to perform the contract, and if it was one on which the firm stood to make money he would presumably do so.

3. Suppose the Employer exercised its right to terminate under cl 63(1) because of some breach of contract by the Contractor, but the breach was not sufficiently serious to justify termination at common law. If cl 63 contained no further provision on the point, would the Employer be entitled to damages for any additional costs incurred in getting another contractor to finish the work? See above, p 428.

4. In fact a further subclause purports to spell out the compensation to which the Employer will be entitled. In effect it attempts to give the Employer in any case of termination the same amount as it would get by way of damages if its termination had been justified at common law. There is some doubt whether this is effective: see below, p 510.

Suppose that a party has considerable doubt whether the other will perform when the time comes: a seller, for instance, has heard that the buyer is having financial difficulties, or discovers that the buyer has not paid him for goods delivered under a separate contract, and is worried about delivering on credit. What can he do?

Sale of Goods Act 1979

Section 41
(1) Subject to this Act, the unpaid seller of goods who is in possession of them is entitled to retain possession of them until payment or tender of the price in the following cases:—
. . . (c) where the buyer becomes insolvent.

Suppose the problem is that he has to build a special machine for the buyer, which will have no value to anyone else if the buyer defaults, and the buyer has already failed to make an advance payment. How could you devise an agreement which would safeguard the seller? You may like to consider the following:

> Terms of payment are usually net cash monthly account but we reserve the right at any time before delivery to enquire as to the customer's credit standing and to require cash before delivery if we see fit.

(P. J. Hare Ltd.)

Do you think that English law should adopt the same approach as the UCC?:

Uniform Commercial Code

§2–609. Right to adequate assurance of performance
(1) A contract for sale imposes an obligation on each party that the other's expectation of receiving due performance will not be impaired. When reasonable grounds for insecurity arise with respect to the performance of either party the other may in writing demand adequate assurance of due performance and until he receives such assurance may if commercially reasonable suspend any performance for which he has not already received the agreed return.
(2) Between merchants the reasonableness of grounds for insecurity and the adequacy of any assurance offered shall be determined according to commercial standards.
(3) Acceptance of any improper delivery or payment does not prejudice the aggrieved party's right to demand adequate assurance of future performance.
(4) After receipt of a justified demand failure to provide within a reasonable time not exceeding thirty days such assurance of due performance as is adequate under the circumstances of the particular case is a repudiation of the contract.

Official comment
. . . 4. What constitutes 'adequate' assurance of due performance is subject to the same test of factual conditions. For example, where the buyer can make use of a defective delivery, a mere promise by a seller of good repute that he is giving the matter his attention and that the defect will not be repeated, is normally sufficient. Under the same circumstances, however, a similar statement by a known corner-cutter might well be considered insufficient without the posting of a guaranty or, if so demanded by the buyer, a speedy replacement of the delivery involved. By the same token where a delivery has defects, even though easily curable, which interfere with easy use by the buyer, no verbal assurance can be deemed adequate which is not accompanied by replacement, repair, money-allowance, or other commercially reasonable cure.

(j) Relief against forfeiture

In certain cases a party who has committed a default which would normally entitle the other party to terminate the contract and repossess property from the defaulter may be given a last chance to cure his default. This may be done by requiring a formal procedure before the property is recovered, or by giving the defaulter relief.

Consumer Credit Act 1974

Section 87: Need for default notice
(1) Service of a notice on the debtor or hirer in accordance with section 88 (a 'default notice') is necessary before the creditor or owner can become entitled, by reason of any breach by the debtor or hirer of a regulated agreement,—
  (a) to terminate the agreement, or
  (b) to demand earlier payment of any sum, or
  (c) to recover possession of any goods or land, or
  (d) to treat any right conferred on the debtor or hirer by the agreement as terminated, restricted or deferred, or
  (e) to enforce any security.
(2) Subsection (1) does not prevent the creditor from treating the right to draw upon any credit as restricted or deferred, and taking such steps as may be necessary to make the restriction or deferment effective. . . .

Section 88: Contents and effect of default notice
(1) The default notice must be in the prescribed form and specify—
  (a) the nature of the alleged breach;
  (b) if the breach is capable of remedy, what action is required to remedy it and the date before which that action is to be taken;
  (c) if the breach is not capable of remedy, the sum (if any) required to be paid as compensation for the breach, and the date before which it is to be paid.
(2) A date specified under subsection (1) must not be less than seven days after the date of service of the default notice, and the creditor or owner shall not take action such as is mentioned in section 87(1) before the date so specified or (if no requirement is made under subsection (1)) before those seven days have elapsed.
(3) The default notice must not treat as a breach failure to comply with a provision of the agreement which becomes operative only on breach of some other provision, but if the breach of that other provision is not duly remedied or compensation demanded under subsection (1) is not duly paid, or (where no requirement is made under subsection (1)) if the seven days mentioned in subsection (2) have elapsed, the creditor or owner may treat the failure as a breach and section 87(1) shall not apply to it.
(4) The default notice must contain information in the prescribed terms about the consequences of failure to comply with it.
(5) A default notice making a requirement under subsection (1) may include a provision for the taking of action such as is mentioned in section 87(1) at any time after the restriction imposed by subsection (2) will cease, together with a statement that the provision will be ineffective if the breach is duly remedied or the compensation duly paid.

Section 89: Compliance with default notice
If before the date specified for that purpose in the default notice the debtor or hirer takes the action specified under section 88(1)(b) or (c) the breach shall be treated as not having occurred.

Section 90: Retaking of protected hire-purchase etc. goods
(1) At any time when—
  (a) the debtor is in breach of a regulated hire-purchase or a regulated conditional sale agreement relating to goods, and
  (b) the debtor has paid to the creditor one-third or more of the total price of the goods, and
  (c) the property in the goods remains in the creditor,
the creditor is not entitled to recover possession of the goods from the debtor except on an order of the court. . . .
(7) Goods falling within this section are in this Act referred to as 'protected goods'.

Section 91: Consequences of breach of s 90
If goods are recovered by the creditor in contravention of section 90—
  (a) the regulated agreement, if not previously terminated, shall terminate, and
  (b) the debtor shall be released from all liability under the agreement, and shall be entitled to recover from the creditor all sums paid by the debtor under the agreement.

EXTENSION OF TIME

Section 129: Time orders
(1) If it appears to the court just to do so—
  (a) on an application for an enforcement order; or
  (b) on an application made by a debtor or hirer under this paragraph after service on him of—
    (i) a default notice, or
    (ii) a notice under section 76(1) or 98(1); or
  (c) in an action brought by a creditor or owner to enforce a regulated agreement or any security, or recover possession of any goods or land to which a regulated agreement relates,
the court may make an order under this section (a 'time order').
(2) A time order shall provide for one or both of the following, as the court considers just—
  (a) the payment by the debtor or hirer or any surety of any sum owed under a regulated agreement or a security by such instalments, payable at such times, as the court, having regard to the means of the debtor or hirer and any surety, considers reasonable;
  (b) the remedying by the debtor or hirer of any breach of a regulated agreement (other than non-payment of money) within such period as the court may specify.

NOTE

Compare the procedures governing the forfeiture of leases for non-payment of rent (governed by the Common Law Procedure Act 1852, ss 210–212) or other breaches of covenant (Law of Property Act 1925, s 146).

In addition to these statutory powers to grant relief there is a more general equitable power to grant relief to a defaulter who stands to forfeit some proprietary or possessory interest but who is ready and able to cure his default. Nearly all the cases involve contracts for the sale of land where the price is payable in instalments and the purchaser is let into possession, with a provision for the termination of the agreement and the forfeiture of sums already paid in the event of a default. The defaulting purchaser must be ready and willing to pay the sums overdue with interest, and the vendor's costs; the court can then grant him specific performance, if the conveyance would be due when the payments in question are made, or restrain the vendor from terminating the contract. The purchaser need not be able to pay the whole sum due immediately, if he can do so within the time the court is prepared to allow: *Starside Properties Ltd v Mustapha* [1974] 2 All ER 567. However, it may be the case that relief against forfeiture is available only to a defaulter who is willing and able ultimately to cure his default. If he cannot do this, it is not clear that there is any power to order the return of the money forfeited. This at least seems to be the case where the contract provides for the forfeiture of money which has been paid by the defaulting party to the innocent party (see below, p 522). Whether it may also apply when the contract gives the innocent party a right to re-enter land sold is not clear. In the recent case of *Jobson v Johnson* [1989] 1 All ER 621 a contract for the sale of shares in Southend United Football Club provided that if the purchaser defaulted in paying instalments of the price, he would transfer a number of shares back to the vendor at a fixed price, which may have been less than their value. The Court of Appeal gave relief in the form of an order that if the shares were worth more than the instalments and the interest due, the shares should be sold and the plaintiff be paid only the instalments and interest. However the clause seems to have been treated as a form of penalty clause for which similar relief is usual (see below, p 508).

The House of Lords has held that the jurisdiction to grant relief against forfeiture is confined to cases where a proprietary or possessory right is to be forfeited. It does not apply to contracts of which specific performance would not be ordered. Thus a time-charterer of a ship who has failed to pay instalments of hire in time cannot invoke the jurisdiction to prevent the owner from withdrawing the ship under the 'withdrawal clause' (see above, p 48): *Scandinavian Trading Tanker Co AB v Flota Petrolera Ecuatoriana, The Scaptrade* [1983] 2 All ER 763. See also *Sport International Bussum BV v Inter-Footwear Ltd* [1984] 2 All ER 321 and Harpum (1984) 100 LQR 369. (Note that a timecharter does not involve the charterer having possessory rights over the ship: it is essentially a contract for the services of the ship. Specific performance would not be granted of a timecharter.)

(k) Reprise: flexibility or certainty?

'Breach and Remedy for the Tender of Non-conforming Goods' by Priest (1978) 91 Harv LR 960, 963, 965, 967–968

Once the contract is found to have been breached by a non-conforming tender, the law provides the buyer two possible remedies. He may call off the sale and return the goods to the seller, or he may keep the goods and seek damages for the non-conformity. The costs imposed by these two remedies can be classified into two categories. First, there are allocative costs—the transfer of real resources from one or both of the parties to the outside world. Freight and insurance for reshipment, administrative costs of resale, and fees for attorneys involved in dispute resolution fall into this category. Second are distributive costs, which consist of transfers of resources *between* the parties, as when one party recovers damages from the other. Ordinarily, the minimization of allocative costs will benefit the parties regardless of the distribution of costs between them. However, the distribution of costs will affect allocative costs because each party will strive to minimize his personal share of the joint costs, even if his effort increases joint costs. In fact, in any dispute over the interpretation of a contract, the parties will expend resources in negotiation or litigation, thereby reducing the joint value of the transaction. In the text that follows, the conditions for minimizing the allocative costs of a remedy are first analyzed apart from the effects of the distribution of costs. Then the causes and effects of the distribution of costs between the parties are analyzed separately. . . .

Although the comparison of the costs of rescission and damages appears complicated, it can be simplified. Parties wishing to maximize the *joint* value of the transaction will prefer return of the goods to damages whenever the goods have a greater value in the seller's hands than in the buyer's. The value of the goods in the seller's hands is their market value less the seller's costs of retrieval and resale. The value of the goods in the buyer's hands is the greater of (1) their market value less the buyer's costs of resale, or (2) their value to the buyer after adaptation less the costs of adapting them. If the parties seek to conserve costs, they might first compare the value of the defective goods to the buyer with the market value of the goods. Where the loss from the defect is less to the buyer than to the market, returning the goods is generally not the cheaper remedy. If, however, the value to the buyer of the defective goods is less than the market value, the parties would agree to return the goods to the seller if the seller's costs of resale were lower than the buyer's by an amount greater than the retrieval costs. If the buyer's business involves the sale of defective as well as conforming goods, the buyer's and the seller's costs of resale may be equivalent, so that retrieval costs tip the balance in favor of a damage remedy. However, if the buyer is a consumer or is engaged solely in manufacturing, the value of managerial time necessary to resell the defective goods may be substantial. Then the advantages of the original seller—superior information about potential customers for defective goods and a superior distribution system—may offset the costs of retrieval and make rescission the preferable remedy. . . .

Where the price of the goods declines after formation of the contract, the buyer has an incentive to conjure up defects or to exaggerate the materiality of real defects, and to demand rescission rather than damages, regardless of which remedy minimizes allocative costs. A similar incentive exists when the buyer realizes that he has chosen an unsuitable product. As long as the legal rules governing breach and remedy are sufficiently manipulable to offer the buyer a significant opportunity for distributional benefits, he will expend resources in negotiation or litigation in an attempt to gain them. Indeed, a rational buyer will spend nearly as much as the amount of the market price decline, discounted by his probability of prevailing in court.

Two conclusions may be drawn from this analysis. First, courts may reduce the parties' expenditures in attempts to gain distributional benefits by making legal rules certain in application. As legal rules became more certain, the probability of each party's manipulating them to his advantage decreases, and hence he is willing to spend less in such an effort. Second, the parties' expenditures in attempts to achieve private benefits sometimes may be greater than the savings achieved by choosing the remedy which otherwise would minimize allocative costs. For example, suppose that the market price of the goods has dropped $10 since contract formation, that the nonconformity in the goods is obviously trivial, that the buyer's and seller's resale costs are small and equal, and that the cost of shipment from buyer to seller is $4. If the buyer can rescind, the net cost to the parties is the $4 shipment cost, and the buyer avoids the market loss. If the buyer must accept damages, the net cost to the parties is just the cost of determining the buyer's damages, which is zero because the triviality of the defect is obvious. Thus damages are the more efficient remedy. However, if the legal rules for choosing the remedy are manipulable, in the case where the parties have equal probabilities of prevailing (50% each), the buyer may expend up to $5 on litigation attempting to avoid his market loss by rescission. And the *seller* may invest up to $5 in litigation trying to avoid bearing the loss which he thought he contracted away. In such a case, the joint expenditure on litigation may be $10, while the savings from avoiding reshipment is only $4. Thus the remedy of damages remains the more efficient, but its true value is never realized unless the legal rules are certain enough to discourage expensive legal disputes.

If the parties to a sale were to negotiate a remedy for a non-conforming tender explicitly, they probably would not limit themselves to an absolute choice between rescission and damages, but would structure a more flexible remedy which would preserve the allocation of risk implicit in a contract of sale at a fixed price. Where allocative costs can be minimized by rescission, the parties would maintain the distribution of risk by allowing the seller to repair the defective tender or to offset the decline in market price against the purchase price to be returned to the buyer. Either such remedy retains the cost advantages of the seller's resale or repair of the defective goods without disturbing the contractual allocation of risk. Similarly, where the goods prove unsuitable to the buyer despite the triviality of the defects, the allocation of risk can be maintained if the buyer reimburses the seller for retrieving and reselling the goods, as well as for depreciation. Even with such flexible remedies, however, there will still be the incentive of distributional benefits as long as the contract is not enforced with certainty. Moreover, the cost of uncertainty will exist whether these remedies are created by the parties or enforced by a court. Since the cost of uncertainty is inevitable and difficult to estimate, the flexibility of legal rules will always make it difficult to determine the most efficient remedy.

Although the courts now apply more flexible rules when dealing with constructive conditions, we have seen that sometimes the implied conditions under the Sale of Goods Act 1979 allow a party to escape an unprofitable contract because of a relatively unimportant breach by the other party. Should the Act be amended?

'Sale and supply of goods' (Law Commission No 160, Cmnd 137, 1987)

2.26 A criticism of the classification of most of the implied terms in the Sale of Goods Act as 'conditions' is that it leads to inflexibility and to a danger that the obligation of the seller to supply goods of the appropriate quality will be watered down. If a defect is a minor one the court may be reluctant to allow rejection and so, under the present law, may be tempted to hold that there is no breach at all of the implied term as to quality. . . . [For example,] . . . in *Cehave NV v Bremer Handelsgesellschaft mbH* Lord Denning MR said that the implied condition was broken only if the defect was so serious that a commercial man would have thought that the buyer should be able to reject the goods. These cases illustrate the difficulties to which the rigid classification gives rise, and lower courts are bound by the precedents thus created. There has, moreover, been express criticism of the inflexibility of the present law as to compliance with description.

4.1. . . . The terms implied by sections 13 to 15 of the 1979 Act are capable of being broken in ways some of which may be very serious but some of which may be very slight. The classification of a term with such a flexible content as a 'condition' with the inflexible result that in all cases the buyer has the right to terminate the contract as well as claim damages can give rise to unfairness. On the one hand, the right to terminate a contract for a very slight breach which can easily be remedied may seem unjust on the seller whose loss might far exceed the cost of remedying the defect. On the other hand, the remedy of rejection is so powerful that it can be counterproductive. A court faced with a claim to reject which it considers thoroughly unreasonable may come to the conclusion that there was no breach of contract at all: the buyer cannot then even recover damages. What the court cannot do in the case of breach of condition is to award damages but at the same time decide that the breach was too slight to entitle the buyer to reject the goods. It is a case of 'rejectability or nothing'. Thus the strength of the buyer's remedy may actually work against his interests.

4.2 We considered in the Consultative Document whether the solution to this problem was to recommend the creation of a new term that goods would be free from all minor defects. Breach of this term would give rise only to a right to damages. We rejected that solution in the Consultative Document and consultation has confirmed us in that view. Such a term would be undesirable where the buyer was a consumer because it would weaken his bargaining position excessively, and for consumers and non-consumers alike there would be too much uncertainty about what was a 'minor defect'.

4.3 The question then asked by the Consultative Document was what the remedy should be when there was a breach of one of the statutory implied terms as to quality. Here, we suggested, there was a distinction to be drawn between the interests of the consumer and those of the non-consumer. . . .

4.4 . . . [T]he consumer is almost always buying goods for domestic use or consumption and not for the purpose of making a profit out of them; he will not usually be content with defective goods when he intended to buy perfect goods, even if the price were reduced or he were compensated in some way. If he wants to retain defective goods he can always keep them and claim damages. But should he ever be prevented from rejecting the goods and terminating the contract when this is what he wants to do? The consumer will not usually be in a position easily to dispose of defective goods and if he keeps them it may be difficult to quantify what his loss is in money terms, especially if the defect is only minor. The seller is also likely to be in a stronger bargaining position than the consumer buyer: the buyer may in practice have to drop his claim or accept less than his due. Given that the overwhelming majority of consumer disputes are not taken to court, or even to lawyers, the relative strength of the bargaining position of each party is, in our view, a factor of critical importance. Even if compensation were agreed, this would often still not be an adequate remedy for the consumer. What he wanted was goods of the proper quality at the full price, not defective goods at a lower price. It must be made as easy as possible for the consumer to get defective goods replaced by sound ones (if, as is so often the case, this is what he is prepared to agree to) or to get his money back (if this is what he insists on).

4.5 It seems to us that these considerations do not apply with the same force to most non-consumer transactions. Non-consumers who are in the business of dealing in goods are usually able to dispose of goods of different qualities through access to the appropriate markets. A breach of contract by the seller can usually be measured in monetary terms and then taken into account in calculating profits. The motive for rejection of goods may well differ between consumers and non-consumers. The consumer is unlikely to attempt to reject goods because of a fall in their market price. He rejects goods because he wants perfect goods, not defective ones. The non-consumer will also, of course, sometimes wish to reject goods for this reason. Not infrequently, however, the non-consumer who deals in goods uses their alleged non-conformity as his excuse for rejection: his real motive is that the market price of the goods has fallen. When prices fall it will be commercially advantageous to him to get rid of the expensive goods in his hands and perhaps then replace them with similar goods, bought at the lower price. The diminution in value caused by the quality defect may be trifling; the diminution caused by the fall in the market price may be immense. Is it just in those circumstances to allow the buyer to reject the goods and terminate the contract so as to cause the loss due to the change in the market to fall on the seller and not on himself?

4.6 Any distinction between the position of consumers and non-consumers may be objected to on the ground that it will be unfair to those near the borderline. We recognise and must accept that any definition of 'consumer' and 'non-consumer' is likely to give rise to some difficult borderline cases. We recognise that there are some powerful consumers who are in practice in a stronger bargaining position than their suppliers. There are also many non-consumers to whom the arguments in the preceding paragraph do not apply. Moreover, those arguments apply with special force to dealers in some types of goods only. They apply with little force, for example, to a retailer who makes his profit from a standard mark-up of goods sold at a standard price, and only slightly (if at all) to the non-consumer who buys goods in which he does not deal. An example of the latter is, perhaps, the small corner shop which buys an item of equipment such as a refrigerator for use in the shop. This type of non-consumer is probably in very much the same position as an individual consumer if the refrigerator proves to be defective. . . .

2. Policy for consumers

4.10 . . .It is, of course, very common in practice for a buyer and seller to agree that the goods should be repaired or replaced free of charge. Some might say that there are circumstances in which it would be unreasonable for the buyer to insist on rejecting the goods when the seller is prepared to replace them or remedy the [defect].

4.11 In the Consultative Document we used the word 'cure' to describe the remedy of repair or replacement. We said that this procedure should be encouraged and we put forward for discussion three possible schemes of remedies based upon the notion of 'cure'. Although the schemes differed in details, their essential feature was that in some instances a seller would have the right to 'cure' any defect but that if he did not do so the buyer could reject. The buyer would thus never have been required to keep defective goods but the seller could, if he wanted, have prevented rejection by correcting the defect or offering replacement goods. . . .

. . .

4.13 On consultation there was much support for our suggested scheme of 'cure'. However, two principal, and formidable, lines of objection emerged. First, it was suggested that the scheme was generally too adverse to consumers' interests because it gave the supplier a ground upon which he could argue that the buyer was not entitled to return defective goods and claim the price back. Secondly, we had recognised in the Consultative Document that the scheme left many questions unanswered. . . .

4.14 We have decided not to recommend a 'cure' scheme for consumer transactions, although not all of us are without regret on the matter. We are, in short, not sufficiently confident that such a scheme would be more beneficial to buyers and sellers generally than is the present law. . . .

We have reached the conclusion, therefore, that, for the consumer transaction, the regime which applies must be a simple one. Such is the present law. In legal theory the consumer has the absolute right to reject for any defect. True, he may seldom exercise that right, almost always being prepared to accept repair or replacement. However, if the seller is unreasonable it is against that legal background that the discussion takes place. Any legal ground upon which rejection might arguably be resisted, however weak such ground might be on the facts, gives the seller a potential weapon with which to undermine the position of the ordinary consumer. Sometimes, moreover, what the law is believed to be is more important than what it is. There should be no ambiguity or misunderstanding about the rights of the consumer buyer.

4.15 We have therefore decided to recommend the retention of the present law so far as concerns the consumer buyer's right to reject the goods and terminate the contract for breach of the statutory implied terms in sections 13 to 15 of the Sale of Goods Act. . . .

3. Policy for non-consumers

4.16 . . . So far as non-consumer buyers are concerned, however, our conclusions are different. The reasons of policy applicable to consumers do not apply to non-consumers. Such buyers cannot as a general rule be presumed to be in a weak bargaining position as against their sellers, and there is less objection to leaving them with non-conforming goods in their hands in an appropriate case, especially because they will still have a claim for damages (which in many cases will be fairly easy to quantify).

4.17 In the Consultative Document we discussed a number of possible ways of modifying the rights of the non-consumer buyer. Of these we provisionally rejected all but one, and those we rejected received little support on consultation. First, we rejected the idea that there should be a list of the circumstances in which rejection or (as the case may be) non-rejection would be permitted. The circumstances of sale transactions are so infinitely variable that any set of rules would both be extremely lengthy and yet incomplete. Secondly, we rejected any idea of a statutory right to 'cure', as we had provisionally proposed for consumers. Now that we are not recommending such a regime for consumers, the case for recommending it for non-consumers is even weaker than it was at the time we made our provisional recommendations. We do not wish to do anything to stop non-consumers from coming to their own agreement about 'curing' defects and, indeed, cure provisions (sometimes very detailed) are common in many types of commercial contract. The question, however, was whether there should be a statutory 'cure' regime in all cases and, for the reasons given in the Consultative Document, which were largely endorsed on consultation, we make no such recommendation. Thirdly, we rejected the idea that a non-consumer buyer should be entitled to reject goods only where damages would not be an adequate remedy. The effect of such a recommendation would be, we thought, that rejection would hardly ever be permissible; damages would in almost all cases be held to be an adequate remedy for a commercial buyer. Not only had there been no call for such a drastic change in the policy of the Act but we ourselves did not think such a change was desirable. Fourthly, we considered whether non-consumers should be entitled to reject only when the breach was very serious. For example, the test could have been taken from the *Hongkong Fir* case: was the breach so serious as to frustrate the contract? Such a test would in substance be a reversal of the present law for rejection would be permissible only in the most extreme cases. Notwithstanding that an express term relating to the quality of goods has been held by the Court of Appeal to carry these remedies, in the Consultative Document we expressed the provisional view that so severe a test was not appropriate for the statutory implied terms. This view has been confirmed on consultation and we do not recommend the major alteration of the law which would result from its adoption.

4.18 We did not think, therefore, that there was need for more than a slight change in the law. What was required was no more than a modification which would, in substance, prevent rejection in bad faith, where the breach was really so insignificant that, as a matter of justice, rejection should not be permitted. To introduce a general duty of good faith into the law relating to the sale of goods might perhaps be desirable but could not be justified by the particular problem which we had under examination. Moreover, if such a duty were to be introduced the question would also have to be asked whether the duty should not extend across the entire range of contract law.

4.19 The proposal we favoured in the Consultative Document aimed to preserve the present law as far as possible whilst lessening the risk of its abuse. Our provisional proposal was that in a non-consumer sale 'the buyer ought to be entitled to reject the goods for breach of any one of the terms implied by section 13 to 15 of the Sale of Goods Act unless the seller can show that the nature and consequences of the breach are so slight that rejection would be unreasonable'. In making this proposal we stressed that the buyer's motive in seeking to reject the goods and treat the contract as repudiated would not be relevant.

4.20 In the Consultative Document we said that we were concerned lest any such modification of the absolute right to reject defective goods should create undesirable uncertainty. Consultation has not affirmed this concern. . .

4.21 The *Law Commission's recommendations* apply to England and Wales. They are that for the non-consumer the statutory implied quality terms should remain as conditions but that the Act should provide that where the breach is so slight that it would be unreasonable for the buyer to reject the goods, the breach is not to be treated as a breach of condition but may be treated as a breach of warranty. The effect of this will be that the buyer will not be able to reject the goods but will only be able to claim damages. . . .

. . .

4.23 Both Commissions recognise that to introduce any modification of the absolute right to reject is to introduce a measure of uncertainty. As so often happens where reform of the law is concerned, a balance has to be struck. On the one hand is the benefit of certainty: on the other is the benefit of justice. We have concluded that the uncertainty will be more apparent than real and is a price worth paying. Parties will, of course, be able to provide, either expressly or by implication, that there shall be an absolute right to reject in any particular circumstances. Moreover, in the appropriate circumstances there will be no difficulty in inferring such an intention.

4.24 A particular example of such circumstances is that in many commercial situations it would be normal to infer an intention that any breach of a time clause, however slight, would justify rejection of the goods and termination of the contract. We do not expect our recommendations to have any effect on such time clauses. We have no doubt that it would continue to be the intention of the parties that any breach, however slight, of such a clause would give rise to a right to reject the goods and terminate the contract; and that when the contract was construed against its commercial matrix, a court would have no difficulty in so holding.

. . .

6.18 In the Consultative Document we raised three questions about [the rules contained in Sale of Goods Act 1979, s 30.]

6.19 *The first question* was whether the special regime of remedies which we proposed in the Consultative Document for breach of the implied terms contained in sections 13 to 15 of the 1979 Act should also apply to delivery of the wrong quantity of goods. Our provisional view was that it should not. We saw no obvious reason why the Act should not contain a number of specific and strict rules about delivery of the wrong quantity, which might differ in effect from the rules on breach of the implied terms.

6.20 We remain of this view. We think, however, that a refinement of our proposal for the restriction on the right to reject in non-consumer cases is desirable where a wrong quantity of goods is delivered to the buyer. Where a wrong quantity is delivered to the buyer he has at present the right to reject the *whole* of the goods, no matter how slight the shortfall or excess. Where there is an excess, he also has the right to reject the excess only. The Law Commission's *recommendation* for England and Wales is that the right to reject an excess should in all cases be preserved, but that where the non-consumer is delivered a wrong quantity of goods, and the shortfall or excess is so slight that it would be unreasonable to reject the *whole*, then he should be barred from so doing.

(I) The nature of termination

Photo Production Ltd v Securicor Transport Ltd [1980] 1 All ER 556, House of Lords

(The facts of this case are set out below, p 695. The issue was whether the termination of a contract prevents an exclusion clause applying to the event relied on as the ground for termination. As we shall see in chapter 34, the Court of Appeal had held in a number of cases that, if the innocent party terminated the contract because of a fundamental breach by the other, that got rid of any exclusion or limitation clauses which would otherwise have governed the defaulter's liability. The argument seemed to be that because the contract had come to an end, the clauses had ceased to apply. The House of Lords had said, obiter, in the *Suisse Atlantique* case (below, p 692) that this doctrine was unsound as well as commercially inconvenient, but the Court of Appeal had continued to apply it. In the *Photo Production* case the House of Lords decisively rejected it.)

Lord Diplock. . . . A basic principle of the common law of contract, to which there are no exceptions that are relevant in the instant case, is that parties to a contract are free to determine for themselves what primary obligations they will accept. They may state these in express words in the contract itself, and, where they do, the statement is determinative; but in practice a commercial contract never states all the primary obligations of the parties in full; many are left to be incorporated by implication of law from the legal nature of the contract into which the parties are entering. But if the parties wish to reject or modify primary obligations which would otherwise be so incorporated, they are fully at liberty to do so by express words.

Leaving aside those comparatively rare cases in which the court is able to enforce a primary obligation by decreeing specific performance of it, breaches of primary obligations give rise to substituted secondary obligations on the part of the party in default, and, in some cases, may entitle the other party to be relieved from further performance of his own primary obligations. These secondary obligations of the contract breaker and any concomitant relief of the other party from his own primary obligations also arise by implication of law, generally common law, but sometimes statute, as in the case of codifying statutes passed at the turn of the century, notably the Sale of Goods Act 1893. The contract, however, is just as much the source of secondary obligations as it is of primary obligations; and like primary obligations that are implied by law secondary obligations too can be modified by agreement between the parties, although, for reasons to be mentioned later, they cannot, in my view, be totally excluded. In the instant case, the only secondary obligations and concomitant reliefs that are applicable arise by implication of the common law as modified by the express words of the contract.

Every failure to perform a primary obligation is a breach of contract. The secondary obligation on the part of the contract breaker to which it gives rise by implication of the common law is to pay monetary compensation to the other party for the loss sustained by him in consequence of the breach; but, with two exceptions, the primary obligations of both parties so far as they have not yet been fully performed remain unchanged. This secondary obligation to pay compensation (damages) for non-performance of primary obligations I will call the 'general secondary obligation'. It applies in the cases of the two exceptions as well.

The exceptions are: (1) where the event resulting from the failure by one party to perform a primary obligation has the effect of depriving the other party of substantially the whole benefit which it was the intention of the parties that he should obtain from the contract, the party not in default may elect to put an end to all primary obligations of both parties remaining unperformed (if the expression 'fundamental breach' is to be retained, it should, in the interests of clarity, be confined to this exception); (2) where the contracting parties have agreed, whether by express words or by implication of law, that *any* failure by one party to perform a particular primary obligation ('condition' in the nomenclature of the Sale of Goods Act 1893), irrespective of the gravity of the event that has in fact resulted from the breach, shall entitle the other party to elect to put an end to all primary obligations of both parties remaining unperformed (in the interests of clarity, the nomenclature of the Sale of Goods Act 1893, 'breach of condition', should be reserved for this exception).

Where such an election is made (a) there is substituted by implication of law for the primary obligations of the party in default which remain unperformed a secondary obligation to pay monetary compensation to the other party for the loss sustained by him in consequence of their non-performance in the future and (b) the unperformed primary obligations of that other party are discharged. This secondary obligation is additional to the general secondary obligation; I will call it 'the anticipatory secondary obligation'.

In cases falling within the first exception, fundamental breach, the anticipatory secondary obligation arises under contracts of all kinds by implication of the common law, except to the extent that it is excluded or modified by the express words of the contract. In cases falling within the second exception, breach of condition, the anticipatory secondary obligation generally arises under particular kinds of contracts by implication of statute law; though in the case of 'deviation' from the contract voyage under a contract of carriage of goods by sea it arises by implication of the common law. The anticipatory secondary obligation in these cases too can be excluded or modified by express words.

When there has been a fundamental breach or breach of condition, the coming to an end of the primary obligations of both parties to the contract at the election of the party not in default is often referred to as the 'determination' or 'rescission' of the contract or, as in the Sale of Goods Act 1893, 'treating the contract as repudiated'. The first two of these expressions, however, are misleading unless it is borne in mind that for the unperformed primary obligations of the party in default there are substituted by operation of law what I have called the secondary obligations.

The bringing to an end of all primary obligations under the contract may also leave the parties in a relationship, typically that of bailor and bailee, in which they owe to one another by operation of law fresh primary obligations of which the contract is not the source; but no such relationship is involved in the instant case.

I have left out of account in this analysis as irrelevant to the instant case an arbitration or choice of forum clause. This does not come into operation until a party to the contract claims that a primary obligation of the other party has not been performed; and its relationship to other obligations of which the contract is the source was dealt with by this House in *Heyman v Darwins Ltd*.

(For further extracts from this case, see below, p 695.)

NOTES

1. You may not find Diplock's explanation easy to follow, but the basic idea is simple enough. A contract contains 'primary obligations'—what each party is to do. When the innocent party terminates, the original obligation on the defaulting party is replaced by the ('secondary') obligation to pay damages—damages to compensate for any breaches which occurred before termination and to compensate for the fact that the defaulting party is now not going to perform the remainder of the contract ('anticipatory secondary obligation')—eg the cost of getting another contractor to finish the job. Just as the parties can agree what their primary obligations are, so they can fix their secondary obligations, eg by limiting the damages to so much. What they have agreed continues to govern their liability after termination, because it defines that liability.

2. Diplock says that in cases of breach of condition, the anticipatory secondary obligation generally arises by implication of statute law. No doubt he was thinking of the implied conditions under the Sale of Goods Act, but it must be remembered that there are other examples of conditions at common law: see *Bunge v Tradax*, above, p 438.

3. Diplock refers to cases in which termination of the contract leaves the parties in a bailment relationship. A bailment occurs when one party is in possession of another party's goods, whether or not there is a contract between them (eg a finder is a bailee). The bailee owes the bailor various duties: see further below, p 691.

(m) Loss of the right to terminate

Allen v Robles [1969] 3 All ER 154, Court of Appeal

The defendant had a policy of motor insurance with the third party; the policy provided that the insured must notify any claim within five days, at the risk of forfeiture of the policy. The defendant drove negligently, injuring the plaintiff and damaging his property, but he failed to inform the third party insurers for two months. The insurers were willing to indemnify the plaintiff for the personal injury, but not for the damage to his property, but they did not inform the defendant of this until over four months after they had been informed of the claim. Mocatta J held that the insurers had lost the right to repudiate their liability under the policy and held that they were liable to indemnify the defendant in full.

Fenton Atkinson LJ. . . . In dealing with this matter, the learned judge held that there had been a breach of the condition by the defendant and, that being so, the third party had the right to elect whether to repudiate liability to indemnify or whether to accept liability to indemnify; but he went on to hold that they had to make up their minds which they were going to do within a reasonable time, and, if they failed within a reasonable time to make up their minds one way or the other, they would thereby lose the right of election and would be compelled to accept liability to indemnify the defendant. He went on to hold that the delay until 29th November was of such a length of time that it was more than a reasonable time and that by that date they had lost their right to refuse to indemnify the defendant; and it is against that view of the law of the learned judge that this appeal is now brought.

Counsel for the third party has cited to us, in particular *Clough v London and North Western Rly Co* and, in particular, a passage set out in the judgment of the court. The law is there set out in this way, and it has been approved since and one finds it so stated in leading textbooks, such as *Chitty on Contract*. It is not necessary, I think, to set out the facts of the case in this judgment, but this is the passage:

> '. . . we agree with what seems to be the opinion of all the judges below, that if it can be shewn that the London Pianoforte Company have at any time after knowledge of the fraud, either by express words or by unequivocal acts, affirmed the contract, their election has been determined forever. But we differ from them in this, that we think the party defrauded may keep the question open so long as he does nothing to affirm the contract.'

In my view the position was this, that when the third party through their agents, their solicitors, discovered: (a) that there was a claim; and (b) that the defendant was in breach of his condition, they were in a position then either to elect by refusing to indemnify or to accept a liability to indemnify, or it was open to them to delay their decision, particularly in view of their letter of 10th August 1967, and mere lapse of time, in my view, on the facts of this case, would not lose them their right ultimately to decide to refuse to indemnify. The lapse of time would only operate against them if thereby there was prejudice to the defendant or if in some way rights of third parties intervened or if their delay was so long that the court felt able to say that the delay in itself was of such a length as to be evidence that they had in truth decided to accept liability. None of these possibilities arise here.

[Phillimore and Danckwerts LJJ agreed.]

Appeal allowed.

NOTES

1. A similar approach to the question was employed in *The Antaios* [1983] 3 All ER 777, CA; affirmed on other grounds [1984] 3 All ER 229, HL.
2. In *Peyman v Lanjani* [1985] Ch 457 the Court of Appeal held that there could be no affirmation unless the victim knew not only of the breach but also that it gave the right to terminate. However, if he gives the appearance of affirming and the other party acts on that apparent affirmation, the victim will be estopped by it irrespective of his knowledge. (Compare the *Hannah Blumenthal*, above, p 168.)
3. Special rules about loss of the right to rescind apply to contracts for the sale of goods.

Sale of Goods Act 1979

Section 34
(1) Where goods are delivered to the buyer, and he has not previously examined them, he is not deemed to have accepted them until he has had a reasonable opportunity of examining them for the purpose of ascertaining whether they are in conformity with the contract.
(2) Unless otherwise agreed, when the seller tenders delivery of goods to the buyer, he is bound on request to afford the buyer a reasonable opportunity of examining the goods for the purpose of ascertaining whether they are in conformity with the contract.

Section 35
(1) The buyer is deemed to have accepted the goods when he intimates to the seller that he has accepted them, or (except where section 34 above otherwise provides) when the goods have been delivered to him and he does any act in relation to them which is inconsistent with the ownership of the seller, or when after the lapse of a reasonable time he retains the goods without intimating to the seller that he has rejected them.

NOTES

1. 'Acceptance' under ss 34 and 35 is nothing to do with 'offer and acceptance'; it deals with whether it is too late for the buyer to reject the goods.

2. The buyer who 'intimates' to the seller that he accepts loses the right to reject even though he has not had a reasonable opportunity to examine the goods. It seems not to matter whether the buyer knew he had a right to reject or whether the seller has acted on the intimation; contrast *Peyman v Lanjani*. The Law Commission has recommended that this be changed because of the problem of buyers who sign 'acceptance notes' when goods are delivered without appreciating the consequences. Any clause in a consumer contract purporting to exclude the new rule would be void; in a non-consumer contract it would be valid if it were fair and reasonable (see below, p 718). (Law Commission Report No 160, *Sale and Supply of Goods* (Cmnd 137, 1987), paras 5.20–.25.)

3. The intricacies of 'acts inconsistent with the ownership of the seller' can be left to books on sale of goods, but it has been suggested that one such act is asking for goods to be repaired. (It might also amount to affirmation: see above, p 294). As the Law Commission said,

> If this be so, then buyers would be best advised *not* to allow the seller to try to put the goods right, but to insist on rejecting . . . we think that informal attempts at cure should be encouraged.

The Commission recommended that a request for repair should not, of itself, amount to acceptance. (Ibid, paras 5.27–.29.)

4. In *Bernstein v Pamson Motors (Golders Green) Ltd* [1987] 2 All ER 220 the engine of a new car had seized up after only 140 miles. It was held that the car was not merchantable, but that as the buyer had had the car for nearly a month, a reasonable time had elapsed under s 35 and he could no longer reject it. For much of the month the buyer had been ill and unable to drive the car. Rougier J said (at p 230):

> . . . [W]hat is a reasonable time in the circumstances? And here the 1979 Act ceases to be helpful. By s 59 'a reasonable time' is defined as a question of fact, no more, as if it could be anything else.
>
> The submission made on behalf of the defendants is that in the context of the sale of [a] new motor car a reasonable time must entail a reasonable time to inspect and try out the car *generally* rather than with an eye to any specific defect, and that to project the period further would be artificial and contrary to the general legal proposition that there should, whenever possible, be finality in commercial transactions. At first I regret to say this proposition got a hostile reception on the ground that a mere 140-odd miles, and some three weeks, part of which were occupied by illness, were not nearly enough to afford the plaintiff any opportunity of discovering this wholly latent defect.
>
> However, it was pointed out, and in my view rightly, that the whole concept of discovery of any *particular* defect and subsequent affirmation of the contract was only material in contracts of hire purchase and that there was nothing in the Sale of Goods Act 1979 to justify any analogous approach. This distinction was clearly stated by Webster J in the recent case of *Laurelgates Ltd v Lombard North Central Ltd* (1983) 133 NLJ 720.
>
> In effect, it was argued, the wording of s 35 of the 1979 Act creates its own implied affirmation, as it were, by stating merely that once a buyer has had the goods for a reasonable time, *not*, be it noted, related to the opportunity to discover any particular defect, he is deemed to have accepted them. I think that this submission is correct.
>
> In my judgment, the nature of the particular defect, discovered ex post facto, and the speed with which it might have been discovered, are irrelevant to the concept of reasonable time in s 35 as drafted. That section seems to me to be directed solely to what is a reasonable practical interval in commercial terms between a buyer receiving the goods and his ability to send them back, taking into consideration from his point of view the nature of the goods and their function, and from the point of view of the seller the commercial desirability of being able to close his ledger reasonably soon after the transaction is complete. The complexity of the intended function of the goods is clearly of prime consideration here. What is a reasonable time in relation to a bicycle would hardly suffice for a nuclear submarine.
>
> Turning to the facts of the present case one asks whether some three weeks and 140-odd

miles constitute a reasonable time after taking delivery of a new motor car? I am bound to
say that I think the answer is Yes. . . .

Subsequently in *Rogers v Parish (Scarborough) Ltd* (above, p 330) the
Court of Appeal allowed a buyer to reject an unmerchantable Range
Rover after having had it some months. Acceptance was not argued and
the case was different from *Bernstein* in that the Range Rover had been
defective from the start; the sellers' efforts at repair had failed. However
it is understood that an appeal in the *Bernstein* case was settled at the
doors of the court, so there may 'be a view' that it is incorrect.

5. Do you think the result of *Bernstein* was fair? Bear in mind that, after the
   engine had been rebuilt, the car was 'as good as new'. Why would a
   consumer still want to reject it and, if he were permitted to do so, who
   would ultimately bear the cost (ie the difference between the original
   price and the resale value of the repaired car)? For discussion of whether
   consumers should have a long-term right to reject, see Law Commission
   No 160, paras 5.6–.13.

CHAPTER 23
Damages

(a) The basic measure of recovery

The basic measure of damages for breach of contract was described in chapter 2: so far as money can do it, the plaintiff is to be placed in the same situation as if the contract had been performed (*Robinson v Harman* (1848) 1 Exch 850 at 855). This is subject to two general qualifications: the mitigation rule, which provides that the plaintiff will not be allowed to recover for losses which could have been avoided by taking reasonable steps; and the remoteness rule, under which the plaintiff will not recover for any unusual loss unless the possibility of such a loss occurring was contemplated by the parties when the contract was made. In *British Westinghouse Electric and Manufacturing Co Ltd v Underground Electric Rlys Co of London Ltd* [1912] AC 673 Viscount Haldane LC stated the general principles thus (at pp 688–689):

> In order to come to a conclusion on the question as to damages thus raised, it is essential to bear in mind certain propositions which I think are well established. In some of the cases there are expressions as to the principles governing the measure of general damages which at first sight seem difficult to harmonise. The apparent discrepancies are, however, mainly due to the varying nature of the particular questions submitted for decision. The quantum of damage is a question of fact, and the only guidance which the law can give is to lay down general principles which afford at times but scanty assistance in dealing with particular cases. The judges who give guidance to juries in these cases have necessarily to look at their special character, and to mould for the purposes of different kinds of claim the expression of the general principles which apply to them, and this is apt to give rise to an appearance of ambiguity. Subject to these observations I think that there are certain broad principles, which are quite well settled. The first is that, as far as possible, he who has proved a breach of a bargain to supply what he contracted to get is to be placed, as far as money can do it, in as good a situation as if the contract had been performed. The fundamental basis is thus compensation for pecuniary loss naturally flowing from the breach; but this first principle is qualified by a second, which imposes on a plaintiff the duty of taking all reasonable steps to mitigate the loss consequent on the breach, and debars him from claiming in respect of any part of the damage which is due to his neglect to take such steps.

(This case is considered in detail below, p 487.)

In this introductory subsection we will look briefly at how the rules of mitigation and remoteness affect the recovery of damages before considering in some detail the nature of the losses which are recoverable in contract. Remoteness and mitigation will be considered in more detail in subsections (b) and (c).

Sale of Goods Act 1979

. . .

Section 50
(1) Where the buyer wrongfully neglects or refuses to accept and pay for the goods, the seller may maintain an action against him for damages for non-acceptance.
(2) The measure of damages is the estimated loss directly and naturally resulting, in the ordinary course of events, from the buyer's breach of contract.
(3) Where there is an available market for the goods in question the measure of damages is prima facie to be ascertained by the difference between the contract price and the market or current price at the time or times when the goods ought to have been accepted or (if no time was fixed for acceptance) at the time of the refusal to accept.

Section 51
(1) Where the seller wrongfully neglects or refuses to deliver the goods to the buyer, the buyer may maintain an action against the seller for damages for non-delivery.
(2) The measure of damages is the estimated loss directly and naturally resulting, in the ordinary course of events, from the seller's breach of contract.
(3) Where there is an available market for the goods in question the measure of damages is prima facie to be ascertained by the difference between the contract price and the market or current price of the goods at the time or times when they ought to have been delivered or (if no time was fixed) at the time of the refusal to deliver.

NOTES

1. There is 'an available market' if goods of the contract description can be readily bought or sold: see below, p 492.
2. Why, when there is an available market for the goods, are the damages prima facie the difference between contract and market prices at the date for delivery? Do you see what is meant when it is said that the measures of damages set out in these subsections incorporates the principle of mitigation (eg *McGregor on Damages* (15th edn) paras 297–303)?
3. If there is no available market, the damages will be assessed according to the general principles. Thus if the seller fails to deliver and the buyer cannot obtain substitute goods in the market, the buyer may recover consequential losses that are suffered as a result – for instance, loss of profit from production or loss of profit on a resale. However the loss must not be too remote: see the next case.

Hadley v Baxendale (1854) 9 Exch 341, Exchequer

Where two parties have made a contract, which one of them has broken, the damages which the other party ought to receive in respect of such breach of contract should be such as may fairly and reasonably be considered either arising naturally, ie according to the usual course of things, from such breach of contract itself, or such as may reasonably be supposed to have been in the contemplation of both parties at the time thay made the contract, as the probable result of the breach of it.—Where the plaintiffs, the owners of a flour mill, sent a broken iron shaft to an office of the defendants, who were common carriers, to be conveyed by them, and the defendants' clerk, who attended at the office, was told that the mill was stopped, that the shaft must be delivered immediately, and that a special entry, if necessary, must be made to hasten its delivery; and the delivery of the broken shaft to the consignee, to whom it had been sent by the plaintiffs as a pattern, by which to make a new shaft, was delayed for an unreasonable time; in consequence of which, the plaintiffs did not receive the new shaft for some days after the time they ought to have received it, and they were consequently unable to work their mill from want of the new shaft, and thereby incurred a loss of profits:—Held, that, under the circumstances, such loss could not be recovered in an action against the defendants as common carriers.

The judgment of the Court was now delivered by

Alderson B. We think that there ought to be a new trial in this case; but, in so doing, we deem it to be expedient and necessary to state explicitly the rule which the Judge, at the next trial, ought, in our opinion, to direct the jury to be governed by when they estimate the damages. . . .

Now we think the proper rule in such a case as the present is this:—Where two parties have made a contract which one of them has broken, the damages which the other party ought to receive in respect of such breach of contract should be such as may fairly and reasonably be considered either arising naturally, ie, according to the usual course of things, from such breach of contract itself, or such as may reasonably be supposed to have been in the contemplation of both parties, at the time they made the contract, as the probable result of the breach of it. Now, if the special circumstances under which the contract was actually made were communicated by the plaintiffs to the defendants, and thus known to both parties, the damages resulting from the breach of such a contract, which they would reasonably contemplate, would be the amount of injury which would ordinarily follow from a breach of contract under these special circumstances so known and communicated. But, on the other hand, if these special circumstances were wholly unknown to the party breaking the contract, he, at the most, could only be supposed to have had in his contemplation the amount of injury which would arise generally, and in the great multitude of cases not affected by any special circumstances, from such a breach of contract. For, had the special circumstances been known, the parties might have specially provided for the breach of contract by special terms as to the damage in that case; and of this advantage it would be very unjust to deprive them. Now the above principles are those by which we think the jury ought to be guided in estimating the damages arising out of any breach of contract. Now, in the present case, if we are to apply the principles above laid down, we find that the only circumstances here communicated by the plaintiffs to the defendants at the time the contract was made, were, that the article to be carried was the broken shaft of a mill, and that the plaintiffs were the millers of that mill. But how do these circumstances shew reasonably that the profits of the mill must be stopped by an unreasonable delay in the delivery of the broken shaft by the carrier to the third person? Suppose the plaintiffs had another shaft in their possession put up or putting up at the time, and that they only wished to send back the broken shaft to the engineer who made it; it is clear that this would be quite consistent with the above circumstances, and yet the unreasonable delay in the delivery would have no effect upon the intermediate profits of the mill. Or, again, suppose that, at the time of the delivery to the carrier, the machinery of the mill had been in other respects defective, then, also, the same results would follow. Here it is true that the shaft was actually sent back to serve as a model for a new one, and that the want of a new one was the only cause of the stoppage of the mill, and that the loss of profits really arose from not sending down the new shaft in proper time, and that this arose from the delay in delivering the broken one to serve as a model. But it is obvious that, in the great multitude of cases of millers sending off broken shafts to third persons by a carrier under ordinary circumstances, such consequences would not, in all probability, have occurred; and these special circumstances were here never communicated by the plaintiffs to the defendants. It follows, therefore, that the loss of profits here cannot reasonably be considered such a consequence of the breach of contract as could have been fairly and reasonably contemplated by both the parties when they made this contract. For such loss would neither have flowed naturally from the breach of this contract in the great multitude of such cases occurring under ordinary circumstances, nor were the special circumstances, which, perhaps, would have made it a reasonable and natural consequence of such breach of contract, communicated to or known by the defendants. . . . There must therefore be a new trial . . .

NOTES

1. It has been held that the headnote states the facts wrongly: if the plaintiffs had told the defendants' clerk that the mill was stopped, they should have recovered. See *Victoria Laundry (Windsor) Ltd v Newman Industries Ltd* [1949] 2 KB 528, 537–538.
2. This case is considered in more detail below, p 475.

3. Subject to the rules of mitigation and remoteness, the innocent party can normally recover damages for all the loss suffered as a result of the breach of contract. This will include any wasted expenditure, any expenditure reasonably incurred in mitigating loss and any loss of profit. In an appropriate case the plaintiff will recover damages for all of these items. Thus in *Hydraulic Engineering Co Ltd v McHaffie, Goslett & Co* (1878) 4 QBD 670 the defendants had contracted to make a 'gun', which they knew was to form part of a 'gunpowder pile driver' that the plaintiffs had contracted to build for Justice. The defendants delivered late, which prevented the plaintiffs delivering the finished machine on time, and Justice refused to take it. The plaintiffs were permitted to recover the expenditure they had wasted in making other parts of the machine (which was 'useless except as old iron', having been built specially), the cost of painting it to preserve it and the reasonable net profit they would have made on the contract with Justice. For further consideration of these various heads of damage, see below, p 470.

'The reliance interest in contract damages' by Fuller and Perdue (1936) 46 Yale LJ 52, 52–56

We are still all too willing to embrace the conceit that it is possible to manipulate legal concepts without the orientation which comes from the simple inquiry: toward what end is this activity directed? Nietzsche's observation, that the most common stupidity consists in forgetting what one is trying to do, retains a discomforting relevance to legal science.

In no field is this more true than in that of damages. In the assessment of damages the law tends to be conceived, not as a purposive ordering of human affairs, but as a kind of juristic mensuration. The language of the decisions sounds in terms not of command but of discovery. We *measure* the *extent* of the injury; we *determine* whether it was *caused* by the defendant's act; we *ascertain* whether the plaintiff has included the *same item* of damage twice in his complaint. One unfamiliar with the unstated premises which language of this sort conceals might almost be led to suppose that Rochester produces some ingenious instrument by which these calculations are accomplished.

. . . For example, one frequently finds the 'normal' rule of contract damages (which awards to the promisee the value of the expectancy, 'the lost profit') treated as a mere corollary of a more fundamental principle, that the purpose of granting damages is to make 'compensation' for injury. Yet in this case we 'compensate' the plaintiff by giving him something he never had. This seems on the face of things a queer kind of compensation. We can, to be sure, make the term 'compensation' seem appropriate by saying that the defendant's breach 'deprived' the plaintiff of the expectancy. But this is in essence only a metaphorical statement of the effect of the legal rule. In actuality the loss which the plaintiff suffers (deprivation of the expectancy) is not a datum of nature but the reflection of a normative order. It appears as a 'loss' only by reference to an unstated *ought*. Consequently, when the law gauges damages by the value of the promised performance it is not merely measuring a quantum, but is seeking an end, however vaguely conceived this end may be.

It is for this reason that it is impossible to separate the law of contract damages from the larger body of motives and policies which constitutes the general law of contracts. . . .

THE PURPOSES PURSUED IN AWARDING CONTRACT DAMAGES

It is convenient to distinguish three principal purposes which may be pursued in awarding contract damages. These purposes, and the situations in which they become appropriate, may be stated briefly as follows:

First, the plaintiff has in reliance on the promise of the defendant conferred some value on the defendant. The defendant fails to perform his promise. The court may force the defendant to disgorge the value he received from the plaintiff. The object here may be termed the prevention of gain by the defaulting promisor at the expense of the promisee; more briefly, the prevention of unjust enrichment. The interest protected may be called the *restitution interest*. For our present purposes it is quite immaterial how the suit in such a case be classified, whether as contractual or quasi-contractual, whether as a suit to enforce the contract or as a suit based upon a rescission of the contract. These questions relate to the superstructure of the law, not to the basic policies with which we are concerned.

Secondly, the plaintiff has in reliance on the promise of the defendant changed his position. For example, the buyer under a contract for the sale of land has incurred expense in the investigation of the seller's title, or has neglected the opportunity to enter other contracts. We may award damages to the plaintiff for the purpose of undoing the harm which his reliance on the defendant's promise has caused him. Our object is to put him in as good a position as he was in before the promise was made. The interest protected in this case may be called the *reliance interest*.

Thirdly, without insisting on reliance by the promisee or enrichment of the promisor, we may seek to give the promisee the value of the expectancy which the promise created. We may in a suit for specific performance actually compel the defendant to render the promised performance to the plaintiff, or, in a suit for damages, we may make the defendant pay the money value of this performance. Here our object is to put the plaintiff in as good a position as he would have occupied had the defendant performed his promise. The interest protected in this case we may call the *expectation interest*.

It will be observed that what we have called the *restitution interest* unites two elements: (1) reliance by the promisee, (2) a resultant gain to the promisor. It may for some purposes be necessary to separate these elements. In some cases a defaulting promisor may after his breach be left with an unjust gain which was not taken from the promisee (a third party furnished the consideration), or which was not the result of reliance by the promisee (the promisor violated a promise not to appropriate the promisee's goods). Even in those cases where the promisor's gain results from the promisee's reliance it may happen that damages will be assessed somewhat differently, depending on whether we take the promisor's gain or the promisee's loss as the standard of measurement. Generally, however, in the cases we shall be discussing, gain by the promisor will be accompanied by a corresponding and, so far as its legal measurement is concerned, identical loss to the promisee, so that for our purposes the most workable classification is one which presupposes in the restitution interest a correlation of promisor's gain and promisee's loss. If, as we shall assume, the gain involved in the restitution interest results from and is identical with the plaintiff's loss through reliance, then the restitution interest is merely a special case of the reliance interest; all of the cases coming under the restitution interest will be covered by the reliance interest, and the reliance interest will be broader than the restitution interest only to the extent that it includes cases where the plaintiff has relied on the defendant's promise without enriching the defendant.

It should not be supposed that the distinction here taken between the reliance and expectation interests coincides with that sometimes taken between 'losses caused' (damnum emergens) and 'gains prevented' (lucrum cessans). In the first place, though reliance ordinarily results in 'losses' of an affirmative nature (expenditures of labor and money) it is also true that opportunities for gain may be foregone in reliance on a promise. Hence the reliance interest must be interpreted as at least potentially covering 'gains prevented' as well as 'losses caused'. (Whether 'gains prevented' through reliance on a promise are properly compensable in damages is a question not here determined. Obviously, certain scruples concerning 'causality' and 'foreseeability' are suggested. It is enough for our present purpose to note that there is nothing in the definition of the reliance interest itself which would exclude items of this sort from consideration.) On the other hand, it is not possible to make the expectation interest entirely synonymous with 'gains prevented'. The disappointment of an expectancy often entails losses of a positive character.

(A further extract from this classic article will be found below, p 562.)

NOTES

1. You will recollect that earlier we drew a distinction between the losses which are recoverable in tort and those which are recoverable in contract. The former compensate the plaintiff for 'out of pocket' loss, the latter will give this plus loss of profit. Beware of assuming that tort damages cannot include compensation for 'loss of expectation'. A tortfeasor may have to compensate the victim for loss of expectation of life, or for loss of profit which the victim would have been able to make, for instance by using the

property which the tortfeasor has destroyed. These expectations, however, were not created by the tortfeasor: they existed beforehand and were destroyed by him. A tort such as a negligent misrepresentation may engender expectations, that the misrepresentation is true, but the victim may not recover damages for loss of this expectation. In contract, the expectations generated by the contract are protected. See the example given above, p 299.

2. Later in the article Fuller notes that sometimes in reliance on the contract the plaintiff will have passed up another opportunity to contract with someone else. Lost opportunity is compensable in tort—for instance, damages for personal injury will include damages for the loss of the opportunity to earn. If the plaintiff would have made the same profit from the opportunity she passed over as she should have done on the contract itself, there will be no difference between expectation loss and reliance loss.

3. If you think about typical tort cases, you will see that Fuller's analysis is actually incomplete. If a plaintiff suffers personal injury or damage to property she can recover for it whether the action is in tort or contract, but it seems odd to describe the injury as 'reliance' loss. Equally she can recover expenses reasonably incurred in mitigating the loss (eg medical expenses or the cost of making a substitute transaction). These are not incurred in reliance on the contract either. We term them 'incidental' loss.

4. It is only recently that the English courts have begun to adopt Fuller's terminology (see below, p 470). Often damages for breach of contract will be calculated by methods which seem to avoid splitting them up in this way. For instance, if a buyer fails to accept goods the seller has built for it and the seller resells the goods to someone else, the damages will normally be the difference between the original contract price and the resale price (cf Sale of Goods Act 1979, s 50(3), above, p 464). Nonetheless Fuller's analysis is a useful way of sorting out what losses the plaintiff is compensated for. For instance, suppose that the contract price for the goods were £10,000 and the goods had cost the seller £9,000 to build (including overheads). If the price at which the seller manages to resell is £9,400 and it cost £100 to arrange the resale, the damages will be £700 (£10,000 + £100 − £9,400). It is clear that we are going beyond putting the plaintiff back into its pre-contractual position by reimbursing its out of pocket loss: we are giving damages for loss of expectation too.

5. The English courts do not use a restitution measure in assessing contract *damages*: the traditional approach looks at what the plaintiff has lost, not what the defendant has gained (see below, p 472). Usually this benefits the plaintiff because its expenditure will be at least equal to and possibly higher than the gain to the defendant. However, the net effect is that the plaintiff recovers at least the value of any benefit conferred, plus any further wasted expenditure and loss of profit. The restitution measure is used by the courts when the plaintiff cannot claim damages (eg where there was no contract, above, p 224, or when the contract has been frustrated, above, p 365). In addition, the victim of a breach of contract may sometimes opt to claim in restitution instead of claiming damages: see below, p 551.

6. In American law the plaintiff is sometimes confined to claiming reliance loss even though the claim is for breach of contract: for instance, when

the claim is based on the reliance principle stated in s 90 of the Restatement (above, p 151). In English law the plaintiff is always entitled in theory to damages for loss of expectation if this can be proved. In practice damages for breach of contract will not always include any expectation element. Firstly, the plaintiff will frequently be able to earn the same amount of profit on a substitute contract with someone else, and the mitigation rule will then rule out recovery of damages for loss of profit. (Some of the implications of this for contract theory are explored below, p 569.) Secondly, the plaintiff may fail to prove that it lost any profit. An example is provided by *McRae v Commonwealth Disposals Commission* (the facts of this case are set out above, p 373; it will be remembered that the High Court of Australia found that the Commission had sold McRae the wreck of an oil tanker, which the court held that they had promised was on the Jourmand Reef). McRae claimed loss of profit. This was disallowed on the ground that as the Commission had not promised to deliver a tanker of any specified size, nor any oil, the claim for loss of profit was too speculative, but it allowed McRae the cost of equipping a salvage expedition.

Anglia Television Ltd v Reed [1971] 3 All ER 690, Court of Appeal

The plaintiff television company decided to make a film for television, and engaged the defendant, Robert Reed, to play the leading role. Later Reed found himelf unable to come to England, and he repudiated the contract at the last moment. The plaintiffs could not obtain a suitable substitute, and they cancelled the film. They claimed for their wasted expenditure, part of which (hiring other members of the team) had been incurred before the contract with Reed had been made. The master held Reed liable for this part of the expenditure and he appealed.

Lord Denning MR. . . . . It seems to me that a plaintiff in such a case as this has an election: he can either claim for his loss of profits; or for his wasted expenditure. But he must elect between them. He cannot claim both. If he has not suffered any loss of profits—or if he cannot prove what his profits would have been—he can claim in the alternative the expenditure which has been thrown away, that is, wasted, by reason of the breach. That is shown by *Cullinane v British 'Rema' Manufacturing Co Ltd.*

If the plaintiff claims the wasted expenditure, he is not limited to the expenditure incurred *after* the contract was concluded. He can claim also the expenditure incurred *before* the contract, provided that it was such as would reasonably be in the contemplation of the parties as likely to be wasted if the contract was broken. Applying that principle here, it is plain that, when Mr Reed entered into this contract, he must have known perfectly well that much expenditure had already been incurred on director's fees and the like. He must have contemplated—or, at any rate, it is reasonably to be imputed to him—that if he broke his contract, all that expenditure would be wasted, whether or not it was incurred before or after the contract. He must pay damages for all the expenditure so wasted and thrown away. This view is supported by the recent decision of Brightman J in *Lloyd v Stanbury*. There was a contract for the sale of land. In anticipation of the contract—and before it was concluded—the purchaser went to much expense in moving a caravan to the site and in getting his furniture there. The seller afterwards entered into a contract to sell the land to the purchaser, but afterwards broke his contract. The land had not increased in value, so the purchaser could not claim for any loss of profit. But Brightman J held that he could recover the cost of moving the caravan and furniture, because it was 'within the contemplation of the parties when the contract was signed'. That decision is in accord with the correct principle, namely, that wasted expenditure can be recovered when it is wasted by reason of the defendant's breach of contract. It is true that, if the defendant had never entered into the contract, he would not be liable, and the expenditure would have been incurred by the plaintiff without redress; but the defendant having made his contract and broken it, it does not lie in his mouth to say he is not liable, when it was because of his breach that the expenditure has been wasted.

I think the master was quite right and this appeal should be dismissed.

Phillimore LJ. I agree.

Megaw LJ. I also agree.

Appeal dismissed.

NOTES

1. Perhaps the plaintiffs did not claim lost profit because (except in the case where a film is sold to other stations) it is very hard to show what profit is made on a film made for television; the company's earnings are derived from the advertising shown before, during and after the film.
2. *Cullinane v British 'Rema' Manufacturing Co Ltd* [1954] 1 QB 292 is cited for the proposition that the plaintiff cannot claim *both* wasted expenditure and lost profit. If gross profit is meant, that must be correct, as if the contract had been performed the expenditure would have to have been paid for out of the gross profits, and to award both would be to give double recovery. If the proposition means that the plaintiff cannot recover the wasted expenditure and the net profit he would have earned at the end of the day had the contract been fulfilled, it seems inconsistent with principle as well as with the *Hydraulic Engineering* case (above, p 466): and in any event the court did not in fact decide that; see Macleod [1970] JBL 19.
3. What if the plaintiff had made a 'bad bargain' in the sense that its out of pocket expenditure was greater than the amount it would have received if the contract had been performed?

C & P Haulage v Middleton [1983] 3 All ER 94, Court of Appeal

The appellant was given a licence to occupy premises on a renewable six-monthly basis, and he incurred expenditure in making the premises suitable for his work, even though it was expressly provided that fixtures put in by him were not to be removed at the end of the licence. He was wrongfully ejected from the premises by the licensor ten weeks before a six-months' term was up; but he obtained the local authority's permission to use his own garage instead, and continued to do this for more than ten weeks. He claimed the cost of the improvements effected by him to the premises, but the trial judge awarded him only nominal damages.

Ackner LJ. . . . The judge approached the case essentially on this basis, that the accepted principle in relation to the assessment of damages for breach of contract was to put the plaintiff in the same position, as far as one could, as he would have been in if the contract had been performed; and, in order to evaluate whether if the contract had been performed what was the nature, if any, of the damage that he should be entitled to claim, one had to look at the consequences of the breach of contract.

The consequences of this breach of contract were that, so far from the appellant suffering any damage as a result of being excluded from the premises ten weeks earlier than would lawfully have been the case, thanks to the tolerance of the planning authorities, he had in effect been saved the payment which was likely to be between £60 and £100 a week which he would have had to have paid for the use of the respondents' premises. He accordingly came to the conclusion that if he was to award the damages claimed he would be putting the appellant in a better position than would have been the case if the contract had been lawfully determined.

The case which was at the forefront of counsel for the appellant's submissions before the judge and before us as well is *Anglia Television Ltd v Reed* . . .

Lord Denning MR was not contemplating what has been referred to subsequently as the 'bad bargain' case, a case in which a plaintiff has entered into a loss-making contract or, I would include, an otherwise disadvantageous contract. He was considering a case where it would not be possible to establish any loss of profits because the situation could not be prophesied had the defendant complied with his contractual obligations. . . . [The appellant] is not claiming for the loss of his bargain, which would involve being put in the position that he would have been in if the contract has been performed. He is not asking to be put in that position. He is asking to be put in the position he would have been in if the contract had never been made at all. If the contract had never been made at all, then he would not have incurred these expenses, and that is the essential approach he adopts in mounting this claim; because, if the right approach is that he should be put in the position in which he would have been had the contract been performed, then it follows that he suffered no damage. He lost his entitlement to a further ten weeks of occupation after 5 October, and during that period he involved himself in no loss of profit, because he found other accommodation, and in no increased expense, in fact the contrary, because he returned immediately to his own garage, thereby saving whatever would have been the agreed figure which he would have to have paid the respondents. . . .

The case which I have found of assistance, and I am grateful to counsel for their research, is *Bowlay Logging Ltd v Domtar Ltd*. It is a case in the British Columbia Supreme Court. Berger J, in a very careful and detailed judgment, goes through various English and American authorities and refers to the leading textbook writers, and I will only quote a small part of his judgment. He refers to the work of Professor L L Fuller and William R Perdue Jr in 'The Reliance Interest in Contract Damages' (1936) 46 Yale LJ:

> 'We will not in a suit for reimbursement for losses incurred in reliance on a contract knowingly put the plaintiff in a better position than he would have occupied had the contract been fully performed.'

Berger J then refers to a case in 1949, *L Albert & Son v Armstrong Rubber Co*, in which Learned Hand CJ, speaking for the Circuit Court of Appeals, Second Circuit, 'held that on a claim for compensation for expenses in part performance the defendant was entitled to deduct whatever he could prove the plaintiff would have lost if the contract had been fully performed'.

What Berger J had to consider was this (at 105):

> 'The parties entered into a contract whereby the plaintiff would cut timber under the defendant's timber sale, and the defendant would be responsible for hauling the timber away from the site of the timber sale. The plaintiff claimed the defendant was in breach of the contract as the defendant had not supplied sufficient trucks to make the plaintiff's operation, which was losing money, viable, and claimed not for loss of profits but for compensation for expenditures. The defendant argued that the plaintiff's operation lost money not because of a lack of trucks but because of the plaintiff's inefficiency, and, further, that even if the defendant had breached the contract the plaintiff should not be awarded damages because its operation would have lost money in any case.'

This submission was clearly accepted because the plaintiff was awarded only nominal damages and Berger J said:

> 'The law of contract compensates a plaintiff for damages resulting from the defendant's breach; it does not compensate a plaintiff for damages resulting from his making a bad bargain. Where it can be seen that the plaintiff would have incurred a loss on the contract as a whole, the expenses he has incurred are losses flowing from entering into the contract, not losses flowing from the defendant's breach. In these circumstances, the true consequence of the defendant's breach is that the plaintiff is released from his obligation to complete the contract—or in other words, he is saved from incurring further losses. If the law of contract were to move from compensating for the consequences of breach to compensating for the consequences of entering into contracts, the law would run contrary to the normal expectations of the world of commerce. The burden of risk would be shifted from the plaintiff to the defendant. The defendant would become the insurer of the plaintiff's enterprise. Moreover, the amount of the damages would increase not in relation to the gravity or consequences of the breach but in relation to the inefficiency with which the plaintiff carried out the contract. The greater his expenses owing to inefficiency, the greater the damages. The fundamental principle upon which damages are measured under the law of contract is restitutio in integrum. The principle contended for here by the plaintiff would entail the award of damages not to compensate the plaintiff but to punish the defendant.'

It is urged here that the garage itself was merely an element in the appellant's business: it was not a profit-making entity on its own. Nevertheless, if as a result of being kept out of these premises the appellant had found no other premises to go to for a period of time, his claim would clearly have been a claim for such a loss of profit as he could establish his business suffered.

In my judgment, the approach of Berger J is the correct one. It is not the function of the courts where there is a breach of contract knowingly, as this would be the case, to put the plaintiff in a better financial position than if the contract had been properly performed. In this case the appellant, if he was right in his claim, would indeed be in a better position because, as I have already indicated, had the contract been lawfully determined, as it could have been in the middle of December, there would have been no question of his recovering these expenses. . . .

Fox LJ. . . . The present case seems to me to be quite different both from *Anglia Television Ltd v Reed* and from *Lloyd v Stanbury* in that, while it is true that the expenditure could in a sense be said to be wasted in consequence of the breach of contract, it was equally likely to be wasted if there had been no breach, because the respondents wanted to get the appellant out and could terminate the licence at quite short notice. A high risk of waste was from the very first inherent in the nature of the contract itself, breach or no breach. The reality of the matter is that the waste resulted from what was, on the appellant's side, a very unsatisfactory and dangerous bargain.

I agree with Ackner LJ that the appeal must be dismissed.

Appeal dismissed.

NOTES

1. The fact that the plaintiff suffered no net loss in this case seems to have flowed partly from the bad initial bargain (see Fox LJ) and partly from the favourable arrangements made subsequently (see Ackner LJ and below, p 486).
2. In *CCC Films (London) Ltd v Impact Quadrant Films Ltd* [1984] 3 All ER 298, Hutchison J held (i) that the plaintiff could claim reliance loss when he could not prove a profit even though the difficulty of proof was not caused by the defendant's breach, as it had been in *McRae's* case; and (ii), following a dictum of Learned Hand CJ in the *Albert* case, that it was for the defendant to prove that the plaintiff would not have recouped his expenditure even if the contract had been performed.
3. These cases seem to follow from the general principle that the plaintiff is entitled to damages only for the loss which the defendant's breach has caused.

Tito v Waddell (No 2) [1977] Ch 106 at 332, Megarry V-C

(For the facts of this case, see below, p 497.)

Megarry V-C. . . . In the absence of any clear authority on the matter before me, I think I must consider it as a matter of principle. I do this in relation to the breach of a contract to do work on the land of another, whether to build, repair, replant or anything else: and I put it very broadly. First, it is fundamental to all questions of damages that they are to compensate the plaintiff for his loss or injury by putting him as nearly as possible in the same position as he would have been in had he not suffered the wrong. The question is not one of making the defendant disgorge what he has saved by committing the wrong, but one of compensating the plaintiff. In the words of O'Connor LJ in *Murphy v Wexford County Council* [1921] 2 IR 230, at 240:

> 'You are not to enrich the party aggrieved; you are not to impoverish him; you are, so far as money can, to leave him in the same position as before.'

Second, if the plaintiff has suffered monetary loss, as by a reduction in the value of his property by reason of the wrong, that is plainly a loss that he is entitled to be recouped. On the other hand, if the defendant has saved himself money, as by not doing what he has contracted to do, that does not of itself entitle the plaintiff to recover the saving as damages; for it by no means necessarily follows that what the defendant has saved the plaintiff has lost.

NOTES

1. In the Scots case of *Teacher v Calder* (1899) 1 F (HL) 39 a party broke a contract to invest money in a timber business and instead put it into a distillery. It was held that the innocent party was entitled to damages only for the loss caused to him by the breach; he could not claim the much greater profit that the guilty party had made from the distillery. In certain very limited circumstances it is possible for the plaintiff to bring an action in restitution to recover the profit the defendant has made through breaking the contract. See below, p 553.

2. Punitive or exemplary damages may be awarded for a breach of contract that is also a tort, but not, it seems, for a mere breach of contract: *Perera v Vandiyar* [1953] 1 All ER 1109.

3. Why is it that contract damages include compensation for 'expectation' losses as well as out of pocket loss? And why is the victim confined to recovering his loss, even if the breach has enabled the guilty party to make a greater profit—might that not actually encourage a party to break the contract if he do so profitably? Why not grant the victim specific performance, if that is still feasible, or allow him to recover any profit the guilty party has made through breaking the contract?

'Economic Analysis of Law' by Posner (2nd edn), pp 88–92

When a breach of contract is established, the issue becomes one of the proper remedy. A starting point for analysis is Holmes's view that it is not the policy of the law to compel adherence to contracts but only to require each party to choose between performing in accordance with the contract and compensating the other party for an injury resulting from a failure to perform. This view contains an important economic insight. In many cases it is uneconomical to induce the completion of a contract after it has been breached. I agree to purchase 100,000 widgets custom-ground for use as components in a machine that I manufacture. After I have taken delivery of 10,000, the market for my machine collapses. I promptly notify my supplier that I am terminating the contract, and admit that my termination is a breach of the contract. When notified of the termination he has not yet begun the custom grinding of the other 90,000 widgets, but he informs me that he intends to complete his performance under the contract and bill me accordingly. The custom-ground widgets have no use other than in my machine, and a negligible scrap value. Plainly, to grant the supplier any remedy that induced him to complete the contract after the breach would result in a waste of resources. The law is alert to this danger and, under the doctrine of mitigation of damages, would refuse to permit the supplier to recover any costs he incurred in continuing production after my notice of termination.

Let us change the facts. I need 100,000 custom-ground widgets for my machine but the supplier, after producing 50,000, is forced to suspend production because of a mechanical failure. Other suppliers are in a position to supply the remaining widgets that I need, but I insist that the original supplier complete his performance of the contract. If the law compels completion, the supplier will probably have to make arrangements with other widget producers to complete his contract with me. But it may be more costly for him to procure an alternative supplier than for me to do so directly; indeed, were it cheaper for him than for me, he would do it voluntarily in order to minimize his liability for breach of contract. To compel completion of the contract would again result in a waste of resources and again the law does not compel completion but remits the victim to a simple damages remedy.

The problem exposed in the foregoing example is a quite general one. It results from the fact, remarked earlier, that contract remedies are frequently invoked in cases where there is no presumption that an exchange pursuant to the (defective) contract would in fact increase value (for example, cases of defective communication). Here we clearly do not want a remedy that will induce the party made liable to complete the exchange.

The objective of giving the party to a contract an incentive to fulfil his promise unless the result would be an inefficient use of resources (the production of the unwanted widgets in the first example, the roundabout procurement of a substitute supplier in the second) can usually be achieved by allowing the victim of a breach to recover his expected profit on the transaction. If the supplier in the first example receives his expected profit from completing the 10,000 widgets, he will have no incentive to produce the remaining 90,000. We do not want him to produce them; no one wants them. In the second example, if I receive my expected profit from dealing with the original supplier, I become indifferent to whether he completes his performance.

In these examples the breach was in a sense involuntary. It was committed only to avert a larger loss. The breaching party would have been happier had there been no occasion to commit a breach. But in some cases a party would be tempted to breach the contract simply because his profit from breach would exceed his expected profit from completion of the contract. If his profit from breach would also exceed the expected profit to the other party from completion of the contract, and if damages are limited to loss of expected profit, there will be an incentive to commit a breach. There should be. The opportunity cost of completion to the breaching party is the profit that he would make from a breach, and if it is greater than his profit from completion, then completion will involve a loss to him. If that loss is greater than the gain to the other party from completion, breach would be value-maximizing and should be encouraged. And because the victim of the breach is made whole for his loss, he is indifferent; hence encouraging breaches in these circumstances will not deter people from entering into contracts in the future.

An arithmetical illustration may be helpful here. I sign a contract to deliver 100,000 custom-ground widgets at $.10 apiece to A, for use in his boiler factory. After I have delivered 10,000, B comes to me, explains that he desperately needs 25,000 custom-ground widgets at once since otherwise he will be forced to close his pianola factory at great cost, and offers me $.15 apiece for 25,000 widgets. I sell him the widgets and as a result do not complete timely delivery to A, who sustains $1000 in lost profits from my breach. Having obtained an additional profit of $1250 on the sale to B, I am better off even after reimbursing A for his loss. Society is also better off. Since B was willing to pay me $.15 per widget, it must mean that each widget was worth at least $.15 to him. But it was worth only $.14 to A—the $.10 that he paid plus his expected profit of $.04 ($1000 divided by 25,000). Thus the breach resulted in a transfer of the 25,000 widgets from a less to a more valuable use. To be sure, had I refused to sell to B, he could have gone to A and negotiated an assignment of part of A's contract with me to him. But this would have introduced an additional step and so imposed additional transaction costs.

Thus far the emphasis has been on the economic importance of not awarding damages in excess of the lost expectation. It is equally important, however, not to award less than the expectation loss. Suppose A contracts to sell B for $100,000 a machine that is worth $110,000 to B, ie, that would yield him a profit of $10,000. Before delivery C comes to A and offers him $109,000 for the machine promised B. A would be tempted to breach were he not liable to B for B's loss of expected profit. Given that measure of damages, C will not be able to induce a breach of A's contract with B unless he offers B more than $110,000, thereby indicating that the machine really is worth more to him than to B. The expectation rule thus assures that the machine ends up where it is most valuable.

One superficially attractive alternative to measuring contract damages by loss of expectation (ie, lost profits) is to measure them by the reliance loss, especially in cases where liability is imposed not to induce performance but to penalize careless behavior. And even in the case where the breach is deliberate, it is arguable that expectation damages may overcompensate the victim of the breach. Suppose I sign a contract to deliver 10,000 widgets in six months, and the day after the contract is signed I default. The buyer's reliance loss—the sum of the costs he has irretrievably incurred as a result of the contract—is, let us say, zero, but his lost profit $1,000. Why should he be allowed to reap a windfall gain by the use of a measure of damages that does not correspond to any actual social cost?

One answer has already been given: the lost-profit measure is necessary to assure that the only breaches made are those that promote efficiency. But there is another answer: that on average, though not in every case, the lost-profit method will give a better approximation than the reliance measure to the actual social costs of contract breach. In a long-run competitive equilibrium, the total revenues of the sellers in a market are just equal to their total costs; there are no 'profits' in the economic sense. What law and accounting call profits are frequently not profits in that sense at all, but rather reimbursement of the costs of capital, of entrepreneurial effort, and of other inputs. These items of cost are excluded by the reliance measure of damages, which will therefore tend to understate the true social costs of breach.

(b) Remoteness of damage

Hadley v Baxendale (1854) 9 Exch 341 (above, p 464)

NOTES

1. What is the usual consequence of a few days' delay in delivering a broken millshaft?
2. A good example of the way in which the remoteness rule operates is *Victoria Laundry (Windsor) Ltd v Newman Industries Ltd* [1949] 2 KB 528. The defendants, an engineering company, agreed to sell a boiler to the plaintiffs, who ran a laundry, not knowing that the plaintiffs intended to use the boiler to fulfil some highly lucrative government dyeing contracts. The boiler was damaged while it was being dismantled for transport to the plaintiffs, and it was delivered late. The plaintiffs claimed for loss of profit on the dyeing contracts. Streatfield J refused the plaintiffs any damages for loss of profits. In the Court of Appeal Asquith LJ pointed out that the degree of knowledge about what losses are likely will vary from one context to another:

A carrier commonly knows less than a seller about the purposes for which the buyer or consignee needs the goods or about 'other special circumstances' which may cause exceptional loss if due delivery is withheld.

Here the defendants had not been told about the dyeing contracts and could not be expected to know about them; but it must have been obvious that in all probability the buyers wanted the boiler for immediate use in their laundering business. Asquith LJ said:

. . . [I]n cases of breach of contract the aggrieved party is only entitled to recover such part of the loss actually resulting as was at the time of the contract reasonably foreseeable as liable to result from the breach. What was at that time reasonably foreseeable depends on the knowledge then possessed by the parties, or, at all events, by the party who later commits the breach. For this purpose, knowledge 'possessed' is of two kinds—one imputed, the other actual. Everyone, as a reasonable person, is taken to know the 'ordinary course of things' and consequently what loss is liable to result from a breach of that ordinary course. This is the subject-matter of the 'first rule' in *Hadley v Baxendale* but to this knowledge, which a contract-breaker is assumed to possess whether he actually possesses it or not, there may have to be added in a particular case knowledge which he actually possesses of special circumstances outside the 'ordinary course of things' of such a kind that a breach in those special circumstances would be liable to cause more loss. Such a case attracts the operation of the 'second rule' so as to make additional loss also recoverable. In order to make the contract-breaker liable under either rule it is not necessary that he should actually have asked himself what loss is liable to result from a breach. As has often been pointed out, parties at the time of contracting contemplate, not the breach of the contract, but its performance. It suffices that, if he had considered the question, he would as a reasonable man have concluded that the loss in question was liable to result: see certain observations of Lord du Parcq in *Monarch Steamship Co, Ltd v A/B Karlshamns Oljefabriker*. Nor, finally, to make a particular loss recoverable, need it be proved that on a given state of knowledge the defendant could, as a reasonable man, foresee that a breach must necessarily result in that loss. It is enough if he could foresee it was likely so to result. It is enough, to borrow from the language of Lord du Parcq in the same case, if the loss (or some factor without which it would not have occurred) is a 'serious possibility' or a 'real danger'. For short, we have used the word 'liable' to result. Possibly the colloquialism 'on the cards' indicates the shade of meaning with some approach to accuracy.

Thus the defendants were not liable for loss of the dyeing contracts but should be liable for the amount of profit the plaintiffs would have made using the boiler for normal laundering. The fact that they actually would not have used it for this purpose but for the more profitable dyeing work did not prevent them recovering the normal profits. (See also *Cory v Thames Ironworks Co* (1868) LR 3 QB 181.)

'Economic Analysis of Law' by Posner (2nd edn), pp 94–95

Foreseeability of damage

The economic rationale of contract damages is nicely illustrated by the famous rule of *Hadley v Baxendale* that the breaching party is liable only for the foreseeable consequences of the breach. Consider the following variant of the facts in that case. A commercial photographer purchases a roll of film to take pictures of the Himalayas for a magazine. The cost of development of the film by the manufacturer is included in the purchasing price. The photographer incurs heavy expenses (including the hire of an airplane) to complete the assignment. He mails the film to the manufacturer but it is mislaid in the developing room and never found.

Compare the incentive effects of allowing the photographer to recover his full losses and of limiting him to recovery of the price of the film. The first alternative creates little incentive to avoid similar losses in the future. The photographer will take no precautions, being indifferent as to successful completion of his assignment or receipt of adequate compensation for its failure. The manufacturer of the film will probably not take additional precautions either; the aggregate costs of such freak losses are probably too small to justify substantial efforts to prevent them. The second alternative, in contrast, should induce the photographer to take precautions that turn out to be at once inexpensive and effective: using two rolls of film or requesting special handling when he sends in the roll to be developed.

The general principle illustrated by this example is that where a risk of loss is known to only one party to the contract, the other party is not liable for the loss if it occurs. This principle induces the party with knowledge of the risk either to take any appropriate precautions himself or, if he believes that the other party might be the more efficient loss avoider, to disclose the risk to that party and pay him to assume it. In this way incentives are generated to deal with the risk in the most efficient fashion.

This principle is not applied, however, where what is unforeseeable is the other party's lost profit. Suppose I offer you $40,000 for a house that has a market value of $50,000, you accept the offer but later breach, and I sue you for $10,000, my lost profit. You would not be permitted to defend on the ground that you had no reason to think that the transaction was such a profitable one for me. Any other rule would make it difficult for a good bargainer to collect damages unless he made disclosures that would reduce the advantage of being a good bargainer—disclosures that would prevent the buyer from appropriating the gains from his efforts to identify a resource that was seriously undervalued in its present use. The *Hadley* principle is thus confined, and rightly so, to 'consequential' damages, ie damages unrelated to the profit from the contract.

The one case where application of the *Hadley* principle could produce an inefficient result in a setting of consequential damages is that of monopoly. If the film manufacturer in our variant of the facts of *Hadley* had a monopoly of film, he could use the information the photographer would have to disclose in order to shift the risk of loss to him to discriminate against the photographer in the price charged for the film more effectively than he otherwise could; the information would indicate that the photographer's demand for the film was far less elastic than that of the amateur photographers who comprise the great bulk of the manufacturer's customers (why would it indicate this?) This use of the information would discourage risk shifting in some cases where the manufacturer was in fact the superior risk bearer.

Thus the defendant is liable for unusual losses only if it knew of them or was warned of them by the plaintiff when the contract was made. At one time it was said that the special circumstances 'must have been brought home . . . in such circumstances that the defendant impliedly undertook to bear any special loss referable to a breach': *British Columbia and Vancouver's Island Spar, Lumber and Sawmill Co Ltd v Nettleship* (1868) LR 3 CP 499 at 509. This has been rejected by the Court of Appeal: *GKN Centrax Gears Ltd v Matbro Ltd* [1976] 2 Lloyd's Rep 555. Should a mere notice to the defendant be sufficient to increase its liability?

'Hadley v Baxendale: a Study in the Industrialization of the Law' by Danzig (1975) 4 JLS 249, 279–283

Whether viewed as a simple 'notice' or a more exacting 'contemplation' requirement, however, this portion of the rule in *Hadley v Baxendale* runs counter to the tide of an industrializing economy. It was already somewhat out of date when expressed in the Exchequer opinion. For in *Hadley v Baxendale* the court spoke as though entrepreneurs were universally flexible enough and enterprises small enough for individuals to be able to serve 'notice' over the counter of specialized needs calling for unusual arrangements. But in mass-transaction situations a seller cannot plausibly engage in an individualized 'contemplation' of the consequencs of breach and a subsequent tailoring of a transaction. In the course of his conversion of a family business into a modern industrial enterprise, Baxendale made Pickfords itself into an operation where the contemplation branch of the rule in *Hadley v Baxendale* was no longer viable. Even in the 1820's the Pickfords' operations were 'highly complex'.

> The bulk of Pickfords' traffic was of an intermediate kind, which came on to the main north-south route from east and west. This was directed to certain staging points, sorted, and thence dispatched to its destination. Cross-traffic of this kind was tricky to organize, and required very clear methods of procedure. According to Joseph Baxendale, then a senior partner in Pickfords, a cargo of 15 tons might involve up to 150 consignees and thus the same number of invoices.

By 1865 the business had grown to the point where it left that contemporary chronicler of industry, Henry Mayhew, without words to 'convey . . . to the reader's mind a fair impression of the gigantic scale upon which the operations of the firm are conducted'. This was 'an enormous mercantile establishment with a huge staff of busy clerks, messengers and porters. . . . It is divided into innumerable departments, the employees in each of which find it as much as they can comfortably do to master its details without troubling themselves about any other'.

A century later most enterprises fragment and standardize operations in just this way. This development—and the law's recognition of it—makes it self-evidently impossible to serve legally cognizable notice on, for example, an airline that a scheduled flight is of special importance or on the telephone company that uninterrupted service is particularly vital at a particular point in a firm's business cycle. . . .

The inadequacies of the rule are masked by still more fundamental phenomena which render the case of very limited relevance to the present economy. At least in mass-transaction situations, the modern enterprise manager is not concerned with his corporation's liability as it arises from a particular transaction, but rather with liability when averaged over the full run of transactions of a given type. In the mass-production situation the run of these transactions will average his consequential-damages pay-out in a way far more predictable than a jury's guesses about the pay-out. In other words, for this type of entrepreneur—a type already emerging at the time of *Hadley v Baxendale*, and far more prevalent today—there is no need for the law to provide protection from the aberrational customer; his own market and self-insurance capacities are great enough to do the job. . . .

It is only for small-volume sellers, those who deal in custom-made transactions or with a small number of customers—ie, for those transactions most like early nineteenth century commerce—that the rule invented in *Hadley v Baxendale* is arguably of commercial significance. . . .

Even within this realm, however, it can be doubted that the rule much effects economic life. It is doubtful that it affects information flow at the time of the making of the contract, because by hypothesis the parties are not very accurate or self-conscious planners. A more sophisticated rationale for the rule in this context might focus on its effect on a seller not at the time of his entering a contract, but rather at the time of his deciding whether to voluntarily breach or to risk breaching. Only at that time and only where an option exists as to whether to breach or to increase the risk of breach, does it seem likely that a seller who has not opted for a limitation of liability clause will consult a lawyer, and consequently be affected by the legal rules. It can be argued that the societal gain from the rule in *Hadley v Baxendale* stems from its improvement of the seller's calculus about whether to breach in this situation.

To put this observation in context, consider the position of a truck owner, A, who has a contract to sell his truck to B, and assume that B would suffer a 'normal' net loss of $200 if the truck were not made available as scheduled. If C arrives on the scene and bids to preempt the truck for an urgent need, A can estimate the damages he will 'normally' owe B. He will presumably sell to C only if the new sale price will exceed the old sale price plus $200 in damages. If C is willing to buy for such a high price, it is to everybody's advantage to let him do so. C benefits because he values the truck more highly than he values the money he is paying for it; B benefits because he receives his expected profits by way of damages; A benefits because he makes more money, even after paying damages than he would have made had the truck not been sold to C. Society benefits because one party, C, has gained while no other party has lost. If B were in an abnormal situation and so expected to suffer greater damages than $200, the rule of *Hadley v Baxendale* would coerce him into signalling these higher damages, so that the proper damage calculation and subsequent truck allocation would be made. Thus, in theory, by facilitating an accurate calculus of breach, the rule optimizes resource allocation.

But if this is its modern rationale, it is apparent that considerable thought ought to be given to restructuring the rule. Resting the seller's liability on whether the type of damages incurred was 'normal' (or, in the UCC's words, whether it was a type of damage of which the seller had 'reason to know'), seems undesirable because it lets an all-or-nothing decision ride on an indicator about which many sellers cannot, at the time of breach, speculate with confidence. Further, if the recoverability of a type of damages is established, a seller may often have no reasonable basis for determining the magnitude of the damages involved. On this dimension—obviously critical to any calculus of the care warranted to avoid breach—the rule has nothing to say. Lastly, if the rule were truly finely geared to optimizing the allocation of resources, it would place its emphasis on the damage known to the seller at the time of breach, rather than at the time of contract, at least where the breach was voluntary. When the rule was framed stress had to be placed on communication at the time of the making of a contract because that was the only occasion on which information exchange could be coerced without fear of imposing enormous transaction costs. Now the telephone and vastly improved telegraphic facilities make it possible to mandate discussion at the time of breach. Would it be desirable to move the focus of the rule to this point? On this question, some empirical evidence would be desirable. Do the average transaction costs associated with information exchange at the time of the contract multiplied by the number of instances in which such information is exchanged exceed the average transaction costs of information exchange at the time of voluntary breach multiplied by the number of occasions when breach is seriously considered? If so, there is much to be said for a revision in the rule.

NOTES

1. In *Kemp v Intasun Holidays Ltd* [1987] 2 FTLR 234, a case involving a package holiday contract, it was said that a merely casual remark about the plaintiff's medical condition should not fix the tour operator with additional liability. Shouldn't a deliberate notice suffice? Isn't it up to the company to create procedures by which special needs are taken into account—or bear the risk of not doing so?

2. Danzig's article is a fascinating historical study of *Hadley v Baxendale* and deserves reading in full.

3. Furmston rings up his local taxi driver and books a taxi to drive him to the airport at 7 am the next day. He tells the driver that it is most important, as he is flying to New York to sign a multi-million dollar contract. The taxi driver oversleeps, Furmston misses his flight and loses his deal. Is the driver liable? Would it, or should it, make any difference if the fare is fixed by law?

In *Koufos v C Czarnikow Ltd, The Heron II* [1969] 1 AC 350 the chartered ship deviated, with the result that it reached its destination nine days later than it would otherwise have done, and the market value of the cargo of sugar had fallen in the meantime. The House of Lords held that the shipowner was liable for this loss, which arose in the usual course of things; but stressed that, in an action for breach of contract, the mere fact that a loss is foreseeable is insufficient. Lord Reid said of the decision in *Hadley v Baxendale* (pp 385–386):

I am satisfed that the court did not intend that every type of damage which was reasonably foreseeable by the parties when the contract was made should either be considered as arising naturally, ie, in the usual course of things, or be supposed to have been in the contemplation of the parties. Indeed the decision makes it clear that a type of damage which was plainly foreseeable as a real possibility but which would only occur in a small minority of cases cannot be regarded as arising in the usual course of things or be supposed to have been in the contemplation of the parties: the parties are not supposed to contemplate as grounds for the recovery of damage any types of loss or damage which, on the knowledge available to the defendant, would appear to him as only likely to occur in a small minority of cases.

In cases like *Hadley v Baxendale* or the present case it is not enough that in fact the plaintiff's loss was directly caused by the defendant's breach of contract. It clearly was so caused in both. The crucial question is whether, on the information available to the defendant when the contract was made, he should, or the reasonable man in his position would, have realised that such loss was sufficiently likely to result from the breach of contract to make it proper to hold that the loss flowed naturally from the breach or that loss of that kind should have been within his contemplation.

The modern rule in tort is quite different and it imposes a much wider liability. The defendant will be liable for any type of damage which is reasonably foreseeable as liable to happen even in the most unusual case, unless the risk is so small that a reasonable man would in the whole circumstances feel justified in neglecting it; and there is good reason for the difference. In contract, if one party wishes to protect himself against a risk which to the other party would appear unusual, he can direct the other party's attention to it before the contract is made, and I need not stop to consider in what circumstances the other party will then be held to have accepted responsibility in that event. In tort, however, there is no opportunity for the injured party to protect himself in that way, and the tortfeasor cannot reasonably complain if he has to pay for some very unusual but nevertheless foreseeable damage which results from his wrongdoing. I have no doubt that today a tortfeasor would be held liable for a type of damage as unlikely as was the stoppage of Hadley's Mill for lack of a crank shaft: to any one with the knowledge the carrier had that may have seemed unlikely, but the chance of it happening would have been seen to be far from negligible. But it does not at all follow that *Hadley v Baxendale* would today be differently decided.

If Asquith LJ in the *Victoria Laundry* case intended to go further than this, he was wrong; in particular, the use of the expression 'on the cards' was to be deprecated.

The House of Lords were insistent that for a loss to be recoverable in contract, it must be more probable than is required in tort. Does Posner's analysis suggest why this might be so?

In *H Parsons (Livestock) Ltd v Uttley Ingham & Co Ltd* [1978] QB 791, the plaintiffs, who were pig farmers, bought a food storage hopper from the defendant manufacturers. When they were erecting the hopper, the defendants omitted to unseal a ventilator on top of the hopper; the ventilator could not be seen from the ground. The pignuts stored in the hopper became mouldy because of the lack of ventilation, and many of the pigs to which the nuts were fed died of a rare intestinal infection, E coli. The plaintiffs claimed for the loss of the pigs and lost sales. Swanwick J held that at the time of the contract neither the farmers nor the manufacturers would reasonably have contemplated as a serious possibility that feeding mouldy pignuts to the pigs would cause this illness in the pigs; but he held that this was irrelevant: the defendants had failed to supply a hopper that was reasonably fit for the purpose, some illness in the pigs was foreseeable and the defendants were liable for all the losses directly caused. The Court of Appeal upheld this decision, but on differing grounds. Lord Denning MR held that a distinction should be drawn in contract, as in tort, between physical damage and mere loss of profit. Loss of profit should be subject to *Hadley v Baxendale*; but physical damage should be recoverable even if it were only foreseeable as a slight possibility, and so the defendants should be liable. Scarman LJ, with whose reasoning Orr LJ agreed, said that the cases did not support this distinction. He considered that the difference between contract and tort was 'semantic, not substantial', but that anyway under either rule it was not necessary that the degree of injury be contemplated. It was sufficient that some physical harm to the pigs would have been anticipated.

'The Contract-Tort Boundary and the Economics of Insurance' by Bishop (1983) 12 JLS 241, 254–256, 259

[Bishop points out that the remoteness rule in tort prevents a negligent defendant from liability for losses which are 'events of very low probability'. He says that there is no clear economic rationale for the rule, but that there may be other justifications, such as that we simply think it unjust to a tortfeasor to make him pay for losses he could not have foreseen. He goes on to discuss the remoteness rule in contract]:

Lord Reid also used the expression 'not unlikely' as a test. Lord Reid gave as reason for the difference between tort and contract the fact that 'in contract, if one party wishes to protect himself against a risk which to the other party would appear unusual, he can direct the other party's attention to it before the contract is made. . . . But in tort there is no opportunity for the injured party to protect himself in that way. . . .' Reid's view is widely, and correctly, regarded as the normal explanation for the difference. It has, however, ramifications so far not generally appreciated, which are pursued here.

The line of cases *Hadley v Baxendale, British Columbia Saw-Mill Co v Nettleship, Victoria Laundry*, and *Heron II* concerns a matter that is usually irrelevant in tort (at least as between strangers): the efficient transfer of information. The law of contract denies recovery to a plaintiff when four conditions are met:

1. The plaintiff possessed information unknown to the defendant.
2. The defendant, had he possessed that information, might have altered his behavior so as to make his breach less likely to occur.
3. The plaintiff could have conveyed the information to the defendant cheaply. (This condition is not mentioned in the cases, though it is clear that it is assumed by the courts to be fulfilled. Of course it is normally *not* fulfilled in tort.)
4. The plaintiff did not do so.

A good example of these rules in operation is the *Victoria Laundry* case. The defendant manufacturer of boilers contracted to supply them to the plaintiff laundry. In breach of contract the manufacturer delivered late. The laundry sought to recover damages for profit lost on an unusually lucrative dyeing contract. The court limited the plaintiff to such damages as would be normal in a case of this kind.

Less clear is *Heron II*. There the plaintiff charterer under a charterparty to transport sugar to a well known sugar market complained that the shipowner had in breach of contract delayed arrival in port by ten days. In the interim the price of sugar fell. The court held the shipowner liable for the loss. Lord Reid thought that the circumstances (that the charterer might well wish to sell on arrival) ought to have been so clear to the shipowner that the latter ought to have realized the risk without explicit warning. This case is near the line, with everything depending on the circumstances the parties were in. If the circumstances were clear, then to require an explicit warning of the obvious would be wasteful of resources (here labor and time).

I take no position on the doctrinal controversy about whether affirmative assumption of risk or merely notice of risk is needed to found liability. I doubt that it really matters very much. Sometimes merely receiving notice, particularly notice of strikingly unusual risks, will be tantamount to affirmative assumption and sometimes not. It is unlikely that a uniform general rule for such cases would be appropriate. It seems that courts treat this, sensibly I think, as depending on the facts of each case.

The central point here is that where the four conditions above are met, the value of the information to the defendant is greater than the cost to the plaintiff of conveying that information to him. To encourage such efficient transfers of information is the purpose of the contract remoteness rule of *Hadley v Baxendale*.

Note that the first limb of the rule in *Hadley* fits easily into this scheme. The normal case is one in which no information needs to be conveyed, since the defendant, knowing normal business conditions, already knows as much as the plaintiff. To require the plaintiff to inform the defendant of normal conditions would be inefficient, because the cost of transactions here, though low, is not zero. Any expenditure on information transfer is only wasted.

It might seem that there is a casus omissus. Consider the case where the consequence of the defendant's breach normally would be a certain loss but in fact is less. Then it seems the plaintiff has no incentive to transfer the information, even though the information would be valuable in that it would allow the defendant to spend less in essential reliance. Such transfer would be efficient: the marginal social value of expenditure on breach avoidance is lower and so less should be spent. But in fact there is no casus omissus. The plaintiff has sufficient incentive to inform the defendant, wholly without legal compulsion, if such information transfer is in fact cost justified. The reason is that the plaintiff can obtain a lower price for the defendant's performance if he informs the defendant of the limited damages for breach. The price is lower because such a contract is cheaper to perform than is a 'normal' contract. This incentive will induce parties to act efficiently in the case of unusually inexpensive breach as well as in the case of unusually expensive breach.

It should be clear that the function of remoteness in the *Hadley v Baxendale* line of contract cases is very different from the function of remoteness in tort. The tort measure of foreseeability seeks to define as too remote an event that no one would anticipate at all—one to which the ordinary observer would assign near zero probability. The contract measure of foreseeability will include as too remote many consequences which are merely unusual—ones that have quite substantial probabilities of occurring. The defining characteristics of an event that is too remote for the purposes of contract are those set out in conditions 1–4 above. These conditions have nothing to do with unforeseeability in the sense of very low probability. If this analysis is correct, it follows that Lord Scarman was wrong to suggest, as he did in *Parsons v Uttley*, that the differences between contract and tort remoteness are semantic only.

. . . [T]he desirability of the *Hadley* (contract) standard as opposed to the *Wagon Mound* (tort) standard for remoteness does *not* depend on any distinction between financial as against physical loss. Rather it depends on information asymmetry. That asymmetry was present in *Hadley*, *Victoria Laundry*, and *Heron II* and can be present in some physical loss cases. It happened not to be present in *Parsons v Uttley*. [NB. Swanwick J's finding that neither would reasonably have contemplated this illness.] We should not allow its absence to mislead us into a doctrine that allows potential victims to refrain from disclosing important information to potential injurers in cases where they have such information and could easily provide it.

NOTE

A further problem over *Parsons v Uttley* is this: if it was foreseeable that some harm might come to the pigs through feeding them mouldy nuts, why were the farmers not contributorily negligent, or the cause of their own injury? See further below, p 485.

(c) Mitigation

(i) Losses that could have been avoided by reasonable steps

We have already looked at the basic idea of mitigation (above, p 463). To quote Viscount Haldane in the *British Westinghouse* case again:

> I think that there are certain broad principles, which are quite well settled. The first is that, as far as possible, he who has proved a breach of a bargain to supply what he contracted to get is to be placed, as far as money can do it, in as good a situation as if the contract had been performed. The fundamental basis is thus compensation for pecuniary loss naturally flowing from the breach; but this first principle is qualified by a second, which imposes on a plaintiff the duty of taking all reasonable steps to mitigate the loss consequent on the breach, and debars him from claiming in respect of any part of the damage which is due to his neglect to take such steps. In the words of James LJ in *Dunkirk Colliery Co v Lever*:
>
> > 'The person who has broken the contract is not to be exposed to additional cost by reason of the plaintiffs not having done what they ought to have done as reasonable men, and the plaintiffs not being under any obligation to do anything otherwise than in the ordinary course of business.'

As James LJ indicates, this second principle does not impose on the plaintiff an obligation to take any step which a reasonable and prudent man would not ordinarily take in the course of his business.

Thus if a seller fails to deliver, the buyer is normally expected to repurchase in the market in order to fill its commitments, and it will not recover any loss resulting from its failure to do so, such as loss of profit on a subsale. Thus in practical terms the innocent party is expected to act positively to reduce its own loss. But it need only do what is reasonable. For instance, it need not 'go hunting the globe' for snake skins which are not readily available (*Lesters Leather and Skin Co Ltd v Home and Overseas Brokers Ltd* (1948) 64 TLR 569).

Suppose that the victim takes what at the time seems a reasonable step to reduce his loss, but it turns out that some other method of mitigating would have been better? In *Gebruder Metelmann GmbH & Co v NBR (London) Ltd* [1984] 1 Lloyd's Rep 614 this occurred, and the Court of Appeal allowed the victim's claim for the expenses of mitigating. Browne-Wilkinson LJ said (at p 634):

> Metelmann is entitled to be compensated for the additional damage flowing from the attempt to mitigate . . . If there are two methods of mitigating damage, both of which are practicable and reasonable in the circumstances known to the innocent party at the time the mitigating action is required, it is not possible to say that the innocent party acted unreasonably in selecting one of these methods just because, in the light of later events, it turns out that the loss would have been less had the other method been adopted.

The mitigation rule seems to have a clear economic rationale of encouraging the parties to avoid unnecessary waste. (For a full analysis see Goetz and Scott (1983) 96 Virginia LR 967.) We shall see, however, that sometimes this rationale seems to be lost sight of.

Payzu Ltd v Saunders [1918–19] All ER Rep 219, Court of Appeal

The defendant had agreed to sell the plaintiffs a quantity of silk on terms that permitted payment a month after delivery, but after some delays in payment she unjustifiably refused to make any further deliveries except for cash. The plaintiffs accepted this repudiation of the contract. The market price had risen considerably, and the plaintiffs were in fact unable to obtain the silk elsewhere. They claimed the difference between the contract price and the market price on the day they accepted the defendant's repudiation. McCardie J held that they had acted unreasonably in refusing the defendant's offer, and they could not recover more than they would have lost if they had accepted this offer.

Bankes LJ. . . . It is plain that the question what is reasonable for a person to do in mitigation of his damages cannot be a question of law, but must be one of fact in the circumstances of each particular case. There may be cases where as matter of fact it would be unreasonable to expect a plaintiff in view of the treatment he has received from the defendant to consider an offer made. If he had been rendering personal services and had been dismissed after being accused in presence of others of being a thief, and if after that his employer had offered to take him back into his service, most persons would think he would be justified in refusing the offer, and that it would be unreasonable to ask him in this way to mitigate the damages in an action of wrongful dismissal. But that is not to state a principle of law, but a conclusion of fact to be arrived at on a consideration of all the circumstances of the case. Counsel for the plaintiffs complained that the defendant had treated his clients so badly that it would be unreasonable to expect them to listen to any proposition that she might make. I do not agree. In my opinion each party to the contract was ready to accuse the other of conduct unworthy of a high commercial reputation, and there was nothing to justify the plaintiffs in refusing to consider the defendant's offer. I think the learned judge came to a right conclusion on the facts, and that the appeal must be dismissed.

[Scrutton LJ and Eve J concurred.]

NOTE

It is not clear whether the plaintiffs in this case were claiming the difference between the contract and market prices because, if the silk had been delivered, they would have been able to resell it at a profit; or whether they were claiming it as a surrogate for other forms of consequential loss (for instance, they had to break a contract to a sub-buyer when they could not obtain the silk, but they did not claim this as an item of loss because the sub-sale was not contemplated by the parties). But whatever the real loss was, did the plaintiffs' action make the defendant any worse off? Suppose the contract price was £x, and by the date the defendant's repudiation was accepted the market price was £x+y. If the plaintiffs had taken the silk offered for cash, the defendant would have received £x. If they bought in the market for £x+y, and were allowed to recover £y from the defendant, wouldn't the latter's financial position be just the same, as she could sell the original silk in the market at £x+y? So why refuse the plaintiffs' claim? See Bridge (1989) 105 LQR 398.

A question which is closely connected to mitigation is the date by which damages should be assessed.

In a case where a seller of goods has failed to deliver, and there is an available market, the prima facie measure laid down in the Sale of Goods Act 1979, s 51(3) (above, p 464) is the difference between the contract price and the market price at the date for delivery. When would it be appropriate to assess the damages by some later date? In *Johnson v Agnew* [1979] 1 All ER 883 at 896, Lord Wilberforce said:

The general principle for the assessment of damages is compensatory, ie that the innocent party is to be placed, so far as money can do so, in the same position as if the contract had been performed. Where the contract is one of sale, this principle normally leads to assessment of damages as at the date of the breach, a principle recognised and embodied in s 51 of the Sale of Goods Act 1893. But this is not an absolute rule; if to follow it would give rise to injustice, the court has power to fix such other date as may be appropriate in the circumstances.

In cases where a breach of a contract for sale has occurred, and the innocent party reasonably continues to try to have the contract completed, it would to me appear more logical and just rather than tie him to the date of the original breach, to assess damages as at the date when (otherwise than by his default) the contract is lost. Support for this approach is to be found in the cases.

At what date should damages be assessed in a case of anticipatory repudiation? See the next case.

Melachrino v Nickoll & Knight [1920] 1 KB 693

The sellers repudiated the contract, and the buyers accepted the repudiation, on 14 December, when the market price was above the contract price. The buyers did not buy against the sellers. By the time stipulated for delivery the market price had fallen below the contract price. The buyers claimed damages based on the difference between the contract and market prices on 14 December.

Bailhache J. Section 51 [see above, p 464] does not in terms deal with an anticipatory breach, and in the case of a breach by effluxion of time it is clear that it makes no difference to the measure of damages whether a buyer goes into the market or is content to take the difference in price without troubling to buy against the defaulting seller. The question to be decided is whether the same rule applies in the case of an anticipatory breach.

An anticipatory breach occurs when the seller refuses to deliver before the contractual time for delivery has arrived and the buyer accepts his refusal as a breach of contract.

In that case the following rules are well established, subject of course to any express provisions to the contrary in any particular contract.

Immediately upon the anticipatory breach the buyer may bring his action whether he buys against the seller or not.

It is the duty of the buyer to go into the market and buy against the defaulting seller if a reasonable opportunity offers. This is expressed by the phrase 'It is the buyer's duty to mitigate damages'. In that event the damages are assessed with reference to the market price on the date of the repurchase. If the buyer does not perform his duty in this respect the seller is none the less entitled to have damages assessed as at the date when a fresh contract might and ought to have been made.

As a corollary to this rule the buyer may if he pleases go into the market and buy against the seller: as he is bound to do so to mitigate damages, so he is entitled to do so to cover himself against his commitments or to secure the goods. In that case again the damages are assessed with reference to the market price at the date of the repurchase.

It is also settled law that when default is made by the seller by refusal to deliver within the contract time the buyer is under no duty to accept the repudiation and buy against him but may claim the difference between the contract price and the market price at the date when under the contract the goods should have been delivered.

It looks therefore at first sight as though the date at which the difference between the contract price and the market price ought to be taken for the assessment of damages when the buyer does not buy against the seller should follow by analogy the rule adopted where the buyer goes into the market and buys, or where the breach is failure to deliver at the due date and should be at or about the date when the buyer intimates his acceptance of the repudiation though he does not actually go into the market against the seller. If so, in this case, the date would be about December 14, when the buyer claimed arbitration and so the arbitrators have found.

As against this line of reasoning it must be remembered that the object of damages is to place a person whose contract is broken in as nearly as possible the same position as if it had been performed. This result is secured by measuring damages either at the date of the repurchase, in the case of repurchase on an anticipatory breach, or at the date when the goods ought to have been delivered when there is no anticipatory breach whether there is a repurchase or not. In these cases the buyer gets a new contract as nearly as may be like the broken contract and the defaulting seller pays the extra expense incurred by the buyer in restoring his position.

Where however there is an anticipatory breach but no buying against the defaulting seller, and the price falls below the contract price between the date of the anticipatory breach and the date when the goods ought to have been delivered, the adoption of the date of the anticipatory breach as the date at which the market price ought to be taken would put the buyer in a better position than if his contract had been duly performed. He would if that date were adopted be given a profit and retain his money wherewith to buy the goods if so minded on the fall of the market. It would be in effect, to use a homely phrase, to allow him to eat his cake and have it. Perhaps it is better to avoid figures of speech however picturesque and to say, to make a profit from the anticipatory breach while the contract if duly performed would have shown a loss—a position which is I think irreconcilable with the principles upon which damages are awarded as between buyer and seller.

In my opinion the true rule is that where there is an anticipatory breach by a seller to deliver goods for which there is a market at a fixed date the buyer without buying against the seller may bring his action at once, but that if he does so his damages must be assessed with reference to the market price of the goods at the time when they ought to have been delivered under the contract. If the action comes to trial before the contractual date for delivery has arrived the Court must arrive at that price as best it can.

To this rule there is one exception for the benefit of the defaulting seller—namely, that if he can show that the buyer acted unreasonably in not buying against him the date to be taken is the date at which the buyer ought to have gone into the market to mitigate damages.

I have discussed the position on principle apart from authority because, in my limited experience, I do not remember a case precisely like this.

The result in this case is that the damages are nominal.

NOTE

The rule that there is no duty on the victim of an anticipatory repudiation to mitigate his damages if he does not wish to accept the repudiation was applied in *Shindler v Northern Raincoat Co Ltd* [1960] 2 All ER 239. If the victim were under a duty to mitigate before the date for performance, his choice whether to accept or ignore the repudiation would be fettered, which the courts have tried to avoid. But see further below, p 544.

(ii) Contributory negligence

Mitigation refers to actions which the victim took or might have taken *after* the breach, to reduce his loss. What if the loss was caused partly by a breach and partly his own contemporaneous action? In the law of tort, such problems are dealt with by the doctrine of contributory negligence. At common law, contributory negligence was a complete defence, but since 1945 it has been a ground for reducing the plaintiff's damages.

Law Reform (Contributory Negligence) Act 1945

Section 1. Apportionment of liability in case of contributory negligence
(1) Where any person suffers damage as the result partly of his own fault and partly of the fault of any other person or persons, a claim in respect of that damage shall not be defeated by reason of the fault of the person suffering the damage, but the damages recoverable in respect thereof shall be reduced to such extent as the court thinks just and equitable having regard to the claimant's share in the responsibility for the damage . . .

Section 4. Interpretation
The following expressions have the meanings hereby respectively assigned to them, that is to say—
'fault' means negligence, breach of statutory duty or other act or omission which gives rise to a liability in tort or would, apart from this Act, give rise to the defence of contributory negligence.

In relation to contract, there are two questions. The first is whether the Act applies so that the court has power to apportion liability. The second is, if the Act does not apply, does the contributory negligence operate to defeat the plaintiff's claim altogether?

In order to decide whether the Act applies, it is necessary to distinguish three situations:

(1) The defendant is in breach of a strict contractual duty.

(2) The defendant is in breach of a duty of care imposed by the contract. There is no corresponding duty in tort.

(3) The defendant was in breach of a contractual duty of care and a duty of care in tort.

It has been held that the Act applies to the third situation. In *Sayers v Harlow UDC* [1958] 2 All ER 342 the plaintiff found herself locked in a public lavatory. She attempted to climb out by standing on the toilet roll holder which rotated, causing her to fall and suffer personal injury. The Court of Appeal applied the Act and reduced her damages. Apparently the question whether the Act applied to a breach of contract was not fully argued, but the Court of Appeal has recently confirmed that it does apply to this category of case: *Forsikringsaktieselskapet Vesta v Butcher* [1988] 2 All ER 43 (affd on other grounds [1989] 1 All ER 402).

The Act does not apply to category (1) cases: *Basildon District Council v J E Lesser (Properties) Ltd* [1985] 1 All ER 20. This is because the defendant's conduct does not fall within the definition of 'fault' in s 4, 'negligence, breach of statutory duty or other act or omission giving rise to a liability in tort'. (The second limb of s 4, acts 'giving rise to the defence of contributory negligence', refers to the plaintiff's conduct.) It is irrelevant that the breach of the strict duty was in fact brought about by the defendant's negligence: Paull J in *Quinn v Burch Bros (Builders) Ltd* [1966] 2 QB 370 at 378–9.

It seems probable that the Act does not apply to the second category of case either. In the *Forsikrings* case (at p 49) O'Connor LJ said:

> . . . the words in s 4 'which gives rise to a liability in tort' define the kind or type of negligence which is to rank as 'fault' when considering 'the fault of any other person or persons'.

If the Act does not apply, it is not altogether clear whether the common law doctrine of contributory negligence (under which contributory negligence was a complete defence) may operate to defeat the plaintiff, but the courts reach the same result by treating the injury as being caused solely by the plaintiff's own fault. For example, in *Quinn v Burch Bros* the defendants failed to provide the plaintiff plasterer with a stepladder, so he used a trestle, folded up and leant against the wall. He did not 'foot' the trestle, and it slipped, causing him injury. Paull J held that the injury was caused solely by his own action, and his decision was affirmed on appeal [1966] 2 QB 370 at 381. A recent House of Lords case contains dicta suggesting that this will apply unless the defendant has warranted that the plaintiff need not take the very precautions at issue: *Lambert v Lewis* [1982] AC 225.

Both *Quinn* and *Lambert* were cases where the breach was clearly known to the plaintiff, who then acted carelessly. Suppose Beale takes his car to a garage, which fits a new master cylinder to the braking system, but without any fault on the garage's part the cylinder fitted is defective and the brakes fail, injuring Beale: would the garage escape liability if it could show that the reasonable driver would have realized from the fact that the brake pedal would go all the way to the floor that the system was defective? Wouldn't it make sense to give the courts power to apportion in such a case? See Law Commission Working Paper No 114, *Contributory Negligence as a Defence in Contract* (1990).

(iii) Savings actually made

The plaintiff should not be awarded damages for more loss than he has suffered, and thus any savings that he has been able to make should be taken into account. Thus if the seller of a machine which is being custom-built for the buyer accepts a repudiation by the buyer and ceases work on the machine, he will not recover damages for the full contract price: any savings in labour and materials will be deducted, or he would be overcompensated. Similarly, if an employee is wrongfully dismissed, savings in tax should be taken into account. If the lost income was taxable, but the damages are not, damages should only be awarded for the net loss of income: *British Transport Commission v Gourley* [1956] AC 185. Where the damages are also taxable, there appears to be some disagreement over how the tax should be taken into account. In *Parsons v BNM Laboratories Ltd* [1964] 1 QB 95 the Court of Appeal had expressed the view that neither amount of tax should be taken into account, thus achieving rough justice and saving a great deal of time. However, in *Shove v Downs Surgical plc* [1984] 1 All ER 7 Sheen J estimated the plaintiff's net loss of income after deduction of tax and then added an amount equivalent to the estimated tax. It appears that *Parsons* was not cited to Sheen J.

British Westinghouse Electric and Manufacturing Co Ltd v Underground Electric Railways Co of London Ltd [1911–13] All ER Rep 63, House of Lords

The appellants contracted to supply the respondents with turbines of a specified efficiency, but the machines supplied failed to meet the specification. The respondents used the machines for a time, but later replaced them with Parsons turbines. These were so much more efficient that the cost of installing and running them was less than the cost of running the Westinghouse machines would have been, even if the latter had performed as specified. In an arbitration the appellants sought to recover the unpaid balance of the contract price; the respondents counterclaimed for the increased running costs of the appellants' machines during the period they were working and the cost of replacing them with the Parsons machines. The arbitrator allowed the first item of the counterclaim, and stated a special case for the opinion of the court on the second.

Viscount Haldane LC. . . . The arbitrator appears to me to have found clearly that the effect of the superiority of the Parsons' machines and efficiency in reducing working expenses was in point of fact such that all loss was extinguished and that actually the respondents made a profit by the course which they took. They were doubtless not bound to purchase machines of a greater kilowatt power than those originally contracted for, but they in fact took the wise course in the circumstances of doing so, with pecuniary advantage to themselves. They had, moreover, used the appellants' machines for several years, and had recovered compensation for the loss incurred by reason of these machines not being during these years up to the standard required by the contract. After that period the arbitrator found that it was reasonable and prudent to take the course which they actually did in purchasing the more powerful machines, and that all the remaining loss and damages was thereby wiped out.

[The Lord Chancellor then set out the general principles on which damages for breach of contract are assessed, see above, pp 463 and 481. He continued:]

. . . But when, in the course of his business, [the plaintiff] has taken action arising out of the transaction, which action has diminished his loss, the effect in actual diminution of the loss which he has suffered may be taken into account, even though there was no duty on him to act.

Staniforth v Lyall illustrates this rule. In that case the defendants had chartered a ship to New Zealand, where they were to load her, or by an agent there to give the plaintiff, the owner, notice that they abandoned the adventure, in which case they were to pay £500. The ship went to New Zealand, but found neither agent nor cargo there, and the captain chose to make a circuitous voyage home by way of Batavia. This voyage, after making every allowance for increased expense and loss of time, was more profitable than the original venture to New Zealand would have been. The Court of Common Pleas decided that the action was to be viewed as one for a breach of contract to put the cargo on board the plaintiff's vessel for which the plaintiff was entitled to recover all the damages which he had incurred, but that he was bound to bring into account, in ascertaining the damages arising from the breach, the advantages which had accrued to him because of the course which he had chosen to adopt. I think that this decision illustrates a principle which has been recognised in other cases that, provided the course taken to protect himself, by the plaintiff, in such an action was one which a reasonable and prudent person might in the ordinary conduct of business properly have taken, and in fact did take whether bound to or not, a jury or an arbitrator may properly look at the whole of the facts and ascertain the result in estimating the quantum of damage.

I think that the principle which applies here is that which makes it right for the jury or arbitrator to look at what actually happened, and to balance loss and gain. The transaction was not res inter alios acta, but one in which the person whose contract was broken took a reasonable and prudent course arising quite naturally out of the circumstances in which he was placed by the breach. Apart from the breach of contract, the lapse of time had rendered the appellants' machines obsolete, and men of business would be doing the only thing which they could properly do in replacing them with new and up-to-date machines. The arbitrator does not in his finding of fact lay any stress on the increase in kilowatt power of the new machines, and I think that the proper inference is that such increase was regarded by him as a natural and prudent course followed by those whose object was to avoid further loss, and that it formed part of a continuous dealing with the situation in which they found themselves, and was not an independent or disconnected transaction. For the reasons which I have given I think that the questions of law stated by the arbitrator in the Special Case have been wrongly answered by the courts below.

[Lords Ashbourne, Macnaghten and Atkinson concurred.]

Appeal allowed.

NOTES

1. In *Harbutt's Plasticine Ltd v Wayne Tank and Pump Co Ltd* [1970] 1 QB 447 the plaintiffs' factory was burned down as a result of the defendants' breach of contract. The plaintiffs recovered the full cost of rebuilding, although this was greater than the value of the old factory. Widgery LJ said (at pp 472–473):

   I must now turn to the issues raised as to the measure of damage. The distinction between those cases in which the measure of damage is the cost of repair of the damaged article, and those in which it is the diminution in value of the article, is not clearly defined. In my opinion each case depends on its own facts, it being remembered, first, that the purpose of the award of damages is to restore the plaintiff to his position before the loss occurred, and secondly, that the plaintiff must act reasonably to mitigate his loss. If the article damaged is a motor car of popular make, the plaintiff cannot charge the defendant with the cost of repair when it is cheaper to buy a similar car on the market. On the other hand, if no substitute for the damaged article is available and no reasonable alternative can be provided, the plaintiff should be entitled to the cost of repair. It was clear in the present case that it was reasonable for the plaintiffs to rebuild their factory, because there was no other way in which they could carry on their business and retain their labour force. The plaintiffs rebuilt their factory to a substantially different design, and if this had involved expenditure beyond the cost of replacing the old, the difference might not have been recoverable, but there is no suggestion of this here. Nor do I accept that the plaintiffs must give credit under the heading of 'betterment' for the fact that their new factory is modern in design and materials. To do so would be the equivalent of forcing the plaintiffs to invest their money in the modernising of their plant which might be highly inconvenient for them. Accordingly I agree with the sum allowed by the trial judge as the cost of replacement.

2. This case has been overruled but on another point: see below, p 697. Widgery LJ's dictum was applied in *Bacon v Cooper (Metals) Ltd* [1982] 1 All ER 397, where the defendant had supplied the wrong kind of scrap metal to the plaintiff and the metal broke the rotor arm of the plaintiff's fragmentizer. The plaintiff could not obtain a used rotor arm, so he bought a new one. Although rotor arms only last some seven years, and the broken one was three-and-a-quarter years old, Cantley J held that the plaintiff was entitled to the full cost of a new arm without giving credit for the fact that it would last longer: there was no certainty that the plaintiff would have bought a new rotor when the broken one wore out, as the fragmentizer itself might well be outmoded by then.

3. Why were the defendants credited with the savings in the *British Westinghouse* case, but not with the increased value of the replacement in the other two cases? If Harbutts had planned to sell the factory in the foreseeable future, would the result have been different?

(d) Quantification

Markets and other contracts

Slater v Hoyle & Smith Ltd [1920] 2 KB 11, Court of Appeal

The sellers of 3,000 pieces of unbleached cotton cloth delivered 1,625 pieces which were below the required quality, and the buyers, who had contracted to resell the goods, justifiably refused to accept further deliveries. In respect of the 1,375 pieces not delivered the buyers claimed loss of profit on the sub-sale, but Greer J awarded them only nominal damages because the market price had fallen below the contract price. The 1,625 pieces they had passed to the sub-buyers with no reduction in price, but in respect of these Greer J awarded the difference in value between the goods as they should have been and as they were actually delivered. The sellers appealed.

Scrutton LJ. . . . [T]he judge has refused to make the sellers pay the profits which the buyers might have made by supplying sound goods from this contract under their second sub-contract, but the sellers, though freed from liability for the higher price of the second sub-contract, desire to take advantage of the lower price of the first sub-contract. Can they do so? It is well settled that damages for non-delivery or delay in delivery of goods, where there is a market price, do not include damages for the loss of any particular contract unless that contract has been in contemplation of the parties to the original contract: *Horne v Midland Rly Co*. The value of the goods in the market independently of any circumstances peculiar to the plaintiff is to be taken: *Great Western Rly Co v Redmayne*; *Williams v Reynolds* per Blackburn J. If the plaintiff has a profitable contract to sell goods, and there is a market, he can supply himself with the goods by purchasing in the market; and he is then left without the goods he should have received under the original contract and has lost their market value. But suppose his sub-contract is at a price below instead of above the market price, so that, if he delivers goods under the sub-contract, he loses. Can his damages be limited by the amount he would have received on the sub-contract? On the above reasoning it would seem not. He could supply the sub-contract by buying in the market, and then should have goods delivered to him of a certain market value, which he has lost because they were not delivered. This has been decided in the case of non-delivery of goods by the Court of Appeal in *Rodocanachi v Milburn*, and by the House of Lords in *Williams v Agius* where *Rodocanachi v Milburn* was approved. . . . A had not delivered coals which he had sold at 16s 3d a ton to W. At the time when they should have been delivered the market price was 23s 6d; but W had sold a similar quantity and description of coals at 19s; the question was whether A ought to pay 7s 3d a ton damages, or only 2s 9d a ton, being the amount W would have received if he had fulfilled his sub-contract. The House of Lords held the damages were 7s 3d a ton, approving *Rodocanachi v Milburn*, and Lord Dunedin held that the defaulting seller is neither mulct in damages for the extra profit the buyer would have got owing to a forward sale at over the market price, nor can he take benefit of the fact that the buyer has made a forward sale at under the market price. He put the case as a dilemma: 'The truth is that the respondents' argument leaves them in a dilemma. Either the sub-sale was of the identical article which was the subject of the principal sale or it was not. If it was not, it is absurd to suppose that a contract with a third party as to something else, just because it is the same kind of thing, can reduce the damages which the unsatisfied buyer is entitled to recover under the original contract. If, on the other hand, the sub-sale is of the selfsame thing or things as is or are the subject of the principal sale, then ex hypothesi the default of the seller in the original sale is going to bring about an enforced default on the part of the original buyer and subsequent seller. And how can it ever be known that the damages recoverable under that contract will be calculable in precisely the same way as in the original contract? All that will depend upon what the sub-buyer will be able to make out. The only safe plan is, therefore, in the original contract, to take the difference of market price as the measure of damages and to leave the sub-contract and the breach thereof to be worked out by those whom it directly concerns.'

Now apply these principles to the delivery of goods not sound but damaged. The only difference appears to be that in the case of non-delivery the buyer has not got the goods and has not paid their contract price; what he has lost is the difference between the market price of the goods and the contract price he would have to pay to get them. If the goods are delivered damaged, he has got goods and has paid the contract price; what he has not got is sound goods, and his loss is therefore the difference between the market value of sound goods and the market value of these damaged goods. Again, sub-contracts do not come into account, for the buyer is under no obligation to use these goods for his sub-contract; he may buy in the market, and he will then be left with goods damaged to a certain extent at the then market price of such goods instead of sound goods at the then market price of sound goods. The difference between the two market prices should be the measure of damages. If the buyer delivers under the sub-contract the damaged goods and has to pay damages, these damages will not be the measure of damages. As Lord Dunedin says: 'How can it ever be known that the damages recoverable under that contract will be calculable in precisely the same way as in the original contract?' If these damages are greater than the difference in market price of sound and damaged goods, they will clearly not be recoverable. The result seems the same if they are less; it is res inter alios acta: 'circumstances peculiar to the plaintiff', which cannot affect his claim one way or the other. If the buyer is lucky enough, for reasons with which the seller has nothing to do, to get his goods through on the sub-contract without a claim against him, this on principle cannot affect his claim against the seller any more than the fact that he had to pay very large damages on his sub-contract would affect his original seller.

In support, however, of the proposition that the sellers could be relieved by what took place under the sub-contract, the case of *Wertheim v Chicoutimi Pulp Co* was relied on. This is a decision of Privy Council, and though not technically binding on us, is of course entitled to the greatest respect. It was a claim for delay in delivery. The contract was to deliver wood pulp in November, 1900, when the market price was 70s a ton. The pulp was delivered in July, 1901, when the market price was 42s 6d a ton; but the buyer had made a sub-contract for sale at 65s a ton. The Privy Council only gave the buyer 5s a ton damages. It is difficult to see how this fits in with the principles above stated. If the buyer had made a sub-contract at 30s a ton and only received that sum, it seems clear that the Privy Council would not have given him 40s but only 27s 6d a ton, for they would have said the seller had nothing to do with the sub-contract. If the buyer had made a forward contract at 80s, and lost it, the Privy Council would not have given him 37s 6d, but only 27s 6d: *Horne v Midland Rly Co*; again for the reason that the seller had no concern with matters peculiar to the buyer. The buyer was under no obligation to deliver the contract goods on the sub-contract. If he had bought other goods and used them for the sub-contract, he would have been left with goods delivered at a time when the market price was 42s 6d, instead of when it was 70s, and would have recovered 27s 6d. Lord Atkinson says that in the case of non-delivery the price at which the purchaser might in anticipation of delivery have resold the goods is properly treated, where no question of loss of profit arises, as an entirely irrelevant matter. It is always so treated, as I understand the law, unless the buyer can affect the seller with such notice of the sub-contract as makes him liable for loss by its non-fulfilment. But he goes on to say that the existence of a sub-contract shows that the real value of the goods is more than the market value and the loss he sustains must be measured by that price. I respectfully think that all the English decisions show that a plaintiff cannot measure the real value of what he has lost by reference to a contract peculiar to himself, for which the defendant is not responsible, and that his loss therefore is not measured by that price.

Wertheim v Chicoutimi Pulp Co was a case of delay in delivery and not, as the present, a case of delivery of inferior goods. I should myself have thought the principles applying to these two cases were the same as those applying to non-delivery, and that the Privy Council judgment was erroneous as departing from those principles. But at any rate it does not decide the case of delivery of inferior goods instead of sound goods, which appears to me the same as the case of non-delivery of any goods at all. It is true that on these principles the plaintiff may recover more than an indemnity. English law freqently gives him less than his real loss. The plaintiff in *Horne v Midland Rly Co*, a case of delay, certainly sustained a real loss greater than the amount he recovered. The plaintiff in *British Columbia Saw-Mill Co v Nettleship*, a case of non-delivery, certainly recovered much less than his real loss. He sometimes recovers more than his real loss. The plaintiffs in *Salford Corporation v Lever* recovered their real damage twice. The rules of English law do not always give exact indemnity, and in this case I think they do not.

For these reasons I think that Greer J was right in disregarding the fact that the buyers, for reasons we do not know, were able to deliver inferior goods under their sub-contract without having to pay damages, just as he would have been right in disregarding the fact if they had had to pay larger damages than the difference in market value.

In my view the appeal should be dismissed with costs.

[Warrington and Bankes LJJ delivered concurring judgments.]

Appeal dismissed.

NOTES

1. If the buyer has resold the goods to a sub-buyer at more than the market price, and the seller fails to deliver (or delivers late, with the result that the sub-sale is lost), Scrutton says that the buyer cannot recover more than the difference between the contract and market prices. Why not?

2. Sometimes the buyer will have resold the specific parcel of goods (eg 3,000 tons wheat *ex Challenger*). If so, he will not be able to buy a replacement in the market. Normally, however, the courts treat this case in the same way, holding that a resale of the specific parcel was not reasonably contemplated. For an exception where the form of contract used contemplated resale of the specific cargo, and loss of profit on the resale was allowed, see *Re R & H Hall Ltd & W H Pim Jr & Co's Arbitration* (1928) 139 LT 50.

3. Scrutton continues that if the resale is at *less* than the market price it will still be ignored. What reason did Lord Dunedin give for this in *Williams Bros v E T Agius Ltd* [1914] AC 510? (Hint: think about the possible liability of the buyer to the sub-buyer.)

4. Scrutton then applies the same principles to a case of delivery of defective goods: damages are to be based on the difference between the market value the goods should have had, and their actual value. But if the buyer has resold the goods to a sub-buyer, who accepts them and does not claim on the buyer despite the defect, what justifies not reducing the buyer's damages accordingly? (Hint: could the buyer have made this 'advantageous' sub-sale anyway?)

5. Other commentators agree that the *Wertheim* case is hard to fit with general principle (eg Treitel, pp 731–732). Assuming that the buyer had simply resold an equivalent quantity of goods to the sub-buyer, the sub-sale should be ignored because the buyer could have made this advantageous deal quite apart from the main sale. If, on the other hand, he had resold the exact same cargo of pulp before the breach occurred, he would not be able to resell it in the market but would have to supply it to the sub-buyer, and he might be liable to the sub-buyer for late delivery: again the sub-sale price should be ignored for the reasons given by Lord Dunedin in *Williams v Agius*.

W L Thompson v R Robinson (Gunmakers) Ltd [1955] 1 All ER 154, Upjohn J

The defendants wrongfully repudiated a contract to buy a Standard Vanguard car from the plaintiff dealers. The plaintiffs returned the car to their suppliers, who did not seek compensation. The price of the cars was fixed by the manufacturer, and the dealers would have received a profit of £61 on the sale. The plaintiffs claimed this loss of profit. It was shown that locally there was a smaller demand for Standard Vanguards than there were cars available, though it was not shown that this was true nationally.

Upjohn J. . . . The plaintiffs say that the true measure of damages in those circumstances is no more, no less, than their loss of profit, £61. The defendants say: 'No, the loss is nominal, for you could have sold the car to another customer or you could do what, in fact, you did do, which was to get your suppliers to release you, and you have suffered no damage.'

The law is not really in doubt. It is set out in the Sale of Goods Act, 1893, s 50 [see above, p 464]. That was declaratory of the existing law and the general principle which has been observed in all cases I take conveniently from the speech of Viscount Haldane LC, in *British Westinghouse Electric & Manufacturing Co, Ltd v Underground Electric Rlys Co of London, Ltd*. Viscount Haldane LC said:

'Subject to these observations I think that there are certain broad principles which are quite well settled. The first is that, as far as possible, he who has proved a breach of a bargain to supply what he contracted to get is to be placed, as far as money can do it, in as good a situation as if the contract had been performed.'

That is the general rule.

Apart altogether from authority and statute, it would seem to me on the facts to be quite plain that the plaintiffs' loss in this case is the loss of their bargain. They have sold one Vanguard less than they otherwise would. The plaintiffs, as the defendants must have known, are in business as dealers in motor cars and make their profit in buying and selling motor cars, and what they have lost is their profit on the sale of this Vanguard. There is no authority exactly in point in this country, although it seems to me that the principle to be applied is a clear one. It is to be found in *Re Vic Mill, Ltd* in which the supplier was to supply certain machines which he had to make and they were to be made to the particular specification of the purchaser although they were of a type generally in common use. It was not, as the present case is, a sale by a motor dealer of a standardised product. The purchaser repudiated his order, and with a view to mitigating damages the supplier, on getting another order for somewhat similar machinery, very sensibly made such alterations as were necessary to the machinery that he had made for the original purchaser and sold the machinery so altered to the second purchaser. His costs of doing that were comparatively trivial. It was said by the supplier that the measure of his damages was the loss of his bargain; by the purchaser that the measure of damages was merely the cost of the conversion of the machinery for the second purchaser and his slight loss on the re-sale . . . Buckley LJ put the matter succinctly in this way . . .:

'As regards No 1, where the goods were manufactured, the respondents are, I think, entitled to both profits, because they were not bound to give the appellants the benefit of another order that the respondents had received. The respondents were left with these goods on their hands. They altered them and sold them to another buyer, but they could have made, and would otherwise, I suppose, have made, other goods for that buyer, and not employed these goods for that purpose. If they had done so, they would have made both profits.'

It seems to me that in principle that covers this case. True the motor car in question was not sold to another purchaser, but the plaintiffs did what was reasonable, they got out of their bargain with George Thompson, Ltd, but they sold one less Vanguard, and lost their profit on that transaction. . .

The main case, however, put by the defendants is this: they submit that s 50 of the Sale of Goods Act, 1893, applies, because they say there is an available market for the goods in question, and in that available market we know that the price of the Vanguard is fixed. It is fixed by the manufacturers. Therefore, they say the measure of damages must necessarily be little more than nominal. Had the plaintiffs kept the car and sold it to another at a later stage, no doubt they would have been entitled to the costs of storage in the meantime, possibly interest on their money laid out, and so on, but, as they in fact mitigated damages by getting out of the contract, damages are nil.

Counsel for the defendants said that the market now must be treated as a market or fair in a limited or technical sense. It is curious that there is a comparative absence of authority on the meaning of the phrase 'available market', because one would have thought there would have been many cases, but the researches of counsel have only disclosed one authority on s 50. It is *Dunkirk Colliery Co v Lever*, a decision of the Court of Appeal. The facts were far removed from the facts before me, and I do not think that I need recite them. It will be sufficient if I read an extract from the judgment of James LJ. He said (9 Ch D at p 24):

'Under those circumstances the only thing that we can do is to send it back to the referee with an intimation that we are of opinion upon the facts (agreeing with the Master of the Rolls in that respect), that the facts do not warrant the application of the principle mentioned in the award, namely, that there was what may be properly called a market. What I understand by a market in such a case as this is, that when the defendant refused to take the three hundred tons the first week or the first month, the plaintiffs might have sent it in waggons somewhere else, where they could sell it, just as they sell corn on the Exchange, or cotton at Liverpool: that is to say, that there was a fair market where they could have found a purchaser either by themselves or through some agent at some particular place. That is my notion of the meaning of a market under those circumstances.'

If that be the right principle to apply, it was proved that there is nothing in the nature of a market like a Cotton Exchange or Baltic or Stock Exchange, or anything of the sort, for the sale of new motor cars. . . .

I think that . . . the decision of the Court of Appeal in *Dunkirk Colliery Co v Lever* is binding on me, and, therefore, unless one finds something in the nature of a market in the sense used by James LJ, s 50(3) has no further application. However, the point seems to me of somewhat academic interest in this case, because, if one gives to the word 'market' an extended meaning, in my view on the facts which I have to consider, a precisely similar result is reached.

Had the matter been res integra, I think I should have found that an 'available market' merely means that the situation in the particular trade in the particular area was such that the particular goods could freely be sold, and that there was a demand sufficient to absorb readily all the goods that were thrust on it, so that if a purchaser defaulted the goods in question could readily be disposed of. Indeed, such was the situation in the motor trade until very recently. It was, of course, notorious that dealers all over the country had long waiting lists for new motor cars. People put their names down and had to wait five or six years, and whenever a car was spared by the manufacturer from export it was snatched at. If any purchaser fell out, there were many waiting to take his place, and it was conceded that if those circumstances were still applicable to the Vanguard motor car, the claim for damages must necessarily have been purely nominal. But on the assumed facts, circumstances had changed in relation to Vanguard motor cars, and in March, 1954, there was not a demand in the East Riding which could readily absorb all the Vanguard motor cars available for sale. If a purchaser defaulted, that sale was lost and there was no means of readily disposing of the Vanguard contracted to be sold, so that there was not, even on the extended definition, an available market. But there is this further consideration: even if I accepted the defendants' broad argument that one must now look at the market as being the whole conspectus of trade, organisation and marketing, I have to remember that s 50 provides only a prima facie rule, and, if on investigation of the facts, one finds that it is unjust to apply that rule, in the light of the general principles mentioned above it is not to be applied. In this case, as I said in the earlier part of my judgment, it seems to me plain almost beyond argument that, in fact, the loss to the plaintiff is £61. Accordingly, however one interprets s 50, it seems to me on the facts that I have to consider one reaches the same result.

There will be judgment for the plaintiffs for £61 1s 9d, but the order must incorporate an undertaking by the plaintiffs to indemnify the defendants against their costs of this action. There must be a mutual set-off between the costs and the sum of £61.

Judgment for the plaintiffs.

NOTES

1. In *Charter v Sullivan* [1957] 2 QB 117 the buyer repudiated a contract to buy a Hillman Minx, which was then sold by the dealers to another customer. The dealers' manager admitted that they could sell all the Hillman Minx cars they could get, and the Court of Appeal held that they were entitled to nominal damages only.

2. The situation in the *Thompson* case is often referred to as a problem of 'lost volume'. The dealer counts on receiving the mark-up on a certain number of sales to contribute to his fixed overheads and, at the end of the day, his profit. If because of the buyer's default the seller makes fewer sales than he otherwise would have done, he has lost the contribution from the lost sale.

Lazenby Garages Ltd v Wright [1976] 2 All ER 770, Court of Appeal

Lord Denning MR. Mr Wright works on the land. On 19th February 1974 he went to the showrooms of motor dealers called Lazenby Garages Ltd. He saw some secondhand cars there. He agreed to buy a BMW 2002. He signed a contract to pay £1,670 for it. It was to be delivered to him on 1st March 1974. He went back home to his wife and told her about it. She persuaded him not to buy it. So next day he went back to the garage and said he would not have it after all. They kept it there offering it for resale. Two months later on 23rd April 1974 they resold it for £1,770, that is for £100 more than Mr Wright was going to pay.

Notwithstanding this advantageous resale, the garage sued Mr Wright for damages. They produced evidence that they had themselves bought the car secondhand on 14th February 1974, that is five days before Mr Wright had come in and agreed to buy it. They said that they had bought it for £1,325. He had agreed to buy it from them for £1,670, so they had lost £345 and they claimed that sum as damages.

In answer Mr Wright said: 'You haven't lost anything; you've sold it for a higher price'. The garage people said that they were dealers in secondhand cars; that they had had a number of cars of this sort of age and type, BMW 2002s; and that they had lost the sale of another car. They said that, if Mr Wright had taken this car, they would have been able to sell one of those other cars to the purchaser. So they had sold one car less and were entitled to profit accordingly.

The judge thought that they had not proved that they had sold one car less, but that there was a 50:50 chance that they would have sold an extra car. So he gave them damages for half the sum claimed. Instead of £345 he gave them £172.50.

Now there is an appeal to this court. The cases show that if there are a number of new cars, all exactly of the same kind, available for sale, and the dealers can prove that they sold one car less than they otherwise would have done, they would be entitled to damages amounting to their loss of profit on the one car: see the judgment of Upjohn J in *W L Thompson v Robinson* (*Gunmakers*) *Ltd*. The same has been held in the United States: *Torkomian v Russell* and *Stewart v Hansen*; in Canada, *Mason & Risch Ltd v Christner*, and in Australia, *Cameron v Campbell & Worthington*.

But it is entirely different in the case of a secondhand car. Each secondhand car is different from the next, even though it is the same make. The sales manager of the garage admitted in evidence that some secondhand cars, of the same make, even of the same year, may sell better than others of the same year. Some may sell quickly, others sluggishly. You simply cannot tell why. But they are all different.

In the circumstances the cases about new cars do not apply. We have simply to apply to s 50 of the Sale of Goods Act 1893. There is no 'available market' for secondhand cars. So its not sub-s (3) but sub-s (2). The measure of damages is the estimated loss directly and naturally resulting in the ordinary course of events from the buyer's breach of contract. That throws us back to the test of what could reasonably be expected to be in the contemplation of the parties as a natural consequence of the breach. The buyer in this case could not have contemplated that the dealer would sell one car less. At most he would contemplate that, if they resold this very car at a lower price, they would suffer by reason of that lower price and should recover the difference. But if they resold this very car at a higher price, they would suffer no loss. Seeing that these plaintiffs resold this car for £100 more than the sale to Mr Wright, they clearly suffered no damage at all.

In my opinion the appeal should be allowed and judgment entered for the defendant, Mr Wright.

Lawton LJ. In the course of argument counsel for the plaintiffs accepted that if a dealer was selling an article which is a unique article, for example if a secondhand car dealer was selling a vintage car, or if an antique dealer was selling a picture, then, if there were a repudiation by a buyer of a contract entered into, the damages would be the particular loss which was sustained on that transaction, and nothing more.

At the other end of the scale, the courts had to consider the principles accepted in a line of cases, of which the most recent one is probably *W L Thompson Ltd v Robinson* (*Gunmakers*) *Ltd*. As Lord Denning MR has pointed out, when the goods are not unique, but are mass-produced, different considerations may apply from those which apply when an article is unique.

The problem in this case is whether a secondhand car of the type with which we are concerned, namely a BMW 2002, petrol injected, was a unique article. The evidence from the plaintiffs' own sales manager shows that it was; he put the matter in this way: 'No one can say what makes a secondhand car sellable. It is the same with new cars. Cars vary as to date, mileage, sound of engine, wear and tear, upholstery etc'. Then, a few answers later, he said: 'In a secondhand showroom each car is different.' In other words, he was saying that secondhand cars are, from their very nature, unique. In those circumstances it seems to me that the *Thompson* type of case has no application to the circumstances of this particular case.

I agree that the appeal should be allowed.

[Bridge LJ concurred.]

NOTES

1. The trial judge recognized that with second-hand cars one cannot be sure that the second buyer would have bought another car if the car he actually bought was not available, having been sold to the defendant: but he thought there was a chance of it and therefore reduced the damages accordingly. Why was that inappropriate?
2. The Court of Appeal described the car as 'unique', but it is very doubtful that it was 'unique' enough that a buyer of it could have obtained specific performance (see below, p 525).
3. Even with new goods, lost volume claims seem to be fairly rare. Why might this be? See 'Micro-economics and the Lost-Volume Seller' (1973) 24 Case W Res LR 712.

(e) Problem cases

(i) Non-payment of money

The common law has developed two special rules about the non-payment of money, both of which are generally regarded as unsatisfactory. The first is that where the defendant's breach simply consists of a failure to pay money, the loss is normally to be measured in terms of the amount of money unpaid. (For a fuller discussion see Ogus, *The Law of Damages*, pp 304–307.) A plaintiff might often plausibly argue that if the defendant had paid on time, he would have put the money to profitable use. A possible answer to this (consistent perhaps with English law's general meanness to impecunious plaintiffs, see *Dredger Liesbosch (Owners) v SS Edison (Owners)* [1933] AC 449) would be that the plaintiff could have used his own money, or have borrowed money, to achieve the same result. But firstly, this is often not the case, as is shown by *Trans-Trust SPRL v Danubian Trading* (above, p 411): the plaintiff may have no other money and be unable to borrow. There the Court of Appeal managed to side-step the rule, by treating the failure to open the credit as being more than a mere failure to pay money. Secondly, whether the plaintiff planned to use the unpaid money in this way or simply to invest it, he will lose interest, and it is at this point that the second rule comes into play.

The second rule is that as a general rule, debts do not carry interest, so that a debtor who pays late discharges his obligation by paying the sum originally due. This rule was treated as well settled by the House of Lords in *London, Chatham and Dover Rly Co v South Eastern Rly Co* [1893] AC 429, though without enthusiasm. With modern rates of interest and inflation, this rule is quite unfairly advantageous to debtors. It was cogently criticised by the Law Commission in its report on Interest in 1978 (Law Commission No 88, Cmnd 7229), which recommended legislation substantially designed to reverse it. The House of Lords, however, reaffirmed the rule in *President of India v La Pintada Cia Navegacion SA* [1984] 2 All ER 773. All the members of the House thought that the rule was unsatisfactory, but they were unanimous that it must be reversed by statute and not by them. The principal reason for this cautious approach was that Parliament had considered the matter in 1982 (see below) and had not accepted the Law Commission's proposals in full (for a heart-rending account by the Lord Chancellor of his inability to move his cabinet colleagues further on the matter, see Hansard, 429 HL Official Report (5th series) cols 165–174 (6 April 1982)).

This decision of the House of Lords makes it necessary to consider carefully the precise scope of the rule, and the qualifications upon it. The starting point must be the two rules mentioned: where there is a failure to pay money, only the amount due is recoverable, and the debtor may discharge his obligation by paying this amount without interest. To this there are a number of exceptions:

(1) The parties may expressly agree that the debt shall carry interest. This is, of course, very common.

(2) The court may decide that the parties have implicitly agreed to pay interest: see *Minter v Welsh Health Technical Services Organization* (1980) 13 BLR 1.

(3) Under the Law Reform (Miscellaneous Provisions) Act 1934, s 3, the court was given a wide discretion to award interest on claims pursued to judgment. This applies to judgments on both debts and other damages claims. This statute suffered a grave defect, however, in that it only applied where the court delivered judgment. If the debtor paid the original sum in full even in the middle of the trial, he avoided having to pay interest. This rule was changed by the Administration of Justice Act 1982, s 15 (amending the Supreme Court Act 1981, s 35A): the court can now award interest so long as money was outstanding at the time proceedings were commenced. This still leaves it open to the debtor to escape liability for interest by paying the original sum just before proceedings are commenced, which may be several years after the debt was incurred. (It was the limited nature of this reform which persuaded the House of Lords that Parliament had not intended to make a more far-reaching change.)

(4) However, in certain circumstances it appears that, if the debtor knows when he makes the contract that the creditor is depending on receipt of the money for some particular purpose, and that the creditor has no other funds available, the debtor may be liable in damages for either the creditor's loss on the frustrated purpose (as in the *Trans-Trust* case), or, if the creditor does manage to borrow the money elsewhere, for the interest paid by the creditor. In *Wadsworth v Lydall* [1981] 2 All ER 401 the purchaser of land had agreed to pay £10,000 by a fixed date, knowing that the vendor was going to use the money to make a down payment on another piece of land. The purchaser paid only £7,200, and the vendor had to borrow the remaining £2,800 in order to make the down payment on time. The Court of Appeal held that the vendor could recover as part of his damages the interest he had had to pay on the £2,800. This case was expressly (and enthusiastically) approved by the House of Lords in the *President of India* case; it was treated as an application of the second rule in *Hadley v Baxendale*, that is, as dependent on the debtor's special knowledge of facts making the loss likely. But in a contract context, the debtor will usually know that if he pays late he will increase the creditor's borrowing, or will deprive him of the chance to invest the money and earn interest. The practical effect of the endorsement of *Wadsworth v Lydall* may be to take away from debtors most of the advantage conceded to them by the refusal to reverse the 'no interest' rule.

(ii) Failure to make title to land – a problem no longer?

Until very recently there was an ancient and exceptional rule, confirmed by the House of Lords in *Bain v Fothergill* (1874) LR 7 HL 158, which provided that the vendor of land who, without any fault on his part, was unable to show good title, was liable to the purchaser for the purchaser's costs in investigating title but not for the loss of bargain. It has been argued that this rule was a survivor from the days when no damages were awarded for loss of bargain (Atiyah, *Rise and Fall of Freedom of Contract* (1979), p 203), but it is not at all clear that earlier law did refuse such damages in other types of contract (see Baker (1980) 43 MLR 467). Whatever its origin, the courts tended to limit the application of the rule in *Bain v Fothergill*. It did not apply when the vendor was unwilling to make proper efforts to make title (*Malhotra v Choudhury* [1980] Ch 52), nor did it apply to 'matters of conveyancing', an obscure phrase which seems to refer to obligations which are separate from the obligation to make title, for instance the obligation to deliver vacant possession (see *Wroth v Tyler* [1974] Ch 30). The rule was criticised as outmoded: see Sydenham, 'The Anomalous Rule in *Bain v Fothergill*' (1977) 41 Conv 341; Emery, 'In Defence of the rule in *Bain v Fothergill*' (1978) 42 Conv 338; Law Commission No 166, *Transfer of Land: the rule in Bain v Fothergill* (Cm 192, 1987). It was abolished by Law of Property (Miscellaneous Provisions) Act 1989, s 3.

(iii) Difference in value or cost of completion?

Tito v Waddell (No 2) [1977] Ch 106 at 328, Megarry V-C

Only a small part of this long and complex case is presented here. Phosphate had been mined on Ocean Island under an agreement made in 1913 with the Banaban landowners. The agreement provided that the mining company (whose rights and obligations had now vested in the British Phosphate Commissioners) would return all worked out lands to the owners, and would 'replant such lands—wherever possible—with coconuts and other food-bearing trees, both in the lands already worked out and in those to be worked out'. In 1942 the island had been occupied by the Japanese, who killed or deported most of the inhabitants and devastated the island. After the war the surviving Banabans were resettled on the island of Rabi, some 1,500 miles away. This is a much larger island, unaffected by mining, whereas Ocean island is five-sixths mined. The Banabans brought an action in which, inter alia, they claimed damages.

Megarry V-C:

(a) BASIS. Mr Macdonald's primary contention was that the measure of damages was the cost of doing the work of replanting, limited to $A73,140 per acre. His secondary contention was that the measure of damages was a suitable proportion of the cost of replanting, to represent the sum which the British Phosphate Commissioners would have paid in order to be released from the obligation to replant. In a helpful summary of his submissions on this part of the case which he put in on Day 101, he worked out some figures on the assumption that the one third for which he had contended in argument was the suitable proportion. These contentions were, of course, made in relation to the extensive replanting obligations that he claimed and I have rejected; but in principle they must apply to the lesser obligation that I have held to exist.

Mr MacCrindle, on the other hand, contended that even if the action were not premature by reason of the failure of the resident commissioner to specify trees and shrubs, and was not barred on any other ground, the damages should be either nominal or minimal. His basic submission was that the proper measure of damages was not the cost of doing the work, but was the diminution in the market value of the land by reason of the work not having been done. Mr Macdonald's secondary contention, based on what British Phosphate Commissioners would have paid for being released from the obligation to replant, had not been put forward at that stage. But Mr Browne-Wilkinson met it on behalf of the British Phosphate Commissioners in his speech in reply; and he contended that this mode of assessment was inapplicable in cases such as this.

I shall take first the rival contentions of the cost of doing the work, and the diminution in the market value. The two approaches are exemplified by *Joyner v Weeks* and *Wigsell v School for Indigent Blind* respectively: both were cited to the House of Lords in *Conquest v Ebbetts*. In *Joyner v Weeks*, the action was by a landlord against the tenant, brought not during the term but at the end of it, for damages for breach of a covenant to keep the demised premises in repair, and to deliver them up in repair. The Court of Appeal held that the ordinary rule was that the damages recoverable were the cost of doing the repairs, and that there was nothing in the facts of the case which made that rule inapplicable. . .

Wigsell's case related to the purchase of 12 acres of land intended for a projected asylum. In the conveyance the purchasers covenanted with the vendor that they would keep their land enclosed on all sides which abutted on the vendor's land with a brick wall or an iron railing seven feet high. The conveyance also gave the vendor, his heirs and assigns a right of pre-emption if the purchasers did not require the land for a blind school or asylum, and desired within 10 years to sell all or any of it. Six years later the purchasers decided not to use any of the land for their projected asylum, and offered it back to the executors of the vendor, who had died in the meantime; but the offer was declined. No wall or fence had been erected, and the executors then sued the purchasers for damages for breach of covenant. The cost of erecting the wall or fence was far greater than the diminution in the value of the vendor's land by reason of the breach.

In delivering the judgment of a Queen's Bench Divisional Court, consisting of himself and Cave J, Field J said . . . that if the plaintiffs had really wished to have the wall built, they would have sued for specific performance; and if the court had thought damages an inadequate remedy, it could have ordered specific performance. Instead, the plaintiffs had elected to sue for damages. They would be under no obligation to spend the money on building the wall, and probably they would never think of such expenditure, which seemed to the court to be a simple waste of money. The effect of suing for damages was to entitle them to the amount of the difference between the state of the plaintiffs on the breach of the contract and what this would have been if the contract had been performed. . . .

Pausing there, it is clear that in some cases of a contract to do work to the plaintiff's land the measure of damages for breach is the reduction in value of the plaintiff's interest in the land, and in other cases it is the cost of doing the work. But which? . . .

For reasons that will appear, I do not think that the question falls to be determined by whether the plaintiff sues for damages or whether he sues for specific performance, even though *McGregor on Damages* appears to put the matter on this point, at any rate to a considerable extent: see at pp 493, 526. Plainly it may be important whether or not the plaintiff is claiming specific performance: but I do not think it can be decisive. Suppose that a recluse sells some of his land on terms that the purchaser will erect a high wall that will enclose most of the vendor's land: the wall is not built, and so the vendor builds a wall himself and then sues for damages. His land may be worth more on the market without the wall than with it, but I cannot see that either this or the fact that he is not suing for specific performance ought to debar him from obtaining damages equal to the cost of building the wall. Whether the wall to be taken for this purpose is the actual wall, if reasonable, or the contractual wall, I need not discuss. If, without erecting the wall, he sues merely for damages, but establishes that he will spend the money on erecting a wall, preferring to have nothing more to do with the faithless purchaser, I do not see why the result should not be the same.

Again, some contracts for alterations to buildings, or for their demolition, might not, if carried out, enhance the market value of the land, and sometimes would reduce it. The tastes and desires of the owner may be wholly out of step with the ideas of those who constitute the market; yet I cannot see why eccentricity of taste should debar him from obtaining substantial damages unless he sues for specific performance. Per contra, if the plaintiff has suffered little or no monetary loss in the reduction of value of his land, and he has no intention of applying any damages towards carrying out the work contracted for, or its equivalent, I cannot see why he should recover the cost of doing work which will never be done. It would be a mere pretence to say that this cost was a loss and so should be recoverable as damages.

In the absence of any clear authority on the matter before me, I think I must consider it as a matter of principle. I do this in relation to the breach of a contract to do work on the land of another, whether to build, repair, replant or anything else: and I put it very broadly. First, it is fundamental to all questions of damages that they are to compensate the plaintiff for his loss or injury by putting him as nearly as possible in the same position as he would have been in had he not suffered the wrong. The question is not one of making the defendant disgorge what he has saved by committing the wrong, but one of compensating the plaintiff. In the words of O'Connor LJ in *Murphy v Wexford County Council* [1921] 2 IR 230, 240:

'You are not to enrich the party aggrieved; you are not to impoverish him; you are, so far as money can, to leave him in the same position as before.'

Second, if the plaintiff has suffered monetary loss, as by a reduction in the value of his property by reason of the wrong, that is plainly a loss that he is entitled to be recouped. On the other hand, if the defendant has saved himself money, as by not doing what he has contracted to do, that does not of itself entitle the plaintiff to recover the savings as damages; for it by no means necessarily follows that what the defendant has saved the plaintiff has lost.

Third, if the plaintiff can establish that his loss consists of or includes the cost of doing work which in breach of contract the defendant has failed to do, then he can recover as damages a sum equivalent to that cost. It is for the plaintiff to establish this: the essential question is what his loss is.

Fourth, the plaintiff may establish that the cost of doing the work constitutes part or all of his loss in a variety of ways. The work may already have been done before he sues. Thus he may have had it done himself, as in *Jones v Herxheimer*. Alternatively, he may be able to establish that the work will be done. This, I think, must depend on all the circumstances, and not merely on whether he sues for specific performance. An action for specific performance is doubtless one way of manifesting a sufficient intention that the work shall be done: but there are others.
. . . [I]f the circumstances fail to indicate sufficiently that the work will be done, the court might accept an undertaking by the plaintiff to do the work; and this, as in the business tenancy cases, would surely 'compel fixity of intention'. Whatever the circumstances, if the plaintiff establishes that the contractual work has been or will be done, then in all normal circumstances it seems to me that he has shown that the cost of doing it is, or is part of, his loss, and is recoverable as damages. Even if it is open to question whether the plaintiff will do the work, the cost of doing it may afford a starting figure, though it should be scaled down according to the circumstances, the real question being that of the loss to the plaintiff: see *Smiley v Townshend* [1950] 2 KB 311, 322, per Denning LJ. In the words of Denning J in *Westminster (Duke) v Swinton* [1948] 1 KB 524, 534, 'The real question in each case is: What damage has the plaintiff really suffered from the breach?' In the end, the question seems to me to come down to a very short point. The cost is a loss if it is shown to be a loss.

There is a fifth point. In most cases there can be no certainty about the doing of work which has not yet been done. A lessee bound by covenant to his lessor to do the work may be released from his covenant, or may have his liability compounded on payment of less than the cost of doing that work, as was envisaged by Lord Herschell in *Conquest v Ebbetts* [1896] AC 490, 494. The local authority may decide not to enforce the statutory obligation, or the court may release a litigant from his undertaking. A plaintiff who had a firm and settled intention to do the work may later find that supervening events have weakened or destroyed his resolve.

I do not think that the plaintiffs' rights are affected by any such absence of certainty. . . .

I turn to Mr Macdonald's secondary contention, founded on a suitable proportion of the cost of replanting as representing what the British Phosphate Commissioners would have paid to be released from their obligation to replant. This contention did not emerge until very late in the proceedings. It was on Day 96 that Mr Macdonald first cited *Wrotham Park Estate Co Ltd v Parkside Homes Ltd* and *Bracewell v Appleby*, on which he relied. In the former case, houses had been built on land without the prior approval of the plaintiffs which a restrictive covenant made requisite. On the facts of the case a mandatory injunction to demolish the houses was refused, and damages in substitution therefore were held to be recoverable under the Act of 1858. Brightman J resolved the difficult question of the appropriate quantum of damages by holding that the plaintiffs should recover 5 per cent of the defendants' expected profit from their venture. In *Bracewell v Appleby*, Graham J applied the same principle where the right in question was not a consent under a restrictive covenant, but an easement of way.

I find great difficulty in seeing how these cases help Mr Macdonald. If the plaintiff has the right to prevent some act being done without his consent, and the defendant does the act without seeking that consent, the plaintiff has suffered a loss in that the defendant has taken without paying for it something for which the plaintiff could have required payment, namely, the right to do the act. The court therefore makes the defendant pay what he ought to have paid the plaintiff, for that is what the plaintiff has lost. The basis of computation is not, it will be observed, in any way directly related to wasted expenditure or other loss that the defendant is escaping by reason of an injunction being refused: it is the loss that the plaintiff has suffered by the defendant not having observed the obligation to obtain the plaintiff's consent. Where the obligation is contractual, that loss is the loss caused to the plaintiff by breach of contract.

In the present case, the loss caused to the plaintiffs by the British Phosphate Commissioners' failure to replant is the diminution in the value of their land resulting from that failure, or, if it is established that the land would be replanted, the cost of replanting. In the latter case, no doubt, the British Phosphate Commissioners might well have been willing to pay something to be released from their obligation to replant, though that something would probably be rather less than the total estimated cost of replanting. But the point is that not unless the British Phosphate Commissioners would be liable to replant or pay damages equal to the cost of replanting would there be any liability from which the British Phosphate Commissioners would seek release on the basis of paying a sum equal to the discounted cost of replanting. If Mr Macdonald establishes that liability, he does not need his less favourable secondary contention: if Mr Macdonald fails to establish that liability, there is no foundation on which to base his secondary contention. Of course, until it has been determined whether or not some burden exists, the person who would be subject to that burden may always be willing to pay something to be relieved of the risk: but I do not think that this can affect the measure of damages in the case which determines that the burden does exist. In any case, the two authorities in question seem to me to be a long way away from a case where the issue is not one of invading the property rights of another without consent, but of breach of a contract to replant his land.

(b) QUANTUM. I return, then, to Mr Macdonald's primary contention. Have the plaintiffs shown that the cost of replanting represents the loss to them caused by the failure to perform the replanting obligation? Only one answer to that question seems possible, and that is No. The plaintiffs own small scattered plots of land; there is nothing to establish that the owners of neighbouring plots of land, who are not parties to these proceedings, would procure the replanting of their plots rather than keep any damages for themselves or other purposes; the Banabans are now well established in Rabi, over 1,500 miles away; and there they have an island over 10 times the size and unaffected by mining, as contrasted with the much smaller Ocean Island with some five-sixths of it mined.

NOTE

Megarry V-C's approach was applied in *Radford v De Froberville* [1978] 1 All ER 33. In that case the defendant had failed to perform a covenant to build a wall on her land along the boundary with the plaintiff's land, and had resold the land. Oliver J held that the plaintiff was entitled to the cost of building a wall on his side of the boundary, irrespective of whether it would increase the value of the property, and even though the plaintiff did not live on his property. It was sufficient that he had clearly established his intention to build the wall.

(iv) Non-pecuniary losses

In *Addis v Gramophone Co Ltd* [1909] AC 488 the plaintiff was employed as manager of the defendants' business in Calcutta. He could be dismissed on six months' notice. The defendants gave him six months' notice and at the same time appointed a successor, taking steps to prevent the plaintiff acting any longer as manager. A jury awarded the plaintiff £340 for loss of commissions and £600 for wrongful dismissal. The House of Lords allowed the first head, but not the second: the plaintiff could only recover his salary for the six months, and no more. Lord Loreburn said (at p 491):

'If there be a dismissal without notice the employer must pay an indemnity; but that indemnity cannot include compensation either for the injured feelings of the servant, or for the loss he may sustain from the fact that his having been dismissed of itself makes it more difficult for him to obtain fresh employment.'

The second part of Lord Loreburn's statement may respectfully be doubted: it is well established that an actor who is wrongfully not permitted to appear may recover for 'the loss of the opportunity of impressing the public with his artistic value and so enhancing or maintaining his reputation': *Withers v General Theatre Corpn Ltd* [1933] 2 KB 536, at 554. The first part of the statement, however, was treated by the Court of Appeal in *Groom v Crocker* [1939] 1 KB 194 as conclusive authority against giving general damages in contract for loss of reputation or injured feelings. In that case solicitors had, without consulting the plaintiff, entered a defence on his behalf admitting negligence in a motoring accident which had been wholly the fault of the other driver. As the insurers who had nominated the solicitors paid the damages assessed against the plaintiff, he recovered only nominal damages from the solicitors. (The Court of Appeal considered that any action against the solicitor must be in contract, not in tort. This view is no longer followed: *Midland Bank Ltd v Hett, Stubbs and Kemp* [1979] Ch 384.)

Jarvis v Swans Tours Ltd [1973] 1 All ER 71, Court of Appeal

The plaintiff booked a winter sports holiday which the defendants advertised in their brochure as 'a Houseparty in Morliap', with 'special resident host' . . . 'Welcome party . . . afternoon tea and cakes . . . Yodler evening'. It was stated that ski-packs would be available, and added, 'You will be in for a great time'. The Houseparty consisted of 13 people for the first week and only the plaintiff for the second, when there was no representative at the hotel; there was no welcoming party; full length skis were only available for two days; the cake for tea was only crisps and dry nutcake; the yodeller was a local man who sang a few songs in his working clothes. The plaintiff claimed damages for breach of a contract to provide the holiday promised. The trial judge awarded him £31.72, and he appealed.

Lord Denning MR. . . . What is the legal position? I think that the statements in the brochure were representations or warranties. The breaches of them give Mr Jarvis a right to damages. It is not necessary to decide whether they were representations or warranties; because, since the Misrepresentation Act 1967, there is a remedy in damages for misrepresentation as well as for breach of warranty.

The one question in the case is: what is the amount of damages? The judge seems to have taken the difference in value between what he paid for and what he got. He said that he intended to give 'the difference between the two values and no other damages' under any other head. He thought that Mr Jarvis had got half of what he paid for. So the judge gave him half the amount which he had paid, namely, £31.72. Mr Jarvis appeals to this court. He says that the damages ought to have been much more. . . .

What is the right way of assessing damages? It has often been said that on a breach of contract damages cannot be given for mental distress. Thus in *Hamlin v Great Northern Railway Co* Pollock CB said that damages cannot be given 'for the disappointment of mind occasioned by the breach of contract'. And in *Hobbs v London & South Western Railway Co* Mellor J said that—

'. . . for the mere inconvenience, such as annoyance and loss of temper, or vexation, or for being disappointed in a particular thing which you have set your mind upon, without real physical inconvenience resulting, you cannot recover damages.'

The courts in those days only allowed the plaintiff to recover damages if he suffered physical inconvenience, such as, having to walk five miles home, as in *Hobbs'* case; or to live in an overcrowded house: see *Bailey v Bullock.*

I think that those limitations are out of date. In a proper case damages for mental distress can be recovered in contract, just as damages for shock can be recovered in tort. One such case is a contract for a holiday, or any other contract to provide entertainment and enjoyment. If the contracting party breaks his contract, damages can be given for the disappointment, the distress, the upset and frustration caused by the breach. I know that it is difficult to assess in terms of money, but it is no more difficult than the assessment which the courts have to make every day in personal injury cases for loss of amenities. Take the present case. Mr Jarvis has only a fortnight's holiday in the year. He books it far ahead, and looks forward to it all that time. He ought to be compensated for the loss of it.

A good illustration was given by Edmund Davies LJ in the course of the argument. He put the case of a man who has taken a ticket for Glyndbourne. It is the only night on which he can get there. He hires a car to take him. The car does not turn up. His damages are not limited to the mere cost of the ticket. He is entitled to general damages for the disappointment he has suffered and the loss of the entertainment which he should have had. Here, Mr Jarvis's fortnight's winter holiday has been a grave disappointment. It is true that he was conveyed to Switzerland and back and had meals and bed in the hotel. But that is not what he went for. He went to enjoy himself with all the facilities which the defendants said he would have. He is entitled to damages for the lack of those facilities, and for his loss of enjoyment. . . . I think the damages in this case should be the sum of £125. I would allow the appeal accordingly.

[Edmund Davies LJ and Stephenson LJ delivered concurring judgments.]

Appeal allowed.

NOTES

1. Is Lord Denning's statement that it does not matter whether the damages are for breach of contract or for misrepresentation correct? Is the plaintiff recovering reliance loss or loss of expectation?
2. Some commentators referred to the damages in *Jarvis*'s case as exemplary (eg Yates (1973) 36 MLR 535). Do you agree?
3. In *Heywood v Wellers* [1976] 1 All ER 300 the plaintiff employed the defendant solicitors to obtain an injunction to prevent a man molesting her. The solicitors were negligent in conducting the litigation, in particular in failing to bring the man before the court when he again molested the plaintiff, with the result that he molested her twice more. The Court of Appeal held that she was entitled to damages for mental distress, which was the very thing that she was employing the solicitors to protect her from.
4. In *Cox v Philips Industries Ltd* [1976] 1 WLR 638 the plaintiff suffered depression and ill health after his employer, in breach of contract, took away his responsibilities and gave him no work to do, though he was still paid his salary. In *Bliss v South East Thames Regional Health Authority* ((1983) Times, 13 December) Farquharson J awarded the plaintiff orthopaedic surgeon damages for distress, frustration and vexation after the defendants had, in breach of contract, required him to submit to a medical examination by a psychiatrist and, when he refused, suspended him from duty: but this part of the decision was reversed by the Court of Appeal [1985] IRLR 308 as contrary to *Addis v Gramophone Co. Cox's* case was overruled.

'Contract Remedies and the Consumer Surplus' by Harris, Ogus and Phillips (1979) 95 LQR 581

In *Radford v De Froberville* the existence of the wall on the new boundary of his land was worth more to the plaintiff than the increase which the wall would make to the market value of the land; it was argued that he valued the particular architectural style and privacy it afforded more highly than would the average purchaser of the land. This is an example of what economists refer to as 'consumer surplus', the excess utility or subjective value obtained from a 'good' over and above the utility associated with its market price. The concept of consumer surplus is important in any attempt to measure consumer losses because, unlike firms, consumers make purchases for the pleasure or utility they confer; this utility has no necessary relationship with the price paid, and is of quite a different order from market prices or business profits. It is, of course, difficult to measure utility, but generally economists avoid the conceptual problem by measuring utility in terms of the maximum amount a consumer would pay for a particular purchase. For instance, if a purchaser can buy a plot of land for £1,000, when he would be prepared to pay up to £1,500 for it, the extra £500 represents his 'consumer surplus'. Without using this term, an intending bidder at an auction thinks in this way when he decides before-hand what is the maximum bid he is prepared to make: the difference between any lower price he pays and the higher price he is prepared to pay measures the consumer surplus expected at that time. Therefore willingness to pay, rather than market price, is the appropriate measure for estimating the value of a purchase, and the consumer surplus is the difference between this value and the market price.

Consumer surplus may arise from services as well as from the possession of land or goods. Thus, a holiday is generally worth more to the tourist than the price he has to pay for it, and the value to the family of wedding photographs exceeds their price. These illustrations show how individuals value performance of non-commercial contracts. However, consumer surplus has its analogue in commercial cases where profit rather than utility is the aim of the contract: the market price may underestimate the value of a good to the firm which buys it, and the surplus value above the market price will be represented by its contribution to profit-making. Lawyers are used to handling claims for loss of profits following the breach of a commercial contract. This article seeks to clarify the corresponding concept of the consumer surplus in the case of consumer contracts: both are relevant to the proper assessment of the expectation interest of the promisee.

. . . Within the framework of these remedies, there are various means whereby account may be taken of consumer surplus. First, the court has a discretionary power to force the promisor to perform (specific performance) (Section C). Secondly, it may indirectly achieve the same result by awarding the promisee such money as will enable him to employ a third party to perform (reinstatement damages) (Section D). Thirdly, either in exercise of its equitable jurisdiction to grant damages in lieu of specific relief (Section F), or in satisfaction of the plaintiff's common law *right* to damages upon a breach of contract (Section E), the court may attempt itelf to evaluate the consumer surplus by awarding a sum designed to compensate for that category of loss. . .

While, as will appear, the courts are in some situations prepared to adopt one of these remedies which does recognise the consumer surplus (though the recognition is rarely explicit), in many other situations they are not willing to do so, with the result that the plaintiff is, we would argue, under-compensated. This inhibition may lie in the common law's refusal to recognise consumer contracts as a separate category from commercial contracts: when claims for sums above the market price are made, judges have been accustomed to think only in terms of loss of profits or similar commercial interests and not in terms of loss of utility. Some categories of consumer contract have for long been recognised (eg landlord and tenant, hire purchase) but it is only more recently that the legislature has begun to recognise the need for general categories of consumer contracts in order to develop rules designed for such transactions. In some, typically civilian, systems, commercial and private contracts are separately categorised: the result, we believe, has been a greater readiness to compensate for the consumer surplus, either through specific relief or as reflected in an award of damages. A second inhibiting factor in the common law has been the fear that selection of one of the remedies may over-compensate the plaintiff or, as it is sometimes said, confer on him a 'windfall'. This would occur, for example, if an award of damages based on the cost of reinstatement in a case such as *Radford* were not actually spent on building the wall, but put to some other use. Thirdly, it can be objected that actual performance of the contractual undertaking would result in 'economic waste'. This may be the case, for example, where the cost of that performance would exceed the utility which the plaintiff expected to obtain on its completion. Thus, where premises are not built to specification, the plaintiff may (in preference to specific performance) be said to accept them in their present state and receive in compensation a small sum which is less than the cost of modifying them. The award of a sum which is in between the diminution in value and the cost of performance would increase the combined utilities of the parties.

C. *Specific Performance*

As regards the sale of chattels, the presumption that specific performance will not be available may be supplanted in the case of those which are 'unique', 'when there is, over and above the market value, that which has been called the *pretium affectionis*', and also, 'in the case of chattels which, though not unique, possess a special and peculiar value to the plaintiff'. This latter statement of principle could be interpreted in the light of the consumer surplus concept to mean that whenever, following the seller's failure to deliver a chattel, an award of damages would not enable the buyer to obtain a similar consumer surplus through a substitute purchase, the courts will be willing to grant specific performance. The reported cases show that specific performance has been ordered of contracts to buy a rare jewel, china vases, particular stones from Old Westminster Bridge, and an ornamental door designed by the famous architect Adam.

D. *Substitute Performance: damages assessed as the cost of completion or reinstatement by a third party*

One possible remedy is to secure what was promised by the indirect means of awarding damages to the promisee based on what it would cost him to obtain performance (or completion of performance) of the contractual undertaking by a third party. As with an order of specific performance, such a remedy would inevitably secure for the promisee any consumer surplus from which he would have benefited under performance of the contractual promise. The substitute or reinstatement approach has the added advantage of avoiding the problems of supervision which may arise under a specific performance order.

. . . [I]n some cases the court has to decide between two competing methods of assessing those damages: the measure based on the completion or reinstatement cost and that based on the difference between the market value of the defendant's performance in its defective or incomplete state and the market value of the performance if it had properly been completed. Again, although the matter is rarely made explicit, an intuitive perception of the consumer surplus problem is evident from the way in which the courts have selected as between these modes of compensation: they have tended to choose the alternative which they instinctively feel is closer to the plaintiff's 'real loss', *viz* the reinstatement measure when there is a substantial loss of consumer surplus, and the diminution in market value measure when there is no substantial loss of consumer surplus. This may be inferred from some of the reasons which have been offered for preferring the reinstatement measure. Thus it has been said that the plaintiff is entitled to the reasonable cost of having the remedial work done if in all the circumstances it is (or was) reasonable for him to insist on having the work done—and either (a) he has actually had the work done, or (b) he undertakes to have it done, or (c) he shows a 'sufficient intention' to have the work done if he receives damages on this basis. The implication of these requirements is that the court will have sufficient evidence from which it can assume that the plaintiff had an interest in performance which exceeded its market value. In the *Radford* case, it will be recalled, the plaintiff could show that the wall would fulfil 'a functional purpose', namely, 'that of enclosing and preserving the privacy of [his] land by a permanent boundary feature constructed in an acceptable architectural style'; and the judge was 'entirely satisfied that the plaintiff genuinely wants this work done and that he intends to expend any damages awarded on carrying it out'. In North America, the reinstatement measure has also been preferred where assessment of the difference in market value was too speculative and, perhaps more significantly, where there was no difference in market value between the performance as promised and that in fact executed, but where the difference is regarded by the plaintiff as of some importance: here the courts seem concerned to preserve some sanction for contract-breaking.

Conversely, the diminution measure has been preferred where the court suspects that the plaintiff does not really want the remedial work to be done but is merely hoping to inflate his damages award, or where it considers that the cost of the remedial work would be grossly and unfairly out of all proportion to the benefit to be obtained (thus amounting to economic waste). In so far as a court is correct in its estimation that the plaintiff's consumer surplus is not more than marginal, there can be no complaint with this approach, but to the extent that it is substituting its own ideas of what the plaintiff's utility *should* have been for what it was, the approach is clearly unsatisfactory. This may be amply demonstrated by the recent decision in *Tito v Waddell (No 2)* (the *Ocean Island* case). . . .

Megarry V-C rejected the plaintiffs' claim not only to specific performance but also to damages based on the cost of reinstating the land. Instead, he applied the diminution measure, though, as he himself admitted, this was largely a matter of guesswork since there was no market for worked-out plots of land in Ocean Island. Refusal of the reinstatement measure (claimed to be A$73,140 per acre) was justified on the grounds that: (i) since the islanders were now established on another island some 1,500, miles away, they had not established that the cost of replanting represented the 'loss' suffered by them on breach and (ii) the Vice-Chancellor was not convinced that they intended to spend the damages on replanting the plots.

It is difficult, on the facts of the case, to accept the implication of this reasoning that the islanders (though now living elsewhere) did not have a substantial consumer surplus in the replanted land, but one can sympathise with the predicament of the judge who felt himself constrained by his interpretation of the law to make the choice between an award of damages based on the cost of reinstatement and one based on £75 an acre (his evaluation of the diminution loss). We shall argue below that in such circumstances awards of damages might properly be made somewhere between the two extremes. For the present, we must consider the consequences of the decision actually reached in the *Ocean Island* case.

In the first place, it should be clear that a large 'benefit' was thereby conferred on the British Phosphate Commissioners. Future increases in labour and other costs arising from replanting were clearly within the risks assumed by the Commissioners' predecessor when the original undertaking was given and escalation in these costs would have been balanced against expected increases in the value of the phosphate to be sold. The result of the judgment, however, is that the Commissioners have been allowed to enjoy all the benefits of the islanders' predecessors' obligations under the contracts, while avoiding the cost of their corresponding obligations to replant.

Secondly, a delicate question is raised as to the relationship between this decision and the doctrine of frustration. It is trite law that a party may be relieved of his contractual obligations only when supervening events have rendered performance impossible, or at least have robbed the contract of its original purpose. But the mere inflation of the costs of performance, even when unforeseeable, has never been a sufficient ground for invoking the doctrine of frustration. It seems anomalous that a result which the law refuses to reach via this doctrine can nevertheless be arrived at indirectly through the process of assessing damages.

The solution to the problem confronted in the *Ocean Island* case and in others where actual reinstatement is either impossible or the court regards its cost as grossly unreasonable in the light of the benefit to be obtained would be a principle by which the damages could be fixed *above* the difference in market values but *below* the cost of reinstatement. There are two ways in which the matter could be approached. The court might attempt to evaluate the plaintiff's loss of consumer surplus. The method of doing this will be considered below. The second alternative would not deal directly with the question of consumer surplus but would provide a justification for ignoring it. It would be to allocate the benefit which accrues to the promisor from the saving he has made in not performing his contractual obligation. Hitherto, the courts seemed to have been concerned that the *promisee* should not make an undeserved 'profit' if damages are awarded on the reinstatement basis but the money is used for some other purpose. This assumes that the only question is whether the promisee 'deserves' to benefit from the 'windfall'; it fails to take into account that when there is a substantial difference between the diminution in market value and the cost of reinstatement, there may be a 'windfall' which must be 'awarded' to one party or the other. In the *Ocean Island* case, Megarry V-C in effect 'awarded' all the windfalls to the defendants, the contract-breakers, without (apparently) considering the possibility of dividing it between the parties. A fair allocation between the parties would strike a balance between their respective interests (following the analogies of unjust enrichment in the law on Restitution) and at the same time would provide the court with a justification for not attempting to compensate for the loss of the expected consumer surplus: the division of the windfall would be in lieu of such compensation, since it would often produce as damages a sum which exceeds the plaintiff's own valuation of his lost consumer surplus. . . .

E. *Damages for Non-Pecuniary Loss*

The common law systems have traditionally been hesitant to award non-pecuniary damages for breach of contract. This may again be attributed to the failure to distinguish between commercial and consumer contracts and to recognise that almost by definition the latter are concerned with the transfer to the promisee of a benefit to be enjoyed rather than a marketable good. But the absence of the award from the reported cases may also be explained by the fact that in most situations it is assumed that the promisee can avoid the loss by obtaining equivalent satisfaction from a substitute. In other words, the problem would arise only where such substitution was not available [as in *Jarvis v Swans Tours*]. . . .

F. *Damages in lieu of specific performance (Lord Cairns' Act)*

Under the Chancery Amendment Act 1858 (Lord Cairns' Act), a court of Equity was empowered to award damages in addition to, or in substitution for, specific performance where it had jurisdiction to grant such specific relief. This power still exists, and in certain respects equitable damages may be awarded in situations not recognised by common law; but the House of Lords has recently held that the Act does not provide for the assessment of damages on any new basis. However, the fact that equitable damages are granted *in lieu* of specific performance, with the consequent object of putting the plaintiff in the position he would have been in if specific relief had been ordered, suggests that to be an adequate substitute they should take account of the consumer surplus. It is difficult to find direct support for this proposition in the reported cases, but where equitable damages have been awarded in lieu of an injunction (a form of specific relief analogous to that of specific performance), they have been assessed at the 'proper and fair price' which the plaintiffs (albeit reluctantly) would have been willing to accept for the loss of an amenity attached to the beneficial use of property. (See *Bracewell v Appleby* [1975] Ch 408, 419–420.] This formulation may be related to the concept of consumer surplus: both are based on an individual's personal evaluation of an asset, although the courts evidently prefer to quantify this by reference to what the reasonable man in the plaintiff's position would have been prepared to accept.

G. *Limits to Damages Awards: Mitigation and Remoteness*

There are a number of doctrines in the law which limit the amount of damages which may be awarded for breach of contract . . . the mitigation principle can be applied to the additional value of the promise to the promisee, the consumer surplus. If a substitute which is reasonably available to the promisee would confer on him utility as great as that resulting from performance of the original contract, clearly there is no loss of consumer surplus. [Further] the loss must be such as to have been within the reasonable expectation of the parties as 'not unlikely' to arise on the breach of contract, as judged at the time of the making of the contract.

H. *The Assessment of Damages for Loss of Consumer Surplus (Whether at Common Law or Equity)*

Although economics can elucidate the concept of consumer surplus, it can offer little guidance on the methods by which a third party, such as a court, could assess in money the value of a lost consumer surplus. . . .

The closest approach to the economist's concept of consumer surplus is found in cases where the plaintiff has been wrongfully deprived of an amenity attached to the beneficial use of land. Thus, where the defendant broke a covenant not to develop land for building purposes except in strict accordance with a plan approved by the plaintiffs, but the judge decided not to grant an injunction for the demolition of the houses erected in breach of the covenant, he concluded that 'a just substitute for a mandatory injunction would be in such a sum of money as might reasonably have been demanded by the plaintiffs from [the defendant] as a quid pro quo for relaxing the covenant.' [*Wrotham Park Estate Co Ltd v Parkside Homes Ltd* [1974] 1 WLR 798] In another case, which was concerned with the use of a right of way for a purpose not envisaged by the original grant, the court fixed the damages at the 'proper and fair price' which the plaintiffs, 'albeit reluctantly, would have been willing to accept for granting the more extensive right of way, *viz* 'as compensating them for loss of amenity and increased user.' [*Bracewell v Appleby*, above] In the case of the vendor's breach of a contract to sell a house to the defendant for the purpose of his own occupation, a convenient approach would be to fix a percentage of the agreed price as damages for loss of the purchaser's expected consumer surplus.

A second approach to the assessment of damages would be for the court to fix an arbitrary sum to provide some utility to replace that lost by the breach of contract. In personal injury cases, the injured person's own subjective valuation of his lost utility is ignored, and the courts have fixed arbitrary, conventional, sums to compensate for the loss of part of the body, for pain and suffering, or for reduction in the expectation of life. . . .

J. *Formal Remedies and Informal Bargains*

The [following] possibilities may provide satisfactory solutions to the consumer surplus problem:

    (a) directly compelling performance of the contractual obligation by an order for specific performance or an injunction;

    (b) indirectly compelling performance of the contractual obligation by awarding the promisee the cost of performance (or of completing performance) coupled with an undertaking that the damages will be spent for this purpose;

    (c) awarding the promisee a sum of money by way of damages (at common law or in equity) which attempts to compensate him for the loss of consumer surplus. . . .

A major problem with an order for specific performance (or an order for reinstatement damages linked with an undertaking to carry out the substance of the contract) is that the remedy may appear to be wasteful. The promisee may prefer to receive a sum of money which is less than the cost of performance, a solution which would also be to the promisor's advantage. This is most obviously the case when work carried out has not been to specification, but the cost of remedying it would be out of all proportion to the loss of consumer surplus. However, it is not to be assumed that in all cases an order for specific performance will in fact be executed or that such a failure thwarts the aims of the law. An order is not normally executed by the court of its own initiative: it is usually necessary for the party for whose benefit it is granted to return to court to complain of non-compliance and to seek execution, typically through the contempt process. Unless, therefore, there are considerations of public policy which render compliance essential, the promisee is entitled to waive or 'sell' his right to specific relief. He will, of course, ordinarily only be prepared to do so when he is offered a price high enough to compensate him for his expected loss from performance (which would include his consumer surplus); this loss will probably exceed the objective value of the benefit derived from performance (*viz* normally the market value). Viewed from this perspective, specific performance may be characterised as a formal declaration by the court that the promisee's interest in performance is absolute in the sense that he cannot be forced against his will to convert it into a monetary equivalent, but that at the same time it remains a negotiable asset in that he can, if he wishes, surrender it to the promisee for valuable consideration.

. . . Given a situation in which the plaintiff would prefer a monetary sum to performance, the question arises whether the appropriate amount should best be arrived at by the process of a compromise after a specific performance order or, rather, by limiting his remedy to damages. In the former case the parties themselves will be evaluating the consumer surplus; in the latter it will result from a judicial determination. The theoretical considerations which ought to be weighed when judging the merits of the two approaches include the following.

First, there is the problem of uncertainty. Even if the sum awarded or agreed upon will be the same, individuals generally prefer a more rather than less certain path in reaching the final result. The problem with an order for specific performance is that, unless the case falls within one of the well-known categories where the order is regularly made, there will be considerable uncertainty as to whether specific performance will be decreed (in contrast to the damages remedy to which the promisee is entitled as of right). . . .

A second problem concerns transaction costs, which include those expenses necessary to reaching the final solution. The damages solution may involve lower legal costs since there will not be a second stage of negotiations (as with the specific performance approach); on the other hand, the parties will incur the expense of collecting evidence relating to the loss.

A third factor relates to the bargaining position of the parties. The 'absolute' nature of the promisee's right, following a specific performance order, may lead to the problem of so-called 'hold-out': he may be tempted to extort from the promisor a sum which approaches as nearly as possible the cost of implementation, thereby exceeding the value he sets on his consumer surplus. In the situation where a settlement is reached on a damages claim, the parties will arrive at a compromise between two limits representing the estimate each has of the likely judicial award: to the extent that that award takes account of the consumer surplus, the bargaining limits should be located close to that figure, or in any event should not be weighted in favour of one party rather than the other. After a specific performance decree, however, the bargaining limits clearly favour the promisee: he will not be prepared to accept a sum less than his evalution of the consumer surplus. The upper limit will be the cost of performance and, if it be assumed that anything above the consumer's evaluation of the benefit will constitute overcompensation, then any bargain struck above the minimum will be subject to that criticism. The extent of overcompensation will depend on the relative bargaining strength of the two parties: the 'hold-out' strategy of the promisee may be tempered by the possibility of actual performance by the promisor (*ex hypothesi* not giving the promisee what he wants). Nevertheless some might regard the probability of overcompensation as an overwhelming objection to the specific performance approach, thus suggesting that the judge should only adopt such an approach when he estimates that the plaintiff's subjective valuation approaches the cost of performance. In any event the risk of overcompensation must be balanced against the risk of undercompensation which may result from the difficulty inherent in evaluating the consumer surplus. Indeed, from a perspective which has been described above, what is at stake is the amount of the windfall which the promisor receives from the court's decision that he will not be compelled to perform, and any 'overcompensation' received by the promisee may be regarded as his share in the 'windfall.'

NOTE

Rea, 'Nonpecuniary loss and breach of contract' (1982) 11 J Legal Studies 35 argues that awarding full compensation for nonpecuniary losses in cases like *Jarvis v Swan Tours* may overcompensate the plaintiff and thus be inefficient. His point is that in many cases what is lost is irreplaceable. If it were simply a question of deciding whether or not to take out insurance against a random event causing the same loss, the rational person would not insure or would do so at a lower level. Where the supplier can influence the probability of a breach of contract leading to loss (as Swan clearly could) there is a conflict between the provision of optimal insurance for the buyer and providing an incentive for the supplier to take optimal precautions. Some liability must be imposed on defaulting suppliers or they will have inadequate incentives to take efficient precautions; but the amount of liability need only be what is adequate to ensure that the proper precautions are taken, not the full nonpecuniary loss. Thus the damages should be somewhere between the optimal amount of insurance and the full nonpecuniary loss which was suffered. Full compensation should be given only when the breach was wilful (as is in fact the rule in some US jurisdictions).

(f) Agreed damages, deposits and forfeitures

(i) Agreed damages

Dunlop Pneumatic Tyre Co Ltd v New Garage and Motor Co Ltd [1915] AC 79, House of Lords

The appellants sold motor tyres, covers and tubes to the respondent dealers, who agreed, inter alia, not to sell or offer the goods to any private customers or to any co-operative society at less than the appellants' current list prices, nor to sell to any person whose supplies the appellants had decided to suspend, and to pay the sum of £5 per tyre by way of liquidated damages for every tyre cover or tube sold or offered in breach of the agreement. The respondents sold a tyre cover to a cooperative society at less than the list price, and the appellants claimed the agreed sum.

Lord Dunedin. . . . I shall content myself with stating succinctly the various propositions which I think are deducible from the decisions which rank as authoritative:—

1. Though the parties to a contract who use the words 'penalty' or 'liquidated damages' may prima facie be supposed to mean what they say, yet the expression used is not conclusive. The Court must find out whether the payment stipulated is in truth a penalty or liquidated damages. This doctrine may be said to be found passim in nearly every case.

2. The essence of a penalty is a payment of money stipulated as in terrorem of the offending party; the essence of liquidated damages is a genuine covenanted pre-estimate of damage (*Clydebank Engineering and Shipbuilding Co v Don Jose Ramos Yzquierdo y Castaneda*).

3. The question whether a sum stipulated is penalty or liquidated damages is a question of construction to be decided upon the terms and inherent circumstances of each particular contract, judged of as at the time of the making of the contract, not as at the time of the breach (*Public Works Commissioner v Hills* and *Webster v Bosanquet*).

4. To assist this task of construction various tests have been suggested, which if applicable to the case under consideration may prove helpful, or even conclusive. Such are:

(a) It will be held to be penalty if the sum stipulated for is extravagant and unconscionable in amount in comparison with the greatest loss that could conceivably be proved to have followed from the breach. (Illustration given by Lord Halsbury in *Clydebank Case.*)

(b) It will be held to be a penalty if the breach consists only in not paying a sum of money, and the sum stipulated is a sum greater than the sum which ought to have been paid. (*Kemble v Farren*). This though one of the most ancient instances is truly a corollary to the last test. Whether it had its historical origin in the doctrine of the common law that when A promised to pay B a sum of money on a certain day and did not do so, B could only recover the sum with, in certain cases, interest, but could never recover further damages for non-timeous payment, or whether it was a survival of the time when equity reformed unconscionable bargains merely because they were unconscionable—a subject which much exercised Jessel MR in *Wallis v Smith*—is probably more interesting than material.

(c) There is a presumption (but no more) that it is penalty when 'a single lump sum is made payable by way of compensation, on the occurrence of one or more or all of several events, some of which may occasion serious and others but trifling damage' (Lord Watson in *Lord Elphinstone v Monkland Iron and Coal Co*).

On the other hand:

(d) It is no obstacle to the sum stipulated being a genuine pre-estimate of damages, that the consequences of the breach are such as to make precise pre-estimation almost an impossibility. On the contrary, that is just the situation when it is probable that pre-estimated damage was the true bargain between the parties (*Clydebank Case*, Lord Halsbury; *Webster v Bosanquet*, Lord Mersey).

Turning now to the facts of the case, it is evident that the damage apprehended by the appellants owing to the breaking of the agreement was an indirect and not a direct damage. So long as they got their price from the respondents for each article sold, it could not matter to them directly what the respondents did with it. Indirectly it did. Accordingly, the agreement is headed 'Price Maintenance Agreement', and the way in which the appellants would be damaged if prices were cut is clearly explained in evidence by Mr Baisley, and no successful attempt is made to controvert that evidence. But though damage as a whole from such a practice would be certain, yet damage from any one sale would be impossible to forecast. It is just, therefore, one of those cases where it seems quite reasonable for parties to contract that they should estimate that damage at a certain figure, and provided that figure is not extravagant there would seem no reason to suspect that it is not truly a bargain to assess damages, but rather a penalty to be held in terrorem.

The argument of the respondents was really based on two heads. They overpressed, in my judgment, the dictum of Lord Watson in *Lord Elphinstone's Case*, reading it as if he had said that the matter was conclusive, instead of saying, as he did, that it raised a presumption, and they relied strongly on the case of *Willson v Love*.

Now, in the first place, I have considerable doubt whether the stipulated payment here can fairly be said to deal with breaches, 'some of which'—I am quoting Lord Watson's words—'may occasion serious and others but trifling damage'. As a mere matter of construction, I doubt whether clause 5 applies to anything but sales below price. But I will assume that it does. None the less the mischief, as I have already pointed out, is an indirect mischief, and I see no data on which, as a matter of construction, I could settle in my own mind that the indirect damage from selling a cover would differ in magnitude from the indirect damage from selling a tube; or that the indirect damage from a cutting-price sale would differ from the indirect damage from supply at a full price to a hostile, because prohibited, agent. You cannot weigh such things in a chemical balance. The character of the agricultural land which was ruined by slag heaps in *Elphinstone's Case* was not all the same, but no objection was raised by Lord Watson to applying an overhead rate per acre, the sum not being in itself unconscionable.

I think *Elphinstone's Case*, or rather the dicta in it, do go this length, that if there are various breaches to which one indiscriminate sum to be paid in breach is applied, then the strength of the chain must be taken at its weakest link. If you can clearly see that the loss on one particular breach could never amount to the stipulated sum, then you may come to the conclusion that the sum is penalty. But further than this it does not go; so, for the reasons already stated, I do not think the present case forms an instance of what I have just expressed.

As regards *Willson's Case*, I do not think it material to consider whether it was well decided on the facts. For it was decided on the view of the facts that the manurial value of straw and of hay were known ascertainable quantities as at the time of the bargain, and radically different, so that the damage resulting from the want of one could never be the same as the damage resulting from the want of the other.

[Lord Atkinson, Lord Parker of Waddington and Lord Parmoor delivered concurring judgments.]

Appeal allowed.

NOTES

1. In *Willson v Love* [1896] 1 QB 626, 65 LJQB 474 (referred to in the *Dunlop* case) a lease of a farm provided that the lessees should not sell hay or straw off the premises during the last twelve months of the term, and that they should pay an additional rent of £3 for every ton of either so sold. Evidence was given that the manurial value of hay was over 15s per

ton, but that of straw less than 5s per ton. The additional rent was held to be a penalty.

2. If the clause is a valid liquidated damages clause, the sum stipulated is recoverable upon the relevant breach, even though the actual loss is less or even nil. In *Clydebank Engineering and Shipbuilding Co v Castaneda* [1905] AC 6, 74 LJPC 1, HL the sellers of four torpedo boats which they had delivered late argued that they should not have to pay liquidated damages to the buyers, the Spanish navy, on the ground that if the boats had been delivered in time, they would have shared the same fate as the rest of the Spanish navy, which had been sent to the bottom of the Atlantic by the American navy. The House of Lords rejected this argument as absurd.

3. Equally, if the clause is valid it does not matter that the real loss suffered by the innocent party is greater than the stipulated sum: only the sum is recoverable. It is interesting to note that an agreed damages clause may be valid even though the sum is deliberately set at *less* than the estimated loss: *Cellulose Acetate Silk Co Ltd v Widnes Foundry (1925) Ltd* [1933] AC 20, 101 LJKB 694.

4. If the clause is invalid as a penalty, the innocent party may recover his actual loss, at least if it is less than the stipulated sum: see Hudson (1974) 90 LQR 31; Gordon 90 LQR 296; Hudson (1975) 91 LQR 25; Barton (1976) 92 LQR 20.

5. The penalty rules also apply to provisions which stipulate that if a party breaks the contract he must retransfer property to the seller: *Jobson v Johnson* (noted above, p 451).

6. It is not clear whether it is permissible to stipulate for liquidated damages for a loss which might not be recoverable at common law, such as non-pecuniary loss. In *Robophone Facilities Ltd v Blank* [1966] 3 All ER 128 at 142–143, Diplock LJ suggested that a clause would be valid if it were a genuine pre-estimate of a loss which would not normally be recoverable because it was outside the ordinary course of things under the first limb of *Hadley v Baxendale*, but that was because the clause would put the other on notice of the amount of loss. The next case suggests a restrictive attitude towards losses which cannot normally be recovered.

Lombard North Central plc v Butterworth [1987] 1 All ER 267, Court of Appeal

The plaintiffs, a finance company, leased a computer to the defendant for a period of five years on payment of an initial sum of £584.05 and 19 subsequent quarterly instalments of the same amount. Clause 2(*a*) of the hiring agreement made punctual payment of each instalment of the essence of the agreement and under cl 5 failure to make due and punctual payment entitled the plaintiffs to terminate the agreement. By cl 6 the plaintiffs were entitled on termination to all arrears of instalments and all future instalments which would have fallen due had the agreement not been terminated. Although the defendant paid the first two instalments promptly, the next three were paid very belatedly, and on four occasions payment made by direct debit was recalled by the bank. When the sixth instalment was six weeks overdue the plaintiffs wrote to the defendant terminating the agreement. Subsequently the plaintiffs recovered possession of the computer and sold it for only £172.88. The plaintiffs brought an action against the defendant claiming the amount of the unpaid sixth instalment and the 13 future instalments or, alternatively, damages for breach of contract. They then applied for and obtained summary judgment under RSC Ord 14 for damages to be assessed. In assessing the damages the master held that the defendant had by his conduct repudiated the contract and accordingly the plaintiffs were entitled to recover damages in respect of all future instalments less certain credits. The defendant appealed, contending that he ought not to be held liable for more than the amount due and unpaid at the date of termination. . . .

Mustill LJ. . . . The Hiring agreement contained the following material provisions:

'THE LESSEE . . . AGREES . . .

2(a) to pay to the lessor: (i) punctually and without previous demand the rentals set out in Part 3 of the Schedule together with Value Added Tax thereon punctual payment of each which shall be of the essence of this Lease . . .

5. IN THE EVENT THAT (*a*) the Lessee shall (i) make default in the due and punctual payment of any of the rentals or of any sum of money payable to the Lessor hereunder or any part thereof . . . then upon the happening of such event . . . the Lessor's consent to the Lessee's possession of the Goods shall determine forthwith without any notice being given by the Lessor, and the Lessor may terminate this Lease either by notice in writing, or by taking possession of the Goods . . .

6. IN THE EVENT that the Lessor's consent to the Lessee's possession of the goods shall be determined under clause 5 hereof (*a*) the Lessee shall pay forthwith to the Lessor: (1) all arrears of rentals; and (ii) all further rentals which would but for the determination of the Lessor's consent to the Lessee's possession of the Goods have fallen due to the end of the fixed period of this Lease less a discount thereon for accelerated payment at the rate of 5 per cent per annum; and (iii) damages for any breach of this Lease and all expenses and costs incurred by the Lessor in retaking possession of the Goods and/or enforcing the Lessor's rights under this Lease together with such Value Added Tax as shall be legally payable thereon; (*b*) the Lessor shall be entitled to exercise any one or more of the rights and remedies provided for in clause 5 and sub clause (*a*) of this clause and the determination of the Lessor's consent to the Lessee's possession of the Goods shall not affect or prejudice such rights and remedies and the Lessee shall be and remain liable to perform all outstanding liabilities under this Lease notwithstanding that the Lessor may have taken possession of the Goods and/or exercised one or more of the rights and remedies of the Lessor; (*c*) any right or remedy to which the Lessor is or may become entitled under this Lease or in consequence of the Lessee's conduct may be enforced from time to time separately or concurrently with any other right or remedy given by this Lease or now or hereafter provided for or arising by operation of law so that such rights and remedies are not exclusive of the other or others of them but are cumulative' . . .

Three issues were canvassed before us. (1) Is cl 6 of the agreement to be disregarded, on the ground that it creates a penalty? (Strictly speaking, this issue does not arise, since the judgment was for damages to be assessed, but cl 6 was relied on by the plaintiffs before the master and in this court, without objection.) (2) Apart from cl 2(*a*) of the agreement, was the master correct in holding that the conduct of the defendant amounted to a wrongful repudiation of the contract, and that the sum claimed was recoverable in damages? (3) Does the provision in cl 2(*a*) of the agreement that time for payment of the instalments was of the essence have the effect of making the defendant's late payment of the outstanding instalments a repudiatory breach?

As to the first two issues, I need say only that I have had the advantage of reading in draft the judgment to be delivered by Nicholls LJ, and that I am in such entire agreement with his conclusions and reasons that it is unnecessary to add any observations of my own.

. . .

The reason why I am impelled to hold that the plaintiffs' contentions are well-founded can most conveniently be set out in a series of propositions. (1) Where a breach goes to the root of the contract, the injured party may elect to put an end to the contract. Thereupon both sides are relieved from those obligations which remain unperformed. (2) If he does so elect, the injured party is entitled to compensation for (a) any breaches which occurred before the contract was terminated and (b) the loss of his opportunity to receive performance of the promisor's outstanding obligations. (3) Certain categories of obligation, often called conditions, have the property that any breach of them is treated as going to the root of the contract. On the occurrence of any breach of condition, the injured party can elect to terminate and claim damages, whatever the gravity of the breach. (4) It is possible by express provision in the contract to make a term a condition, even if it would not be so in the absence of such a provision. (5) A stipulation that time is of the essence, in relation to a particular contractual term, denotes that timely performance is a condition of the contract. The consequence is that delay in performance is treated as going to the root of the contract, without regard to the magnitude of the breach. (6) It follows that where a promisor fails to give timely performance of an obligation in respect of which time is expressly stated to be of the essence, the injured party may elect to terminate and recover damages in respect of the promisor's outstanding obligations, without regard to the magnitude of the breach. (7) A term of the contract prescribing what damages are to be recoverable when a contract is terminated for a breach of condition is open to being struck down as a penalty, if it is not a genuine covenanted pre-estimate of the damage, in the same way as a clause which prescribes the measure for any other type of breach. No doubt the position is the same where the clause is ranked as a condition by virtue of an express provision in the contract. (8) A clause expressly assigning a particular obligation to the category of condition is not a clause which purports to fix the damages for breaches of the obligation, and is not subject to the law governing penalty clauses. (9) Thus, although in the present case cl 6 is to be struck down as a penalty, cl 2(*a*)(i) remains enforceable. The plaintiffs were entitled to terminate the contract independently of cl 5, and to recover damages for loss of the future instalments. This loss was correctly computed by the master.

These bare propositions call for comment. The first three are uncontroversial. The fourth was not, I believe, challenged before us, but I would in any event regard it as indisputable. . . .

The fifth proposition is a matter of terminology, and has been more taken for granted than discussed. That making time of the essence is the same as making timely performance a condition was, however, expressly stated by Megaw and Browne LJJ in *Bunge Corp v Tradax SA* [above, p 438], and the same proposition is implicit in the leading speeches of Lord Wilberforce and Lord Roskill in the House of Lords.

The sixth proposition is a combination of the first five. There appears to be no direct authority for it, and it is right to say that most of the cases on the significance of time being of the essence have been concerned with the right of the injured party to be discharged, rather than the principles on which its damages are to be computed. Nevertheless, it is axiomatic that a person who establishes a breach of condition can terminate and claim damages for loss of the bargain, and I know of no authority which suggests that the position is any different where late performance is made into a breach of condition by a stipulation that time is of the essence.

I return to the propositions stated above. The seventh is uncontroversial, and I would add only the rider that when deciding on the penal nature of a clause which prescribes a measure of recovery for damages resulting from a termination founded on a breach of condition, the comparison should be with the common law measure, namely with the loss to the promisee resulting from the loss of his bargain. If the contract permits him to treat the contract as repudiated, the fact that the breach is comparatively minor should in my view play no part in the equation.

I believe that the real controversy in the present case centres on the eighth proposition. I will repeat it. A clause expressly assigning a particular obligation to the category of condition is not a clause which purports to fix the damages for breach of the obligation, and is not subject to the law governing penalty clauses. I acknowledge, of course, that by promoting a term into the category where all breaches are ranked as breaches of condition, the parties indirectly bring about a situation where, for breaches which are relatively small, the injured party is enabled to recover damages as on the loss of the bargain, whereas without the stipulation his measure of recovery would be different. But I am unable to accept that this permits the court to strike down as a penalty the clause which brings about this promotion. To do so would be to reverse the current of more than 100 years' doctrine, which permits the parties to treat as a condition something which would not otherwise be so. I am not prepared to take this step.

For these reasons I conclude that the plaintiffs are entitled to retain the damages which the master has awarded. This is not a result which I view with much satisfaction, partly because the plaintiffs have achieved by one means a result which the law of penalties might have prevented them from achieving by another and partly because if the line of argument under cl 2 had been developed from the outset, the defendant might have found an answer based on waiver which the court is now precluded from assessing, for want of the necessary facts. Nevertheless, it is the answer to which, in my view, the authorities clearly point. Accordingly, I would dismiss the appeal.

Nicholls LJ. Shortly stated, the two issues raised on this appeal are whether the sums payable under cl 6 of the lease agreement constituted a penalty and, if so, whether the conduct of the hirer (the defendant) amounted to a repudiation of the agreement that was accepted by the owner (the plaintiffs).

The claim under cl 6
On the first issue, the criticism of cl 6 advanced on behalf of the defendant was confined to the absence of provision giving credit for the net amount of the price obtained by the plaintiffs on any resale of the goods effected by it after retaking possession. Argument in this court took place on the footing that the presence or absence of such a provision, which I shall call a 'resale price allowance', was crucial on the penalty point, counsel for the defendant putting forward the omission of such an allowance as the fundamental objection to the clause.

If this were right, and cl 6 would be unobjectionable if it included a resale price allowance, it could only be because cl 6, with the addition of a provision for such an allowance, would represent a genuine estimate of the loss likely to be suffered in this case by the plaintiffs. It is on this footing that the clause would be enforceable. In that event the sum of £6,869.97 claimed in the action with interest, would have been payable by the defendant (because in arriving at that sum the plaintiffs in fact gave credit for the net resale price of the computer, even though cl 6 did not require this). The sum of £6,869.97 is made up of one instalment in arrear (£585.05, plus £87.61 value added tax) and 13 future instalments (£7,592.65) less the net proceeds of sale (£172.85) and less also an allowance for accelerated receipt of the future instalments (£1,221.49). But, on the other hand, according to this argument advanced for the defendant, if cl 6 is struck down as a penalty because of the absence of a resale price allowance, the consequence in law is that nothing is recoverable by the plaintiffs except the one unpaid instalment (£585.05 plus value added tax) and interest thereon.

In my view these two alternative conclusions have only to be set beside each other for their mutual incompatibility to be evident. As Lord Denning pointed out in *Bridge v Campbell Discount Co Ltd*, when equity granted relief against a penalty it always required the recipient of its favours, as a condition of relief, to pay the damage which the other party had really sustained. If a genuine estimate of the damage really sustained by the plaintiffs here produces the sum of £6,869.97, how can the striking down of cl 6 as a penalty because of the omission of a resale price allowance somehow result in him recovering only £585.05?

As I see it, the answer to this question is to be found in the assumption underlying the argument of the defendant that cl 6 with the addition of a resale price allowance would not be a penalty. In my view, in the absence of a repudiatory breach, that assumption is misconceived. The ratio of the decision of this court in *Financings Ltd v Baldock* [above, p 428] was that when an owner determines a hire-purchase agreement in exercise of a right so to do given him by the agreement, in the absence of repudiation he can recover damages for any breaches up to the date of termination but not thereafter, and a 'minimum payment' clause which purports to oblige the hirer to pay larger sums than this is unenforceable as a penalty.

This principle has since been applied in several decisions of this court, including *Brady v St Margaret's Trust Ltd, Charterhouse Credit Co Ltd v Tolly, United Dominions Trust (Commercial) Ltd v Ennis* and *Capital Finance Co Ltd v Donati*.

Of these I refer to one only, *Capital Finance Co Ltd v Donati*. There the court applied the principle in a hire-purchase case where on determination of the hiring, the owner having power to determine the hiring if the hirer made default in the punctual payment of any instalment, a minimum payment clause came into operation that was substantially similar to cl 6 save that, unlike cl 6, it did give credit to the hirer for any sum recovered on the sale of the Fiat car subject to that agreement. The sum expressed to be payable comprised the arrears of hire rent up to the date of termination, any expenses incurred by the owner in recovering possession of the car, and also the amount of the owner's loss on the transaction which was agreed as being the difference between the hire-purchase price and the total of (i) the net proceeds of sale of the car, (ii) the initial payment and the instalments paid by the hirer and (iii) a sum representing a reasonable proportion of the charges shown in the schedule applicable to that part of the hire-purchase price which the owner would by operation of the clause receive prematurely. Cairns LJ pointed out that while there was a difference of opinion in *Financings Ltd v Baldock* as to the proper measure of damages in a case of repudiation, all members of the court held that in the absence of repudiation the common law measure of damages was limited to the overdue instalments and interest thereon and that the provision for additional damages was a penalty clause. He said (I read from the transcript):

'The clause in the present case does differentiate between an early and a late breach by providing for the deduction of a reasonable proportion of the charges, but it makes no distinction between the most trivial breach (for example, delay of a few days in the payment of one instalment) and a repudiatory breach. It purports to assess 'the owners' loss on the transaction' and the method of assessment shows that what is meant is that the owners are to be recompensed for all the consequences of the hirer's breach and of their own election to determine the hiring. This could only be free from the element of penalty if the whole of this loss could be said to result from the breach, which would be contrary to the ratio decidendi of *Financings Ltd v Baldock*.'

In my view, applying the principle enunciated in *Financings Ltd v Baldock* to this case leads inescapably to the conclusion that in the absence of a repudiatory breach cl 6(a) is a penalty in so far as it purports to oblige the defendant, regardless of the seriousness or triviality of the breach which led to the plaintiffs terminating the agreement by retaking possession of the computer, to make a payment, albeit a discounted payment, in respect of rental instalments which had not accrued due prior to 20 December 1982.

From what I have said it will be apparent that I consider that, in the absence of a repudiatory breach, the outcome of this issue is not dependent on the inclusion or exclusion of a resale price allowance, and indeed the legal result would have been the same if cl 6 had contained a resale price allowance.

I consider below whether there was a repudiatory breach in this case, but for completeness I add here that it was accepted by counsel for the plaintiffs (and, in my view, rightly so) that if cl 6(*a*) was unenforceable as a penalty, the provisions in cl 6(*b*) would not assist the plaintiffs in this case.

[Nicholls LJ held that, apart from cl 2(a), the hirers had not repudiated the contract; but he accepted, 'as presently advised', that cl 2(a) made their default into a breach of condition for the reasons given by Mustill LJ. He continued:]

I have to say that I view the impact of that principle in this case with considerable dissatisfaction, for this reason. As already mentioned, the principle applied in *Financings Ltd v Baldock* was that when an owner determines a hire-purchase agreement in exercise of a power so to do given him by the agreement on non-payment of instalments, he can recover damages for any breaches up to the date of termination but (in the absence of repudiation) not thereafter. There is no practical difference between (1) an agreement containing such a power and (2) an agreement containing a provision to the effect that time for payment of each instalment is of the essence, so that any breach will go to the root of the contract. The difference between these two agreements is one of drafting form, and wholly without substance. Yet under an agreement drafted in the first form, the owner's damages claim arising on his exercise of the power of termination is confined to damages for breaches up to the date of termination, whereas under an agreement drafted in the second form the owner's damages claim, arising on his acceptance of an identical breach as a repudiation of the agreement, will extend to damages for loss of the whole transaction.

Nevertheless, as at present advised, I can see no escape from the conclusion that such is the present state of the law. This conclusion emasculates the decision in *Financings Ltd v Baldock*, for it means that a skilled draftsman can easily side-step the effect of that decision. Indeed, that is what has occurred here. . . .

For these reasons, I too would dismiss this appeal.

Lawton LJ. I have read in draft the judgments of Mustill and Nicholls LJJ; I agree and have nothing to add.

Appeal dismissed.

NOTES

1. This decision makes avoidance of the rule in *Financings v Baldock* (above, p 428) relatively easy. Should 'condition precedent' clauses be subject to some control? (It is conceivable that they might be caught by Unfair Contract Terms Act 1977 s 3(2)(b)(ii), below p 716, but this is a 'long shot'.)
2. How much had Lombard actually lost?

3. Presumably they would have lost the same amount (as a matter of fact, even if not as a matter of law) even if prompt payment had not been a condition precedent. Why should they not be permitted to stipulate for liquidated damages to reimburse them that loss? (They should of course allow for the resale value of the goods.)

4. Clause 63(1) of the Institution of Civil Engineers conditions of contract (reproduced above, p. 448) permits the employer to determine the contract for various breaches by the contractor, not all of which would justify termination at common law. Cl 63 goes on to provide:

> (4) If the Employer shall enter and expel the Contractor under this Clause he shall not be liable to pay the Contractor any money on account of the Contract until the expiration of the Period of Maintenance and thereafter until the costs of completion and maintenance damages for delay in completion (if any) and all other expenses incurred by the Employer have been ascertained and the amount thereof certified by the Engineer. The Contractor shall then be entitled to receive only such sum or sums (if any) as the Engineer may certify would have been due to him upon due completion by him after deducting the said amount. But if such amount shall exceed the sum which would have been payable to the Contractor on due completion by him then the Contractor shall upon demand pay to the Employer the amount of such excess and it shall be deemed a debt due by the Contractor to the Employer and shall be recoverable accordingly.

Suppose the Employer determines the contract for a breach which was not sufficiently serious to justify termination at common law, and, after some inevitable delay, employs another contractor to finish the work. Can the Employer recover the extra cost and compensation for delay from the original Contractor?

'Liquidated Damages in California' by Sweet (1972) 60 Calif LR 84, 86–89

A. Reasons for liquidated damages provisions

As the norm has changed from negotiated contract to adhesion contract, the reasons for employing liquidated damages clauses have changed, and accompanying this has been a change in judicial attitude toward enforcement. First, consider the use of liquidation clauses in the model of a negotiated contract. Both contracting parties often wish to control their risk exposure, and permitting them to do so encourages risk-taking. The performing party may also wish to avoid the feared irrationality of the judicial process in determining actual damages. He may also be fearful that the court will give insufficient consideration to legitimate excuses for nonperformance, that the court may be unduly sympathetic to plaintiff's claim that any loss he incurred should be paid for by the party whose nonperformance caused the loss, or that the court may consider contract breach an immoral act.

There are also reasons why the nonperforming party as well may wish to use a liquidated damages clause. Sometimes a breach will cause damage, but the amount of damages cannot be proven under damage rules. For example, in wartime procurement contracts it may be impossible to establish the damages caused by delayed or defective performance by the contractor. Without an enforceable clause purporting to liquidate damages, the nonperforming party may fear that the performing party will have insufficient incentive to perform if the latter realizes that damages he has caused are not sufficiently provable to be collected. Such a clause is a penalty in that its principal function is to coerce performance. Yet if it is reasonable—not disproportionate to actual, although unprovable, damages or to the contract price—it will be enforced. Without a liquidated damages clause there is also a danger the contractor may recover the full contract price despite a breach that caused some unprovable losses. Thus while the nonperforming party may be motivated principally by the penalty aspects of the clause, he may to a lesser degree be motivated by the desire to prevent what appears to him to be unjust enrichment.

Liquidated damages clauses may also be inserted to improve upon what the parties believe to be a deficiency in the litigation process: the cost and difficulty of judicially proving damages. Through a liquidation clause the parties attempt to use contract to settle the amount of damages involved and thus improve the normal rules of damages. Also, when the clause is phrased in such a way as to indicate that the breaching party will pay a specified amount if a particular breach occurs, troublesome problems involved in proving causation and foreseeability may be avoided. This was extremely helpful, for example, in wartime procurement contracts, where not only was it almost impossible to establish the amount of damages, but it was equally impossible to establish that delayed or defective performance by the contractor caused any particular loss and that the loss was reasonably foreseeable at the time the contract was made. Finally, the parties may feel that if they truly agree on damages in advance, it is unlikely that either would later dispute the amount of damages recoverable as the result of his breach.

In the adhesion contract situation there are some similarities in objectives; the desire to control the irrationality and expense of the litigation process and the need to know the extent of risk exposure are still involved. There are, however, obvious additional objectives of the stronger party. He can dictate the terms of the contract; if he is the performing party, he is likely to use the contract clause to limit his exposure almost to the vanishing point, and if he is the nonperforming party, he may try to use a penalty clause to coerce performance, or he may try to use a genuine liquidation clause to make vindication of his legal rights as convenient and inexpensive as possible. In the adhesion context, then, the stronger party may try to limit his own liability and to set an agreed amount that is sufficiently high to coerce performance. In the event performance is not rendered, the clause may obtain a settlement or win the case.

B. Judicial responses to liquidated damages provisions

Moving from the reasons why liquidated damages clauses are used by the parties, let us consider what motivates courts to uphold or reject these clauses. Some courts undoubtedly are persuaded by the argument that the parties have paid their money and taken their chances. Since the parties have assumed certain risks, courts often see no particular reason to relieve them from the risks they have taken. Treating the liquidated damages clauses as any other, such courts uphold the clauses to reward the party who has guessed best on the question of damages. Other courts enforce these clauses because they believe that protecting the reasonable expectations of the contracting parties encourages risk-taking and assists in planning. Still other courts look at the contract as a package and enforce the liquidation clause because they feel that the party attacking the clause has received benefits under the contract. This is especially likely when such a clause is directly related to the contract price. For example, in one important case, a gun manufacturer offered to supply guns at different prices depending upon when delivery had to be made. The government chose the quickest delivery at the highest price. Nonenforcement of the delay-damage liquidation clause in this case would have disturbed the package arrangement and created unjust enrichment.

Courts also enforce these clauses because they believe liquidated damages clauses help the courts achieve just results. Sometimes the computation of damages in litigation is no better than a guess; as long as the amount selected by the parties is within a reasonable range, the courts feel that enforcing the amount selected is likely to be as fair as any amount determined by the court. Furthermore, courts believe that if such agreements are enforced, at least in theory the use of such clauses should expand, resulting in fewer breaches, fewer law suits, fewer or easier trials, and in many cases, at least as just a result.

Finally, courts recognize that enforcement of these clauses can cure defects in the litigation process. For example, the requirements as to certainty may seem too restrictive. A court may enforce a liquidation clause to ensure that a party will get a just recovery that might otherwise be denied him because he cannot establish the loss with sufficient certainty.

Many purported liquidated damages clauses, however, are not enforced. The traditional rationale for nonenforcement is that courts will not aid in coercion, oppression, or unjust enrichment; courts seek only to compensate, and enforcement of penalty clauses is contrary to that purpose. Thus, enforcement of a clause not based upon an estimate of proper compensation would cause an unconscionable result.

Refusal to enforce these clauses may recognize the protection contracting parties need from their own unfortunate optimism and their failure to consider in advance the possibility that subsequent events may affect their performance.

NOTES

1. How many of the advantages of liquidated damages would be lost if the party in breach were permitted to challenge the clause in the light of the actual loss, as the shipbuilders in the *Clydebank* case tried to do?
2. In practice, liquidated damages for delay are commonly found coupled with an extension of time clause, giving the seller (or in a construction

contract the contractor) the right to extra time if he is delayed by matters outside the control of either party (eg bad weather or industrial disputes) or by acts of the buyer or employer (eg ordering changes in the goods or work, or failing to make drawings available promptly). These clauses serve two functions. The more obvious one is to protect the contractor from liability for delay: without the clause his obligation to deliver or complete on time would be strict, save insofar as he was prevented from performing promptly by the other party. The second function is in just such cases of prevention. In a series of cases in the last century it was held that if a contractor is prevented from attaining the completion date by a breach by the employer or by compliance with some order of the employer, the latter cannot claim *any* liquidated damages, even for periods of delay that indubitably were the contractor's fault: see *Holme v Guppy* (1838) 3 M & W 387; *Dodd v Churton* [1897] 1 QB 562. The extension of time clause permits the completion date to be moved back, and thus operates to preserve the liquidated damages machinery.

'Contracts between Businessmen' (1975) 2 Brit J Law & Society 45 at 55

It was only in the specifically negotiated contracts that liquidated damages clauses (clauses agreeing in advance the compensation payable for late delivery) were found. These clauses appear to be convenient ways both of encouraging timely performance and of avoiding disputes about compensation, and are commonly thought by lawyers to be attractive to the business community, but the criticisms made to us may explain why they are not more commonly used, particularly in standard conditions. Sellers clearly wished to avoid any liability for delay, but in most cases of negotiated sales they could not get away with excluding their liability altogether as they attempt to do in their 'back of order' conditions. They might therefore prefer a liquidated damages clause instead of full liability at common law. But this would not be the case if they thought that the customer was unlikely to press any claim for consequential loss, for instance because of a close relationship between the two firms, or was unlikely to be able to prove any loss, for instance because the project for which the goods were required was almost certain to be running late, or because the goods were required for a non-profit making purpose such as 'defence'.

Buyers might have been expected to favour liquidated damages just to avoid having to prove their losses. But again there were criticisms. Firstly, sellers would not usually accept liquidated damages clauses unless delays caused by *force majeure* were excepted, and *force majeure* clauses were so wide that the buyer would receive no compensation for much of the delay. Several buyers said that they preferred to preserve their common law rights even though they would not usually exercise them. Secondly, the administrative costs of enforcing liquidated damages clauses are relatively high because keeping track of delays and investigating the causes requires a lot of manpower.

Nor when a liquidated damages clause had been agreed did buyers seem very keen to make use of the remedy. We were told that often a negotiated settlement would be reached under which only part of the sum due would be paid. This seems to destroy one advantage of the device, and apparently another advantage was also sometimes thrown away: the buyer can normally 'set off' liquidated damages due against the price and pay only the balance, yet we were told of a buyer claiming liquidated damages long after paying the price in full. Our impression is that in the area of delay at least the main reason for liquidated damages was not to obtain compensation but to discipline the other party. One experienced officer told us that he favoured liquidated damages not because he wanted damages but because he wanted a realistic delivery date in the first place and to be told of any likely delay well in advance; in negotiated contracts he would ensure that the operation of the *force majeure* clause excusing the seller was conditioned on prompt notification of the excusable delay.

Thus in both negotiated and non-negotiated contract situations, late delivery seems to be regarded as primarily a commercial problem to be solved commercially rather than a legal problem susceptible to solution by the use of planning. Not surprisingly most buyers and sellers seemed to regard delivery dates as targets rather than firm promises.

Why are penalty clauses not enforceable?

'Efficiency Implications of Penalties and Liquidated Damages' by Rea (1984) 13 JLS 147, at 147–161

Why should freely negotiated contract provisions that specify damages in the event of breach not be enforced? Posner has called this doctrine 'a major unexplained puzzle in the economic theory of the common law.' Previous economic explanations of the doctrine are not convincing . . .

The economic analysis of contracts suggests that damages for breach of contract serve two primary functions, assuming that there is no reliance. First, they provide an incentive for one party to take into account the losses suffered by the other when the former takes precautions against breach or decides whether deliberately to breach a contract. Second, the damages allocate risk between the two parties. The more risk-averse party can, in effect, buy some insurance from the less risk-averse party. The damages may be specified by the parties at the time of the contracting or determined by the courts at the time of breach. The economic literature on contract law usually assumes that the court provides the implicit terms of a contract, including the amount of damages, that the parties to the contract would have agreed to if contracting had been costless. By providing efficient implicit terms in contracts, courts reduce the costs of exchange. The perplexing aspect of the penalties-liquidated damages distinction is that there is a conflict between the apparent, but express, intention of the parties and the subsequent action of the courts. . .

IV.   EX ANTE DETERMINATION OF DAMAGES

This section considers whether there are any circumstances in which the parties may wish to negotiate damages that exceed the actual loss. The basic principles of efficient damages can be illustrated with a simple model which I have discussed elsewhere. In that model a risk-neutral seller (the promisor) sells a product or service to a risk-averse buyer (the promisee). The product may fail to provide the anticipated service, imposing losses on the buyer. When the specific cause of breach, such as change in production cost, careless seller behavior, or a better offer by a third party, is not observable, the damage measure must be a compromise between the amount that will provide optimal insurance and the amount that will provide efficient seller breach or seller precautions against breach. If both the buyer and the seller are risk averse, the damges will also reflect risk sharing between the buyer and seller. The factors that influence the damage level are evaluated below, paying particular attention to the relationship between predetermined damages and the actual loss.

A. Risk Aversion

If the seller is risk neutral and the buyer is risk averse, it is beneficial to both parties for the seller to insure the buyer. The desired amount of insurance, ignoring incentives, will equal the actual loss when there are no nonpecuniary losses, as would be the case in a commercial setting. Damages in excess of full compensation would not appeal to a risk-averse buyer because he would face an unwanted variation in his income, depending on whether the product failed. He would not wish to pay a higher price for the product (to cover the added insurance cost) in order to increase risk.

If the buyer were risk preferring, a clause that specified damages in excess of losses would provide an opportunity to gamble . . .

It seems likely that the parties to most contracts are risk averse or at least risk neutral. None of the commentators has pointed out a case in which gambling was the motivation for unreasonable damages, and it is unlikely that a preference for risk prevails in the commercial world.

Goetz and Scott argue that the court's unwillingness to compensate nonpecuniary losses following breach of contract has led courts to under-compensate victims of breach and has induced contracting parties to attempt to contract around the courts' rules. Goetz and Scott conclude that damage clauses calling for apparently excessive payments should be enforced in order to insure these losses. However, I have shown that it is usually irrational to insure such losses [see above, p 507]. The insurance decision involves transferring income from the state of the world in which the contract is not breached (a higher price will be paid for the contract) to the state of the world in which the contract is breached (damages will be received if breach occurs). If the loss is nonpecuniary, it is likely that the utility of the additional income in the breach state will fall short of the utility of the forgone income in the nonbreach state.

Consequently nonpecuniary losses would not usually be fully compensated in an efficient contract. Therefore there will be few situations in which nonpecuniary losses provide an explanation for damages that are viewed as unreasonable by courts.

[Rea then considers the 'risk' of random higher offers from third parties and concludes that this does not explain stipulations for unreasonable damages either.]

B. Moral Hazard

Clarkson, Miller, and Muris (henceforth referred to as CMM) and Muris claim that economic efficiency requires that the courts not enforce damage clauses in situations in which the nonbreaching party can influence the probability of breach and will benefit from breach. Their argument does not explain why damages would deliberately be set in excess of losses. Moral hazard, which arises because the buyer's precautions cannot be unobserved, will be taken into account at the time of the bargain and will lead to a reduction in the predetermined damage level below the actual damages.

C. Imperfect Enforcement

Borrowing from the literature on enforcement of criminal laws, one can argue that damages should be punitive when the costs of detection or enforcement are such that breachers will be penalized with a probability less than one. For example, the breach may be costly to detect in franchise contracts. The franchisor is interested in maintaining quality of service, but it is costly to monitor continually the quality of all of the franchisees. Termination of the contract by the franchisor, imposing a substantial loss on the franchisee, may be an efficient method of encouraging quality. The same analysis would apply to termination-at-will employment contracts. Terminations of franchises and employment have not typically been challenged as penalties. It does not seem likely that breaches will go undetected in the kinds of cases which occur most frequently, such as delay in completion of a construction contract.

D. Penalties as a Signal

In many situations the promisor may know the probability of breach but the promisee may not. In the second edition of his text Posner points out that penalties promote efficient exchange by signaling a party's intention to honor his contracts. Although no one ever knows for sure that he will honor a contract, those who know that they are more likely to honor than others will find it less costly to agree to penalty clauses. If buyers cannot differentiate low risk from high risk sellers, a seller's acceptance of a penalty clause is a signal of a low probability of breach . . .

Even if signaling is the primary motive for damage clauses, there does not appear to be any reason a signal would involve a damage clause in excess of the actual loss. This can be demonstrated by considering a situation in which (*a*) there is only one type of customer with one type of loss, (*b*) there are numerous sellers who have different degrees of reliability, and (*c*) sellers can signal their reliability by offering guarantees or liquidated damages. If the damages equal the actual loss, the extent of reliability becomes irrelevant for the buyer. He will simply choose the lowest-cost seller offering full compensation in the event of breach. Sellers of less reliable products with the same manufacturing cost will not be able to compete in the market. The low-cost sellers, taking into account the buyers' losses, can drive the others out of the market without offering damages in excess of actual losses. . . .

In the next example consider a market in which buyers have different amounts of losses resulting from product failure. Sellers will offer different guarantees and degrees of reliability, depending on the type of buyer. An individual who expects to sustain a loss L_1 . . . will purchase from the reliable seller, and those expecting only loss L_2 (less than L_1) will buy from the unreliable seller. Other sellers with higher costs for a given level of liquidated damages cannot survive in the market. Again, there is no reason a seller would signal reliability by offering damages in excess of the actual loss. Such a contract would always be inferior to a contract which compensates the buyer for his actual loss . . .

E. Probability of Breach Incorrectly Estimated

If the buyer overestimates the probability of breach or the seller underestimates the probability of breach, the buyer will find it desirable to buy more than full insurance. Cooter suggests that this leads to inefficiency. However, it is not necessarily true that both parties can be made better off by limiting damages to full compensation. A mandatory change in damages will lead to adjustments in precautions against breach which could make the parties worse off.

Misperception of risk explains why two parties might agree to penalty clauses, but it does not explain why courts refuse to enforce these clauses while at the same time underliquidated damages are enforced. Underliquidated damages would arise when the buyer underestimates the probability of breach and/or the seller overestimates the probability. Usually the buyer must assume that the seller has better information concerning the probability of breach and will be wise to specify that damages equal the actual loss.

F. Measurement Problems

When the buyer perceives that he will suffer a loss as a result of a breach of contract but realizes that the actual amount of the loss will be difficult to prove, he may wish to specify the damages at the time that the contract is signed. There is no incentive for him to overstate the loss because this would add to the contract price. At the same time he would not want to underestimate the loss because this would increase the risk that he would bear. After a breach, the victim has an incentive to exaggerate his loss, and the cost of negotiating a settlement or going to trial is high when losses cannot be easily measured. The expected sum of ex ante and ex post transaction costs may be reduced by predetermining damages, particularly if the probability of breach is high. The common law and the U.C.C. recognize the useful role of predetermined damages in situations in which losses are difficult to measure or prove, and courts have been inclined to enforce damage clauses in those situations.

G. Conclusion on Ex Ante Unreasonableness

The discussion in this section has indicated that the parties to a contract are unlikely to agree ex ante to damages that exceed the expected loss. It is rational to agree to excess damages when the optimal insurance amount exceeds full compensation, when only a fraction of the breaches can be detected, when the promisee is overly pessimistic, or when the promisor is overly optimistic. These circumstances are likely to be infrequent. On the other hand, predetermined damages may be set below the expected loss if the promisee wishes to bear some of the risk, if he can influence the probability of breach, if his losses are below average, or if he has non-pecuniary losses. Damages may also be set below the actual losses if the promisee underestimates the probability or size of loss or the promisor overestimates the probability of loss.

What can the court conclude in a situation in which damages are ex ante unreasonably large? There are at least four possible explanations for such a conclusion. First, the excess damages may have been optimal. In light of the discussion above this seems unlikely.

A second explanation for a finding of unreasonable damages is that the court made an incorrect evaluation of the loss. Although it is tempting to conclude that the existence of the clause is prima facie evidence of the court's mistake, much of the law rests on the assumption that courts can measure losses with a sufficient degree of accuracy to justify the court's intervention. The penalty doctrine implicitly recognizes the possibility of court error by tending to enforce damage clauses when the loss is difficult to evaluate. Furthermore, damages not ordinarily awarded, such as attorney's fees, are recognized as losses when a damage clause is evaluated.

A third explanation is that there has been a procedural deficiency in the formation of the contract. For example, one party may not have realized the implications of the damage clause. Such a situation is more likely to arise when one party is an unsophisticated customer than in a commercial setting.

A fourth explanation for excess damages is that the parties, although knowledgeable, made a mistake about the nature of the contract, the possible loss, the probability of loss, or the implications of the damage clause. It is argued below that the mistake is likely to be mutual.

The third and fourth explanations for excess damages seem the most reasonable. Consequently it might be efficient for courts to use unreasonable ex ante damages as evidence of unconscionability or mistake, given the difficulty of observing these two problems.

. . . Although the penalty doctrine addresses the substance of a contract, the existence of ex ante unreasonable clauses may be evidence of procedural unconscionability. Given the difficulty of detecting unconscionability, evidence of excessive damages may be a useful indicator of its existence.

REFERENCES

Clarkson, Muller and Muris, 'Liquidated Damages v Penalties: Sense or Nonsense?' [1978] Wisconsin LR 351.

Goetz and Scott, 'Liquidated Damages, Penalties and the Just Compensation Principle' (1977) 77 Col LR 554.

Muris, 'Opportunistic Behaviour and the Law of Contracts' (1981) 65 Minnesota LR 521.

In the cases discussed so far the sum alleged to be a penalty has been payable in the event of a breach of contract. It is quite common to provide for the payment of money on an event which is not a breach. It has usually been held that the penalty rules apply only when the event which triggers the obligation to pay is a breach of contract.

This distinction has been the basis of a number of hire-purchase cases. In a typical hire-purchase contract (for an example, see above, p 54) the owner (the finance company) is entitled to bring the contract to an end in a number of events, some of which involve breaches of contract (eg repudiation by the hirer) and some of which do not (the hirer's death or bankruptcy). In addition the hirer is usually given an option to terminate the contract. Usually the agreement provides for the same consequences in all these cases: the hirer has to make further payments to bring the total paid up to a pre-determined figure, often two-thirds of the total price. The Court of Appeal has consistently held that a hirer who breaks the contract by failing to pay an instalment can argue that the clause is penal, but that one who exercises his option to return the goods cannot.

The House of Lords was given the opportunity to decide the question in *Bridge v Campbell Discount Co Ltd* [1962] AC 600, but refused to do so in any helpful fashion. In that case the hirer had written to the owner: 'I am very sorry but I will not be able to pay any more payments on the Bedford Dormobile'. In the Court of Appeal this letter was treated as an exercise of the hirer's option to return the goods, and the minimum payment provision was held enforceable. The House of Lords (Viscount Simonds dissenting) held that the letter was not an exercise of the option but a repudiation, and had no difficulty in holding the clause penal, since, in Lord Radcliffe's words, 'it is a sliding scale of compensation, but a scale that slides in the wrong direction'. The shorter the time the hirer had kept the vehicle, the less the owners would lose through its depreciation, but the more the hirer would have to pay after termination.

This left it unnecessary to decide whether the Court of Appeal was right that the penalty rules did not apply if the hirer merely exercised the option. Viscount Simonds and Lord Morton thought they were; Lords Denning and Devlin, though for different reasons, thought they were wrong. Lord Radcliffe did not reach a definite view. However, the question came before the House again, though in a very different factual context, in *Export Credits Guarantee Department v Universal Oil Products Co* [1983] 2 All ER 205. This case arose out of a complex series of multi-partite contracts for the construction of an oil refinery in Newfoundland. The project was financed by a banking consortium, which advanced money to pay for the construction being done by the defendants, in exchange for promissory notes issued by the Newfoundland companies for whom the refinery was being built. The plaintiffs, ECGD, guaranteed payment of these promissory notes to the bank, in exchange for a premium paid by the defendants. One of the terms of the guarantee was that if the Newfoundland companies failed to honour a promissory note 'at a time when' the defendants were in breach of the agreements (including the construction contract), and ECGD had to pay the banking consortium, the defendants would reimburse ECGD for the sums so paid. ECGD had to pay some £39m to the banking consortium because of the promissory notes being dishonoured, and they brought an action for that amount against the defendants, alleging that at the time the payments were made the defendants had been in breach of the construction contract. The defendants argued that the reimbursement clause was a penalty clause and unenforceable, but the House of Lords held that the clause could not be a penalty: the sum was not payable on a breach of contract as between the plaintiffs, ECGD, and the defendants.

The case is puzzling, because it is not clear what the defendants hoped to gain by showing that the clause was subject to the penalty rules: the amount payable seems to have been exactly what ECGD had had to pay out, even if the default on the promissory notes, and thus the amount of the payment to the banking consortium, was not related to the loss caused by the defendants' breach of the construction contract.

(ii) Advance payments, deposits and forfeitures

What is the position if the contract provides that one party will pay money to the other in advance, and after this payment has been made or has fallen due, the contract is justifiably terminated by one party because of the other party's breach?

(a) Advance payments by innocent party
If the money has been paid and the party *to whom it has been paid* is the party who has broken the contract, the party who has paid can recover the money, either in an action for damages or in an action for restitution (see chapter 25). If the money is due but has not been paid by the innocent party, it will normally cease to be payable (though the innocent party might be liable in damages for any loss caused by the failure to pay promptly).

(b) Advance payments by party in breach
If *the party who has paid the money* is the party in breach, it is important to draw a distinction between payments on account, on the one hand, and deposits and money paid under provisions which state that in the event of default it is to be forfeited, on the other.

(i) Payments on account
In contracts of sale, the usual rule is that advance payments on account may be recovered, though the seller can set off its actual loss: *Dies v British and International Mining and Finance Corpn Ltd* [1939] 1 KB 724. In *Hyundai Heavy Industries Co Ltd v Papadopoulos* [1980] 2 All ER 29 the House of Lords said that advance payments made in a shipbuilding contract could not be recovered. The distinction has been explained as follows. In a contract of sale the seller's right to the money is conditional on the subsequent performance by delivery; but in the shipbuilding case the money was viewed as unconditional payment for the work already in progress (see *McDonald v Dennys Lascelles Ltd* (1933) 48 CLR 457, 476–478 and Beatson (1981) 97 LQR 389). In *Rover International Ltd v Cannon Film Sales Ltd (No 3)* [1989] 3 All ER 423 Kerr LJ said (pp 439–440):

> The question is whether there was any consideration in the nature of part performance for which the instalment was payable, as in the *Hyundai Heavy Industries* case, or whether the instalment was payable in advance of any performance which was required from [the defaulting party].

He pointed out that in this context, as in the *Fibrosa* case (above, p 365), consideration refers to the promised performance, not the promise itself.

If the instalment is due but has not yet been paid at the date the contract is terminated, and if it had been paid it would be returnable under the rule just stated, it ceases to be payable (ibid).

(ii) Deposits and money paid subject to forfeiture
A deposit is a sum paid in advance which the payee may keep if the payor defaults. The general rule appears to be that the payee can keep the whole of the deposit, even though it exceeds the loss he suffers as a result of the breach: *Howe v Smith* (1884) 27 Ch D 89. If the deposit is due but has not been paid, the innocent party may recover it. In *Damon Cia Naviera SA v Hapag-Lloyd International SA, The Blankenstein* [1985] 1 All ER 475 the contract provided for the payment of a deposit of 10%, or $236,500, upon execution of a formal agreement. The buyers repudiated the contract before execution of the formal agreement and the Court of Appeal held, by a majority, that the sellers could recover damages of the same amount to compensate them for loss of the deposit. The seller's overall loss was a mere $60,000.

The rule that the money may be kept even though it exceeds the innocent party's loss seems to apply also to money paid under provisions for it to be forfeited in case of default: *Mayson v Clouet* [1924] AC 980. But while the courts continue to enforce deposits stringently (eg *The Blankenstein*—though it is of course possible that at the time the contract was made a 10% deposit was a pre-estimate of the seller's likely loss), the courts' treatment of forfeiture clauses has not been wholly consistent. They look very much like penalties paid in advance, and in *Public Works Comr v Hills* [1906] AC 368 the Privy Council granted a contractor in default relief against forfeiture of 'security deposits' given to the employer, ordering that the employer should return all but the actual amount of its loss. This case was recently cited with approval in *Jobson v Johnson* (noted above, p 451).

In *Stockloser v Johnson* [1954] 1 QB 476 Denning and Somervell LJJ said that there was a general equitable power to grant relief against forfeiture in cases where land or goods were sold on credit, with a provision for repossession and forfeiture of payments made should the buyer default (though they held that on the facts there was no forfeiture: though the plaintiff had forfeited the instalments of the price paid, he had in the meantime derived profits from the machinery sold to him, and these he did not have to return). Romer LJ, however, held that in the absence of fraud, sharp conduct or unconscionable conduct, there was no jurisdiction to grant relief against forfeiture if the defaulting party was not ready and willing to perform his part of the contract. A more general jurisdiction existed only if the defaulter was now prepared to perform, when he could be given extra time (see above, p 449 ff). Subsequent cases involving goods have followed Romer LJ: see *Galbraith v Mitchenall Estates Ltd* [1965] 2 QB 473.

However, one of the most common cases of a deposit is the deposit (customarily 10% of the price) paid by a purchaser of land when contracts are exchanged. It has recently been decided that in such cases the court has power to order a return of the deposit under the Law of Property Act 1925, s 49(2). This provides:

Where the court refuses to grant specific performance of the contract, or in any action for the return of a deposit, the court may, if it thinks fit, order the repayment of any deposit.

It had been thought that the section only gave jurisdiction to order the return of a deposit to a purchaser who was not in default, where for some reason the court refused to grant the vendor specific performance, but in *Universal Corpn v Five Ways Properties Ltd* [1979] 1 All ER 552 the Court of Appeal rejected this approach, holding that the section conferred an unqualified discretion to do justice as between vendor and purchaser. The section was applied to allow a defaulting purchaser to recover his deposit, less the losses actually incurred by the vendors, in *Dimsdale Developments (South East) Ltd v De Haan* (1983) 47 P & CR 1.

In other cases, it appears to be the law still that the innocent party may retain the deposit even though it greatly exceeds his loss, projected or actual.

It seems strange enough that the innocent party is entitled to retain a deposit, or forfeit payments made, even though the effect is to penalize the party in breach; stranger still that the innocent party can recover damages as well if the loss he suffers exceeds the deposit: *Lock v Bell* [1931] 1 Ch 35. What justification is there for permitting the innocent party to retain it without enquiring whether or not it is a penalty? The only distinction between a deposit or forfeiture clause and a penalty clause seems to be that the party in breach has already parted with his money. The Law Commission, in its Working Paper No 61, 'Penalty Clauses and Forfeiture of Monies Paid', provisionally concluded that the fact that a deposit is paid in advance is not sufficient to bring home to the payor that it may be lost if he defaults, and that deposits and clauses providing for the forfeiture of payments made should be subject to the penalty rules (paras 57–67).

CHAPTER 24
Literal enforcement

(a) Specific performance and injunction

Falcke v Gray (1859) 4 Drew 651, Kindersley V-C

The defendant let her house to the plaintiff for six months, and gave him the option of purchasing at the end of the term certain articles of furniture at a valuation. Among the articles were what counsel described as 'a couple of large Oriental jars, with great ugly Chinese pictures upon them'. The valuer admitted that he was ignorant of the value of the vases, but a sum of £40 was eventually agreed on, although the defendant said in her evidence that she had been left the jars by a lady who had, she understood, been offered £100 for them by King George IV. The defendant was later offered £200 for the jars by a purchaser, to whom she had explained what had happened, and she accepted that offer. The plaintiff obtained an ex parte injunction against the defendant and the second purchaser, and then sought specific performance.

The Vice-Chancellor [Sir R. T. Kindersley] (after stating the facts above stated). The first ground of defence is that, this being a bill for the specific performance of a contract for the purchase of chattels, this Court will not interfere. But I am of opinion that the Court will not refuse to interfere simply because the contract relates to chattels, and that if there were no other objection the contract in this case is such a contract as the Court would specifically perform.

What is the difference in the view of the Court between realty and personalty in respect to the question whether the Court will interfere or not? Upon what principle does the Court decree specific performance of any contract whatever? Lord Redesdale in *Harnett v Yeilding* says: 'Whether Courts of Equity in their determinations on this subject have always considered what was the original foundation for decrees of this nature I very much doubt. I believe that from something of habit, decrees of this kind have been carried to an extent which has tended to injustice. Unquestionably the original foundation of these decrees was simply this, that damages at law would not give the party the compensation to which he was entitled; that is, would not put him in a situation as beneficial to him as if the agreement were specifically performed'. So that the principle on which a Court of Equity proceeds is this. A Court of law gives damages for the non-performance, but a Court of Equity says 'that is not sufficient—justice is not satisfied by that remedy'; and, therefore, a Court of Equity will decree specific performance because a mere compensation in damages is not a sufficient remedy and satisfaction for the loss of the performance of the contract.

Now why should that principle apply less to chattels? If in a contract for chattels damages will be a sufficient compensation, the party is left to that remedy. Thus if a contract is for the purchase of a certain quantity of coals, stock &c, this Court will not decree specific performance, because a person can go into the market and buy similar articles and get damages for any difference in the price of the articles in a Court of law. But if damages would not be a sufficient compensation, the principle, on which a Court of Equity decrees specific performance, is just as applicable to a contract for the sale and purchase of chattels, as to a contract for the sale and purchase of land.

In the present case the contract is for the purchase of articles of unusual beauty, rarity and distinction, so that damages would not be an adequate compensation for non-performance; and I am of opinion that a contract for articles of such a description is such a contract as this Court will enforce; and, in the absence of all other objection, I should have no hesitation in decreeing specific performance.

NOTES

1. The purchaser's claim for specific performance was in fact denied in this case on the grounds that the consideration was inadequate, but there is some doubt whether the case is still supportable on this point: see Spry, *Equitable Remedies* (3rd edn), p 186.

2. The second purchaser would be bound to hand over the jars if the plaintiff could get specific performance, since he took with notice of the plaintiff's claim. See further below, p 842.

Société des Industries Metallurgiques SA v The Bronx Engineering Co Ltd [1975] 1 Lloyd's Rep 465, Court of Appeal

The sellers of a machine which they had built for the buyers alleged that the buyers had repudiated the contract, and advised them that it would be resold to a Canadian buyer. The buyers obtained an ex parte injunction restraining the sellers from removing the machine from the jurisdiction, but the judge refused to continue it until trial of the action. The Court of Appeal held that they would make an assumption that the buyers would succeed at trial in establishing a breach by the sellers: the question was thus whether specific performance would be granted at trial.

Lord Edmund Davies. . . . [T]he granting of such an injunction as is sought in the present case . . . is governed by s 52 of the Sale of Goods Act, 1893. That section enables the Court 'if it thinks fit' to order specific performance of a contract to deliver 'specific or ascertained goods'. For present purposes I understand the parties to accept that the machinery in question was 'ascertained goods' within the meaning of the section. But it is established law that such an order will not be made if damages would fully compensate the party wronged: *Whiteley Ltd v Hilt*. The crux of the present application accordingly, as I see it, is whether it is proper to draw the conclusion that damages would not or might not duly compensate the plaintiffs if they establish a contractual breach by the defendants. That the subject-matter was not 'an ordinary article of commerce' is not open to doubt. That if they succeed the plaintiffs might well recover very substantial damages is certainly on the cards. But the defendants are not the only manufacturers of such machinery, and it lacks, in my judgment, the unique quality of such articles as that which was the subject-matter of the specific performance decree made in, for example, *Behnke v Bede Shipping Co Ltd*. That case is commonly cited in the textbooks as supporting the proposition that specific performance will be ordered of a contract for the sale of a ship, but merely to say that is to put the matter too broadly. It is of some importance to note that it was not just any ship, for, as Mr Justice Wright said . . .

'. . . in the present case there is evidence that the *City* was of peculiar and practically unique value to the plaintiff. She was a cheap vessel, being old, having been built in 1892, but her engines and boilers were practically new and such as to satisfy the German regulations, and hence the plaintiff could, as a German shipowner, have her at once put on the German register. A very experienced ship valuer has said that he knew of only one other comparable ship, but that could now have been sold. The plaintiff wants the ship for immediate use, and I do not think damages would be an adequate compensation.'

By way of contrast with that case, the real substance of the plaintiffs' claim here is that were they now obliged to go to another manufacturer, they would probably have to wait another 9–12 months before they could get delivery of such new machinery and that, by reason of that delay and other factors, they would stand to lose a substantial sum. There has been no suggestion of financial inability in the defendants to satisfy such a money judgment (whatever its dimensions) as might be awarded against them to cover all such items of damages as the plaintiffs could legitimately rely upon. While sympathizing with the dilemma in which the plaintiffs find themselves, I see nothing which removes this case from the ordinary run of cases arising out of commercial contracts where damages are claimed. Of course, if the plaintiffs are right, the delay that has arisen by reason of the assumed breach of the defendants will go to inflate their damages; the greater the delay the plaintiffs experience in getting such new machinery (despite their best efforts), the greater the potential liability of the defendants in the event of the plaintiffs' succeeding. But for my part I cannot see that, whatever be the balance of convenience of the parties to which reference has been made, the case is one which, on the authorities, justifies the defendants now being restrained from disposing of the machinery in question as they seek to do and claim they are entitled to do, the plaintiffs, on the other hand, meanwhile seeking to compel the defendants until the trial of the action in what must inevitably be the not very near future to maintain this machinery in store at an expense which runs into several thousand pounds a month. The defendants do undoubtedly run the risk of ultimately being mulcted in what may well be a most substantial sum, but that is a risk which they are seemingly prepared to take and, in my judgment, they must be left free to do so.

[Lord Justice Buckley delivered a concurring judgment; Lord Justice Ormrod concurred.]

Appeal dismissed.

NOTE

What distinction is there between this case and *Behnke v Bede*? Couldn't Behnke have had another ship fitted out so as to be registrable in Germany within a few months?

Sale of Goods Act 1979

Section 52: Specific performance

(1) In any action for breach of contract to deliver specific or ascertained goods the court may, if it thinks fit, on the plaintiff's application, by its judgment or decree direct that the contract shall be performed specifically, without giving the defendant the option of retaining the goods on payment of damages.
(2) The plaintiff's application may be made at any time before judgment or decree.
(3) The judgment or decree may be unconditional, or on such terms and conditions as to damages, payment of the price and otherwise as seem just to the court.
(4) The provisions of this section shall be deemed to be supplementary to, and not in derogation of, the right of specific implement in Scotland.

Sky Petroleum Ltd v VIP Petroleum Ltd [1974] 1 WLR 576, Goulding J

The defendants had agreed to sell the plaintiffs the latters' entire requirements of petrol and diesel fuel for the plaintiffs' filling stations, at fixed prices and with a minimum annual quantity being stipulated. During an oil crisis, when the plaintiffs had no prospect of finding an alternative source of supply, the defendants purported to terminate the contract on the ground that the plaintiffs had exceeded the credit provisions in the contract. The plaintiffs sought an interim injunction to restrain the defendants from withholding supplies.

Goulding J. . . . . Now I come to the most serious hurdle in the way of the plaintiffs which is the well-known doctrine that the court refuses specific performance of a contract to sell and purchase chattels not specific or ascertained. That is a well-established and salutary rule, and I am entirely unconvinced by Mr Christie, for the plaintiffs, when he tells me that an injunction in the form sought by him would not be specific enforcement at all. The matter is one of substance and not of form, and it is, in my judgment, quite plain that I am, for the time being, specifically enforcing the contract if I grant an injunction. However, the ratio behind the rule is, as I believe, that under the ordinary contract for the sale of non-specific goods, damages are a sufficient remedy. That, to my mind, is lacking in the circumstances of the present case. The evidence suggests, and indeed it is common knowledge that the petroleum market is in an unusual state in which a would-be buyer cannot go out into the market and contract with another seller, possibly at some sacrifice as to price. Here, the defendants appear for practical purposes to be the plaintiffs' sole means of keeping their business going, and I am prepared so far to depart from the general rule as to try to preserve the position under the contract until a later date. I therefore propose to grant an injunction.

NOTES

1. Were the goods ascertained in this case? Suppose that the defendants had decided not to deliver petroleum to any buyer, but to stockpile it because they thought the price would rise. Could the plaintiffs have obtained an order of specific performance for the contract quantity?

2. The 'adequacy of damages test' is frequently applied when the plaintiff seeks an injunction, as well as when specific performance is sought. In *Evans Marshall & Co Ltd v Bertola SA* [1973] 1 WLR 349 at 379–380, Sachs LJ said:

> The standard question in relation to the grant of an injunction, 'Are damages an adequate remedy?', might perhaps, in the light of the authorities of recent years, be rewritten: 'Is it just, in all the circumstances, that a plaintiff should be confined to his remedy in damages?'
>
> The courts have repeatedly recognised that there can be claims under contracts in which, as here, it is unjust to confine a plaintiff to his damages for their breach. Great difficulty in estimating these damages is one factor that can be and has been taken into account. Another factor is the creation of certain areas of damage which cannot be taken into monetary account in a common law action for breach of contract: loss of goodwill and trade reputation are examples—see also, in another sphere, the judgment of Jenkins LJ in *Vine v National Dock Labour Board* which, albeit a dissenting judgment, was unanimously adopted in toto in the House of Lords. Generally, indeed, the grant of injunctions in contract cases stems from such factors. . . .
>
> So far the question of adequacy of damages has been discussed on the footing that if judgment was recovered the sum awarded would be paid. But whenever the adequacy of damages falls to be considered in this class of case, there arises the further question—are the defendants good for the money?

3. Although the *Sky Petroleum* case suggests a slightly more liberal attitude towards specific performance than earlier cases do, it is still the rule that a plaintiff will not get specific performance unless damages would not be an adequate remedy. Why?

'Specific Performance' by Kronman (1978) 45 U Chicago LR 351, 357–363, 365–369

The most important common feature of these diverse cases on specific performance is the central role played by the idea of 'uniqueness'. If the 'subject matter of [a] contract is unique in character and cannot be duplicated' or if obtaining 'a substantial equivalent involves difficulty, delay, and inconvenience', a court will be more apt to compel specific performance. 'The fact that such a duplicate or equivalent cannot be so obtained does not necessarily show that money damages are not an adequate remedy, but is a fact that tends strongly in that direction'. Conversely, if the subject matter of a contract is such that 'its substantial equivalent for all practical purposes is readily obtainable from others than the defendant in exchange for a money payment, this fact will usually in the absence of other factors be sufficient to show that money damages are an adequate remedy for breach'. . . .

In common discourse 'unique' means without a substitute or equivalent. In the framework of conventional economic analysis, however, the concept of uniqueness is troublesome. . . .

. . . [E]very good has substitutes, even if only very poor ones. Because all goods compete for consumer attention, a substantial change in the relative price of any good always affects the consumption of other goods. Economists are interested in determining how great a change in the price of one good is required to effect a change of given magnitude in the consumption of certain other goods. But these are really questions of degree, resting on the underlying assumption—fundamental to economic theory—that all goods are ultimately commensurable. If this assumption is accepted, the idea of a unique good loses meaning.

This point may be illustrated by a case that under present law would almost certainly be held to involve a unique good. Suppose that A contracts with Sotheby's to purchase the handwritten manuscript of Hobbes's *Leviathan*. If Sotheby's refuses to perform—perhaps because it has a more attractive offer from someone else—A will undoubtedly be disappointed. Yet no matter how strong his affection for Hobbes, it is likely there are other things that would make A just as happy as getting the manuscript for the contract price. For example, A may be indifferent between purchasing the manuscript at the specified price and having twenty-five hours of violin lessons for the same amount. If so, then A will be fully compensated for the loss he suffers by Sotheby's breach upon receiving the difference between the cost of twenty-five hours worth of violin lessons and the contract price. However, despite the fact that the manuscript has an economic substitute, a court would be likely to order specific performance of the contract (assuming Sotheby's still had the manuscript in its possession) on the ground that the subject matter of the contract is unique.

Pursuing the matter further, it is not difficult to see why A's money damages remedy is likely to be inadequate and on the basis of this insight to develop an economic justification for the uniqueness test. Under a money damages rule, a court must calculate the amount Sotheby's is required to pay A to give A the benefit of his bargain. The amount necessary to fully compensate A is equal to the amount he requires to obtain an appropriate substitute. So in fixing the amount Sotheby's must pay A, the court must first determine what things A would regard as substitutes and then how much of any particular substitute would be required to compensate him for his loss.

In the hypothetical case, however, it would be very difficult and expensive for a court to acquire the information necessary to make these determinations. Perhaps some information of this sort would be produced by the parties. For example, A could introduce evidence to establish a past pattern of consumption from which the court might draw an inference as to what would be a satisfactory substitute for the manuscript. Sotheby's could then attempt to rebut the evidence and establish some alternative theory of preferences and substitutes. But of course it would be time-consuming to produce information this way, and any inference a court might draw on the basis of such information would be most uncertain.

Moreover, this uncertainty cannot be avoided by simply looking to the selling price of other manuscripts or even the expected resale price of the Hobbes manuscript itself (unless, of course, A is a professional dealer). It would be risky to infer the value A places on the Hobbes manuscript from the value placed on it by others, and riskier still to infer it from the value others place on the manuscripts of, for example, Harrington's *Oceana* or Locke's *Second Treatise*. If a court attempts to calculate A's money damages on the basis of such information, there is a substantial probability that the award will miss the mark and be either under- or over-compensatory.

Of course, if a court could accurately identify a substitute for the manuscript, it could disregard the fact that A may value the manuscript in excess of the price that he, or anyone else, has agreed to pay for it. But where it is difficult to identify a satisfactory substitute (as I assume it is here), the goal of compensation requires that an effort be made to determine the value the promisee places on the promisor's performance, as distinct from what the promisee, or anyone else, has offered to pay for it.

Although it is true in a certain sense that all goods compete in the market—that every good has substitutes—this is an empty truth. What matters, in measuring money damages, is the volume, refinement, and reliability of the available information about substitutes for the subject matter of the breached contract. When the relevant information is thin and unreliable, there is a substantial risk that an award of money damages will either exceed or fall short of the promisee's actual loss. Of course this risk can always be reduced—but only at great cost when reliable information is difficult to obtain. Conversely, when there is a great deal of consumer behavior generating abundant and highly dependable information about substitutes, the risk of error in measuring the promisee's loss may be reduced at much smaller cost. In asserting that the subject matter of a particular contract is unique and has no established market value, a court is really saying that it cannot obtain, at reasonable cost, enough information about substitutes to permit it to calculate an award of money damages without imposing an unacceptably high risk of undercompensation on the injured promisee. Conceived in this way, the uniqueness test seems economically sound. . . .

The conclusion to be drawn from this analysis is a simple one. Whenever a court calculates money damages, there is some risk that it will undercompensate the injured party. But the magnitude of this risk is inversely related to the completeness and reliability of the information on which the court bases its award. At one extreme, where there is a well-developed market generating evidence of substitutability, this risk is minimal. At the other extreme, where there is no market or at most a few isolated transactions, this risk is substantial. There is a point between these two extremes at which the risk becomes unacceptably large (or, what amounts to the same thing, at which the risk can only be reduced by incurring unacceptable costs). This is the point separating those contracts that are specifically enforceable from those that are not—the point to which the uniqueness test obliquely refers. . . .

A second, essentially economic, justification for the uniqueness test consists in showing that the test draws the line between specific performance and money damages in the way that most contracting parties would draw it were they free to make their own rules concerning remedies for breach and had they deliberated about the matter at the time of contracting. If this is true, the uniqueness test promotes efficiency by reducing the costs of negotiating contracts. In general, this way of thinking about the rules of contract law requires consideration of the *ex ante* interests of parties engaged in a hypothetical bargaining process, struggling with a problem of rational choice under conditions of uncertainty. As I shall attempt to show in the next section, an analysis based upon *ex ante* considerations does suggest, if only somewhat tentatively, that contracting parties would be more likely to provide for specific performance where the subject matter of their contract is unique, and for money damages where it is not. . . .

When would the parties to a contract freely agree to a judicially enforceable provision giving the promisee an option to specifically enforce the other party's promise? Other things equal a promisee will always prefer to have such a provision included in the contract for it gives him an additional right which he would not otherwise possess. Other things equal, a promisor will always prefer a contract without such a provision—a contract , in other words, which he may unilaterally breach on the condition that he make a subsequent compensatory payment to the promisee. Consequently, a promisee intent upon writing a specific performance provision—a property rule—into the contract will have to pay to secure the promisor's consent. Similarly, a promisor must make a payment of some sort in order to exclude a provision for specific enforcement from the contract. If and only if the benefit which the promisee realizes from a specific performance provision exceeds the cost of the provision to the promisor will the provision be included in the final contract.

When the subject matter of a contract is unique, the risk is greater that the promisee's money damage remedy will be under-compensatory. Since a right to compel specific performance reduces the risk, promisees—as a class—should be willing to pay more for a provision giving them a right of this sort when there is no developed market generating information about the value of the subject matter of their contract.

However, if a specific performance provision is likely to be more beneficial to a promisee when the subject matter of his contract is unique, it is also likely to be more costly to his promisor under the same circumstances. In the first place, a right in the promisee to compel specific performance increases the probability of costly negotiations for transfer of the promisee's contract rights. This of course always reinforces the promisor's preference for a money damages rule. However, a promisor is likely to regard this reason as especially compelling where the subject matter of his contract is unique, since the lack of information about substitutes will almost certainly make the parties' negotiations longer and more complicated and thus more costly.

Second, if the promisee is entitled to specifically enforce the promisor's obligation, the promisor who wishes to breach will have to make a release payment to the promisee and buy his way out of the contract. The amount of the release payment demanded by the promisee will be greater than what the promisor would have to pay the promisee under a money damages rule. This is so whether or not the subject matter of the contract is unique. But the difference between what the promisee would accept in exchange for a release and what he may be expected to receive under a court-administered money damages rule is likely to be larger where the subject matter of his contract is unique, because the risk that court-awarded damages will be undercompensatory is greater. For these two reasons, a specific performance provision will be more expensive to the promisor when the subject matter of his contract is unique.

Thus far, it would appear that the benefits to the promisee and the costs to the promisor of a specific performance provision are proportional; both are greater when the subject matter of the contract is unique. There is, however, an additional consideration influencing their *ex ante* deliberations that provides some basis for thinking that the parties to a contract will be more likely to provide for specific performance when the subject matter of their agreement is unique.

The cost of a specific performance provision to the promisor will be determined, in part, by his own estimate of the likelihood that he will want to breach the contract. If he fully intends to perform, and thinks breach unlikely, a promisor will be less hostile to a contract with a specific performance provision than he would otherwise be. One important factor influencing the promisor's thinking in this regard is the probability that he will receive a better offer for his goods or services in the interim between formation of the contract and performance. The higher the probability, the greater the likelihood he will want to breach. The probability of receiving an attractive alternative offer may be especially low where the subject matter of the contract is unique. In this case there is by definition no developed market, transactions are spotty at best, and therefore a promisor will often justifiably think it highly unlikely that he will receive any alternative offer (let alone a better one) for the promised goods or services. Indeed, where the subject matter of his contract is genuinely unique, a promisor may estimate the likelihood of a preferable alternative offer as close to zero, and thus be nearly indifferent as to what remedies the promisee will enjoy in the highly unlikely event of breach.

Although the promisor thinks breach highly improbable, the promisee may not. Despite the promisor's insistence that he intends to perform, the promisee may be skeptical. As long as he is anxious about the promisor's performance, the promisee will be concerned about the adequacy of his own remedies, and where the subject matter of his contract is unique he will likely have a decided preference for a contract that gives him the right to specifically enforce the other party's promise. Consequently, in the case of a contract or a unique good or service, the benefits the promisee derives from a specific performance provision are apt to outweigh its costs to the promisor, who, free of doubts about his own reliability, may regard the inclusion of such a provision as a relatively costless way of enticing the promisee to enter the contract on advantageous terms.

In the case of a contract for non-unique goods or services, by contrast, the existence of a developed market increases the likelihood that the promisor will receive alternative offers before he has performed the contract. The promisor will therefore be anxious to retain the freedom and flexibility enjoyed under a money damages rule.

Moreover, the promisor will be especially anxious in this case to avoid the additional transaction costs that would be incurred if he had to negotiate a voluntary transfer of the promisee's contract rights. Although these costs will tend to be smaller where the subject matter of the contract is not unique, they can never be less than some fixed minimum (the cost of contacting the promisee, notifying him of an intention to breach, obtaining a release statement of some sort, and so on). Where there is an established market in the goods or services involved, prices will ordinarily be grouped rather closely around a single point. The probability is therefore greater that any alternative offer the promisor does receive will not be sufficiently high to cover the cost of negotiating a release plus the amount he must pay the promisee for the release. Thus the likelihood increases that a promisor who has agreed to a specific performance provision will find himself in the undesirable position of having to decline an alternative offer that he would accept under a money damages rule. In some cases the alternative offer will cover the release payment but will be refused solely because the transaction costs of negotiating a transfer of the promisee's contract rights are prohibitively high. The promisor should therefore be willing to make a small payment to the promisee, perhaps in the form of a slightly reduced contract price, in order to exclude a specific performance provision and thus avoid these potential transaction costs. Because the transaction costs avoided by the promisor would not have benefited the promisee, the latter will be better off with the reduced contract price if he regards the risk of undercompensation under a money damages rule as minimal. The promisee will generally regard this risk as slight where there is a developed market generating information about suitable substitutes.

In sum, promisors and promisees will typically favor a money damages rule if the subject matter of their contract is not unique. When the contract is for unique goods or services, on the other hand, the benefit to the promisee of a specific performance provision is likely to be substantial and the promisor may well regard his own breach as only a remote possibility, so the opposite conclusion seems more plausible. There is thus some basis for believing the uniqueness test reflects the typical solution that contracting parties would arrange for themselves in light of their *ex ante* interests.

'The Case for Specific Performance' by Schwartz (1979) 89 Yale LJ 271, 280–289

[Kronman argues that] in the unique goods case the parties would be expected to agree to a specific performance remedy; the promisee wants the remedy, whereas the promisor is indifferent. In the non-unique goods case, on the other hand, the parties would probably negotiate for a damage remedy, because damages would adequately protect the promisee, while the promisor would want to be free to accept more favorable offers.

Analysis of the equilibria in 'developed' and 'undeveloped markets' and their reactions to exogenous shocks suggests, however, that the promisors of unique goods care more about retaining the option of breach than do promisors of nonunique goods. Respecting equilibria, Professor Kronman equates an undeveloped market with a market in which unique goods are sold. This is misleading because unique goods markets often are well organized; the antique market provides an example. Such markets have two distinguishing features. First, they are usually characterized by greater price dispersion than obtains in the market equilibria for roughly fungible goods. In addition, sellers of unique goods face a lower 'rate of arrival' of potential buyers than do sellers of roughly fungible goods. These two phenomena are related; a high 'buyer arrival' rate implies extensive comparison shopping among firms, whereas the degree of price dispersion a market can sustain varies inversely with the amount of comparison shopping. Sellers of unique goods face a relatively low buyer arrival rate because each item they sell is highly differentiated; consequently, relatively few potential customers for such items exist. Also, search costs are comparatively higher for unique goods; locating them can be difficult, and the sellers often are geographically dispersed. Further, analyzing the quality of particular unique goods and comparing different goods usually are more time-consuming than searching for roughly fungible goods.

A promisor/seller in an 'undeveloped market'—a market in which unique goods are sold—thus faces a lower arrival rate of potential buyers together with the resultant higher degree of price dispersion than a promisor in a developed market. The promisor of unique goods consequently has grounds to believe that the offers he receives are to some extent random, and that later offers could be much higher than earlier ones. This promisor thus prefers damages to specific performance because the damages remedy preserves his freedom to breach.

This conclusion is reinforced by an examination of the differing reactions of 'developed' and 'undeveloped' markets to exogenous shocks. Exogenous shocks help to explain why promisors might receive better offers between the time they contract and the time they are supposed to render performance. This phenomenon needs explanation because a vendor of goods or services is generally assumed to sell to all of his purchasers on the same terms. Price discrimination is often unlawful and its costs in mass transactions exceed the gains it produces. Customers generally know whether a firm offers the same terms to all and are unlikely to make offers that exceed the going price. In addition, firms that negotiate contracts on an individual basis have a strong incentive not to breach, even if they receive better offers, in order to maintain goodwill. In what circumstances, then, will promisors receive and accept better offers?

The most frequent situation in which these circumstances arise is when there is an unexpected and dramatic increase in demand. The increase in demand will exert an upward pressure on prices. In the case of nonunique goods, this pressure is partially relieved by the ability of sellers to increase output. Unique goods, however, are in inelastic supply; only a few Rembrandts exist, and an increase in demand will not increase their number. In consequence, when buyers demand more of a unique item, the primary response of sellers is to increase the price; they can expand output only slightly, if at all.

The argument . . . can be clarified by a diagram.

FIGURE I   FIGURE II

In both figures, an increase in demand is represented by a similar shift in the demand curve from D to D'. In Figure 1, however, supply (S) is inelastic; no matter how great the shift in demand, little more of the good is supplied. Thus almost the full force of the demand shift is translated into the price increase. In Figure 2, supply is elastic, so that output expands considerably and the price increase is more moderate.

Specific performance

Therefore, when demand unexpectedly increases, a promisor in a unique goods market could command higher prices than a promisor in a nonunique goods market. The seller of unique goods, when the contract is negotiated, thus has a strong incentive to preserve his freedom to breach. A seller of nonunique goods, by contrast, will probably have to compete with many other vendors for any new business that a demand increase generates, and the resultant price rise will be relatively modest. Thus he will care less about preserving his freedom to breach in response to demand shifts. In sum, if the promisor's preference for specific performance or damages is assumed to be determined solely by whether the performance at issue is unique, the promisor would not choose specific performance in situations in which the law now routinely grants it.

B. Post-breach negotiations

The second efficiency argument for restricting the availability of specific performance is that making specific performance freely available would generate higher post-breach negotiation costs than the damage remedy now generates. For example, suppose that a buyer (B1) contracts with a seller (S) to buy a widget for $100. Prior to delivery, demand unexpectedly increases. The widget market is temporarily in disequilibrium as buyers make offers at different prices. While the market is in disequilibrium, a second buyer (B2) makes a contract with S to purchase the same widget for $130. Subsequently, the new equilibrium price for widgets is $115. If specific performance is available in this case, B1 is likely to demand it, in order to compel S to pay him some of the profit that S will make from breaching. B1 could, for example, insist on specific performance unless S pays him $20 ($15 in substitution damages plus a $5 premium). If S agrees, B1 can cover at $115, and be better off by $5 than he would have been under the damage remedy, which would have given him only the difference between the cover price and the contract price ($15). Whenever S's better offer is higher than the new market price, the seller has an incentive to breach, and the first buyer has an incentive to threaten specific performance in order to capture some of the seller's gains from breach.

The post-breach negotiations between S and B1 represent a 'dead-weight' efficiency loss; the negotiations serve only to redistribute wealth between S and B1, without generating additional social wealth. If society is indifferent as to whether sellers or buyers as a group profit from an increase in demand, the law should seek to eliminate this efficiency loss. Limiting buyers to the damage remedy apparently does so by foreclosing post-breach negotiations.

This analysis is incomplete, however. Negotiations costs are also generated when B1 attempts to collect damages. If the negotiations by which first buyers (B1 here) capture a portion of their sellers' profits from breach are less costly than the negotiations (or lawsuits) by which first buyers recover the market contract differential, then specific performance would generate lower post-breach negotiations costs than damages. This seems unlikely, however. The difference between the contract and market prices is often easily determined, and breaching sellers have an incentive to pay it promptly so as not to have their extra profit consumed by lawyers' fees. By contrast, if buyers can threaten specific performance and thereby seek to capture some of the sellers' profits from breach, sellers will bargain hard to keep as much of the profits as they can. Therefore, the damage remedy would probably result in quick payments by breaching sellers while the specific performance remedy would probably give rise to difficult negotiations. Thus the post-breach negotiation costs associated with the specific performance remedy would seem to be greater than those associated with the damage remedy.

This analysis makes the crucial assumption, however, that the first buyer, B1, has access to the market at a significantly lower cost than the seller; though both pay the same market price for the substitute, B1 is assumed to have much lower cover costs. If this assumption is false, specific performance would not give rise to post-breach negotiations. Consider the illustration again. Suppose that B1 can obtain specific performance, but that S can cover as conveniently as B1. If B1 insists on a conveyance, S would buy another widget in the market for $115 and deliver on his contracts with both B1 and B2. A total of three transactions would result: S-B1; S-B2; S2-S (S's purchase of a second widget). None of these transactions involves post-breach negotiations. Thus if sellers can cover conveniently, the specific performance remedy does not generate post-breach negotiation costs.

The issue, then, is whether sellers and buyers generally have similar cover costs. Analysis suggests that they do. Sellers as well as buyers have incentives to learn market conditions. Because sellers have to 'check the competition,' they will have a good knowledge of market prices and quality ranges. Also, when a buyer needs goods or services tailored to his own needs, he will be able to find such goods or services more cheaply than sellers in general could, for they would first have to ascertain the buyer's needs before going into the market. However, in situations in which the seller and the first buyer have already negotiated a contract, the seller is likely to have as much information about the buyer's needs as the buyer has. Moreover, in some markets, such as those for complex machines and services, sellers are likely to have a comparative advantage over buyers in evaluating the probable quality of performance and thus would have lower cover costs. Therefore, no basis exists for assuming that buyers generally have significantly lower cover costs than sellers. It follows that expanding the availability of specific performance would not generate higher post-breach negotiation costs than the damage remedy.

[A number of] serious objections may be made to this conclusion: (i) differential cover costs sometimes help induce breach, and their existence leads to higher post-breach negotiation costs under specific performance than under damages; (ii) in some cases, sellers cannot cover at all . . .

The first objection assumes that sellers breach partly because their cover costs are higher than those of their buyers; it then argues that when cover costs do diverge, allowing specific performance seemingly is less efficient than having damages be the sole remedy. Returning to the widget hypothetical, let Cb = the first buyer's (B1's) cover costs; Cs = the seller's cover costs. Assume that S has higher cover costs than B1, ie, Cs > Cb. If specific performance were available, B1 could threaten to obtain it, so as to force S to pay him part of the cover cost differential, Cs − Cb. If B1 made a credible threat, S would be better off negotiating than covering. Because only the availability of specific performance enables B1 to force this negotiation, one could argue that it is less efficient than having damages as the sole remedy.

This objection is incorrect, even if differential cover costs influence seller decisions to breach. A credible threat by B1 to seek specific performance would usually require preparing or initiating a lawsuit. This would entail costs of lost business time, lost goodwill and lawyer's fees, and these costs usually exceed any cover cost differential (Cs − Cb) that may exist. This is because the magnitude of cover costs—and hence of the differential—are low in relation to legal costs. Locating and arranging for substitute transactions are routine, relatively inexpensive business activities. Since the legal and related costs necessary for a credible threat commonly exceed the cover cost differential, it would rarely pay buyers to threaten specific performance to capture part of this differential. Thus no post-breach negotiations would be engendered by any differences in the parties' cover costs.

The second objection to the conclusion that post-breach negotiation costs are no higher under specific performance than under damages follows from the fact that in some cases sellers cannot cover at all. In these cases, buyers can always compel post-breach negotiations by threatening specific performance. There are two situations in which a seller cannot cover: if he is a monopolist or if the goods are unique. In either event, the first buyer would also be unable to cover. If neither the seller nor the first buyer can cover, no reason exists to believe that there would be higher post-breach negotiation costs with specific performance than with damages. If specific performance were available, B1 and S would negotiate over B1's share of the profit that S's deal with B2 would generate, or B1 would insist on a conveyance from S and then sell to B2. If only the damages remedy is available, B1 would negotiate with S respecting his expected net gain from performance rather than over the contract market difference, because he could not purchase a substitute. This expected gain is often difficult to calculate, and easy for the buyer to exaggerate. There is no reason to believe the negotiations or litigation over this gain would be less costly than the negotiations over division of the profit that B2's offer creates, or the costs of a second conveyance between B1 and B2. Thus even when the seller cannot cover, specific performance has not been shown to generate higher post-breach negotiation costs than damages. Moreover, when neither party can cover—the case under discussion—buyers have a right to specific performance under current law.

NOTE

Commenting on Schwartz's article, Muris [1982] Duke LJ 1053 notes (at pp 1062–1066):

Schwartz also asserts that even if cover costs do differ, post-breach negotiations will not occur. He argues that the buyer must make a credible threat before the seller will negotiate, that such a threat will usually require preparing or initiating a lawsuit, and that, because legal costs will usually exceed the differential in cover costs, credible threats will be rare. Although these factors will reduce the costs of specific performance, such costs will not be eliminated or even rendered trivial. Because the seller will be uncertain concerning the facts and the buyer's intentions, the seller cannot be positive that any buyer threat to seek specific performance is idle. A threat costs the buyer far less than a lawsuit would, and the possibility of future breaches by sellers may encourage the buyer to expend considerable resources to demonstrate his willingness to seek the specific remedy. Even when the probability of the seller successfully 'calling the buyer's bluff' is high, resources will still be spent in the bluffing game that would not be spent under a damage rule. Further, the possibility of the buyer's threat being carried out may cause the seller to cover even if the buyer has lower cover costs. At minimum, the possibility of specific performance increases uncertainty because its use will not be automatic. Increased uncertainty necessarily raises costs to those who prefer more certainty to less. . . . [E]ven when the market price is not obvious, in at least some of these cases, requiring specific performance is a more costly remedy than awarding damages. The non-breacher whose loss is less than the cost of correcting the defect in performance has incentive to bargain over specific performance to obtain part of the difference between the correction cost and his loss.

The resources spent negotiating over specific performance or determining the market price are limited by the expected return on the 'investment' in negotiation. In the case of the market price, well-defined rules of law exist to guide the parties, setting reasonable lower and upper bounds that limit the return from the investment. In the case of specific performance, however, no such rules exist. The spread, therefore, is potentially as large as the cost of correcting the defects minus the difference between the contract price of what was promised and the market price of what was delivered (an amount equalling the non-breaching party's damage if subjective value is not relevant). Moreover, even with specific performance, the parties will probably spend some resources to estimate the market price and thereby find the lower boundary of a possible settlement. These resources will probably not be as great as they are when the market price is determined in court, but they need not be trivial. Therefore, the size of the amount the parties will bargain over if specific performance is allowed—the cost of correcting the defects minus the market-based damages—will sometimes exceed the amount in dispute if specific performance is not allowed.

If specific performance is not allowed, the only dispute is between the upper and lower reasonable estimates for the market price. Thus, in some cases, allowing specific performance will give parties an incentive to spend more on deciding the amount of the 'bribe' that the breacher must pay than they would spend in determining the market price. Although in the aggregate parties may not always spend up to expected gains, the higher expected return from negotiating specific performance creates a tendency to have higher expenditures in such cases. No empirical information exists on the frequency of the cases in which the disputed amount regarding the market price is less than the amount over which the parties will bargain with specific performance. Thus uncertainty, as well as the knowledge that even with specific performance parties will spend resources on estimating the market price, places on a weak foundation the assertion that freely granting specific performance will not on balance raise costs compared to the current law.

'Efficient Breach of Contract: Circles in the Sky' by Macneil (1982) 68 Vir LR 947, 957

Whether an expectation damages rule or a specific performance rule is more efficient depends entirely upon the relative transaction costs of operating under the rules. Where, as will most generally be the case, transaction costs under either rule will exceed gross efficiency gains made possible by scrapping one contract in favor of another, each rule is equally (in)efficient. Where both rules will permit substituting a more productive contract for a less productive contract, the difference in efficiency of the rules will be measured exactly by the difference in their respective transaction costs. Where one rule will permit substitution and the other will not, the difference in efficiency will be measured by the difference in respective transaction costs, but subject to an upper limit consisting of the hypothetical net efficiency gain under the rule with the lower transaction costs. None of the transaction costs can be deduced by use of the microeconomic model, but can only be determined inductively from empirical evidence.

In addition to the 'adequacy of damages' rule, there are a number of other restrictions on the availability of specific performance. It is convenient to take the first two together, since they seem to be interconnected. The first is that, traditionally, an order of specific performance would not be granted of a contract which was to be carried out over a period of time. Thus in *Ryan v Mutual Tontine Westminster Chambers Association* [1983] 1 Ch 116 the court refused to order specific performance of a contract to provide portering service for a flat. The usual explanation is that the court has no way of supervising performance. The second is that specific performance will not be granted of a contract involving personal services.

C H Giles Co v Morris [1972] 1 WLR 307

The contract was for, among other things, the reorganization of a company and the sale of certain of its shares to the plaintiff company. Clause 2 provided that the vendors would procure the appointment of Mr Giles as Managing Director of a company (Invincible) for five years.

Megarry J. . . . What I have to consider is whether the presence in the agreement of clause 2(f), providing for Mr Giles to enter into a service agreement with Invincible in the form of the draft annexed to the contract, prevents the court from decreeing specific performance of the entire agreement, including that subclause. It will be observed that there is no question of the plaintiff seeking to enforce any order of the court which will compel any of the defendants to carry out, either as employer or employee, any personal services. The order made is an order to procure 'the execution by the company of the engrossment' of the service agreement. The question is whether such an order falls within the principle that the court will not decree specific performance of a contract for personal services.

On the face of it the answer must be No. There is no question of the execution of the decree requiring constant superintendence by the court of a continuous series of acts such as arose in *Ryan v Mutual Tontine Westminster Chambers Association*, a case that was mentioned but not cited during argument. All that the decree requires in this respect is the procuring of a single act, namely, the execution of the service agreement. When that has been done, the question of any breach of the service agreement and any remedies for that breach is one between Invincible and Mr Giles and not between Invincible and the plaintiff. Invincible, too, is a party neither to the contract nor to the action.

The distinction between an order to perform a contract for services and an order to procure the execution of such a contract seems to me to be sound both in principle and on authority. I do not think that the mere fact that the contract to be made is one of which the court would not decree specific performance is a ground for refusing to decree that the contract be entered into. During the argument Mr Harman cited *Fry on Specific Performance*, 6th edn (1921), pp 50, 51, in support of the proposition that the court will not order specific performance of a contract of hiring and service. This, however, is not the whole of the story: and if one turns on to pp 388 to 390 one finds *Ryan's* case cited, together with certain other cases. To one of the latter, *Wilson v West Hartlepool Railway Co*, I drew the attention of counsel towards the conclusion of Mr Neill's argument.

. . . Knight Bruce LJ said . . .:

'I agree that there may be and have been cases in which it may well be and has been held that there may, under a bill for specific performance of a contract, be a decree against a defendant to execute a deed containing covenants on his part to do acts of which, from their nature, specific performance could not directly be enforced. But the present I think not a case of that description.'

As Turner LJ held not only that the agreement did contemplate the execution of a further deed, but also that the execution of such a deed should be specifically enforced, I think it is clear that both members of the court took the view that specific performance may be decreed of an agreement to execute an instrument even if the obligations under that instrument would not be specifically enforced. It is true that the ground on which specific performance was resisted in that case was not that the further instrument related to acts of personal service but that it was too indefinite in its obligations, requiring a contracting party to use a particular railway 'in preference to all others', 'whenever reasonably practicable', and 'for the longest distance it is reasonably capable of use'. However, in this context I can see no sensible distinction between this objection to specific performance and an objection based on the performance of personal services; and I do not think that the judgments support any such distinction.

That is not the only authority to this effect. Thus there is *Granville v Betts* of which *Fry* says, at p 389: 'The real contract here which the court enforces is a contract to execute the deed'; and see *Stocker v Wedderburn*. So too in *Wilson v Wilson* Lord St Leonards said:

'it does not at all follow, because the court of equity compels the appellant in this case to enter into a covenant that he will not, by the force of ecclesiastical censures, compel restitution of his conjugal rights, that the court would enjoin him from breaking that covenant which he has entered into; the court, I apprehend, would leave him to answer any action that might be brought for damages upon the covenant.'

Indeed, were the rule otherwise, I do not see why a lessor could not resist specific performance of a contract to grant a lease if that lease contained any term of which specific performance would not be granted, such a provision like that in *Ryan's* case for the services of a porter, or for repairs; yet he cannot: see *Paxton v Newton*.

There is a further consideration. The obligation to enter into a service agreement is merely one part of a contract which deals with many other matters; and that obligation is the only part of that complex which is said not to be specifically enforceable. Now there is authority for saying that the mere presence in a contract of one provision which, by itself, would not be specifically enforceable (because, for example, it requires the performance of personal services) does not prevent the contract as a whole from being specifically enforced. This is so even if the obligation to perform personal services could be enforced only, for instance, by ordering sequestration: see *Fortescue v Lostwithiel and Fowey Railway Co; Fry on Specific Performance* 6th edn (1921), p 53. In such cases, the contract must be regarded as a whole, and the court may refuse to let the disadvantages and difficulties of specifically enforcing the obligation to perform personal services outweigh the suitability of the rest of the contract for specific performance, and the desirability of the contract as a whole being enforced. After all, pacta sunt servanda.

One day, perhaps, the courts will look again at the so-called rule that contracts for personal services or involving the continuous performance of services will not be specifically enforced. Such a rule is plainly not absolute and without exception, nor do I think that it can be based on any narrow consideration such as difficulties of constant superintendence by the court. Mandatory injunctions are by no means unknown, and there is normally no question of the court having to send its officers to supervise the performance of the order of the court. Prohibitory injunctions are common, and again there is no direct supervision by the court. Performance of each type of injunction is normally secured by the realisation of the person enjoined that he is liable to be punished for contempt if evidence of his disobedience to the order is put before the court; and if the injunction is prohibitory, actual committal will usually, so long as it continues, make disobedience impossible. If instead the order is for specific performance of a contract for personal services, a similar machinery of enforcement could be employed, again without there being any question of supervision by any officer of the court. The reasons why the court is reluctant to decree specific performance of a contract for personal services (and I would regard it as a strong reluctance rather than a rule) are, I think, more complex and more firmly bottomed on human nature. If a singer contracts to sing, there could be no doubt be proceedings for committal if, ordered to sing, the singer remained obstinately dumb. But if instead the singer sang flat, or sharp, or too fast, or too slowly, or too loudly, or too quietly, or resorted to a dozen of the manifestations of temperament traditionally associated with some singers, the threat of committal would reveal itself as a most unsatisfactory weapon: for who could say whether the imperfections of performance were natural or self-induced? To make an order with such possibilities of evasion would be vain; and so the order will not be made. However, not all contracts of personal service or for the continuous performance of services are as dependent as this on matters of opinion and judgment, nor do all such contracts involve the same degree of the daily impact of person upon person. In general, no doubt, the inconvenience and mischief of decreeing specific performance of most of such contracts will greatly outweigh the advantages, and specific performance will be refused. But I do not think that it should be assumed that as soon as any element of personal service or continuous services can be discerned in a contract the court will, without more, refuse specific performance. Of course, a requirement for the continuous performance of services has the disadvantage that repeated breaches may engender repeated applications to the court for enforcement. But so may many injunctions; and the prospects of repetition, although an important consideration, ought not to be allowed to negative a right. As is so often the case in equity, the matter is one of the balance of advantage and disadvantage in relation to the particular obligations in question: and the fact that the balance will usually lie on one side does not turn this probability into a rule. The present case, of course, is a fortiori, since the contract of which specific performance has been decreed requires not the performance of personal services or any continuous series of acts, but merely procuring the execution of an agreement which contains a provision for such services or acts.

It follows that in my judgment the agreement is specifically enforceable, the consent order was properly made, and the advice given by junior counsel that there was no defence to the action on this score was sound advice. In those circumstances, I can see no defence to the plaintiff's motion to enforce the order.

NOTE

In *Posner v Scott-Lewis* [1986] 3 All ER 513 Mervyn Davies J, relying on what Megarry had said, granted specific performance of a term in a contract that required the defendant to appoint a porter. He said (at p 521):

> Whether or not an order for specific performance should be made seems to me to depend on the following considerations: (a) is there a sufficient definition of what has to be done in order to comply with the order of the court; (b) will enforcing compliance involve superintendence by the court to an unacceptable degree; and (c) what are the respective prejudices or hardships that will be suffered by the parties if the order is made or not made?
>
> As to (a), one may in this case sufficiently define what has to be done by the defendants by ordering the defendants, within say two months, to employ a porter to be resident at Danes Court for the purpose of carrying out the cl 3(11) duties. It is to be borne in mind that there is still a vacant flat available for a resident porter. As to (b), I do not see that such an order will occasion any protracted superintendence by the court. If the defendants without good cause fail to comply with the order in due time, then the plaintiffs can take appropriate enforcement proceedings against the defendants. As to (c), I see no hardship or prejudice resulting to the defendants from the order. They will simply be performing what they have promised to do and what has been carried out by the lessors over the past 20 years.

While this case is certainly not an abandonment of the 'supervision' rule, it does suggest some relaxation of it. In fact at least one exception to the rule has been recognised for a long time. In *Wolverhampton Corpn v Emmons* [1901] 1 KB 515 at 524–525, Romer J stated it thus:

> There is no doubt that as a general rule the Court will not enforce specific performance of a building contract, but an exception from the rule has been recognised. It has, I think, for some time been held that, in order to bring himself within that exception, a plaintiff must establish three things. The first is that the building work, of which he seeks to enforce the performance, is defined by the contract; that is to say, that the particulars of the work are so far definitely ascertained that the Court can sufficiently see what is the exact nature of the work of which it is asked to order the performance. The second is that the plaintiff has a substantial interest in having the contract performed, which is of such a nature that he cannot adequately be compensated for breach of the contract by damages. The third is that the defendant has by the contract obtained possession of land on which the work is contracted to be done.

In *Carpenters Estates Ltd v Davies* [1940] Ch 160 Farwell J held that the defendant need not have acquired the land under the contract in question. In that case a vendor of land had undertaken to do work on adjacent land she retained. Why is specific performance available because the work is to be done on the defendant's land? It appears that, even if the work is to be done on the defendant's land, an order will not be made unless damages would be inadequate for other reasons as well. What sort of damages could be awarded in such circumstances?

There has also been some relaxation of the rule that contracts for personal services will not be specifically enforced. As we shall see shortly, there is a 'companion' rule that the court will not grant an injunction that would amount to ordering specific performance of an employment contract. However in *Hill v CA Parsons Ltd* [1972] Ch 305 the Court of Appeal issued an injunction to restrain an employer from dismissing an employee wrongfully. Both parties wished the relationship to continue, but union pressure caused the employer to threaten dismissal of the employee shortly before he was due to retire and shortly before the coming into force of the Industrial Relations Act 1971, which would have given the employee some protection. It was subsequently emphasised that the case was exceptional, see *Chappell v Times Newspapers Ltd* [1975] 1 WLR 482 at 501, 503, 506; but an injunction was issued in *Powell v Brent London Borough Council* [1987] IRLR

466. The plaintiff applied for promotion to the post of Principal Benefits Officer. After interviews, she was told that she had been selected and she reported to her new place of employment. It was then alleged that the selection procedure had not complied with the Borough's equal opportunity code of practice and she was instructed to return to her previous post. She refused. Although the Borough strongly opposed her continuing in her job, it was stated that her superiors had complete confidence in her and that her return would cause no friction with those with whom she would be working. The Court of Appeal granted an interlocutory injunction. Ralph Gibson LJ stated (at p 473):

> For my part on this issue I have reached the conclusion that the decision of Mr Justice Knox cannot stand. I have reached that conclusion with hesitation because it seems to me essentially unlikely for a plaintiff to be able to satisfy the court that, despite strenuous opposition by her employers to her continuing in her job, nevertheless there subsists the necessary confidence between her and her employers to justify the making of an injunction. The fact of the opposition is likely in my view to be a true indication of the absence of confidence, but as I said at the outset I think this is a most unusual case.
>
> First I must state the principle which must, I think, guide our decision. It is clear to me that part of the basis of the general rule against specific performance of contracts of service is that mutual confidence is normally a necessary condition for the satisfactory working of a contract of service. If one party refuses to allow the relationship to continue the mutual confidence is almost certainly missing. Mr Justice Knox referred to the judgment of Lord Justice Geoffrey Lane (as he then was) in *Chappell v Times Newspapers Ltd* [1975] IRLR 90 at p 95.
>
> For my part I am not able to derive much assistance from the words 'complete confidence' for the purposes of this case. I prefer to state what I think the applicable principle to be in this way. Having regard to the decision in *Hill v Parsons* and to the long-standing general rule of practice to which *Hill v Parsons* was an exception, the court will not by injunction require an employer to let a servant continue in his employment, when the employer has sought to terminate that employment and to prevent the servant carrying out his work under the contract, unless it is clear on the evidence not only that it is otherwise just to make such a requirement but also that there exists sufficient confidence on the part of the employer in the servant's ability and other necessary attributes for it to be reasonable to make the order. Sufficiency of confidence must be judged by reference to the circumstances of the case, including the nature of the work, the people with whom the work must be done and the likely effect upon the employer and the employer's operations if the employer is required by injunction to suffer the plaintiff to continue in the work.

Would it be fair to say that the 'contract for personal service rule' was developed in the context of employment by individuals or small organisations and is not necessarily appropriate to employment within a very large organisation? How many unusual cases must there be before the exception becomes a rule?

Specific performance, which is a discretionary remedy, may also be refused on other equitable grounds, such as hardship to the defendant. For a recent case involving hardship, see *Patel v Ali* [1984] Ch 283, where the vendor of a house had, since the sale, become disabled and heavily dependent for help on neighbours whom she would lose if she had to move. Goulding J refused to grant specific performance, leaving the purchasers to their remedy in damages. Other grounds on which specific performance may be refused are delay ('laches') and mistake (not amounting to a mistake preventing the formation of a contract) on the part of the defendant (see above, p 232).

The court may also refuse to grant specific performance of an obligation which is due to be performed before the plaintiff's own performance, if when the time comes for the plaintiff to perform, specific performance will not be available against him. The point seems to be that it might be unfair to force the defendant to go to the expense of performing, only to find that later the plaintiff will not do so, and in addition is perhaps unable to pay any damages: the defendant might have preferred not to perform and to pay damages, which at that stage will be lower, because the plaintiff has not had to perform. The rule is often called the 'mutuality rule', but this name can be misleading, because it is not the case that specific performance will never be granted to a plaintiff against whom it could not be ordered. If the plaintiff has already performed, it is immaterial that an order could not have been made against him: *Price v Strange* [1978] Ch 337. Even where the plaintiff has not performed, and it will not be possible to order him to do so when the time comes, the problem may be solved by taking security from the plaintiff, see *Langen & Wind Ltd v Bell* [1972] Ch 685.

Warner Bros Pictures Inc v Nelson [1937] 1 KB 209

The defendant, the film star Bette Davis, entered into a contract with the plaintiffs on 27 December 1934 for fifty-two weeks, extendable at the plaintiffs' option up till 1942, to render her exclusive services as a motion picture and/or legitimate stage actress to the plaintiffs, and to perform solely and exclusively for them. In June 1936 the defendant, in admitted breach of contract, refused to be further bound, came to England and entered into a contract to act in a film for another company.

The plaintiffs sought an injunction to restrain the defendant 'from rendering without the written consent of the plaintiffs . . . any services for or in any motion picture or stage production or productions of any person, firm or corporation other than the plaintiffs'.

Branson J. . . . It is conceded that our Courts will not enforce a positive covenant of personal service; and specific performance of the positive covenants by the defendant to serve the plaintiffs is not asked in the present case. The practice of the Court of Chancery in relation to the enforcement of negative covenants is stated on the highest authority by Lord Cairns in the House of Lords in *Doherty v Allman*. His Lordship says: 'My Lords, if there had been a negative covenant, I apprehend, according to well-settled practice, a Court of Equity would have had no discretion to exercise. If parties, for valuable consideration, with their eyes open, contract that a particular thing shall not be done, all that a Court of Equity has to do is to say, by way of injunction, that which the parties have already said by way of covenant, that the thing shall not be done; and in such case the injunction does nothing more than give the sanction of the process of the Court to that which already is the contract between the parties. It is not then a question of the balance of convenience or inconvenience, or of the amount of damage or of injury—it is the specific performance, by the Court, of that negative bargain which the parties have made, with their eyes open, between themselves.'

That was not a case of a contract of personal service; but the same principle had already been applied to such a contract by Lord St Leonards in *Lumley v Wagner*. The Lord Chancellor used the following language: 'Wherever this Court has not proper jurisdiction to enforce specific performance, it operates to bind men's consciences, as far as they can be bound, to a true and literal performance of their agreements; and it will not suffer them to depart from their contracts at their pleasure, leaving the party with whom they have contracted to the mere chance of any damages which a jury may give. The exercise of the jurisdiction has, I believe, had a wholesome tendency towards the maintenance of that good faith which exists in this country to a much greater degree perhaps than in any other; and although the jurisdiction is not to be extended, yet a Judge would desert his duty who did not act up to what his predecessors have handed down as the rule for his guidance in the administration of such an equity.'

The defendant, having broken her positive undertakings in the contract without any cause or excuse which she was prepared to support in the witness-box, contends that she cannot be enjoined from breaking the negative covenants also. The mere fact that a covenant which the Court would not enforce, if expressed in positive form, is expressed in the negative instead, will not induce the Court to enforce it.

. . . The Court will attend to the substance and not to the form of the covenant. Nor will the Court, true to the principle that specific performance of a contract of personal service will never be ordered, grant an injunction in the case of such a contract to enforce negative covenants if the effect of so doing would be to drive the defendant either to starvation or to specific performance of the positive covenants: see *Whitwood Chemical Co v Hardman* . . . but this is subject to a further consideration. An injunction is a discretionary remedy, and the Court in granting it may limit it to what the Court considers reasonable in all the circumstances of the case.

This appears from the judgment of the Court of Appeal in *William Robinson & Co, Ld v Heuer*. The particular covenant in that case is set out at p 452 and provides that 'Heuer shall not during this engagement, without the previous consent in writing of the said W. Robinson & Co, Ltd', and so forth, 'carry on or be engaged either directly or indirectly, as principal, agent, servant, or otherwise, in any trade, business, or calling, either relating to goods of any description sold or manufactured by the said W. Robinson & Co, Ld . . . or in any other business whatsoever'.

. . . [T]he Court there proceeded to sever the covenants and to grant an injunction, not to restrain the defendant from carrying on any other business whatsoever, but framed so as to give what was felt to be a reasonable protection to the plaintiffs and no more. The plaintiffs waived an option which they possessed to extend the period of service for an extra five years, and the injunction then was granted for the remaining period of unextended time.

It is said that this case is no longer the law, but that *Attwood v Lamont* has decided that no such severance is permissible. I do not agree. *Attwood v Lamont* was a case where the covenants were held void as in restraint of trade. There is all the difference in the world between declining to make an illegal covenant good by neglecting that which makes it contrary to law and exercising a discretion as to how far the Court will enforce a valid convenant by injunction. The latter was done in the Court of Appeal in *William Robinson & Co v Heuer*, the former in *Attwood v Lamont*.

The case before me is, therefore, one in which it would be proper to grant an injunction unless to do so would in the circumstances be tantamount to ordering the defendant to perform her contract or remain idle or unless damages would be the more appropriate remedy.

With regard to the first of these considerations, it would, of course, be impossible to grant an injunction covering all the negative covenants in the contract. That would, indeed, force the defendant to perform her contract or remain idle; but this objection is removed by the restricted form in which the injunction is sought. It is confined to forbidding the defendant, without the consent of the plaintiffs, to render any services for or in any motion picture or stage production for any one other than the plaintiffs.

It was also urged that the difference between what the defendant can earn as a film artiste and what she might expect to earn by any other form of activity is so great that she will in effect be driven to perform her contract. That is not the criterion adopted in any of the decided cases. The defendant is stated to be a person of intelligence, capacity and means, and no evidence was adduced to show that, if enjoined from doing the specified acts otherwise than for the plaintiffs, she will not be able to employ herself both usefully and remuneratively in other spheres of activity, though not as remuneratively as in her special line. She will not be driven, although she may be tempted, to perform the contract, and the fact that she may be so tempted is no objection to the grant of an injunction.

With regard to the question whether damages is not the more appropriate remedy, I have the uncontradicted evidence of the plaintiffs as to the difficulty of estimating the damages which they may suffer from the breach by the defendant of her contract. I think it is not inappropriate to refer to the fact that, in the contract between the parties, in clause 22, there is a formal admission by the defendant that her services, being 'of a special, unique, extraordinary and intellectual character' gives them a particular value 'the loss of which cannot be reasonably or adequately compensated in damages' and that a breach may 'cost the producer great and irreparable injury and damage', and the artiste expressly agrees that the producer shall be entitled to the remedy of injunction. Of course, parties cannot contract themselves out of the law; but it assists, at all events, on the question of evidence as to the applicability of an injunction in the present case, to find the parties formally recognizing that in cases of this kind injunction is a more appropriate remedy than damages.

Furthermore, in the case of *Grimston v Cuningham*, which was also a case in which a theatrical manager was attempting to enforce against an actor a negative stipulation against going elsewhere, Wills J granted an injunction, and used the following language: 'This is an agreement of a kind which is pre-eminently subject to the interference of the Court by injunction, for in cases of this nature it very often happens that the injury suffered in consequence of the breach of the agreement would be out of all proportion to any pecuniary damages which could be proved or assessed by a jury. The circumstance affords a strong reason in favour of exercising the discretion of the Court by granting an injunction'.

I think that that applies to the present case also, and that an injunction should be granted in regard to the specified services.

Then comes the question as to the period for which the injunction should operate. The period of the contract, now that the plaintiffs have undertaken not as from October 16, 1936, to exercise the rights of suspension conferred upon them by clause 23 thereof, will, if they exercise their options to prolong it, extend to about May, 1942. As I read the judgment of the Court of Appeal in *Robinson v Heuer* the Court should make the period such as to give reasonable protection and no more to the plaintiffs against the ill effects to them of the defendant's breach of contract. The evidence as to that was perhaps necessarily somewhat vague. The main difficulty that the plaintiffs apprehend is that the defendant might appear in other films whilst the films already made by them and not yet shown are in the market for sale or hire and thus depreciate their value. I think that if the injunction is in force during the continuance of the contract or for three years from now, whichever period is the shorter, that will substantially meet the case.

NOTES

1. For all practical purposes, didn't this amount to ordering Bette Davis to work for Warner Bros? Compare *Page One Records Ltd v Britton* [1968] 1 WLR 157 at 167.

2. The quotation from *Doherty v Allman* (1878) 3 App Cas 709 seems to suggest that adequacy of damages is irrelevant if there is an express negative stipulation. Why should this be? In practice, adequacy of damages is often taken into account even when there is a negative stipulation, eg *Decro-Wall International SA v Practitioners in Marketing Ltd* [1971] 2 All ER 216.

3. It appears that in contracts for employment an injunction will not be granted merely to restrain the employee from working for another employer unless there is an express negative covenant: *Whitwood Chemical Co v Hardman* [1891] 2 Ch 416. This does not apply to other contracts: the court may restrain the defendant from some act implicitly inconsistent with his contractual obligations. In *Bower v Bantam Investments Ltd* [1972] 1 WLR 1120 at 1124–1125, Goff J said:

Where a positive contract is in substance negative the court may grant an injunction: see *Metropolitan Electric Supply Co Ltd v Ginder*. It will be observed there that the substance was indeed negative as there was no contract to take the supply of electricity. Buckley J (referring to the decision of Fry J in *Donnell v Bennett*) said:

'He says this at the beginning of his judgment, after reading or referring to the passage in Lord Selborne's judgment to which I have referred: "that the court ought to look at what is the nature of the contract between the parties; that if the contract as a whole is the subject of equitable jurisdiction, then an injunction may be granted in support of the contract, whether it contain or does not contain a negative stipulation." I think this is such a contract, because it appears to me that the contract for this present purpose is not one for the supply by the plaintiffs to the defendant of electricity—he is not bound to take any. The contract really is a contract, the whole of which is in substance the negative part of it, that he will take the whole from them, involving that he will not take any from anybody else. I therefore think that the fact that the contract is affirmative in form and not negative in form is no ground for refusing an injunction.'

[Moreover] . . . it is clear that in some cases the court will grant an injunction restraining a breach of a negative provision which is part of a positive contract, and moreover, of a contract which is not capable of specific performance: see *Wolverhampton and Walsall Railway Co v London and North-Western Railway Co* and *Catt v Tourle*, particularly per Giffard LJ.

Further, except probably in cases of contracts of personal service and, I think, fiduciary agency as to which special considerations apply, it is not necessary in my judgment to found an express negative covenant; an implied one will suffice: see the interlocutory observation of Buckley J in *Metropolitan Electric Supply Co Ltd v Ginder*, and, as to the requirement of an express covenant in the particular cases mentioned, see the judgment at p 807.

However, in my view, to found a claim for relief by way of injunction it is necessary to point to something specific which a defendant has by implication agreed not to do. The mere fact that his conduct or proposed conduct is inconsistent with his obligations under the contract is not sufficient, although, of course, if he does so act, that may well be in itself a breach of contract giving rise to an immediate right to damages as in *Stirling v Maitland*. This, in my judgment, follows from the basic principle that an injunction will never be granted unless it is clear and certain exactly what a defendant may not do.

(b) Action for sums due under the contract

In contrast to the restrictive attitude towards specific performance, a defendant who has failed to pay money will routinely be forced to pay.

Sale of Goods Act 1979

Section 49: Action for price
(1) Where, under a contract of sale, the property in the goods has passed to the buyer and he wrongfully neglects or refuses to pay for the goods according to the terms of the contract, the seller may maintain an action against him for the price of the goods.
(2) Where, under a contract of sale, the price is payable on a day certain irrespective of delivery and the buyer wrongfully neglects or refuses to pay such price, the seller may maintain an action for the price, although the property in the goods has not passed and the goods have not been appropriated to the contract.

NOTES

1. Thus if the seller has delivered goods to the buyer and the buyer has failed to pay for them, the seller's remedy is to sue for the price. (Note that there are procedural advantages in suing for a 'liquidated' sum rather than 'unliquidated' damages, as you can apply for summary judgment.)
2. Note that the seller's right is only a personal one against the buyer. Under the general law, once the property has passed and the goods have been delivered to the buyer, the seller cannot exercise any right against the goods themselves (such as seizing them). If the buyer is insolvent, a personal right against it may be of little value, so sellers often attempt to preserve a right to repossess the goods. A common way of doing this is by a 'reservation of title' or 'Romalpa' clause. The simplest form of clause is a provision that the goods will remain the seller's property until paid for. See *Aluminium Industrie Vaassen BV v Romalpa Aluminium Ltd* [1976] 2 All ER 552 (the first case on such a clause) and *Clough Mill Ltd v Martin* [1984] 3 All ER 982 (which explains how a simple clause operates).
3. Under a contract for the sale of goods it is quite common for the property in the goods to pass before delivery: in the case of specific goods which are in a state ready to be delivered, the normal presumption (under s 17 and s 18 rule 1) is that the property passes at the time the contract is made. In such a case, what is the practical effect of allowing a seller to sue a defaulting buyer for the price, rather than having to accept the buyer's repudiation and sue for damages? Is the outcome always a sensible one, given that the buyer may have no use for the goods? See Atiyah, *Sale of Goods* (7th edn, pp 369–370).
4. However, if the buyer repudiates *before* the property has passed to him, the seller cannot pass it to him and recover the price. For instance, if a seller under a cif contract (one in which the seller's obligation is not actually to deliver the goods to the buyer, but to ship them to a named port and to deliver to the buyer the shipping documents, namely a bill of lading, an

invoice and an insurance policy covering the voyage: see above, p 53) has reserved the right of disposal of the goods by providing that he will deliver the documents only against cash, it seems he cannot hold the documents for the repudiating buyer and sue for the price: *Colley v Overseas Exporters* [1921] 3 KB 302. Contrast this with the outcome of the next case.

White & Carter (Councils) Ltd v McGregor [1961] 3 All ER 1178, House of Lords

The appellants made litter bins, on which they placed advertisements, and supplied them to local authorities. The respondent's sales manager entered a contract for the respondent's business to be so advertised for three years. The same day the respondent repudiated the agreement, but the appellants made the advertisements and displayed them throughout the three-year period. They sued the respondent for the payments due under the contract.

Lord Reid. . . . The general rule cannot be in doubt. It was settled in Scotland at least as early as 1848 and it has been authoritatively stated time and again in both Scotland and England. If one party to a contract repudiates it in the sense of making it clear to the other party that he refuses or will refuse to carry out his part of the contract, the other party, the innocent party, has an option. He may accept that repudiation and sue for damages for breach of contract whether or not the time for performance has come; or he may if he chooses disregard or refuse to accept it and then the contract remains in full effect.

. . . I need not refer to the numerous authorities. They are not disputed by the respondent but he points out that in all of them the party who refused to accept the repudiation had no active duties under the contract. The innocent party's option is generally said to be to *wait* until the date of performance and then to claim damages estimated as at that date. There is no case in which it is said that he may, in face of the repudiation, go on and incur useless expense in performing the contract and then claim the contract price. The option, it is argued, is merely as to the date as at which damages are to be assessed. Developing this argument, the respondent points out that in most cases the innocent party cannot complete the contract himself without the other party doing, allowing or accepting something, and that it is purely fortuitous that the appellants can do so in this case. In most cases by refusing co-operation the party in breach can compel the innocent party to restrict his claim to damages. Then it was said that even where the innocent party can complete the contract without such co-operation it is against the public interest that he should be allowed to do so. An example was developed in argument. A company might engage an expert to go abroad and prepare an elaborate report and then repudiate the contract before anything was done. To allow such an expert then to waste thousands of pounds in preparing the report cannot be right if a much smaller sum of damages would give him full compensation for his loss. It would merely enable the expert to extort a settlement giving him far more than reasonable compensation.

The respondent founds on the decision of the First Division in *Langford & Co Ltd v Dutch*. There an advertising contractor agreed to exhibit a film for a year. Four days after this agreement was made the advertiser repudiated it but, as in the present case, the contractor refused to accept the repudiation and proceeded to exhibit the film and sue for the contract price. The sheriff-substitute dismissed the action as irrelevant and his decision was affirmed on appeal. In the course of a short opinion the Lord President (Lord Cooper) said:

'. . . The pursuers could not force the defender to accept a year's advertisement which she did not want, though they could of course claim damages for her breach of contract. On the averments the only reasonable and proper course, which the pursuers should have adopted, would have been to treat the defender as having repudiated the contract and as being on that account liable in damages, the measure of which we are, of course, not in a position to discuss.'

The Lord President cited no authority and I am in doubt what principle he had in mind. . . .

. . . We must now decide whether that case was rightly decided. In my judgment it was not. It could only be supported on one or other of two grounds. It might be said that, because in most cases the circumstances are such that an innocent party is unable to complete the contract and earn the contract price without the assent or co-operation of the other party, therefore in cases where he can do so he should not be allowed to do so. I can see no justification for that.

The other ground would be that there is some general equitable principle or element of public policy which requires this limitation of the contractual rights of the innocent party. It may well be that, if it can be shown that a person has no legitimate interest, financial or otherwise, in performing the contract rather than claiming damages, he ought not to be allowed to saddle the other party with an additional burden with no benefit to himself. If a party has no interest to enforce a stipulation he cannot in general enforce it: so it might be said that if a party has no interest to insist on a particular remedy he ought not to be allowed to insist on it. And, just as a party is not allowed to enforce a penalty, so he ought not to be allowed to penalise the other party by taking one course when another is equally advantageous to him. If I may revert to the example which I gave of a company engaging an expert to prepare an elaborate report and then repudiating before anything was done, it might be that the company could show that the expert had no substantial or legitimate interest in carrying out the work rather than accepting damages: I would think that the de minimis principle would apply in determining whether his interest was substantial and that he might have a legitimate interest other than an immediate financial interest. But if the expert had no such interest then that might be regarded as a proper case for the exercise of the general equitable jurisdiction of the court. But that is not this case. Here the respondent did not set out to prove that the appellants had no legitimate interest in completing the contract and claiming the contract price rather than claiming damages, there is nothing in the findings of fact to support such a case, and it seems improbable that any such case could have been proved. It is, in my judgment, impossible to say that the appellants should be deprived of their right to claim the contract price merely because the benefit to them as against claiming damages and reletting their advertising space might be small in comparison with the loss to the respondent: that is the most that could be said in favour of the respondent. Parliament has on many occasions relieved parties from certain kinds of improvident or oppressive contracts, but the common law can only do that in very limited circumstances. Accordingly, I am unable to avoid the conclusion that this appeal must be allowed and the case remitted so that decree can be pronounced as craved in the initial writ.

Lord Morton of Henryton [dissenting] . . . It is well established that repudiation by one party does not put an end to a contract. The other party can say 'I hold you to your contract, which still remains in force'. What, then, is his remedy if the repudiating party persists in his repudiation and refuses to carry out his part of the contract? The contract has been broken. The innocent party is entitled to be compensated by damages for any loss which he has suffered by reason of the breach, and in a limited class of cases the court will decree specific implement. The law of Scotland provides no other remedy for a breach of contract, and there is no reported case which decides that the innocent party may act as the appellants have acted. The present case is one in which specific implement could not be decreed, since the only obligation of the respondent under the contract was to pay a sum of money for services to be rendered by the appellants. Yet the appellants are claiming a kind of inverted specific implement of the contract. They first insist on performing their part of the contract, against the will of the other party, and then claim that he must perform his part and pay the contract price for unwanted services. In my opinion, my Lords, the appellants' only remedy was damages, and they were bound to take steps to minimise their loss, according to a well-established rule of law. Far from doing this, having incurred no expense at the date of the repudiation, they made no attempt to procure another advertiser, but deliberately went on to incur expense and perform unwanted services with the intention of creating a money debt which did not exist at the date of the repudiation.

[Lord Keith of Avonholm also delivered a dissenting judgment.]

Lord Hodson . . . It is settled as a fundamental rule of the law of contract that repudiation by one of the parties to a contract does not itself discharge it. See the speech of Viscount Simon LC in *Heyman v Darwins, Ltd* citing with approval the following sentence from a judgment of Scrutton LJ in *Golding v London & Edinburgh Insurance Co, Ltd*:

'I have never been able to understand what effect repudiation by one party has unless the other party accepts [the repudiation].'

In *Howard v Pickford Tool Co, Ltd* Asquith LJ said: 'An unaccepted repudiation is a thing writ in water and of no value to anybody: it confers no legal rights of any sort or kind'. These are English cases but that the law of Scotland is the same is, I think, clear from the authorities, of which I need only refer to one, namely, *Howie v Anderson* where language to the same effect is to be found in the opinions of the Lord President and Lord Moncrieff.

It follows that, if, as here, there was no acceptance, the contract remains alive for the benefit of both parties and the party who has repudiated can change his mind but it does not follow that the party at the receiving end of the proffered repudiation is bound to accept it before the time for performance and is left to his remedy in damages for breach.

Counsel for the respondent did not seek to dispute the general proposition of law to which I have referred but sought to argue that if at the date of performance by the innocent party the guilty party maintains his refusal to accept performance and the innocent party does not accept the repudiation, although the contract still survives, it does not survive so far as the right of the innocent party to perform it is concerned but survives only for the purpose of enforcing remedies open to him by way of damages or specific implement. This produces an impossible result; if the innocent party is deprived of some of his rights it involves putting an end to the contract except in cases, unlike this, where, in the exercise of the court's discretion, the remedy of specific implement is available.

The true position is that the contract survives and does so not only where specific implement is available. When the assistance of the court is not required the innocent party can choose whether he will accept repudiation and sue for damages for anticipatory breach or await the date of performance by the guilty party. Then, if there is failure in performance, his rights are preserved.

It may be unfortunate that the appellants have saddled themselves with an unwanted contract causing an apparent waste of time and money. No doubt this aspect impressed the Court of Session but there is no equity which can assist the respondent. It is trite that equity will not rewrite an improvident contract where there is no disability on either side. There is no duty laid on a party to a subsisting contract to vary it at the behest of the other party so as to deprive himself of the benefit given to him by the contract. To hold otherwise would be to introduce a novel equitable doctrine that a party was not to be held to his contract unless the court in a given instance thought it reasonable so to do. In this case it would make an action for debt a claim for a discretionary remedy. This would introduce an uncertainty into the field of contract which appears to be unsupported by authority either in English or Scottish law save for the one case on which the Court of Session founded its opinion and which must, in my judgment, be taken to have been wrongly decided.

[Lord Tucker agreed with the reasoning of Lord Hodson.]

Appeal allowed.

NOTES

1. Lord Reid points out that in many cases, the innocent party will not be able to carry out his performance without the co-operation of the repudiating party. This was considered further by Megarry J in *Hounslow London Borough v Twickenham Garden Development Ltd* [1970] 3 All ER 326. Considering the application of the *White & Carter* case to a building contract, the judge said:

   . . . Quite apart from questions of active co-operation, cases where one party is lawfully in possession of property of the other seem to me to raise issues not before the House of Lords in the *White* case. Suppose that A, who owns a large and valuable painting, contracts with B, a picture restorer, to restore it over a period of three months. Before the work is begun. A receives a handsome offer from C to purchase the picture, subject to immediate delivery of the picture in its unrestored state, C having grave suspicions of B's competence. If the work of restoration is to be done in A's house, he can effectually exclude B by refusing to admit him to the house; without A's 'co-operation' to this extent B cannot perform his contract. But what if the picture stands in A's locked barn, the key of which he has lent to B so that he may come and go freely, or if the picture has been removed to B's premises? Can B insist in these cases in performing his contract, even though this makes it impossible for A to accept C's offer? In the case of the barn, A's co-operation may perhaps be said to be requisite to the extent of not barring B's path to the barn or putting another lock on the door; but if the picture is on B's premises, no active co-operation by A is needed. Nevertheless, the picture is A's property, and I find it difficult to believe that Lord Reid intended to restrict the concept of 'co-operation' to active co-operation. In the *White* case, no co-operation by the proprietor, either active or passive, was required; the contract could be performed by the agent wholly without reference to the proprietor or his property. The case was far removed from that of a property owner being forced to stand impotently aside while a perhaps ill-advised contract is executed on property of his which he has delivered into the possession of the other party, and is powerless to retrieve.

   Accordingly, I do not think that the *White* case has any application to the case before me.

In the Canadian case of *Finelli v Dee* [1968] 1 OR 676, 76 DLR(2d) 393 a houseowner repudiated a contract to have his driveway surfaced. The builder entered and did the work without notice while the owner was

away. It was held that the builder could not recover the price: without deciding whether the builder's licence to enter the land had been revoked, the court held that he was not entitled to do the work without giving notice.
2. A wrongfully dismissed employee cannot keep himself available for work and recover his wages. (There were at one time indications that a doctrine of 'constructive service', as it was called, might develop, but the idea was ultimately rejected, see Freedland, *Contract of Employment* (1976), p 294.) How would you explain the different outcome?
3. Lord Reid also suggests that the innocent party may not be able to carry out the contract and recover the price after a repudiation if he has no substantial or legitimate interest in doing so. Did the other members of the House accept this?
4. What is the distinction between the example given of the expert going abroad and preparing his report and the facts of the *White & Carter* case? A possible difference, though not one stated in any of the judgments, is that the pursuers in *White & Carter* could not have relet the space to any other client—they were 'lost volume sellers'. See Diamond, (1978) 11 Melbourne ULR 573 at 575–576.

The legitimate interest point has remained controversial. In *Attica Sea Carriers Corpn v Ferrostaal Poseidon Bulk Reederei GmbH, The Puerto Buitrago* [1976] 1 Lloyd's Rep 250 it appears to have been accepted by all the members of the Court of Appeal, but it is not clear that the principle formed part of the *ratio* of the case. The charterers of a ship by demise (a form of charter under which the charterer takes over the management of the ship) were obliged to return her at the end of the charter in as good condition as when she was delivered to them. In the event, the repairs would have cost more than the ship would have been worth even when repaired, so the charterers returned her unrepaired, admitting liability for damages. It was held that the owners could not have the ship repaired and meanwhile continue to charge the charterers hire. The principal ground for the decision was that the obligation to repair was not a condition precedent to the right to redeliver. However, the court added that the owners would also fail for other reasons: the redelivery was in any event effective notwithstanding the fact that the vessel had not been repaired; the charter could not continue without the charterers' co-operation; and, finally, the owners had no legitimate interest in claiming the hire rather than in taking the ship back and claiming damages.

The legitimate interest point seems also to have been accepted by Kerr J in *The Odenfeld* [1978] 2 Lloyd's Rep 357, though only as applicable

'. . . in extreme cases, viz, where damages would be an adequate remedy *and* where an election to keep the contract alive would be wholly unreasonable'.

(at p 374). Kerr J held that the innocent party in that case, the owners under a time charter, did have a legitimate interest in continuing with the contract, because it would be difficult to find other employment for the ship, termination of the charter would put them into breach of other contracts and the damages would be hard to assess.

Clea Shipping Corpn v Bulk Oil International Ltd, The Alaskan Trader [1984] 1 All ER 129, Lloyd J

By a time charter dated 19 October 1979 the owners chartered a vessel to the charterers for a period of approximately 24 months. After the vessel had been in service for nearly a year, the vessel suffered a serious engine breakdown and it became apparent that the repairs would take several months. The charterers then indicated that they had no further use for the vessel but the owners nevertheless went ahead with the repairs at a cost of £800,000. The repairs were completed on 7 April 1981. The owners then informed the charterers that the vessel was once again at their disposal, but the charters declined to give the master of the vessel any orders since they regarded the charterparty as having come to an end. The owners refused to treat the charterers' conduct as a repudiation of the charterparty and maintained the vessel at anchor with a full crew ready to sail until the time charter expired in December 1981. Hire was paid throughout the period from 7 April until December 1981, first under a letter of credit opened in favour of the owners and thereafter by the charterers themselves without prejudice. When the charterparty came to an end the question whether the charterers could recover the hire paid for the period from April to December 1981 was referred to arbitration. The charterers contended that the owners ought to have accepted the charterers' conduct as a repudiation of the charterparty and confined their claim to damages. The owners contended that in the case of repudiation the innocent party had an unfettered right to elect whether to accept or refuse the repudiation and accordingly they were entitled to keep the vessel at the disposal of the charterers throughout the period and to retain the hire. The arbitrator found that the owners had no legitimate interest in pursuing their claim for hire rather than a claim for damages. He held that the owners ought to have accepted the charterers' repudiation by midnight on 8 April 1981 with a view to mitigating their damage and accordingly that the charterers were entitled to recover the hire, while remaining liable for damages. The owners appealed.

Lloyd J. . . . . [The arbitrator said:]

'I am satisfied that this commercial absurdity is not justified by a proper interpretation of the decided cases. I consider that the analogy of a contract between Master and servant applies more closely to a timecharter than the analogy of a simple debt. The Owner supplies the vessel and crew; the Charterer supplies fuel oil, pays disbursements and gives orders. The Charterers were also able to satisfy me that at that stage the Owners had no legitimate interest in pursuing their claim for hire rather than a claim for damages. In these respects the present case differs materially from the case of *White & Carter v McGregor*, and is more closely analogous to the case of *The Puerto Buitrago*, where the judgments of Lord Denning MR and Lord Orr are particularly in point.'

It seems to me that the arbitrator is here distinguishing clearly between the two observations or limitations on the general principle to which Lord Reid had drawn attention in his speech. He is saying that a time charter is more analogous to a contract between master and servant than a simple debt, ie that it is a contract which calls for co-operation between both parties. He is also saying ('The charterers were *also* able to satisfy me . . .') that the owners had no legitimate interest in pursuing their claim for hire as distinct from damages. I will take the legitimate interest point first.

In addition to arguing that what Lord Reid had said about legitimate interest was only a quotation from counsel, and in any event obiter, arguments with which I have already dealt, counsel for the owners, submitted that Lord Reid was, quite simply, wrong. It seems to me that it would be difficult for me to take that view in the light of what was said by all three members of the Court of Appeal in *The Puerto Buitrago*. Whether one takes Lord Reid's language, which was adopted by Orr and Browne LJJ in *The Puerto Buitrago*, or Lord Denning MR's language in that case ('in all reason'), or Kerr J's language in *The Odenfeld* ('wholly unreasonable . . . quite unrealistic, unreasonable and untenable'), there comes a point at which the court will cease, on general equitable principles, to allow the innocent party to enforce his contract according to its strict legal terms. How one defines that point is obviously a matter of some difficulty, for it involves drawing a line between conduct which is merely unreasonable (see per Lord Reid in *White & Carter v McGregor*, criticising the Lord President in *Langford & Co Ltd v Dutch*) and conduct which is *wholly* unreasonable (see per Kerr J in *The Odenfeld*) . . . But however difficult it may be to define the point, that there *is* such a point seems to me to have been accepted both by the Court of Appeal in *The Puerto Buitrago* and by Kerr J in *The Odenfeld*.

I appreciate that the House of Lords has recently re-emphasised the importance of certainty in commercial contracts, when holding that there is no equitable jurisdiction to relieve against the consequences of the withdrawal clause in a time charter: see *Scandinavian Trading Tanker Co AB v Flota Petrolera Ecuatoriana, The Scaptrade*. I appreciate, too, that the importance of certainty was one of the main reasons urged by Lord Hodson in *White & Carter v McGregor* in upholding the innocent party's unfettered right to elect. But, for reasons already mentioned, it seems to me that this court is bound to hold that there is *some* fetter, if only in extreme cases; and for want of a better way of describing that fetter, it is safest for this court to use the language of Lord Reid, which, as I have already said, was adopted by a majority of the Court of Appeal in *The Puerto Buitrago*.

. . . Counsel for the owners argued that the finding must be wrong in law. The arbitrator must have misunderstood what was said by Lord Reid, or applied the wrong test. But I could only accept that submission if the conclusion reached by the arbitrator was one which no reasonable arbitrator could have reached applying the right test. I cannot take that view. Indeed I can well understand why the arbitrator reached the conclusion he did. It is of course quite unnecessary for me to say whether I would have reached the same conclusion on the facts myself; nor by saying even that, do I mean to imply that I would have reached a different conclusion. It was the arbitrator who heard the evidence over many days, not me. It was for him to decide.

Counsel for the owners then turned to the further reasons given by the arbitrator which I have mentioned earlier in this judgment. But counsel was unable to extract any error of law or any mistake in approach. The arbitrator analysed in detail the main grounds on which it could be said that the owners were justified in continuing to claim hire, rather than damages, namely the requirements of the bank, the difficulty in assessing damages and the difficulty in obtaining alternative employment. These are all matters which were considered by Kerr J in *The Odenfeld*. For example, on the question of damages the arbitrator said:

'I did not accept that the assessment of damages in fact presented any special difficulty, or that the poor prospects of obtaining alternative employment would preclude the Owners from obtaining substantial damages. It was a matter of evidence.'

On the difficulty of assessing damages therefore, as on the other matters, the arbitrator reached, as he was entitled, a different view on the facts than did Kerr J in *The Odenfeld*. I cannot begin to say that he was wrong in law. . . .

I turn last to the alternative ground on which the arbitrator based his decision, that this was a contract which called for co-operation between the parties, and therefore fell within Lord Reid's first limitation. Counsel for the charterers argued that a time charter is a contract for services, to be performed by the owners through the master and crew, and through the use of their vessel. As a contract for services, it is, as Lord Diplock pointed out in *The Scaptrade*—

'the very prototype of a contract of which before the fusion of law and equity a court would never grant specific performance . . .'

As in any other contract for services the owners earn their remuneration by performing the services required. If they are wrongfully prevented from performing any services, then, as in any other contract for services, the only remedy lies in damages. The fact that the owners' remuneration in this case, called hire, is payable in advance makes no difference. Counsel for the owners, on the other hand, argued that the owners earned their hire simply by holding the vessel and the services of their master and crew at the charterers' disposal. He concedes that in the case of master and servant, where the master has wrongfully dismissed the servant, the servant cannot earn remuneration by holding himself at the disposal of his master. He is confined to his remedy in damages. But counsel for the owners submits that a time charter is different. In view of my decision on the legitimate interest point, it is unnecessary for me to decide between these rival arguments, or to explore the nature of a time charter contract any further. All I will say is that, at first blush, there seemed much to be said for the argument of counsel for the charterers. I say no more, because in *The Odenfeld* Kerr J found a similar argument unimpressive.

For the reasons I have given I would dismiss the owners' appeal and uphold the award.

Appeal dismissed. Leave to appeal granted

NOTES

1. What do you think constitutes a 'legitimate interest'? In *The Odenfeld* Kerr J held that the owners were justified in carrying on with the charter because they would otherwise have to break other contracts under which they had assigned the hire. In *The Alaskan Trader* the owners had assigned the hire payments to the bank to which the ship was mortgaged. In view of the difficulty of re-letting the ship, might they be forgiven for feeling they had a legitimate interest in claiming the hire?

2. The behaviour of the parties in this case seems clearly inefficient, in that if the ship could have been re-let, both parties could have been better off. Why do you think that they did not bargain their way to a solution under which the ship was re-let, and the charterers paid the owners a sum somewhere between the full hire under the original charter and the amount payable as damages (viz the difference between the charter rate and the rate at which the ship was re-let)? Does the extract from Priest, 'Breach and Remedy for the Tender of Non-conforming Goods' (above, p 452) suggest any reason?

Restitutionary remedies

The victim of a breach of contract who has justifiably terminated because of it may, instead of claiming damages, opt to claim in restitution for the return of any money paid or for the value of services rendered to the party in breach.

Money paid may be recovered provided that there has been a total failure of consideration—ie the party in breach did not perform at all or the victim has justifiably rejected the performance. See the *Fibrosa* case, noted above, p 365.

Whincup v Hughes (1871) LR 6 CP 78

The plaintiff apprenticed his son to a watchmaker and jeweller for the term of six years, paying to the master a premium of 25*l*. The master duly instructed the apprentice for a year, and then died. The plaintiff sought, in an action against the master's executrix for money had and received, to recover the whole or some part of the premium, on the ground of failure of consideration:—

Bovill CJ. This is an action brought to recover a part of the premium paid upon the execution of an apprenticeship deed, on the ground of failure of consideration. The general rule of law is, that where a contract has been in part performed no part of the money paid under such contract can be recovered back. There may be some cases of partial performance which form exceptions to this rule, as, for instance, if there were a contract to deliver ten sacks of wheat and six only were delivered, the price of the remaining four might be recovered back. But there the consideration is clearly severable.

. . . The contract having been in part performed, it would seem that the general rule must apply unless the consideration be in its nature apportionable. I am at a loss to see on what principle such apportionment could be made. It could not properly be made with reference to the proportion which the period during which the apprentice was instructed bears to the whole term. In the early part of the term the teaching would be most onerous, and the services of the apprentice of little value; as time went on his services would probably be worth more, and he would require less teaching.

NOTE

In *Ebrahim Dawood Ltd v Heath (Est 1927) Ltd* [1961] 2 Lloyd's Rep 512 McNair J held that a buyer who had justifiably rejected part of a consignment of steel sheets for which he had paid in advance was entitled to recover a proportionate part of the money. The seller had argued that the buyer's only remedy was to claim damages, but McNair J pointed out that the result would be:

. . . that if—let us take the figure in this case—the market price at the time of the delivery conformed to £70 against the contract price of £73 10s, there would be recovered on this argument only £70 per ton and not £73 10s per ton, leaving a profit of £3 10s in the pockets of the seller.

Another reason why the innocent party may prefer to recover the price paid than to sue for damages is that an action for a liquidated sum is generally speaking quicker and cheaper to bring than a claim for damages.

In Working Paper No 65, *Pecuniary Restitution on Breach of Contract*, the Law Commission had provisionally proposed extending the right to recover money paid to cases of partial failure of consideration. In the ensuing report (No 121, 1983), Part III, the proposal was dropped.

If the innocent party has performed work before he terminates the contract he may, as an alternative to damages, claim a quantum meruit for the value of the work done. The best known example is probably *Planche v Colburn* (1831) 8 Bing 14. The plaintiff had been employed to write a book on armour for a series to be called 'The Juvenile Library'. After he had written several chapters the defendant cancelled the series. The plaintiff justifiably refused the defendant's offer to publish the work separately and terminated the contract. He recovered the value of his wasted work from the publisher, even though it does not appear that he had delivered any of the manuscript before the publisher repudiated the contract.

Slowey v Lodder (1901) 20 NZLR 321

The plaintiff was wrongly prevented by the defendants from completing a construction contract. At first instance, Edwards J had held that the measure of damages for breach of contract and on a quantum meruit was the same. In the Court of Appeal:

Williams J. . . . Is, then, the plaintiff entitled to recover on a *quantum meruit*? and, if so, on what principle ought the amount which he can recover to be fixed? The law is stated by Mr J. W. Smith, in the notes to *Cutter v Powell* in *Smith's Leading Cases*, as follows:

> 'It is submitted that it is an invariably true proposition that, wherever one of the parties to a special contract not under seal has in an unqualified manner refused to perform his side of the contract, or has disabled himself from performing it by his own act, the other party has thereupon a right to elect to rescind it, and may, on doing so, immediately sue on a *quantum meruit* for anything which he had done under it before the rescission.'

Mr Smith's notes to the leading cases are classical: they are cited in every text-book, and references to them appear frequently in the judgments of the Courts in England. The doctrine above laid down has been universally recognised. . . .

That a plaintiff in a case like the present can recover on a *quantum meruit* is fully recognised in the case of *Appleby v Myers*. . . .

But it is contended that the result must be the same whether a plaintiff sues upon the special contract or upon a *quantum meruit*. If the result must be the same, how can it profit a plaintiff to have—what he certainly has—an alternative remedy? If, however, the principle on which a plaintiff becomes entitled to sue on a *quantum meruit* is considered but for a moment, it is obvious that the amount he can recover must be estimated in a different way from the amount he could recover if he sued for a breach of the special contract. If the plaintiff sues on the contract, treating it as still open, he is entitled, and the defendant is entitled, to place before the jury what the result would have been if the plaintiff had been allowed to complete the contract. If the plaintiff can show that by the action of the defendant he has been prevented from making in the future a large profit, he is entitled to recover for the loss of that profit. So, if the defendant can show that, taking the ultimate result of the contract, the plaintiff has been deprived of no profit, and has possibly been saved from loss, then, though the breach by the defendant may have been wrongful, the damages would properly be nominal. But a *quantum meruit* is different. The right to sue on it rests on this: that the defendant has done something which is equivalent to an abandonment of the contract on his part. Then the right arises for the plaintiff to say, 'You have abandoned the contract. So be it; let the contract be rescinded. But you have in your hands the fruits of my labour: pay me for the work I have done and the materials I have supplied.' . . .

The judgment of the Court of Appeal, including specifically this point, was affirmed by the Privy Council: [1904] AC 442, at 453.

NOTES

1. Just as where a plaintiff wishes to recover money paid, it seems obviously advantageous for the plaintiff who was working under a losing contract to claim a quantum meruit rather than damages. In *Boomer v Muir* 24 P 2d 570 (California, 1924) a contractor who built part of a dam before justifiably terminating the contract was held to be entitled to recover on a quantum meruit more than the contract price which would have been payable had he finished the work. Do you think that is right? See Goff & Jones, *Restitution* (3rd edn), pp 467–468.
2. Can you see any reason why a contractor who stood to make a normal profit if he had been allowed to complete the work, might prefer to claim on a quantum meruit rather than claim damages?
3. Even in cases which are less extreme than *Boomer v Muir*, it seems that the result of allowing the plaintiff to recover the money he has paid, or to recover the value of the services he has rendered, may be to allow him to escape a bad bargain. If he is allowed to recover all that he has paid out or spent, he may come out better off than if the contract had been performed. This is just what the courts have refused to allow when the plaintiff is claiming reliance loss (see above, p 470). Do you see any justification for allowing it when the plaintiff is claiming restitution?
4. Under the law at present, a party who has performed work cannot claim its value if the contract was terminated because of *his* breach: above, p 418.

In certain circumstances, for instance when the party in breach owes a fiduciary duty to the innocent party, the latter may bring an action in restitution and recover the profit the defendant has made through breaking the contract. It has been argued that this remedy should be more widely available. See Jones, 'Recovery of benefits gained by breach of contract' (1983) 99 LQR 443; Birks, 'Restitutionary remedies for breach of contract' [1987] LMCLQ 421.

Could allowing the plaintiff to recover the profit the defendant has made through breach be justified in terms of economic efficiency? If restitutionary recovery were permitted, what behaviour would you expect from a party who is presented with the opportunity to make a greater profit if he can avoid performing the existing contract?

Section 6
Contract theory

Contract theory

You will now have studied enough contract law for us to be able to turn to various theoretical issues. Contract theory is concerned with a number of distinct but related questions. One is why we regard promises as *morally* binding; another, why our legal system treats some promises at least as *legally* binding; a third, whether the central principle of contract law is really the enforcement of promises, or whether this is merely the incidental result of rules which are primarily aimed at liability on some other basis, such as compensation of reliance.

The first question is primarily one of moral philosophy. It has been argued plausibly that philosophical discussion has been impoverished by a failure to refer to the vast body of legal materials illustrating the difficulties in the view that promises are 'usually binding'. Whatever the answer to the first question, most legal systems, and certainly English law, do not enforce all promises which are morally binding.

Space precludes anything but a very small selection of readings on contract theory, with notes simply providing references for further reading. We start with a piece that provides a good summary of the literature up to 1933, and follow with a number of pieces which represent current viewpoints and reflect current controversies. We should stress that we do not agree with some of them!

'The Basis of Contract' by Cohen (1933) 46 Harv LR 553, 571–589, 591–592

III. THE JUSTIFICATION OF CONTRACT LAW

A. The sanctity of promises
Contract law is commonly supposed to enforce promises. Why should promises be enforced?

The simplest answer is that of the intuitionists, namely, that promises are sacred *per se*, that there is something inherently despicable about not keeping a promise, and that a properly organized society should not tolerate this. This may also be said to be the common man's theory.

. . . If, then, we find ourselves in a state of society in which men are, as a matter of fact, repelled by the breaking of promises and feel that such practice should be discouraged or minimized, that is a primary fact which the law must not ignore.

But while this intuitionist theory contains an element of truth, it is clearly inadequate. No legal system does or can attempt to enforce all promises. Not even the canon law held all promises to be sacred. And when we come to draw a distinction between those promises which should be and those which should not be enforced, the intuitionist theory, that all promises should be kept, gives us no light or guiding principle.

Similar to the intuitionist theory is the view of Kantians like Reinach that the duty to keep one's promise is one without which rational society would be impossible. There can be no doubt that from an empirical or historical point of view, the ability to rely on the promises of others adds to the confidence necessary for social intercourse and enterprise. But as an absolute proposition this is untenable. The actual world, which assuredly is among the possible ones, is not one in which all promises are kept, and there are many people—not necessarily diplomats—who prefer a world in which they and others occasionally depart from the truth and go back on some promise. It is indeed very doubtful whether there are many who would prefer to live in an entirely rigid world in which one would be obliged to keep *all* one's promises instead of the present more viable system, in which a vaguely fair proportion is sufficient. Many of us indeed would shudder at the idea of being bound by every promise, no matter how foolish, without any chance of letting increased wisdom undo past foolishness. Certainly, some freedom to change one's mind is necessary for free intercourse between those who lack omniscience.

For this reason we cannot accept Dean Pound's theory that all promises in the course of business should be enforced. He seems to me undoubtedly right in his insistence that promises constitute modern wealth and that their enforcement is thus a necessity of maintaining wealth as a basis of civilization. My bank's promise to pay the checks drawn to my account not only constitutes my wealth but puts it into a more manageable form than that of my personal possession of certain goods or even gold. Still, business men as a whole do not wish the law to enforce every promise. Many business transactions, such as those on a stock or produce exchange, could not be carried on unless we could rely on a mere verbal agreement or hasty memorandum. But other transactions, like those of real estate, are more complicated and would become too risky if we were bound by every chance promise that escapes us. Negotiations would be checked by such fear. In such cases men do not want to be bound until the final stage, when some formality like the signing of papers gives one the feeling of security, of having taken proper precautions. The issue obviously depends upon such factors as the relative simplicity of a given transaction, the speed with which it must be concluded, and the availability of necessary information. . . .

B. The will theory of contract

According to the classical view, the law of contract gives expression to and protects the will of the parties, for the will is something inherently worthy of respect. Hence such authorities as Savigny, Windshield, Pothier, Planiol, Pollock, Salmond, and Langdell hold that the first essential of a contract is the agreement of wills, or the meeting of minds.

The metaphysical difficulties of this view have often been pointed out. Minds or wills are not in themselves existing things that we can look at and recognize. We are restricted in our earthly experience to the observation of the changes or actions of more or less animated bodies in time and space; and disembodied minds or wills are beyond the scope and reach of earthly law. But while this objection has become familiar, it has not been very effective. The force of the old ideas, embodied in the traditional language, has not always been overcome even by those who like Langdell and Salmond profess to recognize the fictional element in the will theory.

Another line of objection can be found in the incompatibility of the classical theory with the consequences that the law attaches to an offer. Suppose that I offer to buy certain goods from A at a given price, and, following his refusal, give him a week's time to reconsider it. If I change my mind the next day but fail to notify him, a contractual obligation will none the less arise if five days later he notifies me that he has accepted my terms. Here obviously there is never a moment of time when the two parties are actually in agreement or of one mind. Yet no one denies that the resulting rights and duties are identical with those called contractual. It does not help the classical theory to say that I am under a legal duty to notify A (the offeree) and that if I fail to perform this duty in the proper way, the law will treat my change of mind as a nullity, *as if* it had never happened. The phrase italicized indicates that we are moving in the realm of fiction (or better, rights and duties imposed by law) and not in the realm of fact. No one denies that the contractual obligation should attach in this case; but there is in point of fact no actual agreement or meeting of minds. The latter, then, is not always necessary for a legal contract.

The logical inconsistency of the classical theory is not cured if we say that the law protects not the will but the expression or declaration of the will. Suppose that in the case mentioned I make a solemn declaration of the revocation of my offer, or write a letter but fail to communicate it. The law, in refusing to give effect to my declared revocation, is not protecting my expressed will, but is enforcing a duty on me in the interest of the general security of business transactions.

A more important objection to the theory that every contract expresses the consensus or agreed wills of the two parties is the fact that most litigation in this field arises precisely because of the advent of conditions that the two parties did not foresee when they entered into the transaction. Litigation usually reveals the absence of genuine agreement between the parties *ab initio*. If both parties had foreseen the difficulty, provision would have been made for it in the beginning when the contract was drawn up. . . .

The obvious limitations of the will theory of contract have caused a reaction that takes the form of positivism or behaviorism: Away with the whole notion of will!—the only realities are specific acts to which the law attaches certain consequences, that is, if you do something by word of mouth, by writing, or by any other act that someone else takes as a promise, then the latter can, under certain conditions, bring an action. In its extreme form, this appears in what Dean Pound calls the state of strict law, which, like everything called primitive, is always with us. A developed system of law, however, must draw some distinction between voluntary and involuntary acts. Mr Justice Holmes thinks that even a dog discriminates between one who stumbles over him and one who kicks him. The whole of the modern law of contract, it may be argued, thus does and should respond to the need of greater or finer discrimination in regard to the intentional character of acts. The law of error, duress, and fraud in contract would be unintelligible apart from such distinction.

C. The injurious-reliance theory

Though this seems the favorite theory today, it has not as yet been adequately formulated, and many of those who subscribe to it fall back on the will theory when they come to discuss special topics in the law of contract. The essence of the theory, however, is clear enough. Contractual liability arises (or should arise) only where (1) someone makes a promise explicitly in words or implicitly by some act, (2) someone else relies on it, and (3) suffers some loss thereby.

This theory appeals to the general moral feeling that not only ought promises to be kept, but that anyone innocently injured by relying on them is entitled to have the loss 'made good' by the one who thus caused it. If, as Schopenhauer has maintained, the sense of wrong is the ultimate human source of the law, then to base the obligations of the promise on the injury of the one who has relied on it, is to appeal to something really fundamental.

This theory also appeals to modern legal theorists because it seems to be entirely objective and social. It does not ask the court to examine the intention of the promisor. Instead, the court is asked to consider whether what the defendant has said or done is such that reasonable people generally do rely on it under the circumstances. The resulting loss can be directly proved and, to some extent, even measured. In emphasizing the element of injury resulting from the breach, the whole question of contract is integrated in the larger realm of obligations, and this tends to put our issues in the right perspective and to correct the misleading artificial distinctions between breach of contract and other civil wrongs or torts.

Nevertheless, this theory is not entirely consistent with existing law, nor does it give an altogether satisfactory account of what the law should do.

Contractual obligation is not coextensive with injurious reliance because (1) there are instances of both injury and reliance for which there is no contractual obligation, and (2) there are cases of such obligation where there is no reliance or injury.

(1) Clearly, not all cases of injury resulting from reliance on the word or act of another are actionable, and the theory before us offers no clue as to what distinguishes those which are. There is, first, the whole class of instances of definite financial injury caused by reliance on an explicit promise made in social relations, such as dinner parties and the like. . . .

Even clearer are those cases where someone advertises goods for sale or a position to be filled, and, when I come, tells me that he has changed his mind. . . .

(2) In formal contracts, such as promises under seal, stipulation in court, and the like, it is clearly not necessary for the promisee to prove reliance and injury. . . . To be sure, where the law recognizes no loss, only nominal damages are usually awarded. But the fact that the plaintiff receives judgment is of practical, as well as of theoretic, importance. Clearly, the law favors the carrying-out of promises even in cases where there is no actual reliance or actual loss from nonperformance.

(3) Finally, the recovery that the law allows to the injured promisee is not determined by what he lost in relying on the promise, but rather by what he would have gained if the promise had been kept. There are obviously many cases where the injured party is substantially no worse after the breach than if the contract had never been made. He has thus not been in fact injured. And yet he may recover heavy damages if he would have gained heavily by the performance of the contract. The policy of the law, then, is not merely to redress injuries but also to protect certain kinds of expectation by making men live up to certain promises.

There can be no question about the soundness of the injurious-reliance theory in accounting for a dominant phase of the law of contract, and the foregoing difficulties may thus seem petty. But they do call attention to fundamental obscurities in the very idea of 'reliance' as well as in the criteria of 'injury'. The injurious-reliance theory, like others, calls attention to a necessary element but does not give an adequate account of the whole of the law of contract. Its merits become clearer when its claims are properly limited.

D. The equivalent theory

Popular sentiment generally favors the enforcement of those promises which involve some *quid pro quo*. It is generally considered unfair that after A has given something of value or rendered B some service, B should fail to render anything in return. Even if what A did was by way of gift, B owes him gratitude and should express it in some appropriate way. And if, in addition, B has promised to pay A for the value of services received, the moral sense of the community condemns B's failure to do so as even more unfair. The demand for justice behind the law is but an elaboration of such feelings of what is fair and unfair.

The equivalent theory of contract has the advantage of being supported by this popular sentiment. This sentiment also explains the primacy of *real* contracts.

While a legal theory must not ignore common sense, it must also go beyond it. For common sense, while generally sound at its core, is almost always vague and inadequate. Common sentiment, for instance, demands an equivalent. But what things are equivalent? It is easy to answer this in regard to goods or services that have a standard market value. But how shall we measure things that are dissimilar in nature, or in a market where monopolistic or other factors prevent a fair or just price? Modern law therefore professes to abandon the effort of more primitive systems to enforce material fairness within the contract. The parties to the contract must themselves determine what is fair. Thereby, however, the law loses a good deal of support in the moral sense of the community. . . .

. . . Consideration is in effect a formality, like an oath, the affixing of a seal, or a stipulation in court.

E. Formalism in contract

The recognition of the formal character of consideration may help us to appreciate the historical myopia of those who speak of seal as 'importing' consideration. Promises under seal were binding (because of the formality) long before the doctrine of consideration was ever heard of. The history of forms and ceremonies in the law of contract offers an illuminating chapter in human psychology or anthropology. We are apt to dismiss the early Roman ceremonies of *mancipatio, nexum*, and *sponsio*, the Anglo-Saxon *wed* and *borh*, or the Frankish ceremonies of *arramitio, wadiatio*, and of the *festuca*, as peculiar to primitive society. But reflection shows that our modern practices of shaking hands to close a bargain, signing papers, and protesting a note are, like the taking of an oath on assuming office, not only designed to make evidence secure, but are in large part also expressions of the fundamental human need for formality and ceremony, to make sharp distinctions where otherwise lines of demarcation would not be so clearly apprehended.

Ceremonies are the channels that the stream of social life creates by its ceaseless flow through the sands of human circumstances. Psychologically, they are habits; socially, they are customary ways of doing things; and ethically, they have what Jellinek has called the normative power of the actual, that is, they control what we do by creating a standard of respectability or a pattern to which we feel bound to conform. . . .

F. Contract and the distribution of risks

Mr Justice Holmes has suggested that a legal promise may be viewed as a wager: I assure you of a certain event (which may or may not be within my control) and I pay in case of failure.

This view has not found much favor. . . .

Nevertheless, when taken in a wider sense in connection with Mr Justice Holmes's general philosophy concerning the risk in all human affairs, his theory is illuminating and important.

All human transactions are directed to a future that is never free from elements of uncertainty. Every one of our ventures, therefore, involves the taking of a risk. When I board a train to go home I am betting my life that I will get to my destination. Now a contract or agreement may be viewed as an agreement for the distribution of anticipated gains or losses. If I agree to sell certain goods or services I expect that I shall be paid in good United States money and that with this money I shall be able to acquire certain other goods. I do not generally take into account the possibility that the purchasing power of the American dollar may be radically reduced when I receive my pay. That contingency is generally not thought of or else deemed too remote, yet certain bondholders do think of it and specify payment in gold of a certain standard. Now the human power to foresee all the consequences of an agreement is limited, even if we suppose that the two parties understand each other's meaning to begin with. Disputes or disagreements are therefore bound to come up; and the law of contract may thus be viewed as an attempt to determine the rights and duties of the two parties under circumstances that were not anticipated exactly in the same way by the two contracting parties, or at any rate were not expressly provided for in an unambiguous way. One can therefore say that the court's adjudication supplements the original contract as a method of distributing gains and losses.

From this point of view, we may look upon the law of contract as a number of rules according to which courts distribute gains and losses according to the equities of such cases; and the pretense that the result follows exclusively from the agreement of the two parties is fictional. Just as the process of interpreting a statute is really a process of subsidiary legislation, so is the interpretation of a contract really a method of supplementing the original agreement by such provisions as are necessary to determine the point at issue.

If we view the law of contract as directed to strengthening the security of transactions by enabling men to rely more fully on promises, we see only one phase of its actual workings. The other phase is the determination of the rights of the contracting parties as to contingencies that they have not foreseen, and for which they have not provided. In this latter respect the law of contract is a way of enforcing some kind of distributive justice within the legal system. And technical doctrines of contract may thus be viewed as a set of rules that will systematize decisions in this field and thus give lawyers and their clients some guidance in the problem of anticipating future decisions. Thus, for instance, if the question arises as to who should suffer a loss caused by the destruction of goods in transit, the technical doctrine of when title passes enables us to deal with the problem more definitely. In any case, the essential problem of the law of contract is the problem of distribution of risks. The other phase, namely, the assurance that what the parties have actually agreed on will be fulfilled, is a limiting principle.

IV. CONTRACT AND SOVEREIGNTY

. . . This task of formulating a comprehensive theory of contract, that shall do justice to its many sources and various phases, is one that I shall not undertake here. But I wish to emphasize certain considerations that supplement the theories discussed so far.

The cardinal error of the traditional individualistic theories of contract is their way of speaking as if the law does nothing but put into effect what the contracting parties originally agreed on. The best that can be said for this is that it may sometimes be true. But even if that were more generally the case, we should still have to attach more importance to the factor of enforcement than the prevailing theories do. The fact, then, that in the general run of transactions people do not resort to actual litigation, is certainly in part due to the fact that they know in a general way what will be the outcome of that process. The law of contract, then, through judges, sheriffs, or marshals puts the sovereign power of the state at the disposal of one party to be exercised over the other party. It thus grants a limited sovereignty to the former.

From this point of view the law of contract may be viewed as a subsidiary branch of public law, as a body of rules according to which the sovereign power of the state will be exercised as between the parties to a more or less voluntary transaction.

The first rules of public law, generally called constitutional law, regulate the conduct of the chief state officials by indicating the scope of their powers. Within this scope legislatures use their discretion or wisdom to enact certain statutes; and judges, by following precedents, elaborate certain rules as to when and how the power of the state shall be exercised. Among these rules we have the laws of partnership, leases, agreements for services, contracts of surety or insurances, and the like. Now, just as the rules of constitutional law are general and leave blanks to be filled in by the legislature, courts, and administrative officials (whose rules and habitual practices are law to those over whom they have authority), so do the rules of contracts allow men to formulate for themselves, within the prescribed limits, certain rights and duties governing certain transactions between them; and when the parties have thus formulated their agreements, the latter become a part of the law of the land, just as much as do treaties between our nation and others, compacts between states, contracts between a state or division thereof and a private corporation, or the grant of a pension to the widow of a former president. . . .

If, then, the law of contract confers sovereignty on one party over another (by putting the state's forces at the disposal of the former), the question naturally arises: For what purposes and under what circumstances shall that power be conferred? Adherents of the classical theory have recognized that legal enforcement serves to protect and encourage transactions that require credit or reliance on the promises of others. But we also need care that the power of the state be not used for unconscionable purposes, such as helping those who exploit the dire need or weakness of their fellows. Usury laws have recognized that he who is under economic necessity is not really free. To put no restrictions on the freedom to contract would logically lead not to a maximum of individual liberty but to contracts of slavery, into which, experience shows, men will 'voluntarily' enter under economic pressure—a pressure that is largely conditioned by the laws of property. Regulations, therefore, involving some restrictions on the freedom to contract are as necessary to real liberty as traffic restrictions are necessary to assure real freedom in the general use of our highways. . . .

We may thus view the law of contract not only as a branch of public law but also as having a function somewhat parallel to that of the criminal law. Both serve to standardize conduct by penalizing departures from the legal norm. Not only by decrees of specific performance or by awards of damages, but also by treating certain contracts as void or voidable and thus withholding its support from those who do not conform to its prescribed forms, does the law of contract in fact impose penalties. Thus even when certain practices like gambling, illicit sex relations, or agreements in restraint of trade are not criminal offences, the law regards them with sufficient disfavor to refuse them the protection of its enforcing machinery.

The function of the law of contract in promoting the standardization of transactions is at all times an important one. . . .

There is no inherent reason for rejecting the view that the roots of the law of contract are many rather than one. Agreements and promises are enforced to enable people to rely on them as a rule and thus make the path of enterprise more secure; but in this connection the law must also go beyond the original intention of the parties to settle controversies as to the distribution of gains and losses that the parties did not anticipate in the same way. Some recognition must always be given to the will or intention of those who made the contract, but the law must always have regard for the *general* effects of classes of transactions, and it cannot free men from the necessity of acting at their peril when they do not know the consequences that the law will attach to their acts—and this needs to be emphasized in any attempt to formulate a rational theory. The law is a going concern and like all social institutions is governed by habit. It therefore will continue to enforce promises and agreements, for no better reason than they have been enforced and there is no sufficient countervailing consideration to force or justify a break with the established habit that has become the basis of social expectancies. Legal and other habits are not always deliberately formed to serve a definite purpose. Certain forms or ceremonies arise under special circumstances but continue to appeal to us through the principle of economy of effort: it is generally easier to use the existing forms than to break with them and adopt new ones. Of course old forms may become inconvenient or positive hindrances. They are then whittled away by pious fiction or violently changed by revolutionary legislation. In general, however, the ancient truth that men are creatures of habit will put us on guard against the vain assumption that we can get rid of formalism in the law of contract or anywhere else. We may flatter ourselves on getting rid of seal or other ancient binding ceremony. But we must remember that these forms seemed as naturally obligatory to our fathers as the signing of papers or the administering of oaths seems to us today.

In arguing for their indispensability we may recognize that not all forms are perfectly congenial or responsive to the need of the life that pulses through them. And as men become more enlightened they become more ready to discard, as well as employ, diverse instruments or vessels. Wisdom is not attained either by blind acceptance or blind rejection. We need a discriminating evaluation of what exists and what is possible; and this is something to which we can apply Spinoza's dictum: All things excellent are as difficult as they are rare.

NOTES

1. The views of Holmes referred to will be found in *The Common Law* (1882), pp 297–303. They are further discussed by Buckland, 'The Nature of Contractual Obligation' (1944) 8 CLJ 247.
2. The reliance theory was developed further in the classic piece that follows.

'The Reliance Interest on Contract Damages' by Fuller and Perdue (1936) 46 Yale LJ 52, 57–65

(An extract from the first few pages of this article will be found above, pp 466–467. The present extract is a continuation.)

Why should the law ever protect the expectation interest?

Perhaps the most obvious answer to this question is one which we may label 'psychological'. This answer would run something as follows: The breach of a promise arouses in the promisee a sense of injury. This feeling is not confined to cases where the promisee has relied on the promise. Whether or not he has actually changed his position because of the promise, the promise has formed an attitude of expectancy such that a breach of the promise causes him to feel that he has been 'deprived' of something which was 'his'. Since this sentiment is a relatively uniform one, the law has no occasion to go back of it. It accepts it as a datum and builds its rule about it.

The difficulty with this expectation is that the law does in fact go back of the sense of injury which the breach of a promise engenders. No legal system attempts to invest with juristic sanction all promises. Some rule or combination of rules effects a sifting out for enforcement of those promises deemed important enough to society to justify the law's concern with them. Whatever the principles which control this sifting out process may be, they are not convertible into terms of the degree of resentment which the breach of a particular kind of promise arouses. Therefore, though it may be assumed that the impulse to assuage disappointment is one shared by those who make and influence the law, this impulse can hardly be regarded as the key which solves the whole problem of the protection accorded by the law to the expectation interest.

A second possible explanation for the rule protecting the expectancy may be found in the much-discussed 'will theory' of contract law. This theory views the contracting parties as exercising, so to speak, a legislative power, so that the legal enforcement of a contract becomes merely an implementing by the state of a kind of private law already established by the parties. If A has made, in proper form, a promise to pay B one thousand dollars, we compel A to pay this sum simply because the rule or *lex* set up by the parties calls for this payment. *Uti lingua nun cupassit, ita jus esto.*

It is not necessary to discuss here the contribution which the will theory is capable of making to a philosophy of contract law. Certainly some borrowings from the theory are discernible in most attempts to rationalize the bases of contract liability. It is enough to note here that while the will theory undoubtedly has some bearing on the problem of contract damages, it cannot be regarded as dictating in all cases a recovery of the expectancy. If a contract represents a kind of private law, it is a law which usually says nothing at all about what shall be done when it is violated. . . .

A third and more promising solution of our difficulty lies in an economic or institutional approach. The essence of a credit economy lies in the fact that it tends to eliminate the distinction between present and future (promised) goods. Expectations of future values become, for purposes of trade, present values. In a society in which credit has become a significant and pervasive institution, it is inevitable that the expectancy created by an enforceable promise should be regarded as a kind of property, and breach of the promise as an injury to that property. In such a society the breach of a promise works an 'actual' diminution of the promisee's assets—'actual' in the sense that it would be so appraised according to modes of thought which enter into the very fiber of our economic system. That the promisee had not 'used' the property which the promise represents (had not relied on the promise) is as immaterial as the question whether the plaintiff in trespass *quare clausum fregit* was using his property at the time it was encroached upon. The analogy to ordinary forms of property goes further, for even in a suit for trespass the recovery is reduced accordingly. Ordinary property differs from a contract right chiefly in the fact that it lies within the power of more persons to work a direct injury to the expectancy it represents. It is generally only the promisor or some one working through or upon him who is able to injure the contract expectancy in a direct enough manner to make expedient legal intervention.

The most obvious objection which can be made to the economic or institutional explanation is that it involves a *petitio principii*. A promise has present value, why? Because the law enforces it. 'The expectancy', regarded as a present value, is not the cause of legal intervention but the consequence of it. This objection may be reinforced by a reference to legal history. Promises were enforced long before there was anything corresponding to a general system of 'credit', and recovery was from the beginning measured by the value of the promised performance, the 'agreed price'. It may therefore be argued that the 'credit system' when it finally emerged was itself in large part built on the foundations of a juristic development which preceded it.

The view just suggested asserts the primacy of law over economics; it sees law not as the creature but as the creator of social institutions. The shift of emphasis thus implied suggests the possibility of a fourth explanation for the law's protection of the unrelied-on expectancy, which we may call *juristic*. This explanation would seek a justification for the normal rule of recovery in some policy consciously pursued by courts and other lawmakers. It would assume that courts have protected the expectation interest because they have considered it wise to do so, not through a blind acquiescence in habitual ways of thinking and feeling, or through an equally blind deference to the individual will. Approaching a problem from this point of view, we are forced to find not a mere explanation for the rule in the form of some sentimental, volitional, or institutional datum, but articulate reasons for its existence.

What reasons can be advanced? In the first place, even if our interest were confined to protecting promisees against an out-of-pocket loss, it would still be possible to justify the rule granting the value of the expectancy, both as a cure for, and as a prophylaxis against, losses of this sort.

It is a cure for these losses in the sense that it offers the measure of recovery most likely to reimburse the plaintiff for the (often very numerous and very difficult to prove) individual acts and forbearances which make up his total reliance on the contract. If we take into account 'gains prevented' by reliance, that is, losses involved in foregoing the opportunity to enter other contracts, the notion that the rule protecting the expectancy is adopted as the most effective means of compensating for detrimental reliance seems not at all far-fetched. Physicians with an extensive practice often charge their patients the full office call fee for broken appointments. Such a charge looks on the face of things like a claim to the promised fee; it seems to be based on the 'expectation interest'. Yet the physician making the charge will quite justifiably regard it as compensation for the loss of the opportunity to gain a similar fee from a different patient. This foregoing of other opportunities is involved to some extent in entering most contracts, and the impossibility of subjecting this type of reliance to any kind of measurement may justify a categorical rule granting the value of the expectancy as the most effective way of compensating for such losses.

But, as we have suggested, the rule measuring damages by the expectancy may also be regarded as a prophylaxis against the losses resulting from detrimental reliance. Whatever tends to discourage breach of contract tends to prevent the losses occasioned through reliance. Since the expectation interest furnishes a more easily administered measure of recovery than the reliance interest, it will in practice offer a more effective sanction against contract breach. It is therefore possible to view the rule measuring damages by the expectancy in a quasi-criminal aspect, its purpose being not so much to compensate the promisee as to penalize breach of promise by the promisor. The rule enforcing the unrelied-on promise finds the same justification, on this theory, as an ordinance which fines a man for driving through a stop-light when no other vehicle is in sight.

In seeking justification for the rule granting the value of the expectancy there is no need, however, to restrict ourselves by the assumption, hitherto made, that the rule can only be intended to cure or prevent the losses caused by reliance. A justification can be developed from a less negative point of view. It may be said that there is not only a policy in favor of preventing and undoing the harms resulting from reliance, but also a policy in favor of promoting and facilitating reliance on business agreements. As in the case of the stop-light ordinance we are interested not only in preventing collisions but in speeding traffic. Agreements can accomplish little, either for their makers or for society, unless they are made the basis for action. When business agreements are not only made but are also acted on, the division of labor is facilitated, goods find their way to the places where they are most needed, and economic activity is generally stimulated. These advantages would be threatened by any rule which limited legal protection to the reliance interest. Such a rule would in practice tend to discourage reliance. The difficulties in proving reliance and subjecting it to pecuniary measurement are such that the business man knowing, or sensing, that these obstacles stood in the way of judicial relief would hesitate to rely on a promise in any case where the legal sanction was of significance to him. To encourage reliance we must therefore dispense with its proof. For this reason it has been found wise to make recovery on a promise independent of reliance, both in the sense that in some cases the promise is enforced though not relied on (as in the bilateral business agreement) and in the sense that recovery is not limited to the detriment incurred in reliance.

The jurisitic explanation in its final form is then twofold. It rests the protection accorded the expectancy on (1) the need for curing and preventing the harms occasioned by reliance, and (2) on the need for facilitating reliance on business agreements. From this spelling out of a possible juristic explanation, it is clear that there is no incompatibility between it and the economic or institutional explanation. They view the same phenomenon from two different aspects. The essence of both of them lies in the word 'credit'. The economic explanation views credit from its institutional side; the juristic explanation views it from its rational side. The economic view sees credit as an accepted way of living; the juristic view invites us to explore the considerations of utility which underlie this way of living, and the part which conscious human direction has played in bringing it into being.

The way in which these two points of view supplement one another becomes clearer when we examine separately the economic implications of the two aspects of the juristic explanation. If we rest the legal argument for measuring damages by the expectancy on the ground that this procedure offers the most satisfactory means of compensating the plaintiff for the loss of other opportunities to contract, it is clear that the force of the argument will depend entirely upon the existing economic environment. It would be most forceful in a hypothetical society in which all values were available on the market and where all markets were 'perfect' in the economic sense. In such a society there would be no difference between the reliance interest and the expectation interest. The plaintiff's loss in foregoing to enter another contract would be identical with the expectation value of the contract he did make. The argument that granting the value of the expectancy merely compensates for that loss, loses force to the extent that actual conditions depart from those of such a hypothetical society. These observations make it clear why the development of open markets for goods tends to carry in its wake the view that a contract claim is a kind of property. . . . He who by entering one contract passes by the opportunity to accomplish the same end elsewhere will not be inclined to regard contract breach lightly or as a mere matter of private morality. The consciousness of what is foregone reinforces the notion that the contract creates a 'right' and that the contract claim is itself a species of property.

If, on the other hand, we found the juristic explanation on the desire to promote reliance on contracts, it is not difficult again to trace a correspondence between the legal view and the actual conditions of economic life. In general our courts and our economic institutions attribute special significance to the same types of promises. The bilateral business agreement is, generally speaking, the only type of informal contract our courts are willing to enforce without proof that reliance has occurred—simply for the sake of facilitating reliance. This is, by no accident, precisely the kind of contract (the 'exchange', 'bargain', 'trade', 'deal') which furnishes the indispensable and pervasive framework for the 'unmanaged' portions of our economic activity.

The inference is therefore justified that the ends of the law of contracts and those of our economic system show an essential correspondence. One may explain this either on the ground that the law (mere superstructure and ideology) reflects inertly the conditions of economic life, or on the ground that economic activity has fitted itself into the rational framework of the law. Neither explanation would be true. In fact we are dealing with a situation in which law and society have interacted. The law measures damages by the expectancy *in part* because society views the expectancy as a present value; society views the expectancy as a present value *in part* because the law (for reasons more or less consciously articulated) gives protection to the expectancy.

The combined juristic and economic explanation which has just been developed may seem vulnerable to one serious objection. This lies in the fact that the 'normal' rule, which measures damages by the expectancy, has been frequently applied to promises of a type having no conceivable relation to 'the credit system', the division of labor, or the organization of economic activity. . . .

Is the application of the 'normal' rule of damages to non-bargain promises then an unanswerable refutation of the explanation which we have attempted of the rule? We think not. In the first place, it is obviously possible that the courts have, through force of habit, given a broader application to the rule than a philosophic inquiry into its possible bases would justify. In the second place, it is by no means clear, from the decisions at any rate, that the rule of recovery in the case of these 'non-bargain' promises *is* necessarily that which measures damages by the expectancy.

NOTES

1. Fuller and Perdue go on to show that in the American cases, the further the contract is from being a bargain, the stronger the tendency to limit recovery to reliance losses.

2. Fuller's analysis cannot be applied directly to English law, which as we have seen does not openly enforce gratuitous promises merely because they have been relied on, and under which damages for breach of contract are almost always said to be damages for loss of expectation. But Atiyah has questioned whether the classical model of the voluntarily-assumed and bargained-for obligation, protected by the award of expectation damages, really represents English law accurately.

'Promises, Obligations and The Law of Contract' by Atiyah on Essays in Contract (1986), pp. 19–31, 33–41

. . . To what extent is it true to say that contractual liabilities arise from agreement or promises or depend on the voluntary assumption of obligation? I want to begin by suggesting that the power of the classical model here derives largely from its stress on the executory contract. If two parties do exchange promises to carry out some performance at a future date, and if, immediately on the exchange of promises, a binding legal obligation comes at once into existence, then it seems inexorably to follow that the obligation is created by the agreement, by the intention of the parties. If they have done nothing to implement the agreement, if no actions have followed the exchange of promises, then manifestly the legal obligation cannot arise from anything except the exchange of promises. Thus far the classical model appears to be impregnable. But closer examination suggests that the area of impregnability is really rather small.

The first point to note is that wholly executory contracts are rarer, more ephemeral in practice, and somewhat less binding than the classical model of Contract would suggest. In the classical model . . . the executory transaction lies at the very heart of Contract. It is precisely because the classical model largely defines Contract in terms of executory transactions that it necessarily locates the source of contractual liability in what the parties intend rather than in what they do. But large numbers of contracts are regularly made in which the making and the performance, or at least part performance, are simultaneous or practically simultaneous events. Consider such simple transactions as the boarding of a bus, or a purchase of goods in a supermarket, or a loan of money. Is it really sensible to characterise these transactions as agreements or exchanges of promises? Is it meaningful or useful to claim that a person who boards a bus is promising to pay his fare? If so, would it not be just as meaningful to say that when he descends from the bus and crosses the road he promises to cross with all due care for the safety of other road users? I do not, of course, deny that all these transactions involve some element of voluntary conduct. People do not generally board buses, buy goods in a supermarket, or borrow money in their sleep. But they involve much else besides voluntary conduct. They usually involve the rendering of some benefit, or actions of detrimental reliance, or both. A person who is carried by a bus from point A to point B after voluntarily boarding the bus can normally be presumed to have derived some benefit from the arrangements. Does his liability to pay his fare have nothing to do with this element of benefit?

Consider next the possibility of detrimental reliance by the promisee. Is it not manifest that a person who has actually worsened his position by reliance on a promise has a more powerful case for redress than one who has not worsened his position by reliance on the promise at all? . . .

. . . [I]n morality and in law the rendering of benefits and actions of detriment reliance can give rise to oblitations even where there was no promise at all. The law of restitution is almost entirely concerned with situations in which one party is entitled to recompense for a benefit received by another from him, or at his expense even though the latter made no promise to pay for it. . . .

And so far I have said nothing about one of the most obvious bodies of legal doctrine which is not easy to reconcile with the theory that contractual and promissory obligations rest on voluntary obligation. I refer, of course, to the so-called 'objective-test' theory of contractual liability. Every law student is taught from his earliest days that contractual intent is not really what it seems; actual subjective intent is normally irrelevant. It is the appearance, the manifestation of intent that matters. Whenever a person is held bound by a promise or a contract contrary to his actual intent or understanding, it is plain that the liability is based not on some notion of a voluntary assumption of obligation, but on something else. And most frequently it will be found that that something else is the element of reasonable reliance. One party relies on a reasonable construction of an offer, or he accepts an offer, reasonably thinking it is still open when the offeror has revoked it but failed to communicate his revocation. All this is standard stuff but I suggest that cases of this type have for too long been regarded as of marginal importance only, as not affecting the fundamental basis and theory of liability. In a simple world of simple promises and contracts this might have been an acceptable perspective. But the arrival of written contracts and above all the standard printed form has surely rendered this approach much less defensible. A party who signs an elaborate printed document is almost invariably held bound by it not because of anything he intended; he is bound in the teeth of his intention and understandings except in some very exceptional cases of fraud or the like. The truth is he is bound not so much because of what he intends but because of what he does. Like the man who is bound to pay his fare because he boards a bus, the man who signs a written contract is liable because of what he does rather than what he intends. And he is liable because of what he does for the good reason that other parties are likely to rely upon what he does in ways which are reasonable and even necessary by the standards of our society.

What I suggest then, is that whatever benefits are obtained, wherever acts of reasonable reliance take place, obligations may arise, both morally and in law. . . . Now I want next to suggest that these cases of benefits received or of action in reliance, are more common than is suggested by our conventional image of the legal world. In conventional contract theory, the paradigm of contract is the executory arrangement. Executory contract theory has totally subsumed liabilities and obligations which arise from the receipt of benefits or from acts of reasonable reliance. But in practice, the wholly executory transaction is nothing like such a paradigm as it appears in the books, I have already said something of the difficulties involved in the very concept of a paradigm in this context, but the most cursory look at the world and at the law will reveal that many types of transactions do not fit the model of the wholly executory arrangement at all. Vast numbers of transactions are not in any real sense binding prior to something being *done* by one or both of the parties. This may partly reflect the fact that lawyers have traditionally implied promises very easily from transactions, and that in consequence today there are many situations in which the lawyer would assert that an executory arrangement involves implied mutual promises while the parties themselves might very well deny that they promised anything at all. The language of consumer transactions, in particular, is not couched in terms of promises. People 'book' holidays, or air reservations, they 'order' goods, they 'accept' estimates, and so on. Even in business circles this sort of terminology is more common than the express language of promises and undertakings. Whether language of this kind is treated as creating an obligation is traditionally thought of as depending upon whether the language is tantamount to being promissory. But it is at least arguable that in many cases of this nature the reality is otherwise. Frequently, both in law and in moral discourse we appear to determine whether there should be an obligation first, and then decide how the language should be constructed afterwards. And it follows that the existence or non-existence of the obligation is then being decided independently of the existence of any promise. . . .

Now I must repeat that I am not arguing that consent, promise, intention, voluntary conduct, are irrelevant to the creation of obligations even where an element of reciprocal benefit is present, or some act of reasonable reliance has taken place. In the first place, where liability arises out of conduct rather than from the voluntary assumption of an obligation, the conduct itself is usually of a voluntary character. Even if liability on a part-executed arrangement can properly be said to be benefit-based rather than promise-based, a man is normally entitled to choose what benefits he will accept—normally, though by no means invariably. Similarly, with reliance-based liability; it is normally open to a person to warn others that they are not to rely upon him, but must trust to their own judgment. Obviously this raises difficulty where a person wants to have his cake and eat it, where he wants to influence others to behave in a certain manner but wants also to disclaim responsibility for their doing so. There is little doubt that in such circumstances the trend is towards insisting on the imposition of responsibility. The striking down of exemption clauses and disclaimers of liability are evidence of the unacceptability of these attempts to have things both ways. This trend may reflect the increased emphasis on reliance and the declining stress on free choice.

But secondly, and much more important, I would argue that even where obligations can be said to be primarily benefit-based or reliance-based, explicit promises may have a valuable role to play. I referred earlier to the conventional wisdom of English common lawyers which some decades ago suggested that the only rational function of the doctrine of consideration was to serve as evidence of the seriousness of a promise. I now want to suggest that the truth lies more closely in the precise converse of this assertion. Where obligations arise out of the rendering of benefits or from acts of reasonable reliance, the presence of an explicit promise may, I suggest, serve valuable evidentiary purposes. Consider the simple example of a loan of money which I referred to earlier as an illustration of a liability which could not, without distortion, be viewed as purely promissory. The presence of an explicit promise may nevertheless serve valuable evidentiary purposes. First, it helps to avoid doubt about the nature of the transaction. The possibility of a gift is ruled out by the express promise to repay. Then it helps clarify who the parties to the transaction may be, for the handing of money by A to B may create a loan from X to Y where A and B are acting as agents or in a transaction of any complexity. An explicit promise may resolve any ambiguities about such matters. Then again an explicit promise may help settle many minor or ancillary terms, and it is worth reflecting on how and why this is the case. Suppose, for example, that the borrower promises to repay the loan with interest at a specified rate. In the sort of society we live in, it can be taken for granted that a loan should normally carry some rate of interest, and in the absence of an agreed rate, the fixing of the rate would fall to the court in the last resort. What would the court do? The court would, of course, endeavour to fix on a just or reasonable rate of interest having regard to all the circumstances. Here again, therefore, the explicit promise to pay a specified rate does not seem to create the obligation, which would exist anyhow, but to give it precision. And the reason why it gives it precision is, surely, that it functions very like a conclusive admission. If the court is to search for a fair and reasonable rate of interest, the rate which the borrower has agreed to pay is good evidence that that is in fact the fair and reasonable rate. Good evidence, but not, at least not always, conclusive evidence. For if the agreed rate of interest is extortionate, or if it has been obtained by fraud or misrepresentation the promise to pay will not bind.

There are, indeed, some cases in which the evidentiary value of promises has already been distinctly recognised by the courts. Naturally enough, given the classical model of Contract, these cases concern situations in which an independent legal obligation already exists. For example, where a person promises to pay for valuable services previously rendered to him—the so-called past consideration cases—the promise may be treated as evidence of the value of those services. And again, where services are rendered in pursuance of a contract which turns out to be invalid for some technical reason, the value of the services may nevertheless be recovered and the contract can be treated as evidence of that value.

It may, of course, be said that these cases are no illustration of the general nature of contractual liability, but on the contrary serve to illustrate the difference between contractual and other forms of liability. For (it may be urged) the whole point of contractual liability is to permit parties to determine conclusively their own obligations. The promise creates the liability, and does not merely evidence it. In non-contractual cases, *per contra*, the duty is in the first instance created by the law; and the promise cannot be treated as creating the obligation. But I suggest that this analysis is the result of treating the executory contract as the paradigm of contract, the heritage of the classical law which I have already criticised. In the part-executed transaction, as I have argued, it is in fact frequently the case that there would be a liability even apart from any express or implied promise. Promises are not a necessary condition of the existence of a liability or the creation of an obligation. The performance by one party of acts which are beneficial to the other, the rendering of services to another, for instance, would normally be thought of as creating some sort of obligation even in the absence of a promise. Similarly, acts of reasonable reliance would often create liability in tort, or by way of trust, or other equitable obligation, even where there is no express or implied promise. Indeed, did not the whole law of trusts arise because property was entrusted to other hands, usually no doubt because of some understanding that the trustee would behave in a certain fashion? In circumstances of this kind, therefore, where obligations would normally be thought of as arising from what has been done, rather than from what has been said, there seems to me no difficulty in regarding promises as having primarily an evidentiary role.

Treating explicit promises as prima-facie evidence, and as strong prima-facie evidence of the fairness of a transaction, of the appropriate price to be paid for goods and services, is an indispensable tool of efficient administration in a free market society. For any other rule would leave it open to a dissatisfied party to any and every transaction to appeal to a judge to upset an agreed price and fix a new one. But, it may be urged, the law does not treat promises as only prima-facie evidence of the fairness of a transaction, or of the terms which should bind the parties; in most circumstances, a promise is treated as conclusive of these matters. If I am right in thinking that the role of the promise is thus limited it is incumbent on me to explain why promises are normally treated as conclusive of most of these questions, and this task I attempt in Essay 5. Here I will content myself with pointing out that promises are never treated as wholly conclusive in law. All promises and contracts are defeasible in *some* circumstances. A promise or agreement extorted by violence is no evidence of the fairness of a transaction, and is therefore naturally set aside by the courts. Promises given as a result of certain types of mistake may likewise be set aside. Alternatively, the courts may uphold the validity of the exchange but adjust the obligations of the parties (for example by implying appropriate terms) so as to ensure, so far as possible, that the exchange is a fair or reasonable one, despite the disparity between the literal obligations assumed by the parties. But the *extent* of the indefeasibility of a promise, the *extent* to which it is to be treated as a conclusive admission of the fairness and reasonableness of the terms of an exchange, is a much less simple proposition. The extent to which the courts and the law are prepared to go in treating promises as defeasible, or merely as prima-facie rather than conclusive evidence of the fairness of an exchange, is obviously something determined by the degree of paternalism which commends itself to the society and the judiciary in question. A society which believes in allowing the skilful and knowledgeable to reap the rewards of their skill and knowledge is likely to have a higher regard for the sanctity of promises than a society which wishes to protect the weak and foolish from the skilful and knowledgeable. As we shall see, this point is a good deal more important in the case of executory transactions.

Now as we know, in modern law, all this is different. A plaintiff is unquestionably entitled to expectation damages for breach of an executory contract, without any actual consideration passing. There is no need to show any actual benefit, any detrimental reliance. The modern law is squared with the doctrine of consideration by saying that the mere promises constitute consideration for each other. That indeed was what judges had been saying since the time of Elizabeth I, but it has not generally been perceived what an enormous difference has come over the practical import of this formula. For in the reign of Elizabeth I, a promise was good consideration for a promise precisely because both promises had to be performed. In our modern law, a plaintiff's promise is good consideration for the defendant's promise even though the plaintiff is discharged from performing his promise by the defendant's breach. It is only since these rules grew up, therefore, that liability on the wholly executory contract has truly become promise-based, rather than benefit or reliance-based.

But although this form of liability must be treated as promise-based, we are entitled to ask how extensive it is in relation to the rest of the law, and whether it deserves to occupy the central role in Contract and even in promissory theory that it occupies today. It is, I think, worth observing that wholly executory contracts are generally nothing like as binding in practice as legal theory might suggest. Consumers and even business men often expect to be able to cancel executory agreements with the minimum of penalty, paying perhaps only for actual expenses laid out in reliance on the promise. And such reliance expenditures would by definition, not exist if the arrangement were still wholly executory. And even in strict law, it must be stressed that the expectations protected by executory contracts are limited. They are not generally expectations of performance but expectations of profit. Where there is no difference in the market price of the goods or services which are the subject of the contract, and the market price of comparable goods or services, the contract may in law be broken with impunity. In practice this must comprise a high proportion of cases in which executory arrangements are broken. Then again, the binding force of wholly executory contracts is normally of an ephemeral nature. Executory contracts do not normally remain executory for very long. Even if made well before the time for performance, the whole purpose of making them is frequently to enable the parties to make preliminary arrangements in confident reliance on reciprocal performance. Thus action in reliance is likely to follow hard on the heels of the making of most executory contracts, and it is only in the rare cases where cancellation is sought very soon after making the contract, or where, despite the lapse of some longer period of time no action in reliance has been commenced, that the source of the obligation has to be rested in the promise alone. Whatever the paradigm of actual Contract may be, there can be no doubt that the paradigm of *a breach of contract* is not the breach of a wholly executory contract. And this surely reflects the intention of most parties who enter into executory contracts. The primary purpose of making such a contract is usually to agree upon the terms which are to regulate a contemplated exchange, when and if it is carried through; it is surely—in most instances—a subordinate and less obvious purpose that the contract binds both parties to see that the exchange is indeed carried through.

. . . The modern, and perhaps even, by now, the traditional legal view would probably be that promises and executory contracts give rise to reasonable expectations and that it is the function of the law to protect reasonable expectations. But this is itself a somewhat circular justification. We all have a large number of expectations, many of which are perfectly reasonable, but only a few of them are protected by the law. Besides, the reasonableness of an expectation is itself something which turns largely upon whether it is in fact protected. If the law did not protect expectations arising from a wholly executory arrangement, then it would be less reasonable to entertain such expectations, or at any rate to entertain them as entitlements. . . .

Then again, the explanation appears to prove too much. For reasonable expectations may arise from assertions or representations of fact as much as from promises. Yet the law seldom or never protects such expectations unless and until they have been acted upon. If we can, as I think we should, conceptually equate the idea of action in reliance on representations with the notion of detrimental reliance as a consideration in the case of promises, then we must recognise that representations can only give rise to a contractual-type obligation in the case of a part-executed transaction. And this remains true even in the extreme case of fraud. No matter what expectations are thereby generated a person who tells a downright and deliberate falsehood is not subject to legal obligations unless and until someone suffers loss through acting upon it. Indeed, even when it is acted upon, it is widely thought that the measure of any consequent liability is fixed by the extent of the reliance losses and not by the expectations generated. This, at least, is said to be the measure of damages in tort for fraud, although it is certainly not the measure in cases classified as warranty or estoppel. It is, perhaps, possible that the explanation for this otherwise puzzling distinction between the law's treatment of promises and assertions lies in the too ready acceptance of the idea that words or conduct are in practice easily classifiable as the one or the other. Perhaps the reality is that in more cases than lawyers are willing to admit, words or conduct are classified as promises or assertions precisely because in the particular circumstances the expectations aroused are, or are not, felt worthy of protection. But if this is the case, then it is clear that we cannot defend the protection of bare expectations by pointing to the fact that they derived from a promise. . . .

The second possible argument for upholding executory contracts is the argument from principle. Executory contracts are made so that the parties can rely upon each other and take the necessary preliminary steps to performance. The whole point of such contracts is that they invite reliance. Therefore, it may be urged, *even if there has in fact been no reliance yet*, it is desirable that the principle of upholding the sanctity of contracts should be maintained.

Supporters of this argument, however, must explain why a shift in the onus of proof would not meet the case. . . .

The third possible argument in support of the executory contract concerns the case where the contract is a deliberate exercise in risk allocation. Where the primary purpose of a contract is to shift a risk of some future possibility from one party to another, and where, in particular, the risk is thereby shifted to a party who in a commercial sense is better able to take the risk, or to take avoiding action against the risk eventuating, there appears to be a strong economic case for the executory contract. I believe that this argument lies at the heart of the historical development of the binding executory contract in English law, but it is imperative to note the limits upon its application. It is very far from being true that all contracts, even all executory contracts, are exercises in risk allocation. Frequently, it is the interpretation of the law which converts a simple postponed exchange into a risk-allocation exercise, rather than any deliberate intent of the parties. . . . It is also far from being always the case that the purpose of an executory contract is to shift a risk to a party whose business it is to handle such risks and who can, therefore, be assumed to be generally more efficient at handling them . . .

. . . I must now observe that if the primary justification for the enforcement of executory contracts is that they are risk-allocation devices, then it follows that the enforcement of such contracts raises profoundly value-laden questions. The justification for the executory contract becomes, in effect, an economic justification, an argument for greater economic efficiency. The purpose of enforcing such contracts is that of facilitating the use of greater skill, intelligence, foresight, knowledge and perhaps even resources by those who possess these advantages. To the extent that the law refuses to recognise the binding force of executory transactions in order to protect the weak, the foolish, the improvident or those who lack bargaining power, it must necessarily weaken the incentives and indeed the power of those not suffering these disadvantages . . .

. . . The economic arguments for the binding executory contract, like those in favour of the institution of property itself, involve a tendency to a perpetuation of existing inequalities. To strike down, or limit the binding force of executory contracts in order to protect some people from their own folly or ignorance is, by contrast, a redistributive device, and like all such devices must impose costs as well as benefits.

The fourth argument, which I have left to the last, for the binding executory contract is the moral argument. It is simple and appealing to argue that promises are morally obligatory, and that this remains the case whether they have been paid for, or relied upon or not. But as the case for the morally binding nature of promises is examined more closely, it bears a curious resemblance to the case for the binding nature of legal contracts rather than offering an independent reason in support of the law. One of the most commonly adduced reasons for arguing that promises are morally binding is that they have a tendency to be relied upon. We then find it being argued that, if that is the only justification, it is a somewhat circular one. For if, promises were not binding, they might not be relied upon. And again, it is argued that if the tendency to rely on promises is the source of their binding character, what of the case where reliance is distinctly disproved? . . .

. . . [W]hen all is said, I do not find the moral contribution to the problem to be a very satisfying one. For moralists and philosophers, like the lawyers themselves, have not generally perceived the need to separate off the wholly executory arrangement for independent justification. Virtually all discussion of the source of contractual and promissory obligation, in law and in morality, has failed to draw the all important distinction between promises and contracts which rest purely in intention, and promises and contracts which depend partly on action. Surely, nobody can doubt that morally speaking promises are more strongly binding where payment has already been received, or where there is a clear and significant act in reliance which would worsen the position of the promisee if the promise were not performed. And just as I have suggested that, in the law of part executed contracts, explicit promises may play a useful evidentiary role, so it may be suggested that promises themselves are frequently of an evidentiary character. The purpose of a promise, far from being, as is so often assumed, to create some wholly independent source of an obligation, is frequently to bolster up an already existing duty. Promises help to clarify, to qualify, to give precision to moral obligations, many of which already exist or would arise anyhow from the performance of acts which are contemplated or invited by the promise. The promise which is given without *any* independent reason for it is a peculiarity, just as the wholly executory contract is a legal peculiarity. Is it pure coincidence that the phrase, a 'gratuitous promise' means both promise without payment and a promise without reason? Could it then be that the refusal of English law to recognise the binding force of executory gratuitous promises is not the peculiarity, the idiosyncrasy it has so long been thought to be? Might it not be that the real oddity lies in the belief that a bare promise creates a moral obligation and should create a legal obligation, without any inquiry into the reason for which the promise was given, or the effect that the promise has had?

These arguments, of course, require much greater development than they can be given here; but enough has been said to show that, if they stand up to further examination, they should suffice to dethrone the executory contract from the central place which it occupies in contract theory. The consequences of this would be to require some drastic redrawing of the lines of the conceptual structure of contractual and promissory obligation. In the first place, the distinction between contract and restitution would surely come crashing to the ground . . .

A similar fate may well await the distinction between contract and tort when once the executory contract is removed from the central place in the law of obligations. I have already suggested that our nineteenth-century heritage has led us to place undue emphasis on the extent to which contractual obligations depend upon intentions and the voluntary assumption of liability. But is it not equally true that, perhaps by way of reaction, tort theory has swung too far in the opposite direction? In their reaction away from contract, lawyers and judges have tended to stress the positive nature of tortious liability. Tort duties are imposed by law, not assumed by the parties. They are the reflection of society's standards of fairness and reasonableness and not the result of deliberate submission to a mutual binding arrangement, and so on. I want to suggest that all this has tended to draw far too sharp a line between contract and tort.

NOTES

1. These views underlie much of Atiyah's *Rise and Fall of Freedom of Contract* (1979). They are developed further in his *Promises, Morals and Law* (1981). An instructive review of the first book from an historical viewpoint will be found in (1980) 43 MLR 467 (Baker); and the second is usefully reviewed in (1982) 95 Harvard LR 916 (Raz) and (1982) 98 LQR 470 (Simpson).

2. Do you agree with Atiyah's analysis? Does he put too much emphasis on 'marginal' cases and not pay enough attention to cases involving commercial contracts? Aren't most of these conscious attempts to allocate a variety of risks?

3. Atiyah's views, which were first published in (1978) 94 LQR 413, have not gone unchallenged: see Raz (1982) 95 Harvard LR 916; Birks [1983] Current Legal Problems 141; Burrows (1983) 99 LQR 216. Atiyah replies to his critics in *Essays in Contract* pp 43–56.

4. The view that contractual liability has become almost indistinguishable from liability in tort and restitution was expressed even more forcibly by Gilmore in *The Death of Contract* (1974). Gilmore argued that classical contract law was the artificial creation of academics (Christopher Columbus Langdell of Harvard, who produced the first casebook on contracts, got most of the blame). Gilmore concluded (at pp 87–88 and 90):

Speaking descriptively, we might say that what is happening is that 'contract' is being reabsorbed into the mainstream of 'tort.' Until the general theory of contract was hurriedly run up late in the nineteenth century, tort had always been our residual category of civil liability. As the contract rules dissolve, it is becoming so again. It should be pointed out that the theory of tort into which contract is being reabsorbed is itself a much more expansive theory of liability than was the theory of tort from which contract was artificially separated a hundred years ago.

We have had more than one occasion to notice the insistence of the classical theorists on the sharp differentiation between contract and tort—the refusal to admit any liability in 'contract' until the formal requisites of offer, acceptance and consideration had been satisfied, the dogma that only 'bargained-for' detriment or benefit could count as consideration, and notably, the limitations on damage recovery. Classical contract theory might well be described as an attempt to stake out an enclave within the general domain of tort. The dykes which were set up to protect the enclave have, it is clear enough, been crumbling at a progressively rapid rate. With the growth of the ideas of quasi-contract and unjust enrichment, classical consideration theory was breached on the benefit side. With the growth of the promissory estoppel idea, it was breached on the detriment side. We are fast approaching the point where, to prevent unjust enrichment, any benefit received by a defendant must be paid for unless it was clearly meant as a gift; where any detriment reasonably incurred by a plaintiff in reliance on a defendant's assurances must be recompensed. When that point is reached, there is really no longer any viable distinction between liability in contract and liability in tort. . . .

I have occasionally suggested to my students that a desirable reform in legal education would be to merge the first-year course in Contracts and Torts into a single course which we could call Contorts. Perhaps the same suggestion would be a good one when the time comes for the third round of Restatements.

5. Partly as a response to Atiyah and Gilmore, Fried in 1981 attempted to justify contract law in terms of what he called the 'promise principle'. A short extract from his work follows.

'Contract as Promise: A Theory of Contractual Obligations' by Fried (1981) pp 14–21, 69–73

THE MORAL OBLIGATION OF PROMISE

Once I have invoked the institution of promising, why exactly is it wrong for me then to break my promise?

My argument so far does not answer that question. The institution of promising is a way for me to bind myself to another so that the other may expect a future performance, and binding myself in this way is something that I may want to be able to do. But this by itself does not show that I am morally obligated to perform my promise at a later time if to do so proves inconvenient or costly. That there should be a system of currency also increases my options and is useful to me, but this does not show why I should not use counterfeit money if I can get away with it. In just the same way the usefulness of promising in general does not show why I should not take advantage of it in a particular case and yet fail to keep my promise. That the convention would cease to function in the long run, would cease to provide benefits if everyone felt free to violate it, is hardly an answer to the question of why I should keep a particular promise on a particular occasion.

David Lewis has shown that a convention that it would be in each person's interest to observe if everyone else observed it will be established and maintained without any special mechanisms of commitment or enforcement. Starting with simple conventions (for example that if a telephone conversation is disconnected, the person who initiated the call is the one who calls back) Lewis extends his argument to the case of language. Now promising is different, since (unlike language, where it is overwhelmingly in the interest of all that everyone comply with linguistic conventions, even when language is used to deceive) it will often be in the interest of the promisor *not* to conform to the convention when it comes time to render his performance. Therefore individual self-interest is not enough to sustain the convention, and some additional ground is needed to keep it from unraveling. There are two principal candidates: external sanctions and moral obligation.

David Hume sought to combine these two by proposing that the external sanction of public opprobrium, of loss of reputation for honesty, which society attaches to promise-breaking, is internalized, becomes instinctual, and accounts for the sense of the moral obligation of promise. Though Hume offers a possible anthropological or psychological account of how people feel about promises, his is not a satisfactory *moral* argument. Assume that I can get away with breaking my promise (the promisee is dead), and I am now asking why I should keep it anyway in the face of some personal inconvenience. Hume's account of obligation is more like an argument *against* my keeping the promise, for it tells me how any feelings of obligation that I may harbor have come to lodge in my psyche and thus is the first step toward ridding me of such inconvenient prejudices.

Considerations of self-interest cannot supply the moral basis of my obligation to keep a promise. By an analogous argument neither can considerations of utility. For however sincerely and impartially I may apply the utilitarian injunction to consider at each step how I might increase the sum of happiness or utility in the world, it will allow me to break my promise whenever the balance of advantage (including, of course, my own advantage) tips in that direction. The possible damage to the institution of promising is only one factor in the calculation. Other factors are the alternative good I might do by breaking my promise, whether and by how many people the breach might be discovered, what the actual effect on confidence of such a breach would be. There is no a priori reason for believing that an individual's calculations will come out in favor of keeping the promise always, sometimes, or most of the time.

Rule-utilitarianism seeks to offer a way out of this conundrum. The individual's moral obligation is determined not by what the best action at a particular moment would be, but by the rule it would be best for him to follow. It has, I believe, been demonstrated that this position is incoherent: Either rule-utilitarianism requires that rules be followed in a particular case even where the result would not be best all things considered, and so the utilitarian aspect of rule-utilitarianism is abandoned; or the obligation to follow the rule is so qualified as to collapse into act-utilitarianism after all. There is, however, a version of rule-utilitarianism that makes a great deal of sense. In this version the utilitarian does not instruct us what our individual moral obligations are but rather instructs legislators what the best rules are. If legislation is our focus, then the contradictions of rule-utilitarianism do not arise, since we are instructing those whose decisions can *only* take the form of issuing rules. From that perspective there is obvious utility to rules establishing and enforcing promissory obligations. Since I am concerned now with the question of individual obligation, that is, moral obligation, this legislative perspective on the argument is not available to me.

The obligation to keep a promise is grounded not in arguments of utility but in respect for individual autonomy and in trust. Autonomy and trust are grounds for the institution of promising as well, but the argument for *individual* obligation is not the same. Individual obligation is only a step away, but the step must be taken. An individual is morally bound to keep his promises because he has intentionally invoked a convention whose function it is to give grounds—moral grounds—for another to expect the promised performance. To renege is to abuse a confidence he was free to invite or not, and which he intentionally did invite. To abuse that confidence now is like (but only *like*) lying: the abuse of a shared social institution that is intended to invoke the bonds of trust. A liar and a promise-breaker each *use* another person. In both speech and promising there is an invitation to the other to trust, to make himself vulnerable; the liar and the promise-breaker then abuse that trust. The obligation to keep a promise is thus similar to but more constraining than the obligation to tell the truth. To avoid lying you need only believe in the truth of what you say when you say it, but a promise binds into the future, well past the moment when the promise is made. There will, of course, be great social utility to a general regime of trust and confidence in promises and truthfulness. But this just shows that a regime of mutual respect allows men and women to accomplish what in a jungle of restrained self-interest could not be accomplished. If this advantage is to be firmly established, there must exist a ground for mutual confidence deeper than and independent of the social utility it permits.

The utilitarian counting the advantages affirms the general importance of enforcing *contracts*. The moralist of duty, however, sees *promising* as a device that free, moral individuals have fashioned on the premise of mutual trust, and which gathers its moral force from that premise. The moralist of duty thus posits a general obligation to keep promises, of which the obligation of contract will be only a special case—that special case in which certain promises have attained legal as well as moral force. But since a contract is first of all a promise, the contract must be kept because a promise must be kept.

To summarize: There exists a convention that defines the practice of promising and its entailments. This convention provides a way that a person may create expectations in others. By virtue of the basic Kantian principles of trust and respect, it is wrong to invoke that convention in order to make a promise, and then to break it.

. . .

WHAT A PROMISE IS WORTH

If I make a promise to you, I should do as I promise; and if I fail to keep my promise, it is fair that I should be made to hand over the equivalent of the promised performance. In contract doctrine this proposition appears as the expectation measure of damages for breach. The expectation standard gives the victim of a breach no more or less than he would have had had there been no breach—in other words, he gets the benefit of his bargain. Two alternative measures of damage, reliance and restitution, express the different notions that if a person has relied on a promise and been hurt, that hurt must be made good; and that if a contract-breaker has obtained goods or services, he must be made to pay a fair (just?) price for them. Consider three cases:

II-A. I enter your antique shop on a quiet afternoon and agree in writing to buy an expensive chest I see there, the price being about three times what you paid for it a short time ago. When I get home I repent of my decision, and within half an hour of my visit—before any other customer has come to your store—I telephone to say I no longer want the chest.

II-B. Same as above, except in the meantime you have waxed and polished the chest and had your delivery van bring it to my door.

II-C. Same as above, except I have the use of the chest for six months, while your shop is closed for renovations.

To require me to pay for the chest in case II-A (or, if you resell it, to pay any profit you lost, including lost business volume) is to give you your expectation, the benefit of your bargain. In II-B if all I must compensate is your effort I am reimbursing your reliance, and in II-C to force me to pay a fair price for the use I have had of the chest is to focus on making me pay for, restore, an actual benefit I have received.

The assault on the classical conception of contract, the concept I call contract as promise, has centered on the connection—taken as canonical for some hundred years—between contract law and expectation damages. To focus the attack on this connection is indeed strategic. As the critics recognize and as I have just stated, to the extent that contract is grounded in promise, it seems natural to measure relief by the expectation, that is, by the promise itself. If that link can be threatened, then contract itself may be grounded elsewhere than in promise, elsewhere than in the will of the parties.

The insistence on reliance or benefit is related to disputes about the nature of promising. As I have argued, reliance on a promise cannot alone explain its force: There is reliance because a promise is binding, and not the other way around. But if a person is bound by his promise and not by the harm the promisee may have suffered in reliance on it, then what he is bound to is just its performance. Put simply, I am bound to do what I promised you I would do—or I am bound to put you in as good a position as if I had done so. To bind me to do no more than to reimburse your reliance is to excuse me to that extent from the obligation I undertook. If your reliance is less than your expectation (in case II-A there is no reliance), then to that extent a reliance standard excuses me from the very obligation I undertook and so weakens the force of an obligation I chose to assume. Since by hypothesis I chose to assume the obligation in its stronger form (that is, to render the performance promised), the reliance rule indeed precludes me from incurring the very obligation I chose to undertake at the time of promising. The most compelling of the arguments for resisting this conclusion and for urging that we settle for reliance is the sense that it is sometimes harsh and ungenerous to insist on the full measure of expectancy. (This is part of Atiyah's thrust when he designates the expectation standard as an aspect of the rigid Victorian promissory morality.) The harshness comes about because in the event the promisor finds the obligation he assumed too burdensome.

This distress may be analyzed into three forms: (1) The promisor regrets having to pay for what he has bought (which may only have been the satisfaction of promising a gift or the thrill of buying a lottery ticket or stock option), though he would readily do the same thing again. I take it that this kind of regret merits no sympathy at all. Indeed if we gave in to it we would frustrate the promisor's ability to engage in his own continuing projects and so the promisor's plea is, strictly speaking, self-contradictory. (2) The promisor regrets his promise because he was mistaken about the nature of the burdens he was assuming—the purchaser in case II-A thought he would find the money for the antique but in fact his savings are depleted, or perhaps the chest is not as old nor as valuable as he had imagined, or his house has burned down and he no longer needs it. All of these regrets are based on mistaken assumptions about the facts as they are or as they turn out to be. As we shall see . . ., the doctrines of mistake, frustration, and impossibility provide grounds for mitigating the effect of the promise principle without at all undermining it.

Finally there is the most troublesome ground of regret: (3) The promisor made no mistake about the facts or probabilities at all, but now that it has come time to perform he no longer values the promise as highly as when he made it. He regrets the promise because he regrets the value judgment that led him to make it. He concludes that the purchase of an expensive antique is an extravagance. Compassion may lead a promisee to release an obligation in such a case, but he releases as an act of generosity, not as a duty, and certainly not because the promisor's repentance destroys the force of the original obligation. The intuitive reason for holding fast is that such repentence should be the promisor's own responsibility, not one he can shift onto others. It seems too easy a way of getting out of one's obligations. Yet our intuition does not depend on suspicions of insincerity alone. Rather we feel that holding people to their obligations is a way of taking them seriously and thus of giving the concept of sincerity itself serious content. Taking this intuition to a more abstract level, I would say that respect for others as free and rational requires taking seriously their capacity to determine their own values. I invoke again the distinction between the right and the good. The right defines the concept of the self as choosing its own conception of the good. Others must respect our capacity as free and rational persons to choose our own good, and that respect means allowing persons to take responsibility for the good they choose. And, of course, that choosing self is not an instantaneous self but one extended in time, so that to respect those determinations of the self is to respect their persistence over time. If we decline to take seriously the assumption of an obligation because we do not take seriously the promisor's prior conception of the good that led him to assume it, to that extent we do not take him seriously as a person. We infantilize him, as we do quite properly when we release the very young from the consequences of their choices.

Since contracts invoke and are invoked by promises, it is not surprising that the law came to impose on the promises it recognized the same incidents as morality demands. The connection between contract and the expectation principle is so palpable that there is reason to doubt that its legal recognition is a relatively recent invention. It is true that over the last two centuries citizens in the liberal democracies have become increasingly free to dispose of their talents, labor, and property as seems best to them. The freedom to bind oneself contractually to a future disposition is an important and striking example of this freedom (the freedom to make testamentary dispositions or to make whatever present use of one's effort or goods one desires are other examples), because in a promise one is taking responsibility not only for one's present self but for one's future self. But this does not argue that the promise principle itself is a novelty—surely Cicero's, Pufendorf's and Grotius's discussions of it show that it is not—but only that its use has expanded greatly over the years.

. . .

FILLING THE GAPS

It would be irrational to ignore the gaps in contracts, to refuse to fill them. It would be irrational not to recognize contractual accidents and to refuse to make adjustments when they occur. The gaps cannot be filled, the adjustments cannot be governed, by the promise principle. We have already encountered the two competing residuary principles of civil obligation that take over when promise gives out: the tort principle to compensate for harm done, and the restitution principle for benefits conferred. Each of these has some application, but only a limited or puzzling one, to the cases that concern us. If a contracting party has knowingly concealed or negligently overlooked an eventuality that sharply alters the risks—for example, if the owner in the *Stees* case knew or easily could have learned of the difficult condition of his land—we may force him to bear the resulting loss for that reason. If a party has conferred benefits (built something, paid in advance) under a contract that subsequently fails because of frustration, the benefit should be paid for or returned. In the cases arising out of the cancellation of the coronation, for instance, the rooms overlooking the procession route were valuable just for that purpose and could be rented again when the coronation was rescheduled. To allow the owners to collect twice would have been preposterous. (But what if there had been no later procession?)

Unfortunately in many cases both parties are harmed, neither is at fault, neither benefits. The half-built house is destroyed by an earthquake. The half-built machine is rendered useless by government regulation. The program printed for the canceled yacht race is of no interest to anyone. In such situations a distinct third principle for apportioning loss and gain comes into play: the principle of sharing.

. . . [The solution that the parties must in such cases share losses relating to their frustrated contract] has problems. Is not the contractual enterprise just that enterprise in which mutual obligations have been willingly undertaken; and yet do not contractual accidents occur precisely because no mutual engagements have been made; so that we are constructing a kind of nonconsensual penumbra around the consensual core? In terms of what do we construct this penumbra? Not in terms of the wills or promises of the parties. Obviously some standard of sharing *external* to the intention of the parties must control. But if the law is free to impose standards external to the intention of contractual parties to the end of fairly dividing up losses in the case of a contractual accident, does this not show that principles of sharing are available potentially to allocate burdens and benefits among any set of citizens at all? If so, then not only is the contractual nexus unnecessary to create the focusing predicate *for* sharing, sharing itself may be seen as so powerful a principle as to overwhelm that nexus reversing the effects of agreements even where there has been no accident.

We need not go this far. Those in concrete or personal relations must have a greater care for each other than those who stand to each other in the abstract relation of fellow citizens, or fellow man. By this principle family members and friends are owed and may engross a greater measure of our concern than abstract justice prescribes. By this principle too, direct or intentional harm constitutes a wrong. Making another person the object of your intention, a step along the way in your plans, particularizes that person and forms a concrete relation between you and him. Typically such concrete relations are freely chosen. Though some family ties are not chosen, ties of friendship are, and, as to harm, the intention to harm a specified other person (stranger or not) is quintessentially voluntary.

A contractual relation is a good example of a concrete relation that may give rise to a more focused duty to share another's good or ill fortune. The relation is, after all, freely chosen. Indeed this is the same idea as that the contractual parties are in a common enterprise—an enterprise they chose to enter. True, the bond does extend beyond the explicit terms of the contract, since the problems we are concerned with are by hypothesis not explicitly disposed of in the contract. The contract does, however, also imply a limit to the obligation. If I have furnished machinery to your factory over the years I am to some unspecified further degree involved in your manufacturing endeavor, but surely not in the misfortunes that befall you in some unrelated speculation, or in your family travails. If I have agreed to sell you a small standard part, an extension cord or a light bulb, my implication in your venture (and yours in mine) will have very little penumbra beyond the actual agreement of sale. Thus in filling the gaps it is natural to look to the agreement itself for some sense of the nature and extent of the common enterprise. Since actual intent is (by hypothesis) missing, a court respects the autonomy of the parties so far as possible by construing an allocation of burdens and benefits that reasonable persons would have made in this kind of arrangement. (It treats the contract as a kind of charter or constitution for the parties' relation.) This is, as I argued earlier, an inquiry with unavoidably normative elements: 'Reasonable' parties do not merely seek to accomplish rational objectives; they do so constrained by norms of fairness and honesty. Finally, this recourse to principles of sharing to fill the gaps does not threaten to overwhelm the promissory principle, for the simple reason that the parties are quite free to control the meaning and extent of their relation by the contract itself.

NOTE

Fried's book was reviewed by Atiyah in (1981) 95 Harvard LR 509. Atiyah was not persuaded. He argues, for instance, that Fried's account of damages pays insufficient attention to mitigation, which means that what the party who breaks his promise has to pay is often much less than he promised. A more fundamental criticism is that Fried has to admit that a considerable number of contract doctrines, such as common mistake and frustration, cannot be justified in terms of the promise principle; other principles are being brought in. Atiyah says this 'calls into question how often judicial decisions in contractual disputes can be attributed to the promise principle.' (at p 516.)

'The Economics of Contract Law' by Kronman and Posner (above, p 71)

The law-and-economics literature, of which this book contains many extracts, represents a rather different viewpoint. Atiyah certainly does not accept all its assumptions (see his *Essays on Contract*, chapter 7). We find economic analysis useful because it seems to provide insights into the way that the rules of law may affect the behaviour of contracting parties. We are very aware however that it begs a number of very important questions. We have chosen two short extracts from a scathing (and typically amusing) review of the first edition of Posner's *Economic Analysis of Law* by Arthur Leff to illustrate just two of the problems.

'Economic analysis of law: some realism about nominalism' by Leff (1974) 60 Virginia LR 451, 456–458 and 478–479

To follow this initially attractive development in legal criticism (for purposes both of admiration and scorn), one will have to master the critical early moves. The first and most basic is 'the assumption that man is a rational maximizer of his ends in life. . . ' As Posner points out, this assumption 'is no stronger than that most people in most affairs of life are guided by what they conceive to be their self-interest and that they choose means reasonably (not perfectly) designed to promote it.' In connection with this assumption, several 'fundamental economic concepts' emerge. 'The first is that of the inverse relation between price charged and quantity demanded.' The second is the economist's definition of cost, 'the price that the resources consumed in making (and selling) the seller's product would command in their next best use—the alternative price.'

The third basic concept, which is also derived from reflection on how self-interested people react to a change in their surroundings, is the tendency of resources to gravitate toward their highest valued uses if exchange is permitted. . . . By a process of voluntary exchange, resources are shifted to those uses in which the value to the consumer, as measured by the consumer's willingness to pay, is highest. When resources are being used where their value is greatest, we may say that they are being employed efficiently.

Now it must immediately be noted, and never forgotten, that these basic propositions are really not empirical propositions at all. They are all generated by 'reflection' on an 'assumption' about choice under scarcity and rational maximization. While Posner states that 'there is abundant evidence that theories derived from those assumptions have considerable power in predicting how people in fact behave,' he cites none. And it is in fact unnecessary to cite any, for the propositions are not empirically falsifiable at all.

Efficiency is a technical term: it means exploiting economic resources in such a way that human satisfaction *as measured by aggregate consumer willingness to pay* for goods and services is maximized. Value too is defined by willingness to pay.

In other words, since people are rationally self-interested, what they do shows what they value, and their willingness to pay for what they value is proof of their rational self-interest. Nothing merely empirical could get in the way of such a structure because it is definitional. That is why the assumptions can predict how people behave: in *these* terms there is no other way they can behave. If, for instance, a society dentist raises his prices and thereby increases his gross volume of business, it is no violation of the principle of inverse relation between price and quantity. It only proves that the buyers now perceive that they are buying something else which they now value more highly, 'society dentistry,' say, rather than 'mere' dentistry. And if circularity isn't sufficient, the weak version of the rational maximization formula ('most people in most affairs of life . . . choose means reasonably (not perfectly) designed. . . .') has the effect of chewing up and spitting out any discordant empirical data anyway. Any puzzling observation fed into that kind of definition will always be able to find a 'most,' or a 'reasonably,' way out.

Thus what people do is good, and its goodness can be determined by looking at what it is they do. In place of the more arbitrary normative 'goods' of Formalism, *and* in place of the more complicated empirical 'goods' of Realism, stands the simple definitionally circular 'value' of Posner's book. If human desire itself becomes normative (in the sense that it cannot be criticized), and if human desire is made definitionally identical with certain human acts, then those human acts are also beyond criticism in normative or efficiency terms; everyone is doing as best he can exactly what he set out to do which, by definition, is 'good' for him. In those terms, it is not at all surprising that economic analyses have 'considerable power in predicting how people in fact behave.'

Despite the use of terms like 'value' and 'efficiency,' economics cannot tell us how society should be managed. Efficiency is a technical term: it means exploiting economic resources in such a way that human satisfaction as measured by aggregate consumer willingness to pay for goods and services is maximized. Value too is defined by willingness to pay. Willingness to pay is in turn a function of the existing distribution of income and wealth in the society. Were income and wealth distributed in a different pattern, the pattern of demands might also be different and efficiency would require a different deployment of our economic resources. The economist cannot tell us whether the existing distribution of income and wealth is just, although he may be able to tell us something about the costs of altering it as well as about the distributive consequences of various policies. Nor can he tell us whether, assuming the existing distribution is just, consumer satisfaction should be the dominant value of society. The economist's competence in a discussion of the legal system is limited to predicting the effect of legal rules and arrangements on value and efficiency, in their strict technical sense, and on the existing distribution of income and wealth.

In such a system whatever is, is. If you do not 'buy' something, you are *unwilling* to do so. There is no place for the word or concept 'unable'. Thus, in this system, there is nothing which is coerced. For instance, let us say that a starving man approaches a loaf of bread held by an armed baker. Another potential buyer is there. The baker institutes an auction; he wants cash only (having too great doubts about the starveling's health to be interested in granting credit). The poor man gropes in his pockets and comes up with a dollar. The other bidder immediately takes out $1.01 and makes off with the bread. Now under Posner's definitional system we must say that the 'value' of the bread was no more than a dollar to the poor man because he was 'unwilling' to pay more than that. An observer not bound within that particular definitional structure might find it somehow much more illuminating to characterize the poor man's failure as being the result of being unable to pay more than a dollar. But one cannot, consistent with Posner's system, say any such thing. One's actual power is irrelevant.

If, as Atiyah and Gilmore argue, contract is beginning to look more and more like tort, in that liability is being imposed when it cannot realistically be said that the party 'voluntarily assumed' it, the distinction between private, voluntarily assumed obligations and public, imposed obligations is called into question. Is there really such a distinction? Some argue not.

'An Essay in the Deconstruction of Contract Doctrine' by Dalton (1985) 94 Yale LJ 997, 1015–1019

Hertzog v Hertzog [29 Pa 465], decided by the Pennsylvania Supreme Court in 1857, is reputedly the first American case to distinguish the quasi-contract from the implied-in-fact contract. The themes and method of analysis present in *Hertzog* still reverberate in the treatment of implied contract found in the *Second Restatement* and in modern case law.

In *Hertzog*, an adult son lived and worked with his father until his father's death, at which point the son sued the estate for compensation for services rendered. The trial judge instructed the jury that John Hertzog could recover only if an employment contract existed between father and son. Two witnesses gave testimony that could be interpreted as evidence of such an agreement: One Stamm testified that he 'heard the old man say he would pay John for the labour he had done,' while one Roderick swore that the father 'said he intended to make John safe.' The jury found for John, and the defendant appealed, successfully.

Pennsylvania Supreme Court Justice Lowrie begins the opinion by distinguishing express, implied-in-fact, and implied-in-law contracts. In advancing this categorization, Lowrie particularly criticized Blackstone for failing to distinguish the implied-in-fact from the implied-in-law contract.

Blackstone had suggested that '[i]mplied [contracts] are such as reason and justice dictate; and which, therefore, the law presumes that every man undertakes to perform.' Lowrie, true to his advanced understanding of the implications of the will theory of contract, observes, 'There is some looseness of thought in supposing that reason and justice ever dictate any contracts between parties, or impose such upon them. All true contracts grow out of the intentions of the parties to transactions, and are dictated only by their mutual and accordant wills.' The only 'contracts' that reason and justice dictate, according to Lowrie, are '*constructive* contracts' in which the contract is 'mere fiction', a form adopted solely to enforce a duty independent of intention. 'In one,' says Lowrie, 'the duty defines the contract; in the other, the contract defines the duty.'

Lowrie offers this definition of quasi-contract:

[W]henever, not our variant notions of reason and justice, but the common sense and common justice of the country, and therefore the common law or statute law, impose upon any one a duty, irrespective of contract, and allow it to be enforced by a contract remedy, [this is] a case of [quasi-] contract.

For Justice Lowrie, quasi-contract, unlike contract proper, reflects public norms. Public norms, however, require legitimation and Lowrie offers two types—one positivist, the other dependent on natural law. The norms are 'positively' binding because they are part of the body of common law or statute recognized as authoritative. They are 'naturally' binding because they reflect 'common sense and common justice.' While Lowrie distinguishes these public obligations from obligations based on consent, he invokes consent to legitimize public norms: Consent underlies his distinction between '*variant* notions of reason and justice' and '*common* sense and *common* justice.'

Lowrie avoids the need to devote more time and attention in *Hertzog* to quasi-contract by stating that '[i]n the present case there is no pretence of a constructive contract, but only of a proper one, either express or implied.' The focus of the opinion, then, is on whether John Hertzog can demonstrate the existence of a contract by words spoken or by an account of the relationship and circumstances.

As to the express contract, Lowrie explicitly uses the parties' relationship and their circumstances to 'frame' the words spoken in such a way that they become words of 'non-contract' instead of contract:

> The court told the jury that a contract of hiring might be inferred from the evidence of Stamm and Roderick. Yet these witnesses add nothing to the facts already recited, except that the father told them, shortly before his death, that he intended to pay his son for his work. This is no making of a contract or admission of one; but rather the contrary. It admits that the son deserved some reward from his father, but not that he had a contract for any.'

The father-son relationship clearly influences Lowrie's conclusion. *Hertzog* thus illustrates that words of intentions are inconclusive until they are shaped by a judicial reading of the context in which they are uttered. Even the paradigmatically self-sufficient 'express' contract, in which 'the terms of the agreement are openly uttered and avowed at the time of the making,' is invaded by 'publicness' in its interpretation and enforcement.

In regard to the implied-in-fact contract, Lowrie says that '[t]he law ordinarily presumes or implies a contract whenever this is necessary to account for other relations found to have existed between the parties.' In *Hertzog*, Lowrie's willingness to find an employment contract will therefore turn on whether the parties are related: He assumes that strangers assist one another only on the expectation of reward, whereas precisely the opposite is true of employment between intimates.

Lowrie thus bases his conclusion that no implied contract exists almost entirely upon 'the customs of society' and commonly accepted notions about human nature in general and family relationships in particular. But his reliance on such customs and commonalities hopelessly undermines his distinction between contracts implied-in-fact and quasi-contracts. Lowrie's treatment of the absence of a contract proper could just as easily be read as an account of the absence of a quasi-contract. Plainly he has decided that common sense and common justice demand a finding that no contract exists here. The advantage of his contractual analysis is that it permits public considerations to be introduced as if they were private, without the elaborate scrutiny of their source and justification that a quasi-contractual analysis would require.

Lowrie's concluding ruminations about the jury's finding for the son ironically illustrate his obliviousness to the 'publicness' of his analysis:

> The difficulty in trying causes of this kind often arises from juries supposing that, because they have the decision of the cause, therefore they may decide according to general principles of honesty and fairness, without reference to the law of the case. But this is a despotic power, and is lodged with no portion of this government.
>
> Their verdict may, in fact, declare what is honest between the parties, and yet it may be a mere usurpation of power, and thus be an effort to correct one evil by a greater one. Citizens have a right to form connexions on their own terms and to be judged accordingly. When parties claim by contract, the contract proved must be the rule by which their rights are to be decided. To judge them by any other rule is to interfere with the liberty of the citizen.

This moralizing might be more convincing if the judge had not just exercised, in the guise of fact-finding, the type of state power he now labels 'despotic.'

In resolving this dispute, then, Lowrie proves incapable of sustaining the distinction between public and private on which he places so much emphasis. He asserts that the intrusion of the state into the relationships of private individuals is generally undesirable. He suggests that in extreme circumstances such intrusion can be justified, provided we impose only those obligations grounded both in community standards and in positive promulgation. In normal circumstances, however, contract law is purely about the intentions of the parties. Disciplined and rational judges, aware of the limitations of their authority, are better equipped to discern these intentions than undisciplined and irrational juries who confuse their sense of what is fair and honest with what the parties had in mind. But when it comes to deciding the case, Lowrie uses standards that were neither explicitly adopted by the parties nor promulgated by the state. In determining that the relationship between the parties was not contractual, he invokes common understandings about the context of the agreement to transform words of agreement into evidence of non-contract. In so doing he avoids the problem of power by appearing to endorse the parties' own choice that their relationship be without legal consequence, and avoids the problem of knowledge by presenting his own normative interpretation of the situation as nothing more than a transparent reading of the parties' intentions.

One does not have to be a radical to accept that frequently contractual liability is not really based on the party having voluntarily assumed it: eg above, p 318. If liability is 'imposed' by the courts, what policies and what values are the courts adopting? You may like to read again the extracts from Adams and Brownsword and Collins (above, pp 63–70).

To the extent that contract law enforces what the parties have agreed, it is still clearly concerned with obligations that were voluntarily assumed. In section 8 'Policing the bargain' and to some extent in section 7 'Changing the bargain', we will be particularly concerned with questions of whether the apparent agreement reached was indeed voluntary. What does 'voluntary' mean?

'Contract law and Distributive Justice' by Kronman (1980) 89 Yale LJ 472, 477–483

But when is an agreement voluntary? For a libertarian, committed to the notion that all voluntary agreements must be enforced, the widest view of voluntariness is almost surely unacceptable. Suppose that I sign a contract to sell my house for $5,000 after being physically threatened by the buyer. It is possible to characterize my agreements as voluntary in one sense: after considering the alternatives, I have concluded that my self-interest is best served by signing and have deliberately implemented a perfectly rational decision by doing precisely that. Described in this general way, my agreement to sell appears in the same light that it would if, for example, I had not been threatened but signed the contract because I thought $5,000 a good price for the house. Under this description, however, my act of signing will be involuntary only if it is not motivated by a decision of any sort at all on my part. Such would be the case, for example, if the purchaser forcibly grabbed my hand and guided it over the document himself, or commanded me to sign the contract while I was in an hypnotic state.

There is, of course, nothing logically absurd about drawing the line between voluntary and involuntary agreements at this point, but I doubt most libertarians would wish to do so. Among other things, defining voluntariness in this way conflicts with deeply entrenched notions of moral responsibility. In assessing the voluntariness of an agreement, it is not enough merely to determine that the agreement was motivated by a deliberate decision of some sort; we also want to know something about the circumstances under which it was given. But if this is true, the problem of drawing a line between agreements that are voluntary and agreements that are not—a problem the libertarian must confront if the idea of voluntary exchange is to have any meaning at all—can be understood as the problem of specifying the conditions that must be present before we will consider an agreement to have been voluntarily concluded. Put differently, unless the libertarian is prepared to accept a very broad concept of voluntariness, which equates voluntary agreement with rational choice, he must specify the various circumstances under which even a deliberately given, rational agreement will be held to have been coerced.

B. *Advantage-Taking*

Whenever a promisor complains that his agreement was coerced and therefore ought not to be enforced, he should be understood as claiming that the agreement was given under circumstances that rendered it involuntary. In making an argument of this sort, a promisor may point to many different circumstances or conditions: he may say, for example that his agreement was involuntary because he lacked the mental and emotional capacities required to appreciate its consequences; or a promisor may claim that he was threatened or deceived by the other party, or that his agreement was given at a time he was hard-pressed for cash and therefore had no choice but to accept the terms proposed by the promisee; or a promisor may assert that his agreement was involuntary because he, unlike the other party, was ignorant of certain facts which, if known at the time of contracting, would have led him to make a different agreement or no agreement at all; or he may say that the other party had a monopoly of some scarce resource—the only water hole or the best cow or the strongest shoulders in town—a monopoly which enabled him to dictate terms of sale to the promisor, making their agreement what is sometimes called a 'contract of adhesion.'

In some of these cases, the circumstances allegedly making the promisor's agreement involuntary is an incapacity of the promisor himself—his insanity, youth, ignorance or impecuniousness. In others, the involuntariness of the promisor's agreement is attributable to an act by the other party—a fraudulent deception or threat of physical harm. Finally, in some cases, it is the other party's monopolization of a scarce resource and the market power he enjoys as a result which (it is claimed) renders the promisor's agreement involuntary. In each case, however, the promisor is asserting that his agreement, although deliberately given, lacked voluntariness because of the circumstances under which it was made—circumstances that in one way or another restricted his range of alternatives to a point where the promisor's choice could be said to be free in name only.

The problem, of course, is to determine when the circumstances under which an agreement is given deprive it of its voluntariness in this sense. In my view, this problem is equivalent to another—the problem of determining which of the many forms of advantage-taking possible in exchange relationships are compatible with the libertarian conception of individual freedom. The latter way of stating the problem may appear to raise new and distinct issues but in fact it does not. In each of the hypothetical cases considered above, the promisee enjoys an advantage of some sort which he has attempted to exploit for his own benefit. The advantage may consist in his superior information, intellect, or judgment, in the monopoly he enjoys with regard to a particular resource, or in his possession of a powerful instrument of violence or a gift for deception. In each of these cases, the fundamental question is whether the promisee should be permitted to exploit his advantage to the detriment of the other party, or whether permitting him to do so will deprive the other party of the freedom that is necessary, from a libertarian point of view, to make his promise truly involuntary and therefore binding.

The term 'advantage-taking' is often used in a pejorative fashion, to refer to conduct we find morally objectionable or think the law should disallow. I mean the term to be understood in a broader sense, however, as including even those methods of gain the law allows and morality accepts (or perhaps even approves). In this broad sense, there is advantage-taking in every contractual exchange. Indeed, in mutually advantageous exchanges, there is advantage-taking by both parties. Suppose I have a cow you want, and you have a horse I want, and we agree to exchange our animals. The fact that you want my cow gives me an advantage I can exploit by insisting that you give me your horse in return. Your ownership of the horse gives you a symmetrical advantage over me. Each of us exploits the advantage we possess and—in this transaction at least—are both made better off as a result. This might seem to make my broad conception of advantage-taking empty or trivial. There is, however, an important reason for using the term in the unconventionally broad way that I do. By using the term to refer to *all* types of advantage-taking—those we tolerate as well as those we do not—attention is focused more sharply on the need to explain why the illicit methods of gain for which we normally reserve the term are thought to be objectionable.

In order to give meaningful content to the idea of voluntary exchange, a libertarian theory of contract law must provide an explanation of precisely this sort. However, although some principle or rule is needed as a basis for deciding which forms of advantage-taking should be allowed and which should not be, it is unclear what this principle or rule might be. Suppose, for example, that my neighbor threatens to shoot me unless I agree to buy his house. If there is one thing which must be treated as a condition for voluntary exchange, it is the absence of direct physical compulsion of the sort involved in this first case. But suppose that instead of threatening me with physical harm, the seller merely lies to me about the house—he tells me, for example, that water pipes inaccessibly buried beneath the basement are copper when in fact he knows them to be made of iron, an inferior material. Ought such advantage-taking be allowed? While it is possible to justify advantage-taking of this sort on the grounds that only physical coercion should be disallowed, there is no good reason for making *this* distinction the decisive one. Moreover, even if one fastens on the physical nature of the advantage-taking act, explicit misrepresentation can be characterized by saying that the misrepresentation is communicated by soundwaves which stimulate an auditory response in the listener which in turn provokes a neural change that causes him to sign the contract. This may be fanciful, but it suggests that with enough imagination any form of advantage-taking can be characterized as a physical intrusion, and the question of when such a characterization is appropriate cannot be answered by simply repeating that it is the physical nature of the act which makes it objectionable.

At this point, many will be tempted to acknowledge explicit misrepresentation as an illegitimate form of advantage-taking, but insist that the line be drawn there—limiting the conditions necessary for voluntary exchange to two (absense of physical coercion and fraud). Suppose, however, that the seller makes no threats and tells no lies, but does say things that, although true, are meant to encourage me to draw a false conclusion about the condition of the house and to inspect the premises less carefully than I might otherwise. (The seller tells me, for example, that the house has been inspected by an exterminator from the Acme Termite Company every six months for the last ten years, which is true, but neglects to inform me that during his last visit the exterminator discovered a termite infestation which the seller has failed to cure.) But telling me only certain things about the house, and not others, the seller intends to throw me off the track and thereby take advantage of my ignorance and naiveté. The same is true if he tells me nothing at all, but simply fails to reveal a defect he knows I am unaware of—a case of pure nondisclosure.

Should this last form of advantage-taking be allowed? At this point, undoubtedly, many will be inclined to say I have only myself to blame for drawing an incorrect inference from the seller's truthful representations and for failing to take precautionary measures such as having the house inspected by an expert. But why is this a good reason for holding me to my bargain here, but not in the previous cases as well? I can, for example, protect myself against the risk that I will be forced to sign a contract at gunpoint by hiring a bodyguard to accompany me wherever I go; and I can protect myself against the danger of explicit misrepresentation by requiring the other party to take a lie detector test or, more simply, by insisting that he warrant the house to be free of pests or any other possible defect that happens to concern me. Why isn't my failure to protect myself in these cases a good reason for enforcing the agreement I have made?

In attempting to sort out these various forms of advantage-taking, a number of distinctions suggest themselves—for example, the distinction between physical and non-physical advantage-taking, or between those forms of advantage-taking that can be prevented by the victim and those that cannot. None, however, provides a principled basis for determining which forms of advantage-taking ought to be allowed. Each can be interpreted in different ways, yielding different results, and the distinctions themselves provide no guidance in deciding which of the competing interpretations is the right one. An independent principle of some sort is required to determine the scope and relevance of these distinctions, and consequently it is that principle, whatever it might be, rather than the distinctions themselves that explains why we ought to allow some forms of advantage-taking but not others.

Some writers argue that the pursuit of 'freedom of contract' leaves so much room for manoevre that it is 'incoherent'.

'Distributive and Paternalist Motives in Contract and Tort Law' by Kennedy (1982) 41 Maryland LR 563, 580–583

3. The Critique of Freedom of Contract as Incoherent and Therefore Incapable of Determining Outcomes—The real problem with freedom of contract is that neither its principles, nor its principles supplemented by common moral understanding, nor its principles supplemented by historical practice, are definite enough to tell the decision maker what to do when asked to change or even just to elaborate the existing law of agreements. This is not to say the principles or the actual elaborated body of law have *no* meaning and no influence. Of course they have both. But of course there are also gaps, conflicts, and ambiguities, and in an area like that of the law of agreements the parties themselves will often have a motive for drafting themselves into these areas of uncertainty.

Confronted with a choice, the decision maker will have available two sets of stereotypical policy arguments. One 'altruist' set of arguments suggests that he should resolve the gap, conflict, or ambiguity by requiring a party who injures the other to pay compensation, and also that he should allow a liberal law of excuse when the injuring party claims to be somehow not really responsible. The other 'individualist' set of arguments emphasizes that the injured party should have looked out for himself, rather than demanding that the other renounce freedom of action, and that the party seeking excuse should have avoided binding himself to obligations he couldn't fulfill.

The arguments on each side take different forms—some are utilitarian, others appeal to rights or fairness, still others work by evoking stylized images of the social world, or by appealing to common moral sentiments, like self-sacrifice and self-reliance. Because the arguments are symmetrical, few in number, and repeated endlessly in different legal contexts, the legally sophisticated decision maker is unlikely to see them as *in themselves* powerful determinants of his own views about proper outcomes.

The experience of gaps, conflicts, and ambiguities within the institution of freedom of contract, and of the availability of two rhetorical modes for arguing about proper resolution of such situations, puts in question the whole structure of rules. Our decision maker has the power to modify the law of agreements as well as to specify it where there is doubt. The same problem of being 'unmoored' that exists when all agree the case is one of first impression exists as well whenever someone asks him to look at a *settled* rule as open to question and objection. There will be arguments in favor of changing the status quo in the direction of more altruism, and others in favor of restricting the range of duty to give actors more freedom. The system as a whole is radically undetermined, at least when viewed as the product of a rational decision process rather than of the brute facts of economic or social or political power.

We have seen already that through the constitutive exceptions for fraud, duress, incapacity and 'no intent to be bound,' the law of freedom of contract claimed to resolve basic issues of distribution and paternalism. Yet these constitutive exceptions refer ultimately to the abstract notion of voluntariness or freedom, which is among the most manipulable and internally contradictory in the legal repertoire. The historical treatment of the issues has produced a mass of conflicting precedents and ambiguous pseudo-resolutions. The flow of social and technological development means that new cases arise regularly, and the new cases may be very important in a practical way even if they seem to be about mere details of the law. It follows that even if he accepts without question that he should put into effect the distributive and paternalist outcome mandated by freedom of contract, the decision maker cannot do so, because the mandate is just too vague.

For example, without doing violence to the notion of voluntariness as it has been worked out in the law, the decision maker could adopt a hard-nosed, self-reliant, individualist posture that shrinks the defenses of fraud and duress almost to nothing. At the other extreme, he could require the slightly stronger or slightly better-informed party to give away all his advantage if he doesn't want to see the agreement invalidated when he tries to enforce it later. If we cut back the rules far enough, we would arrive at something like the state of nature—legalized theft. If we extended them far enough, we would jeopardize the enforceability of the whole range of bargains that define a mixed capitalist economy (capital/labor, business/consumer, and small/large business deals). In either extreme case, we would have departed from freedom of contract—the concept has some meaning and imposes some loose limits. But staying well within those limits, the decision maker's choices in the definition of voluntariness can have substantial distributive effect.

Take the case of fraud. When two parties are bargaining over the distribution of a transaction surplus, information is a crucial element of power, particularly information about the real properties of the commodity in question or about market circumstances affecting its value to others than the two involved. Suppose you know, but the buyer does not know, that the war has ended so that the value of your merchandise is almost certain to fall precipitously as peacetime trade is restored. Do you have to tell the other about the peace treaty? If so, you'll make less from the deal, and he'll make more, than if you could keep silent. Suppose the other party asks you outright if you have any news. Can you keep silent? Evade? Can you put out an advertisement quoting the war-time price 'because of current conditions,' when you know those conditions have ceased to exist?

One way to understand this issue is in terms of the extent of private property in information. As we push the law of fraud from caveat emptor to liability for concealment, then to liability for negligent failure to disclose, to liability for non-negligent failure to disclose and finally to a duty to generate the information as well as to share it, we are 'socializing' a resource. The result will be to reduce the bargaining power of one party vis-à-vis the other, and to change the distribution of transaction surplus between them. This will be the case whether or not the market is competitive. When we make sellers, for example, reveal information detrimental to their position, we reduce the demand for the product at any given price. As a result of having the new information, some people won't transact at all. Those who do transact will pay less now that they know more. All buyers regard themselves as better off with the information than they would be without it. Their new knowledge brings about a price reduction that directly reduces the welfare of sellers.

The decision maker might resolve issues of this kind without reference to the distributive consequences. He could try to determine, for example, the intrinsic fairness or morality of withholding information, without looking at the division of transaction surplus between the parties. Or he could do an analysis of property rights in information based on a theory of the 'original position' rather than on concern about the particular parties before him. There would be nothing irrational about such an approach. And it would be no more and no less consistent with freedom of contract than to undertake a careful analysis in terms of distributive objectives each time a rule came up for consideration. The demise of freedom of contract as a powerful, operative determinant of legal outcomes does not require the decision maker to embrace distributive motives. It merely permits him to do so without appearing to violate a basic institutional arrangement. The supposedly basic arrangement no longer tells him what to do one way or another.

This development has rendered obsolete the old debate between those who adored and those who abhorred the 'strict logic' of free contract. The social or collective principle that the opponents put forward as an alternative to contract turns out to have been well established *within* contract from the very beginning. It is possible, for example, to argue on the most technical grounds for strict scrutiny of the voluntariness of consumer agreements, and for compulsory terms and set prices wherever voluntariness is in doubt. If one takes this approach seriously, there is little of the reformers' program that can't be restated as the implementation of freedom of contract, rather than its displacement by a new regime.

We end with a piece that claims that a major purpose of the law of contract is to justify existing power relations within society.

'Contract law as ideology' by Gabel and Feinman, in The Politics of law (ed Kairys), chapter 8

The recent rise of right-wing forces in the United States has been brought about in large part through the shaping and manipulation of collective fantasies. Among the most powerful of these fantasies is a resurgence of what one might call the utopian imagery of freedom of contract . . .

For this resurgent ideology to enjoy a temporary measure of success, it makes no difference that it is based upon a lie. The truth is that those of us living in the United States today cannot actually achieve our desire for increased personal power, for freedom, and for genuine social connection and equality so long as we are trapped within ubiquitous hierarchies that leave us feeling powerless, alienated from one another, and stupefied by the routines of everyday activities . . .

A principal vehicle for the transmission of such ideological imagery has been and continues to be 'the law.' In order to understand the present and historical function of the legal system, and of contract law as a part of this system, one must grasp the relationship between the utopian images transmitted through legal ideas and the socioeconomic context that these ideas serve to justify. In this essay, we provide a brief introduction to a method for understanding this ideological power of law by tracing the relationship between the history of contract law and the development of capitalism over the last two hundred years.

CONTRACT LAW IN THE EIGHTEENTH CENTURY

Eighteenth-century contract law would be barely recognizable to the modern lawyer. The vision of eighteenth-century contract law was not the enforcement of private agreements but the implementation of customary practices and traditional norms. Indeed, in his *Commentaries on the Law of England*, written in the 1760s, Sir William Blackstone did not consider contracts to be a separate body of law at all.

In part, contracts was that portion of the law of property concerning the transfer of title to specific things from one person to another—the process by which 'my horse' became 'your horse.' . . .

In all types of contracts cases, the substantive fairness of the agreement or relation was subject to scrutiny by a lay jury applying community standards of justice. If a physician sued for his fee or a seller of goods for her price, the jury could decide that even an amount agreed to by the parties was excessive and inequitable, and so award a smaller sum instead.

Thus, eighteenth-century contract law was hostile to commercial enterprise. The traditional image of the world presented by contract law regarded the enforcement of market transactions as often illegitimate, so a seller could never be guaranteed the price he or she had bargained for, and liability might be imposed in the absence of agreement when required by popular notions of fairness. Such a system could exist because the development of a system of production founded upon universal competition in national and world markets had not yet fully emerged, and the political world-view that justified the relatively static property relations of traditional, pre-capitalist society had not yet been entirely overturned.

Between the latter part of the eighteenth century and the middle of the nineteenth century, both the economic and political foundations of eighteenth-century contract law were, in Marx's phrase, 'burst asunder.' In this period the system of economic and social relations known as free-market capitalism achieved a full development . . .

CONTRACT LAW IN THE NINETEENTH CENTURY

In the nineteenth century, the key changes in society were its split into capital-owning and nonowning classes, and the dissolution of traditional patterns of social relations . . .

The social meaning of work, property, and community were increasingly fragmented as socioeconomic processes based on competition and individual self-interest reorganized the social universe . . .

How could people have been persuaded or forced to accept such massive disruptions in their lives? One vehicle of persuasion was the law of contracts, which generated a new ideological imagery that sought to give legitimacy to the new order. To speak of 'ideological imagery' is to imply that there is a reality behind the image that is concealed and even denied by the image. The reality was the new system of oppressive and alienating economic and social relations. Contract law denied the nature of the system by creating an imagery that made the oppression and alienation appear to be the consequences of what the people themselves desired.

Denial and legitimation were accomplished by representing reality in ideal terms, as if things were the way they were because the people wished them to be so. This representation was not the product of conspiratorial manipulation by power-mad lawyers and judges. Instead, the legal elites tended to identify with the structure of the social and economic order because of what they perceived to be their privileged position within it, and they expressed the legitimacy of that structure when arguing and deciding cases in their professional roles. During this period important members of the bench and bar associated themselves emotionally and intellectually with the capitalist transformation and became imbued with the 'logic' of the new system. In arguing and deciding cases, they fit the situation presented within that logic to resolve the conflict represented by the dispute at issue. Those resolutions tended to legitimate the basic social relations, no matter how unjust, oppressive and alienating they actually were. In the process of resolving many cases, legal concepts were built up that embodied the new social relations. The result was a system of contract law that appeared to shape economic affairs according to normative principles but that was, in fact, only a recast form of the underlying socioeconomic relations.

The legitimating image of classical contract law in the nineteenth century was the ideal of free competition as the consequence of wholly voluntary interactions among many private persons, all of whom were in their nature free and equal to one another. From one point of view this was simple truth, for the practical meaning of the market system was that people conceived of as interchangeable productive units ('equality') had unfettered mobility ('freedom') in the market. From another point of view, however, this was denial and apology. It did not take account of the practical limitations on market freedom and equality arising from class position or unequal distribution of wealth. It also ignored other meanings of freedom and equality having to do with the realization of human spirit and potential through work and community. The legitimation of the free market was achieved by seizing upon a narrow economic notion of freedom and equality, and fusing it in the public mind with the genuine meaning . . .

The results in [some nineteenth century] cases may seem unfair or irrational today, but to the judges of the time they were neither. The courts could not easily have intervened to protect a party or to remedy unfairness without violating the ideological image that the source of social obligation rests only upon the bargain that the parties themselves have evinced, not upon the community's version of justice. This imagery, drawn as it was from the exigencies of competitive exchange, served to deny the oppressive character of the market and the lack of real personal liberty experienced by people in their private and work lives. Most important, it served to deny that there was a system at all that was coercively shaping and constricting the social world, because the imagery made it appear that this world was simply the perpetual realization of an infinite number of free choices made by an infinite number of voluntary actors.

CONTRACT LAW IN THE TWENTIETH CENTURY

Today judges applying contemporary contract law would probably reach different results in these cases . . .

Contemporary contract law views these cases differently not because twentieth-century judges are wiser or smarter than their nineteenth-century counterparts, or because a new and more equitable style of legal reasoning has somehow sprung into being through a progressive maturation of the judicial mind. The old rules disintegrated for the same reason they were conceived: there has been a transformation of social and economic life that has brought about a parallel transformation in the ideological imagery required to justify it.

The transformation from the nineteenth-century to the twentieth-century forms of American capitalism was the consequence of a variety of factors that can only be summarized here: competition among businesses produced ever larger concentrations of capital within fewer and fewer companies; workers organized in response to their collective dependence on these emerging monopolies and challenged in a revolutionary way the myths of freedom and equality; exploitation of the Third World, advancing technology, and efficient organization of production facilitated the partial assimilation of the American labor movement, allowing for the payment of higher wages while deflecting more radical labor demands; this increase in the level of wages, the use of part of the economic surplus for unemployment insurance, Social Security, and other types of welfare benefits, and the greater psychological control of consumer purchases through the mass media helped to alleviate the system's persistent tendency toward underconsumption. The basic requirement for understanding contemporary contract law is to look at the socioeconomic system thus produced and to observe its transformation, through the medium of law, into an imaginary construct that attempts to secure the system's appearance of legitimacy.

The essential characteristic of contemporary capitalism is the substitution of integration and coordination in the economy for the unbridled competition of the free market. Coordination is accomplished first by monopolistic corporations that are vertically and horizontally integrated (meaning there are but a few 'horizontal' corporations at the top of the major industries that own the capital that controls 'vertically' production and distribution in each industry); and second, by a massive involvement of the state in regulating and stabilizing the system. In place of the unrestricted mobility of productive units that characterized the operation of the market in the nineteenth century, we now have integration, coordination, and cooperation to above all maintain systemic stability through an ever more pervasive and efficient administration.

A brief look at the dominant American industry, the automobile industry, will illustrate. The industry is composed of three giant companies and one smaller firm, which account for three fourths of the vehicles sold annually. The firms are vertically integrated in fact. . . .

The rise of the coordinated economy has created a major problem for the law—how to transform the ideology of 'freedom and equality' and its adjunct, 'freedom of contract,' into a new image that might retain the legitimating power of the older images while modifying them to conform more closely to the actual organization of daily life in the era of monopoly capitalism. The strategy for solving this problem has been to transform contract law into a relatively uniform code for business transactions that is predominantly defined not by the individualist principle of unregulated free competition but by the more collective principle of competition regulated by trade custom. Since most 'trades' (whatever nostalgia for a bygone era that term may evoke) are actually integrated production networks subject to supervision by dominant firms, the modern law of contracts is able to retain the legitimating features of private agreement while effectuating the regulatory and stabilizing component that is a central principle of the contemporary economy . . .

[S]ometimes consumers and other parties with little economic power can be protected from the more outrageous excesses of economic predators. In sum, people are conceived to be partners in a moral community where equity and the balancing of interests according to standards of fair dealing have supplanted the primitive era, when every moral tie was dissolved in 'the icy waters of egotistical calculation.' And the state as passive enforcer of private transactions has become the state as active enforcer of the newly conceived notion of the general welfare.

CONCLUSION

. . . This is a very different explanation of the role of contract law from liberal or leftist instrumental analyses, which suggest that particular rules of law or particular results 'helped' capitalists by providing a framework for legal enforcement of market activity. Instrumental analyses of contract law confuse the role of direct force with the role of law in the development of sociohistorical processes. Social processes like 'free-market capitalism' do not get 'enforced' by 'laws.' Rather, these processes are accepted through social conditioning, through the collective internalization of practical norms that have their foundation in concrete socioeconomic reality. Since these norms are alienating and oppressive, the process of collective conditioning requires the constant threat of force and the occasional use of it. For example, if you fail to perform your part of a bargain, it *may* be the case that a sheriff with a gun will attach your bank account to pay the aggrieved party his or her damages. The occasional deployment of direct force serves to maintain the status quo as well as to get people to accept its legitimacy.

'The law' does not enforce anything, however, because the law is nothing but ideas and the images they signify. Its purpose is to justify practical norms (and in so doing to help constitute them by contributing to the collective conditioning process). One important way that this justification process occurs is through judicial opinions. Judicial opinions 'work' as ideology by a rhetorical process in which oppressive practical norms are encoded as 'general rules' with ideological content; these 'rules' then serve as the basis for a logic ('legal reasoning') that supposedly determines the outcome of the lawsuit. The key social function of the opinion, however, is not to be found in the outcome and the use of state power which may follow from it, but in the rhetorical structure of the opinion itself, in the legitimation of the practical norm that occurs through the application of it in the form of a 'legal rule.' That enforcement of bargains was much more likely to occur under nineteenth-century contract law than under eighteenth-century law is, of course true; but this does not mean that the function of nineteenth-century contract law was to 'enforce bargains.' The reverse expresses the truth more accurately—that the enforcement of bargains functioned to permit the elaboration of contract law as legitimating ideology.

The central point to understand from this is that contract law today constitutes an elaborate attempt to conceal what is going on in the world. . . .

Most of the time the socioeconomic system operates without any need for law as such because people at every level have been imbued with its inevitability and necessity. When the system breaks down and conflicts arise, a legal case comes into being. This is the 'moment' of legal ideology, the moment at which lawyers and judges in *their* narrow, functional roles seek to justify the normal functioning of the system by resolving the conflict through an idealized way of thinking about it.

But this also can be the moment for struggle against the narrow limits imposed in law on genuine values such as freedom, equality, moral community, and good faith. By questioning whether the legal system helps or hinders the actual realization of those values in a meaningful sense in everyday life, the critical approach permits us to expose the illegitimacy of the system and to explore the possibility of a different order of things.

Section 7
Changing the bargain

CHAPTER 27

Rescission, variation, waiver and promissory estoppel

(a) The setting

It is not surprising to find that with any contract running over a period of time, it is quite common for the parties to agree on some adjustment to the contract terms. Many contracts, particularly longer-term contracts, contain elaborate clauses providing for adjustment, and we shall look at some of these in the next chapter. However, we have seen already that a great deal of contracting takes place with a minimal degree of planning for future contingencies, even quite likely contingencies.

'Non-contractual relations in business' by Macaulay (see above p 301)

Some at least of the lack of planning is due to the difficulty of foreseeing in advance what problems may arise and what will be the most appropriate solutions; some is because the cost of agreeing mechanisms of adjustment does not seem worth incurring when the likelihood of the contingency is low. The latter would explain why adjustment mechanisms are much more common in longer-term contracts: see chapter 28.

As we saw in Section 4, a great deal of contract law is concerned with where the losses caused by such unplanned-for contingencies should fall. In some cases the parties will simply rely on the general law to settle their dispute. At a guess, however, it is equally or more common for a solution to be reached by an ad hoc ageement, and it is with these that this section is primarily concerned.

Adjusting for such contingencies is not the only reason why a contract may be renegotiated, however. An agreement running over a period of time may give a party the scope for 'opportunism', by taking advantage of the other's circumstances to threaten a breach of contract unless the deal is renegotiated in his favour. Frequently the opportunity for such extortion arises from the operation of the contract itself. Even if the parties met on an equal footing originally, when the time for performance draws near one party may be heavily dependent on the other: he may face serious losses if he does not get the other's performance and has nowhere that he can readily obtain a substitute. The old case of *Stilk v Myrick* (above, p 102) suggests the possibilities graphically, though it may be that the master's promise in that case was entirely voluntary (for an American case where the crew reached the fishing grounds and then refused to go on fishing unless their pay was increased see *Alaska Packers' Association v Domenico*, discussed below, p 601).

In the case where the contract is adjusted to deal with an unplanned-for contingency, the reasons for upholding or not upholding the contract modification clearly differ markedly from those in the extortion case. Until fairly recently, however, it has not been clear that English law would treat the two cases differently.

(b) Basic concepts

The traditional approach of English law was that for a renegotiation to be effective to change the contract terms in such a way that neither party could go back on the new agreement, there had to be all the elements which would be required if a fresh binding contract were being made—in other words, offer and acceptance, intention to create legal relations and consideration or a deed under seal. If these elements were present, the change was irrevocable; if they were not, it was of no effect. For the reasons suggested, this approach was too rigid to work satisfactorily, and there has been considerable departure from the traditional position. Some of this involves paying lip-service to the traditional rules but apparently distorting them, some the development of an alternative basis on which a promised change in the contract terms may become binding, through waiver or (what some think is indistinguishable) promissory estoppel. These developments lead to more changes in the contract terms becoming irrevocably binding, because neither a deed nor consideration for the promised change may be required. At the same time, however, it has been found that the traditional doctrine upholds changes that should not be enforced, and the doctrine of economic duress has developed to cope with this.

The starting point of any enquiry into whether the terms of a contract have effectively been changed remains: did the parties agree on the alleged change, and was their agreement made by deed or supported by consideration? If yes, it will be binding unless it can be upset on the ground of economic duress or any of the other grounds upon which contracts generally may be invalidated. If there was no consideration, the inquiry shifts to waiver/ promissory estoppel.

'Changes' in the contract may be divided into three types:

(1) *rescission*, where each party releases the other from liability to perform his outstanding obligations under the contract. Sometimes rescission involves each party returning benefits received under the contract, but an agreement simply to release outstanding obligations on each side will also operate as a rescission: in this case, it is sometimes called 'abandonment'. Rescission or abandonment requires agreement and consideration or a deed. It may be followed immediately by the making of a new contract ('rescission and replacement').

(2) *variation*, where the parties agree that the terms of the contract will be changed. It is sometimes said that an effective variation produces a permanent change in the contract terms, but this can be misleading, as sometimes the agreement is that the changed terms shall apply for a limited period only. Rather the point is that to be fully effective a variation requires agreement and consideration just like a fresh contract, and if these are present the variation cannot be withdrawn unilaterally by either party.

(3) *waiver*, in contrast, is where one party states or indicates by his conduct

that he will not exercise some remedy available to him under the contract, or will not insist on his full contractual rights, without there being any consideration for his promise. A purported variation that fails for want of consideration may also be treated as a waiver. As we shall see, even on the traditional view a waiver could have some interim effect, but it would not normally lead to an irrevocable loss of rights by the waiving party, because the waiver could be withdrawn. The doctrinal development referred to above has taken the form of limiting the circumstances in which withdrawal is permissible.

(c) Discharge or variation by contract

(i) Was there agreement?

The Hannah Blumenthal [1983] 1 All ER 34, House of Lords (above, p 168)

NOTE

In *Allied Marine Transport Ltd v Vale do Rio Navegacao SA, The Leonidas D* [1983] 3 All ER 737, at 741, Mustill J summarized the effect of the decision in *The Hannah Blumenthal* thus:

Principles
  Without going in great detail into matters which have already been thoroughly explored in previous cases, including those already cited, and *Birkett v James*, I believe that the relevant principles can now be summarised as follows.
  (1) An arbitration agreement creates mutual promises to submit to arbitration all disputes falling within the stated category, and to abide by the award of the arbitrator in respect of disputes actually referred to him.
  (2) On the happening of three successive events, viz (a) the making by one party of a claim falling within the arbitration agreement and (b) the invoking of the arbitration agreement in respect of the dispute raised by that claim and (c) the appointment of an arbitrator in respect of the dispute, there comes into existence a series of mutual contractual relationships between the parties inter se, and between each party and the arbitrator. I will for convenience refer to the group of relationships between the parties as 'the reference'.
  (3) As with any other bilateral contractual relationship, both the arbitration agreement and the reference are capable of discharge by consent.
  (4) The reference may be terminated by consent, leaving the arbitration agreement intact.
  (5) A consent to discharge the reference may be inferred from prolonged inactivity on both sides.
  (6) Discharge by consent inferred from inactivity may take place in two situations: (i) where each party conducts himself so as to evince to the other party an intention to treat the reference as ended; (ii) where the conduct of B is such as to lead A reasonably to believe that B intends to treat the reference as ended, and A alters his position in reliance on that belief. This second way of procuring a consensual discharge of the reference represents the important addition to the law brought about by the speeches in the House of Lords in *The Hannah Blumenthal* to which I have already referred.
  (7) In neither of these two situations is it material to examine the actual subjective belief and intention of B.
  (8) In situation (i), since the test is objective, it is necessary to look only at the conduct of each party actually brought to the notice of the other. But in situation (ii) the court must investigate the state of A's mind at the relevant time. The oral evidence of A will be admissible on this question. So also will be evidence of his actions at the time, even if these were not brought to the attention of B.

In *The Leonidas D*, the question was whether the parties had abandoned merely the reference to arbitration, or had abandoned the whole claim.

Mustill J held that the charterers, by commencing arbitation but then totally stopping, tacitly represented that they did not intend to pursue the claim, and the owners, whose response (with one exception, which the judge held was neutral) had been 'a complete blank', had accepted the tacit offer of abandonment. The Court of Appeal disagreed: neither offer and acceptance, nor a represenation, could be inferred from the parties' silence, which was equivocal (see above, p 182).

(ii) Rescission and replacement or variation?

There are a number of cases on the question of whether the parties intended to rescind the existing contract and replace it with a new one, or to vary the existing contract. Some involve the Statute of Frauds (see above, p 131). Under this a contract which was unenforceable unless evidenced in writing, could equally not effectively be varied unless the variation was also evidenced in writing; but it could be rescinded by a purely oral agreement. If the parties orally agreed to some alteration in the original contract, should the oral agreement be treated as an ineffective attempt to vary the contract, or as a rescission of it, so that the parties end up with no contract? An example of this problem is *Morris v Baron & Co* [1918] AC 1. A similar problem arose in *United Dominions Corpn (Jamaica) Ltd v Shoucair* [1969] 1 AC 340. The Moneylending Law of Jamaica provided that no contract for repayment of money lent and no security given was enforceable unless a memorandum in writing containing all the terms of the contract was signed by the borrower before the money was lent or the security given. The appellants had lent the respondent £55,000 on a mortgage, and later had written raising the interest on the loan from 9% to 11%. The respondent wrote acknowledging this, but later he defaulted, and the question was whether the original mortgage remained enforceable. The Privy Council adopted the approach used by the House of Lords in *Morris v Baron & Co*. Lord Devlin said (at p 348):

> . . . the view adopted by the House of Lords . . . is based on the intentions of the parties. They cannot have that which presumably they wanted, that is, the old agreement as amended; so the court has to make up its mind which comes nearer to their intention—to leave them with an unamended agreement or without any agreement at all . . . If the new agreement reveals an intention to rescind the old, the old goes; and if it does not, the old agreement remains in force and unamended.

It was held that the original mortgage remained in force.

(iii) Was there consideration?

There have been evident changes during the last 100 years in what will be recognised as consideration for a promise to change the terms of a contract. These changes do not make it easier to state the present law.

Foakes v Beer (1884) [1881–5] All ER Rep 106, House of Lords

The respondent brought an action against the appellant and obtained judgment for a specific sum. Later the parties made a written agreement by which they agreed that, in consideration of the appellant paying part of the sum due on signing the agreement and the remainder by equal half-yearly instalments, the respondent undertook not to take any proceedings on the judgment. The appellant paid all the instalments, and after the payment of the last one the respondent claimed interest from the date of the judgment. The House of Lords were divided on whether the agreement made amounted to a promise to forgo interest, but held that in any event such a promise would be unenforceable.

The Earl of Selborne LC . . . But the question remains whether the agreement is capable of being legally enforced. Not being under seal, it cannot be legally enforced against the respondent unless she received consideration for it from the appellant, or unless, though without consideration, it operates by way of accord and satisfaction, so as to extinguish the claim for interest. What is the consideration? On the face of the agreement none is expressed except a present payment of £500 on account and in part of the larger debt then due and payable by law under the judgment. The appellant did not contract to pay the future instalments of £150 each at the times therein mentioned; much less did he give any new security in the shape of negotiable paper, or in any other form. The promise de futuro was only that of the respondent, that, if the half-yearly payments of £150 each were regularly paid, she would 'take no proceedings whatever on the judgment'. No doubt, if the appellant had been under no antecedent obligation to pay the whole debt, his fulfilment of the condition might have imported some consideration on his part for that promise. But he was under that antecedent obligation; and payment at those deferred dates, by the forbearance and indulgence of the creditor, of the residue of the principal debt and costs could not, in my opinion, be a consideration for the relinquishment of interest and discharge of the judgment unless the payment of the £500 at the time of signing the agreement was such a consideration.

As to accord and satisfaction, in point of fact there could be no complete satisfaction so long as any future instalment remained payable; and I do not see how any new payments on account could operate in law as a satisfaction ad interim conditionally upon other payments being afterwards duly made, unless there was a consideration sufficient to support the agreement while still unexecuted. Nor was anything in fact done by the respondent in this case, on the receipt of the last payment, which could be tantamount to an acquittance, if the agreement did not previously bind her. The question, therefore, is nakedly raised by this appeal whether your Lordships are now prepared, not only to overrule as contrary to law the doctrine stated by Sir Edward Coke to have been laid down by all the judges of the Common Pleas in *Pinnel's Case* in 1602, and repeated in his note to Littleton, s 344 . . ., but to treat a prospective agreement, not under seal, for satisfaction of a debt by a series of payments on account to a total amount less than the whole debt, as binding in law, provided those payments are regularly made, the case not being one of a composition with a common debtor agreed to inter se by several creditors. . . .

The distinction between the effect of a deed under seal and that of an agreement by parol, or by writing not under seal, may seem arbitrary, but is established in our law; nor is it really unreasonable or practically inconvenient that the law should require particular solemnities to give to a gratuitous contract the force of a binding obligation. If the question be, as in the actual state of the law I think it is, whether consideration is or is not given in a case of this kind by the debtor who pays down part of the debt presently due from him, for a promise by the creditor to relinquish, after certain further payments on account, the residue of the debt, I cannot say that I think consideration is given, in the sense in which I have always understood that word as used in our law. It might be, and indeed I think it would be, an improvement in our law, if a release or acquittance of the whole debt on payment of any sum which the creditor might be content to receive by way of accord and satisfaction, though less than the whole, were held to be generally binding, though not under seal; nor should I be unwilling to see equal force given to a prospective agreement like the present, in writing, though not under seal; but I think it impossible, without refinements which practically alter the sense of the word, to treat such a release or acquittance as supported by any new consideration proceeding from the debtor.

All the authorities subsequent to *Cumber v Wane* which were relied upon by the appellant, such as *Sibree v Tripp*, *Curlewis v Clark*, and *Goddard v O'Brien*, have proceeded upon the distinction that, by giving negotiable paper or otherwise, there had been some new consideration for a new agreement, distinct from mere money payments in or towards discharge of the original liability. I think it unnecessary to go through those cases, or to examine the particular grounds upon which each of them was decided. There are no such facts in the case now before your Lordships. What is called 'any benefit, or even any legal possibility of benefit', in Mr Smith's notes to *Cumber v Wane* (1 Smith, LC, 8th edn, 366) is not, as I conceive, that sort of benefit which a creditor may derive from getting payment of part of the money due to him from a debtor who might otherwise keep him at arm's length, or possibly become insolvent, but is some independent benefit, actual or contingent, of a kind which in law might be a good and valuable consideration for any other sort of agreement not under seal. My conclusion is that the order appealed from should be affirmed and the appeal dismissed with costs and I so move your Lordships.

Lord Blackburn. . . . I think, therefore, that it is necessary to consider the ground on which the Court of Appeal based their judgment, and to say whether the agreement can be enforced. I construe it as accepting and taking £500 in satisfaction of the whole £2,090 19s, subject to the condition that, unless the balance of the principal debt was paid by the instalments, the whole might be enforced with interest. If instead of £500 in money it had been a horse valued at £500, or a promissory note for £500, the authorities are that it would have been a good satisfaction, but it is said to be otherwise as it was money. This is a question, I think, of difficulty. Lord Coke says (Co Litt 212 b):

'Where the condition is for payment of £20, the obligor or feoffor cannot at the time appointed pay a lesser sum in satisfaction of the whole, because it is apparent that a lesser sum of money cannot be a satisfaction of a greater. . . . If the obligor or feoffor pay a lesser sum, either before the day or at another place than is limited by the conditions, and the obligee or feofee receiveth it, this is a good satisfaction.'

For this he cites *Pinnel's Case*. That was an action on a bond for £16, conditional for the payment of £8 10s on Nov 11, 1600. Plea, that defendant, at plaintiff's request, before the said day, to wit, on Oct 1, paid to the plaintiff £5 2s 2d, which the plaintiff accepted in full satisfaction of the £8 10s. The plaintiff had judgment for the insufficient pleading. But, though this was so, Lord Coke reports that it was resolved by the whole Court of Common Pleas,

'that payment of a lesser sum on the day in satisfaction of a greater cannot be any satisfaction for the whole, because it appears to the judges that by no possibility a lesser sum can be a satisfaction to the plaintiff for a greater sum; but the gift of a horse, a hawk, or a robe, etc, in satisfaction is good, for it shall be intended that a horse, hawk, or robe might be more beneficial to the plaintiff than the money in respect of some circumstance, or otherwise the plaintiff would not have accepted of it in satisfaction. But when the whole sum is due, by no intendment the acceptance of a parcel can be a satisfaction to the plaintiff; but in the case at Bar it was resolved that the payment and acceptance of parcel before the day in satisfaction of the whole would be a good satisfaction in regard of circumstance of time; for peradventure parcel of it before the day would be more beneficial to him than the whole at the day, and the value of the satisfaction is not material; so if I am bound in £20 to pay you £10 at Westminster, and you request me to pay £5 at the day at York, and you will accept it in full satisfaction for the whole £10, it is a good satisfaction for the whole, for the expenses to pay it at York is sufficient satisfaction.'

There are two things here resolved. First, that where a matter paid and accepted in satisfaction of a debt certain might by any possibility be more beneficial to the creditor than his debt, the court will not inquire into the adequacy of the consideration. If the creditor, without any fraud, accepted it in satisfaction when it was not a sufficient satisfaction, it was his own fault; and that payment before the day might be more beneficial, and consequently that the plea was in substance good; and this must have been decided in the case. There is a second point stated to have been resolved, namely,

'that payment of a lesser sum on the day cannot be any satisfaction of the whole, because it appears to the judges that by no possibility a lesser sum can be a satisfaction to the plaintiff for a greater sum.'

This was certainly not necessary for the decision of the case; but, though the resolution of the Court of Common Pleas was only a dictum, it seems to me clear that Lord Coke deliberately adopted the dictum, and the great weight of his authority makes it necessary to be cautious before saying that what he deliberately adopted as law was a mistake, and though I cannot find that in any subsequent case this dictum has been made the ground of the decision, except in *Fitch v Sutton*, as to which I shall make some remarks later, and in *Down v Hatcher*, as to which Parke, B, in *Cooper v Parker* said, 'Whenever the question may arise as to whether *Down v Hatcher* is good law, I should have a great deal to say against it', yet there certainly are cases in which great judges have treated the dictum in *Pinnel's Case* as good law.

For instance, in *Sibree v Tripp*, Parke B, says (15 M & W at p 33):

'it is clear that if the claim be a liquidated and ascertained sum, payment of part cannot be satisfaction of the whole, although it may, under certain circumstances, be evidence of a gift of the remainder.'

Alderson, B, in the same case says (ibid at pp 37, 38):

'It is undoubtedly true that payment of a portion of a liquidated demand, in the same manner as the whole liquidated demand ought to be paid, is payment only in part, because it is not one bargain but two, viz., payment of part, and an agreement without consideration to give up the residue. The courts might very well have held the contrary, and have left the matter to the agreement of the parties, but undoubtedly the law is so settled.'

After such strong expressions of opinion, I doubt much whether any judge sitting in a court of first instance would be justified in treating the question as open. But, as this has very seldom, if at all, been the ground of the decision, even in a court of first instance, and certainly never been the ground of a decision in the Court of Exchequer Chamber, still less in this House, I did think it open to your Lordships' House to re-consider this question. Notwithstanding the very high authority of Lord Coke, I think it is not the fact that to accept prompt payment of a part only of a liquidated demand can never be more beneficial than to insist on payment of the whole. And if it be not the fact, it cannot be apparent to the judges. . . .

What principally weighs with me in thinking that Lord Coke made a mistake of fact is my conviction that all men of business, whether merchants or tradesmen, do every day recognise and act on the ground that prompt payment of a part of their demand may be more beneficial to them than it would be to insist on their rights and enforce payment of the whole. Even where the debtor is perfectly solvent, and sure to pay at last, this often is so. Where the credit of the debtor is doubtful it must be more so. I had persuaded myself that there was no such long-continued action on this dictum as to render it improper in this House to re-consider the question. I had written my reasons for so thinking; but, as they were not satisfactory to the other noble and learned Lords who heard the case, I do not now repeat them nor persist in them. I assent to the judgment proposed, though it is not that which I had originally thought proper.

[Lords Watson and Fitzgerald delivered concurring judgments.]

Appeal dismissed.

NOTES

1. A agrees to sell a widget to B for £100. Before delivery or payment the parties agree to cancel the contract. Is there consideration?
2. A agrees to sell a widget to B for £100, payment to be made within thirty days of delivery. After delivery but before payment they agree that the contract should be cancelled if B returns the widget, which he does. Is there consideration?
3. A agrees to sell a 'standard' widget to B for £100. Before delivery they agree that A will fit the widget with an extra gadget and B will pay £110. Is there consideration?
4. A agrees to sell a widget to B for delivery in six months' time, at £100 plus the percentage change recorded in the index of retail prices between the dates of contract and delivery. A week later they agree to change the price to a fixed price of £105. Is there consideration?
5. A agrees to sell a 'standard' widget to B for £100. Before delivery they agree that A will supply the widget fitted with a gadget at no extra charge. Is there consideration?
6. A agrees to sell B a basic model car for £6,000. Before delivery A agrees to supply a 'super deluxe' model at no extra charge. Is this an ineffective variation of the existing contract, or is the original contract rescinded and replaced by a new one?
7. How sensible is it to require consideration in a case like *Foakes v Beer*? Why was Lord Blackburn so hesitant in following *Pinnel's Case*? In

chapter 7 we examined the factors that might underly the requirement of consideration when a fresh contract is being made; how many of them apply when an existing contract is being changed?

'Consideration and Form' by Fuller (1941) 41 Col LR 799, 821

. . . [I]f we look at the problem now under discussion from the standpoint of the cautionary function of form it will be apparent that there is a difference between releasing a claim and creating a claim by a promise. The release of a claim, even if made orally, carries with it normally a sense of deprivation which is lacking in the case of a promise. Where words have this effect, where they tend to produce a psychological wrench on the speaker, they satisfy the desideratum of inducing deliberation as well as a writing or a seal.

In fact a number of exceptions to the rule in *Foakes v Beer* have grown up. One, that there would be consideration if the creditor accepted a cheque or negotiable instrument for less than the amount of the debt, is discussed further in *D & C Builders Ltd v Rees* (below, p 599). A second is that if the holder of a bill of exchange or promissory note (see below, p 835) at or after its maturity, writes unconditionally renouncing his rights against any person liable on it, the latter is discharged (Bills of Exchange Act 1882, s 62). A third is referred to by the Lord Chancellor in his judgment: if a debtor enters a composition agreement with his creditors, whereby he agrees to pay each of them a proportion of what is due, no creditor can later turn round and sue the debtor for the balance of the debt: *Goods v Cheesman* (1831) 2 B & Ad 328. It is hard to see that there is any consideration in this case if there is none when a single creditor agrees to accept party payment in full satisfaction. A fourth exception is that if the creditor agrees to accept payment from a third party in discharge of the debt, he cannot sue the debtor for the balance. This was applied in *Hirachand Punamchand v Temple* [1911] 2 KB 330. Lieutenant Temple had given the plaintiffs a promissory note in exchange for money lent. His father offered them a draft for a lesser amount in full satisfaction, and they accepted it. The Court of Appeal held that they could not recover the balance from Lieutenant Temple. Three separate explanations seem to be given: (1) the promissory note became extinct, just as if the creditor had renounced it; (2) there was a binding contract between the creditor and the father that the creditor would not sue the son, and it would be an abuse of the process of the court to permit the creditor to sue (compare *Snelling v John G Snelling Ltd*, below, p 828); (3) it would be fraud on the father to bring an action for the debt. The last resort at least looks pretty fictitious: it is not normally fraud to change your mind and break your promise.

Stilk v Myrick (above, p 102)

Williams v Roffey Bros & Nicholls (Contractors) Ltd (above, p 103)

NOTES

1. It seems that *Foakes v Beer* was not cited in *Williams v Roffey Bros* and the two cases may be distinguished on the ground that a promise to release part of a debt is different from promising to pay more for performance of an existing contractual obligation. But if the House of Lords had adopted the same approach as the majority of the Court of

Appeal in *Williams v Roffey Bros*, do you think Mrs Beer would have been bound by her promise? Would you need to know any extra facts in order to decide?

2. Whatever the present state of the 'existing contractual duty' rule, the cases which follow were decided on the basis that a promise to release part of a debt if the debtor pays the rest is made without consideration, unless one of the exceptions noted above applies.

D & C Builders Ltd v Rees [1966] 2 QB 617, Court of Appeal

The plaintiffs were a two-man firm of jobbing builders, who had done work on the defendant's premises. The account for this came to some £732, of which the defendant had paid only £250. The plaintiffs were facing bankruptcy if they were not paid the balance, but the defendant's wife, who was acting for him, refused to pay more than £300, alleging that the workmanship was bad. Because of their financial straits, which the defendant's wife allegedly knew about, the plaintiffs reluctantly accepted a cheque for £300, marked 'in completion of account'. They later brought an action for the balance. On a preliminary issue of whether there was a binding settlement, the trial judge held that there was not, and the defendant appealed.

Danckwerts LJ. . . . *Foakes v Beer*, applying the decision in *Pinnel's Case* settled definitely the rule of law that payment of a lesser sum than the amount of a debt due cannot be a satisfaction of the debt, unless there is some benefit to the creditor added so that there is an accord and satisfaction.

In *Foakes v Beer*, Lord Selborne, while approving *Cumber v Wane*, did not overrule the cases which appear to differ from *Cumber v Wane*, saying:

'All the authorities subsequent to *Cumber v Wane*, which were relied upon by the appellant at your Lordships' Bar (such as *Sibree v Tripp, Curlewis v Clark* and *Goddard v O'Brien*) have proceeded upon the distinction, that, by giving negotiable paper or otherwise there had been some new consideration for a new agreement, distinct from mere money payments in or towards discharge of the original liability.'

Lord Selborne was distinguishing those cases before the House.

But the giving of a cheque of the debtor for a smaller amount than the sum due is very different from 'the gift of a horse, hawk, or robe, etc' mentioned in *Pinnel's Case*. I accept that the cheque of some other person than the debtor, in appropriate circumstances, may be the basis of an accord and satisfaction, but I cannot see how in the year 1965 the debtor's own cheque for a smaller sum can be better than payment of the whole amount of the debt in cash. The cheque is only conditional payment, it may be difficult to cash, or it may be returned by the bank with the letters 'RD' [Refer to Drawer] upon it, unpaid. I think that *Goddard v O'Brien*, either was wrongly decided or should not be followed in the circumstances of today.

I agree also that, in the circumstances of the present case, there was no true accord. The Rees really behaved very badly. They knew of the plaintiffs' financial difficulties and used their awkward situation to intimidate them. The plaintiffs did not wish to accept the sum of £300 in discharge of the debt of £482, but were desperate to get some money. It would appear also that the defendant and his wife misled the plaintiffs as to their own financial position. Rees, in his evidence, said: 'In June (1964) I could have paid £700 odd. I could have settled the whole bill'. There is no evidence that by August, or even by November, their financial situation had deteriorated so that they could not pay the £482.

In my view the county court judge was right in applying the rule in *Foakes v Beer*, and I would dismiss the appeal.

[Winn LJ delivered a concurring judgment.]

Appeal dismissed.

(Lord Denning decided this case on a different ground: extracts from his judgment are printed below, p 608).

'Gratuitous promises in economics and law' by Posner (1977) 6 JLS 411, at 421–424

(NB Posner is discussing US law, which is different to English law in this area, but the economic ideas are still relevant.)

E. Contract modification

Often it is possible for a party to make a binding promise, unsupported by any fresh consideration, to modify a term of an existing contract. For example, the payor in a construction contract might agree to pay a higher price to a builder who had encountered unexpected soil conditions. The motives for such promises are various: to gain a reputation for 'fair dealing' (really risk sharing), to avoid driving the promisee into bankruptcy (which might prevent his completing performance or raise the cost of his doing so), or even to be altruistic (the contingency giving rise to modification may have dramatically altered the relative wealth position of the parties). In any event, the stakes are often substantial in such cases, while the increment in utility to the promisor may also be substantial because of the length of time over which optimal performance may extend.

Consider the example of the house purchaser who promises the builder a higher than contract price because the builder has encountered some unexpected difficulty which may make it impossible to complete the contract at the agreed price. If the purchaser merely declares his intention of paying the builder a higher price, but is free to renege, the builder may decide not to complete performance but instead to take his chances in bankruptcy court. Yet the promisor dare not pay him the extra price in advance in exchange for the builder's promise to continue, for if the contractor is financially shaky for other reasons, the prepayment may end up in the hands of a trustee in bankruptcy, with the purchaser relegated to the status of an unsecured creditor. This is a clear case where the enforcement of a promise not supported by fresh consideration enhances the welfare of the promisor.

The facts of a real case upholding enforceability of such a promise, *Goebel v Linn*, are rather similar to those of the last example. The defendants were brewers who had a contract with the plaintiff in the case, an ice company, to supply them with ice at a price not to exceed $2 a ton. An unusually mild winter ruined the local ice 'crop' and the ice company informed the defendants that it would not continue to supply them with ice at the contract price. The defendants had a large stock of beer on hand that would spoil without refrigeration, and therefore agreed to pay the ice company $3.50 to continue the supply of ice under the contract. The defendants later repudiated the agreement and the ice company sued. In upholding the plaintiff's claim, the court observed that the defendants

> 'chose for reasons which they must have deemed sufficient at the time to submit to the company's demand and pay the increased price rather than rely upon their strict rights under the existing contract. . . . Suppose, for example, the defendants had satisfied themselves that the ice company under the very extraordinary circumstances of the entire failure of the local crop of ice must be ruined if their existing contracts were to be insisted upon, and must be utterly unable to respond in damages; it is plain that then, whether they chose to rely upon their contract or not, it could have been of little or no value to them. Unexpected and extraordinary circumstances had rendered the contract worthless; and they must make a new arrangement, or, in insisting on holding the ice company to the existing contract, they would ruin the ice company and thereby at the same time ruin themselves.'

The result in this case has been criticized on the ground that it exposes promisees to extortion. In economic terms, the making of a contract may confer on the seller a monopoly vis-à-vis the buyer which the seller can exploit by threatening to terminate the contract unless the buyer agrees to pay a higher price than originally agreed upon. The court in *Goebel* was aware of this danger but found that the ice company's claim was not extortionate in this case. This raises the question, however, whether extortion can be given a meaningful definition in the modification setting. To answer this question, it is helpful to distinguish three situations in which modification might be sought:

1. Nothing has changed since the contract was made, but the promisor, realizing that the remedies for breach of contract would not fully compensate the promisee, gives the promisee the unhappy choice of either paying the promisor more to complete the contract or pursuing his legal remedies.

2. Something has changed since the contract signing: the promisee has given up alternative sources of supply or otherwise increased his dependence on the promisor. If modification is permitted the promisor can extract a monopoly rent from the promisee.

3. Something has changed since the contract signing: an unexpected event which, as in *Goebel v Linn*, prevents the (willing) promisor from completing the promised performance without a modification of the contract.

The third case is the clearest for allowing modification. The inability of a willing promisor to complete performance removes the factor of strategic behavior that is present in cases one and two. No exploitation of a monopoly position or of the inadequacy of contractual remedies is involved in allowing modification in the third case. The first case might also seem one where modification should be allowed, on the basis of Holmes's 'bad man' theory of contract law which has close affinities with the economic approach. The legal obligation of a promisor is to perform or pay damages. If the promisee wants more—wants in effect specific performance— he must pay extra for it. That is all that *seems* to be involved in the first case but if we pause to ask why the promisee in the first case would ever agree to pay extra, we shall see that the first case is in reality a version of the second, the monopoly case. If the promisee in the first case has equally good alternative sources of supply, or at least no worse than he had when he made the original contract, he will have no incentive to pay a premium above the contract price for the promisor to perform as agreed; he will allow the promisor to breach and turn elsewhere. He will pay the premium only if his dependence on the promisor has increased since the signing of the contract, ie, only if the contract gave the promisor a monopoly position vis-à-vis the promisee.

Alaska Packers' Ass'n v Domenico was such a case. The plaintiffs (technically 'libelants') hired out as sailors and fishermen to the defendant (appellant), but soon after beginning work stopped and threatened to quit unless their wages were raised above the agreed amount. Defendant's agent agreed to pay the higher wage demanded but defendant later reneged. The court refused to enforce the modified contract, noting that

> 'the libelants agreed in writing, for a certain stated compensation, to render their services to the appellant in remote waters where the season for conducting fishing operations is extremely short, and in which enterprise the appellant had a large amount of money invested; and, after having entered upon the discharge of their contract, and at a time when it was impossible for the appellant to secure other men in their places, the libelants, without any valid cause, absolutely refused to continue the services they were under contract to perform unless the appellant would consent to pay them more money.'

This seems a clear case where the motive for the modification was simply to exploit a monopoly position conferred on the promisors by the circumstances of the contract. It might seem that the promisee would have been in even worse shape if the men had quit as they threatened to do. However, since their only motive for threatening to quit was to extract a higher wage, there was probably little danger of their actually quitting. The danger would have been truly negligible had they known that they could not extract an enforceable commitment to pay them a higher wage.

The court in *Alaska Packers'* criticized the earlier result in *Goebel v Linn*, yet the cases are readily distinguishable, with the help of economic analysis. In *Goebel*, without a modification the promisor might well have terminated the contract, so the modification conferred a real benefit on the promisee. But in *Alaska Packers'* the likelihood of termination was much less since the threat to terminate was not a response to external conditions genuinely impairing the promisor's ability to honor the contract but merely a strategic ploy designed to exploit a monopoly position. A firm rule of nonenforceability in such cases solves the monopoly problem and thereby facilitates the making of contractual arrangements in which the promisee will be dependent on the good faith of the promisor.

One can relate this distinction back to the basic theme of this paper by noting that one effect of enforcing the kind of modification attempted in the *Alaska Packers'* case would be to reduce the benefits of contracting to people in the same situation as the plaintiffs in that case. Seamen thereafter could not expect to be promised a high wage in exchange for agreeing to work for a stated period at that wage, since the employer would know that the seamen were not obliged to honor their promise but could at any time 'hold him up' for a higher wage. In a different form, this is the same problem as that of the man who derives little value from promising a future gift because the promise is not binding on him.

An intermediate case between the involuntary threat to terminate (*Goebel v Linn*) and the monopolistic (*Alaska Packers' Ass'n v Domenico*) is that of a promisor who threatens to terminate only because a third party has offered him a higher price for his goods. Because the higher price is a genuine opportunity cost of continued compliance with the contract, the promisor should be allowed to terminate subject only to his obligation to make good the promisee's loss from the breach, and hence he should be allowed to negotiate with the promisee over a modification that will compensate the promisor for the lost opportunity. This was the result in *Schwartzreich v Bauman-Basch, Inc.*

In the cases presented so far the problem has been whether there was any consideration for the creditor's promise to accept less than was due in full satisfaction, and it is clear that in some of the cases at least the requirement of consideration operated to protect the creditor from extortion. Needless to say, the presence of consideration does not indicate the absence of extortion by the debtor. True, a debtor bent on extortion may not commonly make any concession to the creditor in return—but what if he does, perhaps because he is advised to do so? It is to deal with this problem that the doctrine of economic duress has been developed. We will consider it in Section 8.

As Posner suggests, however, there are situations where it makes perfectly good sense to enforce the creditor's promise even though it was made without consideration (though below, p 616, it is argued that it may not be sensible to enforce modifications as readily as Posner suggests). One situation which might seem worthy is where the debtor acts in reliance on the creditor's promise, as in the case of *Jorden v Money* which we looked at in chapter 7 (above, p 136). There the debtor pleaded estoppel, but the plea failed because the creditor had not made any representation of fact, only a promise. You will remember that Atiyah has argued that in the nineteenth century an otherwise gratuitous promise which had been relied on would be treated as having been made for good consideration, and that *Money* only failed because the resulting contract was unenforceable under the Statue of Frauds (see above, p 149). Whether this thesis is correct or not, the modern law appears to be that the act must have been expressly or impliedly requested by the promisor for it to constitute consideration: *Combe v Combe* (above, p 139).

You will also remember that in the *High Trees* case Denning J suggested a new principle that would make a gratuitous promise binding if it was intended to be and was acted on. *Combe* held that this could not create new obligations where none had existed before, but left open the possibility that the principle might apply to gratuitous promises to give up existing contractual or other rights. It is to this that we now turn. One of the sources from which Denning derived his doctrine was a line of cases on waiver.

(d) Waiver

An example of waiver is provided by *Hickman v Haynes* (1875) LR 10 CP 598. The buyer of a quantity of iron under a written contract (at that time the contract had to be evidenced in writing as the goods were worth more than £10, see above, p 131) orally requested the seller to defer delivery, which the seller did; but after protracted delays on the buyer's part, the seller brought an action for non-delivery. The buyer argued that he was not liable because there had only been an ineffective oral variation of the original contract, and the seller had not tendered delivery at the proper time, but the court not surprisingly rejected this. The buyer had asked for extra time, and could not complain that the seller had not delivered on the original date; and the damages should be assessed by the date at which the seller terminated the contract.

Charles Rickards Ltd v Oppenheim [1950] 1 All ER 420, Court of Appeal

The defendant had agreed to buy a Rolls-Royce chassis, which was to be fitted with a coach-built body and delivered to him by 20 March 1948. The car was not delivered on time, but the defendant pressed for delivery. On 29 June the defendant gave notice that if the car was not delivered within four weeks he would not accept it. The car was ready in October, and the defendant refused to take it.

Denning LJ. . . . . It is clear on the findings of the judge that there was an initial stipulation making time of the essence of the contract between the plaintiffs and the defendant, namely, that it was to be completed 'in six, or, at the most, seven months'. Counsel for the plaintiffs did not seek to disturb that finding—indeed, he could not successfully have done so—but he said that that stipulation was waived. His argument was that, the stipulated time having been waived, the time became at large, and that thereupon the plaintiffs' only obligation was to deliver within a reasonable time. He said that, in accordance with well-known authorities, 'a reasonable time' meant a reasonable time in the circumstances as they actually existed, ie, that the plaintiffs would not exceed a reasonable time if they were prevented from delivering by causes outside their control, such as strikes or the impossibility of getting parts, and so forth, and that, on the evidence in this case, it could not be said that a reasonable time was in that sense exceeded. He cited the well-known words of Lord Watson in *Hick v Raymond and Reid* to support the view that in this case, on the evidence, a reasonable time had not been exceeded. If this had been originally a contract without any stipulation in regard to time, and, therefore, with only the implication of reasonable time, it may be that the plaintiffs could have said that they had fulfilled the contract, but, in my opinion, the case is very different when there was an initial contract, making time of the essence, of 'six or, at the most, seven months'. I agree that that initial time was waived by reason of the requests for delivery which the defendant made after March, 1948, and that, if delivery had been tendered in compliance with those requests, the defendant could not have refused to accept. Supposing, for instance, delivery had been tendered in April, May, or June, 1948, the defendant would have had no answer. It would be true that the plaintiffs could not aver and prove that they were ready and willing to deliver in accordance with the original contract. They would have had, in effect, to rely on the waiver almost as a cause of action. At one time there would have been theoretical difficulties about their doing that. It would be said that there was no consideration, or, if the contract was for the sale of goods, that there was nothing in writing to support the variation. *Plevins v Downing*, coupled with what was said in *Besseler, Waechter Glover & Co v South Derwent Coal Co Ltd* gave rise to a good deal of difficulty on that score, but all those difficulties are swept away now. If the defendant, as he did, led the plaintiffs to believe that he would not insist on the stipulation as to time, and that, if they carried out the work, he would accept it, and they did it, he could not afterwards set up the stipulation in regard to time against them. Whether it be called waiver or forbearance on his part, or an agreed variation or substituted performance, does not matter. It is a kind of estoppel. By his conduct he made a promise not to insist on his strict legal rights. That promise was intended to be binding, intended to be acted on, and was, in fact, acted on. He cannot afterwards go back on it. That, I think, follows from *Panoutsos v Raymond Hadley Corpn of New York*, a decision of this court, and it was also anticipated in *Bruner v Moore*. It is a particular application of the principle which I endeavoured to state in *Central London Property Trust, Ltd v High Trees House, Ltd.*

Therefore, if the matter stopped there, the plaintiffs could have said that, notwithstanding that more than seven months had elapsed, the defendant was bound to accept, but the matter does not stop there, because delivery was not given in compliance with the requests of the defendant. Time and time again the defendant pressed for delivery, time and time again he was assured that he would have early delivery, but he never got satisfaction, and eventually at the end of June he gave notice saying that, unless the car was delivered by July 25, he would not accept it. The question thus arises whether he was entitled to give such a notice, making time of the essence, and that is the question which counsel for the plaintiffs has argued before us. He agrees that, if this is a contract for the sale of goods, the defendant could give such a notice. He accepted the statement of McCardie, J in *Hartley v Hymans*, as accurately stating the law in regard to the sale of goods, but he said that that statement did not apply to contracts for work and labour. He said that no notice making time of the essence could be given in regard to contracts for work and labour. The judge thought that the contract was one for the sale of goods, but, in my view, it is unnecessary to determine whether it was a contract for the sale of goods or a contract for work and labour, because, whichever it was, the defendant was entitled to give a notice bringing the matter to a head. It would be most unreasonable if, having been lenient and having waived the initial expressed time, he should thereby have prevented himself from ever thereafter insisting on reasonably quick delivery. In my judgment, he was entitled to give a reasonable notice making time of the essence of the matter. Adequate protection to the suppliers is given by the requirement that the notice should be reasonable.

The next question, therefore, is: Was this a reasonable notice? Counsel for the plaintiffs argued that it was not. He said that a reasonable notice must give sufficient time for the work then outstanding to be completed, and that, on the evidence in this case, four weeks was not a reasonable time because it would, and did, in fact, require three and a half months to complete it. In my opinion, however, the words of Lord Parker of Waddington in *Stickney v Keeble* apply to such a case as the present, just as much as they do to a contract for the sale of land. Lord Parker said . . .:

'In considering whether the time so limited is a reasonable time the court will consider all the circumstances of the case. No doubt what remains to be done at the date of the notice is of importance, but it is by no means the only relevant fact. The fact that the purchaser has continually been pressing for completion, or has before given similar notices which he has waived, or that it is specially important to him to obtain early completion, are equally relevant facts . . .'

To that statement I would add, in the present case, the fact that the original contract made time of the essence. In this case, not only did the defendant press continually for delivery, not only was he given promises of speedy delivery, but, on the very day before he gave the notice, he was told by the sub-contractors' manager, who was in charge of the work, that it would be ready within two weeks. He than gave a four weeks' notice. The judge found that it was a reasonable notice and, in my judgment, there is no ground on which this court could in any way differ from that finding. The reasonableness of the notice must, of course, be judged at the time at which it is given. It cannot be held to be a bad notice because, after it is given, the suppliers find themselves in unanticipated difficulties in making delivery.

The notice of June 29, 1948, was, therefore, a perfectly good notice so as to make time of the essence of the contract.

[Singleton LJ delivered a concurring judgment, Bucknill LJ concurred.]

Appeal dismissed.

NOTES

1. Although Denning LJ cites *High Trees*, the decision in the *Charles Rickards* case does not depend on that case: it follows dicta in *Panoutsos v Raymond Hadley Corpn* [1917] 2 KB 473.
2. If the car had been delivered on 1 April the buyer would have had to accept it: *Panoutsos*.
3. Did the buyer waive his *right* to prompt delivery, or only his *remedy* of termination? If he had received and accepted the car on 1 April, could he have recovered damages for late delivery?

Hughes v Metropolitan Railway Company (1877) 2 App Cas 439, House of Lords

Under a lease the tenant was obliged to repair the premises. The landlord was entitled to give the tenant six months notice to carry out any repairs and, if the tenant failed to do the repairs within that time, to forfeit the lease. The landlord served a notice, but the tenant commenced negotiations to sell the lease to the landlord, stating that in the meantime it would not commence the repairs. The negotiations broke down, and when a few days later the six months expired the landlord claimed that the lease was forfeited. The Court of Appeal, reversing the court below, held that the plaintiff's action of ejectment should be stayed.

Lord Cairns LC. . . . It was not argued at your Lordship's Bar, and it could not be argued, that there was any right of a Court of Equity, or any practice of a Court of Equity, to give relief in cases of this kind, by way of mercy, or by way merely of saving property from forfeiture, but it is the first principle upon which all Courts of Equity proceed, that if parties who have entered into definite and distinct terms involving certain legal results—certain penalties or legal forfeiture—afterwards by their own act or with their own consent enter upon a course of negotiation which has the effect of leading one of the parties to suppose that the strict rights arising under the contract will not be enforced, or will be kept in suspense, or held in abeyance, the person who otherwise might have enforced those rights will not be allowed to enforce them where it would be inequitable having regard to the dealings which have thus taken place between the parties. My Lords, I repeat that I attribute to the Appellant no intention here to take advantage of, to lay a trap for, or to lull into false security those with whom he was dealing; but it appears to me that both parties by entering upon the negotiation which they entered upon, made it an inequitable thing that the exact period of six months dating from the month of October should afterwards be measured out as against the Respondents as the period during which the repairs must be executed.

I therefore propose to your Lordships that the decree which is appealed against should be affirmed, and the present appeal dismissed with costs.

Lord Selborne . . . I think the consequence is that which Lord Justice Baggallay derives from it. He says that the circumstances 'were of a character to lead the company to consider that the notice to repair was at any rate suspended for some period of time', at least until the 31st of December. What is the meaning, in the view of a Court of Equity, of suspending a notice to repair? Manifestly that during that time the notice is not to be operative. What is the reasonable result of that in the circumstances of this case? Why, when the notice is to become operative, the same will be a reasonable time for the execution of the repairs which would have been a reasonable time if the notice had been given at that period, that is, six months from at least the 31st of December, 1874.

[Lords Blackburn and O'Hagan delivered concurring judgments; Lord Gordon concurred.]

Appeal dismissed.

NOTES

1. Do you see any inconsistency between this decision and either *Jorden v Money* or *Foakes v Beer*?
2. Is Lord Cairns' statement of 'the first principle upon which all courts of equity proceed' *ratio*, in the sense of being no broader than was necessary for the decision?
3. In *Birmingham and District Land Co v London and North Western Rly Co* (1888) 40 ChD 268 a building lease was determinable if the tenant had not built on the land by 30 November 1885. As a railway bill affecting the land was pending, the landlord told the tenant to put off building, and the land had not been built on when the railway later acquired the land subject to the lease. Its argument that the tenant had lost his interest in the land through non-building was rejected. Lord Justices Cotton and Lindley simply applied Lord Cairns' statement. Bowen LJ said:

Now, it was suggested by Mr Clare that that proposition only applied to cases where penal rights in the nature of fortfeiture, or analogous to those of forfeiture, were sought to be enforced. I entirely fail to see any such possible distinction. The principle has nothing to do with forfeiture. It is a principle which lies outside forfeiture, and everything connected with forfeiture, as will be seen in a moment of reflection. It was applied in *Hughes v Metropolitan Railway Company* in a case in which equity could not relieve against forfeiture upon the mere ground that it was a forfeiture, but could interfere only because there had been something in the nature of acquiescence, or negotiations between the parties, which made it inequitable to allow the forfeiture to be enforced. The truth is that the proposition is wider than cases of forfeiture. It seems to me to amount to this, that if persons who have contractual rights against others induce by their conduct those against whom they have such rights to believe that such rights will either not be enforced or will be kept in suspense or abeyance for some particular time, those persons will not be allowed by a Court of Equity to enforce the rights until such time has elapsed, without all events placing the parties in the same position as they were before. That is the principle to be applied. I will not say it is not a principle that was recognised by Courts of Law as well as of Equity. It is not necessary to consider how far it was always a principle of common law. Applying that principle to the facts here, I think nobody can come to any but one conclusion, viz, that Mr Boulton (and the railway company took subject to his liabilities) had induced the Plaintiff company reasonably to believe that time would not run against them as regards the building agreements, and that he would not enforce his rights as regards time for building, until a reasonable period had elapsed after they should have received notice from him. As soon as the railway company served notice to treat the reasonable time it seems to me necessarily began to run.

What did he mean by saying that the proposition is wider than cases of forfeiture?

Central London Property Trust Ltd v High Trees House Ltd (above, p 137)

NOTES

1. Is the obiter dictum that the rent was reduced to £1,250 during the war consistent with *Foakes v Beer*?
2. Do the *Hughes* and *Birmingham* cases support the dictum? What was being waived in those cases? In *High Trees*?

Combe v Combe (above, p 139)

NOTES

1. Is this case saying that the *High Trees* principle cannot be used by a plaintiff? Suppose the landlord company had threatened to evict the tenant company during the war on the ground that the full rent had not been paid: could the tenant have obtained an injunction to prevent it? If so, when can the *High Trees* principle be relied on? (See the argument of the sellers in *The Post Chaser*, noted below p 612, that the buyers' failure to live up to its representation entitled them to damages. This argument failed for other reasons.)
2. Thus it seems that if an employer promises to let a builder off some of the work the builder had promised to do, without reducing the price, the doctrine of promissory estoppel might apply; but not if the employer promises to pay the builder 10% extra for completing the original work. In *Williams v Roffey Bros* (above, p 103) it was not argued that promissory estoppel applied, but Russell LJ said:

I would have welcomed the development of argument, if it could have been properly raised in this court, on the basis that there was here an estoppel and that the defendants, in the circumstances prevailing, were precluded from raising the defence that their promise to pay the extra £10,300 was not binding.

In contrast, Glidewell LJ said:

. . . the application of the doctrine of promissory estoppel to facts such as those of the present case has not yet been fully developed: see eg the judgment of Lloyd J in *The Proodos C* [1981] 3 All ER 189 at 191.

In *Tool Metal Manufacturing Co Ltd v Tungsten Electric Co Ltd* [1955] 2 All ER 657, HL, TMMC had granted TECO a licence to deal with patented hard metal alloys. The licence commenced in 1937 and was to continue until

1947, subject to determination by either party on six months' notice. TECO were to pay a royalty on any similar material it used not supplied by TMMC, and by clause 5 they were also to pay 'compensation' if the amount of such material used by them in any month exceeded a named quota. The compensation was to be at 30% of the net value of the excess material. During the war TMMC voluntarily agreed in the national interest to forego compensation and accept a flat royalty of 10%, it being contemplated that some new agreement, possibly not including compensation, should be entered after the war. No compensation was paid after the end of 1939. In 1944 TMMC submitted a draft agreement with a compensation provision to TECO, which rejected it; and in 1945 TECO brought an action against TMMC for fraud and breach of contract, alleging that it had been agreed that no compensation should be payable after 1939. In March 1945 TMMC counterclaimed for compensation from June 1945, though not for the period 1940–May 1945.

The Court of Appeal held, affirming on this point the judgment of Devlin J (1952) 69 RPC 108, that there was no contract to end compensation, only a temporary arrangement to suspend its payment pending a new agreement. This arrangement could not be terminated without reasonable notice and (allowing the appeal on this point) reasonable notice had not been given: the presentation of the draft agreement was not sufficient. Somervell LJ dropped the hint that nine months might be sufficient notice, and accordingly TMMC commenced another action claiming compensation as from 1 January 1947, relying on the delivery of the counterclaim in the first action as reasonable notice.

In the second action the House of Lords held that the delivery of the counterclaim was sufficient notice to enable TMMC to claim compensation payments once more. The decision was confined, however, to that point: because of the principle of res judicata it was not open to the House to reopen the first decision of the Court of Appeal, even if it thought the decision had been wrong. Lord Tucker said (at p 674):

> . . . the parties to the present action are estopped from disputing the correctness of the decision of the Court of Appeal in the first action to the effect that circumstances existed which gave rise to the application of the equitable principle in *Hughes v Metropolitan Rly Co* and that no sufficient intimation to terminate the period of suspension of payment had been given prior to the counterclaim in that action, but it would be wrong, in my opinion, if the view were to prevail that your Lordships in the present case are tacitly accepting the correctness of that decision.

Further discussion will be found in Gordon [1963] CLJ 222; Wilson [1965] CLJ 93.

E A Ajayi v R T Briscoe (Nigeria) Ltd [1964] 3 All ER 556, Privy Council

The owners had let some lorries on hire-purchase to the defendant, who had experienced difficulty in getting them serviced. The owners consented (in a letter dated 22 July) to the defendant 'withholding instalments due [on the lorries] as long as they are withdrawn from active service'. The owners later sued to recover the instalments due, and on appeal the defendant pleaded promissory estoppel. The Privy Council held that this did not defeat the owners' claim, as the defendant had not proved that the lorries remained unavailable for use after they had been repaired.

Lord Hodson. . . . The hire-purchaser's final contention was that having altered his position in the manner indicated the owners never gave notice that the period of suspension was at an end before issuing their summons and that accordingly the lorries never having been returned or made available for service he was entitled to rely on the equitable defence as defined by Bowen LJ in the *Birmingham and District Land Co* case. Alternatively he went further and contended on the authority of the cases of *Central London Property Trust, Ltd v High Trees House, Ltd* and *Combe v Combe* that the promise given by the letter of 22 July was irrevocable unless the lorries were made available for service and that, since this never happened, the owners cannot enforce their claim.

Their lordships are of opinion that the principle of law as defined by Bowen LJ has been confirmed by the House of Lords in the case of the *Tool Metal Manufacturing Co, Ltd v Tungsten Electric Co, Ltd*, where the authorities were reviewed, and no encouragement was given to the view that the principle was capable of extension so as to create rights in the promisee for which he had given no consideration. The principle, which has been described as quasi estoppel and perhaps more aptly as promissory estoppel, is that when one party to a contract in the absence of fresh consideration agrees not to enforce his rights an equity will be raised in favour of the other party. This equity is, however, subject to the qualification (a) that the other party has altered his position, (b) that the promisor can resile from his promise on giving reasonable notice, which need not be a formal notice, giving the promisee a reasonable opportunity of resuming his position, (c) the promise only becomes final and irrevocable if the promisee cannot resume his position.

. . . It would not be just to the owners to remit the matter either for a new trial or for a decision to be given at this late stage on facts which have not been expressly found. Their lordships agree with the Federal Supreme Court in thinking that an application to that end should be rejected, especially as the defence sought to be raised is of a suspensory or delaying nature and not of itself decisive to defeat the owners' claim for all time.

[Lord Morris of Borth-y-Gest and Lord Guest concurred.]

Appeal dismissed.

NOTES

1. What does 'resile from his promise' mean? Can the creditor ultimately get all that was originally due to him?
2. In this case the promise made by the creditor was only that the debtor could *defer* paying some instalments, not that he need not make them at all.

D & C Builders Ltd v Rees (For the facts and the judgments of the majority, see above, p 599)

Lord Denning MR concurred in holding that the cheque had been accepted only as conditional payment, and continued:

. . . in point of law payment of a lesser sum, whether by cash or by cheque, is no discharge of a greater sum.

This doctrine of the common law has come under heavy fire . . . The harshness of the common law has been relieved . . . [he quoted Lord Cairns in *Hughes v Metropolitan Rly Co* and continued]:

It is worth noticing that the principle may be applied, not only so as to suspend strict legal rights, but also so as to preclude the enforcement of them . . .

In applying this principle, however, we must note the qualification: The creditor is only barred from his legal rights when it would be *inequitable* for him to insist upon them. Where there has been a *true accord*, under which the creditor voluntarily agrees to accept a lesser sum in satisfaction, and the debtor *acts upon* that accord by paying the lesser sum and the creditor accepts it, then it is inequitable for the creditor afterwards to insist on the balance. But he is not bound unless there has been truly an accord between them.

In the present case, on the facts as found by the judge, it seems to me that there was no true accord. The debtor's wife held the creditor to ransom. . . .

In my opinion there is no reason in law or equity why the creditor should not enforce the full amount of the debt due to him. I would, therefore, dismiss this appeal.

NOTES

1. To what extent is the rule put forward in this judgment different from that Denning suggested in *High Trees* itself?
2. Is Denning correct to say that the earlier decisions cover precluding the creditor from ever enforcing his rights?

W J Alan & Co Ltd v El Nasr Export and Import Co [1972] 2 All ER 127, Court of Appeal

The sellers made two contracts for the sale of coffee to the buyers, shipment in the first to be in September/October and in the second October/November, at 262 shillings Kenyan per cwt. Payment was to be by confirmed irrevocable letter of credit in Kenyan shillings. The credit opened was not in accordance with the contract in that it was opened in sterling, which was then at parity with Kenyan currency, and was valid only until 5 October. Nonetheless the sellers drew on the credit for the shipment under the first contract, and for another shipment of part of the second contract quantity, and negotiated for the credit to be extended to cover shipment of the remainder in November. The second shipment was made on 16 November, and the sellers prepared an invoice made out in sterling. Before they had presented this to the bank, sterling was devalued on 18 November. The sellers presented the invoice and were paid in sterling, but they claimed the difference between what they were paid and the original contract price for the quantity of the last shipment in Kenyan shillings, which had not been devalued.

Lord Denning MR. . . .

Variation or waiver

All that I have said so far relates to a 'conforming' letter of credit; that is, one which is in accordance with the stipulations in the contract of sale. But in many cases—and our present case is one—the letter of credit does not conform. Then negotiations may take place as a result of which the letter of credit is modified so as to be satisfactory to the seller. Alternatively, the seller may be content to accept the letter of credit as satisfactory, as it is, without modification. Once this happens, then the letter of credit is to be regarded as if it were a conforming letter of credit. It will rank accordingly as conditional payment.

There are two cases on this subject. One is *Panoutsos v Raymond Hadley Corpn of New York*, but the facts are only to be found fully set out in Commercial Cases. The other is *Enrico Furst & Co v W E Fischer Ltd*. In each of those cases the letter of credit did not conform to the contract of sale. In each case the non-conformity was in that it was not a confirmed credit. But the sellers took no objection to the letter of credit on that score. On the contrary, they asked for the letter of credit to be extended; and it was extended. In each case the seller sought afterwards to cancel the contract on the ground that the letter of credit was not in conformity with the contract. In each case the court held that they could not do so.

What is the true basis of those decisions? Is it a variation of the original contract or a waiver of the strict rights thereunder or a promissory estoppel precluding the seller from insisting on his strict rights or what else? In *Enrico Furst* Diplock J said it was a 'classic case of waiver'. I agree with him. It is an instance of the general principle which was first enunciated by Lord Cairns LC in *Hughes v Metropolitan Railway Co*, and rescued from oblivion by *Central London Property Trust Ltd v High Trees House Ltd*. The principle is much wider than waiver itself; but waiver is a good instance of its application. The principle of waiver is simply this: if one party, by his conduct, leads another to believe that the strict rights arising under the contract will not be insisted on, intending that the other should act on that belief, and he does act on it, then the first party will not afterwards be allowed to insist on the strict legal rights when it would be inequitable for him to do so: see *Plasticmoda Societa Per Azioni v Davidsons (Manchester) Ltd.* There may be no consideration moving from him who benefits by the waiver. There may be no detriment to him by acting on it. There may be nothing in writing. Nevertheless, the one who waives his strict rights cannot afterwards insist on them. His strict rights are at any rate suspended so long as the waiver lasts. He may on occasion be able to revert to his strict legal rights for the future by giving reasonable notice in that behalf, or otherwise making it plain by his conduct that he will thereafter insist on them: see *Tool Metal Manufacturing Co Ltd v Tungsten Electric Co Ltd.* But there are cases where no withdrawal is possible. It may be too late to withdraw; or it cannot be done without injustice to the other party. In that event he is bound by his waiver. He will not be allowed to revert to his strict legal rights. He can only enforce them subject to the waiver he has made.

Instances of these principles are ready to hand in contracts for the sale of goods. A seller may, by his conduct, lead the buyer to believe that he is not insisting on the stipulated time for exercising an option: see *Bruner v Moore.* A buyer may, by requesting delivery, lead the seller to believe that he is not insisting on the contractual time for delivery: see *Charles Rickards Ltd v Oppenheim.* A seller may, by his conduct, lead the buyer to believe that he will not insist on a confirmed letter of credit: see *Plasticmoda,* but will accept an unconfirmed one instead: see *Panoutsos v Raymond Hadley Corpn of New York* and *Enrico Furst v Fischer.* A seller may accept a less sum for his goods than the contracted price, thus inducing him to believe that he will not enforce payment of the balance: see *Central London Property Trust Ltd v High Trees House Ltd* and *D & C Builders Ltd v Rees.* In none of these cases does the party who acts on the belief suffer any detriment. It is not a detriment, but a benefit to him, to have an extension of time or to pay less, or as the case may be. Nevertheless, he has conducted his affairs on the basis that he has that benefit and it would not be equitable now to deprive him of it.

The judge rejected this doctrine because, he said, 'there is no evidence of the [buyers] having acted to their detriment'. I know that it has been suggested in some quarters that there must be detriment. But I can find no support for it in the authorities cited by the judge. The nearest approach to it is the statement of Viscount Simonds in the *Tool Metal* case that the other must have been led 'to alter his position', which was adopted by Lord Hodson in *Emmanuel Ayodeji Ajayi v R T Briscoe (Nigeria) Ltd.* But that only means that he must have been led to act differently from what he otherwise would have done. And, if you study the cases in which the doctrine has been applied, you will see that all that is required is that the one should have '*acted* on the belief induced by the other party'. That is how Lord Cohen put it in the *Tool Metal* case, and is how I would put it myself.

The judge also rejected the doctrine because of something which was said in the recent case of *Woodhouse v Nigerian Produce Marketing Co Ltd* about estoppel; but no question of waiver arose there; no question of letters of credit; or anything of that kind. It has no application here and neither counsel relied in any way on it before us.

Conclusion

Applying the principle here, it seems to me that the sellers, by their conduct, waived the right to have payment by means of a letter of credit in Kenyan currency and accepted instead a letter of credit in sterling. It was, when given, conditional payment; with the result that, on being duly honoured (as it was) the payment was no longer conditional. It became absolute, and dated back to the time when the letter of credit was given and acted on. The sellers have, therefore, received payment of the price and cannot recover more.

Megaw LJ. . . . The first issue is whether in the original contract, the contract of 13 July 1967, the money of account was initially Kenyan currency or sterling. To my mind, Orr J was right, for the reasons given by him, in holding that when that contract was made the money of account was Kenyan. The fact that it was expressed in a form which was appropriate for Kenyan currency and was not appropriate for sterling must outweigh, and far outweigh, the various indications relied on by the buyers as pointing to sterling. However, in my judgment the currency of account was subsequently varied from Kenyan currency to sterling. That being so, the sellers have been paid the full amount to which they are entitled and they have no valid claim against the buyers.

The contract of sale contained its own express provision for payment, which I have already quoted in full. I repeat the essential words: 'Payment: by confirmed, irrevocable letter of credit . . .' There is nothing else in the contract, at least in its express terms, which adds to, subtracts from, or qualifies that contractual provision as to payment of the price. It was the buyers' obligation to procure that a bank should offer to the sellers its confirmation of an irrevocable credit which would provide for payment of the contract price as specified in the contract of sale, against delivery to the bank of the proper documents.

The offer made by the confirming bank, as I have already said, did not comply, in several respects, with what the sellers were entitled to require. However, the only non-conforming aspect of the offer which I regard as relevant for the purposes of this appeal is the term of the offer in respect of currency. That, in my view, is not only relevant, it is vital. The confirming bank's offer, made to the sellers with the knowledge of, and on the instructions of, the buyers, was an offer which involved sterling, not merely as the currency of payment, but as the currency of account, in respect of that transaction. The sellers accepted the conforming bank's offer, including its terms as to currency, by submitting invoices and drafts with the form and contents which I have already described.

As I see it, the necessary consequence of that offer and acceptance of a sterling credit is that the original term of the contract of sale as to the money of account was varied from Kenyan currency to sterling. The payment, and the sole payment, stipulated by the contract of sale was by the letter of credit. The buyers, through the confirming bank, had opened a letter of credit which did not conform, because it provided sterling as the money of account. The sellers accepted that offer by making use of the credit to receive payment for a part of the contractual goods. By that acceptance, as the sellers must be deemed to have known, not only did the confirming bank become irrevocably bound by the terms of the offer (and by no other terms), but so also did the buyers become bound. Not only did they incur legal obligations as a result of the sellers' acceptance—for example, an obligation to indemnify the bank—but also the buyers could not thereafter have turned round and said to the sellers (for example, if Kenyan currency had been devalued against sterling) that the bank would thereafter pay less for the contractual goods than the promised sterling payment of £262 per ton. If the buyers could not revert unilaterally to the original currency of account, once they had offered a variation which had been accepted by conduct, neither could the sellers so revert. The contract had been varied in that respect.

The sellers, however, contend that they were, indeed, entitled to make use of the non-conforming letter of credit offered to them, without impairing their rights for the future under the original terms of the contract, if and when they chose to revert. They seek to rely on the analogy of a sale of goods contract where the goods are deliverable by instalments, and one instalment falls short of the prescribed quality. The buyer is not obliged, even if in law he could do so, to treat the contract as repudiated. He is not, it is said, even obliged to complain. But he is in no way precluded from insisting that for future instalments of the goods the seller shall conform with the precise terms of the contract as to quality. That is not, in my opinion, a true analogy. The relevant transaction here is not one of instalments. It is a once-for-all transaction. It is the establishment of a credit which is to cover the whole of the payment for the whole of the contract. Once it has been accepted by the sellers, the bank is committed, and is committed in accordance with its accepted terms, and no other terms. Once the credit is established and accepted it is unalterable, except with the consent of all the parties concerned, all of whose legal rights and liabilities have necessarily been affected by the establishment of the credit. Hence the sellers cannot escape from the consequences of the acceptance of the offered credit by any argument that their apparent acceptance involved merely a temporary acquiescence which they could revoke or abandon at will, or on giving notice. It was an acceptance which, once made, related to the totality of the letter of credit transaction; and the letter of credit transaction was, by the contract of sale, the one and only contractual provision for payment. When the letter of credit was accepted as a transaction in sterling as the currency of account, the price under the sale of contract could not remain as Kenyan currency.

For the buyers it was submitted further that, if there were not here a variation of the contract, there was at least a waiver, which the sellers could not, or did not properly revoke. I do not propose to go into that submission at any length. On analysis, it covers much the same field as the question of variation. In my view, if there were no variation, the buyers would still be entitled to succeed on the ground of waiver. The relevant principle is, in my opinion, that which was stated by Lord Cairns LC in *Hughes v Metropolitan Railway Co*. The acceptance by the sellers of the sterling credit was, as I have said, a once-for-all acceptance. It was not a concession for a specified period of time or one which the sellers could operate as long as they chose and thereafter unilaterally abrogate; any more than the buyers would have been entitled to alter the terms of the credit or to have demanded a refund from the sellers if, after this credit had been partly used, the relative values of the currencies had changed in the opposite way. . . .

Stephenson LJ. I agree that this appeal succeeds on the second point of variation or waiver for reasons which I shall state in my own words, although they add little or nothing to what Lord Denning MR and Megaw LJ have already said.

The currency of account fixed by the contract of sale was clearly Kenya shillings and not sterling. I agree with the judge in attaching importance to the use of the abbreviation 'Shs', recognised as denoting Kenya shillings by the schedule to the Central Bank of Kenya Act 1966. It stamps Kenya on the contract as the money of account almost as 'schillings' would stamp Austria on it. Unlike the judge, I also attach importance to the presumption created by s 21 of the same Act, which does not seem to me to have been displaced by the agreement between buyers and sellers.

The letter of credit varied the currency of account in the events that happened from Kenya shillings to pounds sterling . . .

By not objecting to the non-conforming letter of credit, by obtaining payment on it in sterling from the bank and by extending it the sellers clearly accepted and agreed to it and were treated as having done so not only by the bank but by the buyers, who may be presumed (although there was no evidence about it) to have paid charges and incurred liabilities such as a liability to indemnify the bank. The sellers never indicated any reservations about the change from Kenya shillings to pounds sterling or asked for any adjustment, probably for the simple reason that they considered sterling as good as Kenya shillings if not better. When after devaluation of sterling they invoiced the balance of the goods against part payment of the balance of the price and claimed the difference created by devaluation from the buyers, they were attempting to assert a liability which, whether by variation or waiver, they had allowed the buyers to alter.

I agree also with the views expressed by Lord Denning MR on the first point that this confirmed irrevocable letter of credit operated as a conditional payment of the price which, when honoured, discharged the buyers' debt to the sellers. And I agree further that this would in the ordinary way be the effect of such a letter of credit being issued and accepted by the seller in performance of a contract of sale which does not stipulate expressly or impliedly that its issue and acceptance should have a different effect. But on the second point I would leave open the question whether the action of the other party induced by the party who 'waives' his contractual rights can be any alteration of his position, as Lord Denning MR has said, or must, as the judge thought, be an alteration to his detriment, or for the worse, in some sense. In this case the buyers did, I think, contrary to the judge's view, act to their detriment on the sellers' waiver, if that is what it was, and the contract was varied for good consideration, which may be another way of saying the same thing; so that I need not, and do not, express a concluded opinion on that controversial question.

Appeal allowed.

NOTES

1. The majority said there was a binding variation in this case. What was the consideration?

2. Does the Court of Appeal accept the *High Trees* principle as good law? With what qualifications, if any?

3. Was there any detrimental reliance on the representation in *Hughes* or *Birmingham*? See the definition of detrimental reliance given by Dixon J in *Grundt's* case, above, p 135. What would the tenants in *Hughes* or *Birmingham* have done if the landlords had not made the representations they did? If the landlords were now allowed to enforce their original rights, would the tenants be in the same position as before the representations had not been made, or worse off? What about in *High Trees*?

4. In *Société Italo-Belge pour le Commerce et l'Industrie SA v Palm and Vegetable Oils (Malaysia) Sdn Bhd, The Post Chaser* [1982] 1 All ER 19 the sellers of a quantity of palm oil were obliged to make a declaration of which ship was carrying the oil. They made the declaration out of time, but the buyers made no protest: instead they requested the sellers to hand the shipping documents to sub-buyers. However, when two days later the sub-buyers rejected the documents, the buyers in turn rejected them the same day, and the sellers were forced to sell the oil elsewhere at a loss. The sellers did not argue that the buyers by taking the documents had

elected to accept them in performance (cf above, p 460); they accepted that the buyers' rejection was effective. But they argued that the buyers had represented that they would not exercise their right of rejection and that doing so later was a breach of contract for which the sellers were entitled to damages. Robert Goff J said (pp 26–27):

> I approach the matter as follows. The fundamental principle is that stated by Lord Cairns LC, viz that the representor will not be allowed to enforce his rights 'where it would be inequitable having regard to the dealings which have thus taken place between the parties.' To establish such inequity, it is not necessary to show detriment; indeed, the representee may have benefited from the representation, and yet it may be inequitable, at least without reasonable notice, for the representor to enforce his legal rights. Take the facts of *Central London Property Trust Ltd v High Trees House Ltd*, the case in which Denning J breathed new life into the doctrine of equitable estoppel. The representation was by a lessor to the effect that he would be content to accept a reduced rent. In such a case, although the lessee has benefited from the reduction in rent, it may well be inequitable for the lessor to insist on his legal right to the unpaid rent, because the lessee has conducted his affairs on the basis that he would only have to pay rent at the lower rate; and a court might well think it right to conclude that only after reasonable notice could the lessor return to charging rent at the higher rate specified in the lease. Furthermore it would be open to the court, in any particular case, to infer from the circumstances of the case that the representee must have conducted his affairs in such a way that it would be inequitable for the representor to enforce his rights, or to do so without reasonable notice. But it does not follow that in every case in which the representee has acted, or failed to act, in reliance on the representation, it will be inequitable for the representor to enforce his rights for the nature of the action, or inaction, may be insufficient to give rise to the equity, in which event a necessary requirement stated by Lord Cairns LC for the application of the doctrine would not have been fulfilled.
>
> This, in my judgment, is the principle which I have to apply in the present case. Here, all that happened was that the sellers, through Kievit, presented the documents on the same day as the buyers made their representation; and within two days the documents were rejected. Now on these simple facts, although it is plain that the sellers did actively rely on the buyers' representation, and did conduct their affairs in reliance on it, by presenting the documents, I cannot see anything which would render it inequitable for the buyers thereafter to enforce their legal right to reject the documents. In particular, having regard to the very short time which elapsed between the date of the representation and the date of presentation of the documents on the one hand and the date of rejection on the other hand, I cannot see that, in the absence of any evidence that the sellers' position had been prejudiced by reason of their action in reliance on the representation, it is possible to infer that they suffered any such prejudice. In these circumstances, a necessary element for the application of the doctrine of equitable estoppel is lacking; and I decide this point in favour of the buyers.

5. *Should* the debtor have to prove detrimental reliance? Sometimes detrimental reliance seems the factor that justifies holding the creditor to his or her promise, (compare *Jorden v Money*, above, p 136); but not always. If the concession is properly viewed as an attempt by the parties to deal with a situation that was not provided for in the original contract, it should be regarded as an extension of the original agreement—the original contract did not provide for all eventualities, now one of the gaps has been filled in by the parties themselves. The original agreement was enforceable as soon as made, without either party having to rely to his detriment on it: why shouldn't the same be true of the supplementary agreement?

6. It may be hard for the debtor to show exactly how it has relied on the promise to its detriment when 'it has conducted its affairs on the basis that it would only have to pay rent at the lower rate', as Robert Goff J put it. Is the point that detriment is presumed after a significant period of time has elapsed? (Compare Fuller's argument about proving reliance, above, p 562 ff.)

7. *Woodhouse AC Israel Cocoa Ltd SA v Nigerian Produce Marketing Co Ltd* [1972] AC 741 was another case involving the devaluation of sterling, but here the House of Lords held that the sellers could claim the sterling equivalent of the original contract price, which had been expressed in Nigerian pounds: the sellers had said that 'payment may be made in pounds sterling in London or in £N in Lagos', but that was a statement only that they would accept *payment* in sterling of the sterling equivalent of the price calculated in Nigerian pounds. Even if the statement was ambiguous, to found a promissory estoppel there had to be a clear and unequivocal representation. Lord Hailsham said:

> Counsel for the appellants was asked whether he knew of any case in which an ambiguous statement had ever formed the basis of a purely promissory estoppel, as contended for here, as distinct from estoppel of a more familiar type based on factual misrepresentation. He candidly replied that he did not. I do not find this surprising, since it would really be an astonishing thing if, in the case of a genuine misunderstanding as to the meaning of an offer, the offeree could obtain by means of the doctrine of promissory estoppel something that he must fail to obtain under the conventional law of contract. I share the feeling of incredulity expressed by Lord Denning MR in the course of his judgment when he said:
>
> > 'If the judge be right, it leads to this extraordinary consequence: a letter which is not sufficient to *vary* a contract is, nevertheless, sufficient to work an *estoppel*, which will have the same effect as a *variation*'.
>
> There seem to me to be so many and such conclusive reasons for dismissing this appeal that it may be thought a work of supererogation to add yet another. But basically I feel convinced that there was never here any real room for the doctrine of estoppel at all. If the exchange letter was not variation, I believe it was nothing. The appellants asked for a variation in the mode of discharge of a contract of sale. If the proposal meant what they claimed, and was accepted and acted on, I venture to think that the respondents would have been bound by their acceptance at least until they gave reasonable notice to terminate, and I imagine that a modern court would have found no difficulty in discovering consideration for such a promise. Businessmen know their own business best even when they appear to grant an indulgence, and in the present case I do not think that there would have been insuperable difficulty in spelling out consideration from the earlier correspondence. If, however, the two letters were insufficiently unambiguous and precise to form the basis, if accepted, for a variation in the contract I do not think their combined effect is sufficiently unambiguous or precise to form the basis of an estoppel which would produce the result of reducing the purchase price by no less than 14 per cent against a vendor who had never consciously agreed to the proposition.
>
> I desire to add that the time may soon come when the whole sequence of cases based on promissory estoppel since the war, beginning with *Central London Property Trust Ltd v High Trees House Ltd*, may need to be reviewed and reduced to a coherent body of doctrine by the courts. I do not mean to say that any are to be regarded with suspicion. But, as is common with an expanding doctrine, they do raise problems of coherent exposition which have never been systematically explored. However this may be, we are not in a position to carry out this exploration here and in the present proceedings. It is sufficient to say here that, for the reasons I have given above, I would dismiss this appeal with costs.

8. It is interesting to contrast this insistence that a clear promise (or at least an unambiguous representation) is needed for promissory estoppel with the cases on proprietary estoppel, in which something less clear seems to suffice: see above, p 144.

9. Could an explanation be that in promissory estoppel the promise itself may be taken to have affected the promisor's right to revert to the original state of affairs, unless any reliance by the promisee is disproved (as in *The Post Chaser*); but that a proprietary estoppel only comes into play when it is shown that the other party has acted to its detriment on the representation, so that the courts are less insistent that the representation be a clear one?

In *Brikom Investments Ltd v Carr* [1979] 2 All ER 753 the landlords of four blocks of flats offered to sell 99-year leases to their sitting tenants. At the time the roofs of each block were in need of repair and the landlords made oral representations to the tenants that the landlords would repair the roofs at their own expense. The leases which were subsequently signed provided that the tenants would contribute to maintenance expenses incurred by the landlords. The landlords had the roofs repaired and then claimed contributions from the tenants (in some cases the assignees of the original tenants who had been given the assurances), who refused to pay. The Court of Appeal upheld the judgment of the county court that the landlords' claim should be dismissed. All three members of the court agreed that the landlord's assurance amounted to a collateral contract with each tenant. The assignees were also protected as after the first day in the county court the original tenants who had assigned their leases had also assigned the benefits of any collateral contract to their successors.

However the main ground on which Lord Denning MR rested his judgment was that both the original tenants and their assignees could rely on promissory estoppel. Roskill LJ refused to decide the case on promissory estoppel but held that, in addition to the collateral contract, both original tenants and assignees were protected by what he described as 'a plain waiver by the landlords of their right to claim the cost of these repairs from these tenants'. He said:

I do not rest my decision on any question of promissory estoppel; and I do not think it necessary on the facts of this case to investigate the jurisprudential basis of that doctrine in order to arrive at which I conceive to be the right decision. It is necessary to do no more than to apply that which was said by the House of Lords and especially by Lord Cairns LC in *Hughes v Metropolitan Railway Co.*

I adopt what was said by Sir Alexander Turner in the third edition of *Spencer Bower on Estoppel* [3rd edn, 1977, pp 383, para 349] . . . I would respectfully add to that that it would be wrong to extend the doctrine of promissory estoppel, whatever its precise limits at the present day, to the extent of abolishing in this back-handed way the doctrine of consideration . . .

It seems to me in the present case that counsel for the tenants' argument (in so far as it rests on promissory estoppel) involves taking that doctrine a great deal further than it has hitherto been taken.

. . .

I think it necessary to go no further than what Lord Cairns LC said in *Hughes v Metropolitan Railway Co* where the matter was put not as one of promissory estoppel but as a matter of contract law or equity (call it which you will):

[Roskill LJ quoted an extract from the judgment of Lord Cairns (see above, p 605) and continued:]

For my own part, I would respectfully prefer to regard that as an illustration of contractual variation of strict contractual rights. But it could equally well be put as an illustration of equity relieving from the consequences of strict adherence to the letter of the lease.

But, whichever is the right way of putting it, ever since *Hughes v Metropolitan Railway Co*, through a long line of cases of which there are many examples in the books, one finds that where parties have made a contract which provides one thing and where, by a subsequent course of dealing, the parties have worked that contract out in such a way that one party leads the other to believe that the strict rights under that contract will not be adhered to, the courts will not allow that party who has led the other to think the strict rights will not be adhered, suddenly to seek to enforce those strict rights against him. That seems to me to be precisely what the landlords are trying to do here.

Cumming-Bruce LJ agreed that the appeal should be dismissed for the reasons given by Roskill LJ. Do you agree that on the facts this case was governed by *Hughes v Metropolitan Railway Co*? If not, what difference is there between promissory estoppel and the doctrine of waiver as applied by Roskill LJ?

'The Law of Contract Modifications: The Uncertain Quest for a Benchmark of Enforceability' by Aivazian, Trebilcock and Penny (1984) 22 Osgoode Hall LJ 173, at 187–205

We assume a rather prosaic objective for the law on modifications: minimizing transaction costs, and proceed to develop an economic framework that attempts to identify the variables that must be taken into account in formulating legal rules that advance this objective.

We shall follow Posner and initially distinguish two alternative sets of cases in which contract modifications might be sought. In one set of cases there are no changes in the underlying economic conditions governing the initial contract except that the promisee has acquired some monopoly power *ex post* and exploits this power by forcing higher returns than provided for in the initial contract. Posner argues for the non-enforcement of contract modifications in such cases. The second set of cases is characterized by changes in the underlying economic conditions, or the emergence of new information about the underlying economic conditions governing the contract which prevent or inhibit the promisee from completing the promised performance without a modification of the contract. Posner argues that modification is justified in such cases because without that ability mutually advantageous exchanges may be precluded. . . .

Consider now the first set of cases. For these cases *ex post* contract modification is a zero sum game. What one party gains the other loses—in other words there is, by assumption, no room for co-operative recontracting. Assume an economic environment characterized by zero transaction costs, rational expectations and complete information about all contingencies. Assume also that the contract is initially drawn up under perfectly competitive conditions. We will argue that in such an environment whether the law enforces contract modifications is irrelevant from a resource perspective and has no bearing on the economic welfare of the contracting parties. All that is required is that the law be *unambiguous*.

Suppose the law does enforce contract modifications. Then the terms of the initial contract will reflect the optimal future (*ex post*) strategy of the promisee. Suppose the promisor initially enters into the contract recognizing that the promisee's optimal future strategy will be to force higher returns through contract modifications. Since the law will enforce such modifications, the initial contract terms will be adjusted to reflect these future payoffs to the promisee. Potential extortionary monopoly rents will thus be fully impounded—given perfect competition and rational expectations—into *ex ante* contract terms. As long as the promisee's optimal *ex post* strategy (whether opportunistic or not) is unique, it will be fully reflected in the initial contract in this rational expectations environment.

Suppose, on the other hand, that the law does *not* enforce contract modifications. Then the initial contractual terms will be adjusted so that the return to the promisee, under the contract, will exceed his return in the previous case by a margin which exactly corresponds to the present value of the extortionary monopoly rents that would have accrued to the promisee if contract modifications were allowed and the promisee's optimal *ex post* strategy was to act opportunistically . . .

However, if there are positive transactions costs, then the choice of legal regime may have a significant influence on resource allocation. Initial analysis suggests that a law which unambiguously disallows contract modifications will generally be more efficient. Such a law economizes on the transaction costs that would otherwise be incurred in a regime that allowed contract modification. These costs not only include the direct costs associated with contract modifications (contract renegotiations take time and absorb other resources), but also those associated with various contractual and institutional arrangements designed to forestall opportunistic behaviour. These latter costs include those of writing, monitoring and enforcing detailed contractual provisions to penalize or constrain opportunism, as well as the costs of the resources expended by the promisee (for example bonding costs) to convince the promisor that he will not behave opportunistically. It is in the promisee's interest to incur such costs (which limit his potential opportunism) in a regime that allows contract modifications to induce an optimal initial level of mutually advantageous contracts. However, such costs engender a reduction in the initial exchange opportunity since the exchange process is more costly. . . .

In short, in cases where contract modifications occur purely and simply as a result of changes in the strategic circumstances of the contracting parties, the enforcement or non-enforcement of modified contracts in a zero transaction costs environment with complete information about future contingencies and rational expectations will have no bearing on resource allocation or economic welfare. In an environment with positive transaction costs or incomplete information, a law which disallows contract modifications will economize on transaction costs and maximize the gains from contractual agreements. Hence, efficiency considerations dictate that contract modifications in this context be non-enforceable.

The second set of cases in which contract modifications may be sought (supervening changes in the economic environment of the contract) are those in which modifications can represent mutually advantageous positive-sum games . . .

If recontracting between the parties in a particular *ex post* state of nature is mutually advantageous, then it will occur, leading to an optimal restructuring of contractual terms. These considerations suggest that contract modifications are necessary for the attainment of Pareto efficiency and should be allowed by law in this second set of cases. However, as we will see, such a conclusion is premature since there are additional considerations that bear on the problem . . .

Where the contract has specifically assigned certain risks, the presumption should be that they have been assigned to the superior (that is, most efficient) risk bearer and, moreover, that he has been adequately compensated for bearing them, thus removing any distributional objections to leaving him to bear the costs. Where the contract is not explicit about the allocation of a given risk, it seems a reasonable presumptive rule of interpretation to assume that the parties intended for it to be borne by the superior risk bearer and that it has simply been impounded in the categoric terms of the contract. In either case, the party bearing such risks should not be permitted to subsequently reallocate them to the other party by contract modification, taking advantage of limitations in the relief available to the party on breach in order to induce the modification.

If the law allows contract modifications, it imposes at least part of the risk of adverse outcomes on the promisor. To the extent that the promisee can modify risks by his activities, and there is imperfect monitoring of his activities by the promisor, a moral hazard problem will arise. The promisee will have incentives to increase his risk exposure (relative to the case where he fully bears the risks) over time by devoting fewer resources to risk prevention than is optimal and increasing the probability of occurrence of adverse states (for example, bankruptcy) in which contract modifications may be necessary. Thus, the enforcement of contract modifications may generate inappropriate incentives over time that affect the probabilities of alternative outcomes or states of nature. Inappropriate incentives are created not only for the immediate contracting parties but, even more importantly, for future contracting parties in similar circumstances. . . .

In effect, we view enforceable modifications as a substitute for the doctrine of frustration: contracting parties, facing the occurrence of some intervening event that substantially affects the cost of performance may, under some circumstances, rearrange their contractual rights and obligations either through invocation of the assistance of the courts pursuant to the doctrine of frustration or through private recontracting. In other cases, while the underlying factual circumstances of the contract may not have changed, new information about those circumstances may have been uncovered. The parties may have contracted on the basis of incomplete or inaccurate information about the underlying factual environment of the contract. This situation is the domain of the doctrine of mistake. The economic considerations bearing on permissible rearrangements by virtue of contract modifications, the doctrine of frustration, or the doctrine of mistake would seem to be similar . . .

However, in applying this approach both to frustration and modification cases, several problems must be acknowledged. First, the contract may not clearly assign given risks and an objective inquiry into who is the superior risk bearer may sometimes be indeterminate (for example, one party may have superior ability to appraise the probability of a particular event occurring, but the other party may have superior ability to appraise the magnitude of the costs entailed if it does). . . .

Another problem may arise in cases where it may be feasible to identify clearly the superior risk bearer but the risk in question is very remote. . . . if the risk is remote enough, that is, carries a very low probability, the effects of assigning it to one party or the other may have little effect on contractual behaviour because the *expected* (that is, *ex ante*) costs to whoever bears the risk are so small as to warrant very little, if anything, in the way of efficient precautionary responses.

Taking these two problematic cases together—(a) indeterminacy in the identification of the superior risk bearer, and (b) highly remote risks—it can be argued that these are the transactional domains where contractual modifications should be permitted. In both cases, permitting modifications enables the party to whom a modification is proposed to capture some of the static gains from recontracting by avoiding losses he may well sustain in the event of a breach. Losses in dynamic efficiency associated with a rule that permits subsequent reassignment of initially efficiently assigned risks are likely to be small, in the first case because we cannot determine with confidence what is an efficient allocation of risks, and in the second case because while this can be detemined, disturbing the efficient allocation of risks will have little impact on the long-run behaviour of contracting parties at large while enabling the static gains for the immediate parties from recontracting, which may be significant, to be realized.

Permitting modifications in these two classes of cases, in effect, permits a flexible form of risk sharing by the contracting partners. Assuming the parties to be risk averse and the risk in question one that neither can readily control or insure against, contract modification may reduce the variance in possible contractual outcomes for the parties and thus be Pareto efficient. A countervailing consideration is, of course, that the promisor now is exposed to the risk of strategic behaviour by the promisee designed to exploit or manipulate these two exceptions and to the adjudication costs attendant on courts attempting to apply rules that do not supply knife-edged sharpness in the characterization of situations as falling within or outside given rules or exceptions thereto . . .

Posner endorses the result in [*Goebel v Linn*] case on the basis of his distinction between modifications entered into where there has been a change in underlying circumstances and those where there has not. However, our emphasis on efficient risk allocation suggests a more cautious approach to evaluating the correctness of this decision. If mild winters were one of the occupational hazards of running an ice business during the era in question, the ice company would seem clearly to be the superior risk bearer, both in terms of risk reduction (for example, making different inventory or stand-by sub-contractual arrangements) and in terms of risk insurance (that is, being better able to appraise the impact of climatic variations on the supply of ice and adjusting the initial contractual fixed price accordingly). Only where the winter in question was quite out of the ordinary so that the gains from recontracting were likely to outweigh the long-run costs of moral hazard problems associated with permitting recontracting in these circumstances, could one support the decision. Otherwise, permitting recontracting is inefficient.

(e) An inchoate (incoherent?) principle

We saw earlier (above, p 436) that normally a party who terminates a contract, giving a reason that in law does not justify his action, may nonetheless be held to be justified if in fact there was some other ground on which he was entitled to terminate, even if he was unaware of it at the time. This rule may now be subject to some restriction.

Panchaud Frères SA v Etablissements General Grain Co [1970] 1 Lloyd's Rep 53, Court of Appeal

Five-and-a-half thousand tons of maize were sold under a contract that required shipment by the end of July. The maize was in fact shipped in August, but the bill of lading stated July as the month of shipment. Careful examination of the certificate of quality would have revealed the truth, but the buyers did not notice this. They accepted the documents, but later purported to reject the goods on wholly insufficient grounds. Only some three years later, when they were attempting to recover the price they had paid, did they first raise the point about the date of shipment. The Court of Appeal held it was too late to do so.

Lord Denning MR. . . . The present case is not a case of 'waiver' strictly so called. It is a case of estoppel by conduct. The basis of it is that a man has so conducted himself that it would be unfair or unjust to allow him to depart from a particular state of affairs which another has taken to be settled or correct, see the cases I referred to in *Central Newbury Car Auctions Ltd v Unity Finance Ltd and Another, Mercury Motors, Third Parties.* Applied to the rejection of goods, the principle may be stated thus: If a man, who is entitled to reject goods on a certain ground, so conducts himself as to lead the other to believe that he is not relying on that ground, then he cannot afterwards set it up as a ground of rejection, when it would be unfair or unjust to allow him so to do.

Winn LJ. . . . In my own judgment it does not seem possible in this case to say affirmatively that there was here either a fresh agreement, to rescind or vary the original contract, or anything which, within the scope of the doctrine as hitherto enunciated, could be described as an estoppel or a quasi estoppel. I respectfully agree with my Lord that what one has here is something perhaps in our law not yet wholly developed as a separate doctrine—which is more in the nature of a requirement of fair conduct—a criterion of what is fair conduct between the parties. There may be an inchoate doctrine stemming from the manifest convenience of consistency in pragmatic affairs, negativing any liberty to blow hot and cold in commercial conduct.

NOTES

1. The basis of this decision is elusive: see Treitel, pp. 661–662. In *Procter & Gamble Philippine Manufacturing Corpn v Peter Cremer GmbH & Co* [1988] 3 All ER 843 Hirst J reviewed the case and the explanations of it given in subsequent cases, and concluded (at p 852):

   Perhaps the best lesson to be drawn from all this subsequent commentary is that no distinctive principle of law can be distilled from the *Panchaud* case, which . . . is so often cited as an authority of the last resort.

2. A useful survey of the field of waiver and promissory estoppel will be found in Dugdale and Yates 'Variation, Waiver and Estoppel—a Reappraisal' (1976) 39 MLR 680.

CHAPTER 28
Adjustments in longer-term contracts

Many contracts are designed to run over a period of time, and it may be difficult to predict in advance how such matters as the costs of performing or the parties' needs may change during the period. It is very common for the parties to attempt to build a degree of flexibility into the agreement by the use of various types of clause. An obvious example is a price fluctuation clause, under which the price to be paid will vary as certain costs involved in performing (eg the cost of labour or materials) change. Another is a clause allowing one party to change what is to be done by the other.

ICE Conditions of Contract (5th edn) cll 51–52

ALTERATIONS ADDITIONS AND OMISSIONS

51. (1) *Ordered variations.* The Engineer shall order any variation to any part of the Works that may in his opinion be necessary for the completion of the Works and shall have power to order any variation that for any other reason shall in his opinion be desirable for the satisfactory completion and functioning of the Works. Such variations may include additions omissions substitutions alterations changes in quality form character kind position dimension level or line and changes in the specified sequence method or timing of construction (if any).

(2) *Ordered variations to be in writing.* No such variation shall be made by the Contractor without an order by the Engineer. All such orders shall be given in writing provided that if for any reason the Engineer shall find it necessary to give any such order orally in the first instance the Contractor shall comply with such oral order. Such oral order shall be confirmed in writing by the Engineer as soon as is possible in the circumstances. If the Contractor shall confirm in writing to the Engineer any oral order by the Engineer and such confirmation shall not be contradicted in writing by the Engineer forthwith it shall be deemed to be an order in writing by the Engineer. No variation ordered or deemed to be ordered in writing in accordance with sub-clauses (1) and (2) of this Clause shall in any way vitiate or invalidate the Contract but the value (if any) of all such variations shall be taken into account in ascertaining the amount of the Contract Price.

(3) *Changes in quantities.* No order in writing shall be required for increase or decrease in the quantity of any work where such increase or decrease is not the result of an order given under this Clause but is the result of the quantities exceeding or being less than those stated in the Bill of Quantities.

52. (1) *Valuation of ordered variations.* The value of all variations ordered by the Engineer in accordance with Clause 51 shall be ascertained by the Engineer after consultation with the Contractor in accordance with the following principles. Where work is of similar character and executed under similar conditions to work priced in the Bill of Quantities it shall be valued at such rates and prices contained therein as may be applicable. Where work is not of a similar character or is not executed under similar conditions the rates and prices in the Bill of Quantities shall be used as the basis for valuation so far as may be reasonable failing which a fair valuation shall be made. Failing agreement between the Engineer and the Contractor as to any rate or price to be applied in the valuation of any variation the Engineer shall determine the rate or price in accordance with the foregoing principles and he shall notify the Contractor accordingly.

(2) *Engineer to fix rates.* Provided that if the nature or amount of any variation relative to the nature or amount of the whole of the contract work or to any part thereof shall be such that in the opinion of the Engineer or the Contractor any rate or price contained in the Contract for any item of work is by reason of such variation rendered unreasonable or inapplicable either the

Engineer shall give to the Contractor or the Contractor shall give to the Engineer notice before the varied work is commenced or as soon thereafter as is reasonable in all the circumstances that such rate or price should be varied and the Engineer shall fix such rate or price as in the circumstances he shall think reasonable and proper.

(3) *Daywork*. The Engineer may if in his opinion it is necessary or desirable order in writing that any additional or substituted work shall be executed on a daywork basis. The Contractor shall then be paid for such work under the conditions set out in the Daywork Schedule included in the Bill of Quantities and at the rates and prices affixed thereto by him in his Tender and failing the provision of a Daywork Schedule he shall be paid at the rates and prices and under the conditions contained in the 'Schedules of Dayworks carried out incidental to Contract Work' issued by The Federation of Civil Engineering Contractors current at the date of the execution of the Daywork.

NOTES

1. Why insert a clause of this type rather than agree changes in the specification as and when necessary? Can you see why it would be unwise for the employer to count on persuading the original contractor to do the extra work, or get in someone else to do it if he cannot reach agreement?

2. Note that the power to order variations under cl 51 is expressly limited: the variation must 'in his opinion be desirable for the satisfactory completion and functioning of the Works'. Ordering that an item be omitted simply to save money is probably outside the Engineer's powers. Of course, he could try to persuade the contractor to consent to such an omission, but the contractor would be within his rights to refuse to consent unless he was given compensation. A variation which is outside the scope of cl 51 will equally be outside the scope of the valuation mechanisms of cl 52, unless the contractor is prepared to waive his rights and treat it in all respects as a proper variation.

3. Even more broadly phrased variation clauses may be subject to implicit limitations. In *Carr v JA Berriman Pty Ltd* (1953) 27 ALJ 273 the defendant had contracted to erect a factory for the plaintiff; the variation clause provided: 'The Architect may in his absolute discretion and from time to time issue . . . written instructions or written directions . . . in regard to the . . . omission . . . of any work . . .'. The contract provided for the free issue of steel by the plaintiff and its fabrication by the defendant to the architect's instructions. The High Court held that the architect was not entitled to award a contract for the fabrication of the steel to another company. Fullagar J said: 'The words quoted . . . do not . . . authorize him to say that particular items so included shall be carried out not by the builder with whom the contract is made but by some other builder or contractor. The words used do not, in their natural meaning, extend so far, and a power in the architect to hand over at will any part of the contract to another contractor would be a most unreasonable power, which very clear words would be required to confer'. (Compare the cases on the interpretation of exclusion clauses in the next section, especially at pp 682–685.)

4. A converse problem arose in *Sir Lindsay Parkinson & Co Ltd v Comrs of Works and Public Buildings* [1949] 2 KB 632. The contract (as subsequently varied by deed) contemplated work costing some £5 million in the first instance. It provided that the contractor could be ordered to carry out any extras, but that in no circumstances might the contractor's profit (which was estimated as a percentage of the cost) be less than £150,000 or exceed £300,000. A note in the bill of quantities stated: 'It is probable that further work to the value of approximately £500,000 will be

ordered . . .'. The extra work ordered took the cost to £6½ million and the contractor claimed that it was entitled to additional profit. The Court of Appeal allowed the claim, because the extra work was outside the scope of the contract.

5. The decisions in *Carr* and *Lindsay Parkinson* may be viewed as the courts controlling 'opportunism' on the part of contracting parties who are attempting to exploit the terms of the contract. See further below, p 624 and Muris, 'Opportunistic behaviour and the law of contracts' (1981) 65 Minnesota LR 521.

6. Note also that in some circumstances the Engineer may be under an *obligation* to order a variation: he '*shall* order any variation . . . that may in his opinion be necessary'. If, for instance, a design error makes the original specification impossible to reach, the employer will be in breach of contract if the Engineer does not issue a variation order to deal with the problem. The same result was reached in *Holland, Hannen & Cubitts (Northern) Ltd v Welsh Health Technical Services Organization* (1981) 18 BLR 80 even though the variation clause (under the JCT form, 1963 ed) said nothing expressly about any duty to issue a variation order.

The ICE conditions also exhibit another characteristic often found in contracts designed to last over a period of time: decisions as to what is to be done, and how the consequent costs are to be allocated, are left to a third party, in this case the Engineer. He or she is not a party to the contract, and though employed by the Employer he or she is frequently expected to act in an independent manner in administering the contract—for instance, in deciding whether it is necessary to order a variation, or whether a price contained in the Bill of Quantities is applicable to the work ordered. In fact the Engineer's decisions are not final, as if either party is dissatisfied it may seek arbitration, but clearly there is less likely to be dissatisfaction over an 'independent' decision than one taken by the Employer unilaterally, and in addition, most matters can only be arbitrated after completion of the contract.

In what can again be viewed as a move against opportunism, the courts attempt to ensure that the Engineer (or the Architect who is given a parallel role under many building contracts) does act impartially. If the Engineer allows himself or herself to be unduly influenced by the Employer, or simply only has regard to one side's (typically the Employer's) interests, he or she is disqualified. This means that sums which would normally be due to the Contractor if the Engineer has so certified may be recovered without the Engineer's certificate: *Hickman & Co v Roberts* [1913] AC 229. In *Perini Corpn v Commonwealth of Australia* (1969) 12 BLR 82 it was held that the Engineer's failure to act impartially put the *Employer* into breach of contract, so that the Contractor could recover damages for the increased cost it incurred after the Engineer failed to grant extensions of time and the Contractor speeded up work.

In recent years a considerable amount of theoretical work has been done on long-term contractual and other relationships, particularly by Macneil.

'Restatement (Second) of Contracts and Presentiation' by Macneil (1974) 60 Virginia LR 589, 589–596

To presentiate: 'to make or render present in place or time; to cause to be perceived or realized as present.' Presentiation is only a manner in which a person perceives the future's effect on the present; but it depends upon events outside the individual psyche, events viewed as determining the future. Presentiation is thus a recognition that the course of the future is bound by present events, *and* that by those events the future has for many purposes been brought effectively into the present.

Although we are surrounded by this phenomenon, its name was described as rare even forty years ago. Thus it is not surprising that the term was never employed in a traditional contract theory implicitly requiring total presentiation of each contract relation at the time of its formation through offer and acceptance.

A remark made by Anthony Quinn while playing an Eskimo in *The Savage Innocents* (1961) illustrates further the concept of presentiation. One of the two white men with Quinn had fallen through the ice in the midst of a raging blizzard, and Quinn and the other had quickly pulled him out of the water. The victim was freezing to death in spite of the efforts of his friend to slap circulation through his body. Watching the frantic efforts, Quinn said, 'Your friend *is* dead.' It was a perfectly sensible statement even though the doomed man was still breathing, his heart still beating, and his limbs still moving. All the events had occurred which would cause his death, and there was not the slightest chance of avoiding that event.

Because presentiation depends upon recognition of the binding of the future, anything preventing either binding of the future or recognition of that binding frustrates presentiation. Such an impediment is the existence of choice. To the extent that people have choice and we do not know how they will exercise it, the future remains unbound, and cannot be presentiated.

TRADITIONAL CONTRACT LAW AND PRESENTIATION

Several generations ago the German legal scholar, Kohler, said, 'It is the province of the law of obligations to draw the future into the present.' This is precisely what traditional contract law was designed to do, by adding legal sanctions to the bindingness of mutual assent. This aspect of traditional contract law, most highly developed in this country by Williston, was a truly ingenious intellectual creation. Primarily through manipulations of the notion of consent, traditional contract theory created a legal structure which in theory attempted to presentiate not just part of the relation between contracting parties, but virutally all of it. When a subjective meeting of the minds became too narrow a concept upon which to base complete presentiation, the contract structure shifted to an objective theory of contracts, reinforced by such doctrines as the parol evidence rule. Unfortunately, sometimes consent, even objective consent, was too vague in commitment or content to serve as a basis for total presentiation. The relation created by such vague consent was excluded from the realm of contract altogether, leaving the parties with only the legal reinforcement they might find in the law of quasi-contract or torts. Since this was often undesirable, the designers of the structure went to great lengths to infer consent to such things as reasonable times or prices, or to imply conditions and other terms. Faced with inevitable problems of mistakes, impossibility, or other frustration of original goals, the theory utilized implied conditions in an attempt to preserve the facade of initial presentiation by mutual assent. When consent was stretched as far as it reasonably could be or, some would say, farther, then the gap-filling Corpus Juris Contractus took over directly, exemplified by Williston's analysis of impossibility. . .

No one was ever so naive as to believe that contract law could indeed achieve total presentiation, but there are some kinds of contracts where close approximations may be possible. Complete presentiation is most likely to lead to useful outcomes in contracts properly described as discrete transations. These are contracts of short duration, with limited personal interactions, and with precise party measurements of easily measured objects of exchange, for example money and grain. They are transactions requiring a minimum of future cooperative behavior between the parties and not requiring a sharing of benefits or burdens. They bind the two parties tightly and precisely. The parties view such transactions as deals free of entangling strings, and they certainly expect no altruism. The parties see virtually everything connected with such transactions as clearly defined and presentiated. If trouble is anticipated at all, it is anticipated only if someone or something turns out unexpectedly badly. The epitome of discrete contract transactions: two strangers come into town from opposite directions, one walking and one riding a horse. The walker offers to buy the horse, and after brief dickering a deal is struck in which delivery of the horse is to be made at sundown upon the handing over of $10. The two strangers expect to have nothing to do with each other between now and sundown, they expect never to see each other again thereafter, and each has as much feeling for the other as has a Viking trading with a Saxon.

A high degree of presentiation is possible in truly discrete transactions, because it is possible to approach complete mutual planning and to do so at one point in time. This completeness and unity of planning creates a situation where it is reasonable for the parties to bind themselves to stick rigorously by the planning. That in turn permits the application of the legal reinforcing structure of traditional contract law. Because of the close connection of traditional contract law with discrete transactions, it is appropriate to refer to it as transactional contract law.

RELATIONAL CONTRACTS AND PRESENTIATION

Few economic exchanges occur entirely in the discrete transactional pattern. Virtually all economic exchange takes place in circumstances characterized by one or more of the following: The relations are of significant duration (for example, franchising). Close whole person relations form an integral aspect of the relation (employment). The object of exchange typically includes both easily measured quantities (wages) and quantities not easily measured (the projection of personality by an airline stewardess). Many individuals with individual and collective poles of interest are involved in the relation (industrial relations). Future cooperative behavior is anticipated (the players and management of the Oakland Raiders). The benefits and burdens of the relation are to be shared rather than divided and allocated (a law partnership). The bindingness of the relation is limited (again a law partnership in which in theory each member is free to quit almost at will). The entangling strings of friendship, reputation, interdependence, morality, and altruistic desires are integral parts of the relation (a theatrical agent and his clients). Trouble is expected as a matter of course (a collective bargaining agreement). Finally the participants never intend or expect to see the whole future of the relation as presentiated at any single time, but view the relation as an ongoing integration of behavior which will grow and vary with events in a largely unforseeable future (a marriage; a family business).

In circumstances such as the foregoing each exchange no longer stands alone as in the discrete transaction, but is part of a relational web. Since most actual exchanges are at least partially relational, most contracts could be called relational. It is, however, more useful to think of transactional and relational characteristics as creating a spectrum ranging from such extremes as the highly transactional horse selling epitome to the highly relational nuclear family or commune. As one moves towards the relational end of this spectrum presentiation plays a relatively smaller role, since increasing aspects of the relation must be left to future determination. This fact poses problems for contract law.

'Contracts Adjustment of long-term economic relations under classical, neo-classical and relational contract law' by Macneil (1978) 72 Northwestern University LR 854, 859–870, 873–874, 901

Adjustment and Termination of Economic Relations in a System of Discrete Transactions

An economic and legal system dominated by discrete transactions deals with the conflict between various needs for stability and needs for flexibility in ways described below. (The treatment following deals both with present exchanges of existing goods and with forward contracts where exchange is projected into the future. But the latter are assumed to be of a fairly discrete nature, eg, a contract for 100 tons of iron at a fixed price, delivery in one month.)

Planning Flexibility into Economic Relations—Within itself, a discrete transaction is rigid, there being no intention to achieve internal flexibility. Planning for flexibility must, therefore, be achieved outside the confines of the transaction. Consider, for example, a nineteenth century manufacturer of stoves who needs iron to be cast into stove parts but does not know how many stoves he can sell. The required flexibility has to be achieved, in a pattern of discrete transactions, by keeping each iron purchase contract small in amount, thereby permitting adjustments of quantity up or down each time a contract is entered. Thus, the needed flexibility comes from the opportunity to enter or to refrain from entering the market for iron. This market is external to the transaction rather than within it. The epitome of this kind of flexibility is the purchasing of needs for immediate delivery, rather than using any kind of a forward contract for future delivery. Such flexibility is reduced by use of forward contracts; the larger and longer they are, the greater is the reduction.

Dealing with Conflict between Specific Planning and Needs to Adapt to Change Arising Thereafter—Only rarely in a discrete transaction will the items contracted for become useless before the forward contract is performed or become of such lessened value that the buyer either will not want them or will want them in greatly changed form. To put this another way, only rarely will there be *within* the transaction a serious conflict between specific planning and changed needs. To return to the stove manufacturer as an example, seldom will the demand for iron stoves drop so much that the manufacturer comes to regret that he contracted for as much iron as he did.

The discrete transaction technique does not, however, produce a paradise of stability for economic activity; the conflict between specific planning and the need to adapt to change arising thereafter still remains. In those relatively rare cases of difficulties arising while the contract remains unperformed, the conflict exists but is resolved entirely in favor of the specific planning and against the party desiring flexibility.

Preserving Relations When Conflicts Arise—Where the mode of operation is a series of discrete transactions, no significant relations exist to be preserved when conflicts arise. Inside the discrete transaction all that remains is a dispute. Outside the discrete transaction no relation (other than legal rights arising out of the dispute) exists to be preserved. Thus, all that remains is a dispute to be settled or otherwise resolved. The existence of the market that the discrete transactional system presupposes eliminates the necessity for economic relations between the firms to continue in spite of the disputes. That market, rather than continued relations between these particular parties, will supply their future needs. . .

Classical Contract Law and Discrete Transactions

Any contract law system necessarily must implement certain norms. It must permit and encourage participation in exchange, promote reciprocity, reinforce role patterns appropriate to particular kinds of exchange relations, provide limited freedom for exercise of choice, effectuate planning, and harmonize the internal and external matrixes of particular contracts. A contract law system reinforcing discrete contract transactions, however, must add two further goals: enhancing discreteness and enhancing presentiation. . .

A classical contract law system implements these two norms in a number of ways. To implement discreteness, classical law initially treats as irrelevant the identity of the parties to the transaction. Second, it transactionizes or commodifies as much as possible the subject matter of contracts, eg, it turns employment into a short-term commodity by interpreting employment contracts without express terms of duration as terminable at will. Third, it limits strictly the sources to be considered in establishing the substantive content of the transaction. For example, formal communication (eg, writings) controls informal communication (eg, oral statements); linguistic communication controls nonlinguistic communication; and communicated circumstances (to the limited extent that any circumstances outside of 'agreements' are taken into account at all) control noncommunicated circumstances (eg, status). Fourth, only limited contract remedies are available, so that should the initial presentiation fail to materialize because of nonperformance, the consequences are relatively predictable from the beginning and are not open-ended, as they would be, for example, if damages for unforeseeable or psychic losses were allowed. Fifth, classical contract law draws clear lines between being in and not being in a transaction; eg, rigorous and precise rules of offer and acceptance prevail with no half-way houses where only some contract interests are protected or where losses are shared. Finally, the introduction of third parties into the relation is discouraged since multiple poles of interest tend to create discreteness-destroying relations.

Since discreteness enhances the possibility and likelihood of presentiation, all of the foregoing implementations of discreteness by the classical law also tend to enhance presentiation. Other classical law techniques, however, are even more precisely focused on presentiation. The first of these is the equation of the legal effect of a transaction with the promises creating it. This characteristic of classical contract law is commonly explained in terms of freedom of contract, providing maximum scope to the exercise of choice. Nevertheless, a vital consequence of the use of the technique is presentiation of the transaction. Closely related to the first technique is the second: supplying a precise, predictable body of law to deal with all aspects of the transaction not encompassed by the promises. In theory, if not practice, this enables the parties to know exactly what the future holds, no matter what happens to disrupt performance. Finally, stress on expectation remedies, whether specific performance or damages measured by the value of performance, tends to bring the future into the present, since all risks, including market risks, are thereby transferred at the time the 'deal is made.' . . .

VARIATIONS FROM THE DISCRETE TRANSACTION: NEOCLASSICAL CONTRACT LAW

The discrete transaction is at one end of a spectrum, at the other end of which are contractual relations. Were we to push far in the direction of contractual relations, we would come to the firm itself, since a firm is, in significant ways, nothing more than a very complex bundle of contractual relations. It is not my intention at this point to push that far, but rather to confine consideration of adjustment and termination of long-term economic relations to those where it is clear that the contractual relations are *between* firms rather than *within* a firm. They are, even in traditional terms, contracts. Again, this section will be organized around variations of the questions appearing in the introduction.

Planning Flexibility into Long-Term Contractual Relations and the Neoclassical Response

Two common characteristics of long-term contracts are the existence of gaps in their planning and the presence of a range of processes and techniques used by contract planners to create flexibility in lieu of either leaving gaps or trying to plan rigidly. Prior to exploring the legal response to such planning, an examination of the major types of planning for flexibility used in modern American contracts is in order.

Standards—The use of a standard uncontrolled by either of the parties to plan the contractual relation is very common. One important example is the provision in many collective bargaining agreements for adjustments of wages to reflect fluctuations in the Consumer Price Index. . .

Direct Third-Party Determination of Performance—The role of the architect under form construction contracts of the American Institute of Architects (AIA) provides a good example of direct third-party determination of the performace. The architect is responsible for determining many aspects of the performance relation, including everything from 'general administration' of the contract and making final decisions 'in matters relating to artistic effect' to approving the contractor's selection of a superintendent. . . .

A particularly important and increasingly used technique for third-party determination of performance content is arbitration. Arbitration is best known for its utilization in resolving 'rights disputes,'—disputes about existing rights, usually growing out of existing contracts and always substantially defined and narrowed by law at the time the arbitration takes place. Planning for the arbitration or rights disputes is an important aspect of risk planning. But arbitration is also used for filling gaps in performance planning, eg, in industrial relations where the inability of management and labor to negotiate on their own the performance terms of a collective bargaining agreement is known as an 'interest dispute.' Collective bargaining agreements are not, however, the only agreements that leave open issues relating to future performance and provide for their arbitration: For example, certain joint ventures among design professionals may leave important aspects open to arbitration to provide necessary flexibility.

Interest disputes and hence their arbitration are inherently more open-ended than rights disputes. . .

One-Party Control of Terms—Rather than use external standards or independent third parties, the contract may provide that one of the parties to the contract will define, directly or indirectly, parts of the relation. . .

Agreement to Agree—A flexible technique used more often than one might initially expect is an 'agreement to agree.'. . .

. . .

Conflict between Specific Planning and Needs for Flexibility: The Neoclassical Response

As a general proposition in American neoclassical contract law, specific planning in contractual relations governs in spite of changes in circumstances making such planning undesirable to one of the parties. The same principle of freedom of contract leading to this result permits the parties, however, to adjust their relations by subsequent agreement. A description of these processes and some of the legal considerations follows.

Adjustments of existing contractual relations occur in numerous ways. Performance itself is a kind of adjustment from original planning. Even meticulous performance of the most explicit planning transforms figments of the imagination, however precise, into a new, and therefore different, reality. A set of blueprints and specifications, however detailed, and a newly built house simply are not the same. Less explicit planning is changed even more by performance. For example, the vaguely articulated duties of a secretary are made concrete by his or her actual performance of a day's work. Perhaps this is merely a way of saying that planning is inherently filled with gaps, and that performance fills the gaps, thereby altering the relations as originally planned.

Events outside the performance of the parties also may effect adjustments in contractual relationships. The five dollars per hour promised an employee for his work in 1977 is not the same when paid in November 1977 as it was when promised at the beginning of the year; inflation and other economic developments have seen to that. More or less drastic changes in outside circumstances constantly effect contractual adjustments, however firmly the parties may appear to be holding to their original course.

Nonperformance by one of the parties without the consent of the other also alters contractual relations, although in a way different from performance. This is true no matter how many powers are available to the other party to redress the situation.

Another kind of adjustment occurring in any contractual relation is that based either on mutual agreement or on unilateral concession by one of the parties of a planned right beneficial to him. These alterations, additions, subtractions, terminations, and other changes from original planning may take place at any time during any contractual relation. This is vividly illustrated by various processes of collective bargaining, including periodic renegotiation of the 'whole' contract.

When disputes arise out of contractual relations after adjustment by mutual assent or concession, does the original planning or the adjusted planning govern? . . .

. . .

Somewhere along the line of increasing duration and complexity, trying to force changes into a pattern of original consent becomes both too difficult and too unrewarding to justify the effort, and the contractual relation escapes the bounds of the neoclassical system. That system is replaced by very different adjustment processes of an ongoing-administrative kind in which discreteness and presentation become merely two of the factors of decision, not the theoretical touchstones. Moreover, the substantive relation of change to the status quo has now altered from what happens in some kind of a market external to the contract to what can be achieved through the political and social processes of the relation, internal and external. This includes internal and external dispute-resolution structures. At this point, the relation has become a minisociety with a vast array of norms beyond the norms centred on exchange and its immediate processes.

'Contract analysis: the transaction cost approach' by Williamson, in Burrows and Veljanovski, The Economic Approach to Law (1981) at pp 41–46, 50–54

My transaction cost approach follows Commons by making the transaction the basic unit of analysis. Also, like Commons, I am interested in the design of institutions, legal and otherwise, that serve to promote the renewal or continuity of exchange relations. I follow Coase by regarding the firm as an important alternative to the market for governing economic activity, and I share Hayek's views on the limits of human agents and on the importance of organizing transactions in such a way as to realize more assuredly the productive values embedded in idiosyncratic human and physical assets. To be sure, legal rules and market processes remain important under this extended view of contract, but informal procedures and nonmarket organization also perform important governance functions. Moreover, and crucially to the exercise, *governance structures are matched with transactional attributes in a discriminating way* under the transaction cost approach to contracting set out here . . .

A three-way classification of contracts

Although there is a widespread agreement that the discrete-transaction paradigm—'sharp in by clear agreement; sharp out by clear performance' (Macneil, 1974, p 738)—has served both law and economics well, there is increasing awareness that many contractual relations are not of this well-defined kind. A deeper understanding of the nature of contract has emerged as the legal-rule emphasis associated with the study of discrete contracting has given way to a more general concern with the contractual purposes to be served.

Ian Macneil, in a series of thoughtful and wide-ranging essays on contract, usefully distinguishes between discrete and relational transactions (*see* Macneil, 1976; 1978). He further supplies twelve different 'concepts' with respect to which these differ. Serious problems of recognition and application are posed by such a rich classificatory apparatus. More useful for my purposes is the three-way classification of contracts that Macneil offers in a more recent article, where classical, neoclassical and relational categories of contract law are recognized.

Classical contract law

As Macneil (1978) observes, any system of contract law has the purpose of facilitating exchange. What is distinctive about classical contract law is that it attempts to do this by enhancing discreteness and intensifying 'presentation' (ibid, p 862), where the presentation has reference to efforts to 'make or render present in place or time; to cause to be perceived or realized as present'. The economic counterpart to complete presentiation is contingent-claims contracting, which entails comprehensive contracting in which all relevant future contingencies pertaining to the supply of a good or service are described and discounted with respect to both likelihood and futurity.

Classical contract law endeavours to implement discreteness and presentiation in several ways. For one thing, the identity of the parties to a transaction is treated as irrelevant. In this respect it corresponds exactly with the 'ideal' market transaction in economics. Secondly, the nature of the agreement is carefully delimited and the more formal features govern when formal (for example, written) and informal (for example, oral) terms are contested. Thirdly, remedies are narrowly prescribed such that, 'should the initial presentiation fail to materialize because of nonperformance, the consequences are relatively predictable from the beginning and are not open-ended'. Additionally, third-party participation is discouraged (Macneil, 1978, p 864). The emphasis, thus, is on legal rules, formal documents and self-liquidating transactions.

Neoclassical contract law
Not every transaction fits comfortably into the classical contracting scheme. In particular, long-term contracts executed under conditions of uncertainty are ones for which complete presentiation is apt to be prohibitively costly if not impossible. Problems of several kinds arise. First, not all future contingencies for which adaptations are required can be anticipated at the outset. Secondly, the appropriate adaptations will not be evident for many contingencies until the circumstances materialize. Thirdly, except where changes in states of the world are unambiguous, hard contracting between autonomous parties may well give rise to veridical disputes when state-contingent claims are made. In a world in which (at least some) parties are inclined to be opportunistic, whose representations are to be believed?

Faced with the prospective breakdown of classical contracting in these circumstances, three options are available. One would be to forego such transactions altogether. A second would be to remove these transactions from the market and organize them internally: adaptive, sequential decision making would then be implemented under common ownership and with the assistance of hierarchical incentive and control systems. Third, a different contracting relation that preserves trading but provides for additional governance structure might be devised. This last choice brings us to what Macneil refers to as neoclassical contracting.

As Macneil observes, 'two common characteristics of long-term contracts are the existence of gaps in their planning and the presence of a range of processes and techniques used by contract planners to create flexibility in lieu of either leaving gaps or trying to plan rigidly.' (ibid, p 865). Third-party assistance in resolving disputes and evaluating performance often has advantages over litigation in serving these functions of flexibility and gap filling . . .

A recognition that the world is complex, that agreements are incomplete and that some contracts will never be reached unless both parties have confidence in the settlement machinery thus characterizes neoclassical contract law . . .

Relational contracting
The pressures to sustain continuing relations 'have led to the spin-off of many subject areas from the classical, and later the neoclassical contract law system, eg, much of corporate law and collective bargaining' (Macneil, 1978, p 885). Thus, progressively increasing the 'duration and complexity' of contract has resulted in the displacement of even neoclassical adjustment processes by adjustment processes of a more thoroughly transaction-specific, ongoing-administrative kind (ibid, p 901). The fiction of discreteness is fully displaced as the relation takes on the properties of 'a minisociety with a vast array of norms beyond those centred on the exchange and its immediate processes' (ibid). By contrast with the neoclassical system, in which the reference point for effecting adaptations remains the original agreement, the reference point under a truly relational approach is the 'entire relation as it has developed . . . [through] time. This may or may not include an 'original agreement'; and if it does, may or may not result in great deference being given to it'. (ibid, p 890).

TRANSACTION COST ECONOMICS

Macneil's three-way discussion of contracts discloses that contracts are a good deal more varied and complex than is commonly realized. It furthermore suggests that governance structures— the institutional matrix within which transactions are negotiated and executed—vary with the nature of the transaction. But the critical dimensions of contract are not expressly identified, and the purposes of governance are not stated. The harmonizing of interests that would otherwise give [way] to antagonistic subgoal pursuits appears to be an important governance function but this is not explicit in his discussion . . .

Behavioural assumptions

Bounded rationality and opportunism are the central behavioural assumptions upon which the transaction cost approach is based. Bounded rationality, which should not be confused with irrationality, refers to 'a condition in which human agents are '*intendedly* rational, but only *limitedly* so' (Simon, 1961) . . .

Opportunism extends the usual motivational assumption of self-interest to make allowance for self-interest with guile. Thus, whereas bounded rationality suggests decision-making less complex than the usual assumption of hyperrationality, opportunism suggests calculating behaviour that is more sophisticated than the usual assumption of simple self-interest. Opportunism refers to 'making false or empty, that is, self-disbelieved threats or promises' (Goffman, 1969), cutting corners for undisclosed personal advantage, covering-up tracks and the like.

Dimensionalizing

The puzzle of vertical integration is that under conventional assumptions it is an anomaly: if the costs of operating competitive markets are zero, 'as is usually assumed in our theoretical analysis' . . . why integrate? Coase, in his 1937 paper (p 336), took exception to the usual assumption and argued that vertical integration permitted the firm to economize on the 'cost of negotiating and concluding' many separate intermediate product market contracts by substituting a flexible employment agreement. Inasmuch, however, as the factors that were responsible for differential transaction costs in the intermediate product market were not identified, the argument lacked testable implications. Why not use a flexible employment agreement to organize all transactions rather than just some? Until such time as the transaction cost argument was able to explain the organization of transactions in a discriminating way, it remained rather tautological. . . . Coase's observation (1972, p 63), some twenty-five years later, that his 1937 article was 'much cited and little used' is presumably explained by the failure to operationalize the issues over that interval.

. . . [T]he critical dimensions for describing transactions, and hence for assigning some to markets and others to internal organization, are:

(1) uncertainty;
(2) the frequency with which transactions recur;
(3) the degree to which durable transaction-specific investments are required to realize least-cost supply.

The main governance modes to which transactions need to be matched are:

(1) markets (with varying degrees of adjudicatory support);
(2) internal organization;
(3) an intermediate form of bilateral exchange referred to as 'obligational market contracting'.

Transactions for which internal organization is well-suited are those that involve recurrent exchange in the face of a nontrivial degree of uncertainty and for which transaction-specific investments are incurred. Since internal organization requires the development of a specialized governance structure, the cost of which must be amortized across the transactions organized thereunder, it is rarely economical to organize infrequent (or occasional) transactions internally. Likewise, transactions for which uncertainty is low require little adaptation and hence little governance. Unspecialized market structures commonly work well for these. It should not be inferred, however, that markets function poorly wherever high frequency or great uncertainty, either individually or in combination, appear. On the contrary, except when *transaction-specific investments* are involved, neither frequency nor uncertainty, individually or in combination, would justify the creation of internal organization (with its associated transaction-specific governance structure).

Considering the importance that I attach to transaction-specific investments, some explication is needed. The crucial issue is the degree to which durable, nonmarketable expenses are incurred. Items that are unspecialized among users pose few hazards, since buyers in these circumstances can easily turn to alternative sources, and suppliers can sell output intended for one buyer to other buyers without difficulty. Nonmarketability problems arise when the *specific identity* of the parties has important cost-bearing consequences. Transactions of this kind will be referred to as idiosyncratic.

Occasionally the identity of the parties is important from the outset, as when a buyer induces a supplier to invest in specialized physical capital of a transaction-specific kind. Inasmuch as the value of this capital in other uses is, by definition, much smaller than the specialized use for which it has been intended, the supplier is effectively 'locked into' the transaction to a significant degree. This is symmetrical, moreover, in that the buyer cannot turn to alternative sources of supply and obtain the item on favourable terms, since the cost of supply from unspecialized capital is presumably great. The buyer is thus committed to the transaction as well.

Ordinarily, however, there is more to idiosyncratic exchange than specialized physical capital. Human-capital investments that are transaction-specific commonly occur as well. Specialized training and learning-by-doing economies in production operations are illustrations. Except when these investments are transferable to alternative suppliers at low cost, which is rare, the benefits of the set-up costs can be realized only so long as the relationship between the buyer and seller of the intermediate product is maintained . . .

Governance structures
Three broad types of governance structures will be considered: non-transaction-specific, semi-specific, and highly specific. The market is the classic nonspecific governance structure within which 'faceless buyers and sellers . . . meet . . . for an instant to exchange standardized goods at equilibrium prices'. . . . By contrast, highly specific structures are tailored to the special needs of the transaction. Identity here clearly matters. Semi-specific structures, naturally, fall in between. Several propositions are suggested immediately.

(1) Highly standardized transactions are not apt to require a specialized governance structure.
(2) Only recurrent transactions will support a highly specialized governance structure.
(3) Although occasional transactions of a nonstandardized kind will not support a transaction-specific governance structure, they require special attention nonetheless.

In terms of Macneil's three-way classification of contract, classical contracting presumably applies to all standardized transactions (whatever the frequency), relational contracting develops for transactions of a recurring and nonstandardized kind and neoclassical contracting is needed for occasional, nonstandardized transactions.

Market governance: classical contracting
Market governance is the main governance structure for nonspecific transactions of both occasional and recurrent contracting. . . .

The assumptions of the discrete-contracting paradigm are rather well satisfied for transactions where markets serve as a main governance mode. Thus the specific identity of the parties is of negligible importance, substantive content is determined by reference to formal terms of the contract and legal rules. Market alternatives are mainly what protect each party against opportunism by his opposite . . .

Trilateral governance: neoclassical contracting
. . . The interests of the principals in sustaining the relations are especially great for highly idiosyncratic transactions.

Market relief is thus unsatisfactory. Often the set-up costs of a transaction-specific governance structure cannot be recovered for occasional transactions. Given the limits of classical contract law for sustaining these transactions on the one hand, and the prohibitive cost of transaction-specific (bilateral) governance on the other, an intermediate institutional form is evidently needed.

Neoclassical contract law has many of the sought-after qualities. Thus rather than resort immediately to strict reliance on litigation—with its transaction-rupturing features—*third-party assistance* (arbitration) in resolving disputes and evaluating performance is employed instead. (Thus use of the architect as a relatively independent expert to determine the content of form construction contracts is an example; Macneil, 1978, p 866.) . . .

Transaction-specific governance: relational contracting

. . . [1.] *Bilateral governance: obligational contracting.* Highly idiosyncratic transactions are ones where the human and physical assets required for production are extensively specialized, so there are no obvious scale economies to be realized through interfirm trading that the buyer (or seller) is unable to realize himself through vertical integration. . . .

. . . Inasmuch as the interests of the parties will commonly be at variance when adaptation proposals (originated by either party) are made, a dilemma is evidently posed.

On the one hand, both parties have an incentive to sustain the relationship rather than to permit it to unravel, the object being to avoid the sacrifice of valued transaction-specific economies. On the other hand, each party appropriates a separate profit stream and cannot be expected to accede readily to any proposal to adapt the contract. What is needed, evidently, is some way for delaring admissible dimensions for adjustment such that flexibility is provided under terms in which both parties have confidence. This can be accomplished partly by, first, recognizing that the hazards of opportunism vary with the type of adaptation proposed and, secondly, restricting adjustments to those where the hazards are least. But the spirit within which adaptations are effected is equally important.

Quantity adjustments have much better incentive-compatibility properties than do price adjustments. For one thing, price adjustments have an unfortunate zero-sum quality, whereas proposals to increase, decrease or delay delivery do not. . . .

[2] *Unified governance: internal organization.* Incentives for trading weaken as transactions become progressively more idiosyncratic. The reason is that as the specialized human and physical assets become more specialized to a single use, and hence less transferable to other uses, economies of scale can be as fully realized by the buyer as by an outside supplier. The choice of organizing mode then turns on which mode has superior adaptive properties . . . vertical integration will invariably appear in these circumstances. . . .

NOTE

Many of the references in the above have been omitted. Those remaining are as follows:

COASE, R. H. (1937), The nature of the firm, *Economica NS*, **4**, 336–405, repr. in *Readings in Price Theory* (1952). (G. J. Stigler and K. E. Bouldings, eds), Homewood, Ill: Richard D. Irwin Inc.

COASE, R. H. (1972), Industrial organization: a proposal for research, in *Policy Issues and Research Opportunities in Industrial Organization*, 59–73, (V. R. Fuchs, ed), New York: National Bureau of Economic Research.

COMMONS, J. R. (1934), *Institutional Economics*, Madison: University of Wisconsin Press.

GOFFMANN, I. (1969) *Strategic Interaction*, Philadelphia: University of Pennsylvania Press.

GOLDBERG, V. P. (1976), Toward an expanded theory of contract, *Journal of Economic Issues*, **10**, 45–61.

HAYEK, F. (1945), The use of knowledge in society, *American Economic Review*, **35**, 519–530.

MACNEIL I. R. (1974), The many futures of contract, *Southern California Law Review*, **47**, 691–816.

MACNEIL I. R. (1978), Contracts: adjustment of long-term economic relations under classical, neoclassical and relational contract law, *Northwestern University Law Review*, **72**, no 6, 854–905.

SIMON, H. A. (1961), *Administrative Behaviour*, 2nd ed, p xxiv, New York: The Macmillan Company.

Section 8
Policing the bargain

CHAPTER 29
Duress

'Unconscionability: A Critical Reappraisal' by Epstein (1975) 18 J Law & Econ 293, 293–294

The classical conception of contract at common law had as its first premise the belief that private agreements should be enforced in accordance with their terms. That premise of course was subject to important qualifications. Promises procured by fraud, duress, or undue influence were not generally enforced by the courts; and the same was true with certain exceptions of promises made by infants and incompetents. Again, agreements that had as their object illegal ends were usually not enforced, as, for example, in cases of bribes of public officials or contracts to kill third persons. Yet even after these exceptions are taken into account, there was still one ground on which the initial premise could not be challenged: the terms of private agreements could not be set aside because the court found them to be harsh, unconscionable, or unjust. The reasonableness of the terms of a private agreement was the business of the parties to that agreement. True, there were numerous cases in which the language of the contract stood in need of judicial interpretation, but once that task was done there was no place for a court to impose upon the parties its own views about their rights and duties. 'Public policy' was an 'unruly horse', to be mounted only in exceptional cases and then only with care.

This general regime of freedom of contract can be defended from two points of view. One defense is utilitarian. So long as the tort law protects the interests of strangers to the agreement, its enforcement will tend to maximize the welfare of the parties to it, and therefore the good of the society as a whole. The alternative defense is on libertarian grounds. One of the first functions of the law is to guarantee to individuals a sphere of influence in which they will be able to operate, without having to justify themselves to the state or to third parties: if one individual is entitled to do within the confines of the tort law what he pleases with what he owns, then two individuals who operate with those same constraints should have the same right with respect to their mutual affairs against the rest of the world.

Whatever its merits, however, it is fair to say that this traditional view of the law of contract has been in general retreat in recent years. That decline is reflected in part in the cool reception given to doctrines of laissez-faire, its economic counterpart, since the late nineteenth century, or at least since the New Deal. The total 'hands off' policy with respect to economic matters is regarded as incorrect in most political discussions almost as a matter of course and the same view is taken, moreover, toward a more subtle form of laissez-faire that views all government interference in economic matters as an evil until shown to be good. Instead, the opposite point of view is increasingly urged: market solutions—those which presuppose a regime of freedom of contract—are sure to be inadequate, and the only question worth debating concerns the appropriate form of public intervention. That attitude has, moreover, worked its way (as these things usually happen) into the fabric of the legal system, for today, more than ever, courts are willing to set aside the provisions of private agreements.

One of the major conceptual tools used by courts in their assault upon private agreements has been the doctrine of unconscionability. That doctrine has a place in contract law, but it is not the one usually assigned it by its advocates. The doctrine should not, in my view, allow courts to act as roving commissions to set aside those agreements whose substantive terms they find objectionable. . . .

We suggested in the Introduction (see p 60 ff.) that many rules of contract law are to a greater or lesser extent concerned with ensuring the fairness of contracts. (For a fuller account, see Atiyah, *Essays on Contract* (1986), chap 11.) In this section we will look at various rules which are openly concerned with fairness, first in relation to contracts in general and then in

635

relation to standard form contracts and exemption clauses. There are a number of distinct (though sometimes overlapping) doctrines in this area, and as we look at each it is important to ask a number of questions. In what way is the contract supposedly unfair? Does the unfairness lie in the way that the contract was made, ie 'procedural unfairness'? Or does it lie in the terms of the resulting contract, 'substantive unfairness'? Or is there a combination of the two? (The distinction between procedural and substantive unfairness is adopted from a famous article by Leff in (1967) 115 U Pa LR 485 on s 2–302 of the UCC, see below, p 673, and has now found its way into English case law, see below, p 662.) If substantive unfairness is involved, what precisely is wrong: is one party being overcharged or underpaid, or is something else wrong? If relief is given, what form does it take?

Barton v Armstrong [1975] 2 All ER 465, Privy Council

B, the managing director of a company, executed on its behalf a deed by which the company agreed to pay $140,000 to A, its chairman, and to buy A's shares from him for $180,000, in order to get him off the board of the company. He did this at least partly for commercial reasons, but the trial judge also found that A had threatened to have B killed if he did not make the arrangements. B later tried to have the deed set aside for duress, but the Court of Appeal of New South Wales, affirming the decision at first instance, held that the onus was on B to show that he would not have signed the deed but for the threats, and he had failed to discharge that onus. B appealed.

Lord Cross. . . . Their Lordships turn now to consider the question of law which provoked a difference of opinion in the Court of Appeal Division. It is hardly surprising that there is no direct authority on the point, for if A threatens B with death if he does not execute some document and B, who takes A's threats seriously, executes the document it can be only in the most unusual circumstances that there can be any doubt whether the threats operated to induce him to execute the document. But this is a most unusual case and the findings of fact made below do undoubtedly raise the question whether it was necessary for Barton in order to obtain relief to establish that he would not have executed the deed in question but for the threats. In answering this question in favour of Barton Jacobs JA relied both on a number of old common law authorities on the subject of 'duress' and also—by way of analogy—on later decisions in equity with regard to the avoidance of deeds on the ground of fraud. Their Lordships do not think that the common law authorities are of any real assistance for it seems most unlikely that the authors of the statements relied on had the sort of problem which has arisen here in mind at all. On the other hand they think that the conclusion to which Jacobs JA came was right and that it is supported by the equity decisions. The scope of common law duress was very limited and at a comparatively early date equity began to grant relief in cases where the disposition in question had been procured by the exercise of pressure which the Chancellor considered to be illegitimate—although it did not amount to common law duress. There was a parallel development in the field of dispositions induced by fraud. At common law the only remedy available to the man defrauded was an action for deceit but equity in the same period in which it was building up the doctrine of 'undue influence' came to entertain proceedings to set aside dispositions which had been obtained by fraud: see Holdworth's History of English Law [vol V, pp 328–329]. There is an obvious analogy between setting aside a disposition for duress or undue influence and setting it aside for fraud. In each case—to quote the words of Holmes J in *Fairbanks v Snow*—'the party has been subjected to an improper motive for action'. Again the similarity of the effect in law of metus and dolus in connection with dispositions of property is noted by Stair in his *Institutions of the Law of Scotland*. Had Armstrong made a fraudulent misrepresentation to Barton for the purpose of inducing him to execute the deed of 17th January 1967 the answer to the problem which has arisen would have been clear. If it were established that Barton did not allow the representation to affect his judgment then he could not make it a ground for relief even though the representation was designed and known by Barton to be designed to affect his judgment. If on the other hand Barton relied on the misrepresentation Armstrong could not have defeated his claim to relief by showing that there were other more weighty causes which contributed to his decision to execute the deed, for in this field the court does not allow an examination into the relative importance of contributory causes. 'Once make out that there has been anything like deception, and no contract resting in any degree on that foundation can stand' (per Lord Cranworth LJ in *Reynell v Sprye*; see also the other cases referred to in Cheshire and Fifoot's Law of Contract). Their Lordships think that the same rule should apply in cases of duress and that if Armstrong's threats were 'a' reason for Barton's executing the deed he is entitled to relief even though he might well have entered into the contract if Armstrong had uttered no threats to induce him to do so. . . . The proper inference to be drawn from the facts found is, their Lordships think, that though it may be that Barton would have executed the documents even if Armstrong had made no threats and exerted no unlawful pressure to induce him to do so the threats and unlawful pressure in fact contributed to his decision to sign the documents and to recommend their execution by Landmark and the other parties to them. It may be, of course, that Barton's fear of Armstrong had evaporated before he issued his writ in this action but Armstrong—understandably enough—expressly disclaimed reliance on the defence of delay on Barton's part in repudiating the deed.

In the result therefore the appeal should be allowed and a declaration made that the deeds in question were executed by Barton under duress and are void so far as concerns him. . . .

Dissenting judgment by **Lord Wilberforce** and **Lord Simon of Glaisdale.**

. . . The action is one to set aside an apparently complete and valid agreement on the ground of duress. The basis of the plaintiff's claim is, thus, that though there was apparent consent there was no true consent to the agreement: that the agreement was not voluntary.

This involves consideration of what the law regards as voluntary, or its opposite; for in life, including the life of commerce and finance, many acts are done under pressure, sometimes overwhelming pressure, so that one can say that the actor had no choice but to act. Absence of choice in this sense does not negate consent in law; for this the pressure must be one of a kind which the law does not regard as legitimate. Thus, out of the various means by which consent may be obtained—advice, persuasion, influence, inducement, representation, commercial pressure—the law has come to select some which it will not accept as a reason for voluntary action: fraud, abuse of relation of confidence, undue influence, duress or coercion. In this the law, under the influence of equity, has developed from the old common law conception of duress—threat to life and limb—and it has arrived at the modern generalisation expressed by Holmes J—'subjected to an improper motive for action' (*Fairbanks v Snow*).

In an action such as the present, then, the first step required of the plaintiff is to show that some illegitimate means of persuasion was used. That there were threats to Barton's life was found by the judge, though he did not accept Barton's evidence in important respects. We shall return to this point in detail later.

The next necessary step would be to establish the relationship between the illegitimate means used and the action taken. For the purposes of the present case (reserving our opinion as to cases which may arise in other contexts) we are prepared to accept, as the formula most favourable to Barton, the test proposed by the majority, namely that the illegitimate means used was *a* reason (not *the* reason, nor the *predominant* reason nor the *clinching* reason) why the complainant acted as he did. We are also prepared to accept that a decisive answer is not obtainable by asking the question whether the contract would have been made even if there had been no threats because, even if the answer to this question is affirmative, that does not prove that the contract was not made because of the threats.

Assuming therefore that what has to be decided is whether the illegitimate means used was a reason why the complainant acted as he did, it follows that his reason for acting must (unless the case is one of automatism which this is not) be a conscious reason so that the complainant can give evidence of it: 'I acted because I was forced'. If his evidence is honest and accepted, that will normally conclude the issue. If, moreover, he gives evidence, it is necessary for the court to evaluate his evidence by testing it against his credibility and his actions.

In this case Barton gave evidence—his was, for practical purposes, the only evidence supporting his case. The judge rejected it in important respects and accepted it in others. The issues as to Barton's motivations were issues purely of fact (that motivation is a question of fact hardly needs authority, but see *Cox v Smail* per Cussen J); the findings as to motivation were largely, if not entirely, findings as to credibility. It would be difficult to find matters more peculiarly than these within the field of the trial judge who saw both contestants in the box, and who dealt carefully and at length with the credibility, or lack of credibility, of each of them. . . .

The judge's findings were also accepted, after careful examination by Taylor A-JA: '. . . the conclusion', he finds, 'that Barton entered into this agreement because he wanted to and from commercial motives only is, I think, undoubtedly correct'.

The appeal cannot succeed unless these most explicit findings are overturned. We consider that no basis exists for doing so.

NOTES

1. Barton had the deed set aside: in other words, duress is a ground on which an executed contract may be set aside. Equally a 'gift' made under duress may be set aside.
2. Although Lord Cross refers to the deeds as 'void', it seems likely that a contract made under duress is voidable. Cross also refers to 'setting aside' the contract, as for fraud, and the dissenting speeches seem to treat duress as making the contract voidable. In cases of economic duress it has been held that the contract is voidable and that the right to have it set aside may be lost through affirmation or delay: below, p 639.
3. Presumably the contract would equally be voidable if the threat were to destroy or damage the plaintiff's property wantonly: see *The Siboen and the Sibotre* (below, p 640).

As we suggested in the last section, it has recently been recognized that there may be other forms of duress besides threats of physical injury or damage. Relief was given as early as the eighteenth century when a payment was made in order to avert a wrongful seizure or detention of the plaintiff's goods; the recent cases recognize that relief may also be given when the threat is to break a contract in circumstances which will cause the party threatened severe economic loss.

But these new categories of duress raise new problems. Why shouldn't the victim refuse to pay up, and sue in damages for any loss the threatening party causes him by carrying out the threat? What if the other party is acting in the honest belief that he is entitled to detain the plaintiff's goods, or to refuse to perform his contract? What if the plaintiff is not much influenced by the threat, and agrees to pay up primarily because he does not want the bother of contesting the claim?

Maskell v Horner [1915] 3 KB 106, Court of Appeal

The plaintiff was a dealer in produce who carried on business near Spitalfields market. The defendant, the owner of the market, demanded tolls from him, and when the plaintiff refused, seized the plaintiff's goods. Thereafter, the plaintiff paid the tolls, always under protest, for some twelve years; whenever he challenged the defendant's right to the tolls, seizure or threatened seizure followed. After it had been decided in another case that the tolls were unlawful, the plaintiff sought to recover the money.

Lord Reading CJ. . . . [T]he plaintiff asserts that he paid the money not voluntarily but under the pressure of actual or threatened seizure of his goods, and that he is therefore entitled to recover it as money had and received. If the facts proved support this assertion the plaintiff would, in my opinion, be entitled to succeed in this action.

If a person with knowledge of the facts pays money, which he is not in law bound to pay, and in circumstances implying that he is paying it voluntarily to close the transaction, he cannot recover it. Such a payment is in law like a gift, and the transaction cannot be reopened. If a person pays money, which he is not bound to pay, under the compulsion of urgent and pressing necessity or of seizure, actual or threatened, of his goods he can recover it as money had and received. The money is paid not under duress in the strict sense of the term, as that implies duress of person, but under the pressure of seizure or detention of goods which is analogous to that of duress. Payment under such pressure establishes that the payment is not made voluntarily to close the transaction (per Lord Abinger CB and per Parke B in *Atlee v Backhouse*). The payment is made for the purpose of averting a threatened evil and is made not with the intention of giving up a right but under immediate necessity and with the intention of preserving the right to dispute the legality of the demand (per Tindal CJ in *Valpy v Manley*). There are numerous instances in the books of successful claims in this form of action to recover money paid to relieve goods from seizure. Other familiar instances are cases such as *Parker v Great Western Rly Co*, where the money was paid to the railway company under protest in order to induce them to carry goods which they were refusing to carry except at rates in excess of those they were legally entitled to demand. These payments were made throughout a period of twelve months, always accompanied by the assertion that they were made under protest, and it was held that the plaintiffs were entitled to recover the excess payments as money had and received, on the ground that the payments were made under the compulsion of urgent and pressing necessity. That case was approved in *Great Western Rly Co v Sutton*, when the judges were summoned to the House of Lords to give their opinion. Willes J, in stating his view of the law, said: 'When a man pays more than he is bound to do by law for the performance of a duty which the law says is owed to him for nothing, or for less than he has paid, there is a compulsion or concussion in respect of which he is entitled to recover the excess by condictio indebiti, or action for money had and received. This is every day's practice as to excess freight.' That is a clear and accurate statement in accordance with the views expressed by Blackburn J in the same case and adopted by the House of Lords. It treats such claims made in this form of action as matters of ordinary practice and beyond discussion. (See also per Lord Chelmsford in *Lancashire and Yorkshire Rly Co v Gidlow*.) . . .

Pickford LJ. . . . The second ground of claim is that the payments were not voluntary payments, but were made under protest and to avoid seizure of the plantiff's goods. I do not think that the mere fact that a payment is made under protest is enough to entitle the payer to recover it back, but if it be shown that it was made under circumstances which show that the payer intends to resist the claim and yields to it merely for the purpose of relieving himself from the inconvenience of having his goods sold the money can be recovered back, and the fact of a protest is some indication that it is so made.

I do not think there need be an express notice or declaration of the intention to resist if it is properly indicated by all the circumstances.

Payment to avoid a seizure or (subject to a point taken by the defendant's counsel) a threatened seizure is an involuntary payment and can be recovered back: *Valpy v Manley*. . . .

[Buckley LJ delivered a concurring judgment.]

Appeal allowed.

NOTE

Is saying that the payment is recoverable unless it was made 'voluntarily to close the transaction' the same as saying that relief will be given unless the party threatened was not influenced by the threat at all (cf *Barton v Armstrong*), or does the party threatened have to show something more?

North Ocean Shipping Co v Hyundai Construction Co, The Atlantic Baron [1978] 3 All ER 1170, Mocatta J

Shipbuilders agreed to build a tanker for the owners at a price which was fixed (except in certain events which did not occur). The price was payable in five instalments, and the builders opened a 'reverse' letter of credit to secure repayment of the instalments in the event of their default. After the first instalment had been paid, the dollar was devalued and the builders threatened not to deliver unless the remaining instalments were increased by 10%. The owners were advised that there was no legal basis for the claim, but were anxious that they might lose a favourable charter they had arranged for the vessel to Shell, and in a telex dated 28 June 1973 they agreed to pay the extra

10% 'to maintain an amicable relationship and without prejudice to our rights'. They requested the builders to increase the reverse letter of credit by a corresponding percentage. The builders did this and delivered the tanker; the owners paid the final instalment, and took delivery, without protest. Some eight months later the owners claimed the return of the 10% extra; it was suggested that they did not seek its return earlier because they were concerned that delivery of a sister ship also being built for them might be affected, but the arbitrators found that this fear was groundless. Mocatta J held that preserving 'amicable relations' could not amount to consideration; but that there was no obligation on the builders to increase the letter of credit if the price were increased, and doing so was consideration for the promise to pay the extra 10%. He continued:

Mocatta J. . . . Having reached the conclusion that there was consideration for the agreement made on 28th and 29th June 1973 I must next consider whether even if that agreement, varying the terms of the original shipbuilding contract of 10th April 1972, was made under a threat to break that original contract and the various increased instalments were made consequentially under the varied agreement, the increased sums can be recovered as money had and received. Counsel for the owners submitted that they could be, provided they were involuntary payments and not made, albeit perhaps with some grumbling, to close the transaction.

Certainly this is the well-established position if payments are made, for example, to avoid the wrongful seizure of goods where there is no prior agreement to make such payments. The best known English case to this effect is probably *Maskell v Horner*. . . .

There has been considerable discussion in the books whether, if an agreement is made under duress of goods to pay a sum of money and there is some consideration for the agreement, the excess sum can be recovered. The authority for this suggested distinction is *Skeate v Beale*. It was there said by Lord Denman CJ that an agreement was not void because it was made under duress of goods, the distinction between that case and the cases of money paid to recover goods wrongfully seized being said to be obvious in that the agreement was not compulsorily but voluntarily entered into. In the slightly later case of *Wakefield v Newbon*, Lord Denman CJ referred to cases such as *Skeate v Beale* as 'that class where the parties have come to a voluntary settlement of their concerns, and have chosen to pay what is found due'. Kerr J in *The Siboen and The Sibotre*, gave strong expression to the view that the suggested distinction based on *Skeate v Beale* would not be observed today. He said, though obiter, that *Skeate v Beale* would not justify a decision that—

'if, for instance, I should be compelled to sign a lease or some other contract for a nominal but legally sufficient consideration under an imminent threat of having my house burnt down or a valuable picture slashed, though without any threat of physical violence to anyone, I do not think the law would uphold the agreement'.

I was referred to a number of cases decided overseas: *Nixon v Furphy, Knutson v Bourkes Syndicate* and *Re Hooper and Grass' Contract*, all of which have a similarity to *Close v Phipps*. Perhaps their greatest importance, however, is the quotation in the first mentioned from the judgment of Isaacs J in *Smith v William Charlick Ltd*, where he said:

'It is conceded that the only ground on which the promise to repay could be implied is "compulsion". The payment is said by the respondent not to have been "voluntary" but "forced" from it within the contemplation of the law . . . "Compulsion" in relation to a payment of which refund is sought, and whether it is also variously called "coercion", "extortion", "exaction" or "force", includes every species of duress or conduct analogous to duress, actual or threatened, exacted by or on behalf of the payee and applied to the person or the property or any right of the person who pays . . . Such compulsion is a legal wrong, and the law provides a remedy by raising a fictional promise to repay'.

These cases do not, however, expressly deal with the position arising when the threat or compulsion results in a new or varied contract. This was, or something very like it, however, the position in *T A Sundell & Sons Pty Ltd v Emm Yannoulatos (Overseas) Pty Ltd*. In that case the plaintiff had originally entered into a contract to buy from the defendant a quantity of galvanised iron at £100 15s a ton and had established a letter of credit in favour of the defendant seller accordingly. The iron was to come from France and some months after the contract had been entered into the seller said that an increase in price of probably £27 was inevitable and requested that the letter of credit be increased, otherwise the plaintiff would not get his iron. Eventually the buyer on 17th April sent the seller a fresh order for the same quantity of iron at £140 per ton, but asking the seller to acknowledge that the buyer should have the right to contend that the original contract required the seller to supply the iron at £109 15s a ton. The buyer amended and increased his letter of credit accordingly, but the seller in acknowledging the buyer's letter did not accept the terms laid down in it. Eventually the iron arrived before the argument had been resolved and full use was made of the increased letter of credit.

The buyer thereafter sued to recover the excess he had paid through the increased letter of credit as having been paid under 'practical compulsion'. The first point taken in answer to this was that the original contract was varied or superseded by a new contract made on 17th April and that accordingly the buyer was obliged thereunder to pay. This argument failed since the court found there was no consideration for the provision of the increased letter of credit. The second point argued was that a payment could not be said to have been made under 'practical compulsion' where a threat was made by the payee to withhold from the payer a contractual right as distinct from a right of possession of property, a statutory right or some proprietary right. This it was argued would be to break new ground and would be contrary to what was said by Lord Sumner in *Sinclair v Brougham* against extending the action for money had and received. These arguments were rejected by the court who cited the passage from the judgment of Isaacs J, set out above emphasising by italics the words 'or any right' of the person paying under compulsion. It would seem, therefore, that the Australian courts would be prepared to allow the recovery of excess money paid, even under a new contract, as the result of a threat to break an earlier contract, since the threat or compulsion would be applied to the original contractual right of the party subject to the compulsion or economic duress. This also seems to be the view in the United States, where this was one of the grounds of decision in *King Construction Company v Smith Electric Co*. This view also accords with what was said in *D & C Builders Ltd v Rees* per Lord Denning MR: 'No person can insist on a settlement procured by intimidation.'

Before proceeding further it may be useful to summarise the conclusions I have so far reached. First, I do not take the view that the recovery of money paid under duress other than to the person is necessarily limited to duress to goods falling within one of the categories hitherto established by the English cases. I would respectfully follow and adopt the broad statement of principle laid down by Isaacs J cited earlier and frequently quoted and applied in the Australian cases. Secondly, from this it follows that the compulsion may take the form of 'economic duress' if the necessary facts are proved. A threat to break a contract may amount to such 'economic duress'. Thirdly, if there has been such a form of duress leading to a contract for consideration, I think that contract is a voidable one which can be avoided and the excess money paid under it recovered.

I think the facts found in this case do establish that the agreement to increase the price by ten per cent reached at the end of June 1973 was caused by what may be called 'economic duress'. The yard were adamant in insisting on the increased price without having any legal justification for so doing and the owners realised that the yard would not accept anything other than an unqualified agreement to the increase. The owners might have claimed damages in arbitration against the yard with all the inherent unavoidable uncertainties of litigation, but in view of the position of the owners vis-à-vis their relations with Shell it would be unreasonable to hold that this is the course they should have taken: see *Astley v Reynolds*. The owners made a very reasonable offer of arbitration coupled with security for any award in the yard's favour that might be made, but this was refused. They then made their agreement, which can truly I think be said to have been made under compulsion, by the telex of 28th June without prejudice to their rights. I do not consider the yard's ignorance of the Shell charter material. It may well be that had they known of it they would have been even more exigent.

If I am right in the conclusion reached with some doubt earlier that there was consideration for the ten per cent increase agreement reached at the end of June 1973 and if it be right to regard this as having been reached under a kind of duress in the form of economic pressure, then what is said in *Chitty on Contracts*, to which both counsel referred me, is relevant, namely that a contract entered into under duress is voidable and not void—

> 'that a person who has entered into the contract may either affirm or avoid such contract after the duress has ceased; and if he has so voluntarily acted under it with a full knowledge of all the circumstances, he may be held bound on the ground of ratification, or if, after escaping from the duress, he takes no steps to set aside the transaction, he may be found to have affirmed it.'

On appeal in *Ormes v Beadel* and in Kerr J's case there was on the facts action which was held to amount to affirmation or acquiescence in the form of taking part in an arbitration pursuant to the impugned agreement. There is nothing comparable to such action here.

On the other hand, the findings of fact in the special case present difficulties whether one is proceeding on the basis of a voidable agreement reached at the end of June 1973 or whether such agreement was void for want of consideration, and it were necessary in consequence to establish that the payments were made involuntarily and not with the intention of closing the transaction.

I have already stated that no protest of any kind was made by the owners after their telex of 28th June 1973, before their claim in this arbitration on 30th July 1975, which was shortly after, in July of that year, the Atlantic Baroness, a sister ship of the Atlantic Baron, had been tendered, though, as I understand it, she was not accepted and arbitration proceedings in regard to her are in consequence taking place. There was therefore a delay between 27th November 1974, when the Atlantic Baron was delivered and 30th July 1975, before the owners put forward their claim.

The owners were, therefore, free from the duress on 27th November 1974 and took no action by way of protest or otherwise between their important telex of 28th June 1973 and their formal claim for the return of the excess ten per cent paid of 30th July 1975, when they nominated their arbitrator. One cannot dismiss this delay as of no significance, though I would not consider it conclusive by itself. I do not attach any special importance to the lack of protest made at the time of the assignment, since the documents made no reference to the increased ten per cent. However by the time the Atlantic Baron was due for delivery in November 1974 market conditions had changed radically, as is found in the special case and the owners must have been aware of this. The special case finds, as stated earlier, that the owners did not believe that if they made any protest in the protocol of delivery and acceptance the yard would have refused to deliver the vessel or the Atlantic Baroness and had no reason so to believe. Counsel for the owners naturally stressed that in the rather carefully expressed findings in the special case, there is no finding that if at the time of the final payments the owners had withheld payment of the additional ten per cent, the yard would not have delivered the vessel. However, after careful consideration, I have come to the conclusion that the important points here are that (i) since there was no danger at this time in registering a protest, (ii) the final payments were made without any qualification, and (iii) were followed by a delay until 31st July 1975 before the owners put forward their claim, the correct inference to draw, taking an objective view of the facts, is that the action and inaction of the owners can only be regarded as an affirmation of the variation in June 1973 of the terms of the original contract by the agreement to pay the additional ten per cent. In reaching this conclusion I have not, of course, overlooked the findings in the special case [that the owners never intended to affirm the agreement for extra payments] but I do not think that an intention on the part of the owners not to affirm the agreement for the extra payments, not indicated to the yard, can avail them in view of their overt acts. As was said in *Deacon v Transport Regulation Board* in considering whether a payment was made voluntarily or not: 'No secret mental reservation of the doer is material. The question is—what would his conduct indicate to a reasonable man as his mental state'. I think this test is equally applicable to the decision this court has to make whether a voidable contract has been affirmed or not and I have applied this test in reaching the conclusion I have just expressed.

I think I should add very shortly that having considered the many authorities cited, even if I had come to a different conclusion on the issue about consideration, I would have come to the same decision adverse to the owners on the question whether the payments were made voluntarily in the sense of being made to close the transaction.

I accordingly answer the question of law in the negative with the consequences set out in the award.

Judgment for the yard.

Pao On v Lau Yiu Long [1980] AC 614, Privy Council

(For the facts of this case, see above, p 117.)

Lord Scarman. . . . The American Law Institute in its *Restatement of the Law, Contracts*, Chapter 3, section 84(d), has declared that performance (or promise of performance) of a contractual duty owed to a third person is sufficient consideration. This view (which accords with the statement of our law in *New Zealand Shipping Co Ltd v A M Satterthwaite & Co Ltd*) appears to be generally accepted but only in cases where there is no suggestion of unfair economic pressure exerted to induce the making of what *Corbin on Contracts* calls 'the return promise'.

Their Lordships' knowledge of this developing branch of American law is necessarily limited. In their judgment it would be carrying audacity to the point of foolhardiness for them to attempt to extract from the American case law a principle to provide an answer to the question now under consideration. That question, their Lordships repeat is whether, in a case where duress is not established, public policy may nevertheless invalidate the consideration if there has been a threat to repudiate a pre-existing contractual obligation or an unfair use of a dominating bargaining position. Their Lordships' conclusion is that where businessmen are negotiating at arm's length it is unnecessary for the achievement of justice, and unhelpful in the development of the law, to invoke such a rule of public policy. It would also create unacceptable anomaly. It is unnecessary because justice requires that men, who have negotiated at arm's length, be held to their bargains unless it can be shown that their consent was vitiated by fraud, mistake or duress. If a promise is induced by coercion of a man's will, the doctrine of duress suffices to do justice. The party coerced, if he chooses and acts in time, can avoid the contract. If there is no coercion, there can be no reason for avoiding the contract where there is shown to be a real consideration which is otherwise legal.

Such a rule of public policy as is now being considered would be unhelpful because it would render the law uncertain. It would become a question of fact and degree to determine in each case whether there had been, short of duress, an unfair use of a strong bargaining position. It would create anomaly because, if public policy invalidates the consideration, the effect is to make the contract void. But unless the facts are such as to support a plea of 'non est factum', which is not suggested in this case, duress does no more than confer upon the victim the opportunity, if taken in time, to avoid the contract. It would be strange if conduct less than duress could render a contract void, whereas duress does no more than render a contract voidable. Indeed, it is the defendant's case in this appeal that such an anomaly is the correct result. Their case is that the plaintiffs, having lost by cancellation the safeguard of the subsidiary agreement, are without the safeguard of the guarantee because its consideration is contrary to public policy, and that they are debarred from restoration to their position under the subsidiary agreement because the guarantee is void, not voidable. The logical consequence of Mr Leggatt's submission is that the safeguard which all were at all times agreed the plaintiffs should have—the safeguard against fall in value of the shares—has been lost by the application of a rule of public policy. The law is not, in their Lordships' judgment, reduced to countenancing such stark injustice: nor is it necessary, when one bears in mind the protection offered otherwise by the law to one who contracts in ignorance of what he is doing or under duress. Accordingly, the submission that the additional consideration established by the extrinsic evidence is invalid on the ground of public policy is rejected.

The third question
Duress, whatever form it takes, is a coercion of the will so as to vitiate consent. Their Lordships agree with the observation of Kerr J in *Occidental Worldwide Investment Corporation v Skibs A/S Avanti* . . . that in a contractual situation commercial pressure is not enough. There must be present some factor 'which could in law be regarded as a coercion of his will so as to vitiate his consent'. This conception is in line with what was said in this Board's decision in *Barton v Armstrong* by Lord Wilberforce and Lord Simon of Glaisdale—observations with which the majority judgment appears to be in agreement. In determining whether there was a coercion of will such that there was no true consent, it is material to inquire whether the person alleged to have been coerced did or did not protest; whether, at the time he was allegedly coerced into making the contract, he did or did not have an alternative course open to him such as an adequate legal remedy; whether he was independently advised; and whether after entering the contract he took steps to avoid it. All these matters are, as was recognised in *Maskell v Horner*, relevant in determining whether he acted voluntarily or not.

In the present case there is unanimity amongst the judges below that there was no coercion of the first defendant's will. In the Court of Appeal the trial judge's finding (already quoted) that the first defendant considered the matter thoroughly, chose to avoid litigation, and formed the opinion that the risk in giving the guarantee was more apparent than real was upheld. In short, there was commercial pressure, but no coercion. Even if this Board was disposed, which it is not, to take a different view, it would not substitute its opinion for that of the judges below on this question of fact.

It is, therefore, unnecessary for the Board to embark upon an inquiry into the question whether English law recognises a category of duress known as 'economic duress'. But, since the question has been fully argued in this appeal, their Lordships will indicate very briefly the view which they have formed. At common law money paid under economic compulsion could be recovered in an action for money had and received: *Astley v Reynolds*. The compulsion had to be such that the party was deprived of 'his freedom of exercising his will' (see p 916). It is doubtful, however, whether at common law any duress other than duress to the person sufficed to render a contract voidable: see *Blackstone's Commentaries*, Book 1, 12th edn pp 130–131 and *Skeate v Beale*. American law (*Williston on Contracts*, 3rd edn) now recognises that a contract may be avoided on the ground of economic duress. The commercial pressure alleged to constitute such duress must, however, be such that the victim must have entered the contract against his will, must have had no alternative course open to him, and must have been confronted with coercive acts by the party exerting the pressure: *Williston on Contracts*, 3rd edn, vol 13 (1970), section 1603. American judges pay great attention to such evidential matters as the effectiveness of the alternative remedy available, the fact or absence of protest, the availability of independent advice, the benefit received, and the speed with which the victim has sought to avoid the contract. Recently two English judges have recognised that commercial pressure may constitute duress the pressure of which can render a contract voidable: Kerr J in *Occidental Worldwide Investment Corporation v Skibs A/S Avanti* and Mocatta J in *North Ocean Shipping Co Ltd v Hyundai Construction Co Ltd*. Both stressed that the pressure must be such that the victim's consent to the contract was not a voluntary act on his part. In their Lordships' view, there is nothing contrary to principle in recognising economic duress as a factor which may render a contract voidable, provided always that the basis of such recognition is that it must amount to a coercion of will, which vitiates consent. It must be shown that the payment made or the contract entered into was not a voluntary act.

Appeal allowed.

NOTES

1. 'The victim must have had no alternative course open to him.' Why couldn't the owners in *The Atlantic Baron* refuse to pay extra and sue for damages if the contract was broken?

2. In *B & S Contracts and Design Ltd v Victor Green Publications Ltd* [1984] ICR 419 the plaintiffs had contracted to erect an exhibition stand for the defendants at Olympia. The plaintiffs' workmen went on strike and the plaintiffs informed the defendants that the contract would be cancelled unless the latter agreed to contribute £4,500 towards paying the workmen's claims. If the stands were not erected the defendants faced serious losses and claims from exhibitors to whom they had let space, so they paid up, but the Court of Appeal held that the promise had been made when the plaintiffs had the defendants 'over a barrel' and the defendants could deduct the £4,500 they had paid from the final sum due. A promise to pay an additional charge was also held to be ineffective because made under economic duress in *Atlas Express Ltd v Kafco (Importers and Distributors) Ltd* [1989] 1 All ER 641.

3. Is the victim's 'consent vitiated' if he has no alternative remedy, and he makes a promise or does an act he would not have done if the threat had not been made? Or must the pressure have been more overbearing than that? In *Occidental Worldwide Investment Corpn v Skibs A/S Avanti, The Siboen and The Sibotre* [1976] 1 Lloyd's Rep 293, at 334–336, Kerr J was prepared to assume that English law recognises economic duress: he considered that this was an alternative ground for the decision in *D & C Builders v Rees* (above, p 599)—'there was no true accord'. However, he rejected as much too wide counsel's proposition that the defence is made out 'whenever one party to a contract threatens to commit a breach of it and the other party agrees to vary or cancel the contract under this threat because it has no effective legal remedy in respect of the threatened breach and has in this sense been compelled to agree.' The compulsion must deprive the promisor of animus contrahendi, and on the facts the promisor was 'acting under great pressure, but only commercial pressure, and not under anything which in law could be regarded as a coercion of his will so as to vitiate his consent.' In the *B & S Contracts* case Griffiths LJ said ([1984] ICR at p 425):

. . . it is certainly not on every occasion when one of the parties unwillingly agrees to a variation that the law would consider that he had acted by reason of duress.

Contrast *Barton v Armstrong*, above, p 636.

If a threat coupled with commercial pressure is not enough, what is? Is the 'vitiation of consent' test an accurate description of the effect of duress? Compare *Lynch v DPP for Northern Ireland* [1975] 1 All ER 913 at 926a-c, 938h:

Lord Wilberforce. . . . [D]uress in the English law of contract . . . deflects, without destroying, the will of one of the contracting parties. There is still an intention on his part to contract in the apparently consensual terms; but there is coactus volui on his side. The contrast is with non est factum. The contract procured by duress is therefore not void: it is voidable—at the discretion of the party subject to duress.

Lord Simon of Glaisdale. . . . At the present time, whatever the ultimate analysis in jurisprudence may be, the best opinion, as reflected in decisions of judges and in writers, seems to be that duress per minas is something which is superimposed on the other ingredients which by themselves would make up an offence, ie on the act and intention. 'Coactus volui' sums up the combination: the victim completes the act and knows that he is doing so; but the addition of the element of duress prevents the law from treating what he has done as a crime. One may note—and the comparison is satisfactory—that an analogous result is achieved in a civil law context: duress does not destroy the will, for example, to enter into a contract, but prevents the law from accepting what has happened as a contract valid in law (see the Privy Council case of *Barton v Armstrong* and the judgments in the Supreme Court of New South Wales).

On this see the debate: Atiyah 98 LQR 197; Tiplady 99 LQR 188; Atiyah 99 LQR 353.

Universe Tankships Inc of Monrovia v International Transport Workers' Federation [1982] 2 All ER 67, House of Lords

The plaintiffs' ship was blacked by the defendant union ('ITF'). To secure its release the plaintiffs inter alia paid the sum of $6,480 to ITF's welfare fund. They later sought to recover this sum. ITF admitted that it had been paid under economic duress, but argued that the threat had been made in connection with a trade dispute and that they were therefore protected by the immunity against actions in tort conferred by the Trade Union and Labour Relations Act 1974, s 13.

Lord Diplock. . . . My Lords, I turn to the second ground on which repayment of the $6,480 is claimed, which I will call the duress point. It is not disputed that the circumstances in which the ITF demanded that the shipowners should enter into the special agreement and the typescript agreement and should pay the moneys of which the latter documents acknowledge receipt amounted to economic duress on the shipowners; that is to say, it is conceded that the financial consequences to the shipowners of the Universe Sentinel continuing to be rendered off hire under her time charter to Texaco, while the blacking continued, were so catastrophic as to amount to a coercion of the shipowners' will which vitiated their consent to those agreements and to the payments made by them to the ITF. This concession makes it unnecessary for your Lordships to use the instant appeal as the occasion for a general consideration of the developing law of economic duress as a ground for treating contracts as voidable and obtaining restitution of money paid under economic duress as money had and received to the plaintiffs' use. That economic duress may constitute a ground for such redress was recognised, albeit obiter, by the Privy Council in *Pao On v Lau Yiu*. The Board in that case referred with approval to two judgments at first instance in the Commercial Court which recognised that commercial pressure may constitute duress: one by Kerr J in *The Siboen and the Sibotre, Occidental Worldwide Investment Corp v Skibs A/S Avanti*; the other by Mocatta J in *North Ocean Shipping Co Ltd v Hyundai Construction Co Ltd, The Atlantic Baron*, which traces the development of this branch of the law from its origin in the eighteenth and early nineteenth century cases.

It is, however, in my view crucial to the decision of the instant appeal to identify the rationale of this development of the common law. It is not that the party seeking to avoid the contract which he has entered into with another party, or to recover money that he has paid to another party in response to a demand, did not know the nature or the precise terms of the contract at the time when he entered into it or did not understand the purpose for which the payment was demanded. The rationale is that his apparent consent was induced by pressure exercised on him by that other party which the law does not regard as legitimate, with the consequence that the consent is treated in law as revocable unless approbated either expressly or by implication after the illegitimate pressure has ceased to operate on his mind. It is rationale similar to that which underlies the avoidability of contracts entered into and the recovery of money exacted under colour of office, or under undue influence or in consequence of threats of physical duress.

Commercial pressure, in some degree, exists wherever one party to a commercial transaction is in a stronger bargaining position than the other party. It is not, however, in my view, necessary, nor would it be appropriate in the instant appeal, to enter into the general question of the kinds of circumstances, if any, in which commercial pressure, even though it amounts to a coercion of the will of a party in the weaker bargaining position, may be treated as legitimate and, accordingly, as not giving rise to any legal right of redress. In the instant appeal the economic duress complained of was exercised in the field of industrial relations to which very special considerations apply. . . .

Lord Scarman. . . . Before turning to this issue, it is necessary to state, albeit very briefly, my view as to the nature of the modern law of duress.

It is, I think, already established law that economic pressure can in law amount to duress; and that duress, if proved, not only renders voidable a transaction into which a person has entered under its compulsion but is actionable as a tort, if it causes damage or loss: see *Barton v Armstrong* and *Pao On v Lau Yiu*. The authorities on which these two cases were based reveal two elements in the wrong of duress: (1) pressure amounting to compulsion of the will of the victim; and (2) the illegitimacy of the pressure exerted. There must be pressure, the practical effect of which is compulsion or the absence of choice. Compulsion is variously described in the authorities as coercion or the vitiation of consent. The classic case of duress is, however, not the lack of will to submit but the victim's intentional submission arising from the realisation that there is no other practical choice open to him. This is the thread of principle which links the early law of duress (threat to life or limb) with later developments when the law came also to recognise as duress first the threat to property and now the threat to a man's business or trade. The development is well traced in Goff and Jones *The Law of Restitution* (2nd edn, 1978) ch 9.

The absence of choice can be proved in various ways, eg by protest, by the absence of independent advice, or by a declaration of intention to go to law to recover the money paid or the property transferred; see *Maskell v Horner*. But none of these evidential matters goes to the essence of duress. The victim's silence will not assist the bully, if the lack of any practicable choice but to submit is proved. The present case is an excellent illustration. There was no protest at the time, but only a determination to do whatever was needed as rapidly as possible to release the ship. Yet nobody challenges the judge's finding that the owners acted under compulsion. He put it thus:

'It was a matter of the most urgent commercial necessity that the plaintiffs should regain the use of their vessel. They were advised that their prospects of obtaining an injunction were minimal, the vessel would not have been released unless the payment was made, and they sought recovery of the money with sufficient speed once the duress had terminated.'

The real issue in the appeal is, therefore, as to the second element in the wrong duress: was the pressure applied by the ITF in the circumstances of this case one which the law recognises as legitimate? For, as Lord Wilberforce and Lord Simon in *Barton v Armstrong* said: '. . . the pressure must be one of a kind which the law does not regard as legitimate'.

As Lord Wilberforce and Lord Simon remarked, in life, including life in commerce and finance, many acts are done 'under pressure, sometimes overwhelming pressure'; but they are not necessarily done under duress. That depends on whether the circumstances are such that the law regards the pressure as legitimate.

In determining what is legitimate two matters may have to be considered. The first is as to the nature of the pressure. In many cases this will be decisive, though not in every case. And so the second question may have to be considered, namely, the nature of the demand which the pressure is applied to support.

The origin of the doctrine of duress in threats to life or limb, or to property, suggests strongly that the law regards the threat of unlawful action as illegitimate, whatever the demand. Duress can, of course, exist even if the threat is one of lawful action; whether it does so depends on the nature of the demand. Blackmail is often a demand supported by a threat to do what is lawful, eg to report criminal conduct to the police. In many cases, therefore, 'what [one] has to justify is not the threat, but the demand . . .' (see *Thorne v Motor Trade Association*, per Lord Atkin).

The present is a case in which the nature of the demand determines whether the pressure threatened or applied, ie the blacking, was lawful or unlawful. If it was unlawful, it is conceded that the owner acted under duress and can recover. If it was lawful, it is conceded that there was no duress and the sum sought by the owners is irrecoverable. The lawfulness or otherwise of the demand depends on whether it was an act done in contemplation or furtherance of a trade dispute. If it was, it would not be actionable in tort: s 13(1) of the Act. Although no question of tortious liability arises in this case and s 13(1) is not, therefore, directly in point, it is not possible, in my view, to say of acts which are protected by statute from suit in tort that they nevertheless can amount to duress. Parliament having enacted that such acts are not actionable in tort, it would be inconsistent with legislative policy to say that, when the remedy sought is not damages for tort but recovery of money paid, they become unlawful.

In order to determine whether the making of the demand was an act done in contemplation or furtherance of a trade dispute, it is necessary to refer to s 29 which sets out the statutory meaning of 'trade dispute'. . . .

By a majority the House held that the payment was recoverable because it was not 'connected with . . . the terms and conditions of employment' of the crew members so as to constitute a 'trade dispute' within s 29(1) of the Act.

If the 'vitiation of consent' test is not to be used, in what circumstances should the courts allow a plea of duress? Does the good or bad faith of the threatening party matter? Does it matter whether he knew the seriousness of the threatened party's position (see *The Atlantic Baron*)? Does it matter *why* he is threatening to break the contract? Further, do you think that the fairness of the agreement reached may be relevant? It is noticeable that in the *Pao On* case the Laus realised at the time that the initial agreement was very favourable to them, much more so than the arrangement originally contemplated, so that in a sense the second agreement was merely correcting a mistake made by Pao On in negotiating the first. (Compare also the requirement in cases of undue influence that the agreement must be 'manifestly disadvantageous' to the promisor before relief will be given: below, p 651.) At this stage you may find it useful to refer back to Posner, 'Gratuitous Promises in Economics and Law', above p 600, and you may like to compare Uniform Commercial Code s 2–209:

2–209. Modification, Rescission and Waiver
(1) An agreement modifying a contract within this Article needs no consideration to be binding.

. . .

Official Comment
. . . 2 . . . modifications . . . must meet the test of good faith imposed by this Act. The effective use of bad faith to escape performance on the original contract terms is barred, and the extortion of a 'modification' without legitimate commercial reason is ineffective as a violation of the duty of good faith . . . good faith . . . may in some situations require an objectively demonstrable reason for seeking a modification. But such matters as a market shift which makes performance come to involve a loss may provide such a reason even though there is no such unforeseen difficulty as would make out a legal excuse from performance.

NOTE

If the UCC test were applicable to *D & C Builders v Rees*, would the outcome change? What about *The Atlantic Baron*?

CHAPTER 30
Undue pressure and undue influence

An executory or executed contract or gift would also be set aside in equity in certain circumstances. Following the judgment of Cotton LJ in *Allcard v Skinner* (1887) 36 Ch D 145, 171, it is customary to divide the cases in to two broad classes:

> First where the court has been satisfied that the gift was the result of influence expressly used by the donee for the purpose; second, where the relations between the donor and donee have at or shortly before the execution of the gift been such as to raise a presumption that the donee had influence over the donor.

An example of the first class is *Williams v Bayley* (1866) LR 1 HL 200. The respondent's son had given the appellants promissory notes on which he had forged his father's indorsement. The father, threatened by the appellants with criminal prosecution of his son, agreed to make an equitable mortgage in favour of the appellants in exchange for the return of the notes. The House of Lords upheld cancellation of the agreement. At the time, threats of criminal prosecution were thought to be outside the scope of duress at common law; perhaps this case could now be reclassified as one of duress. In practice there is a good deal of overlap between cases of undue pressure like *Williams v Bayley* and undue influence, as undue pressure may be brought to bear by one who is in a confidential relationship with the person pressurized.

Cases of undue influence may be further subdivided. In some situations, for instance between solicitor and client, doctor and patient or religious adviser and disciple, the existence of a 'confidential relationship' is presumed; in others it must be proved.

Lloyds Bank Ltd v Bundy [1974] 3 All ER 757, Court of Appeal

The plaintiff was an elderly farmer who was not well versed in business affairs. His son had formed a plant hire company which was in financial difficulties, and the plaintiff had already given a guarantee and a charge for £7,500 over his farmhouse, which was his only asset, to secure the company's debts to the bank where father, son and the company had their accounts. At that time the plaintiff had consulted his solicitor, who had advised him that this was the most he should commit to the son's business. The company's affairs got worse, and the assistant bank manager and the son went to see the plaintiff. The assistant manager told him that the bank could only continue to support the company if the plaintiff increased the guarantee and charge to £11,000; although he realised that the plaintiff was relying on him for advice, and that the house was his only asset, the assistant manager did not explain the company's position in full. The plaintiff signed the form of guarantee and charge. Later the bank proceeded to enforce the charge and brought an action for possession of the house.

Sir Eric Sachs. . . . As was pointed out in *Tufton v Sperni*, the relationships which result in such a duty must not be circumscribed by reference to defined limits: it is necessary to—

> 'refute the suggestion that, to create the relationship of confidence, the person owing a duty must be found clothed in the recognizable garb of a guardian, trustee, solicitor, priest, doctor, manager, or the like.'

Everything depends on the particular facts, and such a relationship has been held to exist in unusual circumstances as between purchaser and vendor, as between great uncle and adult nephew, and in other widely differing sets of circumstances. Moreover, it is neither feasible nor desirable to attempt closely to define the relationship, or its characteristics, or the demarcation line showing the exact transition point where a relationship that does not entail that duty passes into one that does (cf Ungoed-Thomas J in *Re Craig*).

On the other hand, whilst disclaiming any intention of seeking to catalogue the elements of such a special relationship, it is perhaps of a little assistance to note some of those which have in the past frequently been found to exist where the court had been led to decide that this relationship existed as between adults of sound mind. Such cases tend to arise where someone relies on the guidance or advice of another, where the other is aware of that reliance and where the person on whom reliance is placed obtains, or may well obtain, a benefit from the transaction or has some other interest in it being concluded. In addition, there must, of course, be shown to exist a vital element which in this judgment will for convenience be referred to as confidentiality. It is this element which is so impossible to define and which is a matter for the judgment of the court on the facts of any particular case.

Confidentiality, a relatively little used word, is being here adopted, albeit with some hesitation, to avoid the possible confusion that can arise through referring to 'confidence'. Reliance on advice can in many circumstances be said to import that type of confidence which only results in a common law duty to take care—a duty which may co-exist with but is not coterminous with that of fiduciary care. 'Confidentiality' is intended to convey that extra quality in the relevant confidence that is implicit in the phrase 'confidential relationship' (cf per Lord Chelmsford LC in *Tate v Williamson*, Lindley LJ in *Allcard v Skinner* and Wright J in *Morley v Loughnan*) and may perhaps have something in common with 'confiding' and also 'confidant', when, for instance, referring to someone's 'man of affairs'. It imports some quality beyond that inherent in the confidence that can well exist between trustworthy persons who in business affairs deal with each other at arm's length. It is one of the features of this element that once it exists, influence naturally grows out of it (cf Evershed MR in *Tufton v Sperni*, following Lord Chelmsford LC in *Tate v Williamson*).

It was inevitably conceded on behalf of the bank that the relevant relationship can arise as between banker and customer. Equally, it was inevitably conceded on behalf of the defendant that in the normal course of transactions by which a customer guarantees a third party's obligations, the relationship does not arise. The onus of proof lies on the customer who alleges that in any individual case the line has been crossed and the relationship has arisen.

Before proceeding to examine the position further, it is as well to dispose of some points on which confusion is apt to arise. Of these the first is one which plainly led to misapprehension on the part of the learned county court judge. Undue influence is a phrase which is commonly regarded—even in the eyes of a number of lawyers—as relating solely to occasions when the will of one person has become so dominated by that of another that, to use the learned county court judge's words, 'the person acts as the mere puppet of the dominator'. Such occasions, of course, fall within what Cotton LJ in *Allcard v Skinner* described as the first class of cases to which the doctrine on undue influence applies. There is, however, a second class of such cases. This is referred to by Cotton LJ as follows:

> 'In the second class of cases the Court interferes, not on the ground that any wrongful act has in fact been committed by the donee, but on the ground of public policy, and to prevent the relations which existed between the parties and the influence arising therefrom being abused.'

It is thus to be emphasised that as regards the second class the exercise of the court's jurisdiction to set aside the relevant transaction does *not* depend on proof of one party being 'able to dominate the other as though a puppet' (to use the words again adopted by the learned county court judge when testing whether the defence was established) nor any wrongful intention on the part of the person who gains a benefit from it, but on the concept that once the special relationship has been shown to exist, no benefit can be retained from the transaction unless it has been positively established that the duty of fiduciary care has been entirely fulfilled. To this second class, however, the learned judge never averted and plainly never directed his mind.

It is also to be noted that what constitutes fulfilment of that duty (the second issue in the case now under consideration) depends again on the facts before the court. It may in the particular circumstances entail that the person in whom confidence has been reposed should insist on independent advice being obtained or ensuring in one way or another that the person being asked to execute a document is not insufficiently informed of some factor which could affect his judgment. The duty has been well stated as being one to ensure that the person liable to be influenced has formed 'an independent *and informed* judgment', or to use the phraseology of Lord Evershed MR in *Zamet v Hyman*, 'after full, free *and informed* thought'. (The italics in each case are mine.) As to the difficulties in which a person may be placed and as to what he should do when there is a conflict of interest between him and the person asked to execute a document, see *Bank of Montreal v Stuart*.

Stress was placed in argument for the bank on the effect of the word 'abused' as it appears in the above cited passage in the judgment of Cotton LJ and in other judgments and textbooks. As regards the second class of undue influence, however, that word in the context means no more than that once the existence of a special relationship has been established, then any possible use of the relevant influence is, irrespective of the intentions of the persons possessing it, regarded in relation to the transaction under consideration as an abuse—unless and until the duty of fiduciary care has been shown to be fulfilled or the transaction is shown to be truly for the benefit of the person influenced. This approach is a matter of public policy.

One further point on which potential confusion emerged in the course of the helpful addresses of counsel stemmed from submissions to the effect that Mr Head, the assistant bank manager, should be cleared of all blame in the matter. When one has to deal with claims of breach of either common law or fiduciary care, it is not unusual to find that counsel for a big corporation tends to try and focus the attention of the court on the responsibility of the employee who deals with the particular matter rather than on that of the corporation as an entity. What we are concerned with in the present case is whether the element of confidentiality has been established as against the bank; Mr Head's part in the affair is but one link in a chain of events. Moreover, when it comes to a question of the relevant knowledge which will have to be discussed later in this judgment, it is the knowledge of the bank and not merely the personal knowledge of Mr Head that has to be examined.

Having discussed the nature of the issues to which the learned county court judge should have directed his mind, it is now convenient to turn to the evidence relating to the first of them— whether the special relationship has here been shown to exist at the material time. . . .

The situation was thus one which to any reasonably sensible person, who gave it but a moment's thought, cried aloud the defendant's need for careful independent advice. Over and above the need any man has for counsel when asked to risk his last penny on even an apparently reasonable project, was the need here for informed advice as to whether there was any real chance of the company's affairs becoming viable if the documents were signed. If not, there arose questions such as, what is the use of taking the risk of becoming penniless without benefiting anyone but the bank; is it not better both for you and your son that you, at any rate, should still have some money when the crash comes; and should not the bank at least bind itself to hold its hand for some given period? The answers to such questions could only be given in the light of a worthwhile appraisement of the company's affairs—without which the defendant could not come to an *informed judgment* as to the wisdom of what he was doing.

No such advice to get an independent opinion was given; on the contrary, Mr Head chose to give his own views on the company's affairs and to take this course, though he had at trial to admit: 'I did not explain the company's affairs very fully. I had only just taken over'. (Another answer that escaped entry in the learned judge's original notes.)

On the above recited facts, the breach of the duty to take fiduciary care is manifest. . . .

The existence of the duty and its breach having thus been established, there remains the submission urged by counsel for the bank that whatever independent advice had been obtained, the defendant would have been so obstinately determined to help his son that the documents would anyway have been signed. The point fails for more than one reason, of which it is sufficient to mention two. First, on a question of fact it ignores the point that the independent advice might well have been to the effect that it would benefit the son better in the event of an almost inevitable crash if his father had some money left, after it occurred—advice which could have affected the mind of the defendant. Secondly, once the relevant duty is established, it is contrary to public policy that benefit of the transaction be retained by the person under the duty unless he positively shows that the duty of fiduciary care has been fulfilled; there is normally no room for debate on the issue as to what would have happened had the care been taken. . . .

There remains to mention that counsel for the bank, whilst conceding that the relevant special relationship could arise as between banker and customer, urged in somewhat doom-laden terms that a decision taken against the bank on the facts of this particular case would seriously affect banking practice. With all respect to that submission, it seems necessary to point out that nothing in this judgment affects the duties of a bank in the normal case where it is obtaining a guarantee, and in accordance with standard practice explains to the person about to sign its legal effect and the sums involved. When, however, a bank, as in this case, goes further and advises on more general matters germane to the wisdom of the transaction, that indicates that it may—not necessarily must—be crossing the line into the area of confidentiality so that the court may then have to examine all the facts, including, of course, the history leading up to the transaction, to ascertain whether or not that line has, as here, been crossed. It would indeed be rather odd if a bank which vis-à-vis a customer attained special relationship in some ways akin to that of a 'man of affairs'—something which can be a matter of pride and enhance his local reputation—should not where a conflict of interest has arisen as between itself and the person advised be under the resulting duty now under discussion. Once, as was inevitably conceded, it is possible for a bank to be under that duty, it is, as in the present case, simply a question for 'meticulous examination' of the particular facts to see whether that duty has arisen. On the special facts here it did arise and it has been broken.

The appeal should be allowed.

[Cairns LJ concurred.]

(The judgment of Lord Denning MR will be considered later, p 669)

National Westminster Bank plc v Morgan [1983] 3 All ER 85, Court of Appeal; [1985] 1 All ER 821, House of Lords

The husband, who was an unreliable and improvident businessman, was unable to meet the repayments due under a mortgage secured over the home which he owned jointly with his wife. As a result the then mortgagee commenced proceedings to take possession of the home, and to avert that the husband made refinancing arrangements with a bank. The bank was made aware of the urgency of the matter and, after the husband executed a legal charge in favour of the bank, the bank manager, at the husband's request, called at the home to get the wife to execute it. Unlike the previous occasion when she executed a mortgage over the home, independent legal advice was not given to her before she signed the mortgage. The husband was present at the brief meeting between the bank manager and the wife at the home although she made it clear she would have preferred him to be absent. The wife told the bank manager that she had little faith in her husband's business ventures and that she did not want the legal charge to cover his business liabilities. The bank manager assured her in good faith but incorrectly that the charge only secured the amount advanced to refinance the mortgage. In fact the charge did extend to business advances. The bank obtained an order for possession of the home after the husband and wife fell into arrears with payments. Soon afterwards the husband died without any indebtedness owing to the bank for business advances. The wife appealed against the order for possession contending that she had signed the mortgage because of undue influence from the bank and that therefore the legal charge should be set aside. The Court of Appeal allowed the appeal.

Dunn LJ. . . . [T]he first submission made by counsel for the bank in the course of his able argument was that as the transaction was not disadvantageous to the wife, there could be no relationship of confidence between her and the bank. He relied in particular on a statement by Ungoed-Thomas J in *Re Craig, Meneces v Middleton*. Counsel submitted that the first requirement before the presumption of undue influence could arise was that the transaction should be one that was manifestly disadvantageous to the person influenced, and which called for an explanation by the person influencing. He said that in this case the transaction was not manifestly disadvantageous to the wife. On the contrary, on balance it was to her advantage, because it was the only way in which she could avoid her house being sold on the application of the Abbey National. The admitted fact that the manager gave her wrong advice as to the effect of the charge, ie that it only covered the amount of the loan and interest from the Abbey National, whereas in truth it covered all borrowing and other liabilities of the husband to the bank, was immaterial to the question of undue influence. Those matters might amount to negligent advice, if the bank had sought (which it did not) to recover more than the amount of the Abbey National loan, in which case the wife would have had a complete defence and counterclaim for damages for negligence. But that provided no ground for setting aside the whole transaction.

This point was referred to by Sir Eric Sachs in *Lloyds Bank Ltd v Bundy*. He first cited a passage from the judgment of Cotton LJ in *Allcard v Skinner*:

'"In the second class of cases the Court interferes, not on the ground that any wrongful act has in fact been committed by the donee, but on the ground of public policy, and to prevent the relations which existed between the parties and the influence arising therefrom being abused." . . . Stress was placed in argument for the bank on the effect of the word "abused" as it appears in the above cited passage in the judgments of Cotton LJ and in other judgments and text books. As regards the second class of undue influence, however, that word in the context means no more than that once the existence of the special relationship has been established, then any possible use of the relevant influence is, irrespective of the intentions of the person possessing it, regarded in relation to the transaction under consideration as an abuse—unless and until the duty of fiduciary care has been shown to be fulfilled or the transaction is shown to be truly for the benefit of the person influenced. This approach is a matter of public policy.'

Counsel for the bank submitted that this transaction was truly for the benefit of the wife, but the passage to which I have referred shows that this does not prevent the existence of the confidential relationship arising in the first place. Slade LJ posed the case in argument of a solicitor who bought his client's house at a full and fair valuation. No doubt the relationship of confidence would exist, and there would be a presumption of undue influence. Only if the solicitor could show that the client had formed an independent and informed judgment could the transaction be upheld, and the mere fact that the price was fair would not be enough to discharge this. There might be all sorts of reasons, apart from the price, why the client did not want to sell his house.

It is true that in all the reported cases of undue influence to which we were referred the transactions were disadvantageous to the person influenced, otherwise they would not have sought to set them aside. As Sir Eric Sachs said in the passage I have cited, it is a matter of public policy which requires that once the relationship of confidence is established, then any possible use of the influence is regarded as an abuse. In this case the terms of the mortgage deed itself constituted a possible abuse of the confidential relationship, because they rendered the wife liable for the very thing she did not wish to accept, namely an open-ended liability for the debts of her husband. That was a possible abuse of the relationship, and in the light of it it cannot be said that the transaction was truly for the benefit of the wife. It is right to say that it was conceded before the assistant recorder that there could be no presumption of undue influence unless the transaction was manifestly disadvantageous to the person influenced. If this concession had not been made, the assistant recorder's conclusion might well have been different.

Counsel for the bank accepted that, if contrary to his submission the above proposition was correct and the transaction need not be disadvantageous to the person influenced, then he could not establish that the bank had performed its fiduciary duty, because the wife had not been given the opportunity of obtaining independent legal advice.

That brings me to the nub of the appeal, namely whether a confidential relationship existed. The relevant law is set out in the judgment of Sir Eric Sachs, with which Cairns LJ agreed, in *Lloyds Bank Ltd v Bundy* [see above, p 649].

. . . There can be no doubt that in this case the bank obtained a benefit from the transaction. Banks are not charitable institutions, and the area office would not have approved the transaction unless it considered it to be for the benefit of the bank and its shareholders. So far as the bank was concerned it was a transaction whereby money was lent at commercial rates on ample security. The house was valued at £26,000 and the Abbey National debt with interest stood at £15,600.

Counsel for the bank submitted that this was no more than a transaction at arm's length between trustworthy persons, and did not involve the additional 'indefinable' element of confidentiality. He pointed out that the wife had never used the bank or the manager as her 'man of business', and that the only relationship between them was that of banker and customer, which did not of itself give rise to a confidential relationship. Further the meeting only lasted five minutes, which was insufficient to give rise to the confidential relationship.

In my view the fact that the manager took the document to the wife's house indicates something more than the relationship of banker and customer. When he arrived the wife explained to him that she did not wish to discuss the document in the presence of her husband. On the evidence of the manager himself, the wife was relying on his guidance and advice whether or not she should sign the document. She explained her fears to him in circumstances which, despite the shortness of the interview, must have shown him that she was relying on his advice. Everything that happened during the meeting showed that she was treating the manager as a confidant.

As Sir Eric Sachs said in *Lloyds Bank Ltd v Bundy* each case turns on its own facts. I am not to be taken as saying that every time a bank manager puts a document before a customer to sign, the confidential relationship arises. That would be contrary to the decided cases. But, on the unusual and special facts of this case in my judgment the confidential relationship did exist between the manager, representing the bank, and the wife immediately before she signed the document. Accordingly, the bank having failed to prove that it had fulfilled its fiduciary duty by recommending the wife to take independent legal advice, the presumption of undue influence prevails and the mortgage must be set aside. For those reasons I would allow the appeal.

[Slade LJ delivered a judgment to the same effect. The Bank appealed.]

Lord Scarman. . . . As to the facts, I am far from being persuaded that the trial judge fell into error when he concluded that the relationship between the bank and the wife never went beyond the normal business relationship of banker and customer. Both Dunn and Slade LJ saw the relationship between the bank and the wife as one of confidence in which she was relying on the bank manager's advice. Each recognised the personal honesty, integrity, and good faith of Mr Barrow. Each took the view that the confidentiality of the relationship was such as to impose on him a 'fiduciary duty of care'. It was his duty, in their view, to ensure that the wife had the opportunity to make an independent and informed decision: but he failed to give her any such opportunity. They, therefore, concluded that it was a case for the presumption of undue influence.

My Lords, I believe that Dunn and Slade LJJ were led into a misinterpretation of the facts by their use, as is all too frequent in this branch of the law, of words and phrases such as 'confidence', 'confidentiality', 'fiduciary duty'. There are plenty of confidential relationships which do not give rise to the presumption of undue influence (a notable example is that of husband and wife: see *Bank of Montreal v Stuart*); and there are plenty of non-confidential relationships in which one person relies on the advice of another, eg many contracts for the sale of goods. Nor am I persuaded that the charge, limited as it was by Mr Barrow's declaration to securing the loan to pay off the Abbey National debt and interest during the bridging period, was disadvantageous to the wife. It meant for her the rescue of her home upon the terms sought by her—a short-term loan at a commercial rate of interest. The Court of Appeal has not, therefore, persuaded me that the judge's understanding of the facts was incorrect.

But, further, the view of the law expressed by the Court of Appeal was, as I shall endeavour to show, mistaken. Dunn LJ . . . while accepting that in all the reported cases to which the court was referred the transactions were disadvantageous to the person influenced, took the view that in cases where public policy requires the court to apply the presumption of undue influence there is no need to prove a disadvantageous transaction. Slade LJ also clearly held that it was not necessary to prove a disadvantageous transaction where the relationship of influence was proved to exist. . . .

Like Dunn LJ, I know of no reported authority where the transaction set aside was not to the manifest disadvantage of the person influenced. It would not always be a gift: it can be a 'hard and inequitable' agreement (*Ormes v Beadel*); or a transaction 'immoderate and irrational' (*Bank of Montreal v Stuart*) or 'unconscionable in that it was a sale at an undervalue (*Poosathurai v Kannappa Chettiar*). Whatever the legal character of the transaction, the authorities show that it must constitute a disadvantage sufficiently serious to require evidence to rebut the presumption that in the circumstances of the relationship between the parties it was procured by the exercise of undue influence. In my judgment, therefore, the Court of Appeal erred in law in holding that the presumption of undue influence can arise from the evidence of the relationship of the parties without also evidence that the transaction itself was wrongful in that it constituted an advantage taken of the person subjected to the influence which, failing proof to the contrary, was explicable only on the basis that undue influence had been exercised to procure it.

The principle justifying the court in setting aside a transaction for undue influence can now be seen to have been established by Lindley LJ in *Allcard v Skinner*. It is not a vague 'public policy' but specifically the victimisation of one party by the other. It was stated by Lindley LJ in a famous passage:

'The principle must be examined. What then is the principle? Is it that it is right and expedient to save persons from the consequences of their own folly? or is it that it is right and expedient to save them from being victimised by other people? In my opinion the doctrine of undue influence is founded upon the second of these two principles. Courts of equity have never set aside gifts on the ground of the folly, imprudence, or want of foresight on the part of donors. The courts have always repudiated any such jurisdiction. *Huguenin v Baseley* is itself a clear authority to this effect. It would obviously be to encourage folly, recklessness, extravagance and vice if persons could get back property which they foolishly made away with, whether by giving it to charitable institutions or by bestowing it on less worthy objects. On the other hand, to protect people from being forced, tricked or misled in any way by others into parting with their property is one of the most legitimate objects of all laws; and the equitable doctrine of undue influence has grown out of and been developed by the necessity of grappling with insidious forms of spiritual tyranny and with the infinite varieties of fraud.'

In *Poosathurai v Kannappa Chettiar* LR 47 IA 1, 3 Lord Shaw, after indicating that there was no difference upon the subject of undue influence between the Indian Contract Act 1872 and English law quoted the Indian statutory provision, section 16(3):

'Where a person who is in a position to dominate the will of another enters into a contract with him, and the transaction appears on the face of it, or on the evidence, to be unconscionable, the burden of proving that such contract was not induced by undue influence shall lie upon the person in the position to dominate the will of the other.'

He proceeded (at p 4) to state the principle in a passage of critical importance, which, since, so far as I am aware, the case is not reported elsewhere, I think it helpful to quote in full.

'It must be established that the person in a position of domination has used that position to obtain unfair advantage for himself, and so to cause injury to the person relying upon his authority or aid. Where the relation of influence, as above set forth, has been established, and the second thing is also made clear, namely, that the bargain is with the "influencer", and in itself unconscionable, then the person in a position to use his dominating power has the burden thrown upon him, and it is a heavy burden, of establishing affirmatively that no domination was practised so as to bring about the transaction, but that the grantor of the deed was scrupulously kept separately advised in the independence of a free agent. These general propositions are mentioned because, if laid alongside of the facts of the present case, then it appears that one vital element—perhaps not sufficiently relied on in the court below, and yet essential to the plaintiff's case—is wanting. It is not proved as a fact in the present case that the bargain of sale come to was unconscionable in itself or constituted an advantage unfair to the plaintiff; it is, in short, not established as a matter of fact that the sale was for undervalue.'

The wrongfulness of the transaction must, therefore, be shown: it must be one in which an unfair advantage has been taken of another. The doctrine is not limited to transactions of gift. A commercial relationship can become a relationship in which one party assumes a role of dominating influence over the other. In *Poosathurai's* case the Board recognised that a sale at an undervalue could be a transaction which a court could set aside as unconscionable if it was shown or could be presumed to have been procured by the exercise of undue influence. Similarly a relationship of banker and customer may become one in which the banker acquires a dominating influence. If he does and a manifestly disadvantageous transaction is proved, there would then be room for the court to presume that it resulted from the exercise of undue influence.

This brings me to *Lloyds Bank Ltd v Bundy* . . .

[Lord Scarman referred to the judgment of Lord Denning (for extracts, see below p 669). He then read the last paragraph of Sir Eric Sachs' judgment (see above, pp 650–651).]

This is good sense and good law, though I would prefer to avoid the term 'confidentiality' as a description of the relationship which has to be proved. In truth, as Sir Eric recognised, the relationships which may develop a dominating influence of one over another are infinitely various. There is no substitute in this branch of the law for a 'meticulous examination of the facts'.

A meticulous examination of the facts of the present case reveals that Mr Barrow never 'crossed the line'. Nor was the transaction unfair to the wife. The bank was, therefore, under no duty to ensure that she had independent advice. It was an ordinary banking transaction whereby the wife sought to save her home; and she obtained an honest and truthful explanation of the bank's intention which, notwithstanding the terms of the mortgage deed which in the circumstances the trial judge was right to dismiss as 'essentially theoretical', was correct: for no one has suggested that Mr Barrow or the bank sought to make the wife liable, or to make her home the security, for any debt of her husband other than the loan and interest necessary to save the house from being taken away from them in discharge of their indebtedness to the building society.

For these reasons, I would allow the appeal. In doing so, I would wish to give a warning. There is no precisely defined law setting limits to the equitable jurisdiction of a court to relieve against undue influence. This is the world of doctrine, not of neat and tidy rules. The courts of equity have developed a body of learning enabling relief to be granted where the law has to treat the transaction as unimpeachable unless it can be held to have been procured by undue influence. It is the unimpeachability at law of a disadvantageous transaction which is the starting-point from which the court advances to consider whether the transaction is the product merely of one's own folly or of the undue influence exercised by another. A court in the exercise of this equitable jurisdiction is a court of conscience. Definition is a poor instrument when used to determine whether a transaction is or is not unconscionable: this is a question which depends upon the particular facts of the case.

[Lords Keith, Roskill, Bridge and Brandon all agreed.]

Appeal allowed.

NOTES

1. What is the distinction between this case and *Lloyds Bank Ltd v Bundy*?
2. Lord Scarman says that he would prefer to avoid the word 'confidentiality' as a description of the relationship which has to be proved because other relationships may give rise to a dominating influence. What sort of relationship do you suppose he had in mind? Would equity set aside any contract made under a high degree of persuasion, for instance high pressure sales tactics? Compare Consumer Credit Act 1974, ss 67–68, below p 664.
3. Although Scarman refers to a 'dominating influence', in the second class of case referred to by Cotton LJ (see above, p 648) it is not necessary to show that one party has acquired a dominating influence in order for the presumption of undue influence to arise.

   > It is enough to show that the party in whom the trust and confidence is reposed is in a position to exert influence over him who reposes it.

   (Nourse LJ in *Goldsworthy v Brickell* [1987] Ch 378 at 404.)
4. As the result of the *National Westminster* case it must also be shown that the transaction was 'manifestly disadvantageous' to the person influenced.

   > . . . the presumption is not perfected and remains inoperative until the party who has ceded the trust and confidence makes a gift so large, or enters a transaction so improvident, as not to be reasonably accounted for on the ground of friendship, relationship, charity or other ordinary motives on which men act. Although influence might have been presumed beforehand, it is only then that it is presumed to have been undue.

   (Nourse LJ in *Goldsworthy v Brickell* at p 401.)
5. In the Court of Appeal Dunn LJ said that a client who sold a house to his solicitor at a fair market price might still be able to have the sale set aside. Is this now incorrect? See *Bank of Credit and Commerce International SA v Aboody* [1989] 2 WLR 759 at 777.
6. In *Aboody's* case the Court of Appeal held that the requirement of manifest disadvantage must also be shown in cases falling within Cotton LJ's first class, ie cases of actual undue influence. If actual undue influence has been used, shouldn't the victim have relief even if the contract which resulted was not manifestly disadvantageous in terms of substance?
7. A recurring problem is that a person is induced by undue influence or undue pressure from a spouse or relation to give a guarantee of the spouse's or relation's debts to a third party, eg a bank. The bank will be able to enforce the guarantee unless either it knew of the undue influence or it had 'left it to' the spouse or relation to obtain the signature on the guarantee, so that the spouse or relation was acting as the bank's agent. See *Avon Finance Co Ltd v Bridger* [1985] 2 All ER 281; *Coldunnell v*

Gallon [1986] QB 1184; and *Aboody's* case, above. In *Lloyd's Bank v Bundy* Sir Eric Sachs had referred to the 'duties of a bank in the normal case where it is obtaining a guarantee, and in accordance with standard practice explains to the person about to sign its legal effect . . .' (above, p 651). This probably refers only to a duty not to misrepresent the effect of the guarantee. Would it be too much to require banks when dealing with individual (as opposed to corporate) guarantors to see them on their own and to attempt to check that they are not acting under pressure?

CHAPTER 31
Unconscionable bargains

This chapter deals with an apparent ragbag of cases which all involve further interference with freedom of contract. Some of the cases are old and, some lawyers may think, obsolete; but they may be adaptable to modern day conditions. Moreover it has been suggested that there is an important general principle underlying them all. We shall return to that question and, if there is such a principle, what its content might be, in Chapter 32.

(a) Mortgages

The classical common law forms of lending on the security of land involved a conveyance of the land to the lender with a contractual provision that the land might be redeemed by the repayment of capital and interest. Typically the contractual date of redemption would be relatively soon after the loan, say six months. Equity early held that if the transaction was in substance a mortgage, the borrower (mortgagor) still had an equitable right to redeem after the contractual date had passed. See for example *Howard v Harris* (1683) 1 Vern 190; *Spurgeon v Collier* (1758) 1 Eden 55; *Jennings v Ward* (1705) 2 Vern 520. The reason given for this was that the lender (mortgagee) was adequately protected if he recovered the money lent in full plus interest at the agreed rate, and he should not make a profit beyond this by retaining land worth more. This was no doubt based on an unarticulated assumption that borrowers as a class often needed protection from lenders, and reinforced by the fact that at the time that the doctrine was first developed there were statutory limits (since abolished) on the rates of interest that lenders could charge.

From this beginning, the doctrine gradually developed a number of sub-rules. The question was to be treated as one of substance, so that what was essentially a mortgage could not be dressed up as a conveyance (compare the quite different treatment of hire-purchase, which is essentially a chattel mortgage dressed up as a contract of hire); a transaction which was essentially a mortgage could not be made irredeemable; and a condition rendering redemption illusory or limiting it was invalid: *Fairclough v Swan Brewery* [1912] AC 565; *Salt v Marquis of Northampton* [1892] AC 1. Even an option to the mortgagee to purchase the land was held invalid in *Samuel v Jarrah Timber Co* [1904] AC 323.

Although these rules undoubtedly had roots in considerations of unconscionability, by the early nineteenth century they were being applied even where borrowers and lenders were bargaining on equal terms and at arms' length: see, for example, *Bradley v Carritt* [1903] AC 253, where the holder of shares in a tea company mortgaged the shares to a tea broker and agreed to use his best endeavours to see that the mortgagee should have the sale of all the company's tea, and if the tea was sold through another broker, to pay compensation for the loss of commission. After the mortgagor had redeemed, the tea company changed its broker. The House of Lords held (Lords Lindley and Shand dissenting) that this stipulation was not enforceable as it had some tendency to discourage the mortgagor from disposing of the shares, and was thus an indirect fetter on the right of redemption.

This decision was effectively overruled by *Kreglinger v New Patagonia Meat and Cold Storage Co Ltd* [1914] AC 25, which reached a different result on indistinguishable facts. There a firm of wool brokers lent money to a firm of meat preservers under a contract including a provision that the borrowers would for five years sell all their sheepskins to the lenders, provided the latter were willing to pay the best price offered by anyone else. Lord Parker said:

> . . . there is now no rule in equity which precludes a mortgagee, whether the mortgage be made upon the occasion of a loan or otherwise, from stipulating for any collateral advantage, provided such collateral advantage is not either (1) unfair and unconscionable, or (2) in the nature of a penalty clogging the equity of redemption, or (3) inconsistent with or repugnant to the contractual and equitable right to redeem.

The clause was upheld. Similarly, in *Knightsbridge Estates Trust Ltd v Byrne* [1939] Ch 441 at 457, Sir Wilfred Greene MR said:

> Equity may give relief against contractual terms in a mortgage transaction if they are oppressive or unconscionable . . . But equity does not reform mortgage transactions because they are unreasonable.

In *Multiservice Bookbinding Ltd v Marden* [1979] Ch 84 the lender had stipulated for interest at 2% above (English) bank rate, and also for both the amount of capital to be repaid and the sums due by way of interest to be linked to the movement of the Swiss franc against the pound. Browne-Wilkinson J held that there was no significant inequality of bargaining power as between the borrower and the lender; that it was unreasonable to stipulate for interest at English rates when the capital value was tied to the Swiss franc, since English interest rates reflected in part the current English rate of inflation; but that the transaction was not unconscionable and should be upheld.

(b) Poor and ignorant persons and expectant heirs

In the eighteenth century the Court of Chancery seems regularly to have set aside contracts and dispositions which were unfair, at least where there was gross inadequacy of consideration and some overreaching (see Atiyah, *Rise and Fall of Freedom of Contract* (1979), pp 169–174). One category of cases involved purchases of property at undervalue from poor and ignorant persons: perhaps the best known example is *Evans v Llewellin* (1787) 1 Cox Eq Cas 333. There a man of very modest means was unexpectedly told that he had inherited a share in his sister's estate, and his brother-in-law, who claimed that the sister had not intended the share to go to the plaintiff, offered to buy it from him for 200 guineas. The plaintiff accepted this offer without having time for reflection or to obtain advice. The share was worth much more and the Master of the Rolls set the transaction aside.

Some of the categories of cases, for instance that of sailors who were persuaded to give up their shares in prize money for much smaller amounts of ready cash, seem to have fallen into disuse early, but others survived well into the nineteenth century. In particular there are many cases involving expectant heirs, who either parted with their reversions at much less than their true value, or who borrowed money at exorbitant rates of interest, to be repaid when they came into their inheritances. Such persons were felt to be particularly at risk from unscrupulous money lenders, as they would not care to risk revealing their circumstances to their families by seeking advice from family advisers. In *Earl of Aylesford v Morris* (1873) 8 Ch App 484 at 491, the Lord Chancellor said:

> The result of the decisions is that where a purchase is made from a poor and ignorant man at a considerable undervalue, the vendor having no independent advice, a Court of Equity will set aside the transaction.
>
> This will be done even in the case of property in possession, and *a fortiori* if the interest be reversionary.
>
> The circumstances of poverty and ignorance of the vendor, and absence of independent advice, throw upon the purchaser, when the transaction is impeached the onus of proving, in Lord *Selborne's* words, that the purchase was 'fair, just, and reasonable'.

Fry v Lane (1888) 40 Ch D 312, Kay J

The plaintiffs, two brothers who were a plumber's assistant and a laundry-man, sold their reversionary interests at considerably below the true value, receiving advice only from an inexperienced solicitor who was also acting for the purchaser.

Kay J. . . . I reserved judgment that I might more carefully consider the facts of the case, and the law which is applicable to them since the passing of the statute 31 Vict c 4.

Long before the passing of that Act it was settled that the Court of Chancery would relieve against a sale of or other dealing with a remainder or reversion at an undervalue on that ground alone, and this even where the remainderman was of mature age and accustomed to business: *Wiseman v Beake; Berkley-Freeman v Bishop; Davis v Duke of Marlborough; Earl of Portmore v Taylor; Boothby v Boothby; Foster v Roberts; Beynon v Cook*. In such cases it was held that the onus lay upon the purchaser to shew that he had given the 'fair' value as it was called in *Earl of Aldborough v Trye*, or 'the market value': *Talbot v Staniforth*.

By the 31 Vict c 4, reciting that it was expedient to amend the law as administered in Courts of Equity with respect to sales of reversions, it was enacted (by sect 1) that 'no purchase, made *bonâ fide* and without fraud or unfair dealing, of any reversionary interest in real or personal estate shall hereafter be opened or set aside merely on the ground of undervalue', and by sect 2 the word 'purchase' in the Act is to include 'every kind of contract, conveyance, or assignment, under or by which any beneficial interest in any kind of property may be acquired'. This Act came into operation on the 1st day of January, 1868.

It is obvious that the words 'merely on the ground of undervalue' do not include the case of an undervalue so gross as to amount of itself to evidence of fraud, and in *Earl of Aylesford v Morris* Lord Selborne said that this Act 'leaves undervalue still a material element in cases in which it is not the sole equitable ground for relief. These changes of the law have in no degree whatever altered the *onus probandi* in those cases, which, according to the language of Lord Hardwicke, raise "from the circumstances or conditions of the parties contracting—weakness on one side, usury on the other, or extortion, or advantage taken of that weakness"—a presumption of fraud. 'Fraud,' says Lord Selborne, 'does not here mean deceit or circumvention; it means an unconscientious use of the power arising out of these circumstances and conditions; and when the relative position of the parties is such as *primâ facie* to raise this presumption, the transaction cannot stand unless the person claiming the benefit of it is able to repel the presumption by contrary evidence, proving it to have been in point of fact fair, just, and reasonable.'

The most common case for the inference of a Court of Equity is that of an expectant heir, reversioner, or remainderman who is just of age, his youth being treated as an important circumstance. Another analogous case is where the vendor is a poor man with imperfect education, as in *Evans v Llewellin; Haygarth v Wearing*. . . .

Sale set aside.

Cresswell v Potter (1968) [1978] 1 WLR 255, Megarry J

The wife left the husband. Later she conveyed to him her half-share in the matrimonial home, in exchange for being released from her liability under the mortgage. The property was worth considerably more than the amount of the mortgage. The husband later sold the property and the wife claimed a half-share in the proceeds of sale.

Megarry J. . . . [Kay J in *Fry v Lane*] laid down three requirements. What has to be considered is, first, whether the plaintiff is poor and ignorant; second, whether the sale was at a considerable undervalue; and third, whether the vendor had independent advice. I am not, of course, suggesting that these are the only circumstances which will suffice; thus there may be circumstances of oppression or abuse of confidence which will invoke the aid of equity. But in the present case only these three requirements are in point. Abuse of confidence, though pleaded, is no longer relied on; and no circumstances of oppression or other matters are alleged. I must therefore consider whether the three requirements laid down in *Fry v Lane* are satisfied.

I think that the plaintiff may fairly be described as falling within whatever is the modern equivalent of 'poor and ignorant'. Eighty years ago, when *Fry v Lane* was decided, social conditions were very different from those which exist today. I do not, however, think that the principle has changed, even though the euphemisms of the 20th century may require the word 'poor' to be replaced by 'a member of the lower income group' or the like, and the word 'ignorant' by 'less highly educated'. The plaintiff has been a van driver for a tobacconist, and is a Post Office telephonist. The evidence of her means is slender. The defendant told me that the plaintiff probably had a little saved, but not much; and there was evidence that her earnings were about the same as the defendant's, and that these were those of a carpenter. The plaintiff also has a legal aid certificate.

In those circumstances I think the plaintiff may properly be described as 'poor' in the sense used in *Fry v Lane*, where it was applied to a laundryman who, in 1888, was earning £1 a week. In this context, as in others, I do not think that 'poverty' is confined to destitution. Further, although no doubt it requires considerable alertness and skill to be a good telephonist, I think that a telephonist can properly be described as 'ignorant' in the context of property transactions in general and the execution of conveyancing documents in particular. I have seen and heard the plaintiff giving evidence, and I have reached the conclusion that she satisfies the requirements of the first head.

The second question is whether the sale was at a 'considerable undervalue'.

[The judge held that the plaintiff was getting 'virtually nothing' from the agreement.]

As for independent advice, from first to last there is no suggestion that the plaintiff had any. The defendant, his solicitor and the inquiry agent stood on one side: on the other the plaintiff stood alone. This was, of course, a conveyancing transaction, and English land law is notoriously complex. I am certainly not saying that other transactions, such as hire-purchase agreements, are free from all difficulty. But the authorities put before me on setting aside dealings at an undervalue all seem to relate to conveyancing transactions, and one may wonder whether the principle is confined to such transactions, and, if so, why? I doubt whether the principle is restricted in this way; and it may be that the explanation is that it is in conveyancing matters that, by long usage, it is regarded as usual, and, indeed, virtually essential, for the parties to have the services of a solicitor. The absence of the aid of a solicitor is thus, as it seems to me, of especial significance if a conveyancing matter is involved. The more usual it is to have a solicitor, the more striking will be his absence, and the more closely will the courts scrutinise what was done.

Mr Balcombe points out that the plaintiff was not bereft of possible legal assistance; for on or before July 28, 1959, when she was having difficulty in getting some furniture and effects from Slate Hall, she consulted a Colchester firm of solicitors, who wrote a letter dated July 28, 1959, that produced the required result. If she wanted legal advice, he said, this shows that she knew how to get it. However, what matters, I think, is not whether she could have obtained proper advice but whether in fact she had it; and she did not. Nobody, of course, can be compelled to obtain independent advice: but I do not think that someone who seeks to uphold what is, to him, an advantageous conveyancing transaction can do so merely by saying that the other party could have obtained independent advice, unless something has been done to bring to the notice of that other party the true nature of the transaction and the need for advice.

At the end of the day, my conclusion is that this transaction cannot stand. In my judgment the plaintiff has made out her case, and so it is for the defendant to prove that the transaction was 'fair, just, and reasonable'. This he has not done.

Accordingly, it seems to me that this action ought to succeed, and subject to discussion of the terms of the appropriate order, I so hold.

Order accordingly.

NOTES

1. *Cresswell v Potter* was considered in *Backhouse v Backhouse* [1978] 1 All ER 1158. In *Watkin v Watson-Smith* (1986) Times, 3 July Hirst J held that 'a desire for a quick sale' could be substituted for 'poverty' and 'old age with its accompanying diminution of physical and mental capacity' for 'ignorance'. He set aside a contract for the sale of land at less than its true value.
2. Suppose a client asks you to act for her in the purchase of a house, and she tells you that the vendor is acting on his own behalf and has not had the house valued. What would you advise?
3. How do these cases differ from those of undue influence?
4. Although there have been few recent cases in England applying the unconscionable bargain doctrine, there have been a fair number in Canada (see, for example, *Morrison v Coast Finance Ltd* (1965) 55 DLR (2d) 710 (British Columbia)), and a recent case in Australia contains a very full discussion: see *Commercial Bank of Australia v Amadio* (1983) 57 ALJR 358 (High Court), which is noted by Hardingham in (1984) 4 Oxford J of Legal Studies 275.
5. It seems that a contract will not be set aside for unconscionability unless there was some form of conscious advantage-taking: see *Hart v O'Connor*, below.

(c) The insane

Sale of Goods Act 1979

Section 3: Capacity to buy and sell
(2) Where necessaries are sold and delivered to a minor or to a person who by reason of mental incapacity or drunkenness is incompetent to contract, he must pay a reasonable price for them.

NOTES

1. This liability is probably restitutionary rather than contractual.
2. Compare *Re Rhodes* (above, p 31).

Hart v O'Connor [1985] 2 All ER 880, PC

In 1977 the appellant entered into an agreement to buy farmland in New Zealand which was the subject matter of a testamentary settlement. The agreement was expressed to be made between the appellant and J, the then sole trustee of the trust estate. The initiative for the sale came from the trust's solicitor and members of the testator's family. All the terms of the agreement were drawn up by the trust's solicitor, including provision for valuation of the property and the nomination of a valuer. The trust's solicitor sent the agreement to the appellant's solicitor's for approval and took it to J for signature. Unknown to the appellant, J was of unsound mind when he signed the agreement. In May 1980 the respondents, the then trustees and beneficiaries of the estate, applied to set aside the agreement on the ground that J was of unsound mind when he entered into it and the contract was unfair to him. The valuer nominated by the trust's solicitor had valued the land at $180,000 as at 1 September 1977, whereas the respondent trustees' valuer later valued the land at $197,000 as at that date. The trial judge held that, although J's unsoundness of mind was not apparent, his unsoundness of mind coupled with the unfairness of the contract which resulted because of the parties' consequent inequality of bargaining position made the contract unenforceable. However, the judge gave judgment for the appellant on the ground that the respondents had been guilty of laches. The New Zealand Court of Appeal allowed an appeal by the respondents. The appellant appealed to the Privy Council.

Lord Brightman. . . . The action came to trial before Cook J and occupied 14 days. The judge delivered a reserved judgment, dismissing the action. He first considered Jack's capacity to contract, and found on a balance of probabilities that Jack did not have contractual ability to enter into the agreement, and would not have had a proper understanding of the matters for decision even if (contrary to the judge's view) they had been adequately explained to him. He then considered the circumstances in which a contract made by a person who lacked mental capacity was liable to be set aside. The traditional view in English law was that it must be proved that the other contracting party knew of or ought to have appreciated such incapacity. Otherwise the contract stood, assuming it was not voidable on equitable principles as an unconscionable bargain. But in *Archer v Cutler* [1980] 1 NZLR 386 it had been decided that a contract made by a person of insufficient mental capacity was voidable at his option not only if the other party knew of or ought to have appreciated his unsoundness of mind, but also if the contract 'was unfair to the person of unsound mind'. *Archer v Cutler*, to which their Lordships will have to refer in detail later, was accepted by both sides and by the judge as a correct statement of the law, and there was no argument on it; in a court of first instance this was almost inevitable . . .

[In *Archer v Cutler* the judge] found that the vendor was suffering from advanced senile dementia at the time of the agreement which rendered her incapable of understanding the bargain, but that the purchaser was unaware of this. The agreement represented a sale at a substantial undervalue. It was held that contractual incapacity was established; that a contract entered into by a person of unsound mind was voidable at that person's option if the other party knew of the incapacity or, whether or not he knew, if the contract was 'unfair' to the person of unsound mind; and that the contract was unfair, the indicia of unfairness being (i) a price significantly below the true value, (ii) the absence of independent legal advice for the vendor and (iii) the difference in bargaining positions resulting from disparity in their respective mental capacities.

If a contract is stigmatised as 'unfair', it may be unfair in one of two ways. It may be unfair by reason of the unfair manner in which it was brought into existence; a contract induced by undue influence is unfair in this sense. It will be convenient to call this 'procedural unfairness'. It may also, in some contexts, be described (accurately or inaccurately) as 'unfair' by reason of the fact that the terms of the contract are more favourable to one party than to the other. In order to distinguish this 'unfairness' from procedural unfairness, it will be convenient to call it 'contractual imbalance'. The two concepts may overlap. Contractual imbalance may be so extreme as to raise a presumption of procedural unfairness, such as undue influence or some other form of victimisation. Equity will relieve a party from a contract which he has been induced to make as a result of victimisation. Equity will not relieve a party from a contract on the ground only that there is contractual imbalance not amounting to unconscionable dealing. Of the three indicia of unfairness relied on by the judge in *Archer v Cutler* (assuming unfairness to have existed) the first was contractual imbalance and the second and third were procedural unfairness.

[Lord Brightman reviewed the cases relied on in *Archer v Cutler* and to *McLaughlin v Daily Telegraph Newspaper Co Ltd*, and continued:]

In the opinion of their Lordships it is perfectly plain that historically a court of equity did not restrain a suit at law on the ground of 'unfairness' unless the conscience of the plaintiff was in some way affected. This might be because of actual fraud (which the courts of common law would equally have remedied) or constructive fraud, ie conduct which falls below the standards demanded by equity, traditionally considered under its more common manifestations of undue influence, abuse of confidence, unconscionable bargains and frauds on a power (cf *Snell's Principles of Equity* (27th edn, 1973) p 545 ff). An unconscionable bargain in this context would be a bargain of an improvident character made by a poor or ignorant person acting without independent advice which cannot be shown to be a fair and reasonable transaction. 'Fraud' in its equitable context does not mean, or is not confined to, deceit: 'it means an unconscientious use of the power arising out of [the] circumstances and conditions [of the contracting parties]': see *Earl of Aylesford v Morris* (1873) 8 Ch App 484 at 490–491, [1861–73] All ER Rep 300 at 303. It is victimisation, which can consist either of the active extortion of a benefit or the passive acceptance of a benefit in unconscionable circumstances.

Their Lordships have not been referred to any authority that a court of equity would restrain a suit at law where there was no victimisation, no taking advantage of another's weakness, and the sole allegation was contractual imbalance with no undertones of constructive fraud. It seems to their Lordships quite illogical to suppose that the courts of common law would have held that a person of unsound mind, whose affliction was not apparent, was nevertheless free of his bargain if a contractual imbalance could be demonstrated which would have been of no avail to him in equity. Nor do their Lordships see a sufficient foundation in the authorities brought to their attention to support any such proposition.

[Lord Brightman then discussed the Australian case of *Tremills v Benyon* and quoted Hodges J (18 VLR 607, at 622–623):]

'There the word "fairly" could not, I think, be referring to a perfect equality of the consideration given by each party to the contract. Again, a little further on, the Vice-Chancellor quotes with approval the following passage from *Story (Equity Jurisprudence* 227):—"The ground upon which courts of equity now interfere to set aside the contracts and other acts, however solemn, of persons who are idiots, lunatics, and otherwise *non compotes mentis*, is fraud." The Vice-Chancellor could not quote, with approval, Story's opinion that the ground on which courts of equity set aside these contracts is *fraud*, if he was deciding that inequality of consideration was a sufficient ground for setting aside such contracts. Again, the Vice-Chancellor a little further on again quotes with approval Story's view (*Equity Jurisprudence* 228) that "If a purchase is made without any knowledge of the incapacity, *and no advantage has been taken*, courts of equity will not interfere to set aside the contract etc." Here again the Vice Chancellor shows that what invalidates these contracts is not mere inequality of consideration, but the taking of an advantage. If an advantage is taken, the contract is not "fair".'

This case appears to their Lordships to be directly contrary to the proposition adopted in *Archer v Cutler*, because it plainly recognises that a contract with an unsuspected lunatic will not be set aside short of equitable fraud.

In the opinion of their Lordships, to accept the proposition enunciated in *Archer v Cutler* that a contract with a person ostensibly sane but actually of unsound mind can be set aside because it is 'unfair' to the person of unsound mind in the sense of contractual imbalance is unsupported by authority, is illogical and would distinguish the law of New Zealand from the law of Australia, as exemplified in *McLaughlin*'s case and *Tremills*'s case, for no good reason, as well as from the law of England from which the law of Australia and New Zealand and other 'common law' countries has stemmed. In so saying their Lordships differ with profound respect from the contrary view so strongly expressed by the New Zealand courts.

To sum the matter up, in the opinion of their Lordships, the validity of a contract entered into by a lunatic who is ostensibly sane is to be judged by the same standards as a contract by a person of sound mind, and is not voidable by the lunatic or his representative by reason of 'unfairness' unless such unfairness amounts to equitable fraud which would have enabled the complaining party to avoid the contract even if he had been sane.

Their Lordships turn finally to issue (c), whether the respondent trustees are entitled to have the contract set aside as an 'unconscionable bargain'. This issue must also be answered in the negative, because the appellant was guilty of no unconscionable conduct. Indeed, as is conceded, he acted with complete innocence throughout. He was unaware of Jack's unsoundness of mind. Jack was ostensibly advised by his own solicitor. The appellant had no means of knowing or cause to suspect that Jack was not in receipt of and acting in accordance with the most full and careful advice. The terms of the bargain were the terms proposed by Jack's solicitor, not terms imposed by the appellant or his solicitor. There was no equitable fraud, no victimisation, no taking advantage, no overreaching or other description of unconscionable doings which might have justified the intervention of equity to restrain an action by the appellant at law. The respondent trustees have in the opinion of their Lordships failed to make out any case for denying to the appellant the benefit of a bargain which struck with complete propriety on his side.

For these reasons their Lordships have tendered to Her Majesty their humble advice that the appeal should be allowed.

NOTE

If during the course of negotiating a contract you make a statement of fact which later is found to be untrue, the other party may (subject to the court's discretion under Misrepresentation Act 1967, s 2(2)) rescind the contract, even though your statement was made not only honestly but with reasonable grounds for believing it to be true.

> Even assuming that moral fraud must be shewn in order to set aside a contract, you have it where a man, having obtained a beneficial contract by a statement which he now knows to be false, insists upon keeping that contract.

(Jessel MR in *Redgrave Hurd*, above, p 286.)

If, on the other hand, you manage to buy a piece of land on very advantageous terms and subsequently you discover that you were dealing with an insane person, or a 'poor and ignorant' person, you can keep the land. Why is there moral fraud in one case but not the other?

(d) Consumer credit

Consumer Credit Act 1974, ss 67, 68

Section 67: Cancellable agreements
A regulated agreement may be cancelled by the debtor or hirer in accordance with this Part if the antecedent negotiations included oral representations made when in the presence of the debtor or hirer by an individual acting as, or on behalf of, the negotiator, unless—
  (a) the agreement is secured on land, or is a restricted-use credit agreement to finance the purchase of land or is an agreement for a bridging loan in connection with the purchase of land, or
  (b) the unexecuted agreement is signed by the debtor or hirer at premises at which any of the following is carrying on any business (whether on a permanent or temporary basis)—
     (i) the creditor or owner;
     (ii) any party to a linked transaction (other than the debtor or hirer or a relative of his);
     (iii) the negotiator in any antecedent negotiations.

Section 68: Cooling-off period
The debtor or hirer may serve notice of cancellation of a cancellable agreement between his signing of the unexecuted agreement and—
  (a) the end of the fifth day following the day on which he received a copy under section 63(2) or a notice under section 64(1)(b), or
  (b) if (by virtue of regulations made under section 64(4)) section 64(1)(b) does not apply, the end of the fourteenth day following the day on which he signed the unexecuted agreement.

NOTES

1. These provisions apply however good a price the consumer was offered. Why?

2. Why are the provisions limited to sales away from business premises?

3. Why is this right of cancellation limited to transactions involving credit? Do you see any parallel between this and the cases in subsections (a), (b) and (c) above?

4. You will find an explanation and critique of ss 67 and 68 in Cranston, *Consumers and the Law* (2nd edn), pp 192–193.

5. Needless to say, these and other rights given by the Consumer Credit Act will not be of much avail to consumers if they are unaware of their rights. Look at the specimen contract on pp 54–55 above. Section 60 of the Act provides:

(1) The Secretary of State shall make regulations as to the form and content of documents embodying regulated agreements, and the regulations shall contain such provisions as appear to him appropriate with a view to ensuring that the debtor or hirer is made aware of—
    (a) The rights and duties conferred or imposed on him by the agreement,
    (b) the amount and rate of the total charge for credit (in the case of a consumer credit agreement),
    (c) the protection and remedies available to him under this Act, and
    (d) any other matters which, in the opinion of the Secretary of State, it is desirable for him to know about in connection with the agreement.
(2) Regulations under subsection (1) may in particular—
    (a) require specified information to be included in the prescribed manner in documents, and other specified material to be excluded.
    (b) contain requirements to ensure that specified information is clearly brought to the attention of the debtor or hirer, and that one part of a document is not given insufficient or excessive prominence compared with another.

Consumer Credit Act 1974, ss 137(1), 138, 139

Section 137: Extortionate credit bargains
(1) If the court finds a credit bargain extortionate it may reopen the credit agreement so as to do justice between parties.
(2) In this section and sections 138 to 140,—
    (a) 'credit agreement' means any agreement between an individual (the 'debtor') and any other person (the 'creditor') by which the creditor provides the debtor with credit of any amount, and
    (b) 'credit bargain'—
        (i) where no transaction other than the credit agreement is to be taken into account in computing the total charge for credit, means the credit agreement, or
        (ii) where one or more other transactions are to be so taken into account, means the credit agreement and those other transactions, taken together.

Section 138: When bargains are extortionate
(1) A credit bargain is extortionate if it—
    (a) requires the debtor or a relative of his to make payments (whether unconditionally, or on certain contingencies) which are grossly exorbitant, or
    (b) otherwise grossly contravenes ordinary principles of fair dealing.
(2) In determining whether a credit bargain is extortionate regard shall be had to such evidence as is adduced concerning—
    (a) interest rates prevailing at the time it was made,
    (b) the factors mentioned in subsections (3) to (5), and
    (c) any other relevant considerations.
(3) Factors applicable under subsection (2) in relation to the debtor include—
    (a) his age, experience, business capacity and state of health; and

    (b) the degree to which, at the time of making the credit bargain, he was under financial pressure and the nature of that pressure.

(4) Factors applicable under section (2) in relation to the creditor include—

    (a) the degree of risk accepted by him, having regard to the value of any security provided;

    (b) his relationship to the debtor; and

    (c) whether or not a colourable cash price was quoted for any goods or services included in the credit bargain.

(5) Factors applicable under subsection (2) in relation to a linked transaction include the question how far the transaction was reasonably required for the protection of debtor or creditor, or was in the interest of the debtor.

Section 139: Reopening of extortionate agreements

. . .

(2) In reopening the agreement, the court may, for the purpose of relieving the debtor or a surety from payment of any sum in excess of that fairly due and reasonable, by order—

    (a) direct accounts to be taken, or (in Scotland) an accounting to be made, between any persons,

    (b) set aside the whole or part of any obligation imposed on the debtor or a surety by the credit bargain or any related agreement,

    (c) require the creditor to repay the whole or part of any sum paid under the credit bargain or any related agreement by the debtor or a surety, whether paid to the creditor or any other person,

    (d) direct the return to the surety of any property provided for the purposes of the security, or

    (e) alter the terms of the credit agreement or any security instrument.

NOTE

A loan at 48% interest, but made at short notice and on little security, was held not to be extortionate in *Ketley Ltd v Scott* [1981] ICR 241.

(e) Minors

The law of minors', or infants', contracts is very complicated, and space precludes a full consideration of it. Nonetheless a simplified outline provides a useful comparison to the rules governing the relief that may be given to adult contracting parties.

    The general rule is that a minor cannot set aside a contract once he has performed it, but he is not bound to perform his obligations while they remain executory. He can enforce the other party's obligations against him.

    To this general rule that the minor is not bound there are a number of exceptions:

(1) If he is supplied with goods or services which are 'necessaries' for him or (if he is married) his family, he must pay a reasonable sum for them. What is necessary is to be determined by the minor's actual needs at the time, and his position in life: but after one or two rather extravagant decisions by juries of tradesmen (for instance that wild ducks and champagne were necessaries to an undergraduate), it was established that it must first be decided as a matter of law whether the goods or services are capable of being necessaries, before the minor's actual needs are considered.

(2) A minor is also bound to perform contracts of service, apprenticeship and the like, provided the contract taken as a whole is for his benefit.

(3) There are four types of contract which are binding on a minor but which he can repudiate either during his minority or within a reasonable time after it. They are agreements to buy or sell land, or to take or grant a lease of land;

marriage settlements made by him; contracts whereby a minor incurs liability for calls on shares in a company; and partnerships.

These rules raise a number of interesting questions of policy:

(1) A minor is supplied on credit with goods that are 'necessaries' for him. He is liable for their reasonable value, not the contract price. Why?

(2) A minor buys and pays the contract price for something of which he had no need (wild ducks and champagne, say). The minor cannot recover the price he has paid, or even the amount by which the contract price exceeded the fair value of the goods (unless, perhaps, he can bring himself within the class of poor and ignorant persons. This may not be as fanciful as it sounds: in *Fry v Lane* expectant heirs and poor and ignorant persons are treated as a single category.) If he obtains the same goods on credit and eats them he need pay nothing, not even the price of a regular meal. Why?

(3) A minor is not bound by a contract for non-necesssaries or which is not for his benefit, but he can enforce it against the other party. Why?

(4) A minor enters a training contract which is, taken as a whole, for his benefit. He is probably bound even though he has not yet started the training. Why?

(f) Restraint of trade

The doctrine of restraint of trade, which may render a contract wholly or partly void as contrary to public policy, is treated in detail in Section 9. For present purposes it is enough to note that many of the cases do seem to involve protecting an economically weaker party—in particular, an employee—against harsh clauses. In *Schroeder v Macaulay* [1974] 3 All ER 616, at 623, Lord Diplock said:

It is, in my view, salutory to acknowledge that in refusing to enforce provisions of a contract whereby one party agrees for the benefit of the other party to exploit or to refrain from exploiting his own earning-power, the public policy which the court is implementing is not some 19th century economic theory about the benefit to the general public of freedom of trade, but the protection of those whose bargaining power is weak against being forced by those whose bargaining power is stronger to enter into bargains that are unconscionable. Under the influence of Bentham and of laissez-faire the courts in the 19th century abandoned the practice of applying the public policy against unconscionable bargains to contracts generally, as they had formerly done to any contract considered to be usurious; but the policy survived in its application to penalty clauses and to relief against forfeiture and also to the special category of contracts in restraint of trade. If one looks at the reasoning of 19th century judges in cases about contracts in restraint of trade one finds lip service paid to current economic theories but if one looks at what they said in the light of what they did, one finds that they struck down a bargain if they thought it was unconscionable as between the parties to it, and upheld it if they thought that it was not.

So I would hold that the question to be answered as respects a contract in restraint of trade of the kind with which this appeal is concerned is: was the bargain fair? The test of fairness is, no doubt, whether the restrictions are both reasonably necessary for the protection of the legitimate interests of the promisee and commensurate with the benefits secured to the promisor under the contract. For the purpose of this test all the provisions of the contract must be taken into consideration.

(Further extracts from this case will be found below, pp 678 and 785.)

If Lord Diplock's statement was intended to describe every case of restraint of trade where one party agrees to refrain from exploiting his earning power, it is too broad: there are cases of the seller of a business agreeing not to compete with the buyer, or the owner of a business agreeing to sell certain products only, where there is no question of the restraint being unreasonable *as between the parties*. It is struck down because it is inimical to the *public interest* (see below, chapter 38). However, Lord Diplock's statement seems to fit the majority of cases of employees who have accepted restraints on their activities during or, more usually, after their employment. (The other categories Lord Diplock mentions, penalty clauses and relief from forfeiture, were dealt with earlier, above, pp 508 and 449).

CHAPTER 32

A general principle?

(a) Is there a general principle?

In *Lloyds Bank Ltd v Bundy* (above, p 648) Lord Denning MR said:

The general rule

Now let me say at once that in the vast majority of cases a customer who signs a bank guarantee or a charge cannot get out of it. No bargain will be upset which is the result of the ordinary interplay of forces. There are many hard cases which are caught by this rule. Take the case of a poor man who is homeless. He agrees to pay a high rent to a landlord just to get a roof over his head. The common law will not interfere. It is left to Parliament. Next take the case of a borrower in urgent need of money. He borrows it from the bank at high interest and it is guaranteed by a friend. The guarantor gives his bond and gets nothing in return. The common law will not interfere. Parliament has intervened to prevent moneylenders charging excessive interest. But it has never interfered with banks.

Yet there are exceptions to this general rule. There are cases in our books in which the courts will set aside a contract, or a transfer of property, when the parties have not met on equal terms—when the one is so strong in bargaining power and the other so weak—that, as a matter of common fairness, it is not right that the strong should be allowed to push the weak to the wall. Hitherto those exceptional cases have been treated each as a separate category in itself. But I think the time has come when we should seek to find a principle to unite them. I put on one side contracts or transactions which are voidable for fraud or misrepresentation or mistake. All those are governed by settled principles. I go only to those where there has been inequality of bargaining power, such as to merit the intervention of the court.

The categories

The first category is that of 'duress of goods'. A typical case is when a man is in a strong bargaining position by being in possession of the goods of another by virtue of a legal right, such as by way of pawn or pledge or taken in distress. The owner is in a weak position because he is in urgent need of the goods. The stronger demands of the weaker more than is justly due: and he pays it in order to get the goods. Such a transaction is voidable. He can recover the excess: see *Astley v Reynolds* and *Green v Duckett*. To which may be added the cases of 'colore oficii', where a man is in a strong bargaining position by virtue of his official position or public profession. He relies upon it so as to gain from the weaker—who is urgently in need—more than is justly due: see *Pigot's* case cited by Lord Kenyon CJ in *Cartwright v Rowley; Parker v Bristol and Exeter Railway Co* and *Steel v Williams*. In such cases the stronger may make his claim in good faith honestly believing that he is entitled to make his demand. He may not be guilty of any fraud or misrepresentation. The inequality of bargaining power—the strength of the one versus the urgent need of the other—renders the transaction voidable and the money paid to be recovered back: see *Maskell v Horner*.

The second category is that of the 'unconscionable transaction'. A man is so placed as to be in need of special care and protection and yet his weakness is exploited by another far stronger than himself so as to get his property at a gross undervalue. The typical case is that of the 'expectant heir'. But it applies to all cases where a man comes into property, or is expected to come into it—and then being in urgent need—another gives him ready cash for it, greatly below its true worth, and so gets the property transferred to him: see *Evans v Llewellin*. Even though there be no evidence of fraud or misrepresentation, nevertheless the transaction will be set aside: see *Fry v Lane*, where Kay J said:

'The result of the decisions is that where a purchase is made from a poor and ignorant man at a considerable undervalue, *the vendor having no independent advice*, a court of equity will set aside the transaction.'

This second category is said to extend to all cases where an unfair advantage has been gained by an unconscientious use of power by a stronger party against a weaker: see the cases cited in *Halsbury's Laws of England*, 3rd edn, vol 17 (1956), p 682 and, in Canada, *Morrison v Coast Finance Ltd* and *Knupp v Bell*.

The third category is that of 'undue influence' usually so called. These are divided into two classes as stated by Cotton LJ in *Allcard v Skinner*. The first are those where the stronger has been guilty of some fraud or wrongful act—expressly so as to gain some gift or advantage from the weaker. The second are those where the stronger has not been guilty of any wrongful act, but has, through the relationship which existed between him and the weaker, gained some gift or advantage for himself. Sometimes the relationship is such as to raise a presumption of undue influence, such as parent over child, solicitor over client, doctor over patient, spiritual adviser over follower. At other times a relationship of confidence must be proved to exist. But to all of them the general principal obtains which was stated by Lord Chelmsford LC in *Tate v Williamson*:

'Wherever two persons stand in such a relation that, while it continues, confidence is necessarily reposed by one, and the influence which naturally grows out of that confidence is possessed by the other, and this confidence is abused, or the influence is exerted to obtain an advantage at the expense of the confiding party, the person so availing himself of his position will not be permitted to retain the advantage, although the transaction could not have been impeached if no such confidential relation had existed.'

Such a case was *Tufton v Sperni*.

The fourth category is that of 'undue pressure'. The most apposite of that is *Williams v Bayley*, where a son forged his father's name to a promissory note and, by means of it, raised money from the bank of which they were both customers. The bank said to the father, in effect: 'Take your choice—give us security for your son's debt. If you do take that on yourself, then it will all go smoothly: if you do not, we shall be bound to exercise pressure.' Thereupon the father charged his property to the bank with payment of the note. The House of Lords held that the charge was invalid because of undue pressure exerted by the bank. Lord Westbury said,

'A contract to give security for the debt of another, which is a contract without consideration, is above all things, a contract that should be based upon the free and voluntary agency of the individual who enters into it.'

Other instances of undue pressure are where one party stipulates for an unfair advantage to which the other has no option but to submit. As where an employer—the stronger party—has employed a builder—the weaker party—to do work for him. When the builder asked for payment of sums properly due (so as to pay his workmen) the employer refused to pay unless he was given some added advantage. Stuart V-C said: 'Where an agreement, hard and inequitable in itself, has been exacted under circumstances of pressure on the part of the person who exacts it, this court will set it aside'; see *Ormes v Beadel* and *D & C Builders Ltd v Rees*.

The fifth category is that of salvage agreements. When a vessel is in danger of sinking and seeks help, the rescuer is in a strong bargaining position. The vessel in distress is in urgent need. The parties cannot be truly said to be on equal terms. The Court of Admiralty have always recognised that fact. The 'fundamental rule' is

'if the parties have made an agreement, the court will enforce it, unless it be manifestly unfair and unjust; but if it be manifestly unfair and unjust, the court will disregard it and decree what is fair and just.'

See *Akerblom v Price, per* Brett LJ, applied in a striking case *The Port Caledonia and The Anna*, when the rescuer refused to help with a rope unless he was paid £1,000.

The general principles

Gathering all together, I would suggest that through all these instances there runs a single thread. They rest on 'inequality of bargaining power'. By virtue of it, the English law gives relief to one who, without independent advice, enters into a contract upon terms which are very unfair or transfers property for a consideration which is grossly inadequate, when his bargaining power is grievously impaired by reason of his own needs or desires, or by his own ignorance or infirmity, coupled with undue influences or pressures brought to bear on him by or for the benefit of the other. When I used the word 'undue' I do not mean to suggest that the principle depends on proof of any wrongdoing. The one who stipulates for an unfair advantage may be moved solely by his own self-interest, unconscious of the distress he is bringing to the other. I have also avoided any reference to the will of the one being 'dominated' or 'overcome' by the other. One who is in extreme need may knowingly consent to a most improvident bargain, solely to relieve the straits in which he finds himself. Again, I do not mean to suggest that every transaction is saved by independent advice. But the absence of it may be fatal. With these explanations, I hope this principle will be found to reconcile the cases. Applying it to the present case, I would notice these points:

(1) The consideration moving from the bank was grossly inadequate. The son's company was in serious difficulty. The overdraft was at its limit of £10,000. The bank considered that its existing security was insufficient. In order to get further security, it asked the father to charge the house—his sole asset—to the uttermost. It was worth £10,000. The charge was for £11,000. That was for the benefit of the bank. But not at all for the benefit of the father, or indeed for the company. The bank did not promise to continue the overdraft or to increase it. On the contrary, it required the overdraft to be reduced. All that the company gained was a short respite from impending doom.

(2) The relationship between the bank and the father was one of trust and confidence. The bank knew that the father relied on it implicitly to advise him about the transaction. The father trusted the bank. This gave the bank much influence on the father. Yet the bank failed in that trust. It allowed the father to charge the house to his ruin.

(3) The relationship between the father and the son was one where the father's natural affection had much influence on him. He would naturally desire to accede to his son's request. He trusted his son.

(4) There was a conflict of interest between the bank and the father. Yet the bank did not realise it. Nor did it suggest that the father should get independent advice. If the father had gone to his solicitor—or to any man of business—there is no doubt that any one of them would say: 'You must not enter into this transaction. You are giving up your house, your sole remaining asset, for no benefit to you. The company is in such a parlous state that you must not do it.'

These considerations seem to me to bring this case within the principles I have stated. But, in case that principle is wrong, I would also say that the case falls within the category of undue influence of the second class stated by Cotton LJ in *Allcard v Skinner*. I have no doubt that the assistant bank manager acted in the utmost good faith and was straightforward and genuine. Indeed the father said so. But beyond doubt he was acting in the interests of the bank—to get further security for a bad debt. There was such a relationship of trust and confidence between them that the bank ought not to have swept up his sole remaining asset into its hands—for nothing—without his having independent advice. I would therefore allow this appeal.

Sir Eric Sachs commented:

As regards the wider areas covered in masterly survey in the judgment of Lord Denning MR, but not raised arguendo, I do not venture to express an opinion—though having some sympathy with the views that the courts should be able to give relief to a party who has been subject to undue pressure as defined in the concluding passage of his judgment on that point.

NOTES

1. It appears unlikely that any general principle will be recognized in English law in the near future. In *National Westminster Bank plc v Morgan* (above, p 651) Lord Scarman said ([1985] 1 All ER at p 830):

Lord Denning MR believed that the doctrine of undue influence could be subsumed under a general principle that English courts will grant relief where there has been 'inequality of bargaining power'. . . . He deliberately avoided reference to the will of one party being dominated or overcome by another. The majority of the court did not follow him; they based their decision on the orthodox view of the doctrine as expounded in *Allcard v Skinner*. This opinion of the Master of the Rolls, therefore, was not the ground of the court's decision, which has to be found in the view of the majority, for whom Sir Eric Sachs delivered the leading judgment.

Nor has counsel for the respondent sought to rely on Lord Denning's general principle: and, in my view, he was right not to do so. The doctrine of undue influence has been sufficiently developed not to need the support of a principle which by its formulation in the language of the law of contract is not appropriate to cover transactions of gift where there is no bargain. The fact of an unequal bargain will, of course, be a relevant feature in some cases of undue influence. But it can never become an appropriate basis of principle of an equitable doctrine which is concerned with transactions 'not to be reasonably accounted for on the ground of friendship, relationship, charity, or other ordinary motives on which ordinary men act' (Lindley LJ in *Allcard v Skinner*). And even in the field of contract I question whether there is any need in the modern law to erect a general principle of relief against inequality of bargaining power. Parliament has undertaken the task (and it is essentially a legislative task) of enacting such restrictions on freedom of contract as are in its judgment necessary to relieve against the mischief: for example, the hire-purchase and consumer protection legislation, of which the Supply of Goods (Implied Terms) Act 1973, Consumer Credit Act 1974, Consumer Safety Act 1978, Supply of Goods and Services Act 1982 and Insurance Companies Act 1982 are examples. I doubt whether the courts should assume the burden of formulating further restrictions.

2. In *Burmah Oil Co Ltd v Governor of the Bank of England* (1981) (noted 125 Sol Jo 528), Burmah's main asset was a large shareholding in British Petroleum (BP). The quoted Stock Exchange price of BP shares fell, causing Burmah grave financial embarrassment, as their own borrowings were structured in such a way as to be dependent on higher BP shares. Burmah approached the Bank of England for help. The Bank consulted the government. The Government would probably not have wanted to see Burmah go into liquidation, or to see its BP shares fall into foreign hands. The Bank bought the BP shares. In due course the quoted price of BP shares rose very considerably, and Burmah brought an action claiming to set aside the transaction on the ground that the Bank had taken unfair advantage of inequality of bargaining power between the parties. Walton J was clearly sceptical as to whether Denning's judgment in *Lloyd's Bank Ltd v Bundy* represented English law, but held that in any case the facts did not come within the principle. Burmah were at all times advised by expert lawyers and merchant bankers, and could not have obtained a better price for their shares elsewhere (to sell such a large block of shares on the Stock Exchange at one time would depress the price dramatically, so a sale to a single buyer was very desirable, but it was not proved that there was any other buyer in field). The Bank's terms were tough, but not unconscionably so, given that Burmah's difficulties were largely of its own making and that public money was being provided for the rescue of Burmah and its shareholders. Nor were Burmah in a gravely unequal bargaining position, since although in financial difficulties, they could see that the Bank and the government would not wish to see a large company collapse, and were thus under pressure to come up with a rescue package.

   Suppose the Bank had intimated informally that it would give generous terms, and on the strength of that Burmah had given up other offers; but when it was too late to revive these other offers, the Bank had reduced its offer to below the level of the other offers. Should Burmah be able to avoid the agreement, or part of it? On what terms? Is 'inequality of bargaining power' a useful concept to help decide this sort of case, or do you need such concepts as good faith bargaining and misrepresentation?

3. Academic commentators have not all been so dismissive. For instance, Waddams, 'Unconscionability in Contracts' (1976) 39 MLR 369 also suggests that there is a single principle running through the cases mentioned, and calls for the recognition of a general principle.

4. Denning's general principle has been accepted by a number of courts in Canada (see Enman, 'Doctrines of Unconscionability in England, Canada and the Commonwealth' (1987) 16 Anglo-Am. LR 191).

5. A more general doctrine has been adopted in many of the United States. Uniform Commercial Code s 2–302 provides:

Unconscionable contract or clause
(1) If the court as a matter of law finds the contract or any clause of the contract to have been unconscionable at the time it was made the court may refuse to enforce the contract, or it may enforce the remainder of the contract without the unconscionable clause, or it may so limit the application of any unconscionable clause as to avoid any unconscionable result.

Article two of the UCC applies only to 'transactions in goods', but some courts have applied an analogous doctrine to other contracts, and Restatement 2d s 208 adopts a similar provision for application to any contract.

(b) Possible advantages of a general doctrine

Is English law defective in not recognizing any general doctrine of unconscionability? Firstly, are there any agreements which are manifestly 'unfair' in some sense but which the courts cannot strike down under any of the existing doctrines? Slayton, 'The Unequal Bargain Doctrine' (1976) 22 McGill LJ 94, at 106, says:

How does the unequal bargain doctrine differ from that of undue influence? The traditional view is that the latter applies either when undue influence resulting in a contract that would not otherwise have been made can be proved as a fact, or when a confidential relationship exists leading to a duty of fiduciary care and giving rise to a presumption of undue influence which is not rebutted. In my opinion, under the unequal bargain doctrine as set forth by Lord Denning (1) no confidential relationship or duty of fiduciary care is necessary, and (2) undue influence need not be proved as a fact, but will be presumed when bargaining power is impaired and the terms are very unfair or consideration grossly inadequate. If this is so, then clearly a new doctrine of momentous scope has been introduced into the law of contract.

Secondly, could a general doctrine be given a sufficiently coherent content that it would be a workable tool, with criteria that would give an answer in each case without an unacceptable degree of uncertainty? Take Lord Denning MR's formulation in *Lloyds Bank Ltd v Bundy* (above, p 670) and test it against the existing categories. He seems to envisage the following criteria:
(1) The terms of the contract must be very unfair or the consideration inadequate;
(2) The bargaining power of the party must have been impaired by necessity, ignorance, or infirmity;
(3) The other party, or someone else on his behalf, must have used undue pressure or influence. This need not be conscious, but the pressure must emanate from him, not from a general situation like a housing shortage;
(4) Independent advice will not always save a transaction but its absence is usually fatal.

How do these fit the five categories of case Denning relied on? The other ones we have looked at? Other instances of 'unfair contracts' that you can envisage?

'Economic Criteria of Unconscionability' by Trebilcock, in Studies in Contract Law, (ed Reiter and Swan), pp 390–396, 404–408

In fashioning economically defensible criteria of unconscionability, it is submitted that two criteria are central. First, if the market in which the transaction occurs is *structurally impaired*, this may provide grounds for judicial intervention by way of preventing the enforcement of such a transaction. Secondly, even in cases where the transaction in question is entered into in a structurally sound market, the market may be *informationally-impaired*, thus rendering the transaction suspect. It is proposed to examine each of these two concepts in turn.

(b) Structurally impaired markets

What is contemplated here is the case of a market which is so structurally impaired as to preclude the behaviour of one or other of the parties to a contract being effectively disciplined in his behaviour towards the other party by market (competitive) forces. Two subsets of circumstances can be identified in this respect. First, there is the case of what might be called situational (or 'spot') monopolies where special circumstances have arisen giving one contracting party abnormal market power with respect to the other, albeit perhaps not in relation to other parties in the same market. The second is what might be called market-wide monopolies where it is claimed that one contracting party is the victim of abnormal market power possessed by the other and obtaining, on a relatively pervasive and durable basis, throughout the whole of the market in question.

(i) *Situational monopolies*

This class of case is approximately coterminous with those circumstances often considered as falling under the doctrine of duress. . . .

As the scope of the doctrine of duress has moved from the narrow case of physical threats to less clearly specified cases of 'economic duress', it has become more important to define precisely what it is that will constitute unacceptable forms of coercion. The failure to articulate the essence of the concept of duress in meaningful economic terms has led courts to rely on a variety of dubiously useful criteria. For example, in the *Occidental* case, the emphasis on whether the coercion had vitiated the consent of the party pleading duress seems unhelpful. In any operational sense, clearly consent has been forthcoming to the transaction. Indeed, even in the physical threat cases, the consent of the party threatened is entirely real. To attach significance to the absence of a protest by a party to an allegedly coerced argeement, as was also suggested in *Occidental*, again seems of doubtful soundness if it was clear that a protest would be futile. Yet again, to talk of these transactions as 'one-sided' is also unhelpful, because even in the extreme example of a contract induced by physical threat, there are substantial mutual advantages to the transaction. Finally, to attach redemptive significance to the presence of independent advice in a situation where it is acknowledged that the presence of independent advice does 'nothing to expand the choices open' to the party alleging duress seems again mistaken.

It is submitted that the relevant test in all of the so-called duress cases is whether the conduct of the party against whom the doctrine is pleaded was as to remove from, or to take advantage of the absence of, effective access by the other party to a workably competitive range of alternative chioces. For example, in the salvage cases, what may be objectionable about the terms exacted by a tug owner from the owner or captain of a sinking ship is that the latter faces no realistic alternative suppliers of the demanded service. Similarly, in cases where one contracting party threatens to suspend performance unless the other party agrees to a variation in the contract. Here, again, the latter may face a form of situational monopoly if the nature of the contract and the stage of performance is such that he cannot readily obtain an alternative supplier to complete the contract, (and is unlikely to obtain full compensation through a damages award). While, as will be argued later in this study, a judicial doctrine of unconscionability can play only a very limited role in redressing distributional imbalances in the marketplace, it is possible that in particular circumstances the fact of poverty may create situational monopolies which other parties can exploit. For example, in *D and C Builders Ltd v Rees*. . . .

The extension of the doctrine of duress to any form of monopolistic threat would seem a promising and defensible line of development for the doctrine to take. Beyond rationalizing all the various classes of cases hitherto subsumed under the doctrine of duress, a doctrine so functionally defined has the advantage of posing a relatively realistic inquiry for the courts to embark upon. In cases of situational monopolies, the circumstances directly surrounding the particular transaction between the two parties in question will generally yield reliable inferences as to the extent of the monopoly power possessed by one in relation to the other. This is in sharp and significant contrast to the problems posed in cases of market-wide monopolies, discussed below. On the other hand, several cautions need to be added.

First, despite the monopoly that exists in these cases some of these transactions may be value maximizing; what has happened is that the monopolist has taken all or almost all the consumer surplus in rents (eg, in the salvage cases). Thus, these transactions may not be so much allocatively inefficient as distributively 'unfair'. What makes them distributively unfair cannot avoid a value judgment, although economic analysis might suggest some caution in intervention where excessive profits merely signal a transition to a new equilibrium or where excessively blunt intervention may eliminate incentives to supply the product or service in question. Second, in a number of the standard duress cases, the circumstances are more accurately characterized, economically, not as simple monopolies but as bilateral monopolies. For example, even in the salvage cases, depending on the circumstances, it may be the case that both the owners of the tug and the vessel in distress each possess abnormal market power in relation to the other. That is to say, the tug owner may be the only supplier of salvage services readily accessible to the distressed vessel, but in turn, the distressed vessel may be the only one readily available demander of the tug's services. As economic theorizing has shown, in bilateral monopoly situations the outcomes of the resulting bargaining processes are somewhat indeterminate in terms of a competitive market benchmark. The implications of this for a judicial doctrine of unconscionability is that it will sometimes be difficult to determine whether resulting contracts are optimal in any relevant economic sense. However, apart from 'fairness' considerations, one potential advantage of a properly fashioned intervention here is that the social waste (inefficiency) that is often generated by strategic behaviour in bilateral monopoly situations might be reduced. Thus, for example, excessive investments in bargaining activities, as in the recent Amoco Cadiz incident where protracted salvage negotiations led to the foundering of an oil tanker, might be discouraged.

(ii) Market-wide monopolies
Here, the case differs from situational monopolies because of the difficulty facing a court in making reliable determinations of abnormal market power simply by looking at the relationship and interactions between the two parties to a contested contract. Claims of abuse of market power can only be validated by extensive inquiry into the structure of the entire market in which the transaction has taken place. The difficulties facing a court in this context are well illustrated by the decision of the House of Lords in *Macaulay v Schroeder Publishing Co Ltd.* . . . [For details of this case and Trebilcock's comments on it, see below, p 785ff.]

It is submitted that the difficulties exemplified in the decision in *Macaulay v Schroeder Publishing Co* suggest extreme caution on the part of courts in withholding contract enforcement on the grounds of inequality of bargaining power involving alleged abuses of market-wide monopoly power. First, inferences of such monopolies are frequently likely to be drawn incorrectly by the courts. Secondly, even where correctly drawn, the courts do not have at their disposal the remedial instruments required to foreclose all second-order, substitution, effects.

(c) Informationally-impaired markets
In this context, it is proposed to examine three classes of situations where a party to a contract may have entered into it with imperfect information; first, the case where that party lacks a normal capacity for processing information; second, the case where one party to a contract possesses material information which has not been disposed to the other party to the contract prior to formation; third, the case of standard form contracts containing clauses which have not been read, or understood by the parties to such contracts. . . . As was suggested earlier in this essay, current rules bearing on contractual invalidity, such as those relating to contractual capacity, involve arbitrary boundary lines which make them at the same time both over and under inclusive. To take the case of rules of incapacity governing infants' contracts, it is clear that some infants who are able to take advantage of these rules to avoid contract performance have as much information-processing capacity as many adults who would be held bound on the same contracts. Conversely, there are some adults who are likely to be afflicted by the same lack of information-processing capacity as is exhibited by less mature infants. Setting aside the problems associated with the over inclusive nature of current rules on capacity and instead focusing on their under inclusive character, it is useful to 'decompose' the concept of infancy into some set of physiological characteristics which might then be extrapolated into a set of guidelines for the courts in applying the doctrine of unconscionability to transactions involving adults. . . .

More difficult issues are posed by cases where the source of the impaired information-processing capacity cannot be so precisely identified. For example, in door-to-door sale transactions, where a party is induced to buy something that, on mature reflection, he does not really want or has agreed to pay an excessive price for, or in the dance studio type situation, where a party is induced to sign up for many more dancing lessons than, on mature reflection, were really wanted, the argument can be made that in these situations psychological vulnerabilities are particularly amenable to exploitation, although care is called for in not casting the doctrine in so expansive a form that it loses all focus and rigour. Obviously, if the courts are to avoid a pervasively interventionist role in the market-place as second guessers of people's bargains and if the costs of error and uncertainty that would be engendered by such a role are to be contained, there should be some costs to non-excusable incompetence in participating in market transactions, and thus, conversely, appropriate incentives to develop some threshold level of competence.

The doctrine of unconscionability, as it applies to the foregoing cases of impaired ability to process information, seems to be playing a very useful and defensible role. The scope of the inquiry posed for the courts by the doctrine in this context seems a relatively manageable one, given that typically the courts need only to examine the circumstances immediately surrounding the particular transaction in question, the charactertistics of the parties, and the nature of the relationship between them. They are not called on to embark upon extensive inquiries into conditions generally in the relevant market beyond establishing, where possible, a market norm against which the values exchanged in the transaction in question can be measured.

However, it is important that the doctrine be seen as a constrained tool of intervention and not the basis for unfettered judicial second-guessing of market participants. The constraints that ought to be particularly noted are: first, the courts, wisely, have generally insisted on a conjunction of a substantial divergence between the consideration received by the party seeking relief and the consideration available from elsewhere in the market and some quite specifically identifiable source of impairment in the information-processing powers of the party seeking relief which prevented him from capturing the benefits of those market alternatives. This constraint on the doctrine, of course, differentiates it from rules on the incapacity of infants where an infant may avoid a contract for non-necessaries even if the consideration which he has received under it comports entirely with relevant market norms. Second, even where this conjunction of circumstances is present, it should probably be treated as doing no more than raising a strong presumption of unconscionability which the other party to the transaction should be at liberty to attempt to rebut. This is particularly important in family-type transactions where what to an outsider might seem a grossly inadequate consideration passing from one party to another may be explained by eg donative intentions or the provision of non-market type services such as eg, companionship. Third, to the extent that the party seeking relief is not able to identify any precise source of impairment to his information-processing capabilities, to that extent the court should insist on more rigorous proof of the market norm against which the applicant seeks to have the inadequacy of consideration provided under the impinged transaction measured. Thus . . . the court might wish to insist, first, on a very substantial disparity between the consideration obtained under the contract and the consideration otherwise available in the market and, second, on very rigorous proof as to the existence and availability to the plaintiff of these market alternatives. Fourth, it is axiomatic that if a person who would otherwise be entitled to relief under the criteria outlined above nevertheless has the advantage of independent legal or similar advice, the presence of an agent with presumably normal information-processing capabilities fully answers any claim for relief by the applicant.

(Further extracts from Trebilcock will be found in the sections on standard form contracts and exemption clauses, below, pp 700–703 and on illegality, below, pp 786–789.)

NOTES

1. Trebilcock characterises the typical duress case as a 'situational monopoly'. How would you describe Denning's case of the poor man who is homeless and has to pay a high rent? Should contract law intervene to upset the bargain in the latter case?
2. Cases of minors' contracts and contracts with insane persons fit into Trebilcock's second category of 'informationally impaired markets'. We shall see another very important example of this with standard form contracts: see below, p 700 ff.
3. How would you apply Trebilcock's analysis to undue influence?
4. Do you think English law should introduce a broad doctrine of unconscionability?

Standard form contracts

'Contracts of Adhesion—Some thoughts about Freedom of Contract' by Kessler (1943) Col LR 629, at 631–632

The development of large scale enterprise with its mass production and mass distribution made a new type of contract inevitable—the standardized mass contract. A standardized contract, once its contents have been formulated by a business firm, is used in every bargain dealing with the same product or service. The individuality of the parties which so frequently gave color to the old type contract has disappeared. The stereotyped contract of today reflects the impersonality of the market. It has reached its greatest perfection in the different types of contracts used on the various exchanges. Once the usefulness of these contracts was discovered and perfected in the transportation, insurance, and banking business, their use spread into all other fields of large scale enterprise, into international as well as national trade, and into labor relations. It is to be noted that uniformity of terms of contracts typically recurring in a business enterprise is an important factor in the exact calculation of risks. Risks which are difficult to calculate can be excluded altogether. Unforeseeable contingencies affecting performance, such as strikes, fire, and transportation difficulties can be taken care of. The standard clauses in insurance policies are the most striking illustrations of successful attempts on the part of business enterprises to select and control risks assumed under a contract. The insurance business probably deserves credit also for having first realized the full importance of the so-called 'juridical risk', the danger that a court or jury may be swayed by 'irrational factors', to decide against a powerful defendant. Ingenious clauses have been the result. Once their practical utility was proven, they were made use of in other lines of business. It is highly probable that the desire to avoid juridical risks has been a motivating factor in the widespread use of warranty clauses in the machine industry limiting the common law remedies of the buyer to breach of an implied warranty of quality and particularly excluding his right to claim damages. The same is true for arbitration clauses in international trade. Standardized contracts have thus become an important means of excluding or controlling the 'irrational factor' in litigation. In this respect they are a true reflection of the spirit of our time with its hostility to irrational factors in the judicial process, and they belong in the same category as codifications and restatements.

In so far as the reduction of costs of production and distribution thus achieved is reflected in reduced prices, society as a whole ultimately benefits from the use of standard contracts. And there can be no doubt that this has been the case to a considerable extent. The use of standard contracts has, however, another aspect which has become increasingly important. Standard contracts are typically used by enterprises with strong bargaining power. The weaker party, in need of the goods or services. is frequently not in a position to shop around for better terms, either because the author of the standard contract has a monopoly (natural or artificial) or because all competitors use the same clauses. His contractual intention is but a subjection more or less voluntary to terms dictated by the stronger party, terms whose consequences are often understood only in a vague way, if at all. Thus, standardized contracts are frequently contracts of adhesion; they are *à prendre ou à laisser*. Not infrequently the weaker party to a prospective contract even agrees in advance not to retract his offer while the offeree reserves for himself the power to accept or refuse, or he submits to terms or change of terms which will be communicated to him later. To be sure, the latter type of clauses regularly provide for a power to disaffirm, but as a practical matter they are acquiesced in frequently, thus becoming part of the 'living law'. Lastly, standardized contracts have also been used to control and regulate the distribution of goods from producer all the way down to the ultimate consumer. They have become one of the many devices to build up and strengthen industrial empires.

NOTE

It has been said that Kessler's analysis represents what has been termed the 'exploitation theory' of standardized contracts (See Priest (1981) 80 Yale LJ 1267, at 1299–1302. An extreme statement of the exploitation theory will be found in Kahn-Freund, Introduction to Renner, *The Institutions of Private Law* (1949) pp 38–39). We shall see later (pp 700ff) that there is good reason to doubt whether the exploitation analysis is an accurate description of the effects of the use of standard form contracts by business concerns. However this approach has been very influential among academics and the judiciary both in England and the US.

A Schroeder Music Publishing Co Ltd v Macaulay [1974] 3 All ER 616, House of Lords

Lord Diplock. . . . Standard forms of contracts are of two kinds. The first, of very ancient origin, are those which set out the terms on which mercantile transactions of common occurrence are to be carried out. Examples are bills of lading, charterparties, policies of insurance, contracts of sale in the commodity markets. The standard clauses in these contracts have been settled over the years by negotiation by representatives of the commercial interests involved and have been widely adopted because experience has shown that they facilitate the conduct of trade. Contracts of these kinds affect not only the actual parties to them but also others who may have a commercial interest in the transactions to which they relate, as buyers or sellers, charterers or shipowners, insurers or bankers. If fairness or reasonableness were relevant to their enforceability the fact that they are widely used by parties whose bargaining power is fairly matched would raise a strong presumption that their terms are fair and reasonable.

The same presumption, however, does not apply to the other kind of standard form of contract. This is of comparatively modern origin. It is the result of the concentration of particular kinds of business in relatively few hands. The ticket cases in the 19th century provide what are probably the first examples. The terms of this kind of standard form of contract have not been the subject of negotiation between the parties to it, or approved by any organisation representing the interests of the weaker party. They have been dictated by the party whose bargaining power, either exercised alone or in conjunction with others providing similar goods or services, enables him to say: 'If you want these goods or services at all, these are the only terms on which they are obtainable. Take it or leave it.'

To be in a position to adopt this attitude towards a party desirous of entering into a contract to obtain goods or services provides a classic instance of superior bargaining power.

CHAPTER 34
Exclusion clauses

The problem with standard form contracts is that they may contain apparently unfair terms. In particular they frequently contain exclusion or limitation clauses, clauses which exclude some right which one of the parties would otherwise have had under the common law, or reduce the remedies available to him. Both the courts and the legislature in England have been particularly concerned with such clauses, and in this chapter we shall examine the rules which have been developed. Other types of term found in standard form contracts such as clauses permitting termination and repossession of property can also operate harshly, and we have seen already examples of statutory controls over such clauses in consumer credit agreements (above, p 450).

Many types of exclusion (or 'exemption') and limitation clauses are found. Here are some examples:

(1) *Limiting the compensation for a breach of contract*
'. . . provided always that our total liability for loss, damage or injury shall not exceed the total value of the contract' (*Harbutts 'Plasticine' Ltd v Wayne Tank and Pump Co Ltd* [1970] 1 QB 447, noted above, p 488).

(2) *Limiting the remedies available*
'Whatever the difference of the shipment may be in value from the grade, type or description specified . . . such question shall not . . . entitle the buyers to reject the delivery or any part thereof' (*J Aron & Co Inc v Comptoir Wegimont* [1921] 3 KB 435).

(3) *Limiting the time during which a remedy is available*
'The goods delivered shall be deemed to be in all respects in accordance with the contract . . . unless the sellers shall within 14 days after the arrival of the goods . . . receive notice . . .' (*Beck & Co v Symanowski* [1924] AC 43).

(4) *Imposing a condition on the remedy*
'. . . limited to making good at its factory any part or parts thereof which shall . . . be returned to it with transportation charges prepaid'.

(5) *Excluding normal rules of evidence*
'. . . the Final Certificate . . . shall constitute conclusive evidence for all purposes and in any proceedings whatsoever . . . that the contractor has completed the design of the works and completed the works . . . in all respects in accordance with the contract' (I Chem E conditions of contract for process plant, 1st ed).

(6) *Excluding express or implied terms*
'No condition or warranty that the vehicle is roadworthy or as to its age, condition or fitness for any purpose is given by the owner or implied herein' (*Karsales (Harrow) Ltd v Wallis* [1956] 2 All ER 866, below, p 689).

(7) *Giving one party a broad discretion over the manner or the substance of performance*

'Steamers, sailing dates, rates and itineraries are subject to change without notice' (*Anglo-Continental Holidays Ltd v Typaldos Lines (London) Ltd* [1967] 2 Lloyd's Rep 61; see further below, p 716).

Further examples will be found in the cases which follow.

As with contract law generally, there is not a great deal of empirical evidence on the use of exclusion clauses. Yates conducted a small survey in Bristol and Manchester on the use of clauses in contracts between commercial organizations and in consumer contracts: see Yates, *Exclusion Clauses in Contracts* (2nd edn), pp 24–30. See also Livermore [1986] JBL 90.

You will find that the courts tend to be hostile to exclusion clauses and frequently find a means to avoid having to give effect to them.

'Second Report on Exemption Clauses in Contracts' (No 69) (Law Commission) (1975) paras 11, 146

THE CASE FOR CONTROL

11. It is clear that exemption clauses are much used both in dealings with private individuals and in purely commercial transactions. We are in no doubt that in many cases they operate against the public interest and that the prevailing judicial attitude of suspicion, or indeed of hostility, to such clauses is well founded. All too often they are introduced in ways which result in the party affected by them remaining ignorant of their presence or import until it is too late. That party, even if he knows of the exemption clause, will often be unable to appreciate what he may lose by accepting it. In any case, he may not have sufficient bargaining strength to refuse to accept it. The result is that the risk of carelessness or of failure to achieve satisfactory standards of performance is thrown on to the party who is not responsible for it or who is unable to guard against it. Moreover, by excluding liability for such carelessness or failure, the economic pressures to maintain high standards of performance are reduced. There is no doubt that the misuse of these clauses is objectionable. Some are unjustified. Others, however, may operate fairly or unfairly, efficiently or inefficiently, depending on the circumstances; for example, the cost and practicability of insurance may be factors in determining how liability should be apportioned between two contracting parties. The problem of devising satisfactory methods of controlling the use of these clauses, and indeed of identifying some of them, has proved both difficult and complicated.

146. . . . We do not propose to define exemption clauses in general terms; we regard this expression not as a legal term of art but as a convenient label for a number of provisions which may be mischievous in broadly the same way. Their mischief is that they deprive or may deprive the person against whom they may be invoked either of certain specific rights which social policy requires that he should have (for example the right of a buyer in a consumer sale to be supplied with goods of merchantable quality, or the right of a person to whom a service has been supplied to a reasonable standard of care and skill on the part of the supplier) or of rights which the promisee reasonably believed that the promisor had conferred upon him.

NOTES

1. These passages seem to identify three distinct problems with exclusion clauses. First, the party affected may remain 'ignorant of their presence or import until it is too late.' The commentary to UCC s 2–302 (above, p 673) terms this 'unfair surprise'. Sometimes references to 'inequality of bargaining power' seem to refer to this problem: it might be better to call it 'inequality of information' or 'inequality of bargaining sophistication.' Compare the extracts from Trebilcock, above pp 673–676 and below pp 700–703.

2. Secondly, the party 'may not have sufficient bargaining strength to refuse to accept it.' This is lack of bargaining power in a different and more accurate sense – the party does not have enough influence to get the terms changed. It seems to be this which Lord Diplock was referring to (above, p 678), though below we shall question whether he was right to attribute the problem to 'the concentration of particular kinds of business in relatively few hands' (see below, p 700).

3. Thirdly, the clauses may deprive the party 'of certain specific rights which social policy requires that he should have.' As you read the pages which follow, you may like to ponder on what rights fall into this category, and on how this statement is to be reconciled with the notion of freedom of contract.

The cases which follow are ones applying the common law rules about exemption clauses; for the most part this involves applying strict construction to the wording of the clause. They demonstrate the courts' hostility, in that some of the constructions seem rather strained, but because this common law 'control' over exemption clauses as an indirect one, the court frequently avoids having to articulate the reasons for its hostility. It is not always clear on what ground the hostility is based. As you read each case you should ask yourself: what is the purpose of this clause? Is it objectionable or acceptable? Why? Is it objectionable in *any* circumstances, or just in the circumstances of this case? To take up some of the points made in the extracts from the Law Commission Report, is the problem that the party affected did not know of the clause? That he would not have understood it to have the effect contended for? That he could not have obtained what he wanted without the clause? Or that the clause deprives him of some specific right which 'social policy requires that he should have?' What would have been the effect on the contract as a whole if one party had insisted on the clause being deleted? If the court by one means or another refuses to give effect to the clause, what will be the effect on similar contracts in the future?

In subsection (b) we will examine some of these questions from an economic viewpoint before, in subsection (c), we look at the statutory controls which have been brought in to supplement the common law.

The theme of how the controls over exemption clauses can be reconciled with freedom of contract is one which will recur often. It is important not only at the theoretical level but also at the technical one. How far can the parties make their own contract, rather than having to select one of a number of standardised 'contract types', each with its own 'central obligations' which cannot necessarily be altered?

At the technical level, the debate usually appears in this form: should an exclusion or limitation clause be treated as a kind of defensive mechanism which operates to restrict 'normal liability' and which may be 'disallowed' in certain circumstances; or should it be treated as defining what is being undertaken in the first place, so that it should be given equal weight to the other terms of the contract?

It has been argued that an exclusion clause merely defines what is being undertaken and should be given equal weight to the other terms of the contract: see Coote, *Exception Clauses* (1964), especially chaps 1 and 8, and Lord Diplock's speech in the *Photo Productions* case (above, p 457). Normally the courts have tended not to take this approach but view exclusion clauses as defensive and to be given second place to the positive obligations under the contract. Thus exclusion clauses are usually interpreted narrowly, so as to leave the positive obligations as far as possible unaffected. The main statute, the Unfair Contract Terms Act 1977 (UCTA), takes the same line: in certain situations exclusion clauses are invalidated, leaving the parties subject to the 'normal liability'.

As the extract from the Law Commission report suggests, there are often very good reasons for doing this; but on occasion this approach might result in the contract becoming rather different to what either party envisaged. A farmer who has sold a horse as 'warranted sound except for hunting' might have just cause for complaint if, as the result of judicial or statutory intervention, she were made liable for providing a hunter, just as an insurance company which had insured a car against damage 'except when used for rallying or motor sport' would if it were made to pay out for damage incurred during a race. We shall see instances of the courts recognising this and switching their approach, so that the clause is regarded as a part of the definition of what was being undertaken (see eg below, p 687). The extent to which the UCTA leaves the parties free to define their own responsibilities is not wholly clear (see below, pp 707–708).

In the sections which follow it is assumed that the exclusion clause has been incorporated into the contract, for instance by forming part of a signed written contract, or by reasonable notice: see above, pp 267–277).

(a) The common law approach to exclusion clauses: interpretation

An exclusion clause will always be construed narrowly, against the party who put it forward (contra proferentem). In addition to cases applying this general approach, we shall look at a number which employ specific 'rules of construction', or, more properly, interpretative devices, to limit the application of the clause.

An example of the general contra preferentem rule being applied is *Andrews Bros (Bournemouth) Ltd v Singer & Co Ltd* [1934] 1 KB 17. In that case the plaintiffs were appointed by the defendants as dealers for 'new Singer cars'. They contracted to buy a number of such cars under an agreement which provided, inter alia, that 'all conditions, warranties and liabilities implied by statute, common law or otherwise are excluded'. The defendants delivered a car which was not strictly a 'new' car, as it had already been driven a considerable mileage to be shown to another customer. The Court of Appeal held that the defendants could not rely on the clause, which dealt only with implied terms, since the obligation to deliver a new car was an *express* term.

In *Beck & Co v Symanowski & Co* [1924] AC 43 clause 5 of a contract for the sale of reels of sewing cotton provided that the goods delivered should be deemed to be in all respects in accordance with the contract unless the sellers were notified within 14 days of delivery. After 18 months the buyers complained that on average each reel contained only 188 yards of cotton instead of the stipulated 200. The House of Lords held that the sellers were not protected by clause 5, which referred to 'goods delivered', whereas the buyers were complaining that a portion of the goods had not been delivered.

A particular application of the contra preferentem approach is found in a group of cases involving the question of whether the clause covers negligence. In *White v John Warwick & Co Ltd* [1953] 2 All ER 1021, the plaintiff hired a bicycle from the defendants. Clause 11 of the Agreement provided:

Nothing in this agreement shall render the owners liable for any personal injuries . . .

The plaintiff was thrown from the bicycle and injured when the saddle tilted as he was riding it. The Court of Appeal held that the defendants were liable for negligence: cl 11 excluded their strict liability in contract, but they were also under a duty in tort to take reasonable care, and cl 11 did not cover that.

Hollier v Rambler Motors (AMC) Ltd [1972] 1 All ER 399, Court of Appeal

The plaintiff took his car to a garage for repairs, as he had done on several previous occasions. Normally he signed a form which provided:

The company is not responsible for damage caused by fire to customers' cars on the premises.

On the occasion in question he did not sign the form. His car was damaged in a fire caused by the negligence of the garage. The court held that the form was not incorporated into the contract by a previous course of dealing (see above, p 273).

Salmon LJ. . . . That really disposes of this appeal, but in case I am wrong on the view that I have formed, without any hesitation I may say, that the course of dealing did not import the so-called exclusion clause, I think I should deal with the point as to whether or not the words on the bottom of the form, had they been incorporated in the contract, would have excluded the defendants' liability to compensate the plaintiff for damage to the plaintiff's car by a fire which had been caused by the defendant's own negligence. It is well settled that a clause excluding liability for negligence should make its meaning plain on its face to any ordinarily literate and sensible person. The easiest way of doing that, of course, is to state expressly that the garage, tradesman or merchant, as the case may be, will not be responsible for any damage caused by his own negligence. No doubt merchants, tradesmen, garage proprietors and the like are a little shy of writing in an exclusion clause quite so bluntly as that. Clearly it would not tend to attract customers, and might even put many off. I am not saying that an exclusion clause cannot be effective to exclude negligence unless it does so expressly, but in order for the clause to be effective the language should be so plain that it clearly bears that meaning. I do not think that defendants should be allowed to shelter behind language which might lull the customer into a false sense of security by letting him think—unless perhaps he happens to be a lawyer—that he would have redress against the person with whom he was dealing for any damage which he, the customer, might suffer by the negligence of that person.

The principles stated by Scrutton LJ with his usual clarity in *Rutter v Palmer*:

'For the present purposes a rougher test will serve. In construing an exemption clause certain general rules may be applied: First the defendant is not exempted from liability for the negligence of his servants unless adequate words are used; secondly, the liability of the defendant apart from the exempting words must be ascertained; then the particular clause in question must be considered; and if the only liability of the party pleading the exemption is a liability for negligence, the clause will more readily operate to exempt him.'

Scrutton LJ was far too great a lawyer, and had far too much robust common sense, if I may be permitted to say so, to put it higher than that 'if the only liability of the party pleading the exemption is a liability for negligence, the clause will more readily operate to exempt him.' He does not say that 'if the only liability of the party pleading the exemption is a liability for negligence, the clause will necessarily exempt him'. After all, there are many cases in the books dealing with exemption clauses, and in every case it comes down to a question of construing the alleged exemption clause which is then before the court. It seems to me that in *Rutter v Palmer*, although the word 'negligence' was never used in the exemption clause, the exemption clause would have conveyed to any ordinary, literate and sensible person that the garage in that case was inserting a clause in the contract which excluded their liability for the negligence of their drivers. The clause being considered in that case—and it was without doubt incorporated in the contract—was: 'Customers' cars are driven by your staff at customers' sole risk . . .' Any ordinary man knows that when a car is damaged it is not infrequently damaged because the driver has driven it negligently. He also knows, I suppose, that if he sends it to a garage and a driver in the employ of the garage takes the car on the road for some purpose in connection with the work which the customer had entrusted the garage to do, the garage could not conceivably be liable for the car being damaged in an accident unless the driver was at fault. It follows that no sensible man could have thought that the words in that case had any meaning except that the garage would not be liable for the negligence of their own drivers. That is a typical case where, on the construction of the clause in question, the meaning for which the defendant was there contending was the obvious meaning of the clause.

The next case to which I wish to refer is the well-known case of *Alderslade v Hendon Laundry Ltd*. In that case articles were sent by the plaintiff to the defendants' laundry to be washed, and they were lost. In an action by the plaintiff against the defendants for damages, the defendants relied on the following condition to limit their liability: 'The maximum amount allowed for lost or damaged article is 20 times the charge made for laundering'. Again, this was a case where negligence was not expressly excluded. The question was: what do the words mean? I have no doubt that they would mean to the ordinary housewife who was sending her washing to the laundry that, if the goods were lost or damaged in the course of being washed through the negligence of the laundry, the laundry would not be liable for more than 20 times the charge made for the laundering. I say that for this reason. It is, I think, obvious that when a laundry loses or damages goods it is almost invariably because there has been some neglect or default on the part of the laundry. It is said that thieves break in and steal, and the goods (in that case handkerchiefs) might have been stolen by thieves. That of course is possible, but I should hardly think that a laundry would be a great allurement to burglars. It is a little far-fetched to think of burglars breaking into a laundry to steal the washing when there are banks, jewellers, post offices, factories, offices and homes likely to contain money and articles far more attractive to burglars. I think that the ordinary sensible housewife, or indeed anyone else who sends washing to the laundry, reading that clause must have appreciated that almost always when goods are lost or damaged it is because of the laundry's negligence, and, therefore, this clause could apply only to limit the liability of the laundry, when they were in fault or negligent.

But counsel for the defendants has drawn our attention to the words used by Lord Greene MR in delivering the leading judgment in this court, and he contends that Lord Greene MR was in fact making a considerable extension to the law as laid down by Scrutton LJ in *Rutter v Palmer*. For this proposition he relies on the following passage in Lord Greene MR's judgment.

'The effect of those authorities can I think be stated as follows: where the head of damage in respect of which limitation of liability is sought to be imposed by such a clause is one which rests on negligence and nothing else, the clause must be construed as extending to that head of damage, because if it were not so construed it would lack subject-matter.'

If one takes that work 'must' au pied de la lettre that passage does support counsel for the defendants' contention. However, we are not here construing a statute, but a passage in an unreserved judgment of the Master of the Rolls, who was clearly intending no more than to restate the effect of the authorities as they then stood. It is to be observed that MacKinnon LJ, who gave the other judgment in this court, relied on the rule or principle which he said was very admirably stated by Scrutton LJ in *Rutter v Palmer*. He said:

'Applying that principle to the facts of this case, I think that this clause does avail to protect the proprietor of the laundry in respect of liability for negligence, which must be assumed to be the cause of these handkerchiefs having disappeared.'

And clearly it did, for the reasons that I have already given. I do not think that Lord Greene MR was intending to extend the law in the sense for which counsel for the defendants contends. If it were so extended, it would make the law entirely artificial by ignoring that rules of construction are merely our guides and not our masters; in the end you are driven back to construing the clause in question to see what it means. Applying the principles laid down by Scrutton LJ, they lead to the result at which the court arrived at in *Alderslade v Hendon Laundry Ltd*. In my judgment these principles lead to a very different result in the present case. The words are: 'The Company is not responsible for damage caused by fire to customer's cars on the premises'. What would that mean to any ordinary literate and sensible car owner? I do not suppose that any such, unless he is a trained lawyer, has an intimate or, indeed, any knowledge of the liability of bailees in law. If you asked the ordinary man or woman: 'Supposing you send your car to the garage to be repaired, and there is a fire, would you suppose that the garage would be liable?', I should be surprised if many of them did not answer, quite wrongly. 'Of course they are liable if there is a fire'. Others might be more cautious and say, 'Well, I had better ask my solicitor', or, 'I do not know. I suppose they may well be liable'. That is the crucial difference, to my mind, between this case and *Alderslade v Hendon Laundry Ltd* and *Rutter v Palmer*. In those two cases, any ordinary man or woman reading the conditions would have known that all that was being excluded was the negligence of the laundry, in the one case, and the garage, in the other. But here I think the ordinary man or woman would be equally surprised and horrified to learn that if the garage was so negligent that a fire was caused which damaged their car, they would be without remedy because of the words in the condition. I can quite understand that the ordinary man or woman would consider that, because of these words, the mere fact that there was a fire would not make the garage liable. Fires can occur from a large variety of causes, only one of which is negligence on the part of the occupier of the premises, and that is by no means the most frequent cause. The ordinary man would I think say to himself: 'Well, what they are telling me is that if there is a fire due to any cause other than their own negligence they are not responsible for it'. To my mind, if the defendants were seeking to exclude their responsibility for a fire caused by their own negligence, they ought to have done so in far plainer language than the language here used. In my view, the words of the condition would be understood as being meant to be a warning to the customer that if a fire does occur at the garage which damages the car, and is not caused by the negligence of the garage owner, then the garage owner is not responsible for damage.

[Stamp LJ and Latey J delivered concurring judgments.]

Appeal allowed.

NOTE

This case did not escape criticism when it was decided (see Barendt (1972) 35 MLR 644), and it *might* not be decided the same way today on the construction point: as we shall see (below, p 699), the House of Lords has recently deplored strained construction, which is not so necessary now that the courts have power to hold a clause unreasonable under the Unfair Contract Terms Act 1977 (hereafter UCTA). However the general approach of reading the clause as it might appear to the intelligent layman is attractive—indeed UCTA itself seems to take this approach in one section (see below, pp 716–717) and it is arguable that some of the other cases on construction rest on a similar basis (eg the 'main purpose' rule, below, p 686).

J Evans & Son (Portsmouth) Ltd v Andrea Merzario Ltd [1976] 2 All ER 930, Court of Appeal

(For additional facts, see above, p 163.) The defendants had orally promised to arrange that the container holding the plaintiff's goods would be stored below decks. The contract was held to be partly oral and partly on the standard conditions of the forwarding trade, which exempted the defendants from liability for loss or damage to the goods unless it occurred while the goods were in their actual custody and by reason of their wilful neglect or default. Clause 4 provided:

Subject to express instructions in writing given by the customer, the Company reserves to itself complete freedom in respect of the means, route and procedure to be followed in the handling and transportation of goods.

Roskill LJ. . . . It is suggested that even so these exemption clauses apply. I ventured to ask counsel for the defendants what the position would have been if when the defendants' first quotation had come along there had been stamped on the face of that quotation: 'No containers to be shipped on deck'; and this container had then been shipped on deck. He bravely said that the exemption clauses would still have applied. With great respect, I think that is an impossible argument. In the words which Devlin J used in *Firestone Tyre & Rubber Co Ltd v Vokins & Co Ltd*, and approved by Lord Denning MR in *Mendelssohn v Normand Ltd*, the defendants' promise that the container would be shipped on deck would be wholly illusory.

. . . It is a question of construction. Interpreting the contract as I find it to have been, I feel driven to the conclusion that none of these exemption clauses can be applied, because one has to treat the promise that no container would be shipped on deck as overriding any question of exempting condition. Otherwise, as I have already said, the promise would be illusory.

NOTES

1. Could the principle invoked by Roskill LJ be used if the clauses had merely been inconsistent with some term that would normally be *implied* into the contract?
2. Could the principle have been used if the only clause had said, 'in the event of the goods being carried on deck, whether through our carelessness or otherwise, our liability for loss or damage to the goods shall be limited to $500 per container'?
3. Roskill LJ treats both clauses as exemption clauses. Is that strictly correct in the case of clause 4? See below, p 716.
4. This case involves two express terms of the contract which are inconsistent with each other. The court treats the positive oral promise (to load the container below decks) as overriding the printed clause. Are there any circumstances in which it would be more appropriate to treat the printed clauses as paramount? (That was the effect of the judgment at first instance, see above, p 163.)
5. What if two printed clauses, one positive and one an exception clause, are inconsistent with each other? At least when the contract is between businesses, the courts have on occasion applied the exception clause even though it has the effect of depriving the other clause of any meaning: eg *Istros SS (Owner) v F W Dahlstroem & Co* [1931] 1 KB 247. (See above, p 682 and below, pp 687–688.)

Glynn v Margetson & Co [1893] AC 351, House of Lords

The plaintiff shipped oranges at Malaga for carriage to Liverpool under a printed bill of lading which stated that the ship should have 'liberty to proceed to and stay at any port or ports in any station in the Mediterranean, Levant, Black Sea, or Adriatic, or on the coasts of Africa, Spain, Portugal, France, Great Britain or Ireland, for the purposes of delivering coals, cargo or passengers, or for any other purpose whatsoever.' The ship left Malaga and proceeded to a port 350 miles further away from Liverpool to pick up a cargo. Because of the delay the oranges arrived at Liverpool damaged.

Lord Herschell LC. . . . My Lords, the main object and intent, as I have said, of this charterparty is the carriage of oranges from Malaga to Liverpool. That is the matter with which the shipper is concerned, and it seems to me that it would be to defeat what is the manifest object and intention of such a contract to hold that it was entered into with a power to the shipowner to proceed anywhere that he pleased, to trade in any manner that he pleased, and to arrive at the port at which the oranges were to be delivered when he pleased.

Then is there any rule of law which compels the construction contended for? I think there is not. Where general words are used in a printed form which are obviously intended to apply, so far as they are applicable, to the circumstances of a particular contract, which particular contract is to be embodied in or introduced into that printed form, I think you are justified in looking at the main object and intent of the contract and in limiting the general words used, having in view that object and intent. Therefore, it seems to me that the construction contended for would be an unreasonable one, and there is no difficulty in construing this clause to apply to a liberty in the performance of the stipulated voyage to call at a particular port or ports in the course of the voyage. That port or those ports would differ according to what the stipulated voyage was, inasmuch as at the time when this document was framed the parties who framed it did not know what the particular voyage would be, and intended it to be equally used whatever that voyage is. The ports a visit to which would be justified under this contract would, no doubt, differ according to the particular voyage stipulated for between the shipper and the shipowner; but it must, in my view, be a liberty consistent with the main object of the contract—a liberty only to proceed to and stay at the ports which are in the course of the voyage. . . .

I move your Lordships that this appeal be dismissed with costs.

Lord Halsbury. . . . My Lords, I am entirely of the same opinion. It seems to me that in construing this document, which is a contract of carriage between the parties, one must in the first instance look at the whole of the instrument and not at one part of it only. Looking at the whole of the instrument, and seeing what one must regard, for a reason which I will give in a moment, as its main purpose, one must reject words, indeed the whole provisions, if they are inconsistent with what one assumes to be the main purpose of the contract. The main purpose of the contract was to take on board at one port and to deliver at another port a perishable cargo. . . .

My Lords, I also concur with my noble and learned friend on the woolsack that the particular words which give the liberty are to be construed to refer to a liberty to deliver in the course of a voyage which has been agreed upon between the parties. . . .

Lords Macnaghten and Shand concurred.

Appeal dismissed.

NOTES

1. Would the decision have been the same if the cargo had not been perishable?
2. Why view the contract as essentially one to carry a perishable cargo, rather than essentially one to have the cargo carried to Liverpool by tramp steamer (ie a ship that 'tramps' from port to port in search of cargo)? Do you suppose the decision would have been different if it wasn't apparent that the goods were perishable and the carrier hadn't known that they were?
3. Do you think the decision would have been the same if the liberty to deviate clause had not been part of a printed form, but part of a contract specially typed up after negotiation?
4. Note that the contract itself makes no reference to any obligation to go directly to the port of discharge. The court is striking out the clause as inconsistent with the *implicit* main purpose of the contract: ie the court implies a term that the ship will go direct and then strikes the clause down as inconsistent with the implied term.
5. How does the court decide whether a clause is inconsistent with the main purpose, and therefore to be rejected, and when it is merely a qualification to or definition of what is being undertaken by the carrier? In *GH Renton & Co Ltd v Palmyra Trading Corpn of Panama* [1957] AC 149 timber was shipped under bills of lading from Canada to London and Hull 'or as near

thereunto as the vessel may safely get . . .'. By cl 14(c) of the bills it was provided that in the event of strikes preventing discharge at the named port, 'the master may discharge the cargo at . . . any other safe and convenient port.' Cl 14(f) stated: 'The discharge of any cargo under the provisions of this clause shall be deemed due fulfilment of the contract.' London and Hull were closed by strikes and the cargo was discharged at Hamburg; the carrier refused to accept responsibility for not arranging for it to be forwarded to England. It was argued that the clause deeming delivery at Hamburg to be due fulfilment of the contract was inconsistent with the main purpose of the contract, but the House of Lords rejected the argument for reasons given by Jenkins LJ in the Court of Appeal:

> It seems to me that there is a material difference between a deviation clause purporting to enable the shipowners to delay indefinitely the performance of the contract voyage simply because they choose to do so, and provisions such as those contained in clause 14(c) and (f) in the present case, which are applicable and operative only in the event of the occurrence of certain specified emergencies. The distinction is between a power given to one of the parties which, if construed literally, would in effect enable that party to nullify the contract at will, and a special provision stating what the rights and obligations of the parties are to be in the event of obstacles beyond the control of either arising to prevent or impede the performance of the contract in accordance with its primary terms.

Gibaud v Great Eastern Rly Co [1921] 2 KB 426, Court of Appeal

The plaintiff left his bicycle at one of the defendants' stations, and received in return a ticket containing the usual provision limiting liability unless the value of the goods was declared to be in excess of £5. The bicycle was not put in the cloakroom but left in the booking hall, from where it was stolen.

Scrutton LJ. . . . [It was argued] that the appellant was not bound by the conditions relieving the company from liability, because the company had not kept the bicycle in the place in which they had contracted to keep it. The principle is well known, and perhaps *Lilley v Doubleday* is the best illustration, that if you undertake to do a thing in a certain way, or to keep a thing in a certain place, with certain conditions protecting it, and have broken the contract by not doing the thing contracted for in the way contracted for, or not keeping the article in the place in which you have contracted to keep it, you cannot rely on the conditions which were only intended to protect you if you carried out the contract in the way in which you had contracted to do it. In *Lilley v Doubleday* the defendant had contracted to warehouse certain goods at the main warehouse. He warehoused part of them at another place and, without negligence on his part, they were lost from the other place. It was held that though he would have been protected if the good had been lost without negligence from the place where he contracted to keep them, he lost that protection when he warehoused them in a place where he had not contracted to keep them. *Lilley v Doubleday* and *Davis v Garrett* were approved by this Court in *James Morrison & Co v Shaw, Savill, & Albion Co.*

Having stated this principle, Scrutton LJ went on to hold that it did not apply to the facts of the case, since the contract should be treated as one to receive the bicycle, not one to keep it in the cloakroom.

Lord Sterndale MR and Younger LJ concurred.

NOTE

The interpretative device Scrutton LJ describes is often called the 'four corners rule', or 'quasi deviation'. Be careful not to confuse it with deviation proper: the four corners rule is one of construction only, unlike deviation proper (see below, p 691). Both seem to be confined to contracts of bailment.

Pinnock Bros v Lewis & Peat Ltd [1923] 1 KB 690

The plaintiffs bought from the defendants East African copra cake, which they resold to B, who resold to dealers, who resold to a farmer who used it for feeding cattle. The cake was so contaminated with castor beans as to be poisonous, and the cattle became ill. Each buyer sued his seller, and in the action by the plaintiffs the defendants relied on an exclusion clause.

Roche J. . . . . The next defence raised was based on the clause of the contract which provides that 'the goods are not warranted free from defect rendering same unmerchantable which would not be apparent on reasonable examination, any statute or rule of law to the contrary notwithstanding'. In my view, where a substance quite different from that contracted for has been delivered, that clause has no application, as such a difference of substance cannot be said to constitute a 'defect'. It was said for the defendants that the admixture of castor beans and copra cake was so common that the presence of the castor beans could not be regarded as otherwise than a 'defect'. Upon the facts I am against this contention, and I hold that the delivery in this case could not be properly described as copra cake at all. That is sufficient to dispose of the defendants' contention, and it is therefore unnecessary to decide whether if there was a defect it was latent. If it were necessary to decide the point I should hold that the defect was not latent, for, in my opinion, that word is only applicable to such a defect as is not discoverable by the exercise of reasonable care. I think this defect, if it could be so called, could have been discovered by the exercise of reasonable care.

Judgment for the plaintiffs.

NOTE

This device is sometimes called the 'total non-performance rule', and sometimes (for reasons which will emerge later), 'breach of fundamental term'. You will find another application of it in *Karsales (Harrow) Ltd v Wallis* (below). In a recent case the House of Lords warned against taking the device too far, and refused to apply it in a case where the seed supplied produced not cabbages, as it should have done, but only little floppy green plants: a clause limiting the suppliers' liability for consequential loss arising from the use of the seeds was still applicable, as seeds had been supplied, even if the seeds were commercially valueless. However the device itself was not said to be wrong, and presumably it would have prevented the sellers relying on the clause if what had been supplied turned out to be little chips of wood or sand. See *George Mitchell Ltd v Finney Lock Seeds Ltd* (below, p 720).

From the cases you have read, how may different interpretative devices can you identify? (You may like to check your answer against Coote [1970] CLJ 221, at 238.)

The cases you have read so far were decided on the basis of construction of the contract, ie wording of the clause. In a series of cases in the 1950s and early 1960s, however, some judges went beyond the construction approach and held that a party who had committed a 'fundamental breach' or 'breach of a fundamental term' could not rely on an exclusion clause no matter how widely it was worded. See Denning LJ's judgment in the next case.

Karsales (Harrow) Ltd v Wallis [1956] 1 WLR 936, Court of Appeal

A man named Stinton offered a Buick car to Wallis, the defendant. Wallis wished to buy it, but could only afford to do so on credit. Stinton was not a dealer and could not arrange hire-purchase directly, so he sold the car to Karsales, who sold it to a finance company who let it on hire-purchase to Wallis. Stinton retained possession of the car throughout, but when he delivered it to Wallis the cylinder head had been removed, the valves in the engine had been burnt out, two of the pistons had been broken, the tyres had been damaged and the radio removed. The car was towed to Wallis' premises late at night. Wallis refused to accept the car and got Stinton to take it away. The finance company got Karsales to take over the hire-purchase agreement, and Karsales sued Wallis for arrears. Karsales relied on cl 3(g):

> No condition or warranty that the vehicle is roadworthy, or as to its age, condition or fitness for purpose is given by the owner or implied herein.

The county court judge gave judgment for the plaintiffs.

Denning LJ. . . . The law about exempting clauses has been much developed in recent years, at any rate about printed exempting clauses, which so often pass unread. Notwithstanding earlier cases which might suggest the contrary, it is now settled that exempting clauses of this kind, no matter how widely they are expressed, only avail the party when he is carrying out his contract in its essential respects. He is not allowed to use them as a cover for misconduct or indifference or to enable him to turn a blind eye to his obligations. They do not avail him when he is guilty of a breach which goes to the root of the contract. The thing to do is to look at the contract apart from the exempting clauses and see what are the terms, express or implied, which impose an obligation on the party. If he has been guilty of a breach of those obligations in a respect which goes to the very root of the contract, he cannot rely on the exempting clauses. I would refer in this regard to what was said by Roche J in the 'copra cake' case (*Pinnock Brothers v Lewis & Peat Ltd*) and the judgments of Devlin J in *Alexander v Railway Executive* and *Smeaton Hanscomb & Co Ltd v Sassoon I Setty, Son & Co (No 1)* and the recent case in this court of *J Spurling Ltd v Bradshaw* and the cases there mentioned. The principle is sometimes said to be that the party cannot rely on an exempting clause when he delivers something 'different in kind' from that contracted for, or has broken a 'fundamental term' or a 'fundamental contractual obligation', but these are, I think, all comprehended by the general principle that a breach which goes to the root of the contract disentitles the party from relying on the exempting clause. In the present case the lender was in breach of the implied obligation that I have mentioned. When the defendant inspected the car before signing the application form, the car was in excellent condition and would go: whereas the car which was subsequently delivered to him was no doubt the same car, but it was in a deplorable state and would not go. That breach went, I think, to the root of the contract and disentitles the lender from relying on the exempting clause.

Birkett LJ. . . . The defendant said: 'The original Buick car is the car I had seen before and which I would like to have.' Clearly it was the duty of the finance company in those circumstances, having regard to the history, to supply to the defendant a 'car', in the ordinary sense of that term, and not something that needed towing, because in the true meaning of words a car that would not go was not a car at all; and on the evidence before the county court judge that was the kind of article which was supplied.

Parker LJ. . . . [H]owever extensive the exception clause may be, it has no application if there has been a breach of a fundamental te 1. We were referred to a number of cases, the most recent of which, I think, is that decideu by Devlin J, *Smeaton Hanscomb & Co Ltd v Sassoon I Setty, Son & Co (No 1)*, in which Devlin J said:

> 'It is no doubt, a principle of construction that exceptions are to be construed as not being applicable for the protection of those for whose benefit they are inserted if the beneficiary has committed a breach of a fundamental term of the contract; . . . I do not think that what is a fundamental term has ever been closely defined. It must be something, I think, narrower than a condition of the contract, for it would be limiting the exceptions too much to say that they applied only to breaches of warranty. It is, I think, something which underlies the whole contract so that, if it is not complied with, the performance becomes something totally different from that which the contract contemplates.'

Applying that to the facts of this case it seems to me that the vehicle delivered in effect is not properly described (as the agreement describes it) as a motor vehicle, 'Buick', giving the chassis and engine number. By that I am not saying that every defect in a car which renders it for the moment unusable on the road amounts to a breach of a fundamental term; but where, as here, a vehicle is delivered incapable of self-propulsion except after a complete overhaul and in the condition referred to by my Lord, it seems to me that it is abundantly clear that there was a breach of a fundamental term and that, accordingly, the exceptions in clause 3(g) do not apply.

I think the same result is achieved by saying, in effect, that what was delivered was not what was contracted for . . . *Andrews Brothers (Bournemouth) Ltd v Singer & Co Ltd* might well have been decided on the basis that there had been a breach of a fundamental term. In that case the contract was for the sale of new Singer cars, and again there was an elaborate exception clause. Scrutton LJ in that case held that, there being an express term that what was sold was a new Singer car, and there having been a breach of that express term, the exception clauses dealing with implied conditions and warranties had no application.

Appeal allowed.

NOTE

Did the Lord Justices decide the case on the same or different grounds?

As the new doctrine did not depend on the wording, or construction, of the contract it became known as the 'substantive doctrine'. It was derived from a series of cases on carriage of goods by sea, the 'deviation' cases, in which it was held that a carrier who departed from the agreed route lost the benefit of the exception clauses in his contract. The carrier thus became liable to pay for any subsequent loss of or damage to the goods, unless he could show either that the loss must have occurred even if he had stayed on course, or that the owner of the goods had, with full knowledge of the deviation, affirmed the contract. The loss might be quite unconnected with the deviation: in *Joseph Thorley Ltd v Orchis SS Co Ltd* [1907] 1 KB 660 the ship had deviated but had returned to its original route without incident; the goods were damaged while being unloaded. Nonetheless it was held that the deviation prevented the normal exceptions applying to any subsequent loss, and the carrier was liable. The best explanation of this strict rule rests on the carrier's status as a bailee who has exceeded his authority (see Coote, *Exception Clauses*, chapter 6); but in *Hain SS Co v Tate & Lyle Ltd* [1936] 2 All ER 597 the House of Lords explained it in terms of deviation being a breach of condition entitling the owner to put an end to the contract, with the result that the exception clauses were no longer in force when the loss occurred. This ignored the point that normally a contract remains in force, despite a breach of condition, until the innocent party elects to terminate it (see above, p 457), whereas in most of the deviation cases the owner did not know of the deviation, and thus could not have elected to terminate, until after the loss occurred. However, once the deviation rule had been explained as resting on the general law of contract, it was then applied to contracts generally. Further, it was quietly forgotten that the deviation cases depended on there being a deviation, depriving the carrier of his protective clauses, prior to the loss complained of; the two were elided and the rule produced that a party who had committed a very serious, or 'fundamental', breach of contract was ipso facto disentitled from relying on any exclusion clause whatever the clause said (see further, Coote, chapter 8).

In addition there was doubt as to what constituted a fundamental breach or breach of fundamental term. One definition was given by Devlin J in *Smeaton Hanscomb & Co Ltd v Sassoon I Setty, Son & Co* [1953] 1 WLR 1468, at 1470 (quoted by Parker LJ in *Karsales*, above). It is reminiscent of the 'total non-performance' cases we looked at earlier. However it is not easy to see the difference between a breach making the performance totally different and a breach 'depriving the innocent party of the substance of what he contracted for', ie a breach of condition (though it must be admitted that not all breaches of the implied conditions under SGA seem to have a very serious effect: see above, p 329). Certainly in some cases breach of condition and fundamental breach seem to have been treated as interchangeable: eg *J Spurling Ltd v Bradshaw* [1956] 2 All ER 121.

Suisse Atlantique Société d'Armement Maritime SA v NY Rotterdamsche Kolen Centrale [1967] 1 AC 361, House of Lords

In December 1956 the respondents agreed to charter a ship from the appellants for coal-carrying voyages from the US to Europe, 'for a total of two years consecutive voyages'. (Thus the owners would be paid according to the freight earned, so that it was in their interest that the ship should make as many voyages as possible.) The charter provided laytime, and fixed demurrage at $1,000 per day (for an explanation of these terms, see above, p 52). Between October 1957 and the end of the charter the ship made eight round trips. The owners claimed that if loading and discharging had been carried out within the laytime, a further six voyages could have been made, and they claimed damages for the lost freight. The charterers contended that their liability was limited to the demurrage. (At one point the owners were minded to terminate the charter, but in fact they allowed it to continue under a 'without prejudice' agreement.)

The owners failed before Mocatta J and the Court of Appeal. In the House of Lords they raised for the first time the argument that the charterers had committed a fundamental breach and could not rely on the demurrage clause. The House of Lords held that no fundamental breach had been committed, and in any event a demurrage clause was a form of liquidated damages, not an exclusion clause. The House went on to express its view on the 'substantive doctrine' of fundamental breach.

Viscount Dilhorne. . . . In a number of cases (eg *Smeaton Hanscomb & Co v Sassoon I Setty, Son & Co (No 1); Karsales (Harrow) Ltd v Wallis; Yeoman Credit Ltd v Apps; Astley Industrial Trust Ltd v Grimley; Charterhouse Credit Co Ltd v Tolly;* and *UGS Finance Ltd v National Mortgage Bank of Greece and National Bank of Greece, SA.*) there are judicial observations to the effect that exempting clauses, no matter how widely they are drawn, only avail a party when he is carrying out the contract in its essential respects. In my view, it is not right to say that the law prohibits and nullifies a clause exempting or limiting liability for a fundamental breach or breach of a fundamental term. Such a rule of law would involve a restriction on freedom of contract and in the older cases I can find no trace of it.

In each case not only have the terms and scope of the exempting clause to be considered but also the contract as a whole. In the cases I have cited above, I think that, on construction of the contract as a whole, it is apparent that the exempting clauses were not intended to give exemption from the consequences of the fundamental breach. . . .

I think that the legal position was most clearly and accurately stated by Pearson LJ in *UGS Finance Ltd.* He said:

'As to the question of "fundamental breach", I think there is a rule of construction that normally an exception or exclusion clause or similar provision in a contract should be construed as not applying to a situation created by a fundamental breach of contract. This is not an independent rule of law imposed by the court on the parties willy-nilly in disregard of their contractual intention. On the contrary it is a rule of construction based on the presumed intention of the contracting parties. It involves the implication of a term to give to the contract that business efficacy which the parties as reasonable men must have intended it to have. This rule of construction is not new in principle but it has become prominent in recent

years in consequence of the tendency to have standard forms of contract containing exceptions clauses drawn in extravagantly wide terms, which would produce absurd results if
applied literally.'

Lord Reid. . . . In my view no such [substantive] rule of law ought to be adopted. I do not take
that view merely because any such rule is new or because it goes beyond what can be done by
developing or adapting existing principles. Courts have often introduced new rules when, in
their view, they were required by public policy. In former times when Parliament seldom
amended the common law, that could hardly have been avoided. And there are recent
examples although, for reasons which I gave in *Shaw v Director of Public Prosecutions*, I think
that this power ought now to be used sparingly. But my main reason is that this rule would not
be a satisfactory solution of the problem which undoubtedly exists.

Exemption clauses differ greatly in many respects. Probably the most objectionable are
found in the complex standard conditions which are now so common. In the ordinary way the
customer has no time to read them, and if he did read them he would probably not understand
them. And if he did understand and object to any of them, he would generally be told he could
take it or leave it. And if he then went to another supplier the result would be the same. Freedom
to contract must surely imply some choice or room for bargaining.

At the other extreme is the case where parties are bargaining on terms of equality and a
stringent exemption clause is accepted for a quid pro quo or other good reason. But this rule
appears to treat all cases alike. There is no indication in the recent cases that the courts are to
consider whether the exemption is fair in all the circumstances or is harsh and unconscionable or
whether it was freely agreed by the customer. And it does not seem to me to be satisfactory that
the decision must always go one way if, eg, defects in a car or other goods are just sufficient to
make the breach of contract a fundamental breach, but must always go the other way if the
defects fall just short of that. This is a complex problem which intimately affects millions of
people and it appears to me that its solution should be left to Parliament. If your Lordships
reject this new rule there will certainly be a need for urgent legislative action but that is not
beyond reasonable expectation. . . .

Lord Wilberforce. . . . Next for consideration is the argument based on 'fundamental breach'
or, which is presumably the same thing, a breach going 'to the root of the contract'. These
expressions are used in the cases to denote two quite different things, namely, (i) a performance
totally different from that which the contract contemplates, (ii) a breach of contract more
serious than one which would entitle the other party merely to damages and which (at least)
would entitle him to refuse performance or further performance under the contract.

Both of these situations have long been familiar in the English law of contract; and it will have
to be considered whether the conception of 'fundamental breach' extends beyond them. What
is certain is that to use the expression without distinguishing to which of these, or to what other,
situations it refers is to invite confusion.

The importance of the difference between these meanings lies in this, that they relate to two
separate questions which may arise in relation to any contract. These are (as to (i)) whether an
'exceptions' clause contained in the contract applies as regards a particular breach and (as to
(ii)) whether one party is entitled to elect to refuse further performance.

The appellants, in their submission that exceptions clauses do not apply to 'fundamental
breaches' or 'repudiations' confuse these two questions. There is in fact no necessary coincidence between the two kinds of (so-called fundamental) breach. For, though it may be true
generally, if the contract contains a wide exceptions clause, that a breach sufficiently serious to
take the case outside that clause, will also give the other party the right to refuse further
performance, it is not the case, necessarily, that a breach of the latter character has the former
consequence. An act which, apart from the exceptions clause, might be a breach sufficiently
serious to justify refusal of further performance, may be reduced in effect, or made not a breach
at all, by the terms of the clause.

The present case is concerned with the application of what may be said (with what justice will
be later considered) to be an exceptions clause to a possible type of 'fundamental breach'. I
treat the words 'exceptions clause' as covering broadly such clauses in a contract as profess to
exclude or limit, either quantitatively or as to the time within which action must be taken, the
right of the injured party to bring an action for damages. Such a clause must, ex hypothesi,
reflect the contemplation of the parties that a breach of contract, or what apart from the clause
would be a breach of contract, may be committed, otherwise the clause would not be there; but
the question remains open in any case whether there is a limit to the type of breach which they
have in mind. One may safely say that the parties cannot, in a contract, have contemplated that
the clause should have so wide an ambit as in effect to deprive one party's stipulations of all
contractual force; to do so would be to reduce the contract to a mere declaration of intent. To

this extent it may be correct to say that there is a rule of law against the application of an exceptions clause to a particular type of breach. But short of this it must be a question of contractual intention whether a particular breach is covered or not and the courts are entitled to insist, as they do, that the more radical the breach the clearer must the language be if it is to be covered. As Lord Parmoor said in *Cunard Steamship Co Ltd v Buerger* in relation to exception clauses:

> '[they] do not apply when . . . loss or damage has occurred outside the route or voyage contemplated by the parties when they entered the contract of carriage, unless the intention that such limitations should apply is expressed in clear and unambiguous language.'

And in *The Cap Palos* Atkin LJ similarly said:

> 'I am far from saying that a contractor may not make a valid contract that he is not to be liable for any failure to perform his contract, including even wilful default; but he must use very clear words to express that purpose . . .'

In application to more radical breaches of contract, the courts have sometimes stated the principle as being that a 'total breach of the contract' disentitles a party to rely on exceptions clauses. This formulation has its use so long as one understands it to mean that the clause cannot be taken to refer to such a breach but it is not a universal solvent: for it leaves to be decided what is meant by a 'total' breach for this purpose—a departure from the contract? but how great a departure?; a delivery of something or a performance different from that promised? but how different? No formula will solve this type of question and one must look individually at the nature of the contract, the character of the breach and its effect upon future performance and expectation and make a judicial estimation of the final result. . . .

The conception, therefore, of 'fundamental breach' as one which, through ascertainment of the parties' contractual intention, falls outside an exceptions clause is well recognised and comprehensible. Is there any need, or authority, in relation to exceptions clauses, for extension of it beyond this? In my opinion there is not. The principle that the contractual intention is to be ascertained—not just grammatically from words used, but by consideration of those words in relation to commercial purpose (or other purpose according to the type of contract)—is surely flexible enough, and though it may be the case that adhesion contracts give rise to particular difficulties in ascertaining or attributing a contractual intent, which may require a special solution, those difficulties need not be imported into the general law of contract nor be permitted to deform it.

The only new category of 'fundamental breach' which in this context I understand to have been suggested is one of 'deliberate' breaches. . . . The 'deliberate' character of a breach cannot, in my opinion, of itself give to a breach of contract a 'fundamental' character, in either sense of that word. Some deliberate breaches there may be of a minor character which can appropriately be sanctioned by damages: some may be, on construction, within an exceptions clause (for example, a deliberate delay for one day in loading). This is not to say the 'deliberateness' may not be a relevant factor: depending on what the party in breach 'deliberately' intended to do, it may be possible to say that the parties never contemplated that such a breach would be excused or limited: and a deliberate breach may give rise to a right for the innocent party to refuse further performance because it indicates the other party's attitude towards future performance. All these arguments fit without difficulty into the general principle: to create a special rule for deliberate acts is unnecessary and may lead astray.

[Lords Upjohn and Hodson delivered concurring judgments. An extract from Lord Upjohn's judgment, discussing the meaning of fundamental breach, will be found above, p 435.]

Appeal dismissed.

NOTES

1. What, if anything, was wrong with the substantive doctrine?
2. The House of Lords cited with approval many of the cases on construction already referred to. Thus although it seemed to reject the substantive doctrine of fundamental breach, and insisted that the parties were free to determine for themselves what liability they should have even in cases of serious breach, it did not reject the approach which many of the earlier cases adopted of favouring the positive obligations to the defensive clauses.

3. How much practical difference is there between the constructive and substantive rules? Could the hire-purchase company in *Karsales v Wallis* have drafted a clause which on otherwise similar facts would have entitled them to claim the price?

The judgments of Lords Reid and Upjohn in the *Suisse Atlantique* case, while apparently denying the substantive doctrine, contained passages which could be interpreted as suggesting that had the contract in the *Suisse Atlantique* case not been affirmed but terminated, exemption clauses would have ceased to apply (one of the relevant passages is reproduced below, p 696). These dicta were seized upon by the CA in *Harbutts' 'Plasticine' Ltd v Wayne Tank and Pump Co Ltd* [1970] 1 QB 447 as showing that the substantive rule still applied if the contract had been terminated. Lord Denning MR summarized his view thus:

> Before leaving this part of the case, I would just like to say what, in my opinion, is the result of the *Suisse Atlantique* case. It affirms the long line of cases in this court that when one party has been guilty of a fundamental breach of the contract, that is, a breach which goes to the very root of it, and the other side accepts it, so that the contract comes to an end . . . then the guilty party cannot rely on an exception or limitation clause to escape from his liability for the breach.
>
> If the innocent party, on getting to know of the breach, does not accept it, but keeps the contract in being . . . then it is a matter of construction whether the guilty party can rely on the exception or limitation clause . . .

This approach was followed in a number of other cases, and one case, *Wathes (Western) Ltd v Austins (Menswear) Ltd* [1976] 1 Lloyd's Rep 14, has been interpreted as applying the substantive doctrine even when the contract had been affirmed after the breach (see 98 LQR 172).

Photo Production Ltd v Securicor Transport Ltd [1980] 1 All ER 556, House of Lords

Lord Wilberforce. My Lords, this appeal arises from the destruction by fire of a factory owned by the respondents ('Photo Productions') involving loss and damage agreed to amount to £615,000. The question is whether the appellants ('Securicor') are liable to the respondents for this sum.

Securicor are a company which provides security services. In 1968 they entered into a contract with Photo Productions by which for a charge of £8 15s 0d (old currency) per week it agreed to 'provide their Night Patrol Service whereby four visits per night shall be made seven nights per week and two visits shall be made during the afternoon of Saturday and four visits shall be made during the day of Sunday'. The contract incorporated printed standard conditions which, in some circumstances, might exclude or limit Securicor's liability. The questions in this appeal are (i) whether these conditions can be invoked at all in the events which happened and (ii) if so, whether either the exclusion provision, or a provision limiting liability, can be applied on the facts. The trial judge (MacKenna J) decided these issues in favour of Securicor. The Court of Appeal decided issue (i) in Photo Productions' favour invoking the doctrine of fundamental breach. Waller LJ in addition would have decided for Photo Productions on issue (ii).

What happened was that on a Sunday night the duty employee of Securicor was one Musgrove. It was not suggested that he was unsuitable for the job or that Securicor were negligent in employing him. He visited the factory at the correct time, but when inside he deliberately started a fire by throwing a match onto some cartons. The fire got out of control and a large part of the premises was burnt down. Though what he did was deliberate, it was not established that he intended to destroy the factory. The judge's finding was in these words:

> 'Whether Musgrove intended to light only a small fire (which was the very least he meant to do) or whether he intended to cause much more serious damage, and, in either case, what was the reason for his act, are mysteries I am unable to solve.'

This, and it is important to bear in mind when considering the judgments in the Court of Appeal, falls short of a finding that Musgrove deliberately burnt or intended to burn Photo Productions' factory.

The condition on which Securicor relies reads, relevantly, as follows:

> 'Under no circumstances shall the Company [Securicor] be responsible for any injurious act or default by any employee of the Company unless such act or default could have been foreseen and avoided by the exercise of due diligence on the part of the Company as his employer; nor, in any event, shall the Company be held responsible for; (a) Any loss suffered by the customer through burglary, theft, fire or any other cause, except insofar as such loss is solely attributable to the negligence of the Company's employees acting within the course of their employment . . .'

There are further provisions limiting to stated amounts the liability of Securicor on which it relies in the alternative if held not to be totally exempt.

It is first necessary to decide on the correct approach to a case such as this where it is sought to invoke an exception or limitation clause in the contract. The approach of Lord Denning MR in the Court of Appeal was to consider first whether the breach was 'fundamental'. If so, he said, the court itself deprives the party of the benefit of an exemption or limitation clause. Shaw and Waller LJJ substantially followed him in this argument.

Lord Denning MR in this was following the earlier decision of the Court of Appeal, and in particular his own judgment in *Harbutt's Plasticine Ltd v Wayne Tank and Pump Co Ltd.* . . .

My Lords, whatever the intrinsic merit of this doctrine, as to which I shall have something to say later, it is clear to me that so far from following this House's decision in the *Suisse Atlantique* case it is directly opposed to it and that the whole purpose and tenor of the *Suisse Atlantique* case was to repudiate it. The lengthy, and perhaps I may say sometimes indigestible speeches of their Lordships, are correctly summarised in the headnote—

> '(3) That the question whether an exceptions clause was applicable where there was a fundamental breach of contract was one of the true construction of the contract.'

That there was any rule of law by which exception clauses are eliminated, or deprived of effect, regardless of their terms, was clearly not the view of Viscount Dilhorne, Lord Hodson or myself. The passages invoked for the contrary view of a rule of law consist only of short extracts from two of the speeches, on any view a minority. But the case for the doctrine does not even go so far as that. Lord Reid, in my respectful opinion, and I recognise that I may not be the best judge of this matter, in his speech read as a whole, cannot be claimed as a supporter of a rule of law.

. . . His conclusion is stated thus: 'In my view no such rule of law ought to be adopted', adding that there is room for legislative reform.

My Lords, in the light of this, the passage from the *Suisse Atlantique* case cited by Lord Denning MR has to be considered. For convenience I restate it:

> 'If fundamental breach is established, the next question is what effect, if any, that has on the applicability of other terms of the contract. This question has often arisen with regard to clauses excluding liability, in whole or in part, of the party in breach. I do not think that there is generally much difficulty where the innocent party has elected to treat the breach as a repudiation, bring the contract to an end and sue for damages. Then the whole contract has ceased to exist including the exclusion clause, and I do not see how that clause can then be used to exclude an action for loss which will be suffered by the innocent party after it has ceased to exist, such as loss of the profit which would have accrued if the contract had run its full term.'

It is with the utmost reluctance that, not forgetting the 'beams' that may exist elsewhere, I have to detect here a mote of ambiguity or perhaps even of inconsistency. What is referred to is 'loss which will be suffered by the innocent party after [the contract] has ceased to exist' and I venture to think that all that is being said, rather elliptically, relates only to what is to happen in the future, and is not a proposition as to the immediate consequences caused by the breach; if it were, that would be inconsistent with the full and reasoned discussion which follows.

It is only because of Lord Reid's great authority in the law that I have found it necessary to embark on what in the end may be superfluous analysis. For I am convinced that, with the possible exception of Lord Upjohn whose critical passage, when read in full, is somewhat ambiguous, their Lordships, fairly read, can only be taken to have rejected those suggestions for a rule of law which had appeared in the Court of Appeal and to have firmly stated the question is one of construction, not merely of course of the exclusion clause alone, but of the whole contract.

Much has been written about the *Suisse Atlantique* case. Each speech has been subjected to various degrees of analysis and criticism, much of it constructive. Speaking for myself I am conscious of imperfections of terminology, though sometimes in good company. But I do not think that I should be conducing to the clarity of the law by adding to what was already too ample a discussion a further analysis which in turn would have to be interpreted. I have no second thoughts as to the main proposition that the question whether, and to what extent, an exclusion clause is to be applied to a fundamental breach, or a breach of a fundamental term, or indeed to any breach of contract, is a matter of construction of the contract. Many difficult questions arise and will continue to arise in the infinitely varied situations in which contracts come to be breached: by repudiatory breaches, accepted or not, anticipatory breaches, by breaches of conditions or of various terms and whether by negligent, or deliberate, action, or otherwise. But there are ample resources in the normal rules of contract law for dealing with these without the superimposition of a judicially invented rule of law. I am content to leave the matter there with some supplementary observations.

1. The doctrine of 'fundamental breach' in spite of its imperfections and doubtful parentage has served a useful purpose. There were a large number of problems, productive of injustice, in which it was worse than unsatisfactory to leave exception clauses to operate. Lord Reid referred to these in the *Suisse Atlantique* case, pointing out at the same time that the doctrine of fundamental breach was a dubious specific. But since then Parliament has taken a hand: it has passed the Unfair Contract Terms Act 1977. This Act applies to consumer contracts and those based on standard terms and enables exception clauses to be applied with regard to what is just and reasonable. It is significant that Parliament refrained from legislating over the whole field of contract. After this Act, in commercial matters generally, when the parties are not of unequal bargaining power, and when risks are normally borne by insurance, not only is the case for judicial intervention undemonstrated, but there is everything to be said, and this seems to have been Parliament's intention, for leaving the parties free to apportion the risks as they think fit and for respecting their decisions.

At the stage of negotiation as to the consequences of a breach, there is everything to be said for allowing the parties to estimate their respective claims according to the contractual provisions they have themselves made, rather than facing them with a legal complex so uncertain as the doctrine of fundamental breach must be. What, for example, would have been the position of Photo Productions' factory if instead of being destroyed it had been damaged, slightly or moderately or severely? At what point does the doctrine (with what logical justification I have not understood) decide, ex post facto, that the breach was (factually) fundamental before going on to ask whether legally it is to be regarded as fundamental? How is the date of 'termination' to be fixed? It it the date of the incident causing the damage, or the date of the innocent party's election, or some other date? All these difficulties arise from the doctrine and are left unsolved by it.

At the judicial stage there is still more to be said for leaving cases to be decided straight-forwardly on what the parties have bargained for rather than on analysis, which becomes progressively more refined, of decisions in other cases leading to inevitable appeals. The learned judge was able to decide this case on normal principles of contractual law with minimal citation of authority. I am sure that most commercial judges have wished to be able to do the same (cf *The Angelia, Trade and Transport Inc v Iino Kaiun Kaisha Ltd*, per Kerr J). In my opinion they can and should.

2. *Harbutt's Plasticine Ltd v Wayne Tank and Pump Co Ltd* must clearly be overruled. It would be enough to put that on its radical inconsistency with the *Suisse Atlantique* case. But even if the matter were res integra I would find the decision to be based on unsatisfactory reasoning as to the 'termination' of the contract and the effect of 'termination' on the plaintiffs' claim for damage. I have, indeed, been unable to understand how the doctrine can be reconciled with the well accepted principle of law, stated by the highest modern authority, that when in the context of a breach of contract one speaks of 'termination' what is meant is no more than that the innocent party or, in some cases, both parties are excused from further perform-ance. Damages, in such cases, are then claimed under the contract, so what reason in principle can there be for disregarding what the contract itself says about damages, whether it 'liquidates' them, or limits them, or excludes them? These difficulties arise in part from uncertain or inconsistent terminology. A vast number of expressions are used to describe situations where a breach has been committed by one party of such a character as to entitle the other party to refuse further performance: discharge, rescission, termination, the contract is at an end, or dead, or displaced; clauses cannot survive, or simply go. I have come to think that some of these difficulties can be avoided; in particular the use of 'rescission', even if distinguished from rescission ab initio, as an equivalent for discharge, though justifiable in some contexts (see *Johnson v Agnew*) may lead to confusion in others. To plead for complete uniformity may be to

cry for the moon. But what can and ought to be avoided is to make use of these confusions in order to produce a concealed and unreasoned legal innovation: to pass, for example, from saying that a party, victim of a breach of contract, is entitled to refuse further performance, to saying that he may treat the contract as at an end, or as rescinded, and to draw from this the proposition, which is not analytical but one of policy, that all or (arbitrarily) some of the clauses of the contract lose, automatically, their force, regardless of intention.

If this process is discontinued the way is free to use such words as 'discharge' or 'termination' consistently with principles as stated by modern authority which *Harbutt*'s case disregards. I venture with apology to relate the classic passages. In *Heyman v Darwins Ltd* Lord Porter said:

> 'To say that the contract is rescinded or has come to an end or has ceased to exist may in individual cases convey the truth with sufficient accuracy, but the fuller expression that the injured party is thereby absolved from future performance of his obligations under the contract is a more exact description of the position. Strictly speaking, to say that, upon acceptance of the renunciation of a contract, the contract is rescinded is incorrect. In such a case the injured party may accept the renunciation as a breach going to the root of the whole of the consideration. By that acceptance he is discharged from further performance and may bring an action for damages, but the contract itself is not rescinded.'

Similarly Lord Macmillan; see also *Boston Deep Sea Fishing and Ice Co Ltd v Ansell* per Bowen LJ. In *Moschi v Lep Air Services Ltd* my noble and learned friend Lord Diplock drew a distinction (relevant for that case) between primary obligations under a contract, which on 'rescission' generally come to an end, and secondary obligations which may then arise. Among the latter he included an obligation to pay compensation, ie damages. And he stated in terms that this latter obligation 'is just as much an obligation arising from the contract as are the primary obligations that it replaces'. My noble and learned friend has developed this line of thought in an enlightening manner in his opinion which I have now had the benefit of reading.

These passages I believe to state correctly the modern law of contract in the relevant respects; they demonstrate that the whole foundation of *Harbutt*'s case is unsound. A fortiori, in addition to *Harbutt*'s case there must be overruled *Wathes (Western) Ltd v Austins (Menswear) Ltd* which sought to apply the doctrine of fundamental breach to a case where, by election of the innocent party, the contract had not been terminated, an impossible acrobatic, yet necessarily engendered by the doctrine. Similarly, *Charterhouse Credit Co Ltd v Tolly* must be overruled, though the result might have been reached on construction of the contract.

3. I must add to this, by way of exception to the decision not to 'gloss' the *Suisse Atlantique*, a brief observation on the deviation cases, since some reliance has been placed on them, particularly on the decision of this House in *Hain Steamship Co Ltd v Tate & Lyle Ltd* (so earlier than the *Suisse Atlantique*) in the support of the *Harbutt* doctrine. I suggested in the *Suisse Atlantique* that these cases can be regarded as proceeding on normal principles applicable to the law of contract generally, viz that it is a matter of the parties' intentions whether and to what extent clauses in shipping contracts can be applied after a deviation, ie a departure from the contractually agreed voyage or adventure. It may be preferable that they should be considered as a body of authority sui generis with special rules derived from historical and commercial reasons. What on either view they cannot do is to lay down different rules as to contracts generally from those later stated by this House in *Heyman v Darwins Ltd*.

4. It is not necessary to review fully the numerous cases in which the doctrine of fundamental breach has been applied or discussed. Many of these have now been superseded by the Unfair Contract Terms Act 1977. Others, as decisions, may be justified as depending on the construction of the contract (cf *Levison v Patent Steam Carpet Cleaning Co Ltd*) in the light of well-known principles such as that stated in *Alderslade v Hendon Laundry Ltd*.

In this situation the present case has to be decided. As a preliminary, the nature of the contract has to be understood. Securicor undertook to provide a service of periodical visits for a very modest charge which works out at 26p per visit. It did not agree to provide equipment. It would have no knowledge of the value of Photo Productions' factory; that, and the efficacy of their fire precautions, would be known to Photo Productions. In these circumstances nobody could consider it unreasonable that as between these two equal parties the risk assumed by Securicor should be a modest one, and that Photo Productions should carry the substantial risk of damage or destruction.

The duty of Securicor was, as stated, to provide a service. There must be implied an obligation to use care in selecting their patrolmen, to take care of the keys and, I would think, to operate the service with due and proper regard to the safety and security of the premises. The breach of duty committed by Securicor lay in a failure to discharge this latter obligation. Alternatively it could be put on a vicarious responsibility for the wrongful act of Musgrove, viz starting a fire on the premises; Securicor would be responsible for this on the principle stated in

Morris v C W Martin & Sons Ltd. This being the breach, does condition 1 apply? It is drafted in strong terms, 'Under no circumstances, any injurious act or default by an employee'. These words have to be approached with the aid of the cardinal rules of construction that they must be read contra proferentem and that in order to escape from the consequences of one's own wrongdoing, or that of one's servant, clear words are necessary. I think that these words are clear. Photo Productions in fact relied on them for an argument that since they exempted from negligence they must be taken as not exempting from the consequence of deliberate acts. But this is a perversion of the rule that if a clause can cover something other than negligence it will not be applied to negligence. Whether, in addition to negligence, it covers other, eg deliberate, acts, remains a matter of construction requiring, of course, clear words. I am of opinion that it does and, being free to construe and apply the clause, I must hold that liability is excluded. On this part of the case I agree with the judge and adopt his reasons for judgment. I would allow the appeal.

[Lords Diplock, Salmon, Keith and Scarman also delivered judgments in favour of the appellants. Extracts from Lord Diplock's judgment will be found above, pp 457–458.]

Appeal allowed.

NOTE

In *Ailsa Craig Fishing Co Ltd v Malvern Fishing Co Ltd* [1983] 1 All ER 101 the appellants were the owners of a fishing boat which sank in Aberdeen harbour. At the time the respondents, Securicor, were required by contract with a fishing boat owners association of which the appellants were members to provide a security service in the harbour, and specifically for the appellants' vessel. There was a clause in that contract limiting the respondents' liability to £1,000. The appellants argued that the clause should not avail the respondents as they had totally failed to provide any security cover at all, but the House of Lords held that their liability was still limited to £1,000. Lord Wilberforce said (at pp 102–103):

. . . one must not strive to create ambiguities by strained construction, as I think the appellants have striven to do. The relevant words must be given, if possible, their natural, plain meaning. Clauses of limitation are not regarded by the courts with the same hostility as clauses of exclusion; this is because they must be related to other contractual terms, in particular to the risks to which the defending party may be exposed, the remuneration which he receives and possibly also the opportunity of the other party to insure.

(b) The problem with exclusion clauses

The cases on exclusion clauses at common law should have provided you with a good idea of what is involved. Before looking at the statutory controls, it seems sensible to return to the question raised at the beginning of the chapter, namely, what are the problems with exemption clauses, and why are such apparently harsh clauses so commonly found in standard form contracts? If some sort of answer can be given, that will give a framework for evaluating the statutory controls, and some guidance on how it might be appropriate for the courts to apply the reasonableness test that many clauses are now subjected to by the Unfair Contract Terms Act 1977.

You may like to start by looking again at the extract from Kessler and Lord Diplock's judgment in *A Schroeder Music Publishing Co Ltd v Macaulay* (above, pp 677–678).

'An economic approach to unconscionability' by Trebilcock in Studies in Contract Law (ed Reiter and Swan) pp 398–400, 412–421.

While recognizing that the assumptions underlying [Lord Diplock's] analysis of the use of standard form contracts have enjoyed considerable academic currency, it is submitted that they are fallacious. First, the proposition that the use of consumer standard-form contracts is the result of the concentration of market power is entirely without factual foundation. The reason why such contracts are used is exactly the same as for their use in the commercial context, that is to 'facilitate the conduct of trade', or in economic terms, to reduce transaction costs. If an agreement had to be negotiated and drafted from scratch every time a relatively standard transaction was entered into the costs of transacting for all parties involved would escalate dramatically. Moreover, it is a matter of common observation that standard forms are used (for this reason) in countless contexts where no significant degree of market concentration exists. Dry-cleaners have standard form dry-cleaning agreements, hotels standard registration forms, credit-grantors standard financing agreements, insurance companies standard life, fire, and automobile insurance policies, real estate agents standard sale and purchase agreements, landlords standard leases, restaurants set menu and price lists, and, for that matter, department and grocery stores set product ranges and price terms. The fact that in these cases a supplier's products are offered on a take-it-or-leave-it basis is evidence not of market power but of a recognition that neither producer nor consumer interests are served by incurring the costs involved in negotiating separately every transaction. Moreover, even the presence of dickering betwen parties, standing alone, is ambiguous as between the presence or absence of competition. Dickering may, for example, be merely a reflection of attempts by a monopolist to price discriminate among consumers by ascertaining and exploiting different demand elasticities. The use of standard forms is a totally spurious proxy for the existence of market power. The real measure of market power is not whether a supplier presents his terms on a take-it-or-leave-it basis but whether the consumer, if he decides to 'leave it' has available to him a workably competitive range of alternative sources of supply. Whether this is or is not so simply cannot be derived intuitively from the fact that a particular supplier is offering non-negotiable standard-form terms. It is a matter for independent inquiry. If the market is workably competitive, any supplier offering uncompetitive standard-form terms will have to reformulate his total package of price and non-price terms to prevent consumers (at least consumers at the margin, which are the decisive consideration in such a market) from switching their business to other competitors.

It is, of course, true that general use of common standard-form contracts throughout an industry may, on occasion, be evidence of cartelization. But here one must be discriminating. If a reasonable choice of different packages of price and non-price terms is available in the market, albeit all through the medium of different standard-form contracts, then obviously the allegation of a 'fix' will not stand up. Even where all contracts are the same, in perfectly competitive markets where the product is homogeneous, commonality of terms is what one would expect to find (for example, the wheat market). Every supplier simply 'takes' his price and probably other terms from the market and is powerless to vary them. In a perfectly competitive market, with many sellers and many buyers each supplying or demanding too insignificant a share of total market output to influence terms, all participants, sellers and buyers, are necessarily confronted with a take-it-or-leave-it proposition. Thus uniformity of terms, standing alone, is ambiguous as between the presence or absence of competition. . . .

(iii) *Information problems with standard form contracts*
Courts and commentators alike have commonly taken the view of standard form contracts that the party who draws them up has a disproportionate bargaining power in terms of his ability to impose terms involuntarily on the other party. To use Lord Reid's language in *Suisse Atlantique*, 'the consumer has not time to read [standard form clauses], and if he did read them, he would probably not understand them. And if he did understand and object to any of them, he would generally be told he could take it or leave it'. Assuming for the purposes of argument that Lord Reid correctly describes the typical bargaining process entailed when a consumer enters into a contract with a supplier on standard form terms, does it follow that the supplier has an unconstrained ability to impose uncompensated risks unilaterally on an uninformed consumer? We have already examined the market structure argument in this respect, and rejected it. However, the issue remains whether information imperfections afflicting a consumer in this context are such as to lead to unconscionable contractual outcomes even in structurally sound markets. The disclaimer clause/fundamental breach cases are the classic example of the courts attempting to struggle with the answer to this question. A number of difficult conceptual issues are raised by the question of the abuse of bargaining power through differential information about the content of standard form contracts.

First, even in cases where Lord Reid's theorem is factually accurate, it does not follow that the supplier has unconstrained bargaining power to impose any terms that he wishes on a consumer. One of the most important determinants of whether contract terms in such circumstances might be considered fair, in the sense of having been effectively disciplined by market forces, is whether at the *margin* of the market, there are *enough* consumers who are sensitive to the content of these clauses to bring effective pressure to bear on suppliers to modify them in an acceptable way. Non-economists often overlook the importance of marginal analysis in this context. For example, if only 10 per cent of the buyers of insurance policies or dry-cleaning services studied all terms scrupulously before contracting and were influenced in their choice of policy by their evaluation of the so-called fine print clauses, and if no supplier of insurance or dry-cleaning services was able to 'term discriminate' between these consumers and other consumers in the market, there would be strong competitive pressures on each supplier to adjust the terms of his contracts so as to avoid losing this potential business. Perhaps more important than the impact of marginal consumers on the initial formulation of standard form contract terms is their impact on the subsequent enforcement of these terms. For example, no matter how draconian the exculpatory clauses in insurance polices or dry-cleaning contracts, few, if any, suppliers in either market will be able to survive the market reactions likely to be engendered by a supplier treating these clauses as defining the limits of his required performance. A dry cleaner who loses or ruins half the suits that are brought in for cleaning is likely to find little long-term solace in exculpatory clauses on his dry-cleaning tickets (even if enforceable).

A recognition of the importance of the marginal consumer confronts a court with intractable factual issues pertaining to how 'thick' the margin of sophisticated consumers is in the relevant market and how well a supplier is able to discriminate in favour of those consumers and against the inframarginal consumers. Both issues are difficult. As in the case of market-wide monopolies, the first issue requires evidence and analysis of conditions prevailing throughout the market in question. The question of whether discrimination is occurring on a non-cost justified basis is one of the most notoriously difficult issues in the whole of anti-trust law. A supplier, in deciding whether to avail himself of terms in a contract which excuse sub-normal performance will have to reckon with a potential consumer reaction that treats this as tantamount to contractual non-performance. This may take the form of threats to initiate legal proceedings, threats to withdraw future business, or threats to undermine the supplier's credibility with other potential customers. It is primarily consumers who cannot make credible threats of these kinds, and who can be identified and thus discriminated against by suppliers at economic cost, who are most vulnerable to overreaching through standard form contracts.

In the light of these factors, it can be appreciated that the courts face a real problem in looking at the fairness of a standard form contract in the context of some particular transaction and assuming that simply because the particular consumer had not studied, understood, or negotiated about, the terms, the supplier was free of effective constraints on the terms included in the transaction or, as importantly, on the performance called for thereunder. Again, the ability of the court to weigh these kinds of market-wide considerations may be very limited.

Second, even if a court were to decide that a particular market was functioning imperfectly because of information breakdowns in that market, the appropriate remedial response on the part of the courts is by no means clear. One line of attack on fine-print clauses in standard form contracts, based on perceived aberrations in the bargaining process, derives from the so-called Coase theorem. This theorem asserts that, in a world of zero transaction costs, irrespective of the legal allocation of risks, the mutual interests of the parties will tend to lead them to bargain their way to the most efficient allocation of risks, that is, the risk allocation that maximizes the joint value of their respective resources, in which state, in a Pareto optimal sense, both parties are better off. If, on the other hand, transaction costs are significant, at least in relation to the stakes involved, allocative efficiency may not be achieved through voluntary exchange, and liability rules may be justified which attempt to simulate the market outcomes that would have occurred had frictionless exchange been possible.

The Coase theorem does not permit of a straightforward application to the standard-form contractual setting, for, unlike many tort cases where *a priori* bargaining over risk allocation is impossible, in standard-form contracts some voluntary interaction, by definition, occurs. One implication from this is that in those areas of a transaction where bargaining does typically occur, one might often expect to find adjustments made which are designed to offset any legal allocations of risks in areas of the transaction where information and transaction costs arguably prevent negotiation. Thus, importantly, in this context, the general balance of advantage between the parties may not be significantly affected by the law's intervention.

From broadly these premises, Goldberg has argued that in the case of standard-form insurance policies, the costs to the consumer of obtaining, processing, and evaluating information about the implications of 'hidden', subsidiary clauses in such contracts will tend to direct competitive forces, even in workably competitive markets, away from the subject-matter of these clauses and towards broader price-quantity comparisons. The result of such a process may be harsh-term-low-price policies, whereas many consumers, in the absence of information and transaction costs, may have preferred an easier-term-higher-price combination. Thus, bargaining processes are distorted. This may be so, Goldberg argues, even though the industry is making no supra-competitive profits. Therefore the argument goes, the industry would be made no worse off, and many consumers might be made better off, by liability rules designed to produce the mix of terms that would have been reached by the parties in a world without information or transaction costs. Unlike rules designed to improve the quality of available information discussed below, these rules would take information markets as given and simply regulate the substantive contents of contracts.

There are several difficulties with Goldberg's argument. First, even assuming that information and transaction costs relative to the stakes involved in matters dealt with in subsidiary terms (for example, the termination and assignment provisions in *Macaulay*) are as high as Goldberg asserts, how does one determine whether more or fewer consumers will be advantaged under a legal reallocation of risks which produces an easier-term-high-price contract and displaces previous harsher-term-lower-price combinations, given that on Goldberg's hypothesis, information costs are such that consumers' true preferences can never be revealed?

If the answer to this is that in fact one must look for some kind of revealed preference on the part of the general body of affected consumers, say in the form of transactions which reallocate offered risks which a minority of consumers are left bearing (unwittingly), then one is conceding that transaction costs are not generally so high as to prevent voluntary reallocation of risks, and firms in the industry will have an incentive to reflect the generally preferred combination of terms in adjustments to their standard-form contracts, thus avoiding needless transaction costs.

A further factor unaccounted for in Goldberg's analysis, as in that of other critics of standard-form contracts who point to the absence of subjective consumer consent to all contractual terms, is the price that most consumers attach to uncertainty. Making the usual assumption that most consumers are risk-averse, consumers who sign contracts containing clauses which have been drafted by the other party with his advantage obviously in mind and which they do not understand will reflect their aversion to the assumption of undetermined, but intuitively adverse, risk allocations by discounting the consideration they are prepared to offer for entering into such contracts.

Finally, if courts were to impose liability rules on parties to standard form contracts on Goldberg's rationale, then *ex post ad hoc* judicial interventions cannot fairly take the form simply of invalidating 'harsh' clauses. In addition, other clauses will have to be reworked to compensate the supplier for the expanded package of contractual benefits which he is now providing to the consumer. In effect, this form of judicial policing of standard-form contracts should strictly involve reformulating whole contracts. If substantive intervention is to occur, this may argue for general, *ex ante*, legislative intervention where 'harsh' terms are invalidated and the market is permitted to take care of consequential adjustments to other terms.

Even if the preferred policy response is not outright prohibition or replacement of certain terms, but rather conditional prohibition in the sense that terms are only prohibited if they fail to meet some test of comprehensibility (rules against unfair surprise), another difficult set of issues must be faced. Even if one were to assume that some of the more common categories of standard form contracts, eg conditional sales contracts, insurance contracts, were all printed in large print and written in English that anybody with a grade 6 education and modest intelligence could read, it is not clear that this would prove an effective response to the information problem in many cases. Intuitively, one suspects many consumers would continue not to read most of these kinds of contracts in any detail before signing them. When one asks why, many consumers probably rely in part on the constraints imposed by other consumers at the margin (ie, they let the market shop for them). More importantly, they are probably recognizing that the information problem they often face is not figuring out what particular clauses mean in the sense of how they are allocating certain risks, but instead the problem of relating that information in a meaningful way to their personal circumstances. For example, in the case of an insurance policy which allocates risks in different ways between myself and my insurance company, I may understand perfectly how the policy allocates those risks, but what I may have difficulty in assessing is how likely it is that certain risks may materialize, and if they do, what kinds of costs are likely to be entailed. Thus, how likely is it, as a matter of probability, that my house will catch on fire, and if it does, how much damage is likely to be done? If there are exemptions for earthquakes, Acts of God, fires caused in certain ways, certain classes of property, etc, my problem lies in assessing whether my personal circumstances at any given time during the currency of the policy will fall within one of these clauses and what costs will be entailed for me if it does. This is not information which can be conveyed by the policy, or at least not easily, and as between the insurance company and myself, this may be information to which I have superior access (no matter how difficult), relative to the insurance company (which may in part explain why coverage for certain kinds of risks is excluded). Moreover, even if all clauses in all insurance policies were clearly written, I would face a formidable task in comparing alternative offerings, which involves figuring out a net worth for the various policies given different patterns of coverage and exemption. Again, it is difficult to see how improving the clarity or conspicuousness of what are at present fine print clauses can address this problem. In other words, it is one thing to acquire relevant information; it may be quite another thing to process it effectively. . . .

III Distributive considerations in the application of the doctrine of unconscionability
In the course of this essay, circumstances have been identified where lack of endowments might well lead to circumstances which justify intervention by the courts to prevent contract enforcement. For example, it was pointed out that poverty may in some cases be conducive to the creation of situational monopolies. Secondly, poverty as it manifests itself in illiteracy, lack of education, or lack of experience with market activity may provide grounds for intervention on the grounds of impaired information-processing ability. However, outside limited cases of this kind, this essay has not suggested distributive considerations as a major underpinning for a judicial doctrine of unconscionability. It is important to elaborate on why this view has been taken.

First, while it is clear that poor people often will be compelled, eg, to enter into consumer credit transactions at very high rates of interest, or to rent accommodation of very low quality, it is not at all clear that this apparently differential treatment of poor people in the marketplace is in any way attributable to objectionable behaviour on the part of the suppliers who deal with them. Even though the demand on the part of poor people for necessities of life may be highly inelastic, ie, unresponsive to price, given their resources, it does not follow from that fact alone that they will be exploited. Exploitation will only occur, in the sense of a charging of supra-competitive prices etc, if there are restrictions on supply in the relevant markets. Studies of low-income markets disclose with remarkable consistency that the rates of return earned by merchants in these markets are entirely normal. Thus, however objectionable the distributive outcomes from these markets, the source of the problem does not lie with the supply side of the market but instead with the simple fact of lack of endowments and the implications this carries for successful participation in market activity. Moreover, the objectionable conditions are not amenable to abatement by judicial intervention which prevents contract enforcement. As again many studies of low-income markets have shown, this simply produces substitution effects, with resources being moved away from low income consumers in such markets. For example, consumer credit will be withdrawn from low income consumers if constraints are imposed on the interest rates that can be charged or collection remedies that can be invoked. Rental accommodation is withdrawn from such markets if rent controls are imposed at below competitive levels. Thus, acknowledging both that suppliers in such markets are not the source of the problem, and judicial intervention in contract enforcement will not alleviate the problem and indeed will often aggravate it, it is submitted that the doctrine of unconscionability should not be given a significant realm of application in this context.

Beyond the conventional proverty context, there is a question of whether despite no clear evidence of a structurally or informationally impaired market, and no clear evidence of a substantial divergence between a party's returns from a contract and returns otherwise available from similar transactions in the market, . . . it might still be plausible to conclude, in the case of a particular transaction, that the values exchanged are so disproportionate to each other than in some sense the bargain is distributively 'unfair'.

As Leff has pointed out, the concept of substantive unfairness in the sense of a judicially perceived non-equivalence in the values exchanged by contracting parties, poses real conceptual difficulties following a determination of (1) no abnormal market power and (2) no aberrations in the process of contract formation. Almost by definition, the outcome of such a process cannot be unfair.

NOTES

1. For an explanation of the Coase theorem, see above, p 75.
2. Some economists have assumed that the invisible hand of the market will 'take care of' any problems over unacceptable clauses. Thus Posner writes:

> If one seller offers unattractive terms to a purchaser, a competing seller, desiring to obtain the sale for himself, will offer more attractive terms. The process should continue until the terms are optimal from the purchaser's standpoint. Thus, the purchaser who is offered a printed contract on a take-it-or-leave-it basis does have a real choice: he can refuse to sign, knowing that if better terms are possible another seller will offer them to him.

(*Economic Analysis of Law* (2nd ed), p 85). The article by Goldberg referred to, 'Institutional change and the quasi-invisible hand' 17 J Law & Econ 461 offers a convincing explanation of how transactions costs (here the cost of obtaining and processing information about contract terms) may result in inefficiencies even in competitive markets, with the result that harsh clauses persist.

3. Goldberg argues that customers will tend to shop in terms of price alone. Why? What information processing problems are customers likely to face?

4. What is the result of these information problems? Are customers being exploited in terms of monopoly pricing? If not, are the contracts which are made not efficient?

5. Both the Law Commission (above, p 680) and Lord Reid (above, p 693) make the point that even a consumer who is aware of the clause in question may have no choice but to accept it or do without the goods or service. In the light of the analysis presented, is this surprising? To produce a 'one-off' contract for him would often be very expensive—so much so that he will seldom be prepared to pay the extra cost. On the other hand, as Schwartz, 'Seller unequal bargaining power and the judicial process' (1974) 49 Ind LJ 367, at 370–371, remarks:

> Although it may be difficult to establish whether an individual buyer could or could not have affected a particular term, it is generally true that most buyers will be able to avoid any one term, if they concentrate their entire resources on doing so.

6. Even where the supplier using standard terms is a monopolist, there is no particular reason to think that the terms on which he will offer goods or services will be harsher, except that he will charge more for them: see Schwartz, ibid, pp 380–381.

7. Goldberg argues that suppliers cut costs by putting more and more risks onto the customers via the harsh standard terms. Are there any constraints on how far suppliers will go in this? What constraints?

8. Trebilcock suggests that it only needs a margin of customers to shop around for there to be pressure on suppliers to offer better terms to all. Thus even if there were no negotiations over the clause between the individual parties, it does not follow that the apparently harsh clause is in fact inefficient. It is possible that the contract represents the balance between risk and price that the 'active margin' of customers prefers. The question must be whether there is a 'thick enough' margin of aware customers to have had any impact.

9. It seems unlikely that a court will have any direct evidence about the 'thickness of the margin'. How might a court try to work this out? Is it relevant whether the clause has ever been the subject of negotiation between, say, suppliers and purchasers' trade or consumer associations? Whether the clause is one that relates to a well-known risk? Whether it is obvious in the documents and easy to understand?

10. Trebilcock distinguishes the question of whether the clause is included in the initial contract from whether it is relied on later by the supplier. (His example is bizarre: a dry cleaner which ruined half the suits would go out of business clause or no clause. What is important is whether when something does go wrong, the supplier 'stands on its rights'.) As he points out, there is much greater scope for discrimination between customers here. As we shall see, the courts have sometimes been harsh on suppliers who discriminate in this way (see below, p 720 ff).

(c) Statutory controls

Until 1977 the statutory controls over the use of exemption clauses, though going back as far as the Canals and Railways Act of 1854, were piecemeal: only certain types of clause were controlled, either by allowing them only if reasonable (under the 1854 Act, limitations of liability had to be reasonable) or by making them of no effect (for example, exclusions of liability for death or personal injury of passengers in a public service vehicle, under the Road Traffic Act 1960). In 1973 the Supply of Goods (Implied Terms) Act controlled the exclusion or restriction of liability for breach of terms implied under the SGA: these provisions were then incorporated into the Unfair Contract Terms Act 1977 (s 6). This Act does not, as we shall see, touch every exemption clause in every type of contract, but it does impose fairly sweeping controls. It seems easiest to take the sections not in the order in which they appear in the Act, but grouped according to their subject matter, starting with the sections derived from the 1973 Act.

As we go through the Act (hereafter referred to as UCTA, as before), we can ask questions at two levels: firstly at the technical level, on the exact effect of the UCTA, and secondly at the policy level: why is this type of clause controlled or banned?

(i) Obligations as to correspondence with description, quality, etc in supply of goods: ss 6(2), (3); 7(1), (2), (3)

Section 6
(2) As against a person dealing as a consumer, liability for breach of the obligations arising from—
  (a) section 13, 14 or 15 of the 1979 Act (seller's implied undertakings as to conformity of goods with description or sample, or as to their quality or fitness for a particular purpose);
  (b) section 9, 10 or 11 of the 1973 Act (the corresponding things in relation to hire-purchase),
cannot be excluded or restricted by reference to any contract term.
(3) As against a person dealing otherwise than as consumer, the liability specified in subsection (2) above can be excluded or restricted by reference to a contract term, but only in so far as the term satisfies the requirement of reasonableness.

Section 7
(1) Where the possession or ownership of goods passes under or in pursuance of a contract not governed by the law of sale of goods or hire-purchase, subsections (2) to (4) below apply as regards the effect (if any) to be given to contract terms excluding or restricting liability for breach of obligation arising by implication of law from the nature of the contract.
(2) As against a person dealing as consumer, liability in respect of the goods' correspondence

with description or sample, or their quality or fitness for any particular purpose, cannot be excluded or restricted by reference to any such term.

(3) As against a person dealing otherwise than as consumer, that liability can be excluded or restricted by reference to such a term, but only in so far as the term satisfies the requirement of reasonableness.

NOTES

1. Section 6 replaces the corresponding provisions of the 1973 Act. Section 7 is new, and covers the supply of goods under contracts of hire, work and materials (such as a building contract or a contract to repair a car) and exchange (or barter).

2. Both sections draw a crucial distinction between consumer and non-consumer contracts. The definition of 'dealing as a consumer' is in s 12.

   Section 12
   (1) A party to a contract 'deals as consumer' in relation to another party if—
      (a) he neither makes the contract in the course of a business nor holds himself out as doing so; and
      (b) the other party does make the contract in the course of a business; and
      (c) in the case of a contract governed by the law of sale of goods or hire-purchase, or by section 7 of this Act, the goods passing under or in pursuance of the contract are of a type ordinarily supplied for private use or consumption.
   (2) But on a sale by auction or by competitive tender the buyer is not in any circumstances to be regarded as dealing as consumer.
   (3) Subject to this, it is for those claiming that a party does not deal as consumer to show that he does not.

   Suppose Furmston buys a mini-bus, without revealing to the dealer that he is not buying it for business but to transport his family. Is he dealing as a consumer? Suppose Beale goes to a cash and carry to buy a large tub of honey for his children, and presents a trade card to obtain a discount. Is he dealing as a consumer?

3. It has been held that a contract may be a consumer sale even though the buyer is a business. In *R & B Customs Brokers Co Ltd v United Dominions Trust Ltd* [1988] 1 All ER 847 the plaintiffs bought from the defendant finance company a car supplied to it by a motor dealer. The plaintiff, a private company, bought the car for the personal and business use of its directors. It had done the same two or three times before. The conditional sale contract between the plaintiff and defendant excluded any implied conditions as to the condition or quality of the car or to its fitness for purpose. The car leaked. The Court of Appeal held that there was a breach of s 14(3), unless that section was excluded by the terms of the contract; and that the plaintiff company was dealing as a consumer, so that the obligations under s 14(3) could not be excluded. The court reached this surprising conclusion by applying the same test as is used to decide whether a false description has been applied in the course of a business under the Trade Description Act 1968: if the transaction is only incidental to the business activity, rather than integral to it, it is not done 'in the course of a business' unless a degree of regularity is established, which had not been shown on the facts.

   Whether this is a sensible outcome may, with respect, be doubted. It is true that many small businesses have no more influence in the market, and are no more sophisticated as bargainers, than private consumers; but the Court of Appeal's approach means that any occasional and 'incidental' purchase by a business of goods 'of a type ordinarily supplied for private use or consumption' will be a consumer sale, however large and sophisticated the buyer. The buyer might also have considerable bargaining power which it could use to obtain better terms, for while it will only count as a consumer if it makes occasional purchases of the type of goods in question, there is nothing to prevent it being a very large customer of the seller for other purchases.

4. Section 6(4) provides:

> (4) The liabilities referred to in this section are not only the business liabilities defined by section 1(3), but include those arising under any contract of sale of goods or hire-purchase agreement.

Thus, although broadly speaking UCTA affects only business liability, in this case a clause in a private sale might be affected. Note however that by s 12 such a sale could not be a consumer sale, so a reasonableness test under s 6(3) would apply; and only attempts to exclude liability for correspondence with description or sample (and title, see next note) would be affected, as the implied terms as to merchantability and fitness for purpose apply only to sales made in the course of a business. Of course a private seller may give *express* undertakings on these matters, but s 6 does not prevent him excluding or restricting his liability in respect of express undertakings.

5. Under s 6(1) the implied obligations as to title cannot be excluded in any contract of sale or hire-purchase, whether consumer or non-consumer. Under s 7(3A) and (4) the prohibition on the exclusion of the implied obligations as to title in other contracts is not absolute but is subject to the reasonableness test.

6. What counts as an exclusion or restriction of liability for breach of the relevant obligation? Section 13 provides:

> (1) To the extent that this Part of this Act prevents the exclusion or restriction of any liability it also prevents—
>   (a) making the liability or its enforcement subject to restrictive or onerous conditions;
>   (b) excluding or restricting any right or remedy in respect of the liability, or subjecting a person to any prejudice in consequence of his pursuing any such right or remedy;
>   (c) excluding or restricting rules of evidence or procedure;
> and (to that extent) sections 2 and 5 to 7 also prevent excluding or restricting liability by reference to terms and notices which exclude or restrict the relevant obligation or duty.
> (2) But an agreement in writing to submit present or future differences to arbitration is not to be treated under this Part of this Act as excluding or restricting any liability.

You have already seen examples of (a), (b) and (c): see the specimen clauses on p 679 above, numbers (4), (2) and (5) respectively. The last part of s 13(1) is intended to deal with the argument we noted earlier (pp 681–682) that a possible effect of an exclusion clause is to define the duties under the contract rather than to act as a partial or total defence. For instance, if a contract of sale contains a clause which states that the seller will not be liable for any defect rendering the goods unmerchantable beyond the cost of repairing or replacing the goods, there is obviously still an obligation on the seller to deliver goods of merchantable quality, but its liability for breach is restricted. If, on the other hand, the clause states that there is no implied undertaking as to merchantability, it might be argued that the clause is not 'excluding or restricting' liability for breach of s 14 because there is no liability under s 14 to exclude. s 13(1) brings this clause within the scope of the Act. However, it has been argued forcefully that s 13 is actually draconian in effect, in that it may prevent the parties defining the type of transaction which they wish to enter. Suppose Beale, acting in the course of a business, wants to sell Bishop, a consumer, an old machine which Beale has never used and which he knows nothing about, without taking any responsibility for its quality. Bishop agrees to a sale on this basis at a suitably reduced price. If they express their agreement by using the clause just given as an example, is it caught by s 6(2)? Or can the operation of s 6(2) be avoided by saying that quite apart from the clause, there would in the circumstances be no obligation as to merchantability, and s 6(2) is to be confined to the case where there would be an obligation *but for the clause in question*? See Yates, *Exclusion Clauses in Contracts* (2nd edn) p 78.

7. Why is the exclusion or restriction of these obligations totally banned in consumer contracts? How common was it for retail sellers and others dealing with consumers to exclude this type of liability? If it was common, why, and how serious a matter was it? Even if it is right to prevent the total *exclusion* of these obligations, does it make sense to prevent the retailer excluding *any* of the liability, even for consequential loss? Suppose a defective appliance causes a fire: the retailer may have no idea of what is likely to be damaged, while the consumer may already have insurance on the property damaged. On some of these questions you may like to consider the following extract and the notes which follow:

'First Report on Exemption Clauses in Contracts' (No 24) (Law Commission) (1969)

68. On the strength of the evidence which they had collected, the Molony Committee declared themselves compelled to view the practice of contracting out as a general threat to consumer interest, in the sense that 'heavy and irrecoverable loss may fall upon the consumer who is unlucky enough to get a defective article.' . . . [The Working Party] found an overriding argument in favour of prohibiting 'contracting out'. The mischief was that this practice enabled well-organised commerce 'consistently to impose unfair terms on the consumer and to deny him what the law means him to have'. On the whole, the consumer did not even know how he was being treated; but where he was alive to the position, he found it difficult and sometimes impossible to avoid submitting to the terms of business universally adopted, because he had no bargaining power of sufficient weight. This being the essence of the case for intervention in support of the consuming public, the Molony Committee endorsed the soundness of the case and accepted the need to ban 'contracting out'. . . .

69. The evidence collected by the Working Party showed that contracting out of the statutory conditions and warranties has continued to be a source of dissatisfaction to consumers. Representatives of the consumer interest have suggested that for the most part the situation has not changed in its essentials during the years which have elapsed since the Molony Committee's inquiry, although it is conceded that there has been a measure of improvement. In the motor vehicle trade contracting out, though still widespread, no longer appears to be 'universal'. Similarly, it has been said that in respect of electrical and mechanical appliances there has been a less 'general' tendency to introduce sweeping exemption clauses. In some cases it would seem that improvements have flowed from the pressure both of the Consumer Council and of other associations and groups representing consumers combined with the work of trade associations and the lead given by certain traders.

. . .

73. Before reaching the conclusion that the Molony Committee's proposal for a general ban on exemption clauses in sales to private consumers was justified and entitled to support, the Working Party considered and rejected a number of other possible solutions. One suggestion was that there should be certain exceptions to the ban on contracting out—for instance, that the exclusion of consequential damage should be permissible, at least in certain specified classes of

sale. This was rejected not only because of the difficulty of defining the exceptions, but also because it was felt that as between the retailer and private consumer the burden of liability under the implied conditions and warranties should fall upon the retailer. Secondly, it was argued that assuming that there was merit in the suggestion that the law should cater for exceptional cases, the only realistic alternative to an unqualified ban was a general test for reasonableness exercisable by the courts on the model of section 3 of the Misrepresentation Act 1967; but this solution was also rejected, on the ground that it would import an element of uncertainty into sales to private consumers whereas certainty and simplicity were of predominant importance in that area of commerce.

. . .

79. . . . [I]t is clear to us that there is widespread public misunderstanding and uncertainty about the purchaser's legal rights against the retailer where the manufacturer's 'guarantee' is offered and accepted. It is our view that legislation, in addition to providing a remedy against effective and oppressive contracting out, can perform the important function of clarifying the legal position of the private consumer. Whatever rights a buyer may have against the manufacturer, and they may be valuable rights, it may be the local retailer rather than the distant (possibly overseas) manufacturer with whom the buyer can most conveniently discuss a complaint and perhaps come to terms, or, in the last resort, litigate his claim. In our view the rights of the private consumer against his seller under the statutory conditions and warranties should be expressly and clearly maintained and safeguarded by the law.

NOTES

1. In what sense are exclusion clauses even in a consumer contract 'unfair'? Do they indicate that consumers are being exploited in the sense that they are being overcharged for what they are receiving? As Trebilcock (above, p 700) points out, standard form contracts with exclusion clauses are not just in trades where there is a monopoly or even a high concentration; and if Goldberg's explanation (above, p 704) of their prevalence is correct, they represent 'value of money', in the sense that they are used by businesses as a way of reducing costs to keep prices down to a competitive level. It is rather that the clauses are not necessarily the terms on which the consumer would have liked to do business had he or she the choice.
2. 'On the whole, the consumer did not even know how he was being treated'. In what sense is this unfair? Suppose a consumer buys a used car from a dealer and shortly afterwards the engine blows up. He then discovers that the contract he signed excludes any liability on the part of the dealer. Assuming the clause to be valid, how would it be unfair? How would the consumer have acted had he or she known the clause was there? Even if the consumer would not have been able to go to another dealer who offered better terms, there are a number of possibilities.
   (a) He might have had the car checked by an independent mechanic before buying it.
   (b) He might have taken out 'extended warranty cover' (a form of insurance).
   (c) He might have refused to pay so much for the car, or if the seller would not reduce the price, have bought a cheaper one, so as to give himself some cash in hand to meet repair bills.
   (d) He might have decided to buy a newer, more reliable, car.
   (e) He might have decided not to buy a car at all.
   (f) He might have gone ahead anyway (he may not mind taking this kind of risk). Leaving case (f) aside, is the unfairness in the clause that it was unexpected, and in reliance on there being some kind of warranty

protecting him the consumer has failed to take steps that would have safeguarded his position at least in part? What if he had assumed that there was no warranty even though he hadn't read the contract?

3. If this were the full extent of the problem, would it be necessary to do more than require that the clause be obvious and immediately comprehensible to the ordinary consumer? Apparently there is more to it: 'where he was alive to the position, he found it difficult and sometimes impossible to avoid submitting to the terms of business universally adopted, because he had no bargaining power of sufficient weight'. Suppose that Furmston, a consumer at least dimly aware of the legal position, tries to buy a lawnmower from Beale Ltd. Beale offers him a contract containing exclusion clauses, and when Furmston replies that he would prefer to have more generous terms (even if that means paying more), Beale tells Furmston to take it or leave it. Unless Furmston is a very large customer for lawnmowers, this seems a likely outcome: he has no bargaining power of sufficient weight. But what do we mean by bargaining power in this context? It is not a case of the crafty exploiting the poor and ignorant (cf *Evans v Llewellin*, above p 658), nor of improper persuasion or pressure (compare Chapters 29 and 30). Nor does it seem to be a case of Beale taking advantage of Furmston's necessity when there is no one else to whom Furmston can turn; there is no suggestion that Beale is a monopolist, and anyway a lawnmower is hardly a necessity: Furmston can always get a flock of sheep or junior lecturers to do the job instead. Moreover, is it really likely that Furmston couldn't get better terms *however* much he was prepared to pay? (Look again at the extract from Schwartz, above p 704). We suggested (also on p 704) that the explanation is a great deal less sinister: it is simply too costly to produce and administer a special set of terms for the odd small customer if the vast majority are apparently content with the terms usually offered. It is no more sinister than finding that Beale won't at any reasonable price produce a custom-built mower. Remember Henry Ford and the Model T, available in any colour so long as it's black. But it may be that only the Furmstons of this world ever ask Beale for better terms because no one else is alive to the problem until too late, and actually everyone would be happier paying slightly more for improved terms *if only they understood*. Is the total ban on excluding merchantability obligations trying to prevent this kind of inefficiency?

4. What if there is a substantial number of customers who ask for something better? Look again at Trebilcock (above, p 700). Isn't it very likely that gradually the contractual offerings will improve? Is this perhaps an explanation of the improvement noted by the Law Commission since the time of the Molony report? In other words, as the Consumers Association and others gradually educated consumers into shopping not just in terms of price, the problem might have gone away.

5. Assuming there were no protective legislation, but that there were a sizeable margin of fully informed shoppers in the relevant market, what kind of terms might one expect to find? Would there be no exclusion clauses at all, so that sellers remained fully responsible for any foreseeable loss resulting from the goods not being merchantable, or would there still be some restrictions because both parties found that a more efficient method of dealing with the problem? Priest, 'A theory

of the product warranty' (1981) 90 Yale LJ 1297 develops a theory which helps to explain the content of manufacturers' warranties of products. A commentator, Whitford, summarizes the theory thus:

Professor Priest's 'investment theory' predicts that warranties will contain the same terms that they would contain in a nearly perfect market. According to his investment theory, there are two principal determinants of warranty content in such a market.

First, if the losses from product defects are avoidable through appropriate actions, the warranty will allocate the loss to the party who can avoid it at least cost. Sometimes losses are best avoided through preventive investments—by the manufacturer through investments in product design or quality control, or by the consumer through investments in a search for the product best adapted to the intended use and investments in proper care and maintenance of the product after purchase. In other instances, losses are best avoided through the repair of a malfunctioning product, and either the manufacturer or the consumer can be the least-cost repairer. Whatever the cheapest method of loss avoidance, the investment theory predicts that warranty terms will allocate losses to induce efficient loss avoidance by the efficient loss avoider.

If losses from product defects are not totally avoidable, then the second determinant of warranty content under the investment theory is the effectiveness of the manufacturer as an insurer against losses. For example, if the risk of loss from product defects varies greatly among consumers, due to important differences in the circumstances of each consumer, Priest believes that the manufacturer is a relatively poor insurer because it usually cannot segregate consumers into risk classes as cheaply and effectively as alternative insurers. In these circumstances, the investment theory predicts that manufacturers will limit warranty coverage to those risks that virtually all consumers share, forcing consumers that face greater risks to self-insure or to obtain alternative insurance. Thus, low risk consumers will not pay for more insurance than their circumstances require. Warranties are likely to exclude consequential damages on this basis, for example, if the potential magnitude of consequential damages varies dramatically among consumers.

Whitford is doubtful about the explanatory power of the theory: see 91 Yale LJ 1372. But see Priest's reply, 91 Yale LJ 1386.

Priest is describing the position between manufacturer and consumer, but probably similar factors would apply between retail seller and consumer. In the light of his analysis, how sensible is it to impose a total ban on *any* restriction of liability for non-merchantability in a consumer sale? What sort of effects is such a ban likely to have on (a) product quality and (b) the number of consumers who can afford to buy the goods? Why did the Law Commission recommend a total ban?

6. The Molony Committee found an overriding argument in favour of a prohibition on contracting out, that the latter enabled commerce to deny the consumer 'what the law means him to have'. What assumptions lie beneath this phrase? Simply that the consumer's rights should not be reduced without his informed consent, or that even informed individuals should *not be allowed* to accept certain risks? If so, why not? Good old paternalism? See further below, p 739.

7. Even if a clause is legally ineffective it may mislead the consumer into thinking he has no rights. Under the Fair Trading Act 1973 delegated legislation may be made to prohibit 'consumer trade practices', including the terms and conditions used in contracts and the manner of their communication, which inequitably affect the economic interests of consumers. The Consumer Transactions (Restrictions on Statements) Order 1976 (SI 1976/1813, as amended by 1978/127), makes it a criminal offence to include in a consumer contract of sale an exclusion clause which would be automatically void under UCTA s 6.

(ii) Manufacturers' guarantee of consumer goods: s 5

Section 5
(1) In the case of goods of a type ordinarily supplied for private use or consumption, where loss or damage—
  (a) arises from the goods proving defective while in consumer use; and
  (b) results from the negligence of a person concerned in the manufacture or distribution of the goods,
liability for the loss or damage cannot be excluded or restricted by reference to any contract term or notice contained in or operating by reference to a guarantee of the goods.
(2) For these purposes—
  (a) goods are to be regarded as 'in consumer use' when a person is using them, or has them in his possession for use, otherwise than exclusively for the purposes of a business; and
  (b) anything in writing is a guarantee if it contains or purports to contain some promise or assurance (however worded or presented) that defects will be made good by complete or partial replacement, or by repair, monetary compensation or otherwise.
(3) This section does not apply as between the parties to a contract under or in pursuance of which possession or ownership of the goods passed.

NOTES

1. Beale, a travelling salesman, buys a car primarily for business but he occasionally uses it for private purposes at weekends. While he is on a business trip he has an accident caused by negligence in manufacture. The manufacturers' guarantee purports to exclude the manufacturers' liability in tort. Is the exclusion effective?
2. Bishop buys a toaster for private use. In the box with the toaster was a guarantee card which stated that in consideration of the purchaser of the toaster waiving all other rights against the manufacturer, the manufacturer would repair or replace any faulty machine within twelve months of purchase. Bishop fills in a tear-off acceptance slip and sends it off. Ten months later the toaster breaks down. The manufacturer has been taken over and refuses to honour the guarantee. Can Bishop recover the cost of having the toaster repaired elsewhere by suing on the guarantee?
3. Can Bishop recover the cost of repair from the manufacturer *in tort*? See *Junior Books v Veitchi* (above, p 25). Could a manufacturer who advertised a product as having a year's manufacturer's guarantee be heard to argue that the purchaser did not rely on the manufacturer to produce a non-defective article?
4. The purpose of s 5(3) is simply to prevent an overlap between s 5 and ss 6 and 7.
5. What policy underlies preventing manufacturers excluding *any* type of tort liability in this manner? Is the guarantee likely to be misleading? You may like to consider the following extract from Law Commission, Second Report on Exemption Clauses (No 69) (1975), para 100:

> In our view, the buyer in a consumer sale who accepts such a guarantee is just as much in need of protection against the manufacturer as he is when dealing with the immediate seller. The guarantee is attractive because it offers him a cheap and simple alternative to an action for damages against the seller if the goods are defective. At the time when the buyer accepts it he may not contemplate the possibility of suffering personal injury or damage to his property because the goods are defective or dangerous and, even if he does, he is not in a position to evaluate the relevant advantages of the guarantee on the one hand and the common law remedies on the other. It is obvious that cases can arise in which he will have abandoned rights far more valuable than those he has gained. Such an exemption clause is a potential trap and we think it should be made void.

6. In the US case of *Collins v Uniroyal Inc* 64 NJ 260, 315 A2d 16 (1974) a tyre manufacturer gave a guarantee against *any* blow-out, including those caused not by any defect in the tyre but by 'road hazards'. It excluded any liability for consequential loss under the guarantee. A purchaser suffered personal injury when a road hazard caused a blow-out and the manufacturer was held liable, the court saying that the exclusion was 'unconscionable'. Would the exclusion be valid under UCTA? Do you think the result is a sensible one? See Epstein, 18 J Law & Econ 293.

(iii) Liability for negligence: ss 1(1) and (3), 2(1)–(3)

Section 1
(1) For the purposes of this Part of this Act, 'negligence' means the breach—
  (a) of any obligation, arising from the express or implied terms of a contract, to take reasonable care or exercise reasonable skill in the performance of the contract;
  (b) of any common law duty to take reasonable care or exercise reasonable skill (but not any stricter duty);
  (c) of the common duty of care imposed by the Occupiers' Liability Act 1957 or the Occupiers' Liability Act (Northern Ireland) 1957.

(3) In the case of both contract and tort, sections 2 to 7 apply (except where the contrary is stated in section 6(4)) only to business liability, that is liability for breach of obligations or duties arising—
  (a) from things done or to be done by a person in the course of a business (whether his own business or another's); or
  (b) from the occupation of premises used for business purposes of the occupier;
and references to liability are to be read accordingly but liability of an occupier of premises for breach of an obligation or duty towards a person obtaining access to the premises for recreational or educational purposes, being liability for loss or damage suffered by reason of the dangerous state of the premises, is not a business liability of the occupier unless granting that person such access for the purposes concerned falls within the business purposes of the occupier.

Section 2
(1) A person cannot by reference to any contract term or to a notice given to persons generally or to particular persons exclude or restrict his liability for death or personal injury resulting from negligence.
(2) In the case of other loss or damage, a person cannot so exclude or restrict his liability for negligence except in so far as the term or notice satisfies the requirement of reasonableness.
(3) Where a contract term or notice purports to exclude or restrict liability for negligence a person's agreement to or awareness of it is not of itself to be taken as indicating his voluntary acceptance of any risk.

NOTES

1. The obligation to deliver goods on time under a contract of sale is normally a strict one. In a contract with Beale, Furmston excludes any liability for consequential loss caused by late delivery. He delivers late because he carelessly sends the goods to Bishop. Is the exclusion clause subject to s 2(2)?

2. What counts as a business? There is a partial definition in s 14:

'business' includes a profession and the activities of any government department or local or public authority.

Is a charity shop a business within the Act? A university? A student union? The organizing committee of the annual church fete? What criteria should be applied to determine the question?

3. Any form of clause which has the effect of excluding the 'business' liability of one party to the other for negligence will fall within s 2. In *Phillips Products Ltd v Hyland* [1987] 2 All ER 620 the plaintiffs had hired a JCB and driver (Mr Hyland) from Hamstead. The contract was on the CPA conditions of hire (for the current version, see above, p 39). Cl 8 provided that drivers should:

'for all purposes in connection with their employment in the working of the plant be regarded as the servants or agents of the Hirer who alone shall be responsible for all claims arising in connection with the operation of such plant by the said drivers or operators.'

Hyland negligently damaged the plaintiff's building. Hamstead argued that as the result of this clause it was not vicariously liable for Hyland and that the clause was one that 'transferred' liability, not one that excluded or restricted it. The Court of Appeal held that the clause was caught by s 2(2); if the clause were enforced, the effect would be 'to negative a common law liability in tort which would otherwise admittedly fall on the plant-owner.' Furthermore, cl 8 fell within s 13(1). (The court went on to hold that the clause was unreasonable: see below, p 723. On the question whether this clause always operates to exclude liability, see below, p 718.)

4. As s 1 makes clear, s 2 applies also to purely tortious liability, so that liability for death or personal injury caused in the course of a business can no longer be excluded by notices, etc (cf *Ashdown v Samuel Williams & Sons Ltd* [1957] 1 QB 409.) Until recently there was some doubt whether a disclaimer of liability for the accuracy of a statement, as in *Hedley Byrne v Heller* (above, p 23) is within s 2(2): again the argument is that the disclaimer prevents the liability ever arising, rather than excluding it (cf. above, p 682). In *Smith v Eric S Bush* [1989] 2 All ER 514 the House of Lords rejected this argument: the effect of s 13(1) was to subject the disclaimer to s 2(2). (On the issue of reasonableness see below, p 726.)

5. Why are exclusions of liability for negligence subject to such stringent control? Consider the following from Law Commission Report No 69:

54 . . . It may be said that to permit a person who owes such a duty to contract out of liability for the breach of it is tantamount to giving him a licence to behave carelessly. This, it may be said, is . . . socially inexpedient because it tends to reduce standards of care and competence. . . .

56 . . . [T]he effect on the interests of those it is intended to protect of imposing a complete ban on exemptions from liability for negligence . . . would be to make a person supplying services in the course of his business the insurer of the person to whom a service is supplied (whether the latter is acting in the course of a business or not) against loss or damage due to the negligence of the supplier. There is nothing inherently unreasonable about that, so long as it is the most economical way of providing cover for the customer. Our Working Party were advised, however, by the insurance experts, whose valuable assistance we have already acknowledged in our joint document, that there are many cases in which it is more economical for the person to whom the service is supplied to effect a separate insurance. In one way or the other, it is said, the customer must always pay for the insurance cover in the form either of an extra charge or of insurance premiums. If that cover is provided by the supplier, he will either insure his liability with an insurance company or, as some very large undertakings do, act as his own insurer. In either event the cost of insurance will normally be added to the supplier's charges to his customer. If it costs more for the supplier than for the customer to cover the risk of loss or damage, it would pay the customer to agree that the supplier should not be liable, to effect his own insurance and to pay a lower charge for the service. We are told that it is in fact generally cheaper for the customer to insure, at any rate for part of the risk, especially in those cases where he knows, and the supplier cannot know, the limit up to which the insurance is required; in such cases the supplier is very likely to over-insure because he will feel that he has to insure up to the maximum of each claim.

For similar reasons the Law Commission did not recommend a total ban on exclusion or restriction of liability for negligently caused personal injury, but bans in specific cases, including car parks and 'movement by mechanical device', where (para 88) one party is weak in bargaining power and he places a high degree of reliance for his personal safety on the other's lack of negligence. The total ban was inserted in Parliament.

6. Is it true that exclusions of liability for negligence reduce the pressure on the party whose liability is excluded to take optimal precautions? Consider the following extract from Schwartz, 'Private law treatment of defective products in sales situations' (1970) 49 Ind LJ 8, at 21–22:

> The goal of improving product quality has been a part of sales law since at least 1829, when Chief Justice Best explained a decision to impose an implied warranty of fitness on a copper manufacturer as compelled by the court's 'duty . . . to make it the interest of manufacturers and those who sell, to furnish the best article that can be supplied'. [*Jones v Bright* (1829) 5 Bing 533.] In recent years the goal has been rephrased to provide that courts should hold liable the party who can best (ie, more cheaply) reduce the costs of defects. No matter how the goal is phrased, however, it is misguided in bargaining situations, where courts can only achieve what economists refer to as optimality: that level of consumer sovereignty where no buyer can be made better off by further market transactions without making another buyer worse off.
>
> Imposing risks on a party will not, of itself, cause that party to do things differently if risks could be completely shifted, for then change is pointless. Risks, however, cannot be completely shifted. Should a seller raise prices by the risk's value he will lose sales. Sellers must therefore decide whether the loss of profit from raising the price by R is greater or less than the loss caused by avoiding or ameliorating that risk. For example, let P be the price, exclusive of risk costs, and R the risk cost. If the seller disclaims, thereby shifting R to buyers, buyers face a cost of $P + R$; if the seller does not disclaim, and instead charges R's value for bearing it, buyers again face a cost of $P + R$. Whether sellers will avoid risks is determined by whether $P + R > P + A(s)$; that is, whether avoidance cost is cheaper than risk cost. Sellers therefore face the same incentive to avoid defects whether they disclaim or not, for in either case buyers will perceive the total cost as $P + R$, and thus force sellers to compare risk and avoidance costs.
>
> The point is that when buyers can correctly value the risk, nothing is to be gained by shifting that risk to sellers. When buyers cannot value the risk, a shift will not necessarily yield improved products. Assume, for example, that the seller disclaims, that A(s) is $8, R is $5, and that many buyers perceive R as $9. Such buyers will be responding to artificially high prices; hence they will purchase less, thereby possibly inducing the seller to avoid defects. If a court bans the disclaimer, the seller (who presumably can value R) will raise price by $5 rather than avoid defects. If this is done, those buyers who overvalued R will perceive a cost reduction of $4, with the result that purchases will increase and there will be more defective products than before judicial intervention. By the same token, when buyers undervalue risks, sellers who disclaim feel artificially low pressure to do things differently. In that case, banning the disclaimer will then force a price of $P + R$ or $P + A(s)$, either of which will be perceived by buyers who have undervalued R as higher than the costs they previously faced. Matters will then be better since less will be bought, and what is bought may be better made.

Suppose a person thinking of taking a ride on a big dipper is confronted with a choice: he can ride on one for 10p but entirely at his own risk, or on another one whose owner does not disclaim liability for 15p. What information would he need in order to decide which ride to take? How often will a private person have the necessary information when the risk is one of death or personal injury? Is he more likely to have the information where the risk is of damage to his property?

7. Even if your answer to the last question was 'hardly ever', does society have any legitimate interest in preventing a person who is aware of what he or she is doing from accepting an exclusion of a business's liability for death or personal injury? Is the problem perhaps what economists call an 'externality', ie the parties do not bear the full cost of their actions because part of the loss is borne willy-nilly by someone else?

(iv) Other clauses in consumer or standard form contracts: s 3

Section 3

(1) This section applies as between contracting parties where one of them deals as consumer or on the other's written standard terms of business.

(2) As against the party, the other cannot by reference to any contract term—

  (a) when himself in breach of contract, exclude or restrict any liability of his in respect of the breach; or

  (b) claim to be entitled—

      (i) to render a contractual performance substantially different from that which was reasonably expected of him, or

      (ii) in respect of the whole or any part of his contractual obligation, to render no performance at all,

except in so far as (in any of the cases mentioned above in this subsection) the contract term satisfies the requirement of reasonableness.

NOTES

1. 'Written standard terms of business' is not defined. Presumably it includes the printed terms on a purchase order or a sales form used by a business buying from or selling to another, where the form was devised by the company concerned. But would it include the following?

(i) A set of terms regularly used by a firm, but drafted by a trade association (eg the Road Haulage Association conditions of carriage).

(ii) A set of conditions drawn up by a body representing both sides of an industry (eg the Joint Contracts Tribunal form of building contract).

(iii) A term in a contract for the sale of a machine, when the contract was negotiated clause by clause, but the clause in question was adopted without amendment from a 'precedent contract' which the seller always uses in such negotiations and often gets adopted at least in part.

(iv) A clause in a standard purchase order where one of the other terms, the payment clause for example, has been altered for this contract only.

2. Section 13 does not apply to s 3. Instead, if a term operates by defining the initial obligation rather than by excluding a liability, s 3(2)(b) comes into play. Law Commission No 69, paras 141 and 143, explains the problem thus:

> 141. One category . . . comprises those provisions which exclude or restrict the exercise of a right or remedy or any liability arising out of the breach of any obligation, express or implied, in the contract. Here the danger of injustice is aggravated by the fact that the promisee will normally assess the value of the contract on the assumption that it will be performed; he may not pay much attention to the provisions for dealing with the consequences of breach. In our view there is a clear case for imposing some degree of control on clauses of this sort, even when the obligations to which they relate can be ascertained only by reference to the express terms of an agreement between the parties. . . .

> **Other 'exemption clauses'**
> 143. There is another and less easily distinguishable class of provisions. These differ from provisions of the category described at paragraph 141 above in that they are expressed not as excluding or restricting liability for the breach of subsisting obligations but as preventing the obligations to which they relate from arising or as providing that such obligations are to arise only in restricted or qualified form.
> . . . [T]he mischief we wish to control . . . is the likelihood (in the light of the surrounding circumstances including the way in which the contract is expressed) that the promisee might reasonably have misunderstood the extent of the promisor's obligation.

3. Suppose a package holiday contract contains a clause permitting the holiday company to substitute another hotel, or another hotel in another resort, for the one named in the booking form (compare *Anglo-Continental Holidays Ltd v Typaldos*, above, p 680). How should the court ascertain what was reasonably expected? Surely not by the standards of that odious reasonable man, who no doubt reads the small print on everything from his Cornflake packet in the morning to his Bournvita tin at night and suspects the worst at every turn: this would make the section virtually toothless. By the standard of the person who never reads anything he signs? Or by the standard of the person who knows what the contract says but expects the clauses to be applied fairly in the circumstances? If the last, is s 3(2)(b)(i) anything more than a statutory enactment of the main purpose rule?

4. Section 3(2)(b)(ii) is clearly designed to prevent partial or total cancellation. But how is it to be applied? There is no reference to the customer's reasonable expectations here. And if the company reserves the right to cancel the holiday in certain circumstances which have arisen, are they 'rendering no performance at all' 'in respect of . . . their contractual obligation'? Surely their contractual obligation to perform has now ended. To make sense of the subsection, it must be interpreted as meaning, what *would* be the contractual obligation if it were not for the clause in question? But if that is the case, isn't the subsection extremely far-reaching? Wouldn't it catch, for instance, any clause making some performance by the other party an express condition when it wouldn't normally be so, eg 'time of payment in this contract for sale of goods to be of the essence'?

(v) Misrepresentation

Misrepresentation Act 1967, s 3, as amended by UCTA s 8 (see above, p 300)

(vi) Indemnity clauses

Section 4
(1) A person dealing as a consumer cannot by reference to any contract term be made to indemnify another person (whether a party to the contract or not) in respect of liability that may be incurred by the other for negligence or breach of contract, except in so far as the contract term satisfies the requirement of reasonableness.
(2) This section applies whether the liability in question—
   (a) is directly that of the person to be indemnified or is incurred by him vicariously;
   (b) is to the person dealing as consumer or to someone else.

NOTES

1. It is not uncommon for a contract to provide that party A must indemnify party B against any liability B may incur to third parties. For instance, construction work which B is to carry out for A might interfere with a third party's property rights and it seems only right that A should bear the ultimate cost of this. Sometimes A will have to indemnify B against B's liability to a third party caused by B's negligence, or which results from some action which was a breach by B of its contract with A. This may be a perfectly sensible arrangement if A carries insurance and B does not. However such clauses can expose parties to unexpected or unwanted

risks and this section, which was inserted in the draft bill in Parliament, will protect consumers.

2. An indemnity clause which operates in the ways just described is not, strictly speaking, an exemption clause: it transfers liability rather than excluding it. However, if A had to indemnify B against its liability *to A* for negligence or breach of contract, the clause would operate as an exclusion and would fall under s 2, just like the transfer of liability clause in the *Hyland* case (above, p 714). It is interesting to contrast *Hyland* to *Thompson v Lohan (Plant Hire) Ltd* [1987] 2 All ER 631. This case involved the same clause (cl 8) of the CPA conditions, but here the question was whether the owner or the hirer was liable to a third party who had been injured by the negligence of the driver. It was held that the clause was not in this situation 'excluding or restricting' liability for negligence and thus was not within s 2; it was operating as a transfer of liability clause and, as it was not a consumer contract, was not caught by UCTA at all.

(vii) The reasonableness test

There are in fact three separate reasonableness tests under the Act. The first is general: s 11(1), (3) and (5).

Section 11
(1) In relation to a contract term, the requirement of reasonableness for the purposes of this Part of this Act, section 3 of the Misrepresentation Act 1967 and section 3 of the Misrepresentation Act (Northern Ireland) 1967 is that the term shall have been a fair and reasonable one to be included having regard to the circumstances which were, or ought reasonably to have been, known to or in the contemplation of the parties when the contract was made.

(3) In relation to a notice (not being a notice having contractual effect), the requirement of reasonableness under this Act is that it should be fair and reasonable to allow reliance on it, having regard to all the circumstances obtaining when the liability arose or (but for the notice) would have arisen.

(5) It is for those claiming that a contract term or notice satisfies the requirement of reasonableness to show that it does.

The second applies to clauses limiting the amount of compensation recoverable: s 11(4).

Section 11
(4) Where by reference to a contract term or notice a person seeks to restrict liability to a specified sum of money, and the question arises (under this or any other Act) whether the term or notice satisfies the requirement of reasonableness, regard shall be had in particular (but without prejudice to subsection (2) above in the case of contract terms) to—
   (a) the resources which he could expect to be available to him for the purpose of meeting the liability should it arise; and
   (b) how far it was open to him to cover himself by insurance.

The third applies only to clauses caught by ss 6(3) and 7(3) and (4): s 11(2) and Sch 2.

Section 11
(2) In determining for the purposes of section 6 or 7 above whether a contract term satisfies the requirement of reasonableness, regard shall be had in particular to the matters specified in Schedule 2 to this Act; but this subsection does not prevent the court or arbitrator from holding, in accordance with any rule of law, that a term which purports to exclude or restrict any relevant liability is not a term of the contract.

Schedule 2: 'Guidelines' for application of reasonableness test
The matters to which regard is to be had in particular for the purposes of sections 6(3), 7(3) and (4), . . . are any of the following which appear to be relevant—

(a) the strength of the bargaining positions of the parties relative to each other, taking into account (among other things) alternative means by which the customer's requirements could have been met;
(b) whether the customer received an inducement to agree to the term, or in accepting it had an opportunity of entering into a similar contract with other persons, but without having to accept a similar term;
(c) whether the customer knew or ought reasonably to have known of the existence and extent of the term (having regard, among other things, to any custom of the trade and any previous course of dealing between the parties);
(d) where the term excludes or restricts any relevant liability if some condition is not complied with, whether it was reasonable at the time of the contract to expect that compliance with that condition would be practicable;
(e) whether the goods were manufactured, processed or adapted to the special order of the customer.

NOTES

1. Under s 11(1), reasonableness of the clause is to be judged at the time the contract was made. Under the Supply of Goods (Implied Terms) Act 1973 the test had been whether:

   . . . it is shown that it would not be fair or reasonable to allow reliance on the term.

   What difference does this change make? What if a clause which seemed reasonable at the outset actually turns out to operate harshly? What if the business includes an exclusion clause which is wider than is reasonable but it would have been perfectly reasonable to exclude or limit liability for the loss which actually occurred? (See also the *George Mitchell* case, below p 720.) In practice, it seems doubtful whether a court will ever ignore what has actually happened.
2. Can the court save a clause which is unreasonably wide in order to apply it to a situation in which it would have been reasonable to exclude or limit liability? Probably this can only be done if the clause is clearly separable into reasonable and unreasonable bits, each of which can stand alone. (This may explain why some contracts contain overlapping clauses, each one wider than the last!)
3. Section 11(5) puts the burden of proving reasonableness on the party trying to rely on the clause. This also seems to be a change from the earlier statute. It has been argued that even before this, there had been a shift in the courts' attitude: the *Photo Productions* case (above, p 695) had been in favour of allowing businesses to determine their contract terms freely, but the cases on the 1973 Act had appeared to apply the opposite presumption. See Adams and Brownsword, 'The Unfair Contract Terms Act; a decade of discretion' (1988) 104 LQR 94.
4. Although the guidelines in Sch 2 apply only to clauses caught by ss 6 and 7, the courts consider them, or at least the same factors, in other cases: eg *Rees Hough Ltd v Redland Reinforced Plastics Ltd* (1984) 27 BLR 136; *Phillips v Hyland* (below, p 723).
5. What do the guidelines mean and how should they be applied?
   (a): What does the 'strength of the bargaining positions of the parties' refer to?
   (b): If Goldberg's analysis (above, p 704) is correct, don't most customers in effect 'receive an inducement to agree to the term' in the form of a lower price? Or is (b) referring to the customer who accepts the clause as part of a special deal?

(c): Knowledge of the 'existence and extent' of the term seems to cover the questions of whether the customer knows of the clause and understands its meaning. What about the problems of seeing how it may affect him or her (see above, p 715)?

(d): For an example of the operation of (d) see *RW Green Ltd v Cade Bros Farm*, below, p 721.

(e): What difference might it make that the goods were a 'special order'?

In *Levison v Patent Steam Carpet Cleaning Co Ltd* [1978] QB 69, the plaintiffs sent a chinese carpet worth £900 to the defendants for cleaning, and signed a form stating that the maximum value of the carpet was deemed to be £40 and that 'all merchandise is expressly accepted at owner's risk'. The form recommended that owners should insure their goods. The defendants never returned the carpet and were unable to explain its disappearance. The Court of Appeal held that the plaintiffs were entitled to recover the full value of the carpet: the majority held that the words were not clear enough to exclude liability for fundamental breach, and that in the circumstances the burden of proving that the loss was not due to a fundamental breach was on the defendants. Lord Denning held the clause did apply, but was void at common law because it was unreasonable. This is clearly a heretical view of the law, but his view that the clause was unreasonable is puzzling. The carpet was already insured; if the owner had been asked whether he wished to have this form of contract, or one with full liability but a higher charge, which do you think he would have chosen?

George Mitchell (Chesterhall) Ltd v Finney Lock Seeds Ltd [1983] 1 All ER 108, Court of Appeal; [1983] 2 All ER 737, House of Lords

The defendant seed merchants agreed in December 1973 to supply the plaintiff farmers with 30lbs of Dutch winter cabbage seed for £192. An invoice which accompanied the seed when it was delivered, and which was treated as forming part of the contract, contained a clause purporting to limit liability if the seed sold were defective to replacing the seed or refunding the price. It went on to exclude 'all liability for any loss or damage arising from the use of any seeds or plants supplied by us and for any consequential loss or damage arising out of such use . . . or for any other loss or damage whatsoever'.

The plaintiffs planted some 63 acres with the seed, but the seed was of the wrong kind and also unmerchantable, and the crop was a total failure. The plaintiffs claimed compensation of some £63,000 for loss of production.

In the Court of Appeal the majority held that as a matter of construction the clause did not apply: it was not clear enough to protect the sellers from the consequences of their own negligence, and (per Oliver LJ) it did not apply when the sellers had delivered something wholly different in kind from what had been ordered. Lord Denning thought the clause did apply. However, all three judges agreed that in any event the clause was invalid under the Supply of Goods (Implied Terms) Act 1973 (by the date of judgment incorporated into SGA 1979 as s 55) because it was unreasonable.

Kerr LJ. . . . However, even if [the decision on construction] be wrong, I would unhesitatingly also decide this case in favour of the plaintiffs on the ground that it would not be fair or reasonable to allow the defendants to rely on this clause, by applying s 55(4) and (5) in Sch 1 to the Sale of Goods Act 1979. In this regard the balance of fairness and reasonableness appears to me to be overwhelmingly on the side of the plaintiffs, and I will only mention some of the most material facts in this connection.

The plaintiffs have suffered a loss of some £61,000 in terms of money; and in terms of time and labour the productivity of over 60 acres has been wasted for over a year. There was nothing whatever which the plaintiffs could have done to avoid this. As between them and the defendants all the fault lay admittedly on the side of the defendants. Further, farmers do not, and cannot be expected to, insure against this kind of disaster; but suppliers of seeds can. We were referred to a 'Wrong Variety of Seed Indemnity Insurance Scheme', set up under the auspices of the United Kingdom Agricultural Supply Trade Association Ltd (UKASTA), which provides an annual cover of £20,000. Although this particular scheme stipulates the exercise of due diligence on the part of the supplier, I am not persuaded that liability for rare events of this kind cannot be adequately insured against. Nor am I persuaded that the cost of such cover would add significantly to the cost of the seed. Further, although the present exemption clause has been in existence for many decades, the evidence shows that it was never negotiated. In effect, it was simply imposed by the suppliers, and no seed can in practice be bought otherwise than subject to its terms. To limit the suppliers' liability to the price of the seed in all cases, as against the magnitude of the losses which farmers can incur in rare disasters of this kind, appears to me to be a grossly disproportionate and unreasonable allocation of the respective risks. Furthermore, the evidence clearly shows that the clause is not relied on 'to the letter' in practice, and that neither the suppliers nor the farmers expect it to be applied literally. Its existence merely provides a basis for the negotiation of mutually acceptable settlements. Thus, we were told that there had been some inconclusive negotiations in the present case, though no figures were mentioned. However, these negotiations do not matter, since the defendants are now seeking to uphold the clause to the letter. It is on this basis that we have to decide whether reliance on the clause would be fair or reasonable, and in my view the answer is clearly that it would not be.

Furthermore, to my mind there is another, overriding, consideration. It seems to me that this new legislation, the modified version of s 55 of the Sale of Goods Act 1979 and the Unfair Contract Terms Act 1977, was designed for exempting provisions whose meaning is clear. Thus, one of the matters to be taken into account in judging fairness and reasonableness (under s 55(5)(c)) is 'whether the buyer knew or ought reasonably to have known of the . . . extent of the term . . .'. But we have several days of argument about the meaning and effect of the present clause, and it is already clear to what extent opinions may differ about it. I do not think that this is the kind of situation for which this legislation was designed. It was designed for exempting provisions whose meaning is plain. Thus, if the present clause had been headed, for instance, 'Supply of wrong or unmerchantable seed, whether by negligence or otherwise', the defendants' case in relation to fairness and reasonableness would to that extent be strengthened. The effect of the parties' bargain would then be plain. But businessmen do not choose to make plain the meaning of the 'small print' which they use, and often do not themselves know what it really means. In that event they must take the consequences of the uncertainty which their 'small print' has created; and uncertainty involves unfairness to the other side. Perhaps the effect of this new legislation will bring about a welcome change in this respect. But so long as the meaning and effect of such provisions remains shrouded in obscurity unless and until determined by the courts (and to many minds even thereafter), I think that the courts should hold that reliance on such provisions would in any event be unfair and unreasonable.

Finally, I must briefly refer to *R W Green Ltd v Cade Bros Farm* on which counsel strongly relied on behalf of the defendants. In that case, seed potatoes had been sold subject to the standard form of conditions of the National Association of Seed Potato Merchants. These included a time limit for claims, and they also limited the supplier's liability to refunding the contract price. The potatoes were suffering from a virus which was undetectable by either party. Griffiths J held that the exempting provision protected the sellers and that it was neither unfair nor unreasonable for them to rely on it. In the latter regard he used language suggesting that he was merely exercising a discretion, but I do not think that this was his intention. As stated by this court in *Conemsco Ltd v Contrapol Ltd*, a determination under s 55 or under the Unfair Contract Terms Act 1977 constitutes a decision, of mixed fact and law, and not merely the exercise of a discretion. But that case was very different from the present. In particular, no blame attached to either party, and the standard condition had been negotiated within the trade. There was also no basis for argument about its meaning and effect. Further, there was evidence that the buyers could have purchased seed certified by inspectors from the Ministry of Agriculture at a small extra charge, whereas it was accepted on behalf of the defendants in the present case that there was nothing equivalent which the plaintiffs could have done. I therefore do not think that that case assists the defendants here in any way.

In the House of Lords there was unanimous agreement that the clause as a matter of construction did cover the loss. Given that the clause was only one of limitation and not a total exclusion, there was no reason why it should not cover the sellers' negligence; and the clauses applied to seeds 'sold' and 'supplied', which these had been, even if they were not the correct variety of seed. However the House agreed that the clause was unreasonable.

Lord Bridge. . . . My Lords, it seems to me, with all due deference, that the judgments of the trial judge and of Oliver LJ on the common law issue come dangerously near to reintroducing by the back door the doctrine of 'fundamental breach' which this House in the *Photo Production* case had so forcibly evicted by the front. The judge discusses what I may call the 'peas and beans' or 'chalk and cheese' cases, ie those in which it has been held that exemption clauses do not apply where there has been a contract to sell one thing, eg a motor car, and the seller has supplied quite another thing, eg a bicycle. I hasten to add that the judge can in no way be criticised for adopting this approach since counsel appearing for the appellants at the trial had conceded 'that, if what had been delivered had been beetroot seed or carrot seed, he would not be able to rely on the clause'. Different counsel appeared for the appellants in the Court of Appeal, where that concession was withdrawn.

In my opinion, this is not a 'peas and beans' case at all. The relevant condition applies to 'seeds'. Clauses 1 refers to 'seeds sold' and 'seeds agreed to be sold'. Clause 2 refers to 'seeds supplied'. As I have pointed out, Oliver LJ concentrated his attention on the phrase 'seeds agreed to be sold'. I can see no justification, with respect, for allowing this phrase alone t⁻ dictate the interpretation of the relevant condition, still less for treating cl 2 as 'merely a supplement' to cl 1. Clause 2 is perfectly clear and unambiguous. The reference to 'seeds agreed to be sold' as well as to 'seeds sold' in cl 1 reflects the same dichotomy as the definition of 'sale' in the Sale of Goods Act 1979 as including a bargain and sale as well as a sale and delivery. The defective seeds in this case were seeds sold and delivered, just as clearly as they were seeds supplied, by the appellants to the respondents. The relevant condition, read as a whole, unambiguously limits the appellants' liability to replacement of the seeds or refund of the price. It is only possible to read an ambiguity into it by the process of strained construction which was deprecated by Lord Diplock in the *Photo Production* case . . . and by Lord Wilberforce in the *Ailsa Craig* case [1983] 1 All ER 101 at 102.

In holding that the relevant condition was ineffective to limit the appellants' liability for a breach of contract caused by their negligence, Kerr LJ applied the principles stated by Lord Morton giving the judgment of the Privy Council in *Canada Steamship Lines Ltd v R*. Kerr LJ stated correctly that this case was also referred to by Lord Fraser in the *Ailsa Craig* case. He omitted, however, to notice that, as appears from the passage from Lord Fraser's speech which I have already cited, the whole point of Lord Fraser's reference was to express his opinion that the very strict principles laid down in the *Canada Steamship Lines* case as applicable to exclusion and indemnity clauses cannot be applied in their full rigour to limitation clauses. Lord Wilberforce's speech contains a passage to the like effect, and Lord Elwyn-Jones, Lord Salmon and Lord Lowry agreed with both speeches. Having once reached a conclusion in the instant case that the relevant condition unambiguously limited the appellants' liability, I know of no principle of construction which can properly be applied to confine the effect of the limitation to breaches of contract arising without negligence on the part of the appellants. In agreement with Lord Denning MR, I would decide the common law issue in the appellants' favour.

. . . The statutory issue . . . turns on the words in s 55(4) 'to the extent that it is shown that it would not be fair or reasonable to allow reliance on' this restriction of the appellants' liabilities, having regard to the matters referred to in subs (5).

This is the first time your Lordships' House has had to consider a modern statutory provision giving the court power to override contractual terms excluding or restricting liability, which depends on the court's view of what is 'fair and reasonable'. The particular provision of the modified s 55 of the 1979 Act which applies in the instant case is of limited and diminishing importance. But the several provisions of the Unfair Contract Terms Act 1977 which depend on 'the requirement of reasonableness', defined in s 11 by reference to what is 'fair and reasonable', albeit in a different context, are likely to come before the courts with increasing frequency. It may, therefore, be appropriate to consider how an original decision what is 'fair and reasonable' made in the application of any of these provisions should be approached by an appellate court. It would not be accurate to describe such a decision as an exercise of discretion. But a decision under any of the provisions referred to will have this in common with the exercise of a discretion, that, in having regard to the various matters to which the modified s 55(5) of the 1979 Act, or s 11 of the 1977 Act direct attention, the court must entertain a whole range of considerations, put them in the scales on one side or the other and decide at the end of the day on which side the balance comes down. There will sometimes be room for a legitimate difference of judicial opinions as to what the answer should be, where it will be impossible to say that one view is demonstrably wrong and the other demonstrably right. It must follow, in my view, that, when asked to review such a decision on appeal, the appellate court should treat the original decision with the utmost respect and refrain from interference with it unless satisfied that it proceeded on some erroneous principle or was plainly and obviously wrong.

Turning back to the modified s 55 of the 1979 Act, it is common ground that the onus was on the respondents to show that it would not be fair or reasonable to allow the appellants to rely on the relevant condition as limiting their liability. It was argued for the appellants that the court must have regard to the circumstances as at the date of the contract, not after the breach. The basis of the argument was that this was the effect of s 11 of the 1977 Act and that it would be wrong to construe the modified s 55 of the Act as having a different effect. Assuming the premise is correct, the conclusion does not follow. The provisions of the 1977 Act cannot be considered in construing the prior enactments now embodied in the modified s 55 of the 1979 Act. But, in any event, the language of sub-ss (4) and (5) of that section is clear and unambiguous. The question whether it is fair or reasonable to allow reliance on a term excluding or limiting liability for a breach of contract can only arise after the breach. The nature of the breach and the circumstances in which it occurred cannot possibly be excluded from 'all the circumstances of the case' to which regard must be had.

The only other question of construction debated in the course of the argument was the meaning to be attached to the words 'to the extent that' in sub-s (4) and, in particular, whether they permit the court to hold that it would be fair and reasonable to allow partial reliance on a limitation clause and, for example, to decide in the instant case that the respondents should recover, say, half their consequential damage. I incline to the view that, in their context, the words are equivalent to 'in so far as' or 'in circumstances in which' and do not permit the kind of judgment of Solomon illustrated by the example.

But for the purpose of deciding this appeal I find it unnecessary to express a concluded view on this question.

My Lords, at long last I turn to the application of the statutory language to the circumstances of the case. Of the particular matters to which attention is directed by paras (a) to (e) of s 55(5), only those in paras (a) to (c) are relevant. As to para (c), the respondents admittedly knew of the relevant condition (they had dealt with the appellants for many years) and, if they had read it, particularly cl 2, they would, I think, as laymen rather than lawyers, have had no difficulty in understanding what it said. This and the magnitude of the damages claimed in proportion to the price of the seeds sold are factors which weigh in the scales in the appellants' favour.

The question of relative bargaining strength under para (a) and of the opportunity to buy seeds without a limitation of the seedsman's liability under para (b) were interrelated. The evidence was that a similar limitation of liability was universally embodied in the terms of trade between seedsmen and farmers and had been so for very many years. The limitation had never been negotiated between representative bodies but, on the other hand, had not been the subject of any protest by the National Farmers' Union. These factors, if considered in isolation, might have been equivocal. The decisive factor however, appears from the evidence of four witnesses called for the appellants, two independent seedsmen, the chairman of the appellant company, and a director of a sister company (both being wholly-owned subsidiaries of the same parent). They said that it had always been their practice, unsuccessfully attempted in the instant case, to negotiate settlements of farmers' claims for damages in excess of the price of the seeds, if they thought that the claims were 'genuine' and 'justified'. This evidence indicated a clear recognition by seedsmen in general, and the appellants in particular, that reliance on the limitation of liability imposed by the relevant condition would not be fair or reasonable.

Two further factors, if more were needed, weigh the scales in favour of the respondents. The supply of autumn, instead of winter, cabbage seed was due to the negligence of the appellants' sister company. Irrespective of its quality, the autumn variety supplied could not, according to the appellants' own evidence, be grown commercially in East Lothian. Finally, as the trial judge found, seedsmen could insure against the risk of crop failure caused by supply of the wrong variety of seeds without materially increasing the price of seeds.

My Lords, even if I felt doubts about the statutory issue, I should not, for the reasons explained earlier, think it right to interfere with the unanimous original decision of that issue by the Court of Appeal. As it is, I feel no such doubts. If I were making the original decision, I should conclude without hesitation that it would not be fair or reasonable to allow the appellants to rely on the contractual limitation of their liability.

I would dismiss the appeal.

Phillips Products Ltd v Hyland [1987] 2 All ER 620, Court of Appeal

The plaintiffs hired an excavator and driver from the second defendants, the plant owner. The contract, by clause 8, provided that drivers 'supplied by the owner . . . shall for all purposes in connection with their employment in the working of the plant be regarded as the servants or agents of the hirer who alone shall be responsible for all claims arising in connection with the operation of the plant by the . . . drivers.' The driver negligently drove the excavator into collision with and damaged the plaintiffs' building. On the plaintiffs' claim for damages for negligence against the driver and the second defendants, the judge, giving judgment for the plaintiffs, held that clause 8 did not satisfy 'the requirement of reasonableness' in section 2(2) of the Unfair Contract Terms Act 1977 and, accordingly, the second defendants were precluded from relying on the clause as exempting them from liability for negligence.

(On the question whether s 2(2) applied to clause 8, see above, p 714.)

Slade LJ: . . . As the judge pointed out, all the relevant circumstances were known to both parties at that time. The task which he therefore set himself was to examine all the relevant circumstances and then ask himself whether, on the balance of probabilities, he was satisfied that clause 8, in so far as it purported to exclude Hamstead's liability for Mr. Hyland's negligence, was a fair and reasonable term. As to these matters, his conclusions as set out in his judgment were:

'What then were the relevant circumstances? Firstly, the second defendants carried on the business of hiring out plant and operators. In contrast the first defendants were steel stockholders, and as such had no occasion to hire plant except on the odd occasions when they had building work to be done at their premises. There had been apparently only three such occasions: one in 1979, one in July 1980 when the drainage trench was dug and the final occasion when the damage was done in August 1980.

Secondly, the hire was to be for a very short period. It was arranged at very short notice. There was no occasion for the plaintiffs to address their mind to all the details of the hiring agreement, nor did they do so. The inclusion of condition 8 arose because it appeared in the second defendants' printed conditions. It was not the product of any discussion or agreement between the parties.

Thirdly, there was little if any opportunity for the plaintiffs to arrange insurance cover for risks arising from the first defendant's negligence. In so far as the first defendant was to be regarded as the plaintiffs' servant it might have been an easy matter to ensure that the plaintiffs' insurance policies were extended, if necessary, to cover his activities in relation to third party claims. Any businessman customarily insures against such claims. He does not usually insure against damage caused to his own property by his own employees' negligence. Thus to arrange insurance cover for the first defendant would have required time and a special and unusual arrangement with the plaintiffs' insurers.

Fourthly, the plaintiffs played no part in the selection of the first defendant as the operator of the JCB. They had to accept whoever the second defendant sent to drive the machine. Further, although they undoubtedly would have had to, and would have had the right to, tell the JCB operator what job he was required to do, from their previous experience they knew they would be unable in any way to control the way in which the first defendant did the job that he was given. They would not have had the knowledge to exercise such control. All the expertise lay with the first defendant. I do not think condition 8 could possibly be construed as giving control of the manner of operation of the JCB to the plaintiffs. Indeed in the event the first defendant made it perfectly plain to Mr. Pritchard, the plaintiffs' builder, that he would brook no interference in the way he operated his machine.

Those being the surrounding circumstances, was it fair and reasonable that the hire contract should include a condition which relieved the second defendants of all responsibility for damage caused, not to the property of a third party but to the plaintiff's own property, by the negligence of the second defendants' own operators? This was for the plaintiffs in a very real sense a "take it or leave it" situation. They needed a JCB for a simple job at short notice. In dealing with the second defendants they had the choice of taking a JCB operator under a contract containing some 43 written conditions or not taking the JCB at all. The question for me is not a general question whether *any* contract of hire of the JCB could fairly and reasonably exclude such liability, but a much more limited question as to whether *this* contract of hire entered into in these circumstances fairly and reasonably included such an exemption.

I have come to the conclusion that the second defendants have failed to satisfy me that condition 8 was in this respect a fair and reasonable term.'

In approaching the judge's reasons and conclusions on this issue, four points have, in our judgment, to be borne in mind. First, as the judge himself clearly appreciated, the question for the court is not a general question whether or not clause 8 is valid or invalid in the case of any and every contract of hire entered into between a hirer and a plant owner who uses the relevant C.P.A. conditions. The question was and is whether the exclusion of Hamstead's liability for negligence satisfied the requirement of reasonableness imposed by the Act, in relation to *this particular contract*.

Secondly, we have to bear in mind that the relevant circumstances, which were or should have been known to or contemplated by the parties, are those which existed when the contract was made. Section 11(1) is specific on that point. Hence, evidence as to what happened during the performance of the contract must, at best, be treated with great caution. As we have indicated, such evidence was adduced at the trial, apparently without objection. At best, it could probably be used to show, by evidence of conduct and absence of objection to that conduct, what the attitude of the parties would have been in that respect, what they would have contemplated, at the time when they made the contract.

Thirdly, the burden of proof falling upon the owner under section 11(5) of the Act is, in our judgment, of great significance in this case in the light, or rather in the obscurity, of the evidence and the absence of evidence on issues which were, or might have been, relevant on the issue of reasonableness. One particular example is the matter of insurance. The insurance position of all the parties was canvassed to some extent in oral evidence at the trial, but such evidence seems to us to have been singularly imprecise and inconclusive.

Finally, by way of approach to the issue of reasonableness, it is necessary to bear in mind, and strive to comply with, the clear and stern injunction issued to appellate courts by Lord Bridge of Harwich in his speech, concurred in by the other members of the House of Lords in *George Mitchell (Chesterhall) Ltd v Finney Lock Seeds Ltd* [1983] 2 AC 803, 815–816:

'But the several provisions of the Unfair Contract Terms Act 1977 which depend on "the requirement of reasonableness," defined in section 11 by reference to what is "fair and reasonable," albeit in a different context, are likely to come before the courts with increasing frequency. It may, therefore, be appropriate to consider how an original decision as to what is "fair and reasonable" made in the application of any of these provisions should be approached by an appellate court. It would not be accurate to describe such a decision as an exercise of discretion. But a decision under any of the provisions referred to will have this in common with the exercise of a discretion, that, in having regard to the various matters to which . . . section 11 of the Act of 1977 direct[s] attention, the court must entertain a whole range of considerations, put them in the scales on one side or the other, and decide at the end of the day on which side the balance comes down. There will sometimes be room for a legitimate difference of judicial opinion as to what the answer should be, where it will be impossible to say that one view is demonstrably wrong and the other demonstrably right. It must follow, in my view, that, when asked to review such a decision on appeal, the appellate court should treat the original decision with the utmost respect and refrain from interference with it unless satisfied that it proceeded upon some erroneous principle or was plainly and obviously wrong.'

In the context of issue (iii), criticism has been made by Mr. Thompson of some parts of the judge's reasoning. It is said that in some respects he misunderstood or mis-recollected the evidence. Some of the evidence was indeed confused and not easy to follow. It is, in some passages, difficult to be confident what was really meant. It may be that the judge placed more stress than we would think right on the lack of opportunity of Mr. Phillips to study and understand the conditions, and in particular clause 8. But this is the very sort of point to which Lord Bridge referred in saying that there is room for a legitimate difference of judicial opinion.

Against this, there is to be set the fact, as it appeared at the trial, that the general conditions with their 43 clauses were adopted by and used by all the members of the trade association to which Hamstead belonged. (Counsel has told us that there is other material which might alter the picture, but we cannot go beyond the evidence which was in fact before the judge.) Thus, we think he was justified in saying that in dealing with Hamstead this was for Phillips in a very real sense a 'take it or leave it situation.' As he said, they needed a JCB for a simple job at short notice and, in dealing with Hamstead, had the choice of taking a JCB operator under the general conditions or not taking the JCB at all. Even if Mr. Phillips had understood and had been worried by the effect of clause 8 before he arranged for the conclusion of the earlier contracts or before he authorised Mr. Pritchard to conclude the contract in August 1980 now in question, it is reasonable to assume, on the evidence as it stood, that he would not have thought that there was much that he could do about it, except to take the conditions offered.

It is fair to say that we were told that various changes had been made, including the alterations to some of the general conditions since the coming into force of the Act and that the position today might be very different. But Mr. Thompson necessarily and realistically accepts that we have to deal, as the judge had to deal, with the contractual terms as they were and with the facts as to the relevant considerations as they were given in evidence at the trial: not as the terms are now or as the relevant facts might have appeared to be if further evidence had been given.

As appears from the passage which we have cited, other matters which influenced the judge in his decision on unreasonableness, and which we think were clearly relevant factors to be weighed in the balance, were that the hirers could play no part in the selection of the operator who was to do the work. Nor did the general conditions contain any warranty by Hamstead as to his fitness or competence for the job. Furthermore, despite the words in clause 8, 'he shall be under the direction and control of the hirer,' we think it reasonable to infer that the parties, when they made the contract, would have assumed that the operator would be the expert in the management of this machine and that he would not, and could not be expected to, take any instructions from anyone representing the hirers as to the manner in which he would operate the machine to do the job, once the extent and nature of the job had been defined to him by the hirers; in short they would tell him what to do but not how to do it. If such evidence is admissable, which we do not find it necessary to decide, this inferrence would be strongly supported by the evidence of what actually happened on the site before the accident occurred.

It may be that in several respects this is a very special case on its facts, its evidence and its paucity of evidence. But on these facts and on the available evidence, we are wholly unpersuaded that the judge proceeded upon some erroneous principle or was plainly and obviously wrong in his conclusion that Hamstead had not discharged the burden upon them of showing that clause 8 satisfied the requirement of reasonableness in the context of this particular contract of hire. It is important therefore that our conclusion on the particular facts of this case should not be treated as a binding precedent in other cases where similar clauses fall to be considered but the evidence of the surrounding circumstances may be very different. Issue (iii) accordingly has to be answered 'No' and we dismiss this appeal.

Appeal dismissed with costs.

It is not easy to draw general conclusions from these two cases about when a clause will be treated as fair and reasonable. The reluctance to interfere with first instance decisions makes the task of predicting harder. What follows are no more than tentative pointers and suggestions.

(1) In *George Mitchell* Bridge treats the facts that the clause was known to the farmers and easy to understand as in its favour. Compare *The Zinnia* [1984] 2 Lloyd's Rep 211, in which Staughton J commented (at p 222):

> I would have been tempted to hold that all the conditions are unfair and unreasonable for two reasons: first, they are in such small print that one can barely read them; secondly, the draughtsmanship is so convoluted and prolix that one almost needs an LL.B. to understand them. However, neither of those arguments was advanced before me, so I say no more about them.

However it is clear that the fact that a clause is known and understood will not necessarily make it reasonable—in other words, the courts are concerned to do more than prevent unfair surprise.

(2) It is not surprising to find the courts reluctant to allow the exclusion of liability for negligence. As we saw earlier (above, p 305), it will normally be efficient to place liability on the least cost avoider. (Schwartz's argument that excluding liability will not lessen the incentive to perform carefully, noted on p 715, operates only under the very restrictive assumption that information costs are near zero—ie that the buyer can easily get the relevant information. As the note hints, this will seldom be the case.)

(3) Equally, insurance or other mechanisms by which the parties can protect themselves from loss are also crucial. In *Smith v Eric S Bush* [1989] 2 All ER 514 the question was whether it was reasonable for a surveyor, employed by a building soceity to inspect and value a house, to disclaim responsibility to the purchaser to whom the report would be passed and who was paying a fee to the building society to have the valuation made. The House of Lords held that it was not. Lord Griffiths said (at pp 531–532):

> I believe that it is impossible to draw up an exhaustive list of the factors that must be taken into account when a judge is faced with this very difficult decision. Nevertheless, the following matters should, in my view, always be considered.
> (1) Were the parties of equal bargaining power? If the court is dealing with a one-off

situation between parties of equal bargaining power the requirement of reasonableness would be more easily discharged than in a case such as the present where the disclaimer is imposed on the purchaser who has no effective power to object.

(2) In the case of advice, would it have been reasonably practicable to obtain the advice from an alternative source taking into account considerations of costs and time? In the present case it is urged on behalf of the surveyor that it would have been easy for the purchaser to have obtained his own report on the condition of the house, to which the purchaser replies that he would then be required to pay twice for the same advice and that people buying at the bottom end of the market, many of whom will be young first-time buyers, are likely to be under considerable financial pressure without the money to go paying twice for the same service.

(3) How difficult is the task being undertaken for which liability is being excluded? When a very difficult or dangerous undertaking is involved there may be a high risk of failure which would certainly be a pointer towards the reasonableness of excluding liability as a condition of doing the work. A valuation, on the other hand, should present no difficulty if the work is undertaken with reasonable skill and care. It is only defects which are observable by a careful visual examination that have to be taken into account and I cannot see that it places any unreasonable burden on the valuer to require him to accept responsibility for the fairly elementary degree of skill and care involved in observing, following up and reporting on such defects. Surely it is work at the lower end of the surveyor's field of professional expertise.

(4) What are the practical consequences of the decision on the question of reasonableness? This must involve the sums of money potentially at stake and the ability of the parties to bear the loss involved, which, in its turn, raises the question of insurance. There was once a time when it was considered improper even to mention the possible existence of insurance cover in a lawsuit. But those days are long past. Everyone knows that all prudent, professional men carry insurance, and the availability and cost of insurance must be a relevant factor when considering which of two parties should be required to bear the risk of a loss. We are dealing in this case with a loss which will be limited to the value of a modest house and against which it can be expected that the surveyor will be insured. Bearing the loss will be unlikely to cause significant hardship if it has to be borne by the surveyor but it is, on the other hand, quite possible that it will be a financial catastrophe for the purchaser who may be left with a valueless house and no money to buy another. If the law in these circumstances denies the surveyor the right to exclude his liability, it may result in a few more claims but I do not think so poorly of the surveyors' profession as to believe that the floodgates will be opened. There may be some increase in surveyors' insurance premiums which will be passed on to the public, but I cannot think that it will be anything approaching the figures involved in the difference between the Abbey National's offer of a valuation without liability and a valuation with liability discussed in the speech of my noble and learned friend Lord Templeman. The result of denying a surveyor, in the circumstances of this case, the right to exclude liability will result in distributing the risk of his negligence among all house purchasers through an increase in his fees to cover insurance, rather than allowing the whole of the risk to fall on the one unfortunate purchaser.

I would not, however, wish it to be thought that I would consider it unreasonable for professional men in all circumstances to seek to exclude or limit their liability for negligence. Sometimes breathtaking sums of money may turn on professional advice against which it would be impossible for the adviser to obtain adequate insurance cover and which would ruin him if he were to be held personally liable. In these circumstances it may indeed by reasonable to give the advice on a basis of no liability or possibly of liability limited to the extent of the adviser's insurance cover.

In addition to the foregoing four factors, which will always have to be considered, there is in this case the additional feature that the surveyor is only employed in the first place because the purchaser wishes to buy the house and the purchaser in fact provides or contributes to the surveyor's fees. No one has argued that if the purchaser had employed and paid the surveyor himself, it would have been reasonable for the surveyor to exclude liability for negligence, and the present situation is not far removed from that of a direct contract between the surveyor and the purchaser. The evaluation of the foregoing matters leads me to the clear conclusion that it would not be fair and reasonable for the surveyor to be permitted to exclude liability in the circumstances of this case. I would therefore dismiss this appeal.

It must, however, be remembered that this is a decision in respect of a dwelling house of modest value in which it is widely recognised by surveyors that purchasers are in fact relying on their care and skill. It will obviously be of general application in broadly similar circumstances. But I expressly reserve my position of valuations of quite different types of property for mortgage purposes, such as industrial property, large blocks of flats or very expensive houses. In such cases it may well be that the general expectation of the behaviour of the purchaser is quite different. With very large sums of money at stake prudence would seem to demand that the purchaser obtain his own structural survey to guide him in his purchase and, in such circumstances with very much larger sums of money at stake, it may be reasonable for the surveyors valuing on behalf of those who are providing the finance either to exclude or limit their liability to the purchaser.

(4) As Lord Griffiths makes clear, the courts will sometimes assume that the parties are the best judges of their own interests. What is not clear is the extent to which the circumstances of the individual contract will be looked at. In *Hyland* Slade stressed that the court was concerned with the particular contract: but suppose that most firms which use plant hire are in fact already insured against damage to buildings? (This is not purely hypothetical. Probably most plant is hired for work on building sites where the building work done already will be insured by either contractor or employer.) Should a contract which is suitable for the majority of contracting parties be held unreasonable because it wasn't reasonable for the individual plaintiff?

(5) If the terms aren't what the plaintiff wants, why not ask for a change? One factor which seems to recur in the cases is whether the individual would have been able to bargain for better terms. How likely is it that a single individual will be able to do this? What if there is a trade association that could bargain on behalf of its members?

(6) Sometimes a firm can be persuaded to make a concession on terms. In *The Zinnia* [1984] 2 Lloyd's Rep 211, 222–223, Staughton J said:

> The point which was most discussed was the strength of the bargaining positions of the parties relative to each other. This I find to have been, in broad terms, equal. The owners could and apparently did, obtain tenders from a number of other yards. The defendants did from time to time relax some of their standard terms at the request of a particular customer, but that had only happened in the past at the request of customers with more economic power than the present owners. They had never in the past relaxed the exclusion in cl 8(9) of economic loss, or modified cl 8 otherwise than by extending the period of guarantee. But they have never been asked to do so. I do not find that surprising. Commercial men negotiating a contract for the future are not too concerned about the small print if they can secure a guarantee clause which seems to them satisfactory. It is only after a breach has occurred that they may take a different view.
>
> In February, 1980, when this contract was made, the defendants were very busy. They would have been reluctant to make any concession. At other times, when they were short of work, they would have been much more ready to do so. In the circumstances of this case, I do not think that I can take that factor into account, or at any rate give it much weight. It can scarcely have been the intention of Parliament that a clause in a ship repairer's standard terms would be fair and reasonable one week—when the yard had no work and was willing to make concessions if asked—but unfair and unreasonable the following week, when the yard was busy. Relative bargaining power must surely be judged by somewhat broader considerations.

Do you think this is correct? If the plaintiffs had the chance to get better terms but did not try to do so, what does that suggest?

(7) In the *George Mitchell* case the farmers' trade association had never negotiated the clause. What does that suggest? Was Bridge correct to regard the absence of negotiation as 'equivocal'?

(8) It may happen that an unreasonable clause is never taken up in negotiations because it very seldom causes trouble. This may have been the case in *Walker v Boyle* [1982] 1 All ER 634. This case arose out of a contract for the purchase of a house. Before the contract is concluded it is normal for the purchaser's solicitors to address a number of enquiries to the vendor. In this case the vendor was asked if she knew of any disputes regarding the boundaries of the property. She allowed her husband to manage her business affairs, and he replied that he knew of no such disputes. In fact there was a serious boundary dispute with a neighbour but the husband was so convinced that his view of it was correct that he honestly thought there was no dispute. In due course contracts were exchanged on the National Conditions

of Sale (19th ed). Condition 17(1) provided that 'no error, misstatement or omission in any preliminary answer shall annul the sale'. When the purchaser discovered the dispute he brought an action seeking rescission and the return of his deposit. It was argued that Condition 17(1) was unreasonable and of no effect by virtue of the Misrepresentation Act 1967, s 3. Dillon J said:

. . . I do not regard condition 17 as satisfying that requirement in the circumstances of this case. Another way of putting it is that Mrs Boyle has not shown that it does satisfy that requirement.

It has been submitted by counsel for Mrs Boyle that as there were solicitors acting for both parties, it would be a very strong thing to say that any term of the contract which resulted is not a fair and reasonable one in the circumstances. That argument would have great force, no doubt, if the solicitors had specifically directed their minds to the problem and had evolved the clause which was under attack. In fact, however, neither solicitor directed his mind to condition 17, and they have both told me, and they are men of not inconsiderable experience as conveyancing solicitors, that they have never come across a case where any question under condition 17 has arisen. It was submitted that it was the duty of the purchaser's solicitor to advise his client, Mr Walker, of the implications of condition 17 and of the other terms of the contract which Mr Walker was going to enter into, and he must be taken to have discharged that duty and satisfied himself and Mr Walker that the terms were reasonable. It is, of course, the duty of a solicitor to advise his client about any abnormal or unusual term in a contract, but I think it is perfectly normal and proper for a solicitor to use standard forms of conditions of sale such as the National Conditions of Sale. I do not think he is called on to go through the small print of those somewhat lengthy conditions with a tooth-comb every time he is advising a purchaser or to draw the purchaser's attention to every problem which on a careful reading of the conditions might in some circumstance or other conceivably arise. I cannot believe that purchasers of house property throughout the land would be overjoyed at having such lengthy explanations of the National Conditions of Sale ritually foisted on them.

It has also been submitted by counsel for Mrs Boyle that the court should be very slow to hold that a common-form clause like condition 17 is not fair and reasonable. Of course it is true that there are common-form clauses which have been evolved by negotiation between trade associations, associations of merchants or associations of growers or trade unions or other such bodies concerned to protect the rights of their members, which can be regarded as representing what consensus in the trade regards as fair and reasonable. Again, the National Conditions of Sale are not the product of negotiation between such bodies and it is plain from the conditions I have cited in the *Nottingham Patent Brick and Tile Co* case and Clauson J's case of *Charles Hunt Ltd v Palmer* that what now appears in condition 17 has come down through the ages despite very drastic limitations imposed on it by the courts. I do not think it can be said that its precarious survival until 1977 entitles it to the automatic accolade of fairness and reasonableness.

Dillon J ordered the vendor to return the purchaser's deposit. Is it ever reasonable to exclude liability for the inaccuracy of information to which you have already access but the other party does not? For a rather inconclusive discussion on this point see *Howard Marine and Dredging Co Ltd v A Ogden & Sons (Excavations) Ltd* [1978] QB 574.

(9) Even if there is no association representing the customers, does it follow that the business is completely unconstrained in putting into the contract whatever clauses it likes? Go back to Trebilcock's analysis (above, p 700). How can the court distinguish between a clause which is inefficiently harsh and one which (whatever this plaintiff knew or thought about it) represents the balance between risk and price that the 'informed margin' of consumers prefer? Consider this account of *Woodman v Photo Trade Processing Ltd* by Lawson (1981) 131 NLJ 933 at 935:

A reel of film had been given to the defendants for processing. The subject matter was a wedding. Most of the snaps were lost and the defendants pleaded reliance on this clause: 'All photographic materials are accepted on the basis that their value does not exceed the cost of the material itself. Responsibility is limited to the replacement of the films. No liability will be accepted consequential or otherwise, however caused'. Judge Clarke examined both the

Schroeder and *Levison* cases and turned also to the very important House of Lords' decision in *Peek v North Staffordshire Rly Co* (1863) 10 HLCas 473 at 493. This case arose from the terms of the Railway and Canal Traffic Act 1854, which permitted transport undertakings to limit their liability providing they used clauses which were 'just and reasonable'. The clause in issue excluded all liability for loss or damage to fragile goods unless these were declared and insured according to their value. By six to five, the House ruled against this clause: it excluded liability for mistake as well as negligence; the railway had a monopoly which in effect forced the customer to take the company's terms; insurance was available, but only at a rate which could be properly described as 'exorbitant'. The conclusion is irresistible that the same verdict would be reached under the Unfair Contract Terms Act.

The view taken by Judge Clarke was that, having regard to the three cases put before him, the exclusion clause was unreasonable. But before he was prepared to come to a final decision, he felt obliged to consider whether there were alternative means by which the customer's needs could have been met. The judge had recognised that this factor, which appears in the guidelines, contained in Schedule 2 to the Act, was necessarily only to be applied, according to the strict wording of the Act, to contracts for the sale, supply or disposition of goods. Judge Clarke fairly rationalised its application to the case in hand, which involved a contract of services, on the ground that the matters contained in the Schedule were such matters as would usually be taken into account in differing categories of case as well.

The crucial point was that the Code of Practice for the Photographic Industry, as agreed with the Office of Fair Trading, clearly recognised the possibility of a two-tier system of trade: the lower tier would be the present way of trade, with full exclusion of liability; the other possibility would be a more expensive service, but with the processors accepting a greater degree of liability. Such an approach, the judge concluded, was not 'only reasonable but practicable'. For that reason, the defendants, upon whom the burden lay, failed to persuade him that the clause 'satisfies the statutory test of reasonableness'.

Was the clause in this case obscure, or well known and easy to understand? If there were any significant number of consumers who wanted a more expensive service on 'lower risk' terms, why wasn't one already on offer? (Note: a bit of 'Saturday afternoon empiricism' in Leamington by one of your editors suggests that a choice of level of service is now readily available—perhaps as the result of the Code of Practice and this decision. What isn't known is how many people opt for the more expensive service. . .)

(10) The main ground for the decision in the *George Mitchell* case seems to have been that the seed company in practice often did pay compensation. Why did this make a difference? Was there an element of unfair surprise in that the seed company did not waive its defence under the clause and pay up? Why would the seed company ever pay up after putting this clause into the contract? If it were shown that it only ever did so for old-established customers, and the plaintiff were not one of these, would reliance on the clause be unreasonable?

(11) A less charitable explanation for inserting harsh clauses but paying up sometimes anyway is that the company is quite prepared to pay in any 'genuine case' (where the farmer has taken all the correct steps?) but the company wants to decide which is a genuine case and which not itself, rather than leave it to judicial decision or arbitration. See Beale & Dugdale 2 Brit J Law & Society 45, at 57.

(12) Would the outcome of cases like *George Mitchell* be different now that it is the reasonableness of including the clause, not of relying on it, which is the test (see note 1 on p 719 above)? Adams and Brownsword 104 LQR 94, 100, 108–109 argue that this might change the result, but wouldn't it be unreasonable to include a clause that gives the company power to decide?

(viii) Exclusions from the Act

Although the Act is of general application, a number of contracts are specifically excluded from it. A full list will be found in Cheshire and Fifoot, pp 172–173 or Treitel, pp 207–209. Perhaps the most important exclusions are:

(1) contracts relating to the creation, transfer or termination of interests in land;

(2) contracts of insurance;

(3) contracts of charterparty or carriage of goods by sea (except for personal injury liability and as against consumers);

(4) international supply contracts;

(5) contracts where English law is the proper law of the contract only by choice of the parties.

See s 31; s 1(2) and Sch 1; ss 26 and 27.

(ix) Evasion by secondary contract

Section 10

A person is not bound by any contract term prejudicing or taking away rights of his which arise under, or in connection with the performance of, another contract, so far as those rights extend to the enforcement of another's liability which this Part of this Act prevents that other from excluding.

(x) Other statutory controls over exemption clauses

There are a number of enactments controlling the use of exemption clauses in specific types of contracts: a notable example is the Carriage of Goods by Sea Act 1971, which adopts the Hague-Visby Rules. This prevents shipowners excluding certain types of liability towards owners of goods, but explicitly permits the use of other exceptions. The subject is too complex for treatment here: a simple account can be found in Payne and Ivamy, *Carriage of Goods by Sea* (13th edn, pp 193–210). See also below, p 736.

Other examples are:

Defective Premises Act 1972

Section 1

(1) A person taking on work for or in connection with the provision of a dwelling (whether the dwelling is provided by the erection or by the conversion or enlargement of a building) owes a duty—

    (a) if the dwelling is provided to the order of any person, to that person; and

    (b) without prejudice to paragraph (a) above, to every person who acquires an interest (whether legal or equitable) in the dwelling;

to see that the work which he takes on is done in a workmanlike or, as the case may be, professional manner, with proper materials and so that as regards that work the dwelling will be fit for habitation when completed.

Section 6

. . .

(3) Any term of an agreement which purports to exclude or restrict, or has the effect of excluding or restricting, the operation of any of the provisions of this Act, or any liability arising by virtue of any such provision, shall be void.

Consumer Protection Act 1987

Section 7
   The liability of a person by virtue of this Part to a person who has suffered damage caused wholly or partly by a defect in a product, or to a dependant or relative of such a person, shall not be limited or excluded by any contract term, by any notice or by any other provision.

CHAPTER 35

Regulated contracts

The account of contract law given in this book has been largely abstract, that is, concerned with rules which are true of contracts whatever their subject matter. In this it has followed the prevalent Anglo-American pattern of the last hundred years. Discussions of particular contracts have commonly been found in other books—on Sale, Hire Purchase, Labour Law, Insurance and so on. This reflects the prevalent view of English lawyers that we have a law of contract rather than of contracts.

One of the consequences of this approach is to exclude from the general law of contract much of the (statutory) regulation of individual contracts on the basis that what applies only to a special contract is not of general interest. The process of regulation has however been carried very far and indeed some commentators have doubted whether this leaves much of general contract law left. This view seems to us an exaggeration but it is worthwhile to look at some examples of regulation, which we classify according to the rationale for adopting regulation. The list that follows is not exhaustive and no doubt in some cases the examples overlap two or more categories.

(a) 'Necessities' in short supply

In ordinary circumstances market exchange mediated by contract operates to provide necessities such as food. Prices are dictated by supply and demand so that a poor potato crop will lead to higher potato prices. There is nowadays considerable interference with pure market forces but this tends to take the form of encouraging farmers to produce more food than customers will buy at market prices (hence butter mountains and wine lakes). In times of famine and war governments have for millenia tried to hold down the prices of staple foods such as corn, though this has often led simply to the development of black markets. One of the most interesting examples of regulation in this field is rented housing, which has been the subject of legislation in England since 1915. The statutory regime is complex, largely as a result of the need to control attempts by landlords to evade the scheme, for example, by demanding the payment of 'premiums' before letting tenants into possession. (See *Kiriri Cotton Ltd v Dewani*, below, p 767). Under the original scheme rents were frozen. Under the scheme which operated until the coming into force of the Housing Act 1988 (and which still applies to many tenancies) rents were held to a 'fair' level but it was assumed that this would often (usually) be below the level which would be fixed by the market. The rationale for intervention is that landlords will be unfairly enriched and tenants unduly impoverished by payment of the difference between 'market' rents and 'fair' rents. The operation of the scheme has been the subject of extensive economic and political debate. There is no doubt that since 1915 the amount of rented accommodation provided by private landlords has diminished greatly; the critical question is whether this has been caused by the scheme. It can be plausibly argued that landlords as a class will not build houses for rent or continue to rent out houses they already own unless the return is commensurate with that to be expected from other forms of investment. If this is true, regulation may operate in the long run to diminish the supply, thereby exacerbating the problem which it is designed to solve. (Of course all is not so simple since in the long run demand is also not constant and governments have adopted other policies such as tax relief on mortgages which encourage customers for accommodation to move if possible from renting houses to buying them). The Housing Act 1988 introduces changes which attempt to ensure that market rents are reflected in the rents set. Whether it will result in an increased supply of rented accommodation remains to be seen.

(b) Intractable problems of inadequate information

Economists sometimes divide goods into 'search goods' and 'experience goods'. When a potential customer has poor information about the former he searches for it until satisfied. But for some goods search will not do as there is no good way to get information before buying. So here the customer commonly must 'experience' the goods in order to inform himself. Such a practice works satisfactorily enough as a basis for choosing between one brand of instant coffee and another but it is hardly satisfactory if the consumer is to make a once-in-a-lifetime purchase. He may often be able to use other people's experience since reputation will often be the key. In many fields a firm's reputation for good work is one of its most valuable assets which it will not depreciate by cheating customers since the short-term gain is small compared with the long-term loss. But this does not help where no reputation can be built up.

A classic example is the supply of passages to emigrants from Europe to America in the nineteenth century.

The Rise and Fall of Freedom of Contract by Atiyah, pp 337–338

The Passenger Acts
. . . Between 1803 and 1860 a large number of emigrants from England, and more especially, Ireland, took their lives in their hands and boarded an emigrant passenger vessel, usually at Liverpool. In the 1840s as a result of failure of the Irish potato crop, the numbers rose hugely, and between 1844 and 1852 some one and a half million persons sought to cross the Atlantic in search of a better life. Most of the emigrants were very poor, many had worked for months to save up the fare—little as it was—many were illiterate, and nearly all were imposed upon. The conditions on these ships were, at the beginning of the century, appalling. The emigrants were crammed into the ships, sometimes with barely room to stand up, let alone lie down, there were no sanitary facilities of any kind, no privacy, no segregation of the sexes, and no food was provided: the passengers were expected to bring their own. When it ran out, as it might do if the voyage was prolonged, they either starved or bought supplies from the ship's master at enormously inflated prices. Disease was rife, and many ships arrived in America or Canada with rotting corpses littering the decks.
　　The facts first came to light almost by accident, in 1803, when a Select Committee inquiring into the Scottish highlands was fed a great deal of information about the emigrant trade. They were told, for example, of a ship in which three-fifths of the passengers had died, and thirty corpses were found when it arrived. The reaction was instantaneous. A Bill was hastily drafted

and passed without a single voice being raised against it. But the Act did more credit to the heart than to the head of its sponsors. It threw away, indeed, any notion of freedom of contract and constituted what Professor MacDonagh has called a revolutionary breach of this principle. But as I have previously pointed out, in 1803 the principle had barely been formulated, for the equitable jurisdiction at that time provided many forms of redress for poor and ignorant contracting parties who were imposed upon by others. In any event the Act did not work. It was too burdensome on the shipowners, and if it had been enforced, the cost of a passage on an emigrant ship would have been priced beyond the reach of the passengers.

We have also seen how in 1826–7 a Parliamentary Select Committee suddenly woke up to the fact that the Act represented an infringement of the important principle of freedom of contract and secured its repeal and how, almost immediately, new revelations about the appalling conditions in the trade led to more legislation. In 1828 a new Act was passed, more modest in its requirements, and this time, though (it seems) largely by accident, the Act was enforced. This came about because the draftsman of the Act, A. C. Buchanan, was appointed Agent-General for Emigration to Canada; in that capacity he took it on himself to prosecute for breaches of the Act and to present annual reports on his efforts to Parliament. An amending Act of 1835 required the shipowners to pay 1s. per day detention money to passengers waiting for their vessel in Liverpool. This Act also required the ships to carry 'sufficient' medicines for the voyage and to post up price lists for the food on sale to the passengers. As usual it was enforcement which remained the principal problem. The Acts conferred all manner of contractual rights on the passengers, but once aboard the ships there was nothing that anyone could do to enforce his rights. Complaints were often made at the other end, but the survivors were generally only too eager to disembark and get away as fast as they could. It was unthinkable for any of them to wait around at the place of disembarkation in order to bring a civil action for damages. Sir James Stephen, Under-Secretary in the Colonial Office, commented somewhat fatalistically, that 'These Irishmen are not the first, nor will they be the last, to make the discovery that a man may starve and yet have the best right of action that a special pleader could wish for'. But this fatalism did not satisfy everybody, and demands for more rigorous enforcement by the Government were frequent. By 1836–40 even the political economists had quite abandoned their opposition to the legislation and were as keen as anyone to suggest tightening-up of the requirements. A Report on the Acts in 1842 paid lip service to the principle of *laissez-faire*, arguing that Acts of Parliament could not 'supply the want of proper discretion in individuals', but generally speaking these cautionary words had little effect.

An important Act was drafted and carried in 1842, based on the detailed proposals of the new emigration officers. This Act was quite destructive of what remained of freedom of contract. It required a written contract in a prescribed form to be given to the passengers, it required the licensing of brokers and agents, compulsory provision of food for the passengers both on board, and even prior to embarkation, from the day appointed for departure. The Act was drafted with a view to its enforceability and it was enforced. The new Commissioner for Emigration was given power to sue the shipowners in the name, and on behalf of, the passengers, and for some years after the Act was passed the Commissioner was recovering some £1,500 annually on their behalf.

The same reasoning has led many countries to undertake extensive regulation of their tourist industries.

Even when information does spread about goods or services it may spread slowly and unevenly. Much consumer protection legislation arises from this problem and the belief that ordinary contract principles alone will not lead to results which maximise consumer welfare.

Similar problems confront the customer who seeks professional services. It is difficult for a non-lawyer to discover which lawyers are competent to undertake which (if any) kinds of work. In many countries this leads to state-imposed minimum standards. In England the tradition of professional self-regulation is very strong. This has meant little state regulation and also little by way of state granted monopoly. So there is in general nothing to stop a non-doctor from giving medical advice provided he does not hold himself out as a doctor.

(c) Problems with transactions costs

Negotiating contracts takes time and therefore costs money. We have seen that one of the responses to this has been the development of standard form contracts, one of the advantages of which is that contract making can be delegated to relatively low level staff who have no authority other than to use the standard form. Similar considerations enter into the thinking of governments and are one of the reasons for the development of special mandatory regimes for certain kinds of international transaction, particularly international carriage. The best example of this is the Hague Rules, enacted into English law by the Carriage of Goods by Sea Act 1924 (now replaced by the Hague-Visby Rules, enacted by the Carriage of Goods by Sea Act 1971). These rules which form the background to a number of cases in this book (see eg *The Eurymedon* p 818) provide a mandatory regime for carriage of goods by sea under a bill of lading and have been enacted into law by nearly all countries. This means that there will be a very high degree of similarity between all bills of lading, which greatly facilitates dealing with them. Similar developments have followed in relation to international carriage of goods by rail and by road.

It would be an oversimplification to regard the Hague Rules simply in this light; they also represent a compromise between the interests of ship owners and shippers, in that they achieve a set of terms that was apparently seldom achieved by negotiation previously. A person or company sending goods under a bill of lading would normally find it uneconomic to pay the amount that a shipping line would demand to alter its standard terms in his favour—he might well be prepared to pay the extra cost of better standard terms if they were shared by all other shippers too, but he would not pay the cost of arranging a special one-off deal (compare above, p 710). This might be true of a considerable number of shippers, and though their aggregate dissatisfaction with the terms offered would have some influence on the shipping lines, there might not be enough shippers aware of the problem to bring about a change (see above, p 704). Thus high transactions costs seem to have prevented an efficient solution until the adoption of the Hague Rules. This analysis seems to be confirmed by the fact that the Rules do not apply to charterparties: a charter is a larger contract and charterers would find it cost-effective to negotiate over the terms.

(d) Vulnerability to exploitation in long-term relationships

It is often the case that parties enjoy roughly equal bargaining power at the time the contract is entered into but that once the contract is on foot the balance of advantage changes sharply. The classic example is a contract of employment. The individual employee commonly has more options open to him before than after taking the contract of employment. Often the employee will develop skills which are job specific and make him less attractive to other employers; often the decision to accept the post will involve foregoing alternative kinds of training and experience. Further the central place which work plays in most people's lives will mean that employer and employee view termination of the contract in quite a different light.

In the last twenty years regulation of the contract of employment has been extensive. Particularly interesting has been the introduction of the notion of 'unfair dismissal', that is a dismissal which is not wrongful within the terms of the contract of employment but nevertheless contravenes acceptable norms and entitles the employee thereby dismissed to compensation.

(e) Private enforcement costs are too high

Private enforcement of contracts is likely to be effective only where the value of the sum sued for exceeds the likely cost of the action to the plaintiff. This will not be the case where there are many victims of contractual misperformance each of whom suffers a small loss. This is the normal position at the shoddy end of the retail trade and has led to the passing of the Fair Trading Act 1973 under which the Director General of Fair Trading has been given wide powers in respect of 'unfair' consumer trade practices. He may also take steps against persistent contract breakers.

Fair Trading Act 1973

Section 13
In this Act 'consumer trade practice' means any practice which is for the time being carried on in connection with the supply of goods (whether by way of sale or otherwise) to consumers or in connection with the supply of services for consumers and which relates—
   (a) to the terms or conditions (whether as to price or otherwise) on or subject to which goods or services are or are sought to be supplied, or
   (b) to the manner in which those terms or conditions are communicated to persons to whom goods are or are sought to be supplied or for whom services are or are sought to be supplied, or
   (c) to promotion (by advertising, labelling or marking of goods, canvassing or otherwise) of the supply of goods or of the supply of services, or
   (d) to methods of salesmanship employed in dealing with consumers, or
   (e) to the way in which goods are packed or otherwise got up for the purpose of being supplied, or
   (f) to methods of demanding or securing payment for goods or services supplied.

Section 14
(1) Subject to sections 15 and 16 of this Act, the Secretary of State or any other Minister or the Director may refer to the Advisory Committee the question whether a consumer trade practice specified in the reference adversely affects the economic interests of consumers in the United Kingdom. . . .

Section 17
. . .
(2) Where it appears to the Director that a consumer trade practice has the effect, or is likely to have the effect,—
   (a) of misleading consumers as to, or withholding from them adequate information as to, or an adequate record of, their rights and obligations under relevant consumer transactions, or
   (b) of otherwise misleading or confusing consumers with respect to any matter in connection with relevant consumer transactions, or
   (c) of subjecting consumers to undue pressure to enter into relevant consumer transactions, or
   (d) of causing the terms or conditions, on or subject to which consumers enter into relevant consumer transactions, to be so adverse to them as to be inequitable,
any reference made by the Director under section 14 of this Act with respect to that consumer trade practice may, if the Director thinks fit, include proposals for recommending to the Secretary of State that he should exercise his powers under the following provisions of this Part of this Act with respect to that consumer trade practice.
. . .

Section 34

(1) Where it appears to the Director that the person carrying on a business has in the course of that business persisted in a course of conduct which—

    (a) is detrimental to the interests of consumers in the United Kingdom, whether those interests are economic interests or interests in respect of health, safety or other matters, and

    (b) in accordance with the following provisions of the section is to be regarded as unfair to consumers,

the Director shall use his best endeavours, by communication with that person or otherwise, to obtain from him a satisfactory written assurance that he will refrain from continuing that course of conduct and from carrying on any similar course of conduct in the course of that business.

(2) For the purposes of subsection (1)(b) of this section a course of conduct shall be regarded as unfair to consumers if it consists of contraventions of one or more enactments which impose duties, prohibitions or restrictions enforceable by criminal proceedings, whether any such duty, prohibition or restriction is imposed in relation to consumers as such or not and whether the person carrying on the business has or has not been convicted of any offence in respect of any such contravention.

(3) A course of conduct on the part of the person carrying on a business shall also be regarded for those purposes as unfair to consumers if it consists of things done, or omitted to be done, in the course of that business in breach of contract or in breach of a duty (other than a contractual duty) owed to any person by virtue of any enactment or rule of law and enforceable by civil proceedings, whether (in any such case) civil proceedings in respect of the breach of contract or breach of duty have been brought or not.

(4) For the purpose of determining whether it appears to him that a person has persisted in such a course of conduct as is mentioned in subsection (1) of this section, the Director shall have regard to either or both of the following, that is to say—

    (a) complaints received by him, whether from consumers or from other persons;

    (b) any other information collected by or furnished to him, whether by virtue of this Act or otherwise.

Section 35

If, in the circumstances specified in subsection (1) of section 34 of this Act,—

    (a) the Director is unable to obtain from the person in question such an assurance as is mentioned in that subsection, or

    (b) that person has given such an assurance and it appears to the Director that he has failed to observe it,

the Director may bring proceedings against him before the Restrictive Practices Court.

Section 37

(1) Where in any proceedings before the Restrictive Practices Court under section 35 of this Act—

    (a) the Court finds that the person against whom the proceedings are brought (in this section referred to as 'the respondent') has in the course of a business carried on by him persisted in such a course of conduct as is mentioned in section 34(1) of this Act, and

    (b) the respondent does not give an undertaking to the Court under subsection (3) of this section which is accepted by the Court, and

    (c) it appears to the Court that, unless an order is made against the respondent under this section, he is likely to continue that course of conduct or to carry on a similar course of conduct,

the Court may make an order against the respondent under this section.

(2) An order of the Court under this section shall (with such degree of particularity as appears to the Court to be sufficient for the purposes of the order) indicate the nature of the course of conduct to which the finding of the Court under subsection (1)(a) of this section relates, and shall direct the respondent—

    (a) to refrain from continuing that course of conduct, and

    (b) to refrain from carrying on any similar course of conduct in the course of his business.

Further, under the Trade Descriptions Act 1968 it is criminal to attach a false trade description to goods which are offered for sale. Most such false trade descriptions would where a contract was concluded amount to terms of the contract or to representations but there are significant advantages to customers in public rather than private enforcement of standards.

(f) Monopolies, oligopolies and anti-competitive arrangements

Regulation through the common law rules on restraint of trade is discussed below, p 776ff. Since the war these rules have been buttressed by a complex statutory regime operating through the Restrictive Practices Court, the Monopolies and Mergers Commission and the European Commission.

(g) Paternalism

'Paternalism and the Law of Contracts' by Kronman (1983) 92 Yale LJ 763–766, 771–779, 786–787, 797–798

In general, any legal rule that prohibits an action on the ground that it would be contrary to the actor's own welfare is paternalistic. The prohibition against suicide, the requirement that motorcyclists wear helmets, laws that restrict the use of drugs or make education compulsory are all examples of legal paternalism. In this Article, I shall be concerned with one branch of this wide and heterogeneous family of legal rules—those that may properly be regarded as belonging to the law of contracts because the liberty they restrict is the liberty to bind oneself by making a legally enforceable promise.

One (relatively new) example of the kind of restriction I have in mind is the rule invalidating any provision in a residential lease that purports to waive the tenant's right to withhold rent if the property fails to meet certain minimum standards of habitability. Even if a tenant believes that a waiver of this sort would be in his own interest and voluntarily agrees to include it in the lease, the law protects him by refusing to enforce his waiver. The invalidity of contracts of peonage or self-enslavement, of agreements purporting to waive the promisor's right to obtain a divorce or sue for relief under the bankruptcy laws, of provisions conferring on either party a right to specifically enforce their agreement (where no right of this sort exists as a matter of law); the voidability of most contracts made by infants; and the nonwaiveable 'cooling-off' period imposed by law in many consumer transactions all also have, at least in part, a paternalistic objective. Unquestionably, some of these limitations on the enforceability of private agreements also seek to protect the moral and economic interests of third parties and, to this extent, have a nonpaternalistic objective as well. One central purpose of each, however, is to protect the promisor himself by limiting his power to do what the law judges to be against his own interests; this is paternalism, and there is more of it in our law of contracts than one might suspect. . . .

I. Economic Efficiency and Distributive Justice

In many jurisdictions, a nondisclaimable warranty of habitability is now applied, as a matter of law, in every lease of residential property. Because the warranty is nondisclaimable, any agreement a tenant makes to waive its benefits will be unenforceable. It is sometimes said that if tenants were given the power to waive the warranty of habitability they might be tricked or forced into doing so—to their own disadvantage—and that the warranty has been made nondisclaimable in order to protect tenants from themselves.

To the extent the rule barring free waiver of the warranty of habitability is acknowledged to have a paternalistic aim, its justification is a mixed one, turning in part on considerations of efficiency and in part on a conception of distributive justice. . . .

The attack on contracts of adhesion rests upon an unstated conception of distributive fairness; though often overlooked, it is this conception that gives the attack its appeal. Many contracts are contracts of adhesion in the general sense that one party is able to dictate terms to the other, but this alone does not make an agreement objectionable. Suppose, for example that my neighbor owns a painting I happen to covet. I offer him $5000 for it. He responds, '$10,000 and no warranties regarding its authenticity. Take it or leave it.' Clearly, the fact that I lack bargaining power and must adhere to the terms he proposes does not by itself justify a judicial or legislative effort to tip the balance in my favor. The imbalance in this case which stems from the fact that he owns the painting and I do not, is unobjectionable because we do not care how control over the painting is distributed.

We feel differently about the distribution of control over society's available housing stock, and inequalities of bargaining power in this context therefore seem a more appropriate target for judicial or legislative attack. The distribution of housing matters more to us than the distribution of paintings: Only the first is likely to seem important from the standpoint of most theories of distributive justice. Those contracts of adhesion that disturb us do so, then, because they reflect an underlying distribution of power or resources that offends our conception of distributive fairness; when distributive concerns are weak or nonexistent, contracts of adhesion are less troubling and the concept of adhesion itself loses meaning.

It is therefore misleading to describe the nondisclaimable warranty of habitability as simply a device for correcting an imbalance in bargaining power. More accurately, it is an instrument of redistribution that seeks to shift control over housing from one group (landlords) to another (tenants) in a way that furthers the widely shared goal of insuring everyone shelter of at least a minimally decent sort. To achieve this goal, the warranty must be made nondisclaimable, for if it is not, tenants—poor tenants in particular—will routinely be required to waive their rights to habitable premises, thereby restoring whatever distributional inequities exist at the outset. . . .

[Kronman considers and rejects one objection.]

A second objection to using the nondisclaimable warranty of habitability as an instrument of distributive justice has greater force. Even if landlords are barred from disclaiming responsiblity for the habitability of property they rent, as long as they are not similarly prevented from altering other aspects of their contractual relationship with their tenants, they can easily pass along—in the form of an increased rent charge—whatever additional insurance or compliance costs they incur as a result of their expanded warranty liability. To the extent this is true, the tenant must pay for the increased protection the warranty gives him—whether he wants it or not. Landlords, one could argue, are likely to be unaffected by a nondisclaimable warranty of habitability, since they will not bear its cost; by contrast, tenants will have to purchase a form of compulsory insurance and can only be made worse off as a result.

There are two ways of meeting this criticism. The first is to deny the unstated premise on which it rests—that the rule in question must be evaluated from the standpoint of the tenants' own preferences. Even if the costs of complying with the warranty are fully passed along, this only means that some tenants will have to pay for protection they do not want, and this is objectionable only in case the wishes of the tenants themselves should be controlling. But there may be nothing wrong with forcing tenants, including poor tenants, to spend their money on better housing (or more exactly, on insurance against the risk of inadequate housing). We recognize the legitimacy of compulsory insurance in other areas; social security is one example, and the inalienable right to a discharge in bankruptcy is another. Whether we should also recognize it in the area of housing will depend upon the relative importance we attach to this good and our confidence that poor tenants will not discount too sharply the value of housing insurance.

Second, even if we evaluate the warranty of habitability on the basis of what tenants actually want, the pass-along argument sketched above is less persuasive than its initial formulation suggests. The extent to which landlords are able to pass along the increased costs of a nondisclaimable warranty of habitability will depend upon characteristics of the rental market that are contingent and variable and cannot be determined in an a priori fashion. Under certain empirically possible conditions, landlords will be able to pass along only a small portion of these costs and will have to absorb the rest; moreover, if alternative uses of the property are economically unattractive, the added cost to landlords of a nondisclaimable warranty of habitability may cause the number of available rental units to decline only slightly, if at all. When these conditions are satisfied, tenants will receive the benefit of the warranty for less than its full cost and will not be hurt through disinvestment in the rental market. In the limiting case, tenants will get something for nothing, and, short of that, they may get it for less than what they would be willing to pay. If so, they are clearly better off, from their own point of view, under a legal regime that makes the warranty of habitability nondisclaimable.

. . .

II. Personal Integrity

The nondisclaimable warranty of habitability seems best explained by considerations of economic efficiency and distributive justice. There are, however, many paternalistic restrictions in our law of contracts that cannot be wholly, or most convincingly, explained on these same grounds. One important example is the varied group of restrictions intended to prevent an individual from contracting away too large a part of his personal liberty. . . . Even the prohibition against peonage or self-enslavement as well entrenched as it is, permits a variety of employment relationships that exhibit many of the same characteristics. In short, the limits each of these 'absolute' prohibitions imposes on contractual freedom may be approached in varying degrees; the result is a gray zone of increasing restrictiveness, rather than a bright line crisply demarcating the permissible from the impermissible. Still, one wonders, why are there any restrictions at all?

The first step in answering this question is to clarify the meaning of self-enslavement. Every executory contract limits the freedom of the parties by creating an enforceable obligation, on both sides, to perform or pay damages: Once an individual has made a contractually binding commitment, his alternatives are limited to these two (assuming the other party is not himself in breach). The distinguishing mark of a contract of self-enslavement is that it purports to take away the latter alternative. From a legal point of view, it is not the length of service that makes a contract of employment self-enslaving, nor is it the nature of the services to be performed; even a contract of short duration that calls for the performance of routine and unobjectionable tasks is a contract of self-enslavement and therefore legally unenforceable if it bars the employee from substituting money damages for his promised performance. The law will not permit an employee to contract away his right to 'depersonalize' a relationship by paying damages in the event he chooses to breach. Whatever its other terms, an employment contract is enslaving if it gives the employer a right to compel specific performance of the agreement.

An antenuptial agreement waiving the right to sue for divorce can be described as a contract of self-enslavement in just this sense. The parties to a marital contract have considerable freedom to define in advance the nature and extent of their financial responsibilities in the event of a divorce or separation, but neither can give the other the power to compel specific performance by waiving the right to terminate the relationship through divorce. Here, as in the employment context, the right to substitute damages for the actual performance of the contract is inalienable, and any agreement purporting to forfeit this entitlement is invalid as a matter of law.

. . .

III. Judgment and Moral Imagination

In addition to the two forms of paternalism I have described, it is possible to distinguish a third. The restrictions that compose this third group include some that are paternalistic in the most literal sense; I have in mind various limitations on the enforcement of promises made by children and other incompetent persons. These restrictions all differ in one important respect from those I have characterized as prohibitions against self-enslavement. The latter bar certain agreements without qualification: Under no circumstances will the law recognize the validity of a promise to become the slave of another or to abstain from bringing a divorce action against one's spouse. Agreements of this sort are prohibited because of their content; it makes no difference whether they have been entered into impulsively and without consideration of the consequences, or after careful deliberation. By contrast, the class of restrictions I now wish to consider—exemplified by the rule that a child's contracts will generally not be enforced against him—seems primarily concerned with defects in the promisor's reasoning process.

Restrictions belonging to this third class characteristically prohibit the enforcement of agreements only for a time, often referred to as a 'cooling-off' period, after which the restraint is lifted. The imposition of a mandatory cooling-off period insures that the promisor has an opportunity to reflect on his commitment and to withdraw from the contract if he wishes. A temporary suspension of the promisor's contractual powers reduces the likelihood of an overly hasty decision and thus helps counteract what I have described as a defect in his reasoning process; its purpose is to prevent the promisor from binding himself too quickly or while his judgment is impaired. Unlike the prohibition against self-enslavement, however, the imposition of a cooling-off period does not by itself guarantee (or forbid) any particular substantive result. . . .

Conclusion

Our legal system restricts contractual freedom in many ways and for many reasons. Some of these restrictions are paternalistic: Their purpose is to prevent people from harming themselves through their own ill-considered or disadvantageous promises. The paternalistic rules in our law of contracts do not derive, however, from a single principle, nor is there any one idea that best explains them all. In this Article, I have described three different forms of paternalism and have attempted to clarify the philosophical presuppositions that underlie each. I have argued that only the first, the nondisclaimable warranty, can be defended persuasively in economic terms. All three may be justified on moral grounds; in each case, however, the justification turns upon a different principle or ideal: distributive fairness, self-respect, and the value of judgment or moral imagination. The concept of paternalism conceals too much philosophical variety to be useful by itself; it wrongly suggests that all paternalistic restrictions address a single problem and must be justified by a single principle, or not at all.

Section 9
Illegality

Contracts contrary to public policy

The rules in this section are significantly different from those in other sections of the book. The contract is alleged to be defective but this defect is not internal to the contract (absence of consent, fraud, duress etc) but external, that is enforcement of the contract will infringe some policy quite independent of the agreement of the parties. Suppose a Mafia boss hires a hit-man to kill another Mafia boss for $10,000. This has in a sense all the ingredients we look for in a binding contract (agreement, exchange, adequate certainty as to what is to be done and paid) and it is unlikely that there will be inequality of bargaining power since there is no doubt a well-developed and competitive market for contracts of this kind. (Is it significant that in the movies such an arrangement is always described as 'a contract'?). The refusal of courts to enforce such transactions clearly proceeds from general policy considerations which in England are usually referred to as 'public policy'.

It is worth noting that 'public policy' is not the same as 'policy'. The doctrine of 'public policy' was recognized at a time when judges seldom overtly recognized that their decisions were based on policy considerations. The 'policy' considerations relevant to contract law in general have been explained in Section I and are concerned with the question why agreements should be enforced (eg protection of reasonable expectations). 'Public policy' is concerned with special situations where there are compelling reasons for departing from these general considerations.

Not all the cases in this section fit into this pattern of infringing some interest external to the parties. We saw earlier (above, pp 667–668) that some of the restraint of trade cases which we will deal with in chapter 38 below are best explained as attempts to protect a party with weak bargaining power. We deal with them in this section because the legal mechanism used to 'regulate' the contract, the doctrine of public policy, is the same as that used when the contract would adversely affect third parties.

What sort of factor is liable to make a contract illegal as being contrary to public policy? The public policy seems to be derived from two sources. One is the rest of the law: a contract may be illegal because it involves something which is independently unlawful such as a crime or a tort. The other is the courts' own initiative. There are some contracts which are considered to be so inimical to the interest of the public (or sometimes, as explained in the previous paragraph, to the interest of one of the parties) that they should not be enforced.

In fact it is very difficult to maintain this distinction, because even when some crime or tort is involved the question whether the contract is rendered unenforceable is nearly always a question of public policy for the courts. Very occasionally statute explicitly makes some contract illegal and unenforceable (for examples see Treitel, pp 394–395). More usually it is simply some action taken in the course of the contract which is illegal and the court has to decide whether that should affect the contract in addition to creating criminal or tortious liability.

'The Analysis of Illegal Contracts' by Furmston (1966) 16 U of Toronto LJ 267

The purpose of this paper is to show that the question of whether a contract is illegal is one of considerable complexity which demands precise analysis. The conventional emphasis on stating the various social and economic interests which are protected by this branch of the law has obscured the fact that even when it is agreed on all hands that these interests should be protected, their protection may not necessarily demand the invalidation of a given contract. We may illustrate our point for the moment by a very simple case. There is no doubt that the law has a strong policy against murder but this does not necessarily mean that an agreement to commit murder and a contract to sell a gun, which is to be used to commit murder, should be treated in the same way. It may well be that the latter contract is illegal but it is abundantly clear that the two situations do not of necessity demand the same solution. In practice, of course, no one would suggest that the two situations were identical but the normal method of stating the rule obscures the distinction. It is important therefore to consider not merely the various interests involved but also the various ways in which they may be involved with a contractual situation.

We will see that the consequences of the contract involving some illegality vary widely. For instance, where the whole purpose of it is to commit a crime, as in the example of the hit-man, neither party will be able to enforce the contract; whereas some illegal act accidentally committed during the course of performance, such as a taxi breaking the speed limit, may have no effect on the contractual liability at all.

Goodinson v Goodinson [1954] 2 QB 118, Court of Appeal

Somervell LJ. . . . In *Bennett v Bennett*, it was pointed out that there are two kinds of illegality of differing effect. The first is where the illegality is criminal, or contra bonos mores, and in those cases, which I will not attempt to enumerate or further classify, such a provision, if an ingredient in a contract, will invalidate the whole, although there may be many other provisions in it. There is a second kind of illegality which has no such taint; the other terms in the contract stand if the illegal portion can be severed, the illegal portion being a provision which the court, on grounds of public policy, will not enforce. The simplest and most common example of the latter class of illegality is a contract for the sale of a business which contains a provision restricting the vendor from competing in or engaging in trade for a certain period or within a certain area. There are many cases in the books where, without in any way impugning the contract of sale, some provision restricting competition has been regarded as in restraint of trade and contrary to public policy. There are many cases where not only has the main contract to purchase been left standing but part of the clause restricting competition has been allowed to stand.

[Birkett and Romer LJJ delivered concurring judgments.]

NOTE

The cases seem to establish that illegal contracts fall into at least two groups. It may be that more than two groups are required but no case has yet arisen to test this point.

Although the consequences of a contract involving an illegal act or something contrary to public policy vary from situation to situation, it should not be thought that this is because the courts have a simple discretion to do what they think fit. The outcome may be the result of statutory intepretation or of the rules which apply to that class of case. On the other hand the courts often have some leeway in deciding how to classify the facts and will no doubt decide with a view to the result that the classification will produce.

It should be noted that the most draconian rules on illegal contracts are likely to have only a limited deterrent effect, because they will only come into play if the case comes to court. It is true that if a case which on the facts pleaded raises some question of illegality does reach court, the court does not have to wait for the issue to be raised by the parties. It may consider the point of its own motion. It should not do so, however, unless the contract is clearly illegal or the whole of the relevant facts are before it. It should not refuse to enforce a contract, for instance, merely because there is some suggestion that it may be an unreasonable restraint of trade: *Northwestern Salt Co Ltd v Electrolytic Alkali Co Ltd* [1914] AC 461.

What is more serious is that in many cases the parties have every incentive to avoid litigation. For instance a cartel agreement between manufacturers to limit output and keep up prices may be clearly detrimental to the public but the more successful it is the less likely the parties are to bring it to court. Meanwhile third parties who are being injured may not have a remedy unless the contract involves a crime or tort committed against them.

AG of Commonwealth of Australia v Adelaide Steamship Co Ltd [1913] AC 781, Privy Council

Lord Parker of Waddington. . . . . It is only necessary to add that no contract was ever an offence at common law merely because it was in restraint of trade. The parties to such a contract, even if unenforceable, were always at liberty to act on it in the manner agreed. Similarly combinations, not amounting to contracts, in restraint of trade were never unlawful at common law. To make any such contract or combination unlawful it must amount to a criminal conspiracy, and the essence of a criminal conspiracy is a contract or combination to do something unlawful, or something lawful by unlawful means. The right of the individual to carry on his trade or business in the manner he considers best in his own interests involves the right of combining with others in a common course of action, provided such common course of action is undertaken with a single view to the interests of the combining parties and not with a view to injure others (the *Mogul Steamship (Case)*).

NOTE

Although this statement is undoubtedly orthodox it produces results which are not wholly satisfactory. The more effective a combination is in damaging a third party's interests, the less likely the members of it are to bring it before the court. In the *Mogul Steamship* case [1892] AC 25, the defendants, who were members of a shipping association, made arrangements amongst themselves designed to drive the plaintiffs, a shipping company which was not a member of the association, out of the China trade. They gave rebates to shippers who dealt exclusively with them and forbade their agents to have any dealings with the plaintiffs. As a consequence, the plaintiffs were ruined. As between the defendants these arrangements were very likely in restraint of trade but the House of Lords held that they were not actionable by the plaintiffs.

It is clear enough that many illegal contracts must be happily performed by the parties with damage both to other parties and to the public interest. There are signs that in certain cases relief may be given to third parties.

Eastham v Newcastle United Football Club Ltd [1964] Ch 413, Wilberforce J

The plaintiff had a contract with the first defendants. He wished to play for another club. Under the then rules of the Football Assocation and the Football League a retain and transfer system operated which Wilberforce J held in unreasonable restraint of trade. The plaintiff sought a declaration against the club, the Football Association and the Football League. He had no contract with either the association or the league.

Wilberforce J. . . . . [I]s it open to an employee to bring an action for a declaration that the contract between the employers is in restraint of trade? To my mind it would seem unjust if this were not so. The employees are just as much affected and, indeed, aimed at by the employers' agreement as the employers themselves. Their liberty of action in seeking employment is threatened just as much as the liberty of the employers to give them employment, and their liberty to seek employment is considered by the law to be an important public interest. Is the defence of that interest to be left exclusively in the hands of the employers themselves, who have set up the ring against the employees and who have (as here) shown every intention of maintaining it as long as they can; left to the chance that one day there may be a blackleg among the employers who will challenge it? In my judgment to grant a remedy by way of declaration to the persons whose interests are vitally affected would be well within the spirit and intent of the rule as to declaratory judgments . . .

If I am right so far, then the court has jurisdiction to grant a declaratory judgment, not only against the employer who is in contractual relationship with the employee, but also against the association of employers whose rules or regulations place an unjustifiable restraint on his liberty of employment. A case where the employee is himself contractually bound by the employers' rules (as the employee is here, by virtue of registration and the terms of his contract) is a fortiori to the case last mentioned.

NOTE

In this case the plaintiff was simply granted a declaration that the retain and transfer system was in restraint of trade. The declaration did not actually require the defendants to do anything but the Football Association and the Football League did substantially alter the transfer system as a result. In *Nagle v Feilden* (below, p 750) the Court of Appeal thought it not unarguable that the plaintiff might obtain an injunction against the stewards of the Jockey Club. The Jockey Club avoided further litigation by giving Mrs Nagle a licence.

(a) The heads of public policy

What are the grounds on which a contract may be held illegal as against public policy? We have already mentioned that the fact that the contract somehow involves the commission of a crime or tort *may* lead to its illegality. This is a complex topic which we deal within the next chapter. Of the other grounds of public policy, by far the most frequently litigated and well-developed is that the contract is in restraint of trade, and that is dealt with in detail in chapter 38. For reasons of space the other heads of public policy will not be covered in detail. They are summarised here:

(1) Contracts involving or tending to promote sexual immorality: eg *Pearce v Brooks* (1866) LR 1 Exch 213 (coachbuilders could not recover the hire payable for a 'curiously constructed' brougham which they knew that the defendant, a prostitute, intended to use to attract customers).

(2) Contracts tending to undermine marriage. *Fender v St John Mildmay*

[1938] AC 1 is a leading case, although there a contract was upheld (the defendant had promised to marry the plaintiff while he was already married but after a decree nisi of divorce from the earlier marriage had been granted).

Since 'marriages are made in Heaven', is it contrary to public policy to recruit spouses for a fee? There are many seventeenth and eighteenth century cases to that effect. In many (but not all) of them the agreement was disreputable, eg to kidnap an heiress. In the only modern case, *Hermann v Charlesworth* [1905] 2 KB 123, these cases were applied to a matrimonial agency. It may be doubted whether there is any serious danger to the public good in the activities of such organizations.

(3) Contracts which tend adversely to affect the conduct of foreign affairs. There are many cases, particularly from the First World War, of 'trading with the enemy', a rather technical part of the law, perhaps unlikely to be of much interest in the future. A more relevant example is *Foster v Driscoll* [1929] 1 KB 470. The Court of Appeal held that an agreement to smuggle whisky into the United States during Prohibition was illegal.

(4) Contracts to pervert the course of justice. Obviously agreements to pay a juror for a perverse verdict or a witness to tell lies fall within this principle. Less obviously the principle has been held to prohibit agreements to abandon the prosecution of most (though not all) crimes. The modern law turns on the construction of Section 5 of the Criminal Law Act 1967: see Buckley (1974) 3 Anglo-American LR 472.

A related though less serious head is agreements to oust the jurisdiction of the courts. So for instance a club or trade association cannot make itself the final arbiter of the application of its own rules. Traditionally this reasoning was applied to arbitration agreements which made the decision of the arbitrator final, even though such agreements are common in many countries: *Czarnikow v Roth, Schmidt & Co* [1922] 2 KB 478. The Arbitration Act 1979 gives the parties a qualified power to make the arbitrator's decision final even on questions of law. The principal reason for the change was the desire to preserve the importance of London as a centre for international arbitration (see above, p 85).

(5) Contracts tending to encourage corruption in public life. Selling honours is an obvious example: see *Parkinson v College of Ambulance Ltd* [1925] 2 KB 1. The murkier borderlines of this principle—how, for instance, it might apply to some of the activities of lobbyists of MPs and central and local government officials—have not been much explored in the English courts.

(6) Agreements to defraud the Revenue. These may be no more than a specific example of contracts to defraud but they are usually treated as a special class. A regrettably common example is an agreement to pay an increased salary and to call the increase 'expenses'. Such an arrangement makes not only the 'expenses' but also the basic salary irrecoverable: *Miller v Karlinski* (1945) 62 TLR 85.

(7) Contracts to conceal information that ought to be revealed. There are many situations in which a party ought to keep information confidential because he has contracted to do so or because he has acquired it in circumstances which impose a duty of confidence. However where the duty is based on contract and would cover information which in the public interest ought to be revealed, the contract may be illegal: eg *Neville v*

Dominion of Canada News Co Ltd [1915] 3 KB 556 (agreement that newspaper, which purported to give readers advice on investment schemes, would not comment on the plaintiff's scheme held illegal).

(8) Contracts tending to promote religious, sexual or racial discrimination: eg *Nagle v Feilden* [1966] 2 QB 633 (Court of Appeal refused to strike out claim for a declaration that Jockey Club's practice of refusing licences to women trainers was illegal).

Janson v Driefontein Consolidated Mines Ltd [1902] AC 484, House of Lords

Lord Halsbury LC. . . . I do not think that the phrase 'against public policy' is one which in a Court of law explains itself. It does not leave at large to each tribunal to find that a particular contract is against public policy. . . .

But I do not think the law of England does leave the matter so much at large as seems to be assumed. In treating of various branches of the law learned persons have analyzed the sources of the law, and have sometimes expressed their opinion that such and such a provision is bad because it is contrary to public policy; but I deny that any Court can invent a new head of public policy; so a contract for marriage brokerage, the creation of a perpetuity, a contract in restraint of trade, a gaming or wagering contract, or, what is relevant here, the assisting of the King's enemies, are all undoubtedly unlawful things; and you may say that it is because they are contrary to public policy they are unlawful; but it is because these things have been either enacted or assumed to be by the common law unlawful, and not because a judge or Court have a right to declare that such and such things are in his or their view contrary to public policy. Of course, in the application of the principles here insisted on, it is inevitable that the particular case must be decided by a judge; he must find the facts, and he must decide whether the facts so found do or do not come within the principles which I have endeavoured to describe—that is, a principle of public policy, recognised by the law, which the suggested contract is infringing, or is supposed to infringe.

The Law and its Compass by Lord Radcliffe, at pp 46–52, 54–55

In the year 1824 Burrough J, not otherwise a judge of any particular authority, made or repeated the observation: 'Public policy is an unruly horse and dangerous to ride.' Ever since then judges have been reminding each other of this very sensible warning. But, even when the warning has been duly digested, it seems an odd thing that in a nation which, if it lacks the tradition of the *manège*, is yet the national home of the fox-hunt and the enthusiastic patron of horse-racing, the metaphor of the unruly horse should not be accepted as a challenge to the rider instead of as an invitation to remain pedestrian. . . .

One curious product of this judicial suspicion of 'public policy' is the theory that its heads have now been finally determined. The list, it is said, is closed: and though it is a judge's duty, if very cautiously, to give effect to the old rules when facts cry out for it, nothing can permit an extension of the conception to cover new situations and new categories (see, for instance, this question discussed in *Fender v Mildmay*).

[In *Janson v Driefontein*, Lord Halsbury, the Lord Chancellor of the day, made a statement which, psychologically, is of great interest.]

. . . [N]ot only does it make the definite assumption that one branch, at any rate, of the common law had become a completely closed system, not admitting of development, somewhere before the year 1902, but also it expresses very forcibly the idea that the principles of the common law somehow succeeded in establishing themselves by their own force and not because at some date or dates this or that judge or combination of judges took upon themselves to recognize as law what had not hitherto had that recognition. Practically, I doubt whether it will matter very much whether judges do or do not regard themselves as at liberty to 'invent' new heads of public policy. To some extent it is a question of words. Heads of this kind are inevitably a categorization after the event. The instances come first and the classification follows. I should think that there are by now enough instances covering a wide enough conspectus of human conduct to provide all the principles that may be needed to keep the doctrine in working order for those who may think it right to use it in the future.

In *Fender v St John Mildmay* [1938] AC 1 Lord Atkin said:

> In [*Janson v Driefontein*] Lord Halsbury indeed appeared to decide that the categories of public policy are closed, and that the principle could not be invoked anew unless the case could be brought within some principle of public policy already recognized by the law. I do not find, however, that this view received the express assent of the other members of the House; and it seems to me, with respect, too rigid. On the other hand, it fortifies the serious warning illustrated by the passages cited above that the doctrine should only be invoked in clear cases in which the harm to the public is substantially incontestable, and does not depend upon the idiosyncratic inferences of a few judicial minds. I think that this should be regarded as the true guide. In popular language, following the wise aphorism of Sir George Jessel [cited above p 60], the contract should be given the benefit of the doubt.

NOTE

The controversy about whether the heads of public policy are closed is, as Lord Radcliffe observes, rather strange. If judges change law at all it would seem that principles that directly and explicitly reflect current society values must be more and not less prone to change than ordinary rules, many of which are (relatively) value-free.

It is worth observing:

(1) Although there are many statements in the reports which echo Lord Halsbury, it is very difficult to find a case where a judge thought a transaction contrary to public policy but was deterred from so holding by the absence of an available head.

(2) It is clear that existing heads of public policy may be closed down as a result of changes in society values. Contrast *Cowan v Milbourn* (1867) LR 2 Exch 230 and *Bowman v Secular Society* [1917] AC 406.

(b) Policy issues

In a broad sense, to say that a contract is illegal indicates that the court disapproves of it. It is surprisingly difficult to offer a more sophisticated analysis because neither judges nor commentators have often gone further than this. One factor must be to discourage the making of such contracts. It would be fanciful to suppose that the Mafia boss and his contract killer will be influenced by the study of the law on illegal contracts, though there is a (perhaps apocryphal) eighteenth century *Highwayman's* case where the plaintiff sued his partner 'for an account of trading together on Newmarket Heath.' Both plaintiff and defendant were hanged! However there are cases where rational men who knew the law would be less likely to make a contract because they knew it would not be enforced. A good example is *Brown Jenkinson & Co Ltd v Percy Dalton (London) Ltd* (below, p 754).

Another factor is the desire to avoid besmirching the reputation of the court by appearing to involve it in unseemly transactions (see further below, p 770). So, although enforcement or non-enforcement is very unlikely to affect the volume of prostitution, it is rational to say that courts are not provided by taxpayers in order for prostitutes to sue their clients.

Where the contract is wholly executory the court will want to encourage the parties not to perform it. The policy consideration may be different where the contract has been partly performed and one party is seeking not to enforce it but to recover money or property which he has transferred (see below, p 766).

Then there is the question of whether a party who has contracted in excusable ignorance of the illegality should be affected. We shall see that in many if not most cases the courts have contrived to give innocent parties a remedy.

The object of the statute or other rule infringed should be considered. It may be designed to protect one of the parties, and here it may well be right to allow that party some remedy but not the other.

It has also been pointed out that the object of the statute should be looked at each time. For instance, quite a number of the cases involve regulations imposed in times of shortages of goods and labour; presumably where the resources will end up as a result of the decision should also be a factor. (See Treitel in *Crime, Proof and Punishment: Essays in Memory of Sir Rupert Cross* (1981), pp 93–104.)

Contracts involving the commission of a crime or a tort

As suggested earlier, contracts which somehow involve the commission of an unlawful act will be affected in different ways according to the circumstances and the unlawful act may have no effect at all on contractual liability. Many of the rules apply also to other contracts which are contrary to public policy.

(a) Contracts requiring the deliberate commission of a crime or a tort

Scott v Brown Doering McNab & Co [1892] 2 QB 724, Court of Appeal

The plaintiff agreed with the defendant stockbrokers that they would buy shares on the Stock Exchange with a view to inducing the public to believe that there was a real market in the shares. The plaintiff alleged that the defendants instead of buying shares had transferred their own shares to him and sought return of his money. The defendants alleged that the contract was illegal.

Lindley LJ. . . . [T]he correspondence put in evidence by the plaintiff in support of the claim he made at the trial shews conclusively that the sole object of the plaintiff in ordering shares to be bought for him at a premium was to impose upon and to deceive the public by leading the public to suppose that there were buyers of such shares at a premium on the Stock Exchange, when in fact there were none but himself. The plaintiff's purchase was an actual purchase, not a sham purchase; that is true, but it is also true that the sole object of the purchase was to cheat and mislead the public. Under these circumstances, the plaintiff must look elsewhere than to a court of justice for such assistance as he may require against the persons he employed to assist him in his fraud, if the claim to such assistance is based on his illegal contract. Any rights which he may have irrespective of his illegal contract will, of course, be recognised and enforced. But his illegal contract confers no rights on him: see *Pearce v Brooks*. The illegal purpose of the plaintiff distinguishes this case from *Wetherell v Jones*, and others of a similar kind. I am quite aware that what the plaintiff has done is very commonly done; it is done every day. But this is immaterial. Picking pockets and various forms of cheating are common enough, and are nevertheless illegal. The plaintiff was not entitled to judgment in the Court below, and he has no right to a new trial.

[Lopes and A L Smith LJJ delivered judgments to the same effect.]

NOTES

1. The conduct which the parties had agreed on here was directly contrary to public policy. If successful in inducing members of the public to buy shares for more than they were worth it would have been both a crime and a tort.

2. In *Brown Jenkinson & Co Ltd v Percy Dalton (London) Ltd* [1957] 2 QB 621 the defendants wished to ship orange juice to Hamburg. The plaintiffs as agents for the shipowners told the defendants that they would have to 'clause' the Bill of Lading (that is note on the Bill that the goods were not in good order and condition). It is inconvenient for shippers to have to deal with such claused Bills and the defendants asked the shipowners to issue a clean Bill, promising in return to indemnify them against the consequences. The shipowners issued a clean Bill, knowing that the goods were in fact in poor condition. On arrival in Hamburg the barrels of orange juice were leaking and the shipowners had to make good the loss. They sued on the indemnity but were met by the defence that the indemnity contract was illegal since it involved the issue of a Bill of Lading which the shipowners knew to be false with the intention that it be relied on and that this amounted to the tort of deceit. The Court of Appeal (Evershed MR dissenting) upheld this defence.

3. The effect in both *Scott v Brown Doering* and *Brown Jenkinson* was to deny the plaintiff any remedy on the contract, whether to enforce it or to recover money.

4. The parties' conduct in both cases was deliberate with full knowledge of the relevant facts. It is usually irrelevant that the parties did not know the law and therefore did not realise that what they were agreeing on was a crime or tort.

5. What if they did not know the facts that made the conduct wrongful? At common law there will normally be no criminal liability without mens rea but statutory offences may be committed without any criminal intent. The fact that a contract necessarily involves the unintentional commission of a crime does not always make it illegal, see next subsection. Equally some torts may be committed through deliberate actions but without knowing the facts that make the conduct tortious: eg a printer might agree to publish material which he did not know was defamatory. Such a case is also treated differently, see below, p 760.

6. All the cases of deliberate crimes seem to involve fairly serious crimes. It is not at all clear that an agreement which calls for the commission of some minor statutory crime (eg a contract to deliver goods by a certain time which the parties know can only be carried out by parking in a prohibited zone) would be affected at all by the illegality.

(b) Contracts involving other unlawful acts

(i) An outline of the rules

St John Shipping Corpn v Joseph Rank Ltd [1957] 1 QB 267, Devlin J

The defendants chartered the plaintiff's ship to carry grain from the USA to the UK. During the voyage the ship was overloaded in contravention of the Merchant Shipping (Safety and Load Line Conventions) Act 1932. On arrival in the UK the Master was convicted and fined the maximum fine of £1,200. The defendants paid part of the freight but withheld a sum equivalent to the extra freight earned by the overloading. They argued that the plaintiffs could not recover the freight as they had illegally performed the Charterparty.

Devlin J. . . . . It is a misfortune for the defendants that the legal weapon which they are wielding is so much more potent than it need be to achieve their purpose. Believing, rightly or wrongly, that the plaintiffs have deliberately committed a serious infraction of the Act and one which has placed their property in jeopardy, the defendants wish to do no more than to take the profit out of the plaintiff's dealing. But the principle which they invoke for this purpose cares not at all for the element of deliberation or for the gravity of the infraction, and does not adjust the penalty to the profits unjustifiably earned. The defendants cannot succeed unless they claim the right to retain the whole freight and to keep it whether the offence was accidental or deliberate, serious or trivial. The application of this principle to a case such as this is bound to lead to startling results. Mr Wilmers does not seek to avert his gaze from the wide consequences. A shipowner who accidentally overloads by a fraction of an inch will not be able to recover from any of the shippers or consignees a penny of the freight. . . . Carriers by land are in no better position; again Mr Wilmers does not shrink from saying that the owner of a lorry could not recover against the consignees the cost of goods transported in it if in the course of the journey it was driven a mile an hour over its permitted speed. If this is really the law, it is very unenterprising of cargo owners and consignees to wait until a criminal conviction has been secured before denying their liabilities. A service of trained observers on all our main roads would soon pay for itself. An effective patrol of the high seas would probably prove too expensive, but the maintenance of a corps of vigilantes in all principal ports would be well worth while when one considers that the smallest infringement of the statute or a regulation made thereunder would relieve all the cargo owners on the ship from all liability for freight.

Of course, as Mr Wilmers says, one must not be deterred from enunciating the correct principle of law because it may have startling or even calamitous results. But I confess I approach the investigation of a legal proposition which has results of this character with a prejudice in favour of the idea that there may be a flaw in the argument somewhere. . . .

. . . There are two general principles. The first is that a contract which is entered into with the object of committing an illegal act is unenforceable. The application of this principle depends upon proof of the intent, at the time the contract was made, to break the law; if the intent is mutual the contract is not enforceable at all, and, if unilateral, it is unenforceable at the suit of the party who is proved to have it. This principle is not involved here. Whether or not the overloading was deliberate when it was done, there is no proof that it was contemplated when the contract of carriage was made. The second principle is that the court will not enforce a contract which is expressly or impliedly prohibited by statute. If the contract is of this class it does not matter what the intent of the parties is; if the statute prohibits the contract, it is unenforceable whether the parties meant to break the law or not. A significant distinction between the two classes is this. In the former class you have only to look and see what acts the statute prohibits; it does not matter whether or not it prohibits a contract; if a contract is deliberately made to do a prohibited act, that contract will be unenforceable. In the latter class, you have to consider not what acts the statute prohibits, but what contracts it prohibits; but you are not concerned at all with the intent of the parties; if the parties enter into a prohibited contract, that contract is unenforceable. . . .

Two questions are involved. The first—and the one which hitherto has usually settled the matter—is: does the statute mean to prohibit contracts at all? But if this be answered in the affirmative, then one must ask: does this contract belong to the class which the statute intends to prohibit? For example, a person is forbidden by statute from using an unlicensed vehicle on the highway. If one asks oneself whether there is in such an enactment an implied prohibition of all contracts for the use of unlicensed vehicles, the answer may well be that there is, and that contracts of hire would be unenforceable. But if one asks oneself whether there is an implied prohibition of contracts for the carriage of goods by unlicensed vehicles or for the repairing of unlicensed vehicles or for the garaging of unlicensed vehicles, the answer may well be different. The answer might be that collateral contracts of this sort are not within the ambit of the statute.

On Mr Wilmers's third point I take the law from the dictum in *Beresford v Royal Insurance Co Ltd* [below, p 761] that was adopted and applied by Lord Atkin: 'no system of jurisprudence can with reason include amongst the rights which it enforces rights directly resulting to the person asserting them from the crime of that person.' I observe in the first place that in the Court of Appeal in the same case Lord Wright doubted whether this principle applied to all statutory offences. His doubt was referred to by Denning LJ in *Marles v Philip Trant & Sons*, . . . The distinction is much to the point here. The Act of 1932 imposes a penalty which is itself designed to deprive the offender of the benefits of his crime. It would be a curious thing if the operation could be performed twice—once by the criminal law and then again by the civil. It would be curious, too, if in a case in which the magistrates had thought fit to impose only a nominal fine, their decision could, in effect, be overridden in a civil action. But the question whether the rule applies to statutory offences is an important one which I do not wish to decide in the present case. The dicta of Lord Wright and Denning LJ suggest that there are cases where its application would be morally unjustifiable; but it is not clear that they go as far as saying that the application would not be justified in law. I prefer, therefore, to deal with Mr Wilmers's submission in another way.

The rights which cannot be enforced must be those 'directly resulting' from the crime. That means, I think, that for a right to money or to property to be unenforceable the property or money must be identifiable as something to which, but for the crime, the plaintiff would have had no right or title. That cannot be said in this case. The amount of the profit which the plaintiffs made from the crime, that is to say, the amount of freight which, but for the overloading, they could not have earned on this voyage, was, as I have said, £2,295. The quantity of cargo consigned to the defendants was approximately 35 per cent of the whole and, therefore, even if it were permissible to treat the benefit as being divisible pro rata over the whole of the cargo, the amount embodied in the claim against the defendants would not be more than 35 per cent of £2,300. That would not justify the withholding of £2,000. . .

The fact is that in this type of case no claim or part of a claim for freight can be clearly identified as being the excess illegally earned.

Judgment for the plaintiffs.

NOTE

Thus according to Devlin there seem to be three questions:
(i) did the illegal act mean that the contract was expressly or impliedly forbidden by statute?
(ii) did either party intend when the contract was made to perform it illegally?
(iii) is the plaintiff claiming some benefit which is the direct result of an illegal act on his part?
In fact we shall see that Devlin's analysis is incomplete. There are some cases in which a party who had made a perfectly legal contract, and who had no intention of performing it in an illegal manner, in fact did commit some illegal act in the course of performing it and is thereby disabled from enforcing the contract, although not falling within (iii). See below, p 760.

(ii) Is the contract expressly or impliedly forbidden by statute?

Re Mahmoud and Ispahani [1921] 2 KB 716, Court of Appeal

By delegated legislation licences were necessary for either the sale or purchase of linseed oil. The plaintiff sold linseed oil to the defendant. The plaintiff had a licence. Before entering into the contract he asked the defendant whether he had a licence and the defendant said he had. He had not. The defendant later refused to accept delivery and on being sued for damages for non-acceptance argued that the contract was illegal.

Atkin LJ. . . . It is admitted that the Order of the Food Controller, made under the Defence of the Realm Regulations, has the effect of a statute, and the contention is that by that Order the contract in this case was prohibited. When the Court has to deal with the question whether a particular contract or class of contract is prohibited by statute, it may find an express prohibition in the statute, or it may have to infer the prohibition from the fact that the statute imposes a penalty upon the person entering into that class of contract. In the latter case one has to examine very carefully the precise terms of the statute imposing the penalty upon the individual. One may find that the statute imposes a penalty upon an individual, and yet does not prohibit the contract if it is made with a party who is innocent of the offence which is created by the statute. I prefer not to deal with the question of contracts forbidden by the common law as being contrary to public policy, because, despite the great authority of Parke B, I think a question might be raised whether or not it is right to say that those contracts are prohibited by the common law. The right view may be that the common law refuses to enforce them. I think a different set of circumstances may arise in respect of such contracts as those, but here it appears to me to be plain that this particular contract was expressly prohibited by the terms of the Order which imposes the necessity of a compliance with the licence.

[Bankes and Scrutton LJJ delivered judgments to the same effect.]

Judgment for the defendant.

NOTES

1. What was the purpose behind the statute? How could the court best further that purpose?
2. What remedy was the plaintiff seeking? Do you think the court would have denied a remedy if he had delivered the oil and was now seeking to recover payment? Compare p 766 below.

Archbolds (Freightage) Ltd v S Spanglett Ltd [1961] 1 QB 374, Court of Appeal

The defendants owned a number of vans with C licences, entitling them to carry their own goods by road but not to carry the goods of others. They entered into a contract with the plaintiffs, who believed the defendants had A licences, which would have entitled them to carry other people's goods for reward, to carry whisky from London to Leeds. The whisky was stolen in transit owing to the negligence of the defendants' driver. On a claim for damages for loss of the whisky, the defendants pleaded that the contract was illegal.

Pearce LJ. . . . If a contract is expressly or by necessary implication forbidden by statute, or if it is ex facie illegal, or if both parties know that though ex facie legal it can only be performed by illegality or is intended to be performed illegally, the law will not help the plaintiffs in any way that is a direct or indirect enforcement of rights under the contract. And for this purpose both parties are presumed to know the law.

The first question, therefore, is whether this contract of carriage was forbidden by statute. The two cases on which the defendants mainly rely re *In re an Arbitration between Mahmoud and Ispahani* and *J Dennis & Co Ltd v Munn*. In both those cases the plaintiffs were unable to enforce their rights under contracts forbidden by statute. In the former case the statutory order said: 'a person shall not . . . buy or sell . . . [certain] articles . . . except under and in accordance with the terms of a licence.' In the latter case the statutory regulation provided: 'subject to the provisions of this regulation . . . the execution . . . of any operation specified . . . shall be unlawful except in so far as authorised.' In neither case could the plaintiff bring his contract within the exception that alone would have made its subject-matter lawful, namely, by showing the existence of a licence. Therefore, the core of both contracts was the mischief expressly forbidden by the statutory order and the statutory regulation respectively.

In *Mahmoud's* case the object of the order was to prevent (except under licence) a person buying and a person selling, and both parties were liable to penalties. A contract of sale between those persons was therefore expressly forbidden. In *Dennis's* case the object of the regulation was to prevent (except under licence) owners from performing building operations, and builders from carrying out the work for them. Both parties were liable to penalties and a contract between these persons for carrying out an unlawful operation would be forbidden by implication.

The case before us is somewhat different. The carriage of the plaintiffs' whisky was not as such prohibited; the statute merely regulated the means by which carriers should carry goods. Therefore this contract was not expressly forbidden by the statute.

Was it then forbidden by implication? The Road and Rail Traffic Act, 1933, section 1, says: 'no person shall use a goods vehicle on a road for the carriage of goods. . . except under licence', and provides that such use shall be an offence. Did the statute thereby intend to forbid by implication all contracts whose performance must on all the facts (whether known or not) result in a contravention of that section?

The object of the Road and Rail Traffic Act 1933, was not (in this connection) to interfere with the owner of goods or his facilities for transport, but to control those who provided the transport, with a view to promoting its efficiency. Transport of goods was not made illegal but the various licence holders were prohibited from encroaching on one another's territory, the intention of the Act being to provide an orderly and comprehensive service. Penalties were provided for those licence holders who went outside the bounds of their allotted spheres. These penalties apply to those using the vehicle but not to the goods owner. Though the latter could be convicted of aiding and abetting any breach, the restrictions were not aimed at him. Thus a contract of carriage was, in the sense used by Devlin J, 'collateral', and it was not impliedly forbidden by the statute.

This view is supported by common sense and convenience. If the other view were held it would have far-reaching effects. For instance, if a carrier induces me (who am in fact ignorant of any illegality) to entrust goods to him and negligently destroys them, he would only have to show that (though unknown to me) his licence had expired, or did not properly cover the transportation, or that he was uninsured, and I should then be without a remedy against him. Or, again, if I ride in a taxicab and the driver leaves me stranded in some deserted spot, he would only have to show that he was (though unknown to me) unlicensed or uninsured, and I should be without remedy. This appears to me to be an undesirable extension of the implications of a statute.

[Sellers and Devlin LJJ delivered concurring judgments.]

NOTES

1. What factors led the court to hold that the contract was not impliedly prohibited?
2. The result of the *Mahmoud* case was that neither party could enforce the contract. This is not convenient if the statute was intended to protect one of the parties, and in such a case the court will lean in favour of holding that, even if the statute makes it an offence for one party to make the contract, it does not impliedly forbid its performance, so that it can be enforced. Alternatively the court may construe the statute as not preventing the party for whose protection it was intended from enforcing the contract. Thus in *Nash v Halifax Building Society* [1979] 2 All ER 19 the Society was forbidden by s 32 of Building Societies Act 1962 from advancing money on a property subject to a prior mortgage to some other lender; but Browne-Wilkinson J held that this was intended to protect those people who were interested in the Society (whether members or outside creditors) and that the Society could therefore recover the money advanced and enforce its security.
3. Sometimes however the words of the statute are too clear for the court to be able to uphold the contract even though the outcome is unfair and inconvenient. For example, Insurance Companies Act 1974 ss 2 and 83(4) forbid the 'business of effecting and carrying out of contracts of insurance' without authorisation. In *Bedford Insurance Co Ltd v Instituto de Resseguros do Brasil* [1985] QB 966 Parker J held that this rendered insurances policies made without authorisation void. This was approved, obiter, by the Court of Appeal in *Phoenix General Insurance Co of Greece SA v Administratia Asigur arilo de Stat* [1987] 2 All ER 152. Kerr LJ said (at p 176):

The problem is therefore to determine whether or not the 1974 Act prohibits contracts of insurance by necessary implication, since it undoubtedly does not do so expressly. In that context it seems to me that the position can be summarised as follows.
   (i) Where a statute prohibits both parties from concluding or performing a contract when

both or either of them have no authority to do so, the contract is impliedly prohibited: see *Mahmoud and Ispahani*'s case and its analysis by Pearce LJ in the *Archbolds* case with which Devlin LJ agreed.

(ii) But where a statute merely prohibits one party from entering into a contract without authority and/or imposes a penalty on him if he does so (ie a unilateral prohibition) it does not follow that the contract itself is impliedly prohibited so as to render it illegal and void. Whether or not the statute has this effect depends on considerations of public policy in the light of the mischief which the statute is designed to prevent, its language, scope and purpose, the consequences for the innocent party, and any other relevant considerations. The statutes considered in *Cope v Rowlands* and *Cornelius v Phillips* fell on one side of the line; the Food Act 1984 would clearly fall on the other.

(iii) The Insurance Companies Act 1974 only imposes a unilateral prohibition on unauthorised insurers. If this were merely to prohibit them from carrying on 'the business of effecting contracts of insurance' of a class for which they have no authority, then it would clearly be open to the court to hold that considerations of public policy preclude the implication that such contracts are prohibited and void. But unfortunately the unilateral prohibition is not limited to the business of 'effecting contracts of insurance' but extends to the business of 'carrying out contracts of insurance'. This is a form of statutory prohibition, albeit only unilateral, which is not covered by any authority. However, in the same way as Parker J in the *Bedford* case, I can see no convincing escape from the conclusion that this extension of the prohibition has the unfortunate effect that contracts made without authorisation are prohibited by necessary implication and therefore void. Since the statute prohibits the insurer from carrying out the contract (of which the most obvious example is paying claims), how can the insured require the insurer to do an act which is expressly forbidden by statute? And how can a court enforce a contract against an unauthorised insurer when Parliament has expressly prohibited him from carrying it out? In that situation there is simply no room for the introduction of considerations of public policy. As Parker J said in the *Bedford* case:

'. . . once it is concluded that on its true construction the Act prohibited both contract and performance, that is the public policy'.

(iv) It follows that, however reluctantly, I feel bound to agree with the analysis of Parker J in the *Bedford* case and his conclusion that contracts of insurance made by unauthorised insurers are prohibited by the 1974 Act in the sense that they are illegal and void, and therefore unenforceable. In particular, I agree with the following passages which led him to this conclusion:

'The express prohibition is on the carrying on of insurance business of a relevant class, but, as I have already mentioned, the definition in the case of each class begins, "the effecting and carrying out of contracts of insurance". What therefore is prohibited is the carrying on of the business of effecting and performing contracts of insurance of various descriptions in the absence of an authorisation. It is thus both the contracts themselves and the performance of them at which the statute is directed.'

The result was later reversed by statute: Financial Services Act 1986 s 132.

4. There may be cases where, although the statute does not expressly or impliedly prohibit the making of the contract, a contract which necessarily involves the breach of the statute is invalid because it is a contract to commit a crime. So a contract to carry goods to a destination within a time limit which could be achieved only by breaking the speed limit might be illegal as being an inducement to commit a crime.

(iii) Contracts intended to be performed in an illegal way

In *Archbolds v Spanglett* (above, p 757) the plaintiffs were innocent because they did not know the defendants were not properly licensed. Suppose the goods had been delivered safely but the plaintiffs had refused to pay the carriage charges? Compare the *St John Shipping* case (above, p 754).

If the plaintiffs had known when they made the contract that the defendants would carry the goods in an unlicensed vehicle, would they have been able to recover the value of the stolen goods? If not, why not?

Both the *Archbold* and the *St John Shipping* cases involved statutory crimes, but the same rule appears to apply to torts. Thus in *Clay v Yates* (1856) 1 H&N 73 a printer who printed a book before discovering that the dedication to it was libellous. He refused to print the dedication but it was held that he could recover for the work done already (see Treitel, p 338).

The rule that a party who did not intend to perform a contract illegally can enforce it but one who did cannot applies also to some other heads of illegality (eg contracts which promote sexual immorality).

(iv) Contracts which are performed in an illegal manner

Alternatively one party may in the course of performing the contract infringe some statute. So a carrier may break the speed limit without having agreed in advance to do so. In practice illegal performance of this kind is likely to be much more common than prior agreement to perform illegally. This distinction is important for a number of reasons:

(a) Illegal performance alone should not affect the rights of the other party. So if in *Archbolds v Spanglett* all that happened was that the carrier chose to carry the goods in an unlicensed vehicle, that would be no defence to the goods owner's complaint that the carrier had negligently lost the goods.

(b) Illegal performance will not *necessarily* defeat the claim of the party who has performed illegally. This is the point of *St John Shipping Co v Rank* and of the next case.

Marles v Philip Trant & Sons Ltd [1954] 1 QB 29, Court of Appeal

The defendants, seed merchants, bought from a farmer, Mackinnon, wheat, described as spring wheat called Fylgia, and resold part of it to the plaintiffs under the same description. The wheat was not spring wheat and the plaintiffs successfully claimed damages from the defendants. The defendants sought to claim over against Mackinnon. He set up the defence that in delivering the wheat to the plaintiffs, the defendants had failed to supply the statement required by the Seeds Act 1920 and therefore their performance of that contract was illegal.

Denning LJ. The first question which arises in this case is: what is the legal effect of the omission to supply the particulars prescribed under the Seeds Act? The trial judge has held that it turned the contract with the farmer, so far as the seed merchant was concerned, into an illegal contract. The judge so held on the authority of *Anderson Ld v Daniel* and *B & B Viennese Fashions v Losane*, and there are indeed some observations in those cases which warrant him taking that view. But I do not think that they are correct. There can be no doubt that the contract between the seed merchants and the farmer was not unlawful when it was made. If the farmer had repudiated it before the time for delivery arrived, the seed merchants could certainly have sued him for damages. Nor was the contract rendered unlawful simply because the seed was delivered without the prescribed particulars. If it were unlawful, the farmer himself could not have sued upon it as he has done. The truth is that it was not the contract itself which was unlawful, but only the performance of it. The seed merchants performed it in an illegal way in that they omitted to furnish the prescribed particulars. That renders the contract unenforceable by them, but it does not render the contract illegal. Atkin LJ expressed the position with his usual accuracy in *Anderson Ltd v Daniel* when he said simply that the contract was unenforceable. I do not think that the law has ever countenanced the idea that a transaction, lawful when done, can be rendered unlawful by the doctrine of relation back: see *Elliott v Boynton*. . . .

Once rid of the notion that the contract with the farmer was itself illegal, the question becomes: what is the effect of the admitted illegality in performance? It certainly prevents the seed merchants from suing the farmer for the price, but does it prevent them suing their supplier for damages? I think not. There was nothing unlawful in the contract between the seed merchants and their supplier, neither in the formation of it, nor in the performance of it. The seed merchants must therefore be entitled to damages for the breach of it. So far so good, but the difficulty comes when they seek to prove their damages. They want to be indemnified for the damages which they have been ordered to pay to the farmer. To prove those damages, they have to prove the contract with the farmer, and the circumstances under which the damages were awarded. It is said that once they begin to rely on their deliveries to the farmer, they seek aid from their own illegality; and that that is a thing which they are not allowed to do. The maxim is invoked: Ex turpi causa non oritur actio. That maxim must not, however, be carried too far . . . they are entitled to recover. . . .

[Singleton LJ delivered a concurring judgment. Hodson LJ dissented.]

Appeal allowed.

NOTES

1. Was the contract between the seed merchants and the plaintiffs in this case expressly or impliedly forbidden when it was made?
2. Did the seed merchants intend to perform the contract with the plaintiffs in an illegal manner?
3. Note that Denning says that the seed merchants could not have enforced the contract against the plaintiffs because of the illegal act they had committed in performing it. However, they were still able to enforce their contract against the farmer: this was not 'tainted' by the illegality.

There are other suggestions that a party who did not know at the time the contract was made that it was to be performed in an illegal way may be debarred from a remedy if he 'participated' in the illegal act. In *Ashmore Benson Pease & Co Ltd v A V Dawson Ltd* [1973] 2 All ER 856, the plaintiffs made a contract with the defendant, a small haulage company, to carry two 25-ton tube banks to a port for shipment at £55 a trip. The defendants sent articulated lorries to collect the load. These could not legally be used to carry it. The plaintiffs' transport manager and assistant watched the lorries being loaded. One of the lorries toppled during the journey and the load was damaged. There was evidence that the transport manager knew that it was illegal to carry that load on that vehicle. The Court of Appeal held that the plaintiffs' action for damages to the tube bank failed as they had 'participated' in the illegal performance. Obviously the contract's illegal performance disabled the defendant from enforcing it but what might it mean that the plaintiffs 'participated' in the illegal performance? But probably in this case the parties actually intended an illegal method of performance at the outset.

(c) Benefits from deliberate illegal acts

Beresford v Royal Insurance Co Ltd [1938] AC 586, House of Lords

Major Rowlandson had made a contract of life insurance with the defendants. On its true construction the policy covered death brought about by suicide provided it took place more than two years after the policy. Major Rowlandson committed suicide more than two years after taking out the policy. His executors brought an action on the policy.

Lord Atkin. . . . My Lords, I entertain no doubt that on the true construction of this contract the insurance company have agreed with the assured to pay to his executors or assigns on his death the sum assured if he dies by his own hand whether sane or insane after the expiration of one year from the commencement of the assurance. The express protection limited to one year, and the clause as to the policy being indisputable subject to that limited exception seem to make this conclusion inevitable. The respondents' counsel appeared shocked that it should be considered that a reputable company could have intended to make such a contract: but the meaning is clear: and one may assume from what one knows of tariff conditions that it is a usual clause. There is no doubt therefore that on the proper construction of this contract the insurance company promised Major Rowlandson that if he in full possession of his senses intentionally killed himself they would pay his executors or assigns the sum assured.

. . . I think that the principle is that a man is not to be allowed to have recourse to a Court of Justice to claim a benefit from his crime whether under a contract or a gift. No doubt the rule pays regard to the fact that to hold otherwise would in some cases offer an inducement to crime or remove a restraint to crime, and that its effect is to act as a deterrent to crime. But apart from these considerations the absolute rule is that the Courts will not recognize a benefit accruing to a criminal from his crime.

The application of this principle to the present case is not difficult. Deliberate suicide, felo de se, is and always has been regarded in English law as a crime, though by the very nature of it the offender escapes personal punishment. . . . The remaining question is whether the principle applies where the criminal is dead and his personal representative is seeking to recover a benefit which only takes shape after his death. It must be remembered that the money becomes due, if at all, under an agreement made by the deceased during his life for the express purpose of benefiting his estate after his death. During his life he had power of complete testamentary disposition over it. I cannot think the principle of public policy to be so narrow as not to include the increase of the criminal's estate amongst the benefits which he is deprived of by his crime. His executor or administrator claims as his representative, and, as his representative, falls under the same ban.

Anxiety is naturally aroused by the thought that this principle may be invoked so as to destroy the security given to lenders and others by policies of life insurance which are in daily use for that purpose. The question does not directly arise, and I do not think that anything said in this case can be authoritative. But I consider myself free to say that I cannot see that there is any objection to an assignee for value before the suicide enforcing a policy which contains an express promise to pay upon sane suicide, at any rate so far as the payment is to extend to the actual interest of the assignee. It is plain that a lender may himself insure the life of the borrower against sane suicide; and the assignee of the policy is in a similar position so far as public policy is concerned.

. . . It was suggested to us that so far as the doctrine was applied to contracts it would have the effect of making the whole contract illegal. I think that the simple answer is that this is a contract to pay on an event which may happen from many causes, one only of which involves a crime by the assured. The cause is severable and the contract, apart from the criminal cause, is perfectly valid.

[Lord Macmillan delivered a judgment to the same effect and Lords Thankerton and Russell concurred.]

NOTES

1. The rules about illegal performance overlap with but are distinct from the general doctrine that a person should not benefit from his own crime. So Major Rowlandson in *Beresford v Royal Insurance* did not perform the contract of life insurance illegally by committing suicide but he did fall foul of the benefit of a crime rule because suicide was then a crime.
2. The possibility that an initially valid contract of insurance may not be enforceable against the insurance company presents particular problems where the policy is one of liability insurance as the next three cases show.

In *Tinline v White Cross Insurance Association Ltd* [1921] 3 KB 327, the insured took out a third party liability policy in respect of his motor car. While driving the car too fast he knocked down three people, injuring two and killing one, and was convicted of manslaughter. He was sued for damages and sought a declaration that he was entitled to be indemnified by the defendants. Bailhache J held that it was not against public policy to allow recovery on such facts. He pointed out that virtually all motor accidents involving negligence must involve some breach of the criminal law by the negligent driver so that to hold that any crime prevented the insured claiming on the policy would have made the policy nugatory. (Note that third party insurance was not yet mandatory at the date of this case.)

Hardy v Motor Insurers' Bureau [1964] 2 QB 745, Court of Appeal

The plaintiff, a security officer at a large metal works, sought to stop the driver of a van bearing a stolen road fund licence. While the plaintiff was holding on to the van the driver drove off at speed and the plaintiff was seriously injured. The plaintiff brought an action for personal injuries. The driver was not insured but, under an agreement with the Minister of Transport, the MIB indemnifies the victims of uninsured drivers in all cases where the insurance company of an insured driver would be obliged to do so. The MIB argued that a contract to indemnify a driver against the consequences of criminal driving was contrary to public policy.

Lord Denning MR. . . . The policy of insurance which a motorist is required by statute to take out must cover any liability which may be incurred by him arising out of the use of the vehicle by him. It must, I think, be wide enough to cover, in general terms, any use by him of the vehicle, be it an innocent use or a criminal use, or be it a murderous use or a playful use. A policy so taken out by him is good altogether according to its terms. Of course, if the motorist intended from the beginning to make a criminal use of the vehicle—intended to run down people with it or to drive it recklessly and dangerously—and the insurers knew that that was his intention, the policy would be bad in its inception. No one can stipulate for iniquity. But that is never the intention with which such a policy is taken out. At any rate no insurer is ever party to it. So the policy is good in its inception. The question only arises when the motorist afterwards makes a criminal use of the vehicle. The consequences are then these: if the motorist is guilty of a crime involving a wicked and deliberate intent, and he is made to pay damages to an injured person, he is not himself entitled to recover on the policy. But if he does not pay the damages, then the injured third party can recover against the insurers under section 207 of the Road Traffic Act, 1960; for it is a liability which the motorist, under the statute, was required to cover. The injured third party is not affected by the disability which attached to the motorist himself.

So here the liability of Phillips to Hardy was a liability which Phillips was required to cover by a policy of insurance, even though it arose out of his wilful and culpable criminal act. If Phillips had been insured, he himself would be disabled from recovering from the insurers. But the injured third party would not be disabled from recovering from them. Seeing that he was not insured, the Motor Insurers' Bureau must treat the case as if he were. They must pay the injured third party, even though Phillips was guilty of felony. I would therefore dismiss the appeal.

[Pearson and Diplock LJJ delivered concurring judgments.]

Gray v Barr [1971] 2 QB 554, Court of Appeal

The defendant went with a loaded shotgun to the farm of the plaintiff's husband to look for his wife, who had been having an affair with Mr Gray. Mrs Barr was not there but the defendant did not accept Mr Gray's statement to this effect and in a scuffle the shotgun went off and Mr Gray was killed. Mr Barr was subsequently acquitted by a jury of manslaughter. Mrs Gray brought an action under the Fatal Accident Acts and Mr Barr claimed an indemnity from his insurers who argued, inter alia, that recovery would be against public policy.

Geoffrey Lane J held that Mr Barr's claim was barred by public policy. Mr Barr appealed.

Salmon LJ. . . . It is well settled that if a man commits murder or committed felo de se in the days when suicide was still a crime, neither he nor his personal representatives could be entitled to reap any financial benefit from such an act: *In the Estate of Crippen: Beresford v Royal Insurance Co Ltd.* This was because the law recognised that, in the public interest, such acts should be deterred and moreover that it would shock the public conscience if a man could use the courts to enforce a money claim either under a contract or a will by reason of his having committed such acts.

Crimes of violence, particularly when committed with loaded guns, are amongst the worst curses of this age. It is very much in the public interest that they should be deterred. A man, covered by a 'hearth and home' policy such as the present, walks into a bank with a loaded gun. He intends only to frighten and not to shoot the cashier. He slips and accidentally shoots a customer standing by the counter. It would be strange indeed if he could enforce the policy in respect of his liability to that customer. Once you threaten violence with a loaded gun and it goes off it is so easy to plead accident. Evidently it is very difficult for the prosecution to prove the contrary. Although public policy is rightly regarded as an unruly steed which should be cautiously ridden, I am confident that public policy undoubtedly requires that no one who threatens unlawful violence with a loaded gun should be allowed to enforce a claim for indemnity against any liability he may incur as a result of having so acted. I do not intend to lay down any wider proposition. In particular, I am not deciding that a man who has committed manslaughter would, in any circumstances, be prevented from enforcing a contract of indemnity in respect of any liability he may have incurred for causing death or from inheriting under a will or upon the intestacy of anyone whom he has killed. Manslaughter is a crime which varies infinitely in its seriousness.

The cases of *Tinline* [above] and *James* in which it was held that persons convicted of manslaughter for reckless and drunken driving could nevertheless recover indemnity from their insurers, were doubted in *Haseldine v Hosken* but approved by this court in *Marles v Philip Trant & Sons Ltd.* It seems now to be settled law that a motorist can rely on his policy of insurance to indemnify him in respect of his liability for any injuries which he has caused otherwise than on purpose: *Hardy v Motor Insurers' Bureau.* These road traffic cases may be sui generis. In any event, although motor cars have sometimes been called lethal weapons, these cases are not in my view akin to the cases in which injuries are caused in the course of unlawfully threatening a man with a loaded gun. Public policy is not static. Even if the crime of suicide had not been abolished by statute, it may be that today *Beresford's* case would have been differently decided. In any event, threatening violence with a loaded gun would, I am sure, now be generally regarded as much more shocking and necessary to be deterred than what the unfortunate Major Rowlandson did in *Beresford's* case. I am confident that, in any civilised society, public policy requires that anyone who inflicts injuries in the course of such an act shall not be allowed to use the courts of justice for the purpose of enforcing any contract of indemnity in respect of his liability in damages for causing injury by accident.

[Lord Denning MR and Phillimore LJ delivered judgments to the same effect.]

Appeal dismissed.

'Unblinkering the Unruly Horse', by Shand [1972A] CLJ 144, 164

Let us take *Gray v Barr*. Applying the Diplock test, the gravity of Mr Barr's anti-social act was certainly considerable; but there the weighing of the insurers' side of the scales ends. The encouragement of similar anti-social acts, despite the frequent references to deterrence, would in reality be non-existent. Nor would considerations of punishing Mr Barr or abating public outrage be relevant, for in all probability it would not be he who would benefit from the indemnity, but the plaintiffs. On the other side of the scale, the social harm which would be caused by refusal of indemnity, both in the specific case and generally, would be enormous; for not only would the innocent dependants of the deceased be deprived of redress, but the business efficacy of indemnity insurance in cases of this kind, would be undermined. Having received Mr Barr's premiums over the years, all that remained to the insurers was to cover the loss arising from the accident. It is submitted with some confidence that if such broader considerations of public policy were admitted, the result in *Gray v Barr* would be reversed.

NOTE

Do you agree with this criticism?

(d) Summary

To summarise:

(1) Contracts to commit serious crimes or torts deliberately are unenforceable by either party.

(2) Contracts which can only be performed by some other unlawful act, or in the course of performing which some unlawful act is committed, may be expressly or impliedly forbidden by statute.

(3) In other cases, parties who intended to perform in an illegal way when the contract was made will be unable to enforce it.

(4) Parties who commit illegal acts in the course of performance are sometimes disabled from enforcing the contract, but more usually the court takes the view that this would not further the aim of the statute (as in the *St John Shipping* case).

(5) Parties may be unable to claim benefits under the contract if their entitlement is the direct result of their own illegal act.

(6) A party who acted 'innocently', not intending to perform in an illegal way, will often be able to enforce the contract as usual.

What of parties who are innocent but fall within case (2)? See the next section.

(e) Collateral contracts

Strongman (1945) Ltd v Sincock [1955] 2 QB 525, Court of Appeal

Denning LJ. The plaintiffs, Strongman (1945) Ltd, are builders in the county of Cornwall. Two practical men, Mr George and Mr Williams Nicholls, are directors of the company. The defendant, Mr Sincock, is an architect. The builders claim against the architect for building work which they have done for him. The architect admits that the work was done, but he says that the plaintiffs are not entitled to be paid because it was all done illegally.

The architect has no merits at all. In addition to being an architect he was the owner of some buildings in Cornwall, and he employed the builders to convert these buildings into modern dwellings. One was at Penpol, and the other at Greatwood, Mylor. The work done was of the value of £6,359. Licences were obtained for only £2,150. The architect says that the builders cannot recover anything above the licensed figure because it was unlawful. It comes ill from him to say this, when on his own admission he sold these converted dwellings altogether for a sum of £10,650. He said in evidence: 'If I paid the plaintiffs for the work they have done, I should have been left with a very handsome profit.' Not only does he wish to keep that profit, but he also wishes to avoid payment of some £4,000 to the plaintiffs on the ground that it was an unlawful contract. But if the defence is good in law, effect must be given to it.

Let me say first that the builders cannot sue here on the contract to do the work, which was done in 1948 and 1949. At that time it was unlawful under Defence Regulation 56A for the work to be done without a proper licence. Licences were only in force to the amount of £2,150. When work was done to the value of over £6,000 the builders and the architect were all guilty of an offence for which they might have been prosecuted. Under many decisions in this court it has been held that a builder doing work without a licence cannot recover under the contract.

The builders seek to overcome this objection by saying that there was a warranty, or (putting it more accurately) a promise by the architect that he would get supplementary licences, or that if he failed to get them he would stop the work. The builders say that on the faith of that promise they did the work, and as the promise was broken they can recover damages in respect of it. . . .

The second question is whether the builders can recover in law on this collateral promise. The promise itself was not illegal, but it is said that damages cannot be recovered for the breach of it. It is said that, if damages could be recovered, it would be an easy way of getting round the law about illegality. This does not alarm me at all. It is, of course, a settled principle that a man cannot recover for the consequences of his own unlawful act, but this has always been confined to cases where the doer of the act knows it to be unlawful or is himself in some way morally culpable. . . . I think the law is that, although a man may have been guilty of an offence which is absolutely prohibited so that he is answerable in a criminal court, nevertheless if he has been led to commit that offence by the representation or by the promise of another, then in those circumstances he can recover damages for fraud if there is fraud, or for breach of promise or warranty if he prove such to have been given, provided always that he himself has not been guilty of culpable negligence on his part disabling him from that remedy.

Mr Dingle Foot referred us to the observations of this court in *In Re Mahmoud & Ispahani*. On a consideration of that case it seems to me that the court only decided that no action lay upon the contract for the purchase of goods. They did not decide whether there was an action for fraud or breach of promise or warranty: and I do not think that their observations were intended to express any view on the matter.

[Birkett and Romer LJJ agreed.]

NOTES

1. This was a case of statutory illegality to which the principle of 'innocence' apparently does not apply (above, p 755).
2. Do you think this case is distinguishable from *Re Mahmoud and Ispahani* (above, p 756)?
3. Once the work had been done, was anything to be gained by refusing to allow the builder to recover?
4. What was the consideration for the architect's promise?
5. See Wedderburn, 'Collateral Contracts' [1959] CLJ 58 at 73–4.

(f) Recovery of payments or property

The starting point for what follows is that even if neither of the parties can enforce an illegal contract, the contract is not totally ineffective. For instance, property may pass under it from one party to the other just as if it were not illegal, and the seller cannot simply take the goods back. In *Singh v Ali* [1960] AC 167, under regulations made in Malaya in 1945 permits were necessary for the use of motor vehicles for the carriage of goods. Government policy was to restrict the issue of permits to those who had had them before the war. The plaintiff who had not had a permit before the war bought a lorry from the defendant who had. The plaintiff paid for the lorry, took possession of it and operated it for the carriage of goods but under a licence which had been issued to the defendant. If the authorities had been told of this arrangement they would not have issued a permit in relation to the lorry.

In 1956 the defendant removed the lorry from the plaintiff's premises without his consent and refused to return it. The plaintiff sued for its return or its value. The Privy Council held that he was entitled to succeed. The transaction between plaintiff and defendant had been fully carried out and was effective to transfer ownership to the plaintiff. In this case the plaintiff had a claim independent of any question of ownership since he was in possession of the lorry at the time that the defendant wrongfully seized it. If this were not so the lorry could have been seized not only by the defendant but by anyone else in the world. The problem is clearly more difficult if the plaintiff has never been in possession and relies on ownership only.

It does not follow that the buyer would be able to recover the goods from the seller just because the property had passed to the buyer: that would be tantamount to enforcing the contract of sale. But it has been held that the buyer of goods under an illegal contract of sale has the right to sue a third party who wrongfully interferes with the goods (eg by converting them), even though the buyer never had possession of them because they were delivered straight to the third party: *Belvoir Finance Co Ltd v Stapleton* [1971] 1 QB 210. It was reasoned that if the buyer had no action, no one else could sue the third party.

Thus a party who has transferred property under an illegal contract cannot simply get it back. The same applies to money which has been paid over; it now belongs to the other party. No action will be given on the contract, and usually no action in restitution will be allowed either. As it is often put, 'in pari delicto potior est conditio defendentis'—'when the parties are equally guilty, the defendant is in the stronger position'.

However, the parties may not be equally guilty. Firstly, of course, an innocent party may be able to enforce the contract anyway (see above, p 765); but aside from this, the courts also recognise that a party who is technically guilty should sometimes be allowed to recover from the other party. The next two subsections consider these cases.

(i) Weaker parties

Kiriri Cotton Co Ltd v Dewani [1960] AC 192, Privy Council

The appellant company let a flat in Kampala, Uganda to the respondent for a term of seven years and one day and received from him a premium of Shs 10,000. To take premiums was contrary to the terms of the Uganda Rent Restriction Ordinance though neither party thought they were doing anything illegal. The Ordinance made no provision for the recovery of illegal premiums (unlike the corresponding English legislation). The respondent having gone into occupation brought an action to recover the premium. The High Court of Uganda gave judgment for the respondent.

The Court of Appeal for Eastern Africa affirmed the decision. The appellant appealed to Her Majesty in Council.

Lord Denning . . . Their Lordships desire to point out at once that neither party thought they were doing anything illegal. The lease was for more than seven years and it was thought that, on a lease for that length of time, there was nothing wrong in asking for a premium or receiving it.

This was an easy mistake to make . . .

Nevertheless, no matter whether the mistake was excusable or inexcusable, or the premium fair or extortionate, the fact remains that the landlord received a premium contrary to the provisions of the Ordinance: and the question is whether the tenant can recover it back—remembering always that there is nothing in the Uganda Ordinance, comparable to the English Acts, enabling a premium to be recovered back. . . .

It is clear that in the present case the illegal transaction was fully executed and carried out. The money was paid. The lease was granted. It was and still is vested in the plaintiff. In order to recover the premium, therefore, the plaintiff must show that he was not in pari delicto with the defendant. That was, indeed, the way he put his claim in the pleadings. . . .

The issue thus becomes: Was the plaintiff in pari delicto with the defendant? Mr Elwyn Jones, for the appellant, said they were both in pari delicto. The payment was, he said, made voluntarily, under no mistake of fact, and without any extortion, oppression or imposition, and could not be recovered back. True, it was paid under a mistake of law, but that was a mistake common to them both. They were both equally supposed to know the law. They both equally mistook it and were thus in pari delicto. In support of this argument the appellant referred to such well-known cases as *Harse v Pearl Life Assurance Co; William Whiteley Ltd v The King; Evanson v Crooks;* and particularly to *Sharp Brothers & Knight v Chant.*

Their Lordships cannot accept this argument. It is not correct to say that everyone is presumed to know the law. The true proposition is that no man can excuse himself from doing his duty by saying that he did not know the law on the matter. Ignorantia juris neminem excusat. Nor is it correct to say that money paid under a mistake of law can never be recovered back. The true proposition is that money paid under a mistake of law, by itself and without more, cannot be recovered back. James LJ pointed that out in *Rogers v Ingham.* If there is something more in addition to a mistake of law—if there is something in the defendant's conduct which shows that, of the two of them, he is the one primarily responsible for the mistake—then it may be recovered back. Thus, if as between the two of them the duty of observing the law is placed on the shoulders of the one rather than the other—it being imposed on him specially for the protection of the other—then they are not in pari delicto and the money can be recovered back: see *Browning v Morris*, by Lord Mansfield. Likewise, if the responsibility for the mistake lies more on the one than the other—because he has misled the other when he ought to know better—then again they are not in pari delicto and the money can be recovered back; see *Harse v Pearl Life Assurance Co*, by Romer LJ. . . .

Appeal dismissed.

(ii) The locus poenitentiae

Even where the parties are in pari delicto a plaintiff may succeed in recovering his property if he 'repents' before things have gone too far. How far is too far? In *Taylor v Bowers* (1876) 1 QBD 291 Mellish J said:

> If money is paid or goods delivered for an illegal purpose, the person who had so paid the money or delivered the goods may recover them back before the illegal purpose is carried out; but if he waits till the illegal purpose is carried out, or if he seeks to enforce the illegal transaction, in neither case can he maintain an action; the law will not allow that to be done.

Kearley v Thomson (1890) 24 QBD 742, Court of Appeal

Fry LJ. . . . The facts are shortly these:—A petition in bankruptcy was presented by one Baynes against Clarke, and a receiving order was made. The defendants were the solicitors acting for the petitioning creditor. That being the condition of things, the plaintiff, who appears to have been a friend of Clarke, intervened, and on October 6, 1887, Messrs Thomson & Ward, the defendants wrote this letter to the plaintiff Kearley:—'Re Clarke. At the request of Mr Kearley we have received from him the sum of 20*l* on account of our costs herein, and he is to pay us before twelve tomorrow a further sum of 20*l*; and in consideration of this sum of 40*l* we waive all our claim for costs, and undertake not to appear at the bankrupt's public examination, nor to oppose his order of discharge.' That was signed by the defendants. On the following day, it appears that the second sum of 20*l* was paid, and a receipt was given by the defendants in these terms:—'7th October, 1887. Re Clarke. Received of Mr Kearley the further sum of 20*l*, mentioned in our receipt of yesterday.' On the same October 7 the public examination of the bankrupt took place, and, in accordance with the stipulation in the letter of the 6th, at that public examination the defendants did not appear.

The tendency of such a bargain as that entered into between the plaintiff and the defendants is obviously to pervert the course of justice. Although the defendants were under no obligation to appear, they certainly were under an obligation not to contract themselves out of the opportunity of appearing. . . .

As a general rule, where the plaintiff cannot get at the money which he seeks to recover without shewing the illegal contract, he cannot succeed. In such a case the usual rule is potior est conditio possidentis. There is another general rule which may be thus stated, that where there is a voluntary payment of money it cannot be recovered back. It follows in the present case that the plaintiff who paid the 40*l* cannot recover it back without shewing the contract upon which it was paid, and when he shews that he shews an illegal contract. The general rule applicable to such a case is laid down in the very elaborate judgment in *Collins v Blantern* . . . To that general rule there are undoubtedly several exceptions, or apparent exceptions. One of these is the case of oppressor and oppressed, in which case usually the oppressed party may recover the money back from the oppressor. In that class of cases the delictum is not par, and therefore the maxim does not apply. Again, there are other illegalities which arise where a statute has been intended to protect a class of persons, and the person seeking to recover is a member of the protected class. Instances of that description are familiar in the case of contracts void for usury under the old statutes, and other instances are to be found in the books under other statutes, which are, I believe, now repealed, such as those directed against lottery keepers. In these cases of oppressor and oppressed, or of a class protected by statute, the one may recover from the other, notwithstanding that both have been parties to the illegal contract.

There is suggested to us a third exception, which is relied on in the present case, and the authority for which is to be found in the judgment of the Court of Appeal in the case of *Taylor v Bowers*. In that case Mellish, LJ, in delivering judgment, says at p 300: 'If money is paid, or goods delivered for an illegal purpose, the person who has so paid the money or delivered the goods may recover them back before the illegal purpose is carried out.' It is remarkable that this proposition is, as I believe, to be found in no earlier case than *Taylor v Bowers*, which occurred in 1867, and, notwithstanding the very high authority of the learned judge who expressed the law in the terms which I have read. I cannot help saying for myself that I think the extent of the application of that principle, and even the principle itself, may, at some time hereafter, require consideration, if not in this Court, yet in a higher tribunal: and I am glad to find that in expressing that view I have the entire concurrence of the Lord Chief Justice. But even assuming the exceptions to exist, does it apply to the present case? What is the condition of things if the illegal purpose has been carried into effect in a material part, but remains unperformed in another material part? As I have already pointed out in the present case, the contract was that the defendants should not appear at the public examination of the bankrupt or at the application for an order of discharge. It was performed as regards the first; but the other application has not yet been made. Can it be contended that, if the illegal contract has been partly carried into effect and partly remains unperformed, the money can still be recovered? In my judgment it cannot be so contended with success. Let me put an illustration of the doctrine contended for, which was that partial performance did not prevent the recovery of the money. Suppose a payment of 100*l* by A to B on a contract that the latter shall murder C and D. He has murdered C, but not D. Can the money be recovered back? In my opinion it cannot be. I think that case illustrates and determines the present one.

I hold, therefore, that where there has been a partial carrying into effect of an illegal purpose in a substantial manner, it is impossible, though there remains something not performed, that the money paid under that illegal contract can be recovered back.
[Lord Coleridge CJ agreed.]

In *Alexander v Rayson* [1936] 1 KB 169 the defendant agreed to let a flat in Piccadilly from the plaintiff for a rent of £1,200 a year. The contract was embodied in two documents; one a lease with some services for £450 a year and the other an agreement to provide services for £750 a year. The services in the second agreement were much the same as in the first with the addition of the provision of a fridge. The plaintiff intended to show only the first document to the rating authorities in the hope of getting the rateable value of the premises reduced. This scheme was unsuccessful as the fraud was detected. The contract was held illegal as intending to defraud the Revenue (this is not without difficulties; see 16 U of Toronto LJ at 286–8). The Court of Appeal further held that once the plaintiff's illegal purpose had been revealed and frustrated it was too late for him to repent.

'In Pari Delicto' by Grodecki (1955) 71 LQR 254, 265–270

1. *The dignity of the court*

In many judgments there is present a feeling that the court must not be humiliated by an enquiry into base and shameful bargains. Such feeling is amply warranted if these involve gross moral turpitude. But, as Story has pointed out, 'there may be, on the part of the court itself, a necessity of supporting the public interests or public policy, in many cases, however reprehensible the acts of the parties may be.' This explanation alone cannot justify the maxim *in pari delicto*. The oft-stated proposition that the courts 'will not assist an illegal transaction in any respect' is far from self-evident if what is sought is not enforcement of an illegal contract but quasi-contractual recovery of money paid or property delivered under it. . . .

2. *Morality*

The maxim is sometimes regarded as expressing a moral principle; and the plaintiff deprived of his remedy because he is a willing party to a bargain involving moral turpitude. The dictates of an objective moral order prevent the court from entertaining his claim. In other words, he is unworthy of help. . . .

It would seem that the morality embodied in the maxim *in pari delicto*, as applied by the courts, is of a dubious kind. This may be shown in several ways. Relief is denied to a claimant who is unaware of the illegality of the transactions to which he is a party and who is thus morally innocent. On the other hand, the maxim directly benefits the defendant who, as often as not, is more guilty and the initiator of the scheme. It protects his possession of money, goods or land to which, apart from the unlawful and void contract, he has no right whatsoever. It thus allows him to reap the fruits of his own turpitude whilst the punishment of the plaintiff is often out of all proportion to his wrong. Furthermore, if the maxim were truly based on a moral principle, one would expect less attention paid to the accident of one party being the plaintiff and the other defendant. Instead, details of procedure obscure ethical considerations. In all these cases, if realities are faced, it is the defendant who resorts to the illegality to secure for himself an unjust benefit rather than the plaintiff who merely claims his own property. Again, the 'moral' approach would lead the court to distinguish between the party who intends to make a gain out of the illegality and the party who is merely concerned to avoid a loss. This, however, is not the case. . . . The court, therefore, does not inquire into the morality of the parties' conduct since the *delictum*. Finally, if accurate apportionment of blame between the parties were possible it would be called for on moral grounds. In fact, the plaintiff is penalised without any investigation into real culpability.

The maxim *in pari delicto* cannot thus be explained and justified by reference to ethics. It is, indeed, amoral. . . . From a moral point of view the best solution might well be confiscation of the money paid or property delivered under an unlawful contract. St Thomas Aquinas advocated this solution: 'the giver deserves to lose what he gave, wherefore restitution should not be made to him; and, since the receiver acted against the law in receiving, he must not retain the price but must use it for some pious object.' . . .

3. *Public policy*
The third reason sometimes given to explain the application of the maxim is respect for public policy. The following passage from Lord Mansfield's judgment in *Holman v Johnson* may be regarded as the *locus classicus*: 'The objection that a contract is immoral or illegal as between plaintiff and defendant sounds at all times ill in the mouth of the defendant. It is not for his sake, however, that the objection is ever allowed; but it is founded in general principles of policy, which the defendant has the advantage of, contrary to the real justice, as between him and the plaintiff, by accident, if I may so say.'

The doctrine of public policy is invoked in support of the maxim in many cases. Why precisely the public interest is thereby promoted is, however, seldom explained. It may only be assumed that what the courts have in mind is, apart from the punitive, the deterrent and preventive effect of the maxim. Refusal of action leaves the parties at the discretion of one another, with sole reliance upon personal honour. Unlawful transactions become risky and precarious and are thus discouraged. This is by far the most pertinent argument in favour of the maxim *in pari delicto*. The plaintiff's claims are sacrificed in the general interest, but as he is *ex hypothesi* a delinquent the court is not under any obligation to redress his grievance.

Unfortunately, however, just as it came to be assumed that the grant of recovery must be immoral, so it came to be overlooked that in some cases it might have a stronger deterrent effect than its denial. The maxim is directed against the plaintiff, restitution against the defendant. A system under which, in the court's discretion, recovery may be given or refused, whichever happens to further the ends of the law most effectively, would seem to have the best of both worlds. The illegal agreements are rendered even more precarious and the parties still remain at each other's mercy. The hope that the court may exercise its discretion in his favour will often induce the plaintiff to abandon the unlawful bargain before it is fully performed. Moreover, the person to whom money is paid or property delivered is never secure in his possession of them. The merits of restitution as a weapon of social policy are particularly obvious where, as in cases of marriage brokage and evasion of currency regulations, the defendant is conducting an organised unlawful business. It is essential that he, in particular, should be discouraged. His enterprise constitutes a serious social menace and he will always be cunning enough to entice new clients. The value of restitution as a deterrent is recognised by the Rent Restriction Acts in allowing a tenant to recover illegal premiums paid to the landlord . . .

. . . [M]orality and public interest dictated the application of the maxim *in pari delicto*. The truth of this assumption was never questioned.

(iii) Proprietary claims

It is sometimes said that a plaintiff may succeed in recovering property if he can show that he has a right to possession without having to 'reveal' the illegality. This is misleading since, if the plaintiff does not reveal it, the defendant certainly will if it suits his purpose. The crucial point is that if a plaintiff can formulate a claim whose legal reasoning is wholly independent of the illegal contract he will succeed. The classic example is a lease of Blackacre by A to B for 5 years, A knowing that B intends to use Blackacre as a brothel. A cannot sue B for the rent nor can he turn B out for non-payment of the rent but he can turn B out after 5 years because his reversion is independent of the lease.

Taylor v Chester (1869) LR 4 QB 309

Mellor J. In this case the plaintiff declared on the bailment on the half of a 50*l* Bank of England note, to the defendant, to be redelivered on request, alleging a refusal by the defendant to redeliver such half-note. The second count was in detinue for the same half-note[.]

The defendant, after traversing the delivery and detention of the note, and to the second count denying that it was the property of the plaintiff, pleaded separately and specially to both counts, in effect, that the half-note in question had been deposited by the plaintiff with the defendant by way of pledge, to secure the repayment of money due and money then advanced by the defendant to the plaintiff and then due.

The plaintiff joined issue on the defendant's pleas, and also replied specially that the alleged debt or sum, in respect of which the defendant justified the non-delivery and detention of the half-note, was for wine and suppers, supplied by the defendant in a brothel and disorderly house kept by the defendant, for the purpose of being consumed there by the plaintiff and divers prostitutes in a debauch there, to incite them to riotous, disorderly, and immoral conduct, and for money knowingly lent for the purpose of being expended in riot and debauchery and immoral conduct. . . .

The true test for determining whether or not the plaintiff and the defendant were in pari delicto, is by considering whether the plaintiff could make out his case otherwise than through the medium and by the aid of the illegal transaction to which he was himself a party: *Simpson v Bloss* . . . The plaintiff, no doubt, was the owner of the note, but he pledged it by way of security for the price of meat and drink provided for, and money advanced to, him by the defendant. Had the case rested there, and no pleading raised the question of illegality, a valid pledge would have been created, and a special property conferred upon the defendant in the half-note, and the plaintiff could only have recovered by showing payment or a tender of the amount due. In order to get rid of the defence arising from the plea, which set up an existing pledge of the half-note, the plaintiff had recourse to the special replication, in which he was obliged to set forth the immoral and illegal character of the contract upon which the half-note had been deposited. It was, therefore, impossible for him to recover except through the medium and by the aid of an illegal transaction to which he was himself a party. Under such circumstances, the maxim 'in pari delicto potior est conditio possidentis', clearly applies, and is decisive of the case.

Bowmakers Ltd v Barnet Instruments Ltd [1945] KB 65, Court of Appeal

The plaintiffs let machine tools to the defendants under three hire-purchase agreements, each of which was illegal as contravening statutory instruments. The defendants resold the tools which were the subject of the first and third agreements and refused to pay the hire on the second. The plaintiffs sued for conversion. The judgment of the court was delivered by:

Du Parcq LJ. . . . It had to be conceded that the hiring agreements did not in themselves transgress this order, but it was contended, and with much more force, that any illegality which attached to the anterior contract of sale must in the circumstances of this case affect the hiring agreements, since these latter agreements were negotiated by the plaintiffs, the defendants and Smith, acting in concert, with a view to ensuring the payment to Smith of a price which could not legally be paid. It is right to add that neither the plaintiffs nor the defendants had any knowledge of the order, so that, if they erred, their error was involuntary, but this, the defendants say, is immaterial. The defendants obtained possession of the machinery as the result of a bargain to procure the commission of a criminal offence, and hence, it was said, they and the plaintiffs, however venial their offence, had been engaged in nothing less than a criminal conspiracy. The plaintiffs, therefore, should be driven from the judgment seat, with the result, fortunate or unfortunate according to the point of view, that the defendants would escape from the transaction without loss, and without even suffering the reproaches of an uneasy conscience. [His Lordship then set out the order on which the defendants relied as having been infringed by the dealings with the used machine tool which was the subject of the third agreement and continued]: Neither Smith or the plaintiffs had the authority of such a licence to dispose of the machine tool in question. The plaintiffs had, therefore, infringed the order, if not by buying from Smith, certainly by themselves hiring out the chattel to the defendants. The result of this illegality, it was contended, must have the same satisfactory consequences for the defendants as the offence committed in respect of the new machines . . .

The question, then, is whether in the circumstances the plaintiffs are without a remedy. So far as their claim in conversion is concerned, they are not relying on the hiring agreements at all. On the contrary, they are willing to admit for this purpose that they cannot rely on them. They simply say that the machines were their property, and this, we think, cannot be denied. We understand Mr Gallop to concede that the property had passed from Smith to the plaintiffs, and still remained in the plaintiffs at the date of the conversion. At any rate, we have no doubt that this is the legal result of the transaction and we find support for this view in the dicta of Parke B in *Scarfe v Morgan*.

Why then should not the plaintiffs have what is their own? No question of the defendants' rights arises. They do not, and cannot, pretend to have had any legal right to possession of the goods at the date of the conversion. Their counsel has to rely, not on any alleged right of theirs, but on the requirements of public policy. . . . Prima facie, a man is entitled to his own property, and it is not a general principle of our law (as was suggested) that when one man's goods have got into another's possession in consequence of some unlawful dealings between them, the true owner can never be allowed to recover those goods by an action. The necessity of such a principle to the interests and advancement of public policy is certainly not obvious. The suggestion that it exists is not, in our opinion supported by authority. . . .

In our opinion, a man's right to possess his own chattels will as a general rule be enforced against one who, without any claim of right, is detaining them, or has converted them to his own use, even though it may appear either from the pleadings, or in the course of the trial, that the chattels in question came into the defendant's possession by reason of an illegal contract between himself and the plaintiff, provided that the plaintiff does not seek, and is not forced, either to found his claim on the illegal contract or to plead its illegality in order to support his claim.

NOTE

By reselling the machines subject to the first and third agreements the defendant had done an act fundamentally inconsistent with the bailment. This normally results in the bailee's right to possession coming to an end. But in relation to the second agreement the defendant had merely failed to pay the hire. As we have seen, this does not, under the general law, bring the contract to an automatic end; if it amounts to a repudiation, it may give the owner the right to terminate. (See above, p 457.)

'Illegal Contracts and Limited Interests' by Hamson (1949) 10 CLJ 249, 258–259

The question in *Bowmakers' Case* is: 'when can a bailor recover from the bailee under an illegal bailment the chattel bailed or its value?' The simplest answer would no doubt have been to treat an illegal bailment as a bailment at will and to permit the bailor always to recover the chattel upon mere demand. This answer had however been rejected in *Taylor v Chester* despite Herschell's argument; and the court in *Bowmaker's Case* accepts that decision as correct. The bailee accordingly still acquires, by virtue of the illegal bailment, some interest or property in the chattel other than one defeasible merely on demand. In *Bowmaker's Case*, however, the court goes on to hold that the bailor can recover the chattel bailed under an illegal hire purchase contract even though the only wrongful act by the bailee, in one of the instances, was his mere continuance in possession after demand made for the return of the chattel upon his failure to pay some instalments of the hire reserved by the bailment. Those instalments could not, by reason of the illegality, be recovered directly by action against the bailee. The difficulty is that the court, while declaring, as indeed it was bound to, that 'no claim founded on an illegal contract will be enforced' and that 'no technical meaning must be ascribed to the words "founded on an illegal contract"', nevertheless appears to come very close, under cover of an action in tort, to enforcing the terms of the illegal bailment against the defendants.

It is suggested that, despite the court's laudable desire to avoid technicalities, the question who is to keep a chattel which has been the subject of an illegal contract will continue to be decided with the aid of very abstruse technicalities; that the established principle that delivery or conveyance under an illegal contract effects a valid transfer of property or of an interest in property is itself no mean technicality and forms the basis of rules which are therefore likely to have a technical bias; and that in *Bowmakers' Case* perhaps the court applied the technicalities with less consideration than they merited, and with results which both to the technician and to the layman are somewhat startling.

It is further suggested that, if *Bowmakers' Case* is rightly decided, there is now no objection to the lessor also recovering possession of premises demised under an illegal lease upon non-payment of the rent reserved, even if the lease has been executed under seal, provided it contain the normal provision for determination upon non-payment. Before *Bowmakers' Case* the balance of authority was against such a recovery during the period of the term.

'Another look at Bowmakers' by Coote (1972) 35 MLR 38, 42–44

[T]here is no longer anything particularly cynical about the rule stated in the *Bowmakers* case. On the contrary, it makes good sense. Nor is recovery by the owner merely the unmeritorious result of an accident of pleading. What the *Bowmakers* rule means is that he will obtain restitution if his claim is based on rights which belong to him independently of the illegal contract. He will not recover if he has, before suit, effectively transferred his rights away under an executed illegal contract. This, it may be added, is substantially the effect of a dictum by Watermeyer JA of the South African Appellate Division in *Jajbhay v Cassim*, which for many years has appeared in successive editions of Cheshire and Fifoot on *The Law of Contract*. According to that learned judge:

'. . . the Court will not assist a party to recover what he has paid or transferred to defendant in terms of the illegal contract, save in exceptional circumstances, but there is no need to go further and to deprive him of his rights which he has not transferred to defendant.

On this line of reasoning, or something like it, the *Bowmakers* decision has been accepted by many commentators to be correct, so far as agreements 1 and 3 are concerned. The plaintiffs were able to plead their ownership and there was no reason for them to rely in any way on the illegal hire-purchase agreements in order to establish their immediate right to restitution. The explanation offered by the commentators for this latter point was that the defendants' act of selling the tools had automatically revested in the plaintiffs a right to immediate possession. Because of a similarly automatic revesting, the argument runs, the plaintiffs could equally have recovered possession once the term of the bailment contract had expired by effluxion of time. They might even have done so upon default in payment of hire, if the contract had contained a clause which terminated the bailment automatically for non-payment. By the same token, a lessor would be able to recover his land on the expiry of the term of an illegal lease.

. . . But these arguments . . . do not, the critics say, cover the circumstances of the second hire-purchase agreement, for in that case there had been no conversion of the tools, and therefore no automatic termination of the bailment. The defendants had failed to comply with a demand for the return of the tools, but the plaintiffs, to show that they were entitled to make the demand, would have been driven back onto the cesser provisions of the contract. To enable them to recover in those circumstances would be to recognise and enforce a right of termination given them by the illegal contract. Such enforcement would be contrary to the *ex turpi causa* rule.

The fact that this line of reasoning leaves unexplained the Court of Appeal's decision on the second agreement is not its only disadvantage. It rests the court's decision in respect of agreements 1 and 3 on the quite fortuitous circumstance that a conversion of bailed goods, while it apparently does not automatically terminate the bailment contract, does revest an immediate right to possession in the bailor. Not only was this a factor not adverted to by du Parcq LJ when he delivered the judgment of the court; it also has the effect of confining the decision substantially to bailment contracts, since there seems to be no equivalent automatic revesting under the law governing leases. It also seems to exclude the possibility of recovery on repudiatory breach generally, since termination in such cases is ordinarily not automatic but depends on an election by the injured party.

Despite the weight of opinion to the contrary, it is submitted that there do exist at least two ways in which both aspects of the *Bowmakers* decision can be justified. The first finds its basis in the dictum of Watermeyer JA in *Jajbhay v Cassim* which has already been referred to, and in the line of South African cases which derive from it. The other involves a direct application of the principle which the Court of Appeal itself purported to apply in the *Bowmakers* case.

(g) Severance

In many cases where a contract is illegal because it involves some unlawful act, the whole contract is rendered invalid because the illegality affects the substance of the contract. If the illegality relates only to a part of it, the position is less clear. Sometimes it is treated as infecting the whole thing. Thus in *Miller v Karlinski* (1945) 62 TLR 85 a provision in a contract of employment was aimed at defrauding the Revenue (see above, p 749) and this rendered the whole contract invalid. Sometimes however the court will treat the illegal part as severable, leaving the rest of the contract enforceable. This is particularly common with contracts which are in restraint of trade, and severance will be discussed in some detail in the next section. It can also be done with contracts involving unlawful acts if the illegal part can readily be separated out. Thus in *Ailion v Spiekermann* [1976] Ch 158 the vendor of a leasehold interest committed an offence by demanding a premium from the purchasers. The latter were permitted to recover the premium yet could still enforce the rest of the agreement.

CHAPTER 38
Contracts in restraint of trade

As we shall see, the law handles contracts in restraint of trade in a number of ways which are different to the main body of illegal contracts. One is that although competition is usually desirable, it is not a value which in all circumstances outweighs all others. At least since the early eighteenth century, the law has recognized that some contracts in restraint of trade are acceptable. Many of the cases are concerned therefore with striking a balance.

Nordenfelt v Maxim Nordenfelt [1894] AC 535, House of Lords

Lord MacNaghten. My Lords, the appellant, Thorsten Nordenfelt, a Swedish gentleman of much intelligence, as his able address to your Lordships proved, and of great skill in certain branches of mechanical science, had established in England and Sweden a valuable business in connection with the manufacture of quick-firing guns. His customers were comparatively few in number, but his trade was world-wide in extent. He had upon his books almost every monarch and almost every State of any note in the habitable globe. In 1886 Mr Nordenfelt sold his business to a limited company which was formed for the purpose of purchasing it. At the same time and as part of the same transaction he entered into a restrictive covenant with the purchasers intended to protect the business in their hands. In 1888 the purchasers transferred their business to the respondents, a limited company established with the object of combining the Nordenfelt business with a similar business founded by a Mr Maxim. The transfer was made with the concurrence of Mr Nordenfelt. Without his concurrence and co-operation it is plain that it would not have been made at all. On the occasion of the transfer, and as part of the arrangement, Mr Nordenfelt entered into a restrictive covenant with the respondents. This covenant was in some respects wider, in others less wide, than the covenant with the original purchasers. But it was in lieu of, and in substitution for, that covenant, which of course would have been kept alive if Mr Nordenfelt had declined to come into the new arrangement.

In these circumstances I think that the Court of Appeal were right in regarding the covenant which Mr Nordenfelt entered into with the respondents as a covenant made upon the occasion of the sale of his business, and as depending for its validity upon the principles and considerations applicable to such a case.

The stipulation was that Mr Nordenfelt should not, during the term of twenty-five years from the date of the incorporation of the company, if the company should so long continue to carry on business, 'engage except on behalf of the company either directly or indirectly in the trade or business of a manufacturer of guns, gun-mountings or carriages, gun powder explosives or ammunition'—so far the covenant has been held good; then come the words, 'or in any business competing or liable to compete in any way with that for the time being carried on by the company'. A proviso was added to the effect that such restriction should not apply to explosives other than gunpowder, or to subaqueous or submarine boats or torpedoes, or to castings or forgings of steel or iron, or alloys of iron or of copper. The latter part of the covenant, which extends to all competing businesses, may be disregarded. In view of the manifold objects of the company, as set out in their memorandum of association, it was held by the Court of Appeal to be void; and there is no appeal from that part of the decision. The proviso also, I think, may be put aside. It is one of the circumstances to be taken into consideration as bearing upon the question of the reasonableness of the agreement; but it is not, I think, essential to the validity of this covenant. . .

In the age of Queen Elizabeth restraints of trade, whatever they were, general or partial, were thought to be contrary to public policy, and therefore void (*Colgate v Bacheler*). In time, however, it was found that a rule so rigid and far-reaching must seriously interfere with transactions of every-day occurrence. Traders could hardly venture to let their shops out of their own hands; the purchaser of a business was at the mercy of the seller; every apprentice was a possible rival. So the rule was relaxed. It was relaxed as far as the exigencies of trade for the time being required, gradually and not without difficulty, until it came to be recognised that all partial restraints might be good, though it was thought that general restraints, that is, restraints of general application extending throughout the kingdom, must be bad. Why was the relaxation supposed to be thus limited? Simply because nobody imagined in those days that a general restraint could be reasonable, not because there was any inherent or essential distinction between the two cases. . . .

The true view at the present time I think, is this: The public have an interest in every person's carrying on his trade freely: so has the individual. All interference with individual liberty of action in trading, and all restraints of trade of themselves, if there is nothing more, are contrary to public policy, and therefore void. That is the general rule. But there are exceptions: restraints of trade and interference with individual liberty of action may be justified by the special circumstances of a particular case. It is a sufficient justification, and indeed it is the only justification, if the restriction is reasonable—reasonable, that is, in reference to the interests of the parties concerned and reasonable in reference to the interests of the public, so framed and so guarded as to afford adequate protection to the party in whose favour it is imposed, while at the same time it is in no way injurious to the public. That, I think, is the fair result of all the authorities.

. . . I think the restraint in the present case is reasonable in every point of view. . . .

[Lord Herschell LC, Lord Watson, Lord Ashbourne and Lord Morris also delivered judgments in favour of dismissing the appeal.]

Appeal dismissed.

NOTES

1. Although all the members of the Court of Appeal and the House of Lords reached the same conclusion in this case, they did so for a variety of different reasons. Lord Macnaghten's statement has come to be treated as the authoritative starting point of the modern law.

2. It is usually accepted that there are a number of recognised categories of covenant which are in restraint of trade (see further below, p 781). This case illustrates one of the major categories, restraints imposed on competition by the seller of a business.

3. Once it is established (by previous authority or otherwise, see below, p 781ff) that a covenant is in restraint of trade, the covenant will be unenforceable unless it is shown to be reasonable. Thus the burden of proof will be on the buyer of the business.

4. In order to show that a covenant is reasonable, it is usually said that the party seeking to enforce it must show two things: first, that he has some legally recognised interest to protect and second, that the covenant is no wider than is reasonably necessary to protect the interest.

5. What legitimate interest does the buyer of a business have in preventing the seller from competing in the future? Is it to the seller's advantage to be able to make a covenant not to compete? (Hint: how much would you get for the good will of your business if you couldn't be stopped from opening up a new, competing business next door next week?)

6. In *Nordenfelt* why do you think that there was no appeal from the Court of Appeal's decision that the part of the covenant undertaking not to engage 'in any business competing or liable to compete in any way with that for the time being carried on by the company' was invalid? For a further example of a covenant invalid because it covered something the

seller didn't sell see *Vancouver Malt and Sake Brewing Co Ltd v Vancouver Breweries Ltd* [1934] AC 181.

7. Even where the buyer has a legitimate interest to protect, the covenant must be reasonable, eg in area and duration. In practice this overlaps with the legitimate interest question. If Nordenfelt's business had been only in Europe, it could have been said either that a world-wide covenant was unreasonably broad or that the company had no legitimate interest in preventing him competing outside Europe.

Mason v Provident Clothing & Supply Co Ltd [1913] AC 724, House of Lords

Lord Moulton. . . . The law as to covenants in restraint of trade was so carefully and authoritatively formulated in this House in the *Nordenfelt Case* that I do not think it necessary to discuss the numerous authorities cited in the course of the argument in order to ascertain what is the critical question which the Court ought to put to itself in such a case as this. It is as follows: Are the restrictions which the covenant imposes upon the freedom of action of the servant after he has left the service of the master greater than are reasonably necessary for the protection of the master in his business? . . .

The nature of the employment of the appellant in this business was solely to obtain members and collect their instalments. A small district in London was assigned to him, which he canvassed and in which he collected the payments due, and outside that small district he had no duties. His employment was therefore that of a local canvasser and debt collector, and nothing more.

Such being the nature of the employment, it would be reasonable for the employer to protect himself against the danger of his former servant canvassing or collecting for a rival firm in the district in which he had been employed. If he were permitted to do so before the expiry of a reasonably long interval he would be in a position to give to his new employer all the advantages of that personal knowledge of the inhabitants of the locality, and more especially of his former customers, which he had acquired in the service of the respondents and at their expense. Against such a contingency the master might reasonably protect himself, but I can see no further or other protection which he could reasonably demand. If the servant is employed by a rival firm in some district which neither includes that in which he formerly worked for the respondents, nor is immediately adjoining thereto, there is no personal knowledge which he has acquired in his former master's service which can be used to that master's prejudice. . . .

These, then, being the limits of the protection which the master might reasonably insist on, I turn to the covenant in order to see whether it exceeds these limits. . . . [I]t prohibits the appellant from entering into a similar employment within 25 miles of [London] for a period of three years . . . such an area is very far greater than could be reasonably required for the protection of his former employers.

It was suggested in the argument that even if the covenant was, as a whole, too wide, the Court might enforce restrictions which it might consider reasonable (even though they were not expressed in the covenant), provided they were within its ambit. My Lords, I do not doubt that the Court may, and in some cases will, enforce a part of a covenant in restraint of trade, even though taken as a whole the covenant exceeds what is reasonable. But, in my opinion, that ought only to be done in cases where the part so enforceable is clearly severable, and even so only in cases where the excess is of trivial importance, or merely technical, and not a part of the main purport and substance of the clause. It would in my opinion be pessimi exempli if, when an employer had exacted a covenant deliberately framed in unreasonably wide terms, the Courts were to come to his assistance and, by applying their ingenuity and knowledge of the law, carve out of this void covenant the maximum of what he might validly have required. It must be remembered that the real sanction at the back of these covenants is the terror and expense of litigation, in which the servant is usually at a great disadvantage, in view of the longer purse of his master. It is sad to think that in this present case this appellant, whose employment is a comparatively humble one, should have had to go through four Courts before he could free himself from such unreasonable restraints as this covenant imposes, and the hardship imposed by the exaction of unreasonable covenants by employers would be greatly increased if they could continue the practice with the expectation that, having exposed the servant to the anxiety and expense of litigation, the Court would in the end enable them to obtain everything which they could have obtained by acting reasonably. It is evident that those who drafted this covenant aimed at making it a penal rather than a protective covenant, and that they hoped by means of it to paralyse the earning capacilities of the man if and when he left their service, and were not thinking of what would be a reasonable protection to their business, and having so acted they must take the consequences.

[Viscount Haldane LC and Lords Dunedin and Shaw of Dunfermline delivered judgments to the same effect.]

Appeal allowed.

NOTES

1. This is an example of a second major category, covenants by employees not to compete after the end of their employment.
2. In Lord Macnaghten's analysis a valid covenant has to be reasonable both as between the parties and in the public interest. In practice the vast majority of the cases have been decided on the issue of reasonableness as between the parties. This is another example of the unusual nature of the restraint of trade doctrine since reasonableness as between the parties is an internal and not an external matter. As the remarks of Lord Moulton above show, these cases can be regarded as early examples of inequality of bargaining power. (See also above, p 667.)
3. The party who seeks to enforce a covenant in restraint of trade has to show that it is reasonable as between the parties. To do this he has to show that he has a legally recognized interest to protect and that the covenant is no wider than is reasonably necessary to protect it. So in *Mason's* case the employer had a protectable interest in his connection with his customers but the covenant was much too wide. Similarly an employer may be entitled to protect trade secrets.

Herbert Morris Ltd v Saxelby [1916] 1 AC 688, House of Lords

The plaintiffs were the leading manufacturers of hoisting machinery in the UK. The defendant had been employed by them since leaving school. After several years he was given a contract as an engineer for two years certain and thereafter subject to four months' notice on either side. As part of this agreement he covenanted:

that he would not during a period of seven years from his ceasing to be employed by the company, either in the United Kingdom of Great Britain or Ireland, carry on either as principal, agent, servant, or otherwise, alone or jointly or in connection with any other person, firm, or company, or be concerned or assist directly or indirectly, whether for reward or otherwise, in the sale or manufacture of pulley blocks, hand overhead runways, electric overhead runways, or hand overhead travelling cranes . . .

Lord Parker. . . . [F]or a restraint to be reasonable in the interests of the parties it must afford *no more than* adequate protection to the party in whose favour it is imposed. So conceived the test appears to me to be valid both as regards the covenantor and covenantee, for though in one sense no doubt it is contrary to the interests of the covenantor to subject himself to any restraint, still it may be for his advantage to be able so to subject himself in cases where, if he could not do so, he would lose other advantages, such as the possibility of obtaining the best terms on the sale of an existing business or the possibility of obtaining employment or training under competent employers. As long as the restraint to which he subjects himself is no wider than is required for the adequate protection of the person in whose favour it is created, it is in his interest to be able to bind himself for the sake of the indirect advantages he may obtain by so doing. It was at one time thought that, in order to ascertain whether a restraint were reasonable in the interests of the covenantor, the Court ought to weigh the advantages accruing to the covenantor under the contract against the disadvantages imposed upon him by the restraint, but any such process has long since been rejected as impracticable. The Court no longer considers the adequacy of the consideration in any particular case. If it be reasonable that a covenantee should, for his own protection, ask for a restraint, it is in my opinion equally reasonable that the covenantor should be able to subject himself to this restraint. The test of reasonableness is the same in both cases.

My Lords, it appears to me that Lord Macnaghten's statement of the law requires amplification in another respect. If the restraint is to secure no more than 'adequate protection' to the party in whose favour it is imposed, it becomes necessary to consider in each particular case what it is for which and what it is against which protection is required. Otherwise it would be impossible to pass any opinion on the adequacy of the protection. . . . I cannot find any case in which a covenant against competition by a servant or apprentice has, as such, ever been upheld by the Court. Wherever such covenants have been upheld it has been on the ground, not that the servant or apprentice would, by reason of his employment or training, obtain the skill and knowledge necessary to equip him as a possible competitor in the trade, but that he might obtain such personal knowledge of and influence over the customers of his employer, or such an acquaintance with his employer's trade secrets as would enable him, if competition were allowed, to take advantage of his employer's trade connection or utilize information confidentially obtained.

An attempt was, however, made in argument to justify the restraint on the ground that it was no more than adequate for the protection of the plaintiffs' trade connection and trade secrets. I am of opinion that this attempt completely failed. With regard to the plaintiffs' connection, there is little or no evidence that the defendant ever came into personal contact with the plaintiffs' customers. For a period, it is true, he was manager of the London branch of the plaintiffs' business, and for another period sales manager at Loughborough. With the exception of these periods he was employed entirely in the engineering department. Had the restraint been confined to London and Loughborough and a reasonable area round each of these centres, it might possibly have been supported as reasonably necessary to protect the plaintiffs' connection, but a restraint extending over the United Kingdom was obviously too wide in this respect.

With regard to trade secrets, I am not satisfied that the defendant was entrusted with any trade secret in the proper sense of the word at all. Mr Walter boldly argued that the expression trade secrets ought to be extended so as to include everything which Mr Morris claimed to be peculiar to the plaintiffs' method of carrying on their business.

I will assume that the matters referred to by Mr Walter are in fact peculiar to the plaintiffs' business, though I can hardly regard Mr Morris's uncorroborated evidence as very satisfactory proof that the practices in question were unknown to other firms. Still, the manner in which Sargant J dealt with this part of the case appears to me to be unanswerable. Though the defendant had access to the E charts, the L sheets, the drawings of special machines, the costs index, and other documents, all of which may be considered confidential, these documents were far too detailed for the defendant to carry away the contents thereof in his head. All that he could carry away was the general method and character of the scheme of organization practised by the plaintiff company. Such scheme and method can hardly be regarded as a trade secret. The same applies to the plaintiff company's system of standardizing mechanical apparatus capable of being used in more than one class of machine. The nearest approach that I can find in the evidence to anything in the nature of a trade secret is the mention of certain formulae, said to be based on the plaintiffs' experience, and to be more trustworthy than Molesworth's formulae for similar purposes.

[Lords Atkinson, Shaw and Sumner delivered judgments to the same effect.]

Appeal dismissed.

Another category is restrictive trading agreements and the like. In *McEllistrim v Ballymacelligot Co-operative Agricultural and Dairy Society Ltd* [1919] AC 548, the plaintiff was a member of the defendant society which carried on the business of manufacturing butter and cheese from milk supplied by some of its members. The society bound itself to take all milk produced by members' cows within a defined area and members agreed not to sell milk to any other creamery or to anyone who sold milk or manufactured butter for sale. Under the rules it was effectively impossible for a member to leave without the consent of the committee. The House of Lords held (Lord Parmoor dissenting) that this feature combined with the restriction on the selling of milk was wider than reasonably necessary for the protection of the society.

As a means of promoting competition the common law rules on restraint of trade suffered from two defects. First, the question would normally only come before the courts if one of the parties was dissatisfied. Clearly the more cosy a cartel the less the incentive for the parties to fall out amongst themselves (see above, p 747). Secondly, the courts in practice seemed to attach more weight to reasonableness between the parties than to the public interest (this latter defect has in fact been less apparent in more recent cases: see next case). The result has been the adoption of statutory regimes, operating partly through a special court, the Restrictive Practices Court, and partly through a standing commission, the Monopolies and Mergers Commission. These statutory developments overlap and coexist with the common law. In addition competition law is one of the most important parts of the law of the European Communities (for further details on all this see Whish, *Competition Law* (2nd ed, 1989)).

If a case does not fall within one of the recognised categories of restraint of trade, how is it to be determined whether the doctrine applies, so that the covenant must be shown to be reasonable before it can be enforced? This question arose with 'solus agreements'. These are agreements between petrol companies and garage owners, whereby in exchange for finance which is often secured by a mortgage on the premises, the garage owner agrees to buy all its petrol from the petrol company, to keep open at all reasonable times and to extract similar undertakings from anyone to whom it sells the garage. The precedents were confused. It had often (but not always) been assumed that simple 'exclusive dealing contracts' were valid (see Treitel pp 359–360); while restrictive covenants imposed on buyers of land preventing them from using the land for various trades had always been enforced without question.

Esso Petroleum Co Ltd v Harper's Garage (Stourport) Ltd [1968] AC 269, House of Lords

The appellants had entered into agreements with the respondents in relation to two filling stations owned by the respondents. Under the agreements the respondents agreed to buy all their requirements of motor fuels from the appellants at their current list prices. One agreement was to last for 4 years 5 months and the other for 21 years. The respondents wished to shift to another brand of petrol and the appellants sought an injunction to restrain them from doing so.

Lord Reid. . . . . The main argument submitted for the appellant on this matter was that restraint of trade means a personal restraint and does not apply to a restraint on the use of a particular piece of land. Otherwise, it was said, every covenant running with the land which prevents its use for all or for some trading purposes would be a covenant in restraint of trade and therefore unenforceable unless it could be shown to be reasonable and for the protection of some legitimate interest. It was said that the present agreement only prevents the sale of petrol from other suppliers on the site of the Mustow Green Garage: It leaves the respondents free to trade anywhere else in any way they choose. But in many cases a trader trading at a particular place does not have the resources to enable him to begin trading elsewhere as well, and if he did he might find it difficult to find another suitable garage for sale or to get planning permission to open a new filling station on another site. As the whole doctrine of restraint of trade is based on public policy its application ought to depend less on legal niceties or theoretical possibilities than on the practical effect of a restraint in hampering that freedom which it is the policy of the law to protect.

It is true that it would be an innovation to hold that ordinary negative covenants preventing the use of a particular site for trading of all kinds or of a particular kind are within the scope of the doctrine of restraint of trade. I do not think they are. Restraint of trade appears to me to imply that a man contracts to give up some freedom which otherwise he would have had. A person buying or leasing land had no previous right to be there at all, let alone to trade there, and when he takes possession of that land subject to a negative restrictive covenant he gives up no right or freedom which he previously had. . . .

In my view this agreement is within the scope of the doctrine of restraint of trade as it had been developed in English law. Not only have the respondents agreed negatively not to sell other petrol but they have agreed positively to keep this garage open for the sale of the appellants' petrol at all reasonable hours throughout the period of the tie. It was argued that this was merely regulating the respondent's trading and rather promoting than restraining his trade. But regulating a person's existing trade may be a greater restraint than prohibiting him from engaging in a new trade. And a contract to take one's whole supply from one source may be much more hampering than a contract to sell one's whole output to one buyer. I would not attempt to define the dividing line between contracts which are and contracts which are not in restraint of trade, but in my view this contract must be held to be in restraint of trade. So it is necessary to consider whether its provisions can be justified. . . .

Where two experienced traders are bargaining on equal terms and one has agreed to a restraint for reasons which seem good to him the court is in grave danger of stultifying itself if it says that it knows that trader's interest better than he does himself. But there may well be cases where, although the party to be restrained has deliberately accepted the main terms of the contract, he has been at a disadvantage as regards other terms: for example where a set of conditions has been incorporated which has not been the subject of negotiation—there the court may have greater freedom to hold them unreasonable. . . .

What were the appellants' legitimate interests must depend largely on what was the state of affairs in their business and with regard to the distribution and sale of petrol generally. And those are questions of fact to be answered by evidence or common knowledge. In the present case restraint of trade was not pleaded originally and the appellants only received notice that it was to be raised a fortnight before the trial. They may have been wise in not seeking a postponement of the trial when the pleadings were amended. But the result has been that the evidence on this matter is scanty. I think however that it is legitimate to supplement it from the considerable body of reported cases regarding solus agreements and from the facts found in the Report of the Monopolies Commission of July, 1965.

When petrol rationing came to an end in 1950 the large producers began to make agreements, now known as solus agreements, with garage owners under which the garage owner, in return for certain advantages, agreed to sell only the petrol of the producer with whom he made the agreement. Within a short time three-quarters of the filling stations in this country were tied in that way and by the dates of the agreements in this case over 90 per cent. had agreed to ties. It appears that the garage owners were not at a disadvantage in bargaining with the large producing companies as there was intense competition between these companies to obtain these ties. So we can assume that both the garage owners and the companies thought that such ties were to their advantage. And it is not said in this case that all ties are either against the public interest or against the interests of the parties. The respondents' case is that the ties with which we are concerned are for too long periods.

The advantage to the garage owner is that he gets a rebate on the wholesale price of the petrol which he buys and also may get other benefits or financial assistance. The main advantages for the producing company appear to be that distribution is made easier and more economical and that it is assured of a steady outlet for its petrol over a period. As regards distribution, it appears that there were some 35,000 filling stations in this country at the relevant time, of which about a fifth were tied to the appellants. So they only have to distribute to some 7,000 filling stations instead of to a very much larger number if most filling stations sold several brands of petrol. But the main reason why the producing companies want ties for five years and more, instead of ties for one or two years only, seems to be that they can organise their business better if on the average only one-fifth or less of their ties come to an end in any one year. The appellants make a point of the fact that they have invested some £200 millions in refineries and other plant and that they could not have done that unless they could foresee a steady and assured level of sales of their petrol. Most of their ties appear to have been made for periods of between five and 20 years. But we have no evidence as to the precise additional advantage which they derive from a five-year tie as compared with a two-year tie or from a 20-year tie as compared with a five-year tie.

The Court of Appeal held that these ties were for unreasonably long periods. They thought that, if for any reason the respondents ceased to sell the appellants' petrol, the appellants could have found other suitable outlets in the neighbourhood within two or three years. I do not think that that is the right test. In the first place there was no evidence about this and I do not think that it would be practicable to apply this test in practice. It might happen that when the respondents ceased to sell their petrol, the appellants would find such an alternative outlet in a very short time. But, looking to the fact that well over 90 per cent of existing filling stations are tied and that there may be great difficulty in opening a new filling station, it might take a very long time to find an alternative. Any estimate of how long it might take to find suitable alternatives for the respondents' filling stations could be little better than guesswork.

I do not think that the appellants' interest can be regarded so narrowly. They are not so much concerned with any particular outlet as with maintaining a stable system of distribution throughout the country so as to enable their business to be run efficiently and economically. In my view there is sufficient material to justify a decision that ties of less than five years were insufficient, in the circumstances of the trade when these agreements were made, to afford adequate protection to the appellants' legitimate interests. . . . A tie for 21 years stretches far beyond any period for which developments are reasonably foreseeable. Restrictions on the garage owner which might seem tolerable and reasonable in reasonably foreseeable conditions might come to have a very different effect in quite different conditions: the public interest comes in here more strongly.

Lord Wilberforce. . . . The doctrine of restraint of trade (a convenient, if imprecise, expression which I continue to use) is one which has throughout the history of its subject-matter been expressed with considerable generality, if not ambiguity. The best-known general formulations, those of Lord Macnaghten in *Nordenfelt* and of Lord Parker of Waddington in *Adelaide*, adapted and used by Diplock LJ in the Court of Appeal in the *Petrofina* case, speak generally of all restraints of trade without any attempt at a definition. Often we find the words 'restraint of trade' in a single passage used indifferently to denote, on the one hand, in a broad popular sense, any contract which limits the free exercise of trade or business, and, on the other hand, as a term of art covering those contracts which are regarded as offending a rule of public policy. Often, in reported cases, we find that instead of segregating two questions, (i) whether the contract is in restraint of trade, (ii) whether, if so, it is 'reasonable', the courts have fused the two by asking whether the contract is in 'undue restraint of trade' or by a compound finding that it is not satisfied that this contract is really in restraint of trade at all but, if it is, it is reasonable. A well-known textbook describes contracts in restraint of trade as those which 'unreasonably restrict' the rights of a person to carry on his trade or profession. There is no need to regret these tendencies: indeed, to do so, when consideration of this subject has passed through such notable minds from Lord Macclesfield onwards, would indicate a failure to understand its nature. The common law has often (if sometimes unconsciously) thrived on ambiguity and it would be mistaken, even if it were possible, to try to crystallise the rules of this, or any, aspect of public policy into neat propositions. The doctrine of restraint of trade is one to be applied to factual situations with a broad and flexible rule of reason. . . .

This does not mean that the question whether a given agreement is in restraint of trade, in either sense of these words, is nothing more than a question of fact to be individually decided in each case. It is not to be supposed, or encouraged, that a bare allegation that a contract limits a trader's freedom of action exposes a party suing on it to the burden of justification. There will always be certain general categories of contracts as to which it can be said, with some degree of certainty, that the 'doctrine' does or does not apply to them. Positively, there are likely to be certain sensitive areas as to which the law will require in every case the test of reasonableness to be passed: such an area has long been and still is that of contracts between employer and employee as regards the period after the employment has ceased. Negatively, and it is this that concerns us here, there will be types of contract as to which the law should be prepared to say with some confidence that they do not enter into the field of restraint of trade at all.

How, then, can such contracts be defined or at least identified? No exhaustive test can be stated—probably no precise non-exhaustive test. But the development of the law does seem to show that judges have been able to dispense from the necessity of justification under a public policy test of reasonableness such contracts or provisions of contracts as, under contemporary conditions may be found to have passed into the accepted and normal currency of commercial or contractual or conveyancing relations. That such contracts have done so may be taken to show with at least strong prima force that, moulded under the pressures of negotiation, competition and public opinion, they have assumed a form which satisfies the test of public policy as understood by the courts at the time, or, regarding the matter from the point of view of the trade, that the trade in question has assumed such a form that for its health or expansion it requires a degree of regulation. Absolute exemption for restriction or regulation is never obtained: circumstances, social or economic, may have altered, since they obtained acceptance, in such a way as to call for a fresh examination: there may be some exorbitance or special feature in the individual contract which takes it out of the accepted category: but the court must be persuaded of this before it calls upon the relevant party to justify a contract of this kind.

Some such limitation upon the meaning in legal practice of 'restraints of trade' must surely have been present to the minds of Lord Macnaghten and Lord Parker. They cannot have meant to say that any contract which in whatever way restricts a man's liberty to trade was (either historically under the common law, or at the time of which they were speaking) prima facie unenforceable and must be shown to be reasonable. They must have been well aware that areas existed, and always had existed in which limitations of this liberty were not only defensible, but were not seriously open to the charge of restraining trade. Their language, they would surely have said, must be interpreted in relation to commercial practice and common sense.

[Lords Morris, Hodson and Pearce agreed that the shorter agreement was valid but the longer one void.]

NOTES

1. The argument in this case was concerned with two separate issues. Firstly, was the agreement within the category of restraint of trade? Secondly, if it was, was it reasonable? The positive answer to the first question exemplifies the broader view which has recently been taken on this question. It will be seen that, although Lord Reid and Lord Wilberforce answered the first question in the same way, they proposed substantially different tests for arriving at the answer. Lord Morris and Lord Hodson agreed with Lord Reid but his test is open to serious criticism, in particular because it is formalistic and easy to evade. (Heydon, *The Restraint of Trade Doctrine* (1971), pp 55–73). Subsequent cases leave the question obscure: *Cleveland Petroleum Co Ltd v Dartstone Ltd* [1969] 1 All ER 201; *Amoco Australia Pty Ltd v Rocca Bros Motor Engineering Co Pty Ltd* [1975] AC 561, HL; *Alec Lobb (Garages) Ltd v Total Oil (GB) Ltd* [1985] 1 All ER 303, CA; but see the next case.

2. In the *Esso* case the House of Lords attached considerable weight to the public interest question. On this question they relied significantly on a contemporary report of the Monopolies Commission (1965 HC 24), which stated:

379. . . . [We] consider that the solus system for petrol, as such, has led to some reduction in suppliers' costs which has exerted a downward pressure on prices, has had some beneficial effect in producing improvements in petrol stations, does not restrict the motorist's choice of petrol and does not, in practice, lead to the setting up of excessive numbers of petrol stations. It follows from this that we think it perfectly possible to have a system of solus trading in petrol which does not operate against the public interest. In arriving at this preliminary conclusion we have left out of account a number of features of the system as now practised in this country. These are features which are capable of being altered or eliminated without destroying the basis of solus trading. It remains for us to consider whether any of these features should be altered or eliminated, or in other words whether the solus arrangements, as they exist at present, operate or may be expected to operate against the public interest in any particular respects. Broadly the questions which arise in this connection are concerned with the effects upon the public interest of:

  (i) the length of term of solus agreements:

  (ii) the terms and conditions of the loans which are made by petrol suppliers to retailers;

  (iii) the provisions of agreements concerned with the supply of petrol equipment by petrol suppliers;

  (iv) the provisions under which petrol retailers accept restrictions on their trade in other petroleum goods, in particular lubricants;

  (v) the degree of control which is, or may be, exercised by the petrol suppliers over the general conduct of their exclusive retailers' businesses, including trade in tyres, batteries and accessories;

(vi) provisions which restrict the retailer in relation to the sale of his premises, including option clauses and undertakings to obtain the purchaser's acceptance of the exclusive obligations;
(vii) the acquisition and ownership of retail premises by petrol suppliers and the terms upon which these premises are let to tenants;
(viii) arrangements at motorway petrol stations.

It is worth emphasizing that it is difficult for a court trying a restraint of trade case to ensure that all the relevant commercial and economic information is before it. The Monopolies Commission is in a much better position in this respect.

A Schroeder Music Publishing Co Ltd v Macaulay [1974] 3 All ER 616, House of Lords

The respondent, an unknown songwriter of 21, entered into an agreement with the appellants, music publishers, for his exclusive services. He gave the appellants the copyright of all compositions during the term of the contract (5 years) which was extendable for a further 5 years if royalties exceeded £5,000. The agreement was terminable by the publishers on one month's notice but not by the respondent. It was assignable by the publishers but not, without the publishers' consent, by the respondent. The publishers accepted no obligation to publish any of the songs.

The respondent sought a declaration that the contract was contrary to public policy. This was granted by Plowman J and the Court of Appeal. On appeal to the House of Lords:

Lord Reid. . . . The public interest requires in the interests both of the public and of the individual that everyone should be free so far as practicable to earn a livelihood and to give to the public the fruits of his particular abilities. The main question to be considered is whether and how far the operation of the terms of this agreement is likely to conflict with this objective. The respondent is bound to assign to the appellants during a long period the fruits of his musical talent. But what are the appellants bound to do with those fruits? Under the contract nothing. If they do use the songs which the respondent composes they must pay in terms of the contract. But they need not do so. As has been said they may put them in a drawer and leave them there. . . .

It was argued that there must be read into this agreement an obligation on the publisher to act in good faith. I take that to mean that he would be in breach of contract if by reason of some oblique or malicious motive he refrained from publishing work which he would otherwise have published. I very much doubt this but even if it were so it would make little difference. Such a case would seldom occur and then would be difficult to prove.

I agree with the appellants argument to this extent. I do not think that a publisher could reasonably be expected to enter into any positive commitment to publish future work by an unknown composer. Possibly there might be some general undertaking to use his best endeavours to promote the composer's work. But that would probably have to be in such general terms as to be of little use to the composer.

But if no satisfactory positive undertaking by the publisher can be devised, it appears to me to be an unreasonable restraint to tie the composer for this period of years so that his work will be sterilised and he can earn nothing from his abilities as a composer if the publisher chooses not to publish. If there had been in clause 9 any provision entitling the composer to terminate the agreement in such an event the case might have had a very different appearance. But as the agreement stands not only is the composer tied but he cannot recover the copyright of work which the publisher refuses to publish.

It was strenuously argued that the agreement is in standard form, that it has stood the test of time, and that there is no indication that it ever causes injustice. Reference was made to passages in the speeches of Lord Pearce and Lord Wilberforce in the *Esso* case with which I wholly agree. Lord Pearce said:

'It is important that the court, in weighing the question of reasonableness, should give full weight to commercial practices and to the generality of contracts made freely by parties bargaining on equal terms.'

Later Lord Wilberforce said:

'The development of the law does seem to show, however, that judges have been able to dispense from the necessity of justification under a public policy test of reasonableness such contracts or provisions of contracts as, under contemporary conditions, may be found to have passed into the accepted and normal currency of commercial or contractual or conveyancing relations. That such contracts have done so may be taken to show with at least strong prima force that, moulded under the pressures of negotiation, competition and public opinion, they have assumed a form which satisfies the test of public policy as understood by the courts at the time, or, regarding the matter from the point of view of the trade, that the trade in question has assumed such a form that for its health or expansion it requires a degree of regulation.'

But those passages refer to contracts 'made freely by parties bargaining on equal terms' or 'moulded under the pressures of negotiation, competition and public opinion'. I do not find from any evidence in this case, nor does it seem probable, that this form of contract made between a publisher and an unknown composer has been moulded by any pressure of negotiation. Indeed, it appears that established composers who can bargain on equal terms can and do make their own contracts.

Any contract by which a person engages to give his exclusive services to another for a period necessarily involves extensive restriction during that period of the common law right to exercise any lawful activity he chooses in such manner as he thinks best. Normally the doctrine of restraint of trade has no application to such restrictions: they require no justification. But if contractual restrictions appear to be unnecessary or to be reasonably capable of enforcement in an oppressive manner, then they must be justified before they can be enforced.

In the present case the respondent assigned to the appellants 'the full copyright for the whole world' in every musical composition 'composed created or conceived' by him alone or in collaboration with any other person during a period of five or it might be ten years. He received no payment (apart from an initial £50) unless his work was published and the appellants need not publish unless they chose to do so. And if they did not publish he had no right to terminate the agreement or to have any copyrights re-assigned to him. I need not consider whether in any circumstances it would be possible to justify such a one-sided agreement. It is sufficient to say that such evidence as there is falls far short of justification. It must therefore follow that the agreement so far as unperformed is unenforceable.

I would dismiss this appeal.

[Viscount Dilhorne, Lord Diplock, Lord Kilbrandon and Lord Simon concurred.]

Appeal dismissed.

(For extracts from Lord Diplock's judgment see above, pp 667 and 678.)

'An economic approach to unconscionability' by Trebilcock in Studies in Contract Law (ed Reiter and Swan), pp 399–404

NB. Trebilcock treats *Schroeder v Macaulay* as establishing a general doctrine of inequality of bargaining power. Your editors do not accept this, but Trebilcock's comments are illuminating.

For other extracts from this piece, see above pp 673 and 700.

It is clear that the music publishing industry does not conform to all the criteria of a perfectly competitive market, given that the products (that is, the service packages) offered by different suppliers to composers are presumably widely differentiated. Because each package may possess a degree of uniqueness, each supplier may have a small measure of ability to adjust price and output combinations in relation to his differentiated product. But, provided that a substantial measure of substitutability is possible between one supplier's product and those of others, the market is as workably competitive as most real-world markets are likely to be. Moreover, as experience in the anti-trust context has demonstrated, an industry whose products are widely differentiated will almost never be able to sustain a stable cartel, as the possibilities for cheating on agreed price and output restrictions are extensive and largely unpoliceable. This difficulty in the way of effective cartelization is, of course, compounded if the industry comprises many firms and entry barriers are low, both features of the music publishing industry, as we shall see.

The suggestion by Lord Diplock, that consumer standard-form contracts are explicable only on the basis that they are dictated by a party whose bargaining power, either exercised alone (monopolization) or in conjunction with others (cartelization), enables him to adopt the position that these are the only terms on which the product is obtainable, simply does not stand up as a matter of *a priori* analysis. This is not to suggest that monopolization or cartelization may not in fact have been present in *Macaulay*. But not a shred of relevant evidence was adduced on this issue.

In contrast, in the landmark U.S. case on manufacturers' products liability, *Henningsen v Bloomfield Motors Inc*, where the New Jersey Supreme Court struck down as unconscionable certain restrictive provisions in Chrysler's new car warranty, the court relied heavily on the fact that the 'Big Three' automobile manufacturers controlled 93.5 percent of passenger-car production in 1958 and that the warranty was a uniform warranty promulgated by the Automobile Manufacturers Association comprising all the major automobile manufacturers, including Chrysler. Thus the existence of substantial and demonstrated market power and proof of explicit cartelization in relation to warranty terms provided a defensible basis for judicial intervention. The court said: 'The gross inequality of bargaining position occupied by the consumer in the automobile industry is thus apparent. There is no competition among car makers in the area of the express warranty. Where can the car buyer go to negotiate for better protection?' The court in *Macaulay* was in a position to say none of these things. Indeed, had it chosen to examine data on the structure and performance of the music industry (which it did not), it is unlikely that it could have defended contractual invalidation on a monopolization or cartelization rationale. Before looking at this data, one or two preliminary observations are in order.

First, even if market concentration exists, there will be the intractable problem, highlighted in many anti-trust cases, of determining whether, and to what extent, it has produced anti-competitive effects. Relative long-run industry profit rates are sometimes considered an alternative, or additional, indicator of non-competitive behaviour, and may be equally relevant in a case such as *Macaulay*. However, for a variety of reasons, neither the market-concentration test, the profit-rate test, nor related tests, can be readily applied in practice to yield reliable predictions of non-competitive behaviour. Whether in ordinary civil litigation between private parties there will normally be sufficient economic incentive for parties to invest in the complex task of producing reliable economic evidence on the issue of abuse of market power raises further problems.

Secondly, the corporate structure of the defendants in *Macaulay* made it presumptively implausible that they had monopoly power or were playing a dominant firm role in the industry. The defendants were a wholly owned subsidiary of a U.S. parent company, whose sole shareholders and directors were a husband and wife. They were also the sole directors of the defendant subsidiary.

As to aggregate data on the United Kingdom music industry, unfortunately the British Census of Production does not disaggregate the numbers of firms or concentration data for either the music-publishing industry or the record-manufacturing industry. However, to cite suggestive figures, Billboard's 1975–76 International Buyer's Guide lists 428 United Kingdom music publishers (after consolidating affiliates). While the defendants in *Macaulay* appear to have been only in the music-publishing business significant integration between music publishing and record manufacturing has occurred, so that figures on record manufacturers are also worth citing. Billboard lists 276 United Kingdom record and tape manufacturers/distributors/importers (after consolidating affiliates and multiple labels) and 54 independent record producers. These numbers appear to suggest a dynamic and highly competitive music industry, probably comprising more competing firms than several of the industries cited in Lord Diplock's first category.

Because experience has shown that industry type tends to generate similar industry structures across industrialized economics, patterns in the United States music industry are worth brief mention. In 1965, an executive of a United States music publishing house, in a description of the industry, said that there are 'thousands' of music-publishing firms in the United States, one of the reasons being that they can be started up with very little capital: many attorneys know that often the only space required is a file drawer in their office and a telephone answering service. The industry was described as highly volatile, with a large annual turnover of firms. Billboard's 1975–76 International Buyer's Guide lists 1,466 United States music publishers (after consolidating affiliates), 1,027 record manufacturers (after consolidating affiliates and multiple labels), and 404 independent record producers.

It is important that the potential breadth of the decision in *Macaulay* be fully appreciated. Treating standard forms as being merely symptomatic of what Lord Diplock found ultimately objectionable in this case, that is, the exercise of abnormal market-power, the decision, in its broadest construction, appears to be enunciating the rule that any exercise of abnormal market-power, whatever its transactional form, is *prima facie* reviewable by the courts in a civil action.

The intent of the doctrine of inequality of bargaining power, at least as it emerges from *Macaulay*, is clearly to redistribute contractual incidents between contracting parties, for example, to make it less costly for songwriters to secure publishers' services and more costly for publishers to provide them, in other words to adjust the relative values exchanged. What will be its effect?

This is most easily considered by taking two polar market models: a perfectly competitive market and a monopolized market. By assumption, in a perfectly competitive market both for the final product and for intermediate inputs, no excess profits are being made (that is, no profits beyond a reasonable return on capital), so that any reduction in industry profits will also induce a reduction in output and thus intermediate inputs (for example, the work of unknown songwriters). The response of firms in such a market to a cost-increasing rule (for example, all contracts terminate on non-publication) will be to offset this cost increase with an appropriate reduction in the prices they are willing to pay for songwriters' services as a factor input in the production of music or records. In the music-publishing industry, the most obvious way of reducing the price paid for songwriters' services is for firms to cut their royalty rates. Alternatively, or in addition, because of the reduced prospect now of returns on successful composers' efforts (because of greater ease of contractual termination) publishers in their turn will presumably find it no longer rational to make the same investment in promoting unknown songwriters. Probably they will 'carry' high risks for shorter periods before setting them adrift. If this is what unknown songwriters were really demanding, why had not some publishers in the market already found it in their interests to meet that demand? If, going further than regulating termination provisions, royalty rates were also frozen at their previous level by an additional rule, firms would then reduce their demand for this class of writer, perhaps partly substituting the services of more established songwriters by paying them more to produce more, or the services of 'unknown' songwriters from other jurisdictions. Indeed, at the limit, music publishers may demand that composers compensate them directly for their promotional efforts on a composer's behalf, thus inducing a composer (rather than a publisher), in effect, to make an investment in human capital by securing at his own expense the services of an agent (a common arrangement in other contexts). In other words, any attempt to regulate the full wage (that is, the normal wage plus other, non-explicit, 'wage' terms of the contract which regulate returns to the recipient) payable to unknown songwriters will operate like a minimum wage law, perhaps benefiting some writers whose services continue to be retained, and prejudicing others whose services are displaced by substitution away from them and towards other factors of production. The lesson of economics, in this context, is that legal liability rules are unlikely to be able to affect the broad balance of advantage between buyers and sellers.

If the market for the final products of songwriters' service is monopolized, the analysis changes little. A single music-publisher acting as a monopolist in the sale of a songwriter's output is also likely to respond to a cost-increasing rule (for example, termination on non-publication) by reducing royalties or 'carry' periods. He has limited ability (depending on the price elasticity of demand and supply for his product) to pass on increased costs to consumers of the final product, and thus has an incentive to minimize costs similar to firms in a competitive industry. Even assuming supra-competitive profits, further rules which proscribe reductions in royalty rates or other contract variations (that is, increase the full wage to songwriters) will generate similar economic incentives to those facing firms in a competitive industry to make substitutions of other factors. Even the relatively enlightened decision in *Henningsen* fails to address the likely response of automobile manufacturers (assuming monopoly power) to imposed warranty terms of greater stringency than those previously prevailing and whether consumers end up any further ahead in the light of that response.

Only in the situation where a music publisher is acting as a monopsonist (that is, sole buyer) of songwriters' factor-inputs in the production of the final products being marketed by the publisher could rules imposing an increase in the full wage payable to songwriters avoid displacement effects. But problems of identifying such a factor market and of determining the magnitude of an imposed wage increase which is possible without creating displacement effects are acute.

In short, to attempt comprehensive wage rate regulation and control over employment of factors by judicial fiat in an industry like the music publishing industry, with many firms and substantial product differentiation, would make the acknowledged problems of public-utility regulation look easy. But anything short of this is like squeezing putty.

It is submitted that the difficulties exemplified in the decision in *Macaulay v Schroeder Publishing Co* suggest extreme caution on the part of courts in withholding contract enforcement on the grounds of inequality of bargaining power involving alleged abuses of market-wide monopoly power. First, inferences of such monopolies are frequently likely to be drawn incorrectly by the courts. Secondly, even where correctly drawn, the courts do not have at their disposal the remedial instruments required to foreclose all second-order, substitution, effects.

The doctrine of restraint of trade has been applied not only to new types of contract but also to other forms of restriction. In *Pharmaceutical Society of Great Britain v Dickson* [1970] AC 403 the appellant society was the professional body of registered pharmacists. The society had a code of practice which laid down guidance on professional conduct. The society was concerned about the increased selling of non-pharmaceutical goods in chemists' shops and proposed a new ethical rule which was approved by a majority of those attending a specially convened meeting of members. This rule would limit the range of goods which could be sold in existing pharmacies and require new pharmacies to be in physically distinct premises. The respondent, a member, brought an action for a declaration that the motion was ultra vires and contrary to public policy. The Society made no attempt to justify the rule but argued that the restraint of trade doctrine did not apply to rules of professional conduct. The House of Lords rejected the argument and declared the rule invalid.

NOTE

On restraint of trade generally, see Trebilcock, *The Common Law Doctrine of Restraint of Trade*.

A covenant which is in restraint of trade and which has not been shown to be reasonable is void. What is the effect on the rest of the contract? If the covenant forms the major part of the contract, the whole contract will be void. If, as more usually happens, the covenant is a subsidiary part, the convenant is void but the rest of the contract is unaffected.

In *Bennett v Bennett* [1952] 1 KB 249, Court of Appeal, a case involving a wife's covenant not to apply to the court for maintenance, Denning LJ said:

. . . In solving this problem a useful analogy may be drawn from covenants in unreasonable restraint of trade. Such covenants offend public policy, just as the covenants of a wife not to apply to the courts may do. They are not 'illegal', in the sense that a contract to do a prohibited or immoral act is illegal. They are 'unenforceable', in the sense that a contract within the Statute of Frauds is unenforceable for want of writing. These covenants lie somewhere in between. They are invalid and unenforceable. The law does not punish them. It simply takes no notice of them. They are void, not illegal. That is how they were described by the full Court of Exchequer Chamber in *Price v Green*, and by the Court of Appeal in *Evans & Co v Heathcote*.

The presence of a void covenant of this kind does not render the deed totally ineffective. That has been well shown by Professor Cheshire and Mr Fifoot in their book on Contracts, 2nd ed, pp 242–3. The party who is entitled to the benefit of the void covenant, or rather who would have been entitled to the benefit of it if it had been valid, can sue upon the other covenants of the deed which are in his favour; and he can even sue upon the void covenant, if he can sever the good from the bad (*Goldsoll v Goldman*), even to the extent of getting full liquidated damages for a breach of the good part: *Price v Green*. So also the other party, that is, the party who gave the void covenant and is not bound by its restraints, can himself sue upon the covenants in his favour, save only when his void covenant forms the whole, or substantially the whole, consideration for the deed. If the void covenant goes only to part of the consideration, so that it can be ignored and yet leave the rest of the deed a reasonable arrangement between the parties, then the deed stands and can be enforced in every respect save in regard to the void covenant.

That seems to me to be the explanation of *Bishop v Kitchen, Kearney v Whitehaven Colliery Co* and *Czarnikow v Roth, Schmidt & Co.*

A second question concerns the internal reformation of an invalid provision. Suppose a covenantee in a restraint of trade case could have enforced a reasonable restraint but the actual restraint is wider than reasonable. Will the court sever the unreasonable from the reasonable? In *Mason v Provident Clothing* (above, p 778) it will be remembered that the court refused to rewrite the covenant to make it reasonable. What if the covenant could be made reasonable by simply striking out parts of it 'with a blue pencil', as the phrase is?

Goldsoll v Goldman [1915] 1 Ch 292, Court of Appeal

Lord Cozens-Hardy MR. This is an appeal from Neville J, and the question is whether a covenant entered into between Goldsoll and Goldman is unreasonable as it stands, and, if it is, whether it is severable, so that it may be good in part and bad in part. The plaintiffs are carrying on the business of dealers in imitation jewellery. They do not carry on business in real jewellery, and I say this although some of the articles they deal in are made of real gold in which Tecla pearls are set and occasionally the pearls are set in small diamonds. Substantially the business is in imitation jewellery. In 1912 Goldman was carrying on a business in competition with Goldsoll, and the agreement in question was entered into with the object of putting an end to the competition. There was ample consideration for the agreement, and by the clause of the deed which we have to consider Goldman covenanted with Goldsoll that he would not for a period of ten years (which was reduced by a subsequent agreement to two years) 'either solely or jointly with or as agent or employee for any person or company directly or indirectly carry on or be interested in the business of a vendor of or dealer in real or imitation jewellery in the county of London, England, Scotland, Ireland, Wales, or any part of the United Kingdom of Great Britain and Ireland and the Isle of Man or in France, the United States of America, Russia or Spain, or within twenty-five miles of Potsdamerstrasse, Berlin, or St Stefans Kirche, Vienna.' Notwithstanding this covenant Goldman has, according to the finding of the learned judge, been assisting and rendering services to a confederate who is carrying on a business identical to that of the plaintiffs in the same street. It is perfectly clear that there has been a breach of the covenant; but that is not conclusive of the case, for what we have to consider is whether the covenant he has broken can be treated as good either in whole or in part, and can be enforced. On the question of the space covered by the covenant Neville J has held, and I entirely agree with him, that it is unnecessarily large in so far as it is intended to cover not merely the United Kingdom and the Isle of Man but also the foreign countries mentioned in the covenant. He has also held, and his decision is consistent with a long series of authorities, that the covenant can be severed as regards the space covered by it. It is clear that part of the covenant dealing with the area is reasonable, and the learned judge has limited the injunction he has granted to 'the county of London, England, Scotland, Ireland, Wales, or any part of the United Kingdom of Great Britain and Ireland and the Isle of Man.' That such a covenant is severable in this respect has been decided by authorities nearly 200 years old. No objection is taken or could be taken with regard to the limit of time, but the further difficulty has been raised that, while the business of the plaintiffs was, as I said, a business in imitation jewellery, the covenant is against carrying on or being interested in 'the business of a vendor of or dealer in real or imitation jewellery'. It is admitted that the business of a dealer in real jewellery is not the same as that of a dealer in imitation jewellery. There are many shopkeepers who would be insulted if they were asked whether they sold imitation jewellery. That being so, it is difficult to support the whole of this provision, for the covenant must be limited to what is reasonably necessary for the protection of the covenantee's business. Then comes the question whether the doctrine of severability is applicable to this part of the covenant. In my opinion it is, and the covenant is good in so far as it operates to restrain the covenantor from carrying on business in imitation jewellery.

[Swinfen Eady and Kennedy LJJ delivered concurring judgments.]

Appeal dismissed.

Attwood v Lamont [1920] 3 KB 571, Court of Appeal

Younger LJ. . . . [T]he position appears to be that the respondent is the owner of a considerable business at Kidderminster, described in the agreement in question as a business of drapers, tailors and general outfitters. The business is, I presume for convenience, divided into different departments all under the same roof, customers going from one to another, and many customers dealing in all departments. The agreement into which the appellant entered, a printed form which all managers of departments are required to sign with modifications of salary and detail appropriate to the individual case, is indorsed as 'An agreement not to trade in opposition within a radius of 10 miles of Regent House, Kidderminster', and contains a recital 'that the assistant', the appellant, 'has requested the employers to employ him as an assistant in their business at Kidderminster at an annual salary commencing at 208*l* and two and a half per cent commission on turnover above 1000*l* in tailoring department and the employers are only willing to do so upon his entering into the agreement not to trade in opposition with him which is hereinafter expressed' and witnesses 'that in consideration of the employers employing him in the capacity and at the salary aforesaid . . . he will not at any time thereafter . . . carry on or be in any way directly or indirectly concerned in any of the following trades or businesses, that is to say, the trade or business of a tailor, dressmaker, general draper, milliner, hatter, haberdasher, gentlemen's, ladies' or children's outfitter at any place, within a radius of 10 miles of the employers' place of business at Regent House, Kidderminster, aforesaid.' The agreement is expressed to be and is, in my opinion, nothing more than an agreement not to trade in opposition with the employers in any part of their business. It will be broken if the appellant not only carries on but is directly or indirectly concerned in any of the specified businesses; and the period of restriction is to cover the whole life of the appellant, although the employment was itself an employment only for a month certain . . .

. . . That evidence confirms me in the conclusion which I should have drawn from the case generally, that it is the appellant's known personal skill as a cutter which attracts to him the customers to whom he attended when with the respondent, and except that they made his acquaintance when he was in the respondent's service, it was not his position there, but it is his own skill which leads them to desire to have the continued benefit of his services, now that he is in business for himself. The question accordingly is whether in these circumstances, and in view of the principles applicable to them enunciated by the House of Lords, this covenant has any validity. In my opinion, as I have already said, it has none. It was apparently strongly urged in the Divisional Court that the covenant was valid as it stands. The learned judges there held that extending to businesses with which the appellant had had no connection when in the respondent's employment it was manifestly too wide, and they so held.

But the learned judges held also that they were entitled to sever the covenant by limiting it to the business of a tailor, and this they did.

Now I agree with the Master of the Rolls that this was not a case in which upon any principle this severance was permissible. The learned judges of the Divisional Court, I think, took the view that such severance always was permissible when it could be effectively accomplished by the action of a blue pencil. I do not agree. The doctrine of severance has not, I think, gone further than to make it permissible in a case where the covenant is not really a single covenant but is in effect a combination of several distinct covenants. In that case and where the severance can be carried out without the addition or alteration of a word, it is permissible. But in that case only.

Now, here, I think, there is in truth but one covenant for the protection of the respondent's entire business, and not several covenants for the protection of his several businesses. The respondent is, on the evidence, not carrying on several businesses but one business, and, in my opinion, this covenant must stand or fall in its unaltered form.

But, further, I am of opinion that even if this were not so this case is not one in which any severance, even if otherwise technically permissible, ought to be made. In my view the necessary effect of the application of the principle on which *Mason's Case* and *Morris v Saxelby* have both been decided has been to render obsolete the cases in which the Courts have severed these restrictive covenants when acting on the view that being prima facie valid it was their duty to bind the covenantee to them as far as was permissible.

[Lord Sterndale MR delivered a judgment to the same effect. Atkin LJ concurred.]

Appeal allowed.

NOTES

1. What is the distinction between these two cases?
2. For further discussion see Marsh 'The severance of illegality in contract' (1948) 64 LQR 230 and 347.

Section 10
Intermediaries, third parties and assignment

CHAPTER 39
Agency

This section examines the problems which arise in contract law when more than two parties are involved in the making of a contract, or the contract affects more than the immediate parties to it. These cases involve not only contract law but also its relationship to the law of tort and the law of property, and the various rules must be considered together if the functioning of the law is to be understood properly.

We have already seen many contracts which involved agents. The vast majority of contracts are made by agents, at least on one side, as of course, a company can only contract through agents. A complete study of the law of agency is too complex to be covered adequately in a basic contract course. This chapter will merely introduce four fundamental points: the legal effect of the normal situation where a properly authorized agent makes a contract explicitly on behalf of his principal, the types of authority, the consequences of lack of authority and the doctrine of the undisclosed principal.

(a) Intermediary or party?

When a properly authorized agent makes a contract on behalf of his principal, the normal position is that the agent can neither sue nor be sued on the contract, which is between the principal and the third party. However it is not always clear whether a person was contracting as agent or on his own behalf, or both simultaneously. In *The Swan* [1968] 1 Lloyd's Rep 5 the defendant J. D. Rodger owned the fishing vessel *Swan* which he hired to J. D. Rodger Ltd. The two plaintiffs had carried out repairs to *Swan* on instructions, some of which were oral and some on company notepaper signed 'J. D. Rodger, Director'. The plaintiffs sent their accounts to the company, which was unable to pay them. Brandon J said that whether J. D. Rodger was liable as well as the company depended on the intentions of the parties, to be gathered from the words of the agreement and the circumstances. He continued:

> Where such words are not used but the person is merely stated to be an agent, or the word 'agent' is just added after his signature, the result is uncertain, because it is not clear whether the word is used as a qualification or merely as a description: see *Gadd v Houghton and another*, per Lord Justice James; and *Universal Steam Navigation Company, Ltd v James McKelvie & Co*, per Lord Sumner. In general it would seem that in such a case the person does not avoid personal liability, although there may be exceptions to this general rule depending on the other terms of the contract or the surrounding circumstances.

Brandon J held that this case was near the borderline, but that Rodger was personally liable:

> [W]hen a person who is known or correctly assumed to be the owner of a boat, has discussions with a repairing company's manager about repairs to her, it is natural for the manager to assume that, if an order for the repairs is placed, that person will accept personal liability for them as such owner unless he makes the contrary clear beyond doubt.

In contrast see *The Santa Carina* [1977] 1 Lloyd's Rep 478, CA.

In *The Swan*, the result was that both the company and the defendant were liable. Where more than one party is liable on one side of a contract, the liabilities can be of various types, and if the contract makes no express provision the court will have to construe it to decide which was 'intended'. If there are really two separate debts, so that the creditor is entitled to be paid in full by both, the liability is called 'several'. Clearly that was not the situation in *The Swan*. If the creditor is only entitled to a single payment, the liability may be 'joint and several'. Joint liability involves a number of technical rules: in particular, all the parties jointly liable must be joined in any action and on the death of one joint party his liability passes to the other(s). It might be sensible to construe some contracts as having this effect, for instance when the joint debtors were co-trustees, but liability will more often be construed as joint and several, so that the creditor is entitled to payment once only but the technical rules of joint liability do not apply. The court may also have to decide whether the two parties on one side of the contract were *entitled* severally, jointly or jointly and severally: thus had the repairs to *Swan* been carried out defectively or late, the court might have had to decide whether Rodger and the company were each entitled to damages for their separate losses, or, if only one set of damages were payable, whether they were payable to them jointly or jointly and severally. It seems likely that Rodger and the company were liable and entitled jointly and severally; it would be inconvenient, for instance, if the company could not be sued or sue without joining Rodger as co-defendant or co-plaintiff.

(b) Types of authority

It is usually said that there are four types of authority: express, implied, ostensible (or apparent) and usual. Express authority needs no comment. Implied authority is authority to do all that is reasonably incidental to achieving what was expressly authorised, or authority by custom: in either case it may be expressly negatived or limited by the principal. Ostensible authority is a form of estoppel: if the principal by words or conduct indicates that a person has authority to act on his behalf, and the third party contracts with the agent on that basis, the principal is estopped from denying the agent's authority even if in fact the agent was unauthorised. Usual authority applies only where there is an 'undisclosed principal' and will be dealt with in section (d).

Waugh v H B Clifford and Sons Ltd [1982] 1 All ER 1095, Court of Appeal

The buyers of two houses brought an action against the builders claiming damages. Negotiations took place between the parties' solicitors over a compromise under which the builders would repurchase the houses at their current value (disregarding the alleged defects), that value to be fixed by an independant valuer. The builders' solicitors informed their clients of this proposal and stated that they would appoint a valuer unless they received contrary instructions. The builders telephoned instructions not to proceed, but the instructions did not reach the relevant partner until after he had agreed to proceed with the compromise, which the builders then claimed was not binding on them. The buyers obtained specific performance of the repurchase agreement and the builders appealed.

Brightman LJ. . . . The law thus became well established that the solicitor or counsel retained in an action has an *implied* authority as between himself and his client to compromise the suit without reference to the client, provided that the compromise does not involve matter 'collateral to the action'; and *ostensible* authority, as between himself and the opposing litigant, to compromise the suit without actual proof of authority, subject to the same limitations; and that a compromise does not involve 'collateral matter' merely because it contains terms which the court could not have ordered by way of judgment in the action: for example, the return of the piano in *Prestwich v Poley*, the withdrawal of the imputations in *Matthews v Munster* and the highly complicated terms of the compromise in *Little v Spreadbury*.

In none of the cases cited to us has there been any debate on the question whether the implied authority of the advocate or solicitor as between himself and his client is necessarily as extensive as the ostensible authority of the advocate or solicitor vis-à-vis the opposing litigant. The possibility of a difference seems to have been adverted to by Byles J in *Prestwich v Poley*. In my judgment there is every reason to draw a distinction.

Suppose that a defamation action is on foot; that terms of compromise are discussed; and that the defendant's solicitor writes to the plaintiff's solicitor offering to compromise at a figure of £100,000, which the plaintiff desires to accept. It would in my view by officious on the part of the plaintiff's solicitor to demand to be satisfied as to the authority of the defendant's solicitor to make the offer. It is perfectly clear that the defendant's solicitor has *ostensible* authority to compromise on behalf of his client, notwithstanding the large sum involved. It is not incumbent on the plaintiff to seek the signature of the defendant, if an individual, or the seal of the defendant if a corporation, or the signature of a director.

But it does not follow that the defendant's solicitor would have *implied* authority to agree damages on that scale without the agreement of his client. In the light of the solicitor's knowledge of his client's cash position it might be quite unreasonable and indeed grossly negligent for the solicitor to commit his client to such a burden without first inquiring if it were acceptable. But that does not affect the *ostensible* authority of the solicitor to compromise, so as to place the plaintiff at risk if he fails to satisfy himself that the defendant's solicitor has sought the agreement of his client. Such a limitation on the ostensible authority of the solicitor would be unworkable. How is the opposing litigant to estimate on which side of the line a particular case falls?

It follows in my view that a solicitor (or counsel) may in a particular case have ostensible authority vis-à-vis the opposing litigant where he has no implied authority vis-à-vis his client. I see no objection to that. All that the opposing litigant need ask himself when testing the ostensible authority of the solicitor or counsel, is the question whether the compromise contains matter 'collateral to the suit'. The magnitude of the compromise, or the burden which its terms impose on the other party, is irrelevant. But much more than that question may need to be asked by a solicitor when deciding whether he can safely compromise without reference to his client.

If I am right so far, all that has to be considered in the present appeal, which concerns *ostensible* and not *implied* authority, is whether the repurchase of the allegedly defective dwelling houses is properly to be described as matter collateral to the action. For the buyers and their solicitors had no notice of any limitation imposed by the builders on the *ostensible* authority of the builders' solicitors. . . .

I think it would be regrettable if this court were to place too restrictive a limitation on the *ostensible* authority of solicitors and counsel to bind their clients to a compromise. I do not think we should decide that matter is 'collateral' to the action unless it really involves extraneous subject matter . . .

I can see no difference, except in degree and in the importance of the subject matter, between this case and the case of the sale of an imperfect chattel. In an action for damages by the purchaser of a defective chattel, it would be within the *ostensible* authority of the vendor's solicitor to agree terms of compromise involving the handing back of the defective chattel in exchange for the price paid. So it was within the *ostensible* authority of the solicitor in the present case to agree terms of compromise which involved the handing back of the defective houses in return for a price reflecting their current value in proper condition. . . .

I wish to emphasise that I am not saying that the terms of compromise in the present case would have been within the *implied* authority of the builders' solicitors. . . . I would dismiss the appeal.

[Cumming Bruce and Ackner LJJ agreed.]

Appeal dismissed.

NOTE

Brightman LJ contrasts the ostensible authority of the solicitors as between themselves and the buyers with their implied authority as between themselves and the client. What does the latter mean? To put the same question another way, would the builders have any claim against the solicitors, and if so, why?

An act done by an agent who did not have authority at the time may be ratified later by the principal, with retroactive effect: thus if in the meanwhile the third party has repudiated or broken the contract the principal has an action against him. On the other hand it has been held that at common law a principal that was not in existence at the time the agent made the contract cannot subsequently ratify, so that a newly incorporated company cannot ratify prior contracts made by its promoters: *Kelner v Baxter* (1866) LR 2 CP 174. (The contract will take effect as one between the third party and the promoter: Companies Act 1985, s 36C). Also the principal cannot ratify if at the time of purported ratification it could not validly have made the contract itself: thus a principal cannot ratify a contract of insurance after the loss has occurred, *Grover & Grover Ltd v Mathews* [1910] 2 KB 401; for an exception see the Marine Insurance Act 1906, s 86. For a further restriction see below, p 821.

(c) The unauthorised agent

Yonge v Toynbee [1910] 1 KB 215, Court of Appeal

The defendant instructed solicitors to conduct his defence in an action by the plaintiff. Subsequently the defendant was certified as being of unsound mind but the solicitors did not know this; they entered an appearance on his behalf and took various subsequent steps. When the plaintiff was informed of the certification she successfully applied for the appearance and subsequent steps to be struck out, and she also applied for an order that the defendant's solicitors should pay her costs to date on the ground that the solicitors had acted without authority. This the Master refused and the judge in chambers affirmed the refusal.

Buckley LJ. . . . . The interesting and important question in this case is as to the extent to which the principle of *Smout v Ilbery* remains good law after the decision in *Collen v Wright*. . . . I understand *Smout v Ilbery* to hold that . . . where [the agent] originally had authority, but that authority has ceased without his having knowledge, or means of knowledge, that it has ceased he is not liable. . . . I can see no distinction in principle between the case where the agent never had authority and the case where the agent originally had authority, but that authority has ceased without his knowledge or means of knowledge. In the latter case as much as in the former the proposition, I think, is true that without any mala fides he has at the moment of acting represented that he had an authority which in fact he had not. In my opinion he is then liable on an implied contract that he had authority, whether there was fraud or not. That this is the true principle is, I think, shewn by passages which I will quote from judgments in three which I have selected out of the numerous cases upon this subject. In *Collen v Wright* Willes J in giving the judgment of the Court uses the following language: 'I am of opinion that a person who induces another to contract with him, as the agent of a third party, by an unqualified assertion of his being authorized to act as such agent, is answerable to the person who so contracts for any damages which he may sustain by reason of the assertion of authority being untrue. . . . The fact that the professed agent honestly thinks that he has authority affects the moral character of his act; but his moral innocence, so far as the person whom he has induced to contract, in no way aids such person or alleviates the inconvenience and damage which he sustains. The obligation arising in such a case is well expressed by saying that a person professing to contract as agent for another, impliedly, if not expressly, undertakes to or promises the person who enters into such contract, upon the faith of the professed agent being duly authorized, that the authority which he professes to have does in point of fact exist.' This language is equally applicable to each of the two classes of cases to which I have referred. The language is not, in my opinion, consistent with maintaining that which *Smout v Ilbery* had laid down as the true principle, that there must be some wrong or omission of right on the part of the agent in order to make him liable. The question is not as to his honesty or bona fides. His liability arises from an implied undertaking or promise made by him that the authority which he professes to have does in point of fact exist. I can see no difference of principle between the case in which the authority never existed at all and the case in which the authority once existed and has ceased to exist. . . .

This implied contract may, of course, be excluded by the facts of the particular case. If, for instance, the agent proved that at the relevant time he told the party with whom he was contracting that he did not know whether the warrant of attorney under which he was acting was genuine or not, and would not warrant its validity, or that his principal was abroad and he did not know whether he was still living, there will have been no representation upon which the implied contract will arise. This may have been the ratio decidendi in *Smout v Ilbery* as expressed in the passsage 'The continuance of the life of the principal was, under these circumstances, a fact equally within the knowledge of both contracting parties'; and this seems to be the ground upon which *Story on Agency*, s 265a, approves the decision. The husband had left England for China in May, 1839, a time in the history of the world when communication was not what it is now, and the Court seems to have decided upon the ground that the butcher who supplied the goods knew that the facts were such that the wife did not, because she could not, take upon herself to affirm that he was alive. If so, there was no implied contract.

For these reasons I think that the appellant is entitled to succeed and to have an order against the solicitors for damages, and the measure of damage is, no doubt, the amount of the plaintiff's costs thrown away in the action. The appeal, therefore, should be allowed with costs here and below.

[Swinfen Eady J delivered judgment to the same effect and Vaughan Williams LJ concurred.]

Appeal allowed.

NOTES

1. The agent who is made liable on an implied warranty of authority is not liable as if he were principal: he is liable for the loss of rights against the principal. This was explained by Brett MR in *Re National Coffee Palace Co, ex p Panmure* (1883) 24 Ch D 367, at 371–372, thus:

   . . . It has been held that when a person in error assumes that he has authority to make a contract for a principal when he is not really his principal, by assuming that he had authority to bind the principal, he warrants that he had that authority which he represented himself to have. The contract in respect of which damages are claimed is not the contract which the principal would have made, but only a contract to the extent of the warranty. That is shewn clearly by *Collen v Wright*. He contracts that he had authority to bind the principal whereas he had no such authority. . . . the measure of damages [is] what the plaintiff actually lost by losing the particular contract which was to have been made by the alleged principal if the defendant had had the authority he professed to have; in other words, what the plaintiff would have gained by the contract which the defendant warranted should be made. If that be the measure of damages, it does not depend upon the amount which would have been awarded to him in an action against the alleged principal if the contract had been broken by him; that may not be the same amount as what the plaintiff has actually lost. We may test it in this way. If the action were brought against the principal because he had broken the contract, the amount actually recovered would be quite different if he were solvent than if he were insolvent; if he were solvent the plaintiff would recover the whole loss, if he were insolvent he might not recover a shilling.

2. Atiyah, *Essays on Contract* (1986), pp 209–210, comments:

> It is sometimes argued that cases of implied warranty are not 'really' contractual at all; such cases are in fact actions for misrepresentation and would have been brought in tort if the law of torts had been more willing to recognize liability for misrepresentation at an earlier date. There is a germ of truth in this inasmuch as the 'promise' in many actions of this kind is plainly a fiction; the desired result is to impose liability on the agent and this is done by implying a promise. But the explanation is nevertheless not wholly acceptable. For one thing, the liability of the agent is strict; he is liable as for a warranty, and not merely for negligence. Secondly, the measure of damages awarded in these cases is plainly the measure appropriate to contract and not tort; for instance, the plaintiff can recover for loss of his profit in the *Collen v Wright* situation. I now think that these two rules (certainly the second) are mistaken deductions from the assumption that the cause of action ought to be treated as contractual, rather than as tortious, but all this goes to show how expansive the concept of contract is, and what uses it has been put to. If contract can be usefully used to enforce a tortious liability, then it is not surprising if difficulty is found in squeezing all contracts into the concept of bargain.

(d) The undisclosed principal

There is nothing to stop an agent contracting explicitly on someone else's behalf without naming his principal. The third party may not be worried about who the principal is, and if it does concern him he can of course refuse to contract without the identity of the principal being revealed. What however if the agent appears to contract in his own name but is in fact acting on behalf of an 'undisclosed' principal? Under a doctrine which common lawyers usually regard as anomalous, the principal can both sue and be sued on the contract, unless to permit this would be inconsistent with the express terms of the contract or the contract involves some personal element. Thus in *Said v Butt* [1920] 3 KB 497 the plaintiff wished to attend the opening night of a play but knew that the management would refuse an application for a ticket made in his own name because he had made serious and unfounded allegations against members of the theatre staff. He therefore arranged for a friend to buy the ticket without disclosing that it was for the plaintiff. The plaintiff was refused admission to the theatre on the orders of the defendant, the managing director, and the plaintiff claimed damages from him for maliciously procuring a breach of a contract between the plaintiff and the theatre. McCardie J held that the contract for a ticket to the first night was one involving a personal element and that, as the theatre would not have contracted with the plaintiff directly, he could not claim to be an undisclosed principal and could not claim that any breach of contract between him and the theatre had been caused. (Compare *Dyster v Randall & Sons* [1926] Ch 932.)

Keighley, Maxsted & Co v Durant [1900–3] All ER Rep 40, House of Lords

The following statement of facts is taken from the opinion of **Lord Brampton**:
  The appellants, Keighley, Maxsted & Co, were corn merchants at Hull, and one Wright was

their manager and agent. Durant, the respondent, was a corn merchant in London, trading as Bryan, Durant & Co, and one Roberts was a corn merchant at Wakefield. On the morning of May 11, 1898, Roberts received from Durant's brokers a telegram containing an offer from Durant of 500 tons of new white Karachi wheat at 46s per quarter and 500 tons of red wheat at 45s per quarter. Later on the same morning Roberts had an interview with Wright, and told him of Durant's offer, and they agreed that, if Roberts could get the wheat at 45s 3d for the white and 44s 3d for the red, Roberts and Keighleys would become the purchasers on joint account. Roberts, however, was unable to get the wheat at those prices; the proposal, therefore, for a purchase on joint account came to nothing. Between 3 and 4 pm on the same day, Roberts, without any further communication with or authority from Keighleys, and apparently purely on his own separate and sole account, by an interchange of telegrams with Durant's brokers, concluded a contract for the purchase by him, in his own name, from Durant of the whole of the wheat, at 45s 6d for the white and 44s 6d for the red. On the following day, May 12, Roberts met Wright casually at the Manchester Corn Market, and told him that he had bought the wheat at 3d a quarter more than the price they had settled on the previous day. Wright replied he had given too much, but he thought the wheat was worth it, and told him to take it. Roberts did so, but failing to fulfill his contract with Durant the latter sold it at a loss, to recover which this action was commenced by Durant against Roberts and Keighley, Maxsted & Co jointly, upon the suggestion of Roberts that this purchase had been made on joint account. Day J, gave judgment for Keighley, Maxsted & Co, on the ground that they were not parties to the contract, and no subsequent ratification by them could make them liable to sue or be sued upon it, but his judgment was reversed by the Court of Appeal, and Keighley, Maxsted & Co now appealed to the House of Lords.

Lord Macnaghten. . . . As a general rule, only persons who are parties to a contract acting either by themselves or by an authorised agent can sue or be sued on the contract. A stranger cannot enforce the contract, nor can it be enforced against a stranger. That is the rule; but there are exceptions. The most remarkable exception, I think, results from the doctrine of ratification as established in English law. The doctrine is thus stated by Tindal, CJ, in *Wilson v Tumman*:

> 'That an act done, for another, by a person, not assuming to act for himself, but for such other person, though without any precedent authority whatever, becomes the act of the principal, if subsequently ratified by him, is the known and well-established rule of law. In that case the principal is bound by the Act, whether it be for his detriment or his advantage, and whether it be founded on a tort or on a contract to the same effect as by, and with all the consequences which follow from, the same act done by his previous authority.'

And so by a wholesome and convenient fiction a person ratifying the act of another who without authority has made a contract openly and avowedly on his behalf, is deemed to be, though in fact he was not, a party to the contract. Does the fiction cover the case of a person who makes no avowal at all, but assumes to act for himself and for no one else? If Tindal CJ's statement of the law is accurate, it would seem to exclude the case of a person who may intend to act for another, but at the same time keeps his intentions locked up in his own breast; for it cannot be said that a person who so conducts himself does assume to act for anybody but himself.

But ought the doctrine of ratification to be extended to such a case? On principle I should say certainly not. It is, I think, a well-estabished principle in English law that civil obligations are not to be created by or founded upon undisclosed intentions. That is a very old principle. Lord Blackburn, enforcing it in *Brogden v Metropolitan Rail Co*, traces it back to the *Year Books* of Edward IV (17 Edw 4, 2 Term Pasc) and to a quaint judgment of Brian CJ, a great authority in those days, who said:

> 'It is common learning that the thought of a man is not triable, for the Devil has not knowledge of man's thoughts.'

Sir E. Fry quotes the same observation in his work on *Specific Performance* (3rd Edn), s 282. It is, I think, a sound maxim—at least, in its legal aspect—and, in my opinion, it is not to be put aside or disregarded merely because it may be that in a case like the present no injustice might be done to the actual parties to the contract by giving effect to the undisclosed intentions of a would-be agent.

. . . [I]t seems to me to be conclusive against the argument for the respondent, that if his reasoning were sound it would be in his power, on an averment of what was passing in his own mind, to make the contract afterwards, either one for himself only, as in fact it was, or one affecting or binding on another as a contracting party, even although he had no authority for this. The result would be to give one of two contracting parties in his option, merely from what was passing in his own mind, and not disclosed, the power of saying that the contract was his alone, or a contract in which others were bound to him. That I think he certainly cannot do in any case where he had no authority when he made the contract to bind anyone but himself. . . .

Lord Davey. . . . [T]he rule which permits an undisclosed principal to sue and be sued on a contract to which he is not a party, though well settled, is itself an anomaly, and to extend it to the case of a person who accepts the benefit of an undisclosed intention of a party to the contract would, in my opinion, be adding another anomaly to the law, and not correcting an anomaly.

[The other members of the House delivered judgments to similar effect.]

Appeal allowed.

Watteau v Fenwick [1893] 1 QB 346

Lord Coleridge CJ. The judgment which I am about to read has been written by my brother Wills, and I entirely concur in it.

Wills J. The plaintiff sues the defendants for the price of cigars supplied to the Victoria Hotel, Stockton-upon-Tees. The house was kept, not by the defendants, but by a person named Humble, whose name was over the door. The plaintiff gave credit to Humble, and to him alone, and had never heard of the defendants. The business, however, was really the defendants', and they had put Humble into it to manage it for them, and had forbidden him to buy cigars on credit. The cigars, however, were such as would usually be supplied to and dealt in at such an establishment. The learned county court judge held that the defendants were liable. I am of opinion that he was right.

There seems to be less of direct authority on the subject than one would expect. But I think that the Lord Chief Justice during the argument laid down the correct principle, viz, once it is established that the defendant was the real principal, the ordinary doctrine as to principal and agent applies—that the principal is liable for all the acts of the agent which are within the authority usually confided to an agent of that character, notwithstanding limitations, as between the principal and the agent, put upon that authority. It is said that it is only so where there has been a holding out of authority—which cannot be said of a case where the person supplying the goods knew nothing of the existence of a principal. But I do not think so. Otherwise, in every case of undisclosed principal, or at least in every case where the fact of there being a principal was undisclosed, the secret limitation of authority would prevail and defeat the action of the person dealing with the agent and then discovering that he was an agent and had a principal.

But in the case of a dormant partner it is clear law that no limitation of authority as between the dormant and active partner will avail the dormant partner as to things within the ordinary authority of a partner. The law of partnerships is, on such a question, nothing but a branch of the general law of principal and agent, and it appears to me to be undisputed and conclusive on the point now under discussion.

The principle laid down by the Lord Chief Justice, and acted upon by the learned county court judge, appears to be identical with that enunciated in the judgments of Cockburn CJ, and Mellor J, in *Edmunds v Bushell*, the circumstances of which case, though not identical with those of the present, come very near to them. There was no holding out, as the plaintiff knew nothing of the defendant. I appreciate the distinction drawn by Mr Finlay in his argument, but the principle laid down in the judgments referred to, if correct, abundantly covers the present case. I cannot find that any doubt has ever been expressed that it is correct, and I think it is right, and that very mischievous consequences would often result if that principle were not upheld.

In my opinion this appeal ought to be dismissed with costs.

Appeal dismissed.

NOTE

Is it consistent with the approach in the *Keighley* case to make an undisclosed principal liable for something he had not actually authorized (indeed had forbidden), when ex hypothesi the plaintiff knew nothing of him at the time he contracted with the agent? The correctness of this case has often been doubted, but it remains the law: see Treitel, pp 538–539.

A third party who thought that he was dealing with the agent personally might be seriously prejudiced if he found that the agent was acting for an undisclosed principal with whom the third party would not have dealt—for instance because he distrusted him or doubted his credit—and had no rights against the agent personally. For this reason the case of the undisclosed principal is subject to another exceptional rule—the third party can elect to hold the agent liable rather than the principal, and the agent may sue on the contract in turn. As to what constitutes election, see *Clarkson Booker Ltd v Andjel* [1964] 2 QB 775.

CHAPTER 40

Privity and the benefit of a contract between others

We now turn to the question of the extent to which a person who is not a party to a contract can gain rights under it (the benefit) or be adversely affected by it (the burden). This chapter looks at the question of benefits under the original contract, and chapter 41 at the subsequent passing of benefits by assignment. Chapters 42 and 43 then look at questions of burdens.

The cases to be considered fall into two groups. The first group (sections (a) to (e)) raise the question of how a contract between A and B under which A promises to confer a benefit on C can be enforced. It would clearly be inefficient if neither B nor C could enforce the contract against A, as this would allow A to break a deliberate bargain with impunity; but which of them should be able to enforce A's promise, and how? The second group of cases (sections (f) and (g)) involve a rather different problem: to what extent can a contract which purports to be solely between A and B, and not to mention C, but which is to C's advantage, be enforced by him?

(a) The basic rule

Dunlop Pneumatic Tyre Co Ltd v Selfridge & Co Ltd [1915] AC 847, House of Lords

The plaintiffs had sold some of their tyres to Dew & Co, on terms that Dews would not resell them at less than the plaintiffs' list prices and that, if they resold them to trade buyers, they would extract a similar undertaking from the trade buyers. Dews resold the tyres to Selfridge, who agreed to observe the restrictions and to pay to Dunlops £5 for each tyre sold in breach of the agreement. Selfridge supplied tyres to two of their customers at below the list price, and Dunlops sought to recover two sums of £5 each as liquidated damages.

Viscount Haldane LC. . . . My Lords, in the law of England certain principles are fundamental. One is that only a person who is a party to a contract can sue on it. Our law knows nothing of a jus quaesitum tertio arising by way of contract. Such a right may be conferred by way of property, as, for example, under a trust, but it cannot be conferred on a stranger to a contract as a right to enforce the contract in personam. A second principle is that if a person with whom a contract not under seal has been made is to be able to enforce it consideration must have been given by him to the promisor or to some other person at the promisor's request. These two principles are not recognized in the same fashion by the jurisprudence of certain Continental countries or of Scotland, but here they are well established. A third proposition is that a principal not named in the contract may sue upon it if the promisee really contracted as his agent. But again, in order to entitle him so to sue, he must have given consideration either personally or through the promisee, acting as his agent in giving it.

My Lords, in the case before us, I am of opinion that the consideration, the allowance of what was in reality part of the discount to which Messrs Dew, the promisees, were entitled as between themselves and the appellants, was to be given by Messrs Dew on their own account, and was not in substance, any more than in form, an allowance made by the appellants. The case for the appellants is that they permitted and enabled Messrs Dew, with the knowledge and by the desire of the respondents, to sell to the latter on the terms of the contract of January 2, 1912. But it appears to me that even if this is so the answer is conclusive. Messrs Dew sold to the respondents goods which they had a title to obtain from the appellants independently of this contract. The consideration by way of discount under the contract of January 2 was to come wholly out of Messrs Dew's pocket, and neither directly nor indirectly out of that of the appellants. If the appellants enabled them to sell to the respondents on the terms they did, this was not done as any part of the terms of the contract sued on.

No doubt it was provided as part of these terms that the appellants should acquire certain rights, but these rights appear on the face of the contract as jura quaesita tertio, which the appellants could not enforce. Moreover, even if this difficulty can be got over by regarding the appellants as the principals of Messrs Dew in stipulating for the rights in question, the only consideration disclosed by the contract is one given by Messrs Dew, not as their agents, but as principals acting on their own account.

The conclusion to which I have come on the point as to the consideration renders it unnecessary to decide the further question as to whether the appellants can claim that a bargain was made in this contract by Messrs Dew as their agents; a bargain which, apart from the point as to consideration, they could therefore enforce. If it were necessary to express an opinion on this further question, a difficulty as to the position of Messrs Dew would have to be considered. Two contracts—one by a man on his own account as principal, and another by the same man as agent—may be validly comprised in the same piece of paper. But they must be two contracts, and not one as here. I do not think that a man can treat one and the same contract as made by him in two capacities. He cannot be regarded as contracting for himself and for uno flatu.

My Lords, the form of the contract which we have to interpret leaves the appellants in this dilemma, that, if they say that Messrs Dew contracted on their behalf, they gave no consideration, and if they say they gave consideration in the shape of a permission to the respondents to buy, they must set up further stipulations, which are neither to be found in the contract sued upon nor are germane to it, but are really inconsistent with its structure. That contract has been reduced to writing, and it is in the writing that we must look for the whole of the terms made between the parties. These terms cannot, in my opinion consistently with the settled principles of English law, be construed as giving to the appellants any enforceable rights as against the respondents.

I think that the judgment of the Court of Appeal was right, and I move that the appeal be dismissed with costs.

Lord Dunedin. My Lords, I confess that this case is to my mind apt to nip any budding affection which one might have had for the doctrine of consideration. For the effect of that doctrine in the present case is to make it possible for a person to snap his fingers at a bargain deliberately made, a bargain not in itself unfair, and which the person seeking to enforce it has a legitimate interest to enforce. Notwithstanding these considerations I cannot say that I have ever had any doubt that the judgment of the Court of Appeal was right.

[Lord Dunedin referred to Pollock's definition of consideration, above, p 91.]

. . . [S]peaking for myself, I should have no difficulty in the circumstances of this case in holding it proved that the agreement was truly made by Dew as agent for Dunlop, or in other words that Dunlop was the undisclosed principal, and as such can sue on the agreement. None the less, in order to enforce it he must show consideration, as above defined, moving from Dunlop to Selfridge.

In the circumstances, how can he do so? The agreement in question is not an agreement for sale. It is only collateral to an agreement for sale; but that agreement for sale is an agreement entirely between Dew and Selfridge. The tyres, the property in which upon the bargain is transferred to Selfridge, were the property of Dew, not of Dunlop, for Dew under his agreement with Dunlop held these tyres as proprietor, and not as agent. What then did Dunlop do, or forbear to do, in a question with Selfridge? The answer must be, nothing.

To my mind, this ends the case. That there are methods of framing a contract which will cause persons in the position of Selfridge to become bound, I do not doubt. But that has not been done in this instance; and as Dunlop's advisers must have known of the law of consideration, it is their affair that they have not so drawn the contract.

I think the appeal should be dismissed.

[Lords Atkinson, Parker, Sumner and Parmoor also thought the appeal should be dismissed for similar reasons.]

Appeal dismissed.

NOTES

1. The doctrine of privity appears to have become firmly established in the case of *Tweddle v Atkinson* (1861) 1 B & S 393, 30 LJQB 265. In consideration of the intended marriage between his daughter and the plaintiff, Guy made a contract with the plaintiff's father whereby each promised to pay the plaintiff a sum of money. Guy failed to pay and the plaintiff sued his executors. The action was dismissed on the ground that the plaintiff was a stranger to the consideration.

2. It is much disputed whether the doctrine of privity is made up of two rules, as Viscount Haldane seems to suggest, or one, namely that only someone who is party to a bargain can enforce it: see Furmston, 23 MLR 383–384. It is not clear that it makes any practical difference, nor in the opinion of some of your editors that there is any real difference between the two viewpoints: one may 'not be party' to a bargain either because he does not assent to it even though he provides something that could be labelled consideration, or because though he assents he does not provide consideration—or, of course, for both reasons at once. In the *Dunlop* case it seems the lack of consideration was the critical factor: the House of Lords were not convinced that Dews were acting as agents for Dunlops, but said that even if they were (which would make Dunlops 'a party' in the sense of assenting) their claim would fail for want of consideration.

3. Lord Dunedin said he did not doubt that Dunlops could have framed the agreement so as to bind Selfridge. How do you think this could have been done? You may like to return to this question when you have read the rest of the chapter.

4. Could Dews have forced Selfridge to pay the £5 per tyre to Dunlops?

Beswick v Beswick [1968] AC 58, House of Lords

Lord Reid. My Lords, before 1962 the respondent's deceased husband carried on business as a coal merchant. By agreement of March 14, 1962, he assigned to his nephew, the appellant, the assets of the business and the appellant undertook first to pay to him £6 10s per week for the remainder of his life and then to pay to the respondent an annuity of £5 per week in the event of her husband's death. The husband died in November, 1963. Thereupon, the appellant made one payment of £5 to the respondent but he refused to make any further payment to her. The respondent now sues for £175 arrears of the annuity and for an order for specific performance of the continuing obligation to pay the annuity. The Vice-Chancellor of the County Palatine of Lancaster decided against the respondent but the Court of Appeal reversed this decision and, besides ordering payment of the arrears, ordered the appellant to pay to the respondent for the remainder of her life an annuity of £5 per week in accordance with the agreement.

It so happens that the respondent is administratrix of the estate of her deceased husband and she sues both in that capacity and in her personal capacity. So it is necessary to consider her rights in each capacity.

For clarity I think it best to begin by considering a simple case where, in consideration of a sale by A to B, B agrees to pay the price of £1,000 to a third party X. Then the first question appears to me to be whether the parties intended that X should receive the money simply as A's nominee so that he would hold the money for behoof of A and be accountable to to him for it, or whether the parties intended that X should receive the money for his own behoof and be entitled to keep it. That appears to me to be a question of construction of the agreement read in light of all the circumstances which were known to the parties. There have been several decisions involving this question. I am not sure that any conflicts with the view which I have expressed: but if any does, for example, *In re Engelbach's Estate*, I would not agree with it. I think that *In re Schebsman* was rightly decided and that the reasoning of Uthwatt J and the Court of Appeal supports what I have just said. In the present case I think it clear that the parties to the agreement intended that the respondent should receive the weekly sums of £5 in her own behoof and should not be accountable to her deceased husband's estate for them. Indeed the contrary was not argued.

Reverting to my simple example the next question appears to me to be: Where the intention was that X should keep the £1,000 as his own, what is the nature of B's obligation and who is entitled to enforce it? It was not argued that the law of England regards B's obligation as a nullity, and I have not observed in any of the authorities any suggestion that it would be a nullity. There may have been a time when the existence of a right depended on whether there was any means of enforcing it, but today the law would be sadly deficient if one found that, although there is a right, the law provides no means for enforcing it. So this obligation of B must be enforceable either by X or by A. I shall leave aside for the moment the question whether section 56(1) of the Law of Property Act 1925, has any application to such a case, and consider the position at common law.

Lord Denning's view, expressed in this case not for the first time, is that X could enforce this obligation. But the view more commonly held in recent times has been that such a contract confers no right on X and that X could not sue for the £1,000. Leading counsel for the respondent based his case on other grounds, and as I agree that the respondent succeeds on other grounds, this would not be an appropriate case in which to solve this question. It is true that a strong Law Revision Committee recommended so long ago as 1937 (Cmd 5449):

'That where a contract by its express terms purports to confer a benefit directly on a third party it shall be enforceable by the third party in his own name . . .' (p 31).

And, if one had to contemplate a further long period of Parliamentary procrastination, this House might find it necessary to deal with this matter. But if legislation is probable at any early date I would not deal with it in a case where that is not essential. So for the purposes of this case I shall proceed on the footing that the commonly accepted view is right.

What then is A's position? I assume that A has not made himself a trustee for X, because it was not argued in this appeal that any trust had been created. So, if X has no right, A can at any time grant a discharge to B or make some new contract with B. If there were a trust the position would be different. X would have an equitable right and A would be entitled and, indeed, bound to recover the money and account for it to X. And A would have no right to grant a discharge to B. If there is no trust and A wishes to enforce the obligation, how does he set about it? He cannot sue B for the £1,000 because under the contract the money is not payable to him, and, if the contract were performed according to its terms, he would never have any right to get the money. So he must seek to make B pay X.

The argument for the appellant is that A's only remedy is to sue B for damages for B's breach of contract in failing to pay the £1,000 to X. Then the appellant says that A can only recover nominal damages of 40s because the fact that X has not received the money will generally cause no loss to A: he admits that there may be cases where A would suffer damage if X did not receive the money but says that the present is not such a case.

Applying what I have said to the circumstances of the present case, the respondent in her personal capacity has no right to sue, but she has a right as administratrix of her husband's estate to require the appellant to perform his obligation under the agreement. He has refused to do so and he maintains that the respondent's only right is to sue him for damages for breach of his contract. If that were so, I shall assume that he is right in maintaining that the administratrix could then only recover nominal damages because his breach of contract has caused no loss to the estate of her deceased husband.

If that were the only remedy available the result would be grossly unjust. It would mean that the appellant keeps the business which he bought and for which he has only paid a small part of the price which he agreed to pay. He would avoid paying the rest of the price, the annuity to the respondent, by paying a mere 40s damages.

. . . The respondent's second argument is that she is entitled in her capacity of administratrix of her deceased husband's estate to enforce the provision of the agreement for the benefit of herself in her personal capacity, and that a proper way of enforcing that provision is to order specific performance. That would produce a just result, and, unless there is some technical objection, I am of opinion that specific performance ought to be ordered. For the reasons given by your Lordships I would reject the arguments submitted for the appellant that specific performance is not a possible remedy in this case.

Lord Pearce. My Lords, if the annuity had been payable to a third party in the lifetime of Beswick senior and there had been default, he could have sued in respect of the breach. His administratrix is now entitled to stand in his shoes and to sue in respect of the breach which has occurred since his death.

It is argued that the estate can only recover nominal damages and that no other remedy is open, either to the estate or to the personal plaintiff. Such a result would be wholly repugnant to justice and commonsense. And if the argument were right it would show a very serious defect in the law.

In the first place, I do not accept the view that damages must be nominal. Lush LJ in *Lloyd's v Harper* said:

> 'Then the next question which, no doubt, is a very important and substantial one, is, that Lloyd's, having sustained no damage themselves, could not recover for the losses sustained by third parties by reason of the default of Robert Henry Harper as an underwriter. That, to my mind, is a startling and alarming doctrine, and a novelty, because I consider it to be an established rule of law that where a contract is made with A for the benefit of B, A can sue on the contract for the benefit of B, and recover all that B could have recovered if the contract had been made with B himself.'

(See also *Drimmie v Davies*.) I agree with the comment of Windeyer J in the case of *Coulls v Bagot's Executor and Trustee Co Ltd* in the High Court of Australia that the words of Lush LJ cannot be accepted without qualification and regardless of context and also with his statement:

> 'I can see no reason why in such cases the damages which A would suffer upon B's breach of his contract to pay C \$500 would be merely nominal: I think that in accordance with the ordinary rules for the assessment of damages for breach of contract they could be substantial. They would not necessarily be \$500, they could I think be less or more.'

In the present case I think that the damages, if assessed, must be substantial. It is not necessary, however, to consider the amount of damages more closely since this is a case in which, as the Court of Appeal rightly decided, the more appropriate remedy is that of specific performance.

The administratrix is entitled, if she so prefers, to enforce the agreement rather than accept its repudiation, and specific performance is more convenient than action for arrears of payment followed by separate actions as each sum falls due. Moreover, damages for breach would be a less appropriate remedy since the parties to the agreement were intending an annuity for a widow; and a lump sum of damages does not accord with this. And if (contrary to my view) the argument that a derisory sum of damages is all that can be obtained be right, the remedy of damages in this case is manifestly useless.

The present case presents all the features which led the equity courts to apply their remedy of specific performance. The contract was for the sale of a business. The defendant could on his part clearly have obtained specific performance of it if Beswick senior or his administratrix had defaulted. Mutuality is a ground in favour of specific performance.

Moreover, the defendant on his side has received the whole benefit of the contract and it is a matter of conscience for the court to see that he now performs his part of it. Kay J said in *Hart v Hart*:

> '. . . when an agreement for valuable consideration . . . has been partially performed, the court ought to do its utmost to carry out that agreement by a decree for specific performance.'

What, then, is the obstacle to granting specific performance?

It is argued that since the widow personally had no rights which she personally could enforce the court will not make an order which will have the effect of enforcing those rights. I can find no principle to this effect. The condition as to payment of an annuity to the widow personally was valid. The estate (though not the widow personally) can enforce it. Why should the estate be barred from exercising its full contractual rights merely because in doing so it secures justice for the widow who, by a mechanical defect of our law, is unable to assert her own rights? Such a principle would be repugnant to justice and fulfil no other object than that of aiding the wrongdoer. I can find no ground on which such a principle should exist.

[Lords Upjohn, Hodson and Guest agreed that, in her capacity as administratrix, Mrs Beswick was entitled to specific performance.]

Appeal dismissed.

NOTES

1. The extract above omits the second point of the decision, which was that the doctrine of privity of contract was not overturned by the Law of Property Act 1925, s 56(1). The effect of that section is dealt with below, p 814.
2. *Beswick v Beswick* reaffirms that a person who is not a party to a contract cannot enforce it. Who is a party to a contract? Would Mrs Beswick have been able to claim the money in her own name if, for instance, she had signed the agreement? The answer seems to depend on a number of factors. Firstly, she certainly could not claim unless she could show that the agreement was intended to give her a right to the money, rather than merely giving the nephew authority to pay her in discharge of his obligations. The fact of her signature would not be conclusive on this point. In *Coulls v Bagot's Executor and Trustee Co Ltd* (1967) 119 CLR 460 an agreement for royalties for quarrying provided:

> I authorize the . . . Company to pay all money connected with this agreement to my wife, Doris Sophia Coulls and myself, Arthur Leopold Coulls as joint tenants (or tenants in common?) (the one which goes to the living partner) [sic].

It was signed by Mrs Coulls as well as her husband. However the majority of the High Court of Australia held that this was merely a mandate to pay in this manner and was revoked by the husband's death, so that the royalties belonged to his estate. One of the reasons was that the husband said he 'authorised' payment to her, which was incompatible with her having a right. In *Beswick*, however, it was clear that it was intended that Mrs Beswick should have a right to the money: see the judgment of Lord Reid.

Secondly, however, it is doubtful whether the act of signing (even explicitly signing 'as a party') would make Mrs Beswick privy to the contract if (as was the case) she provided no consideration. It is possible that if the nephew had promised his uncle and aunt *jointly*, she might have an enforceable right. A different majority in *Coulls'* case said that the court would not enquire which of the joint promisees had provided the consideration. Thus Barwick CJ said:

> In such a case it cannot lie in the mouth of A, in my opinion, to question whether the consideration which he received for his promise moved from both B and C, or as between themselves, only from one of them.

Support for this in English law may be found in a dictum of Lord Atkin in *McEvoy v Belfast Banking Co Ltd* [1935] AC 24. A customer had deposited funds in the joint names of himself and his infant son, and after his death the money had been taken by his executors. Some time after his majority the son claimed the money from the bank. His claim failed for another reason but Atkin said:

> The suggestion is that where A deposits a sum of money with his bank in the names of A and B, payable to A or B, if B comes to the bank with the deposit receipt he has no right to demand the money from the bank or to sue them if his demand is refused. . . . I have myself no doubt that in such a case B can sue the bank. The contract on the face of it purports to be made with A and B, and I think with them jointly and severally. A purports to make the contract on behalf of B as well as himself and the consideration supports such a contract. If A has actual authority from B to make such a contract, B is a party to the contract ab initio. If he has not actual authority then subject to the ordinary principles of ratification B can ratify the contract purporting to have been made on his behalf and his ratification relates back to the original formation of the contract.

It has been pointed out, however, that these dicta confuse two questions, the promise of consideration and the performance of the promise. It does not matter which of the two actually furnished the consideration; but it is crucial to know whether the joint promisees were both undertaking (in a bilateral contract) to provide it or see that it was provided by the other. If one of two apparently joint promisees was not so undertaking he or she was not a party to the bargain and should have no enforceable right (Coote [1978] CLJ 301). This seems theoretically correct, but it is of course inconsistent with Lord Atkin's dictum at least, because the son had provided no consideration.

Thus it remains uncertain whether Mrs Beswick could have sued on the agreement in her own name even if she had signed it as a joint promisee.

3. How could the sale have been arranged so as to give Mrs Beswick an indisputable right to the £5 per week?

4. Why was the administratrix granted specific performance? Was it to avoid the need for an action every time the nephew failed to pay an instalment? Or because the estate was losing nothing? Or because the estate was losing nothing *and* the nephew would otherwise escape paying the full price for what he had received? Do you think specific performance would have been granted if old Mr Beswick had died before the business had been transferred to the nephew?

(b) Damages on behalf of another

In *Jackson v Horizon Holidays Ltd* [1975] 3 All ER 92 the plaintiff booked a package holiday for himself and his family. The accommodation and facilities provided were not in accordance with the contract, and the plaintiff claimed damages in respect of the loss of the holiday for himself, his wife and his children. The defendants admitted liability but appealed against the trial judge's award of £1,100 damages. The Court of Appeal dismissed the appeal. Lord Denning MR said that the father had made the contract for the benefit of his wife and children and could recover damages for their loss as well as his own; he relied on the dictum of Lush LJ in *Lloyd's v Harper* quoted by Lord Pearce in *Beswick v Beswick*, above, p 808. James LJ said that the father had contracted for a family holiday and had not received one. Orr LJ gave no reasons.

Woodar Investment Development Ltd v Wimpey Construction (UK) Ltd [1980] 1 All ER 571, House of Lords

The main question in this case was whether the purchasers had wrongfully repudiated the contract. The House of Lords held that they had not (see above, p 445). One point that was discussed in argument was, if the purchasers had wrongfully repudiated, what the measure of damages would be, since under the contract £150,000 of the purchase price was to be paid not to the vendors but to Transworld Trade Ltd, a Hong Kong company not directly connected with the vendors.

Lord Wilberforce. . . . . The second issue in this appeal is one of damages. Both courts below have allowed Woodar to recover substantial damages in respect of condition 1 under which £150,000 was payable by Wimpey to Transworld Trade Ltd on completion. On the view which I take of the repudiation issue, this question does not require decision, but in view of the unsatisfactory state in which the law would be if the Court of Appeal's decision were to stand I must add three observations.

1. The majority of the Court of Appeal followed, in the case of Goff LJ with expressed reluctance, its previous decision in *Jackson v Horizon Holidays Ltd*. I am not prepared to dissent from the actual decision in that case. It may be supported either as a broad decision on the measure of damages (per James LJ) or possibly as an example of a type of contract, examples of which are persons contracting for family holidays, ordering meals in restaurants for a party, hiring a taxi for a group, calling for special treatment. As I suggested in *New Zealand Shipping Co Ltd v A M Satterthwaite & Co Ltd*, there are many situations of daily life which do not fit neatly into conceptual analysis, but which require some flexibility in the law of contract. *Jackson's* case may well be one.

I cannot agree with the basis on which Lord Denning MR put his decision in that case. The extract on which he relied from the judgment of Lush LJ in *Lloyd's v Harper* was part of a passage in which Lush LJ was stating as an 'established rule of law' that an agent (sc an insurance broker) may sue on a contract made by him on behalf of the principal (sc the assured) if the contract gives him such a right, and is no authority for the proposition required in *Jackson's* case, still less for the proposition, required here, that, if Woodar made a contract for a sum of money to be paid to Transworld, Woodar can, without showing that it has itself suffered loss or that Woodar was agent or trustee for Transworld, sue for damages for non-payment of that sum. That would certainly not be an established rule of law, nor was it quoted as such authority by Lord Pearce in *Beswick v Beswick*.

2. Assuming that *Jackson's* case was correctly decided (as above), it does not carry the present case, where the factual situation is quite different. I respectfully think therefore that the Court of Appeal need not, and should not have followed it.

3. Whether in a situation such as the present, viz where it is not shown that Woodar was agent or trustee for Transworld, or that Woodar itself sustained any loss, Woodar can recover any damages at all, or any but nominal damages, against Wimpey, and on what principle, is, in my opinion, a question of great doubt and difficulty; no doubt open in this House, but one on which I prefer to reserve my opinion.

[**Lord Russell** agreed with Lord Wilberforce, remarking on *Jackson's* case:]

. . . I do not criticize the outcome of that case: the plaintiff had bought and paid for a high class family holiday; he did not get it, and therefore he was entitled to substantial damages for the failure to supply *him* with one. It is to be observed that the order of the Court of Appeal as drawn up did not suggest that any part of the damages awarded to him were 'for the use and benefit of' any member of his family. It was a special case quite different from the instant case on the Transworld point.

[Lord Keith spoke to the same effect.]

Lord Scarman. . . . It being the view of the majority of the House that there was no repudiation, the appeal must be allowed, with the result that there is no need to consider the other issues raised. But because of its importance, I propose to say a few words on the question of damages.

Woodar agreed to sell the land to Wimpey for £850,000. They also required Wimpey to pay £150,000 to a third party. The covenant for this payment was in the following terms: 'I. Upon completion of the purchase of the whole or any part of the land the purchaser shall pay to Transworld Trade Limited of 25 Jermyn Street, London, SW1 a sum of £150,000'. No relationship of trust or agency was proved to exist between Woodar and Transworld. No doubt, it suited Mr Cornwell to split up the moneys payable under the contract between the two companies; but it is not known, let alone established by evidence (though an intelligent guess is possible) why he did so, or why Woodar desired this money to be paid to Transworld. It is simply a case of B agreeing with A to pay a sum of money to C.

B, in breach of his contract with A, has failed to pay C. C it is said, has no remedy, because the English law of contract recognises no 'jus quaesitum tertio': see *Tweddle v Atkinson*. No doubt, it was for this reason that Transworld is not a party to the suit. A, it is acknowledged, could in certain circumstances obtain specific performance of the promise to pay C: see *Beswick v Beswick*. But, since the contract in the present case is admitted (for reasons which do not fall to be considered by the House) to be no longer in existence, specific performance is not available. A's remedy lies only in an award of damages to himself. It is submitted that, in the absence of any evidence that A has suffered loss by reason of B's failure to pay C, A is only entitled to nominal damages. [Lord Scarman conceded that the authorities cited did not support the Court of Appeal's decision, but called for reform: see below, p 828.]

NOTES

1. Lord Russell's explanation of *Jackson's* case may fit its facts, but suppose the breach had been that, without any negligence on the part of the defendants or the hotel, the family had been supplied with food unfit for human consumption and had suffered personal injury? Could an award of damages for the personal injuries be justified on the basis that the father had been promised good food and had not received it?
2. There are a number of exceptional commercial cases in which a party may recover damages on behalf of others as well as himself and must pay them over to the others. Thus a consignor of goods may insure them for their full value, and recover this if the goods are lost, even though he has only a limited interest in the goods (*Hepburn v A Tomlinson (Hauliers) Ltd* [1966] AC 451). See also *Albacruz (Cargo Owners) v Albazero (owners), The Albazero* [1977] AC 774 at 845.

(c) Qualifications to the privity rule

(i) Trusts

If property is given to a person in trust for another, the beneficiary is treated as equitable owner of the property. It is the the duty of the trustee to take all necessary steps to safeguard the property, including taking action against any third party who is under an obligation to the trust. If he fails to do so, not only can the beneficiary sue the trustee; he can bring an action against the third party, joining the trustee as co-plaintiff if the latter consents and as co-defendant if he does not. In addition to property or money, a chose in action may constitute the 'trust property', and thus it is possible for one contracting party to hold the other's promise on trust for a third party, so giving the third party the right to enforce the promise in the name of the promisee. If in every contract containing a promise for the benefit of a third party, the promise were treated as being held on trust for the third party by the promisee, the doctrine of privity would be circumvented. There were signs in the nineteenth and early twentieth centuries that the courts might take this approach, and it appears to have been sanctioned by the House of Lords in *Les Affreteurs Reunis SA v Leopold Walford (London) Ltd* [1919] AC 801. There a shipowner promised a charterer that he would pay a commission to the broker who had negotiated the charter, and it was held that the charterer held this promise on trust for the broker so that the latter could enforce it. However, the tide of judicial opinion seems to have swung against the implication of trusts in order to overcome the privity doctrine: a trust may be created if the intention to do so is clearly expressed, but one will not be implied. A typical example of this more recent attitude is to be found in the last reported case in which the 'trust device' seems to have been seriously argued, *Green v Russell* [1959] 2 QB 226. An architect had taken out an insurance policy covering accidents sustained by his employees, one of whom died in a fire at the office. In the course of an action by the deceased's mother under the Fatal Accidents Act it became necessary to decide whether the deceased had had an enforceable right to the insurance monies, which had been paid to the deceased's personal representatives.

The Court of Appeal held that he did not, with the result that the payments did not fall to be deducted from the damages in tort. Romer LJ said:

> The suggestion that Russell assumed the position and obligations of a trustee was based primarily on the recital to the policy . . . An intention to provide benefits for someone else, and to pay for them, does not in itself give rise to a trusteeship; and yet that is all that emerges from the recital. Nor does the judge's finding that the existence of the policy was known to the employees in such a manner as to create in them a reasonable expectation of benefit affect the matter. There was nothing to prevent Russell at any time, had he chosen to do so, from surrendering the policy and receiving back a proportionate part of the premium which he had paid. Nor was he under any obligation to pay the renewal premiums each year. The truth is that the benefits payable in pursuance of the policy were sums which the company would become contractually liable to Russell to pay if the insured risks matured; and as Lord Greene MR said in *In Re Schebsman*, to which the judge referred: 'It is not legitimate to import into the contract the idea of a trust when the parties have given no indication that such was their intention. To interpret this contract as creating a trust would, in my judgment, be to disregard the dividing line between the case of a trust and the simple case of a contract made between two persons for the benefit of a third.'

Note that there was no suggestion that the money paid to the personal representatives should be repaid, or paid to the employer. The fact that the third party cannot enforce the promise which was intended to benefit him does not mean that the promisor does not discharge his contractual obligation by paying him, although it will mean that for the purposes of assessing damages the payment was gratuitous, and similarly for tax purposes: *Re Schebsman* [1944] Ch 83.

Thus it is probable that the 'implied trust' device will no longer be accepted by the courts as a means of overcoming the doctrine of privity. However, the exceptional cases already noted in which a party with a limited interest in goods is permitted to insure them on behalf of others interested, recover the full value and hold the excess for the other parties, are still recognized as good law, even though they are sometimes thought of as involving a trust of the insurance policy (see the explanation of Pearson LJ in *A Tomlinson (Hauliers) Ltd v Hepburn* [1966] 1 QB 21 at 51; in the House of Lords Lord Reid gave a different explanation based on the special position of a bailee of goods, [1966] AC 451 at 470–471).

(ii) Statutory exceptions

It must be clear by now that the doctrine of privity can have inconvenient effects, especially in insurance contracts, where it is very common for the policy to provide for coverage of the loss or liability of someone other than the insured, or for money to be paid to someone else. In a number of situations statute now gives the beneficiary a direct right of action.

Married Women's Property Act 1882, s 11
A policy of assurance effected by any man on his own life and expressed to be for the benefit of his wife, or of his children, or of his wife and children, or any of them, or by any woman on her own life, and expressed to be for the benefit of her husband, or of her children, or of her husband and children, or any of them, shall create a trust in favour of the objects therein named, and the moneys payable under any such policy shall not, so long as any object of the trust remains unperformed, form part of the estate of the insured, or be subject to his or her debts.

Marine Insurance Act 1906, s 14(2)
A mortgagee, consignee, or other person having an interest in the subject-matter insured may insure on behalf and for the benefit of other persons interested as well as for his own benefit.

Road Traffic Act 1988, s 148(7)
Notwithstanding anything in any enactment, a person issuing a policy of insurance under section 145 of this Act shall be liable to indemnify the persons or classes of persons specified in the policy in respect of any liability which the policy purports to cover in the case of those persons or classes of persons.

Defective Premises Act 1972, s 1(1)
A person taking on work for or in connection with the provision of a dwelling (whether the dwelling is provided by the erection or by the conversion or enlargement of a building) owes a duty—

  (a) if the dwelling is provided to the order of any person, to that person; and
  (b) without prejudice to paragraph (a) above, to every person who acquires an interest (whether legal or equitable) in the dwelling;
to see that the work which he takes on is done in a workman-like or, as the case may be, professional manner, with proper materials and so that as regards that work the dwelling will be fit for habitation when completed.

Law of Property Act 1925, ss 47(1), 56(1), 205(1)
Section 47 (1). Where after the date of any contract for sale or exchange of property, money becomes payable under any policy of insurance maintained by the vendor in respect of any damage to or destruction of property included in the contract, the money shall, on completion of the contract, be held or receivable by the vendor on behalf of the purchaser and paid by the vendor to the purchaser on completion of the sale or exchange, or so soon thereafter as the same shall be received by the vendor.
Section 56 (1). A person may take an immediate or other interest in land or other property, or the benefit of any condition, right of entry, covenant or agreement over or respecting land or other property, although he may not be named as a party to the conveyance or other instrument.
Section 205 (1). In this Act unless the context otherwise requires, the following expressions have the meaning hereby assigned to them respectively, that is to say . . .
(xx) Property includes any thing in action, and any interest in real or personal property.

Note on Law of Property Act 1925, s 56. In *Beswick v Beswick* the majority of the Court of Appeal (Lord Denning MR, Danckwerts LJ and Salmon LJ leaving the question open) held that Mrs Beswick was entitled to enforce the contract in her own right by virtue of s 56 ([1966] Ch 538, following dicta of Denning in *Drive Yourself Hire Co (London) Ltd v Strutt* and *Smith and Snipes Hall Farm Ltd v River Douglas Catchment Board*. The argument was that s 56 provides that a person not named as a party can take the benefit of an agreement respecting property and that by virtue of s 205, 'property' includes a chose in action such as a debt. Thus it was said that the doctrine of privity of contract had been abolished by statute. The House of Lords were unanimous in holding that s 56 does not have this effect and that Mrs Beswick had no remedy in her own name. It was agreed that the context required that the definition of property given in s 205 should not apply to s 56, but the exact scope of s 56 (fortunately not now of concern to mere contract lawyers) was left unclear. See Treitel, pp 494–496.

(d) Negative benefits, or vicarious immunity

Elder, Dempster & Co v Paterson, Zochonis & Co Ltd [1924] AC 522, House of Lords

The respondents shipped some casks of palm oil under a bill of lading contract, on board a vessel which had been chartered by the appellants from her owners. Normally when goods are shipped under a bill of lading contract in a chartered ship, the contract will be between the shipper and the owners (see above, p 45), and the bill of lading will be issued by the owners or on their behalf. However in this case it was the charterers (who operated a fleet of their own vessels and had chartered this ship to supplement it) who issued the bill of lading in their own name, so that the contract was between the appellants, the charterers, and the respondents, the shippers. The casks were damaged when bags of palm kernels were stowed on top of them. The House of Lords held that the loss was caused not by the ship being unseaworthy but by bad stowage. The result was that the appellants, the charterers, were concededly protected from liability by an exception clause in the bill of lading. The second question the House had to decide was whether the owners, whose servants had actually carried out the stowage, were also protected by the clause.

Viscount Cave. . . . There remains a further question, which arises between the shippers and the shipowners, the Griffiths Lewis Steam Navigation Company. It is contended on behalf of the respondents that, assuming their loss to be due to bad stowage on the part of the master of the ship, the owners are not protected by the conditions of the bill of lading, to which they were not parties, and are accordingly liable in tort for the master's negligence. In support of this contention the respondents rely on such cases as *Martin v Great Indian Peninsula Rly Co; Hayn v Culliford;* and *Meux v Great Eastern Rly Co.* I do not think that this argument should prevail. It was stipulated in the bills of lading that 'the shipowners' should not be liable for any damage arising from other goods by stowage or contract with the goods shipped under the bills of lading; and it appears to me that this was intended to be a stipulation on behalf of all the persons interested in the ship, that is to say, charterers and owners alike. It may be that the owners were not directly parties to the contact; but they took possession of the goods (as Scrutton LJ says) on behalf of and as the agents of the charterers, and so can claim the same protection as their principals.

Viscount Finlay. . . . [T]he act complained of was done in the course of the stowage under the bill of lading, and . . . the bill of lading provided that the owners are not to be liable for bad stowage. If the act complained of had been an independent tort unconnected with the performance of the contract evidenced by the bill of lading, the case would have been different. But when the act is done in the course of rendering the very services provided for in the bill of lading, the limitation on liability therein contained must attach, whatever the form of the action and whether owner or charterer be sued. It would be absurd that the owner of the goods could get rid of the protective clauses of the bill of lading, in respect of all stowage, by suing the owner of the ship in tort. The Court of Appeal were, in my opinion, right in rejecting this contention, which would lead to results so extraordinary as those referred to by Scrutton LJ, in his judgment.

 . . . It may be, that in the circumstances of this case the obligations to be inferred from the reception of the cargo for carriage to the United Kingdom amount to a bailment upon terms, which include the exceptions and limitations of liability stipulated in the known and contemplated form of bill of lading. It may be, that the vessel being placed in the Elder, Dempster & Co's line, the captain signs the bills of lading and takes possession of the cargo only as agent for the charterers, though the time charter recognizes the ship's possessory lien for hire. The former I regard as the preferable view, but, be this as it may, I cannot find here any such bald bailment with unrestricted liability, or such tortious handling entirely independent of contract, as would be necessary to support the contention.

[Lord Dunedin delivered a concurring judgment, Lord Carson concurred.]

Order of the Court of Appeal reversed.

Scruttons Ltd v Midland Silicones Ltd [1962] AC 446, House of Lords

The respondents were consignees, and at the material times owners, of a drum of chemicals bought on terms cif London and consigned to them from America by ship under a bill of lading (dated Mar 26, 1957) signed on behalf of the shipowners. The bill of lading incorporated s 4(5) of the United States Carriage of Goods by Sea Act, 1936, which in the circumstances limited the liability of the shipowners (as carriers), for loss or damage to the goods, to 500 dollars. The bill provided that 'carrier' included 'the ship . . . her owner, operator and demise charterer, and also any . . . person to the extent bound by this bill of lading, whether acting as carrier or bailee'. Section 1(a) of the Act of 1936 (incorporated into the bill of lading) provided that the term 'carrier' included the owner or charterer who entered into a contract of carriage with a shipper.

For some years past the shipowners had employed the appellant stevedores to discharge their vessels at the Port of London and deliver goods to consignees, and the contract (dated in 1952) between the shipowners and the stevedores stated that the stevedores would be responsible for any negligence of themselves or their servants, but should have 'such protection as is afforded by the terms . . . of the bills of lading'. The consignees did not know of the contract of 1952. The stevedores, when handling the drum at the Port of London in the course of their duties regarding unloading and delivery, negligently dropped it causing damage amounting to £593 12s 2d. In an action by the consignees against the stevedores for the sum as damages, the stevedores admitted negligence but contended that they were entitled to limit their liability to 500 dollars (or £179 1s) by virtue of the contract of carriage (evidenced by the bill of lading) between the shipowners and the consignees on the ground of the decision in *Elder, Dempster & Co v Paterson, Zochonis & Co*, or because the shipowners contracted as agents for the stevedores or because there was an implied contract, independent of the bill of lading, between the consignees and the stevedores that the stevedores should have the benefit of the provision limiting liability in the contract of carriage.

Lord Reid. . . . We were informed that questions of this kind frequently arise and that this action had been brought as a test case.

In considering the various arguments for the appellants, I think it is necessary to have in mind certain established principles of the English law of contract. Although I may regret it, I find it impossible to deny the existence of the general rule that a stranger to a contract cannot in a question with either of the contracting parties take advantage of provisions of the contract, even where it is clear from the contract that some provision in it was intended to benefit him. That rule appears to have been crystallised a century ago in *Tweddle v Atkinson* and finally established in this House in *Dunlop Pneumatic Tyre Co Ltd v Selfridge & Co Ltd*. There are, it is true, certain well-established exceptions to that rule—though I am not sure that they are really exceptions and do not arise from other principles. But none of these in any way touches the present case.

The actual words used by Lord Haldane in the *Dunlop* case were made the basis of an argument that, although a stranger to a contract may not be able to sue for any benefit under it, he can rely on the contract as a defence if one of the parties to it sues him in breach of his contractual obligation—that he can use the contract as a shield though not as a sword. I can find no justification for that. If the other contracting party can prevent the breach of contract well and good, but if he cannot I do not see how the stranger can. As was said in *Tweddle v Atkinson*, the stranger cannot 'take advantage' from the contract.

It may be that in a roundabout way the stranger could be protected. If A, wishing to protect X, gives to X an enforceable indemnity, and contracts with B that B will not sue X, informing B of the indemnity, and then B does sue X in breach of his contract with A, it may be that A can recover from B as damages the sum which he has to pay X under the indemnity, X having had to pay it to B. But there is nothing remotely resembling that in the present case.

The appellants in this case seek to get round this rule in three different ways. In the first place, they say that the decision in *Elder, Dempster & Co Ltd v Paterson, Zochonis & Co Ltd* establishes an exception to the rule sufficiently wide to cover the present case. I shall later return to consider this case. Secondly, they say that through the agency of the carrier they were brought into contractual relation with the shipper and that they can now found on that against the consignees, the respondents. And thirdly, they say that there should be inferred from the facts an implied contract, independent of the bill of lading, between them and the respondents. It was not argued that they had not committed a tort in damaging the respondents' goods.

I can see a possibility of success of the agency argument if (first) the bill of lading makes it clear that the stevedore is intended to be protected by the provisions in it which limit liability, (secondly) the bill of lading makes it clear that the carrier, in addition to contracting for these provisions on his own behalf, is also contracting as agent for the stevedores that these provisions should apply to the stevedore, (thirdly) the carrier has authority from the stevedore to do that, or perhaps later ratification by the stevedore would suffice, and (fourthly) that any difficulties about consideration moving from the stevedore were overcome. And then to affect the consignee it would be necessary to show that the provisions of the Bills of Lading Act, 1855, apply.

But again there is nothing of that kind in the present case. I agree with your Lordships that 'carrier' in the bill of lading does not include stevedore, and if that is so I can find nothing in the bill of lading which states or even implies that the parties to it intended the limitation of liability to extend to stevedores. Even if it could be said that reasonable men in the shoes of these parties would have agreed that the stevedores should have this benefit, that would not be enough to make this an implied term of the contract. And even if one could spell out of the bill of lading an intention to benefit the stevedore, there is certainly nothing to indicate that the carrier was contracting as agent for the stevedore in addition to contracting on his own behalf. So it appears to me that the agency argument must fail.

And the implied contract argument seems to me to be equally unsound. From the stevedores' angle, they are employed by the carrier to deal with the goods in the ship. They can assume that the carrier is acting properly in employing them and they need not know whom the goods belong to. There was in their contract with the carrier a provision that they should be protected, but that could not by itself bind the consignee. They might assume that the carrier would obtain protection for them against the consignee and feel aggrieved when they found that the carrier did not or could not do that. But a provision in the contract between them and the carrier is irrelevant in a question between them and the consignee. Then from the consignee's angle they would know that stevedores would be employed to handle their goods, but if they read the bill of lading they would find nothing to show that the shippers had agreed to limit the liability of the stevedores. There is nothing to show that they ever thought about this or that if they had they would have agreed or ought as reasonable men to have agreed to this benefit to the stevedores. I can find no basis in this for implying a contract between them and the stevedores. It cannot be said that such a contract was in any way necessary for business efficiency.

So this case depends on the proper interpretation of the *Elder, Dempster* case. What was there decided is clear enough. The ship was under time charter, the bill of lading made by the shippers and the charterers provided for exemption from liability in the event which happened and this exemption was held to enure to the benefit of the shipowners who were not parties to the bill of lading but whose servant the master caused damage to the shippers' goods by his negligence. The decision is binding on us but I agree that the decision by itself will not avail the present appellants because the facts of this case are very different from those in the *Elder, Dempster* case. For the appellants to succeed it would be necessary to find from the speeches in this House a ratio decidendi which would cover this case and then to follow that ratio decidendi.

I would certainly not lightly disregard or depart from any ratio decidendi of this House. But there are at least three classes of case where I think we are entitled to question or limit it: first, where it is obscure, secondly, where the decision itself is out of line with other authorities or established principles, and thirdly, where it is much wider than was necessary for the decision so that it becomes a question of how far it is proper to distinguish the earlier decision. The first two of these grounds appear to me to apply to the present case.

It can hardly be denied that the ratio decidendi of the *Elder, Dempster* decision is very obscure. . . . [The House of Lords] must all have thought that they were merely applying an established principle to the facts of the particular case.

But when I look for such a principle I cannot find it, and the extensive and able arguments of counsel in this case have failed to discover it. . . . [Scrutton LJ in the Court of Appeal, in the *Elder, Dempster* case] was saying in terms that servants and 'agents' can take advantage of contracts made by their master or 'principal'. I would not dissent from a proposition that something of that kind ought to be the law if that was plainly the intention of the contract, and it may well be that this matter is worthy of consideration by those whose function it is to consider amending the law. But it seems to me much too late to do that judicially.

In such circumstances I do not think that it is my duty to pursue the unrewarding task of seeking to extract a ratio decidendi from what was said in this House in *Elder, Dempster*. Nor is it my duty to seek to rationalise the decision by determining in any other way just how far the scope of the decision should extend. I must treat the decision as an anomalous and unexplained exception to the general principle that a stranger cannot rely for his protection on provisions in a contract to which he is not a party. The decision of this House is authoritative in cases of which the circumstances are not reasonably distinguishable from those which gave rise to the decision. The circumstances in the present case are clearly distinguishable in several respects. Therefore I must decide this case on the established principles of the law of England apart from that decision, and on that basis I have no doubt this appeal must be dismissed.

[**Viscount Simonds** delivered a speech to the same effect, adding: . . .] In the course of this opinion I have already borrowed freely, without acknowledgment, from the judgment of the late Fullager J in *Wilson v Darling Island Stevedoring and Lighterage Co Ltd*. . . . I will quote a passage from it which expresses my own view of *Elder, Dempster*. After referring to a passage in *Carver on the Law of Carriage of Goods by Sea*, 9th ed, at p 294, that learned judge said: 'In my opinion what the *Elder, Dempster* case decided, and all that it decided, is that in such a case, the master having signed the bill of lading, the proper inference is that the shipowner, when he receives the goods into his possession, receives them on the terms of the bill of lading. The same inference might perhaps be drawn in some cases even if the charterer himself signed the bill of lading, but it is unnecessary to consider any such question.' This appears to me to be the only possible generalisation, or if your Lordships think 'rationalisation' an appropriate word, the only possible rationalisation of *Elder, Dempster*, and it is a far cry from the circumstances to which it is sought to apply that decision in the present case. . . .

[Lord Keith of Avonholm and Lord Morris of Borth-y-Gest delivered concurring judgments, Lord Denning dissented.]

Appeal dismissed.

NOTE

The notion of 'vicarious immunity' does however have some force. The point has been made that in some situations it must be that a servant or agent of a contracting party has the same immunity in tort as is enjoyed by his employer or principal, even if he is not mentioned in the agreement which gives the latter the immunity. Thus if a patient in a private hospital were to sign an agreement consenting to surgery, and the surgery were properly carried out by either an employee of the hospital or an independent contractor, it is inconceivable that the patient could sue the surgeon for battery. See Coote, *Exception Clauses*, pp 129–130. Similarly it has been held that an agent who deals with the property of an estate with the consent of the executor does not become an *executor de son tort: Sykes v Sykes* (1870) LR 5 CP 113. Presumably it must now be taken that this principle may protect the stevedore from liability in trespass for simply handling the consignee's goods but does not protect him from liability for negligent damage. But see further below, p 822ff.

New Zealand Shipping Co Ltd v A M Satterthwaite & Co Ltd (The Eurymedon) [1974] 1 All ER 1015, Privy Council

Cargo was shipped on board a vessel at Liverpool by the consignor for transshipment to the plaintiff as consignee in New Zealand, pursuant to a bill of lading issued by agents for the carrier. Clause 1 of the bill of lading [see above, pp 44–45] conferred certain exemptions and immunities on the carrier. The clause further provided: 'It is hereby expressly agreed that no servant or agent of the Carrier (including every independent contractor from time to time employed by the Carrier) shall in any circumstances whatsoever be under any liability what-soever to the Shipper, Consignee or Owner of the goods or to any holder of this Bill of Lading for any loss or damage or delay of whatsoever kind arising or resulting directly or indirectly from any act neglect or default on his part while acting in the course of or in connection with his employment and, without prejudice to the generality of the foregoing provisions in this Clause, every exemption, limitation, condition and liberty herein contained and every right, exemption from liability, defence and immunity of whatsoever nature applicable to the Carrier or to which the Carrier is entitled hereunder shall also be available and shall extend to protect every such servant or agent of the Carrier acting as aforesaid and for the purpose of all the foregoing provisions of this Clause the Carrier is or shall be deemed to be acting as agent or trustee on behalf of and for the benefit of all persons who are or might be his servants or agents from time to time (including independent contractors as aforesaid) and all such persons shall to this extent be or be deemed to be parties to the contract in or evidenced by this Bill of Lading.' The defendant company acted as stevedore for the carrier in New Zealand, being employed as an independent contractor. After the plaintiff had become the holder of the bill of lading, the cargo was damaged as a result of the defendant's negligence during unloading. The plaintiff brought an action against the defendant claiming that the defendant could not escape liability by virtue of the exceptions and immunities conferred on it under the terms of cl 1 of the bill of lading, since it was not a party to the contract.

[Lord Wilberforce, delivering the judgment of the majority, quoted the part of Lord Reid's speech in the *Midland Silicones* case in which Lord Reid stated the prerequisites for success of the 'agency' argument and continued:]

The question in this appeal is whether the contract satisfies these propositions.

Clause 1 of the bill of lading, whatever the defects in its drafting, is clear in its relevant terms. The carrier, on his own account, stipulates for certain exemptions and immunities: among these is that conferred by art III(6) of the Hague Rules which discharges the carrier from all liability for loss or damage unless suit is brought within one year after delivery. In addition to these stipulations on his own account, the carrier as agent for, inter alios, independent contractors stipulates for the same exemptions.

Much was made of the fact that the carrier also contracts as agent for numerous other persons; the relevance of this argument is not apparent. It cannot be disputed that among such independent contractors, for whom, as agent, the carrier contracted, is the appellant company which habitually acts as stevedore in New Zealand by arrangement with the carrier and which is, moreover, the parent company of the carrier. The carrier was, indisputably, authorised by the stevedore to contract as its agent for the purposes of cl 1. All of this is quite straightforward and was accepted by all of the learned judges in New Zealand. The only question was, and is, the fourth question presented by Lord Reid, namely that of consideration.

It was on this point that the Court of Appeal differed from Beattie J, holding that it had not been shown that any consideration for the shipper's promise as to exemption moved from the promisee, ie, the stevedore.

[Lord Wilberforce held that the terms of the bill of lading amounted to an offer by the shipper to the stevedore, made through the agency of the carrier, that if the stevedore unloaded the goods it should have the benefit of the exemption clause. This part of Lord Wilberforce's judgment is reproduced above, pp 101–102. Lord Wilberforce continued:]

But whether one describes the shipper's promise to exempt as an offer to be accepted by performance or as a promise in exchange for an act seems in the present context to be a matter of semantics. The words of Bowen LJ in *Carlill v Carbolic Smoke Ball Co*: 'why should not an offer be made to all the world which is to ripen into a contract with anybody who comes forward and performs the condition?' seem to bridge both conceptions: he certainly seems to draw no distinction between an offer which matures into a contract when accepted and a promise which matures into a contract after performance, and, though in some special contexts (such as in connection with the right to withdraw) some further refinement may be needed, either analysis may be equally valid. On the main point in the appeal, their Lordships are in substantial agreement with Beattie J.

The following other points require mention: 1. In their Lordships' opinion, consideration may quite well be provided by the stevedore, as suggested, even though (or if) it was already under an obligation to discharge to the carrier. (There is no direct evidence of the existence or nature of this obligation, but their Lordships are prepared to assume it.) An agreement to do an act which the promisor is under an existing obligation to a third party to do, may quite well amount to valid consideration and does so in the present case: the promisee obtains the benefit of a direct obligation which he can enforce. This proposition is illustrated and supported by *Scotson v Pegg* . . . which their Lordships consider to be good law.

2. The consignee is entitled to the benefit of, and is bound by, the stipulations in the bill of lading by his acceptance of it and request for delivery of the goods thereunder. This is shown by *Brandt v Liverpool, Brazil and River Plate Steam Navigation Co Ltd*, and a line of earlier cases. The Bills of Lading Act 1855, section 1 (in New Zealand the Mercantile Law Act 1908, section 13) gives partial statutory recognition to this rule, but, where the statute does not apply, as it may well not do in this case, the previously established law remains effective.

3. The stevedore submitted, in the alternative, an argument that, quite apart from contract, exemptions from, or limitation of, liability in tort may be conferred by mere consent on the part of the party who may be injured. As their Lordships consider that the stevedore ought to succeed in contract, they prefer to express no opinion upon this argument: to evaluate it requires elaborate discussion.

4. A clause very similar to the present was given effect by a United States District court in *Carle & Montanari Inc v American Export Isbrandtsen Lines Inc*. The carrier in that case contracted, in an exemption clause, as agent, for, inter alios, all stevedores and other

independent contractors, and although it is no doubt true that the law in the United States is more liberal than ours as regards third party contracts, their Lordships see no reason why the law of the Commonwealth should be more restrictive and technical as regards agency contracts. Commercial considerations should have the same force on both sides of the Pacific.

In the opinion of their Lordships, to give the stevedore the benefit of the exemptions and limitations contained in the bill of lading is to give effect to the clear intentions of a commercial document, and can be given within existing principles. They see no reason to strain the law or the facts in order to defeat these intentions. It should not be overlooked that the effect of denying validity to the clause would be to encourage actions against servants, agents and independent contractors in order to get round exemptions (which are almost invariably and often compulsory) accepted by shippers against carriers, the existence, and presumed efficacy, of which is reflected in the rates of freight. They see no attraction in this consequence.

Their Lordships will humbly advise Her Majesty that the appeal be allowed and the judgment of Beattie J restored. The consignee must pay the costs of the appeal and in the Court of Appeal.

Viscount Dilhorne and Lord Simon dissented. They rejected the theory adopted by the majority, on the grounds that the bill of lading purported to be a bilateral agreement with the stevedores and not an offer of a unilateral contract and that as a bilateral contract it failed for want of consideration: the stevedores were not promising the consignee that they would unload the goods. In effect they held that a document drafted by a skilled lawyer (the clause is known to have been drafted by Lord Roskill while at the Bar) should be treated at face value.

On the alternative argument for the stevedores on which the majority had declined to express an opinion, Lord Simon said:

It is really sufficient to dispose of this proposition in the circumstances of the instant case to say that, were it correct, all five of Lord Reid's conditions, which were common ground between the parties, would be entirely irrelevant: *Midland Silicones* should have been decided the other way.

Furthermore, in my opinion, the stevedore's fourth proposition is inconsistent with both the reasoning and the actual decision in *Cosgrove v Horsfall*. It was argued for the stevedore in *Midland Silicones* that *Cosgrove's* case was wrongly decided; but the decision in *Midland Silicones* was inconsistent with that contention (cf Lord Denning, dissenting), In *Cosgrove's* case, the plaintiff, an employee of a transport company, was travelling in one of their omnibuses on a free pass, when a collision occurred with another of the company's omnibuses, causing the plaintiff injuries. One of the conditions to which the grant of the free pass was subject was that neither the company nor their servants were to be liable to the holder of the pass for personal injury however caused. The plaintiff sued the driver of his omnibus and recovered damages. The defendant's appeal to the Court of Appeal was dismissed, on the ground that the defendant was not a party to the contract between the plaintiff and the company, the condition of exemption from liability not having been imposed by the company as agent for the defendant. On the stevedore's fourth proposition (unlike the first three) agency is quite irrelevant; moreover, the stevedore's fourth proposition, if valid, merely needs rephrasing to fit the facts of *Cosgrove v Horsfall* so that the defendant should have succeeded.

Counsel relied for the stevedore's fourth proposition on the cases where a licence is coupled with a disclaimer of liability and on *Hedley Byrne & Co Ltd v Heller & Partners Ltd*. In all these cases, however, the right or service extended was gratuitous; and obviously any person making a gift can delimit its extent. The cases give no ground, in my opinion, for any such general principle of law as is implicit in the stevedore's fourth proposition, which, if valid, would seem to provide a revolutionary short cut to a jus quaesitum tertio.

Since I cannot accept the stevedore's fourth proposition, it is unnecessary to discuss the fine and difficult distinctions which counsel sought to draw between this proposition and the doctrine of volenti non fit injuria.

NOTES

1. Suppose the stevedores are employed to unload goods which are being carried under a bill of lading containing the same clause as in the *New*

Zealand Shipping case, but they damage the goods before they have started to unload them—eg while unloading other goods belonging to a different party but which are stowed on top of the damaged goods? See *Raymond Burke Motors Ltd v Mersey Docks and Harbour Board Co* [1986] 1 Lloyd's Rep 155.

2. Coote [1981] CLJ 13 asks why it is necessary to establish agency if, as the Privy Council held, the bill of lading contains an offer of a unilateral contract. Could the answer be that the stevedore will not necessarily receive the bill of lading before commencing unloading?

3. What if the stevedores were not only not in the same group of companies as the carrier but had not even been employed by the carriers before the occasion on which the loss or damage occurred? In *Port Jackson Stevedoring Pty Ltd v Salmond & Spraggon Pty (Australia) Ltd, The New York Star* [1980] 3 All ER 257, a case also involving stevedores in the same group as the carriers, the Privy Council emphasised the general principle underlying the earlier decision, Lord Wilberforce saying (at p 261):

> Although, in each case, there will be room for evidence as to the precise relationship of carrier and stevedore and as to the practice at the relevant port, the decision does not support, and their Lordships would not encourage, a search for fine distinctions which would diminish the general applicability, in the light of established commercial practice, of the principle . . .

4. In *Southern Water Authority v Carey* [1985] 2 All ER 1077 the plaintiffs employed a contractor to design and build a sewage works. Subsequently the contractor employed sub-contractors to carry out the works. Clause 30 of the main contract, which was on the Institute of Mechanical Engineers/Institute of Electrical Engineers form, limited the contractor's liability to making good defects which appeared within 12 months of completion and stated:

> (iv) The Contractor's liability under this clause shall be in lieu of any condition or warranty implied by law as to the quality or fitness for any particular purpose of any portion of the Works taken over . . . and save as in this clause expressed neither the Contractor nor his Sub-contractors, servants or agents shall be liable, whether in contract, tort or otherwise in respect of defects in or damage to such portion, or for any injury, damage or loss of whatsoever kind attributable to such defects or damage. For the purposes of this sub-clause the Contractor contracts on his own behalf and on behalf of and as trustee for his Sub-Contractors, servants and agents.

The plaintiff alleged that the works failed because of negligence on the part of the third and fourth defendants, who were sub-contractors. A number of issues were tried as preliminary issues, including whether the third and fourth defendants were protected from liability to the plaintiff in tort by the clause in the main contract. Judge David Smout QC referred to Lord Reid's discussion of the 'agency' argument in the *Midland Silicones* case (above, p 816) and accepted that the clause was intended to protect the sub-contractors and that the contract made it clear that for this purpose the contractor was acting as agent for the sub-contractors. Nor was there any difficulty over consideration. However, there was no evidence that the third and fourth defendants had authorised the contractors to do this; and they could not ratify what had been done afterwards. This was because of a well-established rule that ratification of an act is not possible unless the principal was capable of being ascertained at the time when the act was done. The sub-contractors were only selected after the main contract had been signed. Thus the clause did not protect the third and fourth defendants from liability in tort. This suggests a major weakness in the 'agency device' as a way of conferring immunity on sub-contractors, stevedores and the like; it won't work if at the time of the main contract you haven't decided who they are going to be.

5. However, Judge Smout went on to hold that the existence of the ineffective clause was sufficient to protect the sub-contractors from being liable in tort in the first place. He said (at p 1086):

> In *Junior Books Ltd v Veitchi Co Ltd* Lord Roskill cited the passage from Lord Wilberforce's speech in *Anns v Merton London Borough* to which I have referred and with the agreement of Lord Fraser and Lord Russell expressed the majority view of the House of Lords in his approval of Lord Wilberforce's proposition. Significantly, Lord Roskill added this:
>
> > 'During the argument it was asked what the position would be in a case where there was a relevant exclusion clause in the main contract. My Lords, that question does not arise for decision in the instant appeal, but in principle I would venture the view that such a clause according to the manner in which it was worded might in some circumstances limit the duty of care just as in the *Hedley Byrne* case [1963] 2 All ER 575, [1964] AC 465 the plaintiffs were ultimately defeated by the defendants' disclaimer of responsibility.'
>
> The case has now arisen where there is such a limitation that is directly in point. While the terms of cl 30(vi) may, if literally interpreted, exceed the bounds of common sense the intent is clear, namely that the sub-contractor whose works have been so completed as to be the subject of a valid taking-over certificate should be protected in respect of those works from any liability in tort to the plaintiffs. As the plaintiffs' predecessor did so choose to limit the scope of the sub-contractors' liability, I see no reason why such limitation should not be honoured.

6. It seems that the loss in the *Southern Water* case was purely economic; the sewage works had failed. Compare the next case.

Norwich City Council v Harvey [1989] 1 All ER 1180, Court of Appeal

The plaintiff building owners entered into a contract for the extension of a swimming pool complex under a contract in the JCT standard form of local authority building contract (1963 edition, revised in 1977), cl 20[C] of which provided that 'The existing structures . . . owned by him or for which he is responsible and the Works . . . shall be at the sole risk of the Employer [ie the building owners] as regards loss or damage by fire . . . and the Employer shall maintain adequate insurance against those risks'. The contractor sub-contracted certain roofing work to the defendant sub-contractors, one of whose employees, while using a blowtorch, set fire to both the existing buildings and the new extension. The building owners brought an action against the sub-contractors and their employee claiming damages for negligence. The trial judge dismissed the action and the building owners appealed to the Court of Appeal.

May LJ. . . . The judge held that there was no privity of contract between the employer and the sub-contractors, and also that there was no question of the main contractor acting either as the agent or trustee for the sub-contractors (see his Honour Judge David Smout QC in *Southern Water Authority v Carey*). The judge further declined to act on any analogy with the bailment cases where, as in *Leigh & Sillavan Ltd v Aliakmon Shipping Co Ltd, The Aliakmon*, the contractual exemptions is in the defendant sub-bailee's contract with the bailee. Having considered a number of recent authorities relating to the existence and extent of a duty of care he concluded:

'The matter must be approached as one of principle: is the duty owed by the defendant to the plaintiff qualified by the plaintiffs' contract with the main contractor, or to put it more broadly, by the plaintiffs propounding a scheme whereby they accepted the risk of damage by fire and other perils to their own property—existing structures and contents—and some property which does not belong to them—unfixed materials and goods, the value of which has not been included in any certificate—while requiring the contractor to indemnify them against liabilities arising from the omission or default of both the contractor and of any sub-contractor; then requiring the contractor to insure and to cause any sub-contractor to insure against the liabilities included in the indemnity? I am left in no doubt that the duty in tort owed by the sub-contractor to the employer is so qualified. This appears to me to follow from the passage to which I have referred in *Peabody v Parkinson*, and to be consistent with the approach, albeit on different facts in *Scottish Housing v Wimpey* and *Mark Rowlands v Berni Inns* . . . Each case must turn both on its own facts, and on the authority of *Peabody v Parkinson*, what is just and reasonable.'

I trust I do no injustice to the plaintiffs' argument in this appeal if I put it shortly in this way. There is no dispute between the employer and the main contractor that the former accepted the risk of fire damage: see *James Archdale & Co Ltd v Comservices Ltd* and *Scottish Special Housing Association v Wimpey Construction UK Ltd*. However cl 20[C] does not give rise to any obligation on the employer to indemnify the sub-contractor. That clause is primarily concerned to see that the works were completed. It was intended to operate only for the mutual benefit of the employer and the main contractor. If the judge and the sub-contractors are right, the latter obtain protection which the rules of privity do not provide. Undoubtedly the sub-contractors owed duties of care in respect of damage by fire to other persons and in respect of other property (for instance the lawful visitor, employees of the employer or other buildings outside the site); in those circumstances it is impracticable juridically to draw a sensible line between the plaintiffs on the one hand and others on the other to whom a duty of care was owed. The employer had no effective control over the terms on which the relevant sub-contract was let and no direct contractual control over either the sub-contractors or any employee of theirs.

In addition, the plaintiffs pointed to the position of the first defendant, the sub-contractors' employee. Ex hypothesi he was careless and, even if his employers are held to have owed no duty to the building employers, on what grounds can it be said that the employee himself owed no such duty? In my opinion, however, this particular point does not take the matter very much further. If in principle the sub-contractors owed no specific duty to the building owners in respect of damage by fire, then neither in my opinion can any of their employees have done so.

In reply the defendants contend that the judge was right to hold that in all the circumstances there was no duty of care on the sub-contractors in this case.

The law relevant to the question whether or not a duty of care arises in given circumstances has been considered by the House of Lords and the Privy Council in a number of recent decisions. For present purposes one can start with the dictum from the speech of Lord Wilberforce in *Anns v Merton London Borough* [see above, pp 25–26] . . .

In *Yuen Kun-yeu v A-G of Hong Kong*, the question arose whether the Commissioner of Deposit-taking Companies owed any duty to persons who deposited moneys with a company which he had registered to take reasonable care to ensure that that company's affairs were not being conducted fraudulently, speculatively or to the detriment of its depositors. The opinion of the Privy Council was delivered by Lord Keith. He quoted the familiar passage to which I have already referred from the speech of Lord Wilberforce in *Anns*'s case and after referring to other cases in which the passage had been treated with some reservation, he said:

'Their Lordships venture to think that the two-stage test formulated by Lord Wilberforce for determining the existence of a duty of care in negligence has been elevated to a degree of importance greater than it merits, and greater perhaps than its author intended.'

He then went on to express the approval of their Lordships of the view favoured by Gibbs CJ in the High Court of Australia in *Sutherland Shire Council v Heyman* that Lord Wilberforce meant the expression 'proximity of neighbourhood' to be a composite one importing the whole concept of necessary relationship between the plaintiff and the defendant described by Lord Atkin in *Donoghue v Stevenson*. Lord Keith pointed out that although the foreseeability of harm is a necessary ingredient of such a relationship, it is not the only one and, having quoted from passages from the speech of Lord Atkin in *Donoghue v Stevenson*, he said:

'Lord Atkin clearly had in contemplation that all the circumstances of the case, not only the foreseeability of harm, were appropriate to be taken into account in determining whether a duty of care arose.'

Subsequently he expressed the opinion that the second stage of Lord Wilberforce's test in *Anns v Merton London Borough* was one which would rarely have to be applied. It can arise only in a limited category of cases where, notwithstanding that a case of negligence is made out on a proximity basis, public policy requires that there should be no liability.

In my opinion the present state of the law on the question whether or not a duty of care exists is that, save where there is already authority that in the circumstances there is such a duty, it will only exist in novel situations where not only is there foreseeability of harm, but also such a close and direct relation between the parties concerned, not confined to mere physical proximity, to the extent contemplated by Lord Atkin in his speech in *Donoghue v Stevenson*. Further, a court should also have regard to what it considers just and reasonable in all the circumstances and facts of the case.

In the instant case it is clear that as between the employer and the main contractor the former accepted the risk of damage by fire to its premises arising out of and in the course of the building works. Further, although there was no privity between the employer and the sub-contractor, it is equally clear from the documents passing between the main contractors and the sub-contractors to which I have already referred that the sub-contractors contracted on a like basis. In *Scottish Special Housing Association v Wimpey Construction UK Ltd* the House of Lords had to consider whether, as between the employer and main contractors under a contract in precisely the same terms as those of the instant case, it was in truth intended that the employer should bear the whole risk of damage by fire, even fire caused by the contractor's negligence. The position of sub-contractors was not strictly in issue in the *Scottish Housing* case, which I cannot think the House did not appreciate, but having considered the terms of cll 18, 19 and 20[C] of the same standard form as was used in the instant case Lord Keith, in a speech with which the remainder of their Lordships agreed, said:

> 'I have found it impossible to resist the conclusion that it is intended that the employer shall bear the whole risk of damage by fire, including fire caused by the negligence of the contractor or that of sub-contractors.'

As Lord Keith went on to point out, a similar conclusion was arrived at by the Court of Appeal in England in *James Archdale & Co Ltd v Comservices Ltd*, on the construction of similarly but not identically worded corresponding clauses in a predecessor of the standard form used in the *Scottish Housing* and instant cases. Again the issue only arose in the earlier case as between employer and main contractor, but approaching the question on the basis of what is just and reasonable I do not think that the mere fact that there is no strict privity between the employer and the sub-contractor should prevent the latter from relying on the clear basis on which all the parties contracted in relation to damage to the employer's building caused by fire, even when due to the negligence of the contractors or sub-contractors.

[Croom Johnson and Glidewell LJJ agreed.]

Appeal dismissed.

NOTES

1. Is burning down someone else's building with a blowlamp a 'novel situation'?
2. Doesn't the approach taken here very much resemble the argument which was made by the stevedores in the *New Zealand Shipping* case that exemption from liability in tort could be conferred by mere consent? (See above, p 820). What about Lord Simon's comment that this was inconsistent with *Cosgrove v Horsfall*? See also Furmston 23 MLR 373.
3. It is not safe at present to rely on a clause in the main contract by which a party accepts the risk of damage as sufficient to negate the tortious liability of sub-contractors or employees. We have also seen that the 'agency device' is not a totally sure one. Can you think of any other way in which to protect the third party from liability? Read again Lord Reid's speech in the *Midland Silicones* case (above, p 816) and consider the possibilities raised by the next case.

Gore v Van der Lann [1967] 1 All ER 360, Court of Appeal

The Liverpool Corporation issued in 1963 a 'free pass' on the corporation's buses to the plaintiff, who was about seventy-nine years of age and in receipt of a retirement pension; she made and signed a written application whereby 'in consideration of my being granted a free pass . . . I undertake and agree that the use of such pass by me shall be subject to the conditions overleaf. . . .' These conditions included 'The pass is issued and accepted on the understanding that it merely constitutes and grants a licence to the holder to travel on the [corporation's] buses, with and subject to the conditions that neither the [corporation] nor any of [its] servants or agents responsible for driving, management, control or working of their bus system are to be liable to the holder . . . for loss of life, injury . . . or other loss or damage to property however caused'. The pass itself bore a statement that it was 'issued subject to the conditions of grant set out in the written form of application . . . and upon the express condition that the [corporation] and [its] servants shall be under no liability, either contractual or otherwise, to the pass-holder when boarding, alighting from or being carried on [the corporation's] vehicles'. Subsequently a bus which the plaintiff was boarding moved off, and she fell and was injured. She brought an action for damages against the conductor (who was employed by the corporation), alleging that the accident was due to his negligence in causing the bus to move off while she was boarding. The corporation intervened in the action, asking the court to stay the proceedings, under proviso (b) to s 41 of the Supreme Court of Judicature (Consolidation) Act 1925, on the ground that the plaintiff was bound by the condition in her pass that its servant, the conductor, should not be liable to her.

Wilmer LJ. . . . On behalf of the plaintiff it has been contended that the effect of the plaintiff's application and its acceptance by the corporation was to constitute 'a contract for the conveyance of a passenger in a public service vehicle', which is rendered void by s 151 of the Road Traffic Act 1960. That section provides as follows:

'A contract for the conveyance of a passenger in a public service vehicle shall, so far as it purports to negative or restrict the liability of a person in respect of a claim which may be made against him in respect of the death of, or bodily injury to, the passenger while being carried in, entering or alighting from the vehicle, or purports to impose any conditions with respect to the enforcement of any such liability, be void.'

If this contention is well founded it is obvious that, assuming negligence on the part of the defendant, it effectively demolishes any possible defence to the plaintiff's claim, not only by the defendant but also by the corporation itself. In the circumstances it is tempting to ask why the plaintiff's advisers have seen fit to adopt the tortuous procedure of suing the defendant when there would have been an equally good claim against the corporation. Be that as it may, however, it is plain that if the plaintiff's contention be well founded, the corporation can have no possible ground for seeking to interfere with the prosecution of the present action against the defendant.

In reply to this contention counsel for the corporation relied on the decision of Lord Goddard CJ and of Lord Greene MR, in this court in *Wilkie v London Passenger Transport Board*, as authority for the proposition that the issue by a transport authority of a free pass subject to conditions does not constitute a contract between the holder and the authority, but amounts to no more than the grant of a revocable licence with the condition that, while it is being enjoyed, certain consequences are to follow.

[Wilmer LJ read part of Lord Greene MR's judgment in *Wilkie's* case, including the following:]

'It is clearly nothing but a licence subject to conditions, a very common form of licence, eg, a licence to a neighbour to walk over a field, providing he does not go with a dog. You cannot spell such a thing as being a contract: "I will let you go across my field in consideration of you, as a contracting party, agreeing not to take your dog." In other words, looking at this document shortly and sensibly, it contains no intention to contract.'

[Wilmer LJ continued:]

Wilkie's case, being a decision of this court, is binding on us unless it is distinguishable. I have found the question one of no little difficulty, but I have come to the conclusion, not without some hesitation, that the present case is to be distinguished. The circumstances surrounding the issue of the free pass in the present case were quite different from those in which the pass in *Wilkie's* case was issued. There the pass was issued to an employee of the board as a matter of course as one of the privileges attaching to his employment. There was certainly nothing contractual about it; there was, as Lord Greene said, no contractual animus. In the present case, on the other hand, the pass was issued, not to an employee, but to a stranger, and only in response to a written application. By the terms of the application which she signed the plaintiff specifically undertook and agreed that the use of the pass should be subject to the conditions. The very wording of that which the plaintiff signed was couched in the language of contract. It appears to me that all the elements of contract were present. By signing and submitting her application, the plaintiff, as I see it, was accepting the offer of the corporation to carry her free on its buses subject to the conditions specified. Each party gave good consideration by accepting a detriment in return for the advantages gained. Unlike *Wilkie's* case, the facts of the present case do in my judgment reveal a contractual animus. This conclusion is, of course, fatal to the corporation's application. If, as I think, there was a contract, it is clearly rendered void by s 151 of the Road Traffic Act 1960. There can, therefore, be no obstacle in the way of the plaintiff prosecuting an action for negligence, whether against the corporation or against its employee. The corporation can have no possible ground for seeking to interfere with the plaintiff's right to prosecute her action.

That is sufficient to dispose of the appeal; but I think it right to add that, even if I had thought that the issue of the free pass amounted to no more than the grant of a licence subject to conditions, I should still have arrived at the same conclusion so far as this application is concerned. It is true that the conditions accepted by the plaintiff when she accepted the offer of a free pass included a provision that the employees of the corporation were not to be liable to her for any injury or loss; but I cannot construe this provision as a promise by the plaintiff not to institute proceedings against an employee. If the corporation desired such a promise from the holder of a free pass, it could have said so in clear and unambiguous terms. In my judgment the conditions are to be construed strictly against the corporation which put them forward. It is not enough to say that a promise not to sue the employee is to be implied. At the best for the corporation, the condition relied on is ambiguous, and any ambiguity must be resolved in favour of the plaintiff.

In these circumstances the corporation has not satisfied me that it has any justification for interfering with the plaintiff's prima facie right at common law to bring proceedings against the defendant whom she accuses of negligence. On this ground also I am of opinion that the judge came to the right conclusion, and that the appeal should be dismissed.

Since preparing this judgment I have had the advantage of reading the judgment of Harman LJ. I should desire to express my concurrence with his view that, since it has not been shown that there was any contract between the corporation and the defendant rendering the corporation liable in law to indemnify the defendant, there is no ground on which the corporation could be held to have an interest entitling it to relief under s 41 of the Act of 1925. On this ground, also, in addition to those which I have already set out, I am satisfied that the corporation's application was rightly dismissed.

Harman LJ. (read by Salmon LJ): . . . This question, therefore, is whether before the Supreme Court of Judicature Act, 1873 the corporation would have been entitled to apply to restrain the action. This would have been done by a bill in Chancery. The ground stated is that the prosecution of the action would be a fraud on the corporation, and the fraud alleged apparently is that, if the action succeeded and damages were obtained against the conductor, the corporation would in some way be liable to indemnify him. It is here in my judgment that the case breaks down, for I do not see how the corporation could be liable in law for what would be a tort of its servant. . . .

There is no suggestion in the instant case that there is any contract between the corporation and the defendant making the corporation liable for the torts of the latter, and in its absence I cannot see that the corporation is liable at law and, if not, I think that the corporation has no interest which would entitle it to relief under the section. This seems to me to be in accordance with the opinion expressed in the passage which I have read.

In these circumstances I am of opinion that the judge below was right in refusing the corporation's application. I do not think that the question of the applicability of s 151 of the Road Traffic Act 1960 arises. I therefore propose to express no opinion on the difficult question whether the free pass constituted a contract between the plaintiff and the corporation, or whether it was merely a licence subject to a condition having no contractual effect.

Salmon LJ: I agree with both the judgments which have been delivered.

For my part I have little doubt but that there was a contract between the plaintiff and the Liverpool Corporation. The plaintiff signed an application for a pass on one of the corporation's printed forms, the very language of which is calculated to impress on an applicant that she is entering into a legally binding agreement with the corporation.

'In consideration of my being granted a free pass for use on the buses of Liverpool Corporation, I undertake and agree that the use of such pass by me shall be subject to the conditions overleaf.'

. . . Even had there been no contract in the present case, I would have come to the clear conclusion that the corporation must fail. For the corporation to obtain the relief which it claims, it would be necessary for it to show (as Harman LJ points out) that, before the Supreme Court of Judicature Act 1873, it would have been entitled to apply to the court in Chancery to restrain the plaintiff from bringing her action against the defendant. In order to succeed, the corporation would have had to establish that the action was a fraud on the corporation either (i) because the plaintiff had agreed with the corporation for good consideration not to bring such an action, or (ii) because of some other good reason. As to (i) this presupposes a contractual promise by the plaintiff not to sue the corporation's servant. I do not think that any such promise can be implied. Even if it could, it would mean that there was a contract between the plaintiff and the defendant which, in so far as it purported to negative or restrict the plaintiff's right to sue, would be void under s 151 of the Road Traffic Act 1960. As to (ii), the only other reason for holding that the plaintiff's action could be a fraud on the corporation would be that the corporation would in law be obliged to indemnify its servant, the defendant, against his liability to the plaintiff in negligence. Clearly there is no such legal obligation on the corporation. I appreciate that the corporation would not wish to leave the defendant personally to bear the burden of this action, and moreover that it might face trouble with his trade union if it did so; but this is not, in my view, sufficient to stigmatise the plaintiff's action against the defendant as a fraud on the corporation.

For these reasons I agree that the appeal must be dismissed.

Appeal dismissed.

NOTES

1. In order to succeed, would an intervening party have to show *either* that the plaintiff had promised him not to sue the defendant *or* that he was liable to indemnify the defendant, or must he show both?

2. If you wished to draft a clause that *would* prevent a third party being sued, how would you go about it in the light of this case? Consider the following, which is from the warranty clause of a 'precedent' sales contract for aircraft:

(f) The rights expressly conferred upon the Purchaser by paragraphs (a) and (b) of this Condition are accepted by the Purchaser in place of all other warranties or conditions as to quality or fitness express or implied by law or otherwise and Westland shall not be liable to the Purchaser in contract or for negligence or otherwise in respect of any injury loss damage or expenses which directly or indirectly is caused by or arises out of either:
   (i) any defect in or failure of or unsuitability of any Contract Item or of any component or part replaced repaired or supplied by Westland in pursuance of this Contract; or
   (ii) any advice instruction service training or work given rendered or done by Westland or any employee or agent of Westland in pursuance of or for the purpose of this Contract.
   It is agreed that in the event of the above provision relieving Westland from the unlimited consequences of negligence being rendered ineffective by legislation or by the decision of any Court of competent jurisdiction, the remainder of this paragraph (f) shall remain in full force and effect.

(g) The Purchaser agrees to indemnify Westland against all claims against Westland for which Westland may be liable made by persons in the employment of the Purchaser liability for which would have been excluded by this Condition if such claim had been made by the Purchaser.

(h) In the event of a claim being made by the Purchaser or any person in the employment of the Purchaser against any servant of Westland liability for which would have been excluded by this Condition if such claim had been by the Purchaser against Westland, Westland shall be entitled (if such servant of Westland be liable therefore) to indemnify such servant as aforesaid in respect of such claim and the Purchaser will repay to Westland any sum paid by Westland by reason of such indemnity.

(This clause may be varied in negotiations, particularly in domestic sales.)

3. In *Beswick v Beswick* specific performance was *ordered* because the estate was suffering no loss from the breach. In *Gore*, a stay was *refused* because the Corporation was suffering no loss of a kind recognized by law. Does that strike you as curious?

4. In *Snelling v John G Snelling Ltd* [1973] QB 87 the plaintiff and the second and third defendants were brothers and all directors of the defendant company. The company was financed by substantial loans from all three brothers. As part of an arrangement to borrow money from a finance company, the three brothers made an arrangement between themselves not to seek repayment of their loans during the currency of the loan from the finance company, and that if during this period any of them should voluntarily resign his directorship, he should forfeit the money owing to him. The defendant company was not a party to this agreement between the brothers. Later the plaintiff resigned his directorship and sued the company for repayment of his loan. The other two brothers sought to be joined as defendants and counter-claimed for a declaration that the plaintiff had forfeited the money. Ormrod J held that the defendant brothers were entitled to have his action stayed because it was a breach of the plaintiff's contract with them: unlike *Gore's* case, there was a clearly implicit undertaking by the plaintiff not to sue the company. As all the parties were before the court and the reality was that the plaintiff's action failed, it should be dismissed. Whether the defendant brothers would have been liable to the company or the lender if the plaintiff had been permitted to recover does not appear to have been discussed.

(e) Reform

In many situations the doctrine of privity has been abrogated by statute; in cases of exception clauses it has added a clause (admittedly a complicated one) to contracts; even in the case of positive benefits such as the £5 per week in *Beswick v Beswick* it is relatively easy to avoid the doctrine by careful contract planning. Has the time come to abolish it altogether? Lord Scarman seems to think so: in *Woodar Investment Development Ltd v Wimpey Construction (UK) Ltd* (above, p 810) at 591, he said:

I wish to add nothing to what your Lordships have already said about the authorities which the Court of Appeal cited as leading to the conclusion that Woodar is entitled to substantial damages for Wimpey's failure to pay Transworld. I agree that they do not support the conclusion. But I regret that this House has not yet found the opportunity to reconsider the two rules which effectually prevent A or C recovering that which B, for value, has agreed to provide.

First, the jus quaesitum tertio. I respectfully agree with Lord Reid [in *Beswick v Beswick*] that the denial by English law of a jus quaesitum tertio calls for reconsideration. . . . *Beswick v Beswick* was decided in 1967. It is now 1979; but nothing has been done. If the opportunity arises, I hope the House will reconsider *Tweddle v Atkinson* and the other cases which stand guard over this unjust rule.

Likewise, I believe it open to the House to declare that, in the absence of evidence to show that he has suffered no loss, A, who has contracted for a payment to be made to C, may rely on the fact that he required the payment to be made as prima facie evidence that the promise for which he contracted was a benefit to him and that the measure of his loss in the event of non-payment is the benefit which he intended for C but which has not been received. Whatever the reason, he must have desired the payment to be made to C and he must have been relying on B to make it. If B fails to make the payment, A must find the money from other funds if he is to confer the benefit which he sought by his contract to confer on C. Without expressing a final opinion on a question which is clearly difficult, I think the point is one which does require consideration by your Lordships' House.

Certainly the crude proposition for which Wimpey contends, namely that the state of English law is such that neither C for whom the benefit was intended nor A who contracted for it can recover it if the contract is terminated by B's refusal to perform, calls for review, and now, not 40 years on.

Lord Keith associated himself with these observations. As long ago as 1937 the Law Revision Committee (6th Interim Report (Cmd 5449)), section D, recommended that:

> Where a contract by its express terms purports to confer a benefit directly on a third party it shall be enforceable by the third party in his own name subject to any defences that would have been valid between the contracting parties.
>
> Unless the contract otherwise provides it may be cancelled by the mutual consent of the contracting parties before the third party has adopted it either expressly or by conduct.

In the US many states have abandoned the doctrine of privity, following the famous case of *Lawrence v Fox* 20 NY 268 (Court of Appeals, New York, 1859). Restatement 2d now provides:

§302. Intended and incidental beneficiaries
(1) Unless otherwise agreed between promisor and promisee, a beneficiary of a promise is an intended beneficiary if recognition of a right to performance in the beneficiary is appropriate to effectuate the intention of the parties and either

    (a) the performance of the promise will satisfy an obligation of the promisee to pay money to the beneficiary; or

    (b) the circumstances indicate that the promisee intends to give the beneficiary the benefit of the promised performance.

(2) An incidental beneficiary is a beneficiary who is not an intended beneficiary.

§304. Creation of duty to beneficiary
A promise in a contract creates a duty in the promisor to any intended beneficiary to perform the promise, and the intended beneficiary may enforce the duty.

§307. Remedy of specific performance
Where specific performance is otherwise an appropriate remedy, either the promisee or the beneficiary may maintain a suit for specific enforcement of a duty owed to an intended beneficiary.

§311. Variation of a duty to a beneficiary
(1) Discharge or modification of a duty to an intended beneficiary by conduct of the promisee or by a subsequent agreement between promisor and promisee is ineffective if a term of the promise creating the duty so provides.

(2) In the absence of such a term, the promisor and promisee retain power to discharge or modify the duty by subsequent agreement.

(3) Such a power terminates when the beneficiary, before he receives notification of the discharge or modification, materially changes his position in justifiable reliance on the promise or brings suit on it or manifests assent to it at the request of the promisor or promisee.

(4) If promisee receives consideration for an attempted discharge or modification of the promisor's duty which is ineffective against the beneficiary, the beneficiary can assert a right to the consideration so received. The promisor's duty is discharged to the extent of the amount received by the beneficiary.

§315. Effect of a promise of incidental benefit
An incidental beneficiary acquires by virtue of the promise no right against the promisor or the promisee.

It is not clear either how desirable it would be to adopt such reforms, nor how much practical difference doing so would make. On the first point, when we are discussing positive benefits (rather than exemption clauses), the third party will fall into one of two categories. Either he will be someone to whom the promisee owes a legal obligation, which the promisee intends should be wholly or partly discharged by the promisor's performance (the first Restatement termed such a person a 'creditor beneficiary'), or he will be someone on whom the promisee wished to confer a gift (whom the Restatement termed a 'donee beneficiary'. The Restatement 2d has abandoned the distinction). If he is the former, does he need a right of action against the promisor when he can presumably enforce the original obligation against the promisee? Or does the present law merely require wasteful circuity of action? If he is the latter, is it right to give him rights without doing the same for gratuitous promisees generally? There is of course the point that while the promise may be gratuitous against the third party, it is not gratuitous against the promisee: but would it not be sufficient to ensure that the promisee has adequate remedies against the promisor (see section (b) above) without giving the third party a right of action?

On the second point, it will be observed that the Restatement 2d does not confer a right of action on every third party who will benefit from the promised performance, even if he is explicitly referred to in the contract. The decision whether he is an intended beneficiary is often very difficult and courts have reached different conclusions on very similar facts. See Farnsworth, *Contracts*, s 10(3). To ensure that the third party does acquire rights it is more or less essential to provide so explicitly; but if the contract planner has the degree of sophistication needed to appreciate this, he or she could almost certainly devise an enforceable right under English law too.

Two types of qualification to the basic privity rule need to be considered. One is that the benefits of a contract may *subsequently* be transferred: this is dealt with in the next chapter. The qualifications dealt with here relate to initial entitlement to sue.

(f) Agency

The rules relating to agents acting for disclosed principals do not in theory conflict at all with the doctrine of privity, although they do offer a method of escape from its consequences, provided that the third party whom it is wished to benefit can be said to be providing consideration. The doctrine of the undisclosed principal does seem to infringe on the doctrine of privity: the principal may sue the third party even though the latter had no idea that he was contracting with anyone but the agent. Of course, the third party may equally hold the principal responsible, but a notion of being able to take the benefits if one is made to take the burdens does not explain the rule; the principal can sue the third party even though the latter has not attempted to enforce the contract against the principal. It seems better to regard the doctrine of the undisclosed principal as a straightforward exception to the doctrine of privity.

What, however, is the practical point behind allowing the undisclosed principal to sue the third party, rather than confining his rights to those he had against the agent and allowing only the agent to sue the third party? The original rationale, or at least the effect, seems to have been to allow a person for whom a middleman had been selling goods on credit to recover the price directly from the purchaser if the middleman became insolvent. Equally, since any money paid to the middleman by the purchaser would be the principal's, the latter could recover it from the middleman's trustee in bankruptcy. See Stoljar, *The Law of Agency* (1961), pp 204–211.

(g) Tortious liability and vicarious entitlement

Look again at the extracts from *Donoghue v Stevenson* and the other tort cases printed in Section 1, chapter 2 (above, pp 20–28).

NOTES

1. The basis of the decision in *Donoghue v Stevenson* was that a duty was owed by the manufacturer to the consumer independently of any contract, so that it was fallacious to allege that lack of privity of contract was a bar to the suit. Is there a duty to prevent *any* kind of loss? If not, what kinds of loss must be prevented and in what circumstances? What duty, if any, was owed independently of the contract by the sub-contractors in *Junior Books*?

2. In the normal case, what will be the method of recovery from a nominated sub-contractor who does defective work? As we saw earlier, the fact that a contractor is permitted to delegate work does not relieve him of responsibility if the work is not done properly, and the same is true even if he is required by the contract to delegate the work to a sub-contractor nominated by the employer, at least if he had the right to object to the nominee but did not do so (above, pp 335–338). Thus the employer will be able to recover his loss from the contractor, and the contractor will be able to recover the same amount, plus any other expense to which he was put, from the sub-contractor. You may remember that this was the outcome in the *IBA* case (above, p 163): the difficulty there was that the defect was one of design, which the contractor argued it was not responsible for, but the House of Lords held that it had expressly undertaken responsibility for design in its tender. Why did the employer not sue the contractor in the *Junior Books* case? What is the practical effect of allowing him to bypass privity by suing in tort? Is it rather similar to allowing the employer to come in as an undisclosed principal?

3. Suppose a sub-contractor nominated by the employer (and within the *Junior Books* principle) had simply refused to perform (in breach of contract), and it had cost considerably more to get the work done by another sub-contractor as well as causing delay while the new sub-contract was arranged. Clearly the contractor would be entitled to sue the original sub-contractor for any loss the contractor suffered, including any damages it had to pay to the employer. But if for some reason this 'chain of contracts' failed (for instance because the contractor had gone into liquidation), could the employer sue the sub-contractor *in tort* for the extra amount charged by the new sub-contractor? The cost of the delay caused?

4. Suppose the employer had originally paid £50,000 to have the floor laid by the sub-contractor (under the main contract the sub-contract was probably entered as a 'prime cost' item: that is, the contractor is paid whatever the sub-contractor charges plus a percentage profit to cover his responsibility to manage the sub-contract, etc). If having the floor relaid

cost £75,000, would the employer be able to recover this in full, or would his recovery be limited to the amount he had paid for the 'worthless' floor?

5. As we suggested in chapter 2 (above, pp 27–28), in cases like *Junior Books* and even *Donoghue v Stevenson* tort is being used to some extent as a substitute for contract, as a method of bypassing the privity requirement. Much of the reluctance to expand tortious liability further than *Junior Books* seems to be based on the fear that to allow a remedy in tort would upset the contractual arrangements.

6. In any event, as our notes both here and in the first section of the book have tried to suggest, there remain significant differences between the contractual and tortious liabilities: for instance, tort liability depends on proof of negligence and the damages may be confined to the 'out of pocket' loss. Other questions of the interrelationship of the liabilities remain to be explored. What would or should be the position, for instance, if the cost of relaying a defective floor was itself slight but the consequent loss of production while the work was done were considerable, and the sub-contract contained a valid exemption clause excluding the sub-contractor's liability for any such loss of production? This raises questions which will be explored in Chapter 42 under heading (b) (below, p 838).

7. In note 3 it was said that the contractor could recover his loss from a sub-contractor who failed to perform. This is technically correct, but when a *nominated* sub-contractor 'drops out' in this way it is not at all clear that the contractor's loss includes the extra cost of getting the work done by another, because it is apparently the law that (in the absence of a provision to the contrary) the contractor is not responsible to the employer for this amount. In *North West Metropolitan Regional Hospital Board v T A Bickerton & Son Ltd* [1970] 1 All ER 1039, [1970] 1 WLR 607, HL, which involved a building contract under the JCT form, a nominated sub-contractor went into liquidation and the liquidator refused to carry out the sub-contract, which was then terminated. The employer asked the main contractor to complete the sub-contract work, which it did under protest. It was held by the House of Lords that the main contractor was entitled to the reasonable value of the work he thus had to do, not just the price agreed in the original sub-contract. The reason given was that the main contractor was not even entitled, let alone bound, to do the nominated sub-contract work: it was the duty of the employer to renominate. The practical effect of this decision is extraordinary. The extra cost of getting the work completed falls on the employer, who cannot recover it from the contractor, while the sub-contractor gets away scot-free, since the only person with whom he has a contract, the main contractor, cannot sue him for this loss since he is not suffering it. Many forms of contract which envisage the use of nominated sub-contractors now have express provisions to deal with this problem. The scheme used by the ICE (5th edn) is to make the contractor liable for the extra cost so that he can pass this on to the sub-contractor, but to put the risk of financial failure of the nominated sub-contractor on to the employer by providing that if (despite taking all reasonable steps) the contractor fails to recover in full from the sub-contractor, his liability will be reduced by the amount of the shortfall. The Joint Contracts Tribunal forms of building contract now use a different approach: the contractor is

not liable to the employer, but the nominated sub-contractor gives a direct undertaking to the employer, in consideration of being nominated, that he will do nothing that will give rise to rightful termination of his sub-contract. The practical effect where the sub-contractor goes into liquidation is much the same as under the ICE: the employer may recover the extra cost of getting the work done if the sub-contractor has sufficient assets to pay. The two schemes lead to very different results where it is the *main* contractor who goes into liquidation.

8. When a nominated sub-contractor drops out, there is also likely to be a serious problem of delay while a replacement is found. Whether the contractor is responsible for this in the absence of an express provision is a matter of considerable doubt after the House of Lords decision in *Percy Bilton Ltd v Greater London Council* [1982] 2 All ER 623.

CHAPTER 41

Subsequent assignment of the benefit of a contract

(a) Assignment

Like agency, assignment is a complex subject which cannot be treated in full here. Instead enough of the doctrine will be summarized here to enable the reader to understand the cases which follow.

At common law a debt or other contractual right could not be assigned without the assent of the debtor unless it was a debt due on a negotiable instrument (see below, pp 835–837). It was only possible to transfer contractual rights with the consent of the debtor, either by making a tripartite agreement called a 'novation' between the creditor, the debtor and the new creditor (in strict theory this extinguishes the old contract and substitutes a new one); or by getting the debtor to tell the new creditor that he will pay him, which apparently gives the new creditor the right to recover from the debtor (*Shamia v Joory* [1958] 1 QB 448, [1958] 1 All ER 111).

However equity recognized assignment; if notice was given to the debtor he became liable to pay the assignee and could no longer discharge his obligation by paying the assignor. However, unless the right assigned were a purely equitable one, the assignor had to be joined in any action by the assignee. Among the reasons were the historical procedural ones that equity did not enforce legal choses in action, so the action had to be brought in the assignor's name even if equity would compel him to co-operate; and that if the assignee could enforce the debt in equity, the debtor might be subjected to a second action by the assignor in the then separate common law courts.

The Judicature Act 1873, s 25(6) provided for legal assignment: since there was now only one system of courts the old procedural difficulties were gone. Section 25(6) was replaced by the Law of Property Act 1925, s 136(1), which reads:

Section 136

(1) Any absolute assignment by writing under the hand of the assignor (not purporting to be by way of charge only) of any debt or other legal thing in action, of which express notice in writing has been given to the debtor, trustee or other person from whom the assignor would have been entitled to claim such debt or thing in action, is effectual in law (subject to equities having priority over the right of the assignee) to pass and transfer from the date of such notice—

(a) the legal right to such debt or thing in action;
(b) all legal and other remedies for the same; and
(c) the power to give a good discharge for the same without the concurrence of the assignor:
Provided that, if the debtor, trustee or other person liable in respect of such debt or thing in action has notice—

(a) that the assignment is disputed by the assignor or any person claiming under him; or
(b) of any other opposing or conflicting claims to such debt or thing in action;
he may, if he thinks fit, either call upon the persons making claim thereto to interplead concerning the same, or pay the debt or other thing in action into court under the provisions of the Trustee Act, 1925.

It will be noted that for there to be an effective legal assignment, notice must have been given in writing to the debtor, the assignment must be in writing signed by the assignor and the assignment must be absolute. If an assignment of a legal chose in action fails to meet the second or third requirement it may still be effective, but only as an equitable assignment, with the result that the assignee may have to join the assignor in the action. In these cases there are good substantive reasons for joining the assignor. Where the assignment is not written, he may wish to dispute that he made any assignment (compare the evidentiary functions of the seal and consideration, above p 122). Where the assignment is not absolute but conditional (for instance a debt is assigned as security for a loan until such time as the loan is repaid to the assignee), the court will not be able to determine whom the debtor should pay without having the assignor before the court as well as the assignee, so that the state of accounts between the two of them can be determined. This is an important safeguard for the debtor, who might otherwise pay the wrong party and have to pay all over again. In contrast there can be an absolute assignment even if it is provided that at some future time, when a loan is repaid for instance, the debt shall be reassigned; the reassignment will require a fresh notice to the debtor, so the latter will be in no doubt about whom he should pay. For different reasons the assignment of part of a debt is treated as not absolute; here the problem is that the debtor might want to dispute the existence of a debt and if the assignor and assignee could each recover his part in separate actions, the debtor would have to defend himself twice over.

An equitable chose may be assigned under the statute, or if it is not absolute, in equity; but at all events the assignment must be in writing as this is required of any disposition of an equitable interest (Law of Property Act 1925, s 53(1)(c)).

Not every contractual right can be assigned. Thus if the contract provides that a particular right (eg the contractor's right to money under a building contract) may not be assigned at all, or not without the employer's consent and consent is not obtained, any purported assignment is simply ineffective (*Helstan Securities Ltd v Hertfordshire County Council* [1978] 3 All ER 262). Needless to say, the result may be to put the assignor into breach of contract with the assignee. Equally contracts with a 'personal' element may not be assigned: see for example *Cooper v Micklefield Coal and Lime Co Ltd* (1912) 107 LT 457.

Note that an assignee takes 'subject to equities': ie the debtor can use any defence that he could have used against the assignor against the assignee. This is explored in Chapter 43.

(b) Negotiable instruments

'Law of Property' by Lawson and Rudden (2nd edn), pp 26–32

(i) *Negotiable instruments* The best-known negotiable instruments are the bill of exchange, the promissory note, and the cheque. For the law of property the essential feature of a bill of exchange is that it represents, in physical form, the debt which the buyer owes and the seller owns, and the latter may deal with it just as he may his own books or motorcar. Indeed a negotiable instrument is even more suitable to commerce than either of those things. The quality of *negotiability* means that anyone taking the instrument in good faith and for value obtains a good title despite any defect in the title of the transferor. Thus if, in good faith, you buy my books or car from someone who has stolen them from me you must return them to me and are left—for what it may be worth—to an action against the thief. But a thief can pass to an innocent purchaser a good title to a negotiable instrument.

A simple form of bill of exchange, used nowadays in overseas trade, occurs when goods are sold but are still on their way to the buyer. He will get the documents of title described below. But if the seller does not get the cash at once he will take a bill from the buyer which he can then use as if it were cash.

Bill for £1,000   Accepted 1/1/82   Brian Buyer   London, 1st January 1982

Three months after date pay me or my order the sum of one thousand pounds for value received.

To: Brian Buyer Esq.   Steven Seller

The buyer signs the bill for acceptance, gives it to the seller, and has three months in which to find the money. In the hands of the seller, however, the bill of exchange is an immediately realizable asset. He can endorse it, by writing his name on the back, and transfer it by delivery to anyone he chooses. It can then be passed from hand to hand, the holder being entitled to be paid by Brian Buyer when the three months expires and the bill matures. Assuming that the buyer is solvent, and that there are no particular risks in the transaction, Steven Seller will usually endorse and transfer the bill to a bank. The process is known as 'discounting' because the bank will give him for it an amount based on that sum of money which, invested then, would produce £1,000 on the date the bill matures. Thus, during the three months, the claim represented by the bill is an asset which is growing in value; and we shall see later that, in relation to land, the concept of the 'estate' is used to express in legal terms the vital factor of *time* which determines present values.

The bill can then, on endorsement, pass from hand to hand—from that bank to another, or to a customer. Any holder in due course, that is to say anyone who has physical control of the bill at maturity and has bought in good faith, is entitled to be paid the £1,000 by Brian Buyer, even if it had been stolen on its way to him or even if the buyer had a good defence against the seller, because, for instance, the goods never arrived. In other words any transfer of the bill to a purchaser in good faith is a transfer of the right to receive £1,000 from Brian Buyer.

The example just given is of the very simplest type of bill of exchange. Historically, however, the bill evolved to deal with a rather more sophisticated situation. Suppose that when Brian Buyer contracted to buy goods from Steven Seller he was already owed £1,000 by David Debtor. One way to resolve matters would be for DD to send bullion, notes, or coin to BB, and for him then to send them on to SS—a process both expensive and risky. A much cheaper and safer method, especially if DD and SS live in the same place, is for BB to order DD to pay the money to SS. But for DD to be liable directly to SS he must *accept* this order, and so the bill would look like this:

Bill for £1,000   Accepted 3/1/82   David Debtor   London, 1st January 1982

Three months after date pay **Steven Seller** or order the sum of one thousand pounds for value received.

To: David Debtor Esq.   Brian Buyer

SS can now deal with the bill exactly as described above, and any holder in due course will have a remedy against DD.

Another form of negotiable instrument is the promissory note, which differs from bills in that it is unilateral, that is only one person signs.

£1,000   London, 1st January 1982

I promise to pay **Steven Seller** or order at the Old Bank, Oxford, three months after date the sum of one thousand pounds for value received.

Brian Buyer

Most people have in their pockets at some time or another examples in the shape of Bank of England notes. The result is rather interesting: a private-law obligation under which, to use the above example, BB owes SS £1,000 is performed by payment—that is, by handing over banknotes which themselves bear a promise to pay. This obligation, however, is strictly one of public law and the nature of money will be briefly discussed later.

The same rules as to negotiability apply to the cheque, which is defined by statute as 'a bill of exchange, drawn on a banker, payable on demand'. This definition is likely to confuse the beginner. Admittedly a cheque looks like a bill of exchange.

                                                 1st January 1982
                                Old Bank Ltd.,
                                High Street, Oxford

Pay **Steven Seller**   or order

one thousand pounds/00   £1000.00

                                Brian Buyer

As however, the bank never accepts the order by signing the cheque it is never directly liable to the payee. When the cheque is presented it should, of course, meet it—for the cheque is a bill of exchange *payable on demand*. This obligation, however, is only to the drawer, BB, and arises out of the bank's contract with him; so that if he has neither credit balance nor overdraft facilities the bank need not pay. In fact a cheque is more like a promissory note, that is a promise by the drawer that his bank will pay.

Privity and burdens

The converse of the rule that you cannot sue on a contract to which you are not a party is that you cannot normally have your rights diminished by a contract to which you are not a party. There are however qualifications to this rule, too.

(a) Undisclosed principals

Look again at *Watteau v Fenwick* (above, p 802). It was only when the manager failed to pay for the cigars that the plaintiffs discovered the existence of the principal behind him, but nonetheless the principal was made liable. What is the practical effect of such a decision?

(b) Bailment

Morris v CW Martin & Sons Ltd [1965] 2 All ER 725, Court of Appeal

The plaintiff sent her mink stole to a furrier for cleaning. He told her that ne did not do cleaning, but would arrange for the fur to be cleaned by the defendants. She agreed. The furrier, contracting as principal not agent, arranged with the defendants for them to clean the plaintiff's fur on the current trade conditions, of which the furrier knew. The defendants knew that the fur belonged to a customer of the furrier, but did not know to whom it belonged. The current trade conditions provided that 'goods belonging to customers' on the defendants' premises were held at customers' risk, and that the defendants should 'not be responsible for loss or damage however caused'. The conditions further provided that the defendants should compensate for loss or damage to the goods during processing by reason of the defendants' negligence 'but not by reason of any other cause whatsoever'. M, an employee of the defendants, was given the task of cleaning the fur. He had entered the defendants' employment only recently. They had no reason to suspect his honesty. While the fur was in M's custody he stole it. The plaintiff sued the defendants for damages.

Lord Denning MR . . . [W]hen a principal has in his charge the goods or belongings of another in such circumstances that he is under a duty to take all reasonable precautions to protect them from theft or depredation, then if he entrusts that duty to a servant or agent, he is answerable for the manner in which that servant or agent carries out his duty. If the servant or agent is careless so that they are stolen by a stranger, the master is liable. So also if the servant or agent himself steals them or makes away with them. . . .

So far I have been dealing with the cases where the owner himself has entrusted the goods to the defendant. But here it was not the owner, the plaintiff, who entrusted the fur to the cleaners. She handed it to Mr Beder, who was a bailee for reward. He in turn, with her authority, handed it to the cleaners who were sub-bailees for reward. Mr Beder could clearly himself sue the cleaners for loss of the fur and recover the whole value (see *The Winkfield*), unless the cleaners were protected by some exempting conditions. But can the plaintiff sue the cleaners direct for the misappropriation by their servant? And if she does, can she ignore the exempting conditions?

These are questions of the first importance. At one time the owner of goods who bailed them to another could not sue a third person who had wrongfully lost or damaged or detained the goods. He could only sue the bailee; and the bailee could sue the third person. See the history of the matter fully discussed in *Holmes on the Common Law*, pp 164–180. But now an action does lie by the owner direct against the wrongdoer if he has the right to immediate possession; see *Kahler v Midland Bank Ltd*. Even if he has no right to immediate possession, he can sue for any permanent injury to, or loss of, the goods by a wrongful act of the defendant; see *Mears v London and South Western Ry Co*. But what is a wrongful act as between the owner and the sub-bailee? What is the duty of the sub-bailee to the owner? Is the sub-bailee liable for misappropriation by his servant? There is very little authority on this point. *Pollock and Wright on Possession* say this (at p 169):

> 'If the bailee of a thing sub-bails it by authority . . . and there is no direct privity of contract between the third person and the owner *it would seem that both the owner and the first bailee have concurrently the rights of a bailor against the third person according to the nature of the sub-bailment.*'

By which I take it that if the sub-bailment is for reward, the sub-bailee owes to the owner all the duties of a bailee for reward: and the owner can sue the sub-bailee direct for loss of or damage to the goods; and the sub-bailee (unless he is protected by any exempting conditions) is liable unless he can prove that the loss or damage occurred without his fault or that of his servants. So the plaintiff can sue the defendants direct for the loss of the goods by the misappropriation by their servant, and the cleaners are liable unless they are protected by the exempting conditions.

Now comes the question: Can the defendants rely, as against the plaintiff, on the exempting conditions although there was no contract directly between them and her? There is much to be said on each side. On the one hand, it is hard on the plaintiff if her just claim is defeated by exempting conditions of which she knew nothing and to which she was not a party. On the other hand, it is hard on the defendants if they are held liable to a greater responsibility than they agreed to undertake. As long ago as 1601 Lord Coke advised a bailee to stipulate specially that he would not be responsible for theft; see *Southcote's Case*, a case of theft by a servant. It would be strange if his stipulation was of no avail to him. The answer to the problem lies, I think, in this: the owner is bound by the conditions if he expressly or impliedly consented to the bailee making a sub-bailment containing those conditions, but not otherwise. Suppose the owner of a car lets it out on hire, and the hirer sends it for repair, and the repairer holds it for a lien. The owner is bound by the lien because he impliedly consented to the repairs being done, since they were reasonably incidental to the use of the car; see *Tappendent (trading as English & American Autos) v Artus*. So also if the owner of a ship accepts goods for carriage on a bill of lading containing exempting conditions (ie a 'bailment upon terms') the owner of the goods (although not a party to the contract) is bound by those conditions if he impliedly consented to them as being in 'the known and contemplated form'; see the words of Lord Sumner in *Elder, Dempster & Co Ltd v Paterson, Zochonis & Co, Ltd*, which were regarded by Sir Owen Dixon, CJ, and Fullagar J, as stating the ratio decidendi (see *Wilson v Darling Island Stevedoring and Lighterage Co, Ltd*), with whose judgment Viscount Simonds entirely agreed in *Scruttons, Ltd v Midland Silicones, Ltd* and see also the cases to which I referred in that case.

In this case the plaintiff agreed that Mr Beder should send the fur to the cleaners, and by so doing I think she impliedly consented to his making a contract for cleaning on the terms usually current in the trade. But when I come to study the conditions I do not think that they are sufficient to protect the defendants. We always construe such conditions strictly. Clause 9 applies only to 'goods belonging to customers', that is, goods belonging to Mr Beder, and not to goods belonging to his customers such as the plaintiff. The conditions themselves draw a distinction between 'customer' and 'his own customer'; see cl 16. Clause 14 only applies to 'the loss of or damage to the goods during processing'. The loss here was not during processing. It was before or after processing. Seeing that the conditions do not protect the defendants, I am of opinion that they are liable for the loss due to the theft by their servant.

I would allow the appeal accordingly, and direct judgment to be entered for the value of the stole as found by the judge, viz £200.

[Diplock LJ concurred in the result reached by Lord Denning but for different reasons. He expressed no opinion on Denning's views.]

Salmon LJ. . . . I . . . agree with my lords that the appeal should be allowed. I am anxious, however, to make it plain that the conclusion which I have reached depends on Morrissey being the servant through whom the defendants chose to discharge their duty to take reasonable care of the plaintiff's fur. . . .

I agree with my lords that even if the defendants could rely against the plaintiff on the printed conditions, to which we have been referred, their liability would not be excluded. These conditions are, at any rate, ambiguous; they would have to be strictly construed against the defendants who put them forward, and in my view would not protect them. Accordingly, the difficult question does not arise as to whether or not they apply. As at present advised I am strongly attracted by the view expressed on this topic by Lord Denning MR, but I have formed no concluded opinion upon it.

I would allow the appeal.

Appeal allowed.

NOTES

1. Lord Denning's dicta were applied by Steyn J in *Singer Co (UK) Ltd v Tees and Hartlepool Port Authority* [1988] 2 Lloyd's Rep 164. Singer had employed Bachman to crate a machine from Singer's UK plant and deliver it to a UK port. Bachman delivered the machine to the port authority on the latter's standard terms, which limited the port authority's liability. Singer were aware that this would happen and the judge held that it had impliedly authorised Bachman to enter into a sub-bailment with the port authority on its general conditions.

2. The recognition that a sub-bailee might be protected by its conditions from liability to the bailor was carried one stage further in *Johnson Matthey & Co v Constantine Terminals Ltd* [1976] 2 Lloyd's Rep 215. Carriers ('International') arranged for the shipment of the plaintiffs' silver. They delivered it to the defendants under a contract of bailment which excluded the defendants' liability for loss of the goods except if caused by the defendants' wilful neglect or default. The silver was stolen from the defendants' premises through their negligence, but without their wilful neglect or default. Donaldson J held that, quite apart from any question of authority, the plaintiffs could not recover the value of the silver from them. If the defendants had been guilty of a breach of duty of care to the plaintiffs, the latter could have sued them in tort and the clause in the contract between the defendants and International would have been irrelevant. However:

> . . . [T]here was no duty of care, apart from that arising out of the status of (sub) bailee and that duty was owed not only to the head bailee but also to the owners of the goods.
>
> But the plaintiffs cannot prove the bailment upon which, in my judgment, they must rely, without referring to terms upon which the silver was received by Constantine Terminals from International Express. These terms establish (a) that Constantine Terminals were bailees for reward but also (b) that the implied duties of such a bailee were qualified by exceptions. And, despite Mr Wadsworth's vigorous argument to the contrary, I really do not see how the plaintiffs can rely upon one part of the contract while ignoring the other.

In *Scruttons Ltd v Midland Silicones Ltd* (above, p 815) Lord Denning pointed out that the stevedores had been employed by the carriers on terms that they should 'have such protection as is afforded by the terms, conditions and exceptions of the bill of lading'. As he considered (unlike the majority) that the stevedores *were* intended to be protected by the clauses in the bill, Lord Denning held that this was a second reason why they should not be liable for more than $500. This seems to go even further than the *Johnson Matthey* case. The point is not discussed in the other judgments.

(c) Tort

In *Lumley v Gye* (1853) 2 E & B 216 the plaintiff had engaged Joanna Wagner to sing at the Queen's Theatre for the season, with a stipulation that she should not sing elsewhere during that period without his written consent. The defendant, who knew of this contract, persuaded Miss Wagner to sing for him at Covent Garden instead. The plaintiff obtained an injunction against Miss Wagner (referred to above, p 540), whereupon she left the country; he then claimed damages from the defendant, and succeeded on the ground that the defendant had commited a tort by 'maliciously' (ie intentionally) procuring a breach of the plaintiff's contract with Miss Wagner.

A more recent application of the tort of intentionally inducing a breach of contract is *British Motor Trade Association v Salvadori* [1949] Ch 556. The purchaser of a new car had covenanted with the plaintiffs that he would not resell it within one year without first offering it to them. He sold it to the defendant without first offering it to the plaintiffs. The defendant had notice of the covenant and was held liable to the plaintiffs.

(d) Property

Obviously a contract may result in a transfer of property rights which must be respected by third parties. In some circumstances what starts off as an agreement may also create what the law recognizes as property rights which will then affect third parties. Thus the covenants contained in a lease will bind and entitle successors in title to both landlord and tenant, and under the rule in *Tulk v Moxhay* (1848) 2 Ph 774, the owner of a piece of land may accept a restrictive covenant which will bind his successors in title to the successors in title of the covenantee, provided the latter retain land capable of benefiting from enforcement of the covenant. Outside the realm of real property, however, the law has been most reluctant to recognize parallel 'proprietary' rights. Thus it has been held that an agreement by a buyer of goods that neither he nor any successor in title would sell them at below a price set by the original seller does not create a covenant running with the goods, even when the restriction was clearly marked on the goods: *Taddy & Co v Sterious & Co* [1904] 1 Ch 354, followed by the Court of Appeal in *McGruther v Pitcher* [1904] 2 Ch 306. Some of the reasons for this reluctance appear from the judgment of Brougham LC in *Keppell v Bailey* (1834) 2 My & K 517, where it was held that an agreement by a quarry owner to carry all his stone on the Trevil Railroad was not binding on the quarry owner's successors in title. Lord Brougham said (at pp 534–538):

> . . . But it must not therefore be supposed that incidents of a novel kind can be devised and attached to property at the fancy or caprice of any owner. It is clearly inconvenient both to the science of the law and to the public weal that such a latitude should be given. There can be no harm in allowing the fullest latitude to men in binding themselves and their representatives, that is, their assets real and personal, to answer in damages for breach of their obligations. This tends to no mischief, and is a reasonable liberty to bestow; but great detriment would arise and much confusion of rights if parties were allowed to invent new modes of holding and enjoying real property, and to impress upon their lands and tenements a peculiar character, which should follow them into all hands, however remote. Every close, every messuage, might thus be held in a several fashion; and it would hardly be possible to know what rights the acquisition of any parcel conferred, or what obligations it imposed.

In one class of case a subsequent purchaser of a chattel or even a chose in action may be affected by an earlier contract to which he was not a party: that is where the original contract is specifically enforceable and the subsequent purchaser took with actual or constructive notice of it. This point arose in *Swiss Bank Corpn v Lloyds Bank Ltd* [1979] Ch 548, [1979] 2 All ER 853. It was argued that a borrower (IFT) who had used the loan to acquire securities (the FIBI securities) was under a contractual obligation to the lender to repay the loan out of the proceeds of the securities, and that this was a specifically enforceable obligation which would affect the defendants, to whom the securities had been charged. Browne-Wilkinson J said:

As I have indicated, Mr Scott's first contention is that the plaintiff has at all times had a right specifically enforceable against IFT requiring IFT to employ the FIBI securities in the manner specified in the Bank of England conditions, which right confers a property interest enforceable against Lloyds as subsequent equitable chargee. . . .

Turning now to the legal effect of such a contract, I propose first to set out my understanding of the equitable principles which are involved and to consider how in principle the position should stand as between the plaintiff and Lloyds.

Historically the courts of equity acted in personam. Whether equity was supplementing the common law by giving additional remedies or correcting the common law by imposing a different legal result, the courts of equity intervened by directing the defendant personally to do, or refrain from doing, a specific act. In deciding whether or not to intervene, the courts of equity required first, that the plaintiff should have some enforceable right and, secondly, that the conscience of the defendant was affected in some way so as to make the failure of the defendant to give effect to the plaintiff's rights contrary to justice.

The rights which the plaintiff asserted were normally either contractual rights or rights under a trust. In the realm of contracts equity supplemented the common law by ordering the party in default to perform the contract—instead of merely paying damages. In the realm of trusts equity ordered the legal owner of property, the trustee, specifically to carry out the trust which he had accepted. In matters involving property equity intervened by ordering that the defendant do deal with the property in question in a specific manner, whether the plaintiff's rights were founded in contract or trust.

But, although the basis of the equity jurisdiction was and still is founded on an order in personam, the courts of equity evolved the doctrine that, in the eyes of equity, that which ought to have been done is to be treated as having been done. Thus under a specifically enforceable contract for the sale of land, the purchaser is treated in equity as the owner of the property whether or not an order for specific performance has been made. Again, in the law of trusts the beneficiary is treated as immediately entitled to his interest in the trust property whether or not an order for the execution of the trust has been made against the trustee. In this way the plaintiff's rights, although founded upon the ability of the court to make an order in personam against the other contracting party or the trustee, become an interest in the property itself, an equitable interest. Once the position is reached that an order for specific performance could have been made against the legal owner if the matter had been brought before the court, thereafter the legal owner holds the property shorn of those rights in the property which the courts of equity would decree belong to another.

Once an equitable interest in property is established, thereafter any third party taking that property from the original contracting party or the original trustee only takes it, in the eyes of equity shorn of, or subject to, the equitable interest. But as the right and the remedy is equitable only, the courts of equity would not enforce the equitable interest against the third party unless it was inequitable for him not to give effect to the prior equitable interest. It is on this ground that a subsequent purchaser for value of a legal interest without notice takes free of prior equitable interests.

Therefore, in my judgment, on principle, if as between the plaintiff and IFT there was a contractual obligation to service and repay the loan out of the FIBI securities and that was a specifically enforceable obligation, the plaintiff has an equitable interest in those securities, and Lloyd's, as subsequent equitable chargee, took the FIBI securities subject to the prior equitable interest of the plaintiff.

He went on to hold that there was such an obligation, but on this point he was reversed by the Court of Appeal and the House of Lords agreed: [1982]

AC 584. However Lord Wilberforce said (at p 613) that he did not doubt the correctness of the principles of law stated by the judge.

Even where there is no specifically enforceable right which can be enforced against a subsequent purchaser, it has occasionally been suggested that equity will intervene to protect the rights of a party to the original contract. In *De Mattos v Gibson* (1858) 4 De G & J 276, 28 LJ Ch 498 it was held by the Lord Justices of Appeal that a charterer of a vessel was entitled to an injunction to prevent a subsequent mortgagee of her using her inconsistently with the charter. Knight Bruce LJ expressed himself in terms very reminiscent of *Tulk v Moxhay*:

> Reason and justice seem to prescribe that, at least as a general rule, where a man, by gift or purchase, acquires property from another, with knowledge of a previous contract, lawfully and for valuable consideration made by him with a third person, to use and employ the property for a particular purpose in a specified manner, the acquirer shall not, to the material damage of the third person, in opposition to the contract and inconsistently with it, use and employ the property in a manner not allowable to the giver or seller.

The Lord Chancellor also considered that the charterer might be entitled to an injunction (though he refused one for other reasons) but it is not clear on what basis he thought the charterer entitled. In *Lord Strathcona SS Co Ltd v Dominion Coal Co Ltd* [1926] AC 108, 95 LJPC 71 the Privy Council applied Knight Bruce's dictum and restrained a purchaser of a ship from using her inconsistently with a charter made by a previous owner and of which the purchaser knew when he bought the vessel. This decision has been much criticized as contrary to principle, and in *Port Line Ltd v Ben Line Steamers Ltd* [1958] 2 QB 146 Diplock J refused to follow it. He pointed out however (p 165) that the decision in *De Mattos v Gibson* could have been reached on the basis of *Lumley v Gye* (indeed, he thought that the Lord Chancellor had decided the case on this basis); and the same explanation has been given of the *Lord Strathcona* case (see *Swiss Bank Corpn v Lloyds Bank Ltd* [1979] Ch 548, at 574, reversed without reference to this point: [1982] AC 584). The difference is significant: procuring a breach of contract is a tort of intention, so that the defendant will not be liable unless he knew of the contract, whereas under *Tulk v Moxhay* the defendant will be bound unless he was a good faith purchaser without notice, which might be only constructive.

Assignment and the burden of a contract

It is frequently stated that whereas the benefit of a contract can be assigned, the burden cannot. This is quite true, in that the assignor cannot assign away his liability. It does not mean, however, that the assignee will always be able to insist on the debtor performing without having to worry about whether the debtor is receiving the performance he was due from the assignor. Firstly, as we saw in the previous chapter, an assignee takes subject to equities. Thus the debtor can use against him any defence that would have been available against the assignor, including defences which do not arise until after the assignment provided they arise out of the same contract. The result is that while he still has to look to the assignor to perform his part of the bargain, the debtor may be able to refuse to perform his part unless the assignor has done his—or the assignee will do it for him.

A practical example may make this clearer. In building and engineering contracts it is common to provide that if the contract is terminated by the employer because of a serious breach or insolvency on the part of the contractor, the contractor will assign any sub-contracts to the employer. The intention is to enable the employer to get the project finished using the original sub-contractors. The result of the assignment will be that the employer is owed the duty to perform the sub-contract work, but it is the contractor who is obliged to pay the sub-contractor. Suppose the contractor has not paid for work already done, and will not pay for future work: does the sub-contractor have to perform and sue the contractor? If as is normally the case the sub-contractor has the right to be paid as work progresses, he would ultimately be entitled to refuse to do any more until he is paid, and he can use this as a defence against the employer. The employer must therefore see that the sub-contractor is paid.

If the sub-contractor has been paid for the work that he has done at the date of termination, he may have to continue working without being sure of payment until such time as he is entitled not only to be paid for the future work, but is entitled to *refuse to do any more until he has been paid for what he has done*. At this stage he can effectively insist that the employer pay him, even though it is the dismissed contractor who is theoretically liable to him. It will obviously be easier for the sub-contractor to demand payment if he has a clause in his sub-contract entitling him to suspend work after payment is overdue by a fairly short time, as it will be remembered that in the absence of express provision to the contrary, payment is not treated as a condition of the obligation to do further work (see *Mersey Steel and Iron Co v Naylor, Benzon & Co* (1884) 9 App Cas 434, and above p 436.)

Thus even when it is just a question of ensuring payment for future work, the sub-contractor may find it far from easy to ensure that he is paid; when he has not been paid for what he has done at the date of termination and the contractor is insolvent he may find it next to impossible under the regime apparently envisaged by the standard forms. The terms of the original contract are that payments ultimately destined for the sub-contractor be paid to the contractor, who should then pay them on; and, at least as regards payments due before the main contract was terminated, the contractor's liquidator can demand that the payment still be made to the contractor. If the employer pays the sub-contractor direct, he will have to pay the same sum again to the contractor; if he does not pay, the sub-contractor will have to prove in the insolvency and is unlikely to recover anything. Some forms confer a power on the employer to pay unpaid sub-contractors direct, but as the result of the House of Lords decision in *British Eagle International Airlines Ltd v Compagnie Nationale Air France* [1975] 2 All ER 390 such a clause may well be invalid as against the insolvent creditor as an attempt to alter the statutory priorities of creditors on insolvency. In practice the employer may have to enter a novation with contractor and sub-contractor and agree to shoulder the full burden of paying the sub-contractor.

There seems to be a second way in which an assignee may become liable to the burdens of the contract assigned to him (though without releasing the assignor). This is under what Megarry V-C in *Tito v Waddell (No 2)* [1977] Ch 106 called 'the pure principle of benefit and burden'. In that long and complicated case about Ocean Island, which had been strip-mined of its guano (see above, p 497), one of the questions which arose was whether the British Phosphate Commissioners, to whom the mining licences had been assigned, were under any obligation to replant the island in accordance with the agreement. The judge held that they were. He said (at pp 302–303):

> . . . If the initial transaction has created benefits and burdens which, on its true construction, are distinct, the question whether a person who is not an original party can take one without the other will prima facie depend upon the circumstances in which he comes into the transaction. If, for instance, all that is assigned to him is the benefit of a contract, and the assignor, who is a party to the contract, undertakes to continue to discharge the burdens of it, it would be remarkable if it were to be held that the assignee could not take the benefit without assuming the burden. The circumstances show that the assignee was intended to take only the benefit, and that the burden was intended to be borne in the same way as it had been borne previously.
>
> On the other hand, if the assignee takes as a purported assignee of the whole contract from a company which is on the point of going into liquidation, he undertaking to discharge all the burdens and to indemnify the company, then, unless the benefit and burden principle is to be rejected in its entirety, I would have thought that the circumstances showed that he was not intended to take the benefit without also assuming the burdens, and that the result would accord with the intention, vis-à-vis not only the company but also the persons entitled to enforce those burdens. No doubt the terms of any relevant document would be of major importance: but I would regard the matter as one which has to be determined from the surrounding circumstances as a whole.

This doctrine seems distinct from that discussed in the previous paragraph: it does not seem to be based on the debtors' duty to perform being conditional on receiving what they had been promised by the assignors—the debtors in the case (the land owners) had no outstanding duties.

Index